# Annotated Bibliography
# of Mennonite Writings
# on War and Peace:
# 1930-1980

# Annotated Bibliography
# of Mennonite Writings
# on War and Peace:
# 1930-1980

## Edited by Willard M. Swartley
## and Cornelius J. Dyck

Together with Editorial Assistants
Carol A. N. Martin
Mary Schertz
Priscilla Stuckey-Kauffman

and Research Assistants

Rachel Friesen
Charlie Lord
Evelyn Petkau
Mary Schertz
Priscilla Stuckey-Kauffman

Prepared by the
Institute of Mennonite Studies
Elkhart, Indiana

HERALD PRESS
Scottdale, Pennsylvania
Kitchener, Ontario
1987

**Library of Congress Cataloging-in-Publication Data**
Annotated bibliography of Mennonite writings on war
    and peace, 1930-1980.
        "Prepared by the Institute of Mennonite Studies, Elkhart, Indiana."
        Includes index.
            1. War—Religious aspects—Mennonites—Bibliography.
    2. Peace—Religious aspects—Mennonites—Bibliography.
    3. Mennonites—Doctrines—Bibliography.      1. Swartley,
    Willard M., 1936-          II. Dyck, Cornelius J.
    III.  Institute of Mennonite Studies (Elkhart, Ind.)
    Z7845.M4A56    1987    [BX8128.P4]    016.2618'73    87-14932
    ISBN 0-8361-1292-X

ANNOTATED BIBLIOGRAPHY OF MENNONITE WRITINGS
ON WAR AND PEACE: 1930-1980
Copyright © 1987 by Herald Press, Scottdale, Pa.  15683
        Published simultaneously in Canada by Herald Press,
        Kitchener, Ont.  N2G 4M5. All rights reserved.
Library of Congress Catalog Card Number:
International Standard Book Number: 0-8361-1292-X
Printed in the United States of America
Design by Paula M. Johnson

87 88 89 90 91 92 93 94 95 96 10 9 8 7 6 5 4 3 2 1

# Contents

# Preface

The specific origin of this volume lies in the request of a group of European peace workers during the later stages of the Vietnam War for a bibliography of Mennonite writings on peace. The request was addressed to the Institute of Mennonite Studies (IMS) of which Cornelius J. Dyck was then the director. A brief reply listing several dozen key works met an immediate need, but served also as a stimulus to ask for more. These requests then eventually led to the decision to prepare a comprehensive, annotated bibliography of Mennonite writings on war and peace. This volume is the result. Financial and other considerations extended the process of preparation to nearly fifteen years. When Dyck terminated his administrative work with IMS in 1979 the new director, Willard M. Swartley, actively continued the project to its completion.

Several initial decisions about guiding principles for the project had significant implications. One was the decision to annotate each entry. This required selecting persons with the requisite skills for this. Numerous students were selected, with those giving major time listed on the title page. Another early decision involved selecting the publications to be researched. Some were added later. Another decision was the required length of an article for it to be eligible for inclusion, as will be elaborated below. How are exceptions made if an article is just a little bit too short, but otherwise excellent? We decided to include them, knowing well that this increased the subjectivity of the compilation.

Perhaps the two most significant decisions (or learnings) made had to do with choosing the *terminus a quo* and the categories under which to organize the material. Concerning the first issue, we soon discovered what we had actually known before, that the sixteenth-century Anabaptist convictions about peace had fallen prey to traditionalism, acculturation, social withdrawal, and other corroding influences to such an extent that few writings could be found across the span of several centuries. There are exceptions along the way, of course, even in America during the Revolutionary and Civil Wars as well as World War I, but the pathos lies in their paucity. And when writings did appear they were primarily concerned with Mennonite self-preservation. Here is material, and an era, for much further study and analysis. Since we wanted the bibliography to be in English, we decided to begin with 1930 when the voice of Guy F. Hershberger was beginning to be heard.

Equally sobering, and complex, was the identifying of categories. Are race relations a peace issue? we asked ourselves, and answered yes. What about relief, refugee resettlement, law, social action, and other issues? Again we said yes, but the categories grew as we worked and as we moved into the 1970s. There was no question then about tax resistance as a peace issue, or civil disobedience, or justice, labor unions, amnesty, and development. Even lifestyle loomed as a major peace issue until our bibliography seemed to call for including all of life, even driving our cars, as integral to peacemaking. From a very narrow understanding of peace as meaning (for Mennonites) the avoidance of military service and nonswearing of oaths, we increasingly found our publications moving from a simple stress on obedience to a dynamic approach of witnessing to the truth which is Jesus Christ. Equally encouraging was the evidence that Mennos were no longer off alone in a corner in their peace witness as mission; many others were now a part of this witness. We rejoice and are grateful that many who had never heard of Mennonites truly have become disciples of the Way.

We express our appreciation to those listed on the title page, and also unnamed others, without whose careful help this project would not have been possible. We thank Allen Nice-Webb for preparing the Author Index. To these people and those who gave assistance in various historical libraries (Bethel College, Bluffton College, Conrad Grebel College, Mennonite Historical Library (Goshen), and Menno Simons Historical Library (Eastern Mennonite College), as well as to those agencies and institutions who helped to make this project possible financially, we stand in grateful debt. We thank especially the Mennonite Central Committee Peace Section, the Mennonite Mutual Aid Association Shalom Fund, and the Schowalter Foundation, Inc., for the grants of money they made available for the project. The greater portion of expense—both the cost of the student research and the time given by the editors—was borne by the Institute. We thank in turn the Associated Mennonite Biblical Seminaries for providing subsidy for the work of the Institute.

During 1983-86 Director Swartley undertook the task of editing the approximately 10,000 entries and further classifying them by subject in preparation for entry into the computer database. Carol Martin undertook the painstaking job of entering this volume of material into the computer, including some copy editing in the process. Mary Schertz and Jonathan Beachey also assisted in the copy editing.

The following principles and points of information will enable users of this volume to know its strengths and limitations, as well as the procedures that were followed in its preparation.

1. The goal of this project has been to produce an annotated bibliography of North American Mennonite writings on war and peace in the English language, beginning around 1930 and extending up through 1980, with some selected articles up to the time of publishing. We attempted to include all articles written by Mennonites, published in both Mennonite and other publications. The guideline has been to include all articles of 800 words or more, with a minimum limit of 300 words for pertinent news reports, letters to editors, poetry, and editorials. Letters to editors were to be included only if the entry was judged to make some substantial point other than that in the article itself. In some cases (especially with poetry), items shorter than the minimal limits were included.

2. While the bibliography attempts to include all Mennonite writings, other authors whose writings on war and peace have been published in Mennonite papers and by Mennonite publishers have also been included.

3. Although the intention of the project was to be as exhaustive as possible for the period 1930-80, it would be presumptuous to claim that all relevant items have been included. The fallibility of the researchers, limitations on the part of the editors, both in time and knowledge, and potential short-comings in our use of computer technology require us to claim only approximate comprehensiveness in the final product. It is likely, for example, that some peace theme novels written by Mennonites have been overlooked. We did not attempt to include audiovisuals at all. Even though we made a systematic effort to locate articles written by Mennonites in non-Mennonite journals, it is quite certain that we did not find them all. Some pre-1930 and post-1980 articles have also been included.

4. In relation to the earlier reference to decisions about what constitutes a "peace" article, we have followed the policy of including related articles (such as on abortion and environmental issues) when they specifically are correlated to war and peace. This means that the viewpoint represented in the articles selected on some subsidiary topics may not be fully representative of the Mennonite contribution as a whole to this particular issue. When we were conscious of such inherently slanted representation (for example, by including only those articles on abortion which correlated it with killing in war), we did include some other articles to reflect the range of Mennonite viewpoints. But not all articles on abortion are included.

5. We also had to decide whether a given entry would be printed more than once, since one entry may be related to two or three topics. The policy we followed has been to print the given entry several times if the article and annotation spoke directly to the topic under which it appears. It is hoped that this will make the contribution more user-friendly. Since all of the topics are interrelated, many articles have indirect relationship to six or more of the main topics.

6. Consequently, in using the bibliography one should note the interrelatedness of subject categories. For example, if one wishes to do a thorough study of "Church and State," this would entail examination of items under Conscientious Objection (7), Nationalism (12), Amnesty (11c), Peace Witness (13b), and Nonresistance (13c). Further, it should be noted that it is sometimes difficult to decide under which main entry a subcategory best fits. For example, religious freedom could fit well under either Church and State or Conscientious Objection. Similarly, while Conscientious Objection might be considered to be a subcategory of Alternate Service, we have classified it separately as a main topic. The user should be sure to read the "Guide to Topic Search" which follows this Preface in order to learn which keywords have been included or excluded in the selection of articles and annotations that follow. But editorial judgment, not computer selection, was the final arbiter in deciding which articles belong in each category.

This means that some articles were struck from the selected list either because they didn't qualify thematically or because they related more directly to another topic. Further, topical coding of entries was done in order to make sure certain articles were included, even though they did not contain selected keywords.

7. When a given entry occurs under a subtopic, it is thereby excluded from the main topic of which that subtopic is a part, although exceptions were made if the article speaks significantly to both the main topic and the subtopic. It should also be noted that some main topics might be considered subtopics of other main topics. For example, Nationalism (12) might be considered a subtopic of Church and State (5).

8. We have followed the policy of using inclusive language in the annotations, except where it introduced awkward anachronism. Since the span of time covered by this bibliography predates awareness and concern on this issue, we can only apologize for what may now be considered sexist language as it appears in titles and in a few quotations that appear within the annotation. We have also included women's first names when they were known to us, rather than Mrs. plus a husband's first name.

9. Frequently we encountered divergent forms of an author's name, for example John C. Wenger and J. C. Wenger. We have taken the liberty to choose either the latter form of usage, when that divergence was a matter of inclusion or exclusion of a middle name or initial. By making this decision we were able to place all the articles by the same person immediately next to each other through the computer alphabetized indexing of entries by authors.

10. For style policy we have followed *The Chicago Manual of Style* (University of Chicago Press, 13th edition, 1982). We have used numerous abbreviations, printed at the front of the volume for convenient reference. In deference to computer logic, titles that begin with the word *The* are located in the "T" section. Articles without a named author are listed first in the sequence, alphabetically placed by the first letter of the title. Book review entries have been placed last in a list of entries by the same author.

11. Some entries appear without annotation. The policy has been to annotate all published articles and books as well as master's theses or doctoral dissertations. We have not annotated term papers written for college or seminary classes or archival materials. We tried, but were not completely successful, to collect relevant materials from all the historical libraries of Mennonite institutions of higher learning. We did not attempt to include articles from regional conference papers, nor did we attempt to include holdings from regional conference historical libraries and archives.

12. Since the material has been entered into a computer database, Herald Press will perform the service of running a computer search on any given topic or cluster of topics for the years covered by the Bibliography for a nominal fee. If more than one search is requested, Herald Press will need to negotiate time and fee.

When a project of this magnitude is completed, feelings of elation and celebration arise. As editors we are happy to make this material available to the Mennonite church, to Christian brothers and sisters of all religious denominations interested in the cause of peace, and to the scholarly community worldwide. Our hope and prayer is that the work that has been done will contribute to "the things that make for peace."

—Editors Willard M. Swartley and Cornelius J. Dyck
THE INSTITUTE OF MENNONITE STUDIES
Elkhart, Indiana

# Guide to Topic Search

The following information shows which keywords were called on the computer for the various topics:

1. **Alternative Service**
   A. General

   alternative; alternative service; voluntary service (also VS); I-W (also I-W's, I-WS); social service(s); service—I-W; service program(s); service project(s).

   B. Civilian Public Service

   civilian public service; CPS; CPS—past; CPSC; CPSers.

   C. PAX

   pax

2. **Arms, Armament, and Disarmament**

   arms; modern weapons; threat of war; arms race; nuclear weapons; armament(s); guns; bomb(s); bombing; pentagon; disarmament; detente; arms control; limitations and arms; economic conversion; treaty(ies); salt II(2); nuclear missile(s); nuclear arms; atomic weapons; atomic bomb (armament); nuclear bomb.

3. **Attitudes and Education**

   attitudes; education; values; ideology(ies) (ical) (ology); ideologues; political views; truth; attitude formation; attitude change; propaganda; persuasion; conversion; nonconformity; secular(ization); isolation(ism). Nonconformity was included in this list because it was considered to be an attitude that directly influences one's position on war and peace.

4. **The Bible, Peace, and War**

   Bible and peace; Bible and war; New Testament; Old Testament; kingdom of God; politics of Jesus.

5. **Church and State**

   church and state; church-state; patriotism; citizenship; political participation; politics, voting, freedom (of) conscience; religious freedom; politics; voting; lobbying; government, view of; liberty; dissent.

6. **Civil Disobedience**
   A. General

   civil disobedience; war protest(s); marches; peace march(es); demonstration(s); demonstrators.

   B. War Tax Resistance

   war tax(es); tax and military; Caesar; World Peace Tax Fund.

7. **Conscientious Objection**

conscientious objection(or); CO; CO's; COs'; selective objector(s); selective objection.

8. **International Relations**

international relations; international arbitration; foreign policies.

9. **Justice**

A. General

justice; injustice; human rights; violence; peacekeeping; liberation; power; civil rights; torture; revolution; separatism; riots; repression; oppression; terrorism; terrorists.

B. Abortion

abortion

C. Labor unions

union(s).

D. Law and litigation

law; litigation.

E. Corrections

penal and system; capital punishment; prison; death penalty.

F. Conflict and Conciliation

conflict; conciliation; arbitration; negotiation; crisis and intervention; mediation.

10. **Mennonite Central Committee**

A. General

Mennonite Central Committee; MCC.

B. Development

development; colonialism; imperialism.

C. Relief (famine and hunger)

relief; hunger; famine; MDS.

11. **Military Service**

A. General

military; militant; militarism; defense policy; CIA; compulsory; universal military training; selective service; noncombatant; 1-A; I-A's; I-AO; IAO.

B. Conscription, Registration, and the Draft

conscription; draft; registration; noncooperation; nonregistration; draft resistance.

C. Amnesty

amnesty.

12. **Nationalism**

A. General

nationalism; civil religion; bicentennial.

B. Civilian defense

civil(ian) defense(ce) (se') (se-).

C. Flag

flag salute; flag and American.

13. **Peace**

A. General

peace (excluding all subcategory keywords)

B. Peacemaking, Peace Witness, and Peace Movements

peacemaking; peacemaker(s); practical expression; peace living; peace witness; mission(s); pray(er)(ing); historic peace church(es); church(es) and peace; Dutch peace witness; evangelism; reconciliation; reconciled; spirituality; peace dialogue; Anabaptism; Anabaptist(s); Mennonites and peace/war. This computer call specifically excluded all of the keywords listed in 13b, 13c, 13d and 13e.

C. Nonresistance, Nonviolence, and Pacifism

nonviolence; pacifism(ist); nonresistance(ant); love and enemy(ies); martyr(s); persecution. Again this computer call specifically excluded other keywords in the other subsections of topic 13.

D. Evangelicals, Social Action

evangelical(s); Billy Graham; Mennonites and Billy Graham; social action. The rationale for putting these two topics together as subtopics emerged from the entries themselves. Articles that mentioned social action were often the same articles that discussed evangelicals and their relation to peace witnessing. It should be noted that some entries deal with social action as a topic in itself. Theological interpretation of this combination should not be readily deduced.

E. Women, Peace, and War

women and peace; women and war; women and military.

F. Peace Stories

peace stories. Response to this word depended upon editorial identification of a particular entry with the "Peace Story" code.

G. Christian-Marxist Dialogue

Christian and Marxist; Christian-marxist; East-West; East and West; Prague (for Prague Peace Conference).

14. **Race Relations**

race relations; racism; civil rights; class; desegregation; desegregated; apartheid; native and American(s).

15. **Refugees**

A. General

refugee(s); illegal alien(s); orphans; immigrant(s).

B. Russian Story

Russian story; self-defense; Selbstschutz; Russia(n); Siberia.

16. **War**

A. General

war and warfare (excluding all call signals in all other categories in 16 below); causes; war and economics; just war; churches and war; chaplaincy; war toys; war and slavery.

B. Atomic War, Nuclear War

atomic war; nuclear war; nuclear accident(s).
  C. Postwar
    post-war; post and war.
  D. Communism and Anticommunism
    communism; anticommunism.
17. **Wars**
  A. Revolutionary War
    revolutionary war; American and revolution.
  B. American Civil War
    civil and war.
  C. World War I
    world and war and I.
  D. World War II
    world and war and II.
  E. Southeast Asia
    Vietnam; Viet-nam; Indo-China; Indo China; southeast and Asia; Korea; Korean; Sino-Japanese.
  F. Middle East
    middle east; mideast; mid-east.
  G. Latin and Central America
    Latin America(n); Central America(n); El Salvador(ian).

It is important to note that the editorial process introduced coding of the entries according to the above keywords, even when the words as such did not appear in the entry but the thought or concept was present in the entry. Further, in the first search of each of the categories, many of the entries were deleted because the words by which they were called were used in a sense unrelated to the topic or because that particular entry was more directly related to another major topic or subtopic within the major category. In these cases, choices were made in order to avoid too frequent recurrence of one entry.

# Publications Researched and Annotated

Canadian Mennonite, The
Christian Exponent, The
Christian Leader, The
Christian Living
Christian Monitor
Concern
Conrad Grebel Review, The
Contact (MCC)
CPS Bulletin and Supplement

Daughters of Sarah
Direction

Evangelical Visitor

Fellowship (FOR)
Festival Quarterly
Forum
From Swords to Plowshares

God and Caesar
Gospel Herald
Guidelines for Today

Intercollegiate Peace
   Fellowship Peace Notes
Intercom (MCC)

Journal of Church and Society

Lifework (MCC)

MCC Offender Ministries
   Network Newsletter
MCC Peace Section Newsletter
MCC Peace Section Task Force on
   Women in Church and
   Society Report

MCC Peace Section Washington Memo
Mennonite, The
Mennonite and The Christian
   Evangel, The
Mennonite Brethren Herald
Mennonite Community, The
Mennonite Encyclopedia
Mennonite Historical Bulletin
Mennonite Life
Mennonite Mirror
Mennonite Quarterly Review, The
Mennonite Reporter
Mennonite Weekly Review
Messenger of Truth
Mission Focus

Occasional Papers (IMS)

Peace and Change (COPRED)
Plowshares Monitor
Proceedings of Conference on
   Mennonite Educational and
   Cultural Problems

Sojourners (Post-American)
Sword and Trumpet, The

Voice (WMSC)
Voice, The

War Sufferers Relief Bulletin
With

Youth's Christian Companion, The

# Abbreviations

| | |
|---|---|
| AFSC | American Friends Service Committee |
| AID | Agency for International Development (USA) |
| AMBS | Associated Mennonite Biblical Seminaries |
| AMC | Archives of the Mennonite Church |
| ASC | Alternate Service Work (Canada) |
| | |
| BfC | Bluffton College |
| BeC | Bethel College |
| | |
| *CanMenn* | *The Canadian Mennonite* |
| CGCL | Conrad Grebel College Library |
| *CGR* | *The Conrad Grebel Review* |
| *ChrCent* | *The Christian Century* |
| *ChrEv* | *The Christian Evangel* |
| *ChrExp* | *The Christian Exponent* |
| *ChrLead* | *The Christian Leader* |
| *ChrLiv* | *Christian Living* |
| *ChrMon* | *Christian Monitor* |
| *ChrToday* | *Christianity Today* |
| CMBS/Win | Centre for Mennonite Brethren Studies in Canada (Winnepeg) |
| CO,COs | Conscientious Objector(s) |
| COMBS | Council of Mission Board Secretaries |
| comp. | compiler |
| COPRED | Consortium for Peace Research, Education and Development |
| CPS | Civilian Public Service |
| | |
| DRVN | Democratic Republic of Vietnam |
| | |
| ed. | editor |
| EMC | Eastern Mennonite College |
| *Ev* | *Evangelical Visitor* |
| | |
| FOR | Fellowship of Reconciliation |
| *FQ* | *Festival Quarterly* |
| *FStP* | *From Swords to Plowshares* |

| | |
|---|---|
| GBS | Goshen Biblical Seminary |
| GC | General Conference |
| GCMC | General Conference Mennonite Church |
| *Gft* | *Guidelines for Today* |
| *GH* | *Gospel Herald* |
| | |
| HPC | Historic Peace Churches |
| | |
| I(C)BM | Intercontinental Ballistic Missile |
| IMS | Institute of Mennonite Studies |
| *IPF Notes* | *Intercollegiate Peace Fellowship Peace Notes* |
| | |
| *JChSoc* | *Journal for Church and Society* |
| | |
| MB | Mennonite Brethren |
| *MBH* | *Mennonite Brethren Herald* |
| MBS | Mennonite Biblical Seminary |
| MC | Mennonite Church |
| MCC | Mennonite Central Committee |
| *MCC PS Wash. Memo* | *MCC Peace Section Washington Memo* |
| *MCC PS Newsletter* | *MCC Peace Section Newsletter* |
| *MCC PS TF on Women in Ch. and Soc. Report* | *MCC Peace Section Task Force on Women in Church and Society Report* |
| *MCC WSRB* | *MCC War Sufferers Relief Bulletin* |
| *MCE* | *The Mennonite and the Christian Evangel* |
| *ME* | *Mennonite Encyclopedia* |
| *Menn* | *The Mennonite* |
| *MennComm* | *The Mennonite Community* |
| *MennMirror* | *Mennonite Mirror* |
| *MennRep* | *Mennonite Reporter* (also *CMR: Canadian Mennonite Reporter*) |
| *MennLife* | *Mennonite Life* |
| MLA | Mennonite Library and Archives (Bethel College) |
| MLA | Mennonite Library and Archives |
| MP | Member of Parliament |
| MPH | Mennonite Publishing House |
| *MQR* | *The Mennonite Quarterly Review* |
| MSHL(A) | Menno Simons Historical Library (and Archives), EMC |
| MWC | Mennonite World Conference |
| *MWR* | *Mennonite Weekly Review* |

| | |
|---|---|
| n.d. | no date |
| NLF | National Liberation Front |
| NSBRO | National Service Board for Religious Objectors |
| n.p. | no place or no publisher |
| NT | New Testament |
| *OP* | *Occasional Papers* |
| OT | Old Testament |
| | |
| *PCMCP* | *Proceedings of Conference on Mennonite Cultural Problems* |
| *PlMon* | *Plowshares Monitor* |
| *PostAmer* | *Post-American* (forerunner of *Sojourners*) |
| PPC | Peace Problems Committee (MC) |
| | |
| RCAF | Royal Canadian Air Force |
| *RepConsS* | *The Reporter for Conscience Sake* |
| | |
| SDS | Students for a Democratic Society |
| SS | Sunday School |
| *ST* | *The Sword and Trumpet* |
| | |
| UMT | Universal Military Training |
| UNRWA | United Nations Relief and Welfare Agency |
| | |
| WCC | World Council of Churches |
| WMSC | Women's Missionary and Service Commission (MC) |
| *WSRB* | *War Sufferers Relief Bulletin (MCC)* |
| | |
| *YCC* | *The Youth's Christian Companion* |

# Annotated Bibliography
## of Mennonite Writings
## on War and Peace:
## 1930-1980

# 1
# Alternate Service

## A. General

"Amishman Convicted for Refusing Civilian Work." *RepConsS* 14 (Dec., 1957), 4. Abraham Y. Borntreger, member of Amish-Mennonite church colony at Hazilton, Iowa, contends his religious convictions make alternative service impossible.

"An Announcement by the Peace Problems Committee." *GH* 33 (Nov. 21, 1940), 730-31. Announces the financial needs of the civilian service program, the establishment of NSBRO, and a plan to keep the church informed of matters relating to the draft.

Becker, Lawrence F. "Service Preparation of the Church." *MennLife* 13 (July, 1958), 116-17. A report on the orientation program of the Church of God in Christ, Mennonite for those young men going into I-W service.

Bender, Harold S. "Civilian Defense: In the Midst of War—Thoughts for Nonresistants," (Part 8). *GH* 35 (Mar. 25, 1943), 1105-1106. The Peace Problems Committee recommends that nonresistant Christians not take part in Civilian Defense but find alternate ways of service.

[Bender, Harold S.] "Origins of Alternative Service." *The Reporter* 5 (Mar., 1947), 1, 6-8. A discussion of the beginnings of Mennonite alternative service in Russia after 1870, and the experience of CO's in Russia to the present.

Bender, Paul. "Conscientious Objection to Military Service in North America, South America, and Europe: Legislation, Objection, Alternative Service, and Peace Work." Report to the Sixth Mennonite World Conference, Karlsruhe, Aug. 10-16, 1957. Pp. 10. MHL.

Bender, Paul. "Cooperative Testing Program of Mennonite Colleges and Civilian Public Service." *PCMCP Fourth*, 27-34. North Newton, Kansas. Held at Bluffton, Ohio, Aug. 24-25, 1945. A survey of the issues and problems related to granting academic credit for certain formal educational courses in the CPS camps.

Berg, Ford. "The Inescapable Responsibility in Accepting Deferments." *GH* 41 (July 20, 1948), 667. Is voluntary Christian service a permanent commitment of nonresistant Mennonites, or only something prompted by the government and done in lieu of military service?

Bleyker, Marjorie Den. "They Make Employers Happy." *ChrLiv* 4 (May, 1957), 3-6. Drafted I-W workers in Battleboro, Vermont are respected for their work and their witness.

Brenneman, Sheryl. "It Was Difficult to Practice What We Preached." *Menn* 91 (Nov. 9, 1976), 664-65. Reflects on difficulty encountered by the 7-member summer voluntary service peace team in managing interpersonal conflict.

Brubaker, Tom. "Don't Just Say No." *GH* 62 (May 27, 1969), 474-75. Conscientious objectors in alternative service need the positive motivation of constructive service rather than the negative motivation of escaping military duty to adequately undergird their work experience.

Brunk, Conrad G. "Lewis B. Hershey, A Four-Star General from Pacifist Family." *MennRep* 7 (June 13, 1977), 11. Reflects on the life of Gen. Lewis Hershey, Mennonite descendent, director of Selective Service from 1940-1970, and his contribution to forming alternative service programs.

Brunk, Emily. *Espelkamp: The MCC Shares in Community Building in a New Settlement for German Refugees.* Frankfurt, Germany: MCC, 1951. Pp. 42. MHL. Relates the story of Espelkamp, an initial experiment in resettlement of the refugees of World War II in which both American and European Mennonite youth participated on a Voluntary Service basis.

Buchanan, Roy. "A Personal Testimony." *GH* 63 (May 5, 1970), 408-409. World War I conscientious objector disagrees with the position of draft resisters, describing his positive experiences in obtaining cooperation from the military to perform alternative service.

Burkholder, Marie. "Alternative Service Programs

Available for Mennonites During the Second World War." Term paper for History course, Dec. 4, 1973. Pp. 28. CGCL.

"Canadians Research Wartime Experiences." *RepConsS* 32 (June, 1975), 4. Conrad Grebel College has initiated an oral history project to preserve and deepen understanding of the Canadian Mennonite experience with alternative service in World War II.

"Chicago Area Draft Resisters." *GH* 62 (Oct. 14, 1969), 904. Statistical report on number of draft resisters, participants in alternative service, etc., in 125 churches as reported by the Selective Service system.

"Conference Response to Conscription and Militarism." *GH* 62 (Oct. 7, 1969), 869. An appeal to nonresistant faith, service and alternate service, and noncooperation as the situation may require.

"COs Work for Science and Humanity." *RepConsS* 14 (Aug., 1957), 1-3. Describes the work of one Mennonite volunteer at the National Institute of Health as well as alternative service more generally.

Charles, Howard H. "CO's Around the World." *GH Supplement* 38 (Oct., 1945), 568. A review of conscientious objection to war as an international phenomenon; summarizes CO's experiences with government and service programs.

Charles, Howard H. in collaboration with Jesse W. Hoover. *Before You Decide.* Akron: MCC, 1948. Pp. 70. Alternatives to military service for young people facing the draft discussed in biblical and historical perspective.

Curry, A. Stauffer. "The Future of Alternative Service." *GH* 46 (Sept. 15, 1953), 881, 893. Surveys the possible directions alternative service may take in the future. The church must remain involved with the I-W program if it is not to become secularized and lose its high vision of service.

Dyck, Peter J. "German Conscientious Objectors Enter Service." *GH* 54 (June 20, 1961), 561. An account of the first German alternative service program for CO's, its shortcomings and opportunities.

Dyck, Peter J. "Germany Initiates CO Program." *CanMenn* 9 (May 19, 1961), 1, 10. Says EIRENE, the international peace service organization, must be ready to assist the conscientious objectors and the German government to implement the alternative service program.

Ebersole, Myron. "A History of Mennonite Central Committee Voluntary Service, 1944-1949."

Paper presented to Mennonite History Class, n.d. Pp. 38. MHL.

Ediger, Elmer. "Christian Discipleship in Time of War and Peace." *CanMenn* 2 (May 7, 1954), 6, 7. The Christian's nonresistant stand·is to be expressed both in times of war and in times of peace. Whether we choose voluntary service, prison, or some other alternative requires the guidance of the Spirit and the Christian community.

Ediger, Elmer. "Do CPS Men Favor a Voluntary Service Program for Peacetime?" *CPS Bull* 4 (Oct. 22, 1945), 1-2. Discusses reasons the CPS experience is a beneficial one and raises questions about the shape of a possible voluntary service program.

Ediger, Elmer. "Our Colleges and the Voluntary Service Program in the Present Crisis." *PCMCP Eighth,* 54-61. Newton, Kansas: Herald Book and Printing Co., Inc. Held at Messiah Bible College, Grantham, Pennsylvania, June 14-15, 1951. Colleges and voluntary service must be seen together as part of the response to mounting military training and statism. Discusses many possibilities emerging from this relationship.

Ediger, Elmer. "The Voluntary Service Program." *PCMCP Sixth,* 31-40. North Newton: The Bethel College Press. Held at Goshen College, Goshen, Indiana, Aug. 1-2, 1947. Voluntary service is motivated by Christian teachings and is expressed in a world of need and confusion, during peace as well as war time. The church must continue to develop a well-balanced voluntary service program.

Ediger, Elmer. "Voluntary Service and the Draft." *Menn* 66 (Jan. 23, 1951), 58. Urges CO's to enter the VS grogram now, rather than waiting for the prodding of conscription. The VS program offers much greater opportunities for witness and service than the CPS program did.

Engh, Jeri. "Dick Martin: I-W Mentor in Denver." *ChrLiv* 13 (Jan., 1966), 4-6. I-W counselor reflects on the young men and the services they perform.

Epp, Frank H. "Draft-Age Mennonite Youths Witness in Large Colorado City." *CanMenn* 4 (Feb. 17, 1956), 6-7. A positive analysis of I-W's and their contribution in Denver. CO's serve in a variety of sacrificial jobs and other activities.

Epp, Henry H. "World War II Conscientious Objectors in Discussion with Church Leaders." *CanMenn* 11 (June 14, 1963), 3. A panel reviews the nature of the CO's relationship to the government and the community during World Wars I and II at the Ontario Ministers' Peace Retreat. Includes a summary of questions and answers about alternative service in World War II and the position of the Mennonite church today.

Epp, Merle L. "MCC Voluntary Service, 1946-1955." Paper for Mennonite Missions class, MBS, [Chicago, Ill.], May 9, 1956. Pp. 15 plus charts. AMBS.

Erb, Paul. "Alternative Service." GH 41 (Apr. 13, 1948), 339-40. If universal peacetime conscription is adopted, Mennonites must have creative alternative programs ready to be initiated.

Erb, Paul. "Appraising I-W." GH 46 (Nov. 10, 1953), 1067-68. Summarizes a conference convened to study what has been learned after more than a year of I-W service. The program is not without faults but has been generally successful.

Erb, Paul. "The Draft." GH 41 (July 27, 1948), 683. Because nonresistant Christians have been granted deferments there needs to be a great emphasis on voluntary service to show both our neighbors and our government that such privileges are deserved.

Erb, Paul. "Voluntary Service Is Best." GH 46 (June 30, 1953), 611. While both voluntary service and alternative (earning) service may offer many witness opportunities, VS is a better Christian witness than is earning service because of the financial sacrifice involved.

Ewert, Alden H. "Why Alternate Service." ChrLead 17 (Aug. 1, 1953), 4. Love of neighbors and enemies necessitates total rejection of participation in violence and suggests instead constructive service, e.g., in mental health services or in ministry to war-torn Korea.

"Findings of the I-W Evaluation-Planning Conference; Elkhart, Ind., Apr. 9, 10, 1957." GH 50 (May 21, 1957), 489. The I-W program is proceeding satisfactorily. The failures have been primarily spiritual failures.

Faculty of the Mennonite Brethren Biblical Seminary. "Seminary Faculty Gives Draft Position." ChrLead 43 (July 29, 1980), 12-13. Consensus statement recommends alternative service to military duty but supports positions of noncombatant service and noncooperation as well.

Fast, Henry A. (Review). That There Be Peace: Mennonites in Canada and World War II, ed. by Lawrence Klippenstein. Winnipeg: Manitoba CO Reunion Committee, 1979. Menn 95 (Feb. 12, 1980), 108. Recommends the book as a collection of reflections of alternative service workers.

Franken-Liefrinck, E. "The Work of the Dutch Mennonite Peace Group." CanMenn 5 (Sept. 13, 1957), 4. Dutch Mennonites participate in alternative service and discussion for the cause of peace. Explains provisions for Dutch conscientious objectors and the activities of the Mennonite Peace Group.

Fransen, David Warren. "Mennonites in World War II: The Beginnings of Cooperation and Social Conscience." MennRep 8 (July 10, 1978), 9. Traces differences that existed among Canadian Mennonite groups in considering alternative service programs prior to World War II, and their eventual cooperation in the formation of work camps.

Fransen, David Warren. "The Debate on Alternate Service During World War II." Paper presented to the Institute of Anabaptist-Mennonite Studies, Conrad Grebel College, Oct. 1, 1975. Pp. 28. CGCL.

Franz, Delton, ed. "'Your Tax Dollars at Work.'" MCC PS Wash. Memo 3 (Nov.-Dec., 1971), 1-2. Statistics on taxes used for war and what the same money could buy in human service projects.

Fretz, John L. "Alternate Service Work Camps in Canada." YCC 24, Part 1, (Mar. 21, 1943), 505; Part 2, (Mar. 28, 1943), 518. Description of the work camps in British Colombia, including firefighting and building projects.

Friesen, Duane K. "Service and Politics—an Opinion." Forum (Jan., 1974), 4. Christian service has been seen as bandaging wounds resulting from social evils, but now the importance of social reconstruction, compassionate but also political in nature, is emerging.

Friesen, Werner. "There Ought to be Voluntary Service . . . ." CanMenn 2 (Oct. 8, 1954), 2. Voluntary Service as a way of life enables the church to become the salt of the earth and the light of the world because, as a program growing out of the alternative service experience, it provides a positive answer to war and other social problems.

"Greek Royalty Commends Mennonite I-W Men." RepConsS 12 (Oct., 1955), 3. Queen Frederica's appreciation of I-Ws stems from the enthusiasm of the villagers with whom they are working and the harmony between the I-Ws and the Greek Orthodox Church.

Gaeddert, Albert M. "Should I Register Under the Draft Act?" Menn 63 (July 27, 1948), 3. Accepts the Voluntary Service Program as an appropriate way to serve within the "system" while also recognizing the validity of non-registration for the draft.

Gaeddert, Albert M. "The New Draft Legislation." *Menn* 66 (July 31, 1951), 482. Explains how present programs of relief and service can be expanded to accomodate the CO's who will now be "ordered to work" under the new draft law.

George, Albert. "The VS Scandal." *GH* 64 (Apr. 20, 1971), 354-55. Reprinted from *Agape* (Nov.-Dec., 1970). Raised a Methodist, the writer was converted to Anabaptist nonresistance through Mennonite writings and relationships. Maintains that just as nonresistance is a scandal when considered pragmatically, so VS service is based on the scandal of the uniqueness of Christian conversion and love.

Gingerich, Melvin. "Christian Youth As Humanitarians; Christian Youth and the State." *YCC* 22, Part 8, (May 11, 1941), 566. The biblical basis for humanitarianism calls Christians to be concerned about the social needs of all people. Response can be either by material/money or by giving one's life in service.

Gingerich, Melvin. "Discipleship Expressed in Alternative Service." *The Recovery of the Anabaptist Vision.* Ed. Guy F. Hershberger. Scottdale: Herald Press, 1957, 262-74. A discussion of Mennonite alternative service programs from 1775 to the present, including nineteenth-century Russia.

Glick, Jesse B. "This Is I-W." *YCC* 48 (July 30, 1967), 11. Describes the I-W service program.

Goering, Paul L. "Should We Make Registration the Issue?" *Menn* 63 (June 22, 1948), 3. In contrast to Gordon Kaufman's stance (*Menn,* June 8, 1948), Goering argues that Mennonites could present a more effective witness against war by entering alternative service than by refusing to register.

Goertzen, Don. "We Studied Peace in the Arvada-Denver Area." *Menn* 91 (Nov. 9, 1976), 663-64. Reflections on the Mennonite Peace team work in Denver, Colorado, sponsored by General Conference peace and social concerns office, Mennonite Voluntary Service, and the Arvada Mennonite Church.

Graber, J. D. "To Proclaim or to Serve?" *Mission-Focus* 3 (Jan., 1975), 1-8. Argues that gospel proclamation needs to be in the forefront of missionary strategy, giving social services and charity a secondary place. Inner-motivated self-help will come through the new hope in Christ and will be more effective in solving social ills than the conventional institutional approach.

Gratz, Delbert L. "Peace and Our Heritage." In *Mennonite Community Sourcebook,* 25-33. Ed. Esko Loewen. Akron: MCC, 1946. Pp. 147. MHL. Bibliography of peace literature on such topics

as the principles of nonresistance, the history of the peace witness, alternative service, relief work, etc.

Groh, H. D. "The Peace Witness of the Church." *GH* 51 (May 13, 1958), 452. An account of Mennonite Voluntary Service in the British Isles. There is a real need for the Mennonite church to share the Gospel of peace and goodwill in this part of the world.

Gross, Leonard, comp. "Alternative to War: A Story Through Documents, Part 1." *GH* 65 (Nov. 7, 1972), 899-901; Part 2, (Dec. 26, 1972), 1046-47; 66, Part 3, (Jan. 2, 1973), 10-12; Part 4 (Jan. 9, 1973), 34-36; Part 5, (Jan. 16, 1973), 52-55. Uses contemporary documents to describe the difficulties Mennonites encountered during the Civil War and World War I, as well as the Mennonite response.

Gross, Leonard, ed. "The First World War and Mennonite Nonresistance." *MHB* 33 (July, 1972), 4-10. Series of government and private documents traces Mennonite experiences in the war: correspondence with the Secretary of War on conscientious objection; procedures for military induction and discharge; treatment of COs in detention; public pressure to buy war bonds; government suspicion of tract on nonresistance; germinal ideas for alternative service in reconstruction.

"Historic Peace Churches Meeting in Kitchener." *CanMenn* 2 (Oct. 29, 1954), 1. Topics include: Israel and Christianity, the power of love, relief and voluntary service.

"House Passes Bill and Revises Alternate Service." *GH* 64 (Apr. 20, 1971), 365. Describes significance of the vote to extend the military draft till June, 1973 for the CO.

Hallman, William. "Relief and Social Service as Related to Mennonite Missions." Paper presented to the Mennonite Seminar, Goshen College, Goshen, Ind., 1945. Pp. 16. MHL.

Harder, Geraldine. "Teaching Pilgrim Children Peace and Love." *Builder* 24 (May, 1974), 21-23. Suggestions to help juniors and junior highs focus on peace concerns. Examples from Mennonite history and contemporary Mennonite service programs are used.

Harding, Vincent G. "Conscientious Objection: Is It a Christian Response to Vietnam?" *Builder* 17 (Oct., 1967), 12-13. Questions the adequacy of the I-W program as a response to Jesus' call to love the enemy. Identifies a lack of congruence between objecting to war and accepting military protection of that right to object.

Harmon, Wendell E. "Editorially Speaking . . . ." *CPS Bull Supp* 5 (Sept. 26, 1946), 1, 4. Advocates continuation of the service programs begun during the war to encourage young people to enter full time Christian service.

Hartzler, Levi C. "Our Voluntary Service Program, Principles and Practices, and Relation to our Peace Testimony." *ChrMon* 41 (May, 1949), 142-44. While the Civilian Public Service program served as a model, the peacetime draft law provided the impetus for continued alternative service on a volunteer basis.

Hartzler, Roy. "My Testimony." *RepConsS* 19 (May, 1962), 3. Describes a variety of experiences that were important to personal growth during a two-year term of I-W.

Heisey, J. Wilmer. "If the Draft Dies—What About Voluntary Service?" *EV* 86 (Jan. 10, 1973), 13. Hope is expressed for volunteerism to come into a new and truer perspective rather than die out when the draft expires in 1973.

Hershberger, Guy F. "A Letter to the President Suggesting Alternative Service for Mennonite Youth in Case of War." *YCC* 21 (June 16, 1940) 192. A copy of a letter which was presented to President F. D. Roosevelt by a delegation of Mennonites, Friends, and Brethren on Jan. 9, 1940, states the position of the historic peace churches and the desired care for CO's.

Hershberger, Guy F. "Are Today's I-W Boys Performing 'Greater Works'? Our Peace Witness—In the Wake of May 18." (Part 14). *GH* 60 (Dec. 5, 1967), 1090. Most I-W's give a good account of themselves, but sometimes this kind of service is too easy and is abused.

Hershberger, Guy F. "How Can Mennonites Use Their Freedom for the Performance of Greater Works Than They Are Now Doing? Our Peace Witness—In the Wake of May 18." (Part 15). *GH* 60 (Dec. 12, 1967), 1114. The church should support young men to go into VS rather than I-W service.

Hershberger, Guy F. "How Important Is the Peace Problems Committee?" *GH* 56 (Apr. 23, 1963), 346-47. An historical sketch of the PPC, giving witness to its importance and attempting to raise funds for this program as well as General Conference (MC) involvement in other projects such as PAX, I-W, MCC, etc.

Hershberger, Guy F. "Is Alternative Service Desirable and Possible?" *The Christian's Relation to the State in Time of War*, 16-32. [Goshen, Ind.: Mennonite Historical Society, 1935.] Pp. 32. MHL. Also in *MQR* 9 (Jan., 1935), 20-36. Argues that on the basis of the early church's refusal to participate in war, the apolitical stance of the early Anabaptists and the failure of the Quaker experiment in Pennsylvania, that an alternative to military service completely separate from the government's military effort ought to be set in place prior to another war. Alternative service is desirable as an expression of service to the suffering and needy, and as an example to nations engaged in war.

Hershberger, Guy F. "Questions for Nonresistant Christians." *GH* 33, Parts 1-3, (July 18, 1940), 338; Part 4, (July 25, 1940), 371; Parts 5-7, (Aug. 1, 1940), 386; Parts 8-9, (Aug. 8, 1940), 418; Parts 10-11, (Aug. 15, 1940), 435; Part 12, (Aug. 22, 1940), 450; Part 13, (Aug. 29, 1940), 466-67; Part 14, (Sept. 12, 1940), 514; Part 15-16, (Sept. 19, 1940), 530; Part 17, (Oct. 3, 1940), 562; Part 19-22, (Oct. 31, 1940), 658-59; Part 23, (Nov. 7, 1940), 675; Part 24, (Nov. 28, 1940), 738; Part 25, (Dec. 5, 1940), 754. Series includes such topics as war propaganda, conscription, alternative service, conscientious objection, registration, noncombatant service, etc.

Hershberger, Guy F. "What Shall a Christian Youth Do in Time of War?" *YCC* 18 (June 6, 1937), 600. From the experience in World War I, there seem to be four possible courses of action a person might follow in time of war: regular military service; noncombatant service; complete refusal to participate in the military; alternative Christian service.

Hiebert, Linda Gibson. "The Indochina Project." *Peace Section Newsletter* 9 (June-July, 1979), 3-5. The Indochina Project began in mid-1978 as a cooperative effort between the Mennonite Central Committee and the American Friends Service Committee, with the Center for International Policy joining later. Explains the role and concerns of the project.

Horsch, John. "War Resisters and Conscientious Objectors in European Countries." *GH* 29 (Oct. 8, 1936), 602-603. Factual account of the existing situation in Europe, where alternative civil service is offered by some countries while others imprison CO's who refuse military service.

Horst, John L. "Concerning the New Draft Law." *ChrMon* 43 (July, 1951), 200. Reprints section of the draft law pertaining to conscientious objectors and comments on the possible changes in voluntary service programs.

Horst, John L. "The Draft Law and Voluntary Service." *GH* 41 (Oct. 26, 1948), 1003-1004. Because Mennonite youth have so generously been exempted from the draft, they should make a special effort to enlist in VS programs.

Hostetler, Hugh. "The Challenges of Exemption." *Menn* 63 (Sept. 7, 1948), 11-12. Rather than simply "sitting tight" through exemption, Mennonites could well (1) refuse to register, (2) fight for the repeal of the draft law, and/or (3) expand voluntary service programs.

Hostetter, Douglas and McIntyre, Michael. "The Politics of Charity." *Christian Century* 91 (Sept. 18, 1974), 845-50. Questions the cooperation between Christian charitable programs and US government programs which tie the goals of the church to those of the state. Discussion focused by issues facing Church World Service.

Hull, Robert. "[Proposal for Sabbatical Service.]" *God and Caesar* 6 (Oct., 1980), 3-9. Proposal for Mennonites to covenant with their congregations to perform voluntary service every seven years. Considered both as congregational ministry and as active conscientious objection.

"I-Ws Build Block Upon Block at Enkenbach." *RepConsS* 18 (Nov., 1961), 1. One hundred fifty I-Ws have spent 624,000 work hours to build forty-four houses for refugees in Enkenbach, Germany.

"I-Ws Drink Meals Testing Artificial Diet." *RepConsS* 19 (May, 1962), 1, 4. COs at a Denver hospital are participating in a nutritional study attempting to determine the digestibility of cellulose by humans.

"I-Ws Narrowly Escape Death in the Congo." *RepConsS* 22 (Jan., 1965), 1, 3. Two Mennonite PAX persons resume duties in the Congo (Zaire) after a harrowing episode in Stanleyville in which Dr. Paul Carlson was fatally shot on Nov. 24.

"I-Ws on Demonstration Farm, New Extension Progam, Greece." *RepConsS* 19 (Feb., 1962), 1, 3. This Mennonite I-W team is not only providing practical assistance to the Greek people through extension work, but is contributing to the work of the Greek Orthodox Christians as well.

International Christian Service for Peace in Morocco." *CanMenn* 6 (Aug. 8, 1958), 7. Historic peace churches sponsor a peace project in Morocco consisting of building cattle shelters.

Jost, Arthur. "Editorially Speaking . . . ." *CPS Bull Supp* 5 (Oct. 31, 1946), 1, 3. Proposes guidelines for a voluntary service program as a peacetime outgrowth of the Civilian Public Service program.

Juhnke, William. "Shall We Reverse Our Historic Peace Stand?" *Menn* 56 (Aug. 12, 1941), 2. Mennonite tradition would seem to support alternate service. The church will not force young people into this position but should conduct a massive education program making this position clear.

Karpatkin, Marvin M. "'In the Supreme Court of the United States, October Term, 1969 . . .' Jerry Allen Penner, Petitioner, v. United States of America, Respondent. Petition for a Writ of Certiorari to the US Court of Appeals for the 10th Circuit. Marvin M. Karpatkin and Michael N. Pollet . . . Attorneys for Petitioner." NY: Record Press, 1970. MSHL. Legal case involving the question, among others, whether the petitioner's Selective Service local board discriminated against him, a third-generation Mennonite, by insisting on classifying him I-A-O instead of I-O as requested. Also deals with question of whether I-O classification can be denied on evidence of youthful misbehavior.

Kasper, Arlo. "The I-W in Action." *MennLife* 13 (July, 1958), 106, 107, 120. Describes the work of those who are not able to respond to the call of government for military service and become involved in alternative service in hospitals, etc. Gives an overview of the various types of alternate service—I-W earning, voluntary service, and PAX service.

Kauffman, Milo. "Christian Alternatives to Conscription." *GH* 39 (Jan. 21, 1947), 333. Address given at the 1946 General Conference (MC). Christian alternative service programs should not appear to defy the government. Various forms of service are suggested.

Kaufman, Abraham. Letter to the Editor. *Fellowship* 12 (Nov., 1946), 186. Points out the error in Philip Jacob's statement (*Fellowship* [Oct., 1946]), that the historic peace churches were urged by the War Resisters League to undertake administration of alternative service projects.

Kaufman, Donald D. "Implications of Pax, Relief, and Voluntary Service for World Mission." Paper presented to Mennonite Misions and World Service class, MBS, Chicago, Ill., Nov. 27, 1957. Pp. 35.

Kaufman, Stan. "A Proposal for a Legal Tax Alternative." *God and Caesar* 5 (Aug., 1979), 3-4. A Sunday school class at Rainbow Blvd. Mennonite Church in Kansas City has attempted to take seriously the Minneapolis resolution to work out a possible legal alternative to paying war taxes and proposes a compromise which links the World Peace Tax Fund to a national service program.

Keeler, Richard F. "Why Voluntary Service?" *GH* 61 (Jan. 9, 1968), 34. In light of the privilege of voluntary service as an alternative to Selective Service, the author urges all Christians, especially nonresistant ones, to enter a period of such service, with or without being drafted, as a demonstration of Christian commitment.

Keeney, William E. "New Opportunity for Dutch Draftees." *CanMenn* 15 (Mar. 28, 1967), 1. Report on a new law in the Netherlands enabling draftees to do alternate service in developing countries under certain conditions.

Kehler, Larry. "A Profile of Mennonite Personnel Involved in International Experience." *PCMCP Sixteenth,* 9-39. Held at Hesston, Kansas, 1967. Statistics of Mennonites in service work abroad includes discussion of international service experience as peacemaking.

Kehler, Peter. "Fourth Southeast Asia Reconciliation Work Camp." *GH* 61 (Oct. 15, 1968), 937-38. Describes and reflects on a work camp hosted by Taiwan Mennonites for the purpose of building international cooperation in peacemaking while working on some worthy service project.

Keim, Albert N. "Service or Resistance? The Mennonite Response to Conscription in World War II." *MQR* 52 (Apr., 1978), 141-55. Describes the development of an alternative service program during World War II, and stresses the degree to which such a plan was satisfactory to both nonresistant Mennonites and the Selective Service.

King, Frank. "I-W: Obligation or Opportunity." *YCC* 46 (Dec. 26, 1965), 8. Although I W service was entered into as an obligation, there were many rewarding experiences which turned it into an opportunity.

King, John C. "A Program of Church Expansion Through I-W." Paper presented to Practical Theology Seminar, Goshen College, Goshen, Ind., 1955. Pp. 92. MHL.

Klaassen, David. "Now Is the Time to Speak for Peace." *CanMenn* 15 (July 25, 1967), 1, 2. A Mennonite Brethren Christian Service worker discovers the element of peace in the gospel message which Christians have been called to proclaim. Discovery results in contention that nonresistance must be a way of life and a strategy in all situations; that social evils and peace are intimately related; that the total love strategy has much to do with civil rights and evangelism.

Kliewer, Marion W. "The Drafting of Conscientious Objectors." *Menn* 68 (Mar. 17, 1953). 165, 167. Discusses the present status of the I-W program and points to the peace witness given by the quality of work done by the I-W's.

Koehn, Dennis. "The Case for Alternative Service." In *Mennonites and Conscientious Objection in 1980.* See Topic 7.

Koontz, Ted. "Compulsory National Service or Voluntary Christian Service?" *Menn* 91 (May 18, 1976), 345-46. With the cancellation of proposed draft registration, Koontz analyzes the military's options for securing personnel, focusing on mandatory national service as more unjust than a volunteer army or a return to conscription.

Koop, Robert. "Canadian Military Recruitment: Coating the Bitter with the Sweet." *Lifework* 3 (1979), 14-15. Describes programs run by the Canadian government, such as the cadets, the militia, and a voluntary service program, as efforts aimed toward channeling young people into military participation by disguising the true military purpose of the programs.

Kraybill, Donald B. "Civil Religion vs. New Testament Christianity." *GH* 69 (May 11, 1976), 402-3. Kraybill draws distinctions between American civil religion, which uses religious language to legitimize national policies such as militarism, and New Testament Christianity, which follows the narrow way of Jesus.

Kreider, Alan, ed. "Thoughts from Conference Speakers." *IPF Notes* 6 (June, 1960), 3-10. Detailed summary of addresses on the topics of the Christian witness against militarism through politics, I-W program, and missions.

Kreider, Carl. "The Mennonite Central Committee Relief Training School Held at Goshen College." *ChrMon* 35 (Nov., 1943), 336-37. Development of the training program, negotiation with the Selective Service system, and final cancellation by Congress.

Kreider, Robert S. Letter to the Editor. *Menn* 93 (Jan. 10, 1978), 30. Maintains that Mennonite organizations such as Voluntary Service and Teachers Abroad Program were rooted in Mennonite theology of service, not in reaction to the military draft.

Kreider, Roy. "A Strategy of Witness in the Middle East." *GH* 62 (June 10, 1969), 519-20. "A demonstrated gospel blunts the attack against the gospel, shows the gospel to be superior love: through service projects, through the word of witness, through practical expressions of community."

Landis, Wilmer. "Service Frontiers in Agriculture Surpluses." *PCMCP Fourteenth,* 76-82. N.p. Held at Eastern Mennonite College, Harrisonburg, Virginia, June 6-7, 1963. Agriculture surpluses of produce and talent are available in Mennonite communities to respond to the many service frontiers both at home and abroad.

Lantz, Russell. "The Mennonite Peace Position and the Present Crisis." *Menn* 56 (Apr. 1, 1941), 7-8. Mennonites are committed, historically and biblically, to a program of peace. Today that means doing alternate service even if it becomes very costly for them.

Lapp, John A. (Review). *Letters of a CO from Prison,*

by Timothy W. L. Zimmer. The Judson Press, 1969. *GH* 63 (May 19, 1970), 460. Earlham College student imprisoned for refusing induction into the army or alternative service reflects on the topics of government, faith, revolution, protest, love. Recommended for its insight into the thinking of young American idealists.

Lapp, John E. "Expectations for the I-W Program." *MennLife* 13 (July, 1958), 108, 109, 117. The home and the church must find ways to prepare the youth for loyal and consistent peace witness in times of emergency.

Lapp, John E. "The Challenge of I-W Service." *GH* 55 (Mar. 6, 1962), 217-18. Those in alternative service are challenged to true discipleship, to a witness of love, and to represent Jesus Christ.

Lapp, John E. "The I-W Program and the Church." *GH* 50 (May 21, 1957), 481-82, 499. Cites ways in which I-W can be of real benefit to the church, especially by broadening the church's national and world perspective.

Lederach, James S. "A Case for Mandatory Public Service for Conscientious Objectors." *CGR* 2 (Spring, 1984), 139-48. Argues that nonregistration for the draft is not superior to registration and alternative service as a means to Christian obedience because nonregistration provides the state the same information as does registration—in fact, anything short of subversion similarly serves the state; and the rights that nonregistrants forfeit limit their capacity both to proclaim and to serve. Suggests a program involving longer terms and less pay for COs than military inductees for all persons of draft age; this would have the kind of moral force that nonregistration has as well as expand the benefits of traditional alternative service.

Lehman, David and Doris. "At Home in the City." *ChrLiv* 1 (July, 1954), 4-5, 36-37. Alternative service personnel form new community in Indianapolis, Indiana.

Loewen, Esko. "MCC in Europe Today." *Menn* 70 (Nov. 22, 1955), 728. MCC continues the peace witness via PAX, the Heerewegen Conference Center, the Puidoux conferences, and voluntary service projects.

Lohrenz, Gerhard. "The Beginning of Alternative Service During the Russo-Japanese War (1904-1905)." *MennLife* 26 (July, 1971), 114-16. A brief account of the service of Mennonites in Red Cross field hospitals during the war of 1904-1905 and the attitude their congregations took toward their effort.

Löwen, Kenneth. "The Draft Counselor System." *MennLife* 13 (July, 1958), 114-15. The Draft Counselor System "of providing information, counsel, and representation for I-O registrants has contributed immeasurably to the I-W service program."

"MCC." *RepConsS* 23 (Aug., 1966), 3, 4. Summarizes the work of MCC—focusing on PAX, Voluntary Service, and Teachers Abroad Program.

"MDS Discusses Motivation and Alternative Service." *CanMenn* 6 (Apr. 18, 1958), 1, 10. J. A. Toews, Wilbert Loewen, and Henry Poettcker address Manitoba representatives at the Winnipeg regional meeting of the Mennonite Disaster Service, on the opportunities for alternative service and disaster service.

"Mennonite I-W Group Visited by Ex-President Truman." *RepConsS* 15 (Apr., 1958), 1, 2. Describes the former president's commendation of alternative service project in which volunteers test palatability of various irradiated foods.

"Mennonite Questionnaire Reveals I-W Attitudes." *RepConsS* 12 (Dec., 1955), 4. J. S. Shultz, of Bluffton, has completed a survey of Mennonite and Brethren in Christ I-W persons and their attitudes toward the Civilian Work Program.

"Mennonites Discuss Alternative Service, Nonregistration." *RepConsS* 37 (June, 1980), 2, 4. Two-day conference results in statement asking the Mennonite Church to fully support both registration and nonregistration or noncooperation within its understanding of conscientious objection.

"Mennonites Expand Voluntary Service." *RepConsS* 6 (Nov., 1948), 1, 2. Reports MCC intentions to expand number and kinds of service projects as extension of belief in applied Christian love.

"Mennonites Lead in Alternate Service." *Fellowship* 30 (Nov., 1964), 12. According to a survey completed by the National Service Board of Religious Objectors, Mennonites had the largest total of men in draft age in alternative service of all major US denominations since 1951.

"Mennonites to Open Pa. State Park Project Soon." *RepConsS* 17 (Mar., 1960), 1, 4. New I-W project will develop recreation facilities as well as build models for flood control and conservation.

"Mission Board Speaks on the Peace Corps." *GH* 55 (Sept. 18, 1962), 825. Mennonites should be encouraged to serve through church-administered programs instead of through the Peace Corps.

Martens, Harry E. "Our Youth in Christian Service." *MennLife* 9 (Apr., 1954), 77-79, 96. Reflections on Mennonite peace and service witnesses through PAX and voluntary service.

Martin, Glenn. "The I-W and His Church." *MennLife* 13 (July, 1958), 118-20. I-W personnel provide the occasion for establishing witness centers and churches in urban communities.

Martin, John R. "The National Service Board for Religious Objectors." *RepConsS* 15 (Apr., 1958), 3, 4; (May-June, 1958), 3, 4. Outlines history and describes ongoing program of agency created by historic peace churches to serve as liaison between COs of any persuasion and the Selective Service System.

Martin, John R. and Roth, Willard E. "Peace, Not a Sword." *Builder* 14 (June, 1964), 17-18. A series of six ideas for youth programs designed to help young people grow in their understanding of Christian peace and acquire information about church service programs. Plans include texts, hymn selections, audiovisual resources, etc.

Martin, Luann Habegger. "National Service: Society's Cure or Threat?" *Menn* 91 (Nov. 2, 1976), 638-39. Examines Andrew Young's proposal for noncompulsory youth service, cautioning that it may be co-opted by the military, rather than serving as an alternative to it.

Martin, Luann Habegger. "The National Service Debate." *Forum* 10 (Jan., 1977), 6-8. A summary of a larger report which seeks to provide an in-depth analysis of the current interest in national service programs, reasons why people support or oppose such programs, and possible scenarios for national service.

Mennonite Brethren Church. "Report to the Committee of Reference and Counsel . . . in Relation to the Question of Non-combatant Service." *Yearbook of the 46th General Conference of the Mennonite Brethren Church of North America.* Hillsboro: M.B. Publishing House, 1954, 115-21. A report of intensive study of the issues and conversation with government authorities in Washington. Noncombatant service is to be rejected in favor of alternative service. The report was adopted.

Metzler, Edgar. "Another Alternative for Draft-Age Youth." *GH* 52 (Nov. 17, 1959), 977-78. Metzler offers the alternative of noncooperation with the Selective Service system as a clear and compelling witness of conscientious objection against a militaristic society.

Metzler, Edgar. "Conscription—Is the End in Sight?" *Menn* 79 (May 26, 1964), 342-44. In the context of growing pressures to end the draft, the church must expand its service program.

Metzler, Edgar. "Is Alternate Service a Witness for Peace." *GH* 55 (Dec. 11, 1962), 1060; "Editorial." *Menn* 78 (Apr. 2, 1963), 240. The connection between service and our peace witness has not been clearly seen. The I-W program is very often no peace witness at all but simply a government program administered by Selective Service.

Metzler, Edgar. "Selective Service Act." *GH* 57 (Mar. 17, 1964), 225. Reviews the act and then states that the youth and elders of the church ought to be ready to support VS without the prodding of Uncle Sam.

Metzler, James E. "Is I-W Service?" *YCC* 47 (June 19, 1966), 1. Looks at I-W service with critical eyes. Calls for better leadership, programs to help young people to choose to be an army of goodwill and peace.

Meyers, Willie. "Why I Left Vietnam." *ChrLiv* 15 (Aug., 1968), 6-7. International Voluntary Service worker left Vietnam in order to disassociate himself from the American military presence there.

Miller, Robert W. "What Is MCC Doing in Vietnam?" *ChrLead* 36 (July 10, 1973), 6; *MBH* 12 (Aug. 24, 1973), 17; "What Is Mennonite Central Committee Doing in Vietnam?" *GH* 66 (July 3, 1973), 538; *MennRep* 3 (July 9, 1973), 9.. From 1966-72, MCC was part of Vietnam Christian Service (VNCS), a joint effort of Church World Service, Lutheran World Relief, and MCC, but since Jan., 1973, MCC has been operating its own programs in cooperation with the national church and VNCS. These programs are described in this article.

Mueller, Peter (Review). *That There Be Peace,* by Lawrence Klippenstein. Winnipeg: The Manitoba C.O. Reunion Committee, 1979. Pp. 104. *MBH* 19 (Apr. 25, 1980), 28. Reviewer observes that this collection of memorabilia from Canadian conscientious objectors in alternative service during World War II reveals both courage and cowardice.

"No Alternative Service for CO's in Soviet Russia." *CanMenn* 4 (Apr. 27, 1956), 2. Russia does not wish to make martyrs out of CO's. Hence many are ignored, although some are imprisoned.

Naylor, Phyllis Reynolds. "To Continue Was to Condone." *With* 2 (Feb., 1969), 16. Discusses the resignation of Gene Stoltzfus from International Voluntary Service in Vietnam because he could no longer associate himself with American war policies.

Nelson, Boyd N. "Blame George." *GH* 61 (Jan. 9, 1968), 39. Responding to an article criticizing I-W workers for their lack of sacrifice and commitment, author challenges all Mennonites to separate themselves from the unjust affluence of American life, instead of depending on drafted men to make this witness.

Nelson, Boyd N. "New Look in I-W Services: Love, Peace, Nonresistance, or What." (Part 6) *GH* 53 (Mar. 29, 1960), 281-82. Until all our lives are filled daily with love the I-W program will be a mere mockery.

Nelson, Boyd N. "The Plus Side of Nonresistance." *ChrLiv* 5 (July, 1958), 3-5. Outlines the constructive service work done by people opposed to war.

Nelson, Boyd N. "The Responsibility of Pre-Draft Preparation." *MennLead* 13 (July, 1958), 110-13. Encourages individuals and congregations to help prepare Mennonite youth more adequately for the draft and I-W service.

Neufeld, Elmer. "Mennonite Disaster Service and Civil Defense." *CanMenn* 9 (June 9, 1961), 2. Mennonite Disaster Service is a more appropriate Mennonite response to urgent need than full fledged cooperation with the Civil Defense program.

Neufeld, Robert W. "Contribution of the Bethel Church, Inman, to the I-W Program." Student paper for Our Christian Heritage, Bethel College, Feb., 1959. Pp. 9. MLA/BeC.

Newcomer, Jackie. "Mennonites and Alternative Service." Research paper for Mennonite History and Thought class. 1982 Pp. 12. BfC.

Olsen, Victor. "Selective Service Reviews the I-W Program." *MennLife* 13 (July, 1958), 99-100, 105. Analyzes the successful efforts to mobilize for the CO work program of the Selective Service System those who for religious reasons cannot accept combatant or noncombatant.

Oral History Projects (Alternative Service, World War II) (Archival). Twenty-three oral interviews, cassette tape, not transcribed. CGCL.

Penner, Lydia. "Never Made to Kill Each Other, Says Bishop." *MBH* 15 (Oct. 29, 1976), 15. Ontario bishop who was a CO in World War I negotiated with Canadian government in setting up alternative service during World War II.

Peters, Frank C. "Non-combatant Service Then and Now." *MennLife* 10 (Jan., 1955), 31-35. Development of the alternative service program among Mennonites in Russia.

Peters, Virgil. "The Denver I-W Story." Student paper for Mennonite History, Nov. 18, 1957. Pp. 23. MLA/BeC.

Preheim, Gayle O. "Letter from Vietnam."

*RepConsS* 25 (Feb., 1968), 3, 4. In a letter to his parents, an alternative service worker in Vietnam reflects upon his work and the war with which he lives.

Preheim, Vern. "Mennonite Churches and Returning Service Volunteers." *GH* 65 (Feb. 22, 1972), 177. Service volunteers encounter difficulty upon reentry; they can be helped and they can also make meaningful contributions for further church extension and growth.

"Questions on Alternative Service." *CanMenn* 10 (Nov. 16, 1962), 7, 11. Can I-W be considered a witness for peace?

"Resolutions and Decisions of Conference." *Menn* 65 (Sept. 12, 1950), 608-609. GCMC vigorously reaffirms 1941 peace statement regarding reconciliation and war. Encourages expansion of VS program and cooperation with other Christian peace movements.

(Review). *That There Be Peace,* ed. Lawrence Klippenstein. Manitoba CO Reunion Committee, 1979. *MCC PS Newsletter* 10 (June-July, 1980), 9. The book reports on the alternative service activities of Canadian Mennonite conscientious objectors during World War II.

(Review). *The Mennonite Church in the Second World War,* by Guy F. Hershberger. Scottdale: Mennonite Publishing House, 1951. Pp. 308. *Fellowship* 18 (Nov., 1952), 28. This book is "not only an account of the direct relation of the church to the war, but includes as well chapters on missions, education, relief, voluntary service, and intergroup relations both within and without the Mennonite family."

Reimer, Otto B. "The I-W Program of the Pacific District Conference of the Mennonite Brethren." 1981. Pp. 9. MBBS.

Roth, Willard E., ed. *Is There a Middle Road?* Scottdale: Herald Press, 1964. Pp. 15. Peacemaker Pamphlet No. 5. Bob Baker describes his experience in noncombatant service during World War II to show that such service is not an acceptable alternative to either military duty or a rejection of military duty if one wants to follow Christ's way of love.

Royer, Howard E. "Life Was Good for This Boy." *GH* 64 (Oct. 12, 1971), 848-49. By permission of *Brethren Messenger.* Tribute to a 25-year-old Brethren Voluntary Service worker in Vietnam who refused to participate in war and died a victim of war.

"Six Diener Brothers in Alternative Service." *RepConsS* 5 (Apr., 1947), 5. Six of Amanda and Harry A. Diener's seven sons, all members of the Mennonite Church near Hutchinson, Kan., have been involved with alternative service.

"Stresses Alternative Service as Positive Peace Program." *CanMenn* 2 (Mar. 12, 1954), 2, 3. Erland Waltner addresses the Ontario General Conference Churches. Peace is not human doctrine but is God's. Christian nonresistant love begins in the home and carries over to one's relationships with neighbors, employers, and fellow workers.

Schmidt, H. B. "Mennonites and Alternative Service." *MennLife* 13 (July, 1958), 101-103. An historical account of the steps taken to develop an alternative service program in the US.

Schultz, J. S. *Report of the I-W Program; Evaluation Study of Mennonite and Brethren in Christ I-W Men.* [Akron, Pa.: MCC], 1955. Pp. 72. MHL. Summarizes 1,794 responses to questionnaire administered to 2,847 I-W men. Includes such topics as the I-W work program, I-W personnel's reactions to the program, the church and I-W service, the CO position, the I-W off duty, and the I-W before and after service.

Service Ministries. "Voluntary Service, Its Meaning and Its Ministry." *EV* 83 (Dec. 25, 1970), 10. Voluntary Service is the rediscovery of a "very basic principle—that the Gospel must be propagated by every type of human personality."

Shank, J. Ward. "Issues the Church Faces in Conference and College." *ST* 33 (2nd Qtr., 1965), 26. One of the issues noted is the crisis in service. Interest in social service leads almost invariably into demands for social action, going from forms of actual service into messianic pursuit of social reform.

Shank, J. Ward. "More Social Service." *ST* 25 (2nd Qtr., 1957), 2. Although the church is not unconcerned with the needs of society, it should realize that social gospel and social service represents only a partial gospel.

Shank, J. Ward (Editorial). "Amnesty and Indemnity." *ST* 41 (Nov., 1973), 7. Questions the right of alternative service workers to veteran's benefits, and thus to amnesty as well.

Shank, J. Ward (Editorial). "What Is Social Action?" *ST* 37 (May, 1969), 3. Social action translates Christian benevolence or social service into militancy, or into a movement for reform. The problem with social action is that it is so far removed from the heart of the gospel.

Shantz, Gordon. "Postwar Plans." *YCC* 26 (Feb. 18, 1945), 447, 448. The church will have to be cautious in its postwar plans in the areas of social service and relief work.

Shenk, Phil M. "The Power and Penalty of Moral Dissent." *Sojourners* 9 (July, 1980), 10. Reviews the approved Selective Service draft registration program and the possibilities and penalties of noncooperation.

Sherk, J. Harold. "ASW—Past and Future." N.d. Pp. 4. Conscientious Objectors—Canada; Alternative Service Work. MLA/BeC.

Sherk, J. Harold. "The Alternative Service Law and Its Operation." *MennLife* 13 (July, 1958), 103-105. An explanation of the Universal Military Training Act of 1951 and the place of NSBRO in relation to its operation.

Sherk, J. Harold. "Viet-nam War Protesters." *RepConsS* 24 (Nov., 1967), 1. Reports on various forms of protest against the war including a letter to President Johnson from Gene Stoltzfus and other International Voluntary Service workers in Vietnam.

Smucker, Donovan E. "Mennonite Service Projects in Time of War and Peace." *PCMCP First*, 67-74. North Newton, Kansas: The Bethel College Press. Held at Winona Lake, Indiana, Aug. 7-8, 1942. Service projects do not refer to the traditional mutual aid activities among Mennonite communities, but refer to the works of mercy and service done for non-Mennonite, non-historic peace church, and possibly even non-Christian people. Doctrines of separation and nonconformity must be examined in light of the needs.

Smucker, Donovan E., ed. *The Sociology of Canadian Mennonites, Hutterites and Amish: A Bibliography with Annotations.* Waterloo, Ont.: Wilfried Laurier University Press, 1977. Pp. 232. Subject index includes: alternative service, church and state, conflict, draft-conscription, government, National Socialism, peace, race, war.

Smucker, Donovan E. and Smucker, Barbara Claassen. *A Catechism of Peace in a World at War with a Casebook in Non-violence.* Philadelphia: American Friends Service Committee, n.d. Pp. 24. Presents theses on the evil of war and discusses the role of work camps in modeling peaceful social structures. Reprints case studies in nonviolence, with bibliography.

Storms, Paul L. "Forest Service in British Columbia Service Work Camps." *ChrMon* 35, Part 1, (Oct., 1943), 306-7, 320; Part 2, (Nov., 1943), 334-35. Description of life in the Canadian Alternative Service work camps for conscientious objectors.

Stucky, Peter. "Survey of Attitudes Held by I-W Fellows Toward the Witness Value of I-W Service." Paper for War, Peace, and Revolution class, AMBS, Elkhart, Ind., May 8, 1969. Pp. 3. AMBS.

Studer, Gerald C. Letter to the Editor. *GH* 63 (Aug. 25, 1970), 706-707. Expresses regret that the Mennonite Church approved paying jobs in I-W assignments as alternative service, instead of remaining with nonsalaried PAX or VS work. Supports all forms of draft resistance as valid witnesses to the state.

Swarr, Paul. "I-W Men on the Battle Front." *YCC* 37 (July 22, 1956), 234, 240. I-W's are a vital part of the church's mission program.

Swartzentruber, Dorothy. "The Witness of Voluntary Service." *CanMenn* 3 (Jan. 21, 1955), 2, 4. A discussion of the witness of VS in Europe since its beginning in 1948.

"The Church and Selective Service." *Menn* 84 (Oct. 28, 1969), 646. Mennonites support both noncooperation with Selective Service and established alternative service programs as possible and appropriate expressions of their peace witness, says resolution adopted by the Western District Conference (GCMC) on Oct. 11, 1969.

"The Mennonite Civilian Service Program." *GH* 33 (Jan. 9, 1941), 867, 879. A description of the history and functioning of Civilian Service and the MCC Peace Committee.

"The Position of the Mennonite Church of North America on Peace, War, Military Service, and Patriotism." *Menn* 63 (Oct. 12, 1948), 5-6. The official statement of the GCMC on this subject. Appeals to the biblical basis for love and nonviolence. While refusing military service, Mennonites have shown genuine willingness to render service of national importance in alternative programs.

"The Recollections of A. P." *MennMirr* 8, Part 1, "A Look at a Way of Life that Ended Forever," (Feb., 1979), 9-10; Part 2, "Waiting to Leave as Chaos Follows Chaos," (Mar., 1979), 16-18. Excerpts from the journal of an anonymous Russian Mennonite. Includes accounts of experiences in alternative service during World War I and the Russian Revolution.

Talbott, Basil, Jr. "They Also Serve." *YCC* 47 (Jan. 16, 1966), 8. A reporter talked with an Illinois I-W and other pacifists enrolled in the alternative service program in the Chicago area.

The Reporter, extracted. "Russian CO Reports Alternate Service Still Possible in USSR." *ChrLiv* 3 (Sept., 1956), 11. Review of the status of alternate service in USSR since late 1800s.

Toews, J. B. *et al.* "Questions on Our Nonresistant Witness." *ChrLead* 26 (Oct. 29, 1963), 4-5. Our youth have only two alternatives: service in the army, with combatant and noncombatant service both a part of the war effort; or alternate service under civilian direction.

"University Students Call for Peace Efforts." *CanMenn* 3 (Mar. 11, 1955), 1, 7. Winnipeg university and college students pass resolutions at peace conference calling for greater dissemination of peace literature and preparatory work for satisfactory alternative service in the event of war.

"US Supreme Court Denies Veterans Benefits for CO's." *Forum* A (Apr., 1974), 9. In a recent decision, the US Supreme Court ruled that a conscientious objector who served two years of alternate service is not eligible for veterans' educational benefits.

Unruh, Wilfred J. "An Evaluation of Mennonite Service Programs." *PCMCP Sixteenth,* 143-59. N.p. Held at Hesston College, Hesston, Kansas, June 8-9, 1967. An examination of the philosophy, history, and empirical data of the service programs. The conclusion includes the statement that conscription is probably the single most significant influence in service programs.

"Vietnam Voice: Go Home and Leave Us Alone." *Menn* 85 (June 9, 1970), 388-90. Why most of the fifty foreign voluntary agencies working in South Vietnam do more harm than good.

"What You Do for Church You Do for the Government." *CanMenn* 5 (Sept. 13, 1957), 3. Those in I-W are hailed as serving their government by a Washington official.

Weaver, Henry, Jr. "The I-W Program as Present Day Urban Witness." *PCMCP Tenth,* 45-52. N.p. Held at Mennonite Biblical Seminary, Chicago, Illinois, June 16-17, 1955. Majority of Mennonite I-W men are unprepared for the urban setting in which they are placed. The I-W program offers significant witness in the form of honest careful work and new possibilities for the Mennonite church to understand and respond to the urban setting.

Weaver, John W. "A I-W Looks at the I-W Program." *ChrLiv* 1 (July, 1954), 2. I-W service provides opportunities for showing Christian love, or for mismanaging money and leisure time.

Wenger, Warren M. "Peace—The Vine or the Grape?" *GH* 63 (Jan. 20, 1970), 60-62. While the question of how Mennonites with a peace position rooted in love for the enemy should relate to the popular peace movement is an important one, Mennonites should be giving greater attention to providing adequate structures for conscientious objectors in I-W service.

Wiebe, Rudy H. "Conscription for Military Service." *MBH* 1 (May 11, 1962), 4. The MB Youth Service Program is a most significant witness as an alternative to military service.

Wiggers, Arverd. *History and Report of the 1-W Program of the Church of God in Christ (Mennonite): Covering Nearly Ten Years of Activity from the Fall of 1950-July 1, 1960.* Galva, Ks.: Christian Public Service, Inc., [1960?] Pp. 112. MHL. In addition to summary statement of the work of various units, the report addresses such topics as the relationship with MCC, spirituality in the units, improving our peace witness, etc.

Yake, C. F. "That Trailing Shadow." *YCC* 35 (July 11, 1954), 220. A call for responsible living by the people who are in I-W service.

Yoder, Carroll. "Why Couldn't 'Bontrag' Stay for Always?" *RepConsS* 23 (Feb., 1966), 2, 4. Wilbur Bontrager, an alternative service person from Alden, NY, is building human relations as well as a church and school in the Congo (Zaire).

Yoder, Edward and Smucker, Donovan. *The Christian and Conscription. An Inquiry Designed as a Preface to Action.* Akron: MCC, 1945. Pp. 124. An evaluation of the alternative service experience in World War II and a guide to witness against conscription.

Yoder, Roy. "A Way to Serve." *GH* 63 (Aug. 4, 1970), 646-47. Compares the structures of the Voluntary Service and the Civilian Peace Service programs, encouraging volunteers to enter Voluntary Service because it is integrated with local congregations.

Zook, J. Kore. "Peace and War: A Letter to I-W Men." *GH* 46 (June 16, 1953), 569. I-W personnel have a great responsibility to uphold the Mennonite peace witness.

Zook, Mervin D. "Measurement of Attitudes Toward Religious Conscientious Objectors in Selected Magazines of World War II Years by Evaluative Assertion." MA in Journalism thesis, Indiana University, May, 1969. Pp. 114. BfC., MHL. Concludes that religious magazines treated COs slightly more favorably than nonreligious ones; letters to the editor tended to disagree with favorable view of COs presented in secular magazines but in the religious magazines, which also presented a favorable view of COs, the letters to the editor tended to be supportive; generally the COs choosing noncombatant service were rated higher than those choosing alternative service.

# B. Civilian Public Service

*A Civilian Public Service in the Caribbean* Elgin: Brethren Service Committee, [1945]. Pp. 15. MHL. Includes description of La Plata project sponsored by MCC in Puerto Rico.

*A Year of Civilian Public Service.* Akron, Pa.: Mennonite Central Committee, 1942. Pp. 8. MHL. Pamphlet reviews history of CPS, gives CPS statistics, explains educational and religious life programs, and answers questions about CPS.

A Sister. "My Brother Comes Home from Camp." *ChrMon* 36 (Sept., 1944), 258. Describes the ideological differences among the men in CPS camps and the challenge this presented to Mennonite youth.

Albrecht, Paul. "Civilian Public Service Evaluated By Civilian Public Service Men." *MQR* 22 (Jan., 1948), 5-18. Report of an official study of the CPS experience, together with tables and interpretation.

Albrecht, Paul, *et al.* "On Sequoia Trails." Yearbook of CPS Unit No. 107, Three Rivers, Cal., Nov., 1945. Pp. 56. MHL.

*

Ames, Winslow. "Thoughts of an Outsider on Mennonite Civilian Public Service." *MennLife* 3

(Apr., 1948), 41-42. Non-Mennonite CPS worker comments on aspects of Mennonite culture seen in camp and criticizes peace churches for aiding in conscription through administering CPS.

Baer, Willard A.; Bohrer, Albert E.; Freeyenberger, Arthur; and Friesen, Wilber D. "Our Civilian Public Service Camps—Camp Number 35, North Fork, California." *YCC* 24 (Mar. 7, 1943), 491. Description of CPS Camp No. 35 in North Fork, California.

Bainton, Roland H. "The Churches and War: Historic Attitudes Toward Christian Participation." *Social Action* 11 (Jan. 15, 1945), 5-71. Reviews the three positions of pacifism, just war, and crusade from the first through the twentieth centuries, including World War II. Examines especially 20th-century attitudes. Refers to Anabaptist views in the Reformation, as well as the treatment of conscientious objectors and Civilian Public Service.

Bartel, Roland. "Glimpses of Our Civilian Public Service Camps—The Colorado Springs Camp, Colorado." *YCC* 23 (Feb. 8, 1942), 43. Description of the Colorado Springs CPS Camp.

Bartel, Roland. "Hookworm Control at Crestview,

---

*For additional listing, see Supplement, pp. 717-719.

Florida." *CPS Bull* 1 (Sept. 25, 1942), 1-2. Describes the CPS camp's health promotion work in building privies, digging wells, and screening houses.

Becker, Jeff. "Some Causes for Public Tolerance of Conscientious Objectors in Civilian Public Service." Social Science Seminar paper, Dec., 1980. Pp. 87. MLA/BeC.

Beechy, Atlee. "The Civilian Public Service Experience." *GH* 68 (Dec. 9, 1975), 878-79. Beechy recounts personal remembrances of his CPS work during World War II in the US

Bender, Harold S. *Mennonite Origins in Europe.* Akron: MCC, 1942. Pp. 72. First of a series of six studies published under the title *Mennonites and Their Heritage* for use in Civilian Public Service camps during World War II.

Bender, Harold S. "Support of Dependents of Drafted Men: In the Midst of War—Thoughts for Nonresistants," (Part 9). *GH* 35 (Apr. 8, 1943), 42-43. If the need arises, the whole church should help support dependents of drafted men who are in CPS, according to Scriptural principle and the traditional practice of the Mennonite church.

Bender, Paul. "Cooperative Testing Program of Mennonite Colleges and Civilian Public Service." *PCMCP Fourth,* 27-34. North Newton, Kansas. Held at Bluffton, Ohio, Aug. 24-25, 1945. A survey of the issues and problems related to granting academic credit for certain formal educational courses in the CPS camps.

Benner, Norman. "Our Civilian Public Service Camps—The Camp on the Skyline Drive." *YCC* 24 (June 20, 1943), 615. Description of CPS Camp No. 45 at Luray, Va. One of the largest and most commodious of the camps administered by Mennonite Central Committee.

Blosser, Howard R. "CPS Men, Human Guinea Pigs at University of Illinois." *YCC* 25 (June 4, 1944), 181. Description of a "Guinea Pig Project" using CPS men for a study of the relations between heat, diet, and work.

Braden, Murray, "'Fire on the Mountain.' " *ChrLiv* 12 (April, 1965), 22-24. Reprinted from *Smoke Jumper,* publication of the Missoula, Montana, CPS unit. Conscientious objectors in Civilian Public Service worked as smoke jumpers for forest fires.

Brenneman, Paul, ed. "Ypsi." Yearbook of CPS Unit No. 90, Ypsilanti, Mich., Mar., 1946. Pp. [64.] MHL, MSHL.

Brubaker, Henry G. "Assimilation of GI and CPS Men on the Campuses of Mennonite and Affiliated Colleges." *PCMCP Fifth,* 19-23. Berne, Indiana: The Berne Witness. Held at Freeman, South Dakota, Aug. 27-28, 1946. The assimilation process of GI and CPS men into the collegiate setting must be understood in light of the equal division of men (among General Conference Mennonites) choosing CPS and non-combatant military service. Also the maturity level and the variety of experiences shared by these men must be noted.

"Civilian Public Service Camps—Camp Number 55, Belton, Montana." *YCC* 24 (May 9, 1943), 567. Description of CPS Camp No. 55 at Belton, Mont.

"CPS Evaluation." *RepConsS* 5 (Oct., 1946), 1, 3, 4. Summarizes and excerpts Albert M. Gaeddert's analysis of what the Mennonite church has learned from CPS, an analysis previously published in *MennLife.*

Claassen, Arnold. "Our Civilian Public Service Camps—Camino California." *YCC* 24 (Jan. 31, 1943), 453. Description of the Camino CPS camp in California.

Curry, A. Stauffer. "Church and State." *YCC* 35 (Oct. 31, 1954), 350. Examines some of the criticisms of the CPS program as it relates to the separation of church and state.

"Demobilization." *RepConsS* 3 (Dec 1, 1944), 1, 2; (Jan. 15, 1945), 7, 8. Describes MCC plans to offer CPS personnel educational, vocational, and financial counseling as part of the demobilization process.

Derstine, C. F. "Canadian Civilian 'Conchies' Camp." *YCC* 22 (Dec. 7, 1941), 801. A description of the Canadian Civilian Camps. The Canadian federal government arranged camps "for service of public value to the nation."

Derstine, C. F. "CO's Serving in Mental Hospitals and Life's Most Dangerous Age." *ChrMon* 36 (July, 1944), 222-23. Mennonite interest in mental health has been stimulated by the CPS work in mental hospitals

Derstine, C. F. "From Civilian Conservation Corps to Conscientious Objector Camps." *ChrMon* 36 (Aug., 1944), 253-55. Development of the Depression-time Civilian Conservation Corps and its service as the model for the later CPS program.

Derstine, C. F. "Mennonite Ex-CPS Men Serve in Sixteen Nations." *ChrMon* 39 (Aug., 1947), 255-56. The MCC post-war relief programs have their roots in the Civilian Public Service program.

Derstine, C. F. "One Hundred and Eighteen

Affiliations." *ChrMon* 36 (Feb., 1944), 62-63. Complete listing of the denominations represented in CPS camps, and the implications for witness and camp life.

Derstine, C. F. "Postwar Readjustments." *ChrMon* 38 (June, 1946), 190-91. Those returning from CPS camps will have learnings to offer their home communities.

Dester, Marvin. "The Story of Civilian Public Service Camp No. 64." Student paper for Our Christian Heritage, n.d. Pp. 21. MLA/BeC.

Dick, Mildred. "A Survey of Mennonite Civilian Public Service Camps." Student paper for Constructive English, Feb. 18, 1944. Pp. 24. MLA/BeC.

*Directory of Civilian Public Service.* Washington, DC: National Service Board for Religious Objectors, 1947. Pp. 170. Covers the period May, 1941 to March, 1947 and includes camps, agencies, denominations, and all the drafted men involved in CPS.

Dyck, Peter J. "Our Peace Witness in Relation to Government." Revised from an address given at a Peace Conference, Eden Church, Moundridge, Kansas, June 17, 1956. Pp. 8. MLA/BeC., MHL.

Dyck, Walter H. "The Mutual Responsibility of the Church and Returning Service Men." *Menn* 60 (Nov. 13, 1945), 5-7. A survey of CPS and military servicemen, and others. Centers around the problem of re integrating servicemen into the congregations. There is a wide divergence of opinion as to the attitude of the Mennonite church toward those who chose military service.

Eby, Sarah Ann. "In Tribute to Orie Miller." *ChrLead* 40 (Feb., 1977), 16. Tribute includes Miller's commitment to peace and responses initiated like the CPS program.

Ediger, Elmer. "Do CPS Men Favor a Voluntary Service Program for Peacetime?" *CPS Bull* 4 (Oct. 22, 1945), 1-2. Discusses reasons the CPS experience is a beneficial one and raises questions about the shape of a possible voluntary service program.

Ehresman, Roy and Holdeman, Menno. "Glimpses of Our Mennonite Civilian Public Service Camps—Camp Henry, Illinois." *YCC* 23 (June 28, 1942), 206. Description of the Camp Henry, Illinois, CPS camp.

Erb, Paul. "Looking Forward in CPS." *GH* 39 (Sept. 3, 1946), 483. If there is a peacetime draft, Mennonites should continue to operate CPS camps. The camps should be structured to protect the participants from worldly influences and to offer maximum opportunities

to witness to the Christian way.

Frazer, Heather T. and O'Sullivan, John. "Forgotten Women of World War II: Wives of Conscientious Objectors in Civilian Public Service." *Peace and Change* 5 (Fall, 1978), 46-51. Documents the injustice of the CPS system in the absence of government pay or benefits granted to other enlisted men. Focuses especially on the economic and emotional plight of wives of CPS workers.

French, Paul Comly. *Civilian Public Service.* Washington, DC: National Service Board for Conscientious Objectors, 1942. Pp. 21. MHL. Explains, on the basis of the historical development of the CPS program and on theoretical/philosophical grounds, why religious pacifists assumed the financial responsibility for the operation of the CPS camps when legalistic logic would dictate that this responsibility belonged properly to the US government. Includes references to Mennonites, historic peace churches, etc.

Fretz, J. Winfield. "Our Peace Witness During World War II." *The Power of Love; A Study Manual Adopted for Sunday School Use and for Group Discussion,* pp. 58-96. Ed. Peace Committee of the General Conference Mennonite Church. Newton: Board of Publication, 1947. MHL. Discusses the history and operation of the CPS program, the point of view of those Mennonites who entered military service as chaplains, etc., and the witness of the noncombatants. Concludes that the CPS program was the choice most consistent with Mennonite belief and practice and that the program was an effective witness for peace to the nation, to the community, and to the Mennonite churches.

Fretz, J. Winfield. "Postwar Needs of Civilian Public Service Men." *ChrMon* 36 (June, 1944), 179-80. Findings of an MCC survey of CPS personnel deals largely with financial needs.

Fretz, J. Winfield. "Survey Men's Post-War Interests and Needs." *CPS Bull* 2 (Mar. 8, 1944), 3-4. Preliminary findings of the needs of CPS men after the war.

Gaeddert, Albert M. "What Have We Learned from Civilian Public Service?" *MennLife* 1 (July, 1946), 16-20. An evaluation of the CPS experience in relation to the individual participants, the church, society, and the Anabaptist heritage.

Gascho, Milton (Review). *The Story of the Amish in Civilian Public Service,* ed. David Wagler and Roman Raber. n.p., 1945. Pp. 140. *MHB* 13 (Apr., 1952), 4. Contains: anecdotes of CPS life from Amish CPS workers; opinions from periodicals on the CPS program; and a directory of the Amish in CPS. Reviewer gives favorable recommendation.

Gingerich, David. "The Reform Movement in Civilian Public Service, 1941-1947." Paper presented to Social Science Seminar, Goshen College, Goshen, Ind., May, 1977. Pp. 64. MHL.

Gingerich, Melvin. "Conserving Nature's Resources; Christian Youth and the State." *YCC* 22, Part 7, (Apr. 13, 1941), 530. Explores the question "what should be the attitude of Christian youth towards nature's gift to humankind?" CPS camps provide an opportunity to work at conserving rather than exploiting.

Gingerich, Melvin. *Service for Peace.* Akron: MCC, 1949. Pp. 508. The standard history of Mennonite Civilian Public Service during World War II.

Gingerich, Melvin. "The Life of Simplicity; Christian Youth and the State." *YCC* 23, Part 17, (Jan. 11, 1942), 10. Quality of life in a nation goes down during a war economy. There is a relationship between simple living and response to CPS.

Gingerich, Melvin. "The Use of Leisure Time in Mennonite Communities." *PCMCP Fourth,* 147-62. Held at Bluffton, Ohio, 1945. The Civilian Public Service program takes the lead in developing an interest in hobbies, crafts, and recreation.

Gingerich, Melvin (Archival). Box 18—Peace Committees: General Conference Mennonite, 1935-48; MCC, 1944-48; CPS history, 1938-49. Box 20—Peace Deputation trips. Box 39—Draft; Committee on Armed Service hearing, 1959. Box 40—Civilian Public Service. Box 51—Civil Defense; communism; Congressional Record (debate on universal military training), Feb. 5, 1959; conscientious objectors; Japan Anti-A & H Bomb Conference; Japan and peace. Box 52—peace clippings; peace conferences; Peace Problems Committee reports Puidoux Theological Conference. Box 53—peace and Mennonites. Box 62—"The Christian and Revolution;" church-state relations; communism. Box 64—"Nonresistance and Social Justice;" Peace Institutes; Peace/War. Box 91—Service for Peace; CPS history and correspondence. Goshen, Ind., AMC Hist. Mss. 1-129.

Glass, Esther Eby. "'We Had to Grow Up.'" *ChrLiv* 9 (Apr., 1962), 6-7, 39. Wives of conscientious objectors in CPS share their reflections.

Goering, Jacob D. "Soil Conservation Work at Camp Denison." *CPS Bull* 1 (Nov. 14, 1942), 1-2. CPS men at Camp Denison, Iowa, conserve soil

as a constructive method of serving their country.

Goering, Mrs. Jacob D. "Northfork Cooking School." *ChrMon* 37 (June, 1945), 142. Description of the two-month long cooking school for CPS camp cooks.

Guengerich, Paul. "Our Civilian Public Service Camps—Poudre Canyon Camp at Fort Collins, Colorado." *YCC* 24 (July 25, 1943), 654. Description of Poudre Canyon CPS Camp at Fort Collins.

Hamm, Alfred. "Chosen for Service." Short story about CPS written for Mennonite History, 1960. Pp. 24. MLA/BeC.

Harmon, Wendell E. "Glimpses of Our CPS Camps—The Cascade Locks, Oregon, Camp." *YCC* 23, Part 1, (Oct. 4, 1942), 315; Part 2, *YCC* 23 (Oct. 18, 1942), 325. Description of the Cascade Locks, Ore., CPS camp.

Hartzler, R. L. Letter to the Editor. *Menn* 92 (July 12, 1977), 446. Commends General Lewis Hershey for his wise attitude toward conscientious objection in World War II, showing respect for the Civilian Public Service program and after the war reversing the ban on CO's going overseas, thus making possible the Mennonite contribution to European reconstruction.

Hernley, Elizabeth (Mrs. H. Ralph), "Appetites, Rationing, and Camp Dietitians." *ChrMon* 35 (Aug., 1943), 238-39. CPS camp dietitian describes the food budgeting and preparation aspects of camp life.

Hershberger, Guy F. *Christian Relationships to State and Community.* No. 5 in the *Mennonites and Their Heritage* series. Akron: MCC, 1942. Pp. 108. A study guide prepared for use in Civilian Public Service Camps, with special emphasis on church and state relations.

Hershberger, Guy F. "CPS Guinea Pig Projects Commended." *GH* (Oct. 15, 1946), 639. The CPS guinea pig project conducted at the University of Minnesota beginning in 1943 receives a commendation in the July 15, 1946, Congregational Record.

Hershberger, Guy F. "Questions Raised Concerning the Work of the Committee on Peace and Social Concerns (of the Mennonite Church) and Its Predecessors." Mimeographed, 1967. Goshen: MHL. Summary review of questions raised concerning the work of the CPSC and its predecessors, particularly concerning witness to other Christians, to the state, and to society, with respect to peace and the social implications of the gospel, and concerning inter-Mennonite and inter-denominational cooperation in carrying on this work, 1925-66.

Hershberger, Guy F. "The Mennonite Community: A Syllabus." A course in the Farm and Community School, CPS Camp No. 138, Unit 2, Malcolm, Neb., 1945. Mimeographed. Goshen: MHL. A bibliography of readings sectioned into units exploring various facets of the Mennonite community.

Hiebert, P. C. *Life and Service in the Kingdom of God.* No. 6 in *Mennonites and Their Heritage.* Akron: MCC, 1942. Prepared for use in CPS camps, this study manual emphasizes how all of life is to be a peace witness in kingdom service.

Hirsch, Charles B. "The Civilian Public Service Camp Program in Indiana." *Indiana Magazine of History* 46 (1950), 259-81. CPS program in Indiana, with all its inadequacies, was a distinct imporvement over World War I treatment of COs. Innovations included the recognition of COs of all faiths and an alternative program of military service.

Holsinger, Justus G. *Serving Rural Puerto Rico. A History of Eight Years of Service by the Mennonite Church.* Scottdale, Pa.: Mennonite Publishing House, 1952. Pp. 232. Photographs and text relate the story of the service rendered by the La Plata Mennonite Project in Puerto Rico which originated as a CPS alternative to military service.

Horst, Amos S. "Our Testimony Through the CPS Program." *GH Supplement* 35 (Feb., 1943), 1018-19. The testimony given by those in CPS camps is a testimony against war, to our nonresistant faith, and to Christ as example.

Horst, Irvin B. "Edward Yoder—A Tribute from Civilian Public Service." *GH Supplement* 38 (Aug., 1945), 407. Yoder's thought and writings were much appreciated by those in CPS camps during World War II; his book, *Our Mennonite Heritage,* brought inspiration and challenge to many.

Horst, Irvin B. "Glimpses of Our Mennonite Civilian Public Service Camps—The Grottoes, Virginia, Camp." *YCC* 23 (Jan. 4, 1942), 3, 5, 6. Description of the Grottoes CPS Camp.

Horst, John L. "Maintaining Our Peace Testimony." *ChrMon* 34 (June, 1942), 169. As the size of the army and CPS camps increases, Mennonites should stand firm in their nonresistant witness.

Horst, John L. (Editorial). "Civilian Public Service a Reality." *ChrMon* 33 (June, 1941), 169. Comments on the opening of CPS camps for conscientious objectors.

Hostetler, John Andrew. "The Christian Challenge to Peace." *GH* 38 (Aug. 31, 1945), 412-13. Peace and salvation are inseparable. The CPS program offers an opportunity for true peace testimony to those whose lives are filled with the Spirit of Christ.

Hostetler, John Andrew. "The Peace Challenge of Civilian Public Service." *ChrMon* 37 (Sept., 1945), 230. The CPS program attempts to communicate to society that the personal experience of peace with God affects one's response to war.

Hostetler, Mervin J. "A Time to Remember: Civilian Public Service." *ChrLiv* 18 (May, 1971), 7-9. Impressions of years spent in CPS in World War II, and of the rejection faced as a conscientious objector after the war.

Hunsberger, Willard. *The Franconia Mennonites and War.* Scottdale: Peace and Industrial Relations Committee of Franconia Mennonite Conference, 1951. After briefly surveying the experience of the Franconia Mennonites with the earlier American wars, their experience with World War II is discussed more fully. Some of the topics considered are community reactions to conscientious objectors, a typical day in a CPS camp, the activities of the church during and after the war.

Jacob, Philip E. Letter to the Editor. *Fellowship* 12 (Oct., 1946), 171. Writes about the involvement of the historic peace churches in the origins and development of CPS.

Jost, Arthur. "Editorially Speaking . . . ." *CPS Bull Supp* 5 (Oct. 31, 1946), 1, 3. Proposes guidelines for a voluntary service program as a peacetime outgrowth of the Civilian Public Service program.

Jost, Arthur. "Mennonite Ex-CPS Men Serve in Sixteen Nations." *RepConsS* 5 (Mar., 1947), 1, 4, 5. One-third of current MCC relief workers have experience with CPS.

Kauffman, Roland. "A General Survey of the Soil Conservation-Directed Civilian Public Service Camps in Colorado." Paper presented to History Seminar, Goshen College, Goshen, Ind., Mar. 18, 1976. Pp. 51. MHL.

Kaufman, Abraham. Letter to the Editor. *Fellowship* 12 (Nov., 1946), 186. Points out the error in Philip Jacob's statement (*Fellowship* [Oct., 1946]), that the historic peace churches were urged by the War Resisters League to undertake administration of alternative service projects.

Kaufman, Jerome. "The Work of Our CPS Boys." Student paper for Our Christian Heritage, Feb., 1959. Pp. 12. MLA/BeC.

Kaufman, Velora. "National Importance of Civilian Public Service." Student paper for Church of Our Fathers, 1952. Pp. 5. MLA/BeC.

Keim, Albert N. "The Legacy of Civilian Public Service." *GH* 72 (Aug. 7, 1979), 612-13. With the possibility of military conscription emerging again, the CPS program is presented as a frame of reference for developing a Mennonite response to the present issue.

Keys, Ancel, et.al. *The Biology of Human Starvation*, 2 vols. Minneapolis: University of Minnesota Press, 1950. Pp. 1385. Textbook incorporating data gathered from experiments conducted on a University of Minnesota CPS unit.

Kirchhofer, Delvin. "Glimpses of Our Civilian Public Service Camps—The Sideling Hill, PA., Camp." *YCC* 23 (Aug. 9, 1942), 250, 251, 252. Description of the Sideling Hill, Pa., CPS camp.

Kling, Richard. "A Testimony of Experience and Influence in CPS." *ST* 14 (Oct., 1946), 597. In light of all the undesirable influences in CPS camps, the call for a separate organization is urgent.

Klippenstein, Lawrence. *That There Be Peace: Mennonites in Canada and World War II.* Winnipeg: Manitoba CO Reunion Committee, 1979. Pp. 104. Includes summary of the Canadian Mennonite experience of World War II, photographs of the projects and CPS camp life, newspaper clippings, and personal reminiscences.

Kreider, Charles S. "The Assistant Directors' Training School in Civilian Public Service." *ChrMon* 35 (Feb., 1943), 49, 57, 64. Description of the training sessions for CPS camp administrators and outline of their duties.

Kreider, Charles S. "The Hagerstown Project." *CPS Bull* 1 (Sept. 2, 1942), 1-2. CPS camp experiments with small housing units, soil conservation, and farm management.

Kreider, Robert S. "Educational Values Inherent in the Mennonite Civilian Service Program." *ChrMon* 34 (May, 1942), 144-45. Description of classes and club activities taking place in CPS camps.

Kreider, Robert S. "Educational Values Inherent in the Mennonite Civilian Service Program." *ChrMon* 34, Part 2, (June, 1942), 175-77. Work projects and camp life provide opportunities for learning, fellowship, and testimony to nonresistance.

Kroeker, David. "The Boys from CO Camps Remembered Harold Sherk." *MennRep* 4 (Apr. 1, 1974), 9. Tribute to peacemaker Sherk, outspoken advocate of conscientious objector legislation and pastor to CPS camps.

Landis, Ira D. "When War Clouds Hover Low." *ChrMon* 34 (June, 1942), 171-72, 189. The experience of the children of Israel called to leave Babylon parallels Mennonite migrations and the calling out of Mennonite youth into CPS camps.

Landis, Wilmer. "Service Frontiers in Agriculture Surpluses." *PCMCP Fourteenth*, 76-82. N.p. Held at Eastern Mennonite College, Harrisonburg, Virginia, June 6-7, 1963. Agriculture surpluses of produce and talent are available in Mennonite communities to respond to the many service frontiers both at home and abroad.

Lehman, Carl M. "Has CPS Enlarged Our Concept of Missions?" *CPS Bull Supp* 5 (June 20, 1946), 2, 6. Since all of Christian life has been transformed by Christ, Christian missions is expressing the complete Christian life to other people.

Lehman, Carl M. "Mennonite Civilian Public Service Camps—The Bluffton, Indiana, Camp." *YCC* 23 (Apr. 12, 1942), 118-20. Description of the Bluffton, Ind., CPS camp.

Lehman, Carl M. "The Returning CPS Man." *Menn* 60 (Dec. 11, 1945), 5, 15. Emphasizes the positive contributions CPS makes in helping youth to "separate the chaff from the wheat," be more interested in inter-Mennonite cooperation, and practice daily discipleship.

Lehman, J. Irvin. "Shall We Have Another CPS?" *ST* 16 (2nd Qtr., 1948), 4. Concerned that many of the Mennonite leaders representing Mennonites before the government on issues of military legislation represent Mennonite groups who have largely lost the doctrine of nonresistance.

Lehman, M[artin] C[lifford]. "The Program of the Mennonite Central Committee to Train Relief Workers." *ChrMon* 36 (Feb., 1944), 43. Removal of the training program from Goshen College to mental hospitals, where trainees could continue the CPS work into which they were drafted.

"MCC Postwar Planning." *RepConsS* 2 (May 1, 1944), 3. A survey of CPS camps operated by MCC and Mennonites in other camps indicates that CPS has created interest in further education, that 60 percent of those surveyed plan to farm after CPS, etc.

"MCC Questionnaire." *RepConsS* 4 (June 21, 1946), 3. Progress report on CPS evaluation questionnaires sent to assignees in MCC camps and units.

"Mennonite Civilian Public Service Camps." *YCC*

22, Part 1, "How the Program Came to Be," (Aug. 10, 1941), 667, 672; Part 2, "How the Camps Are Handled," (Aug. 17, 1941), 675, 678; Part 3, "Camp Life," (Aug. 24, 1941), 687; Part 4, "The Challenge to Young Men and the Church," (Aug. 13, 1941), 694; Part 5, "Procedure for Inducting Men into Mennonite Civilian Public Service Camps After They Have Been Placed in Class IV-E," (Sept. 14, 1941), 711, 712. A description of the CPS program.

"Mennonites Stay In." *RepConsS* 4 (Jan. 15, 1946), 1, 3. MCC decides to continue administrating CPS until all persons are released.

Martens, Harry E. "Graduated from Civilian Public Service." *CPS Bull Supp* 6 (Jan. 30, 1947), 1, 3. Nonresistance must be a way of life, not confined to the Civilian Public Service camp.

Mennonite Central Committee. *Twenty-Five Years. The Story of the MCC, 1920-1945.* Akron: MCC, 1945. Pp. 24. An interpretive history of North American Mennonite relief and service activities, including CPS and direct peace activities.

*Mennonite CPS Directory: Supplement to the 1948 Mennonite Yearbook.* Scottdale: Mennonite Publishing House, 1948. Pp. 50. MHL. Contains the names of persons in CPS (US) and ASW (Canada) from the Mennonite Church, the Conservative Amish Mennonite Church, the Old Order Amish Mennonite Church, and the Old Order (Wisler) Mennonite Church.

Mennonite General Conference. "Letter to the President of the United States, Aug. 26, 1941." *GH* 34 (Nov. 13, 1941), 711. General Conference (MC) expression of gratitude for the possibility of the CPS program.

Miller, Edward. "Leaven of Good Will." *CPS Bull Supp* 6 (Dec. 28, 1946), 1, 3. Describes the toy repair and distribution program of the CPS camp in Gulfport, Mississippi.

Miller, Ursula. "'To Keep Thee in All Thy Ways.' " *ChrMon* 36 (July, 1944), 195-96. Story about a young man drafted into CPS camp who reconciles himself to conscientious objector service.

Nelson, Boyd N. "Soil Conservation in Weeping Water." *CPS Bull* 1 (Dec. 7, 1942), 1-3. Describes CPS work in Nebraska to reform the land and prevent soil erosion.

Neufeld, Kenneth. "A Comparison of the CPS Program with the Present I-W Program." Student paper for Our Christian Heritage, Feb., 1959. Pp. 9. MLA/BeC.

"Origin of Alternative Service." *RepConsS* 5 (Mar., 1947), 1, 6-8. Credits the origin of the concept of CPS as an alternative to war to 19th century Russian Mennonites and discusses the Russian Mennonite CO movement.

"Our Civilian Public Service Camps—Developing Prairie Farm Land." *YCC* 24 (Oct. 31, 1943), 763. Description of CPS Camp No. 64 at Terry, Montana.

"Peace Church Conference Set for 1976." *RepConsS* 32 (Dec., 1975), 7. Proposed conference to have historical focus in honor of 1935 meeting of Brethren, Friends, and Mennonites to lay groundwork for cooperation in the CPS program.

Peachey, Shem. "The Scriptural Alternative to War." *GH* 43 (Oct. 24, 1950), 1044. Mennonites should give their peace testimony "in the name of Christ" via church organizations and not first of all through CPS camps as an alternative to military service.

Penner, William. *My Experiences in Camp Life.* Ste. Anne, Manitoba: By the Author, RR 1, Box 91, n.d. Pp. 15. MHL. Reflects upon the CO experience in a CPS camp on Vancouver Island where the men worked on various forestry projects including fire fighting.

Phifer, Gregg. "Smoke Jumper." Yearbook of CPS Unit No. 103, Missoula, Montana, n.d. Pp. 47. MHL.

Preheim, Lynn, ed. *The Voice of Peace.* CPS yearbook, CPS Camp No. 57, Hill City, SD, 1946. Pp. 56. MHL.

Q[Anonymous]. "Letter from a I-A-O." *MCC Bull* 3 (Oct. 8, 1944), 5-6. This letter, written to CPS and AFSC, describes the hateful attitudes and military environment which he (Q) experienced in noncombatant service. Because of his resistance to these attitudes, his colonel rightly decided he belonged in CPS.

(Review). *War, Peace, and Nonresistance,* by Guy F. Hershberger. Scottdale: Herald Press, 1944. Pp. 415. *CPS Bull* 3 (Dec. 22, 1944), 3. Recommends the book for reading by every CPS worker.

Regier, C. C. "A Christian Witness in War and Peace." *MennLife* 4 (Jan., 1949), 17-20. Describes the work of the historic peace churches in setting up the CPS program with Selective Service. Includes history and statistics of the Civilian Public Service program during World War II and post-war relief work.

Regier, Hilda. "A Study of Some of the Publications Produced within CPS Camps During World War II." Student paper for Our Christian Heritage, May 14, 1954. Pp. 18. MLA/BeC.

Reimer, Otto B. "What Was Civilian Public Service?" 1983. Pp. 17. MBBS.

Reimer, Rosella. "Service in the South." *CPS Bull Supp* 5 (Aug. 29, 1946), 2-3. Description of life in the women's CPS camp in Gulfport, Mississippi, and their work among the people of the community.

Report of a meeting called by the Executive Committee of the Virginia Conference with representatives of the General Peace Problems Committee, a member of the Civilian Service Investigating Committee, the Virginia Peace Problems Committee, and other brethren of the Virginia Conference, Mar. 17, 1962. Pp. 117. MSHL.

Rich, Mrs. Willis E. "Marriage in Civilian Public Service." *CPS Bull* 3 (Apr. 22, 1945), 1-2. Drafting young men of marriageable age presents problems for their establishing a home and family life, problems the church may have to help solve.

Rohrer, Mary E. and Rohrer, Peter Lester. *The Story of the Lancaster County Conference Mennonites in Civilian Public Service, with Directory.* [Smoketown, Pa.]: By the Authors, n.d. Pp. 118. MHL. A variety of persons report on such topics as hospital experiences, fire fighting, the women's unit, the "guinea pig" experience, the canning project, the cattle ship experience, etc.

"Soil Conservation as a Work of National Importance." *ChrMon* 33 (May, 1941), 149. NSBRO describes soil conservation as one type of civilian work for conscientious objectors.

Shank, Clarence. "A Mennonite Boy's World War Experience." *YCC* 21, Part 1, "Preliminary Experiences," (Apr. 7, 1940), 106-107; Part 2, "My Trip to Camp Lee, Va," (Apr. 14, 1940), 117-20; Part 3, "First Events in Camp Lee," (Apr. 21, 1940), 128; Part 4, "Going Through the Mustering Office," (Apr. 28, 1940), 135; Part 5, "Entering the 'Holy Hill'," (May 5, 1940), 142; Part 6, "The Six-Month Furlough," (May 19, 1940), 155; Part 7, "The Homeward Look," (May 26, 1940), 163, 168. A Mennonite describes his experience as a conscientious objector during World War I.

Shank, Gladys. "'If Ye Love Me.'" *ChrMon* 36 (Aug., 1944), 226, 249. Story about a young man who struggles with his decision to enter army training instead of CPS camp.

Shank, Luke J. and Shank, James M. *Our Boys in Civilian Public Service of the Washington Co., Md.-Frankline Co., Pa. Conference.* Chambersburg: By the Authors, 1947. Pp. 54. MSHL. Describes types of service, offers evaluative comments from CPSers and biographical sketches of the persons involved with CPS.

Shellenberger, Eunice. *Wings of Decision.* Scottdale: Herald Press, 1951. Pp. 240. Fictional account of a young man facing the draft in World War II, his decision to seek conscientious objector status, and his experiences in Civilian Public Service.

Shelley, Paul. "An Evaluation of Methods of Transmitting Mennonite Ideals." *PCMCP Fourth,* 71-82. North Newton, Kansas: n.p. Held at Bluffton, Ohio, Aug. 24-25, 1945. The evaluation includes the CPS experience and the development of the CO position.

Shetler, Florence Hazel Young. "Responsibilities to Our CPS Program." *GH Supplement* 36 (June, 1943), 230. Many things can be done to help our personnel in CPS—prayer, financial help, sending towels and toiletries, as well as visiting them.

Shetler, Sanford G. "Rethinking Civilian Public Service." *ChrMon* 34 (Dec., 1942), 366; *Menn* 58 (Mar. 2, 1943), 9-10. The US entry into World War II caused CPS men to rethink their reasons for participating in the program.

Shetler, Sanford G. "The Civilian Public Service Program." *ST* 11 (Oct., 1943), 49. States that the purpose is to provide a fair and candid representation of a variety of matters pertaining to Civilian Public Service.

Shetler, Sanford G. "The Future of Civilian Public Service and Relief Work." *ST* 14 (July, 1946), 561. Raises some questions and offers some suggestions about Civilian Public Service and relief.

Shoup, Harry. "Activities of CPS Camp No. 66." *YCC* 24 (Aug. 29, 1943), 695, 696. Description of CPS Camp No. 66 located in Norristown, Pa.

Slabaugh, Dan. "Our Civilian Public Service Camps—In the Black Hills of South Dakota." *YCC* 24 (Oct. 17, 1943), 746, 747. Description of CPS Camp No. 57 in the Black Hills of South Dakota.

Smucker, Donovan E. "Mennonite Service Projects in Time of War and Peace." *PCMCP First,* 67-74. North Newton, Kansas: The Bethel College Press. Held at Winona Lake, Indiana, Aug. 7-8, 1942. Service projects do not refer to the traditional mutual aid activities among Mennonite communities, but refer to the works of mercy and service done for non-Mennonite, non-historic peace church, and possibly even non-Christian people. Doctrines of separation and nonconformity must be examined in light of the needs.

Smucker, Donovan E. "What I Saw in CPS." *GH* 37 (June 2, 1944), 156-57. CPS is a real witness to love over justice in spite of some spiritual shortcomings.

Stauffer, William. "The Rehabilitation of Men in the CPS Camps." *PCMCP Second,* 73-76. North Newton, Kansas: The Bethel College Press. Held at Goshen, Indiana, July 22-23, 1943. Explores the disintegration of rural Mennonite community life as it relates to the CPS program and capital investments in non-Mennonite places.

Stehman, Allen. "Our Civilian Public Service Camps—Weeping Water, Nebraska." *YCC* 23 (Nov. 8, 1942), 354-55. Description of Weeping Water, Nebraska, CPS camp.

Stoltzfus, Glen. "The Origins of Civilian Public Service: A Review of the Negotiations During the Period 1936-1940 Between Government Officials and Representatives of the Historic Peace Churches." Paper for History Seminar, Goshen College, Goshen, Ind., 1956. Pp. 35. MHL.

[Stoltzfus, Grant M., ed.] *Farm and Community School: CPS Camp No. 24, Clearspring, Maryland.* Akron, Pa.: MCC, 1944. Pp. 85. Notes from evening school for CPS personnel which was centered around two major emphases: to develop a Christian philosophy of the rural community; to study practical methods and practices of modern agriculture.

Stoltzfus, Grant M. "Mennonite Youth in the Present Crisis." *YCC* 22 (Dec. 28, 1941), 827, 829-30. CPS camps offer an opportunity for a positive expression of the nonresistant lifestyle.

Stoltzfus, Grant M. "Mental Hospital Experience of Civilian Public Service." *MennLife* 2 (Apr., 1947), 8-10, 15. Describes CPS work in the mental hospitals and the subsequent improvement in mental health care in those institutions.

Stoltzfus, Grant M. "The Meaning of Our CPS Testimony." *YCC* 23 (Dec. 27, 1942), 410-11, 413, 414; *Menn* 57 (Sept. 22, 1942), 8. CPS is an acceptable service to government, a discharge of conscientious duty, a testimony to society, and a seedbed for cultivating a greater Mennonite church.

Storms, Paul L. "Forest Service in British Columbia Service Work Camps." *ChrMon* 35, Part 1, (Oct., 1943), 306-7, 320; Part 2, (Nov., 1943), 334-35. Description of life in the Canadian Alternative Service work camps for conscientious objectors.

Suderman, David H. "Report on Civilian Public Service." *Menn* 60 (June 26, 1945), 5-6. CPS is an expression of the doctrine of nonresistance.

Suderman, David H. "The Returning Civilian Public Service Men." *MennLife* 1 (Jan., 1946), 5-7, 21. An analysis of the CPS camper: discusses pre-camp decision about conscription, camp influences, and adjustment to home community after camp experience.

Swartzentruber, Henry. *The Story of Doris Dean.* [Oakland, Md.]: By the Author, [R. 2, Oakland, Md.], 1980. Pp. 14. MHL. Account of a search for a child lost in the Blue Ridge Mountains in which CPS persons from the Grottos, Va., camp participated.

Swope, Cleo. "Glimpses of Our Mennonite Civilian Public Service Camps—the Denison, Iowa, Camp." *YCC* 23 (May 31, 1942), 171, 173-74. Description of the Denison, Iowa, CPS camp.

"The CPS Vision." *CPS Bull* 3 (Apr. 8, 1945); 4 (Nov. 8, 1945). Ten Civilian Public Service workers offer 250-word statements each on their perceptions of the meaning and purpose of the CPS program. A twelve-part series includes articles from John A. Hostetler, Dallas Voran, Denton Burns, Arthur Jost, Abraham Graber, Dick Hunter, Ellen Harder (response), Elmer Ediger, Grant M. Stoltzfus, Wendell Harmon, Albert M. Gaeddert, Irvin B. Horst (summary).

Taylor, Stanley. *Activities of the Pacifist Conscript.* N.p., n.d. Pp. 56. MHL. General summary of alternative service experience of the historic peace churches. Discusses pacifist ideology, relations with Selective Service, activities in basic camps and with special projects, an evaluation of CPS, etc.

Umble, Roy H. "CPS Study for Credit—NOW." *CPS Bull* 3 (May 8, 1945), 1, 3-4. Describes the educational credits available to CPS workers through classes, correspondence, or tutoring.

Umble, Roy H, ed. *Guide to the Evaluation of Education Experiences in Civilian Public Service.* [Akron, Pa.]: MCC and the Council of Mennonite and Affiliated Colleges, March, 1946. Pp. 144. MHL. A handbook designed to help educational institutions evaluate, and assign academic credit to education received in CPS. Provides information such as course duration, objectives, syllabi, credentials of instructors, etc.

Umble, Roy H. "The Significance of the Educational Experiences of CPS Men." *PCMCP Fourth,* 11-26. North Newton, Kansas. n.p. Held at Bluffton, Ohio, Aug. 24-25, 1945. CPS is a far-reaching and complex educational program of the church. Colleges and other educational institutions need to evaluate their role in post-CPS educational needs.

Unsigned. "CPS Evaluations." *CPS Bull Supp* 6 (Jan.

30, 1947), 1, 3, 4. An ex-CPS director and former CPS workers reflect on the strengths and weaknesses of the program.

Unsigned. "Symposium on Post-War Conscription." *CPS Bull* 3 (Oct. 22, 1944), 5-6. Most of the seven CPS respondents encourage the Mennonite church to continue an alternative service program whether or not peacetime conscription becomes a reality.

Unsigned. "The Mennonite Hope in CPS." *CPS Bull* 1 (Mar. 19, 1943), 1-2. Mennonites view CPS camps as a way to witness to Christ's love, and as a means toward increased faith and good works on the part of CPS draftees.

Vogt, Cornelius W., ed. *Our Story.* CPS yearbook, CPS Camp No. 64, Terry, Mont., 1944. Pp. 37. MSHL.

Wagler, David and Raber, Roman, eds. *The Story of the Amish in Civilian Public Service, with Directory.* Boonsboro, Md.: CPS Camp No. 24, Unit III, 1945. Pp. 145. MHL. Essays relate experiences of various aspects of CPS camp life such as flood clean-up, forestry, fire-fighting, hospital work, human guinea pig experiments, relief work, etc. Directory provides names, addresses, induction dates, projects, etc.

Waltner, Emil J. "Why Should the Mennonite Support the Civilian Public Service Camps." *Menn* 67 (Sept. 15, 1942), 6. The nonresistant position now and in the future makes it imperative that Mennonites support CPS camps.

Weaver, Allen, ed. *Service for Peace.* CPS yearbook, CPS Camp No. 33, Fort Collins, Colo., 1945. Pp. 63. MSHL.

Weaver, Edwin L. "Reflections of a Civilian Public Service Man." *ChrMon* 38 (July, 1946), 209-11, 213. Relates nonparticipation in war to missions effectiveness, spiritual maturity, and respect for the natural environment.

Weaver, Edwin L. "With Negroes in the Deep South." *YCC* 31, Part 1, "Negroes in the United States," (May 28, 1950), 172, 173; Part 2, (June 4, 1950), 180, 181; Part 3, "Colored Quarters and Homes," (June 11, 1950), 188, 189; Part 4, "Making a Living," (June 18, 1950), 196, 197; Part 5, "Family Life," (June 25, 1950), 204, 207; Part 6, (July 2, 1950), 212-14; Part 7, "Negro Traits," (July 16, 1950), 231, 232; Part 8, "Negroes as Individuals," (July 23, 1950), 239, 240; Part 9, "Negro Schools," (July 30, 1950), 243, 244; Part 10, "Negro Churches," (Aug. 6, 1950), 249; Part 11, "Helping the Colored People," (Aug. 13, 1950), 258, 259. The sociology of comtemporary blacks in the Deep South. Draws on personal observations made in Polk County, Florida, where a CPS public health project established contact with the black community.

Weaver, Edwin L. (Review). *Activities of the Pacifist Conscript,* by Stanley Taylor. Paper prepared for seminary, n.d. Pp. 56. *ChrMon* 40 (Jan., 1948), 15. Reviewer observes that the paper discusses the basis of pacifist beliefs and presents information on Civilian Public Service activities.

Weaver, Edwin L. (Review). *Pathways of Peace,* by Leslie Eisan. Elgin: Brethren Publishing House, 1948. Pp. 480. *ChrMon* 41 (July, 1949), 215. Recommends the book as a history of the Civilian Public Service program from the Church of the Brethren perspective.

Weaver, Kenneth, ed. "Files." Yearbook of CPS unit No. 66, Norristown State Hospital, Noristown, Pa., n.d. Pp. 48. MHL.

Wedel, David C. "The Responsibility of the Mennonite Church Toward Her Civilian Public Service Camps." *Menn* 57 (Feb. 3, 1942), 6-8; *ChrMon* 34 (Mar., 1942), 81-82, 93. Since the church has taught nonresistance it should now give financial and moral support to the camps and interpret the camp program to the public. Both church and camp need to develop a technique of nonviolence.

Wherry, Neal M. *Conscientious Objection.* Washington, D.C.: Government Printing Office, 1950. Vol. I, pp. 364. Vol. II, pp. 288. MHL. Chronicles World War II conscientious objection from the government's point of view. Mennonite documents and summaries of Mennonite practices and teachings are found in chapters entitled: "Church Backgrounds of CO's," "Conscientious Objection in American History," "Legislative Provisions on Conscientious Objection." Other chapters offer extensive information about the CPS program—history, assignments, administration, discipline, statistics, etc.

Wilson, Bob, ed. *Of Human Importance.* CPS Yearbook, CPS Camp No. 26, Chicago, Ill., 1946. Pp. 31. MHL.

Wilson, William Jerome. "A Letter from a Noncombatant." *GH* 38 (Aug. 31, 1945), 419-20. Expresses deep regret at having left CPS to become a noncombatant.

Witmer, Austin W. "Is Our CPS Testimony Ringing Clear?" *GH* 38 (Jan. 25, 1946), 821. The Mennonites are being watched closely by the world and must present a message full of peace and joy.

World War II. 134 interviews, some transcribed. Emphasis on Mennonite CO's who did CPS work. ALso includes some civilians (women, pastors) and regulars.MLA/BeC.

Yake, C. F. "What Are You Doing for the National Defense?" *YCC* 22 (Aug. 10, 1941), 668. Explores the issue of what kind of cooperation a Christian can give in a war atmosphere when it is against their conscience to take up arms. People who do not qualify for CPS and have to stay home also have an obligation to sacrifice.

Yoder, Edward. *Our Mennonite Heritage: Mennonites and Their Heritage.* No. 3. Akron: MCC, 1942. This booklet is third in a series of six studies on Mennonite heritage prepared for use in CPS camps. It focuses specifically on doctrinal beliefs

with major emphasis on peace and nonresistance.

Young, Dale and Forrer, David. "Glimpses of Our Civilian Public Service Camps—The Marietta, Ohio, Camp." *YCC* 23 (Mar. 1, 1942), 67, 69. Description of the Marietta, Ohio, CPS camp.

[Zercher, Ray, *et al.*]. "The Seagull." Yearbook of the CPS Unit No. 85, Howard, R.I., 1946. Pp. 62. MHL.

"29 Annual Reunion." *RepConsS* 31 (Nov., 1974), 1, 4. Reports a long-standing and particularly vital CPS reunion.

# C. PAX

Bender, Urie A. *Soldiers of Compassion.* Scottdale: Herald Press, 1969. Pp. 320. The story of PAX, a service program of Mennonite Central Committee for conscientious objectors after World War II, told in first person and case history form.

Bergman, Gene. "An Evaluation of Foreign Service Experience." *PCMCP Sixteenth.* 40-49, N.p. Held at Hesston College, Hesston, Kansas, June 8-9, 1967. A personal experience of being in MCC with the PAX program raised serious questions about the inadequate training and preparation offered before assuming the assignment.

"Church Completion Ends Project." *RepConsS* 17 (Oct., 1960), 3, 4. The dedication of the Mennonite Church in Bechterdissen, Germany, completes another community for refugees built by PAX persons.

Dyck, Peter J. "Seedtime and Harvest in Greece." *RepConsS* 17 (June-July, 1960), 1, 5, 6. Phasing out a PAX program from a given location is a time for reflection upon both achievements and mistakes.

Eby, Sarah Ann. "PAX Dies . . . Yet Lives." *ChrLead* 39 (Apr. 13, 1976), 18. History and description of the PAX program. PAX was started in 1951 to provide Mennonite young men with opportunities for civilian service in response to human need and suffering resulting from war.

Epp, Frank H. (Editorial). "Mobilizing Youth for Peace." *CanMenn* 2 (July 23, 1954), 2. In World War II, Canadians put 7 percent of their human resources toward the war effort while Canadian Mennonites put .2 percent of their human resources toward the peace effort. Encourages, in light of this disparity, more involvement with PAX and other service programs.

Fretz, J. Winfield. "Peace Corps: Child of the Historic Peace Churches." *MennLife* 16 (Oct., 1961), 178-81. Summarizes the origin and nature of the US Peace Corps and compares and contrasts it to PAX.

Friesen, Jake and Friesen, Jane. "PAX: A History of MCC-PAX and Its Service." Paper presented to Mennonite History class, Associated Mennonite Biblical Seminaries, Elkhart, Ind., 1962. Pp. 84. MHL.

Goering, James. "PAX—An Opportunity for Spiritual Service." *ST* 23 (2nd Qtr., 1955), 30. Looks at the various ways PAX can be an opportunity for spiritual service. Unless the PAX program presents a positive testimony to the world, of salvation and the Christian way of life, there is hardly reason to continue it at the expense of the church.

Hartzler, Levi C. "Pax Service, a Church Responsibility." *GH* 45 (May 20, 1952), 496-97. Pax Service offers an opportunity for Christian service which may soon be accepted as alternate service for drafted men. The church can support the positive peace witness of Pax Service with financial contributions.

Hershberger, Guy F. "A New Postwar Peace Movement." *GH Supplement* 39 (Oct., 1946), 639. A report on the "Pax Christi" League, which proposes to end war with the universal signing of the Universal Christian Agreement.

Hershberger, Guy F. "How Important Is the Peace Problems Committee?" *GH* 56 (Apr. 23, 1963), 346-47. An historical sketch of the PPC, giving witness to its importance and attempting to raise funds for this program as well as General Conference (MC) involvement in other projects such as PAX, I-W, MCC, etc.

"I-Ws Narrowly Escape Death in the Congo." *RepConsS* 22 (Jan., 1965), 1, 3. Two Mennonite PAX persons resume duties in the Congo (Zaire) after a harrowing episode in Stanleyville in which Dr. Paul Carlson was fatally shot on Nov. 24.

Jansen, Curtis, "Building for Eternity." *ChrLiv* 1 (Feb., 1954), 4-5, 42-43. The PAX program began as a system for building houses for refugees in Europe.

Janzen, Curtis. "Our PAX Boys in Europe." *MennLife* 9 (Apr., 1954), 80-82. Description of rebuilding and resettlement projects in post-war Europe.

Janzen, Curtis. "PAX in Greece and Other Countries." *Menn* 70 (Mar. 8, 1955), 154-56. A survey of the PAX program designed as an aid for the planning of young people's programs.

Jost, Howard. "Pax: A Mind-Expanding Experience." *GH* 61 (Sept. 10, 1968), 823-24. Pax worker describes his work and activities in Dacca, East Pakistan.

Juhnke, James C. "Pax—Peace Through Love." *MennLife* 16 (July, 1961), 102-104. PAX is welcome outgrowth of the principles of nonresistance, conscientious objection, etc. because it measures success by what is accomplished rather than what is not done.

Kasper, Arlo. "The I-W in Action." *MennLife* 13 (July, 1958), 106, 107, 120. Describes the work of those who are not able to respond to the call of government for military service and become involved in alternative service in hospitals, etc. Gives an overview of the various types of alternate service—I-W earning, voluntary service, and PAX service.

Kaufman, Donald D. "Implications of Pax, Relief, and Voluntary Service for World Mission." Paper presented to Mennonite Misions and World Service class, MBS, Chicago, Ill., Nov. 27, 1957. Pp. 35.

Lind, Loren. "What PAX Does to Our Boys." *ChrLiv* 10 (May, 1963), 12-15, 27. PAX workers face problems of readjustment to their home communities after their terms of service.

Loewen, Esko. "MCC in Europe Today." *Menn* 70 (Nov. 22, 1955), 728. MCC continues the peace witness via PAX, the Heerewegen Conference Center, the Puidoux conferences, and voluntary service projects.

"MCC." *RepConsS* 23 (Aug., 1966), 3, 4. Summarizes the work of MCC—focusing on PAX, Voluntary Service, and Teachers Abroad Program.

Martens, Harry E. "Our Youth in Christian Service." *MennLife* 9 (Apr., 1954), 77-79, 96. Reflections on Mennonite peace and service witnesses through PAX and voluntary service.

"New Opportunities for COs with PAX." *RepConsS* 19 (Sept.-Oct., 1962), 1, 3. In eleven years MCC's PAX personnel have worked constructively for peace in twenty-six countries.

"Paxmen Are Turning Swords into Plowshares." *CanMenn* 11 (May 31, 1963), 10. A report on the creative and constructive work of PAX personnel in twenty overseas countries.

Peachey, Urbane. "What Is a Paxman?" *YCC* 49 (June 9, 1968), 3. Description of the PAX program.

"Short Journey into PAX." *YCC* 43 (Sept. 16, 1962), 6-11. A description of the PAX program.

Studer, Gerald C. Letter to the Editor. *GH* 63 (Aug. 25, 1970), 706-707. Expresses regret that the Mennonite Church approved paying jobs in I-W assignments as alternative service, instead of remaining with nonsalaried PAX or VS work. Supports all forms of draft resistance as valid witnesses to the state.

Wiebe, Herb. "Draft-Age Canadian Gives Impressions of Peace Work." *CanMenn* 4 (July 6, 1956), 3, 4. A PAX worker relates his experience and impressions and also assesses the peace witness being made by PAX workers abroad.

Yoder, Kermit. "A Pax Man's Purpose and Motivation." *GH* 55 (Jan. 16, 1962), 57. Reports conversation between a PAX person and Greek villager on the subject of nonresistance.

# 2
# Arms, Armament, and Disarmament

"A Christian Approach to Nuclear War." *Menn* 77 (Nov. 6, 1962), 707-709. Adapted from the statement by the Church Peace Mission, this article calls on American Christians to renew their hope in the way of peace and to abandon reliance on military might. Includes an urgent plea for the discontinuation of stockpiling of nuclear armaments.

"A Letter to the President." *Menn* 74 (Nov. 3, 1959), 678. Consultative Peace Council urges universal, total disarmament as national policy to be implemented by, for example, the admittance of the People's Republic of China into the United Nations, and the resolution of political problems in such places as Berlin and Laos.

"A Message to the Churches." *GH* 52 (May 19, 1959), 465; "A Message to All Christians," *CanMenn* 7 (May 8, 1959), 2. A statement issued by the 1959 Church Peace Mission Conference calling the church to unequivocally renounce war and take decisive action to break the circle of armament and counter-armament. The use of nuclear weapons, particularly, should be completely renounced.

"A Nearly Non-existent Nonresistance." *CanMenn* 11 (Mar. 8, 1963), 6. Mennonites would rather have war with nuclear weapons than experience communism. In their fear of communism the Mennonites have become followers of Carl McIntire, Billy James Hargis, etc., instead of carrying the peaceful cross of Christ.

"An Urgent Appeal to the Churches." *EV* 90 (May 25, 1977), 6. With this appeal, twenty-five persons at a workshop on the church and militarism call our attention to the surprising silence of the Christian church in the face of mass starvation and nuclear stockpiling and urge the church to respond to these atrocities.

"Arms Sales to Third World Soar." *Menn* 87 (May 2, 1972), 303. Wars are fought in the Third World but the armaments are supplied by the big powers. Includes statistics compiled by a

staff of five researchers over a four-year period.

Abrams, Ray H. *Preachers Present Arms*. Scottdale: Herald Press, 1969. Pp. 330. A revised edition of the 1933 volume documenting the active role of clergy in promoting war, with two additional chapters on World War II and later developments, including the Vietnam War.

Atmosuwito, S. "The Desert: for Peace or War?" *ChrLiv* 8 (July, 1961), 36-37. Options for use of desert lands include development for food production or the testing of nuclear weapons.

Aukerman, Dale. "The Bomb and Christ's Coming." *ChrLiv* 9 (Apr., 1962), 23-24. Reprinted from *Gospel Messenger*. The atomic bomb threatens the future of humanity, but Christ's coming will be the final triumph.

Barrett, Lois. "Varieties of Christian Pacifism." *Menn* 91 (Sept. 7, 1976), 518. Interpretive report on the Fellowship of Reconciliation conference, where pacifists gathered to discuss nuclear arms, Christian participation in the political system.

Bassett, David R. and Miyoko I. "Letter to the *Ann Arbor News*." *God and Caesar* 5 (Feb., 1979), 9. This letter to the editor of the *Ann Arbor News* is included as an example of how letters to the editors of local newspapers can be tools to create awareness of the arms race and the World Peace Tax Fund Act.

Beachy, Alvin J. "Survival Is Not Enough." *Pulpit* 33 (Nov., 1962), 12-15. Sermon preached on "Peace Sunday" urges listeners to judge human life by eternal values such as the worth of each individual and the moral effects of war and violence, instead of trusting in "vengeance weapons" such as the Polaris submarine and neutron bomb, to insure "survival" of "our side."

Beachy, Ezra P. "Bigger Guns or Better Homes." *ChrMon* 23 (Mar., 1931), 75-76. While the US takes initiative in signing peace pacts, it spends nearly three quarters of the national budget on armaments.

Beechy, Atlee (Review). *Vietnam and Armageddon: Peace, War, and the Christian Conscience*, by Robert F. Drinnan. Sheed & Ward, 1970. Pp. 210. *GH* 64 (Apr. 6, 1971), 314. A Catholic priest writing on the morality of war concludes that US and Soviet possession of fantastically destructive nuclear, biological, and chemical weapons renders meaningless the concept of just war.

Bender, Nevin and Swartzendruber, Emanuel. *Nonresistance under Test*. Rosedale, Ohio: Keynote Series No. 1, 1969. Pp. 16. The stories of the two authors who refused to bear arms during World War I.

Bender, Wilbur J. "Pacifism Among the Mennonites, Amish Mennonites, and Schwenkfelders of Pensylvania to 1783." *MQR* 1, Part 1 (July, 1927), 23-40; Part 2 (Oct., 1927), 21-48. Until 1776 these groups succeeded in observing strict nonresistance without too much difficulty. Even during the War of Independence there was general tolerance for them, though many paid fines for not bearing arms and refusing to pay war taxes.

Beyler, Betsy. "Candidates for President: a Comparison." *Forum* 10 (Oct., 1976), 2-5; *MCC PS Wash. Memo* 7 (July-Aug., 1976), 1-7. A comparative analysis of Gerald Ford and Jimmy Carter focusing on their stand on some of the crucial issues: military spending, amnesty, foreign arms sales, nuclear disarmament, nuclear power, and foreign policy.

Beyler, Betsy. "Economic Conversion: Reformulating Guns vs. Butter." *MCC PS Wash. Memo* 10 (Mar.-Apr., 1978), 7-8. Supports the process of converting resources used for military production into facilities for meeting human needs.

Beyler, Betsy. "Indochina Is Still on the Map—and on the Agenda." *MCC PS Wash. Memo* 10 (May-June, 1978), 6-7. US bombing during the war and deplorable post-war conditions have created severe problems for Vietnam, Laos, and Kampuchea.

Beyler, Betsy. "Not a Time for Silence: SALT Debate Calls for Disarmament Witness." *MCC PS Wash. Memo* 11 (Sept.-Oct., 1979), 1-2, 7. Explains several positions on the SALT treaty taken by people who oppose the arms race, and urges constituents to write to Congresspeople to support disarmament.

Beyler, Betsy. "SALT II Not the Only Decision in SALT Debate." *MCC PS Wash. Memo* 11 (May-June, 1979), 1-2. The proposed SALT II agreements do not speak to the government's change in rhetoric from mutual deterrence to the concept of limited nuclear war.

Beyler, Betsy, and Franz, Delton. "After Afghanistan—The Fallout." *MCC PS Wash. Memo* 12 (Jan.-Feb., 1980), 5-6, 8. Calculates the effect of the Soviet invasion of Afghanistan on the SALT II agreements, the arms race, the draft, etc.

Blosser, Don. "The Selling of the Pentagon: A Response." *GH* 64 (July 27, 1971), 636-37. Expresses deep dismay over the ideas and values communicated by the Pentagon as seen in the CBS documentary *The Selling of the Pentagon*. Calls Mennonites to become aware of militaristic tactics and to protest the use of their tax dollars in the Pentagon's propaganda.

Blosser, Richard (Review). *In Solitary Witness*, by Gordon Zahn. Collegeville, Minn.: Liturgical Press, 1964. Pp. 278. "Solitary Witness." *Menn* 94 (Nov. 6, 1979), 668. Briefly describes the book which gives an in-depth study of the life and witness of an Austrian peasant whose religious convictions led him to reject the Nazi movement as anti-Christian and to refuse service in the wars in the 1940's. Point out the book's relevance for North American Christians facing issues of the nuclear arms race and peacetime draft.

Bohn, E. Stanley. Letter to the Editor. *Menn* 95 (July 22, 1980), 449. Responds to a letter criticizing Peter Ediger¡s civil disobedience at Rocky Flats nuclear weapons plant by clarifying the facts about the incident.

Born, Daniel. "Christians Protest 'Movable Holocaust.' " *ChrLead* 41 (May 23, 1978), 18. Report on the demonstration at the Rocky Flats nuclear weapons plant on Apr. 29-30, 1978.

Boserup, Anders and Mack, Andrew. "Nonviolence in National Defense." *PlMon* 2 (Nov., 1979), 5. Reprinted from the introduction to *War Without Weapons: Non-violence in National Defense*, by the same authors. New York: Schocken Books, 1975. Reviews military strategy since the advent of nuclear weapons to show that national security through military means in the nuclear age is a fallacy.

Brandt, Laurie. "South African Crisis Stirs Action in United.Nations and Congress." *MCC PS Wash. Memo* 9 (Nov.-Dec., 1977), 4, 9. The UN arms embargo to South Africa is insufficient protest against the apartheid system.

Brenderhorst, Henk. "Peace Movement Grows With Nuclear Arms Race." *CanMenn* 10 (Sept. 7, 1962), 3, 7. An analysis of the peace movement in the Dutch Mennonite church, where it is a minority position.

Brubacher, Grace. Letter to the Editor. *MennRep* 8 (Dec. 25, 1978), 6. Citing the note of urgency found in the final document from the United Nations General Assembly Special Session on Disarmament, Brubacher urges Mennonites to speak vigorously on behalf of disarmament.

Brubaker, Darrel J. and Sider, Ronald J., eds. *Preaching on Peace.* Philadelphia: Fortress Press, 1982. Pp. 95. A collection of addresses and sermons reflecting the broadening variety of theological perspectives being brought to bear upon such issues of peace as disarmament, attitudes which create peace and the biblical basis for peace.

Bumbaugh, Susan K. "Survey as to the Opinions of the Chiefs of Police and Sheriffs in Ohio Concerning Gun Registration Legislation." 1968. Pp. 15. BfC.

Burkholder, J. Richard. "On Patriotism, Piety, and Peace." *GH* 72 (Aug. 28, 1979), 684-85. The writer reflects on recent experiences including a peace convocation where Pres. Carter was present and a workshop on arms control, calling for a new mood of spiritual and moral conviction.

Burkholder, J. Richard. "Wars and Rumors . . ." *GH* 71 (Jan. 24, 1978), 62-64. Using statistics from global military and social expenditures, Burkholder challenges Christians to speak out against the worldwide armaments buildup.

"Canadian Arms Industry Is Focus of Manitoba Talks." *MennRep* 9 (Oct. 29, 1979), 1. Canada's sustained involvement in the armaments trade was stressed in a three-day series of lectures and interviews by Ernie Regehr in Manitoba Oct. 10-12.

"Church Should Speak on Nuclear Testing." *CanMenn* 6 (Oct. 10, 1958), 9. Dr. Erwin Hiebert supports the Social Concerns Committee of the General Conference Mennonite Church in its concern to speak to the moral and spiritual ramifications of nuclear testing.

"Colorado Pastor Sentenced to Six Months Probation." *MennRep* 9 (Jan. 8, 1979), 1. A report on the testimonies given at the trial of co-pastor, Peter J. Ediger, where he received a sentence of six months' unsupervised probation for trespassing at the Rocky Flats nuclear weapons plant.

"Consumerism and Fear Cited as Reasons for Arms Race." *Menn* 94 (Jan. 2, 1979), 9. MCC Peace Section (US) adopted a resolution on the world arms race. The resolution identifies trust in nuclear weapons as a form of idolatry and calls on people to put their trust in Jesus Christ.

Charles, Bob, and Suderman, Dale. Letter to the Editor. *Menn* 89 (Apr. 23, 1974), 278. Peacemakers must decry the false peace of detente, which is bought at the price of oppression for small and powerless nations.

Charles, Howard H. "Thinking About the Atomic Bomb." *GH Supplement* 38 (Oct., 1945), 566-68. A summary of press reactions to the bombing of Hiroshima and Nagasaki and discussion of the moral implications of the use of the atomic bomb. It is clear that in the face of the atomic bomb, the choice is between a redeemed humanity and total destruction.

Cleveland, Harlan. "Trials and Tests at the UN." *ChrLiv* 12 (Aug., 1965), 14-15, 28-29. The issues of nuclear weapons, unsolicited foreign intervention, human rights, and equality threaten the UN's peacekeeping ability.

Cousins, Norman. "Peace Without Panic." *ChrLiv* 8 (Jan., 1961), 19, 35. Reprinted from *Saturday Review*. Questions the view that the American economy needs the threat of war to stabilize it.

Cunningham, Spencer (photographer). "Conversion Possible." *Forum* 13 (Oct., 1979), 7-9. A photo essay on the 1979 protest against the Rocky Flats nuclear weapons plant near Denver, Colo.

Cunningham, Spencer. "Rocky Flats: Denver's Three-Mile Island." *Menn* 94 (May 29, 1979), 376. The first anniversary protest attracts more than 10,000 who gathered Apr. 28 at the Rocky Flats nuclear weapons facility to call for an end to the manufacture of nuclear weapons.

Davidson, Mike. Letter to the Editor. *MBH* 19 (Dec. 19, 1980), 11, 24. The disarmament movement is a humanistic venture. The best protection against Soviet attack is a strong defense.

Derstine, C. F. "A Lull in the Sino-Japanese Storm." *ChrMon* 24 (Apr., 1932), 126. The treaty between Japan and China has averted the immediate threat of conflict on a larger scale.

Derstine, C. F. "'Disarm or Disappear.' " *ChrMon* 24 (Mar., 1932), 95. The outcome of the Disarmament Conference is critical to the question of impending war.

Derstine, C. F. "Disarmament and Debts." *ChrMon* 25 (Jan., 1933), 31-32. European nations should disarm as planned before requesting cancellation of their war debts.

Derstine, C. F. "Is the Shadow of the Beast Appearing Upon the Horizon." *ChrMon* 27 (Apr., 1935), 126-27. The buildup of armaments and the opposition to conscientious objection are signs of the Antichrist.

Derstine, C. F. "Is War with Russia Inevitable?" *ChrMon* 40 (May, 1948), 158. Analyzes the economic strength of the Soviet Union and exhorts believers to have faith in God in spite of the threat of nuclear war.

Derstine, C. F. "The American Paradox of Building Colleges and Bombs to Blow Them Up." *ChrMon* 31 (Mar., 1939), 94. Comment on the devastation of the Sino-Japanese war and the fact that bombs used by Japan were made in the US.

Derstine, C. F. "The Atom-bombed Animals." *ChrMon* 39 (Aug., 1947), 254-55. The destructiveness of the atomic bomb is identified as the tribulation period in the book of Revelation.

Derstine, C. F. "The Atomic Bomb a Milestone or a Tombstone." *ChrMon* 38 (Jan., 1946), 30-32. The awful power of the atomic bomb should move Christians to greater prayer, repentance, and foreign mission work.

Derstine, C. F. "The United States and Japan, and the 'Scrap Iron'." *ChrMon* 34 (Feb., 1942), 61-62. Modernism as practiced in Germany and greed as seen in US arms trades with Japan helped precipitate the world war, and rejection of both will help the US get out of the war.

Derstine, C. F. "The Unnecessary War." *ChrMon* 42 (Aug., 1950), 254-55. Comment on World War II and the threat of nuclear war.

Derstine, C. F. "The War Question and the Coming Disarmament Conference." *ChrMon* 24 (Jan., 1932), 30. World disarmament is necessary because war wastes lives and economic resources, but the only absolute solution is the gospel.

Dick, Ernie (Review). *A Strategy for Peace*, by Frank H. Epp. Grand Rapids: Eerdmans, 1973. Pp. 128. "Essays 'Point Finger' at Exploitation and Injustice." *MennRep* 4 (Apr. 1, 1974), 8. Although the essays were delivered as addresses in the late 1960s and early 1970s, their message of striving after peace remains timely. Most helpful essays deal with themes of nationalism, dialogue between pacifists and nonpacifists, arms buildup, complicity of the Christian church in making war.

Dourte, Eber. "To Serve the Present Age." *EV* 92 (Jan. 25, 1979), 9. At the semi-annual meeting of the MCC Peace Section, the agenda included reports and discussion on the New Call to Peacemaking, peace education, the World Arms Race and our peace witness, and the possibility of draft for military service.

Driedger, Leo. "Doctrinal Belief: A Major Factor in the Differential Perception of Social Issues." *Sociological Quarterly* 15 (Winter, 1974), 66-80. This survey of clergy (including Mennonite clergy) to determine the correlation between doctrine and positions on social issues includes questions concerning military readiness, bombing of Vietnam, rights of communists, and racial integration.

Driedger, Leo, *et. al.* "War and Rumors of War." *Menn* 78 (Nov. 5, 1963), 664-66. A symposium on war and its meaning for peacemakers. Subjects include children and the bomb, fallout shelters, disarmament, peace witness in service and evangelism, and alternatives to violence.

Dudley, Derwood M. Letter to the Editor. *Menn* 89 (Mar. 12, 1974), 182. The arms buildup is a tribute to human idiocy, since intelligent people would recognize the solidarity of international humanity and the destructive evil of armaments.

Dueck, Dennis. "The Nuclear Debate: A Personal Dilemma." *MennRep* 10 (Sept. 29, 1980), 7. Deals with three major questions regarding nuclear power, one of which is its potential relationship to nuclear weapons proliferation.

Dyck, Anna. "We Experienced Hiroshima," story told by Setsuko Kokubu. *MBH* (Sept. 16, 1977), 6-8. Survivor describes the destruction, illness, and death during and following the bombing of Hiroshima.

"Ellsberg Calls Rocky Flats a 'Harrisburg Waiting to Happen'." *MennRep* 9 (May 28, 1979), 7. Former Pentagon analyst, Daniel Ellsberg, was one of several speakers who addressed a crowd of ten to fifteen thousand people gathered at Rocky Flats nuclear weapons facility to call for an end to the manufacture of nuclear weapons.

Eash-Sutter, Ruth. "Continental Walk." *Lifework* 1 (1978), 6-8. Participant in four of the nine months of the Continental Walk for Disarmament and Social Justice in 1976 reflects on the experience as part of a lifetime commitment to peacemaking.

Eckstein, Fay. "Canadian Initiatives for Disarmament." Term paper for Peace and Conflict Studies course, Apr. 22, 1978. Pp. 22. CGCL.

Ediger, Peter J. "Cain and the Voice of the Lord." *God and Caesar* 1 (Oct., 1975), 1. A poem in which "Cain" symbolizes the arms investment that the "Ameri-Cainized" citizens are making in total disregard to the voice of the Lord who asks, "where is your brother?"

Ediger, Peter J. "Daniel 3 Revisited." *God and Caesar* 1 (Jan., 1975), 1. A paraphrase of Daniel 3, likening the Pentagon to King Nebuchadnezzar showing the faith of some Christians who have refused to worship his "image of steel."

Ediger, Peter J. "Eden Revisited." *God and Caesar* 2 (Oct., 1976), 1. The Christians are likened to Adam and Eve, tempted by the "Security Serpent" to arm themselves and become secure in their own strength, but God punishes them.

Ediger, Peter J. "Hunger and Handwashing." *God and Caesar* 3 (Nov., 1977), 1. Poem concerning how we have tried to quench our hunger with bombs and bullets rather than with the "Word of the Lord."

Ediger, Peter J. "Rocky Flats: 'The Light Keeps Coming On.' " *MennRep* 8 (June 12, 1978), 5. Reflections on the Rocky Flats nuclear weapons plant peace rally, and a call for further Mennonite awareness of the nuclear arms buildup and witness against it.

Ediger, Peter J. "The Golden Calf: 1979—Exodus 32 and April 15." *God and Caesar* 5 (Apr., 1979), 1. The account in Ex. 32 is retold to draw out its parallel with our modern situation, in which the American nation worships the molten image of war weapons.

Elias, Jacob W. "Games Christians Watch." *Menn* 88 (Nov. 20, 1973), 666-68. Links the "sports philosophy" of winning at any cost, even violence, to the realms of life: competition in the business world; political tactics of Watergate; Cambodian bombing.

Eller, Vernard. *King Jesus' Manual of Arms for the 'Armless.* Nashville: Abingdon Press, 1973. Pp. 205. Revised and reprinted by Scottdale: Herald Press, *War and Peace from Genesis to Revelation,* 1981. Makes a case for scriptural unity on pacifism by saying that the Old Testament holy war and Zion traditions, rightly understood, provide the framework within which the New Testament Christians understood Jesus' life, death, and resurrection. The last few chapters apply this concept to the contemporary scene.

Enns, Elizabeth. Letter to the Editor. *MennRep* 10 (Mar. 31, 1980), 6. Registered nurse relates conscientious objection to the taking of fetal life to protesting war, nuclear weapons, and capital punishment.

Epp, Frank H. "A Ban of Nuclear Tests." *CanMenn* 10 (Dec. 7, 1962), 6. As a 17-nation disarmament conference tries to bring about a ban on nuclear weapons tests, the writer supports this step toward peace and asks why it cannot begin at Christmas, 1962.

Epp, Frank H. "A Call to Repentance." *CanMenn* 3 (Aug. 12, 1955), 2. A statement of repentance drawn up by the Fellowship of Reconciliation and concerned individuals on the tenth anniversary of the dropping of the atomic bomb. The nation which developed atomic power for war has the responsibility to develop atomic power for peace.

Epp, Frank H. "A Concert and Banquet: A Day with the Doukhobors." *CanMenn* 13, Part 2, (July 20, 1963), 2. Describes concert featuring peace and disarmament themes.

Epp, Frank H. *A Strategy for Peace: Reflections of a Christian Pacifist.* Grand Rapids: Wm. B. Eerdmans, 1973. Pp. 128. Eleven essays on topics related to war and peace, such as pacifism, militarism, nationalism, social order. Includes essays previously published in other collections, for example: "The Unilateral Disarmament of the Church" (*Peacemakers in a Broken World,* 1969); "American Causes of World War III" (*The Star-Spangled Beaver,* ed. Redekop, 1971); "Evangelism and Peace" (*Probe,* ed. Fairfield, 1972).

Epp, Frank H. "Abolish the Bomb." *CanMenn* 7 (May 8, 1959), 8. Explains why the manufacture and testing of nuclear weapons should be abolished. Nuclear weapons are always dirty and should be banned for every divine and human reason.

Epp, Frank H. "Can We Disarm?" *CanMenn* 12 (Dec. 15, 1964), 7. Although disarmament is possible without economic collapse, it remains unlikely because of the stranglehold the military-industrial complex has on western society.

Epp, Frank H. "Christians Should Witness Against Man's Collective Sins." *CanMenn* 6 (Apr. 25, 1968), 3, 4. The "Ban the Bomb" movement has focused the world's growing protest against the manufacture and testing of nuclear weapons. A Christian position on nuclear weapons is developed from a biblical standpoint.

Epp, Frank H. "H-Bombs on H-Day." *CanMenn* 4 (May 25, 1956), 2. Condemns hydrogen bomb testing in general and the Pentecost Sunday test in particular. "All human and divine values, all sacredness in temporal living has suddenly been erased" when bombs are tested on holy days.

Epp, Frank H. "Makers of Peace." *CanMenn* 6 (Oct. 3, 1958), 2. The United Church of Canada is lauded for its stand for peace. The church has as much to say to government today about nuclear bombs as John the Baptist had to say to Herod about having the wrong wife.

Epp, Frank H. "Nuclear Warheads." *CanMenn* 11 (Aug. 27, 1963), 5. That Canada should acquire nuclear warheads is a tragedy, especially when the decision was made only a few days after the signing of a limited nuclear test ban treaty.

Epp, Frank H. "Nuclear Weapons." *CanMenn* 10 (Feb. 23, 1962), 2. For biblical and practical reasons Canada should not acquire nuclear weapons. Canada's mission to the world would be thwarted by such an acquisition.

Epp, Frank H. "Settling the Peace of the World." *CanMenn* 1 (Nov. 20, 1953), 2. "Guns, tanks, bombs have no place in the defense philosophy of a Christian and shouldn't be considered in a Christian nation." Our best defense is to share our material surpluses with those in need so that they need not turn to communism for an answer to their problems.

Epp, Frank H. "Stop the Nuclear Tests." *CanMenn* 5 (May 31, 1957), 2. Christians should speak prophetically and call for the end of nuclear testing and the stockpiling of nuclear weapons before it is too late.

Epp, Frank H. "The Atomic Bomb Tests." *CanMenn* 3 (May 13, 1955), 2. Good cannot come from nations' testing weapons of mass destruction. While the physical results of atomic testing remain unknown, it is inevitable that this wrong use of resources will reap evil consequences.

Epp, Frank H. "The Atomic Urge Unchecked." *CanMenn* 5 (Apr. 26, 1957), 2. Even though no one wanted it that way the atomic urge has run rampant. Science, education, and religion seem to perpetuate this situation.

Epp, Frank H. "The Folly of Rearmament." *CanMenn* 2 (Dec. 3, 1954), 2. The rearmament of Germany was to be expected in the light of history, where one nation's rearmament means an arms race for all. The Christian message in this situation is the way of the Cross.

Epp, Frank H. "The Unilateral Disarmament of the Church." *Peacemakers in a Broken World.* Ed. John A Lapp. Scottdale: Herald Press, 1969, 126-43. Unilateral disarmament is considered impractical by American society because the rich fear losing their wealth. Epp maintains that Christians must cultivate an understanding of property as a stewardship resource in order to free themselves from dependence on the military for security. The church's unilateral disarmament would be truly a form of peace witness to the state.

Epp, Frank H. (Editorial). "The Atomic Bomb Tests." *CanMenn* 3 (May 13, 1955), 2. A statement on the conflict between A-bombs and Christian hope.

Epp, Frank H. (Editorial). "The Folly of Rearmament." *CanMenn* 2 (Dec. 3, 1954), 2. Speaks of the "foolishness of the cross."

Erb, Paul. "The War Is Not Over." *GH* 38 (Aug. 31, 1945), 411. The war seems to be over but the evils which it was to cure still exist. The Atomic bomb, enormous national debts, and continued conscription are part of the legacy of this war.

Escalona, Sibylle. "Adolescence and the Threat of Nuclear War." *ChrLiv* 13 (Apr., 1966), 26-28. Reprinted from the pamphlet *Children and the Threat of Nuclear War,* 1962, Child Study Association and National Institute of Mental Health. Analysis of the threat of nuclear annihilation on adolescent development.

Everett, Glenn D. "Radiation and Our Children." *ChrLiv* 5 (Feb., 1958), 24-26. Exploring the effects of radiation emitted by nuclear bombs.

Ewert, Claire. "Weapons of Death." *MennRep* 4 (Sept. 16, 1974), 9. Also "Canadian Weapons of Death." *Intercom* 14 (Aug., 1974), 6. Discusses Canada's role in the Vietnam war through its arms sales to the US.

"Firearms Placed on Altar." *GH* 65 (July 18, 1972), 582. United Methodist hand gun owner relinquishes his weapons as "a witness for domestic disarmament in a land of escalating violence."

"Flats Defendants Get Probation." *GH* 72 (Jan. 23, 1979), 62. Report on the sentence of ten defendants who protested at the Rocky Flats nuclear weapons plant near Denver, Colo.

Failing, George E. "Could It Happen Before 1984?" *EV* 91 (Nov. 10, 1978), 15. Reflecting on George Orwell's book, *1984,* the writer suggests the US has chosen the alternative of war over peace probably on the presumption that no viable economy can survive without the sale of arms.

Fransen, Harold. "The North American Military— 2." *Menn* 93 (Apr. 18, 1978), 268. Discusses Canadian complicity in the arms race and the burgeoning military enterprise around the world.

Fransen, Harold. "The Savor of SALT." *Menn* 94 (Oct. 30, 1979), 653. Writer attempts to show the complexities of the SALT II issue and raises the question of where we as Christians endorsing a peace postition give our voice.

Franz, Delton. "A Visit to the Arms Bazaar." *ChrLead* 41 (Nov. 21, 1978), 24; "I Went to an Arms Bazaar." *GH* 71 (Dec. 5, 1978), 945; *Menn* 94 (Jan. 23, 1979), 61. Description of the annual weapons extravaganza sponsored by the Association of the US Army which is designed to entice the US and foreigners to buy the latest, most powerful, and deadly weapons.

Franz, Delton. "Conscription Not Upon Us, But the Arms Race Is." *MCC PS Wash. Memo* 10 (Sept.-

Oct., 1978), 3-4. Disagrees with news releases implying that military conscription is near; urges people to focus their energies on working to halt the arms race.

Franz, Delton. "Here We Go to the Arms Bazaar, Tra-La, Tra-La . . ." *The Other Side* 15 (Jan., 1979), 17-19. A report on a visit to an arms bazaar sponsored by the Association of the United States Army.

Franz, Delton. "Implements of Death at a Washington Bazaar." *EV* 92 (Feb. 10, 1979), 5. Reflections on a visit to the annual weapons extravaganza sponsored by the Association of the United States Army.

Franz, Delton. "President Asks Congress to Double Foreign Arms Aid." *MCC PS Wash. Memo* 7 (Nov.-Dec., 1976), 1-2. Comment on the White House collaboration with the Pentagon in expanding arms sales, with suggested actions Congress should take in limiting the arms budget.

Franz, Delton. "Sounding the Trumpet on Nuclear Arms." *ChrLead* 40 (Apr. 17, 1977), 8. Examines the reality of the nuclear arms issue. Suggestions for individuals, congregations, and conferences on how to begin to respond to these concerns.

Franz, Delton. "The Other Arms Race." *Menn* 84 (Oct. 21, 1969), 640. Information on US arms sales to other countries making continued warfare possible but limiting success in promoting agricultural and educational development.

Franz, Delton. "US Senators Propose Department of Peace." *CanMenn* 16 (Dec. 31, 1968), 1, 2. The proposal is for an umbrella organization for the Agency for International Development, the Peace Corps, and the Arms Control and Disarmament Agency.

Friesen, Duane K. "A Moral Justification for War Tax Resistance." *CGR* 1 (Spring, 1983), 21-28. The case for tax resistance depends on three criteria: that the policy of arms race escalation is a violation of moral law; that persons are obliged to disobey their government when it violates a moral law; that resisting military tax payment is an appropriate point at which to challenge government policy.

Friesen, John R. "Last of a Kind? Thoughts After the Wichita Conference." *MennMirror* 8 (Aug.-Sept., 1978), 14. The expressed purpose of the Mennonite World Conference was fellowship, but the diversity of the participants and some burning issues such as armaments, war, and justice indicate that different levels of working together will be necessary for the future.

Gaede, Don H. "GCs Seek Exemption from Collecting War Taxes." *ChrLead* 42 (Mar. 13, 1979), 22. Report on the special General Conference Mennonite Church conference, held Feb. 9-10, 1979, to "discern the will of God for Christians in their response to militarism and the worldwide arms race."

Gerber, Ellis J. Letter to the Editor. *ChrLiv* 26 (Mar., 1979), 2-3. Nonviolence and pacifism must be instilled into coming generations through limiting children's use of toy guns.

Gingerich, Melvin. "It Seems to Me." *YCC* 37 (Dec. 30, 1956), 424. American missionaries in Japan are faced with questions like "How can you justify the manufacture and use of atomic and hydrogen bombs by Christian America?"

Goering, Jim. "Servanthood for Today: Stopping the Arms Race." *Forum* 13 (Dec., 1979), 1-3. A look at SALT II, the nuclear arms race, and the example of Jesus' life leads this writer to conclude that Christians should be supporting SALT II and should use their influence within the power structure to work for arms control.

Goertzen, Don. "Everything's Going to Blow Up." *Menn* 92 (Oct. 11, 1977), 578-79. Discusses nuclear disarmament issues from the perspective of one involved in peace witness at Rocky Flats plutonium plant in Colorado.

Goertzen, Don and Solo, Pam. "Nuclear Crossroads at Rocky Flats." *Sojourners* 7 (Mar., 1978), 20. Description of the Rocky Flats nuclear weapons plant located near Denver, Colorado.

Goosen, Wally. Letter to the Editor. *MennRep* 8 (Feb. 20, 1978), 6. Interprets Mennonite peace stance as withholding aid from the injured on the battlefield in order to convert people to a peace stance. Maintains that the peace of Christ is available in the midst of flying bombs.

Goossen, Steve. Letter to the Editor. *ChrLead* 41 (May 9, 1978), 10. Resistance to the arms race can be correlated with similar historic protests like the abolitionist movement against slavery.

Graham, Billy. "A Change of Heart." *ChrLead* 42 (Aug. 28, 1979), 5. An interview with Billy Graham where he states his belief that the nation and the world face their own hour of decision about halting the escalation of nuclear weapons.

Graham, Billy, and Tçth, Karçly. " 'Breaking the Dividing Wall of Hostility . . .' " *God and Caesar* 6 (Sept., 1980), 9-11. Reprints of letters between two religious leaders on Christian witness against the arms race.

Habegger, Luann. "Exporting Men, Money, and

Arms." *MCC PS Wash. Memo* 6 (July-Aug., 1974), 1-3. Statistics and comment on US foreign military aid to train military and police forces in policies favoring the US government.

Harms, Menno. Letter to the Editor. *ChrLead* 38 (Oct. 28, 1975), 15. Believes that all the hysteria about law-abiding citizens owning guns is overdone.

Harms, Orlando. "Budget Reflects Priorities." *ChrLead* 38 (Apr. 29, 1975), 24. The national budget reflects that US has a priority to supply guns rather than butter to countries.

Hartzler, H. Harold. "Some Thoughts on the Atomic Bomb." *GH* 38 (Oct. 26, 1945), 570. Moral research lags behind the scientific research which has developed the atomic bomb. Yet new scientific discoveries place greater moral responsibilities upon humankind.

Hassler, Alfred (Review). *The Voyage of the Lucky Dragon,* by Ralph E. Lapp. Harper, 1958. Pp. 200. "The Feel of Fallout." *Fellowship* 24 (July, 1958), 33. Describes how this book is able to personalize the horror and suffering caused by war by telling what happened to twenty-three fishermen when their boat was dusted with radioactive ashes from an American H-bomb test on Mar. 1, 1954. Recommends this book for its ability to awaken the conscience.

Haury, David A. "The Mennonite Congregation of Boston." *MennLife* 34 (Sept., 1979), 24-27. The birth and development of the Mennonite congregation of Boston including their concerns and mission regarding nuclear weapons, the Vietnam war, military service, and war taxes.

Hershberger, Bernie; Bender, Brent; Kauffman, Duane; Yoder, Steve; and Nafziger, Beverly. "A Four-College Comparison of Ethical Ideologies in Relation to Current Moral Issues." *Journal of Psychology and Christianity* 1 (Fall, 1982), 32-39. A study of 207 General Psychology students explores the influence of ideology on responses to specific ethical issues, including such items as the death penalty, the military draft, and nuclear weapons.

Hershberger, Guy F. "August 6: A Day of Intercession." *GH* 52 (1959), 663. On Apr. 16-19, 1959, an international Christian peace conference, held in Prague, designated Aug. 6, the anniversary of the destruction of Hiroshima, as a day of confession, penitence, and intercession for the world. A copy of the summons to intercession is included.

Hershberger, Guy F. "Nuclear Warfare: The Christian Witness to the State." (Part 5). *GH* 53 (Nov. 15, 1960), 1001, 1014. The state with the nuclear bomb is the demonic beast of Rev. 13.

The church should rise up in a mighty witness against this force.

Hershberger, Guy F. "The Supreme Court and Conscientious Objectors." *GH Supplement* 39 (Aug., 1946), 460-61. The court has recently said that one may become a citizen of the US even if one will not bear arms. The court's position on religious liberty, while not unanimous, is nonetheless encouraging.

Hershberger, Guy F. "The Tragedy of the Empty House." *GH* 54 (1961), 733-35. Using Matt. 12:43-45, Hershberger identifies demons worse than communism which threaten the US because of the lack of dependence on God and growing dependence on wealth and power.

Hershberger, Paul. "Editorial." *IPF Notes* 3 (May, 1957), 2, 5-6. Comment on the cold war and the nuclear arms race.

Hertzler, Dan (Editorial). "Playing with Fire." *GH* 72 (Apr. 24, 1979), 352. We need to be responsible with the use of fire and with conserving fuel; especially distressing is the use of fire for destruction, as in the case in the first Trident submarine.

Hester, Hugh B. "Can We Stop War?" *Menn* 76 (May 16, 1961), 324-25. Disarmament is absolutely essential to human survival, according to important American leaders. If nations do not learn to co-exist peacefully they will perish violently.

Hiebert, Erwin N. *The Impact of Atomic Energy.* Newton: Faith and Life Press, 1961. Pp. 302. A history of the development of atomic energy and its impact on scientists, nations, and the church, together with a plea for restricting its use to peaceful purposes.

Hiebert, Erwin N. "The Role of the Scientist as Reconciliator." *PCMCP Fourteenth,* 92-98. N.p. Held at Eastern Mennonite College, Harrisonburg, Virginia, June 6-7, 1963. Evaluation of the position of the scientist to be a potential reconciler between East and West. Modern science can provide a new language and new tools that might adapt to a new formulation of the Christian ethos in various non-Western cultures.

Hiebert, Linda Gibson and Hiebert, Murray. "Why Do You Use Guns?" *MBH* 14 (Oct. 3, 1975), 17: *GH* 68 (Aug. 26, 1975), 599-600; *RepConsS* 23 (Sept., 1975), 2; *Menn* 90 (Sept. 16, 1975), 510. A 13-year-old Vietnamese boy, paralyzed by a grenade, asks this question of soldiers.

Hiebert, Murray and Hiebert, Linda Gibson. "Laos Invites the World to View Damage Caused by War." *MennRep* 8 (Jan. 23, 1978), 2. MCC representatives describe destruction in Laos caused by bombing.

Hirstine, Ed. "What Choice Shall I Make?" *Menn* 54 (Jan. 31, 1939), 9-10. Mennonites should not compromise with the military regarding a possible draft, by accepting a kind of alternative to drilling with guns. Only total nonresistance is sufficient.

Holsinger, Justus G. "Our World at the Crossroads." *GH* 48 (May 17, 1955), 465, 477-78. If the world is to survive its new-found instruments of death, the church will have to recapture, through Jesus Christ, the concept of the sacredness of life.

Horning, Emma. "How a Bomb Transformed Chang." *ChrMon* 23 (May, 1931), 141. Reprinted from *The Gospel Messenger*. Story of a Chinese soldier who leaves the army upon conversion to Christianity.

Hostetler, David E. "Lay that Pistol Down." *GH* 71 (July 4, 1978), 529. A Mennonite who attended the United Nations' Special Session on Disarmament reflects on the limitations of this world congress.

Hostetter, David E. "Carter Administration Seeks Support of Religious Community on SALT II." *Menn* 94 (Nov. 13, 1979), 684. A briefing on SALT II was set up for the religious press in an attempt to both inform and persuade the religious community to support SALT II.

Hostetter, David E. "The Church and SALT II." *GH* 72 (Nov. 6, 1979), 880. The Mennonite Church should take a strong position condemning nuclear weapons of any kind, anywhere. In particular the church needs to respond to SALT II.

Hostetter, Douglas. "In Search of Peace for Vietnam." *With* 4 (July, 1971), 15. A former Mennonite Central Committee worker was asked by the National Student Association to return to Vietnam to help draw up a peace treaty.

Hübner, Harry (Review). *King Jesus' Manual of Arms for the 'Armless,* by Vernard Eller. Nashville: Abingdon Press, 1973. Pp. 205. Also, *Liberation Ethics,* by John M. Swomley. New York: Macmillan, 1972. Pp. 238. *Menn* 88 (Oct. 30, 1973), 628-29. While Eller considers peace activism an unfaithful siezing of the reins of history, a prerogative belonging only to God, Swomley advocates nonviolent revolution as the strategy for liberation. The reviewer believes that Christian faithfulness will include political activism, but that activism will not bring the Kingdom, which is a gift of God.

Hunsberger, Wilson. "Interesting Scenes in Europe; Warsaw—Life Among the Ruins." *ChrMon* 40, Part 5, (Oct., 1948), 308-9. Describes the German bombing of Poland and the present state of the city.

"Japan Christians Ask Abolition of Nuclear Weapons." *CanMenn* 10 (July 6, 1962), 8. A group of Christians in Japan form the Miyazaki Council of Christians for the Abolition of Nuclear Weapons. Their statement was made available to MCC Peace Section by Ferd Ediger.

Janzen, David. "Mennonites and the East-West Conflict." *Christians Between East and West.* Winnipeg: Board of Christian Service, Conference of Mennonites in Canada, [ca. 1965], 40-53. Links the rise of communism with rejection of a false Christianity identifying with the exploiting class. Calls Mennonites to reject anticommunist propaganda as well as trust in nuclear weapons, in order to engage in deeper dialogue with communist people. Paper presented at the Canadian Conference Sessions, Altona, Man., July 20, 1963. Pp. 11. AMBS, MLA/BeC.

Janzen, David H. "My People, I Am Your Security." *Sojourners* 8 (Jan., 1979), 19. Affirmation that a Christian's security comes from God even when the hope for the world is dimmed by the escalating nuclear arms race.

Janzen, William (Review). *Making a Killing: Canada's Arms Industry,* by Ernie Regehr. Toronto: McClelland and Stewart, 1975. Pp. 135. *MennRep* 6 (July 12, 1976), 8. Regehr's documentation of the shape of Canadian armaments policy and business is a contribution to peace.

Kakajima, John. "North Vietnamese Talks About His Church." *MBH* 14 (Apr. 4, 1975), 28. Protestant minister reports on damage to churches by American bombing and discusses the Vietnamese church's task to help the country protect itself.

Keeney, William E. "Dutch Mennonites Discuss Problems of the Nuclear Era." *GH* 56 (July 16, 1963), 609. Report of a conference to consider the Dutch Reformed Church statement on nuclear weapons and the Mennonite response to the issue.

Kehler, Larry. "Arms Sales and Canadian Violence." *CanMenn* 18 (Oct. 2, 1970), 5. Statistical information on Canadian attitudes to violence and the promotion of violence. Asks what the church should do about it.

Kehler, Larry. "Blossoms Amidst the Bursting Bombs." *Menn* 89 (June 25, 1974), 413-14; *MennRep* 4 (July 8, 1974), 7. Initial impressions of conflict-ridden Middle East by member of MCC delegation visiting there.

Kehler, Larry. "Starve the Military Monster." *Menn* 89 (Apr. 30, 1974), 296. Calls Christians to speak forcefully against the arms race by writing to Parliament and Congress and by supporting the April 30 national day of repentance for trusting in military security.

Kent, Katherine McElroy. "A Role for Christians in National Defense?" *CanMenn* 13 (Nov. 9, 1965), 6. Interview with Andrew Brewin, a lay leader of the Anglican church of Canada, delegate to the WCC at New Delhi and a member of Canada's Parliament and of its Special Committee on Defense, in which Brewin explains his interest in getting rid of war and of the arms race, and in national defense problems.

King, Mary Lou. "Moratorium on Atomic Weapons Development?" *GH* 72 (Dec. 4, 1979), 968. Senator Mark Hatfield's amendment to the SALT II treaty is one positive alternative to the insanity of continued stockpiling and development of atomic weapons.

Klaassen, Walter. *What Have You to Do with Peace?* Altona: D. W. Friesen and Sons, Ltd., 1969. Pp. 74. Originally given as lectures designed to help Sunday school teachers teach the basic principles of nonviolence. Covers subjects such as the biblical use of the language of "principalities and powers," the church as the agency of peace, just war doctrine, nuclear war and disarmament issues, and church and state relations.

Koontz, Gayle Gerber. "Moral Responsibility in Technological Warfare." *GH* 65 (Sept. 19, 1972), 762-63. Describes American warfare in Vietnam through dike bombing, forest burning, and cloud-seeding activities, and questions what responsibility Mennonites have to witness against such actions and withhold tax money from them.

Koontz, Ted. "Has SALT II Lost Its Savor?" *Menn* 94 (Dec. 4, 1979), 733; "SALT II Better Than No Salt." *GH* 72 (Sept. 25, 1979), 757. The writer presents a brief argument for the case of SALT II. Although SALT II involves a choice between relative good and evil, we do not need to give up our vision of a world without nuclear catastrophe in order to support SALT II.

Koop, Jake (Review). *Canada and the Nuclear Arms Race,* ed. Ernie Regehr and Simon Rosenblum. Lorimer and Co., 1983. Pp. 268. *CGR* 2 (Spring, 1984), 172-76. Explains that while the articles in the compilation are, with a few exceptions, informed and dispassionate, the book as a whole lacks substantive recognition of the "unpalatable facts" that complete nuclear disarmament could well have the effect of unleashing large-scale conventional warfare. Suggests that we must, rather, learn to make

ethical choices within the reality that even if all nuclear weapons could be destroyed, we can not disinvent them.

Koop, Robert. "Ottawa Report: Is There Hypocrisy in Trudeau's Call for Disarmament?" *MennRep* 8 (June 26, 1978), 7. Comments on Prime Minister Trudeau's recent speech to the United Nations special session on disarmament, noting that while Canada indeed possesses no nuclear weapons, it sells uranium and military equipment freely, and makes huge domestic military expenditures.

Koop, Robert. "Ottawa Report: National Defense, Disarmament and the Neutron Bomb." *MennRep* 8 (Mar. 6, 1978), 7. Recent NATO meeting shows Canada's defense policy is changing from limited defense spending to major increases in armaments and forces.

Koop, Robert. "Transfiguration." *Menn* 93 (Nov. 14, 1978), 671; *MennRep* 8 (Oct. 16, 1978), 8. Discusses the convergence of the church's celebration of Jesus' transfiguration, Aug. 6, with that day in 1945 when Hiroshima was transformed into a city of death by the atomic bomb.

Krahn, David. "The Treaty of Versailles." *CanMenn* 17 (Nov. 14, 1969), 7. Insists that "territorily the Treaty (of Versailles) was not unusually severe; but economically, financially, militarily, and especially morally it was intolerable." Quotes George Goldberg as saying that "the Peace Conference of 1919 . . . was the peace to end peace."

Kraybill, Donald B. "Detours Around Jesus." *The Other Side* 14 (Dec., 1978), 17-21. Examination of some of the major detours that are used to avoid the substance of Jesus' economic message. Biblical Christians must face up to Jesus' strong call for economic conversion.

Kraybill, Donald B. *Facing Nuclear War: A Plea for Christian Witness.* Scottdale and Kitchener: Herald Press, 1982. Pp. 307. Using the tragedy of Hiroshima as a reference point, Kraybill provides clear information on the effects of contemporary nuclear weapons. In light of this "chief moral issue," he analyzes the global political situation and interweaves, with these technological and political analyses, the pertinent biblical perspectives offering guidance to Christian responses to the threat of nuclear war. In the last part of the book he concretizes these responses by suggesting specific actions individuals can take toward peace and explodes some of the excuses commonly given for not taking action.

Kraybill, J. Charles. "Conceit and Folly." *Sojourners* 9 (Apr., 1980), 8-10. Author considers present nuclear waste disposal plans foolish and dangerous. Does not distinguish between the military weapons industry and the commercial power industry in their production and disposal of nuclear wastes.

Kreider, Alan. "Biblical Perspectives on War." *Third Way* 4 (Nov., 1980), 13-14. Brings the Old Testament prophetic insistence—that Israel rely on Yahweh rather than numerical, technological or nonrestricted military strength—to bear upon our modern quest for security in nuclear weapons.

Kreider, Alan. "Swords into Plowshares." *Time to Choose: A Grass Roots Study Guide on the Nuclear Arms Race from a Christian Perspective.* Ed. Martha Keys Barker, et al. Dorset: Celebration Publishing, 1983, 54-88. Summarizes both the just war and pacifist positions and explains why adherents of both positions might together decry nuclear war.

Kreider, Alan. "The Arms Race: The Defense Debate—Nuclear Weaponry and Pacifism." *The Year 2000,* ed. John R. W. Stott. Downers Grove: InterVarsity Press, 1983, 27-55. Pp. 179. Since the security afforded by deterrence policy is neither adequate nor real, and since pacifists and just war theorists agree that nuclear war is indefensible, we ought to unite, despite other differences, in order to search for viable alternatives for conflict resolution.

Kreider, Alan. "The Gospel No to the Bomb." *Dropping the Bomb: The Church and the Bomb Debate,* ed. John Gladwin. London: Hodder and Stoughton, 1985. Pp. 74-95. Technological development, self-righteous rhetoric, and nuclear proliferation are undermining deterrence as a viable nuclear strategy. The values implicit within deterrence undermine it morally. As the stronger party in the nuclear stalemate, the West must take incremental, unilateral steps to reverse the arms race.

Kreider, Carl. "Atomic Bomb Tests." *ChrLiv* 4 (Sept., 1957), 18, 37. In spite of documented damage and death caused by atomic bomb tests, the government continues to defend them on the grounds of defense necessity.

Kreider, Carl. "Defense Against H Bomb." *ChrLiv* 1 (Jan., 1954), 39-40. Military, political, and economic defenses are discussed, as well as some practical suggestions for the Christian nonresistant.

Kreider, Carl. "Disarmament." *ChrLiv* 7 (May, 1960), 18, 37, 39. Arguments outlining the urgency of disarmament.

Kreider, Carl. "Disarmament and Your Job." *ChrLiv* 6 (July, 1959), 6-7. Suggestions for stabilizing the economy with a much lower percentage of defense spending.

Kreider, Carl. "H Bomb Foreign Policy." *ChrLiv* 1 (July, 1954), 35-36. The US atomic bomb test on Bikini Atoll which injured Japanese fishermen raises new fears about US military policy.

Kreider, Carl. "Internationalism or Isolationism?" *Menn Comm* 5 (Feb., 1951), 30, 32. Strongly advocates a Christian internationalism of increased foreign trade and aid, without rearmament and military intervention.

Kreider, Carl. "Japan Becomes an Independent Nation." *Menn Comm* 6 (June, 1952), 30, 33. Problems in US/Japanese relations may develop if US insists upon full Japanese rearmament.

Kreider, Carl. "Losing the Peace." *MennComm* 5 (Oct., 1951), 30, 32. Discussion of post-World War II treaties with Japan, Spain, and Germany that provide for rearmament.

Kreider, Carl. "Nuclear Test Ban Treaty." *ChrLiv* 10 (Oct., 1963), 18-19. Background and analysis of the treaty signed by US, Great Britain, and Soviet Union.

Kreider, Carl. "Outlawing Atomic Bomb Tests." *ChrLiv* 6 (Feb., 1959), 18, 39. Reasons for urging a ban on all further testing of nuclear weapons.

Kreider, Carl. "Rearming Our Ex-Enemies." *ChrLiv* 2 (Jan., 1955), 22, 45. Description of and comment on the agreements providing for rearmament of Japan and Germany.

Kreider, Carl. "Shall We Build Fallout Shelters?" *ChrLiv* 9 (Jan., 1962), 18, 39. Christians' highest calling is not self-preservation, but the promotion of the Kingdom of peace.

Kreider, Carl. "Summit Talks." *ChrLiv* 5 (Apr., 1958), 18, 40. Pros and cons of the proposed meeting of Eastern and Western heads of state to negotiate arms agreements.

Kreider, Carl. "The Japanese Election." *MennComm* 6 (Dec., 1952), 29-31. Japanese rearmament is one of the issues of the election disputes.

Kreider, Carl. "The Mutual Security Treaty with Japan." *ChrLiv* 7 (Sept., 1960), 19, 37. Recent political troubles with Japan over the ratification of the newest defense treaty could lead to war.

Kreider, Carl (Review). *Peace or Atomic War?* by Albert Schweitzer. New York: Henry Holt and Co., 1958. Pp. 47. *ChrLiv* 6 (Sept., 1959), 33. Reviewer observes that Schweitzer presents his objections to testing and production of nuclear weapons simply and clearly.

Kreider, L. C. "The Atomic Age." *Menn* 60 (Aug. 28, 1945), 1-2. A brief description of the development of atomic power, its uses in peace and war, and the Christian attitude toward the atomic bomb.

Kreider, Robert S. "Use of Deadly Force Authorized." *Sojourners* 9 (July, 1979), 36. Meditation on a visit to a Titan II installation of McConnell Air Force Base in Kansas.

Kreider, Robert S. (Review). *The Rule of the Lamb*, by Larry Kehler, and *The Rule of the Sword*, by Charlie Lord. Newton: Faith and Life Press, 1978. *Menn* 93 (Oct. 3, 1978), 573. Enthusiastic recommendation for these readable, information-filled booklets on the war tax question (Kehler) and the arms race and militarization (Lord).

Kroeker, David. "Arms and the Poor: What's a Billion?" *MennRep* 7 (Sept. 19, 1977), 6. Presents statistics of Canada's growing arms industry and calls for a halt to this drain on essential resources and services.

Kroeker, Marvin (Review). *Between the Eagle and the Dove: The Christian and American Foreign Policy*, by Ronald Kirkemo. Downers Grove: InterVarsity, 1976. Pp. 215. *ChrLeader* 40 (Oct. 11, 1977), 11. This "Christian perspective" on such issues as war, nuclear armaments, and international relations is not distinguishable from a "strictly secular" perspective. Therefore the book is neither newly insightful nor compatible with an Anabaptist-Mennonite view.

Kroeker, Walter. "Justice and Rights Issues Occupy MCC Members in Reedley." *MennRep* 9 (Feb. 19, 1979), 1. Among the issues discussed at the MCC annual meeting was aid to Vietnam, justice and human rights overseas, and a paper on militarism calling the church to renounce the development of nuclear weapons and military exports.

Kroeker, Walter.. "What About Our Guns?" *ChrLead* 38 (Sept. 30, 1975), 24. Our concern for human life should extend to issues like gun control.

"Letter from Miyazaki." *Menn* 77 (July 10, 1962), 435. The Miyazaki (Japan) Council of Christians, which includes a Mennonite pastor, appeals to American churches to cooperate in the abolition of nuclear weapons.

"Letter to Members of Congress." *Menn* 54 (Oct. 3, 1939), 3. Peace Committee of the Western District (GCM) says our nation should endeavor to adjust all international tensions by negotiation rather than by force of arms.

Lang, Ehrhardt. "The Bomb." *YCC* 47 (Aug. 7, 1966), 2. Description of some of the events surrounding the bombing of Hiroshima.

Lapp, John A. "A Cease-Fire Is Not a Peace." *ChrLiv* 20 (Mar., 1973), 15, 27. Discussion of the US bombing of Hanoi and the subsequent cease-fire agreement.

Lapp, John A. "A Treaty, But No Peace." *ChrLiv* 26 (May, 1979), 33-35. President Carter's peace mission to Egypt and Israel has resulted in a treaty but not peace because negotiations did not include other essential Arab voices.

Lapp, John A. "Agenda for the Eighties." *ChrLiv* 27 (Feb., 1980), 15, 34. Includes statistics about nuclear weapons proliferation.

Lapp, John A. "Arms Sales: International Epidemic of the Seventies." *ChrLiv* 25 (Mar., 1978), 15, 31. Comment on the expanding international arms market, with a plea for reversing the trend.

Lapp, John A. "Bullets Instead of Bodies: The New Indochina War." *ChrLiv* 19 (Apr., 1972), 18-19. Comment on the new automated and electronic techniques used by the US army in Vietnam.

Lapp, John A. "Is There a 'Security Gap'?" *ChrLiv* 16 (Jan., 1969), 18-19. Comparison of US and Soviet arsenals, with a call for curtailing the arms race.

Lapp, John A. "Nuclear Nightmare." *ChrLiv* 22 (Jan., 1975), 15. Compilation of statistics from Defense Department, comment by American Friends Service Committee, quotations from Henry Kissinger and Dwight D. Eisenhower on the subject of strategic weaponry.

Lapp, John A. "Pentagonism." *ChrLiv* 18 (July, 1971), 18-19. 14 (July, 1967), 18-19. Description of the political and military tensions among the regions in Nigeria. Comment on Pentagon policies and propaganda, including a call for halting its growth.

Lapp, John A. "The Agenda for Jimmy Carter." *ChrLiv* 24 (Mar., 1977), 15, 27. Number one priority is scaling down the arms race, followed by restructuring world power and restoring the democratic balance.

Lapp, John A. "The Antiballistic Missile (ABM)." *ChrLiv* 16 (July, 1969), 18-19. Discussion of the latest defense weapon and the unwillingness of many members of Congress to support it.

Lapp, John A. "The Foreign Policy Debate of 1964." *ChrLiv* 11 (Nov., 1964), 18-19. Contrasting Goldwater's militaristic goals with Fulbright's ideas of international cooperation and arms limitations.

Lapp, John A. "The Meaning of the Pentagon Papers." *ChrLiv* 18 (Sept., 1971), 18-19.

Discussion of the revelations about American policy in Vietnam as found in the Pentagon study.

Lapp, John A. "The Roots of War." *ChrLiv* 25 (Apr., 1978), 14-15. Disarmament alone is not the key to peace; a new social order must be created.

Lapp, John A. "Whatever Happened to Detente?" *ChrLiv* 27 (Apr., 1980), 15, 33. Hawkish rhetoric in Washington threatens to sever the fragile US-Soviet detente of the past decade.

Lapp, John A. (Review). *Foreign Policy in Christian Perspective,* by John C. Bennett. Charles Scribner's Sons, 1966. Pp. 110. *ChrLiv* 13 (Nov., 1966), 28-29. Recommends this examination of the cold war, nuclear weapons, and Vietnam in light of Christian realism.

Lapp, John A. (Review). *The Respectable Murderers: Social Evil and Christian Conscience,* by Paul Hanly Furfey. Herder and Herder, 1966. Pp. 192. *ChrLiv* 15 (Jan., 1968), 33-34. Recommends this discussion of four conspicuous social injustices: American slavery, German genocide of Jews, the mass bombing of noncombatants during World War II, and treatment of the poor.

Lapp, John A. (Review). *Voices from the Plain of Jars,* compiled. Harper & Row, 1972. Pp. 160. *GH* 66 (Nov. 6, 1973), 855. Excerpts from interviews with Laotian peasants who fled the bombing of the Plain of Jars in the 1960s graphically portray peasant life in wartime.

Lapp, Karin and Leichty, Greg. Letter from members of the Ad Hoc Committee on Disarmament to Goshen College faculty, Goshen, Ind., Mar. 3, 1978. Pp. 2. MHL.

Leatherman, Mary. "When Your Child Wants to Play with Guns." *ChrLiv* 25 (July, 1978), 12-14. One family's attempts to deal with war toys and games.

Lederach, John Paul. "Candlelight in the Darkness of Anti-Christ." *Forum* 13 (Dec., 1979), 4-6. Studies the implications that the nuclear arms race and SALT II have for Christian faith and witness.

Lehman, Frances (Review). *North Vietnam: A Documentary,* by John Gerassi. Bobbs-Merrill, 1968. Pp. 200. *ChrLiv* 16 (Nov., 1969), 33-34. Recommends this reporter's presentation of the reality of US bombing in Vietnam.

Lehman, Herbert H. "The Senator Is Disturbed." *Fellowship* 18 (July, 1952), 18-23. The Senator writes about his concerns regarding the Japanese Peace Treaty and includes some of the correspondence he has had encouraging him not to endorse the rearming of Japan.

Lehman, M[artin] C[lifford]. "Need of Shelter; Needs and Conditions in Europe." *ChrMon* 37, Part 4, (Oct., 1945), 256. Bombing and "scorched earth" policy destroy housing and shelter.

Lehman, Melvin L. (Review). *Who Burned the Barn Down?,* drama by I. Merle Good. *ChrLiv* 18 (May, 1971), 36-37. Reviewer observes the play explores the problem of peacemaking in the context of pacifism in personal relations. Lind, Loren. "One Thing to Do About It." *ChrLiv* 11 (Apr., 1964), 2. Editorial suggests books on war, nonviolent racial revolution, nuclear arms, cold war, and poverty, in order to help our minds keep pace with our bodies living in a modern world.

Lind, Loren. "A Great Society to All." *YCC* 47 (Mar. 27, 1966), 6. Description of the various programs of the Great Society. We must also face the question of whether a society that spends the greatest resources for instruments of war can be called great.

Lind, Marcus. "The Battle Is Not Yours But God's." *ST* 47 (Oct., 1979), 11. A Bible study of 2 Chron. 20 looking at the conditions that Judah had to meet before taking up arms.

Lord, Charles R. "And I Saw a Beast Coming Out of the Sea." *Peace Section Newsletter* 9 (May-June, 1978), 4-7. Examines the role and the latest developments associated with the submarine program in the US.

Lord, Charles R. "Building a Submarine for Peace." *Lifework* 4 (1979), 7-8. Describes a high school Sunday School class project of constructing a Trident submarine—a length of rope the length of the sub—as a witness against nuclear weapons.

Lord, Charles R. Letter to the Editor. *ChrLead* 41 (May 9, 1978), 10. Reason for joining Mennonite Brethren was an understanding of the position on peace and nonresistance. Urges a statement of concern on the arms race.

Lord, Charles R. "The Strange Journey of the Killer Bombs." *The Other Side* 15 (Jan., 1979), 23-27. Exploration into the responsibility for weapons that are built in the United States and eventually used to destroy life in other countries.

"MCC Asks Unconditional Outlaw of All Nuclear Weapons." *CanMenn* 6 (May 23, 1958), 1. A joint statement against nuclear weapons is made by Mennonites, Brethren, and Friends.

Makaroff, Sonya. "Civil Disobedience at Comox." *CanMenn* 13 (Aug. 24, 1965), 4. Asks Mennonites to participate in Comox Peace Project '65, an organized protest against the basing of nuclear weapons on Canadian soil.

Martin, Earl S. "Bombs Wait for Viet Farmers." *ChrLead* 36 (July 10, 1973), 4; *Menn* 88 (July 10, 1973), 431; *MennRep* 3 (July 9, 1973), 9; *GH* 66 (July 31, 1973), 589. There is a serious problem for Vietnamese refugees as they move back to the farmland which is littered with live bombs, dud artillery shells, and undetonated mines and booby traps.

Martin, Earl S. "Part of Me Died Today." *ChrLiv* 14 (Feb., 1967), 20. Poem mourning the deaths caused by American bombing in Vietnam.

Marymoon, Pashta. "Canadian Group Advocates War Tax Resistance." *God and Caesar* 5 (Aug., 1979), 6-7. Because modern warfare is more dependent on armaments than on large armies and therefore relies primarily on revenue from taxes, this Canadian group, War Tax Alternatives, strongly encourages war tax resistance.

McSorley, Richard T., S.J. "It's a Sin to Build a Nuclear Weapon." *IPF Notes* 23 (Mar., 1977), 5-7. Reprinted from *Sojourners* (Feb., 1977). Describes the effect of a 20-megaton nuclear weapon and asserts that the possession of and intent to use nuclear weapons is wrong.

Mennonite Central Committee. "Telegram Commends President's Efforts," *GH* 61 (Apr. 23, 1968), 375-76. A telegram commending President Johnson for stopping the bombing of North Vietnam.

Mennonite Central Committee Canada News Service (Review). *Making a Killing: The Truth About the Canadian Arms Industry,* by Ernie Regehr. N.p., n.d. *Forum* 9 (Feb., 1976), 6-7. Summarizes the main thesis of this book: Canada's diplomatic stance as a nation favoring nonviolent solutions is inconsistent with its promotion of Canadian-made arms abroad.

Mennonite Central Committee Peace Section. "A Plea to Resist the Nuclear Arms Race." Adopted Nov. 20, 1981. P. 1. (Located in MCC Peace Section Official Statements folder in MHL.) Urges Mennonite and Brethren in Christ churches to witness against the momentum of the nuclear arms race.

Metzler, Edgar. "Washington Report: Gearing Up for Return of Draft." *MennRep* 10 (Oct. 27, 1980), 7. As plans for draft resumption unfold in Washington, Mennonites must witness to a faith that does not depend on arms for security.

Miller, Ellene. Letter to the Editor. *Menn* 94 (May 1, 1979), 316. The Minneapolis midtriennium conference placed a great deal of emphasis on law, but the church must deal with a "higher law" of compassion, justice, and mercy in responding to all the victims of the arms race and nuclear proliferation.

Miller, Evelyn. "Power to the People." *Builder* 29 (Dec., 1979), 2-7. A reading drama for five persons which raises some of the significant issues of the development of nuclear power and nuclear weapons. Focus on appropriate Christian responses to these issues.

Miller, Levi. "The Nuclear Threat." *Builder* 32 (Jan., 1982), 2-3. Although the historic peace churches have a long history of dealing with such war and peace issues as conscription, the issues of nuclear war are relatively new and require study and action.

Miller, Paul M. (Review). *This Atomic Age and the World of God,* by Wilbur M. Smith. Boston: W. A. Wilde Co., 1948. Pp. 363. *ChrMon* 41 (Mar., 1949), 86-87. Reviewer recommends the book for its study of the implications of releasing nuclear energy and its relating the effects of the bomb to select biblical passages.

Mumaw, David K. Letter to the Editor. *GH* 65 (Dec. 12, 1972), 1020-21. Argues that gun ownership can be consistent with a profession of nonviolence if the gun is used only on animals, not people. Disagrees with the idea that guns breed violence.

Myers, Rosalyn. "Opening Pandora's Box: Which Way Will the US Go on the Neutron Bomb?" *MCC PS Wash. Memo* 9 (July-Aug., 1977), 1-2, 8. A decision to deploy the neutron bomb would seriously threaten the future of arms limitation talks.

"New Call to Peacemaking." *EV* 91 (Nov. 10, 1978), 16. The New Call to Peacemaking, a coalition of the historic peace churches, agreed to carry its concern about military spending, nuclear weapons, arms sales, and related matters to President Carter.

Nelson, Boyd N. (Review). *The Irreversible Decision,* by Robert C. Batchelder. Macmillan, 1965. *ChrLiv* 13 (June, 1966), 34. Recommends this doctoral dissertation tracing the development of the atomic bomb and American military strategy in World War II.

Newcomer, Peggy Kilborn. "Seattle Mennonites Participate in Anti-Trident March." *Menn* 94 (Dec. 4, 1979), 728. At Bangor, Washington, 20 members of the South Seattle Mennonite Church joined hundreds of others on Oct. 28 in a peaceful protest march against the proliferation of nuclear weapons.

Niemoeller, Martin. "The Way of Peace." *GH* 48 (Feb. 15, 1955), 153; *CanMenn* 5 (July 19, 1957), 2. The author talks with three leading German nuclear physicists. The destructive power of the bomb cannot be exaggerated; war is madness. The New Testament's teaching of peace is the only answer.

Nigh, Harold. "A Bright Light on the Testing Grounds of Galilee." *MennRep* 9 (Feb. 5, 1979), 5. The bright light of Jesus is diametrically opposed to the bright light preceding the mushroom cloud of the atomic bomb. This sermon urges us to follow the way of the Prince of Peace.

Nisley, Weldon D. "Nuclear Power and Sin." *Menn* 92 (Oct. 11, 1977), 580-81. Using "nuclear power" to mean the power accompanying possession and use of nuclear weapons, Nisly discusses the morality of nuclear weapons when compared with Jesus' teachings on peacemaking.

"Office Restructured, Clearer Witness Urged at Peace Section Meeting." *GH* 72 (Jan. 2, 1979), 8-9. Report from the annual MCC Peace Section (International) meeting at Hesston, Kansas, in Dec., 1978, where a statement was accepted calling North American Mennonites to give clearer witness to government and other bodies against militarism and the arms race.

"Our Position on Peace." *Menn* 54 (Jan. 17, 1939), 5. A resolution adopted by the Grace Mennonite Church, Lansdale, Pa., in the face of increasing armaments and international tensions. "We cannot sanction war nor conscientiously lend our support to the taking of human life."

Olson, Ted. "An Alternmative Defense Strategy for Canada." *PlMon* 2 (Nov., 1979), 4-5. Suggests Canada look seriously at non-military methods of civilian resistance in order to lessen dependence on American military protection.

Oniga, Akiko. "The Sea of Flames." *YCC* 49 (May 12, 1968), 12. A personal tragedy is shared by an eyewitness of the bombing of Hiroshima.

Ortman, David. Letter to the Editor. *Menn* 92 (Jan. 25, 1977), 61. Reprints letter written to President Carter on "deeply troubling" issues such as development of the Trident undersea missile system, production of the B-1 bomber, and absence of amnesty for war resisters.

Ortman, David. "Nuclear Energy Myths." *Menn* 95 (Jan. 1, 1980), 13. Links nuclear energy development to nuclear weapons building.

"Peace Groups Affirm SALT, Caution President." *Menn* 94 (June 19, 1979), 424. Thirty national organizations, including MCC Peace Section and individuals, urge President Carter not to use promises of new weapons to win Senate votes for the approval of the SALT II Treaty.

"Peace Section (US) Calls for Restraint in Iran Crisis, Supports SALT Amendment." *GH* 72 (Dec. 25, 1979), 1032, 1037. Meeting of MCC Peace Section (US) passed resolutions concerning the US-Iranian crisis, SALT II, and the proposed World Peace Tax Fund on Nov. 30-Dec. 1.

Pauls, Alvin N. Letter to the Editor. *ChrLead* 38 (Nov. 11, 1975), 15. People, not guns, are instruments of all violence.

Peachey, J. Lorne. "Army Men and Dart Guns." *ChrLiv* 22 (Apr., 1975), 39. Editorial recounts family search for a policy toward toys of war and violence.

Peachey, J. Lorne. "For the Good of the People." *ChrLiv* 15 (Feb., 1968), 11, 32. Report of a Pentagon briefing with 45 editors of religious magazines attempting to gain access to facts about Vietnam.

Peachey, Paul L. "Hiroshima: Mecca of World Peace?" *ChrLiv* 6 (Dec., 1959), 12-14. The city is dedicated to peace, but the effects of the atomic bomb remain. Also as paper, n.d. Pp. 4. MLA/BeC.

Peachey, Paul L. "New Ethical Possibility: The Task of 'Post Christendom Ethics'." *New Theology No. 3*, ed. Martin E. Marty and Dean G. Peerman. New York: Macmillan, 1965, 103-117. Discusses, in the context of the break-up of the Constantinian synthesis, the crisis in Christian morality brought about by the development of nuclear weapons and explores the possibility that the community of grace, rather than the natural community, may become re-established as the framework for Christian ethical thought.

Peachey, Paul L. "Peacemaking, a Church Calling." *ChrCent* 80 (July 31, 1963), 952-54. Reflects on an ecumenical peace colloquium which discussed such topics as church-state separation, the church's position toward possession of nuclear weapons, and the church's contribution to the resolution of the East-West conflict.

Peachey, Paul L. (Editorial). "Is There Still Any Point to Conscientious Objection?" *RepConsS* 21 (June, 1964), 2. In order to meet the challenges presented by the threat of nuclear war, the CO position must be based on a less dubious premise than the hope that war will be eradicated through a popular adoption of the CO position.

Peachey, Paul (Review). *Children of the A-Bomb: Testament of the Boys and Girls of Hiroshima,* by Dr. Arata Osada. Uchida Rokakuho Publishing House, 1959. "Book Review of Children of the A-Bomb." *CanMenn* 8 (June 3, 1960), 2, 9. Recommends this book containing the "simple, moving, personal accounts: of some of the Japanese grade school, high school, and college students who lived through the horors of the Hiroshima bombing.

Peachey, Urbane. "Reflections on the UN Special Session on Disarmament." *Peace Section Newsletter* 9 (May-June, 1978), 1-3. Examines some of the limitations and proposals of the United Nations special session on disarmament held in May, 1978.

Peachey, Urbane. "The Violence of Complicity." *Peace Section Newsletter* 8 (Feb., 1977), 5-6. Even though the United States government is increasingly concerned about the proliferation of weapons technology in various parts of the world, United States firms are participating in a diversity of multinational arms schemes.

Penner, Lydia. "Researcher Says Canadian Arms Industry Based on Fallacies." *Peace Section Newsletter* 8 (Apr., 1977), 2-4. The Canadian arms industry is based on the profit motive and the arguments used to rationalize it publicly are fabrications.

Penner, Mrs. H. A. Letter to the Editor. *ChrLead* 41 (June 6, 1978), 11. We ought to believe in a God whose power of love has greater ability than armaments.

Peters, Robert V. "The Heart of the Beast." *Menn* 94 (Sept. 18, 1979), 557. Reports witness of a group of people at the Pentagon against the destruction of nuclear weapons and their call for repentance.

Platt, LaVonne. "On Atoms and Hiroshima Day." *Menn* 95 (Aug. 5, 1980), 465. Laments the creative force turned to destructive force in the atomic bomb.

Ploughshares Study Group, Halifax. "'Get Out of the Arms Race . . .' " *PlMon* 1 (Sept., 1978), 6. Letter to the Canadian prime minister urging a moratorium on sales and production of nuclear weapons by Canada.

Powell, Donald E. Letter to the Editor. *GH* 65 (Nov. 21, 1972), 973. Labels as communist propaganda the idea that guns cause violence. Asserts his intention to use his hunting weapons on criminal intruders if necessary, since God does not intend people to die at the hand of "senseless criminals," but rather to die for Christ's sake.

Preheim, Marion Keeney. "Send Us Young Men Without Guns." *CanMenn* 17 (Aug. 22, 1969), 6. Interview with Lucien Luntadila, a Kimbanguist leader visiting American Mennonite communities.

(Review). *Disarmament Times.* Published by the Non-Governmental Organizations Committee on Disarmament at the UN Headquarters, n.d. *MCC PS Newsletter* 10 (Jan.-Feb., 1980), 9. Discusses the viewpoint of this newspaper reporting regularly and fully on disarmament issues in the United Nations.

Ramalingam, Mrs. M. P. Letter to the Editor. *Menn* 92 (June 21, 1977), 412. Indian Christian calls western missionaries to distinguish allegiance to Christ from allegiance to the economic and political structures of their countries, since western dominance feeds the arms race and breeds dependence.

Ratzlaff, Peter. "Not in the Bomb." *CanMenn* 5 (Aug. 16, 1957), 2. Hope is found in God as international scientific group issues statement against nuclear war.

Redekop, John H. "Looking Backward . . . and also Ahead." *MBH* 17 (Dec. 22, 1978), 10. Ominous signs of the future include stockpiling weapons, Mideast conflict, racism in Africa.

Redekop, John H. "Vietnam, 1976." *MBH* 15 (Mar. 5, 1976), 12. Calls peace-preaching Christians to give massive economic aid for the destruction caused by US bombing.

Redekopp, Orlando. Letter to the Editor. *MBH* 19 (Jan. 18, 1980), 8. Mennonite pacifists should be declaring that arms made in North America and sold to Third World governments are destroying hope for the poor of those nations.

Regehr, Ernie. "Civil War in El Salvador: North America Supports a Repressive Regime." *MennRep* 10 (Dec. 8, 1980), 8. Reports on North American military support of the violently repressive Salvadorian government, and calls for the right to self-rule by the people of El Salvador and an end to foreign arms shipments.

Regehr, Ernie. "Disarmament Week 1980: Canadian Churches Campaign Against the Arms Race." *MennRep* 10 (Nov. 10, 1980), 7. Reviews the major issues addressed by Disarmament Week activities.

Regehr, Ernie. *Making a Killing: Canada's Arms Industry.* Toronto: McClelland and Steward Limited in cooperation with MCC Canada, 1975. Pp. 135. Discusses the exploitation of the international arms market, promoting and marketing the arms industry, and defense research, in an effort to prove the contention that the export of arms is an indefensible pursuit. Appendices include data on Canadian defense industry products, Canadian companies receiving contracts from the US defense department, and grants distributed by the Defense Research Board.

Regehr, Ernie. "Micronesia: Nuclear Laboratory of the Big Powers." *MennRep* 10 (Mar. 31, 1980), 7. Discusses the use of these South Pacific Islands as nuclear weapons test sites by American, French, and British forces who apparently care little for the effects of such operations on the lives of Micronesians.

Regehr, Ernie. *Militarism and the World Military Order: A Study Guide for Churches.* Geneva, Switzerland: Commission of the Churches on International Affairs of the World Council of Churches, 1980. Pp. 69. Discussion in 4 parts: "The Dynamics of Militarism," which deals with such issues as the nuclear arms race, international trade, and the United Nations; "The Fruits of Militarism," which discusses the security question and the social/economic consequences of militarism; "The Roots of Militarism," including external and internal factors; "Militarism and the Response of the Church."

Regehr, Ernie. "The Arms Industry in Canada." *MCC PS Newsletter* 10 (Sept.-Oct., 1980), 6-7. Focuses on the dependence of the Canadian arms industry on US defense decisions and expenditures.

Regehr, Ernie. "The UN Sessions on Disarmament: The Arms Race Continues." *MennRep* 8 (July 24, 1978), 7. Reflects on recent United Nations special sessions on disarmament, noting that no progress was made in curbing expanding arms buildup.

Regehr, Ernie. "Uranium Refineries and the Bomb: Need to Redefine Our Needs." *MennRep* 10 (Aug. 18, 1980), 7. Not the closing down of nuclear power plants but the sealing down of North American consumption will reduce the need for gigantic defense systems and nuclear weapons.

Regehr, Ernie and Thomson, Murray. "Appeal to US and Soviet Leaders." *MCC PS Newsletter* 10 (Sept.-Oct., 1980), 9. Reprinted from *PlMon* (Feb.-Mar., 1980), 2. Letter to Presidents Jimmy Carter and Leonid Brezhnev urging detente and nuclear weapons freeze.

Reimer, Richard. "Facing the Race." *Menn* 76 (Jan. 3, 1961), 5-6. Questions the effectiveness of the usually proposed alternatives to payment of war taxes. Asks for massive direct efforts toward disarmament.

Reimer, Vic. "More Than a Gripe." *Menn* 93 (Apr. 4, 1978), 240. The madness of nuclear weapons calls all Christians to witness against evil powers. Writer encourages Mennonites to participate in the national peaceful demonstration at Rocky Flats against nuclear weapons.

Reimer, Vic. "Nuclear Threat to World Stressed." *Menn* 94 (Jan. 2, 1979), 7. The first nuclear war conference held Dec. 7, 1978, in Washington, DC, discussed the inevitability of nuclear war, how it would start, where it would be fought, and its devastating effects.

Reimer, Vic. "The Arms Race: Playing Games with the Planet." *MennRep* 9 (Jan. 8, 1979), 3. The first nuclear war conference held Dec. 7, 1978, in Washington, DC, featured a panel of scientists, military men, and public affairs analysts, who discussed the threat of a nuclear holocaust.

Reimer, Vic. "The Myths That We Live By Will Change, Says Specialist." *Menn* 94 (Mar. 20, 1979), 215. Speaking at the Mid-America New Call to Peacemaking conference, Mar. 3, at Bethel College, Burns Weston said that among the myths that will need to change are: wealth trickles down to the poor; bigger is better; arms spending helps the economy; and the nation state is the ultimate political structure.

Rempel, Peter H. and Miller, Larry. "Church Life in Russia: Two Impressions by North Americans." *MennRep* 9 (Dec. 10, 1979), 5. These reports from a study tour to Russia include concern over the arms race and the need for sincere peace initiatives by the United States.

Rempel, Ron. "Disarmament—Urgent Agenda for Christians." *MennRep* 10 (Nov. 10, 1980), 6. Urges Mennonites to become actively involved into the disarmament movement, not to allow a two-kingdom theology to lead to passive resignation to nuclear arms buildup.

Rempel, Roy. Letter to the Editor. *MBH* 19 (Dec. 5, 1980), 8. Arms levels and defense spending must be kept where they are to insure against Soviet attack.

Rich, Elaine Sommers and Rich, Ronald. "Christians and Bomb Tests." *Menn* 73 (Mar. 11, 1958), 150-51; *GH* 51 (Mar. 11, 1958), 222-23. Documents the dangers of radioactivity and urges Christians to witness against the immorality of bomb-testing.

Rinks, Riley. Letter to the Editor. *Menn* 88 (Feb. 13, 1973), 110-111. Criticizes the voices faulting Billy Graham for not speaking out against American bombing of Vietnam, since the writer believes government efforts toward a settlement of the war are being hampered by meddling and criticism from "peace" advocates.

Roberts, Marge. Letter to the Editor. *Menn* 94 (Sept. 25, 1979), 574. The writer was sentenced to pay a fine of $1000 for trespassing against the Rocky Flats nuclear weapons plant; she explains in the letter her ongoing participation in a peace witness.

Ruth, John L., ed. "Mennonite Petition to the Assembly." *GH* 68 (Nov. 4, 1975), 800; *Menn* 91 (Jan. 13, 1976), 21. A 1775 Mennonite petition to the Pennsylvania Assembly requesting respect for the position of those who cannot, in good conscience, bear arms.

"Saskatchewan Peace Vigil to Call for Disarmament." *CanMenn* 13 (June 1, 1965), 1, 2. Report on a Doukhobor peace witness at the Dana radar base in Saskatchewan, led by Peter Makaroff. Makaroff wanted to involve the Mennonites but found them too apathetic.

"Seven Arrested at Rocky Flats: Felony Charge Leveled." *Menn* 94 (Oct. 16, 1979), 617. On Sept. 26, seven persons, all members of Christian communities, trespassed on the property surrounding the Rocky Flats nuclear weapons plant near Denver, Colo.

"Statement of Position from Mennonite MP." *MennRep* 9 (Nov. 12, 1979), 7, 8. John Reimer, MP for Kitchener, Ont., responds to a list of questions from the *Mennonite Reporter,* setting forth his position on various issues including arms sales, abortion, and capital punishment.

"Students Fast, Pray, and Protest." *CanMenn* 13 (May 18, 1965), 1. Report on a fast at MBS to show concern for American bombing of North Vietnam.

Sartin, Nancy E. "Any Number Can Run." *YCC* 49 (May 26, 1968), 10. Both the United States and Russia encourage the small arms race by investment, sales, and new systems. All the countries want to be involved.

Sartin, Nancy E. "Battle Tickets—No Money Down." *YCC* 49 (May 12, 1968), 2-5. Conventional arms are a greater threat to peace than nuclear arms because of the increasing international trade with very little regulation.

Sartin, Nancy E. "Pageants and Windmills." *YCC* 49 (June 2, 1968), 11. Survey of the corporate international cartels involved in the conventional arms race.

Schmidt, Linda. "Denver Area Economic Conversion Project Underway." *Peace Section Newsletter* 8 (Nov.-Dec., 1977), 9-10. Describes an organization called the Social and Economic Analysis Corporation (SEAC) which is working on plans for total economic conversion in the greater Denver metropolitan area. Economic conversion is the transition from defense- to civil-related industries and employment.

Schmidt, Linda. "Perpetuating Repression: US Training of Foreign Military and Police." *Peace Section Newsletter* 9 (Jan.-Feb., 1978), 4-8. The training of foreign military and police has been an integral part of the US foreign policy over

the past twenty-five years. The countries which have received large amounts of military and economic aid are the same countries which have been cited most often for human rights violations.

Schmidt, Steven G. Letter to the Editor. *Menn* 88 (Feb. 6, 1973), 93-94. Writer mourns the American bombing of Vietnam, speaking out in order to dissassociate himself from the terrible acts.

Schmucker, Tim. Letter to the Editor. *MennRep* 9 (July 23, 1979), 6. A response to P. J. Sawatzky's letter in the previous issue of *MennRep* arguing that the biblical teachings are not so simple and clear and that the build-up of nuclear arms is costly and destructive.

Schrag, Martin H. "Graham and Stott on Nuclear Weapons." *Menn* 95 (Dec. 2, 1980), 705; *EvVis* 93 (Sept. 10, 1980), 4-5. Comment on recent conclusions by John R. W. Stott and Billy Graham that the nuclear weapons race is madness and that Christians are called to seek salvation, not destruction.

Schrag, Martin H. "The New Call to Peacemaking—Hearing and Heeding the Call." *EV* 91 (Dec. 25, 1978), 5-7. A report on the national meeting of the New Call to Peacemaking held at Green Lake, Wis. Although the US is presently not engaged in a war, the threat of a nuclear holocaust, the possibility of conscription, and the build-up of arms, among other things, all urge us to heed the call to peacemaking.

Schuchardt, John. "A Parable." *God and Caesar* 3 (Nov., 1977), 3-4. Various religious groups consider the suffering of villagers from napalm bombs but do not take personal responsibility by refusing to pay for war, a parallel to religious leaders in the parable of the Good Samaritan.

Sera, Megumi. "Child of the A-Bomb." *ChrLiv* 10 (July, 1963), 28-29. Reprinted from *Children of the A-Bomb,* compiled by Arata Osada. G. P. Putnam's Sons, 1959. A woman from Hiroshima who was a sixth grader when the bomb was dropped describes that day.

Shank, Duane. "Pentagon Announces Discharge Review." *RepConsS* 34 (Apr., 1977), 1, 6. Explains and responds to President Carter's policies dealing with military deserters and veterans receiving other than honorable discharges from the amnesty movement's point of view.

Shank, J. Ward. "The Struggle Over Disarmament." *ST* 29 (1st Qtr., 1961), 3. The motives of disarmament are good but the efforts are futile. The church should be diligent in the task of mission to a lost world rather than spending time working for disarmament.

Shank, J. Ward (Editorial). "Which Way to Peace?" *ST* 48 (Feb., 1980), 6-8. Discusses the Hatfield amendment to the SALT II treaty and cautions against using political action to bring about peace.

Sheats, Ladon. Letter to the Editor. *Menn* 93 (Mar. 7, 1978), 173. Calls attention to Canadian complicity in the arms race.

Sheats, Ladon. *God and Caesar* 4 (June, 1978), 4-5. A poem reflecting on the nonviolent peace witness in which the writer was involved at the Pentagon and describing the three days of action and vigils.

Shenk, Phil M. "A Missile Built on Quicksand." *Sojourners* 9 (May, 1980), 9-10. Description and criticism of the proposed M-X missile system.

Shenk, Phil M. "Faith in the Works." *GH* 72 (Oct. 30, 1979), 851-52. A plea to the Mennonite Church to respond to our present perilous situation, and in particular to the SALT II treaty.

Shenk, Phil M. "Washington for Jesus." *Sojourners* 9 (June, 1980), 10-11. The religious rally in Washington focused on issues such as waning US military power and ignored problems of the arms race and proliferating violence.

Shetler, Sanford G. "Peace and War: The Hydrogen Bomb and Our Peace Testimony." *GH* 48 (Jan. 18, 1955), 57. The witness should be not only against the hydrogen bombs but against all war, all weapons. The world should know we are fighting a spiritual battle.

Sider, Ronald J. "At Arm's Length." *United Evangelical Action* 42 (Mar.-Apr., 1983), 7-8. Supports the nuclear freeze movement because the proposed new weapons systems complicate verification and because the hope that the superpowers can continue to possess nuclear weapons without using them is based on the shaky premises of humanism.

Siebert, Allan. "Mennonite Community Helps Block Uranium Refinery." *MCC PS Newsletter* 10 (Sept.-Oct., 1980), 1-3. Reviews the role of Mennonites in Warman, Saskatchewan, in blocking Eldorado Nuclear Ltd.'s plans to build a uranium refinery there; cites Mennonite concerns for land stewardship and the refinery's link to nuclear weapons proliferation.

Siebert, Allan J. "The Ranks of the Insane." *MBH* 17 (Apr. 28, 1978), 11. Editorial expressing concern for the vast expense of maintaining the arms race.

Smedes, Lewis B. "Who Will Answer?" *Menn* 88 (Jan. 9, 1973), 32. Calls for evangelist Billy Graham, who "has the heart of evangelical middle America in his hands" to speak out on the moral and spiritual issues involved in the massive bombing of Vietnam.

Smith, Willard H. (Review). *The Military Establishment*, by John M. Swomley, Jr. Boston: Beacon Press, 1964. Pp. 266. *MHB* 26 (July, 1956), 8. Recommends the book for its disturbing but accurate thesis that US policy is being increasingly controlled by the Pentagon, disregarding all historical safeguards to prevent such a situation.

Snyder, Brian. "MacGuigan Links Disarmament and Development." *PlMon* 3 (Dec., 1980), 1-2. Reprinted from University of Waterloo *Imprint*. Summarizes a speech given by Canadian External Affairs Minister Mark MacGuigan, and includes an interview with him on Canadian policy on arms sales.

Stoltzfus, Grant M. (Review). *Preachers Present Arms*, by Ray H. Abrams. Scottdale: Herald Press, 1969. Pp. 354. *GH* 62 (Nov. 18, 1969), 1015-16. Discusses the book's impact when it was first published in 1933, and the continuing relevance of its study of the relationship of church and state during wartime.

Stoltzfus, J. Letter to the Editor. *GH* 66 (Feb. 20, 1973), 169. Responding to the Jan. 16 editorial decrying American bombing in Vietnam, the writer attributes the editor's views to a political attempt to smear the newly re-elected president, instead of relying on the gospel of Christ to bring peace.

Stoltzfus, Ruth Ann (Review). *Poor Elephants*, by Yukio Tsuchiya. Tokyo: Kin-no-Hoshi-Sha Company, 1979. *Sojourners* 9 (June, 1980), 33. Observes that the book illustrates for children the horrors of war by describing the killing of Tokyo zoo animals during World War II to prevent them from straying in case of bombing.

Stoner, John K. "A Parable." *EV* 91 (June 25, 1978), 11. A note of warning that we ought to pay attention to the threat of a nuclear war and not sit idly by.

Stoner, John K. Letter to the Editor. *Menn* 93 (Apr. 25, 1978), 284. The unprecedented evil of the nuclear arms race demands that peaceloving people make their objections known, through legal means or through civil disobedience.

Stoner, John K. Letter to the Editor. *EV* 92 (Apr. 25, 1979), 6. Writer describes some of his thoughts on a bumper sticker which says "We Can Stop Nuclear Madness" in an effort to encourage a response to the nuclear arms race.

Stoner, John K. "SALT II: Opiate or Opportunity?" *Peace Section Newsletter* 9 (Feb.-Mar., 1979), 10-11. Reservations about SALT II note that this treaty can be the opiate which drugs people against a keen awareness of the surging momentum of the arms race, rather than a genuine opportunity to further the cause of disarmament.

Stoner, John K. "The Moral Equivalent of Disarmament." *Sojourners* 8 (Feb., 1979), 15. War tax resistance for the church is the moral equivalent of disarmament for the government. Paper originally presented at the New Call to Peacemaking, Green Lake, Wis., Oct., 1978. Pp. 5. MHL.

Stoner, John K. "The West Is Losing Ground." *Menn* 93 (Aug. 8, 1978), 480. Truth and justice, not bombs and weapons delivery systems, are the only adequate weapons against communism.

Stoner, John K. "War Tax Conference: Uneasy Conscience About Paying for Armageddon." *God and Caesar* 1 (Nov., 1975), 2-3. The conference in Kitchener, Ont., sponsored by the Mennonite and Brethren in Christ Churches sought theological and practical discernment on war tax issues. The churches acknowledged the way of peace as their heritage and the growing menace of the world arms race.

Stoner, John K. "War Tax Dilemma: The Arms Race or the Human Race?" *Peace Section Newsletter* 9 (Dec., 1979), 7-8. War tax resistance is not the only way to say that nuclear deterrence is wrong, but it might be one way.

Stoner, John K. (Review). *To Avoid Catastrophe: A Study in Future Nuclear Weapons Policy,* ed. Michael P. Hamilton. Grand Rapids: Eerdmans, 1977. In *ChrLead* 41 (Aug. 15, 1978), 16. Presents a sobering description of being on the brink of nuclear disaster.

Swartz, Carl J. Letter to the Editor. *GH* 65 (Dec. 5, 1972), 996. Since many Mennonites are uncertain of their peace stance, refusing to own guns would be a hypocritical action. Moreover, it would not guarantee that one were a peaceful person on the inside.

Swift, Richard and Regehr, Ernie. "Dubious Sentinel: Canada and the World Military Order." Waterloo, Ont.: "Project Plowshares," Institute for Peace and Conflict Studies, Conrad Grebel College, [1979]. Pp. [40]. MHL. Education kit. Table of Contents: I The World Military Order; II Canadian Military Spending and Waste; III The Arms Trade and the Third World; IV Spheres of Influence; V State of Siege; VI Guide to Action; VII Christian Perspectives on Militarism.

Symposium. "The Christian in the Age of Missiles." *ChrLiv* 6 (July, 1959), 13-14, 40. Seven respondents discuss forms of Christian witness

against the nuclear arms buildup.

"Tent Dwellers Witness at Arms Show." *EV* 92 (Apr. 10, 1979), 13. A group protests "Defense Technology '79," an international military conference and trade show, in Rosemont, Ill., and one member of this group, Doug Wiebe, contributes a poem, "The Second Nativity," which expresses his reflections on nuclear weapons.

"The Atomic Bomb Is No Fun Anymore." *CanMenn* 17 (Mar. 25, 1969), 1, 2. Report of a teach-in on war held in Winnipeg on Mar. 22. Walter Dinsdale, M.P., was one speaker. Frank Epp, William Eichhorst who is dean of the faculty at the Winnipeg Bible Institute, and David Schroeder spoke as well.

"The Empty Tomb at Hiroshima." *CanMenn* 6 (Nov. 28, 1958), 2. Little remains outwardly of the destruction and death caused by the bomb on Hiroshima, but the Memorial Peace Park with its flowers and monuments pleads that war should cease.

Tanase, Takio. "I Want to Say Something." *IPF Notes* 2 (June, 1956), 5-6. Comment on the danger of US and Soviet nuclear weapons testing.

Tanimoto, Kiyoshi. "The Youth of Hiroshima." *YCC* 37 (Feb. 5, 1956), 45, 48. Acts of reconciliation and rebuilding in both Japan and America after the bombing of Hiroshima and Nagasaki.

Teichroeb, Ruth. "From Trident to Life for Humankind." *Menn* 92 (Sept. 27, 1977), 557. Describes nonviolent resistance efforts in Seattle protesting the Trident submarine and nuclear weapons, and challenges Mennonites to take risks in their peace witness.

Thomson, Murray (Review). *Making a Killing: Canada's Arms Industry,* by Ernie Regehr. Toronto: McClelland and Stewart, 1975. *MBH* 15 (Mar. 19, 1976), 26. Recommends this documentation of Canada's involvement in arms production and trade from 1940 to 1974.

Thomson, Murray and Regehr, Ernie. *A Time to Disarm.* Montreal, Que.: Harvest House Ltd., 1978. Pp. 38. Speaks to such issues of disarmament as securing a comprehensive test ban treaty, preventing the spread of nuclear weapons, curbing the growth and use of conventional weapons, and linking disarmament and development.

Thomson, Murray and Regehr, Ernie. "Arms Control and Disarmament: New Initiative from the Third World." *PlMon* 1 (Oct., 1977), 1. Relates the failure of development in Third

World countries to the failure of disarmament in the 1970s.

Thomson, Murray and Regehr, Ernie. "Arms to the Third World." *PlMon* 1 (July, 1977), 1. Statistics and comment on the effect of arms exports by industrialized nations to the Third World.

Thomson, Murray and Regehr, Ernie. "Beginning the Disarmament Process." *PlMon* 1 (Oct., 1977), 3-4. Brief discussion of 13 issues involved in disarmament, taken from the booklet *The Disarmament Process: Where to Begin,* by Robert C. Johansen (Institute for World Order, 1977).

Thomson, Murray and Regehr, Ernie. "Canadian Military Sales." *PlMon* 1 (July, 1977), 5. Documents Canadian arms sales to the Third World and comments on Canada's role in the militarization of the Third World.

Thomson, Murray and Regehr, Ernie. "New Fighter Aircraft Part of $8 Billion Procurement Plans for Canadian Forces." *PlMon* 1 (Apr., 1977), 1. Information and statistics regarding the Canadian government's decision to vastly increase arms expenditures; includes questions about the effectiveness of such a policy.

Thomson, Murray and Regehr, Ernie. "Pious Words, Wayward Deeds." *PlMon* 1 (Oct., 1977), 5-6. Documents Canadian complicity in nuclear weapons export policies while verbally supporting disarmament discussions.

Thomson, Murray and Regehr, Ernie. "Requirements for Progress." *PlMon* 3 (Sept.-Oct., 1980), 1-4. Reprints select paragraphs from the final document of the 1978 UN Special Session on Disarmament as bases for Canadian Disarmament Week activities.

Thomson, Murray and Regehr, Ernie. "SALT II: Symbol of Restraint or Legalized Madness?" *PlMon* 2 (Aug., 1979), 1, 3. Concludes that SALT II provides modest benefits in paving the way for further arms reduction talks, but leaves room for significant arms expansion.

Thomson, Murray and Regehr, Ernie. "Security Through Disarmament." *PlMon* 1 (May, 1978), 1, 6. A look at some of the elements in the world-wide race to modernize conventional weapons and how this contributes to the current arms race.

Thomson, Murray and Regehr, Ernie. "The Election and Canadian Military Policy." *PlMon* 2 (Apr.-May, 1979), 1-2. Challenges the direction of Canadian military policy toward greater spending for military purpose and increased export of armaments.

Thomson, Murray and Regehr, Ernie, eds. "The Nuclear Pacific: Nuclear Laboratory of the Big Powers." Adopted from articles by Peter D. Jones and Giff Johnson. *PlMon* 2 (Feb.-Mar., 1980), 1-4. Reviews the US atomic weapons testing program in the South Pacific and its disastrous effect on the people of Micronesia.

Thomson, Murray and Regehr, Ernie. "Underdevelopment and the Arms Race." *PlMon* 1 (July, 1977), 3-4. Reviews the motivations for arms sales to Third World countries and the economic and political effects of these expenditures on those countries.

"US Volunteer Army 'Succeeding' As Pentagon Juggles Figures." *Forum* (Mar., 1974), 14. The controversy over the adequacy of a volunteer army is presented and the conscientious objector is warned to watch carefully and weigh thoughtfully this allegiance.

Umble, Diane Z. *Choices for Human Justice: How to Care About the Poor, Disabled, Abused, Oppressed.* Harrisonburg, Va.: Choice Books, 1978. Pp. 111. A collection of articles, reprinted from a variety of sources such as *Sojourners,* the *Gospel Herald,* and *The Mennonite,* which focus various justice issues such as the exploitation of native Americans, the penal system, racism, rape and the battering of women, and the arms race.

Unrau, Neil. "Pentagon Vigil: Reflections by a Canadian Mennonite." *MennRep* 10 (Mar. 31, 1980), 5. Participant in a week-long vigil at the Pentagon reflects on the military's commitment to destruction and the church's response.

Unruh, John D. "A World of Madness." *GH* 54 (May 23, 1961), 473-74, 485. A discussion of the futility of the nuclear arms race and its possible results.

Unruh, John D. "Concerning the Nuclear Test-Ban." *MBH* 2 (Aug. 20, 1963), 2, 5. Mennonites should vigorously support the test-ban treaty proposal, in spite of massive national opposition.

Unruh, W. F. "Witness Through Involvement." *Menn* 75 (Apr. 5, 1960), 213. Urges Mennonites to get involved in government, for example, by supporting the "Point Four Youth Corps" proposal and the new moves toward world disarmament.

"Vietnam Workers Urge Cut in Arms Flow." *GH* 67 (July 2, 1974), 536. Reprints the text of a letter from 22 MCC and Eastern Board of Missions workers to congressional committees responsible for military funding in Vietnam. Letter calls for drastic reductions in military hardware to Vietnam.

"Visitors Cite Pervasive Militarism in South

Africa." *Menn* 94 (Dec. 18, 1979), 762. Three South African members of the Africa National Congress visited the MCC-Canada office to give information about the conditions in South Africa and to ask for discontinuation of financial investment in their country and of sale of arms.

"Volunteer to Defuse Vietnam Bombs." *MBH* 12 (Oct. 19, 1973), 15-16. MCC volunteers will be doing exploratory work in the Vietnamese countryside to find ways to help local farmers clear their land of unexploded bombs.

Vigneron, Arman. Letter to the Editor. *Menn* 95 (June 24, 1980), 418. Criticizes the editor for supporting Peter Ediger's civil disobedience at Rocky Flats nuclear weapons plant.

"War Tax Packet." Akron, Pa.: MCC US Peace Section, revised Sept., 1980. MHL. Items added: Kaufman, Donald, "Pay for War While Praying for Peace: Dilemma of Individuals and the Body," pp. 4; Stoner, John K., "The Moral Equivalent of Disarmament," pp. 3; MCC Peace Section, "Mennonite Conferences Speak on War Taxes," pp. 2; Reedy, Janet and Stan, "Personal Experiences," pp. 3; Leatherman, Loretta and Paul, "Personal Experiences," pp. 3; GCMC Resolutions on War Taxes, pp. 2; MCC US Peace Section, *A Guide to Peace Resources* (brochure); Durland, William, "Guidelines on Military Tax Refusal," pp. 2; MCC US Peace Section, "War Tax Resistance: Techniques and Options," pp. 1; Schroeder, David, "Is There a Biblical Case for Civil Disobedience? Is Civil Disobedience Called for in the Specific Case of War Taxes?" pp. 8; MCC US Peace Section, *Resolution on the World Arms Race,* Dec. 1, 1978 (brochure).

Wald, George. "A Generation Unsure that It Has a Future." *MCC PS Wash. Memo* 1 (June, 1969), 7-9. Reprint from *Congressional Record* of an address on the Vietnam war and the threat of nuclear war.

Waltner, James. "Pacifist Witness at Omaha." *Menn* 74 (Aug. 11, 1959), 453-84. Mennonite critique of "Omaha Action," a pacifist protest of the arms race and particularly of construction of ICBM bases. Lists "nonresistant" reservations about such a witness.

Wiebe, Bernie. "Making Peace." *Menn* 93 (Jan. 3, 1978), 16. Calls attention to two peacemaking events of 1977: Egyptian President Sadat's visit to Israel, and the conversion of the Aldridge family of California from nuclear weapons development to nonviolent resistance to arms buildup.

Wiebe, Bernie. "Uneasy About Canada." *Menn* 93 (Jan. 10, 1978), 32. In light of Canadian Mennonite denunciation of Pentagon strategies, Wiebe challenges Mennonites of Canada to examine militarism also in their country.

Wiebe, Katie Funk. "Cheap at Any Price." *GH* 64 (Oct. 12, 1971), 850. Uses the example of Daniel Ellsberg, leaking Pentagon papers to the press in the hopes of stopping the war, to demonstrate moral courage in the face of blind evildoing.

Wiens, Marie K. "Hiroshima: In Search of Peace." *MBH* 16 (Sept. 16, 1977), 7. Hiroshima, a city speaking to peace through shrines and organizations, needs the true peace found through Christ, say two missionaries.

Yake, C. F. "What Are You Doing for the National Defense?" *YCC* 22 (Aug. 10, 1941), 668. Explores the issue of what kind of cooperation a Christian can give in a war atmosphere when it is against their conscience to take up arms. People who do not qualify for CPS and have to stay home also have an obligation to sacrifice.

Yoder, D. R., "M." *ChrLiv* 11 (July, 1964), 19. Short poem on the atomic bomb.

Yoder, Edward. "The Cry for Peace." *GH Supplement* 37 (Dec., 1944), 758-59. The church cannot outline specifics for postwar peace treaties but, because it recognizes the sinfulness of people and nations, it must tell the state what Christ has said about the value of persons.

Yoder, Edward. "Will Pastors Present Arms? Peace Principles from a Scriptural Viewpoint" Part 46. *GH Supplement* 34 (Oct., 1941), 631. So far preachers have been reluctant to support the war effort, but there are signs, unfortunately, that this sentiment is changing.

Yoder, Henry P. and Yoder, Allan. "Possession of Guns and Peace." *GH* 65 (Oct. 31, 1972), 883-84. Mennonites committed to peace and nonviolence should not own guns, since owning such instruments of violence is not consistent with belief in peace, and it hampers a consistent peace witness.

Zook, Al. "A Family Affair." *The Other Side* 103 (Apr., 1980), 24-27; "A Family's Faith Put into Action." *ChrLiv* 27 (Apr., 1980), 23-25. One family's participation in a demonstration against the arms race at the Rocky Flats, Colorado, nuclear weapons plant.

Zook, Gordon. "Militarism and Conscription, an Introduction." *GH* 72 (Oct. 2, 1979), 777. The Mennonite Church statement on militarism and conscription grew from at least four influences: the Acts of the Apostles; the arms race; international fellowship; efforts to reactivate military conscription.

# 3
# Attitudes and Education

"A Christian Declaration on Communism and Anti-Communism." *Menn* 79 (Apr. 28, 1964), 282. A condensed version of the statement adopted by the General Conference of the GCMC in 1962. While rejecting any ideology opposed to the gospel of Jesus, the church rejects also any holy war approach toward communism. The lived gospel of peace is the best answer.

"A Declaration of Christian Faith and Commitment." *ChrMon* 43 (Feb., 1951), 42-43. Statement resulting from study on nonresistance outlines the starting point and suggests methods of peacemaking.

"Applied Nonresistance." Papers read at the Mennonite Conference on Applied Nonresistance, Goshen, Indiana, Apr., 1939. Reprinted from *MQR* 13 (Apr., 1939), 75-154. MHL. Published by Peace Problems Committee, Mennonite General Conference, Scottdale, 1939. Includes Erb, Paul, "Nonresistance and Litigation," 75-82; Bender, H. S., "Church and State in Mennonite History," 83-103; Yoder, Edward, "The Obligation of the Christian to the State—'Render to Caesar,' " 104-122; Gingerich, Melvin, "The Menace of Propaganda and How to Meet It," 123-34; Hershberger, Guy F. "Nonresistance and Industrial Conflict," 135-54.

A Sister. "My Brother Comes Home from Camp." *ChrMon* 36 (Sept., 1944), 258. Describes the ideological differences among the men in CPS camps and the challenge this presented to Mennonite youth.

Akar, John T. "An African Views America." *MennLife* 22 (Jan., 1967), 19-23. Fundamental conflicts and opposing ideologies between Americans and Africans are dealt with from the perspective of an objective and dispassionate nationalist.

Augsburger, David W. "Anger: The Thrust Towards Power." *MBH* 15 (Feb. 6, 1976), 2-3; also in *GH* 68 (Aug. 12, 1975), 557-59. Research compares nonviolent, nonresistant Mennonite management of hostility with that of

Mennonites who are not nonresistant.

Augsburger, David W. "Mennonites Should Lose/ Use Their Tempers." *FQ* 4 (Nov., Dec., 1977, Jan., 1978), 12-13. Relates Mennonite suppression of anger to the history of nonresistance and peacemaking, urging Mennonites to express anger authentically.

"Blessed Are the Peacemakers in Every Community." *MennComm* 3 (June, 1949), 26-27. Dialogue between peace team member and community resident about peace education and practice in all areas of life.

Baehr, Karl. "The Secularization Process Among Mennonites." *PCMCP First*, 35-40. North Newton, Kansas: The Bethel College Press. Held at Winona Lake, Indiana, Aug. 7, 8, 1942. Uses sociological diagrams to discuss the relationship between the Mennonite sect and the larger society. Notes responses to secularization in conservative, moderate, and liberal groups of Mennonites.

Bainton, Roland H. "The Churches and War: Historic Attitudes Toward Christian Participation." *Social Action* 11 (Jan. 15, 1945), 5-71. Reviews the three positions of pacifism, just war, and crusade from the first through the twentieth centuries, including World War II. Examines especially 20th-century attitudes. Refers to Anabaptist views in the Reformation, as well as the treatment of conscientious objectors and Civilian Public Service.

Barrett, Lois. "Living Nonviolently." *Menn* 91 (Sept. 21, 1976), 556. Discusses nonviolence on the interpersonal level, suggesting that loving the enemy breaks the circle of fear and hate.

Barrett, Lois [Janzen]. "Mennonites and Participation in Politics." *Menn* 87 (Nov. 7, 1972), 648, 649; *MennRep* 2 (Nov. 13, 1972), 3. Results of a church member profile show that Mennonites have changed in their views about government and their participation in it.

Barrett, Lois. "Separation from an Ambiguous

World." *Menn* 91 (June 22, 1976), 428. Christian separation from the world means neither isolation nor setting up a Christian government. Giving first loyalty to God means holding a value system that critiques political structures.

Bartel, Peter. "Revolution, Mennonite Style." Paper for War, Peace, and Revolution class, AMBS, Elkhart, Ind. n.d. Pp. 3. AMBS.

Basinger, Carlus. "Education as a Solution for Peace." *Menn* 53, Part 1, (July 12, 1938), 10-11; Part 2, July 19, 1938), 9. Peace education includes disassociation of war from patriotism, a sense of national humility, and a knowledge of the real causes and results of war.

Bauman, John. "Peace is Our Responsibility." *Menn* 66 (July 17, 1951), 447, 449. The winning oration on peace in a contest at Bluffton College states that "procuring peace" is the job of those who understand and live the biblical faith through witness, service, education, and clear obedience to God rather than the state.

Beachy, Alvin J. "Survival Is Not Enough." *Pulpit* 33 (Nov., 1962), 12-15. Sermon preached on "Peace Sunday" urges listeners to judge human life by eternal values such as the worth of each individual and the moral effects of war and violence, instead of trusting in "vengeance weapons" such as the Polaris submarine and neutron bomb, to insure "survival" of "our side."

Beechy, Atlee. "Nurturing Peacemakers." *Builder* 33 (June, 1983), 2-5. Interview with Levi Miller. Originally printed in Feb., 1976, *Builder.*

Beechy, Atlee. "The Fight for Peace." *ChrMon* 25 (Jan., 1933), 12, 20. While the peace movement has produced significant results, further education and Christian awakening are needed before permanent peace is won.

Bender, Bertha Burkholder. "Youth, Church, and State." *YCC* 12, Part 1, (Jan. 4, 1931), 420-21; Part 2, (Jan. 11, 1931), 426-27; Part 3, (Jan. 18, 1931), 434-35; Part 4, (Jan. 25, 1931), 444-45; Part 5, (Feb. 1, 1931), 450, 451, 453; Part 6, (Feb. 8, 1931), 461-62; Part 7, (Feb. 15, 1931), 466-67; Part 8, (Feb. 22, 1931), 479-80; Part 9, (Mar. 1, 1931), 487, 488; Part 10, (Mar. 8, 1931), 491, 493; Part 11, (Mar. 15, 1931), 498, 499; Part 12, (Mar. 22, 1931), 505, 506; Part 13, (Mar. 29, 1931), 515, 517; Part 14, (Apr. 5, 1931), 523, 525; Part 15, (Apr. 12, 1931), 534, 535; Part 16, (Apr. 19, 1931), 539, 541; Part 17, (Apr. 26, 1931), 545-47; Part 18, (May 3, 1931), 559, 560; Part 19, (May 17, 1931), 571, 573; Part 20, (May 31, 1931), 589; Part 21, (June 7, 1931), 595; Part 22, (June 21, 1931), 610; Part 23, (July 5, 1931), 627, 629; Part 24, (July 19, 1931), 645, 646; Part 25, (July 26, 1931), 650, 651; Part 26, (Aug. 2, 1931), 657-59; Part 27, (Aug. 16, 1931), 675-77. Written in a narrative style, the progression of peace-related topics include: the biblical story, the history of the church, issues about responding to government and militarism, e.g., CO status during Civil War and World War I, and Mennonite relief work.

Bender, Harold S. "Outside Influences on Mennonite Thought." *PCMCP Ninth,* 33-41. North Newton, Kansas: The Mennonite Press. Held at Hesston College, Hesston, Kansas, June 18-19, 1953. The era of Mennonite isolationism is part of the past, so Mennonites must be aware of the variety of "outside" influences to which the group has been exposed. Some of these changes have been very revitalizing and necessary, other changes have caused confusion and disunity.

Bender, Harold S. "Peace Problems Committee." *The Mennonite Encyclopedia* IV:130, Scottdale-Newton-Hillsboro Mennonite Publishing Offices, 1959. This MC committee works in peace education, witness to government leaders, and a witness to other Christians. Cf. Bender's article on "Peace Section" (of MCC) on p. 131, *ibid.*

Bender, Harold S. "War Hysteria: In the Midst of War—Thoughts for Nonresistants," (Part 5). *GH* 35 (Mar. 4, 1943), 1050. The Christian should not participate in any "propaganda or activity that tends to promote ill-will."

Bender, Ross T. "Family Life Education." *Builder* 32 (July, 1982), 20-21. Recommends a number of resources helpful to families who wish to teach and practice peace in their homes and communities.

Berg, Ford. "Their Blood Is Upon Us." *GH* 45 (Oct. 28, 1952), 1057, 1069-70. An historical overview of anti-Semitism in Christendom, showing how the attitude of the Christian church during the past 19 centuries made possible the massacre of six million Jews under Hitler in this century.

Bergen, Lois. "Youth Education: Peace Education Is Lifelong Growth." *Builder* 31 (Jan., 1981), 28-29. Lists resources and makes suggestions for helping youth think through their positions on militarism, registration, conscientious objection, biblical peacemaking, etc.

Bergmann, Frank. "Talking About Peace." *MBH* 14 (Jan. 10, 1975), 12-13. MCC (BC) Peace and Service Committee consulted on such topics as peace education, conflict resolution, distribution of wealth, and family ties as compared with Christian fellowship ties.

Berkey, Esther. "Actions of the Indiana-Michigan Mennonite Conference in Reference to

Nonconformity and Nonresistance." Term paper for a Social Science seminar, Goshen College, Goshen, Ind., Mar. 12, 1953. Pp. 36. MHL.

Bethel College Peace Activities. About 65 interviews. Emphasis is on the 1960's and 1970's, including news reports on Bethel's Moratorium Day protest, nonregistration, bellringing, student attitudes, and Women's International League for Peace and Freedom. MLA/BeC.

*Bicentennial Studies for the Church.* Akron, Pa.: Congregational Peace Education Program, 1976. Pp. 31. MHL. Study guide with the option of four or thirteen sessions on such themes as church and state relations, civil religion and evangelism.

Blosser, Don. "But, Daddy." *GH* 65 (June 27, 1972), 542-43. A family visit to Civil War battlefields provides the opportunity to talk with children about the incongruity of Christians believing in and financially supporting war.

Blosser, Don. "The Selling of the Pentagon: A Response." *GH* 64 (July 27, 1971), 636-37. Expresses deep dismay over the ideas and values communicated by the Pentagon as seen in the CBS documentary *The Selling of the Pentagon.* Calls Mennonites to become aware of militaristic tactics and to protest the use of their tax dollars in the Pentagon's propaganda.

Bohn, E. Stanley. "Resources for Peacemaking." *Builder* 18 (Apr., 1968), 15-16. Listing of audio-visual resources prepared for use with series of Sunday school lessons on "Peacemakers in a Broken World." Subjects covered in this listing are: "Introduction to Peacemaking," "Relief and Service as Peacemaking," and "The Peace Witness Itself."

Born, Daniel (Review). *Christian Mission and Social Justice,* by Samuel Escobar and John Driver. Scottdale: Herald Press, 1978. In *ChrLead* 41 (Aug. 15, 1978), 16. The authors explore the range of theological attitudes toward social justice in Latin America.

Born, Daniel (Review). *Twilight of the Saints: Biblical Christianity and Civil Religion in America,* by Robert D. Linder and Richard V. Pierard. Downers Grove, IL: Inter Varsity, 1978. In *ChrLead* 41 (Aug. 15, 1978), 17. Examines the spectrum of attitudes on Christianity vis-a-vis patriotism steeped in religious rhetoric.

Boyer, Dave. Letter to the Editor. *God and Caesar* 5 (Apr., 1979), 8-9. A Catholic pacifist expresses his appreciation to the Mennonite community for support and guidance in taking a pacifist stance and his feeling of isolation in the Catholic community.

Brenneman, Virgil J. Letter to the Editor. *ChrLiv* 15 (Apr., 1968), 35-36. Lists four ways nonresistant Christians view other Christians who do not hold to certain important aspects of the gospel such as non-support of war.

Brunk, Conrad G. "Rediscovering Biblical Nonconformity." *ChrLead* 36 (Oct. 2, 1973) 4. To rediscover nonconformity we must recapture the "spirit" rather than the "form." Surveys the biblical and historical roots of nonconformity in the church.

Burkholder, J. Lawrence. "An Examination of the Mennonite Doctrine of Nonconformity to the World." ThM thesis, Princeton Theological Seminary, 1951. Pp. 221. MHL. Thesis discusses the distinctive Mennonite doctrine and practice of nonconformity to the world in the life of the Swiss Brethren of the Reformation period, the Hutterites and Amish, the Mennonite Church in America. A fourth major section deals with the doctrine and practice of nonresistance as the most essential aspect of nonconformity. Included in this section are such topics as the biblical basis of nonresistance, Mennonite nonresistance in the Revolutionary War, Civil War, World War I and World War II, a comparison of nonresistance with modern religious pacifism, nonresistance and industrial conflict. Concludes that the doctrine of nonconformity has hindered Mennonites from accepting social responsibility and produced a sectarianism which can only be judged theologically, on the basis of whether God has designed the church to lose itself in the world by accepting responsibility for the world.

Burkholder, J. Lawrence. "The Peace Churches as Communities of Discernment." *Christian Century* 80 (Sept. 4, 1963), 1072-75. Discusses the relationship between the structure of the local congregation and its ability to make vital ethical decisions about peace and other issues.

Burkholder, J. Richard and Bender, John. *Children of Peace.* Elgin: The Brethren Press; Nappanee: Evangel Press; Newton: Faith and Life Press; Scottdale: Mennonite Publishing House, 1982. Pp. 160. Theme of book is that peace is a way as well as a goal. The first unit explores the biblical meanings of peace in both their Old Testament and New Testament contexts. The second unit deals with the practice of peace in various areas of life, such as home, community, politics, and the military. The third unit explores the church and state relationship and includes accounts of the ways some people are effectively and creatively witnessing to peace in militaristic and totalitarian countries.

Byler, Dionisio. "Freedom in Christ." *GH* 69 (June 15, 1976), 496-97. Urges American Mennonites to be thankful for their freedom in Christ, not for the political freedoms of a country won through military means.

"Christians Are More Warlike." *CanMenn* 14 (Jan. 11, 1966), 2. A survey of the Canadian Peace Research Institute reveals that Christians as a whole are more warlike in their attitudes than atheists and agnostics. The news report draws other conclusions from the survey.

"Conference on Life and Human Values." Proceedings of Mennonite Medical Association Conference on Abortion. Chicago, Ill, Oct. 5-6, 1973. Pp. 114. MHL. Similarities and dissimilarities between abortion and killing are minor points in some of the discussions. Major addresses include: Bender, Ross T., "The Religious Perspectives," 16-31; Alderfer, Helen, "The Personal Aspects," 40-45; Koontz, Ted, "Social Implications," 55-80; Ewert, Marvin, "Institutional Responsibilities," 86-94; Erb, Paul, "Church Involvement," 104-109.

Carruthers, Andy. Letter to the Editor. *MennRep* 8 (Feb. 6, 1978), 6. Calls Mennonites to political involvement, to leaven government with values of peace and respect for human life.

Chesebro, Scott. "Integrating the Social Sciences and the Church: A Critique." *Direction* 7 (Jan., 1978), 18-25. The relationship between the church and the social sciences should be one of mediation rather than integration.

Clemens, Fred. "The Prussian Mennonites' Attitudes Toward the Loss of Their Military Service Exemption." Paper prepared for history seminar, Goshen College, Goshen, Ind., July 14, 1980. Pp. 33. MHL.

Climenhaga, Arthur M. "The Role of Foreign Service and Foreign Study in Education for World Mission." *PCMCP Fourteenth*, 33-46. N.p. Held at Eastern Mennonite College, Harrisonburg, Virginia, June 6-7, 1963. The church must approach overseas preparation, some of which should take place in college, as one of its many tasks. It will pursue the Great Commission most effectively through ministries like the Teachers Abroad program of MCC.

Cutrell, Ben (Review). *Barriers and Bridges to Brotherhood*, by Haskell M. Miller. Abingdon, 1962. Pp. 192. *ChrLiv* 11 (Feb., 1964), 34. Recommends the book as a manual for intergroup relations and techniques for solving intergroup conflict.

Davis, Abraham. "Ethnic Integration." *The Other Side* 10 (Sept.-Oct., 1974), 48-49. Failure to implement ethnic integration throughout a liberal arts education not only academically and psychologically damages the disadvantaged minority, but it also perpetuates ignorance among American students.

Derstine, C. F. "Why Isms, False Teachings, and Destructive Ideas Flourish." *ChrMon* 33 (Jan., 1941), 30. Not war, but ideas foreign to truth are the real destroyers of human liberty.

Dick, N. S. *The Peacemaker.* Scottdale: Herald Press and Newton: Faith and Life Press, 1972. Pp. 63. A Bible study guide on peacemaking organized into 13 lessons. Topics include the Jesus way, Old Testament wars, the relationship between poverty and militarism, patriotism, servanthood, etc. Resources include films, music, poetry, discussion questions.

Diggers, The (a corporate student group). "Rigorous, Regulated, Rowdy, Religious, and Radical: A Study of Bethel College During World War II." Oral history project for History of Civilization II, Mar. 6, 1974. Pp. 96. MLA/ BeC.

Dourte, Eber. "To Serve the Present Age." *EV* 92 (Jan. 25, 1979), 9. At the semi-annual meeting of the MCC Peace Section, the agenda included reports and discussion on the New Call to Peacemaking, peace education, the World Arms Race and our peace witness, and the possibility of draft for military service.

Drescher, James M. "Is the Peace Ethic Optional for Anabaptists?" *GH* 73 (Oct. 7, 1980), 789. Commitment to the peace ethic, central to the New Testament andn Anabaptist history, should be as much a prerequisite for Mennonite membership as baptism.

Drescher, James M. "Living and Passing on an Ethic." *Builder* 29 (July, 1979), 6-9. Calls the church to recapture a vision of peace as God's way and to make a conscious, consistent and systematic effort to transmit that vision to our children and youth.

Drescher, James M. "Oh Yes—I Guess." *Swords into Plowshares: A Collection of Plays About Peace and Social Justice*, ed. Ingrid Rogers. Elgin: The Brethren Press, 1983, 221-27. A satiric drama in which a draft board questions a young man and finds him unsuitable for the active duty classification he has requested because he possesses too many human and religious values.

Driedger, Leo, ed. *School of Peace.* Newton: Board of Christián Service, GCMC, [1961?]. MHL. Curriculum designed to emphasize peace as a basic teaching of the Bible and our Christian faith. Planned for four sessions. Dick, Nickolas, "Blessed Are the Peacemakers: A Manual for Leaders of Adults," pp. 39; Reusser, James, "Blessed Are the Peacemakers: A Manual for Leaders of Intermediates and Youth," pp. 22; Rich, Elaine Sommers, "Blessed Are the Peacemakers: A Manual for Teachers of Juniors," pp. 17; Harder, Geraldine Gross,

"Loving All the Time: A Manual for Teachers of Primary Children," pp. 41; "Peace School Activity Sheets for Primaries;" "Peace Maker Packet: Juniors."

Driedger, Leo. "Native Rebellion and Mennonite Invasion: An Examination of Two Canadian River Valleys." *MQR* 46 (July, 1972), 290-300. A focus on the Red River Valley in Manitoba in 1869-74 and on the Saskatchewan River Valley in 1884-95 in order to determine in what sense peace-loving Mennonites cooperated with a government using force to drive away native Canadians so that the Mennonites could settle.

Driedger, Leo; Currie, Raymond; and Linden, Lick. "Dualistic and Wholistic Views of God and the World." *Review of Religions Research* 24 (March, 1983), 225-44. Findings support the posited correlation between a dualistic view of God and less interest in social action, and a wholistic view of God and more interest in social action.

Driedger, Leo and Zehr, Dan. "The Mennonite State-Church Trauma: Its Effects on Attitudes of Canadian Students and Leaders." *MQR* 48 (Oct., 1974), 515-26. A sociological analysis of Canadian Mennonite attitudes toward the state and social concerns, and the interpretation of the peace stance, compared across generational and denominational lines.

Dueck, Allan. "Education for Justice." *Direction* 6 (Jan., 1977), 12-20. Christian education includes education for awareness of injustice and the encouragement of Christians to involve themselves in social conflict.

Dyck, Walter H. "Peace: A Study Course in Outline." N.d. Pp. 11. MHL.

Dyck, Walter H.; Smith, C. Henry; Fretz, J. Winfield; and Mast, Russell. *The Power of Love.* Newton: General Conference Board of Publication, 1947. Pp. 136. A study manual on peace for use in Sunday schools and group discussions.

Eby, Omar. "Consultation on Conscience and Conscription: A Personal Impression." *GH* 63 (Jan. 13, 1970), 34-35. Author reflects on the generous support for the position of noncooperation with the draft shown at the recent Chicago Peace Assembly. He affirms resisters, but expresses concern that they not become as tyrannical on this issue as past church leaders on other issues of nonconformity.

Ediger, Elmer and Waltner, Erland, eds.; Wiebe, Willard; Gundy, Wilma; and Dyck, C. J., writers; Jost, Norma and Duerkesen, Roland, assistants. *Youth and Christian Love.* Newton: Mennonite Publication Office, n.d. Pp. 69. Thirteen study lessons for young people on nonresistance as a way of life.

Ediger, Max. "Freedom." *GH* 67 (Oct. 29, 1974), 817-19. Contrasts the spiritual freedom of prisoners of conscience who have refused to compromise their convictions, with the bondage of those enslaved to militarism, apathy, fear, hate.

Engle, T. L. "Attitudes Toward War as Expressed by Amish and Non-Amish Children." *Journal of Educational Psychology* 35 (Apr., 1944), 211-19. Evidence from two measurement instruments, children's essays, and an attitude-toward-war scale, indicates that the Amish children exhibited a statistically significant less favorable attitude toward war than non-Amish children.

Engle, T. L. "Attitudes Toward War as Expressed by Amish and Non-Amish Children: A Follow-Up Study." *The Elementary School Journal* 53 (Feb., 1953), 345-51. Follow-up study indicates that the differences in the attitude toward war between Amish and non-Amish children are less marked than they were eight and a half years earlier.

Entz, Margaret. "The Formation of Political Concepts: Zion Church Board Members." Student paper for US Government course, Elbing, KS, Mar., 1974. Pp. 9. MLA/BeC.

Epp, Frank H. "Christians Between East and West." *Christians Between East and West.* Christian Concerns Series No. 1. Winnipeg: Board of Christian Service, Conference of Mennonites in Canada, [ca. 1965], 7-16. Describes features of communist and anticommunist propaganda which have attracted Mennonites to both camps, then uses the image of Christ to critique the materialism, militarism, power, and propaganda of both perspectives.

Epp, Frank H. "God's Word Stands Above Man's Opinions." *CanMenn* 2 (Oct. 1, 1954), 2. Human opinion must not be confused with biblical truth even as it relates to violence in war time. It is to be regretted that various Christian leaders have advocated "preventive war" against communism in recent times.

Epp, Frank H. "How Dare We Call the President." *CanMenn* 14 (Feb. 1, 1966), 5. A portrayal of attitudes to a government which wars and seeks loyalty which is above loyalty to Christ.

Epp, Frank H. "National Socialism Among Canadian Mennonites in the 1930s." *PCMCP Fifteenth,* 123-31. North Newton, Kansas: The Mennonite Press. Held at Bluffton College, Bluffton, Ohio, June 10-11, 1965. The assumption that the Canadian Mennonite community harbored a certain amount of National Socialism in the 1930s is supported by research of all the issues (1930-39) of a weekly newspaper serving Mennonites who immigrated from Russia in the 1920s. Also at AMBS.

Epp, Frank H. "Peace Mission in Orient Should Be Escalated." *CanMenn* 14 (Apr. 5, 1966), 3. A report on the peace activity, history and present needs of the MCC peace section in Japan. Based on Mar. 1-Apr. 5 tour to Asia, Epp argues that with nationalism's threat to the church in Asia, MCC Peace Section should support more peace education activity in the Far East.

Epp, Frank H. "The Atomic Urge Unchecked." *CanMenn* 5 (Apr. 26, 1957), 2. Even though no one wanted it that way the atomic urge has run rampant. Science, education, and religion seem to perpetuate this situation.

Erb, Alta Mae (Review). *Prudence Crandall, Woman of Courage,* by Elizabeth Yates. Aladdin Books, 1955. *ChrLiv* 3 (Feb., 1956), 33. Recommends this story of a nineteenth-century woman who worked for justice for blacks, especially in education.

Erb, Paul. "Nonconformity in Race Relations." *GH* 48 (June 7, 1955), 531. It is time that the Mennonites declare themselves against racism—a major cause of war. We have too long conformed to the world's sin of racism.

Erb, Paul. "The Nonresistant Personality." *ChrLiv* 1 (July, 1954), 7, 41. The truly nonresistant person is one who cultivates a character of love and meekness.

Erb, Paul. "World War III." *GH* 41 (Apr. 20, 1948), 363. It is not Christian to oppose communism by military pressure even though communism is anti-Christian. The Christian must remember that there is no righteous side in power politics.

"Friends, Brethren, and Mennonites Meet." *RepConsS* 5 (Mar., 1947), 3. Reports a two-day meeting of historic peace churches at Akron, Pa., on "Peace Education in the Home, Sunday School, and the Church."

Fast, Henry A. "The Spiritual Values of Contributing to Relief." *MennLife* 2 (Apr., 1947), 5-7. The author shows the positive side of nonresistance by describing Mennonite relief work as a ministry of reconciliation responding to the hate and destruction of war.

Ford, Leighton. "The Church and Evangelism in a Day of Revolution." *GH* 62, Part 1, (Dec. 9, 1969), 1046-48; Part 2, (Dec. 16, 1969), 1076-78. Contemporary revolutions issue a crucial call to change, but only the Christian message will cause effective, lasting change, because revolutions must grapple with sin. The gospel deals with sin, but one must follow conversion with commitment to social change.

Ford, Leighton. "Violence." *GH* 64 (July 6, 1971), 601. With confession of sin, peace begins within and moves outward in forgiveness, rejecting the violence and hatred of both extreme positions in conflict.

Foreman, Dennis W. "Preparation for Peace." *ChrMon* 40 (Aug., 1948), 235, 243. Guidelines for promoting peace in the face of militaristic propaganda.

Frantz, Margarete. "Last Ship to Freedom." *MBH* 13 (Nov. 29, 1974), 26-28. Russian Mennonite refugee in Germany tries to obtain exit visa by lying about his service in Hitler's army.

Franz, Marian Claassen. "Bucking Sexism in Sunday School." *Daughters of Sarah* (Nov.-Dec., 1980), 5-6. Guidelines on how to avoid the violence of stereotyping and cataloguing persons in Christian education.

Franz, Marian Claassen. "National Turmoil, Our Children, Government." *Builder* 24 (May, 1974), 10-14. Reflects on ways adults can help children understand the world's problems, including war, from an appropriately global, international Christian perspective.

Fretz, J. Winfield. "Why Mennonite Boys Choose Military Service." (Part 2) *Menn* (July 31, 1945), 5-6. The position of drafted men generally reflects the attitudes of their pastors. The census as a whole indicates that the General Conference is losing its doctrine of biblical nonresistance.

Fretz, J. Winfield; Krahn, Cornelius; and Kreider, Robert. "Altruism in Mennonite Life." *Forms and Techniques of Altruistic and Spiritual Growth.* Ed. Pitirim A. Sorokin. Boston: Beacon Press, 1954, 309-328. A description of select examples of Mennonite altruism, including the peace witness, and an analysis of its roots in biblicism and nonconformity.

Friesen, Dorothy. "Meditation on the Despicable and Unimportant." *Sojourners* 7 (Feb., 1978), 22. The people from whom church workers get their information on the environment in which they want to work is reflective of who they think God is and how he works in the world.

Friesen, Duane K. "Peace Studies: What Is It?" Paper presented at the American Society of Christian Ethics, Chicago, Ill., Jan. 19, 1974. Pp. 35. MHL.

Friesen, J. J. "Thoughts on Peace." *GH* 28 (Feb. 27, 1936), 1011. Most peace movements fail to advocate a personal change of heart. It is doubtful whether such peace conferences and education will bring lasting peace.

Friesen, Jacob T. "Ministers: Focus on Peace."

*Builder* 31 (Jan., 1981), 26-27. Column focuses on ideas and resources to assist peace-minded pastoring.

Friesen, Mrs. Dee. Letter to the Editor. *ChrLead* 41 (Jan. 31, 1978), 16. Pacifism is a very privileged position. There are many members of the military who are just as devout and sincere Christians as the "best" Mennonites.

Friesen, Norris. Letter to the Editor. *ChrLead* 41 (May 23, 1978), 15. Appreciates *Leader's* articles on peace to help raise children in the way of peace.

Friesen, Ronald. "A Christian Witness in a World of Economic Disparity." *Forum* 10 (Jan., 1977), 1-3. Conveys the strong negative attitudes of the disadvantaged toward the more wealthy, and presents a rationale for and possible ways of minimizing these economic disparities.

Froese, Arnold. Letter to the Editor. *ChrLead* 41 (June 6, 1978), 10. Praises some statistical conclusions other than those reported in a survey on "What Our Pastors Believe and Teach" on peace (*Leader*, Apr. 25).

Froese, Peter J. "BC Peace Committee Plans Inter-Mennonite Meetings." *CanMenn* 12 (Apr. 28, 1964), 3, 12. Announcement of plans for peace education meetings in the western Canadian provinces for the purpose of strengthening the non-resistant position in the churches.

Funk, John F. *Warfare. Its Evils Our Duty. Addressed to the Mennonite Churches Throughout the United States, and All Others Who Sincerely Seek and Love the Truth.* Chicago: By the Author, 1863. Pp. 16. MHL. Despite the pressures of society and the lure of military glory, let us remain faithful to the example of Jesus, who lived the nonresistant life in every way.

General Conference Mennonite Church. *The Church, the Gospel, and War.* General Conference Peace Study Conference. Eden Mennonite Church, Moundridge, Kans., Apr. 10-11, 1953. Sixteen essays on the theme, together with a report of discussions and findings and two messages—to the congregations of the conference, and to the Christian church at large.

George, Albert. "The VS Scandal." *GH* 64 (Apr. 20, 1971), 354-55. Reprinted from *Agape* (Nov.-Dec., 1970). Raised a Methodist, the writer was converted to Anabaptist nonresistance through Mennonite writings and relationships. Maintains that just as nonresistance is a scandal when considered pragmatically, so VS service is based on the scandal of the uniqueness of Christian conversion and love.

George, Elias. "Ten Things I Wish North American Mennonites Knew About My People." *FQ* 6 (Nov., Dec., 1979, Jan., 1980), 15. Arab Mennonite social studies teacher clarifies misconceptions about Arabs and offers his perspective on the Arab-Israeli conflict and prospects for peace.

Gibble, Kenneth L. "Ethics in War and Peace." *Builder* 18 (June, 1968), 15-16. Explores some of the basic ethical issues facing young men of draft age and suggests ways these youths might be assisted in their process of thinking through these issues for themselves.

Gingerich, Melvin. "As He Thinketh; Christian Youth and the State." *YCC* 23, Part 18, (Feb. 15, 1942), 56. If Christianity is to be a living force, time must be spent in thought and practice.

Gingerich, Melvin. "Honesty; Christian Youth and the State." *YCC* 22, Part 13, (Aug. 17, 1941), 673. To be Christian is to be genuinely truthful. During war especially, there are many stories which are not true about which the Christian has an obligation to seek the truth.

Gingerich, Melvin. "Moral Standards and Military Life." *GH* 55 (July 17, 1962), 625. When persons are trained in the art of killing, other moral values no longer seem absolute or relevant. This problem will not be solved until the immorality of war itself is faced.

Gingerich, Melvin. "Reactions to Revolutions." *GH* 62 (Apr. 8, 1969), 314-15. Outlines three positions commonly taken in response to revolution: 1) advocating violent overthrow of the existing order; 2) conservative reaction which may turn to propaganda of fear; 3) acceptance of change and openness to facts. Advocates the last option for nonresistant Christians.

Gingerich, Melvin. "The Menace of Propaganda and How to Meet It." *MQR* 13 (Apr., 1939), 123-34. A definition of propaganda and its dangers. As a nonresistant people, Mennonites should avoid making careless, unfair, or prejudiced statements; they should critically examine conflicting points of view.

Gingerich, Melvin. "The Mennonite Church in World War II; A Review and Evaluation." *MQR* 25 (July, 1951), 183-200. A summary of the work of the Peace Problems Committee. In spite of intensive peace education between the World Wars, nearly half of the young men drafted in World War II served militarily; most others found it difficult to refrain from compromise.

Gingerich, Melvin. "The Prague Peace Assembly in the Press." *MennLife* 20 (July, 1965), 127-30. This report consists of quotes from secular press releases as well as from reports in religious journals and church papers, including those from Mennonite denominations.

Gingerich, Melvin. "Towards an Understanding of the Jews." *Menn* 63 (Feb. 17, 1948), 3-4. Appeals to Mennonites (who also have known discrimination and persecution) to counteract hate propaganda directed toward Jews. Historical analysis destroys many of the myths perpetuated about the Jewish people.

Gingerich, Melvin. "Ye Are the Salt of the Earth; Christian Youth and the State." *YCC* 22, Part 4 (Jan. 12, 1941), 432. True Christians are the "salt of the earth." While other people may say that nonresistant Christians are not contributing to society, the truth is that nonresistant Christians are those preserving society.

Gingerich, Melvin (Review). *The Church in Communist China: a Protestant Appraisal,* by Francis Price Jones. New York: Friendship Press, n.d. *GH* 55 (Sept. 18, 1962), 825, 836-37. While the church in China has compromised its position, the sincerity of many Chinese Christians must still be recognized. American Christians should seek to show love to Chinese Christians in concrete ways.

Gleysteen, Jan. "Käthe Kollwitz—An Artist's Protest to War." *YCC* 48 (July 9, 1967), 5. The story of Kollwitz, a famous woman artist, whose art reflects her social conscience and pacifist ideology.

Goering, James A. "Martin Luther King and the Gandhian Method of Nonviolent Resistance." *ST* 36 (Oct., 1968), 1. The philosophy of nonviolent resistance embodies enough Christian truth and has done enough good in the past decade in rectifying social ills, that well-meaning but undiscerning Christians may find themselves not only sympathetic to the movement, but actively supporting it without really being aware of its merely semi-Christian aspects.

Graber, Edith Claassen. *Children and Peace.* Newton: Board of Christian Service, General Conference Mennonite Church, n.d. Pp. 15. MHL. Discusses teaching children the basic attitudes for peace. Describes techniques and methods, provides resources, etc.

Graber, Edith Claassen. "Preparing Children for Peace and Non-resistance." *Menn* 68 (June 2, 1953), 342, 347. Deals with tools and methods for teaching children principles of peace and love. Lists Church of the Brethren and Quaker materials already available.

Graber, Eldon W. "Some Questions Concerning Peacetime Conscription." *Menn* 60 (June 3, 1945), 13. Argues that peacetime conscription would not improve the health of the nation. It would neither contribute to discipline or character education nor would it produce the right kind of leaders or technical institutions for peacetime.

*

Graybill, Dave. "Mennonites Reflect on Values After Accident at Nuclear Plant." *GH* 72 (Apr. 24, 1979), 344-45. Individual responses of Mennonites in the area of the Three-Mile Island nuclear plant accident are presented.

Groff, Weyburn W. *Nonviolence: a Comparative Study of Mohandas K. Gandhi and the Mennonite Church on the Subject of Nonviolence.* Unpublished doctoral dissertation, New York Univ., Dept. of Education, 1963. Pp. 242. Using twentieth century sources representing the (Old) Mennonite Church and the collected writings of M. K. Gandhi, the research demonstrates similarities and differences in concept and application in respect to social and political action.

Gustafson, David L. "Shalom, the Dream and the Reality: Curriculum for Advent Through Easter." MA in Peace Studies thesis, AMBS, 1981. Pp. 58. While the shalom theme, one of the major Anabaptist distinctives, has been extensively discussed in academic circles, little of its message has filtered down to the congregations. This adaptation of a shalom lectionary seeks to bring peace teachings into the worship life of the congregation. Outlines the basic teachings for each Sunday and provides one fully developed lesson as an example.

Habegger, Luann. "The Berne, Indiana, Mennonites During World War I." Paper presented to the Mennonite History class, Associated Mennonite Biblical Seminaries, Dec. 23, 1974. Pp. 15. MHL.

Hackman, Walton. "A Time to Speak and a Time for Peace?" *GH* 64 (June 22, 1971), 558-59. Calls Mennonite congregations to use Peace Sunday, June 27, as a time to discuss peace convictions and to plan for sharing them in the surrounding community, since many people are interested in an anti-war position growing out of Christian faith.

Harder, Gary. "An Evaluation of the 'Peacemaker' Series of Mennonite Sunday School Lessons, April 21-June 30, 1968." Paper for War, Peace, and Revolution class, AMBS, Elkhart, Ind., May 8, 1969. Pp. 3. AMBS.

Harder, Geraldine. "Teaching Pilgrim Children Peace and Love." *Builder* 24 (May, 1974), 21-23. Suggestions to help juniors and junior highs focus on peace concerns. Examples from Mennonite history and contemporary Mennonite service programs are used.

*For additional listing, see Supplement, pp. 717-719.

Harder, Geraldine. "Through Children's Eyes: A Report of Discussions on Nonconformity and Nonresistance as Perceived by a Class of Fifth-Graders." *Builder* 18 (Jan., 1968), 6-8. Children's answers to "How are Christians different?" and "Is it wrong to fight back?"

Harder, Leland. "The Political Behavior of Northern Indiana Mennonites." *Indiana Academy of the Social Sciences.* (Third Series.) Proceedings, 1970, Vol. 5, 159-72. A statistical and interpretive study of political attitudes and activities, particularly voting and the political role of the church, compared with respondents in Glock, Ringer, and Babbie study of Episcopalians. Study shows that low political permissiveness on the part of Elkhart Mennonites correlates with high religious commitment, low income, and low education. It appears that "among those who take the Anabaptist vision most seriously are persons who have found some implications in it which lead to political involvement."

Harder, R. R. Letter to the Editor. *CanMenn* 2 (Apr. 9, 1954), 7. A plea for a strong peace education program.

Harding, Vincent G. "When Stokely Met the Presidents: Black Power and Negro Education." *Motive* 27 (Jan., 1967), 4-9. The confrontation of Stokely Carmichael and the presidents of 2 Atlanta black colleges focuses an analysis of several key educational issues of race relations.

Harding, Vincent G. (Review). *The American Revolution*, by James Boggs. Monthly Review Press, 1963. *ChrLiv* 12 (Oct., 1965), 32-33. The book demonstrates that the secular nonconformity movement critiques American middle-class values and searches for justice.

Harshbarger, Emmett L. "A Mennonite Preparedness Program." *Menn* 53 (Dec. 20, 1938), 5-6. A peacemaking response to international strife demands a different sort of preparedness than a military response. Mennonites must prepare themselves for wartime individually, educationally, and by taking part in peace programs.

Harshbarger, Emmett L. "Anti-semitism Before the World War: History Views the Jewish Persecutions" (Part 2). *Menn* 54 (Feb. 21, 1939), 3-4. A brief review of the course of anti-semitism from Old Testament times through the 19th century.

Harshbarger, Emmett L. "Concluding Statements from a Christian Point of View: History View the Jewish Persecutions" (Part 5). *Menn* 54 (May 2, 1939), 1-2. History says Christians can propagandize against and persecute the Jews. Mennonites who live by the Sermon on the Mount cannot join in nor condone this.

Harshbarger, Emmett L. *Propaganda: How to Analyze and Counteract It.* North Newton: By the Author, 1940. Pp. 40. MSHL. Analyzes the purposes, principles, and methods of propaganda as used in support of war and suggests ways to recognize and resist this phenomenon.

Harshbarger, Emmett L. "The Most Common Anti-semitic Arguments: History Views the Jewish Persecutions" (Part 4). *Menn* 54, Part 1, (Mar. 7, 1939), 4-5; Part 2, (Mar. 14, 1939), 8-9; Part 3, (Apr. 25, 1939), 5-6. Refutes the charge that the Jew is to blame for Germany's troubles since the World War; it is a half-truth to say that the Jews dominate the economics of the world; a common argument is that the Jew is the source of all kinds of radicalism.

Harshbarger, Emmett L. "Why Jewish Persecutions? History Views the Jewish Persecutions" (Part 1). *Menn* 54 (Feb. 14, 1939), 2. The basis of anti-semitism is hatred of the foreigner, the person who is different.

Hartman, Wilmer J. "Living Peaceably with Others." *Builder* 20 (Sept., 1970), 21-25. An adult Sunday school lesson utilizing the story of Isaac's conflict with the Philistine herders over a well (Gen. 26) to focus discussion of peacemaking.

Hartzler, Levi C. "Missions and Our Peace Witness." *GH* 46 (Aug. 11, 1953), 769. The true peacemaker is motivated by inner compulsion. For him or her the peace witness is an integral part of the Christian life and witness.

Hasek, K. Gary. "Art and the Peacemaking Church." MA in Peace Studies thesis, AMBS, 1981. Cassette, slides, script (i, 13). A multimedia presentation which utilizes music, slides, and a script to explore what aesthetic concepts such as balance, light, shape, and tension contribute to an understanding of biblical shalom.

Helmuth, David. "Adult Education: Peace Study Materials for the Congregation." *Builder* 31 (Jan., 1981), 20-21. List of resources includes four-session peace emphasis program for youth, a bibliography available from Provident Bookstores, etc.

Helmuth, David and Beechy, Winifred. "MBCM Peace Education Bibliography." Mennonite Board of Congregational Ministries, Elkhart, Ind., Mar., 1980. Pp. 6. MHL.

Hershberger, Bernie; Bender, Brent; Kauffman, Duane; Yoder, Steve; and Nafziger, Beverly. "A Four-College Comparison of Ethical Ideologies in Relation to Current Moral Issues." *Journal of Psychology and Christianity* 1 (Fall, 1982), 32-39. A study of 207 General Psychology students explores the influence of ideology on responses to specific ethical issues, including such items as the death penalty, the military draft, and nuclear weapons.

Hershberger, Guy F. "Christian Attitudes Toward Nuclear Warfare." In *Program Guide*, edited by Arnold Roth, pp. 104-106. Scottdale: Herald Press, 1967. General discussion about attitudes toward war which raise questions about responsible witness to the state.

Hershberger, Guy F. "Christians Must Exercise Good Will Toward All People." *YCC* 19 (May 1, 1938), 143-44. Christians must show a spirit of love and good will toward all races and nations in both times of war and times of peace. This is the only way to respond to propaganda.

Hershberger, Guy F. "False Patriotism." *MQR* 1, Part 1, (Jan., 1927), 9-27; Part 2, (Apr., 1927), 29-45. An exposé of the attitudes and actions of earlier Americans together with an analysis of the dynamics of nationalism.

Hershberger, Guy F. "Mennonite Principles: A Re-Examination." *MennComm* 5 (Dec., 1951), 17-19, 33. Mennonite adherence to nonconformity speaks also to the issue of social justice.

Hershberger, Guy F. "Military Training in Schools and Colleges." *YCC* 19 (Apr. 3, 1938), 111-12. History and description of the military training efforts in US schools and colleges. Mennonite young people should receive their education in Mennonite schools.

Hershberger, Guy F. "Questions for Nonresistant Christians." *GH* 33, Parts 1-3, (July 18, 1940), 338; Part 4, (July 25, 1940), 371; Parts 5-7, (Aug. 1, 1940), 386; Parts 8-9, (Aug. 8, 1940), 418; Parts 10-11, (Aug. 15, 1940), 435; Part 12, (Aug. 22, 1940), 450; Part 13, (Aug. 29, 1940), 466-67; Part 14, (Sept. 12, 1940), 514; Part 15-16, (Sept. 19, 1940), 530; Part 17, (Oct. 3, 1940), 562; Part 19-22, (Oct. 31, 1940), 658-59; Part 23, (Nov. 7, 1940), 675; Part 24, (Nov. 28, 1940), 738; Part 25, (Dec. 5, 1940), 754. Series includes such topics as war propaganda, conscription, alternative service, conscientious objection, registration, noncombatant service, etc.

Hershberger, Guy F. "Report on My Term of Service for the Peace Section of the Mennonite Central Committee, June 10, 1949, to Aug. 21, 1950." Mimeographed. Goshen: MHL. Study of pacifism in Europe, the peace attitudes of European Mennonites and the legal status of conscientious objectors in Europe.

Hershberger, Guy F. "Social Science Textbooks in Mennonite Colleges." *PCMCP Tenth*, 9-22. N.p. Held at Mennonite Biblical Seminary, Chicago, Illinois, June 16-17, 1955. Educators need to approach their social science teaching with the Anabaptist vision. Some suggestions on specific examples once teaching ideas are offered.

Hershberger, Guy F. "The Cross in Personal Relations." *ChrLiv* 6 (July, 1959), 27-29. An unloving spirit among church members invalidates a witness to nonresistance.

Hershberger, Guy F., ed. "The Peace Committee Circular." Bibliography compiled by Peace Committee, Goshen College, Goshen, Ind., Jan., 1931. Pp. 6. MHL. Designed to assist Goshen College graduates teaching in the public schools counteract a "false patriotism: detrimental to international relations.

Hershberger, Guy F. "War Is a Maker of Hatred and Lies." *YCC* 18 (May 2, 1937), 560. War is also a violator of the ninth commandment about bearing false witness. Propaganda is used to stir up people's hatred of the other side.

Hershberger, Guy F. "What Color Is Christ?" In *Program Guide*, ed. Arnold Roth, pp. 149. Scottdale: Herald Press, 1967. Biblical material from which to examine the Mennonite Church's response to race issues.

Hershey, Lynford. "What Is the Mennonite Attitude on Race Relations?" *GH* 64 (Mar. 23, 1971), 262-64. A questionnaire, results, and evaluation of data concerning attitudes towards other races in 58 Mennonite churches.

Hertzler, Daniel. "Gracious Living." *ChrLiv* 19 (Mar., 1972), 40. Editorial redefines "gracious": from modern connotations of elegance to Old Testament meaning of concern for justice.

Hertzler, Daniel. "The War Hysteria." *GH* 73 (July 22, 1980), 592. Criticizes the atmosphere of aggression present in conservative political and religious circles.

Hertzler, Daniel. "Violence and Deception." *GH* 66 (Dec. 11, 1973), 940. Violence and deception go hand in hand, and have become accepted parts of life, as both Watergate and children's cartoons show.

Hertzler, Daniel (Editorial). "Kicking Uncle Sam." *GH* 69 (Apr. 6, 1976), 302. Asserts that since a national government stands opposed to Christ's teachings on selflessness, defenselessness, love, and truth, Christians must separate loyalty to the state from living the way of peace.

Hertzler, Daniel (Editorial). "Sex and Violence." *GH* 70 (Sept. 20, 1977), 712. Comments on the prevalence of sex and violence in the mass media, especially television, and offers suggestions for action by concerned people.

Hess, James R. "Did Mennonite Conservatives Meet Their Waterloo at Assembly '79?" *ST* 47

(Nov., 1979), 8. In analyzing the Mennonite Church General Assembly at Waterloo, Ont., in Aug., 1979, the following are among the concerns raised: the role of women, nonconformity, nonresistance, relationship to minorities, and the relationship between word and deed.

Hess, James R. "Reflections on the Kitchener, Ontario War Tax Convention." *GfT* 11 (Mar.-Apr., 1976), 16-18. Links the refusal to pay war taxes to leftist ideology and subjectivistic hermeneutics.

Hess, James R. "The Washington Peace Seminar." *ST* 44 (July, 1976), 21-23. Criticizes the hostility shown toward business and government leaders, and traces it to those involved in church institutions as compared with those involved in the workday world.

Hobbs, William O. "Maintaining Scriptural Discipline and the Nonresistant Faith." *GH* 35 (Mar. 18, 1943), 1092. Those in the Mennonite church who do not hold to the nonresistant principle should be disciplined so that the church's witness remains clear. Half-hearted attitudes will not maintain this testimony.

Hochstetler, Walter. "Anabaptist Dreams and Menno-Nite-Mares: Some Reflections on Mennonite Attitudes Toward Peace." Paper, 1971. Pp. 5. AMBS.

Honser, Gordon. "Peace Teachers: He Takes His Nap, Fellowships, and Acts." *Builder* 31 (Jan., 1981), 18-19. Peter Ediger, Arvada, Colorado, challenges the church by asking if there can be peace education without peace action.

Horsch, John (Review). *Preachers Present Arms,* by Dr. Ray H. Abrams. Round Table Press, n.d. *ChrMon* 26 (Feb., 1934), 37-39. The book documents the spiritual and moral losses of denominations which supported involvement in World War I.

Horst, John L. (Editorial). "The Next War." *ChrMon* 26 (Feb., 1934), 41. Encourages preaching nonresistance during peacetime so that the church may stand firm in its convictions during the next war.

Hostetler, Adelia L. and Shank, J. R. "The Christian Principle of Peace." *ChrMon* 22 (Dec., 1930), 376-77. Young People's Meeting lesson study guide and comment on the principles of peace and nonresistance.

Hostetler, Nancy Gingrich. "War of Words Destroying Peace." *ChrMon* 23 (Sept., 1931), 268. Verbal conflict destroys peace as surely as armed conflict.

Hostetter, B. Charles. "Christian Love and the World Crisis." *ChrLiv* 1 (Oct., 1954), 8-9. Active Christian love is the only answer to the crises brought on by warring "Christian" nations.

Hostetter, B. Charles. "Christian Love Forgives." *ChrLiv* 2 (Feb., 1955), 32-33. Christian love means forgiveness and mercy, not justice or vengeance.

Hull, Carol. "Peacemaking: A Presence for All Seasons." *Daughters of Sarah* 7 (Nov.-Dec., 1981), 11-15. Hull recounts her personal and spiritual journey as a peacemaker and then summarizes her vision of the New Jerusalem as a reality encompassing elements of respect, forgiveness, sharing, nonviolence, peace education, discipline, and celebration.

Hull, Robert. *Leader's Guide: "Justice and the Christian Witness."* Newton: Faith and Life Press; Scottdale: Herald Press, 1982. Pp. 66. Companion volume to the study report provides suggestions for group activities, lesson plans, a significant number (19) of case studies, and class projects.

"Important Conference Resolutions." *Menn* 53 (Sept. 20, 1938), 3 7. Resolutions 79 83 and 93 of the GCMC refer to Peace Committee reports and initiate actions for peace education and peace conferences.

Jackson, Dave. *Dial 911: Peaceful Christians and Urban Violence, A Leader's Guide for Group Study.* Scottdale: Mennonite Publishing House, 1982. Pp. 47. Provides plans for four sessions with the book, *Dial 911.* Resources include worship suggestions, discussion guides, group activities, and worksheets.

James, J. T. L. "Is Society Responsible for Crime?" *CanMenn* 18 (Mar. 13, 1970), 4, 10. The concern of this article is to consider whether society is acting responsibly towards the criminal, thus dealing with questions: innocent or guilty?; changing the criminal; respectable punishment; and security and education in a prison cell.

Jantz, Harold. "An Agenda for Peace-loving Christians." *MBH* 19 (Nov. 7, 1980), 12. Editorial calling for more peace education in Mennonite Brethren churches.

Jantz, Harold. "Moros in the Peaceable Kingdom." *MBH* 18 (Aug. 10, 1979), 27-28. Christian conversion for the Moro tribe in Paraguay meant seeking peace with enemy groups within their tribe.

Jantz, Sylvia. "Peace Is . . ." *GH* 65 (Mar. 21, 1972), 266. Vignettes of inner turmoil and conflict with neighbors and friends present images of the meaning of peace and peacemaking in the local setting.

Janzen, David. "Mennonites Should Establish a Seminary Chair for Peace." *CanMenn* 17 (Nov. 21, 1969), 11. After a critical analysis of Ralph B. Potter's *War and Moral Discourse,* in which the just war concept is developed as the only hope for effective war morality, Janzen proposes the seminary at Elkhart establish a chair for peace.

Janzen, David. "Tolstoy and Nonresistance." *CanMenn* 5 (Feb. 22, 1957), 2. Janzen points out that Tolstoy, although he based his nonresistance on the Sermon on the Mount, failed to acknowledge grace as a factor in his moral teachings. His moralism was too rational and secular. It lacked Christian mysticism and the concept of revelation. Biblical nonresistance is an active love that permeates the whole of Christian morality.

Janzen, Wilhelm. "Christians Ought to Fight." *CanMenn* 14 (Aug. 30, 1966), 4. Letter to the editor states that Christians do not need carnal weapons but the weapons of truth, righteousness, gospel of peace, and faith.

Juhnke, James C. "Kansas Mennonites During the Spanish-American War." *MennLife* 26 (Apr., 1971), 70-72. Examines attitudes, political mores, and nonresistant viewpoints present among the Mennonites from 1894 to 1900.

Juhnke, James C. "The Agony of Civic Isolation: Mennonites in World War I." *MennLife* 25 (Jan., 1970), 27-33. World War I shattered the easy assumption many Mennonites held that they could be good citizens and good Mennonites at the same time. This experience was influential for clarifying the Mennonite self-identity.

Juhnke, William. "Shall We Reverse Our Historic Peace Stand?" *Menn* 56 (Aug. 12, 1941), 2. Mennonite tradition would seem to support alternate service. The church will not force young people into this position but should conduct a massive education program making this position clear.

Just, Roy. "An Analysis of the Social Distance Reactions of Students from the Three Major American Mennonite Groups." *PCMCP Ninth,* 73-77. North Newton, Kansas: The Mennonite Press. Held at Hesston College, Hesston, Kansas, June 18-19, 1953. Social distance is the amount of sympathetic understanding that exists between a person and a group. Conclusions from the study show that there are differences in the responses of the three major Mennonite groups. The concept of social distance is important in the analysis of Mennonite social attitudes.

*Justice and the Christian Witness: A Study Report and Study Guide.* Newton: Faith and Life Press; Scottdale: Mennonite Publishing House, 1982. Pp. 66. Discusses why and what issues of justice face the church, the character of biblical justice and how the Christian peace witness guides the church's efforts to speak to these issues.

"Krauses Stress Peace in Asia Teaching Mission." *GH* 72 (Jan. 30, 1979), 80. Norman and Ruth Kraus report on their biblical peace teaching mission to India and Indonesia under the sponsorship of MCC Peace Section and overseas services. They conclude that leadership in peace education must come from within Asia.

Kauffman, Beulah. "Family Life Education." *Builder* 31 (Jan., 1981), 24-25. Column focuses on topics such as peace for families in distress, parenting for peace and justice, nonviolence and children, etc.

Kauffman, Daniel. "Attitudes of Nonresistant People Toward War." *GH* 35 (May 21, 1942), 161. As nonresistant people, we are against war because God has commanded us to be peaceful and holy.

Kauffman, Daniel. "Christian Attitudes Toward War." *GH* 29 (Sept. 3, 1936), 482. The Gospel forbids any part in carnal warfare. Obedience to God, not disobedience to governments, determines our attitude towards war.

Kauffman, J. Howard and Harder, Leland. *Anabaptists Four Centuries Later: A Profile of Five Mennonite and Brethren in Christ Denominations.* Scottdale: Herald Press, 1975. Pp. 399. Reports a survey of 3,591 church members. Chapter 8, entitled "Social Ethics," probes participants' adherence to a nonresistant ethic in relation to a variety of issues such as war, race relations, labor-management relations, concern for the poor, capital punishment, etc. Chapter 9, entitled "Political Participation," explores attitudes concerning the church and state relationship as well as other related topics.

Kauffman, Richard A. "Draft Consultation Calls for Peace Education." *ChrLead* 40 (Dec. 20, 1977), 18. Reports on the Consultation on the Draft at Kansas City sponsored by MCC Peace Section (US).

Kauffman, Richard A. and Miller, Levi, eds. "Songs of Shalom: A *With-Builder* Songbook." *Builder* 29 (Dec., 1979), 49-80. Pp. 32. A songbook designed to be removed from the *Builder* and used independently. Twenty-six songs contributed by contemporary composers and lyricists on themes of peace, praise, and community.

Kauffman, S. Duane, comp. "Religious Pacifists and the American Revolution: Selected Readings and Suggested Student Activities." 1975. Pp. 15. MLA/BeC.

Kauffman, S. Duane with Charles, Tom; Hiebert,

John; Miller, Cecelia; and Voran, Miriam. "A Study of Ethical Ideology and Religious Belief Involving Goshen College Students, Faculty, and Church Members of Region IV." 1983. Pp. 31.

Kauffman, S. Duane, with Koshmider, John; Zehr, Terry; and Zook, Avery. "Religion, Altruism, and Kinship: A Study of Sociobiological Theory." *Journal of Psychology and Christianity* 1 (Fall, 1982), 23-31. Study explores relationship between personal religiosity and personal altruism—a trait defined as both soft-core altruism, which is "relatively painless" sharing of oneself, and hard-core altruism, which is giving oneself to non-kin in potentially life-altering ways.

Kauffman, S. Duane and Zook, Avery. "Reply to Mellor and Andre's 'Religions Group Value Patterns and Motive Orientations': Data and Comment." *Journal of Psychology and Theology* 10 (Fall, 1982), 256-58. Study extends prior measurement of value differences between religious groups to identify differences in values within a particular religious group, the Mennonites. Includes data on values such as a world of peace and national security.

Keeney, Lois. "Mennonite Attitudes in the North During the Civil War." Research paper for Anabaptist History class. 1972. Pp. 10. BfC.

Kehler, Larry. "Arms Sales and Canadian Violence." *CanMenn* 18 (Oct. 2, 1970), 5. Statistical information on Canadian attitudes to violence and the promotion of violence. Asks what the church should do about it.

Kehler, Larry. "Beauty and the Beast." *GH* 70 (Jan. 4, 1977), 4-5; *Menn* 92) (Jan. 18, 1977), 45-46; "Beauty and the Beast (Violence and the Children)." *ChrLead* 40 (Feb. 1, 1977), 4. Examines the effects of the violence portrayed in children's TV programs and lists five safeguards for children's use of television.

Kehler, Larry. "Racism Darkens a Beautiful Continent." *Menn* 87 (Mar. 21, 1972), 190-93; *MennRep* 2 (Apr. 17, 1972), 2. Defines apartheid, what it is and how it influences attitudes within the borders of South Africa and beyond.

Keidel, Levi O. "The Shaping Effects of Violence." *GH* 63 (Nov. 17, 1970), 968-69. Outbreaks of violence and revolution reveal what kind of person one really is and mold one further in that direction. Author relates a story of a conflict situation and the reactions of the people involved to back up his conclusion.

Keidel, Levi O. "The Trap." *GH* 62 (Jan. 21, 1969), 50-51. Describes an imaginary dream in which a young Congolese boy searches for an escape from poverty and injustice first through

education, then through guerilla warfare aimed at the overthrow of the corrupt government.

Keim, Ray; Beechy, Atlee; and Beechy, Winifred. *The Church: The Reconciling Community, Leader's Guide.* Scottdale: Mennonite Publishing House; Newton: Faith and Life Press, 1970. Pp. 102. Leader's guide to companion volume offers scripture readings, session outlines, bibliographic and audiovisual resources, etc.

King, Calvin. "The Nonresistance Credibility Gap." *ChrLiv* 14 (July, 1967), 11. Nonresistant Christians must live and die for eternal, not earthly, values.

King, Martin Luther, Jr. "Transformed Nonconformist." *ChrLiv* 11 (Feb., 1964), 9-10, 38. Reprinted from *Strength to Love,* by King; Harper and Row, 1963. Urges nonconformity to the world in matters of nationalism, militarism, racism, and lifestyle.

Kirk, June. Letter to the Editor. *Menn* 88 (Feb. 20, 1973), 127. Disagrees with the enthusiastic review of the film *Sounder* (Jan. 9, 1973), stating that, while the film did portray strong family values, it also portrayed patience and tolerance among blacks of 1938 toward gross oppression, while the real story is that many blacks in 1938 were witnessing nonviolently against maltreatment.

Klaassen, Walter. "The Christian and Peace." Lectures given for Conrad Grebel College Adult Education Programme, Apr.-May, 1968. Pp. 63. CGCL.

Klaassen, Walter. *What Have You to Do with Peace?* Altona: D. W. Friesen and Sons, Ltd., 1969. Pp. 74. Originally given as lectures designed to help Sunday school teachers teach the basic principles of nonviolence. Covers subjects such as the biblical use of the language of "principalities and powers," the church as the agency of peace, just war doctrine, nuclear war and disarmament issues, and church and state relations.

Klaassen, Walter. "Why Should We Care About Draft Resisters?" *CanMenn* 18 (May 22, 1970), 5. Analyzes the dynamics of Mennonite attitudes to the draft refugee and suggests a positive response to the resisters on the basis of Mennonite history.

Klassen, Aaron. "Peace Sunday." *CanMenn* 8 (Nov. 4, 1960), 2. The church might well ponder whether it can separate its peace teachings from its evangelistic outreach and whether or not Christ taught anything which speaks to the issue of war and peace.

Klassen, Bev. "Children's Peace Literature/

Resources." Term paper for Social Issues course, Apr. 18, 1983. Pp. 30. CGCL.

Klassen, D. D. Letter to the Editor. *CanMenn* 4 (Dec. 28, 1956), 2, 9. A reply to John H. Redekop's "Non-Resistance and UN Police Action," (*CanMenn*, Dec. 7, 1956). Klassen reviews church history on church-state relations and asks for strong peace position through education.

Klassen, D. D. Letter to the Editor. *Menn* 90 (Apr. 8, 1975), 230-31. Underscores the need to send Mennonite youth to Mennonite schools teaching peace theology, by citing situations from World War II, when Mennonites graduated from fundamentalist schools which preached going to war as a Christian duty.

Klassen, Mike. "Implementing a Congregational Dialogue on the Draft and National Service." *MCC PS Newsletter* 10 (Mar.-Apr., 1980), 1-5. Paper presented at the Mar., 1980, Assembly on the Draft and National Service suggests methods for effective conscientious objection education in the congregation. Includes extensive bibliography.

Klassen, William. "Revenge of Love." *GH* 55 (Apr. 12, 1962), 361. Christ gave us a way to relate to enemies—the way of love. Christians have perverted discipleship as they have watered down this truth.

Krehbiel, H[enry] P[eter]. *War, Peace, Amity.* Newton: Herald Publishing Co., 1937. Pp. 350. A historical study of the dynamics of war and peace, written in a time of fear of another war as a study guide for church and peace groups. Includes a chapter on "Women and Peace," by Elva Krehbiel Leisy (annotated separately).

Kreider, Carl. "Peace Thought in the Mennonite Church from the Beginning of the World War in Europe, August, 1914, to the Establishment of the War Sufferer's Relief Commission, December, 1917." Paper presented to American History class, 1936. Pp. 34. MHL.

Kreider, Carl. "The Communist and the Christian Approaches to Peace." Paper, International Christian University, Tokyo, Japan, n.d. Pp. 8. MHL. Lectures presented in Tokyo, Japan, 1957. Pp. 8. MLA/BeC.

Kreider, Robert S. "Educational Values Inherent in the Mennonite Civilian Service Program." *ChrMon* 34 (May, 1942), 144-45. Description of classes and club activities taking place in CPS camps.

Kreider, Robert S. "Educational Values Inherent in the Mennonite Civilian Service Program." *ChrMon* 34, Part 2, (June, 1942), 175-77. Work projects and camp life provide opportunities for learning, fellowship, and testimony to nonresistance.

Kreider, Robert S. "How Beautiful Are the Feet." *MBH* 14 (Oct. 31, 1975), 2-3. Peacemaking and peace education are central in the gospel and should be high in the church's priorities.

Kreider, Robert S. "The Beautiful Feet." *GH* 68 (Apr. 15, 1975), 285-86; "How Beautiful Are the Feet: Taking Stock of Our Peacemaking Commitments When the Heat Is Off." *Menn* 90 (Apr. 15, 1975), 237-38. Discusses the need for congregational peace education programs, and the inseparability of peace and evangelism.

Kreider, Robert S. "The Environmental Influences Affecting the Decisions of Mennonite Boys of Draft Age." *PCMCP First,* 75-88. North Newton, Kansas: The Bethel College Press. Held at Winona Lake, Indiana, Aug. 7-8, 1942. Based on the assumption that the behavior of an individual is profoundly affected by environmental factors, e.g., church, home, community, education, and personal associations.

Kroeker, Walter.. "Concern Over Ethics, Pacifism." *ChrLead* 40 (Mar. 29, 1977), 9. Report from the Mennonite Brethren US Board of Reference and Counsel in which racism, peace/war attitudes, and alliance with New Call to Peacemaking were discussed.

Kuhns, Dennis R. "In Response to Violence." *GH* 68 (Apr. 8, 1975), 266-67. The best way to deal with the destructive cycle of violence is for people to take individual responsibility in rejecting violence and following Jesus' way.

Kurtz, Lydia. "Teaching Peace in Botswana." *MennRep* 7 (Apr. 4, 1977), 16. Mennonite teacher in Botswana describes incident with student that allowed her to reinforce peacemaking values.

Kvaraceus, William C. "Tackling Juvenile Delinquency." *YCC* 46 (May 16, 1965), 8. Education, home life, and employment are some of the areas that are crucial in finding answers to juvenile delinquency.

"Letters Call Young People to Become Makers of Peace." *CanMenn* 6 (Jan. 3, 1958), 1, 7. The Canadian Board of Christian Service sent peace literature to 4,000 youth. The literature includes reflections from a nonresistant Japanese Baptist and Erland Waltner.

"Living as Peacemakers." *Builder* 12 (Feb., 1962), 17-18. Four youth program ideas designed to help youth think through the implications of the church's peace theology with respect to practice and witness.

"Love Works in Conflicts' Says Hostetter." *MBH* 10 (May 28, 1971), 18-19. Former MCC worker Doug Hostetter speaks of the effects of propaganda and the American military presence in war-torn Vietnam. Also speaks of the power of love at work in his relationships with the Vietnamese people.

Landes, Carl J. "A Mennonite Peace Program for Local Groups." *Menn* 51 (Apr. 14, 1936), 2-3. Individuals must not only have inner peace but must work for peace in the community and the nation. Specific suggestions are given.

Langenwalter, J. H. *For All Mankind.* North Newton, Ks.: Bethel College Press, 1943. Pp. 48. MHL. A study of the four gospels centered around the theme of peace as a way of life for all with ramification for both attitudes and actions.

Langhofer, Dennis L. "Ethics, The Businessman, and the Church." *Direction* 7 (Jan., 1979), 26-34. The basis for business ethics should be the ethical values held by the church.

Leatherman, Daniel R. "The Political Socialization of Students in Mennonite Secondary Schools." MA thesis in political science, Univ. of Chicago, Chicago, Ill., 1960. Pp. 92. Some of the items used to test the attitudes of Mennonite youth toward political participation were: self-rating on degree of political interest; image of government; current events activity; party preference; and intention to vote when old enough.

Leatherman, John D. "The Story of Non-Resistant Peoples During the World War as Told in the *Goshen Daily Democrat.*" Paper presented to Peace and War Seminar, Goshen College, Goshen, Ind., June, 1940. Pp. 22. MHL.

Lederach, Paul. *Hunger Hurts: How Shall Christians Respond? (Leader's Guide).* Scottdale: Herald Press; Newton: Faith and Life PRess, 1968. Pp. 15. Organizes material of accompanying volume edited by Willard Roth into five teaching sessions and provides a statement of purpose, Bible study, discussion guide, and homework assignment for each lesson.

Lehman, Chester K. "As Applied to the Christian and Civil Government: Bible Teaching on Nonconformity." (Part 7). *GH* 32 (June 15, 1939), 226-27. Christ's Kingdom is primarily spiritual, but since God has ordained government, these powers are used by God. Deals with various problems encountered, e.g., tax payment, office-holding, and the meaning of subjection to government.

Lehman, Ernest. "There Shall Be Wars . . . See That Ye Be Not Troubled." *GH Supplement* 40 (Apr., 1947), 96. There will always be wars but the Christian must not be troubled by this reality. Rather he or she remains sober, watchful, and urgently and steadily active in serving Jesus Christ.

Lehman, M[artin] C[lifford]. "The Philosophical Basis for Mennonite Relief and Non-Resistance." *PCMCP Second,* 95-105. North Newton, Kansas: The Bethel College Press. Held at Goshen, Indiana, July 22-23, 1943. There are internal factors that need to be rediscovered and defined as to theological origin, philosophical implication, and social application which can operate in encouraging cooperation among the various Mennonite groups. These factors should not be related to responding to concerns associated with war.

Lehman, Melvin L. "The Tent." *ChrLiv* 16 (May, 1969), 20-27. Story of young Amish men who refrained from playing a trick of revenge upon city tourists because it was not consistent with the way of peace.

Lehn, Cornelia. *Peace Be with You.* Newton: Faith and Life, 1980. Pp. 126. Fifty-nine stories about peace from the first through the 20th centuries. Intended as a resource for peace education with children.

Leichty, Bruce. "IPF Assembly Reveals 'Folly' of Values." *Forum* 13 (Nov., 1979), 14, 15. The annual Intercollegiate Peace Fellowship assembly, meeting in Hesston, Kans., Oct. 25-27, confronted the participants with the "folly" of the peace witness.

Leis, Vernon. "Our Mandate to Be Peacemakers." *GH* 65 (Feb. 29, 1972), 186-87. Underscoring biblical references, the writer asserts that peacemaking is central to the gospel, based on: Jesus' teaching and ministry; biblical evidence indicating that conversion produces ethical changes; and the fellowship of Christians around the world.

Leisy, Elva Krehbiel. "Women and Peace." *War, Peace, Amity,* by H. P. Krehbiel. Newton: Herald Publishing Co., 1937, 302-315. Reviews the beginnings of women's peace groups and the contributions of individual women around the world. Calls upon women to make their creative impulses felt against the destructiveness of war by working in peace education programs, or by instilling international awareness in their children.

Liechty, C. Daniel. "Political Nonresistance: A Thesis in Christian Ethics." MA in Peace Studies thesis, AMBS, 1978. Pp. 71. An exploration of the OT anti-kingship tradition, a comparison of the political views of Hegel and Marx, and a summary of Christian thinking on the relationship of church and state contribute to a

Christian understanding of the political organism.

Lind, Ivan Reuben. "The Attitude of the (Old) Mennonite Church Toward Labor Unions." *PCMCP Third*, 89-97. North Newton, Kansas: n.p. Held at North Newton, Kansas, Aug. 18-19, 1944. Scriptural bases for the nonresistant position in war can also be applied to the labor situation. Exploration of the attitudes which the Mennonites have taken through the years toward labor organizations.

Lind, Loren. "Nonresistance and You." *Builder* 14 (Jan., 1964), 59-61. A planning guide for a youth program designed to help the participants become enthusiastic about the principle of nonresistance and to find new ways of making the concept meaningful in life.

Lind, Loren. "Second Thoughts About China." *YCC* 47 (May 22, 1966), 8. Inquiry into the attitudes and policies underlying the relationship between the US and China.

Lind, Loren. "Who Gets Propaganda?" *YCC* 43 (Jan. 21, 1962), 5. An analysis of propaganda using international political situations. Suggestions are offered for Christians who are interested in seeking truth.

Lind, Millard C. *Answer to War*. Scottdale: Herald Press, 1952. Pp. 143. Written particularly for young people to show from the Bible and history that God, Christ, and the Church are the answer to war.

Littell, Franklin H. "The New Shape of the Church-State Issue." *MQR* 40 (July, 1966), 179-89. In a time when nation and church tend to fuse toward a culture-religion, we need a church with more devotion and discipline, and secular institutions with more respect for their limited but essential function.

Longacre, James C. "Letter of Concern to All." *GH* 66 (July 17, 1973), 556-57. A call for new peace education efforts for the Mennonite Church, in order to prevent Mennonite assimilation of the militaristic and economically oppressive values of US culture.

Longacre, James C., writer, and Martin, Lawrence, ed. *Citizens of Christ's Kingdom: A Peace Education Resource Guide for Congregational Leaders*. Scottdale, Pa.: Mennonite Publishing House, 1975. Pp. 16. MHL. Organized around 3 themes: biblical foundations for peacemaking; peacemaking in the family and congregation; and peacemaking in the social order.

Longacre, Paul. "Learning About World Hunger." *Builder* 29 (May, 1979), 1-5. An annotated list of audiovisual and print resources to help congregational educators to promote both awareness and response on the issue of world hunger.

Lubosch, Lore. "The Mennonites in Brazil—They Did It Almost Without Help . . . ' " *MennMirror* 1 (Jan., 1972), 10-14. Dr. Boruszenko, economic historian in Curitiba, Brazil, gives a detailed report on the history of Brazil's Mennonites from the emigration from Russia in 1929 to the present, including such aspects as education, economics, and conscription.

Lutz, John A. "Eighteen." *YCC* 40 (Apr. 12, 1959), 235. Mennonite youth have to review seriously what they believe about peace and then make choices reflecting their belief. Prize-winning essay.

"MCC Postwar Planning." *RepConsS* 2 (May 1, 1944), 3. A survey of CPS camps operated by MCC and Mennonites in other camps indicates that CPS has created interest in further education, that 60 percent of those surveyed plan to farm after CPS, etc.

"MCC to Establish Washington Office." *CanMenn* 16 (Feb. 13, 1968), 1. The "office in Washington is not for lobbying. It shall serve as an *observer*, particularly with reference to developments in the federal government, but also in liaison with other church, welfare, and professional agencies. It would analyze and interpret trends which may affect peace, religious liberty, social welfare, education, and related fields."

"Mennonite Questionnaire Reveals I-W Attitudes." *RepConsS* 12 (Dec., 1955), 4. J. S. Shultz, of Bluffton, has completed a survey of Mennonite and Brethren in Christ I-W persons and their attitudes toward the Civilian Work Program.

"Mennonite Race Relations Still at Low." *CanMenn* 18 (Aug. 14, 1970), 4, 12. A report on a study of Mennonite attitudes toward blacks by Denny Weaver includes a historical survey over the last hundred years, an evaluation, and a listing of resources for improving race relations.

MacDonald, Dennis. "The Order of the Shovel." *Post-American* 1 (Fall, 1971), 6. An ethically self-conscious community which is militant in its refusal to be co-opted by the American war involvement, racism, and materialistic values, can be a basis for penetrating society with the message of total redemption in Jesus Christ.

Martin, John R. and Roth, Willard E. "Peace, Not a Sword." *Builder* 14 (June, 1964), 17-18. A series of six ideas for youth programs designed to help young people grow in their understanding of Christian peace and acquire information about church service programs. Plans include texts, hymn selections, audiovisual resources, etc.

Matsuo, Hilda. "Can We Handle All Those Boat People?" *MennMirror* 9 (Sept., 1979), 10. The writer looks at the varying attitudes of Canadians towards Indochinese refugees and points out what two MCC employees have advised—that Canadians should act as peacemakers rather than continuing the more popular route of polarizing the situation in Southeast Asia.

Matty, Maria. "Sanctity of Life Is Theme for Eben-Ezer Education Week." *MennRep* 9 (Dec. 24, 1979), 5. Education week at the Eben-Ezer Mennonite Church of Abbotsford, BC resulted in resolutions on capital punishment, militarism, and abortion.

Mayer, Robert. "At the Grass Roots—The Quest for an Alternative Community: An Historical and Contemporary Model." *Forum* (Oct., 1972), 1-2. Just as the early Anabaptists emphasized small, voluntary human communities which separated themselves from the state and witnessed to the state's injustices, we need to develop a life-style alternative to that of the present, where humanitarian values are primary.

Menninger, William C. "Adapting to Change." *YCC* 43 (Feb. 11, 1962), 5. Adapting to change or long-term threats like war are very important for a mature person.

Menninger, William C. "Getting Along with Others." *YCC* 43 (Mar. 11, 1962), 13. Relating to people means being able to understand and accept people even though they are different from you.

Menninger, William C. "Giving Yourself Away." *YCC* 43 (Mar. 4, 1962), 5. Mature giving includes the giving of self to family, friends, and community. "Causes" are healthy outlets for mature giving.

Menninger, William C. "Learning to Love." *YCC* 43 (Mar. 25, 1962), 5. Love is the most important indication of emotional maturity. Refers to an all-embracing attitude toward the world.

Metzler, Edgar. "Breaking the Cycle." *YCC* 32 (July 29, 1951), 660, 664. The vicious cycle of wars will cease when enough people believe, live, and practice the answer of Christ which is the triumph over conflict by love.

Metzler, Edgar. "Mennonite Witness to the State: Attitudes and Actions, World War I-1956." Paper presented at the Laurelville, Pa., conference on "Nonresistance and Political Responsibility," 1956. N.p.: Peace Problems Committee, 1956, 49-53. MHL. A survey of forty years of Mennonite witness to the state. Primarily a review of the Peace Problems Committee of the (Old) Mennonite Church. The witness "has almost without exception been a matter of petitioning for our [own] rights and privileges."

Metzler, Eric E. "Peacemaking Today." *GH* 73 (July 1, 1980), 524-26. Reflects on American values and Mennonite commitments and compares them with New Testament exhortations to peacemaking.

Metzler, James E. "A Shalom Focus for Christian Education." *Builder* 29 (Nov., 1979), 2-11. Suggests that the theme of Shalom, the colorful "language of God's dreams," could appropriately focus the educational mission of the church because it combines joyful celebration of God's family with a prophetic witness for justice in God's world.

Metzler, James E. "The Radical Generation." *YCC* 49 (May 26, 1968), 8. Challenges Mennonite attitudes and assumptions about the radical generation.

Metzler, James R.[*sic.,* E.] "This Is War!" *GH* 59 (June 14, 1966), 526-27. Describes war's horror, illusion, propaganda, and selfishness; we must represent the concern of Christ in our involvement in the Vietnam war and renounce our attitude of isolation.

Miller, Dorcas S. "What If War Comes." *ChrLiv* 12 (Nov., 1965), 3. Mother faces child's questions about war.

Miller, Ernest F. "Training Young People to Give a Christian Witness in the Face of World Ideologues." *ChrMon* 44 (Aug., 1952), 242-44. Addresses, among others, the issue of militarism.

Miller, Evelyn. "Power to the People." *Builder* 29 (Dec., 1979), 2-7. A reading drama for five persons which raises some of the significant issues of the development of nuclear power and nuclear weapons. Focus on appropriate Christian responses to these issues.

Miller, Levi (Editorial). "Does Peace Education Help?" *Builder* 31 (Jan., 1981), 2-3. Study and reflection upon the biblical materials upon which the peace position is based can move us beyond the peace learnings gained by merely identifying with the Mennonite group.

Miller, Levi (Editorial). "Paul's Letters of Peace." *Builder* 29 (June, 1979), inside front cover. Introduces a new Sunday School peace emphasis utilizing the theme of "Jesus Christ Our Lord" focused by the epistles of Philippians, Ephesians, and Colossians.

Miller, Levi (Editorial). "Teaching Peace." *Builder* 28 (May, 1978), 1. Cites findings of Kauffman and Harder study, *Anabaptists Four Centuries Later* (Herald Press, 1975), on the lack of impact Sunday School participation seems to have had on social concerns and suggests some ways congregations can teach peace.

Miller, Orie O. "Our Peace Policy." *MQR* 3 (Jan., 1929), 26-32. An address delivered to World War I CO's deals with the problem of the ill preparedness of the CO's and puts forth the 1924 three-point program for peace education in the Mennonite Church.

Miller, S. Paul. "Peace Literature for the Mennonite Church in India." Paper presented to Mennonite Seminar and Seminar in Christian Education, AMBS, Elkhart, Ind., 1964. Pp. 35. MHL. With this is bound "Christ's Teaching About War, an Adaptation of the Book *Christ and War* by Millard Lind." Pp. 13.

Miller, Terry. "Types of Religious Beliefs, Level of Education and College Attended in Relation to Payment of War Taxes." Social Science Seminar paper, Mar. 29, 1979. Pp. 39. MLA/BeC.

Miller, Vern. "Christian Theology for Our Time." *Builder* 18 (June, 1968), 10-12. In an article designed to serve as a resource, the last of a series of lessons focused on peacemaking issues, the author suggests relevant Christian theology must be mission-oriented, community-oriented, and people-oriented.

Moore, Warren. "Ethnic Mennonites?" *MennLife* 22 (Jan., 1967), 25-26. Mennonite communities reveal a survival tactic, "the disavowal of values in alien groups and institutions." ". . . What would happen to the concepts, customs, and language of Mennonite-styled Christianity" if Mennonites decided to live in all-black neighborhoods?

Mosemann, John H. "The March of Militarism." *GH* 33 (July 11, 1940), 322. The Christian must guard against allowing his or her attitudes to be shaped by the worldwide spirit of militarism.

"Nuclear Energy, Hot Topic at Peace Section Meeting." *GH* 72 (June 19, 1979), 504-505. Agenda items at the annual MCC Peace Section Meeting in Washington, DC, June 1-2, included proposed draft registration legislation, various peace education projects, and nuclear energy.

Nickel, Arnold. "Peace Committee." *The Mennonite Encyclopedia* IV:130, Scottdale-Newton-Hillsboro Mennonite Publishing Offices, 1959. This committee of the General Conference Mennonite Church promoted peace education and peace witness from World War I until 1950, when it merged with other service committees to form the Board of Christian Service.

Nisly, Paul W. *Children of Peace: Teacher's Guide.* Elgin: The Brethren Press; Nappanee: Evangel Press; Newton: Faith and Life Press; Scottdale: Herald Press, 1982. Pp. 64. Plans 13 sessions for companion volume by J. R. Burkholder and John Bender. Resources offered include discussion guides, background information, and audiovisual aids.

*Of All Nations One People: A Study Guide on Race Relations.* Salunga, Pa.: Peace Committee of the Lancaster Conference of the Mennonite Church, 1972. Pp. 24. MHL. Three lessons designed to help persons recognize their attitudes and work toward greater understanding and empathy with all people—whatever their race.

Oyer, Russell L. "The Philosophy of Pressure in War Propaganda." 1942. Pp. 8. BfC.

"Peace Church Officials Contact State Directors." *RepConsS* 9 (Mar.-Apr., 1952), 6. MCC finds both receptive and punitive attitudes toward COs among contacted state directors of Selective Service.

"Prepare Draft, Peace Materials for Spanish Speaking." *GH* 65 (Sept. 26, 1972), 787. Puerto Rican Mennonites are requesting materials in the Spanish language because of an admitted passive and dormant peace witness.

"Prospects and Programs for Peace in 1937." *Menn* 52 (Jan. 26, 1937), 9. The Peace Committee of the GCMC proposes a peace education program; included is a brief description of peace issues likely to be confronted by Congress in 1937.

Peachey, J. Lorne. "Die Stillen im Lande?" *ChrLiv* 12 (Aug., 1965), 9, 28. Mennonites who align with the militaristic and racist "Radical Right" are in danger of repeating the mistakes of German Mennonites who supported Hitler.

Peachey, J. Lorne. "How Do You Teach Peace to Children?" *GH* 73, Part 1, (Apr. 22, 1980), 329-30; Part 2, (Apr. 29, 1980), 353-55; Part 3, (May 6, 1980), 373-75. Encourages a broad definition of peace as a reconciling lifestyle. Suggests ways in which both home and church can contribute to children's appreciation for peace.

Peachey, J. Lorne. *How to Teach Peace to Children.* Scottdale and Kitchener: Herald Press, 1981. Pp. 32. MHL. Surveys historic peace church writing since World War II on peace education and condenses this wisdom into 20 suggestions for parents and other caretakers. Addresses such issues as war toys, entertainment glorifying violence, competitive vs. cooperative play, international experience, peace projects, etc. Other resources included in the book are a discussion guide and reading list.

Peachey, J. Lorne. "One Way to Teach Peace." *ChrLiv* 26 (Feb., 1979), 31. Editorial recommends extended family relationships for children and parents.

Peachey, J. Lorne. "'What Can I Do.' " *ChrLiv* 14 (Mar., 1967), 11. Suggestions for promoting peace range from volunteer work to hosting international visitors.

Peachey, Paul L. "Identity Crisis Among American Mennonites." *MQR* 42 (Oct., 1968), 243-59. The identity crisis problem is not primarily one of accretions but of mutation in the basic charter, in the structure of belief consciousness, and in the sense of identity which make one a "Mennonite."

Peachey, Paul L. "Our Peace Witness in Europe." *Menn* 65 (June 20, 1950), 439. Mennonite witness can be something of a beacon to other Protestants. Witness must be rooted in the concept of conversion, in which peace characterizes all relationships.

Peachey, Paul L. *The Churches and War.* N.p.: Mennonite General Conference Peace Problems Committee, 1956. Pp. 19. The Christian Youth and War Pamphlets No. 5. Directed toward young men approaching draft age, pamphlet traces the attitudes of the Christian church since the first century toward involvement in war. Includes comments on the just war theory as well as on individual pacifists throughout Christian history.

Peters, Frank C. "Are We Suffering from Compassion Fatigue?" *ChrLead* 39 (Feb. 3, 1976), 2. Caution against letting media overexposure blunt the Christian's response to social concerns. Suggests three levels of aproach to these issues.

Peters, Frank C. "The Christian in a World of Violence." *ChrLead* 22 (Feb. 10, 1959), 4-5, 16. Jesus did not intend truth to be defended with coercion and violence, but with the strength of the Spirit and love of God.

Preheim, Vern. "MCC's Efforts in the Middle East." *GH* 62 (June 10, 1969), 517-18. Describes MCC activities, primarily in Jordan, which range from war relief and reconstruction to education and crafts projects.

Prieb, Wesley. "What Are Our Racial Attitudes?" *Menn* 64 (Jan. 25, 1949), 13-14. As in the area of nonresistance, Mennonites must bring together theology and practice regarding racial attitudes.

Purves, John H. "My Decision on Militarism." *Menn* 67 (Jan. 1, 1952), 11-12. An account of a pilgrimage from the militaristic point of view to persuasion that nonresistance is God's will and way.

Q[Anonymous]. "Letter from a I-A-O." *MCC Bull* 3 (Oct. 8, 1944), 5-6. This letter, written to CPS and AFSC, describes the hateful attitudes and military environment which he (Q) experienced in noncombatant service. Because of his resistance to these attitudes, his colonel rightly decided he belonged in CPS.

(Review). *Disarmament Times.* Published by the Non-Governmental Organizations Committee on Disarmament at the UN Headquarters, n.d. *MCC PS Newsletter* 10 (Jan.-Feb., 1980), 9. Discusses the viewpoint of this newspaper reporting regularly and fully on disarmament issues in the United Nations.

(Review). *The Mennonite Church in the Second World War,* by Guy F. Hershberger. Scottdale: Mennonite Publishing House, 1951. Pp. 308. *Fellowship* 18 (Nov., 1952), 28. This book is "not only an account of the direct relation of the church to the war, but includes as well chapters on missions, education, relief, voluntary service, and intergroup relations both within and without the Mennonite family."

Rasker, A. J. "The German Question and the Quest for Peace." *MennLife* 20 (July, 1965), 122, 123. ". . . The basic Christian views of repentance and willingness to be reconciled are not only essential for a personal Christian life, but are also revelant in the realm of the political life."

Reba Place Fellowship Drama Group. "Good Friday." *Swords into Plowshares: A Collection of Plays About Peace and Social Justice.* Ed. Ingrid Rogers. Elgin: The Brethren Press, 1983, 30-44. Seven scenes dramatizing the passion of Christ and emphasizing the way of suffering love demonstrated by Jesus' attitudes and behaviors through that ordeal.

Redekop, Calvin W. "Peace Resources and People." *ChrLiv* 6 (Aug., 1959), 32-33, 37. Witness to peace through education and living should be the work of local congregations.

Redekop, John H. "A Christian Looks at the '79 Election." *MBH* 18 (Apr. 27, 1979), 2-5. Assesses Christian values in each of the three major parties in Canadian politics.

Redekop, John H. "Above the Law." *MBH* 14 (June 13, 1975), 8. Militant Canadian postal strikers typify an "above the law" stance motivated by self-interest, while nonviolent figures such as Jesus stand above the law because of a higher moral commitment.

Redekop, John H. "Evangelical Christianity . . . and Political Ideology." *ChrLead* 27 (Nov. 10, 1964), 4-5. True Christianity cannot be equated with either the liberal or conservative political orientation. It stands in tension with both.

Redekop, John H. "Prince of Peace and Pacifism." *MBH* 15 (Nov. 26, 1976), 10. Disturbed by attitudes displayed during a peace conference, author urges pacifism as a lifestyle affecting all relationships.

Redekop, John H. "Race Consciousness Generates World Tension." *CanMenn* 3 (Mar. 4, 1955), 2. "One of the best ways to prevent communism or any other despicable 'ism' from exploiting anti-West, anti-Christian attitudes is to eliminate and eradicate the factors which give rise to those attitudes."

Redekop, John H. "Some of My Best Friends Are Americans." *The Star-Spangled Beaver.* Ed. John H. Redekop. Toronto: Peter Martin Assoc. Ltd., 1971, 203-216. Explores reasons behind negative Canadian attitudes toward the US, including the American sense of manifest destiny which resulted from the nationalization of Christianity in the US.

Reed, Kenneth. *Joseph, Put That Gun Down.* Lancaster, Pa.: Good Enterprises, Ltd., 1973. Pp. 34. Two-act play dramatizing the story of the Hochstetler family caught in the French, English, and Indian war of 1754. Contrasts the values of war and peace found in both the Amish and native American cultures.

Regier, Robert. "Attitude of Young People Toward Peace Teaching." *Menn* 66 (Aug. 7, 1951), 494-95, 491. Majority of youth in this GCMC survey, taken by Bethel College students, want to maintain the Mennonite peace stance, but feel that peace education is inadequate in Mennonite churches.

Reimer, Vic. "The Myths That We Live By Will Change, Says Specialist." *Menn* 94 (Mar. 20, 1979), 215. Speaking at the Mid-America New Call to Peacemaking conference, Mar. 3, at Bethel College, Burns Weston said that among the myths that will need to change are: wealth trickles down to the poor; bigger is better; arms spending helps the economy; and the nation state is the ultimate political structure.

Reitz, Herman R. "Evangelism in the Shadow of Peace." *ST* 47 (Mar., 1979), 27. After describing a spiritual conversion, Reitz notes that this pattern seems less and less common in mainstream Mennonite thinking. Attributes this to Mennonite scholars like John H. Yoder and his book *The Politics of Jesus,* which, while not discounting conversion experience, does not place it sequentially before the working out of human reconciliation.

Reitz, Herman R. (Review.) *The Upside-Down Kingdom,* by Don Kraybill. Scottdale: Herald Press, 1978. *ST* 47 (Aug., 1979), 32. This book creates much disturbance for those who tend to confine their nonconformity to the narrow corridors of appearance and recreation.

Rempel, Peter H. "Attitudes to Jews and Nazi Germany in the *Christian Science Monitor,* 1922-1953." Term paper for Canadian minorities course, Dec., 1974. Pp. 24. CGCL.

Rempel, Richard. "The Evolution of Mennonite Political Views." Student paper for Menonite History, Bethel College, Feb., 1962. Pp. 19. MLA/BeC.

Ressler, Lawrence and Peachey, Dean. "A Call to Nonconformity." *GH* 72 (Nov. 6, 1979), 869-70. We need to re-examine our economic system and structures and seek alternatives if we want to seriously address problems such as poverty, hunger, urban decay, and militarism.

Richert, P. H. "Why Conscription in Peacetime . . ." *Menn* 55 (July 30, 1940), 5. Peacetime conscription has more propaganda value than military value and should be opposed as a totalitarian measure.

Rogalski, Edgar. "Titan I Display Prompted Peace Education Efforts." *CanMenn* 13 (Oct. 12, 1965), 1. A Titan I missile display at the Central Ontario Exhibition in Kitchener prompted Bruce and Doug Jutzi to carry out a program of peace education. A group organized by the Jutzi brothers confronted many people at the exhibition about the weapon's threat to world peace.

Roth, John D. "Peace Teachers: She Makes the World a Little Saltier." *Builder* 31 (Jan., 1981), 10-11. Profile of Janet Umble Reedy, Elkhart, Ind., who, as social worker, student, mother, and tax resister, perceives the framework of peace involvement to be those acts which work toward growth in human relation.

Roth, Nadine S. "Claude Follows the Prince of Peace All the Way." *ChrMon* 29 (Dec., 1937), 355-56. Story about a young man and woman's friendship troubled by differing opinions on a Christian response to war.

Roth, Nadine S. "On the Altar." *ChrMon* 27 (Feb., 1935), 35-36. Story about the friendship of two neighbor women strained over the issue of participation in war.

Roth, Wallace. "Public Opinion and Propaganda in Relation to War and Peace." Social Science Seminar paper, Mar. 31, 1966. Pp. 20. MLA/BeC.

"Sixty Winnipeg Layman [*sic*] Will Participate in Peace Seminar." *CanMenn* 12 (Sept. 29, 1964), 12. Peace education effort will involve discussion of such topics as the Bible and peace as well as role plays.

"Social Values are Key to Assimilation." *CanMenn* 15 (Nov. 14, 1967), 4. Report of Lawrence Hart's recent visit to the Elkhart seminary. Greatest contributing factor to lack of understanding between native Americans and their white fellow citizens is the divergence in thinking about social values.

"Soldiers Strong Spiritually and Not Opposed to War." *CanMenn* 14 (Feb. 8, 1966), 6. A report on the involvement in the church by generals in the army and their attitudes to war.

"Statement from the Black Delegates of US Congress on Evangelism." *EV* 83 (Jan. 25, 1970), 6. Statement deals with what it means to be committed to evangelism and seriously concerned about attitudes of prejudice in race relations.

"Students Puzzled by Views of Revolution." *Menn* 84 (Apr. 15, 1969), 252-54. Differing theologies and political theories are presented in order to find an answer to the problems of our time: injustice, war, poverty, inequality, conscription, and violence.

Sawatsky, Rodney J. "History and Ideology: American Mennonite Identity Definition Through History." PhD dissertation, Princeton University, Princeton, NJ, May, 1977. Pp. 332. MHL. Contends that the American Mennonites, from their first expressions of identity in the early 18th century, have always tried to explain who they are and what they are about by means of their history—both among themselves and with their neighbors. Sawatsky traces this usage through the "owning" of the *Martyrs' Mirror*, the work of C. Henry Smith and John Horsch and the identity crisis of the 1920s to the work of Harold S. Bender and the reformation captioned as the "Anabaptist vision." Within this context, the issues of war and peace receive substantive treatment in two sections: the chapter entitled, "Two Wars: The Context of Identity," 122-69; the chapter entitled, "Biblical Nonresistance: An Acceptable Denominational Distinctive," 211-60.

Sawatsky, Rodney J. "The Attitudes of the Canadian Mennonites Toward Communism as Seen in Mennonite Weekly Periodicals." Social Science Sminar paper, Apr., 1965. Pp. 35. MLA/BeC.

Schmidt, Henry J. "Discipleship . . ." *ChrLead* 39 (Sept. 28, 1976), 2. One of the greatest dangers of every generation is to settle for a cheapened version of Christianity rooted more in culture than in biblical truth.

Schmidt, Linda. "Denver Area Economic Conversion Project Underway." *Peace Section Newsletter* 8 (Nov.-Dec., 1977), 9-10. Describes an organization called the Social and Economic Analysis Corporation (SEAC) which is working on plans for total economic conversion in the greater Denver metropolitan area. Economic conversion is the transition from defense- to civil-related industries and employment.

Schmidt, Linda. "Peace Section (US) Opposes Registration; Less Clear About Nuclear Issues." *Menn* 94 (June 26, 1979), 438. MCC Peace Section (US) annual meeting agenda includes proposed draft registration legislation, discussion of various peace education projects, and debate on nuclear energy.

Schrag, Dale R. "The Key in Reconciliation." *Menn* 85 (Nov. 3, 1970), 678. The nature of reconciliation as it relates to our peace witness and our attitudes toward other races or minority groups.

Schrag, Martin H. "Subject to the Higher Powers." *EV* 83 (Feb. 10, 1970), 6. We are helped in clarifying our attitudes to our loyalties to God and nation by reviewing the history of the faith of our forebears.

Schultz, Harold J. "A Christian College: Vision for Peacemaking." *Menn* 88 (Apr. 24, 1973), 266-67. The central focus of a small, Mennonite, liberal arts college on peacemaking and conflict resolution can inform its other commitments: reconciling a fractured Christianity; genuine community with the campus; a philosophy of continuing education.

Seitz, Kathryn F. *A Working Bibliography of Peace Books for Children and Youth.* Harrisonburg: Education Dept., Eastern Mennonite College, 1984. Pp. 20. Lists a variety of peace educational resources—books, games, films, recordings—for use by different age groups, nursery through high school.

Shank, Gladys. "'If Ye Love Me.'" *ChrMon* 36 (Aug., 1944), 226, 249. Story about a young man who struggles with his decision to enter army training instead of CPS camp.

Shank, J. R. "Applied Nonresistance." *ChrMon* 32 (June, 1940), 188. Young People's Meeting study guide focuses on nonresistance in daily living.

Shank, J. R. "Bible Nonresistance, as Applied to Our Present Day." *ChrMon* 28 (June, 1936), 188-89. Young People's Meeting study guide for a lesson on this topic.

Shank, J. R. "'Blessed Are the Peacemakers.'" *ChrMon* 25 (June, 1933), 184-85. Young People's Meeting study guide focuses on living in peace with all people.

Shank, J. R. "'Blessed Are the Peacemakers.'"

*ChrMon* 31 (June, 1939), 188. Young People's Meeting study guide for a lesson on peacemaking.

Shank, J. R. "Loyalty to the Prince of Peace." *ChrMon* 34 (June, 1942), 1889. Young People's Meeting study guide focuses on peace with God and love toward enemies.

Shank, J. R. "Nonresistance in Practice." *ChrMon* 38 (Sept., 1946), 279. Young People's Meeting study guide focuses on overcoming evil with good.

Shank, J. R. "The Christian's Relation to the Government." *ChrMon* 28 (Mar., 1936), 91-92. Young People's Meeting study guide for a lesson on this topic.

Shank, J. R. "The Promotion and Practice of Peace." *ChrMon* 26 (June, 1934), 186-87. Young People's Meeting study guide focuses on peace living.

Shank, J. R. "The Way of Peace." *ChrMon* 29 (June, 1937), 189. Young People's Meeting study guide for a lesson on peace with self, others, and God.

Shank, J. Ward (Editorial). "Nationalism and Anti-Nationalism." *ST* 41 (Apr., 1973), 5. There is no inherent wrong in expressing loyalty and regard for one's country even in the face of its wrongdoing. Rather the sin is in the negativist and antinational attitudes.

Shank, J. Ward (Editorial). "The Teaching of Peace." *ST* 40 (Dec., 1972), 7. In the teaching of peace it is the essential spiritual character which is evidently being neglected, especially in the company of our intellectuals and social actionists.

Shank, J. Ward (Editorial). "What Kind of Peace Education?" *ST* 41 (Sept., 1973), 9. Examines comments about peace education contained in a letter from Franconia Conference Peace and Social Concerns Task Force.

Shelley, Paul. "An Evaluation of Methods of Transmitting Mennonite Ideals." *PCMCP Fourth*, 71-82. North Newton, Kansas: n.p. Held at Bluffton, Ohio, Aug. 24-25, 1945. The evaluation includes the CPS experience and the development of the CO position.

Shelly, Andrew R. "COMBS to Step Up Peace Witness." *CanMenn* 16 (Jan. 16, 1968), 3. At a joint MCC-COMBS meeting in Akron on Dec. 13 it was decided to make Peace Section resources available to all missionaries. It was also felt that new ways must be found to respond to the desire of new churches for resources and help in stimulating peace teaching.

Shelly, Maynard. "Becoming Reconciled." *Builder* 25 (Nov., 1975), 98-103. A Sunday school lesson for adult students which uses the conflict between Joseph and his brothers, Genesis 45-50, to focus contemporary peacemaking concerns.

Shelly, Maynard. "Christians Still Reflect a Racist Society." *Menn* 85 (Sept. 29, 1970), 587, 588. Reports on a study on Mennonite attitudes toward other races from 1886 to 1969 by Denny Weaver, a graduate student in church history at Duke University.

Shenk, Dan, and Garcia, Lupe. "Travels with Neftali." *GH* 69 (Sept. 21, 1976), 714-15. Two writers report on peace education efforts among minority congregations, especially the MCC-sponsored work of Neftali Torres.

Shenk, Stanley C. *Youth and Nonresistance.* Scottdale: Herald Press, 1953. Pp. 63. A series of thirteen lessons for group discussion prepared for the Mennonite Commission for Christian Education.

Sherk, J. Harold. "Some Reflections on an Odyssey." *RepConsS* 21 (Dec., 1964), 1. Reports contacts made with COs of a variety of denominational, ideological and cultural identities on a trip to the West Coast.

Sherk, J. Harold. "The Way to Peace." *RepConsS* 22 (Dec., 1965), 2. Short collection of peace quotations taken from biblical, historical, and literary sources.

Shetler, Sanford G. "Youth in an Age of Revolution." *ST* 35 (June, 1967), 10. In a world of revolution, the youth are both the target of the revolution and a part of the revolution. Suggests some criteria that can be used to evaluate programs and innovations for the youth.

Showalter, Elizabeth A. (Review). *Christians and War*, by Llewelyn Harris. A Plough pamphlet, 1957. Pp. 12. *ChrLiv* 4 (Dec., 1957), 32. Recommends this short survey of Christian stands on war throughout Christian history, written by a member of the Society of Brothers in England.

Showalter, Stuart W. "Coverage of Conscientious Objectors to the Vietnam War: An Analysis of the Editorial Content of American Magazines, 1964-1972." PhD dissertation, Univ. of Texas at Austin, 1975. Pp. 163. MSHL. Study finds that the nation's most widely read and respected popular magazines took seriously their responsibility to defend individual rights because they portrayed COs, certainly an ideological minority during the Vietnam War, positively most of the time.

Showalter, Stuart W. "Six Opinion Magazines' Coverage of Conscientious Objectors to the Vietnam War." Paper presented to the Association for Education in Journalism, San Diego State University. Aug. 18-21, 1974. Pp. 22. MHL.

Sider, Arbutus. "White in a Black School." *The Other Side* 10 (Sept.-Oct., 1974), 27-31. White parents struggle with what it means to have pre-school children in public school education in a predominantly black neighborhood.

Sider, Ronald J., ed. *Cry Justice: The Bible Speaks on Hunger and Poverty.* New York: Paulist Press, 1980. A collection of biblical passages on justice issues accompanied by brief commentary, tables containing information on such topics as the infant mortality rate in different countries, and study questions designed for use by individuals and/or groups.

Sider, Ronald J. "Spirituality and Social Concern." *The Other Side* 9 (Sept.-Oct., 1973), 8-11, 38-41; *GH* 67 (Apr. 23, 1974), 337-40. Spirituality and social concern are a unity—regeneration involves changed attitudes toward poverty, racism, and war; the disciplines of the spirit are essential to social change.

Smith, C. Henry. "Is the General Conference Losing Its Peace Testimony?" *Menn* 57 (July 28, 1942), 1-2. Because of a neglect of peace education the peace doctrine is being lost in the Mennonite churches.

Smith, C. Henry. "Why Do Men Fight?" *Fellowship* 5 (Dec., 1939), 6. Seven FOR members, including Smith, respond to the question of why the people (not the rulers) fight. Smith contends that masses are driven into war by the misguided propaganda of the minority of leaders.

Smith, Wayne LaVelle. "Rockingham County Nonresistance and the First World War." MA thesis, Madison College, Harrisonburg, Va., 1967. Pp. 160. A study of Mennonite and Brethren experiences, attitudes, and activities during World War I. Includes summary of the nonresistant position dating from the Reformation, and a brief look at Mennonite experiences during the Civil War. MSHL.

Smucker, Barbara Claassen. "Are We Preparing for World War III?" *Menn* 59 (Jan. 4, 1944), 7. Our children should know the truth regarding the destructiveness of war and we should not provide them with war toys.

Smucker, Donovan E. "The Influence of Public Schools on Mennonite Ideals and Its Implications for the Future." *PCMCP Second,* 44-66. North Newton, Kansas: The Bethel College Press. Held at Goshen, Indiana, July 22-23, 1943. A survey of the impact of the public school system on Mennonite ideals as interpreted by Mennonites who have graduated from Mennonite colleges. Nonresistance is cited as the most frequently abused ideal.

Spalding, Blanche. "The Library." *Builder* 31 (Jan., 1981), 30. Encourages church librarians to update their peace education resources and makes several recommendations.

Stackley, Muriel Thiessen. *Read Peace, Speak Peace, Teach Peace: A Working Bibliography.* Newton: Faith and Life, 1980. Pp. 190. A partially annotated bibliography of books on peace for children, youth, adults, teachers, families. Includes Mennonite and non-Mennonite authors of books, drama, audio-visuals, and periodicals.

Stoltzfus, Grant M. "Where Have All the Russian Brothers Gone?" *ChrLiv* 19 (May, 1972), 25-30. Discussion of the book *Mennonity* by Russian W. F. Krestyaninov and his treatment of their attitudes toward war and nonresistance.

Stoltzfus, Victor (Review). *Christ and Your Job,* by Alfred P. Klausler. Concordia, 1956. Pp. 145. *The Christian Calling,* by Virgil Vogt. Scottdale: Herald Press, 1961. Pamphlet. *ChrLiv* 9 (Jan., 1962), 33. Reviewer compares and contrasts Lutheran and Mennonite views on the definition of vocational calling and its relation to social concerns and justice.

Stoner, John K. *Bicentennial Studies for the Church.* Akron, Pa.: Congregational Peace Education Program, n.d. Pp. 31. MHL. Includes such topics as the political use of religion, the church as nonviolent witness to justice in a hostile world, true and false prayer, evangelism as witness from a posture of nonviolence and suffering.

Stoner, John K. Letter to the Editor. *EV* 92 (Feb. 10, 1979), 6. In our emphasis on human depravity we consider people more capable of believing lies about our national security based on military strength than the truth about the real basis of security.

Stoner, John K. "The West Is Losing Ground." *Menn* 93 (Aug. 8, 1978), 480. Truth and justice, not bombs and weapons delivery systems, are the only adequate weapons against communism.

Stott, John R. W. "The Balance of the Bible." *ChrLead* 40 (Mar. 1, 1977), 4. Examines three areas of polarity in Christianity, individualism and corporateness, worship and witness, and holiness and worldliness.

Stucky, Gregory J. "Fighting Against the War: The Mennonite *Vorwärts* from 1914 to 1919," *The*

*Kansas Historical Quarterly,* 38 (Summer, 1972), 169-86. Discusses the editorial attitude and coverage of World War I in the MB paper from Hillsboro, KS, including early support for Germany, war propaganda, the dilemma of being German-American during the war, and the conflict encountered by nonresistant Mennonites who refused to buy war bonds. MLA/BeC.

Stucky, Harley J. (Review). *Christianity, Diplomacy, and War,* by Herbert Butterfield. Abingdon-Cokesbury, 1953. Pp. 125. *MennLife* 9 (Oct., 1954), 189-90. Advocates making war more tolerable by removing ideological overtones and limiting objectives.

Stucky, Peter. "Survey of Attitudes Held by I-W Fellows Toward the Witness Value of I-W Service." Paper for War, Peace, and Revolution class, AMBS, Elkhart, Ind., May 8, 1969. Pp. 3. AMBS.

Swartley, Willard M. "Cry for Peace." *Builder* 17 (Dec., 1967), 11-14. A dramatic reading utilizing the resources of Scripture, music, literature, and history to develop the concept of peace as an obedient response to a loving God.

Swartz, Herbert L. (Review). *The Social Conscience of the Evangelical,* by Sherwood Eliot Wirt. New York: Harper and Row, Pub., 1968. *The Voice* 19 (Oct., 1970), 31-32. The way the author deals with the question of war, particularly the Vietnam war, is exemplary of a more general idealization of American values that aborts deep thinking about the issues.

Swift, Richard and Regehr, Ernie. "Dubious Sentinel: Canada and the World Military Order." Waterloo, Ont.: "Project Plowshares," Institute for Peace and Conflict Studies, Conrad Grebel College, [1979]. Pp. [40]. MHL. Education kit. Table of Contents: I The World Military Order; II Canadian Military Spending and Waste; III The Arms Trade and the Third World; IV Spheres of Influence; V State of Siege; VI Guide to Action; VII Christian Perspectives on Militarism.

"Talks on Peace." *CanMenn* 4 (Mar. 2, 1956), 8. Arlan Gaufman takes first place honors in the peace oratorical contest held under the Julius and Olga L. Stucky Peace Oration Fund at Bethel College.

"The Atomic Bomb Is No Fun Anymore." *CanMenn* 17 (Mar. 25, 1969), 1, 2. Report of a teach-in on war held in Winnipeg on Mar. 22. Walter Dinsdale, M.P., was one speaker. Frank Epp, William Eichhorst who is dean of the faculty at the Winnipeg Bible Institute, and David Schroeder spoke as well.

"The Refugee American. . ." *Forum* (Jan., 1971),

A4-A5. Several Mennonites dialogue about their work with American draft dodgers in Ottawa and the problems and attitudes of these Americans.

"Thirty Evangelicals to Discuss War Attitudes." *CanMenn* 11 (July 19, 1963), 1, 9. MCC Peace Section arranges a summer seminar at Winona Lake, Ind.

"Three Hundred Peace Plays to Choose From." *CanMenn* 8 (Sept. 2, 1960), 10. The Board of Christian Service office at Newton makes peace play kits available on a loan basis.

Tarasoff, Koozma J. "Doukhobors and Mennonites—A Comparative Study of Ideological Persistence in Response to the Institution of Militarism." Term paper for Tutorial on the Nature and Dynamics of Plural Societies (Carleton Univ., Ottawa), June, 1975. Pp. 66. CGCL.

Teichroeb, Ruth. "Peace Conversion." Term paper for Peace and Conflict Studies course, Apr., 1978. Pp. 32. CGCL.

Thierstein, J. R. "If War, Will the US Be In It?" *Menn* 54 (May 2, 1939), 2. The US will likely be drawn into the war, particularly because of the propaganda for war in our nation.

Thiessen, Norman. "MB Youth: A Decade Later." *ChrLead* 42 (Dec. 4, 1979), 2. A study of the values of MB youth, including observations on social and political issues.

Thomson, Murray and Regehr, Ernie. "Conversion." *PlMon* 1 (Feb., 1978), 3-5. Statistics and information support the thesis that industrial conversion from military to socially useful production is possible and practical.

Toews, John A. "Cultural Change and Christian Ethics." *The Voice* 15 (Nov.-Dec., 1966), 1. A changing culture demands a periodic reformulation of the Christian answer as well as a periodic reevaluation of the Christian response to various social and political issues.

Toews, Paul. "Some Preliminary Notions on Pacific College and a Peace Model of Education." 1973. Pp. 7. MBBS

Umble, Roy H, ed. *Guide to the Evaluation of Education Experiences in Civilian Public Service.* [Akron, Pa.]: MCC and the Council of Mennonite and Affiliated Colleges, March, 1946. Pp. 144. MHL. A handbook designed to help educational institutions evaluate, and assign academic credit to education received in CPS. Provides information such as course duration, objectives, syllabi, credentials of instructors, etc.

Unrau, Neil. "American Moravian Noncombatancy: A Study in Changing Attitudes." Paper for War, Peace, and Revolution class, AMBS, Elkhart, Ind., n.d. Pp. 17. AMBS.

"Visitors from Hiroshima Share Vision for Peace." *MennRep* 9 (Sept. 17, 1979), 3. Four Japanese from Hiroshima, sponsored by the World Friendship Center in Hiroshima, engaged in a speaking tour in the US, advocating peace education.

Vietnam. 49 interviews. On effects of Vietnam War on Newton, KS, and area communities, including attitudes in Newton High School, Bethel College, churches, Mexican-American community, Halstead, Moundridge, Goessel, Lorraine Ave. Mennonite Church in Wichita. MLA/BeC.

Vogt, Roy. "Ideology Is Sometimes Only Skin Deep . . . Behind the Stone Faces Are Sensitive Hearts and Minds." Part 4. *MennMirror* 6 (Apr., 1977), 6-8. Writer describes two different encounters he has had with military personnel in East Germany when he has been able to penetrate their military mask and learn something about their personal experience in the military.

Vogt, Virgil. "Youth and the Mennonite Tradition." *ChrLiv* 4 (Dec., 1957), 20-21. Recent research on the Goshen College campus reveal this generation's attitudes toward Christian involvement in politics.

Voth, David L. "An Examination of Three Mennonite Theological Alternatives with Special Note of Their Views Toward Participation in Foreign Policy." MA in Peace Studies thesis, AMBS, 1982. Compares the views of John H. Yoder, Gordon D. Kaufman, and Duane K. Friesen on discipleship, the believers' church, and nonresistance in an effort to determine whether Mennonite participation in the foreign policy arm of the government is theologically consistent with Mennonite faith.

Voth, James J. "The Way of Peace as a Way of Life: A Study Guide for Catechetical Instruction." Research project (MDiv), 1980. Pp. 89. MBBS.

Waltner, Emil J. "Difficulties in Applying Non-Conformity in Modern Life." *PCMCP Third,* 53-67. North Newton, Kansas: n.p. Held at North Newton, Kansas, Aug. 18-19, 1944. As people attempt to live a life of nonconformity in modern times, the issue of post-war military training is one of the most challenging.

Ward, Frank G. "Media Resources: Films on War and Peace." *Builder* 23 (May, 1973), 16. Summarizes five imaginative short films created by European and American film makers on the subjects of war and peace.

Waybill, Marjorie Ann. "Children's Education: Peace Education for Younger Children." *Builder* 31 (Jan., 1981), 22-23. Resources and suggestions for working with young children on the issues of peace.

Weaver, Beth. "Peacemaking Is Theme for Fall Course." *MennRep* 9 (Dec. 24, 1979), 15. A description of "The Call to Peacemaking," a course offered in Christian education at the Valleyview Mennonite Church, London, Ont.

Weber, Ralph K. "Basic Approaches in Presenting the Peace Position." *ChrLead* 20 (Nov. 1, 1957), 4-5. Peace education must be woven into the very fabric of the church's ministry; it is integral to Christian faith and life.

Weber, Ralph K. "Peace Teaching in the Local Church." *Menn* 72 (May 7, 1957), 296-97. The peace position is central to the gospel; it must be woven into the very fabric of the church's ministry.

Wenger, A. Grace. "Anabaptist Perspectives on Education." *GH* 68 (Feb. 25, 1975), 137-39. Among distinctive emphases of Anabaptism which must be communicated to each generation is the emphasis on love and nonresistance, which translates in part into "vocation as servanthood."

Wenger, J. C. "Regaining the Early Anabaptist Peace Testimony." *GH* 43 (Aug. 1, 1950), 777-78. A renewed educational effort is needed to revitalize the Mennonite position on nonresistance.

Wenger, J. C. *Separated unto God.* Scottdale: Mennonite Publishing House, 1951. Pp. 350. A plea for Christian simplicity of life and for a scriptural nonconformity to the world. Nonconformity functions as the context for separation from the worldly military nature of political rule, and for nonresistance specifically church and state.

Wenger, James. "Nonresistance: What College Students Think." *ChrLiv* 15 (June, 1968), 9-10. Report on a survey of 150 Mennonite juniors and seniors in college.

Wenger, Linden M. "Trends in Peace Education." *ST* 43 (July, 1975), 1-6. Review of Mennonite peace emphases in this century calls for a greater focus on the biblical basis for peace and less attention to the strategy of conflict resolution.

Wiebe, Bernie. "What Is the Price for Peace?" *The Abundant Life* (Nov., 1967). Altona, Man.: Mennonite Radio Mission. Pp. 15. Four brief radio talks entitled: 1) The War Game; 2) The Hawks and the Doves; 3) Prisoners of War, and 4) War and Peace.

Wiebe, Eric, and Letkemann, Jake. "Peacemaker Workshop Stimulating." *CanMenn* 16 (May 14, 1968), 10. Report on a workshop in British Columbia designed to assist the teaching of the peacemaker Sunday school series.

Wiebe, Katie Funk. "A Conversion to Violence." *MBH* 15 (Feb. 6, 1976), 4; *Menn* 90 (Oct. 28, 1975), 605; *GH* 68 (Nov. 25, 1975), 849; *ChrLead* 38 (Oct. 14, 1975), 19. The acceptance of violence as a way of life may take place in different ways: a Charles Manson follower experienced a conversion, while the American society as a whole slowly drifts toward it.

Wiebe, Katie Funk. "Education for Violence." *CanMenn* 18 (July 31, 1970), 7; *GH* 63 (Nov. 17, 1970), 973. Analyzes the way our culture socializes us to accept violence as a lifestyle. Asks the church for more help in distinguishing spiritual values from those acquired torough the media.

Wiebe, Katie Funk. "Making Peace with Violence." *ChrLead* 40 (Jan. 18, 1977), 17; *GH* 70 (Feb. 8, 1977), 114; *MBH* 16 (Apr. 15, 1977), 32. While American Mennonites reject the violence of war, their rejection of other forms of violence in American society—TV, structural violence, etc.—is not so clear.

Wiebe, Katie Funk. "Taboo Religion." *ChrLead* 36 (Aug. 7, 1973), 19. Looks at a questionnaire that indicates that Mennonite Brethren and Brethren in Christ lean more toward fundamentalism than other Mennonite groups tested, and therefore rank lower in nonresistance, race relations, and social witness.

Wingert, Norman A. "Japan Wants Peace and Education." *ChrLiv* 2 (Jan., 1955), 8-9, 35. Japanese people are opposed to rearming the country.

"Youth Sounds Off on War, Peace." *YCC* 48 (July 16, 1967), 13. Finding of a 20-question form filled out by young people from across the Mennonite church in Canada and the United States.

Yake, C. F. "Patriotism." *YCC* 22 (Apr. 20, 1941), 540. The propaganda machinery fuels the war mentality by stirring up patriotic feelings. Christian patriotism fosters the development of Christian morality, courage, conscience, and character.

Yoder, Delmar R. "A Plea for Nonresistance and Nonconformity." *GH* 72 (Aug. 28, 1979), 696. A questioning of the conservative rank of the "Smoketown 20" over the issue of all Scripture

being of equal importance which would put an end to the Mennonite doctrines of nonresistance and nonconformity.

Yoder, Edward. "Fanning the Fires of Hate." *GH Supplement* 35 (June, 1942), 271. The Christian must not be influenced by those preaching hatred for the enemy.

Yoder, Edward. "Harvest of the Spirit." *GH Supplement* 36 (Oct., 1943), 638. The work of the Spirit in the believer is largely that of producing right social attitudes and relationships.

Yoder, Edward. "Nationalism—A False Faith." *GH Supplement* 37 (Feb., 1945), 942-43. Extreme nationalism neglects and destroys the values needed to preserve humankind.

Yoder, Edward. "Sowing Dragon's Teeth: Peace Principles from a Scriptural Viewpoint." Part 20. *GH* 31 (Oct. 20, 1938), 647. As long as the spirit of revenge governs people and nations there will be no peace.

Yoder, Edward. "The Madness of War: Peace Principles from a Scriptural Viewpoint." Part 16. *GH* 31 (July 21, 1938), 374-75. How does one guard against the irrational spirit of war? By knowing the Word, by realizing the bias of news agencies in wartime, and by recognizing propaganda for what it is.

Yoder, Edward. "The Mind to War: Peace Principles from a Scriptural Viewpoint." Part 5. *GH* 28 (Jan. 16, 1936), 910-11. Modern war is essentially conflict between whole populations. Governments employ propaganda techniques to arouse a populace against the enemy. The Christian must be alert to this.

Yoder, Edward. "The Movies and War-making: Peace Principles from a Scriptural Viewpoint." Part 29. *GH* 32 (Oct. 19, 1939), 638. There is an increasing assault of propaganda through pictures shown in movie houses.

Yoder, Edward. "The Power of Love: Peace Principles from a Scriptural Viewpoint." Part 9. *GH* 29 (Apr. 16, 1937), 78-79. Christian is a "permanent heart set" which does no harm to the neighbor and drives out all fears.

Yoder, Edward. "The Spirit of Forgiveness: Peace Principles from a Scriptural Viewpoint." Part 18. *GH* 31 (July 21, 1938), 374-75. In wartime it is especially important not to hate the person who has committed a wrong act. The Christian forgives.

Yoder, Edward. "War Is Sin: Peace Principles from a Scriptural Viewpoint." Part 3. *GH* 28 (July 18, 1935), 366-67. War is contrary to the teachings of the New Testament. Mennonites should witness to the truth that Jesus Christ has abrogated the Mosaic provision for revenge.

Yoder, John H. "Christian Attitudes to War, Peace, and Revolution: A Companion to Bainton." Printing of classroom lectures and study resource for War, Peace, and Revolution class, Goshen Biblical Seminary, Elkhart, Ind., 1983. Pp. 602. In 26 chapters presents class lectures on war and peace thought in historical perspective, from the biblical to the present periods.

Yoder, John H. "Love Seeketh Not Its Own." *ChrLiv* 3 (Jan., 1956), 26-28. Mennonite nonconformity, historically directed toward baptism, oath, and military service, should now be directed toward economics and our use of money.

Yoder, John H. "Nonconformity and the Nation." *ChrLiv* 2 (Feb., 1955), 8-9, 25, 33. The deeper issue behind conscientious objection to military service is the question of loyalty to the nation or to the Kingdom of God.

Yoder, John H. "The Christian Answer to Communism." *Concern* 10 (Nov., 1961), 26-31. Much of the opposing behavior and attitudes directed toward communism are based on the provincial assumption that the United States is a Christian nation. The Christian answer to communism is repentance for the continuing failure of Christians to obey Christ.

Yoder, John H. "The Original Revolution." *Forum* (Mar., 1971), A-2. God's original revolution involves the creation of a new, distinct community with its own deviant set of values and way of life, which rejects our classical revolutionary strategies.

Yoder, John H. "The Subtle Worldliness." *GH* 47 (Dec. 21, 1954), 1209. Our nonconformity should consist not in ignorance or withdrawal, but in the exercise of independent judgment in matters of a social, economic, and political nature and in continual application of Christian truths.

Yoder, Lloyd. "Nonresistance of Today." *YCC* 17 (Aug. 9, 1936), 249, 250, 255-56. To stand for one's convictions on nonresistance against the majority opinion is an example of a true soldier of Christ. Even with all the peace activity and education, each individual has to search their own heart for this courage.

Yoder, Perry B. "Attitudinal Survey on Church/State Issues." *God and Caesar* 4 (July, 1978), 8-9. A report on the results of an attitude survey which was sent to all General Conference Mennonite congregations to aid in determining the range of attitudes that exist on the war tax issue and several other issues.

Zehr, Daniel. "Teach-In Looks at Religion and International Affairs." *CanMenn* 15 (Oct. 31, 1967), 1, 10. Reflections of attitudes on revolution, war, and the church by prominent leaders in theology, education, and the church from South America, North America, and Africa.

Zehr, John D. "An Analysis of the Attitudes That Mennonites Show Toward Voting." Paper for War, Peace, and Nonresistance class, GBS, Elkhart, Ind., spring, 1966. Pp. 12. AMBS.

Zook, Mervin D. "Measurement of Attitudes Toward Religious Conscientious Objectors in Selected Magazines of World War II Years by Evaluative Assertion." MA in Journalism thesis, Indiana University, May, 1969. Pp. 114. BfC., MHL. Concludes that religious magazines treated COs slightly more favorably than nonreligious ones; letters to the editor tended to disagree with favorable view of COs presented in secular magazines but in the religious magazines, which also presented a favorable view of COs, the letters to the editor tended to be supportive; generally the COs choosing noncombatant service were rated higher than those choosing alternative service.

# 4

# The Bible, Peace, and War

*A Christian Declaration on the Way of Peace.* Newton: Faith and Life Press, 1972. Pp. 24. MHL. Resolution adopted by the GCMC at its triennal session at Fresno, Cal., Aug., 1971. Presented in two sections. The first deals with biblical perspectives on peace; the second with issues of practical application such as the use of resources, citizenship, conscription and military service, and social change.

Adrian, Victor. "The Sword and the Keys of the Kingdom." *The Voice* 14, Part 1, (May-June, 1965), 12; Part 2, (July-Aug., 1945), 4. The article addresses the question: how are we to understand the variation found between the Old Testament and the New Testament in the methods God has ordained to combat evil?

Algrim, Ryan J. "The Lamb Is a Warrior: A Theology of History and Warfare in the Book of Revelation." Paper for War and Peace in the Bible class, AMBS, Elkhart, Ind., Nov. 29, 1981. Pp. 16. AMBS.

Andrews, Robert F. "The Handling of Enemies." *EV* 90 (Aug. 25, 1977), 6. Jesus Christ has offered us a model and principle of loving and giving in relating to our enemies, rather than following the self-serving philosophy in our individual disagreements that we see modeled by dictators.

Arms, George Wells. "The Bible and the War." *ChrMon* 32 (Nov., 1940), 336-37, 346. Reprinted from *The Presbyterian.* The war in Europe shows the failure of modernism, democracy, and Protestantism.

Augsburger, Myron S. "Christian Pacifism." *War: Four Christian Views,* ed. Robert G. Clouse. Downers Grove, Ill.: InterVarsity Press, 1981, 81-97. Pp. 210. Outlines the evangelical premises and perspectives leading to the conclusion that, while Christians may participate in government as long as they do not create a state church, they may not participate in war. The book is composed of articulations of four positions on war: nonresistance, Christian pacifism, the just war,

and the crusade or preventive war. Then each of the presenters comments on the other three discussions. So, in addition to Augsburger's essay on Christian pacifism, he responds from that point of view to the other three views: to nonresistance, 58-63; to just war, 141-45; to the crusade, 175-80.

Augsburger, Myron S. "Facing the Problem." In *Perfect Love and War: A Dialogue on Christian Holiness and the Issues of War and Peace,* 11-20. Ed. Paul Hostetler. Nappanee, IN: Evangel Press, 1974. Outlines five basic points of a New Testament approach to the problem of peace and relates these issues to the underlying consideration, the church and state relationship.

Augsburger, Myron S. "Nonresistance Clarified." *GH* 66 (Nov. 20, 1973), 883-84. Outlines five basic and biblical reasons why evangelical Christians should be pacifists: priority of membership in the kingdom of Christ; the Great Commission, which extends to enemies; Jesus' command to love; the sacredness of human life; the materialistic causes of war.

Augsburger, Myron S. "The Basis of Christian Opposition to War." *GH* 63, Part 1, (Nov. 17, 1970), 960-71; Part 2, (Nov. 24, 1970), 990-91; also in *EV* 84 (Sept. 25, 1971), 4. Christians oppose war on the basis of Christ's revelatory commands. The Christian's loyalty is not to the state but to the Kingdom of Christ, in which Christians arm themselves only with love.

Aukerman, Dale. "Jesus at Blast Center." *ChrLiv* 10 (Sept., 1963), 36-37. Jesus stands in the center of human war and conflict, suffering injury and death with the wounded.

"Biblical Teaching on Nonresistance." *GH* 35 (Nov. 12, 1942), 706. A review of New Testament passages supporting nonresistance, including the sayings of Jesus and the writings of Paul and Peter.

"But I Say to You." *Lifework* 3 (1979), 3-7. Adapted and reprinted from *What Does Christ Say About*

*War,* Peacemaker Pamphlet No. 3, ed. Willard E. Roth. Scottdale: Herald Press, 1964. Pp. 15. Shows that Jesus chose a way of love and nonviolence in his life, and that Christians should pattern their choices on Jesus' example. Includes responses from three Mennonite young people.

Beachy, Alvin J. "The Biblical Basis for Civil Disobedience." *MennLife* 25 (Jan., 1970), 6-11. A review of biblical history leading to the conviction that "there are times in the history of man [sic] when Christians can be obedient to the coming kingdom of God, only as they are civilly disobedient to their earthly rulers."

Beachy, Alvin J. (Review). *The Politics of Jesus,* by John Howard Yoder. Grand Rapids: Wm. B. Eerdmans, 1972. Pp. 176. *Menn* 88 (Oct. 9, 1973), 580-82. Focuses the central theme of Yoder's book as Jesus' normativeness for political ethics and his rejection of violent revolution as bringing the kingdom of God.

Beachy, Moses. "Romans 13:1-7." Research "capsule" for War, Peace, and Revolution class, AMBS, Elkhart, Ind., Apr. 10, 1969. Pp. 4. AMBS.

Beechy, Atlee. *What Mennonites Believe About the Military.* Scottdale, Pa.: Mennonite Publishing House, 1980. Pp. 8. MHL. Also in *With* 13 (Apr., 1980), 32-36. Advises high school students to identify the gap between military recruiters' promises and the reality of military life as well as to consider seriously Christ's call to his disciples to build the kingdom of God.

Beitler, Alan. "Civil Disobedience as Christian Discipleship." Paper for War and Peace in the Bible class, AMBS, Elkhart, Ind., Dec. 7, 1981. Pp. 26. AMBS.

Berg, Ford. "Jesus' Reaction to an Atrocity." *Menn* 63 (Jan. 6, 1948), 5-6. Jesus' call to repentance (Luke 13:1-3) involves the renunciation of violent revolutionary tactics and the turning to the way of suffering love.

Berg, Ford. "Nonresistance Stories Which Are Open to Question." *GH* 43 (Feb. 21, 1950), 179. One needs to proceed with caution when attempting to validate the nonresistant position by an appeal to certain Old Testament stories which have, at first glance, "the nonresistant flavor."

Berkey, E. J. "Bible Teaching on Nonresistance." *GH Supplement* 34 (Oct., 1941), 627-28, 632. Presents the Biblical basis of nonresistance. Israel was blessed in war only when it fought under the direct command of God. The dispensation of the New Testament makes it clear that Christians are called to be nonresistant.

Bicksler, Harriet. "Fortunate Are Those Who Work for Peace." *EV* 91 (Jan. 10, 1978), 10-11. The Keystone Bible Institute's Seminar on Christian Peacemaking and New Call to Peacemaking consider the broader implications of peacemaking now that the draft and Vietnam war are over.

Bicksler, Harriet S. (Review). *Christ and Violence,* by Ronald J. Sider. Scottdale and Kitchener: Herald Press, 1979. *EV* 92, Part 1, (Dec. 25, 1979), 10, 11; Part 2, (Jan. 10, 1980), 8. Contains essays originally presented at the New Call to Peacemaking conferences in Lancaster, Pa., and Green Lake, Wis. Essays look at Jesus' life and teachings as a model for our approach to violence. Part 2 of the review, focusing on chapters 3 and 4, highlights Sider's emphasis on the centrality of the cross and resurrection as a basis for nonviolence.

Bieber, Doreen. "Nationalism vs. the Kingdom of God." *GH* 71 (Jan. 24, 1978), 68-69. Speech, which won second place in the C. Henry Smith Peace Oratorical Contest, suggests that nation-worship leads to war, and war is sin. Also in MHL.

Blosser, Don. "What Did Jesus Say About Killing People?" *GH* 63 (Feb. 10, 1970), 121-23. Discusses passages from the Gospels showing that Jesus forbade armed resistance and killing. Implications of his teaching for today include actively seeking to correct injustices, refusing to trust the protection of the army, and offering sacrificial service.

Blosser, Don. "What Would Jesus Say to Us This Christmas?" *GH* 68 (Dec. 9, 1975), 868-69. The message of Jesus, as found in Old Testament prophets, calls for living in love, justice, forgiveness, and peace.

Bogard, Michael B. "The Righteousness of Yahweh's Judgment in the Holy War Paradigm." Paper, AMBS, Elkhart, Ind., Nov. 30, 1981. Pp. 22. AMBS.

Bohn, Ernest J. *Christian Peace According to the New Testament Peace Teachings Outside the Gospels.* Peace Committee, General Conference Mennonite Church, 1938. Pp. 53. Some New Testament passages, for example, Acts 10; 23:12-35; Rom. 13, might seem to sanction war. However, exegeted carefully and viewed in light of such New Testament themes as the evil nature of war, nonresistant love and the international body of Christ, these texts cannot constitute an argument for the rightness of war.

Brown, Robert McAfee. "We Must Love One Another or Die." *GH* 66 (Dec. 25, 1973), 957-58. Reprinted from *California Living* (Dec. 24, 1967). Behind the manger lies the shadow of the cross, the brutal end of life for one who translated love into justice and refused to believe peace was only an ideal.

Brubaker, Darrel J. and Sider, Ronald J., eds. *Preaching on Peace.* Philadelphia: Fortress Press, 1982. Pp. 95. A collection of addresses and sermons reflecting the broadening variety of theological perspectives being brought to bear upon such issues of peace as disarmament, attitudes which create peace and the biblical basis for peace.

Brunk, George R., I. "Nonresistance." *ST* 2 (Oct., 1930), 20. Examination of "nonresistance" in both the Old Testament and New Testament, based on the premise that God is the same in nature and attributes forever but His law and government have changed with changed conditions.

Brunk, George R., I. "Nonresistance Not the Law of the Old Testament." *ST* 46 (July, 1978), 9-12. Reprinted from *ST* (Oct., 1930), p. 20. Mennonite belief in nonresistance is grounded in the difference between the two covenants represented by the Old and New Testaments.

Brunk, George R., I. "Was Christ a Pacifist?" *ST* 4 (Oct., 1932), 20. A letter to the editor of *The Daily Press* discusses how the ideas of war and peace relate to the old dispensation in the Old Testament and the new dispensation ushered in with the resurrection of Christ.

Burkhalter, Sheldon. "How to Pray for Government." *GH* 68 (Apr. 29, 1975), 325-27. Examining passages from Genesis, Romans, and 1 Timothy, Burkhalter concludes that to properly pray for governemnt is to pray for international peace so that the gospel may advance, not to pronounce a blanket endorsement on government policies.

Burkhalter, Sheldon, et al. *A Mennonite Response, 1776-1976.* Souderton, Pa.:" Franconia Mennonite Conference, 1975. Pp. 16. MHL. Discussion on Mennonite responses during the Revolutionary War and what being citizens in Christ's kingdom means for today. Also includes suggestions for Bible study and congregational action.

Burkholder, H. D. *The Blessed Fruit of the Gospel: An Address Presented at the Quarterly Conference of the Eastern District General Conference of Mennonites by H. D. Burkholder, DD, President of Grace Bible Institute, Omaha, Neb.* Henderson: Service Press, 1954. Pp. 5. MHL. Author relates personal story of his early rejection of nonresistance because those who were preaching the doctrine also denied the Virgin Birth, and his subsequent conversion to biblical pacifism through the arguments presented in Theodore Epp's "Should God's People Partake in War?" Also in MSHL.

Burkholder, J. Richard and Bender, John. *Children of Peace.* Elgin: The Brethren Press; Nappanee: Evangel Press; Newton: Faith and Life Press; Scottdale: Mennonite Publishing House, 1982. Pp. 160. Theme of book is that peace is a way as well as a goal. The first unit explores the biblical meanings of peace in both their Old Testament and New Testament contexts. The second unit deals with the practice of peace in various areas of life, such as home, community, politics, and the military. The third unit explores the church and state relationship and includes accounts of the ways some people are effectively and creatively witnessing to peace in militaristic and totalitarian countries.

Burkholder, J. Richard. (Review). *Mennonite Statements on Peace, 1915-1966,* by Richard C. Detweiler. Scottdale: Herald Press, 1968. Pp. 71. Also *The Christian and Warfare,* by Jacob J. Enz. Scottdale: Herald Press, 1972. Pp. 95. Also *Christian Pacifism in History,* by Geoffrey F. Nuttall. Berkeley: World Without War Council, 1971. Pp. 84. Also *Nevertheless,* by John H. Yoder. Scottdale, Herald Press, 1971. Pp. 144. *MQR* 48 (Apr., 1974), 269-72. Describes, with limited analysis, these four books presenting distinctive perspectives on Christian peace concerns.

Burkholder, Roy (Review). *The Original Revolution,* by John H. Yoder. Scottdale: Herald Press, 1972. Pp. 189. *GH* 66 (Nov. 6, 1973), 855. A helpful collection of Yoder's articles and lectures articulating the conviction that pacifism as practiced by the disciple community is a key to Christian faithfulness and social change.

Buzzard, Harold. "The Basis of Permanent Peace." *ChrMon* 24 (July, 1932), 202-203. True peace is possible only through the principles of Christ, because these principles build moral integrity, not merely outer restraints.

Byler, Raymond. Letter to the Editor. *GH* 64 (May 4, 1971), 410-11. Chastises church members and leaders for having no greater responsibility toward peace than the nonchurched, and Mennonites in particular for silently supporting warfare on the basis of Romans 13.

Charles, Howard H. "Blessed Are the Peacemakers." *Builder* 31 (Jan., 1981), 31-35. The ongoing mission of peacemaking is set out in the context of the salt and light imagery of Matt. 5:13-16, which suggests the positive redemptive function of the new life in Christ.

Charles, Howard H. "The Christian Warfare." *Builder* X [sic, 1] (Nov., 1960), 20, 21. The New Testament clearly teaches that conflict is the life pattern for the followers of Jesus. In this conflict, we must remember both that the decisive victory is already won and that the complete victory over evil awaits the second coming.

Charles, Howard H. "The Conquest and the Problem of Violence." *Builder* 32 (Nov., 1982), 35-39. Summarizes the Old Testament conquest theme and some representative approaches taken to the moral problem raised by the theme before suggesting that Millard Lind has provided some useful guidelines with which to think about the issues in *Yahweh Is a Warrior* (Herald Press, 1980).

Charles, Howard H. "The Kingdom Beyond Caste." *Builder* 14 (Feb., 1964), 17-18. What the Bible teaches about the way of the cross in group relations can and should be applied to the issues of racial conflict: the church "must reach agressively across all barriers with the call of the Gospel."

Charles, Howard H. "The Quest for Peace." *Builder* 18 (June, 1968), 18-19. Summarizes Old Testament and New Testament understandings of peace and concludes that the development of weapons making race suicide possible has underscored the seriousness of the human dilemma but neither essentially changed the nature of that dilemma nor the relevance of the biblical peace message to it.

Charles, Howard H. "The Revolutionary Jesus." *Builder* 26 (Jan., 1976), 29-32. While Jesus was not a revolutionary in the militant nationalistic sense for which S. G. F. Brandon argues, his perception of the will of God and dedication to it were so radical as to be revolutionary in one sense.

Coffman, S. F. "Bible Study: Christian Doctrine." *ChrMon* 39, Part 66: Peace," (Feb., 1947), 50-51; Part 67: "Peace," (Mar., 1947), 80-81; Part 68: "Peace—The Kingdom of Peace," (Apr., 1947), 114-115; Part 69: "The Kingdom of Peace," (May, 1947), 146-47; Part 70: "The Kingdom of Peace," (June, 1947), 176-77. Uses the Old Testament and the Lord's Prayer to show that the Kingdom of God is a kingdom of peace, personally, socially, and eternally. Because peace grows out of righteousness before God, Old Testament law is not a law of vengeance and judgment but a law of peace and goodwill.

"Delegates Agree Bible Teaches Non-Resistance." *CanMenn* 2 (Apr. 16, 1954), 1, 3. Issues discussed at GCMC Peace Study Conference in Winnipeg on Apr. 9-10, 1954, included absolutism, non-combatant service, positive alternatives to war, and the biblical basis of nonresistance.

Derstine, C. F. "Are the Last Days Upon Us?" *ChrMon* 29 (Dec., 1937), 381, 384. Cites the militant forces gathering in many parts of the world in opposition to the peace principles of Christ.

Derstine, C. F. "Babylon, Media-Persia, Greece, Rome, and Succeeding Gentile Nations." *ChrMon* 32 (Aug., 1940), 254-55. Daniel's characterization of the nations as beasts is applied to the nations presently at war.

Derstine, C. F. "Can the Allies Expect to Win the War?" *ChrMon* 34 (Nov., 1942), 350-51. Since neither the Allies nor the Axis is worthy to win, author uses scriptural passages to predict the outcome of the war.

Derstine, C. F. "The Fall of the French Empire." *ChrMon* 32 (Sept., 1940), 287-88. France's defeat by Germany is another step to Armageddon.

Derstine, C. F. "'The World of Tomorrow.'" *ChrMon* 32 (Feb., 1940), 62. Only the Prince of Peace can build a peaceful world.

Derstine, C. F. "What the World Ought to Do." *ChrMon* 32 (Oct., 1940), 318-19. Belief in the Son of God and the practice of social justice and stewardship are biblical prescriptions for a war-torn world.

Derstine, C. F. "World War No. II Proves the Bible to Be True." *ChrMon* 34 (May, 1942), 158-59. The present worldwide conflict bears out the biblical prophecies of the presence of war in this dispensation.

Derstine, James L. "The Problem of War in the Old Testament as Answered by Nonresistant Christians in the *Gospel Herald* and *The Sword and Trumpet* and Various Other Pamphlets and Books." Outline and bibliography presented to Christian Attitudes to War, Peace, and Revolution class, AMBS, Elkhart, Ind., Apr. 10, 1969. Pp. 4. AMBS.

Derstine, Norman. "Peacemakers in a Broken World." *GH* 61 (Jan. 23, 1968), 82-84. Elaborating on the peacemaker beatitude, the author reviews Christian attitudes toward participation in war from the early church through the Reformation, citing also American Mennonite experiences with conscientious objection.

Detweiler, J. F. "Peace!" *GH* 36 (Sept. 30, 1943), 546-47, 555, 557. An examination of Old Testament prophetic writings as to their vision of future world peace. When the prophets spoke of peace they were foretelling the church of Jesus Christ rather than a national world peace.

Detweiler, Richard C. "God's Peace Action—and Ours." *YCC* 49 (Apr. 28, 1968), 7. Incarnation, atonement, resurrection, and community are four aspects of God's peace action. The Christian's peace action is to participate in the ministry of reconciliation.

Detweiler, Richard C. "Peace Is the Will of God." *Peacemakers in a Broken World.* Ed. John A. Lapp. Scottdale: Herald Press, 1969, 67-74. Builds a peace theology on four scriptural assertions: that peace is God's will for humanity; that Jesus Christ is the locus of God's peace action; that Christians should be ministers of reconciliation; that God's action in Christ is the model for Christian peacemaking.

Detweiler, Richard C. "The Founding of Our Nonresistant Faith." *ChrMon* 37 (Apr., 1945), 93, 105. Traces New Testament and 16th-century events to encourage contemporary nonresistant Mennonites in their convictions.

Dick, N. S. *The Peacemaker.* Scottdale: Herald Press and Newton: Faith and Life Press, 1972. Pp. 63. A Bible study guide on peacemaking organized into 13 lessons. Topics include the Jesus way, Old Testament wars, the relationship between poverty and militarism, patriotism, servanthood, etc. Resources include films, music, poetry, discussion questions.

Diener, Harry A. "Peace, Peaceable, Peacemakers." *ChrMon* 43, Part 1, (June, 1951), 169-70; Part 2, (July, 1951), 201-202; Part 3, (Aug., 1951), 233-34. Peace program based on Romans 12 discusses inner peace, peace with friends, peace with enemies, and overcoming evil with good.

Dirks, Victor A. "'War, Peace, and Freedom' a Lutheran Confrontation." *CanMenn* 14 (Nov. 1, 1966), 1, 4. A Mennonite observes that Lutheran young people are confronting American Lutheran Church leadership with peace ideas from the New Testament. The writer recalls Conrad Grebel and the Anabaptists and then considers the peace witness of the present-day Mennonites.

Dirrim, Allen W. "Political Implications of Sixteenth Century Hessian Anabaptism." *MennLife* 19 (Oct., 1964), 179-83. The Anabaptists' striving for a free and separate church and their absolute New Testament ethic, plus real and alleged connections with the Peasants' Revolt in 1525, are reasons why they were not accepted by their contemporaries.

Drescher, James M. "Is the Peace Ethic Optional for Anabaptists?" *GH* 73 (Oct. 7, 1980), 789. Commitment to the peace ethic, central to the New Testament andn Anabaptist history, should be as much a prerequisite for Mennonite membership as baptism.

Drescher, John M. "Validating Our Peace Position." *MBH* 19 (Nov. 7, 1980), 2-3. A valid peace position must be rooted in Christology, supported by personal witness, and not jeopardized by wealth.

Drescher, John M. "Why Christians Shouldn't Carry the Sword." *Christianity Today* 24 (Nov. 7, 1980), 15-17, 20-23. Discusses the theological components of a biblical pacifism, claiming that concepts such as the cosmic Christ, the global appeal of the gospel, and the internationalism of the church imply that a proper national loyalty is a limited loyalty. Bible and peace

Driedger, Leo, ed. *School of Peace.* Newton: Board of Christian Service, GCMC, [1961?]. MHL. Curriculum designed to emphasize peace as a basic teaching of the Bible and our Christian faith. Planned for four sessions. Dick, Nickolas, "Blessed Are the Peacemakers: A Manual for Leaders of Adults," pp. 39; Reusser, James, "Blessed Are the Peacemakers: A Manual for Leaders of Intermediates and Youth," pp. 22; Rich, Elaine Sommers, "Blessed Are the Peacemakers: A Manual for Teachers of Juniors," pp. 17; Harder, Geraldine Gross, "Loving All the Time: A Manual for Teachers of Primary Children," pp. 41; "Peace School Activity Sheets for Primaries," "Peace Maker Packet: Juniors."

Driver, John. *Understanding the Atonement for the Mission of the Church.* Scottdale and Kitchener: Herald Press, 1986. Pp. 286. An extensive study of the various NT ways of describing Christ's atonement. Many of these ways connect atonement directly to peacemaking: victory over evil, vicarious suffering, martyr motif, sacrifice, expiation, reconciliation, and justification. Chapters 13-15 draw out the implications of the atonement for the peace- and community-making mission of the church in the contemporary world.

Dueck, Allan (Review). *War and the Gospel,* by Jean Lasserre. Scottdale: Herald Press, 1962. Pp. 243. *The Voice* 16 (Nov.-Dec., 1967), 22-26. Recommends the book for its thorough theoretical analysis and concrete practicality; says the most stimulating section is the one in which Lasserre "searches for a biblical criterion of political morality."

Durland, William R. *No King But Caesar?* Scottdale: Herald Press, 1975. Pp. 182. Catholic lawyer urges Christians to assume the risk of nonviolence through faith and hope. Argument proceeds in three sections: an examination of the pacifist and nonresistant ethic of the biblical materials, especially the Sermon on the Mount and Isaiah; an historical overview of Christian responses to state violence, from the apostolic peace gospel and the pacifism of the early church, through the Constantinian synthesis to the contemporary confusion; an analysis of that contemporary confusion concerning the demands of God and Caesar, particularly in the context of the Roman Catholic church.

Durnbaugh, Donald F., ed. *On Earth Peace:*

*Discussions on War/Peace Issues Between Friends, Mennonites, Brethren, and European Churches, 1935-1975.* Elgin, Ill.: Brethren Press, 1978. Pp. 412. A collection of documents emphasizing the "Puidoux" Conferences held in Europe on the theme of "The Lordship of Christ Over Church and State" and the contributions made by the historic peace churches to the study processes sponsored by the WCC on the issues of peace and justice. Essays focused on or by Mennonites include: "Principles of Christian Peace and Patriotism—Historic Peace Churches," 30-32; "War Is Contrary to the Will of God—HPC and FOR," 46-72; "God Establishes Both Justice and Peace," (Paul Peachey and members of the Continuation Committee, 1955 and 1958), 108-21; "The Theological Basis of the Christian Witness to the State," John H. Yoder, 136-43; "Discipleship as Witness to the Unity in Christ as Seen by the Dissenters," Paul Peachey, 153-60; "On Divine and Human Justice," John H. Yoder, 197-210; "The Sixth Commandment: Its Significance for the Christian as Citizen and for the Statesman," Warren F. Groff, 211-22; "Church and State According to a Free Church Tradition," John H. Yoder, 279-88; "Response to the Cardiff Report by Brethren, Friends, Mennonites," 353-64, "Jesus and Power," John H. Yoder, 365-72; "Epilogue: The Way Ahead," John H. Yoder, 390-93.

Dyck, C. J. (Review). *The Doctrine of Love and Nonresistance,* by Harley J. Stucky. N.p.: By the Author, 1955. Pp. 60. *MennLife* 10 (Oct., 1955), 192. Booklet places nonresistance in its historical setting in Palestine of Jesus' time and the church of the first three centuries.

Dyck, Edna Krueger. "Peace Teachers: She Studies and Obeys." *Builder* 31 (Jan., 1981), 12-13. The consequences of Cornelia Lehn's commitment to "study the Bible seriously and then to obey the Word" have resulted in a General Conference study process on the issues of tax resistance and a collection of peace stories which she edited entitled *Peace Be With You* (Faith and Life, 1981).

Dyck, Paul. "Peter Stuhlmacher's Contributions to a Biblical Theology of the New Testament." IMS *OP* 9 (1986), 83-94. Summarizing Stuhlmacher's writings on biblical theology, Dyck highlights Stuhlmacher's central point: the Gospels' emphasis on Jesus as Reconciler and Paul's teaching on reconciliation provide the hermeneutical key to the unity of the New Testament.

Dyck, Walter H. "Peace: A Study Course in Outline." N.d. Pp. 11. MHL.

Dyck, Walter H. "The Scriptural Basis of Our Faith." In *The Power of Love: A Study Manual Adapted for Sunday School Use and for Group Discussion.* Pp. 11-37. Edited by the Peace Committee of the General Conference Mennonite Church. Newton: Board of Publication, 1947. MHL. Although God permits wars and other evils, the will of God revealed in Jesus is that evil be overcome by the good expressed and enacted in the obedience of the faithful disciples.

Eby, Omar. "Mennonites from Israel, Arab Territories Convene in Athens." *CanMenn* 17 (July 4, 1969), 1, 2. Report on a meeting of Mennonite personnel in Athens Apr. 10-12 to discuss peace and reconciliation in the Middle East. Participants came from the East Bank, the West Bank, Israel, Lebanon, the US, and Europe. Action was taken to see what could be done about repatriation and resettlement of Arab refugees. First step was for West Bank/Israel personnel to make concrete proposal to the Israeli government. Politics in the Old Testament, myths about Arab countries and Israel and the refugee problem in the Middle East were discussed.

Ediger, Peter J. "America! America!" *GH* 69 (June 29, 1976), 527-28; "America! America! A Litany of Love and Lamentation." *MennRep* 6 (June 28, 1976), 5; *Menn* 91 (June 22, 1976), 413-16. Poem intended for use during worship on July 4 includes allusions from the Declaration of Independence, national hymns, Old Testament prophets, and Martin Luther King, woven into an outcry against American militarism and exploitation, and a prayer for peace.

Ediger, Peter J. "Amos Visits America." *Peacemakers in a Broken World.* Ed. John A. Lapp. Scottdale: Herald Press, 1969, 8-19. Ediger rewrites passages from Amos, placing the contemporary translation parallel to original passages on facing pages, in order to illustrate God's judgment for wealthy and religious Americans who oppress the poor and trust in military protection.

Ediger, Peter J. "An American Version of Luke 12: 16-21." *The Other Side* 13 (July, 1977), 34; *God and Caesar* 3 (Jan., 1977), 1. A paraphrase that concludes that the harm to the earth that comes from weapons is the inheritance of "the nation which lays up massive weapons for itself and is not rich toward God."

Ediger, Peter J. "Cain and the Voice of the Lord." *God and Caesar* 1 (Oct., 1975), 1. A poem in which "Cain" symbolizes the arms investment that the "Ameri-Cainized" citizens are making in total disregard to the voice of the Lord who asks, "where is your brother?"

Ediger, Peter J. "Daniel 3 Revisited." *God and Caesar* 1 (Jan., 1975), 1. A paraphrase of Daniel 3, likening the Pentagon to King Nebuchadnezzar and showing the faith of some Christians who have refused to worship his "image of steel."

Ediger, Peter J. "Eden Revisited." *God and Caesar* 2 (Oct., 1976), 1. The Christians are likened to Adam and Eve, tempted by the "Security Serpent" to arm themselves and become secure in their own strength, but God punishes them.

Ediger, Peter J. "Hunger and Handwashing." *God and Caesar* 3 (Nov., 1977), 1. Poem concerning how we have tried to quench our hunger with bombs and bullets rather than with the "Word of the Lord."

Ediger, Peter J. "Job Revisited: The Bloated Camel and the Needle's Eye." *God and Caesar* 5 (Aug., 1979), 1. Scripture is retold to show that we have succumbed to the power of Satan and forgotten God in our prosperity and national defense.

Ediger, Peter J. "Jonah Revisited . . . Unfinished." *Menn* 94 (Apr. 17, 1979), 285-86. Responds to the Minneapolis midtriennium in verse form comparing Mennonites to Jonah in the whale.

Ediger, Peter J. "Jonah Revisited . . . Unfinished (Still)." *God and Caesar* 6 (Jan., 1980), 7-8. Poem comparing Jonah's mission to the North American Mennonite mission to be a peace witness to US and Canadian governments.

Ediger, Peter J. "The Golden Calf: 1979—Exodus 32 and April 15." *God and Caesar* 5 (Apr., 1979), 1. The account in Ex. 32 is retold to draw out its parallel with our modern situation, in which the American nation worships the molten image of war weapons.

Ediger, Peter J. "The New Creation—Reflections on Revelation and Resurrection." *God and Caesar* 1 (Mar., 1975), 1. Jesus Christ is all-powerful and the kings of the earth have no real power.

Ediger, Peter J. "Which Gospel?" *God and Caesar* 2 (June, 1976), 1. The writer juxtaposes the Gospel of Christ with the gospel of military power.

Edwards, George R. (Review). *The Politics of Jesus,* by John H. Yoder. Grand Rapids: Eerdmans, 1972. Pp. 260. *MQR* 48 (Oct., 1974), 537-38. Commends Yoder's contribution to studies in Christian pacifism and political responsibility, but disagrees with Yoder's conclusions regarding the Year of Jubilee and "revolutionary subordination" in the household codes.

Eller, Vernard. *King Jesus' Manual of Arms for the 'Armless.* Nashville: Abingdon Press, 1973. Pp. 205. Revised and reprinted by Scottdale: Herald Press, *War and Peace from Genesis to Revelation,* 1981. Makes a case for scriptural unity on pacifism by saying that the Old Testament holy war and Zion traditions, rightly understood, provide the framework within which the New

Testament Christians understood Jesus' life, death, and resurrection. The last few chapters apply this concept to the contemporary scene.

Elster, William. "The New Law of Christ and Early Christian Pacifism." IMS *OP* 9 (1986), 108-29. Through citations of primary sources Elster documents that numerous church fathers during the second to fourth centuries used the phrase "the new law of Christ" to refer to specific biblical peace teachings (i.e., beating swords into plowshares and love of enemies.)

Enz, Jacob J. *The Christian and Warfare. The Roots of Pacifism in the Old Testament.* Scottdale: Herald Press, 1972. Pp. 95. Given originally as the Menno Simons Lectures at Bethel College, North Newton, Kans., in 1957. An exegetical-theological analysis of the roots of biblical pacifism in such concepts as creation, covenant, kingdom, incarnation, substitution, proclamation, and messianic hope. From the compassion of Joseph, through the literature of the Suffering Servant, and "the quiet pacifist cosmogony of Genesis 1 and 2" and Isaiah 53, the implicit pacifism in the Old Testament prepares for the explicit pacifism in the New Testament.

Enz, Jacob J. "The Gospel: Daring Fulfillment to Virgil's Prophecy." *Builder* 23 (Dec., 1973), 16-21. Explains how the Gospels both fulfill and challenge the wider expectation of the times, the Pax Romana.

Enz, Jacob J. "The Gospel's Two Crosses." *Menn* 66 (Nov. 13, 1951), 717. The Cross of Christ was a demonstration of Jesus' love for people; the Christian's cross demonstrates that his suffering love continues to "live through us."

Enz, Jacob J. "What Would You Say?" *Menn* 71 (Oct. 2, 1956), 625, 629. The Old Testament, specifically on the question of war, must be interpreted by the Gospels, i.e., by the teachings and life of Jesus.

Epp, Frank H. "Man and His World of War." *GH* 59 (June 28, 1966), 574; *YCC* 47 (July 17, 1966), 2. It is shocking that Christians show the same tendency to believe in military might rather than in love that non-Christians do. This tendency denies the kingdom, love, and cross of Christ.

Epp, Frank H. (Editorial). "Conscription in Canada." *CanMenn* 2 (Nov. 19, 1954), 2. An editorial speaks out against conscription and encourages the way of peace as put forth in the Bible.

Epp, Frank H. (Editorial). "Non-Resistant Love and Evangelism." *CanMenn* 4 (Mar. 9, 1956), 2. Epp asks that the ethic of love in the New Testament not be diluted in the name of evangelism. He sees the two as inseparable.

Epp, George K. (Review). *Peacemakers in a Broken World*, ed. John A. Lapp. Scottdale: Herald Press, 1969. *The Voice* 19 (Apr., 1970), 25-26. Applauds editor's choice of 12 essays representing a solid cross-section of views on the issues of reconciliation in a complex world. Urges readers to examine the essays critically in order to come to greater understanding of the issues.

Epp, Theodore H. *Should God's People Partake in War? A Study on Nonresistance in the Old and New Testaments*. Inman, Kans.: By the Author, n.d. Pp. 25. MHL. While war will continue as long as there is sin, the only warfare permitted to the people of God is spiritual warfare. Material warfare is to be left to those who are not God's people because only God fights for the people of God.

Escobar, Samuel and Driver, John. *Christian Mission and Social Justice*. Institute of Mennonite Studies, Missionary Studies No. 5. Scottdale: Herald Press, 1978. Pp. 112. Four essays bring to bear biblical perspectives and a historical critique derived from a reappraisal of the distinctive Anabaptist experience in the Reformation on the issues of mission and justice today. The application of these perspectives results in seeing missions and justice as necessary complements rather than a polarity. Essays are: "The Need for Historical Awareness;" "The Gospel and the Poor;" "Reform, Revolution, and Missions;" "The Anabaptist Vision and Social Justice."

Ewert, David. "The Signs of the Times." *MBH* 16 (Jan. 7, 1977), 2-5. While Christians should seek to preserve life, war remains as one sign of the interim time between Christ's first coming and the parousia.

Ewert, David. "The Unique Character of Christian Ethics." *Direction* 2 (July, 1973), 66-70. With the sense of "progressive revelation," the books of the Old Testament and New Testament cannot be viewed as standing on one plane. Thus, New Testament Christian ethics are unique, a part of our total experience of God's salvation in Jesus Christ.

Farrell, Frank. "Mennonites Reaffirm Biblicism and Pacifism." *ChrToday* 3 (Sept. 28, 1959), 23, 24, 29. Reports on General Conference and Mennonite Church conferences, summarizing pertinent issues and describing the theological position of the denominations regarding their views of the Bible and ethics of nonresistance.

Fast, Henry A. *Jesus and Human Conflict*. Scottdale: Herald Press, 1959. Pp. 209. An exegetical and theological study of the words of Jesus on peace and nonresistant love.

Ferguson, John. "The Christian Necessity of Pacifism." Chapel address, Goshen College, Goshen, Ind., Jan. 27, 1969. Pp. 3. MHL, MLA/BeC.

Ferguson, John (Review). *The Politics of Jesus*, by John H. Yoder. Grand Rapids: Eerdmans, 1972. Pp. 260. *Fellowship* 40 (Jan., 1974), 23. Summarizes the contents of this book which examines Jesus' model of radical political action.

Fransen, Harold. "The Middle East, 1977-78 (King James Version)." *Menn* 93 (June 27, 1978), 430. Allegorizes the Mideast conflict using Old Testament King James version language, characterizing Israel as trusting in weapons of war rather than in God.

Franz, Delton. "Washington Report: Mortgaging the Future to the Military." *MennRep* 5 (Apr. 14, 1975), 7. Deplores the size of the requested military budget for 1976 and "cold war idealogue" Schlesinger's introduction of the military budget by using scripture.

Franz, Delton. "Washington Report: of Swords and Plowshares." *MennRep* 4 (Apr. 1, 1974), 7. American billions for "swords" compared with pennies for "plowshares"—peacemaking activities such as forestalling world famine—comes under the Isaiah prophecy of woe to those who trust in weapons of war.

Fretz, Clarence Y. "Promoting the Way of Peace." *ST* 38 (Sept., 1970), 1. A careful survey of many of the commandments recorded in the New Testament reveal guidance into the way of peace. The reason peace is lacking today is that many of these divine directives have been overlooked or neglected.

Fretz, Mark. "*Herem* in the Old Testament: A Critical Reading." IMS *OP* 9 (1986), 7-44. A thorough textual study of the uses of *herem* in the O.T. Though the term often refers to the complete slaughter of the enemy, its most basic meaning is "devoted to God." Rooted thus in God's holiness, its use applies not only to warfare but to other aspects of the community's life as well.

Frey, Philemon L. "Nonresistance Taught in the Scriptures." *The Eastern Mennonite School Journal* 18 (Apr., 1940), 18-21. Despite the fact that God permitted the Israelites to practice warfare, the divine intention was, from the very beginning, that God's people should live by the principles of nonresistance.

Friesen, Abraham. "Thomas Müntzer and the Old Testament." *MQR* 47 (Jan., 1973), 5-19. Thomas Müntzer, leader of the peasants' revolt, found inspiration for his vision of the military inauguration of the kingdom of God on earth in

Old Testament accounts of God's elect conquering the Promised Land, and in the dispensational thought of medieval Joachim of Fiore.

Friesen, Dorothy. "In Naboth's Vinyard." *Swords into Plowshares: A Collection of Plays About Peace and Social Justice,* ed. Ingrid Rogers. Elgin: The Brethren Press, 1983, 255-59. One-act play which draws an analogy between the story of Naboth's vinyard in 1 Kings 21 and the injustices being enacted in the Philippines.

Friesen, John. "War and Peace in the Patristic Age." IMS *OP* 9 (1986), 130-54. Traces the development of pacifism from Jesus to Augustine—in its continuity and change— through three main phases: the pacifism of Jesus and the NT teachings expressed in both Greek and Latin writings in the first two centuries; the pacifism of all becomes the pacifism of a few in the third century; and how pacifism is newly understood when the church develops from a persecuted minority to the cohesive cement of the empire in the fourth century.

Friesen, Louise. "God and War." Student paper for Our Christian Heritage, Feb., 1959. Pp. 15. MLA/BeC.

Fundenburg, Harry C. "Military Training Unchristian." *GH* 28 (Nov. 14, 1935), 706-707. Military training, war, and killing of any sort are not sanctioned by the New Testament. The Church of the Brethren has since its beginning opposed war and maintained the principle of nonresistance.

Gaeddert, Albert M., sec., et al. (The Peace Committee of the General Conference Mennonite Church, eds.) *The Power of Love: A Study Manual Adapted for Sunday School Use and for Group Discussion.* Newton, Ks.: The Board of Publication, 1947. Pp. 136. MHL. Four essays prepared to help the churches place greater emphasis on the teaching of New Testament peace principles. Essays are: Dyck, Walter H., "The Scriptural Basis of Our Faith," 11-37; Smith, C. Henry, "The Historical Background," 38-57; Fretz, J. Winfield, "Our Peace Witness During World War II," 58-96; Mast, Russell, "Living the Peace Testimony," 97-122.

Gautsche, Charles. "'Sermons for 76.'" *GH* 69 (Jan. 13, 1976), 17-19. One of the three subjects presented for possible sermons in 1976 is the theme of nationalism and what it means to give primary loyalty to the Kingdom of God rather than to the state.

Giesbrichet, H. (Review). *True Nonresistance Through Christ,* by J. A. Toews. Board of General Welfare and Public Relations of the Mennonite Brethren Church of North America, 1955. *The Voice* 4 (Sept.-Oct., 1955), 18. The fundamental thesis of this book is that Christ, in his life as well as in his teachings, constitutes the most compelling reason for holding so firmly to the doctrine of nonresistance.

Gingerich, Melvin. "Perilous Times; Christian Youth and the State." *YCC* 24, Part 28, (Apr. 4, 1943), 525. There are different opinions on the condition and direction of a society. Thus we must not be dogmatic in interpretation of scripture.

Gingrich, Newton. "Others Must Live—At All Costs to Me." *CanMenn* 18 (Oct. 23, 1970), 7, 10. Biblical basis for social concern and the dynamics involved in making this discussion a lively debate.

Gish, Arthur G. "Sacrificial Love." *Post-American* 3 (Nov., 1974), 9-11. A proper understanding of Jesus' life, death, and resurrection leads to a commitment to nonviolence.

Goering, Jack. "Biblical Issues Raised by War Tax Workshop." *Menn* 86 (Mar. 23, 1971), 190-91. Christian stewardship and a simpler lifestyle must supplement the decision to withhold or reduce taxes as a witness to peace.

Good, Douglas L. "The Politics of Daniel." Paper for War and Peace in the Bible class, AMBS, Elkhart, Ind., Dec. 7, 1981. Pp. 18. AMBS.

Graff, Tom (Review). *The Politics of Jesus,* by John Howard Yoder. Grand Rapids: Eerdmans, 1972. Pp. 260. *MBH* 13 (Jan. 11, 1974), 28. Summarizes this book as a testimony of total submission and obedience to God. Praises the book for its clear, well-developed inductive approach to Scripture.

Graham, Billy. "From the Press: Graham on Vietnam and Watergate." *MennRep* 3 (June 11, 1973), 7. Reprinted from *Christianity Today* (Jan. 19, 1973), 416 and *New York Times* (May 6, 1973), 17. Evangelist Graham states that while the Bible indicates there will always be wars, he has never advocated war. Denies his publicized role as "White House chaplain."

Graham, James R. *Strangers and Pilgrims.* Scottdale: Herald Press, 1951. Pp. 55. Christ's followers must be prepared to witness to his power also through suffering—the way of the cross.

Grimsrud, Ted. *Triumph of the Lamb: A Self-Study Guide to the Book of Revelation.* Scottdale and Kitchener: Herald Press, 1987. A study resource in thirteen lessons which probes the theological depth of Revelation. The textual commentary in each lesson contributes to understanding how God conquers evil and the role the Lamb and the saints play in the victory. Revelation both recognizes the dismaying power of evil and affirms the ultimacy of God's power, justice, and goodness.

Guenther, Allen R. "God's Word to His Unjust People." *MBH* 14 (Feb.. 7, 1975), 6-7. "God's Word to Unjust Societies." *MBH* 14 (Jan. 24, 1975), 8, 29. "The Meaning of Justice." *MBH* 14 (Feb. 21, 1975), 6-7. Book study in Amos focuses on God's judgment of the injustice practiced by Israel and Judah; God's judgment upon the nations practicing injustice; justice and righteousness in their relationship to the oppressed.

Guenther, Allen R. "Possessions: A Biblical Study of the Principle of Reward and Retribution." *Direction* 8 (July, 1979), 27-32. The principle enunciated in the Old Testament, that God would reward obedience with prosperity and punish disobedience with poverty undergoes modification in the course of biblical revelation. The priority which the disciple gives to God's Kingdom is now the Christian indicator of godliness.

"He That Hath No Sword." *Menn* 56 (Oct. 7, 1941), 3, 7 A homiletical exposition of Luke 22:36, claiming that this passage does not justify the militarist's position but rather reveals the absurdity of defense by the sword.

Harder, Gary. "A Preliminary Summary Report on the Positions of Four Mennonite Scholars on the Question of War in the Old Testament." Paper for War, Peace, and Revolution class, AMBS, Elkhart, Ind., Apr. 10, 1969. Pp. 4. AMBS.

Harshbarger, Emmett L. "Anti-semitism Before the World War: History Views the Jewish Persecutions" (Part 2). *Menn* 54 (Feb. 21, 1939), 3-4. A brief review of the course of anti-semitism from Old Testament times through the 19th century.

Hasek, K. Gary. "A Goyim Examines the Religious Basis for Jewish Pacifism." Paper presented to the Theology of Warfare in the Old Testament class, AMBS, Elkhart, Ind., spring, 1981. Pp. 24. AMBS.

Helmuth, David. "Why (Some) Christians Fight for Their Country." *GH* 71 (July 4, 1978), 522-24. Discusses reasons Christians go to war, such as believing the Bible teaches it, or believing the US is a Christian nation, and answers with his personal reasons for not participating in war.

Heppner, Daniel. "The Old Testament and War." *CanMenn* 14 (Feb. 8, 1966), 7. Letter to the editor argues against the idea that the God of the Old Testament condoned war. Encourages belief in doctrine of "progressive revelation of God."

Hershberger, Guy F. "How the American Churches Made Themselves Believe That the World War Was a Holy War." *YCC* 18 (Apr. 4, 1937), 528. Many preachers were misled into thinking that World War I was a "holy war." They failed because they were not rooted in the nonresistant teachings of the Bible.

Hershberger, Guy F. "Peace and War in the New Testament." *MQR* 17 (Apr., 1943), 59-72. The nonresistant way of life is integral to God's purpose for the church; it corresponds with the whole tenor of the Gospel and is to be practiced in our day.

Hershberger, Guy F. "Peace and War in the Old Testament." *MQR* 17 (Jan., 1943), 5-22. Both the Old and New Testaments, carefully read and correctly understo. J, show that the way of peace is God's will; warfare and the spirt of retaliation have no place in the life of the Christian.

Hershberger, Guy F. "Prophets, Priests, and Kings: Civil Religion, Then and Now." Sermon delivered at Trinity Mennonite Church, Mar. 3, 1974, in Glendale, Ariz. Typescript. Goshen: AMC Hist. MSS 1-171 Box 54. Defines civil religion as the form of idolatry in which men give their highest allegiance not to God but to Caesar, and then use worship and religious ceremony for the glorification of Caesar and the state. Traces civil religion from the Old Testament to the modern political situation.

Hershberger, Guy F. "The New Birth: A New Life, A New Social Order." Sermon delivered at Trinity Mennonite Church, June 2, 1974, in Glendale, Ariz. Typescript. Goshen: AMC Hist. MSS 1-171 Box 54. Examines the life and the atoning ministry of Christ which enables Christians to enter into the life of the new social order.

Hershberger, Guy F. *War, Peace, and Nonresistance.* Scottdale: Herald Press, 1944. Pp. 375. For many years the standard work in the field. God has one eternal plan for human conduct: love for God and neighbor. This law forbids one to compel another. One rather meets force with nonresistance. In the Old Testament covenant with Israel, God made a concession to the hardness of human hearts by permitting warfare. In the New Testament, Jesus initiates a new covenant in which believers receive a new heart, enabling them to keep God's fundamental moral law. By going to the cross rather than retaliating, Jesus indeed modeled nonresistance perfectly. The early church at first followed Jesus' nonresistant example but gradually applied it less strictly. After Constantine's conversion, the church abandoned nonresistance as an ideal for all Christians. Small Christian sects however retained it, of whom the Mennonites provide a history extending from the sixteenth century to the present. Because nonresistance renounces all coercion, finds its authority in God's will, and takes sin seriously, one should not confuse it with other types of pacifism. Nonresistance implies that Christians will not take part in coercive state functions, will search for alternatives in the complex industrial, agricultural, and economic conflicts of modern life, and will nurture an attitude of brotherhood toward other races. By bringing healing to society, nonresistance serves society in a more essential way than those who take responsibility for running it.

Hershberger, Guy F. "What Is the Relationship of Our Peace Message to the Gospel? Our Peace Witness—In the Wake of May 18." (Part 16). *GH* 60 (Dec. 19, 1967), 1134. The New Testament teaching on nonresistance is an integral part of the gospel message.

Hershberger, Guy F. "Why Have Many Christians Forgotten the Bible Teachings on Peace?" *YCC* 17 (Mar. 8, 1936), 80. Under Constantine's rule, beginning in 313 A.D., Christianity became a state religion. The union of church and state and the heathen ways of war are still a part of the larger church today.

Hershberger, Guy F. (Review). *The Christian Attitude Toward War,* by Loraine Boettner. Grand Rapids: Wm. B. Eerdmans Publishing Co., 1940. *MQR* 17 (1943), 53-55. Hershberger takes issue with Boettner's arguments that "invariably the Christian pacifist turns out to be a modernist in the church" and that the Scriptures approve warfare for the Christian.

Hershberger, Guy F. (Review). *The Politics of Jesus,* by John H. Yoder. Grand Rapids: Wm. B. Eerdman's Publishing Co., 1972. Pp. 260. *MQR* 48 (Oct., 1974), 534-37. Hershberger credits the book with delineating weak and missing features in the theological-ethical structure that Protestantism has given the New Testament for many years, and summarizes various parts of the book to show how this is done. He urges Yoder, however, on to the next necessary step of providing a new New Testament theological treatise.

Hershberger, Guy F., Metzler, Edgar, and Meyer, Albert J. "Theses on the Christian Witness to the State." Sub-committee report to the Peace Problems Committee of the Mennonite Church, June 22, 1960. Pp. 32. MHL.

Hertzler, Daniel. "Gracious Living." *ChrLiv* 19 (Mar., 1972), 40. Editorial redefines "gracious": from modern connotations of elegance to Old Testament meaning of concern for justice.

Hertzler, Daniel. "The Isaiah Vision." *GH* 67 (July 2, 1974), 544. Isaiah's vision of God standing apart from the military victories or defeats of a people is more profound than the Exodus vision, which viewed God as a great warrior.

Hiebert, Paul G. "The Kingdom Reconciling Humanity." *ChrLead* 41 (Oct. 10, 1978), 7; *MBH* 17 (Oct. 13, 1978), 6-8. Hope that a model of church and mission centered on Christ and God's message of incarnation and reconciliation would focus on the kingdom and ministries to the whole person.

Hilty, Almeta. "The Christian's Attitude Toward War." *YCC* 21 (Sept. 1, 1940), 276, 280. Scripture teaches that the Christian should not participate in carnal warfare. Government and war are permitted by God to do His will.

Hochstetler, Walter. "Jesus' Ethic as a Bridge over Troubled Waters: a Study of Matthew 5:43-48." Paper for War, Peace, and Revolution and Sermon on the Mount classes, AMBS, Elkhart, Ind., May 20, 1970. Pp. 40. AMBS.

Hofer, Shirley. "The Christian Conscience and War Taxes." *God and Caesar* 2 (June, 1976), 10-12. A whimsical dialogue between Moses and the Lord by Art Hoppe illustrates the inconsistencies in biblical and theological interpretation regarding the sixth commandment and the sanctity of human life. The writer also shares results from a survey she took on the war tax issue.

Holdeman, John. *A Treatise on Magistracy and War, Millenium, Holiness, and the Manifestation of Spirits.* Jasper, Mo.: By the Author, 1891. Pp. 303. MHL. Arguments against war based on Old Testament prophetic statements, the spirit of the gospel, the prohibition of Christ, the love commandment, and the two-kingdom theology.

Holderman, George. "A Sure Foundation for Peace." *ChrMon* 27 (June, 1935), 171-72. Cites examples of conflict settled through trust and goodwill to show that New Testament principles do work.

Hoover, Donald J. "The Politics of Jahweh: On the Relationship Between Justice and War Acts." Paper for Warfare in the Old Testament class, AMBS, Elkhart, Ind., Dec. 17, 1977. Pp. 25. AMBS.

Horner, Glen A. (Review). *New Testament Basis for Peacemaking,* by Richard McSorley. Washington, DC: Center for Peace Studies, n.d. Pp. 167. "Deals with Biblical Texts on Quesions of War," *MennRep* 9 (Oct. 29, 1979), 11. This book seriously questions the apparent approval of war by the Christian church, examines the message of the New Testament, and looks at Christian history, refuting questions and theories that indicate war to be of God.

Horsch, John. "The Relation of the Old Testament Scriptures to the New Testament." *ChrMon* 30 (Nov., 1938), 329. The Anabaptists' distinction between the Testaments was basic to their convictions on nonresistance, separation of church and state, etc.

Horst, John L. (Review). *Must Christians Fight? A Scriptural Inquiry,* by Edward Yoder, with Jesse W. Hoover and Harold S. Bender. Akron: Mennonite Central Committee, n.d. *ChrMon* 35 (Dec., 1943), 376. Recommends the book as a thorough discussion of biblical nonresistance and its application to daily living.

Hostetter, C. J., Jr. "The Christian and War." *EV* 82 (Dec. 1, 1969), 3, 4, 13. Summarizes the historical development of the church's changing attitude to war and the relevant teaching of the New Testament on war and discipleship.

Hostetter, C. N., Jr. "The Christian and War." *CanMenn* 3 (June 10, 1955), 6; *Menn* 70 (Aug. 23, 1955), 521-22. A statement on what the New Testament teaches about war for the Christian.

Hostetter, C. N., Jr. *War and the Word: A Study of the Problem of the Christian Conscience and War.* Nappanee, Ind.: E. V. Publishing House, n.d. Pp. 24. MSHL. A study of the problem of the Christian conscience and war.

Howland, Larry O. "Becoming Peacemakers." *GH* 69 (June 29, 1976), 530-31. Former prison inmate testifies that Christians are called to be peacemakers, after the example of Jesus, who showed that conferring peace upon others means to be willing to suffer for them.

Hübner, Harry (Review). *King Jesus' Manual of Arms for the 'Armless,* by Vernard Eller. Nashville: Abingdon Press, 1973. Pp. 205. Also, *Liberation Ethics,* by John M. Swomley. New York: Macmillan, 1972. Pp. 238. *Menn* 88 (Oct. 30, 1973), 628-29. While Eller considers peace activism an unfaithful siezing of the reins of history, a prerogative belonging only to God, Swomley advocates nonviolent revolution as the strategy for liberation. The reviewer believes that Christian faithfulness will include political activism, but that activism will not bring the Kingdom, which is a gift of God.

Hull, Robert. "Day of Yahweh." Paper, n.d. Pp. 13. AMBS.

Hull, Robert and Eccleston, Alan. "A Peace Church Style of Witness." In *Affirm Life: Pay for Peace.* 19-24. Ed. by Maynard Shelly and Ron Flickinger. Newton: Historic Peace Church Task Force on Taxes, 1981. Pp. [87]. MHL. Examines methodology of a variety of New Testament and historic peace church examples of witness to the state and urges that the methods used to frame the peace message be consonant with the message.

"In My Opinion." *CanMenn* 2 (Apr. 23, 1954), 7. Four participants respond positively to the Canadian Peace Study Conference, the first such study group focusing on the teaching of the Bible and the church on peace.

Jantz, Harold. "'I Will Joy in the God of My Salvation.'" *MBH* 18 (Dec. 21, 1979), 13. Fear of the future is one response Christians have to unpleasant world events, typified in Jerry Falwell's urgent pleas for American moral and military might. Alternatively, the article calls for trust and joy in God.

Janzen, David. "The Prince of Peace in the Epistles." *CanMenn* 11 (June 7, 1963), 7. A summary of a Bible study at the Ontario Ministers' Peace Retreat at Five Oaks, Paris.

Janzen, Waldemar. "God as Warrior and Lord: A Conversation with G. E. Wright." *Menn* 91 (Nov. 2, 1976), 640-42. Reprinted from the *Bulletin of the American Schools of Oriental Research* (Dec., 1975). This tribute essay to George Ernest Wright presents a pacifist critique of Wright's use of the "God as Warrior" metaphor.

Janzen, Waldemar. "The Burden of War." *Still in the Image: Essays in Biblical Theology and Anthropology,* by Waldemar Janzen. Newton: Faith and Life Press, Institute of Mennonite Studies Series No. 6, 1982, 173-211. Pp. 226. Three chapters discuss Old Testament warfare. The first explores the extent to which war is topical and problematic in the Old Testament materials. The second takes issue with G. E. Wright's thesis that God as warrior is one aspect of God as Lord by contending that cosmic government is only the final, eschatological activity of the divine—that exile, apparent domination by an oppressive power, is the historical reality. The third chapter (published earlier in the IMS *OP* No. 1, 1981, pp. 3-18) outlines the basic options available on this question: regard the Old Testament as an account of God's victorious rule; see it as the history of the preparation for God's coming rule; or regard it as the history of failure of one form of God's rule. Janzen then aligns himself with the second view and explains why he thinks this position is most viable.

Janzen, Waldemar. "War in the Old Testament." *MQR* 46 (Apr., 1972), 155-66. Outlines Old Testament views of war as a human reality, a result of sin; of God as a Warrior who establishes justice; and of peace as a full reality in the future of God's kingdom.

Janzen, Waldemar (Review). *The Christian and Warfare,* by Jacob J. Enz. Scottdale: Herald Press, 1972. Pp. 93. *Menn* 88 (Feb. 6, 1973), 92.

Reviewer observes that Enz traces the roots of New Testament pacifism in the Old Testament with clear, often poetic, language, but he approaches a "dispensationalism" which favors the New Testament over the Old as a "higher" revelation.

Jess, John D. "Was Jesus a Revolutionary?" *ST* 40 (Aug., 1972), 22. Thesis is that Jesus did not come as a revolutionary as the term is classically defined, but that his mission was to die a sacrificial death so that all who put their trust in him can be saved.

Johnsson, William G. "Jesus—A Revolutionary?" *Menn* 93 (Jan. 31, 1978), 65-67. Traces contours of Jesus' life and ministry, including his nonviolent approach to revolution.

Jost, Connie. Letter to the Editor. *ChrLead* 42 (Oct. 23, 1979), 11. Sees two groups in the Mennonite Brethren constituency: one group that embraces socialism, liberalism, and liberation theology and the other group that believes the Bible as God's Word.

Kauffman, Benjamin K. "They Sound Out the Word." *GH* 60 (May 23, 1967), 458-59. There are so few in "Christian" America against war. Christ taught against all war, including the "just war"; he became a servant, not a fighter.

Kauffman, Daniel. "Christian Attitudes Toward War." *GH* 29 (Sept. 3, 1936), 482. The Gospel forbids any part in carnal warfare. Obedience to God, not disobedience to governments, determines our attitude towards war.

Kauffman, Daniel. "Followers of the Prince of Peace." *GH* 28 (Apr. 18, 1935), 65-66. Mennonites must not only be anti-war but also remember that they should base their peace testimony on the fact that they are followers of the Prince of Peace.

Kauffman, Daniel. "On Peace: Bible Teachings." (Part 3). *GH* 36 (July 15, 1943), 329-30. Outlines scriptural references to "Christ the Prince of Peace" and "apostolic testimonies."

Kauffman, Daniel. "Scriptural Principles Underlying the Doctrine of Nonresistance." *GH* 34 (May 1, 1941), 97-98. The sacredness of human life, the blessedness of peace, the constraining power of love, and the passion for saving lost souls are some of the principles outlined.

Kauffman, Milo. "Was Christ Our Lord Peaceable?" Thesis for BD degree, Northern Baptist Theological Seminary, 1929-1930. Pp. 44. MLA/BeC.

Kauffman, Nancy L. "Justice in the Book of Habakkuk." Paper presented to Theology of Warfare in the Old Testament class, AMBS, Elkhart, Ind., May 26, 1981. Pp. 21. AMBS.

Kauffman, Richard A. "The Christian and the State." *GH* 70 (May 24, 1977), 422-23. Part 19 in a series on the Mennonite Confession of Faith reviews the Old Testament conflict between God and governing authorities and the example of Jesus in seeking a more accurate interpretation of Romans 13.

Kauffman, W. Wallace. Letter to the Editor. *GH* 61 (Aug. 6, 1968), 713. Cites biblical passages to show that God uses war as a form of judgment, and that Christians should pay all taxes.

Kaufman, Gordon D. (Review). *The Non-Violent Cross: A Theology of Revolution and Peace,* by James W. Douglas. Macmillan, 1966. Pp. 301. *Harvard Divinity Bulletin,* New Series 2 (Winter, 1969), 12, 13. Commends this effort to develop a theology of revolution and peace as biblical and moving but regrets that the author fails to analyze the political and social realities.

Keen, Susan H. "The Futility of War." *ChrMon* 36 (Aug., 1944), 229. Comment on the horror of war and its incompatibility with the teachings of Jesus.

Keeney, William E. *Lordship as Servanthood: 13 Lessons on the Biblical Basis for Peacemaking.* Newton: Faith and Life Press, 1975. Pp. 112. A series of lessons on the principles of Christian pacifism designed for either individuals or groups. Central premise: a Christ-centered view of the Bible yields an understanding that the way of the cross embodied by Jesus is to be normative for his disciples. Faithful disciples will take the effects of evil upon themselves and let the grace of God empower them to change evil into good. Other topics discussed within this framework include the kingdom and the church, Old Testament warfare, and the Christian's relation to government.

Keeney, William E. "The Right of Dissent." *GH* 59 (Aug. 9, 1966), 702-704. The roots of this right are found in the Old Testament, in Jesus, and in the American system, among other places. Dissent is desirable because human knowledge is limited and conditioned. The two alternatives to controversy are suppression and apathy.

Kehler, Larry. "Our Christian Civil Responsibility—2." *Menn* 93 (Nov. 28, 1978), 701; *MennRep* 8 (Dec. 11, 1978), 6. Discusses New Testament texts referring to tax payment in preparation for the midtriennium conference discussion on war taxes.

King, Calvin R. "Historical Mennonite Interpretation of Romans 13:1-7, A Study of the *MQR.*" Paper presented to Mennonite History class, Goshen Biblical Seminary, Goshen, Ind., June 1, 1962. MHL.

King, Lauren A. "Why One Quaker Refuses War." *GH* 67 (Apr. 9, 1974), 308-309. In question-and-answer format, the author sets forth his reasons for conscientious objector convictions, which include the basic moral reason, the primacy of God's kingdom, and the teachings and examples of Jesus and the apostles.

Kingsley, Keith. "Politics and the Kingdom of God." *GH* 65 (Oct. 24, 1972), 857-59. Calls Christians to focus their attention on the politics of God's Kingdom, which might be characterized by communities of people committed to nonresistance, economic sharing, marital fidelity, and spiritually and psychologically interdependent relationships, instead of focusing attention on national politics.

Klaassen, Walter. "The Biblical Basis of Nonresistance." *MennLife* 17 (Apr., 1962), 51, 52. The biblical basis of nonresistance is established "not on the basis of a collection of prooftexts" but on the "basis of the total relationship of the Christian to God."

Klaassen, Walter. "The Christian and the State: Biblical and Anabaptist Perspectives." *Menn* 89 (July 9, 1974), 428-29; *Citizens and Disciples: Christian Essays on Nationalism.* Akron: MCC Peace Section, [1974], 10-12. MHL. In both the Old and New Testaments the concepts of "people" and "nation" are distinguished with the concept of "people" taking priority. The majority of Anabaptists also expressed this biblical principle in the doctrine of the "two kingdoms." Finally, while neither the biblical nor Anabaptist traditions can be used as prescriptive law today, these perspectives present models with which to shape contemporary responses to the issues of church and state.

Klassen, J. M. "A Very Peculiar Teaching." *MBH* 15 (Oct. 29, 1976), 2-4, 31. Peace position is at the heart of the gospel. Discusses the view which appeals to the Old Testament for support for participation in war.

Klassen, Randolph. "A Matter of Conscience." *HIS* (Magazine of Inter-Varsity Christian Fellowship) 28 (June, 1968), 14-16, 21. From the examples of Christ and the Scripture, the author argues that a military profession may be consistent with God's will, that lifetaking must be without hate, and that Christians should aid the state's God-given mandate to preserve order in society. Argues that a Christian may carry a draft card and participate in military activities if that person recognizes clearly that his/her first loyalty is to the heavenly King.

Klassen, William. "'A Child of Peace' (Luke 10.6) in First Century Context." *NTStud* 27 (July,

1981), 488-506. Compares New Testament understandings of peace with those of two first-century Stoic philosophers, Musonius Rufus and Epictetus and raises the question of whether the centrality of peace in New Testament proclamation may not have originated in Jesus.

Klassen, William. "Coals of Fire: Sign of Repentance or Revenge?" *NT Studies* 9 (July, 1963), 337-50. "Heaping coals of fire" in Rom. 12:20 is a sign of repentance brought about by an act of love. It is an image, not for nonresistance of evil, but for overcoming evil with good.

Klassen, William. "Jesus and the Zealot Option." *Canadian Journal of Theology* 16 (Spring, 1970), 12-21. An exegetical study which refutes S. G. F. Brandon's thesis that Jesus was a revolutionary connected to the Zealot movement.

Klassen, William. *Love of Enemies: the Way to Peace.* Overtures to Biblical Theology 15. Philadelphia: Fortress Press, 1984. Pp. 145 (+ xiv). This distinctive and timely contribution examines and compares five strands of literature on "love of enemies" and "peace:" Greek thought, the Hebrew Bible, intertestamental Judaism, Jesus (the Gospels), and Paul (his epistles). He argues that neither "pacifism" nor "nonviolence" capture Jesus' message; rather Jesus "had a positive, militant but nonviolent message." Jesus called into being children of peace to carry on his work in prayer, witness, and, if necessary, death for the cause of peace.

Klassen, William. "Love Your Enemy: A Study of the New Testament Teaching on Coping with an Enemy." *MQR* 37 (July, 1963), 147-71 and in *Biblical Realism Confronts the Nations,* ed. Paul Peachey (Fellowship Publications, 1963), 153-83. Surveys briefly the history of interpretation of "love of enemy," then studies its meaning against the Old Testament and Qumran backgrounds, and assesses its meaning in the Gospels and Pauline uses. Examines then the church's faithfulness in light of this teaching.

Klassen, William. "The Novel Element in the Love Commandment of Jesus." *In The New Way of Jesus: Essays Presented to Howard Charles,* ed. William Klassen. Newton: Faith and Life Press, 1980. Pp. 100-114. Shows that Jesus' love command, even love of enemies, has parallels in both earlier Judaism and Hellenism. Jesus' novel contribution was to call together a community to be "children of peace" and to make this a hallmark of their identity (Mt. 5:9) and mission (Lk. 10:6).

Klassen, William. "Man of Courage, Martin Luther King." *Menn* 85 (Apr. 7, 1970), 242-44. The way this one man interpreted the New Testament and what that meant for the civil rights movement can be seen as a standard or test for Mennonite faith and practice.

Klassen, William. "Taxes and the New Testament." *GH* 56 (June 18, 1963), 521, 522. Those protesting against income tax in the US on the basis of the proportion of taxes going into military effort or the size of these taxes cannot appeal to the New Testament. Yet we must attempt to find the will of Christ for today.

Klassen, William. "The Two Swords in Luke 22:35-38." *CanMenn* 2 (Nov. 19, 1954), 2. Klassen's thesis is that Christ is using a simple object lesson to show that to follow him one must be ready to be a social outcast. Absolute love is the prerequisite for the growth and stability of the church.

Klassen, William. "Vengeance in the Apocalypse of John." *Catholic Biblical Quarterly* 28 (July, 1966), 300-311. The wrath of God is central to the Christian faith. Vengeance and retribution are in his hand, not part of the suffering church, even as they were not part of the mission of Jesus.

Klassen, William. "We Must Obey and Pay, But We May Also Protest." *CanMenn* 11 (Apr. 19, 1963), 5. A study of taxes in the New Testament; surveys the biblical mandate for Christians to pay taxes to government.

Kniss, Lloy A. "The Sacredness of Human Life." *ST* 39 (Jan., 1971), 1. Examines the responsibility of Christians regarding the sacredness of human life, the responsibility of the non-Christian, and government regarding the same concern.

Koehn, Brent A. "The Shalom Covenant and Peacemaking." Advanced Peace Studies Seminar paper, Mar. 28, 1979. Pp. 66. MLA/BeC.

Kolb, Noah. "Exegesis of Luke 22:35-38 with Reference to 49-51." Paper for War, Peace, and Revolution class, AMBS, Elkhart, Ind., Apr. 10, 1969. Pp. 3. AMBS.

Kolb, Norman. "Nations on the Verge of Calamity." *ST* 47 (July, 1979), 24. A Bible study from which one learns that national preservation depends on national spirituality and not on national military might.

Koop, Robert. "YHWH's War and the War of the Sons of Light: A Synergism of Holy War." Paper for Dead Sea Scrolls and Theology of War in the Old Testament classes, AMBS, Elkhart, Ind., May, 1977. Pp. 35. AMBS.

Kraus, C. Norman. "A Christian Perspective on Revolution." *GH* 63 (July 21, 1970), 618-19. Calls Christianity which has set itself up as a defender of the status quo to return to the future-oriented perspective of the New Testament in order to faithfully understand and critique both the existing order and social revolutions.

Kraus, C. Norman (Review). *Jesus and the Nonviolent Revolution,* by Andre Trocme. Trans. by Michael H. Shank and Marlin Miller. Scottdale: Herald Press, 1973. Pp. 211. *MQR* 51 (Jan., 1977), 85-86. Trocme presents a convincing thesis that Jesus the Messiah was a nonviolent revolutionary prophet who used the principle of the Jubilee Year and its restoration as the focal point for his ministry. Reviewer observes that while it is a helpful thesis, the author perhaps presses this framework onto too many New Testament texts.

Kraybill, Donald B. "Civil Religion vs. New Testament Christianity." *GH* 69 (May 11, 1976), 402-3. Kraybill draws distinctions between American civil religion, which uses religious language to legitimize national policies such as militarism, and New Testament Christianity, which follows the narrow way of Jesus.

Kraybill, Donald B. *The Upside Down Kingdom.* Scottdale: Herald Press, 1978. Pp. 327. Popularly provocative study of the kingdom of God in the synoptic gospels. Uses the imagery of Luke 3:4-6 to make the point that taking Jesus seriously involves an inversion of the prevailing social order—politically, economically, and socially.

Kraybill, Ron S. "Christmastime and the Foolish Conjunction." *GH* 73 (Dec. 23, 1980), 1027. Comment on the joining of worship and peace in the angelic announcement to the shepherds.

Krehbiel, Henry P[eter]. *War Inconsistent with the Spirit and Teaching of Christ.* Newton: Herald Publishing Co., 1934. Pp. 26. Examines Jesus' teachings and conduct and finds them opposing war, hatred, and resistance. Reprint of an 1894 essay.

Kreider, Alan. "Biblical Perspectives on War." *Third Way* 4 (Nov., 1980), 13-14. Brings the Old Testament prophetic insistence—that Israel rely on Yahweh rather than numerical, technological or nonrestricted military strength—to bear upon our modern quest for security in nuclear weapons.

Kreider, Carl. "The Christian Message of Peace." *Japan Christian Quarterly* 18 (Autumn, 1952), 293-99. Both the teachings of Jesus and his own example call us to practice the way of love and peace, as an answer to those who trust in military power.

Kreider, Evelyn B. "It's Our Turn." *Lifework* 1 (1978), 3-5. Essay on peace outlines the biblical basis for shalom, the nonresistant convictions of

Anabaptists, and the call to be peacemakers today as Christians.

Kreider, Robert S. "A Litany of Violence and Reconciliation." *GH* 61 (Apr. 16, 1968), 346-47; *CanMenn* 16 (Aug. 13, 1968), 13; *MBH* 7 (Mar. 29, 1968), 4-5; *ChrLead* 31 (Mar. 26, 1968), 5, 12. Offsets scripture passages on hope and reconciliation against vignettes of the problems of war, violence, poverty, racial tensions.

Kreider, Robert S. "The Gospel of Christ Is the Gospel of Peace." *CanMenn* 11 (Aug. 20, 1963), 6, 8. According to Colossians 1:15, 20 and 3:15, the motif of peace, love, and reconciliation is an essential part of the gospel.

Kroeker, Werner. "Christian Biblical Teaching on War and Non-resistance." Thesis (BD) North American Baptist Seminary, n.d. Pp. 193. MBBS.

Kuhns, Dennis R. "In Response to Violence." *GH* 68 (Apr. 8, 1975), 266-67. The best way to deal with the destructive cycle of violence is for people to take individual responsibility in rejecting violence and following Jesus' way.

Kuhns, Dennis R. "The King on a Donkey." *GH* 72 (Apr. 3, 1979), 266-67. Jesus is recognized as a King, a man of peace, working to establish God's kingdom in righteousness and peace by God's Spirit at work in us and through us in nonconformity to the world.

Landis, Ira D. "When Nations War: A Study of Habakkuk 2:6-20." *ChrMon* 34 (Apr., 1942), 105-7. God's dealings with Babylon provide an object lesson for the Christian's relationship to the state.

Langenwalter, J. H. *For All Mankind.* North Newton, Ks.: Bethel College Press, 1943. Pp. 48. MHL. A study of the four Gospels centered around the theme of peace as a way of life for all with ramification for both attitudes and actions.

Lapp, George J. "Helps and Hindrances to Peace." *GH* 37 (Sept. 22, 1944), 493. The Christian "stranger and pilgrim" does not participate in war because he or she is part of the kingdom of God and is engaged in spiritual, not carnal, warfare.

Lapp, John A. (Review). *The Concept of Peace,* by John Macquarrie. Harper and Row, 1973. Pp. 82. *GH* 67 (June 11, 1974), 495. Although not a pacifist, Macquarrie presents a biblical vision of peace as healing in both interpersonal and international relations.

Lapp, John A. (Review). *The Politics of Jesus,* by John H. Yoder. Grand Rapids: Eerdmans, 1973. Pp. 260. *FQ* 1 (Spring, 1974), 11; *GH* 67 (Mar.

19, 1974), 255. Considers this work the most important of Yoder's books to date because it begins with the first principles of Christian pacifism—Jesus' life and teachings as norm for biblical ethics.

Lapp, John E. "Maintaining Nonresistance in Doctrine and Practice." *GH* 36 (Sept. 9, 1943), 498-99. Mennonites need to understand both the Old and New Testaments, their relationship, and their teachings on nonresistance. Then practice of these teachings is required.

Lapp, John E. "My Kingdom Is Not of This World." *GH* 68 (Nov. 25, 1975), 846-48. The Christian way to live according to God's Kingdom while on earth is to be nonresistant to existing powers, to overcome evil with good, to raise a prophetic voice on social issues, in faithfulness to a New Testament ethic.

Lapp, John E. *Studies in Nonresistance: An Outline for Study and Reference.* Akron, Pa.: Peace Problems Committee, 1948. Pp. 35. MHL. Outlines a study course for MYF in 12 lessons. Topics covered include Old Testament and New Testament teachings on war and peace, nonresistance in the early church, Anabaptist concepts of nonresistance, the Mennonite experience in America, World War I, World War II, and church and state.

Lapp, John E. "The Christian—A Servant of Reconciliation." *GH* 63 (Dec. 15, 1970), 1034-35. God calls all Christians to follow Jesus in becoming servants of reconciliation, a conviction the author arrives at through examining New Testament passages.

Lapp, John E. "The Third Way of the Gospel." *GH* 61 (Mar. 5, 1968), 204-206. The gospel of salvation by grace through faith demands also ethical commitment to peace and goodwill.

Lasserre, Jean. "War and the Christian Ethic." *CanMenn* 11 (July 12, 1963), 7; *GH* 56 (Aug. 20, 1963), 720. In the New Testament there is no clear distinction between individual and collective, private and political ethics. The New Testament challenges the Christian consistently to a coherent and homogeneous kind of behavior without the duplicity of contradiction.

Lasserre, Jean. *War and the Gospel.* Scottdale: Herald Press, 1962. Pp. 243. Determines, through exegetical and theological analysis, that the Decalogue is the link between the gospel and public morality, the criterion of good by which Christians can judge the actions and commands of the state. Having reached this conclusion, Lasserre then applies the criterion of the sixth commandment to an evaluation of the police and military functions of the state. He concludes that while both law enforcement and defense are legitimate state functions, the death penalty and war are illegitimate ways to perform these functions.

Ledford, Monty. Letter to the Editor. *Menn* 95 (Jan. 1, 1980), 14. Maintains that God does not change, but uses different means to accomplish divine purposes, as can be seen in the Old Testament command to war and the New Testament teaching to refrain from war.

Lehman, Chester K. "As Applied to the Christian and Civil Government: Bible Teaching on Nonconformity." (Part 7). *GH* 32 (June 15, 1939), 226-27. Christ's Kingdom is primarily spiritual, but since God has ordained government, these powers are used by God. Deals with various problems encountered, e.g., tax payment, office-holding, and the meaning of subjection to government.

Lehman, Emmett R. "War and Killing in Both Testaments." *GfT* Series 2, Vol. 3, Part 1, (Oct., 1968), 6-7; Part 2, (Dec., 1968), 15. Supports a two-covenant view by citing Old Testament divine commands for warfare as evidence that nonresistance was not part of God's plan for that time. Roots nonresistance in commitment to Christ and differentiates nonresistance from pacifism.

Lehman, J. Irvin. "A Criticism of the Article 'Peace and War in the Old Testament'." *ST* 11 (July, 1943), 28. Discusses an article in a Jan., 1943, issue of *MQR*. Criticisms revolve around quoting only the part of the scriptures that are relevant to the subject, philosophizing, using false logic and improper analogies.

Lehman, J. Irvin. *God and War*. Scottdale: Mennonite Publishing House, 1942. Pp. 63. Warfare in the Old Testament was in accord with God's basic will. In a future age God will again delegate the administration of vengeance to Christian people.

Lehman, J. Irvin (Editorial). "Biblicist Nonresistance." *ST* 21 (1st Qtr., 1953), 27. Outlines Matthew 5:17-48 as it relates to nonresistance.

Leis, Vernon. "Our Mandate to Be Peacemakers." *GH* 65 (Feb. 29, 1972), 186-87. Underscoring biblical references, the writer asserts that peacemaking is central to the gospel, based on: Jesus' teaching and ministry; biblical evidence indicating that conversion produces ethical changes; and the fellowship of Christians around the world.

Liechty, C. Daniel. "Political Nonresistance: A Thesis in Christian Ethics." MA in Peace Studies thesis, AMBS, 1978. Pp. 71. An exploration of the OT anti-kingship tradition, a comparison of the political views of Hegel and Marx, and a summary of Christian thinking on the relationship of church and state contribute to a Christian understanding of the political organism.

Liechty, C. Daniel. "War in the Old Testament: Three Views." *GH* 71 (May 23, 1978), 408-409; *Menn* 94 (Nov. 6, 1979), 658-59. Examines three types of Mennonite writers on the subject of war in the Old Testament: 1)Those who posit discontinuity between the Old and New Testaments; 2) those who find nonresistance as an ideal presesnt in the Old as well as New Testaments; 3) those who see Israel's trust in a warrior-God instead of a warrior-king as a challenge to military action.

Lind, Ivan Reuben. "The Problem of War in the Old Testament." PhD dissertation, Southwestern Baptist Theological Seminary, Fort Worth, Tx., 1956. Pp. 112. AMBS; BfC. Theorizes that while God's moral law does not change, in the case of the Old Testament, these moral teachings must be interpreted in the light of the maturation of the human vehicle within which the teachings are developed. This theory is then tested against the problem of Old Testament violence and warfare. The study proceeds in three sections: preliminary considerations such as the sovereignty of God, concepts of theocracy and progressive revelation; bloodshed in civil relations; and bloodshed through warfare.

Lind, Marcus. "A Prophet of Grace and Peace." *ST* 47 (June, 1979), 10-13. Elisha's overcoming of evil with good in II Kings 6:23 is a paradigm for present day conflict.

Lind, Marcus. "Abigail, an Advocate of Peace." *ST* 47 (Mar., 1979), 12-14. Comment on I Samuel 25, where Abigail persuades David not to attack her husband Nabal.

Lind, Marcus. "From Carnal Sword to Peaceful Rod." *ST* 48 (May, 1980), 11-14. Moses led the children of Israel, not with a sword of violence, but with the more peaceful symbol of authority, a shepherd's rod.

Lind, Marcus. "How Abram Learned the Way of Peace." *GH* 67 (Apr. 16, 1974), 323-24. Describes Abraham's struggle outlined in Genesis 14 in choosing between the way of peace as represented by the high priest Melchizadek, or the way of war, represented by Bera, king of Sodom.

Lind, Marcus. "Learning from the Bible's First War." *ST* 47 (Jan., 1979), 19-22. Abram's acceptance of Melchizedek's bread and wine instead of Bera's war spoils marked his choice of servanthood rather than violence.

Lind, Marcus. "The Battle Is Not Yours But God's."

*ST* 47 (Oct., 1979), 11. A Bible study of 2 Chron. 20 looking at the conditions that Judah had to meet before taking up arms.

Lind, Marcus. "'The Just Shall Live.'" *ST* 48 (Aug., 1980), 24-27. Justification by faith, which results in nonresistance, is God's reply to violence.

Lind, Marcus. "When the Lord Fought in Battle." *ST* 45 (June, 1977), 11-14. God, not the Israelites, fought their wars as long as they kept covenant.

Lind, Millard C. *Answer to War.* Scottdale: Herald Press, 1952. Pp. 143. Written particularly for young people to show from the Bible and history that God, Christ, and the Church are the answer to war.

Lind, Millard C. "Is There a Biblical Case for Civil Disobedience?" *God and Caesar* 4 (July, 1978), 6-8. An examination and summary of Old Testament texts which set forth the clash between the two mutually exclusive political systems: the kingdom of Yahweh and the rebellious kingdoms of humankind.

Lind, Millard C. "Israeli or Jacobi?" *GH* 62 (June 10, 1969), 514-16. The relevance of the Old Testament to the contemporary Middle East situation lies in the biblical witness to a new community which transcends nationalism.

Lind, Millard C. "Monotheism, Power and Justice: A Study in Isaiah 40-55." *CBQ* 46 (July, 1984), 432-46. By a careful comparison of the trial speeches, the Cyrus poems, and the servant poems, Lind shows that while all three testify to Yahweh's historical and cosmic sovereignty, only the servant poems embody the divine purpose to bring justice to the nations. The servant's work, rooted in Torah-justice, discloses a distinctive understanding of politics and, specifically, the moral quality of Yahweh's rule.

Lind, Millard C. "Over the Nations." Paper presented to Colloquium on Peace Studies, AMBS, Elkhart, Ind., June 5-8, 1972. Pp. 4. MHL.

Lind, Millard C. "Paradigm of Holy War in the Old Testament." *Biblical Research* 16 (1976), 16-31. Develops thesis that belief in Yahweh as heavenly king and divine warrior (meaning that Israel needs neither a king nor an army) is an early and central component of biblical faith.

Lind, Millard C. "Politics of the Spirit." *GH* 65 (Feb. 22, 1972), 169-71. If a theology of personal integrity and a theology of politics are combined according to the Bible, a politics of

power, characterized by self-interest, hypocrisy, and death must come to an end.

Lind, Millard C. "Summary and Critique of Norbert Lohfink's *Gewalt und Gewaltlosigkeit im Alten Testament.*" IMS *OP* 9 (1986), 73-82. Summarizes the contents of the five scholarly essays in Lohfink's book published in 1983 and occasioned by Girard's books on the relation between violence and the sacred (see E. Pries' entry below). While applauding the symposium by Catholic scholars, Lind states that the study focuses too narrowly on the relation of violence to sacrifice; it also misses some essential elements in the Isaiah servant traditions.

Lind, Millard C. "The Old Testament and the Believers' Church." Paper, n.d. Pp. 11. AMBS.

Lind, Millard C. *Yahweh Is a Warrior: The Theology of Warfare in Ancient Israel.* Scottdale, Pa.: Herald Press, 1980. Pp. 232; Consists of an exegetical and descriptive analysis of Hebrew warfare in the Primary History (the materials from Genesis through 2 Kings, minus Ruth). The argument has three major emphases: Yahweh delivered the people of Israel through a prophet rather than a warrior, with Yahweh's intervention in the form of a nature miracle rather than human strategy and battle; the exodus became the basis for a distinctive social order that was prophetic in nature, an order which rejected concepts of kingship based on violent force as representative of divinity; as Israel drifted toward the Ancient Near Eastern standard of kingship grounded in violence, Yahweh's war became directed against Israel itself.

Lind, Millard C. (Review). *The Way to Peace,* by L. John Topel, S.J. Maryknoll: Orbis Books, 1979. Pp. 199. *MissFoc* 8 (Mar., 1980), 19-20. Reviewer discusses Topel's biblical theology and pacifism in his approach to liberation theology.

Lind, Werner Allan. "The Incompatibility of Human Kingship with Jahwism: True or False?" Paper presented to War and Peace in the Bible class, AMBS, Elkhart, Ind., Jan. 30, 1980. Pp. 20. AMBS.

Longacre, James C. "Love and Nonresistance." *GH* 70 (May 17, 1977), 406-407. [No. 18] Examines the Mennonite Confession of Faith (1963) and shows therein the biblical perspective calling all Christians to live according to Jesus' way of love and to witness to peace outside of the church.

Lord, Charles R. "An Exercise in Integration: In *God* We Trust." Paper presented to War and Peace in the Bible class, AMBS, Elkhart, Ind., Jan. 25, 1980. Pp. 21. AMBS.

Lueders, A. J. "War and the Old Testament

Prophets." *GH* 41 (Oct. 19, 1948), 987. The prophets' message was that war is wrong and that peace comes only with the Messiah.

Lugibihl. Jan. "Jesus As Conscientizer." IMS *OP* 9 (1986), 95-107. Informed by Paulo Friere's model of conscientizing the oppressed, Lugibihl shows how Jesus brought new identity, vision, and empowerment to the marginalized of his day, the poor, the tax collectors, and women.

"Mennonite Leaders Meet with Billy Graham." *GH* 54 (Sept. 19, 1961), 824. Some Mennonite leaders meet with Billy Graham to share with him their understanding of the New Testament ethic of love and nonresistance.

"Mennonite Peace Theology Colloquium Papers." From sessions held at St. Paul's School of Theology. Kansas City, Mo., Oct. 8, 1976. Pp. [163]. AMBS. Colloquium focused on Yoder's *The Politics of Jesus* includes: Burkholder, J. R., "Mennonite Social Ethics and *The Politics of Jesus*;" Edwards, George R., "Biblical Interpretation and *The Politics of Jesus*;" Swartley, Willard, "Biblical Interpretation and *The Politics of Jesus*;" Schroeder, David, "Theologizing and *The Politics of Jesus*;" Groff, Warren, "Theologizing and *The Politics of Jesus*;" Stassen, Glen, "Ethical Methodology and *The Politics of Jesus*;" Mouw, Richard, "Political Thought and *The Politics of Jesus*."

Martens, Elmer A. "The Problem of Old Testament Ethics." *Direction* 6 (July, 1977), 23-35. Identifies some of the issues in the task of establishing ethical norms in Old Testament material and also notes that the descriptive task of ethics is challenged by the nature of Old Testament ethical material.

Martin-Adkins, Ron. "Why Christian Pacifism?" *Menn* 95 (Dec. 2, 1980), 694-95. Roots Christian pacifism in God who creates life, Christ's suffering love on the cross, and Christian commitment to the kingdom of God.

Mast, Russell L. "Did Jesus Sanction War?" *Menn* 67, Part 1, (Aug. 5, 1952), 485, 491; Part 2, (Aug. 12, 1952), 504-505. Mast's negative answer grows out of the principles supported in the New Testament: God is sovereign; love must control all relationships; life is supremely sacred; evil is to be overcome only by good.

Matties, Gordon. "Swords or Plowshares? An Inquiry into War and Ethics in the Old Testament." Term paper, 1981. Box 13-D-7. CMBS/Win.

McGrath, William R. *Why We Are Conscientious Objectors to War.* Seymour: Historical Mennonite Faith Publications, n.d. Pp. 54. Uses discussion of scripture passages to answer questions commonly asked of nonresistant Christians,

such as the validity of war in the Old Testament, Christian obedience to government, and early church convictions on war.

McPhee, Arthur G. "Jesus and the Whip." *GfT* 6 (Sept.-Oct., 1971), 3, 5; (Nov.-Dec., 1971), 19. Jesus' chasing the animals out of the temple was a demonstration of his authority, not a sanctioning of violence or war; since Jesus whipped animals, not people, in the temple, the passage cannot be used to justify the use of physical violence.

McPhee, Arthur G. "Scriptural Guidelines on the Way of Peace." *GfT* 6 (Mar.-Apr., 1971), 10-11. Sermon on Matthew 5:43-48 extols love as the way to peace with God and humans.

McPhee, Arthur G. "Why Does God Allow War?" *ST* 42 (Aug., 1974), 1. Suggests that war as a revelation of sin, as a condemnation of sin, and as a manifestation of sin are helpful guides to understanding why God allows war.

Mennonite Central Committee. *The Evangelical Christian and Modern War.* A seminar at Winona Lake, Ind., Aug., 1963. Akron: MCC Peace Section, 1963. Includes seven study papers: Ladd, George E., "The Evangelical Christian and the State;" Backer, Glenn W., "A New Testament Perspective;" Klassen, William, "Biblical Faith and War;" Peachey, Paul, "War and the Christian Witness;" Reid, W. Stanford, "The Christian and Modern War: The Reformed Perspective;" Yoder, John H., "The Christian and War in the Perspective of Historical and Systematic Theology."

Metzler, Eric E. "Peacemaking Today." *GH* 73 (July 1, 1980), 524-26. Reflects on American values and Mennonite commitments and compares them with New Testament exhortations to peacemaking.

Metzler, James E. "Shalom and Mission." MA in Peace Studies thesis, AMBS, 1977. Pp. 127. Reviews the biblical concept of Shalom from both OT and NT perspectives and evaluates Mennonite missions in light of the concept in an effort to suggest a model that integrates shalom as mission.

Miller, Bernice and Berdella. "Justice Shall Roll Down." *Builder* 15 (July, 1965), 10-13. A choral reading arranged from a sermon by Carl Beck that relates the message of Amos to the situation in war-torn Asia.

Miller, John W. "'Holy War' in the Old Testament." *GH* 48 (Mar. 15, 1955), 249-50. The true "Holy War" sought to demonstrate that God, not the arm of flesh, brings victory. Jesus' words, "All who take the sword will perish by the sword," are not only his words but also those of all the true saints in both testaments.

Miller, John W. *The Christian Way: A Guide to the Christian Life Based on the Sermon on the Mount.* Scottdale: Herald Press, 1969. Pp. 136. Study manual on the meaning of the Sermon on the Mount and its significance for Christian living includes discussion of the political aspects of the kingdom of God as well as nonresistance and other topics related to loving one's enemies.

Miller, John W. (Review). *The Christian and Warfare: The Roots of Pacifism in the Old Testament,* by Jacob J. Enz. Herald Press, 1972. Pp. 95. "Pacifism: A Stream in the Ocean of History." *MennRep* 4 (Jan. 21, 1974), 8. The unifying theme of these essays on biblical theology is biblical pacifism, on which Enz focuses in order to demonstrate the unity and direction of biblical materials.

Miller, Paul M. (Review). *This Atomic Age and the Word of God,* by Wilbur M. Smith. Boston: W. A. Wilde Co., 1948. Pp. 363. *ChrMon* 41 (Mar., 1949), 86-87. Reviewer recommends the book for its study of the implications of releasing nuclear energy and its relating the effects of the bomb to select biblical passages.

Mininger, J. D. "Nonresistance." *GH Supplement* 35 (Oct., 1942), 635. An outline of the basis for nonresistance in the Old and New Testaments, and the Christian's relationship to civil government.

Moomaw, Benjamin F. "A Dialogue on the Doctrine of Nonresistance." *Discussion on Trine Immersion by Letter Between Elder Benj. F. Moomaw . . . und Dr. J. J. Jackson . . . ,* by Benjamin F. Moomaw. Singer's Glen, Va.: Joseph Funk's Sons, 1867, 220-74. Using the form of a dialogue between an advocate and an opponent of Christian pacifism, the Brethren author deals with such arguments on nonresistance issues as the New Testament passages on submission to authority, Old Testament warfare, and natural law.

Mosemann, John H. "Must Christians Fight?" *GH* 35 (May 21, 1942), 163. God dealt differently with Israel than with the church. The church also has a different purpose than does the world.

"No Christians in Army Until 170 A.D. - Penner." *CanMenn* 2 (Nov. 12, 1954), 3. G. Groening and Archie Penner address Steinbach Bible conference stressing the teaching of Jesus regarding a personal ethic. No record can be found of early Christians participating in war.

Nestor, Bob A. Letter to the Editor. *ChrLead* 36 (May 29, 1973), 13. To say the Christian cannot participate in the military is certainly without scriptural basis.

Neufeld, John H. "A Comparative Study of Romans 13:1-7; 1 Peter 2:13-17; and 1 Timothy 2:1-3." Paper for War, Peace, and Revolution class, AMBS, Elkhart, Ind., n.d. Pp. 3. AMBS.

Nigh, Harold. "A Bright Light on the Testing Grounds of Galilee." *MennRep* 9 (Feb. 5, 1979), 5. The bright light of Jesus is diametrically opposed to the bright light preceding the mushroom cloud of the atomic bomb. This sermon urges us to follow the way of the Prince of Peace.

Ollenburger, Ben C. (Review). *The Problem of War in the Old Testament,* by Peter C. Craigie. Grand Rapids: Eerdmans, 1978. *ChrLead* 42 (July 31, 1979), 20. Deals with the Old Testament teaching on war by relating it to God's participation in human history and activity in bringing people to salvation.

Ollenburger, Ben. *Zion, The City of the Great King.* Sheffield: JSOT Press, 1987. Written as a doctoral dissertation at Princeton Theological Seminary, this original study identifies the Zion tradition in numerous Psalms and selected Isaiah texts as a distinctive theological emphasis. Though often occurring in the biblical texts together with the royal theology of Davidic kingship, the Zion theology is distinct from and often critical of the kingship ideology. Zion theology extols Yahweh as King and attributes to Yahweh the exclusive perogative of judgment. The Zion symbolism calls Israel to trust in Yahweh's sovereignty and to refuse the proud boastful way of life which seeks military alliances and security through arms and wealth.

Ovensen, Barney. "The Early Christians and War." *GH* 43, Part 1, (Oct. 17, 1950), 1025-27; Part 2, (Oct. 24, 1950), 1051. The early Christians objected to war on the basis of the gospel of Christ. The Old and New Testaments teach that one is to maintain peace with all people.

Ovensen, Barney. "Why It Is NOT Right for a Christian to Fight." *GH* 45, Part 1, (June 17, 1952), 592-93, 605; Part 2, (July 15, 1952), 696-97. Argues against Robert C. McQuilkin's position (*Why It Is Right for a Christian to Fight*) on the grounds that McQuilkin bases too much on the Old Testament and fails to consider sufficiently Christ's command to love the enemy.

"Peace Principles." *GH* 28 (Oct. 3, 1935), 563. Scriptural quotations in support of the nonresistant position are cited as found in the Gospels and in the writings of the apostles.

*Peace or Pieces: Leader's Guide.* Salunga, Pa.: Eastern Mennonite Board of Missions, Voluntary Service Office, 1968. Pp. 18. MHL. Suggestions for leading a Bible study on peace. Includes structures for working with the biblical materials, stimulating group discussion, group action, individual creative expression, and prayer experience.

Peachey, Paul L. "A General Speaks on War." *GH* 48 (June 21, 1955), 585. Fundamentalism and its appeal to the Bible to support war must be scrutinized by Mennonites with the same critical eye that examines liberalism.

Peachey, Paul L., ed. *Biblical Realism Confronts the Nation.* New York: Fellowship Publications, 1963. Pp. 224. Ten Christian scholars summon the church to the discipleship of peace. I. *The Problem:* 1. Paul Peachey, "Church and Nation in Western History;" 2. John Edwin Smylie, "The Christian Church and National Ethos." II. *Old Testament Perspectives:* 3. Lionel A. Whiston, Jr., "God and the Nations: A Study in Old Testament Theology;" 4. Norman K. Gottwald, "Prophetic Faith and Contemporary International Relations." III. *New Testament Perspectives:* 5. George R. Edwards, "Christology and Ethics;" 6. Clinton Morrison, "The Mission of the Church in Relation to Civil Government;" 7. Otto A. Piper, "Conflict and Reconciliation." IV. *Some Proposed Solutions:* 8. Krister Stendahl, "Messianic License;" 9. William Klassen, "Love Your Enemy: A Study of New Testament Teaching on Coping with an Enemy;" 10. John J. Vincent, "Christ's Ministry and Our Discipleship." Summary by the editor, "Toward Recovery."

Peachey, Paul L. "Evangelicals and War." *GH* 48 (Aug. 16, 1955), 777. Those evangelicals who support war usually read the New Testament in the perspective of the Old. The nonresistant Christian reads the Old by way of the New.

Peachey, Paul (Review). *The New Testament Basis of Pacifism,* by G. H. C. Macgregor. NY: FOR, 1954; *The Early Christian Attitude to War,* by C. John Cadoux. London: Headly Bros. Publ., 1919; *The State in the New Testament,* by Oscar Cullmann. NY: Chas. Scribner's Sons, 1956; *The Sword and the Cross,* by Robert M. Grant. NY: MacMillan, 1955; *Church and State from Constantine to Theodosius,* by S. L. Greenslade. London: SCM Press, 1954. "Some New Books on the Early Church and War." *GH* 49 (Sept. 18, 1956), 897, 911. Recommends these books as helpful in identifying the practices of the early church on the issues of church and state.

Peachey, Shem. *Shall America Fight Herself Into Extinction?* Quarryville, Pa.: By the Author, n.d. Pp. 15. MHL. Laments warfare's destruction and calls America's Christians to commit themselves to the teachings of the Sermon on the Mount as a basis for living peacefully with one's neighbors and other nations.

Penner, Archie. *The Christian, the State, and the New Testament.* Scottdale: Herald Press, 1959. Pp. 128.

A biblical-historical study affirming the necessity of the state for the order of society, but locating it outside the perfection of Christ.

Penner, Stephen James. "Peace Strands in Isaiah." Thesis (MDiv), 1979. Pp. 113. MBBS.

Penner, Stephen (Review). *The Problem of War in the Old Testament,* by Peter C. Craigie. Grand Rapids: Eerdmans, 1978. Pp. 125. *Direction* 9 (Apr., 1980), 40. Recommends the book as a discussion of the warrior God motif, the problem of the Bible as revelation, and the relation of the Old and New Testaments.

Peters, Frank C. "The Scriptural Basis for Nonresistance." *ChrLead* 22 (Oct. 20, 1959), 4-5, 18. While Israel was, in a sense, the carrier and promoter of divine justice, the church is clearly the carrier of divine grace and redemptive love.

Peters, Frank C. "Why I Am a Christian Pacifist." *MBH* 15 (July 9, 1976), 7. Bases his position on the history of war, the teachings of Jesus, and the cross.

Peters, Peter H. (Review). *Christ and Violence,* by Ron Sider. Herald Press, 1979. Pp. 105. *MennRep* 10 (Aug. 18, 1980), 8. The book locates Christ's love and suffering for enemies at the heart of the gospel and examines the relationship of subjection to government and nonviolent resistance to governmental injustice.

Petkau, Brian T. "Reconciliation in the Joseph Narrative." Paper presented to Hebrew Exegesis: Law in the Old Testament class, AMBS, Elkhart, Ind., spring, 1981. Pp. 16. AMBS.

Plett, Harvey. "Nonresistance in the Gospel and in Church History." Paper presented to Mennonite History class, GBS, Elkhart, Ind., May 17, 1962. Pp. 51. MHL.

Poettcker, Henry (Review). *Covenant and Community: The Life, Writings, Peace Theology, and Hermeneutics of Pilgram Marpeck,* by William Klassen. Grand Rapids: Eerdmans, 1968. Pp. 211. "Dissertation Is Valuable Book on Pilgram Marpeck." *CanMenn* 17 (Jan. 21, 1969), 5. Draws attention to Klassen's emphasis on Marpeck's interpretation of the relationship between the Old and New Testaments and of the role of the Holy Spirit in interpreting Scripture. The former especially crucially affects the Christian position on participation in war.

Pries, Edmund. "Violence and the Sacred Scapegoat." IMS *OP* 9 (1986), 45-72. Summarizes the writings of René Girard and Raymund Schwager on the intrinsic and universal relationship between human violence and need for sacrifice (a sacred scapegoat) to "bleed" communities from self-destruction.

Schwager, as a Catholic theologian, relates the theory to OT sacrifice and NT views of the atonement.

Purvis, Ralph B. "Shall the Terrible War Which Is Threatening Be the End of the World?" *GH* 32 (Apr. 20, 1939), 70. A biblical study of the problem, with the conclusion that the war will not likely bring the end of the world.

"Religion Teachers Discuss War in the Old Testament." *MennRep* 2 (Oct. 30, 1972), 3. Evidence in Old Testament of the pacifist nature of the community which God had called to be his people.

Ratzlaff, Vernon. "How About Caesar?" *The Voice* 12 (Sept.-Oct., 1968), 8. A biblical assessment of social action and political involvement.

Ratzlaff, Vernon (Review). *King Jesus' Manual of Arms for the 'Armless,* by Vernard Eller. Nashville: Abingdon, 1973. Pp. 205. *Direction* 4 (Oct., 1975), 391-92. Says that beneath the "zany style" of the book lies a basic and rewarding treatment of the biblical perspective on the issues of war and peace.

Ratzlaff, Vernon (Review). *Political Evangelism,* by Richard Mouw. Grand Rapids: Eerdmans, 1973. Pp. 111. *Responsible Revolution,* by J. Verkuyl and H. Nordholt. Grand Rapids: Eerdmans, 1974. Pp. 101. *Politics: A Case for Christian Action,* by R. Linder and R. Pierard. Downers Grover: InterVarsity Press, 1973. Pp. 160. *Direction* 3 (Apr., 1974), 180-82. Of these three books on the subject of the church and state relation, the first is exegetically weak; the second lists the issues but does not develop them well; the third fails to offer a critical perspective on the present political system.

Ratzlaff, Vernon (Review). *The Christian and Warfare,* by Jacob J. Enz. Scottdale: Herald Press, 1972. Pp. 95. *Direction* 1 (July, 1973), 95. Applaud's Enz's "careful theological treatment of biblical themes" but wishes he had dealt with specific Old Testament wars in greater detail.

Reba Place Fellowship Drama Group. "Good Friday." *Swords into Plowshares: A Collection of Plays About Peace and Social Justice.* Ed. Ingrid Rogers. Elgin: The Brethren Press, 1983, 30-44. Seven scenes dramatizing the passion of Christ and emphasizing the way of suffering love demonstrated by Jesus' attitudes and behaviors through that ordeal.

Reedy, Janet Umble. "Christ Is Lord: A Study of the Principalities and Powers." Paper presented to War and Peace in the Bible class, Dec., 1983. Pp. 23. AMBS.

Regier, Dwight. "The Biblical Basis of Dutch Anabaptist Nonresistance." Student paper for Mennonite History, Nov. 29, 1976. Pp. 20. MLA/BeC.

Reschly, Steven D. "Manfred Weippert's Critique of Gerhard von Rad's *Der Heilige Krieg im Alten Israel* (Holy War in Ancient Israel)." Paper presented to War and Peace in the Bible class, AMBS, Elkhart, Ind., May 17, 1979. Pp. 26. AMBS.

Retzlaff, Peter. "Towards an Understanding of War in the OT." Paper presented at the Alberta Sunday School Convention, Calgary First Mennonite Church, Calgary, Alta., Oct. 25, 1969. Pp. 7. AMBS.

Richert, P. H. *A Brief Catechism on Difficult Scripture Passages and Involved Questions on the Use of the Sword.* Newton, 1942. Holds that in the Old Testament time God in some cases delegated the administration of vengeance to Israel, but that in the New Testament era God always reserves this prerogative.

"Sixty Winnipeg Layman [sic] Will Participate in Peace Seminar." *CanMenn* 12 (Sept. 29, 1964), 12. Peace education effort will involve discussion of such topics as the Bible and peace as well as role plays.

Sauder, Menno. *An Introduction to the Pamp[h]let "The Peaceful Kingdom of Christ: An Exposition on the Twentieth Chapter of Revelations [sic]' by Peter Twisk and a Treatise by Several Other Authors Bearing on the Same Subject.* Elmira, Ont.: By the Author, 1943. Pp. 40. MHL. Believes an interpretation of apocalyptic literature that envisions Christ's kingdom as a physical entity can lead to an abandonment of nonresistance in the effort to "help" the vision to fulfillment and, thus, to violation of a basic biblical principle.

Scarano, Dotti. "The Final Truth (Rev. 6:2-8)." *God and Caesar* 2 (Oct., 1976), 8. Based on the biblical text, this poem shows the destructiveness in which we are senselessly engaged.

Schertz, Mary H. "For the Healing of the Nations." Paper presented to War and Peace in the Bible class, AMBS, Elkhart, Ind., Nov. 30, 1981. Pp. 21. AMBS.

Schmidt, George. "Blessed Are the Peacemakers." *Menn* 95 (Mar. 11, 1980), 177. Meditation on the fifth beatitude stresses beginning peacemaking by making the conditions of the first four beatitudes present in one's personal life.

Schrag, Martin H. and Stoner, John K. *The Ministry of Reconciliation.* Nappanee, Ind.: Evangel Press, 1973. Pp. 131. A study of the biblical basis for nonresistance. Reflects that peace begins with the God who is at work in the world. The church is, then, the agency of reconciliation as its members work for change that overcomes sin.

Schroeder, David. "Not Heroes of the Dagger But Soldiers of the Cross." *CanMenn* 1 (Nov., 1953), 6. A creative, active peace will only come about when we give of ourselves. Harmony between Christians with peace emphasis is essential.

Schroeder, David. "The Church Representing the Kingdom." *MBH* 17 (Sept. 29, 1978), 4-6. The church is a sign of the kingdom when it speaks against injustice and manifests in its life the liberating action of God.

Schuchardt, John. "A Parable." *God and Caesar* 3 (Nov., 1977), 3-4. Various religious groups consider the suffering of villagers from napalm bombs but do not take personal responsibility by refusing to pay for war, a parallel to religious leaders in the parable of the Good Samaritan.

Schwarzschild, Steven S. "The Basis of Jewish Pacifism." *GH* 42 (Jan. 17, 1950), 59. Jewish pacifists hold that pacifism is the logical direction of the internal dynamic of Jewish faith and history.

Shank, Aaron M. *Studies in the Doctrine of Nonresistance: A Study Guide.* Myerstown, Pa.: Publication Board of the Eastern Pennsylvania Mennonite Church, [ca. 1974]. Pp. 42. MHL. Series of ten reading and memorization assignments plus detailed lesson outlines includes such topics as Jesus and nonresistance, the Old Testament and nonresistance, the state and nonresistance, etc.

Shank, Henry. "Turn the Other Cheek." *GH* 71 (Jan. 10, 1978), 17-19. Examines Jesus' command in Luke 6:29 to "turn the other cheek," concluding that a contemporary application calls for prophets of God's way to love the enemy of God's truth.

Shank, J. M. "'A Time to Kill and a Time to Heal.'" *ChrMon* 35, Part 1, (July, 1943), 201-3; Part 2, (Aug., 1943), 235-36, 255-56. Comment on Old Testament passages regarding war and killing concludes that war was sometimes the instrument of God's justice. While God commanded Israel to go to war and exercise capital punishment, God has forbidden both for the Christian church.

Shank, J. M. *"A Time to Kill and a Time to Heal:" A Treatise on the Sanctity of Human Life, War and Human Government, and Nonresistance.* N.p.: Mennonite Messianic Mission, 1967. Pp. 24. Citing examples and stories from Genesis to Samuel, the author contends that God in the Old Testament commanded war and capital punishment. As a new dispensation, however, the New Testament forbids both, commanding instead love and nonresistance.

Shank, J. Ward. "Anything and Anybody in the Name of Peace." *ST* 39 (June, 1971), 5. A whole new generation of Mennonites is being schooled in pacifism and social action which is in contrast to the basic principle of nonresistance, based on agape love as set forth in the New Testament.

Shank, J. Ward. "'Honor the King'." *ST* 39 (July, 1971), 8. To properly honor the high officials of government is a New Testament principle that should operate during either peace or war, or under prosperity or depression.

Shank, J. Ward. "The Christian Doctrine of Peace." *ST* 47 (Feb., 1979), 22-24. Comment on Romans 12:17-21 and its contribution to the concepts of peace and nonresistance.

Shank, J. Ward. "The Present Ethical-Psychological Climate—A Challenge for Writers." *ST* 38 (June, 1970), 18. Expresses concern that writers are using selected portions of scripture in application to modern social issues, often without proper regard to sound or consistent exegesis of those texts.

Shank, J. Ward (Editorial). "The Prince of Peace." *ST* 37 (Dec., 1969), 7. Looks at different dispensational views of approaching the Prince of Peace.

Shank, J. Ward (Editorial). "The Prophets of Peace." *ST* 30 (1st Qtr., 1962), 9. Modern application of the verbal exchange between Jeremiah and Hannaniah which shows their fundamental difference in outlook on matters of current events.

Shank, J. Ward (Review). *Christ and Violence,* by Ronald J. Sider. Scottdale: Herald Press, 1979. Pp. 108. *ST* 48 (July, 1980), 28-29. Reviewer observes that rather than serving as a study of Jesus' teachings on war and violence, the book advocates Christian social reform.

Shank, Luke J. "The Prince of Peace." *ChrMon* 39 (Dec., 1947), 359, 378. Sermon on the birth of Jesus emphasizes both the personal and social peace which comes through Jesus.

Shearer, Jon (Review). *Jesus and the Nonviolent Revolution,* by André Trocmé. Scottdale: Herald Press, 1971. Pp. 173. "The Ministry of Jesus: Justice and Redemption Inseparable." *MennRep* 4 (Apr. 29, 1974), Section A, 8. Book focuses on Jesus' ministry of active nonviolence rooted in his inauguration of the Year of Jubilee. Shearer observes it is foundational work for John H. Yoder's *Politics of Jesus.*

Shearer, Vel. "'Make Us Builders of Peace': The

Meaning of Discipleship." *MennRep* 4 (Apr. 15, 1974), 5. Address given at World Day of Prayer focuses on Jesus' teachings on discipleship and his practice of nonresistance, even to the cross.

Shelly, Maynard. *New Call for Peacemakers: A New Call to Peacemaking Study Guide.* Newton: Faith and Life, 1979. Pp. 109. Ten lessons on various aspects of living peacefully such as the biblical bases for peace, the roots of violence, the relationship of evangelism and peacemaking, the politics of servanthood, etc. Each lesson contains a Bible study guide and concludes with items for discussion and further study.

Shelly, Maynard. "No Christmas Card Scenes for Mary when Joseph Defied the Terrorists." *Menn* 91 (Dec. 14, 1976), 736-37; *MennRep* 6 (Dec. 13, 1976), 6. Reminds readers of the political ferment into which Jesus, the Prince of Peace, was born, and of the danger which threatened Mary, Joseph, and the unborn baby from terrorists resisting the Roman census decree.

Shelly, Maynard. "Songs of Men and of Angels." *GH* 70 (Dec. 20, 1977), 944-45; *EV* 90 (Dec. 25, 1977), 4; *MennRep* 7 (Dec. 26, 1977), 6. Describes the vision of peace as the new order of salvation, outlined by the songs of peace sung at Jesus' birth. The biblical use of the word peace carries the idea of a new order, a whole new way of life for people now living on earth, but when we want to escape the way of the cross on earth we twist it to mean "peace in heaven."

Shelly, Maynard. "Suffering Servant and King (3): Weakness as a Way of Life." *MennRep* 7 (Apr. 4, 1977), 6. In Jesus' nonviolence and suffering we see that God works through weakness, not strength.

Shenk, Lois Landis. "A House for David." *Swords into Plowshares: A Collection of Plays About Peace and Social Justice.* Ed. Ingrid Rogers. Elgin: The Brethren Press, 1983, 19-27. Dramatization of the temptation of Jesus in the wilderness explores the reasons Jesus rejected all Satan's "solutions" to the injustice and unfaithfulness Jesus had encountered in his world.

Shenk, Susan E. S. "Israel's Settlement: Conquest, Immigration, or Revolt? An Overview of Gottwald's Critique." Paper presented to War and Peace in the Bible class, AMBS, Elkhart, Ind., 1980. Pp. 23. AMBS.

Sherk, J. Harold. "My Peace I Give to You." Address given at Conference of Brethren, Friends, and Mennonites, Chicago, Ill., Dec. 5-7, 1952. Pp. 4. MHL. Christ and peace. MLA/BeC.

Sherk, J. Harold, comp. "Report of the MCC Peace Section Study Conference." Winona Lake, Ind., Nov. 9-12, 1950. Pp. 149. MHL. Includes: Toews, J. B., "Nonresistance and the Gospel,"

45-50; Wenger, J. C., "Nonresistance and the Gospel," 51-52; Hershberger, Guy F., "The Disciple of Christ and the State," 53-58; Kreider, Robert, "The Disciple of Christ and the State," 59-65; Fretz, J. Winfield, "Nonresistance and the Social Order," 66-72; Good, Noah, "Nonresistance and the Social Order," 73-76; Gingerich, Melvin, "What About the Noncombatant Position?" 77-85; Rempel, J. G., "What About the Noncombatant Position?" 86-90; Hostetter, C. N. Jr., "Our Peace Witness to Christendom," 91-95; Peachey, Paul, "Our Peace Witness to Christendom," 96-100; Smucker, Don, "Nonresistance and Pacifism," 101-108; Fast, H. A., "CPS—Past and Future," 109-112; Sherk, J. Harold, "ASW—Past and Future," 113-16; Graber, J. D., "Nonresistance and Missions," 117-20; Pannabecker, S. F., "Nonresistance and Missions," 121-26; Janzen, A. E., "Nonresistance and Missions," 127-28.

Shetler, Sanford G. (Review). *The Politics of Jesus,* by John Howard Yoder. Grand Rapids: Eerdmans, 1972. *ST* 41 (May, 1973), 33. A comprehensive book with many commendable features. But the author assumes too quickly a thesis establishing Jesus' radical involvement in the social and political structures of the day.

Sider, Ronald J. "A Call for Evangelical Nonviolence." *Christian Century* 93 (Sept. 15, 1976), 753-57. Also in *Mission and the Peace Witness.* Ed. Robert L. Ramseyer. Scottdale and Kitchener: Herald Press, 1979, 52-67. Contends that the biblical understandings of the ministry, cross, and resurrection of Jesus of Nazareth both lead to and are the only proper basis for nonviolent action.

Sider, Ronald J. "An Evangelical Witness for Peace." *Preaching on Peace,* ed. Darrel J. Brubaker and Ronald J. Sider. Philadelphia: Fortress Press, 1982, 25-28. Finds theological basis for evangelical position on peace in the themes of creation and the redemptive work of Jesus of Nazareth.

Sider, Ronald J. "Christ and Power." *International Review of Mission* 69 (Jan., 1980), 8-20. Author appeals to New Testament passages to support his thesis that power is not inherently evil but becomes compatible with the way of the cross when it is exercised for the other's good. Calls the church to actively witness to and resist the evil in government.

Sider, Ronald J., ed. *Cry Justice. The Bible Speaks on Hunger and Poverty.* New York: Paulist Press, 1980. A collection of biblical passages on justice issues accompanied by brief commentary, tables containing information on such topics as the infant mortality rate in different countries, and study questions designed for use by individuals and/or groups.

Sider, Ronald J. "Is God Really on the Side of the Poor?" *Sojourners* 7 (Oct., 1977), 11. Examines how at crucial moments when God displayed his mighty acts in history to reveal his nature and will, God also intervened to liberate the poor and oppressed.

Sider, Ronald J. "Jesus' Resurrection and the Search for Peace and Justice." *Christian Century* 99 (Nov. 3, 1982), 1103-1108. Develops four theses explaining why the bodily resurrection of Jesus is important to the issues of nuclear war: 1) As the foundation for understanding the lordship of Jesus, 2) as source of strength for the struggle for justice, 3) as the clue to the relationship between our work for justice and the shalom of the second coming, and 4) as the base from which to confront the powers.

Sider, Ronald J. "Reconciling Our Enemies." *Sojourners* 8 (Jan., 1979), 14. Jesus' vicarious death for sinful enemies of God lies at the very heart of a Christian's commitment to nonviolence.

Sider, Ronald J. "Resurrection and Liberation: An Evangelical Approach to Social Justice." *The Recovery of Spirit in Higher Education*, ed. Robert Rankin. New York: Seabury Press, 1980, 154-77. Develops three biblical themes as central to the pursuit of justice: the prophetic model, God's identification with the poor, and the bodily resurrection of Jesus of Nazareth as the foundation of hope.

Smith, C. Henry. "The Historical Background." *The Power of Love: A Study Manual Adapted for Sunday School User and for Group Discussion*. Ed. Peace Committee of the GCMC. Newton: Board of Publication, 1947, 38-57. MHL. Brief summary of the belief and practice of nonresistance from the New Testament church through World War I.

Smith, Daniel L. "The Exodus as Revolutionary Pedagogy: A Specific Critique of Aspects in Norman K. Gottwald's *The Tribes of Yahweh*." Paper presented to War and Peace in the Bible class, AMBS, Elkhart, Ind., Jan., 1980. Pp. 21. AMBS.

Smith, Daniel L. "The Military Exemptions of Deuteronomy 20:1-8, An Exegetical Study of a Holy War Motif in Seventh Century Israel." Paper presented to Hebrew Exegesis: Law class, AMBS, Elkhart, Ind., May, 1981. Pp. 29. AMBS.

Smucker, Donovan E. (Review). *Politics of Jesus*, by John H. Yoder. Grand Rapids: Eerdmans, 1972. Pp. 260. "The Jesus Ethic Is a Social Ethic." *MennRep* 3 (Apr. 16, 1973), 8. Yoder uses biblical exegesis, history of theology, and Christian ethics to show that Jesus is normative for Christian social ethics.

Snyder, Elvin V. "Christ, the Basis of Lasting Peace." *ChrMon* 30 (May, 1938), 138-39, 149. Address given at a peace conference stresses spiritual life in Christ as the basis for world peace.

Sperling, Ken (Review). *Christ and Violence*, by Ronald J. Sider. Kitchener: Herald Press, 1979. Pp. 102. *MBH* 19 (Jan. 18, 1980), 28. Recommends the book for its presentation of a biblical basis for nonviolence, plus suggestions for active peacemaking.

Stafford, Chase. "The Anger of God." *ChrLead* 42 (Apr. 24, 1979), 2. Looks at the implications of the fact that even God frequently displayed anger.

Stauffer, John L. "Can We Agree on Nonresistance?" *ST* 47 (June, 1979), 1-3, 26-29. Eight propositions on biblical hermeneutics and the nature of God form the basis of his defense of nonresistance. We must have unity on the philosophy of peace. A major point of disagreement on the basis of nonresistance arises from the question of warfare in the Old Testament. Paper, Harrisonburg, Va., n.d. Pp. 5. MHL.

Stauffer, John L. "Ninety to One." *ST* 27 (3rd Qtr., 1959), 37. The New Testament does not recommend nonresistance as a way of life for the nations of the world.

Stauffer, John L. "Peace and War: Fundamentalists and War." *GH* 46 (Apr. 21, 1953), 369. The nonresistant Christian must separate him- or herself from the Fundamentalists' support of war. Much of the rationale for this support of war comes from the Old Testament.

Stauffer, John L. "Peace Section: Can We Agree?" *GH* 42 (Mar. 15, 1949), 247-48. Nonresistant suffering is a New Testament doctrine. In the Old Testament there are warrior saints, in the New Testament there are martyr-saints.

Stauffer, John L. "The Error of Old Testament Nonresistance." *ST* 6 (2nd Qtr., 1960), 6. The line of argument that nonresistance must have been God's way of life for Israel in the Old Testament brings confusion to an understanding of law and grace.

Stauffer, John L. *The Message of the Scriptures on Nonresistance*. Harrison, Va.: Tract Press, n.d. Pp. 15. MHL. Summarizes New Testament and Old Testament views on war, church and state, etc., as well as the differences between the Testaments on these issues.

Stauffer, John L. "Was Nonresistance God's Plan for Old Testament Saints?" *ST* 13 (May, 1945), 352. Examines the premises of *War, Peace, and*

*Nonresistance* by Guy F. Hershverger. Stauffer's critical response is based on the belief that there is a radical difference between the Old and the New Covenants, which Hershberger does not sufficiently recognize.

Stoltzfus, Gene and Friesen, Dorothy. "Working for Human Rights." *Peace Section Newsletter* 8 (June, 1977), 1-3. Biblical words on justice are firm and consistent throughout the Old and New Testament. People who work for justice are sometimes the object of much criticism. Lists common objections voiced during the Vietnam era that continue to surface.

Stoltzfus, Victor. "Jesus Christ—Revolutionary." *YCC* 43, Part 1, (Oct. 7, 1962), 2; Part 2, (Oct. 14, 1962), 2; Part 3 (Oct. 21, 1962), 2; Part 4 (Oct. 28, 1962), 2; Part 5 (Nov. 4, 1962), 2. Jesus was and is a revolutionary person in His claim to be the Son of God.

Stoner, John K. "Beloved, Do Not Be Surprised: Anabaptists and the State." *Peace Section Newsletter* 8 (Sept.-Oct., 1977), 1-9. Develops the biblical and theological basis for actions and words which witness to the state.

Stoner, John K. "Jesus, Are You Really Serious?" *Lifework* 2 (1979), 3-5. Places Jesus' ministry in the context of national oppression by Rome, emphasizing Jesus' nonviolence as seen through eyes of Peter who hoped for a national revolution.

Stoner, John K. "Loving Confrontation in the Life of Jesus." *Affirm Life. Pay for Peace.* Ed. Maynard Shelly and Ron Flickinger. Newton: Historic Peace Church Task Force on Taxes, 1981, 11-12. Pp. [87]. MHL. The instances in which Jesus confronted the political, religious, and satanic powers of his day reveal that Jesus: did not compromise truth for tranquility; was clear that evil had both cosmic and human dimensions; regarded the law highly but right more highly; took initiative in confronting evil.

Stoner, John K. "Peace and Evangelism." *EV* 86 (Jan. 25, 1973), 5. Three major New Testament themes show the inseparable unity of evangelism and peace: the kingdom, the cross, and the resurrection.

Stoner, John K. (Review). *Does the Bible Teach Pacifism?*, by Robert E. D. Clark. England: Fellowship of Reconciliation, 1976. Pp. 70. *Fellowship* 43 (Sept., 1977), 22. Provides a summary of the contents of the book which gives an affirmative response to its title as well as examining why most of Christendom is not pacifist. Recommends this book for its timely subject and persuasive, original handling of the subject.

Studer, Gerald C. "Conscripts of Christ." *GH* 43

(Sept. 19, 1950), 1. Mennonites hold to the nonresistant faith because Christ, the Apostles, and the early church taught and practiced it. The Old Testament teaching on nonresistance is valid only insofar as it is not contradicted by the New Testament.

Swalm, E. J. "The Prince of Peace in the Gospels." *CanMenn* 13 (Sept. 7, 1965), 9, 15. A Bible study on nonresistance.

Swartley, Willard M. "Answering the Pharisees: A New Testament Study on the Payment of War Taxes." *Sojourners* 8 (Feb., 1979), 18-20. (See last entry on this page for annotation.)

Swartley, Willard M. "How to Interpret the Bible: A Case Study of Romans 13:1-7 and the Payment of Taxes for War." *Seeds* 3, 4 (June, 1984), 28-31. Applies the method proposed in Swartley's *Slavery, Sabbath, War and Women* study to this text and issue.

Swartley, Willard M. "Peacemakers: The Salt of the Earth." *Peacemakers in a Broken World.* Ed. John A. Lapp. Scottdale: Herald Press, 1969, 85-100. Studies biblical teachings on incarnation, atonement, church, government, and morality, concluding that Jesus' life, death, and resurrection are the bases for a peace witness; that the international church is the locus for this witness; and that war is politically as well as morally wrong.

Swartley, Willard M. "Politics and Peace (*Eirēnē*) in Luke's Gospel." *Political Issues in Luke-Acts,* ed. Richard J. Cassidy and Phillip J. Scharper. Maryknoll: Orbis Books, 1983, 18-37. Summarizes the divergent political understandings of Luke's Gospel as developed by Hans Conzelmann, John H. Yoder, and Richard J. Cassidy. After examining Luke's distinctive use of *eirēnē,* Swartley argues that Luke's peace gospel presents a third way. It neither directly opposes the empire and the rulers (Cassidy) nor does it present the gospel as a political apologetic, seeking pacification with Roman rule (Conzelmann).

Swartley, Willard M. "The Bible and War." *Slavery, Sabbath, War, and Women.* Scottdale: Herald Press, 1983, 96-149. Examines the biblical support for both a variety of positions allowing Christian participation in war and a variety of pacifist/nonresistant positions. The chapter concludes with commentary on the hermeneutical issues and problems pertinent to the debate.

Swartley, Willard M. "What Does the New Testament Say About War Taxes?" Condensed by Lois Barrett. *Affirm Life: Pay for Peace.* Ed. Maynard Shelly and Ron Flickinger. Newton: Historic Peace Church Task Force on Taxes, 1981, 7-9. Pp. [87]. MHL. Brief exegetical comments on the tax texts: Matt. 17:24-27; Mark 12:13-17; Luke 23:2; Rom. 13:6-7. Concludes that while these particular texts cannot be used as a rulebook for the issue; application of the basic moral principles of the New Testament indicates that nonpayment can speak a word faithful to the gospel when done as a Christian witness against war. The complete version, available from the Mennonite Board of Congregational Ministries, includes more extensive commentary on the biblical texts.

Swartley, Willard M. and Barrett, Lois. "God's Government and Human Government: The Christian's Relationship to Power and Peace." *MCC PS Newsletter* 12,6 (Nov.-Dec.), 1982. Biblically oriented, the article focuses on the kingship of Yahweh and Jesus and what this means for the way to peace. With exposition of Romans 12—13 and other texts, the call to overcome evil with good becomes the guiding vision in witness to government.

Swartley, Willard M. and Krieder, Alan. "Pacifist Christianity: the Kingdom Way." *Pacifism and War*, ed. Oliver R. Barclay. Leicester: Inter-Varsity Press, 1984. Pp. 38-60. One of seven position essays representing varying positions on war, Swartley and Kreider present the biblical-theological, historical, and ethical bases for the pacifist position as the kingdom way. Both authors have short responses to other essayists: Swartley to Arthur Holmes (pp. 35-37) and Kreider to Sir Frederick Catherwood (pp. 81-84); Holmes responds to the Swartley-Kreider article (pp. 61-67).

Swartley, Willard M. ed. *Essays on War and Peace: Bible and Early Church*. Elkhart: Institute of Mennonite Studies, 1986. Consists of seven essays annotated in the entries by author in this section: Mark Fretz, Edmund Pries, Millard C. Lind, Paul Dyck, Jan Lugibihl, William Elster, and John Friesen.

"The Conflict and the Church." *CanMenn* 9 (Sept. 29, 1961), 6. A biblical basis for "bypassing militarism."

"Their Biblical Teaching Against War." *CanMenn* 2 (Aug. 20, 1954), 7. A personal testimony of how this doctrine became the criteria for joining the Mennonite Church.

Teichert, Lucille. "*Marx and the Bible*: Summary, Critique, Reflections." Paper presented to War and Peace in the Bible class, AMBS, Elkhart, Ind., Dec., 1983. Pp. 33. AMBS.

Temple, Walter H. J. "Topic for Brotherhood for the Month of November, 1938." *Menn* 53 (Nov. 22, 1938), 7-8. New Testament teachings about the sin of war, and the problem of peace today.

*The Christian Nonresistant Way of Life*. Scottdale: Mennonite Publishing House, 1940. Also issued by Peace Problems Committee and Tract Editors of Lancaster Conference District, 1940, and Weaverland Conference, Menn., 1968. Pp. 48. MSIIL. Pamphlet on the biblical basis for the doctrine of nonresistance. Includes such topics as "Christ Our Example under Test," "The Christian and Government" and "The Christian Conscience."

Tiessen, Daniel. "Ahab and Naboth: Some Lessons About Land." *MennRep* 9 (June 25, 1979), 5. The Old Testament story of Ahab and Naboth is strikingly similar to the way in which the white society has claimed the land of the Indians.

Tiessen, Daniel. "Dividing Up the Land: Lessons from the Old Testament." *MennRep* 9 (July 9, 1979), 5. Referring to several of the Old Testament laws regarding the possession of land, this article addresses the issue of Indians being allowed to exercise control over the resources of their land.

Toews, John A. "Non-Resistance in the Old Testament." *ChrLead* 17 (Jan. 15, 1953), 2-3. It has always been the will of God that the people of God walk in the way of peace and love. The foundations for this understanding are laid in the Old Testament.

Toews, John A. *Our Ministry of Reconciliation in a Broken World*. Mennonite Brethren Church Board of Reference and Counsel, [1975]. Pp. 9 (pamphlet). Attached to *ChrLead* 38 (Oct. 28, 1975), 15. Position statement on peace outlines a biblical basis for peacemaking, then discusses its contemporary application in areas of international, national, industrial, racial, and economic conflict. Contends that a Christian attitude toward evil is not an attitude of passive acquiescence but one of positive and effective counteraction expressed in ways consistent with Scriptural principles of limitless love. MHL.

Toews, John A. "The Christian and Armed Combat." Paper, n.d. Pp. 10. MHL.

Toews, John A. "The Christian Debate on War." *Campus Ambassador Magazine* 20, #5, n.d., 11-15, 27. Contends that the life, teaching, and redemptive death of Jesus indicate that those who submit unconditionally to his Lordship cannot participate in armed conflict or war.

Toews, John A. "The Weapons of the Church for World Conquest." *The Voice* 5, Part 1, (Nov.-Dec., 1956), 1; Part 2, (Jan.-Feb., 1957), 1. The world "nonresistance" does not adequately express the positive and powerful nature of our witness of peace and love. Discussion of the weapons of the Christian's warfare.

Toews, John E. "Paul's View of the State." *ChrLead* 41 (Apr. 25, 1978), 5. Examines what Romans 13 says about peace and warfare. Lists several applications of Romans 13 for 20th century Christians.

Toews, John E. and Nickel, Gordon, eds. *The Power of the Lamb*. Winnipeg, and Hillsboro: Kindred press, 1986. Pp. 183. Consisting of thirteen chapters written by seven Mennonite Brethren (John E. Toews, Elmer A. Martens, John Fast, Mervin Dick, Henry Schmidt, Howard J. Loewen and Wesley J. Prieb), this resource for MB congregations is a biblical study of peace theology and peacemaking themes. It includes chapters on "The Lord is a Warrior" (Martens), "The Power of the Lamb" (Prieb), "The Mennonite Brethren Peace Witness" (Schmidt), and two chapters on the contemporary situation of bombs and just war (Loewen) as the context in which biblical peace theology is to be expressed.

Toews, Monroe. *Why I Can't Take Part in Carnal Warfare Since I've Become a Christian*. Hesston: Free Tract and Bible Society, [1962]. Pp. 15. MHL. Argument against war in fulfillment of a promise the author made to God during his tour of duty as an American soldier in Germany during World War II—that if he lived he would spend his days speaking of the love of God and the horrors of war.

Toews, Paul (Review). *The Original Revolution*, by John Howard Yoder. Scottdale: Herald Press, 1971. Pp. 188. *Direction* 1 (Oct., 1972), 134-35. Finds Yoder's analysis of such issues as the questions of "Christ and culture," the relationship between the Old Testament and New Testament on violence, the pacifist options for personal ethics and public policy, etc., to be a significant and helpful treatment.

Trocmé, André. *Jesus and the Nonviolent Revolution*. Trans. Michael H. Shank and Marlin E. Miller. Introduction by Marlin E. Miller. Scottdale: Herald Press, 1973. Pp. 211. Develops the thesis that the social, economic, and political revolution based upon the jubilary law of Moses was central to Jesus' vision and led to the conflict which ended on the cross. The second part of the book surveys the history of violence and nonviolence from Elijah to Herod and identifies a prophetic concept of nonviolent resistance within the broader stream of nationalism and messianism. The last section traces Jesus' expansion of contemporary religious thought by transforming messianic expectations through the choice of nonviolent resistance as his kingdom method.

Twisk, Peter J. *The Peaceful Kingdom of Christ: An Exposition of the Twentieth Chapter of the Book of Revelation*. Trans. John F. Funk. Carthage, Mo.: John Zeiset, 1929. Pp. 34. MHL. Presents the chapter in sections and offers comment on each section.

Ulery, O. B. *Can a Christian Fight?* Nappanee: E. V. Publishing House, n.d. Pp. 14 (pamphlet). Examines biblical passages regarding a Christian's relationship to the state, Old Testament teachings on war, and Jesus' teachings and ministry, and concludes that none can be used to justify Christian participation in war.

Unruh, W. F. "Bible Can't Be Used to Support War." *Menn* 86 (May 25, 1971), 352. Even in the use of the Bible, we ought to consider Jesus Christ to be the Lord and final authority in all interpretation.

Unruh, W. F. "The Gethsemane-Calvary Way of Dealing with Evil." *Menn* 61 (Apr. 2, 1946), 3-4. Sees Jesus' suffering as a redemptive force. Sin is disarmed via suffering.

van de Meusbrugghe, Andre. "A Letter to a Lawyer." *YCC* 36 (Feb. 13, 1955), 51-52, 55. A personal letter stating the biblical basis for the conviction to be a conscientious objector.

Voolstra, Sjouke. "The Search for a Biblical Peace Testimony." *Mission and the Peace Witness*. Ed. Robert L. Ramseyer. Scottdale and Kitchener: Herald Press, 1979, 24-35. An adequate peace theology will interpret the Bible in its social and political context, paying special attention to Old Testament visions of shalom and justice. An authentic peace witness must be active (not merely nonresistant) and community-oriented. Also available as paper, 1977. Pp. 6. MLA/BeC.

Voth, Dennis. Letter to the Editor. *ChrLead* 36 (June 26, 1973), 13. Raises some questions about certain biblical passages and how they are used to justify the Christian's responsibility to defend his country.

Waltner, Erland. "Peace and Your Health." *Menn* 95 (Nov. 25, 1980), 689. Discusses the close proximity of physical health, mental health, and right relationships with God and others in the biblical concept of shalom.

Waltner, Erland. "The Church in the Bible." *Proceedings of the Study Conference on the Believer's Church*. Newton: General Conference Mennonite Church, 1955, 55-72. A study of the nature of the church in the Old and New Testament writing. Shows how the themes of grace and discipleship, faith and love, witness and service, while in preparation in the Old Testament, emerge central in the New Testament.

*War Is Contrary to the Will of God: Statements by the Historic Peace Churches and the International Fellowship of Reconciliation*. Amsterdam: J. H. de

Bussy, July, 1951. Pp. 32. MHL. Introductory statement contends that Christ's call to overcome evil with good will be more effective in the long run than any kind of violent response to problems. The Christian's task is to rediscover and reconstruct in modern language and concrete situations the New Testament kind of warfare against evil. From this central tenet, each of the historic peace churches and the IFOR offers a separate statement emerging from its own tradition and in its own idiom.

Weaver, Amos W. Letter in "Our Readers Say." *GH* 56 (Apr. 2, 1963), 268. Response to John Howard Yoder's "Why I Don't Pay All My Income Taxes [*GH* 56 (Jan. 22, 1963), 81]. Commends Yoder's spirit, but feels he cannot act similarly without violating the New Testament teaching of Christ.

Weaver, Edwin L. "Loyalty to Christ in Wartime." *YCC* 25 (Apr. 23, 1944), 133, 136. The conscience against war is most frequently based on social, economic, or spiritual foundations. For the Christian, opposition to war is based on loyalty to Christ.

Weaver, Edwin L. "The Unnaturalness of War for the Christian." *YCC* 26 (Feb. 25, 1945), 449-50. Both the feelings aroused in warfare and the activities of the soldier are contrary to the example and teaching of Christ. Examples are included.

Wellcome, I. C. *Should Christians Fight?* Scottdale, Pa.: Mennonite Publishing House, 1951. Pp. 53. MHL. Format is a debate between "Demi," representative of those "half-christianized by the Gospel," and "Christian," representative of those to whom Christ's law is supreme—and, who, consequently, believe in nonresistance. Topics discussed within this polemic are Christ's teaching on warfare, obedience to civil law, Old Testament warfare, the standards of the early church, etc.

Wenger, C. D. "Why I Am a CO: In Two Parts." Harrisonburg, VA: By the Author, Box 182, 1947. Pp. [6]. MHL. Two lists of scriptures—one supporting the CO position, the other supporting the authority of scripture.

Wenger, J. C. *Pacifism and Biblical Nonresistance.* Focal Pamphlet No. 15. Scottdale: Herald Press, 1968. Pp. 28. A definition of both pacifism and nonresistance in relation to their understanding of Christ, sin, society, power, etc. with the latter emerging as the preferred biblical teaching.

Wenger, J. C. "The Theology of Pilgrim Marpeck." *MQR* 12 (Oct., 1938), 205-256. A treatise on the relation of the Old and New Testaments, and the impact of this position on the Christian stance of nonparticipation in war.

Wenger, Linden M. "Trends in Peace Education." *ST* 43 (July, 1975), 1-6. Review of Mennonite peace emphases in this century calls for a greater focus on the biblical basis for peace and less attention to the strategy of conflict resolution.

Wenger, Richard. "War and the Christian Ideal." *ChrMon* 37 (Mar., 1945), 57-58. Biblical basis for the nonparticipation of Christians in war, and debate with a contemporary writer allowing the use of force in resisting evil.

Wiebe, Bernie. "The Bible Speaks to Our Search." *Menn* 94 (Feb. 27, 1979), 141. Willard Swartley spoke to the Minneapolis Midtriennium Conference using the Bible as a guide in how to deal with the war tax issue. His three presentations were: "How Christians Solve Difficult Questions," "The Identity of God's People," and "Faithfulness and Witness."

Wiebe, Franz. "A Look at John 2:15." Paper for War, Peace, and Revolution class, AMBS, Elkhart, Ind., n.d. Pp. 2. AMBS.

Wiens, Devon H. "Holy War Theology in the New Testament and its Relationship to the Eschatological Day of the Lord Tradition." PhD dissertation, University of Southern California, Aug., 1967. Pp. 180. MHL. Uses a history of traditions approach to trace and analyze the New Testament appearances of these two motifs. Concludes that the motifs are reinterpreted in aspects of Jesus' death and resurrection, that Jesus becomes the personification of the eschatological day and fights the Holy War *par excellence*.

Yake, C. F. "A Christian's Peace Testimony." *YCC* 28 (Feb. 9, 1947), 364. Biblical basis for the Christian's peace testimony.

Yake, Lois. "The Social Message of the New Testament; The Social Gospel; Growth of a Social Consciousness in the Mennonite Church." Paper presented to Sociology Seminar, Goshen College, Goshen, Ind., Aug., 1947. Pp. 81. MHL.

Yoder, Bruce (Review). *Christ and Violence,* by Ronald Sider. Scottdale: Herald Press, 1979. Pp. 104. *FQ* 6 (Nov., Dec., 1979, Jan., 1980), 9. Filled with unanswered questions, Sider's book sensitizes readers to violent social structures, calling for activist nonviolence based in God's work in Christ on the cross.

Yoder, Dewey. "The Wars of Asa." *GH* 40 (May 20, 1947), 169. "The Old Testament shows beyond a doubt that preparedness for war is a fast and sure road to national calamity."

Yoder, Edward. "A Brief Meditation on Colossians 3:15." *GH Supplement* 35 (Dec., 1942), 830-31.

Peace is not found in humanistic and materialistic speculations, but by doing the will of God.

Yoder, Edward. "Beware of False Prophets." *GH Supplement* 35 (Apr., 1942), 78-80. Points on which Mennonites need to be clear include: the state is provisional, human, and lower than the church. The Christian, therefore, gives all of his or her obedience to the church; Christ taught nonresistance; Christ is superior to the Old Testament; nonresistant Christians will suffer reproach.

Yoder, Edward. "James 3:13-18: Peace Principles from a Scriptural Viewpoint." Part 19. *GH* 31 (Oct. 20, 1938), 646-47. True wisdom knows that God's work is done in the spirit of peace, not in a spirit of fanatical zeal.

Yoder, Edward. "John 18:36." *GH* 30 (Apr. 15, 1937), 79. Jesus' Kingdom is not of this world, nor can force be used to advance it.

Yoder, Edward. "Luke 3:14. Peace Principles from a Scriptural Viewpoint." Part 33. *GH* 32 (Jan. 18, 1940), 912. An appeal to this reference cannot justify military life for a Christian.

Yoder, Edward. "Military Figures in the New Testament: Peace Principles from a Scriptural Viewpoint." Part 39. *GH Supplement* 34 (Apr., 1941), 78. Paul did not mean to sanction the military by his repeated use of military metaphors.

Yoder, Edward. "Note on John 2:13-17." *GH* 29 (Jan. 21, 1937), 927. This passage is an argument against, rather than for, the use of violence.

Yoder, Edward. "Notes on Luke 22:35-38." *GH* 29 (Oct. 15, 1936), 638-39. This passage does not support war.

Yoder, Edward. "Notes on Romans 12:17-21: Peace Principles from a Scriptural Viewpoint." Part 26. *GH* 32 (July 20, 1939), 350-51. Christian faith finds expression as it interacts with people, returning good for evil.

Yoder, Edward. "Old Testament Nonresistance." *GH Supplement* 37 (Oct., 1944), 591. David was nonresistant toward his personal enemies and militant only against God's enemies.

Yoder, Edward. "Peace and War: What the Bible Teaches About War." *GH* 46 (Jan. 20, 1953), 56-57. War is contrary to the teachings of Christ.

Yoder, Edward. "Peace in the New Testament: Peace Principles from a Scriptural Viewpoint." Part 14. *GH* 31 (Apr. 21, 1938), 78. In the New Testament peace is both internal and external.

However, outward peace will not always abound.

Yoder, Edward. "Peace Principles: An Armistice Day Address." *Hesston College and Bible School Bulletin* 17 (Jan., 1931), 3-7. Discusses false foundations for nonresistance, such as weakness or cowardice, then examines the distinction between pacifism based on humanitarian ideals and pacifism based on Christian faith in the power of God to deal with the root of war—sin.

Yoder, Edward. "The Patience of the Saints: Peace Principles from a Scriptural Viewpoint." Part 38. *GH* 33 (Jan. 16, 1941), 909-911. The Bible and history teach that nonresistant suffering is the way of the Christian.

Yoder, Edward. "War Is Sin: Peace Principles from a Scriptural Viewpoint." Part 3. *GH* 28 (July 18, 1935), 366-67. War is contrary to the teachings of the New Testament. Mennonites should witness to the truth that Jesus Christ has abrogated the Mosaic provision for revenge.

Yoder, Edward. "Wars in the Old Testament: Peace Principles from a Scriptural Viewpoint." Part 35. *GH* 33 (July 18, 1940), 365-66. It is questionable that, in the Old Testament, it was God's absolute will that people should engage in carnal conflict.

Yoder, Edward (Review). *Can Christians Fight*, by Guy F. Hershberger. Scottdale: Mennonite Publishing House, n.d. *ChrMon* 32 (Oct., 1940), 305. Reprint of 35 essays on war and peace originally published in the *Youth's Christian Companion*.

Yoder, Edward (Review). *War and the Christian Conscience*, by John Horsch. Scottdale: Mennonite Publishing House, n.d. *ChrMon* 32 (October, 1940), 305. Recommends the book for its demonstration of the scriptural basis for and the reasonableness of nonresistance.

Yoder, Edward and others. *Must Christians Fight? A Scriptural Inquiry*. Akron: MCC, 1943. Pp. 68. MHL. Fifty-six questions and answers on nonresistance, ranging from definition of principles, biblical teaching, the essential, nonresistant character of Christ, apostolic practice of nonresistance, etc., to payment of taxes, relationship to pacifism, separation of church and state, etc.

Yoder, Glen. "Thou Shalt Not Kill; The Sixth Commandment." *GH* 43 (May 9, 1950), 483-84. This commandment and the New Testament ethic of love illustrate that one cannot take the life of a fellow human being.

Yoder, J. Otis. "And the King of the South." *ST* 46 (Jan., 1978), 14. A look at the prophecy in

Daniel 11 and the relationship between Israel and Egypt.

Yoder, J. Otis. "Don't Try It, Russia!" *ST* 40 (Dec., 1972), 25. Examines Ezekiel 38 and concludes that a nation from the North is going to undertake an invasion of Palestine.

Yoder, J. Otis. "The Yom Kippur War." *ST* 42 (Feb., 1974), 29. Analysis of the Oct. 6, 1973, war. Concludes that the Yom Kippur War was another act in the fulfillment of God's purpose for Israel.

Yoder, John H. "A People in the World: Theological Interpretation." *The Concept of the Believers Church.* Ed. James Leo Garrett Jr. Scottdale: Herald Press, 1969, 250-83. Pp. 342. Differentiates the believers' church understanding of the church from the theocratic, or Puritan, and the spiritualist, or Pietist, understanding and contends that the distinctness of the church is essential to the gospel. Then reinterprets Menno Simons' marks of the church—holy living, love, witness, and suffering—and speculates as to how the church might better meet human need by utilizing the believers' church as a model.

Yoder, John H. ". . . And on Earth Peace . . . ." *MennLife* 20 (July, 1965), 108-110. Avoiding the "assumption shared by all kinds of men in our time, that peace can be *made,* the Bible peace is a promise, a practice, a person and a prayer."

Yoder, John H. "Exodus: Probing the Meaning of Liberation." *Sojourners* 5 (Sept., 1976), 26. Contrasts the form, content, and means of liberation in the Bible with liberation theology.

Yoder, John H. "Exodus 20:13—'Thou Shalt Not Kill'." *Interp* 34 (Oct., 1980), 394-99. Interprets the sixth commandment to mean the prohibition of blood vengeance, which expands through historical development and the work of Christ into rejection of all killing by the early Christian community.

Yoder, John H. "Living the Disarmed Life." *Sojourners* 6 (May, 1977), 16. If God's strategy for dealing with his enemies was to love them and give himself for them, it must be ours as well. Christians have been disarmed by God.

Yoder, John H. "Nonconformity and the Nation." *ChrLiv* 2 (Feb., 1955), 8-9, 25, 33. The deeper issue behind conscientious objection to military service is the question of loyalty to the nation or to the Kingdom of God.

Yoder, John H. "Portraits of Christ: The Way of Peace in a World at War." Part 1. *GH* 54 (July 25, 1961), 617-18. Christ's strategy in dealing with his enemies was to love them and give

himself for them. The Christian must do likewise.

Yoder, John H. "Power and the Powerless." *Covenant Quarterly* 36 (Nov., 1978), 29-35. If, as the Bible says, God is on the side of the oppressed and if we want to be on God's side, the answer is not to spiritualize or universalize oppression so that we might be included but to begin dealing with the real ways in which we oppress others.

Yoder, John H. "The Christian and War." *United Evangelical Action* 13 (Oct. 1, 1954), 434, 445 [*sic.* 455]. Just as Jesus did not defend himself but suffered unto death, so we are to love those who treat us unjustly; we share in the triumph of the cross by walking in the way of the cross. Distinguishes between the religious liberal peace position and the biblical peace position.

Yoder, John H. "The Cross of Christ and the Death Penalty." Part 3. *CanMenn* 7 (Oct. 9, 1959), 2. Relates the question of capital punishment to New Testament materials.

Yoder, John H. "The Moral Order and the Death Penalty." Part 2. *CanMenn* 7 (Oct. 2, 1959), 2. Relates the question of capital punishment to Old Testament materials.

Yoder, John H. *The Original Revolution.* Scottdale: Herald Press, 1971. Pp. 129. Excerpts printed in *Post-American* 2 (Sept.-Oct., 1973), 4-5, 14. Excerpts from the book center on the Christian community witnessing without violence to the kingdom of God.

Yoder, John H. *The Politics of Jesus.* Grand Rapids: Wm. B. Eerdmans Publ. Co., 1972. Pp. 260. Yoder shows that Jesus and his proclamation of the Kingdom of God are normative for present social and political ethics. Focuses the discussion especially on pacifism as normative for Christians. Represents a scholarly landmark in the interconnections between biblical studies and theological-ethical methodological reflection.

Yoder, John H. "The Way of the Peacemaker." *Peacemakers in a Broken World.* Ed. John A. Lapp. Scottdale: Herald Press, 1969, 111-25. Outlines major criteria of the "just war" theory, contrasts it with Jesus' example of loving enemies. Argues that Jesus' authority and humanity are to be taken at full value, so that he is the peacemaking example for Christians.

Yoder, John H. "What Do Ye More Than They?" *GH* 66 (Jan. 23, 1973), 72-75. Yoder maintains that the beatitudes, including reconciliation and peacemaking, are not moral demands. They are rather the good news, signs of the wholeness of the kingdom.

Yoder, Perry B. *Shalom: The Bible's Word for Salvation, Justice and Peace.* Newton, KS: Faith and Life Press, 1987. Pp. 174. A thorough study of the biblical meaning of peace (OT and NT), justice, and salvation. God's purpose in establishing justice is to transform situations of oppression into freedom and liberation for the oppressed. Shalom requires justice. Atonement and law are God's design to achieve and maintain justice and shalom. Biblical justice, salvation, and shalom transform social and systemic structures as well as people personally. Reconciliation means *shalom* relationships between humans as well as between humans and God. Yoder contrasts economics of shalom to wealth economics. Since God desires the state to defend the poor, shalom makers must be involved to change "the politics of oppression into the politics of liberation and shalom" (115). Jesus' messianic mission was to establish justice and shalom through love. The church is called to continue Jesus' messianic mission of bringing salvation and shalom to the oppressed.

Yoder, Perry B. "What the Bible Teaches About Peace." *With* 11 (Oct., 1978), 14. A Bible study that shows that the Bible has more to say about peace than speaking against war.

Yoder, Rebecca. "From 'Herem' to 'Anathema': The Participation of God's People in His Judgment." Paper presented to War and Peace in the Bible class, AMBS, Elkhart, Ind., Interterm, 1980. Pp. 19. AMBS. Published as "Old Testament Cherem and New Testament Sentences of Holy Law" in *Occasional Papers* No. 1. Elkhart: IMS, 1981. Shows continuity between the testaments in God's effort to keep the covenant people from evil.

Zehr, Daniel. "Discipleship Includes Peacemaking." *Menn* 92 (July 12, 1977), 433-34; *EV* 90 (Aug. 25, 1977), 10; "Discipleship Includes Peacemaking: Example from the Biblical Record." *MennRep* 7 (Aug. 8, 1977), 5. Jesus' life shows peacemaking to be a daily commitment. Jesus' death and resurrection provide the strategy for the new kingdom, nonviolent peacemaking under Christ's kingship.

Zehr, Daniel. "Inter-Mennonite Peace Retreat Conducted by MCC (Ontario)." *CanMenn* 13 (Sept. 28, 1965), 1, 2, 14. A synopsis of messages and talks on the teaching of peace as portrayed in the Bible and through Christ with an application to the current situation. Edgar Metzler and Frank C. Peters were the main speakers.

Zimmerman, Mrs. Nathan. "War Opposite to Christianity." *GH* 32 (Jan. 18, 1940), 906-907. A biblical study which concludes that although the Old Testament people were under a different dispensation, the New Testament points us in the direction opposite to war.

Zook, J. K. *War. Its Evils and Its Blessings: The Parable of the Tares.* N.p., [1895]. Pp. 30. MHL. Protests that war is not criminal but the tool of God's judgment; while saints living under the new covenant seek no vengeance, those same saints should be content to allow the "ordained powers" to execute God's justice. In this age, after all, the wheat and the tares coexist.

# 5
# Church and State

"A Statement by the Board for Missions on the Rhodesian Situation." *EV* 89 (July 10, 1976), 6-7. Because the position of nonparticipation in political processes is becoming problematic, the Board for Missions of the Brethren in Christ Church has drawn up a statement outlining their response to the situation and sent it to the Bishop of the Rhodesian Brethren in Christ church.

"A Statement of the Position of the General Conference of the Mennonite Church of North America on Peace, War, Military Service, and Patriotism." *Menn* 56 (Sept. 9, 1941), 7-8. The statement approved at the 1941 meeting. "We believe that war is altogether contrary to the teaching and spirit of Christ and the gospel . . . ."

"Amish Win Landmark Court Liberty Decision." *CanMenn* 19 (Jan. 29, 1971), 1, 2. An account of the struggle between the courts and those believing in religious freedom, both the Amish and those supporting their convictions.

"Applied Nonresistance." Papers read at the Mennonite Conference on Applied Nonresistance, Goshen, Indiana, Apr., 1939. Reprinted from *MQR* 13 (Apr., 1939), 75-154. MHL. Published by Peace Problems Committee, Mennonite General Conference, Scottdale, 1939. Includes Erb, Paul, "Nonresistance and Litigation," 75-82; Bender, H. S., "Church and State in Mennonite History," 83-103; Yoder, Edward, "The Obligation of the Christian to the State—'Render to Caesar,' " 104-122; Gingerich, Melvin, "The Menace of Propaganda and How to Meet It," 123-34; Hershberger, Guy F. "Nonresistance and Industrial Conflict," 135-54.

Abrams, Ray H. *Preachers Present Arms.* Scottdale: Herald Press, 1969. Pp. 330. A revised edition of the 1933 volume documenting the active role of clergy in promoting war, with two additional chapters on World War II and later developments, including the Vietnam War.

Adrian, Victor (Review). *War and the Gospel,* by Jean Lasserre. Christian Press, 1962. Pp. 243.

"Moral Standards of Church and State," *MBH* 2 (June 21, 1963), 20. Adrian questions Lasserre's central thesis that "God has established a moral standard for the state, which is not contradictory to that prescribed for the believer."

Alexander, John F. "A Politics of Love." *MBH* 11 (Oct. 20, 1972), 4-6. Contends that the "most important contribution of Christianity to an understanding of politics is its teaching on rebirth."

Anderson, John B. and Penner, Archie. "Get Active Politically: Two Views." *Christianity Today* 20 (March 26, 1976), 10-12. Anderson urges evangelical Christians to become politically involved with the issues of economic injustice while Penner insists that any such involvement must find expression within the limits imposed by the concept of agape love exemplified by Christ.

Augsburger, Myron S. "Christian Pacifism." *War: Four Christian Views,* ed. Robert G. Clouse. Downers Grove, Ill.: InterVarsity Press, 1981, 81-97. Pp. 210. Outlines the evangelical premises and perspectives leading to the conclusion that, while Christians may participate in government as long as they do not create a state church, they may not participate in war. The book is composed of articulations of four positions on war: nonresistance, Christian pacifism, the just war, and the crusade or preventive war. Then each of the presenters comments on the other three discussions. So, in addition to Augsburger's essay on Christian pacifism, he responds from that point of view to the other three views: to nonresistance, 58-63; to just war, 141-45; to the crusade, 175-80.

Augsburger, Myron S. "Facing the Problem." In *Perfect Love and War: A Dialogue on Christian Holiness and the Issues of War and Peace,* 11-20. Ed. Paul Hostetler. Nappanee, IN: Evangel Press, 1974. Outlines five basic points of a New Testament approach to the problem of peace and relates these issues to the underlying consideration, the church and state relationship.

Augsburger, Myron S. *Pilgrim Aflame.* Scottdale: Herald Press, 1967. Pp. 288. Novel portraying the life of Michael Sattler, early Anabaptist leader and probably drafter of the Schleitheim Confession. Discussions of the sword, the oath, and the church and state relationship are developed in the contexts, characters, relationships of the 16th century martyrs of the Radical Reformation.

Augsburger, Myron S. "The Basis of Christian Opposition to War." *GH* 63, Part 1, (Nov. 17, 1970), 960-71; Part 2, (Nov. 24, 1970), 990-91; also in *EV* 84 (Sept. 25, 1971), 4. Christians oppose war on the basis of Christ's revelatory commands. The Christian's loyalty is not to the state but to the Kingdom of Christ, in which Christians arm themselves only with love.

Bainton, Roland H. "The Church of the Restoration." *MennLife* 8 (July, 1953), 136-43. Lecture on the origins of Anabaptism deals with the issues of infant baptism and separation of church and state.

Barrett, Lois. "Disconnecting the CIA Connection." *MBH* 15 (Jan. 9, 1976), 14-15. Relates the issue of foreign missionaries acting as informants for the CIA to the issue of separation of church and state.

Barrett, Lois [Janzen]. "Mennonites and Participation in Politics." *Menn* 87 (Nov. 7, 1972), 648, 649; *MennRep* 2 (Nov. 13, 1972), 3. Results of a church member profile show that Mennonites have changed in their views about government and their participation in it.

Barrett, Lois [Janzen]. "Mennonites Divided on Political Activism." *MBH* 12 (Sept. 21, 1973), 13-14. Preliminary results from the Church Member Profile, a wide-ranging survey of Mennonites, indicates that they still do not have unanimity on the subject of government and Christian involvement.

Barrett, Lois. "Separation from an Ambiguous World." *Menn* 91 (June 22, 1976), 428. Christian separation from the world means neither isolation nor setting up a Christian government. Giving first loyalty to God means holding a value system that critiques political structures.

Barrett, Lois. "Varieties of Christian Pacifism." *Menn* 91 (Sept. 7, 1976), 518. Interpretive report on the Fellowship of Reconciliation conference, where pacifists gathered to discuss nuclear arms, Christian participation in the political system.

Bartel, Lawrence. Letter to the Editor. *Menn* 88

(April 3, 1973), 231. Defends Richard Nixon and Billy Graham against attacks from "partisan political criticisms" by stating that Nixon is keeping his pledge to seek an honorable peace in Vietnam, and that previously hostile nations are now friendly to the US.

Bauer, Evelyn. "Breaking Bottlenecks Around the World." *YCC* 44 (Nov. 24, 1963), 5. The story of Andrew W. Cordier, who for sixteen years was the executive assistant to the Secretary-General of the United Nations. Member of Church of the Brethren.

Bauer, Evelyn. "He Focuses on People—Not Politicians." *YCC* 44 (Dec. 15, 1963), 11. The story of Mark Hatfield, governer of Oregon.

Bauman, Clarence. "An Introduction to Theological Discussion on Christian Participation in War and Related Concerns." Paper presented to Puidoux Theological Conference: The Lordship of Christ over Church and State, n.d. Pp. 9. AMBS.

Bauman, Clarence. *Christian Discipleship.* Newton: Faith and Life Press, n.d., pp. 16. "Christian discipleship . . . is ultimate commitment to incorporate kingdom ethics into kingdom theology in a way often implying that one cannot be in the church and in the world in the same way and at the same time."

Bauman, Clarence. "Recovering the Anabaptist Movement." Paper, n.d. Pp. 17. AMBS.

Bauman, Harvey W. "Our New Relationship to the Government." *GH* 37 (Sept. 8, 1944), 452-53. The experience of salvation means that the Christian becomes subject to all the higher powers, not only those that please him or her. If one cannot submit to a certain ordinance of government, one must submit to the penalty for failure to obey it.

Bauman, John. "Peace is Our Responsibility." *Menn* 66 (July 17, 1951), 447, 449. The winning oration on peace in a contest at Bluffton College states that "procuring peace" is the job of those who understand and live the biblical faith through witness, service, education, and clear obedience to God rather than the state.

Beachy, Alvin J. *The Concept of Grace in the Radical Reformation.* Nieuwkoop: De Graaf, 1977. Pp. 238. In this theological study of the Anabaptist movement, the chapter entitled "Anabaptist or Radical Ethics and the Works of Grace," 153-72, outlines the major points of the Anabaptist ethic: discipleship in conformity with the example of Christ is only possible through the power of the Holy Spirit; while the state has a legitimate place and function, it is limited by the example of Christ which precludes violence; oath-taking is one area in which

Christians must disobey the state, according to the example of Christ; military duty is another area demanding disobedience to the state.

Beachy, Alvin J. (Review). *The Politics of Jesus,* by John Howard Yoder. Grand Rapids: Wm. B. Eerdmans, 1972. Pp. 176. *Menn* 88 (Oct. 9, 1973), 580-82. Focuses the central theme of Yoder's book as Jesus' normativeness for political ethics and his rejection of violent revolution as bringing the kingdom of God.

Beachy, Moses. "Romans 13:1-7." Research "capsule" for War, Peace, and Revolution class, AMBS, Elkhart, Ind., Apr. 10, 1969. Pp. 4. AMBS.

Beachy, Rosemary. "The Mennonites and the State." *MHB* 9 (Oct., 1948), 4. Focuses on separation of church and state as it has been expressed in Mennonite refusal to swear oaths and perform military duty. Reviews US government policies regarding such scruples from 1689 through the Civil War.

Becker, Henry. "Don't Take Nonresistance Too Far!" *CanMenn* 14 (Jan. 4, 1966), 15. Letter to the Editor denouncing *CanMenn* for its criticism of Canadian and US governments.

Beechy, Atlee. "The Unfinished Peace Task in Indochina." *Menn* 89 (May 28, 1974), 360. m In spite of the ceasefire, the US continues to be involved in the Vietnamese conflict in the form of military advisers, equipment, and money. Beechy gives seven suggestions for speaking out against continued US support of the war effort.

Beechy, Atlee. "What Will Happen to the Church When the Troops Leave?" *Christian Herald* 92 (Nov., 1969), 16-18, 23-25. Examines consequences of church and state identification for the missionary-supported church in Vietnam as the US military withdraws.

Beidler, Luke. "Vietnam Missionaries State Position on War." *GH* 60 (Dec. 19, 1967), 1136. A statement prepared by missionaries in Vietnam and addressed to their Vietnamese friends: "We are not here as representatives of any government or government agency . . . . We affirm that the church of Jesus Christ is universal and should not be identified with any particular people or political system."

Bender, Bertha Burkholder. "Youth, Church, and State." *YCC* 12, Part 1, (Jan. 4, 1931), 420-21; Part 2, (Jan. 11, 1931), 426-27; Part 3, (Jan. 18, 1931), 434-35; Part 4, (Jan. 25, 1931), 444-45; Part 5, (Feb. 1, 1931), 450, 451, 453; Part 6, (Feb. 8, 1931), 461-62; Part 7, (Feb. 15, 1931), 466-67; Part 8, (Feb. 22, 1931), 479-80; Part 9, (Mar. 1, 1931), 487, 488; Part 10, (Mar. 8, 1931), 491, 493; Part 11, (Mar. 15, 1931), 498, 499; Part 12, (Mar. 22, 1931), 505, 506; Part 13, (Mar. 29,

1931), 515, 517; Part 14, (Apr. 5, 1931), 523, 525; Part 15, (Apr. 12, 1931), 534, 535; Part 16, (Apr. 19, 1931), 539, 541; Part 17, (Apr. 26, 1931), 545-47; Part 18, (May 3, 1931), 559, 560; Part 19, (May 17, 1931), 571, 573; Part 20, (May 31, 1931), 589; Part 21, (June 7, 1931), 595; Part 22, (June 21, 1931), 610; Part 23, (July 5, 1931), 627, 629; Part 24, (July 19, 1931), 645, 646; Part 25, (July 26, 1931), 650, 651; Part 26, (Aug. 2, 1931), 657-59; Part 27, (Aug. 16, 1931), 675-77. Written in a narrative style, the progression of peace-related topics include: the biblical story, the history of the church, issues about responding to government and militarism, e.g., CO status during Civil War and World War I, and Mennonite relief work.

Bender, Dale. "Relating to Authority—An Anabaptist-Existentialist Alternative." *Forum* (Jan., 1974), 14-15. Anabaptists rebelled against both civil and religious authorities, arguing that religious experience could not be separated from life.

Bender, Harold S. "A Historical Review of the Anabaptist-Mennonite Position and Practice from 1525 to the Present." Paper presented at the MCC Peace Section Study Conference, Chicago, 1958. Pp. 11. MHL, BfC.

Bender, Harold S. "Anabaptist Testimonies on Religious Liberty." *Liberty* 51 (1st quarter, 1956), 10-12. Part 2 of "The Anabaptists and Religious Liberty in the 16th Century," originally published in *Archiv fu*[1]*r* Reformationsgeschichte 44 (1953), 32-50; reprinted in *MQR* 29 (Apr., 1955), 83-100. See either of latter sources for annotation.

Bender, Harold S. "Church and State in Mennonite History." *MQR* 13 (Apr., 1939), 83-103. An historical survey of the relationship of the Mennonite church to the state which focuses on the questions of the Christian's participation in political life and his or her obedience to the state.

Bender, Harold S. "Our Duties and Privileges as Loyal Christian Citizens." *GH* 34 (Jan. 15, 1942), 893, 900; *Menn* 57 (Jan. 27, 1942), 1. Eight guidelines for Mennonite action in wartime which speak to issues of participation in the war effort.

Bender, Harold S. "The Anabaptists and Religious Liberty in the 16th Century." *Archiv fu*[1]*r* Reformationsgeschichte 44 (1953), 32-50. Examines writings from 16th-century Anabaptists advocating religious liberty and concludes their views were grounded in commitments to voluntary church membership and the way of love and suffering instead of force and coercion. [Published as booklet in Facet Book Historical Series, No. 16. Ed. Charles

S. Anderson. Philadelphia: Fortress Press, 1970. Pp. 27.]

Berg, Ford. "The Christian's Obligation to the Government; Based upon Romans 13:1-7." *GH Supplement* 40 (Oct., 1947), 654-56. An analysis of this passage on "subjection to the higher powers" concludes that the obligation to be subject does not mean obedience to every command of government.

Berg, Ford. "The Church, the State, Mennonites, and Mennonite History." *GH* 41 (Feb. 17, 1948), 155. Mennonites have contributed greatly to the theory of the separation of church and state.

Berg, Ford. "The Use of Flags in Worship." *GH* 41 (Mar. 16, 19480, 251, 250. Both our understanding of the Christian's relationship to the state and our concern for simplicity in worship lead to the avoidance of flag displays in places of worship.

Berg, Ford (Review). *The Politics of Repentance*, by André Trocmé. Fellowship Publications, 1953. Pp. 111. "The Fourth Point to the Trinity." *GH* 47 (Jan. 19, 1954), 57. Recommends Trocmé's analysis of the Christian's relationship to government.

Beyler, Betsy. "Candidates for President: a Comparison." *Forum* 10 (Oct., 1976), 2-5; *MCC PS Wash. Memo* 7 (July-Aug., 1976), 1-7. A comparative analysis of Gerald Ford and Jimmy Carter focusing on their stand on some of the crucial issues: military spending, amnesty, foreign arms sales, nuclear disarmament, nuclear power, and foreign policy.

*Bicentennial Studies for the Church.* Akron, Pa.: Congregational Peace Education Program, 1976. Pp. 31. MHL. Study guide with the option of four or thirteen sessions on such themes as church and state relations, civil religion and evangelism.

Bieber, Doreen. "Nationalism vs. the Kingdom of God." *GH* 71 (Jan. 24, 1978), 68-69. Speech, which won second place in the C. Henry Smith Peace Oratorical Contest, suggests that nation-worship leads to war, and war is sin. Also in MHL.

Birky, Merritt. "Allegiance and Where Will the Line Be Drawn?" *GH* 61 (Sept. 3, 1968), 790-91. Asks where a Christian draws the line in refusing to support government policies, citing the large amount of defense spending and militaristically dictated foreign policies.

Birmingham, Egla. "Una Declaracion de Fe y Obligacion Cristiana." Pp. 3. BfC.

Blancke, Fritz. "Anabaptism and the Reformation." *The Recovery of the Anabaptist Vision.* Ed. Guy F. Hershberger. Scottdale: Herald Press, 1957, 57-68. Describes the rise of Anabaptism, showing that it grew out of dissent from Zwingli's reform. Elaborates on the Anabaptist view of "free church," i.e., both the relationship of church and state and the concept of voluntary church membership.

Boll, Noah S. "The Christian's Duty Toward the Election and Our Country in General." *GH* 30 (Dec. 30, 1937), 843, 846. The Christian's prayer is more powerful than his or her vote.

Born, Daniel. "Obeying God Over Caesar." *ChrLead* 43 (Nov. 4, 1980), 12. Encourages readers to consider nonregistration for the draft as a valid Christian response by relating it to other historical circumstances where Christian commitment called for civil disobedience.

Born, Daniel (Review). *Twilight of the Saints: Biblical Christianity and Civil Religion in America,* by Robert D. Linder and Richard V. Pierard. Downers Grove, IL: Inter Varsity, 1978. In *ChrLead* 41 (Aug. 15, 1978), 17. Examines the spectrum of attitudes on Christianity vis-a-vis patriotism steeped in religious rhetoric.

Brandt, Diana (Review). *No King But Caesar? A Catholic Lawyer Looks at Christian Violence,* by William R. Durland. Scottdale: Herald Press, 1975. Pp. 182. Also, *A People of Two Kingdoms: The Political Acculturation of the Kansas Mennonites,* by James C. Juhnke. Newton: Faith and Life Press, 1975. Pp. 215. *Menn* 90 (Oct. 28, 1975), 611-12. Durland, a Catholic lawyer, makes a strong plea for Christian nonviolence, based on Jesus' demand to love neighbors and enemies. Juhnke's study demonstrates that Mennonite nonresistance and apoliticism has persisted to the present, in spite of thorough political acculturation.

Brown, Dale W. "The Free Church of the Future." *Kingdom, Cross, and Community,* ed. John R. Burkholder and Calvin Redekop. Scottdale: Herald Press, 1976, 259-72. Brown suggests guidelines for the free church of the future, including placing more emphasis on faithfulness to Christ's nonresistant way than on pragmatic concerns and greater compassionate, nonviolent involvement in the social order.

Brubacher, Dwight. "Mennonite Nonresistance in Ontario, World War I: The Persecution of a Separate People." Paper presented to Social Science Seminar, Goshen College, Goshen, Ind., May 13, 1976. Pp. 23. MHL.

Brunk, Conrad G. "Reflections on the Anabaptist View of Law and Morality." *CGR* 1 (Spring, 1983), 1-20. Law is never amoral; only within the church can law really reflect Christian justice and Christian love. While the church's ethic cannot truly be put into effect in the state, the ethic should, nevertheless, guide the law of the state because Christians live in both kingdoms and both are orders of law and morality.

Brunk, Conrad G. (Review). *The Rule of the Sword,* by Charlie Lord, and *The Rule of the Lamb,* by Larry Kehler. Both published by Newton: Faith and Life Press, 1978. Pp. 68 each. *MennRep* 23 (Nov. 13, 1978), 10. Study guides on militarism and taxes go beyond the Bible to study current events, history, and politics, in order to arrive at a more complete ethical response.

Brunk, George R., I. "Peace Witness." *ST* 3 (Apr., 1931), 5. Churches that want peace must strangle the demon-child, modernism. The church must leave to Caesar what belongs to Caesar and expend energies to keep the church separate from the world and, if possible, secure exemptions for religious nonresistants, a religious freedom which the constitution guarantees.

Brunk, George R., II. "The Flag Salute Problem." *ST* 12 (Mar., 1944), 123. Examines the position of the church, Supreme Court, and the War Department on the issue of saluting the flag.

Buhr, Martin. "Problems of Peace and War in Taiwan." *CanMenn* 11 (May 24, 1963), 7. An analysis of the tensions existing in Free China, where religious freedom does not extend to pacifists.

Burkhalter, Sheldon. "The Christian and Politics: A Proposal." *GH* 69 (Oct. 26, 1976), 818-19. Supports Christian participation in the voting process because of the Christian calling to witness to society. Presents criteria for judging among political candidates.

Burkholder, J. Lawrence. "An Examination of the Mennonite Doctrine of Nonconformity to the World." ThM thesis, Princeton Theological Seminary, 1951. Pp. 221. MHL. Thesis discusses the distinctive Mennonite doctrine and practice of nonconformity to the world in the life of the Swiss Brethren of the Reformation period, the Hutterites and Amish, the Mennonite Church in America. A fourth major section deals with the doctrine and practice of nonresistance as the most essential aspect of nonconformity. Included in this section are such topics as the biblical basis of nonresistance, Mennonite nonresistance in the Revolutionary War, Civil War, World War I and World War II, a comparison of nonresistance with modern religious pacifism, nonresistance and industrial conflict. Concludes that the doctrine of nonconformity has hindered Mennonites from accepting social responsibility and produced a

sectarianism which can only be judged theologically, on the basis of whether God has designed the church to lose itself in the world by accepting responsibility for the world.

Burkholder, J. Lawrence. "The Problem of Social Responsibility from the Perspective of the Mennonite Church." ThD dissertation, Princeton Theological Seminary, 1958. Pp. 369. MHL. Examines, from a sociology of religion perspective, the acute challenge which the ecumenical doctrine of the responsible society poses for Mennonites caught between a tradition of nonresistant noninvolvement and the pressures of modern culture. After outlining what is meant by social responsibility and why responsibility ethics underscore the fundamental conflict between the absolutism of the way of the cross and the relativities of the social order, the author reviews the relevant theological and ethical themes found in the early Anabaptist formulation of Christianity as discipleship. In subsequent chapters, attention is given to Anabaptism as dissent from the corpus christianum, to the types of social structures promoted by Mennonites historically, and to a summary of Mennonite social outreach. In the final chapters, the author lists the sociological, ethical, and theological factors which the Mennonite Church should consider in constructing an adequate social policy. Concludes that Mennonites must come to understand the inevitability of power in the ethical demand for justice, to recognize the inadequacy of nonresistance as a norm and to include nonviolent resistance in the Mennonite ethic.

Burkholder, J. Lawrence. "The Relation of Agape, the Essential Christian Ethic to Social Structure and Political Action." Term paper, n.d. Pp. 13. MHL.

*

Burkholder, J. Richard. "Forms of Christian Witness to the State: A Mennonite Perspective." Convocation address given at Goshen College, Goshen, Ind., Mar. 12, 1976. Pp. 7. MHL.

Burkholder, J. Richard. "On Patriotism, Piety, and Peace." *GH* 72 (Aug. 28, 1979), 684-85. The writer reflects on recent experiences including a peace convocation where Pres. Carter was present and a workshop on arms control, calling for a new mood of spiritual and moral conviction.

Burkholder, J. Richard and Bender, John. *Children of Peace.* Elgin: The Brethren Press; Nappanee: Evangel Press; Newton: Faith and Life Press; Scottdale: Mennonite Publishing House, 1982. Pp. 160. Theme of book is that peace is a way as well as a goal. The first unit explores the biblical meanings of peace in both their Old Testament and New Testament contexts. The

---

*For additional listing, see Supplement, pp. 717-719.

second unit deals with the practice of peace in various areas of life, such as home, community, politics, and the military. The third unit explores the church and state relationship and includes accounts of the ways some people are effectively and creatively witnessing to peace in militaristic and totalitarian countries.

Burkholder, J. Richard and Redekop, Calvin. *Kingdom, Cross, and Community: Essays on Mennonite Themes in Honor of Guy F. Hershberger.* Scottdale: Herald Press, 1976. Pp. 323. Schlabach, T. F., "To Focus a Mennonite Vision; Gross, L., "History and Community in the Thought of Guy F. Hershberger;" Kreider, R. S., "Discussing the Times;" Lind, Millard C., "Reflections on Biblical Hermeneutics;" Kraus, C. N., "Toward a Theology for the Disciple Community;" Bauman, H. E., "Forms of Covenant Community;" Burkholder, J. L., "Nonresistance, Nonviolent Resistance, and Power;" Burkholder, J. Richard., "A Perspective on Mennonite Ethics;" Juhnke, J. C., "Mennonites in Militarist America;" Redekop, J. H., "The State and the Free Church;" Lapp, J. A., "Civil Religion Is But Old Establishment Writ Large;" LaRocque, E., "The Ethnic Church and the Minority," Smucker, D. E., "Gelassenheit, Entrepeneurs, and Remnants;" Peachey, P., "The Peace Churches as Ecumenical Witness;" Brown, D. W., "The Free Church of the Future;" Hershberger, Guy F., "Our Citizenship Is in Heaven."

Burkholder, Oscar. "The Doctrine of Separation in Relation to the State." *ST* 19 (2nd Qtr., 1951), 24. The believer's attitude to the state should be one of intelligence, sympathy, concern, support, prayer, and obedience.

Burkholder, Oscar. "The Relation of the Ministry to the State." *ST* 13 (May, 1945), 366. Based on Paul's letters to Timothy, the Christian should attend strictly to his own business as an ambassador for Christ, and not limit or hinder his ministry by the doubtful affiliation with the government.

Buttrick, George A. "American Protestantism and European War." *Menn* 54 (Oct. 3, 1939), 4-5. A radio address given one week after the outbreak of World War II explains the duty of American Protestant churches in the face of war.

Byler, Dionisio. "Freedom in Christ." *GH* 69 (June 15, 1976), 496-97. Urges American Mennonites to be thankful for their freedom in Christ, not for the political freedoms of a country won through military means.

Byler, Frank. "A History of the Nonresistant People of Logan and Champaign Counties, 1917-1918." Paper presented to Social Science Seminar, Goshen College, Goshen, Ind., n.d. Pp. 32. MHL.

"Canadians Claim US Imperialism." *CanMenn* 18 (Mar. 13, 1970), 3. Fifty-three American and Canadian Mennonites join to conduct a Christian Citizenship Seminar in New York City. Focusing on each nation's problems (imperialism, poverty, native American policies, external affairs, bureaucracy), an attempt is made to pinpoint the Christian's responsibility as the member of a nation and of the world community.

"Change Hearts on War." *GH* 65 (Sept. 26, 1972), 787. Maintaining that Americans have moved away from the gospel on the question of peace, a Roman Catholic bishop seeks to awaken the people to what is really happening under the guise of patriotism.

"Christianity and Politics: A Convention in California." *CanMenn* 15 (Feb.21, 1967), 1, 11. Evaluates strengths and weaknesses of a NAE convention on peace and politics.

"Christians Belong in Politics, Says Speaker." *ChrLead* 33 (June 16, 1970), 12. An evangelical Christian sees the need for Christians in politics because political issues have moral or spiritual dimensions and Christians "need to show support of the decision-making process by becoming involved."

"Christians to be Lambs, Not Hawks or Doves." *CanMenn* 14 (Dec. 13, 1966), 1, 8, 9. Report on an inter-Mennonite consultation in Minneapolis Dec. 2-4 called by MCC Peace Section to discuss the nature of the Mennonite witness to government.

"Church and Society Conference." Paper, reports, minutes, etc., of General Conference Mennonite Church conference, Chicago, Ill., Oct. 31-Nov. 3, 1961. Two volumes. MHL. Some pertinent commission papers include: "The Christian Church and Civil Defense;" "Christian Labor and Management Relations;" "The Christian in Race Relations;" "The Christian Church and the State;" "The Church, the State, and the Offender."

"Communism and Anti-communism." *Menn* 77 (June 5, 1962), 370-71. The statement of the General Conference Mennonite Church contends that our gospel of love, in word and deed, is for all people. Communism can only be overcome by peaceful witness to Christian truth, not by force and violence.

"Conference on Nonresistance and Political Responsibility." Papers presented and discussion summaries, Laurelville, PA, Sept. 21-22, 1956. Pp. 54. MHL.

Carper, Ruth. "A Study of Church and State in the United States of America." Paper presented to Church History class, Goshen College, Goshen, Ind., 1946. Pp. 44. MHL.

Carruthers, Andy. Letter to the Editor. *MennRep* 8 (Feb. 6, 1978), 6. Calls Mennonites to political involvement, to leaven government with values of peace and respect for human life.

Charles, Howard H. "The World: What Is It?" *Builder* 18 (May, 1968), 18-19. Concise summary of the New Testament meanings attached to the concept of "world." Included are the world as cosmic, as related to human existence, as related to fallen humanity, and also ways in which the term is used temporally and qualitatively.

Christenson, Reo M. "The Church and Public Policy." *GH* 66 (Apr. 3, 1973), 285-88. Reprinted from *Christianity Today.* While the church should condemn social evils, such as war, which are incompatible with the spirit of Jesus, a Christian's primary contribution lies in interpersonal relations, because government and public policy are severely limited in their ability to effect social change.

Classen, Jack G. "When Christmas Came." *RepConsS* 7 (Dec., 1949), 2. The dialectic between church and state is concretized in two anecdotes concerning Russian Mennonite children's efforts to honor Christmas in spite of pressure from peers and teachers.

Companion Forum. "How Can the Christian Best Witness to the State?" *YCC* 43 (Jan. 28, 1962), 8. Several responses to this question by Christian youth.

Conservative Mennonite Conference. "The Church and Civil Government." *GfT* 12 (July-Aug., 1977), 16-17. Position statement on church and state relationships includes statements on war, civil disobedience, payment of war taxes.

Cooper, Clay. "The Church Is Found 'Meddling'." *ST* 34 (3rd Qtr., 1966), 34. The present need is for the church to bow to divine authority, avoid entanglement in worldly disputation like the current socio-political war of words and deeds, and vigorously prosecute her uniquely spiritual mission in the world.

Cornies, Paul. "Canadian Protestantism and Its Conceived Role Within the National Life of Canada, 1900-1914." Essay for History 691 course, Jan. 17, 1975. Pp. 55. CGCL.

Cosens, John. "Issues of Church and State: Selective Tax Evasion: The War Tax." Term paper, Apr. 7, 1981. Box 12-A-5. CMBS/Win.

Cressman, Dave and Anita. "Especially Question the Rhetoric." *Forum* (Mar., 1971), A-4. North American judments about the affairs of other societies need to be questioned, and more particularly, the proposed boycott of Brazil by the Mennonite World Conference in an attempt to affect government policies needs to be re-examined.

Curry, A. Stauffer. "Church and State." *YCC* 35 (Oct. 31, 1954), 350. Examines some of the criticisms of the CPS program as it relates to the separation of church and state.

"Demonstrate Biblical Citizenship." *Menn* 83 (Sept. 10, 1968), 566; "Resolution or *[sic]* Nationalism," *GH* 61 (Nov. 5, 1968), 992-93. The 1968 resolution on nationalism as adopted by the GCMC at the Estes Park conference. A call to Christian internationalism which parallels our contribution to the welfare of the country we live in.

"Dr. H. Bender Speaks to Peace Conference." *CanMenn* 1 (July 3, 1953), 1, 4. J. A. Toews and H. S. Bender address conference sponsored by the Canadian Conference and MB churches. Toews spoke of the purpose of the church as the proclaimation of the salvation of the cross. Bender gave a summary of the history of Mennonite nonresistance and the Christian view of the state.

D. A. S. "The Christian Witness and Conscription." *CPS Bull Supp* 5 (May 16, 1946), 9. Since peacetime conscription would increase militarism and limit freedom of conscience, the church should make its convictions on this issue known to the government.

Decker, Mr. and Mrs. LaVerne. Letter to the Editor. *ChrLead* 39 (Feb. 17, 1976), 12. Christians ought to be the best citizens the United States could have.

DeKoster, Lester. "Anabaptism at 450: A Challenge, A Warning." *ChrToday* 20 (Oct. 24, 1975), 75-78. Commends Anabaptist courage and emphasis on practical consequences of faith, while criticizing consistent pacifism as undermining the state's legitimate use of force to maintain order.

Derstine, C. F. "Conscience as a Bar to Citizenship." *ChrMon* 23 (Aug., 1931), 254. Comment on Supreme Court decision to deny citizenship to two conscientious objectors.

Derstine, C. F. "Fascism—Friend or Foe—Which?" *ChrMon* 25 (Oct., 1933), 318. Hitler's rise to power seems to mean the loss of liberties and perhaps even the advent of war.

Derstine, C. F. "Hitler's Ten Commandments for the German Church." *ChrMon* 26 (Nov., 1934),

351. Deplores the close association of the church and state in Germany.

Derstine, C. F. "Impressions of the Nazi Regime and its Effect on the Churches." *ChrMon* 26 (Jan., 1934), 30-31. Support of U. S. Christians is due the church in Germany for its resistance to the race prejudice and nationalism of the Nazi state church.

Derstine, C. F. "Kidnaping [sic]—The Hauptmann Trial—Capital Punishment." *ChrMon* 27 (Mar., 1935), 94-95. Discusses the attitudes of the church and state toward evildoers.

Derstine, C. F. "Nationalism the Supreme Rival of Christianity." *ChrMon* 30 (Feb., 1938), 61-62. Fascism, Nazism, and communism try to replace devotion to God with loyalty to the state.

Derstine, C. F. "State and Church in Nazi Germany." *ChrMon* 29 (June, 1937), 190. Cites magazine and newspaper articles showing Hitler's attempts to replace Christian faith with state loyalty.

Derstine, C. F. "The Counsel of a Canadian Member of Parliament to Conscientious Objectors of the Future." *ChrMon* 26 (Aug., 1934), 253-54. Former Brethren in Christ minister, now MP, advises Mennonites to retain their non-voting position on politics.

Derstine, C. F. "The Great Controversy Between Christ and Antichrist." *ChrMon* 34 (Oct., 1942), 318-20. Cites examples of Christians refusing to deify the state in seven countries.

Derstine, C. F. "The Image of the Beast—'No King but Caesar." I(CMon 32 (Mar., 1940), 94. Christians in modern times face idolatry in the form of patriotism.

Derstine, C. F. "The State—Absolute, Final, Supreme!" *ChrMon* 30 (Sept., 1938), 290. The great threat of fascism is its claim to total loyalty and obedience.

Derstine, C. F. "The Trail of Blood." *ChrMon* 45 (Oct., 1953), 319. Review of the sufferings of the Anabaptists for their break with the state church.

Derstine, C. F. "Uncle Sam Building a War Machine." *ChrMon* 23 (July, 1931), 221-22. Documents public anti-war sentiment and contrasts it with the recent Supreme Court decision to deny citizenship to two conscientious objectors.

Derstine, C. F. "War! War! War!" *ChrMon* 32 (Dec., 1940), 381. God delegates the use of force to the state, while the church operates by love, so the two must be completely separate for the Christian.

Derstine, C. F. "Why Isms, False Teachings, and Destructive Ideas Flourish." *ChrMon* 33 (Jan., 1941), 30. Not war, but ideas foreign to truth are the real destroyers of human liberty.

Derstine, James L. "Quakers in Pennsylvania Government." Paper for Christian Attitudes to War, Peace, and Revolution class, AMBS, Elkhart, Ind., May 8, 1969. Pp. 3. AMBS.

Detweiler, Richard C. *Mennonite Statements on Peace, 1915-1966: A Historical and Theological Review of Anabaptist-Mennonite Concepts of Peace Witness and Church-State Relations.* Scottdale, Pa.: Herald Press, 1968. Pp. 71. Finds that the Mennonite peace witness has essentially affirmed and restated the historic Anabaptist understandings on these issues while (in the process of relating these concerns to the contemporary situations) intensifying, clarifying, and expanding the early articulations. Includes observations on some of the theological implications of these trends in the recent peace witness.

Dick, Ernie. "Religious Freedom by Default." Term paper for History 499 course, Apr. 1, 1969. Pp. 25. CGCL.

Dirrim, Allen W. "Political Implications of Sixteenth Century Hessian Anabaptism." *MennLife* 19 (Oct., 1964), 179-83. The Anabaptists' striving for a free and separate church and their absolute New Testament ethic, plus real and alleged connections with the Peasants' Revolt in 1525, are reasons why they were not accepted by their contemporaries.

Drescher, John M. "Church, Civil Authorities, and Free Enterprise." *GH* 65 (May 30, 1972), 481. Lutherans and Calvinists in Europe challenge Christians to put the claims of Christ above our political and economic systems.

Drescher, John M. "Disturbing the War." *GH* 62 (Mar. 25, 1969), 269. The church is divided between those who believe it ought to be the conscience of the nation and those who believe it has nothing to say to the government.

Drescher, John M. (Editorial). "Peacemaker Questions." *GH* 61 (July 2, 1968), 585. Interprets "separation of church and state" to mean that the church should be the conscience of society raising questions on issues of military service and payment of war taxes.

Driedger, Leo. "Should Mennonites Hold Office in Government?" Student paper for Great Social Issues, Apr. 30, 1954. Pp. 20. MLA/BeC.

Driedger, Leo; Currie, Raymond; and Linden, Lick.

"Dualistic and Wholistic Views of God and the World." *Review of Religions Research* 24 (March, 1983), 225-44. Findings support the posited correlation between a dualistic view of God and less interest in social action, and a wholistic view of God and more interest in social action.

Driedger, Leo and Zehr, Dan. "The Mennonite State-Church Trauma: Its Effects on Attitudes of Canadian Students and Leaders." *MQR* 48 (Oct., 1974), 515-26. A sociological analysis of Canadian Mennonite attitudes toward the state and social concerns, and the interpretation of the peace stance, compared across generational and denominational lines.

Driediger, Ab Douglas. Letter to the Editor. *MennRep* 9 (Sept. 3, 1979), 6. In response to the third part of John Friesen's series on church-state relations (Aug. 20, 1979), the writer argues that there were many more Mennonite men who accepted full military service in World War II than is commonly believed.

Dueck, Abe. "Church and State: Developments Among Mennonite Brethren in Canada Since World War II." Study paper, Nov. 22, 1980. Box 8-E-1.

Dueck, Abe (Review). *Kingdom, Cross, and Community*, ed. J. R. Burkholder and Calvin Redekop. Scottdale: Herald Press, 1976. Pp. 323. *Direction* 7 (July, 1978), 44-46. This collection of essays is both a fitting tribute to Guy F. Hershberger on his 8th birthday and a laudable attempt to "consciously engage in dialogue with the twentieth century" on such issues as fundamentalism, nonresistance, and church and state relations.

Dueck, Dora. "Mexico Mennonites Return to Canada." *MBH* 14 (Jan. 10, 1975), 22. Mennonites who left Canada to preserve religious and ethnic freedom (including nonparticipation in the military) are returning to Canada for the same reasons.

Dueck, John. "Canadian Mennonites Leave 400-Year Tradition." *MBH* 14 (Nov. 18, 1975), 15-17. Profiles of Mennonites serving as Members of Parliament, with their views on reconciling Mennonite tradition with politics.

Dueck, John. "Forsake 400-Year Tradition; Mennonites Enter Politics by the Dozen." *MennRep* 6 (Jan. 12, 1976), 10-11. Dueck reflects on Mennonite tradition of expressing nonresistance through refusing public office; interviews Canadian Mennonite politicians.

Duerksen, D. D. Letter to the Editor. *MBH* 12 (Sept. 21, 1973), 9. Responding to John Regehr's article (*MBH* [Aug. 24, 1973]) regarding the Christian and politics, the reader suggests seeking positive involvement by speaking to government rather than by striving to become involved in it.

Durland, William R. *No King But Caesar?* Scottdale: Herald Press, 1975. Pp. 182. Catholic lawyer urges Christians to assume the risk of nonviolence through faith and hope. Argument proceeds in three sections: an examination of the pacifist and nonresistant ethic of the biblical materials, especially the Sermon on the Mount and Isaiah; an historical overview of Christian responses to state violence, from the apostolic peace gospel and the pacifism of the early church, through the Constantinian synthesis to the contemporary confusion; an analysis of that contemporary confusion concerning the demands of God and Caesar, particularly in the context of the Roman Catholic church.

Durnbaugh, Donald F., ed. *On Earth Peace: Discussions on War/Peace Issues Between Friends, Mennonites, Brethren, and European Churches, 1935-1975*. Elgin, Ill.: Brethren Press, 1978. Pp. 412. A collection of documents emphasizing the "Puidoux" Conferences held in Europe on the theme of "The Lordship of Christ Over Church and State" and the contributions made by the historic peace churches to the study processes sponsored by the WCC on the issues of peace and justice. Essays focused on or by Mennonites include: "Principles of Christian Peace and Patriotism—Historic Peace Churches," 30-32; "War Is Contrary to the Will of God—HPC and FOR," 46-72; "God Establishes Both Justice and Peace," (Paul Peachey and members of the Continuation Committee, 1955 and 1958), 108-21; "The Theological Basis of the Christian Witness to the State," John H. Yoder, 136-43; "Discipleship as Witness to the Unity in Christ as Seen by the Dissenters," Paul Peachey, 153-60; "On Divine and Human Justice," John H. Yoder, 197-210; "The Sixth Commandment: Its Significance for the Christian as Citizen and for the Statesman," Warren F. Groff, 211-22; "Church and State According to a Free Church Tradition," John H. Yoder, 279-88; "Response to the Cardiff Report by Brethren, Friends, Mennonites," 353-64; "Jesus and Power," John H. Yoder, 365-72; "Epilogue: The Way Ahead," John H. Yoder, 390-93.

Dyck, C. J. "No Politics Lid Put on Brazil Conference." *Menn* 86 (Feb. 23, 1971), 132, 133. Curitiba conversations on locating the Mennonite World Conference show how difficult it is to draw a clear line between religious and social concerns and their political implications.

Dyck, Peter J. "Politics of Small Steps—Will Trust Come?" *Menn* 88 (Aug. 7, 1973), 464-5 Reflects on increased US-Soviet cooperation following Brezhnev's visit to the US, and offers suggestions for "small steps" toward superpowers reconciliation that can be implemented by individuals.

"Evangelicals in Social Action Peace Witness Seminar." Papers presented at EMC, Nov. 30-Dec. 2, 1967. Pp. 71. MSHL. Includes: Hostetter, C. N. Jr., "What Is the Christian Attitude Toward Those Who Are Considered Enemies?"; Hoyt, Herman A., "Is Warfare a Denial of the World-wide Nature of the Church?"; Wenger, J. C., "Pacifism and Biblical Nonresistance;" King, Lauren A., "The Effect of War on Preaching the Gospel;" Wood, James E., Jr., "The Problem of Nationalism in Church-State Relations;" Grounds, Vernon D., "Evangelism and Social Responsibility;" Shenk, Wilbert R., "Christian Responsibility: National and International."

Ebersole, John. "Race, Rhodesia, and the Church." Paper for Church and Race class, AMBS, Elkhart, Ind., May 27, 1971. Pp. 23. AMBS.

Eby, Sarah Ann. "Delegates Explore Peace." *RepConsS* 34 (May, 1977), 1, 6. European and North American Christians meet in W. Germany to discuss how the form of a congregation, which defines the relation between church and state, affects the congregation's peace witness.

Ediger, Elmer. "A Christian's Political Responsibility." *MennLife* 11 (July, 1956), 143-44. More participation in government as well as hesitancy to participate are two movements among those of pacifist persuasion that are gaining influence in Mennonite churches. An analysis of the two views is presented.

Ediger, Elmer. "Conference Held Last March." *IPF Notes* 4 (May, 1958), 1, 3. Summary of the addresses at the annual IPF conference on the topic of the Christian pacifist's responsibility to government.

Ediger, Peter J. "Summer's End." *God and Caesar* 6 (Sept., 1980), 1. Poem outlines choices Mennonites face between serving God and serving a government committed to military might.

Ehlers, Randall. Letter to the Editor. *ChrLead* 36 (Jan. 23, 1973), 17. Support for the military. The liberty and freedom in America are preserved because Americans have fought and died on foreign soil.

Elias, Christine A. Letter to the Editor. *Menn* 94 (Dec. 11, 1979), 750. Believes there are many other issues and principles, aside from the issue of war and peace, which should take priority. We should pray for and support our country rather than going off on a tangent in the name of peace.

Engel, Mrs. Allen. Letter to the Editor. *MBH* 12 (Sept. 21, 1973), 9. Contrary to John Regehr's statement, "Politics not for Christians," God calls some people to be political leaders and they need our prayers and support.

Enns, Mary M. "John Howard Yoder Is Not a Man for Those Who Prefer Complacency." *MennMirror* 9 (Nov., 1979), 12, 13. In a series of symposia at the Univ. of Winnipeg, John Howard Yoder spoke on the subjects of "An Anabaptist View of Political Power," "Mennonite Political Conservatism," and "An Anabaptist View of Liberation Theology."

Enns, Mary M. "Keeping the Faith Alive Behind the Iron Curtain." *MennMirror* 5 (Mar., 1976), 9, 10. A report on the research Walter Sawatsky is doing under MCC in Russia and East European countries with particular attention to the current religious situation.

Epp, Frank H. "A New Nationalism." *CanMenn* 5 (Apr. 5, 1957), 2. Decries the new Canadian nationalism which renounces a world citizenship in favor of a narrower identity based on economics.

Epp, Frank H. "A New Religion: Americanism." *CanMenn* 6 (June 6, 1958), 2. "Americanism makes Christ a political Messiah, and idealizes the American way of life as the Christian way of life." The identity of the church's interest with the development of missiles brings about an adulterous relationship between church and nation.

Epp, Frank H. "Canada's Second Class Citizens." *CanMenn* 4 (Sept. 28, 1956), 2. Indians and Eskimos also were created in the image of God and have a right to first class citizenship. Canadians must repent of their kind of racism.

Epp, Frank H. "Democracy and Christianity." *CanMenn* 2 (Aug. 27, 1954), 2. True Christianity cannot be identified with any political system or ideology. It can only be identified with Christ on the cross.

Epp, Frank H. "How Dare We Call the President." *CanMenn* 14 (Feb. 1, 1966), 5. A portrayal of attitudes to a government which wars and seeks loyalty which is above loyalty to Christ.

Epp, Frank H. "Immorality, Hanging, and H-Bombs." *CanMenn* 5 (June 7, 1957), 2. The church is called to be a prophetic voice and to prick the conscience of the world again and again when it pursues its evil ways. The Spirit is leading the church to an increasing prophetic witness.

Epp, Frank H. Letter to the Editor. *MennRep* 8 (Jan. 23, 1978), 6. Candidate for Canadian federal nomination defends his decision on the basis of

Anabaptist views of church ar..d state and continuity with his own life of conscientious protest and involved activism.

Epp, Frank H. "MCC Group Studies Christian Responsibility to the State." CanMenn 5 (Nov. 22, 1957), 5-6. An indepth report of the study of the questions and implications connected with the pacifist position. The study conference called by MCC Peace Section brought together 59 persons from various Mennonite groups in Canada and the US to work at the difficult questions of the Christian's involvement in politics. Participants included: H. S. Bender, J. Harold Sherk, John Howard Yoder, J. A. Toews, Elmer Neufeld, J. Winfield Fretz, John E. Lapp, and Edgar Metzler.

Epp, Frank H. Mennonites in Canada, 1920-1940: A People's Struggle for Survival, Vol. 2. Toronto: Macmillan of Canada, 1982. Pp. 640. The concluding chapter of this extensive historical survey is entitled "Facing the World" and includes discussion of the issues of war and peace, church and state, Germanism, communism, peace conferences and resolutions.

Epp, Frank H. "National Socialism Among Canadian Mennonites in the 1930s." PCMCP Fifteenth, 123-31. North Newton, Kansas: The Mennonite Press. Held at Bluffton College, Bluffton, Ohio, June 10-11, 1965. The assumption that the Canadian Mennonite community harbored a certain amount of National Socialism in the 1930s is supported by research of all the issues (1930-39) of a weekly newspaper serving Mennonites who immigrated from Russia in the 1920s. Also at AMBS.

Epp, Frank H. "Nothing to Say to the World." CanMenn 4 (Aug. 24, 1956), 2. A critique of the General Conference triennial meeting which had "nothing to say to the world." Mennonites must realize that the world is shrinking and that they must be responsible in the world.

Epp, Frank H. "Participation in Politics." CanMenn 5 (Mar. 15, 1957), 2. Honest discipleship leaves little room for a noninvolvement mentality. If we follow Christ in all areas of our lives the world system will provide the brakes.

Epp, Frank H. "The Christian and National Interest." CanMenn 5 (June 21, 1957), 2. Response is invited to the questions surrounding personal and corporate ethics posed by Dr. Donald Barnhouse in Eternity magazine.

Epp, Frank H. "The Christian Attitude Toward Communism." CanMenn 3 (Jan. 14, 1955), 2. God created all people and wills that all should be saved. Christians, while hating the sins of

communism, are called to love the sinners enslaved by these sins.

Epp, Frank H. "The Church and Canadian Civil Defense." CanMenn 5, Part 1, (Nov. 1, 1957), 2; Part 2, (Nov. 8, 1957), 2; Part 3, (Nov. 15, 1957), 2, 7. Analyzes the civil defense program and Mennonite captivation with it. The church's response to human need does not mean compromising its central doctrine of love.

Epp, Frank H. "The Church and State in America." CanMenn 3 (Oct. 21, 1955), 2. We dare not identify Christianity with the American state any more than with the communist state. The church is to stand before the state as the prophetic voice of God.

Epp, Frank H. "The Conscience of the State." CanMenn 2 (June 4, 1954), 2. The true church of Christ is called upon to exert a Christian influence upon the state today just as Elijah and Daniel voiced the will of God before their leaders.

Epp, Frank H. The Glory and the Shame. Winnipeg: Canadian Mennonite Publishing Association, Inc., 1968. Pp. 79. A reprint of editorials appearing in The Canadian Mennonite in 1967 on the theme "The Past, Present, and Future of the Mennonite Church." N.b. chs. V on "Church and State" and VI on "Communism."

Epp, Frank H. "The Office of Civil Government." CanMenn 3 (June 24, 1955), 2. A reprint of Article XIII, Mennonite Confession of Faith, Dortrecht, April 21, 1632, outlining the purpose of government and the Christian's response to the civil authorities.

Epp, Frank H. "'Wars and Rumors of Wars'." CanMenn 14 (Feb. 8, 1966), 5. One of a series of five letters written by Frank Epp to Henry Becker in response to Becker's denunciation of the CanMenn in the Jan. 4 issue. Epp argues that to justify participation in war because Jesus said there would always be "wars and rumors of wars" is to limit the Lordship of Christ to the church.

Epp, Frank H. "What Your Letter Can Do." CanMenn 3 (Aug. 19, 1955), 2. A call to voice our convictions on societal issues about which we are concerned by writing to the mass media and our elected representatives.

Epp, Frank H. (Editorial). "Participation in Politics." CanMenn 5 (Mar. 15, 1957), 2. Honest discipleship leaves little room for a non-involvement mentality. If we follow Christ, the world will tell us when to stop.

Epp, Frank H. (Editorial). "The Church and State in America." CanMenn 3 (Oct. 21, 1955), 2. While most agree that church and state in communist Russia are "incompatible," fewer recognize the dangers of identifying the church with the state in "blessed America."

Erb, Paul. Letter in "Readers Say" Column. *GH* 59 (Sept. 20, 1966), 849. Comments on an article which advocated the Christian's saying nothing to the state. Does the Lord not have anything to say to the nations that slaughter people? Who will say it if the church does not?

Esau, John A. "The Congressional Debates on the Coming of the Russian Mennonites." Paper presented to the Anabaptist-Mennonite History class, MBS, Elkhart, Ind., June 2, 1961. Pp. 31. AMBS.

Esau, Ken. "The Question of Political Office." Term paper, Mar. 31, 1981. Box 12-A-2. CMBS/Win.

Esau, Mrs. David. Letter to the Editor. *ChrLead* 39 (Jan. 9, 1976), 15. Concerned that this publication has become part of the bandwagon of criticism directed toward the wrongs of the United States.

Estep, William R. "Separation as Sedition: America's Debt to the Anabaptists." *ChrToday* 20 (May 21, 1976), 872-74. Attempts a fair presentation of major Anabaptist tenets, including voluntary church membership, religious liberty, and the corresponding limitation of the state's authority to temporal affairs.

Estes, James M., ed. "Whether Secular Government Has the Right to Wield the Sword in Matters of Faith." *MQR* 49 (Jan., 1975), 22-37. A plea for religious toleration by an anonymous 16th century Lutheran patrician from Nürnberg, calling for neutrality on the part of state authorities toward all religious expressions. Includes historical interpretation by the editor.

Evangelicals for Social Action. "Can My Vote Be Biblical?" *ChrLead* 43 (Oct. 21, 1980), 2-5. Guidelines for making Christ lord of our politics include emphasis on peacemaking and justice for the poor.

Ewert, Norm. Letter to the Editor. *ChrLead* 36 (July 24, 1973), 14. Not only Watergate, but the general philosophy and conduct of the political administration are reasons for concern. The church must continue to respond to the dominant political issue of equitable distribution of goods and services.

"Frank Epp May Have Lost But He's Not Done with Politics." *MennMirror* 9 (Sept., 1979), 7. Epp's effort to gain a Parliament seat, prompted by his concern that Canada find nonviolent ways to solve the unity issue, is an outgrowth of his interest in the Vietnam War and Mideast tensions.

Fast, Donald H. "The Church Versus State." Student paper for Christians and Peace Seminar, May 15, 1964. Pp. 18. MLA/BeC.

Fast, Peter G. "The Russian Mennonites and the State." Paper presented to the Social Science Seminar, Goshen College, Goshen, Ind., May 31, 1949. Pp. 39. MHL.

Fawcett, Joe. Letter to the Editor. *ChrLead* 37 (Apr. 16, 1974), 15. Christians should get involved in US politics.

Fransen, David Warren. "The Jensen Case: A Vital Principle Is at Stake." *MennRep* 6 (Dec. 13, 1976), 7. Discusses reasons Mennonites should not sit by complacently as the Jensens, Jehovah's Witnesses, are denied Canadian citizenship on the basis of conscientious objection to war.

Fransen, Harold. "Cold War Thaw and Mennonite Response." *Menn* 95 (Apr. 1, 1980), 225. Interprets the Soviet invasion of Afghanistan as an attempt to inhibit the rise of a nationalist Islamic state, and calls on Mennonites to take a public peace stance during present cold war politics.

Franz, Delton. "Reflections on Watergate." *ChrLead* 36 (June 26, 1973), 4. Notes some of the good tha may emerge from Watergate.

Franz, Delton. "CIA Reverses Policy on Relation to Missionaries." *ChrLead* 39 (July 20, 1976), 14. Reports on the new regulation issued by the CIA to restrict its agents from initiating contacts with missionaries.

Franz, Delton. "Washington Report: A Watershed in the Corruption of Power." *MennRep* 3 (June 11, 1973), 6-7. Corruption and deceit revealed by the Watergate scandal reminds American Christians that ultimate loyalty must be given to God, not the national leader.

Franz, Delton. "Witness in Washington." *MennLife* 26 (Dec., 1971), 158-59. As Mennonites we continue to minister to the victims of warfare, hunger, and oppression, but now we also need to be concerned with the underlying causes of suffering.

Franz, Delton, ed. "Nixon, McGovern Compared on Key Issues." *MCC PS Wash. Memo* 4 (Sept.-Oct., 1972), 1-4. Comparative analysis of the two presidential candidates on the draft and military spending as well as other social issues.

Franz, Edward W. "Seeking the Mind of Christ in Our Attitude Toward War." *Menn* 51, Part 1, (May 26, 1936), 4-5; Part 2, (June 2, 1936), 2-6.

Our tradition teaches that we must not only be of the mind of Christ in our opposition to war, but that we must apply this principle practically. It is not patriotism but selfishness which leads one into war. When one studies wars it is seen that they are foolish and do not accomplish their goals. Mennonites have numerous opportunities to work with others to bring peace.

Fretz, Clarence Y. "The Separation of the Church from the State." *ST* 36 (May, 1968), 7. God will perform His will in the world through the church rather than through any political or social organization.

Fretz, J. Winfield. "Post-War Problems Facing Mennonites." *Menn* 59 (May 9, 1944), 6-7; *ChrMon* 36 (July, 1944), 200. The post-war world will see great disillusionment and spiritual callousness on the part of the citizenry and increasing totalitarianism on the part of the government. Mennonites must not be complacent in the face of these pressures.

Fretz, J. Winfield. "Should Mennonites Participate in Politics?" *MennLife* 11 (July, 1956), 139, 140. Taking issue with the traditional Mennonite position against political participation, the author contends that because of the fundamental changes that have taken place in society, "many of the original grounds of opposition have been removed."

Frey, Philemon L. "Lessons from the World War: for Conscientious Objectors." *The Eastern Mennonite School Journal* 18 (Apr., 1940), 42-45. Twelve "lessons"—all the way from "In time of war it is best to keep your eyes and ears open and our mouths shut" to "It is best to stay out of politics" to "Nonresistance should be practiced in times of peace as well as in time of war," etc.

Friesen, Dorothy. "The Church in Burma." *Mission-Focus* 7 (Dec., 1979), 61-67. Describes the political, economic, and religious context which the Christian church in Burma is facing. Shows how government action in this country has helped to implement a servanthood theology.

Friesen, Dorothy (Review). *Letters from South Korea.* T. K. Idoc/North America. *Sojourners* 6 (July, 1977, 35. A collection of anonymous letters sparked by a declaration of martial law by Korea's President Park in late 1972.

Friesen, Dorothy and Stoltzfus, Gene. "Christians in China." *The Other Side* 15 (Mar., 1979), 23-24. Report on the health of Christianity in China. Institutionless Christianity in China perhaps more clearly resembles the early church than anything else in the world today.

Friesen, Dorothy and Stoltzfus, Gene. "Philippino Christians Question Graham Crusade." *The Other Side* 13 (Oct., 1977), 78-79. Concludes that the Billy Graham Metro Manila Crusade will be seen as a symbol of the church's collusion with continued American influence and affluence in the Philippines.

Friesen, Dorothy, and Stoltzfus, Gene. "The Church in New China." *EV* 91 (Dec. 10, 1978), 16. In China, there is a determined policy of religious repression, but institutionless Christianity is showing strength; the church that allied itself with power has not been particularly successful.

Friesen, Gerhard. "The Flag in the Church." *Menn* 60 (June 26, 1945), 8. The displaying of national flags in houses of worship betrays the universal and international character of the Gospel. In addition, flag-waving is unnecessary for the genuine patriot, and it indicates that loyalty to country is more important than loyalty to God.

Friesen, Jake. Letter to the Editor. *Intercom* 5 (May-June, 1965), 2-3. Calls attention to inconsistencies in the Mennonite peace witness, such as accepting protection from American military personnel while working in a foreign country.

Friesen, John. "Church-State Relationships: The Development of a Separate People." Part 2. *MennRep* 9 (Aug. 6, 1979), 5. This second article in a 3-part series discusses the development of the church-state relationships of the Anabaptists and their view of "separateness," as they were influenced by the migrations, persecution, and trends in Europe.

Friesen, John. "Church-State Relationships: The Experience in North America." Part 3. *MennRep* 9 (Aug. 20, 1979), 5. A summary of current church-state relations in North America, the factors influencing this relationship, and consideration for the Mennonite church's future relationship to the state.

Friesen, John. "Church-State Relationships: The Experiences of the Anabaptists." Part 1. *MennRep* 9 (July 23, 1979), 5. In this first of a 3-part series the issue of church-state relationships from the viewpoint of 16th-century Anabaptists is discussed.

Friesen, Mrs. Dee. Letter to the Editor. *ChrLead* 41 (Jan. 31, 1978), 16. Pacifism is a very privileged position. There are many members of the military who are just as devout and sincere Christians as the "best" Mennonites.

Friesen, Steven K. "The Rise of Mennonite Social Consciousness, 1899-1905." Paper presented to Seminar in Political and Social History, Bethel College, Newton, Ks., Dec. 9, 1973. Pp. 44. MHL, MLA/BeC.

Froese, Jacob A. and Hofer, Phil. *The Church As Peace Witness: A Resource Manual.* Hillsboro, Ks.: Mennonite Brethren Publishing House, 1975. Pp. 60. MHL. Presents the Mennonite Brethren peace position and suggests ways that position might affect the church in its relations with contemporary society. Topics include biblical foundations, issues of church and state, history of MB peace position, etc.

Funk, Cornelius C. *Escape to Freedom,* trans. and ed. Peter J. Klassen. Hillsboro: Mennonite Brethren Publishing House, 1982. Pp. 124. Personal account of Russian young man who enlists in the medical corps of the Russian army. Describes horrors of war as well as the difficult task of sorting through the chaotic political situation in order to make ethical decisions about one's participation in a changing government.

Funk, John F. "Patriotism and the Mennonites." *Mennonite Historical Bulletin* 40 (Apr., 1979), 5. A letter to the editor of *Bucks County Intelligencer,* April 10, 1865, takes issue with a newspaper article which is written in such a way as to indicate that all Mennonites are very patriotic.

"Government Changes Citizenship Law." *RepConsS* 34 (Mar., 1977), 2. MCC (Canada) influential in eliminating conscientious objection as a barrier to Canadian citizenship.

Gaeddert, Albert M. "An Important Peace Meeting." *Menn* 66 (July 10, 1951), 424. Church agencies affiliated with NSBRO state their concerns to Washington officials and propose a list of the kinds of work they would be willing to do under the new conscription law.

General Conference Mennonite Church. *A Christian Declaration on the Way of Peace.* Newton: Commission on Home Ministries, General Conference Mennonite Church, 1971. Pp. 20. Position statement maintains that peace is grounded in biblical perspectives of love, evangelism, and justice, and it applies to use of resources, views of citizenship and military service, and involvement in social change.

Gerber, Samuel. "Render to Caesar What Is Caesar's and to God What Is God's." Paper for War, Peace, and Revolution class, AMBS, Elkhart, Ind., Apr. 10, 1969. Pp. 3. AMBS.

Gingerich, Melvin. "A Community Leisure Time Program; Christian Youth and the State." *YCC* 25, Part 38, (1944), 339. The theme that continues is that the small Christian community is the foundation of democracy. We need more ideas to help the rural setting be more attractive to its young people.

Gingerich, Melvin. "As We Forgive Our Debtors; Christian Youth and the State." *YCC* 25, Part 32, (Mar. 5, 1944), 74. When the Christian community gives up to the government its responsibility for the physical welfare of its own members, the separation of church and state becomes less clearly marked. Looks at a service of the government in the Federal Reserve Act.

Gingerich, Melvin. "Christian Youth and the State; Christian Youth and the State." *YCC* 24, Part 26, (Jan. 23, 1943), 423. Luther believed that a Christian has two obligations, church and state; they are of equal importance. Nonresistant Christians believe that one should "obey God rather than man."

Gingerich, Melvin. "Citizenship in the Kingdom of God." Sermon, College Mennonite Church, Goshen, Ind., July 1, 1973. Pp. 4. MHL.

Gingerich, Melvin. "Discussing Our Problems; Christian Youth and the State." *YCC* 22, Part 16, (Dec. 7, 1941), 802. The training of our young people in Sunday school clsses, Bible meetings, and other programs should be the kind of experience that will fit them to make a contribution toward solving the complex problems of modern life.

Gingerich, Melvin. "Growing Community Roots; Christian Youth and the State." *YCC* 23, Part 19, (Mar. 15, 1942), 82. People need to have a sense of community. But one has to work at it by learning the historic backgrounds of the people and institutions in each local community.

Gingerich, Melvin. "Political Elections; Christian Youth and the State." *YCC* 21, Part 2, (Dec. 15, 1940), 400. Should respond to political elections with clear, unbiased thinking. The state is only a means to an end. The Christians chief concern is God's kingdom.

Gingerich, Melvin. "Practicing Peace in a Hostile World." *Builder* 12 (June, 1962), 52-53. Worship and sermon suggestions to use in conjunction with patriotic holidays that emphasize peace.

Gingerich, Melvin. "Religious Liberty; Christian Youth and the State." *YCC* 22, Part 12, (Aug. 3, 1941), 658. There have been many great statesmen and thinkers who believed in the spirit of religious liberty that it is essential for a government to understand the concept of "obeying God rather than men."

Gingerich, Melvin. "Reunions; Christian Youth and the State." *YCC* 25, Part 39, (Nov. 19, 1944), 370. Our nation's welfare can be assured only to the extent to which a community spirit and other Christian qualities are cultivated in our society.

Gingerich, Melvin. "Social Security; Christian Youth and the State." *YCC* 24, Part 30, (Aug. 8,

1943), 669. The government's Social Security program is being administered with a desire to help the unfortunate. Secular governments are now doing what churches ought to be doing.

Gingerich, Melvin. "The Christian Community; Christian Youth and the State." YCC 22, Part 15, (Nov. 23, 1941), 789. To the extent that Christian young people help to build friendly, cooperative communities they are promoting the welfare of our nation and civilization.

Gingerich, Melvin. "The Christian's Relation to the State." GH 57 (May 19, 1964), 421-22. Supreme allegiance is given only to God, not to government. While the church will not always be able to submit to the demands of the government, it continues to respect and witness to the government.

Gingerich, Melvin. "The Church of the Middle Ages; Christian Youth and the State." YCC 23, Part 25, (Nov. 1, 1942), 346. The church must remain separate from the world. Thus the church not only condemns war but the set of world conditions that make for war.

Gingerich, Melvin. "The Early Church; Christian Youth and the State." YCC 23, Part 23, (Aug. 2, 1942), 242. The understanding we have about the time of Christ's return may affect how we live in our willingness to share and our willingness to be separated from the world.

Gingerich, Melvin. "The Problem of Leisure; Christian Youth and the State." YCC 25, Part 34, (May 28, 1944), 173. The church rather than local and state governments should furnish the leadership and standards for our leisure time.

Gingerich, Melvin. "True Patriotism." CanMenn 2 (Feb. 5, 1954), 2. "The true patriot is he who, true to democratic beliefs in the sanctity of human life and the reasonableness of mankind, and true to the Bible teachings that the way to overcome evil is through good deeds, teaches constantly the dangers of exalting 'the technique of direct action' and a 'worship of force and bloodshed'."

Gingerich, Melvin. "Using Christian Democracy." YCC 30 (Sept. 11, 1949), 707. Christian principles demand that there be democracy in the Christian community and church.

Gingerich, Melvin. "We Meet Our Government Daily; Christian Youth and the State." YCC 21, Part 1, (Dec. 1, 1940), 379. The services and powers of various government agencies are a part of our daily life. We should have an attitude of gratitude and appreciation for the many blessings that come to us through the channels of government.

Gingerich, Melvin. Youth and Christian Citizenship.

Scottdale: Herald Press, 1949. Pp. 204. A collection of 50 essays written for high school age Christians on a variety of practical citizenship issues raised by the church and state relationship. Topics include nationalism, patriotism, political participation, racism, communism, community vitality, ecology, and more.

Gingerich, Melvin (Archival). Box 18—Peace Committees: General Conference Mennonite, 1935-48; MCC, 1944-48; CPS history, 1938-49. Box 20—Peace Deputation trips. Box 39— Draft; Committee on Armed Service hearing, 1959. Box 40—Civilian Public Service. Box 51— Civil Defense; communism; Congressional Record (debate on universal military training), Feb. 5, 1959; conscientious objectors; Japan Anti-A & H Bomb Conference; Japan and peace. Box 52—peace clippings; peace conferences; Peace Problems Committee reports Puidoux Theological Conference. Box 53—peace and Mennonites. Box 62—"The Christian and Revolution;" church-state relations; communism. Box 64—"Nonresistance and Social Justice;" Peace Institutes; Peace/War. Box 91—Service for Peace; CPS history and correspondence. Goshen, Ind., AMC Hist. Mss. 1-129.

Gingerich, Melvin (Review). The Church in Communist China: a Protestant Appraisal, by Francis Price Jones. New York: Friendship Press, n.d. GH 55 (Sept. 18, 1962), 825, 836-37. While the church in China has compromised its position, the sincerity of many Chinese Christians must still be recognized. American Christians should seek to show love to Chinese Christians in concrete ways.

Gingerich, Ray C. "Jesse Jackson: The Prophet in Politics." Paper presented to the Church and Race class, AMBS, Elkhart, Ind., spring, 1970. Pp. 28. AMBS.

Gingerich, Ray C. "The Sword in the Disputations Between the Swiss Anabaptists and Zwinglian Reformers, 1531-1538." Paper presented to the History of Christian Thought class, AMBS, Elkhart, Ind., spring, 1969. Pp. 24. AMBS.

Gish, Arthur G. Living in Christian Community: A Personal Manifesto. Scottdale: Herald Press, 1979. Pp. 375. Concluding chapters in this handbook for Christian communities are entitled "The Nonconforming Community" and "The Witnessing Community." Topics discussed in these chapters include the church and state, the church and economics, and the "Lamb's War" as the struggle against all that is outside God's intentions for the world, such as militarism, injustice, and oppression.

Gleysteen, Jan. Letter to the Editor. GH 69 (Apr. 27, 1976), 277. As a recently naturalized US citizen, Gleysteen cites realities which show that the US is not a favored Christian nation, and that its national priorities in military expenditures, etc., do not conform to Jesus' way.

Goering, James A. "Democracy or Christocracy?" *ST* 26 (2nd Qtr., 1958), 31. The spirit of democracy and the spirit of Christianity are incompatible.

Goering, James A. "Pilgrims in a Democratic Society." *ST* 33 (1st Qtr., 1965), 30. Although the early Christians were instructed to be good citizens, they were not encouraged to active participation in political, social, or civil causes, whether local or national. Thus the most reasonable course for the nonresistant Christian is personal separation from any involvement in any way in the political life of the civil government under which he or she lives.

Goering, James A. (Review). *War and the Gospel,* by Jean Lasserre. Scottdale: Herald Press, 1962. *ST* 35 (May, 1967), 13. Should be read by everyone who is interested in understanding pacifist and current Mennonite thinking on church and state relations.

Goering, Paul L. "Your Congressman and You." *Menn* 62 (Oct. 21, 1947), 3, 5. Urges Mennonites to express their concerns to Congressmen via 1) personal visits when the Congressperson is "at home," 2) delegations sent to Washington, and 3) writing letters.

Goertz, Hans-Jürgen. "Willy Brandt and the Nobel Peace Prize." *CMR* 1 (Dec. 13, 1971), 9. Reflections on German politics with the observation "that those political parties which have no historic kinship with Christianity have developed a concept of peace, which is more suitable to the radical world peace demands of the gospel of Jesus Christ than the political assumptions and apprehensions of the so-called Christian parties."

Goertzen, Don. "Tightening the Vise." *Sojourners* 6 (Jan., 1977), 8. Notes recent events that indicate a clamping down on Latin American Christians.

Good, Douglas L. "The Politics of Daniel." Paper for War and Peace in the Bible class, AMBS, Elkhart, Ind., Dec. 7, 1981. Pp. 18. AMBS.

Graber, Ralph. "Evaluation of the McCrackin Case as Related to Radical Pacifism." Paper for War, Peace, and Revolution class, AMBS, Elkhart, Ind., Jan., 1961. AMBS.

Graybill, J. Silas. "God and the Nations." *ST* 33 (3rd Qtr., 1965), 31. Examines several things about God and the nations: the responsibility of nations to God, the phrase "this nation under

God," and the secret of a nation's blessings.

Grimsrud, Theodore G. "Foundations for Christian Social Responsibility: Creation, Love, and Justice." MA in Peace Studies thesis, AMBS, 1983. Pp. 135. In the context of the contemporary debate on the subjects of social responsibility and biblical authority, develops three theological themes as a basis for proper Christian participation in society's structures.

Gross, Harold H. "The Christian Dilemma: The Politics of Morality." *MennLife* 23 (Apr., 1968), 59-63. A discussion of conscience, politics, pacifism, and patriotism. The need for sharpening Christian moral sensitivity must be a major concern.

Gross, Wesley. Letter to the Editor. *GH* 66 (July 31, 1973), 596-97. Calls Mennonites to refrain from criticizing governmental policies, since the state "stems the tide of lawlessness" and encourages Christians to spread the gospel. Mennonites should instead simply practice nonresistance.

Gundy, James. "History of Christianity Project." Paper for History of Christianity class, AMBS, Elkhart, Ind., Dec., 1970. Pp. 12. AMBS.

"Historic Peace Church Council Members Meet." *CanMenn* 9 (May 26, 1961), 1, 8. Members of the Council meet in Winnipeg to discuss problems related to citizenship, oaths of allegiance, and Mennonite Disaster Service. A main topic of dicussion was the denial of Canadian citizenship to new Canadians due to their CO position.

"Historic Peace Church Council Will Hold Annual Meeting in Winnipeg." *CanMenn* 10 (Nov. 23, 1962), 1. The annual meeting of the Council, which unites nine Mennonite member groups, focuses on citizenship and service.

Hackman, Walton. "GI Benefits for CO's?" *Forum* (Apr., 1973), 8. The case of a CO applying for veteran's benefits has been appealed to the US Supreme Court and the result of this court decision may confront Mennonite CO's with the question of whether or not they will apply for and accept these benefits.

Harder, Leland. "The Political Behavior of Northern Indiana Mennonites." *Indiana Academy of the Social Sciences.* (Third Series.) Proceedings, 1970, Vol. 5, 159-72. A statistical and interpretive study of political attitudes and activities, particularly voting and the political role of the church, compared with respondents in Glock, Ringer, and Babbie study of Episcopalians. Study shows that low political permissiveness on the part of Elkhart Mennonites correlates with high religious commitment, low income, and low education. It appears that "among those who take the

Anabaptist vision most seriously are persons who have found some implications in it which lead to political involvement."

Harder, M. A. "Shall We Participate in Politics? The Affirmative." N.d. Pp. 5. MLA/BeC.

Harms, Orlando. "Let Us Not Fail Them." *ChrLead* 37 (Sept. 3, 1974), 24. After noting the changes in Washington government, reminds the reader of the Christian's responsibility to uphold the president and those in authority.

Harms, Orlando. "Our Government and We." *ChrLead* 23 (Sept. 20, 1960), 2. Emphasizes the principle that authority is divine; Christians in a democracy, however, should seek to help elect persons "who would rule according to the precepts of God's Word."

Hartzler, Levi C. "We Welcome Franco." *ChrMon* 31 (July, 1939), 205-6. Report of the Mennonite relief work in Spain taken over by victorious Franco.

Hatfield, Mark O. "A Christian and His Political Convictions." *Menn* 85 (Sept. 8, 1970), 536-37. A US senator sees a place for the conservative Christian in the social revolution.

Hatfield, Mark O. "A Senator Speaks His Mind." *MennLife* 26 (Dec.. 1971), 147-48. Mark O. Hatfield, an active Baptist layperson and former professor of political science, relates his convictions as a Christian to the solution of the political problems of today.

Hatfield, Mark O. "Civil Religion." *EV* 86 (Aug. 10, 1973), 4, 5, 11. Senator Hatfield, in his commencement address at Messiah College, warns that the Christian, like every citizen, cannot avoid being political in some sense, but the political realm must be under the authority of Jesus Christ and not of the surrounding culture.

Hatfield, Mark O. "Leadership, Power, and the Purpose of Life." *Menn* 88 (July 24, 1973), 442-44. The Watergate scandal inspires reflection on abuse of power brought on in part by the national idolatry of the presidency, instead of allegiance to God and the biblical vision of God's justice and peace.

Hatfield, Mark O. "Piety and Patriotism." *MBH* 13 (Aug. 9, 1974), 1-4. Since ultimate loyalty belongs to God, not the state, Christians must confront militarism, materialism, and racism. Cites cases of third century pacifist stances.

Haury, David A. "German-Russian Immigrants to Kansas and American Politics." *Kansas History: A Journal of the Central Plains* 3 (Winter, 1980), 226-37. Compares two groups of German-Russian immigrants, one Catholic and one

Mennonite, on issues of political participation in government. Concludes that a variety of cultural and religious factors plus influences from the local environment and its leadership have given shape to the Mennonite and Catholic political experience in Kansas.

Heisey, J. Wilmer. "God's Gift to the American Continent." *EV* 87 (June 10, 1974), 11. The American Indian has a great contribution to make to this country if we can remove the stereotypes and recognize their equal citizenship in the kingdom of God.

Heisy, D. Ray. "On Which Issues Should the Church Witness to the State." Paper, n.d. Pp. 3. MHL.

Henly, Keith R. "The Jim Juhnke Congressional Campaign of 1970." Social Science Seminar paper, Apr. 10, 1975. Pp. 61. MLA/BeC.

Henry, Carl F. H. "The Theology of Revolution." *GfT* 6 (Mar.-Apr., 1971), 11, 16, 19. While pacifist theology oversimplifies the complexity of social problems, revolutionary theology disregards the divinely appointed civil government as the instrument of justice.

Hernley, Catherine. "How the Mennonite Church Began." *ChrMon* 33 (Sept., 1941), 261-62. Narrative describes the Reformation struggle over the issue of a state-controlled or separated church.

Herr, Edwin. "The Christian and Politics: A Query." *GH* 69 (Oct. 26, 1976), 815-16. When Mennonites believe the tasks of the church are reconciliation, redemption, and mercy, while the state's purpose is to administer justice by force, to what extent can Mennonites participate in the state?

Herr, Eli. "Christians Take No Part in Worldly Government." Tract, Lancaster, Pa., 1915. Pp. 32. MHL.

Hershberger, Guy F. "A Newly Discovered Pennsylvania Mennonite Petition of 1755." *MQR* 33 (1959), 143-55. An article containing the exact transcription of the petition which was drawn up by the Pennsylvania Mennonites who feared the implications of their signing earlier declarations of allegiance, fidelity, and abjuration, and who wanted to make clear their nonresistant position.

Hershberger, Guy F. "A Study of Church-State Relations." *GH* 57 (Oct. 13, 1964), 889-90. An announcement of a program to study issues related to church-state theory; includes the MCC Peace Section statement which proposes an outline for this study.

Hershberger, Guy F. "Anabaptist Views on Church

and State—1942." *GfT* 10 (Sept.-Oct., 1975), 14-15. Excerpts from Hershberger's writings on the relation of the nonresistant Christian to the state.

Hershberger, Guy F. "Christian Missions and Colonialism: The Christian Witness to the State." (Part 3). *GH* 53 (Sept. 20, 1960), 826. The identification of missions with paternalistic colonialism is an area in which a stronger witness to the state has been needed in the past. The Christian mission today must still speak out against paternalism and colonialism in word and deed.

Hershberger, Guy F. *Christian Relationships to State and Community.* No. 5 in the *Mennonites and Their Heritage* series. Akron: MCC, 1942. Pp. 108. A study guide prepared for use in Civilian Public Service Camps, with special emphasis on church and state relations.

Hershberger, Guy F. "Church and State: The Mennonite View." Paper presented at the National Association of Evangelicals, 1952. Pp. 6. MHL.

Hershberger, Guy F. "Examples from Mennonite History: The Christian Witness to the State." (Part 1). *GH* 53 (July 26, 1960), 647, 654. The first in a series of articles dealing with how and why the church should speak to the state about the conduct of its affairs. Examples are cited of many Mennonites of the past who have stated what God requires of all individuals, even those in government.

Hershberger, Guy F. "False Patriotism." *MQR* 1, Part 1, (Jan., 1927), 9-27; Part 2, (Apr., 1927), 29-45. An exposé of the attitudes and actions of earlier Americans together with an analysis of the dynamics of nationalism.

Hershberger, Guy F. "From 'God and His People' to 'God and Country'." Typescript; July, 1975. Goshen: AMC Hist. MSS 1-171 Box 54. Explores the question "when a people are in covenant relationship with God, what kind of relationship do they maintain with the fallen powers?" Begins with Abraham and ends with the modern political situation.

Hershberger, Guy F. "Mennonites and Government: A Historical Perspective." In *Our National Government and the Christian Witness: Seminar Report*, pp. 11-16. Sponsored by Mennonite Central Committee Peace Section, Akron, Pa., held at Washington, DC, Apr. 27-29, 1961. While it is clear that participation in public office has serious questions for the nonresistant Christian, it is equally clear that complete aloofness from all concern for the state is not the answer either.

Hershberger, Guy F. "Nationalism and

Internationalism: The Christian Witness to the State." (Part 4). *GH* 53 (Oct. 18, 1960), 913, 924. The Christian will witness for cooperative internationalism as opposed to competitive and conflicting nationalism.

Hershberger, Guy F. *Nonresistance and the State: The Pennslyvania Quaker Experiment in Politics, 1682-1756.* Scottdale: Mennonite Publishing House, 1936. Pp. 48. After examining Penn's "Holy Experiment" the author concludes that if one adheres to the New Testament ethic one must remain detached from the political aspects of the social order.

Hershberger, Guy F. "Nuclear Warfare: The Christian Witness to the State." (Part 5). *GH* 53 (Nov. 15, 1960), 1001, 1014. The state with the nuclear bomb is the demonic beast of Rev. 13. The church should rise up in a mighty witness against this force.

Hershberger, Guy F. "Our Citizenship Is in Heaven." *Kingdom, Cross, and Community.* Ed. John R. Burkholder and Calvin Redekop. Scottdale: Herald Press, 1976, 273-85. Discusses six characteristics of Christians as aliens of the present order: obedient to Great Commission, witness to principalities and powers; work primarily outside the power structure; witness in the spirit of the Suffering Servant; keep mission/evangelism and social service balanced; maintain keen sense of destiny.

Hershberger, Guy F. "Our Citizenship is in Heaven." Sermon delivered at College Mennonite Church, July 18, 1971, in Goshen, Ind. Typescript. Goshen: AMC Hist. MSS 1-171 Box 54. A Christian's citizenship is in heaven. Looks at the role of a heavenly citizen with respect to the church and with respect to visible kings and presidents, the agents of the invisible principalities and powers in heavenly places.

Hershberger, Guy F. "Pacifism and the State in Colonial Pennsylvania." *Church History* 8 (Mar., 1939), 54-74. Analyzes William Penn's "holy experiment" and concludes that pacifism, even if necessarily detached from the political order, contributes to society by establishing a moral witness.

Hershberger, Guy F. "Prophets, Priests, and Kings: Civil Religion, Then and Now." Sermon delivered at Trinity Mennonite Church, Mar. 3, 1974, in Glendale, Ariz. Typescript. Goshen: AMC Hist. MSS 1-171 Box 54. Defines civil religion as the form of idolatry in which men give their highest allegiance not to God but to Caesar, and then use worship and religious ceremony for the glorification of Caesar and the state. Traces civil religion from the Old Testament to the modern political situation.

Hershberger, Guy F. "Questions Raised

Concerning the Work of the Committee on Peace and Social Concerns (of the Mennonite Church) and Its Predecessors." Mimeographed, 1967. Goshen: MHL. Summary review of questions raised concerning the work of the CPSC and its predecessors, particularly concerning witness to other Christians, to the state, and to society, with respect to peace and the social implications of the gospel, and concerning inter-Mennonite and inter-denominational cooperation in carrying on this work, 1925-66.

Hershberger, Guy F. "Religion in Politics and Social Reform." Typescript, 1933. Goshen: AMC Hist. MSS 1-171 Box 12. The religious phase of the story of American civilization is often neglected. Suggests a number of points where political and social phenomena came in vital contact with religion.

Hershberger, Guy F. "The Christian Witness, Catholicism, and a Presidential Year." GH 53 (1960), 841, 861. A recognition of the persecution and treatment of Catholics and a plea to be a witness and testimony to the Catholic people.

Hershberger, Guy F. "The Committee on Peace and Social Concerns and Its Predecessors: A Summary Review of the Witness of the MC to Other Christians, to the State, and to Peace, with Respect to Peace and the Social Implications of the Gospel (1915-1966)." Paper, 1966. Pp. 22. MHL.

Hershberger, Guy F. "The Disciple of Christ and the State." Goshen, IN, n.d. Pp. 6. MLA/BeC.

Hershberger, Guy F., ed. "The Peace Committee Circular." Bibliography compiled by Peace Committee, Goshen College, Goshen, Ind., Jan., 1931. Pp. 6. MHL. Designed to assist Goshen College graduates teaching in the public schools counteract a "false patriotism: detrimental to international relations.

Hershberger, Guy F. "The Pennsylvania Quaker Experiment in Politics, 1682-1756." MQR 10 (Oct., 1936), 187-221. An examination of Quaker political theory and its test in actual practice in colonial Pennsyivania. The withdrawal of Friends from politics in the eighteenth century indicates that the nonresistant Christian will most likely need to remain detached from the political aspects of the social order.

Hershberger, Guy F. "The People of God, Then and Now." GH 67 (Jan. 1, 1974), 6-8. Hershberger briefly recounts the history of the People of God from Abraham to the present noting that the church has taken on a subservient role of "spiritual advisor to power and prestige" and needs to once again assume the role of prophet to nationalism and the glorification of American interests.

Hershberger, Guy F. "The Scriptural Basis: The Christian Witness to the State." (Part 2). GH 53 (Aug. 16, 1960), 713, 725. Because Jesus is Lord of history the powers fall under his judgment. Therefore the Christian has a responsibility to witness to government.

Hershberger, Guy F. The Way of the Cross in Human Relations. Scottdale: Herald Press, 1958. Pp. 424. Having been crucified with Christ, Christians follow Jesus in the way of the cross: they love with a self-giving love. After examining many theological traditions, Hershberger concludes that the Anabaptists most closely approximated this ideal. He then analyzes the organizations that structure modern society, proposes conditions under which Christians can become involved in them, and advocates a role for the church as society's conscience. Yet, because Christians look forward to Christ's consummation of history to establish justice, they depend not upon human efforts.

Hershberger, Guy F. War, Peace, and Nonresistance. Scottdale: Herald Press, 1944. Pp. 375. For many years the standard work in the field. God has one eternal plan for human conduct: love for God and neighbor. This law forbids one to compel another. One rather meets force with nonresistance. In the Old Testament covenant with Israel, God made a concession to the hardness of human hearts by permitting warfare. In the New Testament, Jesus initiates a new covenant in which believers receive a new heart, enabling them to keep God's fundamental moral law. By going to the cross rather than retaliating, Jesus indeed modeled nonresistance perfectly. The early church at first followed Jesus' nonresistant example but gradually applied it less strictly. After Constantine's conversion, the church abandoned nonresistance as an ideal for all Christians. Small Christian sects however retained it, of whom the Mennonites provide a history extending from the sixteenth century to the present. Because nonresistance renounces all coercion, finds its authority in God's will, and takes sin seriously, one should not confuse it with other types of pacifism. Nonresistance implies that Christians will not take part in coercive state functions, will search for alternatives in the complex industrial, agricultural, and economic conflicts of modern life, and will nurture an attitude of brotherhood toward other races. By bringing healing to society, nonresistance serves society in a more essential way than those who take responsibility for running it.

Hershberger, Guy F. "What Did the Early Christians Think About War and State?" YCC 17 (Feb. 2, 1936), 40. The first two hundred years of the Church after Christ show that most Christians believed that killing was wrong. There were many martyrs for peace.

*

Hershberger, Guy F. "What Did the Early Mennonites Say About War and Peace?" *YCC* 17 (Apr. 5, 1936), 112. At the end of the Middle Ages there were many Christians in Europe who questioned the church-state union and its use of warfare. Included in this group were the Waldensians and later the Anabaptists, who believed that the teachings of Jesus on war must be literally obeyed.

Hershberger, Guy F. "What Do the Events Surrounding May 18 Teach Us Concerning a Chauvinistic Spirit in American Life? Our Peace Witness—In the Wake of May 18." (Part 8). *GH* 60 (Oct. 17, 1967), 944. Extreme reactions to a few radical youths' flag-burnings show the false kind of patriotism of many Americans.

Hershberger, Guy F. "Why Have Many Christians Forgotten the Bible Teachings on Peace?" *YCC* 17 (Mar. 8, 1936), 80. Under Constantine's rule, beginning in 313 A.D., Christianity became a state religion. The union of church and state and the heathen ways of war are still a part of the larger church today.

Hershberger, Guy F. (Archival). Boxes 10-19—writings: church history; labor; mutual aid; peace; peace witness; race; *War, Peace, and Nonresistance*—reviews and correspondence. Boxes 23-33—church and state: Study Conference, 1964-65; extremism; War, Peace, Nonresistance class notes; Draft Law 1967, Committee on Peace and Social Concerns. Box 48—capital punishment. Box 54—miscellaneous peace and social concerns. Goshen, Ind. AMC. Hist. Mss. 1-171.

Hershberger, Guy F. (Review). *The New Leviathan,* by Paul Hutchinson. Chicago: Willett, Clark, & Co., 1946. Pp. 233. "The New Leviathan." *GH Supplement* 39 (Aug., 1946), 459-60. While lacking a vigorous biblical approach, the book is a sharp and insightful approach to the question of the church and the totalitarian state.

Hershberger, Guy F., Metzler, Edgar, and Meyer, Albert J. "Theses on the Christian Witness to the State." Sub-committee report to the Peace Problems Committee of the Mennonite Church, June 22, 1960. Pp. 32. MHL.

Hertzler, Daniel. "Can One Vote In Faith?" *GH* 69 (Oct. 26, 1976), 836. Suggests that both voting and not voting may be Christian options, and that a common assumption underlying both points of view is the belief in two Kingdoms—God's and this world's—and that they must be evaluated according to their separate tasks.

Hertzler, Daniel. "Jesus Christ: Our President?" *ChrLiv* 17 (Oct., 1970), 40. A Christian's deepest loyalty belongs to Jesus Christ, not to the state.

Hertzler, Daniel. "Religion and Politics." *ChrLiv* 20 (Aug., 1973), 31. Editorial includes general guidelines for a Christian's relationship to the state.

Hertzler, Daniel. "What the Court Didn't Change." *ChrLiv* 9 (Sept., 1962), 2. Comment on the removal of prayer from public schools and the deeper issue of the relation of government and religion.

Hertzler, Daniel (Editorial). "Kicking Uncle Sam." *GH* 69 (Apr. 6, 1976), 302. Asserts that since a national government stands opposed to Christ's teachings on selflessness, defenselessness, love, and truth, Christians must separate loyalty to the state from living the way of peace.

Hertzler, Daniel (Editorial). "The Politics of the Gospel." *GH* 72 (Jan. 2, 1979), 16. Hertzler suggests a new sense of loyalty is needed to displace the old loyalties, one in which people are willing to seek peace at great personal risk.

Hess, James R. "Church and State Ordained for Separate Functions." *ST* 45 (Jan., 1977), 10-13. Draft registration and war tax payment are examples of proper responses of the Christian toward government.

Hess, James R. "The 1975 Consultation on War Taxes." *ST* 44 (May, 1976), 7-9. Questions the assumptions about the relationship of church and state involved in the discussion of nonpayment of war taxes.

Hess, James R. "The Washington Peace Seminar." *ST* 44 (July, 1976), 21-23. Criticizes the hostility shown toward business and government leaders, and traces it to those involved in church institutions as compared with those involved in the workday world.

Hess, James R. (Review). *Our Star-Spangled Faith,* by Donald B. Kraybill. Scottdale: Herald Press, n.d. Pp. 216. *ST* 45 (Sept., 1977), 22-23. The book calls for avoidance of all civil religion, but the reviewer cautions that this will mean that the state as well as the church will separate religious values from national business.

Hill, Dave. "Dietrich Bonhöffer [sic]—A Witness for Today." *YCC* 47 (Apr. 10, 1966), 2. A sketch of the life and thought of Bonhoeffer.

Hillerbrand, Hans J. "The Anabaptist View of the State." *MQR* 32 (Apr., 1958), 83-110. The office of government is ordained of God to maintain order, to restrain evil, and to protect the good; the state, however, is not meant to violate a person's conscience.

Histand, A. O. "Jesus and the Authorities." *GH* 28 (Aug. 8, 1935), 426. Governments are subject to Jesus and will one day become the "Kingdoms of Our Lord." The government is to be prayed for and obeyed with gratitude for all that the government is doing for the church.

Hodel, Nate J. Letter to the Editor. *ChrLead* 39 (Mar. 16, 1976), 13. Will never further God's kingdom by denouncing and finding fault with the United States.

Hoover, Donald J. "The Politics of Jahweh: On the Relationship Between Justice and War Acts." Paper for Warfare in the Old Testament class, AMBS, Elkhart, Ind., Dec. 17, 1977. Pp. 25. AMBS.

Hornus, Jean-Michel. *It Is Not Lawful for Me to Fight: Early Christian Attitudes Toward War, Violence, and the State,* trans. Alan Kreider and Oliver Coburn. Rev. ed. Scottdale and Kitchener: Herald Press, 1980. Pp. 367. Hornus studies the social, political, and theological framework and extant writings from the first 3 centuries of Christianity to show: Christian teaching consistently opposed military participation; this position was based on commitment to nonviolence, not merely the rejection of idolatry in emperor worship; why this position was abandoned in the 4th century.

Horsch, John. "Balthasar Hubmaier, the Outstanding Defender of Believers' Baptism." *ChrMon* 26 (Oct., 1934), 293-94; edited reprint, *ChrMon* 29 (July, 1937), 197-98. Although he did not preach nonresistance, Hubmaier broke with Zwingli on the issue of infant baptism and rejected a state church model.

Horsch, John. "Liberty of Conscience Versus General Toleration Within the Church." *ChrMon* 22 (Feb., 1930), 38-39, 49. Separation of church and state means that the state will tolerate various religions, and the church will tolerate various political convictions, but the principle of toleration does not apply within the church to doctrinal matters.

Horsch, John. "The Anabaptists." *ChrMon* 31 (Sept., 1939), 260-61. Believers' baptism was the fundamental characteristic of the Anabaptists, and signified their belief in the separation of church and state.

Horsch, John. "The Anabaptists of Münster." *ChrMon* 27 (May, 1935), 134-35. The relationship of church and state is one factor in the Münster story.

Horsch, John. "The Character of the Evangelical Anabaptists as Reported by Contemporary Reformation Writers." *ChrMon* 38 (July, 1946), 197-99. Reprinted from *MQR.* The Anabaptist dissent from state-church Christianity inspired

harsh words from contemporaries.

Horsch, John. "The Debate in Zofingen in 1532." *ChrMon* 24, Part 1, (June, 1932), 165-67; Part 2, (July, 1932), 198-99. Describes the debate between advocates of the Swiss state church and the Swiss Brethren.

Horsch, John. "The Doctrinal Differences Between the Swiss Brethren and Swiss State Church Protestantism." *ChrMon* 22 (Jan., 1930), 6. While the controversy focused on infant baptism, the underlying issue was the relationship of church and state.

Horsch, John. "The Earliest Protestant Leaders on the Principle of Nonresistance." *GH* 31 (Aug. 11, 1938), 426. Both Luther and Zwingli were advocates of nonresistance in the earliest period of the Reformation. This position was lost when they accepted the establishment of a state church.

Horsch, John. "The Early Mennonite Teaching on Liberty of Conscience." *ChrMon* 30 (Oct., 1938), 296-97. "Liberty of conscience" referred to the separation of church and state, or the refusal to force anyone to accept faith.

Horsch, John. "The Origin of Protestant State Churchism." *ChrMon* 32 (Dec., 1940), 358. Brief review of the place of civil authorities in the churches during the Reformation.

Horsch, John. "The Origin of the Mennonite Church." *ChrMon* 25 (Feb., 1933), 38, 52. Recounting of the origin of the Swiss Brethren in 1525 highlights the issue of infant baptism, linked to the relationship of church and state.

Horsch, John. "The Persecution of the Evangelical Anabaptists." *ChrMon* 38 (Aug., 1946), 230-32, 253, 256. Reprinted from *MQR,* Jan., 1938. Relates the persecutions experienced by Anabaptists at the hands of state church leaders.

Horsch, John. "The Relation of the Old Testament Scriptures to the New Testament." *ChrMon* 30 (Nov., 1938), 329. The Anabaptists' distinction between the Testaments was basic to their convictions on nonresistance, separation of church and state, etc.

Horsch, John. "The Spread and Persecution of the Evangelical Baptists." *ChrMon* 25, Part 1, (Aug., 1933), 230-31; Part 2, (Sept., 1933), 260-61, 263; Part 3, (Oct., 1933), 292-94. The progress of the Anabaptist movement threatened the existence of the state church. Briefly mentions nonresistance as a factor in the persecutions.

Horsch, John. "The Swiss Brethren in Canton Berne." *ChrMon* 31, Part 1, (Nov., 1939), 325-26, 340; Part 2, (Dec., 1939), 357-58, 379; *ChrMon*

32, Part 3, (Jan., 1939), 5-6, 23. Reviews the conflict of the Swiss Brethren with the state church in Berne over the separation of church and state.

Horsch, John. "The Swiss Brethren in St. Gallen." *ChrMon* 29, Part 1, (Nov., 1937), 324-25; Part 2, (Dec., 1937), 357-58; *ChrMon* 30, Part 3, (Jan., 1940), 5-6. The spread of Anabaptism in eastern Switzerland and subsequent persecution centered on the issue of believers' baptism and separation of church and state.

Horsch, John. "The Weakness of the Defense of Infant Baptism in the Reformation Period." *ChrMon* 29 (Aug., 1937), 229-30. Zwingli's support for infant baptism was based on his belief in the unity of church and state.

Horst, Samuel. *Mennonites in the Confederacy: A Study in Civil War Pacifism.* Scottdale: Herald Press, 1967. Pp. 148. Documents the variety of ways Mennonites responded to the issues raised by the crisis of the Civil War, such as reluctant cooperation with the military, desertion, flight, choosing prison, working with government officials for legal alternatives, etc. Concludes that the Mennonite witness for peace in this era was not faultless but, nevertheless, significant and sincere. Includes extensive bibliography.

Hostetler, John Andrew. "The Amish and the Public School." *ChrLiv* 3 (Sept., 1956), 4-6, 41-43. Amish conflict with public school systems over their religious right not to send children to school beyond the eighth grade.

Hostetler, John Andrew. (Review). *The Christian in the Modern World,* by T. B. Maston. Broadman Press, 1952. Pp. 144. *ChrLiv* 1 (June, 1954), 29. Reviewer questions the author's approval of Christian involvement in politics.

Hostetter, Douglas and McIntyre, Michael. "The Politics of Charity." *Christian Century* 91 (Sept. 18, 1974), 845-50. Questions the cooperation between Christian charitable programs and US government programs which tie the goals of the church to those of the state. Discussion focused by issues facing Church World Service.

Huber, Clarence. *The Relationship of Church and State.* Crockett, Ky.: Rod and Staff Publishers, ca. 1965. Pp. 23. MHL. Argues against Christian participation in politics or any sort of nonviolent resistance because the state is ordained by God to use the sword against doers of evil.

Huebert, Norman. Letter to the Editor. *ChrLead* 41 (July 18, 1978), 15. Mennonites are progressively entering into the arena of political and social conflict as is evident from the articles

and readers' responses in the *Christian Leader* and other Mennonite periodicals.

Huebner, Bert. "Why Should a Christian Be Interested in Politics?" *MBH* 1 (Apr. 27, 1962), 5. Elected office can be an excellent arena for Christian witness and action regarding social and moral problems.

Hurd, Menno B. "Menno's Opinion." *GH* 69 (Oct. 12, 1976), 782. Compares the 1975 celebration of Anabaptist heritage with the 1976 celebration of the national Bicentennial, and cautions Mennonites to "worship neither at the Liberty Bell in Philadelphia nor the Memorial Shaft in Witmarsum."

Ingrim, Jony L. Letter to the Editor. *ChrLead* 41 (Sept. 12, 1978), 12. There is a place for nationality in Christianity. Thankful that US nationality allows us to do God's work as no other nation in the world does.

"Jost Receives Citizenship." *RepConsS* 12 (May, 1955), 1, 3. After delays, the US Supreme Court decision (Feb. 1, 1954) in favor of CO Arthur Jost's petition for naturalization results in his being granted citizenship.

Jantz, Harold. "A Case for Political Action." *MBH* 18 (Apr. 27, 1979), 13. Editorial reflects on the contributions and cautions involved in a Christian holding political office.

Jantz, Harold. "Depoliticizing Our Aid." *MBH* 18 (Dec. 7, 1979), 10. Editorial expresses the opinion that MCC workers, especially in Southeast Asia, should refrain from becoming involved in political activity.

Jantz, Harold. "New Tax Rules Give Charities Concern." *MBH* 17 (Apr. 28, 1978), 12. Revenue Canada issues guidelines on being political for charitable organizations.

Jantz, Harold. "Rossmere: An Issue That Divides Mennonites." *MBH* 12 (Oct. 5, 1973), 15; *MennMirror* 3 (Nov., 1973), 11, 12. A dispute among Manitoba Mennonites of the Rossmere constituency has been stirred up by the allegations of the defeated Mennonite Conservative candidate, who argues that the election victory of Premier Schreyer should be declared void because the returning officer in the constituency was a Mennonite minister.

Jantz, Harold (Editorial). "Mennonites in Politics." *MBH* 16 (Oct. 28, 1977), 11. Suggests that Mennonite political interest is more concerned with protecting privilege than justice.

Janzen, A. E. "Patriotism, Peace, and War." *ChrLead* 13 (July 1, 1949), 3-4. Christians are devoted to the welfare of all people; because they believe peace is the will of God, they renounce the use of force and violence.

Janzen, Bill and Steiner, Sam. "Politics—Is It for Mennonites?" *With* 9 (Oct., 1976), 6. Mennonites should feel some responsibility toward the political order.

Janzen, David. "Are We Selling Our Birthright?" *CanMenn* 4 (Nov. 9, 1956), 2, 7. To withdraw or to become involved in the affairs of the world is the question. Janzen works with church and secular history in his analysis.

Janzen, David. "Danger Signs on the Road to Brazil." *Menn* 86 (Apr. 13, 1971), 250-51. To bow to the politics-out limitations set by the Brazilian government for the Mennonite World Conference reminds author of a parable in 1 Kings 13.

Janzen, David. "On Politics and Immorality, Communism and Democracy." *CanMenn* 5 (Jan. 4, 1957), 7. In debate with John H. Redekop, Janzen tries to define terms for understanding of nonresistance and the Christian's involvement with the state.

Janzen, William. "Can Conscientious Objectors Be Citizens?" *Menn* 92 (Jan. 4, 1977), 9. Jehovah's Witness conscientious objector relates his views on Christians, war, and politics to an MCC representative assisting him in appealing the Canadian court decision not to grant citizenship because of conscientious objection.

Janzen, William. "MCC's Ottawa Listening Post." *MBH* 14 (Oct. 31, 1975), 9. Describes the MCC (Canada) Ottawa office as a "listening post" because it is an attempt by the church to neither dominate nor withdraw from the state.

Janzen, William. "Opposition to War No Bar to Citizenship." *MBH* 16 (Mar. 4, 1977), 12. The denial of Canadian citizenship to a Jehovah's Witnesses couple refusing military service was the basis for a court ruling guaranteeing citizenship to conscientious objectors.

Jeschke, Marlin. "Render to Caesar or to God?" Address, Mar. 20, 1973. Revision of Peace Assembly Address, Chicago, Nov. 16-18, 1972. Pp. 3. MLA/BeC., MHL.

Juhnke, James C. "A Mennonite Runs for Congress." *MennLife* 26 (Jan., 1971), 8-11. The story of a Mennonite who was asked to run for a national office, the political battle, and its outcome.

Juhnke, James C. *A People of Two Kingdoms: The Political Acculturation of the Kansas Mennonites.* Newton: Faith and Life Press, 1975. Pp. 215. Explains that this process of acculturation was fundamentally shaped by the "abrasive encounter of Mennonite nonresistance with American nationalism" and charts the encounter from the shadows cast on the civic role of the Mennonite German-Americans by the Spanish-American War, through the essential Mennonite-American compatibility of the Progressive Era, through the shattering of that easy course in World War I, through the efforts to bridge the conflict in the inter-war period, to the new phase—characterized by voting and alternative service—during World War II.

Juhnke, James C. "Crisis of Citizenship: Kansas Mennonites in the First World War." *PCMCP Sixteenth,* 101-18. N.p. Held at Hesston College, Hesston, Kansas, June 8-9, 1967. There were many incongruities in nonresistant Mennonite attempts to validate American citizenship. During the early years of the war there was the identification with Germany; in later years, there was an emphasis on "Mennonite" as the primary source of identity for the community.

Juhnke, James C. "Mennonites and a Christian America." *Citizens and Disciples: Christian Essays on Nationalism.* Akron: MCC Peace Section, [1974], 18-20. MHL. Suggests that, instead of vainly trying to escape participation in the political communities, Mennonites would do well to renew the affirmations that Jesus is Lord and that the kingdom of God takes precedence over all earthly nations, and to recover a prophetic witness to the powers more comprehensive than the refusal of military service.

Juhnke, James C. "Mennonites and the Great Compromise." *Menn* 84 (Sept. 23, 1969), 562-64. "From the first World War through the 1960s, American Mennonites and the US government have made a compromise, a deal which has allowed church and state to coexist in peace, harmony, and productivity."

Juhnke, James C. "Our Almost Unused Political Power." *GH* 61 (Jan. 9, 1968), 38-39. Reflects on Mennonite use of political power to defeat proposed changes in the draft laws that would have been unfavorable to conscientious objectors, and urges Mennonites to use this power to influence foreign policy toward de-escalation in Vietnam.

Juhnke, James C. "Politics and Information." *Menn* 87 (Feb. 29, 1972), 152, 153. The issue of political involvement by Mennonites has to do with compromise with evil on the one hand and with a positive potential for a Mennonite witness within government on the other.

Juhnke, James C. "Recently in South Africa." *MBH* 12 (May 4, 1973), 32. Both Billy Graham and a group of American sportsmen recently visited South Africa. Though both visits were clouded by controversy and sensationalism, Graham in some measure communicated the gospel's critique to the white South Africans while the sportsment were completely "duped" by their white hosts.

Juhnke, James C. "What Does the Profile Say?" *MBH* 14 (June 27, 1975), 5-6. The *Anabaptists, Four Centuries Later* (J. Howard Kauffman and Leland Harder) study shows that 10-20 percent of present church members disagree with Anabaptist principles of church and state separation, nonresistance, etc.

Juhnke, Roger, "John P. Franz: An Example of Political Awareness Among the Mennonites." Diggers Oral History project, History of Civilization, Mar. 21, 1972. Pp. 49. MLA/BeC.

Just, Roy. "Which Way Will You Choose?" *ChrLead* 29 (Nov. 8, 1966), 3. Like Jesus, we choose some form of accomodation toward or resistance to the "powers that be."

Jutzi, Robin (Review). *XX Century and Peace,* ed. A. Khomenko. Soviet Peace Committee, n.d. *MennRep* 10 (Sept. 1, 1980), 8. Observes that the official magazine of the Soviet Peace Committee reveals that the Soviets have a particular horror for war but believe that peace is achieved through the presence of a strong military.

Kauffman, Daniel. "The Crisis." *GH* 34 (Dec. 18, 1941), 793. Christians should look to the Scriptures for guidance in time of crisis, avoiding earthly entanglements, being subject to the authorities, and living the nonresistant life.

Kauffman, Daniel. "Thoughts on the Recent Election." *GH* 29 (Nov. 12, 1936), 705-706. Politics is not a realm for Christian people but one must be thankful if he or she lives in a land of law and order.

Kauffman, Ivan and Francis, Dale. "A Mennonite and a Catholic in Dialogue." *CanMenn* 15 (Feb. 21, 1967). Exchange of letters discussing pacifism. Francis, editor of the *Operation Understanding* edition of *Our Sunday Visitor* asks how Mennonites acquit themselves of responsibility for others; Kauffman argues that Mennonite pacifism is theologically, not politically, motivated and points out the conflict between service under Christ and service under the state involved in war.

Kauffman, J. Howard and Harder, Leland *Anabaptists Four Centuries Later: A Profile of Five Mennonite and Brethren in Christ Denominations.* Scottdale: Herald Press, 1975. Pp. 399. Reports a survey of 3,591 church members. Chapter 8, entitled "Social Ethics," probes participants' adherence to a nonresistant ethic in relation to a variety of issues such as war, race relations, labor-management relations, concern for the poor, capital punishment, etc. Chapter 9, entitled "Political Participation," explores attitudes concerning the church and state relationship as well as other related topics.

Kauffman, Ralph C. "The Philosophical Aspects of Mennonitism." *PCMCP Second,* 113-26. North Newton, Kansas: The Bethel College Press. Held at Goshen, Indiana, July 22-23, 1943. Philosophical aspects of Mennonitism are those aspects which can be rationally substantiated. Comments on separation of church and state, materialism as it relates to war, and the sovereignty of God as it relates to personal conscience.

Kauffman, Richard A. "The Christian and the State." *GH* 70 (May 24, 1977), 422-23. Part 19 in a series on the Mennonite Confession of Faith reviews the Old Testament conflict between God and governing authorities and the example of Jesus in seeking a more accurate interpretation of Romans 13.

Kautz, B. B. "Romans XIII." *GH* 28 (Feb. 27, 1936), 1018-19. The apostolic church did not particiapte in government nor did they criticize it. We should follow their example.

Keeney, William E. *Lordship as Servanthood: 13 Lessons on the Biblical Basis for Peacemaking.* Newton: Faith and Life Press, 1975. Pp. 112. A series of lessons on the principles of Christian pacifism designed for either individuals or groups. Central premise: a Christ-centered view of the Bible yields an understanding that the way of the cross embodied by Jesus is to be normative for his disciples. Faithful disciples will take the effects of evil upon themselves and let the grace of God empower them to change evil into good. Other topics discussed within this framework include the kingdom and the church, Old Testament warfare, and the Christian's relation to government.

Keeney, William E. "Mennonite Cooperation with Government Agencies and Programs." *PCMCP Fifteenth,* 62-74. North Newton, Kansas: The Mennonite Press. Held at Bluffton College, Bluffton, Ohio, June 10-11, 1965. In its relationship to a benevolent state, the church must learn to critically distinguish between the areas in which there can be cooperation and the areas in which noncooperation is appropriate. To preserve the prophetic stance of the church, a sense of tension needs to be maintained with the state.

Keeney, William E. "The Right of Dissent." *GH* 59 (Aug. 9, 1966), 702-704. The roots of this right are found in the Old Testament, in Jesus, and in the American system, among other places. Dissent is desirable because human knowledge is limited and conditioned. The two alternatives to controversy are suppression and apathy.

Keeney, William E. "WCC Called to Nonviolent Position." *Menn* 89 (Jan. 1, 1974), 11. Summarizes the statement, "Violence, Nonviolence, and the Struggle for Social Justice," prepared by the historic peace church representatives for the World Council of Churches discussion. Reviews the history of peace church-WCC discussions on the issue of war, and alludes to the broader issues which it touches: christology, biblical interpretation, the relationship of church and state.

Kehler, Larry. "Christ's Lordship and Caesar's." *Menn* 86 (June 15, 1971), 390-93. Eight opinion leaders in the General Conference Mennonite Church in Canada discuss in a two-day encounter the relation between "the Lordship of Christ and our position on peace."

Kehler, Larry. "Conference Takes Fresh Look at Church-State Relationships." *CanMenn* 13 (Oct. 19, 1965), 1, 2, 14. Franklin Littel, Paul Peachey, Al Meyer, and Leo Driedger are represented in this detailed report.

Kehler, Larry. "The Challenge of Peace Witness Is Very Close to Home." *CanMenn* 13 (Feb. 9, 1965), 3. Report on MCC Peace Section's annual meeting in Chicago on Jan. 14. Crucial issue for 1965 is the local church's involvement in peacemaking. Continuation of participation in Prague Peace Conference was proposed and a major study conference on church-state relations, in which MCC Peace Section would be involved, was discussed.

Kehler, Larry. "The Peace Corps and the Church." *GH* 54 (Dec. 5, 1961), 1040. This article outlines the history of the Peace Corps and traces the churches' reaction to it as it evolved.

Keidel, Levi O. *Caught in the Crossfire.* Scottdale and Kitchener: Herald Press, 1979. Pp. 229. Account of the early years of Zaire;s political independence, a period characterized by revolution and tribal warfare, and the ethical dilemmas the church had to face in regard to participation in violence or conscientious objection to it.

King, Calvin R. "Historical Mennonite Interpretation of Romans 13:1-7, A Study of the *MQR.*" Paper presented to Mennonite History class, Goshen Biblical Seminary, Goshen, Ind., June 1, 1962. MHL.

Kingsley, Keith. "Politics and the Kingdom of God." *GH* 65 (Oct. 24, 1972), 857-59. Calls Christians to focus their attention on the politics of God's Kingdom, which might be characterized by communities of people committed to nonresistance, economic sharing, marital fidelity, and spiritually and psychologically interdependent relationships, instead of focusing attention on national politics.

Kingsley, Keith. "Radical Discipleship and Caesar's Politics." *MennRep* 2 (July 24, 1972), 5; (Aug. 7, 1972), 5; (Aug. 21, 1972), 5; (Sept. 4, 1972), 5. A criticism of the "fundamentalist, flag-waving" enthusiasts and of the "liberal, social-action advocates" and of the "Stillen im Lande" over against the "people of God" through whom God builds his kingdom. Paper, Elkhart, Ind., 1971. Pp. 5. MHL.

Klaassen, Gerhard. "Mennonite Participation in Politics." 1959. Pp. 15. MLA/BeC.

Klaassen, Walter. "The Anabaptist Critique of Constantinian Christendom." *MQR* 55 (July, 1981), 218-30. Outlines the emergence and main features of Constantinian Christendom, the Anabaptist identification of infant baptism as the principal link between church and state, and a summary of the Anabaptist critique of the roles and actions of both church and state within a Constantinian model.

Klaassen, Walter. "The Christian and the State: Biblical and Anabaptist Perspectives." *Menn* 89 (July 9, 1974), 428-29; *Citizens and Disciples: Christian Essays on Nationalism.* Akron: MCC Peace Section, [1974], 10-12. MHL. In both the Old and New Testaments the concepts of "people" and "nation" are distinguished with the concept of "people" taking priority. The majority of Anabaptists also expressed this biblical principle in the doctrine of the "two kingdoms." Finally, while neither the biblical nor Anabaptist traditions can be used as prescriptive law today, these perspectives present models with which to shape contemporary responses to the issues of church and state.

Klaassen, Walter. "The Meaning of Anabaptism." *MBH* 14 (Jan. 24, 1975), 6-7. Giving ultimate loyalty to God over social and political powers exercising violence was one of the marks of 16th-century Anabaptists.

Klaassen, Walter. *What Have You to Do with Peace?* Altona: D. W. Friesen and Sons, Ltd., 1969. Pp. 74. Originally given as lectures designed to help Sunday school teachers teach the basic principles of nonviolence. Covers subjects such as the biblical use of the language of "principalities and powers," the church as the agency of peace, just war doctrine, nuclear war and disarmament issues, and church and state relations.

Klaassen, Walter. (Review). *Mennoniten im Dritten Reich: Dokumentation und Deutung,* by Diether Götz Lichdi. Weierhof/Pfalz: *Mennonitischer Geschichtsverein,* 1977. Pp. 248. *MQR* 53 (Jan., 1979), 87-88. An account of the Mennonite response and reaction to national socialism, beginning in 1933.

Klassen, D. D. Letter to the Editor. *CanMenn* 4 (Dec. 28, 1956), 2, 9. A reply to John H. Redekop's "Non-Resistance and UN Police Action," (*CanMenn*, Dec. 7, 1956). Klassen reviews church history on church-state relations and asks for strong peace position through education.

Klassen, D. D. "UN Police Action and Nonresistance." *CanMenn* 4 (Dec. 28, 1956), 2, 9. A reply to John H. Redekop's article, "Nonresistance and UN Police Action." Redekop's questions are based on a confusion over the nature of the separation of church and state.

Klassen, Peter J. (Editorial). "A Time for Decisions." *MBH* 11 (Oct. 20, 1972), 11. Says, "We will need to take up our responsibility as Christian citizens to help run this country the best way we know how."

Klassen, Randolph. "A Matter of Conscience." *HIS* (Magazine of Inter-Varsity Christian Fellowship) 28 (June, 1968), 14-16, 21. From the examples of Christ and the Scripture, the author argues that a military profession may be consistent with God's will, that lifetaking must be without hate, and that Christians should aid the state's God-given mandate to preserve order in society. Argues that a Christian may carry a draft card and participate in military activities if that person recognizes clearly that his/her first loyalty is to the heavenly King.

Klassen, William. "We Must Obey and Pay, But We May Also Protest." *CanMenn* 11 (Apr. 19, 1963), 5. A study of taxes in the New Testament; surveys the biblical mandate for Christians to pay taxes to government.

Kliewer, Gerd Uwe. "Let Us Have Courage to Meet in Brazil." *Menn* 86 (Jan. 26, 1971), 60, 61. What it means to stand on the side of a government and what it can mean to stand on the side of Jesus when governments are not all that good.

Knipscheer, L. D. G. "Renewal of the Doctrine of Nonresistance Among the European Mennonites." *The Witness of the Holy Spirit.* Ed. Cornelius J. Dyck. Elkhart: MWC, 1967, 328-30. Since World War I the Spirit of God is again bringing new life to Mennonites; false patriotism is rapidly giving way to radical obedience and reconciliation.

Kolb, V. C. "The Christian's Duty to the Government." *GH* 36 (Apr. 1, 1943), 2. The Christian should never resist the government but live in complete submission.

Krabill, Willard S. "Vietnam: Soulsick, War-weary, and Divided." *CanMenn* 14 (Feb. 8, 1966), 9; *ChrLead* 29 (Mar. 15, 1966), 3-5. A condensed version of Krabill's report to Elkhart Mennonite churches about the extent and solution of the refugee problem in Vietnam. Includes discussion of the question of Vietnamese national identity and how that question relates to questions of politics, government, and war.

Krahn, Cornelius. "Mennonites in Russia Today Gaining the Favor of the State." *MennRep* 9 (July 23, 1979), 6, 7. A description is given of the situation and conditions under which the Mennonite church in Russia is struggling to preserve its identity.

Kraus, C. Norman. *Christians and the State.* Ed. Paul Peachey, n.p.: Mennonite General Conference. Peace Problems Committee, 1956. Pp. 13. The Christian Youth and War Pamphlets No. 4. Directed to young men approaching draft age, pamphlet encourages them to obey the government but give primary allegiance to God, not the country.

Kraus, C. Norman (Review). *Religious Liberty in the United States: The Development of Church-State Thought Since the Revolutionary Era,* by Elwyn A. Smith. Philadelphia: Fortress Press, 1972. Pp. 386. *MQR* 48 (Jan., 1974), 120. Recommends this interpretive historical essay on the evolution of church-state relations from separation to neutralism, faulting the book for its many typographical errors.

Krause, James R. Letter to the Editor. *Menn* 92 (Apr. 26, 1977), 285. Christian obedience to government is limited, because those in power, being human, carry out God's will only imperfectly. Primary loyalty is to God, who commands love to enemies, even national enemies.

Kraybill, Donald B. "I Pledge Allegiance, But . . ." *ChrLiv* 21 (July, 1974), 26-27. Questions about expressing loyalty to the nation, when patriotism can mean hostile military action against other nations.

Kraybill, Donald B. *Our Star-Spangled Faith.* Scottdale, Pa.: Herald Press, 1976. Pp. 216. An anthology of examples, quotations, slogans, photos that illustrate the historical and contemporary merger of religion and politics that has resulted in an American civil religion that is idolatrous by nature.

Kraybill, Donald B. "Ten Thanks for Watergate." *ChrLiv* 21 (June, 1974), 34. One of the effects of Watergate will be to lessen temptation to equate Christian commitment with religious lipservice by politicians.

Kraybill, Paul N. "The Christian in Modern Africa." Messages and Reports from the Limuru Study Conference, Limuru, Kenya, Mar. 28-Apr. 1, 1962. Pp. 45. MHL. Includes: Jacobs, Don, "The Spirit of the Lamb," 1-4; Neufeld, Elmer, "The Mighty Acts of God," 5-7; Neufeld, Elmer, "The Church—The Body of Christ," 8-11; Miller, Orie O., "Scriptural Position on War Participation—My Personal Testimony," 11-12; Mudenda, Sampson, "The Prophetic Christian in Relation to Local and National Politics," 13-15; Lemma, Daniel, "The Church and the State," 15-16; Kisare, Zedekiah, "Christians in a Newly Independent Country," 17-18; Kisanja, Elijah, "The Mau Mau and Christianity," 19-20; Weaver, Edwin I., "The Ministry of Reconciliation in Africa or Bridges of Forgiveness, Love, and Fellowship," 20-23.

Kreider, Alan. "The Early Church and Warfare." ChrLead 43 (Dec. 30, 1980), 18-19. Historical inquiry into the pacifism of the early church, based on It Is Not Lawful for Me to Fight: Early Christian Attitudes Toward War, Violence, and the State, by Jean-Michel Hornus (Herald Press).

Kreider, Alan. "The Way of Christ." Is Revolution Change? ed. Brian Griffiths. London: Inter-Varsity Press, 1972, 46-69. Both Jesus' rejection of violence as an option and the history of the church and state relationship point to suffering love, embodied by the (minority) church as the method of the true revolution.

Kreider, Alan, ed. "Thoughts from Conference Speakers." IPF Notes 6 (June, 1960), 3-10. Detailed summary of addresses on the topics of the Christian witness against militarism through politics, I-W program, and missions.

Kreider, Alan (Review). It Is Not Lawful for Me to Fight: Early Christian Attitudes Toward War, Nonviolence, and the State, by Jean-Michel Hornus. Revised, ed., trans. A. Kreider and O. Coburn. Scottdale: Herald Press, 1980. Pp. 367. "The Early Church and Warfare." GH 73 (Dec. 2, 1980), 964-65. The experience of the early Christians was more nearly pacifist than not.

Kreider, Carl. "American Leadership." ChrLiv 2 (July, 1955), 22, 11, 19, 46. In material possessions, political influence, and military power, America is one of the world leaders; but secular leadership is transient.

Kreider, Carl. "Civil Rights Here and Abroad." ChrLiv 7 (June, 1960), 18, 23, 39. Racial discrimination in violent form, such as in South Africa, or in the more subtle form of granting voting rights on the basis of race, denies the gospel of Jesus Christ.

Kreider, Carl. "Cuba: Revolt that Failed." ChrLiv 8 (July, 1961), 18, 35. The US-backed revolt in Cuba is a deplorable symbol of Cold War politics.

Kreider, Carl. "President Peron vs. the Catholic Church." ChrLiv 2 (Sept., 1955), 22, 47. The military forces are one source of power for Peron of Argentina.

Kreider, Carl (Review). The Church and Social Responsibility, by J. Richard Spann. Abingdon-Cokesbury, 1953. Pp. 272. ChrLiv 1 (Nov., 1954), 31. Recommends this collection of essays on social problems such as war, church and state, crime, civil rights, etc.

Kreider, Robert S. "A Hymn of Affection for a Land and a People." With 9 (May, 1976), 32. In spite of all the wrong America has done, there are many little things that can stir one's love for one's country.

Kreider, Robert S. "The Anabaptist Conception of the Church in the Russian Mennonite Environment." MQR 25 (Jan., 1951), 17-33. In Russia the Mennonite church moved in the direction of a Volkskirche (state church type) away from a believers' church type, though renewal movements also countered the trend.

Kreider, Robert S. "The Anabaptists and the Civil Authorities of Strasbourg, 1525-1555." Church History 24 (June, 1955), 99-118. Explores issues of the church and state relationship by analyzing the personalities, events, and ideas of a particular historical conflict. Analyzes the Anabaptists' view of the authorities, including their commitment to the separation of church and state, obedience to government when possible, and complete nonresistance.

Kreider, Robert S. "The Anabaptists and the State." The Recovery of the Anabaptist Vision. Ed. Guy F. Hershberger. Scottdale: Herald Press, 1957, 180-93. Discusses the state's view of Anabaptism, which included fear of subversion and breakdown of social order, and Anabaptist views of the state, which call for obedience to God rather than to human authorities.

Kreider, Robert S. "The Christian View in Political Science." PCMCP Eleventh, 43-48. Held at Bethel College, North Newton, Kansas, June 6-7, 1957. Outlines both some broad principles for the development of a Christian view in political science and some practical suggestions that encourage growth in Christian responsibility toward government.

Kreider, Robert S. The Relations of the Anabaptists to the Civil Authorities in Switzerland, 1525-1555. The Univ. of Chicago, Dept. of History, published PhD dissertation, 1952. Pp. 266. A study of the techniques and theories of the several Swiss governments in relation to the challenge of anabaptist dissent, and of anabaptist thought and practice in regard to civil authorities.

Kroeker, Marvin (Review). *Between the Eagle and the Dove: The Christian and American Foreign Policy,* by Ronald Kirkemo. Downers Grove: InterVarsity, 1976. Pp. 215. *ChrLeader* 40 (Oct. 11, 1977), 11. This "Christian perspective" on such issues as war, nuclear armaments, and international relations is not distinguishable from a "strictly secular" perspective. Therefore the book is neither newly insightful nor compatible with an Anabaptist-Mennonite view.

Kroeker, Walter. "Influence in Politics." *The Voice* 20 (Oct., 1971), 15. If we let the force of clear Christian witness operate in and through our lives we will have a great impact on politicians and on legislation.

Kroeker, Walter.. "What About Our Registered Brethren?" *ChrLead* 40 (Apr. 26, 1977), 24. Raises some questions about western attitutdes toward the registered church in the Soviet Union.

"Lecturer Attacks Politicization of Christianity." *Menn* 94 (Mar. 6, 1979), 180. 1978 Keith lecturer, Edward Norman, dean of Peterhouse, Cambridge, criticized efforts by Christian churches to build a more just and peaceful world.

Landis, Ira D. "A New Chapter on the Flag Salute." *GH* 36 (July 29, 1943), 363. Mennonites should be thankful for recent court decisions against the obligatory flag salute.

Landis, Ira D. "When Nations War: A Study of Habakkuk 2:6-20." *ChrMon* 34 (Apr., 1942), 105-7. God's dealings with Babylon provide an object lesson for the Christian's relationship to the state.

Landis, Maurice W. "The Secularization of the Church and Civil Religion, Part 2." *GfT* 8 (Nov.-Dec., 1973), 10-11, 15. By advocating amnesty for those who broke the Selective Service law, the church is violating the principle of separation of church and state and becoming an instrument of lawlessness.

Lapp, Alice W. (Review). *Our Star-Spangled Faith,* by Donald B. Kraybill. Scottdale: Herald Press, 1976. *FQ* 3 (May, June, July, 1976), 4. Kraybill's discussion of patriotism and biblical foundations for respecting government helps clear up the common confusion between loyalty to God and to country.

Lapp, Benjamin F. "The Bicentennial: Two Views. 2. My Attitude Toward My Country." *GH* 69 (Feb. 10, 1976), 103-104. While the Christian's allegiance is to the heavenly kingdom rather than the earthly country, the Christian is also called to be subject to the existing authorities, not to criticize the government in the name of peace.

Lapp, Helen and Sam, "Raising Children in a Bicentennial Year." *ChrLiv* 23 (Sept., 1976), 6-9. Conflict of loyalty experienced by people committed to peace in a year of patriotism.

Lapp, John A. "Civil War in Angola." *ChrLiv* 23 (Feb., 1976), 15-16. Review of Angolan politics, including conflict among three liberation movements.

Lapp, John A. "General Conference Sponsors Church/State Consultation." *GH* 63 (May 19, 1970), 461. Reports and comments on a recent conference on church-state issues which focused on questions of biblical interpretation, institutional ethics, and the lordship of Christ.

Lapp, John A. "Missions, Missionaries, and the Political Process." Paper presented at the GCMC Commission on Overseas Missions, Missionary Retreat, June 26, 1976. Pp. 11. MHL.

Lapp, John A. "Peace Section Not Political." *CanMenn* 19 (Feb. 2, 1971), 2. A concern that the MCC Peace Section not be a political unit but inspire to a life of peace that has political dimensions.

Lapp, John A., ed. *Peacemakers in a Broken World.* Scottdale: Herald Press, 1969. Pp. 159. A discussion of issues relating to peace by twelve Mennonite scholars and the editor under the following headings: I. *Voices of Love:* 1. Peter J. Ediger, "Amos Visits America;" 2. Hubert Schwartzentruber, "The Brokenness of the City;" 3. C. Norman Kraus, "Christian Perspectives on Nationalism, Racism, and Poverty in American Life;" 4. R. Herbert Minnich, "Hunger, Revolution, and the Church;" 5. Atlee Beechy, "Peacemaking in Vietnam." II. *Voices of Faith:* 6. Richard C. Detweiler, "Peace Is the Will of God;" 7. Sanford G. Shetler, "God's Sons Are Peacemakers;" 8. Willard Swartley, "Peacemakers: The Salt of the Earth." III. *Voices of Hope:* 9. Stanley Bohn, "Toward a New Understanding of Nonresistance;" 10. John Howard Yoder, "The Way of the Peacemaker;" 11. Frank H. Epp, "The Unilateral Disarmament of the Church;" 12. J. Lawrence Burkholder, "The Church in a Brave New World." Conclusion: "Peacemaking in a Broken World," by the editor. While all of these essays touch on church-state relations, chapters 6-8 are of special relevance. Questions for study and thought are included.

Lapp, John A. "Seminary Letter Precipitates Intense Brotherly Discourse." *CanMenn* 18 (Mar. 13, 1970), 1, 11. Describes tensions aroused between MCC and the AMBS community over a letter the seminary sent to President Nixon. Also describes the efforts to resolve the conflict and the very solid discussion of the issues of church and state which resulted from the tensions.

Lapp, John A. "The Argentine Nightmare." *ChrLiv* 24 (Feb., 1977), 15-16. Review of Argentine politics, including paramilitary assassinations and armed groups preparing for guerilla warfare.

Lapp, John A. "The Christian and Politics." *ChrLead* 39 (Oct. 26, 1976), 6. Examines several principles that may help as one looks at the faithful Christian and the political process.

Lapp, John A. "The Politics of Terror." *ChrLiv* 21 (Aug., 1974), 15, 27. Torture as a means of political and military intimidation is used by both left-wing and right-wing governments.

Lapp, John A. "The Real Issues in 1972." *ChrLiv* 19 (Nov., 1972), 15, 32. Comments on the religiosity of American politics.

Lapp, John A. "Upheaval in Central America." *ChrLiv* 27 (June, 1980), 15, 34. Review of recent events in Central American politics: victory of the Sandinistas in Nicaragua; murder of Archbishop Oscar Romero in El Salvador.

Lapp, John A. "Why Didn't Mennonites Join the Revolution?" *GH* 69 (Aug. 3, 1976), 594-95. Mennonites objected to the Revolutionary War for three philosophical reasons: 1) The Mennonites were already a community, which the Revolution claimed to bring about; 2) The fall of the church was represented by the dominant churches' support of the war; 3) The revolution distorted good politics.

Lapp, John A. (Review). *Letters of a CO from Prison*, by Timothy W. L. Zimmer. The Judson Press, 1969. *GH* 63 (May 19, 1970), 460. Earlham College student imprisoned for refusing induction into the army or alternative service reflects on the topics of government, faith, revolution, protest, love. Recommended for its insight into the thinking of young American idealists.

Lapp, John E. "Jesus Christ or Caesar?" *GH* 66 (June 12, 1973), 500. The corruption in government evidenced through the Watergate scandal should convince Christians that their first loyalty is to God, not the state.

Lapp, John E. "Study of Church-State Relations." *GH* 61 (Mar. 12, 1968), 236. Announces the formation of a committee to study the church's witness to the state—the Preparatory Commission for the Study of Church-State Relations.

Lapp, John E. "Why I Do Not Vote in Political Elections." *GH* 59 (July 12, 1966), 612-14. One reason for not voting is because one is a conscientious objector to war. Other reasons, as well as a list of obligations to government, are put forth.

Lapp, John E. (Review). *Mennonite Statements on Peace, 1915-1966*, by Richard C. Detweiler. Scottdale: Herald Press, 1968. Pp. 71. *GH* 62 (Apr. 15, 1969), 353. Describes the contents of the booklet, which include an evaluation of the peace witness documents and a review of Mennonite scholarship on views of church and state and Anabaptist historiography in this century.

Lapp, John E.; Hernley, H. Ralph; and Hershberger, Guy F. "Moral Issues in the Election of 1964." *GH* 57 (1964), 826. Christians who vote in the 1964 election must endeavor to find those issues important from the viewpoint of Christian morals and to discover which candidates are most responsive to the claims of Christ. Civil rights and nuclear warfare are two issues considered.

Lauver, Florence B. "The Church's Responsibility Concerning War." *GH* 29 (July 9, 1936), 330-31. The Christian should pray for rulers, pardon enemies, and preach the Gospel that saves souls.

Leatherman, Dan. "Mennonites and the Superpatriots." *ChrLiv* 9 (Mar., 1962), 12-14. Analysis of right-wing extremist tendencies in US society and their contrast with a nonresistant gospel.

Leatherman, Dan. "Survey of (Old) Mennonite Positions on Voting." Paper for War, Peace, and Nonresistance class, AMBS, Elkhart, Ind., Jan. 12, 1961. Pp. 13. AMBS.

Leatherman, Daniel R. "The Political Socialization of Students in Mennonite Secondary Schools." MA thesis in political science, Univ. of Chicago, Chicago, Ill., 1960. Pp. 92. Some of the items used to test the attitudes of Mennonite youth toward political participation were: self-rating on degree of political interest; image of government; current events activity; party preference; and intention to vote when old enough.

Lehman, Celia. "The Middle Man." *Swords into Plowshares: A Collection of Plays About Peace and Social Justice*. Ed. Ingrid Rogers. Elgin: The Brethren Press, 1983, 109-124. A choral reading which explores the issue of civil religion as well as other aspects of the church and state relationship.

Lehman, Chester K. "As Applied to the Christian and Civil Government: Bible Teaching on

Nonconformity." (Part 7). *GH* 32 (June 15, 1939), 226-27. Christ's Kingdom is primarily spiritual, but since God has ordained government, these powers are used by God. Deals with various problems encountered, e.g., tax payment, office-holding, and the meaning of subjection to government.

Lehman, Emmett R. "Basic Concerns in the Anabaptist Position." *GfT* Series 2, 4 (Jan.-Feb., 1969), 15. Discusses three tenets: separation of church and state; nonresistance as the refusal to judge actions of the state; and the difference between nonresistance and pacifism.

Lehman, J. Irvin. "Letter to an Editor." *ST* 34 (1st Qtr., 1966), 32. Reprint of a letter that was addressed to an editor of a local newspaper concerning the Christian's proper involvement in policies of government.

Liechty, C. Daniel. "Political Nonresistance: A Thesis in Christian Ethics." MA in Peace Studies thesis, AMBS, 1978. Pp. 71. An exploration of the OT anti-kingship tradition, a comparison of the political views of Hegel and Marx, and a summary of Christian thinking on the relationship of church and state contribute to a Christian understanding of the political organism.

Lind, Marcus. "The Gospel of God." *ST* 36, Part 1, (Aug., 1968), 14; Part 2, (Dec, 1968), 11; Part 3, (Dec, 1968), 11. A Bible study in the book of Romans on the Christian and the state. Accents the difference between the Christian way of love and governmental force. Shows also how Romans provides an answer to racial prejudice.

Lind, Marcus. "Was Constantine a Sincere Christian?" *ST* 35 (Jan., 1967), 35. Looks at the life and rule of Constantine in light of the implications of the phrase "sincere Christian."

Lind, Millard C. "Monotheism, Power and Justice: A Study in Isaiah 40-55." *CBQ* 46 (July, 1984), 432-46. By a careful comparison of the trial speeches, the Cyrus poems, and the servant poems, Lind shows that while all three testify to Yahweh's historical and cosmic sovereignty, only the servant poems embody the divine purpose to bring justice to the nations. The servant's work, rooted in Torah-justice, discloses a distinctive understanding of politics and, specifically, the moral quality of Yahweh's rule. This distinction between the work of Cyrus and the mission of Israel is foundational for understanding the respective roles of state and church.

Lind, Millard C. "Politics of the Spirit." *GH* 65 (Feb. 22, 1972), 169-71. If a theology of personal integrity and a theology of politics are combined according to the Bible, a politics of power, characterized by self-interest, hypocrisy, and death must come to an end.

Lind, Millard C. "The Old Testament and the Believers' Church." Paper, n.d. Pp. 11. AMBS.

Littell, Franklin H. "The Anabaptist Concept of the Church." *The Recovery of the Anabaptist Vision.* Ed. Guy F. Hershberger. Scottdale: Herald Press, 1957, 119-34. The Anabaptist concept of the church as a "community of discipleship," i.e., a "free church," could provide needed corrective against modern individualism and against capitulation to the state, as in the case of the Nazi regime.

Littell, Franklin H. "The New Shape of the Church-State Issue." *MQR* 40 (July, 1966), 179-89. In a time when nation and church tend to fuse toward a culture-religion, we need a church with more devotion and discipline, and secular institutions with more respect for their limited but essential function.

Loewen, Esko. "Church and State." *MennLife* 11 (July, 1956), 141-42. The Christian's first loyalty is to God; other "duties" are always "assumed in the light of the first loyalty."

Loewen, Esko. "Patriotism and the Christian." *Menn* 73 (Sept. 2, 1958), 534-35. While respecting her or his own national government, the Christian is committed to a universal church and to the total human family. Thus he or she rejects a nationalistic patriotism.

Loewen, Esko. "The Theological Basis of Political Participation or Non-participation." 1957. Pp. 5. MLA/BeC.

Loewen, Mary J. "Persecuted Optimists." Paper presented to Christianity in Russia class, MBS, [Chicago, Ill.], fall, 1951. Pp. 41. AMBS.

Longacre, James C. "Religion and the State: The Contemporary American Scene." *Menn* 89 (July 9, 1974), 430-32; *Citizens and Disciples: Christian Essays on Nationalism.* Akron: MCC Peace Section, [1974], 13-17. Pp. 30. MHL. The American church, by taking the symbols of God's people and relating them to the nation rather than the church, has limited the parameters of faith to personal piety and deprived itself of an identity, a vision, and a mission separate from that of the nation.

"MCC to Establish Washington Office." *CanMenn* 16 (Feb. 13, 1968), 1. The "office in Washington is not for lobbying. It shall serve as an *observer*, particularly with reference to developments in the federal government, but also in liaison with other church, welfare, and professional agencies. It would analyze and interpret trends which may affect peace, religious liberty, social welfare, education, and related fields."

"Mennonites Should Combine Mission and Political Responsibility, Fast Says." *GH* 65 (Nov. 21, 1972), 969. According to German pastor Heinold Fast, the elements of sixteenth-century Anabaptim were mission, social responsibility, and political consciousness. Anabaptists were a political factor. By staying out of the political and social life, Mennonites today become political conformists.

MacMaster, Richard K. *Christian Obedience in Revolutionary Times: The Peace Churches and the American Revolution.* Akron, Pa.: MCC (US) Peace Section, 1976. Pp. 26. MHL. Demonstrates that Mennonites and other Christians committed to peace during the Revolutionary War times conflicted with the government on issues of military service, war taxes, and oaths of allegiance. Discusses their stance and resulting persecution within the context of differing concepts of religious liberty; the sectarian concept of discipleship as a separate and distinct way of life was not understood by a government to whom religious freedom meant the freedom to worship according to the dictates of conscience, not the freedom to live by conscience.

Mann, David W. "A Hermeneutical Study of Peter Rideman on the Question of the Christian's Relationship to Governmental Authority: The Purpose of Government, Christians in Magistracy, and the Payment of Taxes for War." Paper for Theology of the Anabaptist Classics class, [Goshen College, Goshen, Ind.], May 9, 1971. Pp. 25. MHL.

Martens, Bob. Letter to the Editor. *MBH* 13 (Sept. 6, 1974), 9. Not only does the church owe a greater allegiance to God than to the state, the church must also avoid any allegiance with the power of the state.

Martens, Rick. "A Threat to Unity?" *MennMirror* 3 (Nov., 1973), 11, 12. The writer considers the implications for the Mennonite community of the petition that has been filed against the appointment of a Mennonite minister as the returning officer in Rossmere constituency, Manitoba.

Martin, Brenda. "The Relation Between the Historic Peace Churches and the Government of Pennsylvania from 1775 to the Beginning of the Revolutionary War." Paper for History Seminar, Goshen College, Goshen, Ind., Apr. 15, 1975. Pp. 55. MHL.

Martin, Warren B. "Weak Christian: Strong President." *ChrLiv* 8 (Jan., 1961), 28-29. Reprinted from *Christian Century.* Conflict between Christian conscience and political goals.

Martin, Wilmer. "'Subject' in North America." *GH*

71 (July 4, 1978), 518-20. In a season of Canadian and American national holidays, Martin calls all North American Mennonites to be subject to the authorities, after Romans 13, without becoming nationalistic.

Martin, Winston J. "Some Consensus on Church-State Issue." *CanMenn* 18 (May 8, 1970), 1. Committees, delegates of churches, and students from Mennonite colleges of the Mennonite Church (MC) discuss church-state relations. A summary of their discussions in 10 points is shared with the constituency.

Marty, Martin E. "Do-It-Yourself Religion." *ChrLiv* 13 (May, 1966), 28-32. Tenets of general religiosity and how they function in the US in relation to the society and the state.

Mast, Russell L. "The Conscience of a Nation." *MennLife* 22 (Oct., 1967), 147-50. Micah, Amos, Paul, Jesus, and Thomas More are examples of people who helped form the conscience of a nation. Mennonites too must consider their responsibility to their respective nations.

Mast, Russell L. "What Are We Doing to Prevent Another War?" *Menn* 58 (Nov. 2, 1943), 3-4. The Christian must work for those national policies that hold the greatest possibility for preventing another world war.

Matthews, Glenn I. Letter to the Editor. *ChrLead* 39 (Mar. 2, 1976), 11. Regrets so many Mennonites have to be critical of the United States.

Mayer, Robert. "At the Grass Roots—The Quest for an Alternative Community: An Historical and Contemporary Model." *Forum* (Oct., 1972), 1-2. Just as the early Anabaptists emphasized small, voluntary human communities which separated themselves from the state and witnessed to the state's injustices, we need to develop a life-style alternative to that of the present, where humanitarian values are primary.

Mennonite Central Committee. *Report: A New Look at the Church and State Issue.* Akron: Mennonite Central Committee, 1966. Pp. 35. Three documents from the MCC Peace Section study conference held in Chicago, Oct., 1965: Metzler, Edgar, "Why Another Look at Church-State Relations?;" Littell, Franklin H., "The New Shape of the Church-State Issue;" and a findings statement from the conference.

Mennonite Central Committee. "Vietnam Study: Relief Often Tied to Politics, Military." *MennRep* 2 (Oct. 2, 1972), 1. Relief agencies enjoy the benevolences of a government because the latter recognizes a potential in the former to realize its political and military ends.

Mennonite Central Committee News. "Snow Falls

on MCC Agenda." *EV* 90 (Feb. 25, 1977), 7. Among the issues and concerns discussed at the MCC annual meeting in Metamora, Ill., members discussed how MCC should relate to authoritarian governments that deny justice and religious or political freedom to their citizens.

Metzler, Edgar. "A Churchman's Point of View." *RepConsS* 22 (Apr., 1965), 1, 2. Affirms the Supreme Court decision of Mar. 8, 1965, which states that the difference conscience makes in a person's life must be taken seriously whatever the theological source of those convictions.

Metzler, Edgar. "Guessing About the Next Four Years." *MCC PS Wash. Memo* 12 (Nov.-Dec., 1980), 1-2, 6, 9-10. Implications of the Reagan election for peace and justice issues.

Metzler, Edgar. "Mennonite Witness to the State: Attitudes and Actions, World War I-1956." Paper presented at the Laurelville, Pa., conference on "Nonresistance and Political Responsibility," 1956. N.p.: Peace Problems Committee, 1956, 49-53. MHL. A survey of forty years of Mennonite witness to the state. Primarily a review of the Peace Problems Committee of the (Old) Mennonite Church. The witness "has almost without exception been a matter of petitioning for our [own] rights and privileges."

Metzler, Edgar. "Still More Lessons from Indochina." *ChrLiv* 22 (Aug., 1975), 15, 26. Review of Laotian politics and American intervention there.

Metzler, James E. "Vietnam: I Wouldn't Do It Again." *Mission-Focus* 6 (Nov., 1977), 1-3; *GH* 70 (Dec. 13, 1977), 930-32. Because of his association with the political-military machine and American religiosity, the writer states that he would never again serve in an American organization in an area like Vietnam where the United States is involved. He raises critical issues, such as: how mission work aided the South, prolonging war and suffering; how the Mennonite Church in Vietnam did not distinguish itself from other Protestant groups through its peace witness.

Miller, D. D. Letter in "Our Readers Say." *GH* 59 (Feb. 15, 1966), 136. The church should not meddle in the affairs of the government.

Miller, D. D. "The Christian Attitude Toward the Government in Peace and War." *The Eastern Mennonite Journal* 18 (Apr., 1940), 59-63; *GH* 33 (May 23, 1940), 163-64. We ought to submit to every law and every regulation as long as such obedience does not conflict with the Law of God.

Miller, Marlin E. "The Church in the World: A Mennonite Perspective." *The Covenant Quarterly: Lutheran-Conservative Evangelical Dialogue*, ed. Joseph A. Burgess. Chicago: North Park Theol. Seminary, Aug., 1983, 45-50. Some foundational components of a theological understanding of the church's relationship to the world are grace as God's creating love, discipleship as inclusive of both personal and social dimensions, and the distinctive reality of the Christian community.

Miller, Marlin E. (Review). *Pacifism in Europe to 1914*, by Peter Brock. Princeton: Princeton Univ. Press, 1972. Pp. 566. *MQR* 47 (July, 1973), 254-55. Recommends the book as a valuable historical and bibliographical reference, but questions author's use of "separational" and "integrational" typology to characterize Anabaptists/Mennonites and Quakers, respectively.

Miller, Vern. "The Church and Public Policy (Another View)." *GH* 66 (May 15, 1973), 412-13. In response to an earlier article (Apr. 3), pessimistic of Christian influence on social conditions, Miller argues that government programs such as the Peace Corps have a positive moral quality compared to expenditures related to war.

Mohler, Allen R. "Caesar or God?" *GH* 68 (Apr. 8, 1975), 269-70. Christians preserve social morality, not by becoming involved in politics, but by leading people to accept Jesus as Lord.

Mosemann, Clyde R. "The Relationship of Church and State." Paper presented to Church History class, [Goshen College, Goshen, Ind.], May 12, 1950. Pp. 23. MHL.

Moyer, Mark. "Christian Patriotism." *YCC* 23 (1942), 182. True Christian patriotism is that love which Christ manifests in us which makes us willing to sacrifice, to work, to pray, and if need be, to die to free our country from sin and unrighteousness.

Mumaw, John R. "The Church and Principalities and Powers." *ST* 37, Part 1, (July, 1969), 1; Part 2, (Aug., 1969), 14. Responds to the uncertainty as to what actually consitutes the "principalities and powers." Examines the forces of influence that affect the relationship of church and state.

"No Christians in Army Until 170 A.D. - Penner." *CanMenn* 2 (Nov. 12, 1954), 3. G. Groening and Archie Penner address Steinbach Bible conference stressing the teaching of Jesus regarding a personal ethic. No record can be found of early Christians participating in war.

Nation, Mark. "The Politics of Compassion: A Study of Christian Nonviolent Resistance in the Third Reich." MA in Peace Studies thesis, AMBS, 1981. Pp. 115. Summarizes the variety of nonviolent resistance offered by German Christians to both the ideology of the Nazi regime and to Nazi practices such as the persecution of the Jews, euthanasia, and war in order to dispel the notions that violence is inherent in the word "resistance" and that pacifists can be nothing but "passivists" in the face of tyranny.

Neube, T. L. "The Church and the Rhodesia Question." *EV* 89 (Feb. 25, 1976), 6, 7. T. L. Neube, a teacher at Wanezi Mission, outlines his understanding of the historical setting and the current attitude of the church toward the political situation in Rhodesia, noting as well the effect of the church's position on African youth.

Neufeld, David. "Attitude Toward Vietnam: As Found in *Christianity Today*." Paper for War, Peace, and Revolution class, AMBS, Elkhart, Ind., Apr. 4, 1969. Pp. 3. AMBS.

Neufeld, Elmer. "Christian Responsibility in the Political Situation." *MQR* 32 (Apr., 1958), 141-62. When we are thoroughly motivated by the love of the Christ of the cross, our concerns for our neighbors will find appropriate expression in politically relevant actions.

Neufeld, P. L. "Army Officer Played Key Role in Moving Mennonites to Prairies." *MennMirror* 8 (Jan., 1979), 9-10. Describes the efforts Col. J. S. Dennis, Jr., made to bring Mennonites across from Russia to settle on the Canadian prairies following the Russian Revolution.

Neufeld, Walter. "MCC's Nonpolitical Stance." *Menn* 87 (Feb. 22, 1972), 138. Letter to the Editor reacting to Marvin Hein's article (Jan. 25, 1972). Raises critical questions as to the logic of being involved "nonpolitically" at Curitiba. Is this a means of avoiding moral responsibility?

Newton, Kansas Study Group. "The Christian Church and the State." Paper presented at the Church and Society Conference, Chicago, Ill., Oct. 31-Nov. 3, 1961. Pp. 13. AMBS.

Nuckles, Dick. Letter to the Editor. *ChrLead* 42 (Sept. 25, 1979), 15. Seems like the staff of the *Christian Leader* is opposed to patriotism and the American way of life.

Ollenburger, Ben C. "Mennonites, 'Civil Religion,' and the American Bicentennial." An interview with James C. Juhnke. *Direction* 5 (July, 1976), 15-21. It is not the task of the church to abolish civil government and civil religion. Our task is to restore the integrity of the church's symbols as separate and distinct from those of the state.

Ortman, Walter L. Letter to the Editor. *Menn* 89 (Jan. 15, 1974), 46. Since corruption is part of the natural human condition, Christians should not be surprised to find it even in the nation's president. Because God ordains national leaders, Christians should applaud Nixon's aggressive leadership and pray for him, instead of calling for his impeachment.

Osborne, David. "Islamic Resurgence: Something New or Something Old?" *Mission-Focus* 7 (Dec., 1979), 68-69. Discusses the recent Islamic resurgence in Iran which presents both inspiration and danger for Western Christians.

"Peace Church Officials Contact State Directors." *RepConsS* 9 (Mar.-Apr., 1952), 6. MCC finds both receptive and punitive attitudes toward COs among contacted state directors of Selective Service.

"Peace Section Opens Washington Office." *CanMenn* 16 (Sept. 3, 1968), 3. MCC Peace Section's Washington office opened July 1, 1968. The purpose of the office is: to give Mennonites current and accurate information on governmental developments in areas affecting the life and work of Mennonite and Brethren in Christ churches; to equip and assist constituent groups when they want to make statements to the government; and to serve as a source of knowledge on peace and social issues related to government.

"Press Bob Jones U. on Ban of Blacks." *GH* 65 (Oct. 31, 1972), 895. The university is contending that separation of the races is ordained of God and that the government's attempt to penalize the university for this conviction is a violation of religious freedom.

"Proposed Resolution on Nationalism." *Menn* 83 (July 9, 1968), 462-63. A statement proposed for adoption at the 1968 conference of the GCMC. The state has a legitimate, limited function which is to be respected, but to equate the state's action with God's action is idolatrous. One's loyalty and commitment are given first to God who is the Lord of history.

Palmer, Albert W. "The Church and the World Crisis." *Menn* 54 (May 2, 1939), 4-5. What can the church do? It can call the nations together to study the problems of the present world crisis.

Pauls, Jacob F. "A Theology of Separation: A Study in the Writings of Michael Sattler and Peter Rideman." Paper presented to theology of Anabaptist Classics class, AMBS, Elkhart, Ind., May 10, 1971. Pp. 15. MHL.

Peachey, J. Lorne. "In the Shadow of the Dome." *YCC* 46 (May 30, 1965), 7. Fifteenth annual Intercollegiate Peace Fellowship meeting on "The Christian and National Government."

Peachey, J. Lorne. "The Christian and National Government." *CanMenn* 13 (Apr. 20, 1965), 3, 10. Christian leaders and government officials emphasize the need for the Christian to be concerned about what is happening in government and to make her or his opinions about it known.

Peachey, Paul L. "A Message to the President." *GH* 48 (Oct. 18, 1955), 993. Mennonites should witness to God's redeeming grace to all. They should also remind those in authority, whatever their attitude toward grace, that they hold authority under God.

Peachey, Paul L. "Beyond Christian-Communist Strife." *Christianity Today* 3 (Oct. 27, 1958), 15-17, 24. Exposes the theological errors resulting from the identification of Christianity with a particular political system which posits Christianity and communism as alternative world orders.

Peachey, Paul L. "Church and Peace." *GH* 50 (Aug. 27, 1957), 751. A report on the proceedings of the July, 1957, conference at Iserlohn, Germany, on the lordship of Christ over church and state.

Peachey, Paul L. "Constantinian Christendom and the Marx-Engels Phenomenon." *MQR* 55 (July, 1981), 184-97. Identifies the Constantinian marriage of church and society and its remains in the 19th century as a necessary ingredient in Marx's intellectual development and critique of religion.

Peachey, Paul L. "Mennonites Confer on Christianity and Politics." *GH* 49 (Oct. 16, 1956), 993. A report of discussions at the Laurelville Camp, Sept., 1956, along with a review of an interchange between nonpacifist John C. Bennett and three pacifists, including Mennonite Alvin Beachy.

Peachey, Paul L. "New Ethical Possibility: The Task of 'Post Christendom Ethics'." *New Theology No. 3*, ed. Martin E. Marty and Dean G. Peerman. New York: Macmillan, 1965, 103-117. Discusses, in the context of the break-up of the Constantinian synthesis, the crisis in Christian morality brought about by the development of nuclear weapons and explores the possibility that the community of grace, rather than the natural community, may become re-established as the framework for Christian ethical thought.

Peachey, Paul L. "Peacemaking, a Church Calling." *ChrCent* 80 (July 31, 1963), 952-54. Reflects on an ecumenical peace colloquium which discussed such topics as church-state separation, the church's position toward possession of nuclear weapons, and the church's contribution to the resolution of the East-West conflict.

Peachey, Paul L. "The Church and the Hungarian Catastrophe." *GH* 49 (Dec. 18, 1956), 1174. The experience of the Hungarian churches warns us against too close an identification of the church with any social or political order.

Peachey, Paul L. "The Peace Study Conference at Bluffton." *GH* 47 (Sept. 21, 1954), 897. It is highly urgent that Mennonites restudy their concept of church-state relations, particularly as it relates to the peace question.

Peachey, Paul (Review). *The New Testament Basis of Pacifism*, by G. H. C. Macgregor. NY: FOR, 1954; *The Early Christian Attitude to War*, by C. John Cadoux. London: Headly Bros. Publ., 1919; *The State in the New Testament*, by Oscar Cullmann. NY: Chas. Scribner's Sons, 1956; *The Sword and the Cross*, by Robert M. Grant. NY: MacMillan, 1955; *Church and State from Constantine to Theodosius*, by S. L. Greenslade. London: SCM Press, 1954. "Some New Books on the Early Church and War." *GH* 49 (Sept. 18, 1956), 897, 911. Recommends these books as helpful in identifying the practices of the early church on the issues of church and state.

Peachey, Shem. "Christian Ethics and State Ethics." *GfT* 6 (Jan.-Feb., 1971), 17-18. Love, peace, and holiness characterized the early church for the first several centuries, before they began to confuse national interests with Christian commitment.

Peachey, Urbane. "Life in These United States." *Peace Section Newsletter* 8 (Nov.-Dec., 1977), 4-5. Questions whether there is so much preoccupation with the imperfections of other societies that it is too easy to overlook the ills and limitations of the US system.

Peachey, Urbane (Review). *The Power Peddlers*, by Russell Warren Howe and Sarah Hays Trott. Garden City, New York: Doubleday and Co., Inc., 1976, 1977. *Peace Section Newsletter* 9 (Mar.-Apr., 1978), 6-7. An eye-opening account of domestic and foreign lobbying in Washington.

Penner, Alfred. Letter to the Editor. *MBH* 13 (Feb. 22, 1974), 7. In responding to criticism of President Nixon, writer notes that unlike Johnson who escalated the war, Nixon's peace initiatives are well-known.

Penner, Archie. *The Christian, the State, and the New Testament*. Scottdale: Herald Press, 1959. Pp. 128. A biblical-historical study affirming the necessity of the state for the order of society, but locating it outside the perfection of Christ.

Penner, Stephen. Letter to the Editor. *ChrLead* 38 (Apr. 15, 1975), 14. Examines the reality of the phrase "the United States has been generous."

Preheim, Vern, comp. *Background Papers: Church-*

State Study Conference, Chicago, Ill., Oct. 7-9, 1965. Akron: MCC Peace Section, Sept. 9, 1965. Pp. 124. MHL. Includes: Yoder, John H. and others, "Biblical and Historical Perspectives on the Problem," 22-34; Klippenstein, Larry, "The State in the Gospels," 35-47; Leatherman, Dan, et al., "The State and Establishment," 49-62; Dick, Nick, "Views of Church and State in the Ontario Religion-in-the-Schools Controversy," 63-68; "Church-State Relations and Economic Benefits," 69-92; Smith, Tilman, "Bridging the Wall of Separation?" 93-97; Bauman, Harold E., "Decision in Regard to Federal Aid: Excerpt from the Minutes of the Special Meeting of the Mennonite Board of Education, Wabash YMCA, Chicago, Illinois, Feb. 27, 1964," 98-99; "The Christian and National Loyalties," 100-119; "The State and Public Morality," 120-23.

Puidoux Secretariat. *The Puidoux Series of Theological Conferences on the Lordship of Christ Over Church and State. Report of the Second Conference.* Iserlohn, July 28-Aug. 1, 1957. N.p.: Puidoux Secretariat, 1960. Pp. 113. Nine papers, including three by John H. Yoder and Paul Peachey on discipleship and political ethics, with reports of discussions and statement of consensus. (In German.)

Ramer, C. J. "Peter on Civic Behavior." *ST* 39 (July, 1971), 10. Peter's comprehensive guideline for civic behavior is "Honor all men. Love the brotherhood. Fear God. Honor the King."

Ratzlaff, Don (Review). *The Upside-Down Kingdom,* by Donald B. Kraybill. Scottdale: Herald Press, 1978. In *ChrLead* 42 (Mar. 27, 1979), 22. Shows how the shape and form of the new kingdom contrast sharply with the old social order.

Ratzlaff, Vernon. "The Christian and Politics." *MBH* 1 (Apr. 27, 1962), 1, 6. The Christian calling is to witness to the way of love rather than to seek political office.

Ratzlaff, Vernon (Review). *Political Evangelism,* by Richard Mouw. Grand Rapids: Eerdmans, 1973. Pp. 111. *Responsible Revolution,* by J. Verkuyl and H. Nordholt. Grand Rapids: Eerdmans, 1974. Pp. 101. *Politics: A Case for Christian Action,* by R. Linder and R. Pierard. Downers Grover: InterVarsity Press, 1973. Pp. 160. *Direction* 3 (Apr., 1974), 180-82. Of these three books on the subject of the church and state relation, the first is exegetically weak; the second lists the issues but does not develop them well; the third fails to offer a critical perspective on the present political system.

Redekop, Calvin W. "Religion and Society: A State Within a Church." *MQR* 47 (Oct., 1973), 339-57. Examines the social and religious system of Mennonites in Paraguay to prove that a "separationist" model of the church in relation to the state tends to import the entire sociopolitical system into its own ranks, needing to face the problem from within.

Redekop, Calvin W. "The Church for the World." *ChrLiv* 12 (Jan., 1965), 15-17. Reflections on the nature of the free church tradition, including relationship to state and nationalism.

Redekop, John H. "A Christian Looks at the '79 Election." *MBH* 18 (Apr. 27, 1979), 2-5. Assesses Christian values in each of the three major parties in Canadian politics.

Redekop, John H. "A Christian Pacifist Looks at the Expression of Our Peace Witness." *MBH* 7 (Nov. 1, 1968), 7-10. Mennonites have been too hesitant to engage in lobbying or demonstrating for peace; they have not seen peace as integrally related to love and justice.

Redekop, John H. "Christianity and Political Neutralism." *CanMenn* 4 (Aug. 10, 1956), 3, 15. The question is raised as to whether or not Christians can remain neutral in light of the oppression and suffering in the world.

Redekop, John H. "Church and State: A Fresh Look." *CanMenn* 14 (Jan. 18, 1966), 6; *ChrLead* 29 (Apr. 2, 1966), 3-4. Suggests that withdrawal from political life, on the one hand, or "a deeply compromising patriotic commitment, on the other hand, are not the only options for a Christian view of government. Suggests, as a third option, that we might "analyze prayerfully and carefully the various facets of contemporary government and then react in appropriate ways to specific issues."

Redekop, John H. "Clarifying the Call to Consistency." *MBH* 16 (Oct. 14, 1977), 12. Continued concern that MCC policies may be compromising its pacifist, non-political stance.

Redekop, John H. "Evangelical Christianity . . . and Political Ideology." *ChrLead* 27 (Nov. 10, 1964), 4-5. True Christianity cannot be equated with either the liberal or conservative political orientation. It stands in tension with both.

Redekop, John H. "How Christians Should Make Political Decisions." S. F. Coffman Lecture, Minneapolis, Minn., Nov. 19, 1970. Pp. 13. MHL.

Redekop, John H. "How to Be Christian in Politics." *MBH* 16 (Oct. 28, 1977), 6-8. Anabaptist conservative Christianity parts company with political conservatism on such things as super-patriotism, militant nationalism.

Redekop, John H. "Involvement in the Political Order." *ChrLead* 40 (Sept. 27, 1977), 10. A Mennonite Brethren Board of Reference and

Counsel study paper that explores the proper perspectives and guidelines for members of the MB church as to the Christian's involvement in the political order.

Redekop, John H. *Making Political Decisions: A Christian Perspective.* Scottdale: Herald Press, 1972. Pp. 46. Calls Christians to "selective involvement" in the affairs of the state and outlines some guidelines directing Christians toward political sensitivity and such subsequent activity in these matters as appropriate.

Redekop, John H. "Mennonites and Politics in Canada and the USA: The States of the Analysis." Study paper, 1982. Box 10-H-13. CMBS/Win.

Redekop, John H. "Running Away." *MBH* 11 (Dec. 15, 1972), 10. A total withdrawal from politics, from any political involvement, is not only "intrinsically un-Christian" but is also practically impossibile.

Redekop, John H. "Should a Christian Join a Political Party?" *CanMenn* 5 (Nov. 22, 1957), 7. Discusses whether, in the terms of nonresistant Christianity, pacifists can participate in those higher governmental politics that deal in military matters?

[Redekop, John H.] "Should Mennonites Participate in Politics?" Paper, n.d. Pp. 8. MHL.

Redekop, John H. *The American Far Right.* Grand Rapids: Wm. B. Eerdmans, 1968. Pp. 232. A case study of Billy James Hargis and Christian Crusade.

Redekop, John H. "The Church and State." *MBH* 17 (Jan. 6, 1978), 18-19. Christians owe their deepest loyalty to God, but they have the responsibility of respecting and cooperating where possible with the state.

Redekop, John H. "The State." *ChrLead* 40 (Dec. 20, 1977), 12. Examines the role of the state as it is explained in section 14 of the Mennonite Brethren Confession of Faith.

Redekop, John H. "The State and the Free Church." *Kingdom, Cross, and Community.* Ed. John R. Burkholder and Calvin Redekop. Scottdale: Herald Press, 1976, 179-95. Redekop urges Mennonites to develop propositions of selective church involvement in government, based on the following premises: negativism toward government that assumes a "great wall of separation" between church and state is of recent and nonbiblical origin; free church strategy should always be one of influence, not coercion; recent changes in government toward greater participation in decisions reduces its monolithic character.

Redekop, John H. "What Is the Christian Interpretation of World Events?" *CanMenn* 4 (Jan. 6, 1956), 2, 4. World politics are generally based on power and selfishness. Christianity is based on love. The Christian's role is to witness to the state, not to demand discipleship before salvation.

Redekop, John H. (Review). *Church and State in the United States,* by Anson Phelps Stokes and Leo Pfeffer. NY: Harper and Row, 1964. Pp. 660. "Church-State Relations in America." *CanMenn* 13 (Mar. 16, 1965), 8. Recommends the three-volume survey as the standard work in the area. The treatment is both chronological and topical.

Redekopp, Orlando (Review). *Between a Rock and a Hard Place,* by Mark Hatfield. Waco: Word, 1976. *MBH* 15 (Dec. 10, 1976), 30-31. Reviewer observes that Hatfield critiques both a Christian apologist, who condones violence by splitting ethics into personal and private spheres, and a purist, who refuses all violence and withdraws from the political world.

Regehr, Ernie. *Perceptions of Apartheid: The Churches and Political Change in South Africa.* Scottdale: Herald Press; Kitchener: Between the Lines, 1979. Pp. 309. Detailed analysis of racial violence in South Africa. Includes extensive discussion of the church and state relationship in that context as well as a final chapter entitled "Violence/Nonviolence and the Dilemma of the Churches" in which the issues of conscientious objection, as well as other issues of war and peace, are raised.

Regehr, Ernie. "The State, the Church, and the Penal System." *CMR* 1 (Dec. 27, 1971), 7. The responsibility of the Christian community toward the penal system is to influence the government toward granting more concessions and to be the kind of community in which the offender experiences love and forgiveness.

Regehr, John. "Jesus and the State." *Direction* 5 (July, 1976), 30-33. Biblical study on how Jesus related to the civil and political authorities of his day.

Regehr, John. Letter to the Editor. *MBH* 12 (Aug. 24, 1973), 7-8. Explains the rationale behind his view that the Christian has no place in politics.

Reimer, Al. "Questions Raised by the Death of a Mennonite Terrorist." *MennMirror* 9 (Sept., 1979), 22. Two German articles on the death of Elizabeth von Dyck, a young Mennonite terrorist who was gunned down by police in West Germany in May, 1979, are included in this issue. The editor looks at some of the questions they raise about Christian responsibility towards such people and their destructive acts.

Reimer, Ernie M. "Christian Interpretation of World Events." *CanMenn* 4 (Feb. 10, 1956), 2. Reimer disagrees with Redekop's arguments for being aware of and interpreting world events from a Christian perspective.

Reimer, Vic. "Delegates Say Church Should Not Be Tax Collector." *MennRep* 9 (Feb. 19, 1979), 1. Mennonites gathered in Minneapolis Feb. 10-11 to launch a vigorous campaign to exempt the church from acting as a tax collector for the state, a campaign which was prompted by a General Conference employee who requested the church to stop withholding war taxes from her wages.

Rempel, John. Letter to the Editor. *MennRep* 9 (Nov. 26, 1979), 6. In response to the editorial, "Remembrance Day and the Peace Witness" (*MennRep* 9 [Oct. 29, 1979], 6), questions are raised about our strong identification with society rather than placing ourselves in a framework in which Christ and culture are opposed to each other.

Rempel, John. "On Radical Discipleship and Caesar's Politics." *MennRep* 2 (Sept. 18, 1972), 6. Favors a view committed to Christian involvement in politics over the view which hopes that God will work without the people of God becoming directly involved.

Rempel, Richard. "The Evolution of Mennonite Political Views." Student paper for Menonite History, Bethel College, Feb., 1962. Pp. 19. MLA/BeC.

Rinks, Riley. Letter to the Editor. *Menn* 88 (Feb. 13, 1973), 110-111. Criticizes the voices faulting Billy Graham for not speaking out against American bombing of Vietnam, since the writer believes government efforts toward a settlement of the war are being hampered by meddling and criticism from "peace" advocates.

Ritschl, Dietrich. "The Political Misuse of the Concern for Peace." *MennLife* 20 (July, 1965), 110-12. Our concern for peace must go beyond seeking to attain our own ends which often are not only politically based but also politically manipulated.

Rohrer, Charles. *When and Where the Church Met Three Disastrous Defeats.* Elkhart: By the Author, 3140 Idelwild St., 1973. Pp. 23. MHL. The three "defeats" named in the title are the abandonment of pacifism for just war theory in the time of Constantine, the unification of church and state in the Edict of Intolerance at Nicea, and the exchange of immersion water baptism for the sprinkling of babies baptism at the Church Council of Carthage, 418 CE.

Roth, Roy. "Paul's Teaching Concerning the Relationship of the Christian to the State." *GH* *Supplement* 37 (Dec., 1944), 749-50. The Christian should submit to government in what ever form it is found, since government is ordained by God.

Roth, Willard E., ed. *What About Church History?* Scottdale: Herald Press, 1964. Pp. 15. Peacemaker Pamphlet No. 4. Reviews Christian church history up to the Reformation to show that nonparticipation in war, the early church's position, changed to approval of war when the church was joined with the state.

Roth, Willard E., ed. *What Is Christian Citizenship?* Scottdale: Herald Press, 1964. Pp. 15. Peacemaker Pamphlet No. 6. Calls for Christian obedience to government except in those situations where it conflicts with loyalty to God. Identifies peacemaking as practicing true Christian citizenship.

Rutschman, Tom. "Repentance in a Year of Revelry." *GH* 69 (June 29, 1976), 528-29. A call for a fresh analysis of US history and a repentance from military policies and injustices born of mythologizing national history.

"Separated from the State." *CanMenn* 15 (May 9, 1967), 5. Describes Anabaptist view of the state using Menno Simons is the main source.

"Separation of Church and State." Reprint from *The Lutheran Witness.* *GH* 28 (Feb. 20, 1936), 1004. The church receives power from the atoning work of Christ; the state receives power from the sword. Therefore we must distinguish between what is owed to each institution.

"Seventy Will Discuss Duty to the State in Chicago Meeting." *CanMenn* 5 (Sept. 27, 1957), 1. Noted Mennonite speakers address the conference planned by MCC peace section.

"Statement on Position and Practices of the Church of the Brethren in Relation to War." *GH* 42 (May 17, 1949), 475, 484. The Church of the Brethren statement adopted in 1948 presents the church's position on war, freedom of conscience, conscription, and Christian citizenship.

Sanger, S. F. and Hays, D. *The Olive Branch of Peace and Good Will to Men: Anti-War History of the Brethren and Mennonites, the Peace People of the South, During the Civil War 1861-1865.* Elgin: Brethren Publishing House, 1907. Pp. 232. Compilation of personal accounts from Brethren and Mennonites in the Confederacy who refused to participate in the war. Includes treatises on church and state, and the basis for nonresistance; reprints Exemption Act of Confederate Congress.

Sawatsky, Rodney J. (Review). *A People of Two*

*Kingdoms: The Political Acculturation of the Kansas Mennonites,* by James C. Juhnke. North Newton, Kansas: Faith and Life Press, 1975. Pp. 215. *MQR* 50 (Jan., 1976), 72-73. Juhnke defines the dualism of the title as "conflict between the ethic of modern nationalism and the ethic of traditional Mennonitism" characterized by pacifism, apoliticism, and German ethnic identity.

Sawatsky, Walter W. "Power in Church-State Relations in Eastern Europe." *MQR* 55 (July, 1981), 214-17. Testing a thesis formulated by the Lutheran World Federation that the state's power is the primary variable shaping encounters between church and state in Marxist countries, the author reflects on particular meetings of Mennonites with state officials of Yugoslavia, East Germany, and the Soviet Union.

Sawatsky, Walter W. *Soviet Evangelicals Since World War II.* Scottdale and Kitchener: Herald Press, 1981. See especially Chapter 4, "Preaching and Peace."

Sawatzky, P. J. Letter to the Editor. *MennRep* 9 (July 9, 1979), 6. In response to the decision on war taxes made at the General Conference midtriennium, this writer stresses the need for military protection against communism and the biblical teachings to support the government and pay taxes.

Schlabach, Theron F. "To Focus a Mennonite Vision." *Kingdom, Cross, and Community.* Ed. John R. Burkholder and Calvin Redekop. Scottdale: Herald Press, 1976, 15-50. Reviews Guy F. Hershberger's intellectual development and life work of interpreting Mennonite nonresistance in relation to war, industrial relations, church-state relations, community life and mutual aid, and race relations.

Schmidt, Daryl Dean. "The Christian's Relation to the State." Student paper for Christians and Peace Seminar, May 15, 1964. Pp. 30. MLA/BeC.

Schmidt, Linda. "A Brief Layperson's Guide to Southern Africa." *Peace Section Newsletter* 9 (Feb.-Mar., 1979), 5-9. Attempts to provide a brief overview of the history and current political situation in several South African countries.

Schottstaedt, Bruno. "Experience in the German Democratic Republic." *MQR* 55 (July, 1981), 198-213. Author describes experiences in his life leading to his present convictions, then advances theses on Christian participation in and contribution to a socialist society.

Schrag, Martin H. "Subject to the Higher Powers." *EV* 83 (Feb. 10, 1970), 6. We are helped in clarifying our attitudes to our loyalties to God and nation by reviewing the history of the faith of our forebears.

Schrag, Tim. "Mastered by Deceit: The Work of the Exemption Committee of the Western District Conference." Paper presented to World War I Seminar, [Bethel College, North Newton, Ks.], Dec. 12, 1975. Pp. 18. MHL, MLA/BeC.

Schroeder, David. "Nationalism and Internationalism: Ground Rules for a Discussion." *Citizens and Disciples: Christian Essays on Nationalism.* Akron: MCC Peace Section, [1974], 1-3. MHL. Also in *Menn* 89 (July 9, 1974), 426-27. Suggests that there are basic biblical principles that can help to form a frame of reference within which the questions of nationalism and internationalism can be discussed constructively. Schroeder concludes that Christians are called to be citizens of the state also, discerning carefully among national policies which work for and against justice and goodness.

Schroeder, Richard J. "The Cutting Edge." *ChrLead* 37 (Jan. 22, 1974), 17. A military coup in Washington, DC is very unlikely because of the nature of the American government.

Schwartzentruber, Hubert. "A Thought on Patriotism." *GH* 64 (Jan. 12, 1971), 38. Suggests abandoning citizenship in a country like the US, where patriotic people condone war in God's name and favor the rich and powerful more than the poor and needy.

Shank, J. R. "The Christian's Relation to the Government." *ChrMon* 28 (Mar., 1936), 91-92. Young People's Meeting study guide for a lesson on this topic.

Shank, J. Ward. "Church People and Political Office." *ST* 46 (Apr., 1978), 7. The church must exert its influence upon the hearts of men rather than get involved in politics.

Shank, J. Ward. "Due Regard for Civil Law." *ST* 20 (2nd Qtr., 1952), 10. The true child of God will yield obedience where God has required it, whether to the institutions of the home, the church, or the state.

Shank, J. Ward. "'Honor the King'." *ST* 39 (July, 1971), 8. To properly honor the high officials of government is a New Testament principle that should operate during either peace or war, or under prosperity or depression.

Shank, J. Ward. "If We Should Have a Catholic President." *ST* 28 (3rd Qtr., 1960), 3. Explores the many concerns that are associated with the pending possibility of a Catholic president in the United States.

Shank, J. Ward. "Limitations of the Democratic

Process." *ST* 34 (1st Qtr., 1966), 24. Cautions that having lived under democratic institutions, and having enjoyed the blessings of freedom in a wonderful land, the Mennonite Church is prone to confuse democratic institutions and democratic processes with the outworking of Christianity.

Shank, J. Ward. "The Christian and Nationalism." *ST* 38 (Nov., 1970), 4. The dedicated Christian should not be caught up in the wave of revolution. He or she should continue to express loyalty and appreciation to country with the limits of his higher duty to God.

Shank, J. Ward. "The Christian and the State." *ST* 34 (2nd Qtr., 1966), 22. A Bible study on Rom. 13:1-7.

Shank, J. Ward (Editorial). "America! America!" *ST* 42 (May, 1974), 7. As nonresistant Christians, we live in unique relationship to our country—as neither patriots in the ordinary sense nor as radical revolutionaries. We owe our nation a deep loyalty, expressed in productive labor, service to others, and preeminently as stewards of the gospel.

Shank, J. Ward (Editorial). "Nationalism and Anti-Nationalism." *ST* 41 (Apr., 1973), 5. There is no inherent wrong in expressing loyalty and regard for one's country even in the face of its wrongdoing. Rather the sin is in the negativist and antinational attitudes.

Shank, J. Ward (Editorial). "Peace Moratoriums." *ST* 37 (Dec., 1969), 8. Nonresistant Christians need to examine everything that may be advocated in the name of peace. The use of a device like the peace moratorium is the politics of force and contradiction, not of reasoned judgment and orderly appeal.

Shank, J. Ward (Editorial). "The New Conscientious Objector." *ST* 35 (July, 1967), 2. Concern that the broadening definition for conscientious objection presents a serious risk of Mennonites becoming identified with the left wing of American politics and religion.

Shank, J. Ward (Editorial). "The Washington Inquisition." *ST* 42 (Jan., 1974), 5. The Christian response to the turmoil in Washington [Watergate] should be in the calm assurance that God is in ultimate control.

Shank, J. Ward (Editorial). "To Join or Not to Join." *ST* 48 (Jan., 1980), 4-6. Cautions against policies of both liberal peacemaking groups and conservative lobbying groups trying to influence the state to operate by Christian principles.

Shank, J. Ward (Editorial). "What Is Political?" *ST* 39 (June, 1971), 6. Politics has to do with things

relating to human government. Christians should be careful with the use of political tools—protests, lobbying, group pressures, party identification, and the like.

Shank, J. Ward (Editorial). "Which Way to Peace?" *ST* 48 (Feb., 1980), 6-8. Discusses the Hatfield amendment to the SALT II treaty and cautions against using political action to bring about peace.

Shank, J. Ward (Review). *Between a Rock and a Hard Place,* by Mark Hatfield. Waco: Word Books, 1976. Pp. 223. *ST* 46 (Jan., 1978), 26-28. Shares what it is like to be caught between the ideals of the Gospel and the hard demands of modern social and political life. Significant since it articulates ideas that are increasingly influential in Mennonite circles. Reviewer observes the most significant contribution of the book is its analysis of the relationship between the Christian and the state.

Shank, J. Ward (Review). *Christianity and the Class Struggle,* by Harold O. J. Brown. Arlington House, 1970. *ST* 39 (Mar., 1971), 15. The central political reality in the world today is that of class struggle for which the only answer is the Christian message.

Shank, J. Ward (Review). *Pioneers for Peace Through Religion,* by Charles S. McFarland. Fleming H. Revell Co., 1946. Pp. 256. *ChrMon* 39 (Apr., 1947), 119. Study of the religious organizations promoting peace through political channels leads the reviewer to criticize this cooperation of church and state.

Shank, J. Ward (Review). *The Worldly Evangelicals,* by Richard Quebedeaux. Harper and Row, 1978. In *ST* 47 (Jan., 1979), 23. This book focuses upon evangelicals and the evolution of their thought; it helps one to note that the Mennonite church is allowing a liberal, advanced scholarship to reinterpret the Anabaptist vision and in many parts is adopting the program of social radicals.

Shank, R. M. "The Divine Purpose and Relationship of Church and State." *GH* 32 (May 4, 1939), 106-107. Biblical doctrine teaches us that there must be absolute separation between church and state. The Christian is subject to the state, but does not work with or through it.

Shelly, Maynard. "Are the Stars and Stripes in a Different Class?" *Builder* 32 (Nov., 1982), 32-34. Reflects on question asked by Bruno and Ruth Schottstaedt, East German Christians, while on a visit to the United States: "Why is there an American flag in a Mennonite church?"

Shelly, Maynard. "Jesus Called Herod a Fox." *Menn* 85 (Apr. 28, 1970), 304. "On showing proper respect to rulers and those in authority, being a treatise on the Christian stance toward emperors, kings, princes, prime ministers, and presidents . . . ."

Shelly, Maynard. "Jimmy Carter's Faith." *ChrLead* 39 (Sept. 14, 1976), 6. Explores Carter's religion and politics.

Shelly, Maynard. "The Peace That Fails Us." *GH* 61 (May 28, 1968), 479-80. Reports and reflects on an ecumenical Christian Peace Conference held in Prague in which Christians from western nations seemed more able to criticize their governments' actions than Christians from Eastern European countries.

Shenk, N. Gerald. "Social Expectations of Christians in a Marxist State." *MQR* 55 (July, 1981), 231-39. Using Christianity in Yugoslavia as an example, the author describes the social and institutional reorganization of the church effected by the Marxist state, then identifies as authentic a Christianity which works outside of socially powerful institutions but is not content with relegation to the private, mystical sphere.

Shenk, Stanley C. "The Powers that Be." *GH* 41 (Nov. 16, 1948), 1082. The Christian cannot impose the nonresistant ethic on the state. Since the state has been given the sword, it has a right to live by it.

Shenk, Wilbert R. "Authoritarian Governments and Mission." *Mission-Focus* 5 (May, 1977), 6-8. Looks at theological, strategic, policy, and training questions in discussing the problem of missions in a world rapidly moving toward more authoritarian patterns of government.

Shenk, Wilbert R. "The Perils of Propaganda." *CanMenn* 18 (Aug. 28, 1970), 7. Analyzes the ambiguities and pitfalls of the perceived and real relationships between American missionaries and American intelligence gathering. Provides some guidelines for missionaries reporting from and about the countries where they are guests and, therefore, "obliged to be a model of sensitivity and good manners."

Shenk, Wilbert R. "Where Are We in Mission Today: Which Paradigm?" *Mission-Focus* 5 (Sept., 1976), 1-4. In discussing the two Biblical paradigms for mission, i.e., the missionary vision of Israel and that of Christ, the writer notes that we have tended to follow the first paradigm, even in our support or judgment of wars.

Shenk, Wilbert R. (Editorial). "Missions and Politics." *Mission-Focus* 6 (Nov., 1977), 15-16. Briefly discusses some of the positions concerning the relationship between the missionary and the political order, and lessons to learn about it.

Sherk, J. Harold. "Congressman Byron L. Johnson." *ChrLiv* 7 (March, 1960), 22-23, 33. Sketch of a pacifist who was elected to Congress.

Sherk, J. Harold. "That Special Kind of Patriotism." *CanMenn* 13 (Jan. 29, 1965), 1, 2. A Christian view of patriotism.

Sherk, J. Harold. "The Alternative Service Law and Its Operation." *MennLife* 13 (July, 1958), 103-105. An explanation of the Universal Military Training Act of 1951 and the place of NSBRO in relation to its operation.

Shetler, Jan Bender. "Editorial." *IPF Notes* 24 (Nov., 1977), 2-3. Human rights issue in light of the church-state relationship.

Shetler, Sanford G. "Christians Should Vote: Cassels." *GfT* 7 (Sept.-Oct., 1972), 12-13. Disagrees with Louis Cassel's belief that voting is a Christian duty, because the state operates by a different ethics than the church.

Shetler, Sanford G. "Church Politics." *ST* 22 (3rd Qtr., 1954), 24. The church should keep clear of practices which bear even a remote likeness to real politicians' tactics.

Shetler, Sanford G. "'Civil Religion'—Let's Quit the Confusion." *ST* 44 (Oct., 1976), 8-9. From *Guidelines for Today.* Peace activists, while rejecting God-and-country ethics, are instead championing a new kind of civil religion in which the church may scrutinize the government, but not vice versa.

Shetler, Sanford G. "Leftist Group in Dialogue at Goshen." *ST* 34 (2nd Qtr., 1966), 32. Raises questions about having leftist groups like the SDS on the campus of a church-related college such as Goshen.

Shetler, Sanford G. "On Church and State." *GfT* Series I, No. 3 (June, 1966), 1-4. Criticizes political activism such as anti-war efforts on the grounds that it departs from the principle of the separation of church and state as found in biblical materials.

Shetler, Sanford G. "'Political Activities.' " *GfT* 7 (Jan.-Feb., 1972), 16, 19. Christians should not be involved in coercing the state into a certain kind of policy decisionmaking, but they may be involved in social and community activities.

Shetler, Sanford G. (Review). *The Christian as Citizen,* by John C. Bennett. New York, Association Press, 1955. *GfT* 8 (Jan.-Feb., 1973), 16-17. Criticizes Bennett's view that Christians should be concerned with politics and views the book negatively as a moving force behind the theology of socio-political action.

Shetler, Sanford G. (Review). *The Politics of Jesus*, by John Howard Yoder. Grand Rapids: Eerdmans, 1972. *ST* 41 (May, 1973), 33. A comprehensive book with many commendable features. But the author assumes too quickly a thesis establishing Jesus' radical involvement in the social and political structures of the day.

Sider, Ronald J. "Allegiance." *Baker's Dictionary of Christian Ethics*, ed. Carl F. H. Henry. Grand Rapids, MI: Baker Book House Co., 1973, 17. Christian allegiance to God limits one's allegiance to the state.

Sider, Ronald J. "Aside: Where Have All the Liberals Gone?" *The Other Side* 12 (May-June, 1976), 42-44. The essence of liberal theology can be described as when the current culture supplies the operational norms and values for a significant number of evangelicals and mainline church people. Concerns like racism, militarism, civil religion, and unjust economic structures are not spoken to because of the liberal context.

Siebert, Allan J. "Mennonites and Political Power: Yoder Gives Lectures in Winnipeg." *MennRep* 9 (Oct. 1, 1979), 13. John Howard Yoder gave a series of three lectures at the Univ. of Winnipeg, each centering around political themes: "An Anabaptist View of Political Power;" "Mennonite Political Conservatism: Paradox or Contradiction;" and "An Anabaptist View of Liberation Theology."

Siegel, Barry. "A Quiet Killing." *FQ* 8 (May, June, July, 1981), 19-26. Reprinted from *Rolling Stone*, Issue 337. Los Angeles reporter probes thoughtfully into the killing of an Indiana Amish baby by rock-throwing young people. Asks perceptive questions about the relationship between the state and the nonresistant Amish.

Smith, C. Henry. *Smith's Story of the Mennonites*. Fifth edition revised and enlarged by Cornelius Krahn. Newton: Faith and Life Press, 1981. (First edition copyright 1941.) Pp. 589. A comprehensive overview of Mennonites from the 16th century to the present. The theme of nonresistance is woven into the story, while the final chapter, "Witnessing in War and Peace," discusses church-state issues in early America and the World Wars.

Smucker, Donovan E. "Christian Responsibility and the State." *Menn* 65 (June 13, 1950), 414-15. Rejects a rigid dualism between church and state, although the church is always to be engaged in witness to all, including the state, of what ought to be.

Smucker, Donovan E. "Peace and War: Christian Responsibility in the Face of National and International Problems." *GH* 43 (Mar. 21, 1950), 275. The Christian must witness to government if Christ is King. The Christian can become involved in government to the degree which does not force him or her to disobey Christ.

Smucker, Donovan E. "Russian Christianity and Communism." *Menn Comm* 7 (Sept., 1953), 10-11, 34; *Menn* 68 (May 17, 1953), 312-13. Briefly discusses the relationship of church and state in Russia before the communist government, and considers communism a judgment on Christianity.

Smucker, Donovan E. "The Federal Election of 1979: Some Reflections About Politics." *MennRep* 9 (Nov. 12, 1979), 7, 8. Reflections on the Canadian federal election of 1979, politics in general, and how they relate to the Christian faith and witness.

Snyder, John M. "Responsibilities of Christian Citizens." *ST* 39 (July, 1971), 15. Basic to consideration of the responsibilities of Christian citizens in God's ultimate sovereignty over people and nations. Examines the ministry of grace and the ministry of wrath.

Snyder, John M. (Review). *Conflict and Conscience*, by Mark O. Hatfield. Waco: Word Books, 1971. *ST* 40 (Apr., 1972), 14. Brings into focus many legitimate concerns for contemporary committed Christians. Recommended for careful, critical reading by mature persons who are grounded in the scriptural teaching as to the Christian's relation to the state and responsibility toward general society.

Snyder, John M. (Review). *I Pledge Allegiance: Patriotism and the Bible*, by Paul S. Minear. Westminster Press, n.d. Pp. 141. *ST* 44 (May, 1976), 31-32. While the reviewer agrees with the author that much professed Christianity places national interests before Chrsitian commitment, he criticizes the book for mixing biblical perspectives with nonevangelical and humanist viewpoints.

Souder, Elvin. "Problems of a Conscientious Objector in the Legal Practice." *PCMCP Seventh*, 101-12. North Newton, Kansas: The Mennonite Press. Held at Tabor College, Hillsboro, Kansas, June 16-17, 1949. A conscientious objector faces no greater problems of an ethical nature in legal practice than those one might encounter in business. Speaks to questions of law enforcement and the relationship of church and state encountered in legal practice.

Stahl, Omar. "A Christian Encounter in East Berlin." *CanMenn* 14 (Mar. 22, 1966), 7. A report on an exchange of views by representatives of East and West churches on church and state relationships and an agreement to do something for peace together.

Stauffer, James K. "Vietnam Churches Struggle with New Trials." *Menn* 93 (Sept. 19, 1978), 537; *MennRep* 8 (Sept. 18, 1978), 7. Describes freedoms and limitations of the evangelical church in Vietnam since the change in government. Reflects on the church's previous sanctioning of American military policies and its present compromise of church and state separation by allowing some pastors to work on local government committees.

Stauffer, John L. *The Message of the Scriptures on Nonresistance.* Harrison, Va.: Tract Press, n.d. Pp. 15. MHL. Summarizes New Testament and Old Testament views on war, church and state, etc., as well as the differences between the Testaments on these issues.

Steiner, Sam. "Kitchener Germans and National Socialism." Term paper for History 268G course, Mar. 28, 1973. Pp. 22. CGCL.

Steiner, Susan Clemmer. "The July National Holidays." *GH* 69 (June 29, 1976), 525-26. Reflects on Canadian and American national holidays in July, and asserts that, for the Christian, the church, not the nation, is one's primary identity.

Stoltzfus, Ed. "Menno Simons' Theology of the Nonresistant Christian and His Relation to the State." Paper presented to Mennonite History class, [Goshen College, Goshen, Ind.], n.d. Pp. 18. MHL.

Stoltzfus, Grant M. (Review). *Preachers Present Arms,* by Ray H. Abrams. Scottdale: Herald Press, 1969. Pp. 354. *GH* 62 (Nov. 18, 1969), 1015-16. Discusses the book's impact when it was first published in 1933, and the continuing relevance of its study of the relationship of church and state during wartime.

Stoltzfus, J. Letter to the Editor. *GH* 66 (Feb. 20, 1973), 169. Responding to the Jan. 16 editorial decrying American bombing in Vietnam, the writer attributes the editor's views to a political attempt to smear the newly re-elected president, instead of relying on the gospel of Christ to bring peace.

Stoltzfus, Luke G. (Review). *A Strategy for Peace,* by Frank Epp. Grand Rapids: Wm. B. Eerdmans, 1973. *GH* 67 (Oct. 1, 1974), 758. Recommends the book for its fresh approach to issues of nationalism, North American militarism, separation of church and state, a biblical response to communism, evangelism and peace witness.

Stoner, John K. "Caesar and God." *EV* 82 (Dec. 1, 1969), 11. An examination of the conflicting claims of church and state in light of Scripture and in light of the current American situation.

Stoner, John K. (Review). *Between a Rock and a Hard Place,* by Mark Hatfield. Waco, Tex.: Word Books, 1976. Pp. 224. *Menn* 91 (Oct. 26, 1976), 633; *ChrLead* 39 (Aug. 17, 1976), 14. Hatfield prods the church to separate its vision from the destiny of America, examining questions of nuclear war, violence, and patriotism.

Stoner, John K. (Review). *I Pledge Allegiance: Patriotism and the Bible,* by Paul S. Minear. Philadelphia: Geneva Press, 1975. *Menn* 91 (Jan. 13, 1976), 28; *ChrLead* 38 (Oct. 28, 1975), 20; *EV* 88 (Nov. 25, 1975), 12; *MennRep* 5 (Nov. 10, 1975), 10; "A New Understanding of the Powers." *GH* 69 (Jan. 13, 1976), 23. Discusses issues centering around the relationship of church and state in the context of biblical texts, advocating the congregation as the locus for scripture study.

Stucky, Harley J. "Should Mennonites Participate in Government?" *MennLife* 14 (Jan., 1959), 34-38, 12. A professor of history sharpens the issue of the Christian's participation in government by delineating reasons for participation in politics and reasons for not doing so.

Stucky, Harley J. "The Problem of Participation or Non-participation in Politics for a Conscientious Christian." Paper, n.d. Pp. 16. MHL, MLA/BeC.

Stucky, Vernon. Letter to the Editor. *Menn* 95 (Jan. 15, 1980), 46. America's insistence that wars and weapons will bring freedom and security indicates the need for national repentance.

Studer, Gerald C. Letter to the Editor. *GH* 63 (Aug. 25, 1970), 706-707. Expresses regret that the Mennonite Church approved paying jobs in I-W assignments as alternative service, instead of remaining with nonsalaried PAX or VS work. Supports all forms of draft resistance as valid witnesses to the state.

Studer, Gerald C. "The Bicentennial: Two Views. 1. Will a Christian Be a Patriot?" *GH* 69 (Feb. 10, 1976), 102-103; *Menn* 91 (June 22, 1976, 426-27. Christians cannot divide their loyalty between God and the state; they are called to live wholly according to God's kingdom.

Studer, Gerald C. "The Christian and Politics: A Testimony." *GH* 69 (Oct. 26, 1976), 816-17. Because he wants to be known more for his Christian citizenship than his American one, Studer does not vote in political elections.

Studer, Gerald C. "Will a Christian Be Patriotic?" *ChrLead* 39 (Jan. 20, 1976), 5. Christian patriotism notes that it is righteousness not military might that exalts a nation, that it is justice for all, tempered with mercy that gives strength to a nation. A Christian must first give loyalty to Christ.

---

*For additional listing, see Supplement, pp. 717-719.

Stutzman, M. D. "The Christian's Relation to Civil Government." *GH* 28 (Apr. 18, 1935), 77-78. While the Christian is to be nonresistant, it is ordained that civil government wield the sword to execute wrath. The Christian needs to be subject to government, stay out of the political world, uplift the country by high morals, and pray for the state.

Swartley, Willard M. "How to Interpret the Bible: A Case Study of Romans 13: 1-7 and the Payment of Taxes for War." *Seeds* 3, 4 (June, 1984), 28-31. Applies the method proposed in Swartley's *Slavery, Sabbath, War and Women* study to this text and issue.

Swartley, Willard M. "Politics and Peace (*Eirene*) in Luke's Gospel." *Political Issues in Luke-Acts*, ed. Richard J. Cassidy and Phillip J. Scharper. Maryknoll: Orbis Books, 1983. Summarizes the divergent political understandings of Luke's gospel as developed by Hans Conzelmann, John H. Yoder, and Richard J. Cassidy. After examining Luke's distinctive use of *eirene*, Swartley argues that Luke's peace gospel presents a third way. It neither directly opposes the empire and the rulers (Cassidy) nor does it present the gospel as a political apologetic, seeking pacification with Roman rule (Conzelmann).

Swartley, Willard M. "The Christian and Government—Church State Relations." Paper, 1976, revised 1983. Pp. 4. AMBS.

Swartley, Willard M. and Krieder, Alan. "Pacifist Christianity: the Kingdom Way." *Pacifism and War*, ed. Oliver R. Barclay. Leicester: Inter-Varsity Press, 1984. Pp. 38-60. One of seven position essays representing varying positions on war, Swartley and Kreider present the biblical-theological, historical, and ethical bases for the pacifist position as the kingdom way. Both authors have short responses to other essayists: Swartley to Arthur Holmes (pp. 35-37) and Kreider to Sir Frederick Catherwood (pp. 81-84; Holmes responds to the Swartley-Kreider article (pp. 61-67).

Swartz, A. D. "Should a Christian Vote?" *GH* 33 (Dec. 26, 1940), 827-28. As Christ's ambassadors we should not vote but represent his law of love.

Swartzentruber, Anita. "The Argentine Mennonite Church, the State, and Military Service." Paper presented to Mennonite History class, English Clinic, Jan. 16, 1954. Pp. 7. MHL.

"The Christian Witness to the State." *GH* 56 (Apr. 30, 1963), 363. PPC notes that if the state is ordained by God, the people of God ought to give witness to what the purpose of the state really is.

"The Church in the German Democratic Republic." *GH* 72 (July 17, 1979), 562-63. Disillusionment and spiritual and theological disorientation are problems in the GDR churches but they show strength in issues of war and peace.

"The Church Makes Peace in a World Filled with War." *CanMenn* 7 (Jan. 23, 1959), 6. Papers given at Study Conference in Winnipeg on Jan. 9-11, 1959. Archie Penner looks at the problems of church and state, while Harvey Taves regards secularism, not communism, as the enemy.

"The Lordship of Christ over Church and State." *Menn* 70 (Oct. 11, 1955), 632-33. Summary of the Puidoux Theological Conference and its statement on "The Church and Peace."

"The Position of the Mennonite Church of North America on Peace, War, Military Service, and Patriotism." *Menn* 63 (Oct. 12, 1948), 5-6. The official statement of the GCMC on this subject. Appeals to the biblical basis for love and nonviolence. While refusing military service, Mennonites have shown genuine willingness to render service of national importance in alternative programs.

"To Be a Christian Citizen." *With* 3 (Sept., 1970), 24. A report from the Christian Citizenship Seminar by Mennonites who exposed themselves to the political process to think about their responsibilities as Christians to their respective countries, either the United States or Canada.

Tarr, Leslie K. "The Tightly-Shut World of Neo-Fundamentalism." *ChrLead* 41 (Nov. 7, 1978), 2. Covers ten recurring basic tenets and life outlooks of neo-fundamentalism, which is threatening evangelicalism. One of these tenets is the equation of right-wing politics with the appoved Christian political stance.

*The Church, the State, and the Offender*. Newton: Faith and Life Press, Church and Society Series No. 3, 1963. Pp. 24. Explores the biblical and theological premises which bear on the issues of criminal and capital punishment and makes some suggestions as to what might be some Christian responses to the laws, to crime prevention, and to offenders. Prepared by the Peace and Social Concerns Committee of the General Conference Mennonite Church and approved at a study conference in 1961.

Thiessen, Norman. "MB Youth: A Decade Later." *ChrLead* 42 (Dec. 4, 1979), 2. A study of the values of MB youth, including observations on social and political issues.

Toews, John A. "Can the Christian Participate in Government?" *The Voice* 7 (Jan.-Feb., 1958), 4.

Argument against greater participation in government is summarized by stating that the world's problems can be dealt with more effectively by giving an independent witness in word and deed "in the name of Christ."

Toews, John A. *People of the Way: Selected Essays and Adresses*. Ed. Abe J. Dueck, Herbert Giesbrecht, and Allen R. Guenther. Winnipeg, Man.: Historical Committee, Board of Higher Education, Canadian Conference of Mennonite Brethren Churches, 1981. Pp. 245. Memorial collection includes section entitled "Peace and Nonresistance: Crucial Issues for the Church." Essays in this section are: "True Nonresistance," "The Christian and Armed Combat," "The Expression of Our Peace Witness," "The Christian Response to Communism," and "The Christian and the State."

Toews, John B. *Czars, Soviets, and Mennonites*. Newton: Faith and Life Press, 1982. Pp. 221. Analytical and interpretive study of the history of the Mennonites in Russia. While this examination of parochial Mennonitism in the wider socio-political context discusses the church's peace witness, including the church and state relationship, at various points, chapters which deal more explicitly with war/peace issues are: "The Russian Mennonites and World War I," 63-78; "Response to Anarchy," 79-94; "Communism and the Peace Witness," 95-106.

Toews, John E. "Paul's View of the State." *ChrLead* 41 (Apr. 25, 1978), 5. Examines what Romans 13 says about peace and warfare. Lists several applications of Romans 13 for 20th century Christians.

Tripp, Myron. "Civil Liberties for Christian Pacifists." *ChrMon* 39 (July, 1947), 205. Documents cases of US government denial of religious liberty to pacifists in this century.

"US Supreme Court Denies Veterans Benefits for CO's." *Forum* A (Apr., 1974), 9. In a recent decision, the US Supreme Court ruled that a conscientious objector who served two years of alternate service is not eligible for veterans' educational benefits.

Unger, George. "The Church and the World." Paper prepared for the church seminar, Goshen Biblical Seminary, Goshen, Ind., 1956. Pp. 43. MHL.

Unger, George. "The Social Thought of the Early Manitoba Mennonites: 1874-1924." Paper presented to Sociology Seminar, Goshen College, Goshen, Ind., May 22, 1954. Pp. 67. MHL.

Univ. of Waterloo Gazette. "Frank Epp May Have Lost But He's Not Done With Politics."

*MennMirror* 9 (Sept., 1979), 7. In the past, Frank Epp has been involved in issues like Vietnam, Russia, and the Middle East, and now, although he was defeated in his riding in the federal election, he plans to remain involved in the Canadian struggle for unity out of concern for a peaceful resolution.

Unruh, Pamela J. Letter to the Editor. *Menn* 92 (Feb. 22, 1977), 142. The World Peace Tax Fund is an extension of liberal politics which, however well-intentioned, does not remove warmakers from power or curb excessive government spending.

Unruh, Richard. "Classical Patterns of Church-State Relations." *Direction* 5 (July, 1976), 22-26. Discusses the Catholic, Lutheran, Anabaptist, and Reformed models of church-state relations.

Unruh, Richard (Review). *Vision and Betrayal in America*, by John B. Anderson. Waco: Word Books, 1975. In *ChrLead* 39 (Mar. 16, 1975), 15. A call for Americans to recommit themselves to the values of constitutional tradition in the aftermath of Watergate.

Unruh, Richard (Review). *Washington: Christians in the Corridors of Power*, by Edward E. Plowman and James C. Heffley. Wheaton: Tyndale House, 1975. An honest attempt to discover the spiritual changes that are happening among individuals in government.

Unruh, W. F. "Witness Through Involvement." *Menn* 75 (Apr. 5, 1960), 213. Urges Mennonites to get involved in government, for example, by supporting the "Point Four Youth Corps" proposal and the new moves toward world disarmament.

Unsigned. "Probing the Issues of Peace." *ChrLead* 43 (Sept. 9, 1980), 10-12. Reports on five papers dealing with peace issues prepared for the MB convention at Minneapolis.

Unsigned. "The Pacifist's Obligation to the State." *IPF Notes* 4 (Mar., 1958), 3. (IPF Executive Committee, Paul Hershberger, Pres., edits the *Notes*.) Reviews Mennonite participation in government in Europe and North America and the difference of opinion existing on the issue.

"Vietnam Study: Relief Often Tied to Politics, Military." *MennRep* 2 (Oct. 2, 1972), 1. Relief agencies enjoy the benevolences of a government because the latter recognizes a potential in the former to realize its political and military ends.

Van der Wissel, Felix. "The Christian and the State," *Proceedings of the Fourth Mennonite World Conference*. Akron: MCC, 1950. Pp. 252-56. As the state seeks to control the whole of a people's life, the church must again become a suffering, serving, pilgrim people.

Van Houten, Diether H. Letter to the Editor. *ChrLead* 41 (Jan. 31, 1978), 16. There are "born-again" Christians in the military services and many are members of Officers' Christian Fellowship, an internationally affiliated organization with the purpose of witnessing for Christ to the military officer.

Vandezande, Gerald. Letter to the Editor. *MBH* 19 (Apr. 25, 1980), 9. Christians must declare their convictions on peace and justice in order to reform the electoral system.

Varkey, Joseph. "The Christian and Politics: An Analysis." *GH* 69 (Oct. 26, 1976), 817-18. Because the church and the state share common concerns—justice, welfare, etc.— Christians need to contribute to the state's workings in order to find satisfactory solutions to these problems.

Vogt, Roy. "Mennonites in Politics: No Radicals." *MennMirror* 9 (Apr., 1980), 22. Calls upon the growing number of Canadian Mennonites in politics to risk radical Christian action even if that action requires "engaging in unsafe or unpopular politics."

Vogt, Roy. "The RCMP—Does It Matter How They Get Their Man?" *MennMirror* 7 (Feb., 1978), 26. The RCMP, as enforcers of law and order, deserve respect but are no more immune from criticism and prosecution than any other citizen who violates the law.

Vogt, Roy (Editorial). "Who Is a Mennonite?" *MennMirror* 10 (Sept., 1980), 30. Assesses various components of the Mennonite identity, including aspects such as principles of peace and nonviolence, church and state relations.

Vogt, Virgil. "Youth and the Mennonite Tradition." *ChrLiv* 4 (Dec., 1957), 20-21. Recent research on the Goshen College campus reveal this generation's attitudes toward Christian involvement in politics.

Vos, Peter. "Peace in Christian Endeavor." *MCE* 2 (Oct. 1, 1935), 5-6. War exists because Christianity has not been tried. If enough people would refuse to fight it would affect government decisions.

Voth, David L. "An Examination of Three Mennonite Theological Alternatives with Special Note of their Views Toward Participation in Foreign Policy." MA in Peace Studies thesis, AMBS, 1982. Pp. 117. Compares the views of John H. Yoder, Gordon D. Kaufman, and Duane K. Friesen on discipleship, the believers' church, and nonresistance in an effort to determine

whether Mennonite participation in the foreign policy arm of the government is theologically consistent with Mennonite faith.

"War Tax Packet." [Akron, Pa.]: MCC, Feb., 1976. MIIL. Of the seventeen essays in this packet, two are specifically on church-state relations: Klaassen, Walter, "Anabaptism and Church/ Government Issues," pp. 12; and Miller, Marlin, "The Christian's Relationship to the State and Civil Authority," pp. 6.

"Witness in Washington." *CanMenn* 3 (Feb. 25, 1955), 2. Comments on the witness of US Mennonites to the state regarding draft alternatives.

"Who Can Postmark the Stamp of Liberty?" *Lifework* 4 (1979), 2-3. Summarized from articles by Richard K. MacMaster in *Purpose* (Scottdale: 1976). Relates stories of Eve Yoder and John Newcomer of Pennsylvania who stood for peace and liberty during the Revolutionary War.

Waltner, Erland. "An Analysis of the Mennonite Views on the Christian's Relation to the State in the Light of the New Testament." Unpublished ThD dissertation, Eastern Baptist Theological Seminary, 1948. Pp. 273. An exegetical and historical study. The Swiss Brethren and some of their descendents today may have overemphasized the punitive function of the state and neglected its constructive functions. Menno Simons' ideal of "Christian rulers conducting their functions according to the principles of Christ ought not to be dismissed as impossible."

Waltner, Erland. "The Christian and the State." *ChrLead* 24 (Sept. 19, 1961), 4-5, 24. The Christian is to pray for her or his government and be subject to it, in principle, but a Christian witness also involves refusal to give unconditional support, e.g., by war taxes.

Waltner, Erland. "The Mennonite View of the Relation of Church and State." *PCMCP Fourth,* 53-69. North Newton, Kansas: n.p. Held at Bluffton, Ohio, Aug. 24-25, 1945. Times of national crisis focus the conflicting demands of church and state upon the individual. Surveys the Mennonite view of the church, the Mennonite view of the state, and the Mennonite view of the relation of the Christian to the state.

Wasylycia-Leis, Judy. "The Church and Politics: Nonparticipation Is an Inadequate Response." *MennRep* 6 (May 17, 1976), 5. Calls for selective Christian involvement in politics, based on Jesus message of being "doers" of the word.

Weaver, Amos W. "Some Implications of Law and Grace." *ST* 30 (3rd Qtr., 1962), 12. Examines how law and grace functions in the Christian's relationship to society.

Weaver, John W. "Presidents, Prayers, and Breakfasts." *GH* 64 (June 1, 1971), 492-93. Criticizes presidential prayer breakfasts for reinforcing values of militarism and oppressive economic policies, and calls Mennonites to greater courage in "speaking truth to power."

Weidner, Mark. "A Paper on Church and Stae from the Early Church to the Reformation as Viewed from the Witness the Church Has Made to the State." Paper presented to the History of Christianity class, AMBS, Elkhart, Ind., Dec. 12, 1970. Pp. 19. AMBS.

Wenger, J. C. "A Leader Faces Civil Powers." *ST* 46 (Sept., 1978), 1. Relates the story of George R. Brunk facing the Board of Education for the Commonwealth of Virginia about the right of a boy not to salute the flag for conscience' sake.

Wenger, J. C. *Separated unto God.* Scottdale: Mennonite Publishing House, 1951. Pp. 350. A plea for Christian simplicity of life and for a scriptural nonconformity to the world. Nonconformity functions as the context for separation from the worldly military nature of political rule, and for nonresistance specifically church and state.

Wenger, J. C. "The Message of the Mennonite Church." *GH* 63 (Aug. 25, 1970), 697. Summarizes major tenets of Anabaptist leaders, including statements on the relationship of church and state, baptism, and nonviolence.

Wenger, J. C. *The Way of Peace.* Scottdale, Pa.: Herald Press, [1977]. Pp. 70. MHL. Examines peace teachings of Old and New Testaments and traces the history of the doctrine of peace as well as its present status in the larger church. In the last chapter, Wenger summarizes the case for the way of peace along the lines of the sovereignty of God, cross-bearing, internationalism, evangelism, the permissiveness of God, the divine institution of government, the separation of church and state, etc.

Wenger, Linden M. "Sound Philosophy of Church-World Relationship." *ST* 28 (4th Qtr., 1960), 18. The three aspects of a sound philosophy of church-world relationships involve the relationship to the material world, the relationship to the institutions of society, and the relationship to people as individuals.

Wherry, Neal M. *Conscientious Objection.* Washington, D.C.: Government Printing Office, 1950. Vol. I, pp. 364. Vol. II, pp. 288. MHL. Chronicles World War II conscientious objection from the government's point of view. Mennonite documents and summaries of

Mennonite practices and teachings are found in chapters entitled: "Church Backgrounds of CO's," "Conscientious Objection in American History," "Legislative Provisions on Conscientious Objection." Other chapters offer extensive information about the CPS program—history, assignments, administration, discipline, statistics, etc.

Whyte, Frazer. Letter to the Editor. *MennRep* 8 (Jan. 9, 1978), 6. Questions Frank Epp's decision to seek the Federal Liberal nomination, asking how he will remain nonviolent and how he will be able to give first loyalty to God's kingdom.

Wiebe, Don (Review). *Agenda for a Biblical People,* by Jim Wallis. Harper and Row, 1976. Pp. 145. *MBH* 15 (Dec. 24, 1976), 21. Wallis attacks the peace between the Christian church and present economic and military goals of Western capitalism, but reviewer labels his ethics "utopian."

Wiebe, Franz. "The Statelike Functions of the Mennonite Colonies in Paraguay." Paper for War, Peace, and Revolution class, AMBS, Elkhart, Ind., May 8, 1969. Pp. 2. AMBS

Wiebe, Katie Funk. "Finding the Enemy." *ChrLead* 40 (June 7, 1977), 19. A look at H. Berkhof's book *Christ and the Powers* in which a discussion of the cosmic powers and their influence on society is found.

Wiebe, Katie Funk. "No-sweat Christianity." *ChrLead* 40 (Oct. 25, 1977), 17; *MBH* 16 (Oct. 28, 1977), 5. Reflections on hearing a Latin American evangelist challenge the church to break its ties to the state and the military.

Wiebe, Katie Funk. "Two Sides of a Counterfeit Coin." *ChrLead* 39 (Apr. 27, 1976), 19. Looks at how politics gets involved in church decision making. Civil religion in government and politics in church life are two sides of a counterfeit coin.

Wiebe, Katie Funk. "We Can't Escape Politics." *GH* 63 (Sept. 1, 1970), 723. Maintains that since church people are concerned about political issues and that such issues cannot be separated from spiritual concerns, the church should not continue to keep politics at arm's length on the basis of the separation of church and state.

Wiebe, Peter. "The Day I Talked About the Flag." *Builder* 21 (Oct., 1971), 8-9, 12. Speech delivered at dedication of community flag calls audience to enlist in the war commanded by the Man of Sorrows, the Prince of Peace. Includes commentary on community reaction to the speech.

Wiebe, Vernon R. "Authoritarian Governments

and Mission." *ChrLead* 40 (July 5, 1977), 19. Authoritarian governments demand ultimate authority, which may create a difficult atmosphere in which missionaries who are guests have to work.

Wiebe, Vernon R. Letter to the Editor. *ChrLead* 39 (Apr. 13, 1976), 14. Mennonite Brethren have mixed too much of the kingdom of man with the kingdom of God.

Wiens, Martin. "Mennonites and Politics: Participation or Observation." Student paper for Mennonite History, Life and Thought, May 9, 1978. Pp. 11. MLA/BeC.

Wiens, Rudolf P. "Brazil Needs a Concerned Witness." *Menn* 86 (Feb. 16, 1971), 107, 108. A resident of Brazil since 1952, the author explains the relationship between the Brazilian Mennonite church and the Brazilian state.

Wiens, Rudolf P. "Misinformed about Brazil." *Menn* 87 (Apr. 11, 1972), 257, 258. Corrects figures and opinions of American writers about the political, social, and economic situation in Brazil.

Wittmer, S. C. "War and You." *Menn* 53 (Jan. 18, 1938), 4-5. The proper time to express our opinion in opposition to war is before the war starts as we vote and participate in lawmaking.

Yake, C. F. "Democratic Democracy." *YCC* 29 (May 2, 1948), 140, 141. Discussion of the constitutional interpretation and present practice as regards "religious instruction" in the public schools.

Yake, C. F. "Dethroning God." *YCC* 11 (Mar. 9, 1930), 76. The question of citizenship of nonresistant people is an important issue. Comparisons are made between America as a Christian land and Russia as a nation without God.

Yake, C. F. "Freedom for What?" *YCC* 32 (July 1, 1951), 628, 629. A discussion of freedom and liberty, e.g., the political sense, must not obscure the importance of freedom from sin. Destroying communism does not destroy bondage to sin.

Yake, C. F. "On the Spot." *YCC* 35 (Nov. 28, 1954), 380. Freedom of religion to worship God according to the dictates of conscience is tested when it interferes with the United States military.

Yake, C. F. "Patriotism." *YCC* 22 (Apr. 20, 1941), 540. The propaganda machinery fuels the war mentality by stirring up patriotic feelings. Christian patriotism fosters the development of Christian morality, courage, conscience, and character.

Yamada, Takashi. "The Anabaptist Vision and Our World Mission (II)." *Mission-Focus* 4 (Mar., 1976), 7-14. In this discussion of the Anabaptist movement and vision as an attitude of confrontation in world missions, the writer also considers the nonresistant position of Mennonites in world mission.

Yoder, Edward. "Beware of False Prophets." *GH Supplement* 35 (Apr., 1942), 78-80. Points on which Mennonites need to be clear include: the state is provisional, human, and lower than the church. The Christian, therefore, gives all of his or her obedience to the church; Christ taught nonresistance; Christ is superior to the Old Testament; nonresistant Christians will suffer reproach.

Yoder, Edward. "Christ's Kingdom of Truth." *GH Supplement* 37 (Feb., 1945), 942. The truth of Jesus exposes the kingdoms of earth as ultimately powerless.

Yoder, Edward. "Christianity and the State." *MQR* 11 (July, 1937), 171-95. The basic indifference of Jesus and the early church toward the state suggests the separation of Christianity and the state. Mennonites are pessimistic about the value of participation in government.

Yoder, Edward. "Citizenship and War Service: Peace Principles from a Scriptural Viewpoint." Part 25. *GH* 32 (Apr. 20, 1939), 78-79. Some totalitarian trends in this and other countries should make it clear to nonresistant Christians that in times of war their position may well depend on the clearness of their own personal conviction.

Yoder, Edward. "Did Jesus Get Politicaly Involved?" *GfT* 6 (Sept.-Oct., 1971), 2-3. Reprinted from *Mennonites and Their Heritage*, No. 3, Mennonite Central Committee, 1942. Also reprinted in *GfT* 9 (Mar.-Apr., 1974), 18-19, 3, under the title "Jesus in a World of Strife!" Jesus practiced nonresistance and nonparticipation in politics because his kingdom was not of this world.

Yoder, Edward. "Kinds of Pacifists: Peace Principles from a Scriptural Viewpoint." Part 42. *GH Supplement* 34 (July, 1941), 358. There are many kinds of pacifists and several kinds of Christian pacifists. The nonresistant Christian pacifist has no particular advice to give government; the liberal Christian pacifist tries to apply Christ's teaching to politics.

Yoder, Edward. "Origen and War." *GH Supplement* 36 (Aug., 1943), 447. Origen defends the early Christian refusal to participate in warfare and politics.

Yoder, Edward. "The Christian's Duty to Goverment." *GH Supplement* (Aug., 1942), 462-

63. A historical, biblical study showing that Romans 13 is not calling for Christians to obey every commandment of government.

Yoder, Edward. "The Cry for Peace." *GH Supplement* 37 (Dec., 1944), 758-59. The church cannot outline specifics for postwar peace treaties but, because it recognizes the sinfulness of people and nations, it must tell the state what Christ has said about the value of persons.

Yoder, Edward. "The Obligation of the Christian to the State and Community—'Render to Caesar'." *MQR* 13 (Apr., 1939), 104-22. The Christian community, as a loving fellowship, is "a light to the world" and in its scattered life is "a salt to the earth;" while committed to the way of love, it also works through direct social action to improve society.

Yoder, Edward. "Worshipping Satan: Peace Principles from a Scriptural Viewpoint." Part 48. *GH Supplement* 34 (Dec., 1941), 822. Those who want America to defend religious liberty by war are deluding themselves; spiritual values cannot be defended with carnal weapons.

Yoder, Edward (Archival). Box 5: pacifism— indices, booklets, correspondence; Pax Christiana; peace articles, ideas. Box 7: "Christianity and the State;" "The Christian's Attitude Toward Participation in War Activities;" "Compromise with War." Goshen, IN. AMC. Hist. Mss. 1-47.

Yoder, Edward and others. *Must Christians Fight? A Scriptural Inquiry.* Akron: MCC, 1943. Pp. 68. MHL. Fifty-six questions and answers on nonresistance, ranging from definition of principles, biblical teaching, the essential, nonresistant character of Christ, apostolic practice of nonresistance, etc., to payment of taxes, relationship to pacifism, separation of church and state, etc.

Yoder, J. Otis. "One-World Government." *ST* 40 (Feb., 1972), 29. World events indicate that a one-world government is yet to come as predicted in Rev. 13:1-18. This world government will be demonic in origin, religious in purpose, and universal in scope.

Yoder, John H. "Caesar and the Meidung." *MQR* 23 (Apr., 1949), 76-98. A case study in church discipline.

Yoder, John H. "Capital Punishment and Our Witness to Government." *Menn* 78 (June 11, 1963), 390-94. A discussion of the Christian's relation to the state, using capital punishment as a case study.

Yoder, John H. "Discerning the Kingdom of God in the Struggles of the World." *International Review of Missions* 68 (1979), 366-72. Points out the dangers of identifying too easily or too quickly the acts of God with the events of statecraft. Proposes not that we abandon the effort to attach Christian meaning to worldly events, but that we use Jesus' servanthood as the criterion by which we discern that meaning in order to keep the church and state relationship in proper perspective.

Yoder, John H. "How Do Christians Witness to the State?" *GH* 56, Part 1, (May 28, 1963), 461; Part 2, (June 4, 1963), 475; Part 3, (June 11, 1963) 506; Part 4, (June 18, 1963), 522; Part 5, (June 25, 1963), 542. The Christian peace witness is characterized by the inner life of the church, by the service the church renders to people in need, by a human concern for people in government, and by formal testimony at congressional hearings. Whether the exercise of the franchise is or is not an appropriate Christian witness to the state is less clear.

Yoder, John H. "Nonconformity and the Nation." *ChrLiv* 2 (Feb., 1955), 8-9, 25, 33. The deeper issue behind conscientious objection to military service is the question of loyalty to the nation or to the Kingdom of God.

Yoder, John H. "Our Nationality? Christian: The Way of Peace in a World at War." Part 2. *GH* 54 (July 25, 1961), 645-46. No political nation, no geographical homeland, can take precedence over the heavenly citizenship which is given a Christian in the new birth. Nationalism is testing many Christians on this point.

Yoder, John H. "Radical Reformation Ethics in Ecumenical Perspective." *Journal of Ecumenical Studies* 15 (Fall, 1978), 647-61. The constitution of the church as voluntary determines the shape of the Christian community and, thus, the structure of Christian ethical reasoning. Moreover, since this voluntary nature disengages the church from alliances with the sword, wealth, and hierarchy, the substance of a believers' church ethic becomes the rejection of violence.

Yoder, John H. "The Christian Witness and Current Events." *GH* 47 (Aug. 17, 1954), 777. The prophetic aspect of the Christian witness involves a proclamation of God's judgment on the life of non-Christian society and the nation. American involvement in Indo-China and Guatemala prompts this kind of witness.

Yoder, John H. "The Christian Witness to the State." *CanMenn* 9, Part 1, (Mar. 31, 1961), 2-3; Part 2, (Apr. 7, 1961), 2; Part 3, (Apr. 14, 1961), 2, 4; Part 4, (Apr. 21, 1961), 2, 9. An appeal for an undiluted witness that God is sovereign and Lord of history in all areas of our individual and corporate lives.

Yoder, John H. *The Christian Witness to the State.* Newton: Faith and Life Press, LAS Series No. 3, 1964. Pp. 90. Examines the question of whether a Christian pacifist position rooted in christological considerations is relevant to the social order. Concludes that such relevancy is supported by a view of the church and state relationship which recognizes a duality of response—faith or unbelief—but which upholds a unity of norm; God's will for all is the love revealed in Christ. Thus the Christian should speak critically about specific ways the state is misusing its ordination while not presupposing the faith of the person or persons involved in such evils.

Yoder, John H. "The Christian's Responsibility to the State." *MBH* 2 (Dec. 6, 1963), 4-6. The Christian is to be subject to the existing regime, but at the same time, limit this loyalty to the proper business of government and state clearly where this submission ends.

Yoder, John H. "The Hermeneutics of the Anabaptists." *MQR* 41 (Oct., 1967), 291-308. Holds that the distinctive feature in Anabaptist hermeneutics consists of reading the text within the context of congregational discernment, especially congregations committed to obedience and freedom from the state.

Yoder, John H., ed. *The Legacy of Michael Sattler.* Scottdale: Herald Press, 1973. Pp. 191. This collection of the early Anabaptists' writings with editorial comment includes not only article No. 6 of the Schleitheim Confession, from which much of the Mennonite tradition of nonresistance derives, but also references to such related subjects as government, the oath, the sword, etc. See indices, pp. 183ff.

Yoder, John H. "The National Ritual: Biblical Realism and the Elections." *Sojourners* 5 (Oct., 1976), 29. The way one approaches the electoral system may be reflective of one's view of the state, which may lean either to full participation or complete withdrawal. Position advocated is that participation in the electoral system must be reflective of the non-electoral mode of which the criteria are chosen only to witness to the truth.

Yoder, John H. "The Otherness of the Church." *Concern* No. 8, Scottdale: Herald Press, 1960. Reprinted in *MQR* 35 (Oct., 1961), 286-96. The assumption of a Christian world is no longer held. Evaluation of this change and its implications for the free church are examined in the historical context.

Yoder, John H. "The Subtle Worldliness." *GH* 47 (Dec. 21, 1954), 1209. Our nonconformity should consist not in ignorance or withdrawal, but in the exercise of independent judgment in matters of a social, economic, and political nature and in continual application of Christian truths.

Yoder, John H. "The Two Kingdoms." *Christus Victor* 106 (Sept., 1959), 3-7. Challenges the assumption held by the Lutheran two-kingdom theory that agape is, essentially, utopian, ahistorical, and therefore incompatible with order, dissolving any society to which it might be applied.

Yoder, John H. "The Wrath of God and the Love of God." Address delivered at the Historic Peace Churches and International Fellowship of Reconciliation Conference, Beatrice Webb House, England, Sept. 11-14, 1956. Pp. 11. MHL.

Yoder, John H. "When the State Is God." *GH* 46 (Feb. 17, 1953), 153. When the state establishes itself as God, the obedient Christian may suffer and seem to play no evident role in the world.

Yoder, John H. "Why Should a Christian Witness to the State?" *GH* 56, Part 1, (Apr. 30, 1963), 373; Part 2, (May 7, 1963), 381; Part 3, (May 14, 1963), 407; Part 4, (May 21, 1963), 434. Because of concern for the state and the welfare of its people; to be helpful to misguided Christians in government; because the church has been given the ministry of prophecy; because in modern life whatever we do is already a form of witness. Therefore, Christians should endeavor to make their witness positive, intelligent, and scriptural.

Yoder, John H. "Why Speak to Government." *CanMenn* 14 (Dec. 13, 1966), 10; *GH* 59 (Jan. 25, 1966), 73-74. Background paper for the MCC consultation in Minneapolis. We should speak to government because: we love our neighbor; we reject idolatry; the statespersons in North America are church people; we are Christian missionaries; we live in a democracy; we are already involved. In so speaking, what do we say? That God is on the side of humanity; that human beings cannot be trusted to be their own judges; that violence is no basis for social peace.

Yoder, Orrie D. "'Politics' in the Church." *ST* 17 (1st Qtr., 1949), 26. The tactics of worldly politics have no place in the church of Jesus Christ.

Yoder, Orrie D. Letter in "Our Readers Say." *GH* 58 (Oct. 26, 1965), 951. If we are to be nonresistant then we must also maintain a strict separation of church and state.

Yoder, Orrie D. "Peace and War: What Will You Answer God About the Blood Question?" *GH* 42 (Dec. 26, 1949), 1243. The Christian should not take part in war or government.

Yoder, Orrie D. "Unique Privileges of Our Christian Schools." *ST* 30 (1st Qtr., 1962), 21. One of the unique privileges of a Christian school is that it enables the maintenance of the concept of the separation of church and state.

Zahn, Gordon. "The Religious Basis of Dissent." *MQR* 42 (Apr., 1968), 132-43, In the Judeo-Christian heritage the minority religious community, through its prophets, is called to be "a powerful source of social and political dissent."

Zehr, Albert. "Deserter-Evangelist in Tradition of Menno." *CanMenn* 18 (May 22, 1970), 8. John Webb tells a Mennonite congregation in Ontario why he left the army and then, with his wife, fled to Canada. He is disillusioned by a "system which is built on, and nourished by, war and bloodshed, containing a church . . . which blesses the state and prays, 'God grant our men safety, and may they bring back many dead.'"

Zehr, John D. "An Analysis of the Attitudes That Mennonites Show Toward Voting." Paper for War, Peace, and Nonresistance class, GBS, Elkhart, Ind., spring, 1966. Pp. 12. AMBS.

Zehr, Paul M. "After the Shouting." *GH* 69 (Nov. 23, 1976), 907-908. A post-mortem of the US Bicentennial observes its positive as well as negative effects on Mennonites. Among the latter is a greater confusion of church and state.

Zisk, Betty Ann [Hershberger]. "A Pacifist Approach to Civil Government: A Comparison of the Participant Quaker and Non-Participant Mennonite View." BA Thesis, Swarthmore College, Swarthmore, Pa., 1951. Pp. 178. BfC.

Zochert, Donald (Review). *Thaddeus Stevens and the Fight for Negro Rights*, by Milton Metzler. Thomas Y. Crowell Co., 1967. Pp. 231. *ChrLiv* 15 (Feb., 1968), 36-37. Reviewer observes the book's thesis is that while Stevens worked for justice in promoting the 13th, 14th, and 15th amendments to the Constitution, he was politically a contradictory figure.

# 6
# Civil Disobedience

## A. General

Baechler, Gerald W. "Peace Begins with Christ." *GH* 72 (Aug. 28, 1979), 687. All the peace demonstrations and efforts will not be helpful unless peace begins within us and in our daily relationships.

Bartel, R. F. "Prepare Statement on Draft-Dodgers, Protests." *CanMenn* 16 (July 2, 1968), 1, 2. A report on the 37th convention of the Ontario MB Conference held in Kitchener July 14-16 which includes the text of a statement of non-support for US draft-dodgers in Canada and rejection of all MCC involvement in marches and protests.

Beachy, Alvin J. "A Case Study in Civil Disobedience: Pilgram Marbeck." *MennLife* 25 (Jan., 1970), 12-15. Marbeck's life represents "one of the longest records of civil disobedience within the sixteenth century." Brief comparative references are made to Thoreau.

Beachy, Alvin J. "The Biblical Basis for Civil Disobedience." *MennLife* 25 (Jan., 1970), 6-11. A review of biblical history leading to the conviction that "there are times in the history of man [sic] when Christians can be obedient to the coming kingdom of God, only as they are civilly disobedient to their earthly rulers."

Beitler, Alan. "Civil Disobedience as Christian Discipleship." Paper for War and Peace in the Bible class, AMBS, Elkhart, Ind., Dec. 7, 1981. Pp. 26. AMBS.

Bender, Harold S. "When May Christians Disobey the Government?" *GH* 53 (Jan. 12, 1960), 25-26, 44; *GfT* Series 2, 5 (Mar.-Apr., 1970), 16-17. Maintains that draft legislation is a civil, not a military act, and as such, Christians should obey the law and register. The Christian may disobey the government only when the content of an act required by the state is an evil in itself since "the desire to witness to the truth or against an evil cannot be a ground to disobey the requirements of the state which in themselves are not wrong."

Bishop, Elaine L. "Quaker Youth Describes 200-Hour December Fast in Canadian Capital." *CanMenn* 15 (Jan. 17, 1967), 1, 2. Description of a fast in Ottawa from Dec. 23-31, 1966 by Young Friends appealing to Canadians to remember innocent war victims in Vietnam who suffer during the Christmas season.

Bohn, E. Stanley. Letter to the Editor. *Menn* 95 (July 22, 1980), 449. Responds to a letter criticizing Peter Ediger;s civil disobedience at Rocky Flats nuclear weapons plant by clarifying the facts about the incident.

Bontrager, L. "War Questions with their Answers." *GH* 33 (Dec. 12, 1940), 771-72. A call to discipleship and peace, even if this should mean disobeying civil laws.

Born, Daniel. "Christians Protest 'Movable Holocaust.'" *ChrLead* 41 (May 23, 1978), 18. Report on the demonstration at the Rocky Flats nuclear weapons plant on Apr. 29-30, 1978.

Born, Daniel. "Obeying God Over Caesar." *ChrLead* 43 (Nov. 4, 1980), 12. Encourages readers to consider nonregistration for the draft as a valid Christian response by relating it to other historical circumstances where Christian commitment called for civil disobedience.

Breneman, Rose; Good, Luke; Hershey, Mim; Hess, Dan. "An Open Letter to Pastors of College Students." *GH* 63 (Aug. 25, 1970), 700. College students explain their support of peace demonstrations as a witness to the government against war and killing, in response to minister's sermon declaring that Christians should remain separate from government structures.

Brennan, Michael. "Students for a Democratic Society." Paper for class in War, Peace, and Revolution, AMBS, Elkhart, Ind., Apr. 10, 1969. Pp. 4.

Brenneman, Virgil J. "A Voice from the Crowd." *GH* 63 (Jan. 6, 1970), 10-11. Author reflects on his participation in the mass peace demonstration in Washington, DC, and is disturbed that the administration tried to discourage people from participating and deliberately downplayed the size of the crowd and their totally nonviolent spirit. A critical evaluation of this mode of peace witness.

Buckwalter, Clair. Letter to the Editor. *GH* 64 (July 6, 1971), 611. Criticizes *Gospel Herald* reporting of MDS repairing park benches at the Washington Monument because it incorrectly implies that the damage was done by peace demonstrators. Criticizes the MDS action for responding to a peace demonstration as an apparent blessing on Nixon's war policies, when it has not made similar gestures toward reconstruction after race riots.

Burkhalter, Terry. "Demonstrations at the Chicago Democratic Convention." Paper for Christian Attitudes Toward War, Peace, and Revolution class, AMBS, Elkhart, Ind., Apr. 10, 1969. Pp. 3. AMBS.

Charles, Howard H. "Can Civil Disobedience Be Christian?" *Builder* 21 (July, 1971), 19-20. Defines civil disobedience and provides some New Testament, ethical, and theological guidelines to direct consideration of specific acts of civil disobedience.

Conservative Mennonite Conference. "The Church and Civil Government." *GfT* 12 (July-Aug., 1977), 16-17. Position statement on church and state relationships includes statements on war, civil disobedience, payment of war taxes.

Cunningham, Spencer (photographer). "Conversion Possible." *Forum* 13 (Oct., 1979), 7-9. "A photo essay on the 1979 protest against the Rocky Flats nuclear weapons plant near Denver, Colo.

DeBoer, Hans A. "'I Must Disobey Laws Against Democracy and God'—Sibley. *CanMenn* 13, Part 1, (Apr. 13, 1965), 1, 11; Part 2, (Apr. 20, 1965), 11. A Quaker pacifist analyzes student protests, the US involvement in Vietnam, and the nature of the East-West cold war.

DeBoer, Hans A. (Editorial). "A Man Who Talked to the Viet Cong Suggests 15 Responses to Asian War." *CanMenn* 13 (Oct. 5, 1965), 6. Suggestions include taking a critical attitude toward information available through national news services, beginning serious Christian-Marxist dialogue, supporting demonstrations and peace protests against the Vietnam War, etc.

Derstine, C. F. "The Churches and Conscientious Objectors." *ChrMon* 26 (Mar., 1934), 94-95. Christian people who object to war should not only live nonresistantly but take every opportunity to protest the government's refusal to recognize conscientious objectors.

Dick, Mervin. "Reservations: Taking the Military Oath: Practicing Civil Disobedience." Exploring Peace Study, March 19-20, 1980. Pp. 6. MBBS.

Drescher, John M. "Demonstration . . . Then Proclamation." *ChrLead* 42 (May 22, 1979), 24. Before one talks of love and reconciliation, one must make love and reconciliation visible.

Drescher, John M. "Kill Toys Teach the 'Game' of Killing." *MBH* 7 (Nov. 29, 1968), 4-5; *Menn* 83 (Dec. 3, 1968), 746-47. Since replicas of the "machines of violence" contradict the spirit of Jesus, Christians should boycott and protest vigorously against "war toys."

Drescher, John M. "The Game of Killing." *ChrLiv* 15 (Dec., 1968), 9-10. Urges Christians to protest the manufacture and sale of war toys.

Driedger, Leo. "Acceptable and Non-Acceptable Forms of Witness: A Special Study Report on Nonviolence and Civil Disobedience." Leaflet printed by the Canadian Board of Christian Service, Winnipeg, Manitoba, 1966. Pp. 2. Also in *CanMenn* 14 (May 31, 1966), 7-8. Discusses and evaluates the trends in nonviolent protest stimulated by the civil rights movement and the Vietnam war. Analysis includes consideration of Mennonite youth involvement in these trends.

Driedger, Leo. "Non-Violence and Civil Disobedience: Acceptable and Non-acceptable Forms of Witness." *CanMenn* 14 (May 31, 1966), 7, 8. A discussion of several prominent leaders of nonviolence, nonviolent methods used today, new trends in nonviolence etc.

Dyck, A. A. "War Will Always Be With Us." *CanMenn* 18 (Jan. 16, 1970), 5. Participation in the March Against Death (Washington) or in other demonstrations is questioned. Rather than working towards peace in far-off places one must seek to help those who lack peace in one's own neighborhood.

Ediger, Peter J. "The Alpha and the Omega." Dramatic reading presented to the Conference on Conscience, Religion, and Resistance: Civil Disobedience and the Law in the Nuclear Crisis, sponsored by Center on Law and Pacifism, Philadelphia, Pa., n.d. Pp. 7. MHL.

Eitzen, Allan. Letter to the Editor. *GH* 61 (Mar. 5, 1968), 214. Recommends more active peace witnessing, such as a large-scale war tax protest. In light of the fact that the government is becoming immune to verbal dissent.

Eitzen, Ruth. "Can I Have a Part in Change?" *Lifework* 5 (1981), 14. Describes Mennonite protest against slavery which may be seen as "forerunner" of the later abolition movement, and suggests that war is another issue in which small protests could bring overarching change.

Epp, Frank H. "An Evaluation of a Demonstration: A Day with the Doukhobors." *CanMenn* 13, Part 4, (Aug. 3, 1965), 2. Frank Epp reflects on the peace vigil near the RCAF Radar Base at Dana, Sask. on June 27. He concludes that the vigil was a good thing because it championed Jesus Christ as the Prince of Peace.

Epp, Frank H. "Civil Disobedience." *CanMenn* 11 (May 10, 1963), 6. Expresses support for the practice of civil disobedience in desegregation demonstrations in the American South. "It is better to break the law and be right than to keep the law and be wrong."

Epp, Henry H. "The Word of God in the Nuclear Age." *CanMenn* 7 (May 29, 1959), 2. An interpretation of the Church Peace Mission conference at Evanston, Ill. The military chaplaincy, civil disobedience, and nonviolence as a means of social change were among the topics discussed.

"Fifteen Goshen Students Marched in Alabama." *CanMenn* 13 (Apr. 20, 1965), 3, 11. Goshen students and Civil Rights demonstrators have common belief in the uses of nonviolence in the search for justice in race relations.

Fast, Victor. "The March on Washington." *CanMenn* 13 (Dec. 14, 1965), 5. Letter to the editor from participant in the March on Washington in the fall of 1965 for peace in Vietnam. Fast felt that the mass protest was justified because one voice can often not be heard.

Franz, Arthur R. "What Should My Attitude as a Christian Be Toward War?" *MCE* 1 (Aug. 21, 1934), 2-4. The Mennonite church is not now taking an active part in the fight against war and militarism. Those who do not raise a voice of protest against the evils of war are guilty of these evils.

Friesen, Ivan. Letter to the Editor. *God and Caesar* 1 (Oct., 1975), 4-5. Engaging in W-4 Form war tax refusal was a freeing experience from the fear associated with civil disobedience.

Friesen, Richard. "War Protest in Popular Music." Paper for War, Peace, and Revolution class, AMBS, Elkhart, Ind., n.d. Pp. 3. AMBS.

Gleysteen, Jan. "Käthe Kollwitz—An Artist's Protest to War." *YCC* 48 (July 9, 1967), 5. The story of Kollwitz, a famous woman artist, whose art reflects her social conscience and pacifist ideology.

Glockner, Michael W. "Contemporary Protest Songs Interpreted." Paper for War, Peace, and

Revolution class, AMBS, Elkhart, Ind., May 8, 1969. Pp. 3. AMBS.

Hackman, Walton. "The Draft Lottery: An Explanation of a Stopgap Move." *GH* 63 (Jan. 6, 1970), 14-15. Explains the procedures followed in the draft lottery system and contends that, instead of removing the draft's inequities, the changes represent a stopgap move to quiet protest against the draft and war.

Hackman, Walton (Editorial). "No Victory Parades, No Peace Marches." *Intercom* 13 (Nov., 1973), 4. Observes the change in public sentiment from protesting the war in Vietnam to supporting the Middle East war.

Harms, Orlando. "What I Learned in California." *ChrLead* 39 (May 25, 1976), 2. Report on a trip made to California to investigate the practices Mennonite Brethren and others were employing regarding legal and illegal immigrants.

Hershberger, Guy F. "Conscience of Society." *GH* 61 (Feb. 20, 1968), 150-51. [No. 24] In support of his position that the church is the conscience of society, the author lists and describes cases of Mennonite protest against the Vietnam war and efforts toward peacemaking in addressing the problem of segregated urban housing.

Hershberger, Guy F. "Do We Have the Boldness of the Suffering Servant? Our Peace Witness—In the Wake of May 18." (Part 12). *GH* 60 (Nov. 14, 1967), 1039. We must protest war and all social evils by having "boldness without arrogance."

Hershberger, Guy F. "Protest Against Evil." *GH* 61 (Jan. 30, 1968), 104. [No. 22] Asserts that protest against social evils goes hand in hand with preaching the gospel, citing prophetic witness and demonstrations by early Anabaptists.

Hershberger, Guy F. "The Current Upsurge of War Objection." *GH* 61 (Jan. 16, 1968), 57. [No. 20] Writer observes that the growth of anti-war sentiment during wartime is unusual, and that the burgeoning peace movement protesting activities in Vietnam is disturbing to government officials.

Hershberger, Guy F. "What Must We Do if Our Function as the Conscience of Society, and Our Obligation to Protest Against Evil, Is to Be Implemented? Our Peace Witness—In the Wake of May 18." (Part 24). *GH* 61 (Feb. 20, 1968), 150-51. Lists seven ways that Mennonites have protested the Vietnam war, poverty, and racial discrimination.

Hilborn, Jean A. "Positive Protest Through Involvement." *YCC* 49 (June 16, 1968), 2;

*CanMenn* 16 (Mar. 5, 1968), 1. Text of the speech by Jean Hilborn which won the national peace oratorical contest in Canada. A challenge to protest: its positive function arises from involvement in social justice issues. To work for peace is to understand the roots of war.

"Intercollegiate Peace Fellowship Almost Loses Sight of Its Theme." *CanMenn* 17 (Apr. 1, 1969), 1, 2. Report on IPF meeting March 19-22 in Washington, DC, discussing the peacemaker in revolution. Speakers with a wide range of views addressed the meetings. One was a member of SDS, another a former editor of the underground *Washington Free Press,* another was facing trial for refusing conscription. Myron Augsburger said that violent revolution is the old "just war" doctrine in a new garment. Norman Kraus said nonresistance as it is practiced will not see us through the next few decades and it is not biblical. There is no social revolution without conflict, and we must find our place in it.

Janzen, David and Peters, Kay. "Students Protest in Washington." *MennLife* 17 (Apr., 1962), 63-65. "The Bethel [College] students' demonstration for peace in Washington is an example of an active attempt to ameliorate the condition facing the world."

Kaufman, Donald D. "War Taxes: From Personal to Corporate Responsibility." *God and Caesar* 2 (Oct., 1976), 2-3. Excerpts from a larger paper prepared for the Commission on Home Ministries stating that civil disobedience is a necessary Christian witness in the face of wrong.

Klaassen, Walter. "The Nature of the Anabaptist Protest," *MQR* 45 (Oct., 1971), 291-311. A delineation of the main features of the Anabaptist protest in the religious, social, and political context of the time, noting how Catholics and Protestants viewed the protest, and inquiring into Anabaptist consciousness of their protest.

Kraus, C. Norman. Letter in "Our Readers Say." *GH* (Dec. 14, 1965), 1088. As we carry out our mission of mercy in Vietnam we must disassociate ourselves from the war effort. We must let the public and government officials know we are opposed to the war.

Lange, Andrea. "A New Testament Perspective on Civil Disobedience." Paper for War and Peace in the Bible, AMBS, Elkhart, Ind., fall, 1981. Pp. 17. AMBS.

Lapp, John A. (Review). *Democracy, Dissent, and Disorder: The Issues and the Law,* by Robert F. Drinan. Seabury Press, 1969. Pp. 152. *GH* 63 (June 9, 1970), 524. Recommends the book for its insights into legal dimensions of current social protest, including conscientious objection and opposition to the Vietnam war.

Lapp, John E. "The Gospel in Reconciliation of Men." *GH* 61 (Mar. 12, 1968), 228-29. The social implications of the gospel include economic and racial equality and opposition to war.

Leatherman, Daniel R. Letter to the Editor. *GH* 61 (Jan. 23, 1968), 94. Disagrees with Jim Juhnke's conclusion (Jan. 9, 1968, 38-39) that the threat of widespread Mennonite civil disobedience influenced Congress to enact more favorable Selective Service laws. Supports political mobilization on issues such as draft laws, even though such action can be misconstrued as "self-interest."

Leatherman, Loretta. "Taking a Stand." *WMSC Voice* 54 (Dec., 1980), 7. Encourages some form of war tax resistance to protest the dollars being used to finance American military endeavors.

Lehman, Carl M. "Tax Resistance—A Form of Protest?" *Menn* 90 (Oct. 14, 1975), 573-74. While tax resistance may be acceptable for activists and absolutists, the focus of Christian opposition to paying for war should be pressure on Congress to keep military spending down.

Lehman, Emmett R. "Martin Luther King and Civil Disobedience." *GfT* Series 2, Vol. 3 (Apr.-June, 1968), 5-6. King's nonviolent resistance takes obedience to civil authorities too lightly, and thus cannot bring about justice, since order is a prerequisite of justice.

Lehman, Emmett R. "Positive Dissent." *GfT* Series 2, Vol. 3 (Feb., 1968), 5-6. Reprinted also in *GfT* 6 (Sept.-Oct., 1971), 12. All witness to the priority of divine law over human must avoid violence and civil disobedience, since violent dissent cannot bring about justice.

Lehman, Emmett R. "The Fraud of Civil Disobedience." *ST* 35 (July, 1967), 4. Considers civil disobedience from both its moral and legal aspects.

Lehman, Emmett R. "The Rule of Law." *GfT* Series 2, 4 (Nov.-Dec., 1969), 16-17. Civil disobedience for any reason less worthy than preservation of the spiritual life shows disregard of God's command to obey the civil authorities.

Lind, Loren. "A Time to March." *YCC* 47 (Jan. 23, 1966), 6. A description of participating in the march on Washington for Peace in Vietnam.

Lind, Loren. "What Should We Do?" *YCC* 47 (July 3, 1966), 8. Survey of protest responses to the Vietnam War. What should Mennonites do to express their peace witness?

Lind, Millard C. "Is There a Biblical Case for Civil Disobedience?" *God and Caesar* 4 (July, 1978), 6-8. An examination and summary of Old Testament texts which set forth the clash between the two mutually exclusive political systems: the kingdom of Yahweh and the rebellious kingdoms of humankind.

Lind, Millard C. "Is There a Biblical Case for Civil Disobedience?" Paper, n.d. Pp. 15. AMBS.

"Marching Is One Way to Protest." *With* 4 (Oct., 1971), 26. Responses to the question "As a Christian who feels strongly that war is wrong, would you participate in such a march to make your views known?"

Macartney, John, and Conrad, Ron. "Disobedience: Civil, Criminal." *Fellowship* 34 (May, 1968), 19-20. Attempts to provide a guideline for comparing different kinds of disobedience and offers support for civil disobedience.

Makaroff, Sonya. "Civil Disobedience at Comox." *CanMenn* 13 (Aug. 24, 1965), 4. Asks Mennonites to participate in Comox Peace Project '65, an organized protest against the basing of nuclear weapons on Canadian soil.

Martin, Harold S. "Biblical Truth and the Call to Peacemaking." *ST* 47 (June, 1979), 4-5. Maintains that the pacifism which is made popular today through anti-war demonstrations, the New Call to Peacemaking, and the emphasis on nonviolence is not the same as biblical nonresistance. Nonresistant Christians refuse to participate in war, while many pacifists work for political change on the mistaken assumption that human nature is good.

McNamara, Francis J. "Capitol Peace Rally Successful 'Red Move.' " *GfT* Series 2, 5 (Jan.-Feb., 1970), 12, 9. Reprinted from *The Johnstown* [PA] *Tribune Democrat,* December 8, 1969. Claims anti-Vietnam war demonstrations are essentially communist operations.

"Nins Says Western Campaigns Held Dissidents." *Menn* 94 (June 5, 1979), 392. An interview with Russian dissident, Nins, points out that peaceful demonstrations arising out of Christian principles are important.

"Nonviolence and Civil Disobedience." *CanMenn* 14 (Feb. 8, 1966), 8. Report on the reading of a paper by Leo Driedger during Council of Board (GCMC) meeting on Jan. 21. Driedger's paper reviewed biblical and contemporary leaders who practiced civil disobedience, including Hosea, Jesus, and Martin Luther King, and noted that Mennonites in general have not participated in radical civil disobedience. Paper concludes that positive ways to bind society's

wounds should be found but that occasional radical action is needed.

Oliver, John. "Jesus and Subversives." *GH* 64 (Oct. 5, 1971), 820-21. Society in Jesus' day responded to subversives with "undisguised contempt." Jesus, however, responded differently. Perhaps, then, the followers of Jesus ought to reach out to those practicing civil disobedience and other forms of dissent with sensitivity and reconciliation.

Peachey, J. Lorne. "Hup—Left, Right, Left, Right . . . " *ChrLiv* 14 (May, 1967), 11. Report on a peace march organized by Bethel College Peace Club for Armistice Day, 1966.

Penner, P. E. "Christians Should Link with Peace Movement." *CanMenn* 17 (Nov. 28, 1969), 4. Having taken part in the March Against Death, two Canadians explain their motives. They appeal to Christians to join ranks in opposing war and not to repeat the error of the Crusades in the twelfth century.

"Resource Packet on Civil Responsibility." Papers presented at the Civil Responsibility Consultation, AMBS, Elkhart, Ind., June 1-4, 1978, and the War Tax Conference in Kitchener, Ont., Nov., 1975. Pp. [181]. MHL. Includes: Stucky, Ted W. and Toews, Reg, "The Administrative Dimension," 3-12; Lind, Millard, "Is There a Biblical Case for Civil Disobedience (O.T.)?" 13-35; Bauman, Kenneth, "Federal Taxation and the Mennonite Conscience," 36-50; Schroeder, David, "Is Civil Disobedience Called for in the Case of War Taxes," 51-60; Kraybill, J. Elvin, "Nonpayment of Income Taxes for Religious Reasons," 66-76; Yoder, John H., "The Limits of Obedience to Caesar: The Shape of the Problem," 77-91; Keeney, William, "Corporate Action and Individual Conscience," 92-109; Burkholder, J. Lawrence, "Prophetic Criticism and Corporate Responsibility," 110-18; Miller, Marlin E., "The Christian's Relationship to the State and Civil Authority," 126-31; Swartley, Willard M., "The Christian and Payment of War Taxes," 132-48; Kaufman, Donald D., "War Taxes: From Personal to Corporate Responsibility," 149-78; Toews, John E. "Paul's View of the State," 179-81 (reprinted from *ChrLeader,* Apr. 28, 1978).

"Rocky Flats Saga Builds Support During Trial." *Menn* 94 (Jan. 2, 1979), 6. A summary of the eleven-day trial of the ten defendants who were involved in the Rocky Flats protest. They were found guilty of trespassing but were acquitted on the charge of obstructing a public passageway.

Reed, Kenneth; Pawling, Jim; and Rhodes, James. "Setting Our Faces Toward Lockheed." *GH* 73 (June 17, 1980), 491-93. Three Mennonite participants in demonstrations against weapons manufacture explain how their actions relate to their Christian commitment.

Reed, Watford. "How to Cool a Hot Summer." *ChrLiv* 19 (May, 1972), 2-7. How the city of Portland avoided violence and rioting during demonstrations in the summer of 1970.

Regier, Austin. "Civil Disobedience for Christ: A CO's Witness to His Faith." *CanMenn* 14 (Nov. 1, 1966), 8. Regier refused to obey the Selective Service act of 1948 which gave him the right of religious conscientious objection while denying it to others equally conscientious but of different religious persuasion.

Regier, Harold R. "Conference Resolution on War Taxes Passed." *God and Caesar* 3 (Nov., 1977), 2. A resolution calling on congregations and regional conferences of the General Conference Mennonite Church to commit themselves to a serious study of civil disobedience and war tax resistance was passed at triennial conference sessions held in Bluffton, Ohio, July 28-Aug. 3, 1977.

Regier, Harold R. "Congregations to Prepare for Conference on Civil Responsibility." *God and Caesar* 4 (July, 1978), 4-5. A listing of books, papers, and slide sets available to facilitate congregations in their study of civil disobedience and war tax issues in preparation for the special General Conference mid-triennium session.

Regier, Harold R. "Group Initiates Peace Pledge." *God and Caesar* 5 (Feb., 1979), 11-12. The article encourages others to follow the example of a group of persons from the Bethel College Mennonite Church, North Newton, Kans., who have developed a "Peace Pledge" and considered other personal actions to protest war taxes.

Reimer, Vic. "More Than a Gripe." *Menn* 93 (Apr. 4, 1978), 240. The madness of nuclear weapons calls all Christians to witness against evil powers. Writer encourages Mennonites to participate in the national peaceful demonstration at Rocky Flats against nuclear weapons.

Roberts, Marge. Letter to the Editor. *Menn* 92 (May 3, 1977), 300-301. Tax resister explains why she must protest the amount of money the government calls her to contribute to the war machine, and describes the thought-provoking conversations her resistance raises with IRS officials, etc.

"Setting the Record Straight on Billy Graham's War Stand." *CanMenn* 14 (June 7, 1966), 1, 2. Although Billy Graham in a Texas Crusade did *not* appeal to his listeners to support the war in Vietnam, he did contrast those who "protest sin and moral evil" by attending his meeting and the "noisy minority" which protests against the war. This distinction is either careless rhetoric or moral confusion.

Shank, J. Ward. "Civil Noncompliance." *ST* 35 (July, 1967), 1. As a means of social protest, civil disobedience has been badly confused with problems of the Christian conscience. In situations where a Christian must stand upon his rights of conscience perhaps a better term would be "civil noncompliance."

Shank, J. Ward. "The Death of Martin Luther King, Jr." *ST* 36 (June, 1968), 1. Comments on the implications and assessment of the death of King.

Shank, J. Ward (Editorial). "The Ultimate in Civil Disobedience." *ST* 35 (Nov., 1967), 2. The true alternative to civil disobedience is in fidelity and stability, both as Christians in the church and as citizens in the state.

Shank, J. Ward (Editorial). "Voice in the Streets." *ST* 37 (Apr., 1969), 4. Questions the Christian legitimacy of demonstrations and other public forms of protest.

Shelly, Maynard. "Church Bell and Shuffling Feet Rattle Chains of Chauvinism." *CanMenn* 17 (Oct. 31, 1969), 1, 2. Bethel College students and faculty protest the continuation of the Vietnam War. In addition to a 4-day vigil and a march through the streets of Newton, KS, 11 ministers published a letter in the local paper calling on fellow Christians to join in a renewed effort to live as peacemakers.

Shelly, Maynard. "Draft Resistance Makes the Scene." *With* 3 (May, 1970), 28. In addition to alternate service, in 1969 the Mennonite traditions of civil disobedience and martyrdom have come back to take their place as new options in the Mennonite protest against war.

Shelly, Maynard. "Peace Church Baffled by Peace Walk." *CanMenn* 14 (Dec. 13, 1966), 1, 11-18. Historical summary of events leading up to the controversial peace walk by Bethel College students on Nov. 11 and an evaluation of the march itself which includes reactions of Mennonite and non-Mennonite communities.

Shenk, Phil M. "Hope, Faith, and Love." *GH* 70 (May 17, 1977), 401-402. Participant in a "Christians Against Torture" demonstration reflects on the Christian call to witness and hope for national repentance for supporting repressive governments through economic and military aid.

Sherk, J. Harold. "Viet-nam War Protesters." *RepConsS* 24 (Nov., 1967), 1. Reports on various forms of protest against the war including a letter to President Johnson from Gene Stoltzfus and other International Voluntary Service workers in Vietnam.

Shetler, Sanford G. "Martin Luther King, Five Years Later." *GfT* 8 (Mar.-Apr., 1973), 15-16; (May-June, 1973), 7, 17; (July-Aug., 1973), 14-15; (Sept.-Oct., 1973), 12-13; (Nov.-Dec., 1973), 13-14; 9 (Jan.-Feb., 1974), 12-13; (Mar.-Apr., 1974), 13-14; (May-June, 1974), 14-15; (Jul.-Aug., 1974), 13-14. Evaluation of King's leadership and teachings on nonviolence and his position within the nonviolent civil rights movement; traces King's tactics to Thoreau, the Fellowship of Reconciliation, and especially Gandhi; describes civil disobedience; distinguishes between nonviolence and nonresistance. Author claims that the writers King picked as mentors—Kirkegaard, Heidegger, Sartre, Tillich—led him in the direction of humanism rather than toward a theology of salvation through the atonement of Christ.

Shetler, Sanford G. "Pacifism and the War in Vietnam." *GfT* Series I, No. 5 (May, 1967), 1-8. Truly biblical objectors to war and evil should refrain from participating in activities that complicate a peace witness, such as the popular anti-Vietnam war protests.

Smedes, Lewis B. "Dissent and Disruption." *GH* 61 (Apr. 16, 1968), 337. Reprinted from *The Reformed Journal.* Affirms the right to protest unjust American policies in the Vietnam war, but denounces protesters who refuse to respect another's opinion.

Smith, Allan W. Letter to the Editor. *MennRep* 9 (Aug. 20, 1979), 6. Overt civil disobedience is not scriptural, but voluntary protest may be made about war taxes if one feels convicted to do so.

Sprunger-Froese, Mary. "Defendant's Version of the Offense." *Forum* 13 (Oct., 1979), 8-9. An excerpt from Sprunger-Froese's statement which she submitted to Judge John Kane Jr., in federal court in Denver, explaining her convictions and reasons for trespassing at Rocky Flats nuclear plant.

Sprunger-Froese, Mary. Letter to the Editor. *Forum* 13 (Nov., 1979), 16. One of the defendants in the Rocky Flats trial provides some detail on the trial proceedings and thoughts about this kind of peace witness.

Stoner, John K. Letter to the Editor. *Menn* 93 (Apr. 25, 1978), 284. The unprecendented evil of the nuclear arms race demands that peaceloving people make their objections known, through legal means or through civil disobedience.

"The Expression of Our Peace Witness." *MBH* 7 (July 26, 1968), 8-9. A clear peace witness must be given to the state; though we support our government generally, civil disobedience may sometimes be necessary.
*

Toews, Ron. "Capital Punishment and Vietnam." *CanMenn* 14 (May 3, 1966), 5. Letter to the Editor against the abolition of capital punishment in Canada and against peace marches.

Vigneron, Arman. Letter to the Editor. *Menn* 95 (June 24, 1980), 418. Criticizes the editor for supporting Peter Ediger's civil disobedience at Rocky Flats nuclear weapons plant.

"Waging Peace . . ." *ChrLead* 41 (Nov. 7, 1978), 11. Faithfulness to the life and teachings of Christ and the New Testament necessitates active involvement—perhaps to the point of civil disobedience. This is a conclusion reached at the national New Call to Peacemaking conference held in Green Lake, Wis., Oct. 5-8, 1978.

Walters, LeRoy. "The Vietnam Situation. An Open Letter to the Brotherhood." *EV* 79 (Jan. 17, 1966), 19-20. The Christian's first loyalty is to the international community of faith. Therefore we must protest both the Vietnam War itself and recent statements by Billy Graham and President Johnson.

Wiens, P. B. "Protest Marches Are Not Good." *CanMenn* 14 (May 17, 1966), 5, 7. Lists reasons for believing anti-war protest marches are not doing the Mennonites nor their cause of peace any good.

Yoder, Glee. "Obedience to Whom?" *With* 4 (Oct., 1971), 14. Discussion of civil disobedience and the question of highest authority.

Zook, Al. "A Family Affair." *The Other Side* 103 (Apr., 1980), 24-27; "A Family's Faith Put into Action." *ChrLiv* 27 (Apr., 1980), 23-25. One family's participation in a demonstration against the arms race at the Rocky Flats, Colorado, nuclear weapons plant.

---

*For additional listing, see Supplement, pp. 717-719.

# B. War Tax Resistance

"A Call for Congregational Study of Civil Disobedience and War Tax Issues." *God and Caesar* 3 (June, 1977), 2-3. The resolution calls for implementing a study and decision-making process on civil disobedience and war tax issues and will be presented to the triennial conference of the General Conference Mennonite Church in Bluffton, Ohio.

"An Urgent Message to Our Churches from the 1967 Council of Boards." *Menn* 82 (Dec. 12, 1967), 753-54. A statement by the GCMC Council of Boards to their constituency, urging more vigorous witness against the war in Vietnam. Part of this witness would be war tax resistance.

Alderfer, Helen. "A 'Simple' People Questionnaire." *ChrLiv* 19 (Aug., 1972), 27-28. Hard questions about an appropriate standard of living; includes questions on paying war taxes.

Baerg, Henry R. Letter to the Editor. *Menn* 92 (Jan. 11, 1977), 29. Gives six reasons why he considers it wrong to withhold payment of taxes, ranging from belief that Jesus and Paul commanded tax payment, to the assertion that tax monies are the government's responsibility once they are paid.

Baergen, Samuel. "World Peace Tax Fund." *Menn* 94 (Nov. 27, 1979), 717. Reports responses of various senators and congressional represntatives to the issue of a World Peace Tax Fund.

Baergen, Samuel. Letter to the Editor. *Menn* 89 (Mar. 5, 1974), 165-66. Calls for more publicity and letter-writing support for HR 7053, the bill providing for conscientious objection to tax money paid for war.

Baergen, Samuel. Letter to the Editor. *Menn* 90 (May 13, 1975), 310. Encourages support for the World Peace Tax Fund bill by writing letters to Congressional representatives.

Baergen, Samuel. Letter to the Editor. *God and Caesar* 1 (Nov., 1975), 7-8. Writer objects to the form of war tax resistance Ivan Friesen described in a previous letter and encourages us, rather, to all work for the passage of the World Peace Tax Fund bill.

Baergen, Samuel. Letter to the Editor. *God and Caesar* 2 (Oct., 1976), 9-10. This letter raises questions about the lack of support among Mennonites for the World Peace Tax Fund Act.

Balzer, Thayne and Mary Anne. Letter to the Editor. *God and Caesar* 1 (Jan., 1975), 4-5. The writers' personal statement, outlining their reasons for withholding war taxes and also raising questions and suggestions.

Barrett, Lois. "War Taxes: Topic for Midtriennium." *Menn* 92 (Sept. 6, 1977), 501. Reports on the vigorous debate at the General Conference midtriennium over the conference's role in withholding taxes from employees' paychecks, a discussion introduced by Cornelia Lehn's testimony on war taxes.

Barrett, Lois. "War Taxes and Green Lake." *Peace Section Newsletter* 9 (Sept.-Oct., 1978), 7-9. Reflections on the statement on war taxes issued at the national New Call to Peacemaking conference Oct. 5-8 at Green Lake, Wisconsin.

Bassett, David R. and Miyoko I. "Letter to the *Ann Arbor News*." *God and Caesar* 5 (Feb., 1979), 9. This letter to the editor of the *Ann Arbor News* is included as an example of how letters to the editors of local newspapers can be tools to create awareness of the arms race and the World Peace Tax Fund Act.

Bauman, Kenneth G. "Some of Us." *Menn* 94 (Jan. 23, 1979), 64. Those who are opposed to the withholding of war taxes do not feel adequately represented on the issue.

Beachy, Alvin J. "Reflections After Minneapolis— On Legality, Anabaptists, and War Tax Refusal." *God and Caesar* 5 (Apr., 1979), 4-5. Challenges the prevailing assumption that since Anabaptists did not practice any kind of tax resistance, it would be "un-Anabaptist" for us to do so.

Beachy, Rosemary. "Standing for Life." *RepConsS* 35 (Mar., 1978), 1. Outlines several options for persons who want to resist the payment of war taxes.

Beechy, Winifred Nelson. "More War-Tax Opposition." *GH* 72 (Apr. 17, 1979), 330. Report on a seminar held in Goshen, Ind., Mar. 24, 1979, on the moral dilemma faced by Christians who are opposed to war as a method of settling disputes but who involuntarily contribute through war taxes.

Bender, Wilbur J. "Pacifism Among the Mennonites, Amish Mennonites, and Schwenkfelders of Pensylvania to 1783." *MQR* 1, Part 1 (July, 1927), 23-40; Part 2 (Oct., 1927), 21-48. Until 1776 these groups succeeded in observing strict nonresistance without too much difficulty. Even during the War of Independence there was general tolerance for them, though many paid fines for not bearing arms and refusing to pay war taxes.

Bicksler, Harriet S. "Turning Swords into Plowshares: The World Peace Tax Fund." *EvVis* 93 (Dec. 25, 1980), 6-7, 11. Reviews the Brethren in Christ history of conscientious objection in this century and explains the purposes of war tax resistance and the World Peace Tax Fund.

Bowman, David. "Mennonite Nonresistance: A Comparison of Practices in the American Revolution and the War Between the States." Term paper for Anabaptist and Mennonite History, Apr. 6, 1978. Pp. 22. MHL.

Bowman, John G. "It's Not Enough to Pray that Your Money Go for Bridges." *With* 4 (Oct., 1971), 20. Discussion of the war tax issue.

Brenneman, Allen. Letter to the Editor. *God and Caesar* 1 (Jan., 1975), 5-7. A personal statement regarding the writer's pacifist stance on participation in war, including financial participation through taxes.

Brunk, Conrad G. (Review). *The Rule of the Sword,* by Charlie Lord, and *The Rule of the Lamb,* by Larry Kehler. Both published by Newton: Faith and Life Press, 1978. Pp. 68 each. *MennRep* 23 (Nov. 13, 1978), 10. Study guides on militarism and taxes go beyond the Bible to study current events, history, and politics, in order to arrive at a more complete ethical response.

Bukrkuhl, Mathilda. Letter to the Editor. *ChrLead* 42 (May 22, 1979), 15. Until God changes Mark 12 and Romans 13 we will pay our taxes.

Bull, Wendall. "Pilgrimage with IRS." *God and Caesar* 5 (Feb., 1979), 5. A personal account of his experience since 1959 with refusing to pay war tax and leading a life of voluntary poverty.

"CHM Working on Resolution Mandate." *God and Caesar* 1 (Jan., 1975), 3-4. Commission on Home Ministries has received the mandate from the General Conference to work with the war tax issue and invites suggesions and quesions from readers.

"Church Should Not Act as Tax Collector." *GH* 72 (Mar. 6, 1979), 201. At the Minneapolis, Feb. 9-10, special General Conference Meeting, a resolution was passed to launch a vigorous campaign to obtain legal conscientious objection to war taxes.

"Conference Speaks on War Taxes." *God and Caesar* 1 (Jan., 1975), 2-3. The General Conference Mennonite Church at their Aug., 1974 sessions adopted resolutions concerning the pervasiveness of militarism in our society generally and the problem of war taxes particularly.

"Consultation on Civil Responsibility Findings Committee Report." *God and Caesar* 4 (July, 1978), 2-3. A statement drafted and approved by the persons who attended a consultation on civil responsibility in Elkhart, Ind., in June, 1978, urging General Conference congregations to seek ways which will facilitate the expression of convictions held by employees who do not wish their taxes to be withheld.

Christian Living Forum. "Mennonite Families and War Taxes." *ChrLiv* 27 (Sept., 1980), 28-31. Six people respond to the question of paying taxes for defense purposes.

Clemens, Steve. Letter to the Editor. *God and Caesar* 4 (Nov., 1978), 9. Suggests "peace church" institutions should, at least, not withhold the war tax portion of the federal income tax for all employees. Discussion could then decide what should be done with those monies.

Conservative Mennonite Conference. "The Church and Civil Government." *GfT* 12 (July-Aug., 1977), 16-17. Position statement on church and state relationships includes statements on war, civil disobedience, payment of war taxes.

Cosens, John. "Issues of Church and State: Selective Tax Evasion: The War Tax." Term paper, Apr. 7, 1981. Box 12-A-5. CMBS/Win.

Coursey, Eric K. Letter to the Editor. *Menn* 92 (Mar. 29, 1977), 222. Citing passages from Romans, 1 Peter, Titus, and Matthew, writer asserts that the Bible commands Christians to pay all taxes, and that because government is ordained by God, tax resistance is tantamount to resisting God's will.

Davies, Blodwen. "From Militia Tax to Relief." *MennLife* 5 (Oct., 1950), 27-28. A Canadian government exemption for CO's could at one time be attained by paying a government imposed tax. Thomas Reesor helped form the Non-Resistant Movement of Ontario in 1918 which went beyond the government tax by raising $100 for each exempt church member for relief.

Dickinson, Robert E. "What Belongs to Caesar?" *GH* 65 (Apr. 4, 1972), 319. Paying war taxes in order to protect property and job may amount to paying taxes so that others can serve in the military while I refuse to do so.

Diller, Duane A. "Teacher Asks Mennonite School Not to Withhold." *God and Caesar* 5 (July, 1978), 10-11. Reports on a Mennonite school employee's request that the institution discontinue withholding her taxes, and the process followed by the school and the regional conference in responding to her request.

Drescher, James M. "A Letter from Freddy." *Swords into Plowshares: A Collection of Plays About*

*Peace and Social Justice*, ed. Ingrid Rogers. Elgin: The Brethren Press, 1983, 236-41. An 18-year-old son presses his family for consistency by offering them a deal—he won't enroll in military service if they will resist paying the war tax.

Drescher, John M. "Dare We Pay Taxes for War?" *GH* 60 (Oct. 10, 1967), 909. A call for guidance on the question of war taxes in light of the uses of war tax revenues in Vietnam.

Drescher, John M. "Taxes for War." *GH* 65 (June 27, 1972), 545. Issues on the payment of war taxes which are used for killing others are brought close to home by asking pertinent quesions as to the meaning of "Render to Caesar . . . ."

Drescher, John M. (Editorial). "Peacemaker Questions." *GH* 61 (July 2, 1968), 585. Interprets "separation of church and state" to mean that the church should be the conscience of society raising questions on issues of military service and payment of war taxes.

Driedger, Leo. "The Taxes that Go to War." *Menn* 78 (Jan. 15, 1963), 38-39. Expresses uneasiness with complicity in the war effort and gives concrete suggestions for acting on one's opposition to war taxes.

Dyck, Edna Krueger. "Peace Teachers: She Studies and Obeys." *Builder* 31 (Jan., 1981), 12-13. The consequences of Cornelia Lehn's commitment to "study the Bible seriously and then to obey the Word" have resulted in a General Conference study process on the issues of tax resistance and a collection of peace stories which she edited entitled *Peace Be With You* (Faith and Life, 1981).

Dyck, John H. A. "Response to Conrad Brunk, 'Reflections on the Anabaptist View of Law and Morality,' and to Duane K. Friesen, 'A Moral Justification for War Tax Resistance,' *CGR* 1 (Soring, 1983), 1-28." *CGR* 2 (Winter, 1984), 51-56. Questions whether reality supports the assumption by Brunk and Friesen of a common moral norm.

Eccleston, Alan. "Witnessing to Peace—For Ourselves and for Each Other." *God and Caesar* 6 (Sept., 1980), 5-8. Reflections on war tax resistance.

Ediger, Max. "'Give Unto Caesar . . . '" *MennRep* 3 (Feb. 19, 1973), 13. Epic poem draws a connection between payment of taxes and financing war.

Ediger, Peter J. "An Uncanonical Chronicle." *God and Caesar* 2 (Mar., 1976), 1. In prose form, the writer describes how the General Conference Mennonite Church has handled the request to have taxes withheld from salaries of employees who submit such a request.

Ediger, Peter J. "Another Response to War Tax Discussion." Also poem, "Jonah Revisited . . . Unfinished." *MennRep* 9 (Mar. 19, 1979), 5. Likening the Mennonites at the General Conference midtriennium to Jonah in the whale, Ediger shares his feeling about the response to the war tax question.

Ediger, Peter J. "Christ and Caesar: A Ballad of Faith." *Menn* 90 (Oct. 14, 1975), 569-72. Ballad traces the history of Mennonite conscientious objection to war, focusing especially on the dilemma of war tax payment.

Ediger, Peter J. "Conference Commission Wrestles with War Tax Questions." *God and Caesar* 1 (Mar., 1975), 2-3. A recommendation that the Conference "honor the employees' request not to have war taxes withheld from income" was tested by the Commission on Home Ministries of the General Conference Mennonite Church at its annual meeting but did not arrive at concensus.

Ediger, Peter J. "Jonah Revisited . . . Unfinished." *Menn* 94 (Apr. 17, 1979), 285-86. Responds to the Minneapolis midtriennium in verse form comparing Mennonites to Jonah in the whale.

Ediger, Peter J. "Questions After a War Tax Conference." *God and Caesar* 1 (Nov., 1975), 1. A poem asking why the recurring question of war taxes and do we really want to know the answers.

Ediger, Peter J. "Two Dreams." *God and Caesar* 3 (June, 1977), 1. A poem written after the General Board of the Mennonite General Conference refused, for the third time, to honor the request of an employee of the conference not to withhold the war tax portion of her income tax.

Eitzen, Allan. Letter to the Editor. *GH* 61 (Mar. 5, 1968), 214. Recommends more active peace witnessing, such as a large-scale war tax protest, in light of the fact that the government is becoming immune to verbal dissent.

Epp, Albert H. Letter to the Editor. *Menn* 94 (Jan. 30, 1979), 76-77. A pastor writes on behalf of himself and many in his congregation who do not agree with withholding war taxes.

Epp, Frank H. "Giving to Caesar." *CanMenn* 5 (Mar. 22, 1957), 2. Daniel Graber of Goshen, Ind., has called attention to the fact that, through taxation, Mennonites contribute fortunes for war hardware. This is a new question for Mennonites to face, both in the US and in Canada.

Epp, Frank H. "On the Topic of the Tax." *Menn* 76 (Mar. 7, 1961), 151. "Caesar" is not entitled to everything he requests. Conscientious objection to war may call for refusal to pay war taxes.

Epp, Frank H. "T Is for Taxes." *CanMenn* 7 (Apr. 10, 1959), 6. A look at taxation from a biblical perspective. Epp questions unconditional obedience to Caesar in regard to taxes that go for war purposes.

Epp, Frank H. (Editorial). "Giving to Caesar." *CanMenn* 5 (Mar. 22, 1957), 2. Summarizes Daniel Graber's observations about hom much money Elkhart County Mennonites contribute to national defense through war taxes.

Fransen, Harold. "Reflections on Minneapolis: Is the Law of the Land Higher Than God's Law?" *MennRep* 9 (Feb. 19, 1979), 7. Writer reflects on the mood and the process of the General Conference midtriennium which dealt with the question of war taxes.

Franz, Delton. "Channeling War Taxes to Peace." *Sojourners* 6 (Mar., 1977), 21. History and current status of the World Peace Tax Fund.

Franz, Delton. Letter to the Editor. *God and Caesar* 1 (Mar., 1975), 6. Writer shares the views of Congresswoman Pat Schroeder who holds a strong dove position on the military but expresses concerns about the World Peace Tax Fund in that it will divert equal energies of the Mennonite people from helping to actually curb military growth.

Franz, Delton. "Seeking a Consensus of Conscience." *RepConsS* 35 (Dec., 1978), 4. Describes efforts and outcomes of the New Call to Peacemaking's Green Lake, Wis., conference on issues relating to payment of war taxes.

Franz, Delton, ed. "Alternative to War Tax Payments: Citizens Drafting Legislation." *MCC PS Wash. Memo* 4 (Jan.-Feb., 1972), 3-4. Introduces the World Peace Tax Fund bill as authored by a Quaker professor.

Franz, Delton, ed. "'Your Tax Dollars at Work.'" *MCC PS Wash. Memo* 3 (Nov.-Dec., 1971), 1-2. Statistics on taxes used for war and what the same money could buy in human service projects.

Franz, Delton (Editorial). "Conscientious Objectors and War Taxes." *RepConsS* 34 (Apr., 1977), 2, 4. Describes history of the war tax issue and explains present status of the World Peace Tax Fund Act.

Frey, Mark. Letter to the Editor. *God and Caesar* 4 (Nov., 1978), 10. Shares reasons for not supporting the World Peace Tax Fund.

Friedmann, Michael. Letter to the Editor. *Menn* 90 (Nov. 4, 1975), 630. Member of Fellowship of Hope in Elkhart, IN, describes his experinece in war tax resistance and his testimony in tax court.

Friedmann, Michael. Letter to the Editor. *God and Caesar* 6 (Jan., 1980), 11-12. Expresses pessimism over the possibility of legislatively decreasing the amount of money available to the military and calls for increased war tax resistance and nonviolent action at military centers.

Friesen, Duane K. "A Moral Justification for War Tax Resistance." *CGR* 1 (Spring, 1983), 21-28. The case for tax resistance depends on three criteria: that the policy of arms race escalation is a violation of moral law; that persons are obliged to disobey their government when it violates a moral law; that resisting military tax payment is an appropriate point at which to challenge government policy.

Friesen, Duane K. "A Moral Justification for War Tax Resistance." Paper presented to the American Society of Christian Ethics, New York, 1980. Pp. 17. MLA/BeC.

Friesen, Ivan. Letter to the Editor. *God and Caesar* 1 (Oct., 1975), 4-5. Engaging in W-4 Form war tax refusal was a freeing experience from the fear associated with civil disobedience.

Friesen, Jacob T. Letter to the Editor. *Menn* 94 (Feb. 6, 1979), 93. Writer outlines the steps he took to begin a dialogue on peace by withholding a portion of his 1977 income tax.

Gaede, Don H. "GCs Seek Exemption from Collecting War Taxes." *ChrLead* 42 (Mar. 13, 1979), 22. Report on the special General Conference Mennonite Church conference, held Feb. 9-10, 1979, to "discern the will of God for Christians in their response to militarism and the worldwide arms race."

General Conference Mennonite Church. "Resolutions." *Menn* 89 (Sept. 10, 1974), 517. Resolutions from the 40th Triennial Session include a statement giving the war tax question greater priority.
*

Gingerich, Ray C. "Shalom for the '80s." *Builder* 31 (Jan., 1981), 4-9. The challenge for each congregation is to be a model of shalom and congregations need to begin thinking about the implications of this vision for daily life. Also suggests the issues of draft registration and war taxes as appropriate agenda items for this process of reflection.

Gleysteen, Jan (Review). *What Belongs to Caesar?*, by Donald D. Kaufman. Scottdale: Herald Press, 1970. Pp. 128. *GH* 63 (Nov. 10, 1970), 950.

*For additional listing, see Supplement, pp. 717-719.

Recommends the book for its historical and biblical overviews of the question of taxation and its clarifying the issues involved in resisting war tax payment.

Goering, Elmer H. Letter to the Editor. *Menn* 90 (Nov. 18, 19750, 659-60. In response to the question of war tax payment, writer asserts that paying taxes is an obligation Christians owe the government. To support his position he cites the complications which would arise if individuals could refuse payment because they object to the way government spends its money.

Goering, Jack. "Biblical Issues Raised by War Tax Workshop." *Menn* 86 (Mar. 23, 1971), 190-91. Christian stewardship and a simpler lifestyle must supplement the decision to withhold or reduce taxes as a witness to peace.

Goertzen, Arlean L. "Should Christians Pay War Taxes?" *Menn* 85 (Nov. 10, 1970), 682-83. Makes a case for the evil of paying war taxes and recommends action to publicize that position as a witness to the way of Christ.

Goossen, Steve. Letter to the Editor. *ChrLead* 42 (May 22, 1979), 15. Asks how one can pay for the war while uttering a prayer for peace.

Gormly, Walter. "War Tax Resistance News." *God and Caesar* 3 (Nov., 1977), 6-7. A letter, reprinted from the Sept. 2, 1977, issue of *Peacemaker,* intended to convey the power of the IRS as this writer has experienced it.

Graber, Daniel. "Taxes." *Menn* 72 (Mar. 19, 1957), 182-83. The "quiet in the land" should think seriously about the implications of supporting war preparations via taxes. Most Mennonites pay much more in war taxes than they give to the church.

Habegger, David L. "Shall We Pay War Taxes?" *Menn* 87 (Mar. 14, 1972), 182-83. Interprets biblical passages on the Christian's responsibility to pay taxes to government.

Hackman, Walton. "Taxes-for-Peace Fund." *MBH* 12 (Mar. 9, 1973), 9. Contributions to this fund may be one tangible way in which conscientious objectors can express a peace witness through the use of their tax dollars.

Hartzler, R. L. "A Covenant Movement for Peace." *Menn* 86 (Sept. 28, 1971), 577-78, The issues of conscription and the payment of war taxes are secondary; the basic issue is, militarism as a long established, deeply engrained element in national policy.

Haury, David A. "The Mennonite Congregation of Boston." *MennLife* 34 (Sept., 1979), 24-27. The birth and development of the Mennonite congregation of Boston including their concerns and mission regarding nuclear weapons, the Vietnam war, military service, and war taxes.

Hershberger, Guy F. "What Did the Mennonites Do in the American Revolution?" *YCC* 17 (May 31, 1936), 176. The Revolutionary War was a trying experience for nonresistant people. Mennonites did not take up arms, but they were willing to give aid to the suffering. The special war tax issues had a variety of responses.

Hertzler, Daniel. "Death and Taxes." *ChrLiv* 17 (Apr., 1970), 40. Editorial suggesting ways to support life, not war and death, including non-payment of war taxes.

Hertzler, Daniel. "We Commend . . ." *ChrLiv* 19 (Apr., 1972), 40. Salute to good news-makers includes a Lockheed manager who developed a conscience for social justice, and a tax firm studying the question of war tax objection.

Hess, James R. "Church and State Ordained for Separate Functions." *ST* 45 (Jan., 1977), 10-13. Draft registration and war tax payment are examples of proper responses of the Christian toward government.

Hess, James R. "Reflections on the Kitchener, Ontario War Tax Convention." *GfT* 11 (Mar.-Apr., 1976), 16-18. Links the refusal to pay war taxes to leftist ideology and subjectivistic hermeneutics.

Hess, James R. "The 1975 Consultation on War Taxes." *ST* 44 (May, 1976), 7-9. Questions the assumptions about the relationship of church and state involved in the discussion of nonpayment of war taxes.

Hofer, Shirley. "The Christian Conscience and War Taxes." *God and Caesar* 2 (June, 1976), 10-12. A whimsical dialogue between Moses and the Lord by Art Hoppe illustrates the inconsistencies in biblical and theological interpretation regarding the sixth commandment and the sanctity of human life. The writer also shares results from a survey she took on the war tax issue.

Honsaker, Karl and Miriam. Letter to the Editor. *God and Caesar* 2 (June, 1976), 4-5. Contributors share their letter written to IRS explaining why they refuse to pay taxes which help supply weapons for war.

Honsaker, Karl and Miriam. Letter to the Editor. *God and Caesar* 4 (July, 1978), 15. A report on their experience of war tax resistance which began in 1975 when they refused to pay telephone tax.

Hull, Robert. "Historical Roots of a Peace Church Witness." *Affirm Life: Pay for Peace*, ed. Maynard Shelly and Ron Flickinger. Newton: Historic Peace Church Task Force on Taxes, 1981, 13-17. Pp. [87]. MHL. Charts history of historic peace church responses and actions on war tax issues from the French and Indian war, 1754-1763 to the contemporary period—the Vietnam War era, the World Peace Tax Fund (1973), and the General Conference Mennonite Church experience with Cornelia Lehn's request.

"In Trouble Again." *GH* 65 (June 27, 1972), 550. Dorothy Day, age 74, head of the Catholic Worker Movement, refuses to pay taxes supporting the war effort and gives her reasons.

"IRS Sues War Objector Group." *God and Caesar* 4 (June, 1978), 6. In an unprecedented move, the IRS has brought suit against an employer, the Central Committee for Conscientious Objectors, for failure to pay the tax debt allegedly owed by a past employee who refused to pay for reasons of conscience.

Janzen, David. "Pay to Tax-Conscience Fund." *Menn* 86 (Apr. 6, 1971), 236-37. An alternative to supporting war through taxes might be to pay these monies into a tax conscience fund if negotiations do not lead to peace by Jan. 1, 1972.

Janzen, Marie J. (Regier, Frantz). Letter to the Editor. *Menn* 92 (Feb. 15, 1977), 116. Maintains that because of the difference in government structures between Jesus' day and our present democracy, Christians now do have responsibility for requesting taxes to be diverted to constructive, not destructive, ends. Recommends the World Peace Tax Fund.

Jubilee Mennonite Church. "From Conscience to Community." *God and Caesar* 6 (Sept., 1980), 11-12. Congregational letter to the Internal Revenue Service supporting a member who is a war tax resister.

Juhnke, James C. "Youth and Taxes." *Menn* 77 (Apr. 24, 1962), 285-86. We are to be responsible stewards and should not (voluntarily) pay "war taxes" if we object to participation in war.

Kauffman, W. Wallace. Letter to the Editor. *GH* 61 (Aug. 6, 1968), 713. Cites biblical passages to show that God uses war as a form of judgment, and that Christians should pay all taxes.

Kaufman, Donald D. Letter to the Editor. *Menn* 92 (Jan. 11, 1977), 29. Calls for both confrontation and affirmation of one another in the continuing, profitable discussion on war tax payment.

Kaufman, Donald D. Letter to the Editor. *God and Caesar* 3 (Jan., 1977), 9. A letter of encouragement to continue the dialogue and the search for obedience to Christ in the issue of war taxes and to remain motivated by the love of God.

Kaufman, Donald D. Letter to the Editor. *God and Caesar* 5 (Apr., 1979), 9-10. Offers an illustration of how all of us, by paying our war taxes, are contributing to the taking of life in war.

Kaufman, Donald D. "Paying for War." *Sojourners* 6 (Mar., 1977), 16. War tax resistance is a dilemma for both Christian individuals and the church. Examines the withholding dilemma and suggests viable options for responding.

Kaufman, Donald D. *The Tax Dilema: Praying for Peace, Paying for War*. Scottdale: Herald Press, 1978. Explores the contradiction expressed in the title with a view to finding the path of Christian obedience. Illustrates options for war tax resistance with both historical and contemporary examples. Helpful appendices include resources such as hymns, poems, letters, addresses of peace organizations, and audiovisuals list.

Kaufman, Donald D. "War Taxes: From Personal to Corporate Responsibility." *God and Caesar* 2 (Oct., 1976), 2-3. Excerpts from a larger paper prepared for the Commission on Home Ministries stating that civil disobedience is a necessary Christian witness in the face of wrong.

Kaufman, Donald D. "War Taxes and the Christian Response." Research paper for Independent Study in Ethics, AMBS, 1968. Pp. 87. BfC.

Kaufman, Donald D. *What Belongs to Caesar?* Scottdale: Herald Press, 1969. Pp. 128. Seeks to clarify the war tax issue by surveying the history of taxation and the interpretation of several key biblical passages on the issue. Also includes an outline of the argument against the payment of war taxes and a historical survey of nonpayment positions and practices. Concludes by challenging readers to evaluate the payment of war taxes in light of the lordship of Jesus.

Kaufman, Donald D. and Eleanor. "Can Christians Pay for War?" *CanMenn* 7 (June 5, 1959), 2. Copy of a letter to the Internal Revenue Service protesting the use of tax money for military purposes.

Kaufman, Stan. "A Proposal for a Legal Tax Alternative." *God and Caesar* 5 (Aug., 1979), 3-4. A Sunday school class at Rainbow Blvd. Mennonite Church in Kansas City has attempted to take seriously the Minneapolis resolution to work out a possible legal alternative to paying war taxes and proposes a compromise which links the World Peace Tax Fund to a national service program.

Keeney, William E. (Review). *The Rule of the Lamb,* by Larry Kehler. A study Guide on Civil Responsibility. Newton: Faith and Life Press, 1978. Pp. 68. *MennLife* 34 (Sept., 1979), 28-29. Briefly describes this booklet consisting of a series of eight lessons presented in preparation for dealing with the war tax issue at the General Conference Midtriennium (1979). Commends Kehler for his masterful job in selecting the key issues and taking the essence of the consultation papers presented in preparation for the conference.

Keeney, William E. (Review). *The Tax Dilemma: Praying for Peace, Paying for War.* Scottdale: Herald Press, 1978. Pp. 104. *MennLife* 34 (Sept., 1979), 28-29. Describes and critiques this book which argues in favor of nonpayment of war taxes. Acknowledges its helpfulness in raising and examining the issues but also points out some shortcomings.

Kehler, Larry. "Christian Civil Responsibility (4): The Prophets and Managers." *MennRep* 9 (Jan. 8, 1979), 6. The last in a series of four preparatory articles for the General Conference midtriennium addressing a concern raised by the war tax question: what it means to be good stewards of our church-related institutions.

Kehler, Larry. "Our Christian Civil Responsibility—1." *Menn* 93 (Nov. 21, 1978), 685; *MennRep* 8 (Nov. 27, 1978), 6. Urges congregations to study the war tax and militarism questions in preparation for the midtriennium conference in Feb., 1979.

Kehler, Larry. "Our Christian Civil Responsibility—2." *Menn* 93 (Nov. 28, 1978), 701; *MennRep* 8 (Dec. 11, 1978), 6. Discusses New Testament texts referring to tax payment in preparation for the midtriennium conference discussion on war taxes.

Kehler, Larry. "Our Christian Civil Responsibility—3." *Menn* 93 (Dec. 5, 1978), 717; *MennRep* 8 (Dec. 25, 2978), 6. Militarism and war taxes are live issues in Canada as well as the US, needing Mennonite attention and activity, says Kehler, in preparation for the midtrienium conference discussion on these issues.

Kehler, Larry. "Our Christian Civil Responsibility: The Prophets and the Managers." *Menn* 94 (Jan. 2, 1979), 13. The last in a series of four preparatory articles on the war tax question to be discussed at the midtriennium convention of the General Conference. Raises the question of how Mennonites should relate to institutions.

Kellerman, Bill. Letter to the Editor. *God and Caesar*

2 (Mar., 1976), 5-6. Argues against the World Peace Tax Fund, but supports resisting federal taxes.

Klaassen, Walter. *Mennonites and War Taxes.* Newton, Ks.: Faith and Life Press, 1978. Pp. 27. Although history indicates that the early Anabaptists paid their taxes, including war taxes, without objection, the contemporary reality of the degree to which tax money is being used for destructive purpose calls for new sensitivity to an old issue.

Klassen, James R. "Dear Computer:" *Menn* 95 (Feb. 12, 1980), 109; *God and Caesar* 6 (Jan., 1980), 1. Poem reflecting on war tax resistance and the inhumanity of government military policy.

Klassen, James R. Letter to the Editor. *God and Caesar* 4 (June, 1978), 8-10. A copy of the contributor's statement for the IRS 1040 form sent to the President, congresspersons, and IRS Commissioner. Outlines his reasons for claiming a "Nuremberg Principles" tax deduction.

Klassen, James R. "Receives Refund." *God and Caesar* 4 (July, 1980), 14-15. In response to a letter to IRS (*God and Caesar* [June, 1978]) explaining his war tax deduction, the writer received the refund requested. This letter acknowledges the IRS action.

Kliewer, Dean. Letter to the Editor. *ChrLead* 42 (July 31, 1979, 16. Thinks that Mennonite Brethren should join other historic peace churches in examining the issue of war tax resistance.

Konkel, Gus. Letter to the Editor. *Menn* 88 (Apr. 10, 1973), 245. Calls *The Mennonite* to focus less attention on political issues, citing the examples of "copious verbiage on the Vietnam War" and the question of war tax payment as issues where poorly informed opinions fail to grasp the complexity of political issues.

Krehbiel, Jude. Letter to the Editor. *Menn* 94 (Apr. 17, 1979), 284. Expresses concern that a stronger witness of faith to our government did not come out of the Minneapolis midtriennium.

Kreider, Robert S. (Review). *The Rule of the Lamb,* by Larry Kehler, and *The Rule of the Sword,* by Charlie Lord. Newton: Faith and Life Press, 1978. *Menn* 93 (Oct. 3, 1978), 573. Enthusiastic recommendation for these readable, information-filled booklets on the war tax question (Kehler) and the arms race and militarization (Lord).

*

Kroeker, David (Review). *What Belongs to Caesar? A Discussion on the Christian's Response to Payment of*

*War Taxes,* by Donald D. Kaufman. Scottdale: Herald Press, 1969. Pp. 128. *MQR* 46 (Jan., 1972), 91-92. Recommends this study of Christian opposition to paying war taxes for popular reading in congregations on the basis of its clear and easily understood arguments.

Lapp, John A. (Review). *What Belongs to Caesar,* by Donald D. Kaufman. Herald Press, 1970. "What Belongs to Caesar? Sticky War Tax Question." *CanMenn* 18 (Sept. 18, 1970), 7, 8; *GH* 63 (Sept. 15, 1970), 770-71. Major review article recommending Kaufman's study of war taxes for its historical and biblical approach to the question of conscientious objection through nonpayment of taxes.

Leatherman, Loretta. "Taking a Stand." *WMSC Voice* 54 (Dec., 1980), 7. Encourages some form of war tax resistance to protest the dollars being used to finance American military endeavors.

Leatherman, Loretta and Paul. "Our Case for Tax Resistance." *GH* 73 (Apr. 29, 1980), 350-52. In an interview with the MCC Peace Section, the Leathermans describe their reasons for not paying war taxes and their experiences with this practice.

Lehman, Carl M. "I Also Have a Conscience." *Menn* 92 (Feb. 22, 1977), 141. While considering tax resistance an acceptable response to a violated conscience, writer maintains that it is futile, since Internal Revenue collectors do not regulate tax spending. Asserts that most reasons cited for war tax resistance are not well-founded.

Lehman, Carl M. "Tax Resistance—A Form of Protest?" *Menn* 90 (Oct. 14, 1975), 573-74. While tax resistance may be acceptable for activists and absolutists, the focus of Christian opposition to paying for war should be pressure on Congress to keep military spending down.

Lehman, Carl M. "The Parable of Zacatecas." *God and Caesar* 4 (June, 1978), 6. A parable which raises the concern that war tax resistance, even when exercised with the best intentions, must be understood in a larger framework of societal needs.

Lehn, Cornelia. "My Pilgrimage with War Tax Resistance." *Menn* 91 (Nov. 2, 1976), 648. General Conference employee describes her decision to take a stand against war tax payment, concluding she will give sizable amounts of her income to church work, since it is not legally possible for the conference to refuse to withhold her taxes.

Lord, Charles R. *The Rule of the Sword: A Study Guide on Technological Militarism.* Newton, Ks.: Faith and Life Press, 1978. Pp. 72. Lessons designed to clarigy the issues and show how these issues relate to us. Another goal of the guide is to help students develop a background helpful for examination of the questions of civil responsibility and war taxes.

Loss, J. Michael. "We Try to Avoid Supporting the War Machine." *GH* 73 (Apr. 15, 1980), 318. Family reduces their income below taxable level by giving to the work of the church, since wars today depend more on tax money and machines than on personnel.

Lull, Howard W. Letter to the Editor. *God and Caesar* 2 (June, 1976), 5-6. Responding to the questions concerning the payment of war taxes posed in the article, "April 15—Again!" (*God and Caesar* [Mar., 1976]), the writer offers some comments and an editorial note is added explaining the constitutional amendments which allow for tax resistance.

"Meeting Shows Diversity of Views on Militarism." *GH* 72 (Feb. 20, 1979), 167. Report of a meeting of the General Conference Mennonite Church on Feb. 9-10, 1979, in Minneapolis where war tax resistance was discussed.

"Mennonites Examine War Taxes." *RepConsS* 35 [*sic,* 34] (Oct., 1977), 1. Reports discussion in General Conference Mennonite Church on war taxes precipitated by conference employee Cornelia Lehn's request that the portion of her tax used for military purposes not be withheld.

Mace, Jack L. Letter to the Editor. *Menn* 94 (May 1, 1979), 318. Describes his response to the war tax issue: using a "second mile theology of witness," he sends a letter of protest to the IRS with his full payment of taxes and sends an amount equal to the "war taxes" to his representative in government with a letter of witness.

MacMaster, Richard K. *Christian Obedience in Revolutionary Times: The Peace Churches and the American Revolution.* Akron, Pa.: MCC (US) Peace Section, 1976. Pp. 26. MHL. Demonstrates that Mennonites and other Christians committed to peace during the Revolutionary War times conflicted with the government on issues of military service, war taxes, and oaths of allegiance. Discusses their stance and resulting persecution within the context of differing concepts of religious liberty; the sectarian concept of discipleship as a separate and distinct way of life was not understood by a government to whom religious freedom meant the freedom to worship according to the dictates of conscience, not the freedom to live by conscience.

MacMaster, Richard K. "'I'd as Soon Go into the War.'" *GH* 68 (Nov. 18, 1975), 832. Cites the refusal of Mennonites and Quakers in the 1770s to pay taxes intended for the Revolutionary War as an example for present-day Mennonites.

MacMaster, Richard K. "Mennonite Conscience About Taxes." *Menn* 94 (Jan. 9, 1979), 20, 21. Writer points out that Virginia and Pennsylvania Mennonites of the 18th century had "deep-seated scruples of conscience" on the war tax issue.

Magnuson, Lynn J. Letter to the Editor. *God and Caesar* 1 (Nov., 1975), 8-9. Writer explains position on the payment of taxes by sharing a note attached to the IRS Form W-4 stating objection to war and its preparations.

Magnuson, Lynn J. Letter to the Editor. *God and Caesar* 2 (June, 1976), 7. Writer shares his/her experience in dealing with the war tax issue.

Malishchak, Richard. "Some Thoughts on Peace Taxes." *GH* 65 (Oct. 31, 1972), 885-86. Reprinted from *The Reporter for Conscience Sake*. Discusses the World Peace Tax Fund act and its two major advantages: making a provision for positive peace expenditures, and confronting each taxpayer with the possibility of conscientious objection to war taxes by requiring the option to be included in the tax return instruction booklet.

Mann, David W. "A Hermeneutical Study of Peter Rideman on the Question of the Christian's Relationship to Governmental Authority: The Purpose of Government, Christians in Magistracy, and the Payment of Taxes for War." Paper for Theology of the Anabaptist Classics class, [Goshen College, Goshen, Ind.], May 9, 1971. Pp. 25. MHL.

Marymoon, Pashta. "Canadian Group Advocates War Tax Resistance." *God and Caesar* 5 (Aug., 1979), 6-7. Because modern warfare is more dependent on armaments than on large armies and therefore relies primarily on revenue from taxes, this Canadian group, War Tax Alternatives, strongly encourages war tax resistance.

Melcombe, Bob. Letter to the Editor. *God and Caesar* 2 (June, 1976), 7-9. A Canadian shares a letter he included with his income tax return outlining his reasons for not completing the tax return.

Mennonite Central Committee Peace Section. "World Peace Tax Fund . . . Congressional Hearings?" *God and Caesar* 1 (June, 1975), 8. *Washington Memo* (July-Aug., 1975). Supporters of the World Peace Tax Fund Act should be indicating their interest in order for the World Peace Tax Fund witnesses to be able to testify at the Congressional tax reform hearings.

Metzler, Paul R. Letter to the Editor. *GH* 65 (Aug. 8, 1972), 634. Disagrees with writers calling for nonpayment of war taxes, since such a practice violates the New Testament commands to obey the government.

Meyer, Ron. "Reflections on Paying War Taxes." *GH* 65 (May 23, 1972), 465-66. Since 60 to 75 percent of income tax is used as revenue for warfare, the writer outlines various approaches to tax resistance aimed at witnessing against this use of money for military purposes.

Miller, Ellene. Letter to the Editor. *Menn* 94 (May 1, 1979), 316. The Minneapolis midtriennium conference placed a great deal of emphasis on law, but the church must deal with a "higher law" of compassion, justice, and mercy in responding to all the victims of the arms race and nuclear proliferation.

Miller, Marvin and Rachel. "Testimony on Taxes." *GH* 65 (June 27, 1972), 548. A letter to the president of the US about the futility of supporting the war effort by paying war taxes; provides suggestions for supporting the peace effort.

Miller, Terry. "Types of Religious Beliefs, Level of Education and College Attended in Relation to Payment of War Taxes." Social Science Seminar paper, Mar. 29, 1979. Pp. 39. MLA/BeC.

Mueller, Adam. Letter to the Editor. *Menn* 94 (Apr. 17, 1979), 286. Responding to an earlier editorial (Feb. 20), which reports on some ideas expressed by the midtriennium meeting, this writer states that God has only one will for us and unless we do his will, we are exercising our own will.

Mueller, Melanie. "Thirty-Three Identify Themselves as War Tax Resisters." *God and Caesar* 4 (July, 1978), 11-12. Thirty-three persons/families have identified themselves thus far as "war tax resisters" after *God and Caesar* in its June, 1978, issue provided the opportunity for people to do so.

"News from the Peace Front." *Fellowship* 24 (June 1, 1958), 4. News statement reporting that Benjamin Kauffman, a 23-year-old Amish farmer, has been sentenced to eighteen months in prison for refusing to accept a civilian work assignment as a CO in an institution using modern conveniences.

Narowski, Wladyslaw; Johnson, Susan K.; Broersma, Don. "Ann Arbor Group Gives Tax Day Peace Witness." *God and Caesar* 5 (Aug., 1979), 7-8. On Apr. 16, at an Ann Arbor, Mich., demonstration, sponsored by the Ann Arbor War Tax Dissidents, about twenty-five people openly announced their decision not to pay all or part of the federal income tax.

Neufeld, Elmer. "Should the Conference Withhold Taxes for War?" *Menn* 91 (Nov. 2, 1976), 642-48; *God and Caesar* 3 (Jan., 1977), 7-9. Excerpts from a letter by the General Conference president to all General Conference pastors, urging the conference to investigate alternatives to institutional withholding of taxes from employees.

Neufeld, Ernest W. Letter to the Editor. *Menn* 94 (Feb. 6, 1979), 93. Suggests that we return to Minneapolis triennium with an attitude of probing, listening, and seeking as was present at Probe '72.

Nisley, Margaret and Weldon. "War Tax Resistance News." *God and Caesar* 3 (Nov., 1977), 7-9. A letter sent to Bell of Pennsylvania Telephone Co. and IRS explains their conviction behind the contribution to Jubilee Fund of the federal excise tax which the Nisleys withheld.

"Peace Section (US) Calls for Restraint in Iran Crisis, Supports SALT Amendment." *GH* 72 (Dec. 25, 1979), 1032, 1037. Meeting of MCC Peace Section (US) passed resolutions concerning the US-Iranian crisis, SALT II, and the proposed World Peace Tax Fund on Nov. 30-Dec. 1.

Peachey, Dean E. Letter to the Editor. *God and Caesar* 4 (July, 1978), 15-16. Raises the question of the actual effectiveness of the World Peace Tax Fund.

Peachey, J. Lorne. "No Money for War." *ChrLiv* 15 (Jan., 1968), 11. Reports on war tax protesters in various parts of the US.

Pearson, Ed. Letter to the Editor. *God and Caesar* 4 (Nov., 1978), 10. Support for the World Peace Tax Fund must be seen in a larger context of efforts working for peace and justice.

Penner, Archie. "The Christian's Responsibility to the State." *Perfect Love and War,* ed. Paul Hostetler. Nappanee, IN: Evangel Press, 1974, 89-98. Develops, from NT materials, a theological framework with which to work at the question of how a Christian should relate to the government under which she or he lives. Deals briefly with such specific issues as office-holding, payment of taxes, and bearing arms.

Penner, Mark. Letter to the Editor. *Menn* 94 (May 1, 1979), 317. Although opposed to going to war, writer raises concerns about withholding war taxes and the discussions regarding the church posing as a tax collector.

Pomeroy, Wendy and Dirdak, Paul R. Letter to the Editor. *God and Caesar* 2 (Oct., 1976), 11. Copy of a letter sent to IRS which "casts the painful experience of computing war taxes into one of

contemplative religious ritual and Christian witness."

"Refuse Payment of 'Phone Tax.' " *GH* 65 (July 18, 1972), 582. Unitarians counsel members to refuse telephone tax payments and warn them of the consequences.

"Resource Packet on Civil Responsibility." Papers presented at the Civil Responsibility Consultation, AMBS, Elkhart, Ind., June 1-4, 1978, and the War Tax Conference in Kitchener, Ont., Nov., 1975. Pp. [181]. MHL. Includes: Stucky, Ted W. and Toews, Reg, "The Administrative Dimension," 3-12; Lind, Millard, "Is There a Biblical Case for Civil Disobedience (O.T.)?" 13-35; Bauman, Kenneth, "Federal Taxation and the Mennonite Conscience," 36-50; Schroeder, David, "Is Civil Disobedience Called for in the Case of War Taxes," 51-60; Kraybill, J. Elvin, "Nonpayment of Income Taxes for Religious Reasons," 66-76; Yoder, John H., "The Limits of Obedience to Caesar: The Shape of the Problem," 77-91; Keeney, William, "Corporate Action and Individual Conscience," 92-109; Burkholder, J. Lawrence, "Prophetic Criticism and Corporate Responsibility," 110-18; Miller, Marlin E., "The Christian's Relationship to the State and Civil Authority," 126-31; Swartley, Willard M., "The Christian and Payment of War Taxes," 132-48; Kaufman, Donald D., "War Taxes: From Personal to Corporate Responsibility," 149-78; Toews, John E. "Paul's View of the State," 179-81 (reprinted from *ChrLeader,* Apr. 28, 1978).

Reedy, Janet Umble. "Our Day in Court." *God and Caesar* 3 (June, 1977), 3-6. Reedy describes the pilgrimage of tax resistance which has taken her and her husband to the US Tax Court and representatives in Congress.

Rees, Paul S. (Editorial). "Now It Is Official." *ST* 47 (May, 1979), 5. The encouragement of our church agencies to support the World Peace Tax Fund legislation raises many questions about this course of action and the political means being employed.

Regier, Harold R. "April 15—Again!" *God and Caesar* 2 (Mar., 1976), 2. Certain questions that aid in soul searching and dialogue with others on the question of payment of war taxes.

Regier, Harold R. "Conference Resolution on War Taxes Passed." *God and Caesar* 3 (Nov., 1977), 2. A resolution calling on congregations and regional conferences of the General Conference Mennonite Church to commit themselves to a serious study of civil disobedience and war tax resistance was passed at triennial conference sessions held in Bluffton, Ohio, July 28-Aug. 3, 1977.

Regier, Harold R. "Congregation Affirms

Members' War Tax Resistance." *God and Caesar* 5 (Aug., 1979), 5. To encourage other congregations to take similar action, a letter from the church council of the South Seattle Mennonite Church is printed which offers support for their members participating in war tax resistance.

Regier, Harold R. "Congregations to Prepare for Conference on Civil Responsibility." *God and Caesar* 4 (July, 1978), 4-5. A listing of books, papers, and slide sets available to facilitate congregations in their study of civil disobedience and war tax issues in preparation for the special General Conference mid-triennium session.

Regier, Harold R. "General Conference Board Discusses Withholding." *God and Caesar* 2 (Oct., 1976), 3-4. The General Conference Board has devoted much time and energy to a theological debate on the war tax issue and plans to come with a decision or recommendation to the July, 1977, triennial General Conference Mennonite Church session.

Regier, Harold R. "General Conference Board to Discuss Withholding." *God and Caesar* 2 (June, 1976), 3. The General Conference Mennonite Church will use substantial agenda time at their August meeting to discuss the issue of withholding taxes from employees requesting nonwithholding of war taxes.

Regier, Harold R. "Group Initiates Peace Pledge." *God and Caesar* 5 (Feb., 1979), 11-12. The article encourages others to follow the example of a group of persons from the Bethel College Mennonite Church, North Newton, Kans., who have developed a "Peace Pledge" and considered other personal actions to protest war taxes.

Regier, Harold R. "IRS Refuses Dialogue with Mennonites." *God and Caesar* 5 (Feb., 1979), 6. The General Conference Mennonite Church through its Peace and Social Concerns office has requested a meeting with a special IRS "Illegal Tax Protest Study Group" but that request has been denied.

Regier, Harold R. "IRS Studying Tax Protestors." *God and Caesar* 4 (July, 1978), 12. IRS has established a study group to determine the magnitude of illegal tax protest activities around the country.

Regier, Harold R. "MWC Witness at IRS." *God and Caesar* 4 (Nov., 1978), 6. Description of the 24-hour witness and prayer vigil for peace at the Internal Revenue Service office at Wichita during the Mennonite World Conference.

Regier, Harold R. "Reflections Before Minneapolis." *Menn* 94 (Jan. 16, 1979), 48.

Suggests ways the General Conference, at their midtriennium session in Minneapolis, might take corporate responsibility and action on the issue of paying war taxes.

Regier, Harold R. "Reflections of a Retiring Editor." *God and Caesar* 5 (Aug., 1979), 2-3. Upon retiring as editor of this publication, Regier shares some of his thoughts which have grown out of his pilgrimage with war tax resistance.

Regier, Harold R. "Suggestions for War Tax Resistance." *God and Caesar* 2 (Mar., 1976), 2-3. A list of suggested methods people of conscience might use to resist payment of war taxes.

Regier, Harold R. "Tax Resister Named Arvada Woman of the Year." *God and Caesar* 3 (Jan., 1977), 6-7. Marge Roberts, a peace and social concerns activist who participates in the Arvada Mennonite Church, was named the city woman of the year.

Regier, Harold R. "The Church as Tax Collector: Issues and Options." *God and Caesar* 2 (Oct., 1976), 5-6. An examination of the issues that lie behind the war tax issue, what strategies they suggest, and the various responses available to the church.

Regier, Harold R. "US Supreme Court to Hear War Tax Case?" *God and Caesar* 4 (June, 1978), 3. A petition has been made to the US Supreme Court asking it to rule on the constitutionality of requiring conscientious objectors to military taxes to pay those taxes, based on the First Amendment to the Constitution.

Regier, Harold R. "War Taxes Not a Religious Issue?" *God and Caesar* 3 (June, 1977), 6-7. Further challenges in the courts and in Congress are needed to argue against the inconsistency between the US government's recognition that physical participation in war is a violation of religious freedom for conscientious objectors while financial participation is not.

Regier, Harold R. "Wichita Congregation Prepares WPTF Act Resolution." *God and Caesar* 2 (Oct., 1976), 6-7. Members of the Lorraine Avenue Mennonite Church, Wichita, Kansas, have prepared a resolution addressed to the Western District Conference of the General Conference Mennonite Church in support of the World Peace Tax Fund Act.

Reimer, Margaret Loewen. "Christ Versus Caesar; What Was Accomplished at Minneapolis?" *MennRep* 9 (Mar. 5, 1979), 6. The final resolution on war taxes at the General Conference midtriennium in Minneapolis was concerned with legality and raised questions as to what we really are attempting to witness to government and country.

Reimer, Richard. "Facing the Race." *Menn* 76 (Jan. 3, 1961), 5-6. Questions the effectiveness of the usually proposed alternatives to payment of war taxes. Asks for massive direct efforts toward disarmament.

Reimer, Vic. "Delegates Say Church Should Not Be Tax Collector." *MennRep* 9 (Feb. 19, 1979), 1. Mennonites gathered in Minneapolis Feb. 10-11 to launch a vigorous campaign to exempt the church from acting as a tax collector for the state, a campaign which was prompted by a General Conference employee who requested the church to stop withholding war taxes from her wages.

Reimer, Vic. "The Midtriennium: In Which Direction Will the Spirit Move Us Next?" *Menn* 94 (Feb. 22, 1979), 138-41. A report on the General Conference Midtriennium meeting which moved participants toward greater appreciation of the varieties of faithfulness and understanding on the issue of war taxes.

Reitz, Herman R. (Review). *The Tax Dilemma: Praying for Peace, Paying for War,* by Donald D. Kaufman. Scottdale: Herald Press, 1978. Pp. 101. *ST* 47 (Sept., 1979), 26-27. Reviewer notes that the book equates income tax with war tax, but also that the book is not simply anti-war propaganda. Concludes that it is not so much praying for peace and paying for war as it is recognizing the ethical arguments against paying "war taxes" while being aware of the biblical injunctions to pay taxes.

Roberts, Marge. Letter to the Editor. *Menn* 92 (May 3, 1977), 300-301. Tax resister explains why she must protest the amount of money the government calls her to contribute to the war machine, and describes the thought-provoking conversations her resistance raises with IRS officials, etc.

Ruth, Janet. "National Peace Academy." *MCC PS Wash. Memo* 12 (Nov.-Dec., 1980), 7-8. Description, background of, and possible problems with the establishment of a National Academy of Peace and Conflict Resolution..

"Slow Progress Reported by Task Force on Taxes." *GH* 72 (Aug. 21, 1979), 673-74. Report on the progress of the task force mandated by the General Conference Mennonite Church at the Minneapolis meeting to seek legal and administrative avenues for achieving conscientious objector exemption.

"Some Ways of Saying 'No' to War Taxes." *God and Caesar* 1 (Jan., 1975), 7-8. A listing of eight ways in which persons are saying no to war taxes at different levels.

"Supreme Court Opposes War Tax Protest." *Forum* 8 (Dec., 1974), 3. On Oct. 29, 1974, the US Supreme Court in an 8 to 1 decision reversed a US district court ruling which had favored the American Friends Service Committee in a case of refusing to withhold war tax because of religious convictions.

Samuel, Bill. "Income Tax Refusal." *God and Caesar* 4 (Nov., 1978), 7. Discussion of how one can reduce or eliminate federal income tax withholding for the purposes of war tax resistance and the legal reasoning underlying such action.

Sawatzky, P. J. Letter to the Editor. *MennRep* 9 (July 9, 1979), 6. In response to the decision on war taxes made at the General Conference midtriennium, this writer stresses the need for military protection against communism and the biblical teachings to support the government and pay taxes.

Sawatzky, P. J. "The Question of War Taxes." *GfT* 14 (Sept./-Oct., 1979), 17-18. Reprinted "Letter to the Editor," *Mennonite Reporter* (July 9, 1979). Advocates paying all taxes in order to obey the government which preserves freedom by keeping a military check on Soviet communism.

Schmidt, Steven G. Letter to the Editor. *ChrLiv* 20 (Mar., 1973), 28. Speaks out against US military destruction in Vietnam; suggests that opposers of war refuse payment of war taxes.

Schrag, Roger. Letter to the Editor. *ChrLead* 42 (Apr. 24, 1979), 11. War tax resistance is illegal. One who lives in a country obviously must follow the laws of that country.

Schrock, Paul M. (Review). *The Tax Dilemma: Praying for Peace, Paying for War,* by Donald D. Kaufman. Scottdale: Herald Press, 1978. "New Book on War Taxes." *God and Caesar* 5 (Feb., 1979), 8. This book considers the issue of two kingdoms, traces the history of conscientious objection to war taxes and discusses a dozen viable options which Christians can use to witness to their faith and oppose corporate warmaking.

Schuchardt, John. "A Parable." *God and Caesar* 3 (Nov., 1977), 3-4. Various religious groups consider the suffering of villagers from napalm bombs but do not take personal responsibility by refusing to pay for war, a parallel to religious leaders in the parable of the Good Samaritan.

Shank, Aaron M. "Let's Pay Our Taxes." *GfT* 8 (Jan.-Feb., 1973), 17-18. Reprinted from *The Eastern Mennonite Testimony* (Aug., 1972). Responds to arguments against paying war taxes.

Shank, Duane (Editorial). "Now That the Draft Is Over . . . ?" *RepConsS* 32 [sic, 33] (Mar., 1976), 2.

The draft over, NISBCO will work on such issues as military recruitment for the all-volunteer force and war taxes.

Shank, J. Ward. "Question of the Surtax." *ST* 36 (Mar., 1968), 23. Examines the issue of tax monies that are collected by the government to pay for military and war expenditures.

Sheats, Ladon. Letter to the Editor. *God and Caesar* 2 (Mar., 1976), 7. Writer shares his present perceptions and sense of urgency on war tax issues.

Sheats, Ladon. "Who Is Lord of the Castle?" *God and Caesar* 3 (Jan., 1977), 3-5. Excerpts from an article written by the same author reminding us of the grim realities of how the US government uses tax dollars.

Shelly, Andrew R. "Taxes for Military Spending." *GH* 54 (July 18, 1961), 622-23. People should consider giving as much as they can to tax deductible charities rather than to war.

Shelly, Maynard. "A New Call to Tax Resistance." *God and Caesar* 4 (Nov., 1978), 3. Discusses why the approval given to war tax resistance at the Green Lake conference of the New Call to Peacemaking is a "giant step" for Mennonites, Friends, and Brethren.

Shelly, Maynard. "Western District Takes Stand on War Taxes." *Menn* 85 (Nov. 10, 1970), 682-84. Torn apart by loyalties to government and God, Mennonites conclude that withholding war taxes is in the tradition of Mennonite conscientious objection to war.

Shelly, Maynard and Flickinger, Ron. *Affirm Life: Pay for Peace.* Newton: Historic Peace Church Task Force on Taxes, 1981. Pp. [87]. MHL. Handbook for World Peace Tax Fund educators and organizers. Some of the articles are focused more broadly on the war tax issue—exploring biblical dimensions, historical roots of the peace church witness, etc. Others are more specifically focussed on the WPTF—strategies and resources for effective education, definition of terms, commonly asked questions, etc. Articles indexed separately are: Stoner, John K., "Why a War Tax Concern Now?" 5-6; Swartley, Willard, "What Does the New Testament Say About War Taxes?" 7-9; Stoner, John K., "Loving Confrontation in the Life of Jesus," 11-12; Hull, Robert, "Historical Roots of a Peace Church Witness." 13-17; Hull, Robert and Eccleston, Alan, "A Peace Church Style of Witness," 19-24.

Shenk, Phil M. "An Oratorical Essay on the World Peace Tax Fund and Faithfulness." Paper, entry in C. Henry Smith Peace Contest, Washington, DC, May 13, 1977. Pp. 6. MHL.

Shenk, Phil M. "The World Peace Tax Fund: A Faithful Response?" *GH* 70 (Nov. 22, 1977), 893; *Menn* 92 (Dec. 13, 1977), 735. Speech which won first place in the C. Henry Smith Peace Oratorical Contest examines the World Peace Tax Fund, its relation to the gospel of Christ, and its possible effects on the social consciences of persons opposed to war.

Shetler, Sanford G. "That Perennial War Tax Problem." *GfT* 14 (Nov.-Dec., 1979), 15, 18. Nonpayment of war taxes has no biblical foundation.

Shutt, Joyce M. Letter to the Editor. *Menn* 94 (Apr. 17, 1979), 285. The midtriennium conference has shown us that we are not a peace church and that we view peacemaking as incidental to and irrelevant to the preaching and doing of Christ.

Siebert, John (Review). *The Tax Dilemma: Praying for Peace, Paying for War,* by Donald D. Kaufman. Scottdale: Herald Press, 1978. *MBH* 18 (Apr. 27, 1979), 32. Reviewer observes the book's thesis is that pacifists face a moral dilemma in refusing to support war in body while paying taxes which support the defense budget.

Silliman, Markus. Letter to the Editor. *God and Caesar* 2 (Mar., 1976), 5. Writer reveals his search for a firm base for decision making and the dilemma of hurting more helpful government departments by withholding telephone excise tax.

Slabaugh, Dan. "Why I Support the World Peace Tax Fund." *GH* 72 (Apr. 10, 1979), 304-305. The author puts forth his rationale for supporting world peace tax fund legislation which will allow one to legally refrain from contributing to the cost of war and help finance peace programs.

Smith, Allan W. Letter to the Editor. *MennRep* 9 (Aug. 20, 1979), 6. Overt civil disobedience is not scriptural, but voluntary protest may be made about war taxes if one feels convicted to do so.

Smith, Allan W. Letter to the Editor." *GH* 61 (Sept. 3, 1968), 802-803. Advocates paying all taxes, albeit "with grief," since it is commanded by scripture and since it is impossible to withdraw monetary support from all other questionable activities besides war.

Snyder, John M. (Review). *What Belongs to Caesar?* by Donald D. Kauffman. Herald Press, 1969. *ST* 39 (June, 1971), 11. The question posed is timely and calls for consideration of the implications of scriptural teaching in relation to the tax problem. The answers given in this book do not validly take into account all the relevant factors.

Stauffer, J. L. "Nonresistance in War-Time." *GH* 28 (Nov. 7, 1935), 675-76. Excerpts from a pastoral letter to the Lower District in Virginia outline the biblical basis for abstaining from direct or indirect contribution to the war effort. The Christian citizen should continue to pay taxes.

Stauffer, James K. "War Taxes Questioned." *GH* 63 (June 2, 1970), 505. Death and destruction of the innocent in Vietnam raises the question of whether Christians should pay the taxes supporting this war.

Stoltzfus, Victor, comp. "What About Taxes for War Purposes?" *ChrLiv* 8 (July, 1961), 38-39. Reprint of a letter published in the Church of the Brethren's *Gospel Messenger* (Feb. 25, 1961) supporting nonpayment of war taxes.

Stoner, John K. "The Moral Equivalent of Disarmament." *Sojourners* 8 (Feb., 1979), 15. War tax resistance for the church is the moral equivalent of disarmament for the government. Paper originally presented at the New Call to Peacemaking, Green Lake, Wis., Oct., 1978. Pp. 5. MHL.

Stoner, John K. "Uneasy Conscience: Paying for War." *RepConsS* 32 (Nov., 1975), 1, 3. Two-day conference draws 115 Mennonites and Brethren in Christ together to seek practical and theological discernment on war tax issues.

Stoner, John K. "War Tax Conference: Uneasy Conscience About Paying for Armageddon." *God and Caesar* 1 (Nov., 1975), 2-3. The conference in Kitchener, Ont., sponsored by the Mennonite and Brethren in Christ Churches sought theological and practical discernment on war tax issues. The churches acknowledged the way of peace as their heritage and the growing menace of the world arms race.

Stoner, John K. "War Tax Dilemma: The Arms Race or the Human Race?" *Peace Section Newsletter* 9 (Dec., 1979), 7-8. War tax resistance is not the only way to say that nuclear deterrence is wrong, but it might be one way.

Stoner, John K. "Why a War Tax Concern Now?" *Affirm Life: Pay for Peace.* Ed. Maynard Shelly and Ron Flickinger. Newton: Historic Peace Church Task Force on Taxes, 1981, 5-6. Pp. [87]. MHL. Urges church to act now on the tax quesion because "taxation marshalls the wealth of the nation to fuel the engines of war" and if we do not act today there may be no tomorrow.

Strunk, Stephen. Letter to the Editor. *Menn* 92 (Oct. 18, 1977), 604. Questions the practice of war tax resistance, using Matthew 5:39 to show that refusal to pay war taxes is a form of resistance, contradicting Jesus' command to nonresistance.

Sutter, Sam and Mabel. Letter to the Editor. *Menn* 88 (Feb. 27, 1973), 151. Writers submit to *The Mennonite* a copy of the letter they sent with their Internal Revenue Service return, protesting their payment of war taxes and explaining the conscientious objector position of the Mennonite church.

Swartley, Willard M. "Answering the Pharisees: A New Testament Study on the Payment of War Taxes." *Sojourners* 8 (Feb., 1979), 18-20. A New Testament study on the payment of war taxes.

Swartley, Willard M. "How to Interpret the Bible: A Case Study of Romans 13:1-7 and the Payment of Taxes for War." *Seeds* 3, 4 (June, 1984), 28-31. Applies the method proposed in Swartley's *Slavery, Sabbath, War and Women* study to this text and issue.

Swartley, Willard M. "What Does the New Testament Say About War Taxes?" Condensed by Lois Barrett. *Affirm Life: Pay for Peace.* Ed. Maynard Shelly and Ron Flickinger. Newton: Historic Peace Church Task Force on Taxes, 1981, 7-9. Pp. [87]. MHL. Brief exegetical comments on the tax texts: Matt. 17:24-27; Mark 12:13-17; Luke 23:2; Rom. 13:6-7. Concludes that while these particular texts cannot be used as a rulebook for the issue, application of the basic moral principles of the New Testament determines that such witnesses as nonpayment can speak a word faithful to the gospel. The complete version of this paper is available from the Mennonite Board of Congregational Ministries.

"Task Force on War Taxes Rejects Administrative Loophole." *MennRep* 9 (Aug. 20, 1979), 3. The General Conference Mennonite Church task force on taxes rejected the pursuit of administrative avenues for exemption of war taxes and decided that a separate group should work at Canadian tax issues.

"Taxes for Peace Fund Grow." *RepConsS* 35 (Oct., 1973), 4. Reports actions and statements of individual Mennonites, such as James and Anna Juhnke and Marlin Miller, who have resisted payment of war taxes.

"The World Peace Tax Fund Act." *God and Caesar* 1 (Jan., 1975), 8-9. Report indicating the present status of the World Peace Tax Fund, which was developed in 1971 as a legislative proposal to provide a legal alternative to the payment of taxes used for military purposes.

[Transcript of Court Proceedings]. "In the Matter of US vs. Bruce Chrisman." *God and Caesar* 6 (Oct., 1980), 10-18. Transcripts of war tax resister's testimony, summary of the issues at stake, and the "Friend of the Court" argument submitted by the General Conference Mennonite Church.

Unruh, Pamela J. Letter to the Editor. *Menn* 92 (Feb. 22, 1977), 142. The World Peace Tax Fund is an extension of liberal politics which, however well-intentioned, does not remove warmakers from power or curb excessive government spending.

*

Vogt, Roy. "Taxes: Drawing the Line About Rendering Unto Caesar." *MennMirror* 8 (Mar., 1979), 19, 20. Although the final resolution was disappointing, the Minneapolis triennium of the General Conference, which met Feb. 9-10, 1979, dealt with the issue of war taxes and Christian civil responsibility with great passion and fairness.

"War Tax Conference at Kitchener." *God and Caesar* 1 (June, 1975), 2-3. Announcement of a conference for theological and practical discernment on war tax issues sponsored by the General Conference Mennonite Church, Mennonite Church, Brethren in Christ, and the MCC Peace Section to be held in Kitchener, Ont., Oct. 30-Nov. 1.

"War Tax Conference Provides Impetus for Peace Advocates." *Menn* 94 (Sept. 4, 1979), 520. Clergy interested in peace issues are beginning to work together in the twin cities of Minneapolis-St. Paul.

"War Tax Packet." Akron, Pa.: MCC US Peace Section, revised Sept., 1980. MHL. Items added: Kaufman, Donald, "Pay for War While Praying for Peace: Dilemma of Individuals and the Body," pp. 4; Stoner, John K., "The Moral Equivalent of Disarmament," pp. 3; MCC Peace Section, "Mennonite Conferences Speak on War Taxes," pp. 2; Reedy, Janet and Stan, "Personal Experiences," pp. 3; Leatherman, Loretta and Paul, "Personal Experiences," pp. 3; GCMC Resolutions on War Taxes, pp. 2; MCC US Peace Section, *A Guide to Peace Resources* (brochure); Durland, William, "Guidelines on Military Tax Refusal," pp. 2; MCC US Peace Section, "War Tax Resistance: Techniques and Options," pp. 1; Schroeder, David, "Is There a Biblical Case for Civil Disobedience? Is Civil Disobedience Called for in the Specific Case of War Taxes?" pp. 8; MCC US Peace Section, *Resolution on the World Arms Race,* Dec. 1, 1978 (brochure).

"War Tax Packet." [Akron, Pa.]: MCC, Feb., 1976. MHL. Includes: Stoner, John K., "Suggestions for Use of Packet and for Additional Resources," pp. 2; King, Col. Edward L. (retired), "Militarism in Today's Society . . . in the United States, . . . in Canada," pp. 12; Kaufman, Donald D., "A Chronology of Wars Reflecting the 'Anabaptist' Response to War Taxes," pp. 28; Klaassen, Walter, "Anabaptism and Church/Government Issues," pp. 12; Miller, Marlin, "The Christian's Relationship to the State and Civil Authority," pp. 6; Swartley,

Willard, "The Christian and Payment of War Taxes," pp. 18; Hess, James, "The Case for the Payment of All Taxes," pp. 8; Ediger, Peter J., "Christ and Caesar: A Ballad of Faith," pp. 4; Lehman, Carl M., "Tax Resistance—A Form of Protest?" pp. 2; Stoltzfus, Ruth C., "War Tax Research Report: Challenging Withholding Law on First Amendment Grounds," pp. 9; National Council for World Peace Tax Fund, *Support the World Peace Tax Fund* (brochure); National Council for World Peace Tax Fund, "Conscientious Objection for Taxpayers Too?" pp. 1; National Council for World Peace Tax Fund, "Commonly Asked Questions About the World Peace Tax Fund Act," pp. 1; Shank, Duane, "World Peace Tax Fund Act—Some Unanswered Questions," pp. 2; MCC Peace Section, "Taxes for Military Purposes" (brochure); Church of the Brethren Annual Conference, "Taxation for War," pp. 6. Also includes a questionnaire on war taxes and a bibliography on war taxes.

"World Peace Tax Fund Act—Another View." *RepConsS* 32 (May, 1975), 3. Congresswoman Pat Schroeder explains her refusal to cosponsor CPTF to Chris Brown and Delton Franz.

Waltner, Erland. "The Christian and the State." *ChrLead* 24 (Sept. 19, 1961), 4-5, 24. The Christian is to pray for her or his government and be subject to it, in principle, but a Christian witness also involves refusal to give unconditional support, e.g., by war taxes.

War Tax Conference Participants. "War Tax Conference Summary Statement." *God and Caesar* 1 (Nov., 1975), 3-6. A summary statement prepared and approved by the participants at the Kitchener war tax conference with suggestions for actions and responses to the war tax issue by churches, church institutions, or individuals.

Warkentin, B. Alf. "Test War Tax in the Courts." *CanMenn* 10 (Nov. 23, 1962), 6. If Mennonites sincerely believe in nonresistance, they should take every step to bring their belief to the attention of others.

Weidner, Mark; Weidner, Susan; Nisley, Margaret; and Nisley, Weldon. "Tax Resistance Letters." *God and Caesar* 2 (Mar., 1976), 8-9. Parts of two letters to IRS are printed to illustrate two forms of resistance: refusing payment of war taxes while filing form 1040 when taxes are still owed IRS; and filing for refund of war taxes when taxes are withheld by employer.

Werner, Murray. Letter to the Editor. *God and Caesar* 4 (June, 1978), 11. A Canadian contributes a letter he enclosed with his tax return stating his reason for withholding the portion used for military purposes and suggesting a Canadian World Peace Tax Fund.

---

*For additional listing, see Supplement, pp. 717-719.

Werscham, Mary. Letter to the Editor. *God and Caesar* 3 (Nov., 1977), 5-6. A summary of how the writer has tried to witness to her commitment to nonviolence through non-payment of taxes.

Wiebe, Bernie. "The Bible Speaks to Our Search." *Menn* 94 (Feb. 27, 1979), 141. Willard Swartley spoke to the Minneapolis Midtriennium Conference using the Bible as a guide in how to deal with the war tax issue. His three presentations were: "How Christians Solve Difficult Questions," "The Identity of God's People," and "Faithfulness and Witness."

Wiebe, Bernie. "We Found Some Things." *Menn* 94 (Feb. 20, 1979), 136. Report on the midtriennium of the General Conference in Minneapolis Feb. 9-10, 1979, on Christian civil responsibility.

Wiebe, Menno. Letter to the Editor. *God and Caesar* 1 (June, 1975), 7. In response to a previous letter regarding a question on war taxes in Canada, the writer suggests contacting the MCC (Canada) office in Ottawa and reading the book *Making a Killing* by Ernie Regehr.

Yoder, John H. "Do We Believe in Sharing Our Decisions?" *GH* 66 (May 22, 1973), 427. Uses the example of a small group of people committed to withholding some of their war taxes, and their sharing of the concern at the district conference, to commend the process of open discussion and decision making within the wider church fellowship.

Yoder, John H. "The Things That Are Caesar's." *ChrLiv* 7, Part 1, (July, 1960), 4-5, 34; Part 2, (Aug., 1960), 14-17, 39; Part 3, (Sept., 1960), 16-18. Christian witness to the state is necessary because Jesus is Lord; the state must be reminded of its limited place; the evils of oppression and exploitation must be challenged. Our message to all is the call to repentance and faith and to people in government in particular the call to do justice. Awareness of the meaning of Christ's lordship and of the complexity of Caesar's realm can free us from fear of involvement and from dogmas of responsibility.

Yoder, John H. "Why I Don't Pay All My Income Tax." *Sojourners* 6 (Mar., 1977), 11. The concern for war tax resistance is not an effort to be morally immaculate by making absolutely no contribution to the war effort but to testify to the government about its own obligation.

Yoder, Perry B. "Attitudinal Survey on Church/State Issues." *God and Caesar* 4 (July, 1978), 8-9. A report on the results of an attitude survey which was sent to all General Conference Mennonite congregations to aid in determining the range of attitudes that exist on the war tax issue and several other issues.

Yoder, Perry B. "Implementing the War Tax Resolution." *God and Caesar* 3 (Nov., 1977), 2-3. Several projects are underway in following up the resolution concerning war taxes passed at the General Conference Mennonite Church triennial sessions in Bluffton, Summer, 1977.

Yoder, Perry B. "Update on the General Conference's Implementation of the Bluffton War Tax Resolution." *God and Caesar* 4 (June, 1978), 2. In preparation for the General Conference Mennonite Church mid-triennium session on war taxes, an attitude inventory has been mailed to congregations, two study guides are being prepared, and a consultation of church leaders, Bible scholars and theologians, and lawyers is planned.

*

Zarembka, David. Letter to the Editor. *God and Caesar* 6 (Sept., 1980), 12-13. Describes encounter with IRS collector who suggested the option of paying war tax money into the Department of Health and Welfare or the Department of Education.

# 7

# Conscientious Objection

"A League of Recognition of Conscientious Objection." *GH* 62 (Oct. 7, 1969), 876. Summarizes the status of conscientious objection to war in Italy.

"A Message from the Consultation on Conscience and Conscription." *GH* 63 (Jan. 6, 1970), 12-13. Outlines concerns, affirmations, objections, and appeals to obedience in relationship to war and peace drawn up by the Peace Assembly of the MCC Peace Section. Statement affirms both alternative service and noncooperation as valid Christian responses to the draft and encourages the government to grant exemption from military service to selective objectors to war.

"A Simple Questionnaire for CO's." *GH* 65 (Feb. 22, 1972), 176. Formerly containing thirty-one questions, the new form has four questions for applicants who desire CO classification.

"Acting Secretary Reports on Case Work." *RepConsS* 15 (Sept., 1958), 2. John R. Martin reports on cases of conscientious objection which must be worked through the Presidential Appeal Board or the military channels.

"Amishman Released from Prison After Mental Breakdown." *RepConsS* 15 (July, 1958), 3. Judge grants parents' request for release of son who suffered mental illness while serving sentence for conscientious objection.

"Analysis of Draft Census of Five Mennonite Conferences." *GH* 49 (Nov. 20, 1956), 1105. Mennonite Research Foundation reports the CO record of the Mennonite Church in 1952-56 was better than it was in World War II.

"Associate Secretary Appointed to Pastoral Position." *RepConsS* 13 (Dec., 1956), 3. Upon his resignation as Associate Executive Secretary of NSBRO, Edgar Metzler is praised for his excellence in the cause of conscientious objection.

*A Manual of Draft Information for Conscientious*

*Objectors.* Akron, Pa.: MCC Peace Section, 1968. Pp. 206. MHL.

Augsburger, Myron S. "An Answer for Nonresistance." *MBH* 14 (Oct. 31, 1975), 32. Five simple explanations for conscientious objection based on biblical texts.

"Baptist Delegation from Russia Meets Mennonites." *CanMenn* 4 (June 1, 1956), 1, 7. Russian Baptists visiting the Mennonite Biblical Seminary in Chicago describe Mennonite-Baptist cooperation in the Soviet Union and discuss the status of conscientious objection in their country.

"Bishop Appears Before US Committee to Testify on Military Draft Laws." *CanMenn* 15 (May 23, 1967), 1, 5. Text of a statement made by John E. Lapp, MCC Peace Section resentative, before the Armed Services Committee of the US House of Representatives on May 3, 1967. Lapp's requests included: equal liberties for COs of all denominations; equal liberties for all COs of sincere religious convictions; freedom for all sincerely troubled by ethical problems of militarism; abolition of universal military training.

"Boot Camp Teaches Fighting for Peace." *Menn* 86 (Dec. 21, 1971), 768. A pre-draft boot camp is an attempt to introduce young people to how one works for peace as a conscientious objector.

"Brazilian Mennonites Hope for CO Status." *RepConsS* 31 (Nov., 1974), 3. Brazilian Mennonites are negotiating with their government for recognition of their stance on conscientious objection.

"Brethren, Mennonites Ask New NSB." *Fellowship* 13 (July, 1947), 120. A news item stating that the Brethren and Mennonites have decided to sponsor a continuing National Service Board for Conscientious Objectors.

"Brethren-Friends-Mennonites, Others, Protest Inaccurate CO Article." *RepConsS* 11 (Sept., 1954), 1. Reports that a letter has been sent to the editors of *Newsweek* protesting its reference to COs as a "generally unruly lot" in the Aug. 2 issue.

Baer, Isaac. "My Experience as a Conscientious Objector in World War I at Camp Meade, Maryland." Tape recording transcribed by John Kreider, 1962. Pp. 17. MSHL.

Baergen, Samuel. Letter to the Editor. *Menn* 89 (Mar. 5, 1974), 165-66. Calls for more publicity and letter-writing support for HR 7053, the bill providing for conscientious objection to tax money paid for war.

Bainton, Roland H. "The Churches and War: Historic Attitudes Toward Christian Participation." *Social Action* 11 (Jan. 15, 1945), 5-71. Reviews the three positions of pacifism, just war, and crusade from the first through the twentieth centuries, including World War II. Examines especially 20th-century attitudes. Refers to Anabaptist views in the Reformation, as well as the treatment of conscientious objectors and Civilian Public Service.

Baker, Robert J. *Is There a Middle Road?* Scottdale: Herald Press, 1956. Pp. 15. The Christian Youth and War Pamphlets, No. 6. Author recounts his experience in noncombatant service as an attempt to find a middle road between complete participation and nonparticipation in the military. Asserts that true conscientious objectors cannot in good conscience serve noncombatantly.

Barrett, Lois [Janzen]. "Clemency—Now He Sees It; Now He Doesn't." *Menn* 90 (Mar. 11, 1975), 162-63. Relates the story of Steve Trimm, a draft resister who had been refused conscientious objector status and sought to obtain clemency; shows the difficulties inherent in President Ford's "conditional amnesty" program.

Barrett, Lois. "Stand for What You Believe." *With* 13 (Oct., 1980), 14-15. Conscientious objector from World War I and active peace advocate counsels young people to be able to articulate their peace position.

Bassinger, David W. Notebook of names, addresses (handwritten). World War I CO Records. Pp. 19. MSHLA.

Bauman, Clarence. "Conscientious Objection and Alternative Service." *CanMenn* (Mar. 13, 1959), 2, 11; "Conscientious Objection in Germany," *Menn* 74 (Apr. 14, 1959), 231-32. An analysis of the political and social climate of West Germany and how this relates to the pacifist. Traces recent development of legal provisions for conscientiouos objectors and describes the EIRENE program in Morocco, a joint project for the historic peace churches and FOR.

Bauman, Clarence. "Conscientious Objection and the German Draft Law." Paper presented at the Historic Peace Churches and IFOR Conference, Beatrice Webb House, England, Sept. 11-14, 1956. Pp. 12. MHL.

Bauman, Clarence. "Conscientious Objection in Germany." *Fellowship* 25 (Sept., 1959), 29-30. Reports on conscientious objection and alternative service proposals in Germany, highlighting the nature and extent of the involvement of the Mennonites.

Becker, Jeff. "Some Causes for Public Tolerance of Conscientious Objectors in Civilian Public Service." Social Science Seminar paper, Dec., 1980. Pp. 87. MLA/BeC.

Beery, Ward. Lists. World War I CO Records. COs of Camp Lee, Va., Sept., 1917-Dec., 1918; supplemental list to former, Dec. 5, 1918; "Jail Birds," Nov., 1917 (handwritten, xeroxed); and COs of Detachment CO, Jan. 24, 1918. MSHLA.

Beery, Ward. Notebook (handwritten, xeroxed copy). World War I CO Records. Pp. 53. Contains poems, lists of names and addresses, etc. Also list of birthday presents received in 1918, e.g., 1 penny, a ribbon, a pencil, and a safety pin. MSHLA.

Beiler, Edna. "Armed Only with Love." *ChrLiv* 4 (Jan., 1957), 3-5. Conscientious objectors contribute to the welfare of people by constructing houses in Indianapolis.

Beitler, Jim. "How I Came to Be a Conscientious Objector." *With* 4 (July, 1971), 27. Personal experience in military basic training clarified the difference between being a soldier and being a conscientious objector.

Bender, Bertha Burkholder. "Youth, Church, and State." *YCC* 12, Part 1, (Jan. 4, 1931), 420-21; Part 2, (Jan. 11, 1931), 426-27; Part 3, (Jan. 18, 1931), 434-35; Part 4, (Jan. 25, 1931), 444-45; Part 5, (Feb. 1, 1931), 450, 451, 453; Part 6, (Feb. 8, 1931), 461-62; Part 7, (Feb. 15, 1931), 466-67; Part 8, (Feb. 22, 1931), 479-80; Part 9, (Mar. 1, 1931), 487, 488; Part 10, (Mar. 8, 1931), 491, 493; Part 11, (Mar. 15, 1931), 498, 499; Part 12, (Mar. 22, 1931), 505, 506; Part 13, (Mar. 29, 1931), 515, 517; Part 14, (Apr. 5, 1931), 523, 525; Part 15, (Apr. 12, 1931), 534, 535; Part 16, (Apr. 19, 1931), 539, 541; Part 17, (Apr. 26, 1931), 545-47; Part 18, (May 3, 1931), 559, 560; Part 19, (May 17, 1931), 571, 573; Part 20, (May 31, 1931), 589; Part 21, (June 7, 1931), 595; Part 22, (June 21, 1931), 610; Part 23, (July 5, 1931), 627, 629; Part 24, (July 19, 1931), 645, 646; Part 25, (July 26, 1931), 650, 651; Part 26, (Aug. 2, 1931), 657-59; Part 27, (Aug. 16, 1931), 675-77. Written in a narrative style, the progression of peace-related topics include: the biblical story, the history of the church, issues about responding to government and militarism, e.g., CO status during Civil War and World War I, and Mennonite relief work.

[Bender, Harold S.] "Origins of Alternative Service." *The Reporter* 5 (Mar., 1947), 1, 6-8. A discussion of the beginnings of Mennonite alternative service in Russia after 1870, and the experience of CO's in Russia to the present.

Bender, John M. "The Draft: a Personal Statement." *GH* 64 (Apr. 13, 1971), 338. Even after registering with the Selective Service System and taking a CO stand, there are many questions as to what it means to live a nonresistant life. The writer, a Canadian resident in the US, reviews his dilemma of considering nonregistration for the draft in order to refuse cooperation with the war industry.

Bender, Paul. "Conscientious Objection to Military Service in North America, South America, and Europe: Legislation, Objection, Alternative Service, and Peace Work." Report to the Sixth Mennonite World Conference, Karlsruhe, Aug. 10-16, 1957. Pp. 10. MHL.

Bender, Titus. "Peace, Freedom, and Religion." *CanMenn* 15 (Feb. 14, 1967), 5. Letter to the editor makes point about the absurdity of war and the validity of conscientious objection via a short satire involving a father-son conversation.

Bender, Urie A. *Soldiers of Compassion.* Scottdale: Herald Press, 1969. Pp. 320. The story of PAX, a service program of Mennonite Central Committee for conscientious objectors after World War II, told in first person and case history form.

Benner, Rhine W. "First World War." Transcript of interview conducted by Joseph L. Lapp, 1966. Pp. 11. MSHL.

Berg, Ford. "Let Us Tell." *GH Supplement* 40 (Aug., 1947), 463. The Mennonite church should be more aggressive in proclaiming the doctrine of nonresistance. Too often this testimony has been "hidden under a bushel," when it could have been helpful, especially to CO's of other denominations.

Berg, Ford. "The Status of Conscientious Objectors in Europe." *GH* 45 (Jan. 15, 1952), 56-57. A brief survey of nine European countries based on a report by Guy F. Hershberger for the Mennonite Central Committee Peace Section.

Berg, Ford. "What's Happening in the Peace and War Area." *GH* 43 (May 16, 1950), 467, 477. A series of short news items reporting the status and activities of conscientious objectors and war resisters around the world.

Berg, Ford (Review). *Fruit in His Season,* by Helen Corse Barney. N.p., n.d., pp. 134; *The Dagger and the Cross,* by Culbert G. Rutenber. N.p., n.d., pp. 134; *Christianity vs. War,* by John D. Roop. N.p., n.d.; *Conscientious Objection.* Washington, DC: Selective Service System, n.d., pp. 364. "Four New Books of interest to Peace-Minded Folk." *GH* 44 (June 19, 1951), 585, 595. Four perspectives on the issues of war and peace which can better prepare us for the future.

Berg, Nettie. "The Sausage Skins Did It." *MBH* 13 (Jan. 11, 1974), 29-30. Children's story about conscientious objector in army camp who appeased a sergeant's dog with table scraps and befriended the sergeant.

Bergen, Lois. "Youth Education: Peace Education Is Lifelong Growth." *Builder* 31 (Jan., 1981), 28-29. Lists resources and makes suggestions for helping youth think through their positions on militarism, registration, conscientious objection, biblical peacemaking, etc.

Bicksler, Harriet S. "Turning Swords into Plowshares: The World Peace Tax Fund." *EvVis* 93 (Dec. 25, 1980), 6-7, 11. Reviews the Brethren in Christ history of conscientious objection in this century and explains the purposes of war tax resistance and the World Peace Tax Fund.

Birmingham, Egla. "Quien Es El Objetor Por Consciencia? Conscientious Objector Service." Pp. 4. BfC.

Boers, Arthur Paul. "Speaking for the Imprisoned." *MBH* 18 (Apr. 27, 1979), 18-19. Part of Amnesty International's concern for those unjustly imprisoned includes a special concern for conscientious objectors to war.

Bontrager, Marion. "Regan Savage and the Mennonite Dream." *GH* 71 (July 4, 1978), 521. Relates the story of a tank commander who, after six years in the Army, received discharge as a conscientious objector.

Bowman, David. "Mennonite Nonresistance: A Comparison of Practices in the American Revolution and the War Between the States." Term paper for Anabaptist and Mennonite History, Apr. 6, 1978. Pp. 22. MHL.

Braden, Murray. "'Fire on the Mountain.'" *ChrLiv* 12 (April, 1965), 22-24. Reprinted from *Smoke Jumper,* publication of the Missoula, Montana, CPS unit. Conscientious objectors in Civilian Public Service worked as smoke jumpers for forest fires.

Brenneman, Aldine. Diary, World War I CO Records. Handwritten, xeroxed copy. Pp. 37. MSHLA.

Brock, Peter, ed. and trans. "A Polish Anabaptist Against War: The Question of Conscientious Objection in Marcin Czechowic's *Christian Dialogues* of 1575." *MQR* 52 (Oct., 1978), 279-93. Dialogue on nonresistance written by a Polish Anabaptist presents the first detailed and systematic treatment of the subject from a pacifist point of view. Introductory essay describes the development of Polish Anabaptism and the contemporary debate over nonresistance.

Brubacher, Dwight. "Mennonite Nonresistance in Ontario, World War I: The Persecution of a Separate People." Paper presented to Social Science Seminar, Goshen College, Goshen, Ind., May 13, 1976. Pp. 23. MHL.

Brubaker, Jack (Review). *Mennonite Soldier,* by Kenneth Reed. Scottdale: Herald Press, n.d. "Portrait of an Artist: Novel Tells of CO Dilemma in World War I." *MennRep* 5 (Mar. 3, 1975), 8. Reed reflects on his pilgrimage with conscientious objection to war.

Brubaker, Tom. "Don't Just Say No." *GH* 62 (May 27, 1969), 474-75. Conscientious objectors in alternative service need the positive motivation of constructive service rather than the negative motivation of escaping military duty to adequately undergird their work experience.

Brunk, Conrad G. *Conscientious Objectors and the Draft.* Washington, DC: National Interreligious Service Board for Conscientious Objectors, 1972. Pp. 48. MHL. Information pamphlet covering such topics as the tradition of conscientious objection to war, the various alternatives open for those confronted with the draft and some of the moral implications of these alternatives.

Brunk, Harry A. *History of Mennonites in Virginia, 1900-1960.* Verona, Va.: by the author, 1972. Pp. 592. MHL. Contains chapter entitled "Conscientious Objectors in World Wars I & II," 451-66.

Brunk, Harry A. "Virginia Mennonites and the Civil War." *ChrLiv* 8 (July, 1961), 14-17. Experiences of conscientious objectors during the Civil War.

Buchanan, Roy. "A Personal Testimony." *GH* 63 (May 5, 1970), 408-409. World War I conscientious objector disagrees with the position of draft resisters, describing his positive experiences in obtaining cooperation from the military to perform alternative service.

Buchanan, Roy. Letter to the Editor. *GH* 62 (July 1, 1969), 594. World War I conscientious objector describes his experience of finding a response of positive action to the war in relief work in France. Written in response to Tom

Brubaker, "Don't Just Say No" (May 27, 1969).

Buller, Harold. "Why I Am a Conscientious Objector to War." *GH* 42 (Feb. 15, 1949), 155, 165-66; *Menn* 65 (Oct. 24, 1950), 702-703, 711. Seven reasons, with many biblical references, are advanced in support of the CO position. Nonresistance is the heart of the Good News since the nonresistant love of God, the example of Jesus, and the life of the early church all affirm this way of love. Also in BfC., MLA/BeC.

Burkholder, J. Lawrence. "Other Kinds of Conscientious Objectors." *GH* 60 (Feb. 21, 1967), 148, 154; *Menn* 82 (Mar. 28, 1967), 213-15. Says Mennonites need to support, in various ways, nonreligious and selective objectors to war. Urges Mennonites to work for draft legislation recognizing such objectors as CO's.

Burkholder, J. Lawrence. "Profile of a Conscientious Objector." *GH* 73 (Mar. 18, 1980), 217-19. Examines traditionally high expectations on the CO and calls for peacemakers who see the interconnection of all nations and who commit themselves to spiritual growth.

Burkholder, J. Lawrence. "Some Early Nineteenth Century Pacifists." Term paper, n.d. Pp. 13. MHL.

Burkholder, Marlin S. "The Truth About Noncombatant Service." *YCC* 32 (Jan. 21, 1951), 441. A personal testimony to the reality that for a conscientious objector, there is absolutely no difference at all between noncombatant service and regular military service.

Burrell, Curtis E., Jr. "The Conscience of a Heavyweight." *YCC* 48 (Aug. 20, 1967), 10. A discussion of the implications of Muhammad Ali in taking a position of CO.

Byler, Dennis. "Letter to Draft Board." *GH* 63 (June 30, 1970), 586-87. Conscientious objector who chose noncooperation with the draft explains his reasons for opposing participation in war or any of its accompanying machinery.

Byler, Frank. "A History of the Nonresistant People of Logan and Champaign Counties, 1917-1918." Paper presented to Social Science Seminar, Goshen College, Goshen, Ind., n.d. Pp. 32. MHL.

"Can Conscientious Objectors Work in War Industry?" *GH* 35 (June 25, 1942), 282. PPC asserts that it is inconsistent for a person who claims conscientious objector status to participate in a war industry.

"Church Should Not Act as Tax Collector." *GH* 72 (Mar. 6, 1979), 201. At the Minneapolis, Feb. 9-10, special General Conference Meeting, a resolution was passed to launch a vigorous campaign to obtain legal conscientious objection to war taxes.

"CO Confined in Mental Hospital for 29 Years." *GH* 65 (Jan. 11, 1972), 27. Reprinted from *The Reporter for Conscience Sake* (Nov., 1971). The story of a black CO who was wrongly institutionalized in a mental health facility as a result of the legal complications of his pacifist position on "Roosevelt's War."

"CO Kidnapped by Vietnamese Communists." *RepConsS* 19 (July, 1962), 1, 3. Describes the kidnapping of Daniel Gerber, member of the Kidron Mennonite Church, along with two other American church workers from a leprosarium near Banmethnot, Vietnam.

"CO News." *Fellowship* 25 (Feb. 1, 1959), 3. Statement carrying news that the Belgian Mennonites have appealed to the parliament for legal recognition of conscientious objection.

"CO's in Spain Seek New Law." *MennRep* 9 (Dec. 10, 1979), 2. International support is necessary for a law which would meet some of the demands of Spanish conscientious objectors.

"Congress Looks at the Conscience Objector." Washington, DC: National Service Boards for Religious Objectors, 1943. Pp. 96. Transcripts of Senate and House Committee hearings relating to conscientious objectors to war from 1940-1943.

"COs Forced to Stay in Barracks Without Food." *RepConsS* 13 (June-July, 1956), 1, 3. Five Amish men serving prison sentences as a result of conscientious objection are punished for refusing to wear clothing prohibited by their church.

"COs Work for Science and Humanity." *RepConsS* 14 (Aug., 1957), 1-3. Describes the work of one Mennonite volunteer at the National Institute of Health as well as alternative service more generally.

"Counsel to Mennonite Young Men Regarding the Selective Training and Service Act of 1940 as it Applies to Conscientious Objectors." *GH* 33 (Oct. 10, 1940), 603-604. PPC summarizes certain aspects of the act and adds a personal message to the youth who will be facing conscription.

Catton, Bruce. "Draft More Liberal Than in 1917 Toward Conscientious Objectors." *Goshen News* n.d., 16. Describes the Selective Service registration process for conscientious objectors (during World War II). Includes photo of a Mennonite from Pa. registering.

Charles, Howard H. "CO's Around the World."

*GH Supplement* 38 (Oct., 1945), 568. A review of conscientious objection to war as an international phenomenon; summarizes CO's experiences with government and service programs.

Charles, Howard H. "Do CO's Have Civil Rights?" *GH Supplement* 38 (Aug., 1945), 407-408. A description of recent attempts to deprive CO's of their personal and civil rights and a number of court cases crucial to the definition of the legal basis of the civil rights of religious objectors.

Conrad, Tom. "Counsel Decides Against Military Chaplaincy." *ChrLead* 39 (Mar. 30, 1976), 10. The Board of Reference and Counsel decided that the US Mennonite Brethren Conference will not try to place men in the military chaplaincy because that might harm the church's historic position on peace and conscientious objection.

Conscientious Objection in Spain. 40 Interviews in Spanish or Catalonian by John Paul Lederach, 1979. Some English transcriptions. MLA/BeC.

Quan, Helen C. "A Flag Over His Grave." *Menn* 92 (June 28, 1977), 418-19. Tribute to the author's father, John T. Neufeld, a conscientious objector in World War II and pastor of Grace Mennonite Church in Chicago.

Crouse, Susan Kay. "The Conscientious Objector: His Right to a Conscience." Research paper for American Religion: The Sacred and the Civil class. 1980. Pp. 12. BfC.

Davies, Blodwen. "From Militia Tax to Relief." *MennLife* 5 (Oct., 1950), 27-28. A Canadian government exemption for CO's could at one time be attained by paying a government imposed tax. Thomas Reesor helped form the Non-Resistant Movement of Ontario in 1918 which went beyond the government tax by raising $100 for each exempt church member for relief.

Delph, Prisca. "As the Stars." *ChrMon* 35 (Jan., 1943), 2, 4. Story about a young woman whose fiancee goes to camp as a conscientious objector.

Derstine, C. F. "British Treatment of CO's." *ChrMon* 38 (May, 1946), 159-60. British laws governing conscientious objectors in World War II were tolerant by comparison to American laws.

Derstine, C. F. "Camps for 'Conchies' Without Uniforms, Who Never Handle a Gun." *ChrMon* 33 (Sept., 1941), 286-88. Excerpts from newspapers commenting on the conscientious objector camp experiment.

Derstine, C. F. "Canadian Conscientious Objectors in Camp." *GH* 35 (Aug. 13, 1942), 426-27. Describes the situation and needs of CO's in Canadian camps. The government, church, and home share responsibility for the support of these men and their families.

Derstine, C. F. "CO's in World War I and World War II." *ChrMon* 36 (May, 1944), 158-59. Comparison of Selective Service regulations and penalties for refusing to comply in World Wars I and II.

Derstine, C. F. "CO's Serving in Mental Hospitals and Life's Most Dangerous Age." *ChrMon* 36 (July, 1944), 222-23. Mennonite interest in mental health has been stimulated by the CPS work in mental hospitals

Derstine, C. F. "'Conchies' in the Northland." *ChrMon* 36 (Apr., 1944), 126-27. Describes the conscientious objector camps of northern Ontario.

Derstine, C. F. "Conscience as a Bar to Citizenship." *ChrMon* 23 (Aug., 1931), 254. Comment on Supreme Court decision to deny citizenship to two conscientious objectors.

Derstine, C. F. "Conscription and Conscientious Objectors." *ChrMon* 32 (May, 1940), 158-59. Reviews the government attitude toward conscientious objection during World War I and strongly advocates the position to youth in World War II.

Derstine, C. F. "England Calls the CO's 'Conchies.'" *ChrMon* 32 (Mar., 1940), 94-95. England takes lenient attitude toward conscientious objectors in World War II.

Derstine, C. F. "From Civilian Conservation Corps to Conscientious Objector Camps." *ChrMon* 36 (Aug., 1944), 253-55. Development of the Depression-time Civilian Conservation Corps and its service as the model for the later CPS program.

Derstine, C. F. "Is the Shadow of the Beast Appearing Upon the Horizon." *ChrMon* 27 (Apr., 1935), 126-27. The buildup of armaments and the opposition to conscientious objection are signs of the Antichrist.

Derstine, C. F. "Nearly Five Thousand Conscientious Objectors Classified IV-E." *ChrMon* 41 (June, 1949), 190-91. Notes and statistics on the treatment of conscientious objectors in the US.

Derstine, C. F. "The Christian and War" *ChrMon* 35 (June, 1943), 190-91. Reprinted message advocating the conscientious objector position by J. A. Huffman, the Dean of Religion, Taylor University and President of the Winona Lake School of Theology.

Derstine, C. F. "The Churches and Conscientious Objectors." *ChrMon* 26 (Mar., 1934), 94-95. Christian people who object to war should not only live nonresistantly but take every opportunity to protest the government's refusal to recognize conscientious objectors.

Derstine, C. F. "The Counsel of a Canadian Member of Parliament to Conscientious Objectors of the Future." *ChrMon* 26 (Aug., 1934), 253-54. Former Brethren in Christ minister, now MP, advises Mennonites to retain their non-voting position on politics.

Derstine, C. F. "The High Cost of Killing." *ChrMon* 33 (Jan., 1941), 31. While the world pours time, money, and lives into the world war, conscientious objectors should be active in prayer and sacrificial living.

Derstine, C. F. "The Schweitzer CO Case." *ChrMon* 36 (Jan., 1944), 30. Reprinted article from *The Reporter* (Washington, D.C.) describes a schoolteacher fired for his conscientious objector stance.

Derstine, C. F. "Uncle Sam Building a War Machine." *ChrMon* 23 (July, 1931), 221-22. Documents public anti-war sentiment and contrasts it with the recent Supreme Court decision to deny citizenship to two conscientious objectors.

Derstine, C. F. "'What If Everybody Were a CO?'" *ChrMon* 38 (July, 1946), 222-23. Faith in God and fellow human beings is the best safety policy.

Derstine, C. F. "What the Soldier Said." *ChrMon* 28 (Feb., 1936), 62-63. In the face of war's destructiveness, peaceloving Christians should take a firm stand against participating in war.

Derstine, Norman. "Peacemakers in a Broken World." *GH* 61 (Jan. 23, 1968), 82-84. Elaborating on the peacemaker beatitude, the author reviews Christian attitudes toward participation in war from the early church through the Reformation, citing also American Mennonite experiences with conscientious objection.

Drange, E. R. "Reminiscences of War Experiences." *GH* 27 (Mar. 21, 1935), 1087. A recounting of one CO's personal opportunities for witness during wartime, and his conclusion that only a complete surrender of the will to God can lead one to live a highly Christian life in all times and situations.

Drescher, James M. "A Letter from Freddy." *Swords into Plowshares: A Collection of Plays About*

*Peace and Social Justice,* ed. Ingrid Rogers. Elgin: The Brethren Press, 1983, 236-41. An 18-year-old son presses his family for consistency by offering them a deal—he won't enroll in military service if they will resist paying the war tax.

Drescher, James M. "Oh Yes—I Guess." *Swords into Plowshares: A Collection of Plays About Peace and Social Justice,* ed. Ingrid Rogers. Elgin: The Brethren Press, 1983, 221-27. A satiric drama in which a draft board questions a young man and finds him unsuitable for the active duty classification he has requested because he possesses too many human and religious values.

Dueck, Dora (Review). *Mennonite Soldier,* by Kenneth Reed. Scottdale: Herald Press, 1974. Pp. 518. *MBH* 14 (Mar. 7, 1975), 27. Recommends this novel about two Mennonite brothers' responses to the draft: one joins the army; the other takes a conscientious objector stance.

Dyck, Peter J. "German Conscientious Objectors Enter Service." *GH* 54 (June 20, 1961), 561. An account of the first German alternative service program for CO's, its shortcomings and opportunities.

Dyck, Peter J. "Germany Initiates CO Program." *CanMenn* 9 (May 19, 1961), 1, 10. Says EIRENE, the international peace service organization, must be ready to assist the conscientious objectors and the German government to implement the alternative service program.

Ediger, Elmer. "Voluntary Service and the Draft." *Menn* 66 (Jan. 23, 1951), 58. Urges CO's to enter the VS grogram now, rather than waiting for the prodding of conscription. The VS program offers much greater opportunities for witness and service than the CPS program did.

Ediger, Peter J. "Christ and Caesar: A Ballad of Faith." *Menn* 90 (Oct. 14, 1975), 569-72. Ballad traces the history of Mennonite conscientious objection to war, focusing especially on the dilemma of war tax payment.

Enns, Elizabeth. Letter to the Editor. *MennRep* 10 (Mar. 31, 1980), 6. Registered nurse relates conscientious objection to the taking of fetal life to protesting war, nuclear weapons, and capital punishment.

Epp, Frank H. ". . . My Own History Allows Me No Escape." *I Would Like to Dodge the Draft-Dodgers But . . . ,* ed. Frank H. Epp. Waterloo and Winnipeg: Conrad Press, 1970, 8-19. Pp. 95. Reminds readers that the 1967 movement of American war resisters to Canada has an antecedent in the 1917 movement of Mennonite conscientious objector families to Canada in order to escape persecution and harrassment in the US.

Epp, Frank H. "A Convict, a CO, and a Soldier." *CanMenn* 3 (Mar. 18, 1955), 2. A newspaper clipping illustrates an interesting paradox in our society, where killing is rewarded in some situations (war) and punished in others (murder), while CO's are imprisoned for refusing to kill!

Epp, Frank H. "CO's or PM's." *CanMenn* 5 (Dec. 13, 1957), 2. "We are called to actively engage in peacemaking, to act as shock absorbers to the evil of the world, to help relieve the pressures which generate war."

Epp, Frank H. "Draft-Age Mennonite Youths Witness in Large Colorado City." *CanMenn* 4 (Feb. 17, 1956), 6-7. A positive analysis of I-W's and their contribution in Denver. CO's serve in a variety of sacrificial jobs and other activities.

Epp, Frank H. "On the Topic of the Tax." *Menn* 76 (Mar. 7, 1961), 151. "Caesar" is not entitled to everything he requests. Conscientious objection to war may call for refusal to pay war taxes.

Epp, Frank H. (Editorial). "CO's or PM's." *CanMenn* 5 (Dec. 13, 1957), 2. A call to be peacemakers today, not only CO's of World Wars I and II.

Epp, Henry H. "World War II Conscientious Objectors in Discussion with Church Leaders." *CanMenn* 11 (June 14, 1963), 3. A panel reviews the nature of the CO's relationship to the government and the community during World Wars I and II at the Ontario Ministers' Peace Retreat. Includes a summary of questions and answers about alternative service in World War II and the position of the Mennonite church today.

Evert, J. G. "The Other Side: A Plea for Fair Play to the COs by a Mennonite." Paper, n.d. Pp. 4. MHL.

"Five Mennonite COs Convicted of Draft Violation." *RepConsS* 13 (Dec., 1956), 1, 3. Expressing personal distress, Philadelphia judge sentences five Lancaster County men for various types of conscientious objection.

Fast, Henry A. "Revisiting Camp Funston." *GH* 72 (Feb. 14, 1978), 129-30; *Menn* 92 (Aug. 9, 1977) 474. A World War I conscientious objector reflects on the witness he and others made against war at this military camp in Kansas.

Fast, Henry A. (Review). *That There Be Peace: Mennonites in Canada and World War II,* ed. by Lawrence Klippenstein. Winnipeg: Manitoba CO Reunion Committee, 1979. *Menn* 95 (Feb. 12, 1980), 108. Recommends the book as a collection of reflections of alternative service workers.

Fast, Henry A. (Review). *Voices Against War: A Guide to the Schowalter Oral History Collection on World War I Conscientious Objection,* by Keith L. Sprunger, James C. Juhnke, and John D. Waltner. N. Newton, Kansas: Bethel College, 1973. *Menn* 89 (Oct. 29, 1974), 628. A valuable guide to a priceless collection of conscientious objector experiences recorded on tape, the book and the collection should stimulate further research.

Fast, Jack. Letter to the Editor. *ChrLead* 43 (Dec. 16, 1980), 21. Criticizes conscientious objectors for pushing their views on others and lacking respect for persons with other points of view.

Franken-Liefrinck, E. "The Work of the Dutch Mennonite Peace Group." *CanMenn* 5 (Sept. 13, 1957), 4. Dutch Mennonites participate in alternative service and discussion for the cause of peace. Explains provisions for Dutch conscientious objectors and the activities of the Mennonite Peace Group.

Fransen, David Warren. "Canadian Mennonites and Conscientious Objectors in World War II." MA in History Thesis, Univ. of Waterloo, Waterloo, Ont., 1977. Pp. 204. MHL. Canadian Mennonites' experience on the CO issue in World War II involved internal and external struggle. The internal struggle was the effort to establish unity among the congregations on the nonresistant position. Fransen analyzes both the organizational development toward unity and the forces shaping this development—such as traditions, personalities, language, regionalism, etc. The external struggle was the effort to negotiate, with the government, an alternative to military service that had integrity for the Mennonite churches and for the government.

Fransen, David Warren. "The Jensen Case: A Vital Principle Is at Stake." *MennRep* 6 (Dec. 13, 1976), 7. Discusses reasons Mennonites should not sit by complacently as the Jensens, Jehovah's Witnesses, are denied Canadian citizenship on the basis of conscientious objection to war.

Franz, Delton (Editorial). "Conscientious Objectors and War Taxes." *RepConsS* 34 (Apr., 1977), 2, 4. Describes history of the war tax issue and explains present status of the World Peace Tax Fund Act.

Frazer, Heather T. and O'Sullivan, John. "Forgotten Women of World War II: Wives of Conscientious Objectors in Civilian Public Service." *Peace and Change* 5 (Fall, 1978), 46-51. Documents the injustice of the CPS system in the absence of government pay or benefits granted to other enlisted men. Focuses especially on the economic and emotional plight of wives of CPS workers.

French, Paul Comly. *Civilian Public Service.* Washington, DC: National Service Board for Conscientious Objectors, 1942. Pp. 21. MHL. Explains, on the basis of the historical development of the CPS program and on theoretical/philosophical grounds, why religious pacifists assumed the financial responsibility for the operation of the CPS camps when legalistic logic would dictate that this responsibility belonged properly to the US government. Includes references to Mennonites, historic peace churches, etc.

Fretz, J. Winfield. "Conscientious Objectors and City Life." *Menn* 57 (June 2, 1942), 3-4. The economic anmd psychological pressures to conform in the city are almost too great for the individual conscientious objector to withstand. Strong rural communities are the hope of the Mennonite future.

Fretz, J. Winfield. "Mennonite Speaks Out." *Fellowship* 5 (Nov., 1939), 18. Declares his position, based on reasons of conscience, against participating in war or supporting it.

Fretz, J. Winfield. "The Draft Status of General Conference Men in World War II." (Part 1) *Menn* 60 (July 24, 1945), 1-2. A summary, with tables, of the Peace Committee's census of draft-age men. Of the drafted men about 27 percent were CO's, 18 percent had I-AO status, and 55 percent enlisted as I-A's.

Frey, Philemon L. "Lessons from the World War: for Conscientious Objectors." *The Eastern Mennonite School Journal* 18 (Apr., 1940), 42-45. Twelve "lessons"—all the way from "In time of war it is best to keep our eyes and ears open and our mouths shut" to "It is best to stay out of politics" to "Nonresistance should be practiced in times of peace as well as in time of war," etc.

Frey, Philemon L. "The Answer Is 'No.' " *GH* 71 (July 4, 1978), 526-27. Conscientious objector from two world wars reflects on Jesus' resounding "No" to the disciples' question about smiting with the sword, discussing his personal reasons for conscientious objection.

"Germany Sends CO's to School." *GH* 65 (Jan. 18, 1972), 64. The course of studies for CO's, mostly with the equivalent of a junior college degree, is primarily: first aid, social problems, and the search for world peace.

"Government Changes Citizenship Law." *RepConsS* 34 (Mar., 1977), 2. MCC (Canada) influential in eliminating conscientious objection as a barrier to Canadian citizenship.

Gaeddert, Albert M. "The New Draft Legislation." *Menn* 66 (July 31, 1951), 482. Explains how present programs of relief and service can be expanded to accomodate the CO's who will now be "ordered to work" under the new draft law.

Gallardo, Jose. "The Status of Conscientious Objectors in Spain." *Peace Section Newsletter* 8 (Nov.-Dec., 1977), 5-8. A former pastor of a Spanish church in Belgium summarizes the history, present situation, and his contacts with conscientious objectors in Spain.

Gering, William. *I Must Go: A Play in One Act.* Newton: Faith and Life Press, 1961. Pp. 22. Jim, a college sophomore in a state school, struggles with what it means to be a conscientious objector in an environment that is neither sympathetic nor supportive. Setting is the era of the Korean conflict.

Gerlach, Horst. "Before the German Draft Board." *YCC* 42 (Sept. 24, 1961), 613. A man's testimony on his CO position befor the German draft board.

Gillespie, Malcolm. "Three-Year Struggle." *YCC* 47 (July 3, 1966), 5. A conscientious objector convinces the court only after a grueling three-year struggle and wins the I-O classification.

Gingerich, Melvin. "Majorities and Minorites; Christian Youth and the State." *YCC* 22, Part 5, (Feb. 2, 1941), 449. One accusation against the CO position is that it thinks it is the only "in step" position. CO's do not need to apologize for their position.

Gingerich, Melvin. "Mennonite Central Committee Assignment in Japan, 1955-57." Reports of MCC Peace Section representative, Goshen, Ind., 1962. Pp. 57. MHL. Sixfold mission included working with Mennonite and Brethren missionaries to correlate the peace message with the Gospel; making contact with the Japanese Christian peace movement; production of peace literature; building a peace library; studying the problem of legal recognition for the CO position in Japan; and visiting Formosa and Korea to evaluate potential for similar peace-oriented work there.

Gingerich, Melvin. "The Measure of Love; Christian Youth and the State." *YCC* 22, Part 6, (Feb. 23, 1941), 478. There are numerous ways to give our lives for fellow humans. CO's should be willing to risk everything in order to do relief work to alleviate human suffering.

Gingerich, Melvin. *What of Noncombatant Service? A Study of Alternatives Facing the Conscientious Objector.* Scottdale: Herald Press, 1949. Pp. 48. MSHL. Concludes that the demands of the love ethic are such that Christians must refuse any

participation in an organization, such as the military, whose purpose is to kill those for whom Christ died.

Gingerich, Melvin (Archival). Box 18—Peace Committees: General Conference Mennonite, 1935-48; MCC, 1944-48; CPS history, 1938-49. Box 20—Peace Deputation trips. Box 39—Draft; Committee on Armed Service hearing, 1959. Box 40—Civilian Public Service. Box 51—Civil Defense; communism; Congressional Record (debate on universal military training), Feb. 5, 1959; conscientious objectors; Japan Anti-A & H Bomb Conference; Japan and peace. Box 52—peace clippings; peace conferences; Peace Problems Committee reports Puidoux Theological Conference. Box 53—peace and Mennonites. Box 62—"The Christian and Revolution;" church-state relations; communism. Box 64—"Nonresistance and Social Justice;" Peace Institutes; Peace/War. Box 91—Service for Peace; CPS history and correspondence. Goshen, Ind., AMC Hist. Mss. 1-129.

Glass, Esther Eby. "'We Had to Grow Up.'" *ChrLiv* 9 (Apr., 1962), 6-7, 39. Wives of conscientious objectors in CPS share their reflections.

Glick, Lester J. "How Starvation Would Affect You." *ChrLiv* 10 (Mar., 1963), 12-13. Thirty-five conscientious objectors volunteer for semi-starvation diet at the University of Minnesota in 1944.

Goering, Paul L. "Proposed Registration Act Endangers CO's." *Menn* 65 (Mar. 14, 1950), 178-79. An analysis of the Manpower Registration Act. Mennonites are urged to write Congress protesting the proposed elimination of certain provisions for CO's.

Goering, Paul L. and Fretz, J. Winfield (Review). *The Theological Basis of Christian Pacifism,* by Charles E. Raven. New York: Fellowship Pub., 1951, pp. 87; *The Dagger and the Cross,* by Culbert G. Rutenber. New York: Fellowship Pub., 1950, pp. 134; *Conscientious Objection,* Special Monograph No. 11 by Selective Service. Washington, DC: Government Printing Office, n.d., Vol. I, pp. 342, Vol. II, pp. 288; *Conscription of Conscience; the American State and the Conscientious Objector, 1940-1947,* by Mulford Q. Sibley and Philip E. Jacob. Ithaca: Cornell U. Press, 1952, pp. 580. "The Conscientious Objector in Recent Literature." *MennLife* 8 (Jan., 1953), 43-46. Reviewers recommend these four books on pacifism and the conscientious objector as "significant."

Goertz, Duane and Edwards, Carl, comp. "Court Martial Records of 131 Conscientious Objectors During World War I." Summer, 1975. MHL (microfilm, 3 rolls). Research project consisting of 98 case files, gathered from Army records and National Archives, documenting litigations involving CO's representing various branches of Mennonites. Materials include memorandae, forms, handwritten notes, transcripts of questioning, sentences, personal testimony, etc.

Good, I. Merle. "A Conscientious Objector's View of the Bicentennial." *FQ* 3 (May, June, July, 1976), 2. Reprinted from *The Washington Post*, (1976). Sketches Mennonite history of conscientious objection to war, and outlines the dilemma facing Mennonites condemned by wider society for not joining wholeheartedly in celebrating the American Revolution.

Graber, C. L. "Experiences of a Conscientious Objector." *GH* 28 (Apr. 18, 1935), 79-80. An address at the Conference on Peace and War. The writer recounts some of the persecutions he was subjected to in training camp during World War I.

Graber, Richard D. "The Evolution of the Treatment of the Conscientious Objectors by the War Department During the First World War." Paper presented to the Social Science Seminar, Goshen College, Goshen, Ind., June, 1957.

Gross, Leonard, ed. "Civil War CO Documents." *MHB* 34 (Apr., 1973), 6. Publishes documents pertaining to Samuel Guengerich of Pennsylvania and his requested exemption from military duty.

Gross, Leonard, ed. "The First World War and Mennonite Nonresistance." *MHB* 33 (July, 1972), 4-10. Series of government and private documents traces Mennonite experiences in the war: correspondence with the Secretary of War on conscientious objection; procedures for military induction and discharge; treatment of COs in detention; public pressure to buy war bonds; government suspicion of tract on nonresistance; germinal ideas for alternative service in reconstruction.

Gross, William G. and Gross, Samuel G. "A Civil War Letter." *MHB* 23 (July, 1962), 5. Letter from twin brothers in Pennsylvania in 1862 describes provisions made by the North for conscientious objectors. The writers identified themselves with the American people as being punished by God for the sins of the nation.

"Historic Peace Church Council Members Meet." *CanMenn* 9 (May 26, 1961), 1, 8. Members of the Council meet in Winnipeg to discuss problems related to citizenship, oaths of allegiance, and Mennonite Disaster Service. A main topic of dicussion was the denial of Canadian citizenship to new Canadians due to their CO position.

"House Committee Hears Peace Tax Proposal."

*RepConsS* 32 [*sic*, 33] (Mar., 1976), 1, 6. Spokespersons from the Catholic, Quaker, Brethren, Mennonite, and Unitarian faiths speak to House Ways and Means Committee in favor of extending CO rights to the tax laws.

"House Passes Bill and Revises Alternate Service." *GH* 64 (Apr. 20, 1971), 365. Describes significance of the vote to extend the military draft till June, 1973 for the CO.

"How to Register as a Conscientious Objector." *With* 2 (Mar., 1969), 11. A look at the steps necessary to receive a CO classification.

"Hunting and Speeding No Basis for Denial of CO Claim." *RepConsS* 12 (May, 1955), 1. The Circuit Court of Appeals reverses the conviction of John W. Rempel, Nebr., on the basis that sporadic deviations from Mennonite church practices do not justify denial of CO status.

Habegger, Luann. "The Berne, Indiana, Mennonites During World War I." Paper presented to the Mennonite History class, Associated Mennonite Biblical Seminaries, Dec. 23, 1974. Pp. 15. MHL.

Hackman, Walton. "A Conscientious Objector Becomes a Military Chaplain—for a Day." *GH* 64 (Jan. 5, 1971), 18-19. Peace Section representative describes a day spent at Fitzsimmons Army Base: his discussions with army chaplains on the issue of just war, and his conversations with injured soldiers just returned from Vietnam.

Hackman, Walton. "GI Benefits for CO's?" *Forum* (Apr., 1973), 8. The case of a CO applying for veteran's benefits has been appealed to the US Supreme Court and the result of this court decision may confront Mennonite CO's with the question of whether or not they will apply for and accept these benefits.

Hackman, Walton. "Giving for Peace." *Menn* 88 (Dec. 18, 1973), 734. Encourages alternative giving for Christmas to people such as families of civilian prisoners in South Vietnam, imprisoned conscientious objectors, war resisters exiled in Canada, and political refugees from Chile.

Hackman, Walton. "Penner Case Acquitted, and Prayers Answered." *GH* 63 (Aug. 11, 1970), 671; *EV* 83 (Aug. 25, 1970), 13. Reviews the story of an Oklahoma Mennonite conscientious objector who was refused CO status, prosecuted, convicted, and sentenced for refusing to comply with induction orders, and whose conviction was reversed on recommendation by the Solicitor General of the Supreme Court.

Hackman, Walton. "Taxes-for-Peace Fund." *MBH*

12 (Mar. 9, 1973), 9. Contributions to this fund may be one tangible way in which conscientious objectors can express a peace witness through the use of their tax dollars.

Handrich, Rick L. "My God, My Country, and My Fellowman." *GH* 61 (Oct. 15, 1968), 930-31. Conscientious objector serving as research subject at an army hospital explains why he decided to enter the military in a noncombatant role.

Harder, Leland. "Mennonites and Contemporary Cultural Change." *The Lordship of Christ (Proceedings of the Seventh Mennonite World Conference.* Ed. Cornelius J. Dyck. Elkhart: MWC, 1962, 440-51. Includes a study of conscientious objection in the General Conference Mennonite Church. An inverse correlation was found to exist between evangelism and nonresistance. Includes three tables and one graph.

Harder, Marvin. "The Supreme Court and the CO." *MennLife* 7 (Oct., 1952), 185-87. On the basis of case studies the writer concludes that the pacifist in America must look to Congress and not to the courts for support.

Harding, Vincent G. "Conscientious Objection: Is It a Christian Response to Vietnam?" *Builder* 17 (Oct., 1967), 12-13. Questions the adequacy of the I-W program as a response to Jesus' call to love the enemy. Identifies a lack of congruence between objecting to war and accepting military protection of that right to object.

Harley, Isaiah Buckwalter. "Goshen's Attitude Toward Conscientious Objectors as Reflected in the News and Editorial Columns of the *Goshen Daily News Times,* Apr. 1, 1917-Nov. 11, 1918." Paper presented to the Peace and War Seminar, Goshen College, Goshen, Ind., n.d. Pp. 15. MHL.

Harris, Arthur S., Jr. "That's All You Need to Know." *ChrLiv* 4 (Mar., 1957), 16-17, 36. Conscientious objector learns a simple view of war and peace from a fellow worker in a CO camp during World War II.

Harshbarger, Emmett L. "Delegates from Historic Peace Churches Visit the President." *Menn* 55 (Jan. 23, 1940), 3-4. Report on a delegation seeking to secure a satisfactory program for conscientious objectors. Included is a statement presented to the president.

Hartman, O. E. "An Original Draft Resister." *ST* 42 (June, 1974), 24. Taped interview of a personal account of someone who, when subject to the draft as a young man during World War I, solved his problem of conscientious objection to the war by living in the woods.

Hartman, Peter S. "Civil War Reminiscences."

*MQR* 3 (July, 1929), 203-19. A record of personal experiences and observations among the Mennonite objectors under the Confederate government in Virginia.

Hartzler, Jonas S. *Mennonites in the World War or Nonresistance Under Test.* Scottdale: Mennonite Publishing House, 1922. Pp. 246. MHL. Treatment of the World War I conscientious objector experience includes analysis of the issues, summaries of meetings and position papers, descriptions of camp life and life in the disciplinary barracks, congregational reaction, and relief work.

Hartzler, R. L. Letter to the Editor. *Menn* 92 (July 12, 1977), 446. Commends General Lewis Hershey for his wise attitude toward conscientious objection in World War II, showing respect for the Civilian Public Service program and after the war reversing the ban on CO's going overseas, thus making possible the Mennonite contribution to European reconstruction.

Heatwole, Reuben Joseph. "Reminiscences of Civil War Days." *GH* 51 (Aug. 19, 1958), 782. Heatwole relates his boyhood memories of the experience of those opposed to fighting in the Civil War.

Hernley, Elam R. "My Experiences During the World War." *ChrMon* 31, Part 1, (Nov., 1939), 332-33; Part 2, (Dec., 1939), 363, 373; *ChrMon* 32, Part 3, (Jan., 1940), 10-11; Part 4, (Feb., 1940), 42-43; Part 5, (Mar., 1940), 75, 77; Part 6, (Apr., 1940), 105; Part 7, (May, 1940), 140-41. World War I CO reports his experience as a prisoner in the guardhouse of an army camp, his transfer to a CO detachment, his term on farm furlough, and his discharge from the camp.

Hernley, Elam R. "What It Meant to Be a Conscientious Objector in the World War." *YCC* 20 (Nov. 5, 1939), 769. Among some of the things shared: to be a conscientious objector in the World War meant a testing of nonresistance, an opportunity to witness for Christ, and an appreciation for Christian fellowship.

Hershberger, Guy F. "A Letter to the President Suggesting Alternative Service for Mennonite Youth in Case of War." *YCC* 21 (June 16, 1940), 192. A copy of a letter which was presented to President F. D. Roosevelt by a delegation of Mennonites, Friends, and Brethren on Jan. 9, 1940, states the position of the historic peace churches and the desired care for CO's.

Hershberger, Guy F. "Conscientious Objector." *Encyclopaedia Britannica* 6 (1973), 366-68. Coauthor, John Moss. A description of "conscientious objector," written as an encyclopedia entry.

Hershberger, Guy F. "Conscientious Objector." *ME* I (1955), 692-99. Surveys the history of the conscientious objector position in both Europe and North America.

Hershberger, Guy F. *Conscientious Objectors in Europe.* Washington, DC: National Service Board for Religious Objectors, 1952. Excerpt from "Report on My Term of Service for the Peace Section of the Mennonite Central Committee, June 10, 1949 to Aug. 21, 1950." Excerpts from an extensive report given to Mennonite Central Committee on a study of the status of conscientious objection in Europe.

Hershberger, Guy F. "Conscientious Objectors in Prison." *GH Supplement* 39 (Aug., 1946), 460. There is growing support for the policy of granting amnesty to the war objectors still in prison. Many of these persons have been imprisoned unjustly.

Hershberger, Guy F. "Current Status of COs in Europe Described by Mennonite Scholar." *RepConsS* 7 (Sept.-Oct., 1951), 6, 7; (Nov.-Dec., 1951), 4; 8 (May, 1952), 5. Reports the legal status of COs by countries, describes peace societies and identifies peace leaders working in these countries.

Hershberger, Guy F. "French Conscientious Objectors: Henri Roser." *YCC* 21 (Oct. 13, 1940), 328. The French military laws have made no provision for exemption of conscientious objectors. Roser served four years in prison for being a CO.

Hershberger, Guy F. "French Conscientious Objectors: Philippe and Pierre Vernier." *YCC* 21 (Oct. 27, 1940), 344. The story and testimony of two brothers who were CO's in France.

Hershberger, Guy F. "Labor Union Relations: The Basis of Understanding." *ChrLiv* 2 (Mar., 1955), 26. Copy of the alternative union card expressing the Basis of Understanding bewtween Mennonite and Brethren in Chrsit churches and any given labor union on the question of conscientious objector employees.

Hershberger, Guy F. "Military Conscription and the Conscientious Objector." *YCC* 20 (Dec. 10, 1939), 809-10. Description of the Selective Service plan for conscription. The official committees of the church can only do so much. The individual must decide on the hard questions about being a CO.

Hershberger, Guy F. *Military Conscription and the Conscientious Objector: A World-Wide Survey.* Akron: Mennonite Central Committee Peace Section, 1962. A survey country by country outlining the status of military conscription and the conscientious objector in each.

Hershberger, Guy F. "Military Conscription and the Conscientious Objector: A World-Wide Survey, with Special Reference to Mennonites." Paper presented at the Seventh Mennonite World Conference, Kitchener, Ont., Aug. 7, 1962. Mimeographed. Goshen: MHL. Pp. 38. Reports on draft laws in the worldwide Mennonite experience. Concluding comments focus on the status of the nonresistant teaching on the mission field.

Hershberger, Guy F. "Objectors to War in England." *YCC* 21 (Sept. 29, 1940), 312. There are many pacifist groups in England that maintain a CO position toward the war. The English government is fairly tolerant in their provisions.

Hershberger, Guy F. "Our Peace Witness—In the Light of May 18." *GH* 61 (Jan. 9, 1968), 33. [No. 19] Recommends that a Mennonite attitude toward "unjust war objectors" should be one of respect and encouragement, without compromising a more thorough nonresistant position.

Hershberger, Guy F. "Our Peace Witness—In the Wake of May 18." *GH* 61 (Jan. 2, 1968), 7. [No. 18] Discusses "unjust war objectors," persons who may be opposed to some but not all wars, and raises the question whether draft boards should recognize such persons as conscientious objectors.

Hershberger, Guy F. "Questions for Nonresistant Christians." *GH* 33, Parts 1-3, (July 18, 1940), 338; Part 4, (July 25, 1940), 371; Parts 5-7, (Aug. 1, 1940), 386; Parts 8-9, (Aug. 8, 1940), 418; Parts 10-11, (Aug. 15, 1940), 435; Part 12, (Aug. 22, 1940), 450; Part 13, (Aug. 29, 1940), 466-67; Part 14, (Sept. 12, 1940), 514; Part 15-16, (Sept. 19, 1940), 530; Part 17, (Oct. 3, 1940), 562; Part 19-22, (Oct. 31, 1940), 658-59; Part 23, (Nov. 7, 1940), 675; Part 24, (Nov. 28, 1940), 738; Part 25, (Dec. 5, 1940), 754. Series includes such topics as war propaganda, conscription, alternative service, conscientious objection, registration, noncombatant service, etc.

Hershberger, Guy F. "Relations with Labor Organizations." *ChrLiv* 1 (Dec., 1954), 36. Survey of provisions possible for conscientious objectors to labor unions.

Hershberger, Guy F. "Report on My Term of Service for the Peace Section of the Mennonite Central Committee, June 10, 1949, to Aug. 21, 1950." Mimeographed. Goshen: MHL. Study of pacifism in Europe, the peace attitudes of European Mennonites and the legal status of conscientious objectors in Europe.

Hershberger, Guy F. "Says Truman Pardons Pendergast Note-Stealers, But Not CO's" *GH* 39 (1946), 640. A report on F. E. Spicer's letter printed in the *Kansas City Star* which questions Truman's pardoning of note-stealers but refusing to pardon conscientious objectors.

Hershberger, Guy F. "The Methodist Church and the Conscientious Objector." *YCC* 21 (Sept. 15, 1940), 296. The Methodist Church is one of the many groups who are giving attention to and support for the CO position. The US government has taken into account the nonresistant stand of these churches not among the historic peace churches in the Bukke-Wadsworth military conscription bill.

Hershberger, Guy F. "The Supreme Court and Conscientious Objectors." *GH Supplement* 39 (Aug., 1946), 460-61. The court has recently said that one may become a citizen of the US even if one will not bear arms. The court's position on religious liberty, while not unanimous, is nonetheless encouraging.

Hershberger, Guy F. "What Changes Does the New Draft Law Actually Make With Respect to Conscientious Objectors? Our Peace Witness—In the Wake of May 18." (Part 3). *GH* 60 (Sept. 19, 1967), 847. The definition of a CO and the appeal procedure were changed.

Hershberger, Guy F. "What Happened on May 18, 1967? Our Peace Witness—In the Wake of May 18." (Part 1). *GH* 60 (Sept. 5, 1967), 803-804. The news report was published that Congress was considering a bill calling for the induction of CO's into the military forces.

Hershberger, Guy F. "Why Does the New Draft Law (1967) Change the Definition of a Conscientious Objector? Our Peace Witness—In the Wake of May 18." (Part 5). *GH* 60 (Sept. 26, 1967), 874. Congress sought to narrow the definition of conscientious objector but actually broadened it.

Hershberger, Guy F. "Why Does the New Draft Law (1967) Change the Appeal Procedure for Conscientious Objectors? Our Peace Witness—In the Wake of May 18." (Part 6). *GH* 60 (Oct. 3, 1967), 889. It is believed that the new procedure will save time.

Hershberger, Guy F. "Why Was It Proposed to Induct Conscientious Objectors into the Armed Forces? Our Peace Witness—In the Wake of May 18." (Part 7). *GH* 60 (Oct. 10, 1967), 918. The temper of Congress and the desire to control "phony CO's" led to the proposal.

Hershberger, Guy F. "World Wide Report on Military Draft and CO's." In *The Lordship of Christ: Proceedings of the Seventh Mennonite World Conference*, ed. C. J. Dyck, pp. 544-48. Scottdale:

Mennonite Publishing House, 1962. Held at Kitchener, Ont., Aug. 1-7, 1962. Surveys the status of the military draft and conscientious objector's position in countries where Mennonites reside.

Hershberger, Guy F. (Review). *Conscription of Conscience: The American State and the Conscientious Objector, 1940-1947*, by Melford Q. Sibley and Philip E. Jacob. Ithaca: Cornell University Press, 1952. Pp. 580. *MQR* 27 (1953), 351-55. Summarizes the book's story of conscription and the CO in World War II as seen through the eyes of authors whose primary interest is in civil liberties rather than the New Testament way of nonresistant love. Harshberger raises the question of whether the two causes of social justice and nonresistant love can be served best by the more militant type of pacifist or the way of MCC. Considers this book helpful in raising this issue into sharp focus.

Hershberger, Guy F. (Review). *"Hey! Yellowbacks!" The War Diary of a Conscientious Objector*, by Ernest I. Meyer. New York: John Day Co., 1930. In *MQR* 5 (1931), 72-77. This book contains the memoirs of a Univ. of Wisconsin undergraduate who was inducted into the United States Army against his will in 1918.

Hertzler, Daniel. "John Woolman or the Bootlegger." *GH* 73 (July 15, 1980), 468. Reflects on the variety of Mennonite opinion on the question of conscientious objection and cites the Quaker Woolman and his refusal to own slaves.

Hertzler, Daniel. "The Legacy of Timothy Lee Yoder." *GH* 69 (Aug. 24, 1976), 642. Reprints the letter written to the draft board requesting a conscientious objection classification by a Mennonite high school senior later killed in a car accident.

Hess, Mahlon. "Essential Elements of Conscientious Objection." *YCC* 23 (May 10, 1942), 147, 150. Essential qualifications for a conscientious objector are honest convictions, consistent life, and a vital Christian experience.

Hiebert, Susan. "In Time of Crisis: How Two Responded." *MennRep* 4 (Feb. 18, 1974), 9. Two Canadian conscientious objectors reflect on two major life crises: World War II and contracting polio.

Hirsch, Charles B. "The Civilian Public Service Camp Program in Indiana." *Indiana Magazine of History* 46 (1950), 259-81. CPS program in Indiana, with all its inadequacies, was a distinct improvement over World War I treatment of COs. Innovations included the recognition of COs of all faiths and an alternative program of military service.

Hofer, David. "The Martyrdom of Joseph and

Michael Hofer." Paper translated from the German by Franz Wiebe, 1974. Pp. 4. MHL.

Hooley, E. M. *The 1918 Christmas Eve Man of the Hour at Leavenworth: Written by a Mennonite Who Was Entrapped in that Riot.* n.p., [1960]. Pp. 13. MHL. World War I conscientious objector sentenced to 10 years at Leavenworth relates, with considerable awe, the story of how Col. Sedgwick Rice quelled a prison riot using no force other than the strength of his presence and the respect he had acquired among the prisoners.

Hoover, Jesse W. and Orie O. Miller. "The Civilian Bond Purchase Plan." *Menn* 57 (July 21, 1942), 1-4. A description of efforts on the part of MCC, NSBRO, the Friends, and the Brethren to work with the US Treasury Department to provide an alternative to war bonds for conscientious objectors.

Horsch, John. "Conscientious Objectors to Military Service in European Countries." *GH* 29 (Feb. 18, 1937), 996-97. A summary of the most recent information on conscientious objection in Europe, including statistics about those imprisoned in a number of countries.

Horsch, John. *War and the Christian Conscience.* Scottdale: Mennonite Publishing House, [1938]. Pp. 16. MHL. Laments the fact that while most varieties of Christianity admit that war is sin, a conscience against participation in war is lacking. Contends, in contrast to these other denominations, that conscientious objection to war is a Christian essential.

Horsch, John. "War Resisters and Conscientious Objectors in European Countries." *GH* 29 (Oct. 8, 1936), 602-603. Factual account of the existing situation in Europe, where alternative civil service is offered by some countries while others imprison CO's who refuse military service.

Horst, John L. "Concerning the New Draft Law." *ChrMon* 43 (July, 1951), 200. Reprints section of the draft law pertaining to conscientious objectors and comments on the possible changes in voluntary service programs.

Horst, John L. "Selective Service Act of 1948." *GH* 41 (Aug. 10, 1948), 732. A review of the Selective Service Act which inaugurated the draft in 1948. Outlines the provisions made for the deferment of conscientious objectors.

Hostetler, Mervin J. "A Time to Remember: Civilian Public Service." *ChrLiv* 18 (May, 1971), 7-9. Impressions of years spent in CPS in World War II, and of the rejection faced as a conscientious objector after the war.

Hull, Robert. "[Proposal for Sabbatical Service.]" *God and Caesar* 6 (Oct., 1980), 3-9. Proposal for Mennonites to covenant with their congregations to perform voluntary service every seven years. Considered both as congregational ministry and as active conscientious objection.

Hunsberger, Willard. *The Franconia Mennonites and War.* Scottdale: Peace and Industrial Relations Committee of Franconia Mennonite Conference, 1951. After briefly surveying the experience of the Franconia Mennonites with the earlier American wars, their experience with World War II is discussed more fully. Some of the topics considered are community reactions to conscientious objectors, a typical day in a CPS camp, the activities of the church during and after the war.

"Increasing Approval of CO's by the Public." *Menn* 60 (July 17, 1945), 1. Interprets the Office of Public Opinion Research reports of 1944 and 1945 which show that public opinion is increasingly more favorable toward conscientious objectors.

"IRS Sues War Objector Group." *God and Caesar* 4 (June, 1978), 6. In an unprecedented move, the IRS has brought suit against an employer, the Central Committee for Conscientious Objectors, for failure to pay the tax debt allegedly owed by a past employee who refused to pay for reasons of conscience.

"Items and Comments." *GH* 64 (Apr. 12, 1971), 340. The US Supreme Court rules 8 to 1 that the basic test in order to receive CO status is whether opposition applied to war is general or particular.

"J. Harold Sherk Retires as Executive Secretary of the NSBRO; Warren W. Hoover Elected." *RepConsS* 26 (July, 1969), 3. Sherk is recognized for twenty years of service in the cause of conscientious objection.

"Jewish Pacifist Proposes Mid-East Confederation." *CanMenn* 17 (Sept. 19, 1969), 4. A conscientious objector to war, Mr. Abileah objects to the erection of a Jewish state with national sovereignty and proposes a confederation of three states, Jordan, Arab Palestine, and Israel—with a federal capital in Jerusalem. "Political solutions depend on economic solutions," says Abileah.

"Jost Receives Citizenship." *RepConsS* 12 (May, 1955), 1, 3. After delays, the US Supreme Court decision (Feb. 1, 1954) in favor of CO Arthur Jost's petition for naturalization results in his being granted citizenship.

"Judge Rules Indian Case Dismissed." *GH* 65 (July 18, 1972), 582. A native American of the Chippewa tribe makes successful case for CO status on basis of his tribal religious beliefs and the fact that the US-Chippewa treaty requires the tribe to "live in peace."

Jantz, Harold. "Conscience Doesn't Count, Says Labor Board." *MBH* 13 (May 31, 1974), 16-17; *MennMirror* 3 (Summer, 1974), 22. Two nurses in Manitoba who requested exemption from membership and dues in the Nurses' Association on the basis of conscientious objection were turned down by the Labor Board. Includes a letter written by the editor to the Premier of Manitoba requesting him to investigate this decision.

Jantz, Harold. "Court Recognizes Funk's Beliefs on Union." *GH* 69 (Jan. 27, 1976), 70; *MBH* 15 (Jan. 23, 1976), 12. Reports on the case of Henry Funk of Manitoba, who opposed union membership on grounds of conscientious objection, and who won his case in the Manitoba Court of Appeals.

Jantz, Harold. "Labour Board Rejects Conscientious Objector." *Menn* 89 (Nov. 5, 1974), 649; *MennMirror* 4 (Nov., 1974), 11, 12; *MBH* 13 (Oct. 18, 1974), 10. Relates the case of Henry Funk of Niverville, Man., who refused to sign a union membership application for reasons of conscience and was consequently fired from his place of work.

Jantz, Harold. "Mennonites Struggle with Union Membership." *MBH* 14 (Dec. 12, 1975), 13-15. In a paper presented to MCC (Manitoba) annual meeting, Harold Jantz urged congregations to support conscientious objectors to union membership.

Janzen, David. Letter to the Editor. *MennRep* 7 (Jan. 10, 1977), 6. Maintains that MCC should not help the Jehovah's Witnesses family, Jensens, gain Canadian citizenship thus far denied on grounds of their conscientious objection to war, since to help JW's become members of an institution the denomination regards as Satanic would be morally wrong, and because conscientious objection is a special, not general, right, granted by the Canadian government only to members of peace churches.

Janzen, David. "The Anabaptists (4): What Is Happening to the Believers' Church?" *MennRep* 5 (Sept. 15, 1975), 5. Challenges Mennonites to remain faithful to prophetic Anabaptist stances on conscientious objection from killing, and discipleship practiced according to the Sermon on the Mount.

Janzen, William. "Can Conscientious Objectors Be Citizens?" *Menn* 92 (Jan. 4, 1977), 9. Jehovah's Witness conscientious objector relates his views on Christians, war, and politics to an MCC representative assisting him in appealing the Canadian court decision not to grant citizenship because of conscientious objection.

Janzen, William. "Canadian Government Changes Law to Favour Conscientious Objectors." *Peace Section Newsletter* 8 (Apr., 1977), 5-6. The Canadian government has made a change in the citizenship law which says in effect that Canada does accept as citizens people who are conscientious objectors by reason of their religion and that their citizenship is not conditional upon acceptance of obligations to Canada in wartime.

Janzen, William. Letter to the Editor. *MennRep* 7 (Feb. 21, 1977), 6. Defends and explains MCC intervention in the Jensen case, conscientious objectors who were denied Canadian citizenship for reasons of conscientious objection to war.

Janzen, William. "Opposition to War No Bar to Citizenship." *MBH* 16 (Mar. 4, 1977), 12. The denial of Canadian citizenship to a Jehovah's Witnesses was the basis for a court ruling guaranteeing citizenship to conscientious objectors.

Juhnke, James C. "Bibles and Bullets; Military Conscription in South Africa." *MennRep* 2 (May 1, 1972), 2. Draft ruling in South Africa includes whites and excludes blacks, but what of the conscientious objectors?

Juhnke, James C. "CO's and Chemical Warfare in the First World War." *MHB* 30 (1969), 4. Quotes from and comments upon documents from the Office of the Chief of Staff which show certain officials proposed that conscientious objectors be assigned to work in gas manufacturing plants instead of in agriculture.

Juhnke, James C. "Pax—Peace Through Love." *MennLife* 16 (July, 1961), 102-104. PAX is welcome outgrowth of the principles of nonresistance, conscientious objection, etc. because it measures success by what is accomplished rather than what is not done.

Juhnke, Roger. "The Perils of Conscientious Objection: An Oral History Study of a 1944 Event." *MennLife* 34 (Sept., 1979), 4-9. Juhnke tells and examines the story of an unusual bus ride to Fort Leavenworth in which six CO were harrassed by a number of inductees in 1944.

Kauffman, Edward. "Is the Conscientious Objector Living in a Dream World?" *GH* 37 (Aug. 4, 1944), 341. The CO realizes what kind of world one lives in, but one is only in the world, not of it.

Kauffman, Ivan. "Congress and Conscientious

Objectors." *GH* 60 (June 13, 1967), 537-38. Kauffman reports on the effort to induct all CO's into the military.

Kauffman, Ivan. "Congress Decision on CO Provisions Influenced by Peace Section Testimony." *CanMenn* 15 (June 6, 1967), 2. A proposed bill, which would have been a return to the provisions for CO's that were in effect in World War I, was changed to one with little difference from the present law. The change was due to MCC Peace Section testimony.

Kauffman, Nelson E. "Giving Needed Witness." *GH* 64 (Aug. 24, 1971), 700. Calls Mennonites to greater peace witness in the public media, in light of the numbers of youth from other denominations searching for counsel on conscientious objection.

Kauffmann, Joel. *The Weight*. Scottdale, Pa.: Herald Press, 1980. Pp. 146. Jon Springer, whose father is a Mennonite minister, turns eighteen during the summer after his high school graduation. The time is the Vietnam era and he must decide whether to register for conscientious objector status or to follow the example of some peers as well as community sentiment and register I-A. The questions with which he struggles as the peacemaker model of church and family teaching becomes his own choice are "the weight." Novel for young adults.

Keeney, William E. "European Christian Peace Activities Expand. *Menn* 89 (Jan. 22, 1974), 56-57; *MennRep* 4 (Feb. 18, 1974), 7. Examines the disparate, yet growing, peace groups in Europe, the status of conscientious objection in various European countries, areas of concern among peace groups, and the progress of peace educational research, suggesting possible Mennonite contributions to these efforts.

Keeney, William E. "The Pilgrimage of a CO." Autobiographical. N.d. Pp. 64. MLA/BeC.

Kehler, Larry. "Swiss Conscientious Objectors Are Examined by Psychiatrist." *CanMenn* 11 (Apr. 5, 1963), 1, 12. The publication of a newsletter by the International Mennonite Peace Committee highlights the treatment of conscientious objectors in Holland, Switzerland, Germany, Austria, and France.

Keidel, Levi O. *Caught in the Crossfire*. Scottdale and Kitchener: Herald Press, 1979. Pp. 229. Account of the early years of Zaire;s political independence, a period characterized by revolution and tribal warfare, and the ethical dilemmas the church had to face in regard to participation in violence or conscientious objection to it.

King, John C. "A Program of Church Expansion Through I-W." Paper presented to Practical Theology Seminar, Goshen College, Goshen, Ind., 1955. Pp. 92. MHL.

King, Lauren A. "Why One Quaker Refuses War." *GH* 67 (Apr. 9, 1974), 308-309. In question-and-answer format, the author sets forth his reasons for conscientious objector convictions, which include the basic moral reason, the primacy of God's kingdom, and the teachings and examples of Jesus and the apostles.

Klaassen, Walter. ". . . Christianity Demands a Positive Response." *I Would Like to Dodge the Draft-Dodgers But . . .*, ed. Frank H. Epp. Waterloo and Winnipeg: Conrad Press, 1970, 61-67. Pp. 95. Contends that Mennonite resistance to supporting draft-dodgers is both inconsistent with our history as conscientious objectors and incompatible with the words and attitudes of Jesus.

Klassen, F. V. Letter to the Editor. *MBH* 15 (Apr. 2, 1976), 10. A stand in favor of capital punishment cannot be reconciled with conscientious objection.

Klassen, James R. "There Is Another Way." Student peace oration, 1966. Pp. 7. MLA/BeC.

Klassen, Mike. "Implementing a Congregational Dialogue on the Draft and National Service." *MCC PS Newsletter* 10 (Mar.-Apr., 1980), 1-5. Paper presented at the Mar., 1980, Assembly on the Draft and National Service suggests methods for effective conscientious objection education in the congregation. Includes extensive bibliography.

Klassen, William. "Mennonite Witness on the Line: An Attempt at Clarifying the Issues." *MennRep* 6 (Aug. 23, 1976), 7. Criticizes Mennonite Brethren Member of Parliament Jake Epp for his stance favoring capital punishment, observing that it is not consistent with Mennonite conscientious objection to violence in other forms, such as labor union strikes.

Kliewer, Marion W. "The Drafting of Conscientious Objectors." *Menn* 68 (Mar. 17, 1953). 165, 167. Discusses the present status of the I-W program and points to the peace witness given by the quality of work done by the I-W's.

Klippenstein, Lawrence. *That There Be Peace: Mennonites in Canada and World War II*. Winnipeg: Manitoba CO Reunion Committee, 1979. Pp. 104. Includes summary of the Canadian Mennonite experience of World War II, photographs of the projects and CPS camp life, newspaper clippings, and personal reminiscences.

Kniss, Lloy A. *I Couldn't Fight: The Story of a CO in*

*World War I*. Scottdale, Pa.: Herald Press, 1971. Pp. 47. Portrays the ridicule and hardship experienced by a World War I CO as a result of his steadfast refusal to cooperate with the military system in the military training camps into which he had been forced.

Kniss, Lloy A. *Why I Couldn't Fight*. Harrisonburg, Va.: Christian Light Publications, 1974. Pp. 72. Uses experiences as a World War I CO to explain and defend the nonresistant position.

Koontz, Ted. "No Opportunity to Be Given for CO Registration." *Menn* 90 (Dec. 9, 1975), 705. Describes pending Selective Service plans for draft registration, which at the inital stage include no place for registering conscientious objection.

Kratz, James D. "Mennonites and Military Service in Argentina." *GH* 66 (Oct. 16, 1973), 790-91. Relates the story of Dennis Byler, US and Argentine citizen, who was drafted in Argentina while serving in a missions assignment. His conscientious objector stance is helping to sensitize the conscience of the Argentine church.

Kreider, Lucille. *The Friendly Way: A One-Act Play in Three Scenes*. Newton: Faith and Life Press, 1961. Pp. 22. Set in 1917, the drama depicts some of the struggles experienced by a Quaker family as the son refuses to join the military and, instead, volunteers for relief work in Beirut, where his nonresistant ideals are tested.

Kremer, Russell. "Conscientious Objection in Antebellum America." Paper presented to the class US History, 1789-1877, at Goshen College, Goshen, Ind., fall, 1974. Pp. 23. MHL.

Kroeker, David. "The Boys from CO Camps Remembered Harold Sherk." *MennRep* 4 (Apr. 1, 1974), 9. Tribute to peacemaker Sherk, outspoken advocate of conscientious objector legislation and pastor to CPS camps.

Kroeker, David (Review). *I Would Like to Dodge the Draft-Dodgers But . . .*, ed. Frank H. Epp. Winnipeg and Waterloo: Conrad Press, 1970. Pp. 95. *MQR* 46 (Jan., 1972), 92-93. Selected essays on the peace position, conscientious objection, treatment of war deserters, and biblical foundations call Canadian churches and Mennonites in particular to assist American draft resisters in Canada.

Landes, Carl J. "A Call to Rural Fellowship Members." *Fellowship* 7 (Feb., 1941), 30. The Fellowship of Reconciliation Council has provided for a Rural Secretary for the next six months to serve rural pacifists in America.

Landes, Carl J. "An Open Letter to My Government." *Menn* 53 (Feb. 15, 1938), 5-6.

Declares that he will not accept any service supporting the impending war.

Landes, Carl J. "Why I Cannot Accept Non-Combatant Service." *Menn* 56 (Mar. 4, 1941), 9. Essential reason for refusing noncombatant service is that there is no *basic* difference between combatant and noncombatant service.

Landis, Cliff. "A Soldier for Christ." Paper entered in the Horsch History Essay Contest, [Kidron, Ohio], May 1, 1973. Pp. 5. MHL.

Lapp, John A. ". . . The New Militarism Makes Its Harsh Demands." *I Would Like to Dodge the Draft-dodgers But . . .*. Ed. Frank H. Epp. Waterloo and Winnipeg: Conrad Press, 1070, 21-26. Pp. 95. Assesses the contemporary conscription process, outlines the options available to conscientious objectors and the varieties of positions labeled CO, and discusses reformation of the draft laws.

Lapp, John A. (Review). *Conscience in America: A Documentary History of Conscientious Objection in America, 1757-1967*, ed. Lillian Schlissel. E. P. Dutton and Co., 1968. Pp. 444. *ChrLiv* 16 (June, 1969), 37. Recommends this compilation of documents concerning conscientious objection in America.

Lapp, John A. (Review). *Democracy, Dissent, and Disorder: The Issues and the Law*, by Robert F. Drinan. Seabury Press, 1969. Pp. 152. *GH* 63 (June 9, 1970), 524. Recommends the book for its insights into legal dimensions of current social protest, including conscientious objection and opposition to the Vietnam war.

Lapp, John A. (Review). *Letters of a CO from Prison*, by Timothy W. L. Zimmer. The Judson Press, 1969. *GH* 63 (May 19, 1970), 460. Earlham College student imprisoned for refusing induction into the army or alternative service reflects on the topics of government, faith, revolution, protest, love. Recommended for its insight into the thinking of young American idealists.

Lapp, John A. (Review). *The Draft?*, by the Peace Education Committee of the American Friends Service Committee. Hill and Wang, 1968. Pp. 112. *ChrLiv* 16 (Feb., 1969), 36. Reviewer notes that the author opposes national service, whether civilian or military, and makes a case for the "selective objector."

Lapp, John A. (Review). *What Belongs to Caesar*, by Donald D. Kaufman. Herald Press, 1970. "What Belongs to Caesar? Sticky War Tax Question." *CanMenn* 18 (Sept. 18, 1970), 7, 8; *GH* 63 (Sept. 15, 1970), 770-71. Major review article recommending Kaufman's study of war taxes for its historical and biblical approach to the question of conscientious objection through nonpayment of taxes.

Lapp, John E. "Why I Do Not Vote in Political Elections." *GH* 59 (July 12, 1966), 612-14. One reason for not voting is because one is a conscientious objector to war. Other reasons, as well as a list of obligations to government, are put forth.

Lapp, Joseph L. "The United States vs. Mennonite Ministers." Term paper presented to EMC History Seminar, June 2, 1966. Pp. 28. MSHL.

Leatherman, Noah H. *Diary Kept by Noah H. Leatherman While in Camp During World War I.* Linden, Alberta: Aaron L. Toews, 1951. Pp. 86. MHL. A day to day account gives a detailed portrait of life as a World War I CO including prison experience at Fort Leavenworth. Materials include journal reflections, menus, schedules, letters, and essays.

Lederach, James S. "A Case for Mandatory Public Service for Conscientious Objectors." *CGR* 2 (Spring, 1984), 139-48. Argues that nonregistration for the draft is not superior to registration and alternative service as a means to Christian obedience because nonregistration provides the state the same information as does registration—in fact, anything short of subversion similarly serves the state; and the rights that nonregistrants forfeit limit their capacity both to proclaim and to serve. Suggests a program involving longer terms and less pay for COs than military inductees for all persons of draft age; this would have the kind of moral force that nonregistration has as wel as expand the benefits of traditional alternative service.

Lederach, John Paul. "The So-Called Pacifists: A Study of Nonviolence in Spain." Social Science Seminar paper, Mar., 1980. Pp. 97. MLA/BeC.

Lehman, Emmett R. "Wyzanski Decision Is Significant." *GH* 62 (May 20, 1969), 461. Reports and discusses this District Court judge's ruling that conscientious objectors outside of religious traditions may be eligible for exemption from military duty.

Lehman, Eric. "Experiences of Mennonite Conscientious Objectors in Camp Sherman During World War I." Paper, Central Christian High School, Kidron, Ohio, May 30, 1977. MHL.

Lehman, J. Irvin. "Questions and Answers on Nonresistance." *ST* 18 (4th Qtr., 1950), 21. Nonresistance is discussed between an inquiring conscientious objector and a minister.

Lehman, James O. "The Mennonites of Maryland During the Revolutionary War." *MQR* 50 (July, 1976), 200-229. Describes the geographical, cultural, religious, and political setting of Maryland Mennonites in the late 18th century, their responses to the Revolutionary War fermemt, and the conflict they faced as conscientious objectors during the war.

Lind, Millard C. *Christ and War.* Ed. Paul Peachey, n.p.: Mennonite General Conference Peace Problems Committee, 1956. Pp. 19. The Christian Youth and War Pamphlets No. 3. Pamphlet directed to young men approaching draft age enjoins them to follow Christ by following the way of nonresistant love, even toward national enemies.

Lind, Miriam Sieber, "A Time to Say No," as told by Roy Buchanan. *ChrLiv* 7 (Sept., 1960), 6-10, 34-35; 7 (Oct., 1960), 12-15, 34; 7 (Nov., 1960), 14-17, 19, 33-34; 7 (Dec., 1960), 22-25, 32-33; 8 (Jan., 1961), 24-27, 34. Experiences of a conscientious objector during World War I: draft; imprisonment in guardhouse; discrimination ; persecution; reconstruction work in France.

Lind, Suzanne. "Mothers of South African COs Send Message to Mennonite Women." *WMSC Voice* 54 (Sept., 1980), 8-9. Beryl Moll and Dorothy Steele, mothers of Peter Moll and Richard Steele, reflect on what their sons' decisions for conscientious objection have meant in their own experiences.

Lott, John C. "The Christian, His Country, His Conscience, an Apology for Noncooperation." *CanMenn* 17 (Oct. 24, 1969), 6, 8. An American army deserter preaches a sermon in the Ottawa Mennonite Church. Besides sharing his pilgrimage, he says: war cannot be Christianized; a Christian cannot be a murderer; the highest allegiance is to God; a CO cannot be a soldier, etc.

"MCC, Peace Conference Topics for Rev. G. Rempel." *CanMenn* 2 (Jan. 22, 1954), 8. Rempel reports on the Detroit Peace Conference and the annual meeting of the Mennonite Central Committee, encouraging the churches to continue their relief programs and peace witness. Strong statements on biblical nonresistance are reported. The problem of the fundamentalists and the peace witness is brought out in an example of the Old Fashioned Revival Hour refusing donations from Mennonite COs.

"MCC (Manitoba) Asks for Stronger CO Provisions in Labor Act." *RepConsS* 32 (Mar., 1975), 5. Request prompted by Labor Board's denial of eight recent applications for exemption from union membership for reasons of conscientious objection.

"Mennonites Discuss Alternative Service, Nonregistration." *RepConsS* 37 (June, 1980), 2, 4.

Two-day conference results in statement asking the Mennonite Church to fully support both registration and nonregistration or noncooperation within its understanding of conscientious objection.

MacMaster, Richard K.; with Horst, Samuel L. and Ulle, Robert F. *Conscience in Crisis: Mennonites and other Peace Churches in America, 1739-1789; Interpretation and Documents.* Scottdale and Kitchener: Herald Press, 1979. Pp. 576. Sourcebook of Mennonites in 18th-century America, focusing especially on Mennonite experience in the Revolutionary War. Includes documents on relations with Native Americans, conscientious objection, nationalism, religious liberty, etc.

Malishchak, Richard. "Some Thoughts on Peace Taxes." *GH* 65 (Oct. 31, 1972), 885-86. Reprinted from *The Reporter for Conscience Sake.* Discusses the World Peace Tax Fund act and its two major advantages: making a provision for positive peace expenditures, and confronting each taxpayer with the possibility of conscientious objection to war taxes by requiring the option to be included in the tax return instruction booklet.

Malishchak, Richard (Review). *I Couldn't Fight,* by Lloy A. Kniss. Herald Press, 1971. Pp. 47. *RepConsS* 28 (Dec., 1971), 5. The testimony of a World War I CO lends perspective to the contemporary issues of conscientious objection.

Martens, Wilfred. "When Stuart Talked About Peace." *With* 4 (Oct., 1971), 34. The experience of a salutatorian who selected and gave as his topic, "Why I Am a Conscientious Objector."

Martin, Ernest H. Private papers and letters from fellow imprisoned COs (Maurice Hess and Robert E. Fox). Lists: religious COs imprisoned at the US Disciplinary Barracks, Ft. Leavenworth, Ks., published by J. D. Mininger, 200 S. 7th, Kansas City, Ks., Mar. 10, 1919; Mennonite CO of World War I, reported to Mennonite Research Foundation. MSHLA.

Martin, John R. "The National Service Board for Religious Objectors." *RepConsS* 15 (Apr., 1958), 3, 4; (May-June, 1958), 3, 4. Outlines history and describes ongoing program of agency created by historic peace churches to serve as liaison between COs of any persuasion and the Selective Service System.

Martin, John R. "We Speak for the CO." *ChrLiv* 5 (Aug., 1958), 6-8. The origin and function of the National Service Board for Religious Objectors.

Martin, Willard. "World War I Conscientious Objectors in Fort Leavenworth." Paper presented to History Seminar, Goshen College, Goshen, Ind., May 30, 1957. Pp. 44. MHL.

Mast, C. Z. "Imprisonment of Amish in the Revolutionary War." *ChrMon* 44 (May, 1952), 151; *MHB* 13 (Jan., 1952), 6-7. Relates the story of several nonresistant Amish men imprisoned in Reading, Pa. during the Revolutionary War, who were saved from execution by the intervention of a local minister of the German Reformed Church.

Mast, C. Z. "Releasing of Early Amish under Severe Trial." Unpublished paper, n.d. Pp. 4. MHL.

McGrath, William R. *Why We Are Conscientious Objectors to War.* Seymour: Historical Mennonite Faith Publications, n.d. Pp. 54. Uses discussion of scripture passages to answer questions commonly asked of nonresistant Christians, such as the validity of war in the Old Testament, Christian obedience to government, and early church convictions on war.

Mennonite Central Committee. "Statement on Conscription for Military Training, and Provisions for Conscientious Objectors," *GH* 38 (Dec. 21, 1945), 733-34. A statement submitted to the House Military Affairs Committee. Expresses opposition to any program of compulsory military training, and support for provisions for conscientious objectors in case such legislation is passed.

Mennonite Central Committee (US). "Statement on World Tensions and the Draft." Adopted Jan. 24, 1980. P. 1. (Located in MCC Peace Section Official Statements folder in MHL.) Urges young Mennonite men and women to register their conscientious objector convictions with the Peacemaker Registration Program in response to proposed military conscription.

Mennonite Central Committee Peace Section. "A Christian Declaration on Amnesty." *GH* 66 (May 15, 1973), 413-14; *Menn* 88 (Apr. 24, 1973), 268-69. Based on the belief that peace and reconciliation are at the heart of the gospel, the Peace Section urges adopting a "general amnesty" to cover all types of conscientious objectors, an action that would help to bind up the wounds of the Vietnam war.

*Mennonites and Conscientious Objection in 1980.* Akron, Pa.: MCC US Peace Section, 1980. Pp. 95. MHL. Papers presented at the MCC US Peace Section Assembly on the Draft and National Service, Mar. 27-29, 1980, at Goshen, Ind. Includes: Blosser, Don, "Biblical Principles and Government Conscription: The Mennonite Dilemma;" Juhnke, James, "The Response of Christians to Conscription in United States History;" Franz, Delton, "Current Legislative Proposals and Their Implications for Conscientious Objectors;" Beals, J. Duane, "The Case for Selective Participation in Military Service;" Martin, Charles D., "The Case for

Noncombatant Military Service;" Beechy, Winifred, "The Case for Alternative Service;" Koehn, Dennis, "A Call to Conscientious Resistance;" Graff, Tom, "The Case for Emigration;" Neufeld, Elmer, "Mennonite Response to Conscription: A Majority Response and Variations from It;" Klassen, Mike, "Implementing a Congregational Dialogue on the Draft and National Service."

Metzler, Edgar. "Another Alternative for Draft-Age Youth." *GH* 52 (Nov. 17, 1959), 977-78. Metzler offers the alternative of noncooperation with the Selective Service system as a clear and compelling witness of conscientious objection against a militaristic society.

Metzler, Edgar. "How Recent Draft Changes Affect the CO." *CanMenn* 13 (Sept. 28, 1965), 3, 16. No change in status of conscientious objectors is expected. Increased draft calls will have same consequences for CO's as for non-CO's.

Metzler, Edgar. Letter to the Editor. *GH* 48 (Dec. 6, 1955), 1154. "Now that our position as conscientious objectors to the draft is generally recognized, has the time come to extend our witness to a more positive conscientious objection to militarism in general?"

Metzler, Edgar. "Selective Conscientious Objectors." *GH* 60 (Mar. 14, 1967), 233. NSBRO and MCC Peace Section support the concern for the civil rights of religious selective objectors. This support was declared on Nov. 19-20, 1965.

Miller, Clyde E. "Where Do I Still Fall Short?" *GH* 61 (Jan. 2, 1968), 10-11. The distinction between a sincere and an insincere CO is found in the superior service rendered by the former. Suggests that the world food crisis presents a test for Mennonite sincerity and calls for *all* Mennonites to become involved with this need.

Miller, Ernest H. "Experiences of a CO in World War I." Paper, Chesapeake, Va., Oct., 1972. Pp. 14. MSHLA.

Miller, Ernest H. "I Tried to Be Reasonable." *GH* 67 (Jan. 22, 1974), 72-74. Conscientious objector in World War I relates his experiences in Camp Funston, Kansas, and a short time in Leavenworth Prison.

Miller, John W. "Are CO's Dangerous?" *GH* 47 (Feb. 16, 1954), 153; *Menn* 69 (Mar. 30, 1954), 197. The world has stopped hating CO's. Can we survive this new tolerance? Does lack of persecution indicate a lack of discipleship?

Miller, Levi (Review). *Mennonites and Conscientious Objection in 1980,* Mennonite Central Committee, 1980. Pp. 95. *FQ* 7 (Nov., Dec., 1980,

Jan., 1981), 9. Publishes papers presented at the MCC Peace Section Assembly on the Draft and National Service, 1980, in Goshen, Ind. Reviewer assesses its main purpose as informing interested persons of Mennonite thinking, since the book bears typewritten copy and no particular editing to draw it into a volume.

Miller, Orie O. "Our Peace Policy." *MQR* 3 (Jan., 1929), 26-32. An address delivered to World War I CO's deals with the problem of the ill preparedness of the CO's and puts forth the 1924 three-point program for peace education in the Mennonite Church.

Miller, Orie O. "The Peace Witness Then and Now." *RepConsS* 23 (Feb., 1966), 2. Briefly reviews the history of the relationship between COs and governments in England, Canada, and the US in order to give thanks for current freedoms.

Miller, Ursula. "'To Keep Thee in All Thy Ways.' " *ChrMon* 36 (July, 1944), 195-96. Story about a young man drafted into CPS camp who reconciles himself to conscientious objector service.

Mohr, Roberta. "I Resisted Nonresistance." *ChrLiv* 16 (Apr., 1969), 20-21. Wife of conscientious objector faces her disagreement with his position.

Morrow, Brent. Letter to the Editor. *ChrLead* 43 (June 3, 1980), 14-15. Contends that the I-A-O noncombatant position is a viable option for conscientious objectors.

Moshier, Edwin A. "CO—COnscience or COward?" *GH* 59 (Aug. 23, 1966), 754. If we will deserve the CO position we must become channels of love wherever we work. Too often we are granted the CO classification without having the proper inner convictions.

Mueller, Peter (Review). *Another Part of the War: The Camp Simon Story,* by Gordon C. Zahn. Amherst: U. of Mass. Press, 1979. Pp. 240. *MBH* 19 (Apr. 25, 1980), 28-29. Recommends this sociological study of Catholic conscientious objectors in a US forestry camp during World War II.

Mueller, Peter (Review). *That There Be Peace,* by Lawrence Klippenstein. Winnipeg: The Manitoba C.O. Reunion Committee, 1979. Pp. 104. *MBH* 19 (Apr. 25, 1980), 28. Reviewer observes that this collection of memorabilia from Canadian conscientious objectors in alternative service during World War II reveals both courage and cowardice.

Mumaw, Adam H. "My Experience as

Conscientious Objector in World War I." Paper. Pp. 12. MSHLA.

Mumaw, John R. World War I papers. Lists names of CO's, Camp Lalor, Kentucky, 1918. MSHLA.

Mumaw, John R. (Archives). Archive box of papers labeled "World War I Conscientious objectors, Private Papers." Box includes materials (diaries, photographs, and miscellaneous records) from a variety of persons: Adam H. Mumaw from Ohio at Camp Taylor, Louisville, KY; Ernest H. Miller; Aldine Brenneman; Asa M. Hartzler; Lloy Kniss; David H. Ranck; Ward Beery; and John G. Meyers from Camp Lee, VA; and David W. Basinger (including a list of CO's imprisoned at Fort Leavenworth, Kansas, 1918-19). MSHL.

Musser, Daniel. *Nonresistance Asserted: Or the Kingdom of Christ and the Kingdom of This World Separated, and No Concord Between Christ and Belial.* Lancaster: Elias Barr and Co., 1864. Pp. 74. MHL. Argues the biblical basis of nonresistance and contends, in regard to the pending draft, that to pay another person to go to war in one's place is just as wrong as actually going to war one's self.

"New Opportunities for COs with PAX." *RepConsS* 19 (Sept.-Oct., 1962), 1, 3. In eleven years MCC's PAX personnel have worked constructively for peace in twenty-six countries.

"News from the Peace Front." *Fellowship* 24 (June 1, 1958), 4. News statement reporting that Benjamin Kauffman, a 23-year-old Amish farmer, has been sentenced to eighteen months in prison for refusing to accept a civilian work assignment as a CO in an institution using modern conveniences.

"No Alternative Service for CO's in Soviet Russia." *CanMenn* 4 (Apr. 27, 1956), 2. Russia does not wish to make martyrs out of CO's. Hence many are ignored, although some are imprisoned.

Neufeld, Elmer. "Three Mennonites in Prison." *CanMenn* 2 (June 25, 1954), 2. The testimony of three men who refused induction into the US armed forces.

Neufeld, Roger C. Letter to the Editor. *ChrLead* 36 (Apr. 3, 1973), 13. People who have applied for the conscientious objector classification should not have to feel any guilt for the Vietnam war

Newcomer, Frank C. "Nonresistance under Test—Experiences of CO's During the World War." *YCC* 21 (Feb. 25, 1940), 58, 59, 64. The World War was a time of severe testing of the Mennonite doctrine of nonresistance. Present conditions are moving toward a possible US

involvement in the war. Are Mennonite youth ready to respond?

Nickel, J. W. "The Canadian Conscientious Objector." *MennLead* 3 (Jan., 1948), 24-28. A picture of Canadian camp life. The problems and frustrations of the CO's are related with an emphasis on the inadequate instruction on nonresistance.

"Objector Troubles Conscience of a Judge." *Menn* 86 (June 29, 1971), 426. How much punishment is to be given to one who has acted according to his or her conscience? The judge: "You are the tragedy of our time, young man; or, maybe, you are the light in the darkness."

"Orie O. Miller (1892-1977)." *RepConsS* 34 (Jan., 1977), 2. Miller is remembered for his leadership in the activities and issues of conscientious objection.

"Origin of Alternative Service." *RepConsS* 5 (Mar., 1947), 1, 6-8. Credits the origin of the concept of CPS as an alternative to war to 19th century Russian Mennonites and discusses the Russian Mennonite CO movement.

Olsen, Victor. "Selective Service Reviews the I-W Program." *MennLife* 13 (July, 1958), 99-100, 105. Analyzes the successful efforts to mobilize for the CO work program of the Selective Service System those who for religious reasons cannot accept combatant or noncombatant.

"Peace and War: A French Conscientious Objector." *GH* 43 (Aug. 15, 1950), 810-11. A brief biography of Jean Widmer who became a CO in the military.

"Peace Church Officials Contact State Directors." *RepConsS* 9 (Mar.-Apr., 1952), 6. MCC finds both receptive and punitive attitudes toward COs among contacted state directors of Selective Service.

"Prison Brutality Bared in Amish CO's Ordeal." *Fellowship* 22 (Sept., 1956), 25. This news release states that what was first reported as a "hunger strike" by five Amish CO's at a W. Va. prison camp has been exposed as an act of prison brutality.

Peachey, J. Lorne. "Speaking Out." *ChrLiv* 16 (Apr., 1969), 11. Joe Hertzler, pastor in Iowa City, wrote of his conscientious objector position in *The Daily Iowan,* student newspaper of the University of Iowa.

Peachey, Paul L. "The Cost of Conscience." *GH* 50 (Aug. 6, 1957), 703. A collection of items pertaining to CO's and pacifism from many countries.

Peachey, Paul L. (Editorial). "Is There Still Any

Point to Conscientious Objection?" *RepConsS* 21 (June, 1964), 2. In order to meet the challenges presented by the threat of nuclear war, the CO position must be based on a less dubious premise than the hope that war will be eradicated through a popular adoption of the CO position.

Penner, Lydia. "E. J. Swalm: A Life Dedicated to Peace." *MennRep* 6 (Aug. 23, 1976), 9. Describes the life and thoughts of this Brethren in Christ bishop who has devoted his life to teaching conscientious objection.

Penner, Lydia. "Never Made to Kill Each Other, Says Bishop." *MBH* 15 (Oct. 29, 1976), 15. Ontario bishop who was a CO in World War I negotiated with Canadian government in setting up alternative service during World War II.

Penner, Lydia. "The Peacemaker." *EV* 89 (Aug. 25, 1976), 11. Rev. E. J. Swalm, a bishop of the Brethren in Christ Church in Ontario and minister for fifty-six years, has dedicated his life to teaching conscientious objection and opposition to war.

Penner, Peter (Review). *That There Be Peace: Mennonites in Canada and World War II,* ed. Lawrence Klippenstein. Winnipeg, Man.: The Manitoba CO Reunion Committee, 1979. Pp. 104. *MQR* 55 (July, 1981), 271. Recalls the Christian witness of young Manitobans whose unpopular stance benefited themselves and their fellow Canadians.

Penner, William. *My Experiences in Camp Life.* Ste. Anne, Manitoba: By the Author, RR 1, Box 91, n.d. Pp. 15. MHL. Reflects upon the CO experience in a CPS camp on Vancouver Island where the men worked on various forestry projects including fire fighting.

Perry, Shawn, ed. *Words of Conscience: Religious Statements on Conscientious Objection.* Washington, DC: National Interreligious Service Board for Conscientious Objectors, 1980. 9th ed. Official and unofficial statements by Catholic, Protestant, Jewish, Krishna, Muslim, Buddhist, and American Indian groups. Includes essays on war and conscientious objection, and a section on nuclear pacifism. Some earlier editions have been edited by Mennonites (e.g., Michael L. Yoder, 4th ed.; J. Harold Sherk, 6th ed.; Gerald E. Shenk, 7th ed., etc.) and have included some Mennonite statements.

Preheim, Marion Keeney. "The People of Peace." *ChrLiv* 23 (July, 1976), 34-35. How the author first learned about conscientious objection and how it affected her life.

Pringle, Cyrus. "A Quaker Against the Civil War." *ChrLiv* 10, Part I: (Sept., 1963), 15-17, 38; Part II: (Oct., 1963), 24-25, 40. Adapted from *The Civil War Diary of Cyrus Pringle,* with foreword by Henry J. Cadbury, Pendle Hill Pamphlets, Wallingford, Pa. Experiences and thoughts of a conscientious objector who would not comply in the Union army camp.

(Review). *That There Be Peace,* ed. Lawrence Klippenstein. Manitoba CO Reunion Committee, 1979. *MCC PS Newsletter* 10 (June-July, 1980), 9. The book reports on the alternative service activities of Canadian Mennonite conscientious objectors during World War II.

(Review). *Why I Couldn't Fight,* by Lloy A. Kniss. N.p., n.d. *GfT* 10 (Jan.-Feb., 1975), 14-15. World War I conscientious objector explains his position. Reviewer recommends the book because it distinguishes between pacifism and biblical nonresistance.

Ranck, David H. Diary, World War I CO Records. Handwritten, xeroxed copy. Pp. 79. MSHLA. Contains extensive name, address list.

Ray-Crichton, Jim. "The Military: A View from the Inside." *Lifework* 5 (1981), 3-5. Former Coast Guard draftee describes his reactions to basic training and navy policies and his decision not to participate in the military, based on Chrsitian convictions.

Redekop, John H. "Penner vs. Beaver County Draft Board." *MBH* 9 (Aug. 21, 1970), 8. MCC assists a CO from Oklahoma to make his stand before the courts. Article discusses how one can learn from this encounter.

Redekop, John H. "The Dodgers." *MBH* 7 (June 14, 1968), 2. Those who migrate because of conscientious objection to conscription merit our sympathetic understanding and assistance.

Redekop, John H. "The Farmer and the Faith." *MBH* 16 (Sept. 30, 1977), 10. Pacifists should support the cause of the Amish in the milk shipping controversy because it is a case of pacifist conscientious objection.

Redekop, John H. "The New Conscientious Objectors." *MBH* 14 (Mar. 21, 1975), 8, Although Canadian youths do not face the draft, other forms of conscientious objection are being practiced, such as noncooperation with unions or forced tax evasion.

Reed, Kenneth. *Mennonite Soldier.* Scottdale, Pa.: Herald Press, 1974. Pp. 518. Novel uses the prodigal son motif to order this story of two brothers, Ira and Mastie Stoltzfus, and their different responses to the moral dilemmas posed for them by World War I. Ira, the older brother, remains true to the Mennonite Church position and endures camp life and a prison term as a CO. Mastie joins the army and is sent to fight on the French front. In addition to following these two stories, the novel also portrays the divisive effects of the war upon the Pennsylvania community that is home to the Stoltzfuses.

Regehr, Ernie. "Conscientious Objection in South Africa." *GH* 68 (Dec. 9, 1975), 872-73; *MennRep* 5 (May 12, 1975), A7. Examines a resolution by the South African Council of Churches to consider conscientious objection as a means of refusing to support apartheid. Considers the resolution a "modest beginning," since it denounces violence only when supporting an unjust cause.

Regehr, Ernie. "Conscientious Objection: Escape from or Challenge to Militarism?" *MennRep* 10 (Mar. 3, 1980), 8. Reprinted from *MCC PS Newsletter* 10 (Mar.-Apr., 1980), 8-9. Author contends that conscientious objection can be used to combat social evil, and cites the South African Council of Churches' resolution on conscientious objection as an example.

Regehr, Ernie. *Perceptions of Apartheid: The Churches and Political Change in South Africa.* Scottdale: Herald Press; Kitchener: Between the Lines, 1979. Pp. 309. Detailed analysis of racial violence in South Africa. Includes extensive discussion of the church and state relationship in that context as well as a final chapter entitled "Violence/Nonviolence and the Dilemma of the Churches" in which the issues of conscientious objection, as well as other issues of war and peace, are raised.

Regier, Austin. "Civil Disobedience for Christ: A CO's Witness to His Faith." *CanMenn* 14 (Nov. 1, 1966), 8. Regier refused to obey the Selective Service act of 1948 which gave him the right of religious conscientious objection while denying it to others equally conscientious but of different religious persuasion.

Regier, Harold R. "Minneapolis Conference Calls for Tax Withholding Exemption." *God and Caesar* 5 (Apr., 1979), 2-3. Although a clear commitment to tax resistance as individuals or institutions was not made, the General Conference Mid-Triennium took a small but significant step in agreeing that tax resistance is a valid concern and that the conference should seek conscientious objector exemption from collecting taxes for the state.

Regier, Harold R. "US Supreme Court to Hear War Tax Case?" *God and Caesar* 4 (June, 1978), 3. A petition has been made to the US Supreme Court asking it to rule on the constitutionality of requiring conscientious objectors to military taxes to pay those taxes, based on the First Amendment to the Constitution.

Regier, Harold R. "War Taxes Not a Religious Issue?" *God and Caesar* 3 (June, 1977), 6-7. Further challenges in the courts and in Congress are needed to argue against the inconsistency between the US government's recognition that physical participation in war is a violation of religious freedom for conscientious objectors while financial participation is not.

Reimer, Paul. "Conscientious Objectors at Fort Leavenworth Prison During World War I: A Mennonite Perspective." Social Science Seminar paper, Apr., 1973. Pp. 41. MLA/BeC.

*Remembering: Stories of Peacemakers.* Akron, Pa.: MCC Peace Section, 1982. Pp. 59. MHL. Stories, readings, and short plays for use in churches and schools. Topics included are conscientious objection in World War I, World War II, and the Vietnam War, as well as an interview with a South African conscientious objector.

Rensberger, David and Lois. "The Case of David Rensberger, 22." *ChrLiv* 18 (Sept., 1971), 2-6. Draft resister and his mother speak on the eve of his sentencing.

Rosenberger, David. "Were the Conscientious Objectors Fairly Treated in World War I?" Pp. 16. BfC.

Roth, Nadine S. "Claude Follows the Prince of Peace All the Way." *ChrMon* 29 (Dec., 1937), 355-56. Story about a young man and woman's friendship troubled by differing opinions on a Christian response to war.

Roth, Nadine S. "On the Altar." *ChrMon* 27 (Feb., 1935), 35-36. Story about the friendship of two neighbor women strained over the issue of participation in war.

"Slow Progress Reported by Task Force on Taxes." *GH* 72 (Aug. 21, 1979), 673-74. Report on the progress of the task force mandated by the General Conference Mennonite Church at the Minneapolis meeting to seek legal and administrative avenues for achieving conscientious objector exemption.

"Soil Conservation as a Work of National Importance." *ChrMon* 33 (May, 1941), 149. NSBRO describes soil conservation as one type of civilian work for conscientious objectors.

"Study on Conscientious Objectors and Volunteers." *MennMirror* 5 (Oct., 1975), 12. A brief summary of a news item found in a West German publication which points out basic personality differences between volunteers to the Federal Army and conscientious objectors.

"Supreme Court Broadens Definition of Religious Conscientious Objection." *CanMenn* 13 (Sept. 14,

1965), 2. An MCC report on a US Supreme Court ruling concerning religious conscientious objection. MCC is urging the government to recognize freedom of conscience without attempting to require a particular theological point of view.

"Swiss Mennonite Refuses to Do Military Service." RepConsS 27 (Mar., 1970), 4. Michael Gerber, in refusing to serve in the army medical corps, has become the first Swiss Mennonite in many years to take a CO position.

Santiago, Lydia Esther. "Peace and War: A Personal Experience with Nonresistance." GH 43 (Nov. 21, 1950), 1147. Santiago explains how she encountered nonresistance and conscientious objectors in World War II in Puerto Rico.

Sauder, Bill. "Employment Regardless of Race or Religion." ChrLiv 12 (Sept., 1965), 18-19. Provisions of Title VII of the Civil Rights Act of 1964 will affect job discrimination because of conscientious objection to war.

Sawatsky, Rodney J. (Review). Voices Against War: A Guide to the Schowalter Oral History Collection on World War I Conscientious Objection, ed. Keith L. Sprunger, James C. Juhnke, and John D. Waltner. North Newton, Kansas: Bethel College, 1973. Pp. 100. MQR 50 (Jan., 1976), 69-70. Reviewer considers this book a valuable research aid to the important collection of Mennonite oral history, and he calls for greater historical analysis of the collected data.

Schlabach, Theron F., ed. "An Account by Jakob Waldner: Diary of a Conscientious Objector in World War I." MQR 48 (Jan., 1974), 73-111. The diary of a Hutterite conscientious objector demonstrates belief in two strictly separate kingdoms, with unswerving loyalty to the kingdom of God rather than to the nation.

Schmidt, Allen. Experiences of Allen Schmidt During World War I. Hesston, Ks.: Gospel Publishers, [1972]. MHL. Series of letters from a conscientious objector, sentenced to 25 years in Fort Leavenworth, to his family and friends.

Schmidt, John F. "Probing the Impact of World War I." MennLife 26 (Dec., 1971), 161, 162. Interviews with people who were CO's during World War I are being taped for preservation in the Bethel College Historical Library.

Schmidt, Linda. "Somewhat Cool but Sometimes Boiling: World War II's Effect on Bethel-Newton Relations." Paper presented to History of Civilization class, Bethel College, North Newton, Ks., 1974. Pp. 12. MHL.

Schrader, Don. Letter to the Editor. GH 70 (May 24, 1977), 429-30. Call for Christian conscientious objectors to take a stand against capital punishment as an extension of their nonresistant convictions, and to attack the causes of social violence.

Schrag, Duane. "Two Twentieth-Century Mennonite Martyrs." Menn 90 (Oct. 28, 1975), 613. Quotes from Werner Forssmann's Experiments on Myself (St. Martin's Press), which tells of the execution of two Mennonite men by Nazis for conscientious objection.

Schrag, Paul. "Mennonites and United States Conscientious Objector Laws." Student paper for Mennonite History, Life and Thought, Jan., 1983. Pp. 23. MLA/BeC.

Schrock, Paul M. (Review). The Tax Dilemma: Praying for Peace, Paying for War, by Donald D. Kaufman. Scottdale: Herald Press, 1978. "New Book on War Taxes." God and Caesar 5 (Feb., 1979), 8. This book considers the issue of two kingdoms, traces the history of conscientious objection to war taxes and discusses a dozen viable options which Christians can use to witness to their faith and oppose corporate warmaking.

Schultz, J. S. "Contributions to World Peace by the Historic Peace Churches." Paper, Bluffton, Ohio, [1957]. Pp. 15. MLA/BeC., MHL.

Schultz, J. S. Report of the I-W Program; Evaluation Study of Mennonite and Brethren in Christ I-W Men. [Akron, Pa.: MCC], 1955. Pp. 72. MHL. Summarizes 1,794 responses to questionnaire administered to 2,847 I-W men. Includes such topics as the I-W work program, I-W personnel's reactions to the program, the church and I-W service, the CO position, the I-W off duty, and the I-W before and after service.

Shank, Clarence. "A Mennonite Boy's World War Experience." YCC 21, Part 1, "Preliminary Experiences, (Apr. 7, 1940), 106-107; Part 2, "My Trip to Camp Lee, Va," (Apr. 14, 1940), 117-20; Part 3, "First Events in Camp Lee;" (Apr. 21, 1940), 128; Part 4, "Going Through the Mustering Office," (Apr. 28, 1940), 135; Part 5, "Entering the 'Holy Hill';" (May 5, 1940), 142; Part 6, "The Six-Month Furlough," (May 19, 1940), 155; Part 7, "The Homeward Look," (May 26, 1940), 163, 168. A Mennonite describes his experience as a conscientious objector during World War I.

Shank, Duane. "An Open Letter to Selective Service." RepConsS 27 (May, 1970), 1. An eighteen-year-old refuses to register with the SSS on the grounds that to accept any classification from Selective Service System indicates participation in the "war machine."

Shank, Duane. "COs and the Draft." RepConsS 32

[*sic*, 33] (May, 1976), 5. Ford Foundation "Information Paper" provides data on inequities and inconsistencies in handling of CO applications by local Selective Service personnel.

Shank, Duane. "Pardons for Some." *RepConsS* 32 [*sic*, 33] (May, 1976), 1, 3. Discusses the Democratic Party plank favoring pardons for those whose conscientious objection to the Vietnam War resulted in Selective Service violations.

Shank, J. Ward (Editorial). "The New Conscientious Objector." *ST* 35 (July, 1967), 2. Concern that the broadening definition for conscientious objection presents a serious risk of Mennonites becoming identified with the left wing of American politics and religion.

Shellenberger, Eunice. *Wings of Decision*. Scottdale: Herald Press, 1951. Pp. 240. Fictional account of a young man facing the draft in World War II, his decision to seek conscientious objector status, and his experiences in Civilian Public Service.

Shelley, Paul. "An Evaluation of Methods of Transmitting Mennonite Ideals." *PCMCP Fourth*, 71-82. North Newton, Kansas: n.p. Held at Bluffton, Ohio, Aug. 24-25, 1945. The evaluation includes the CPS experience and the development of the CO position.

Shelly, Andrew R. "Thinking Things Through about Being a CO." Pamphlet written for the young men of Stirling Avenue Mennonite Church, Kitchener, Ontario, [194__]. Pp. 14. MHL.

Shelly, Maynard. "Western District Takes Stand on War Taxes." *Menn* 85 (Nov. 10, 1970), 682-84. Torn apart by loyalties to government and God, Mennonites conclude that withholding war taxes is in the tradition of Mennonite conscientious objection to war.

Shenk, Gerald E. "Increase in Conscientious Objection a Worldwide Phenomenon." *GH* 64 (Oct. 5, 1971), 828. Reports on the treatment of conscientious objectors in Spain and other countries not recognizing conscientious objection to war, and the increasing numbers of COs in those countries in which it is a legally recognized alternative.

Shenk, Gerald E., ed. *Religious Statements on Conscientious Objection*. Washington, DC: National Religious Service Board for Conscientious Objectors, 1970. Pp. 72. MSHL. A compilation of over sixty statements on conscientious objection from a variety of denominational and humanitarian viewpoints.

Shenk, Gerald E. *Supplement to "Religious Statements*

*on Conscientious Objection."* Washington, DC: National Religious Service Board for Conscientious Objectors. Pp. 19. MSHL. Adds such views as those of the American Indians, Buddhists, Moslems, Gandhi, Martin Luther King, etc.

Sherk, J. Harold. "Belgian COs Win Recognition." *RepConsS* 21 (Aug., 1964), 1. A fourteen-year process to secure provisions for COs in Belgium has resulted in the passage of two laws favorable to conscientious objection.

Sherk, J. Harold. "COs in the News." *RepConsS* 25 (Feb., 1968), 1, 2. Summarizes the plights of several COs with various religious orientations who have attempted to witness for peace in a variety of ways.

Sherk, J. Harold. "Draft Prospects and Problems." *RepConsS* 22 (Oct., 1965), 1, 4. Assesses CO situation for US citizens in light of the draft call increase announced by President Johnson on July 28.

Sherk, J. Harold. "NSBRO Comments." *RepConsS* 22 (Apr., 1965), 1, 3, 4. Discusses the Mar. 8, 1965 Supreme Court decision in favor of Seeger, Jakobsen, and Peter.

Sherk, J. Harold. "Some Reflections on an Odyssey." *RepConsS* 21 (Dec., 1964), 1. Reports contacts made with COs of a variety of denominational, ideological and cultural identities on a trip to the West Coast.

Sherk, J. Harold (Editorial). "From Where I Sit." *RepConsS* 20 (Feb., 1963), 2. Decries the religious test for COs and conscription as infringements of religious freedom.

Sherk, J. Harold (Editorial). "From Where I Sit: Too Easy?" *RepConsS* 20 (Nov., 1963), 2. Declares that making CO status more difficult to obtain is not the solution to the problem of the small number of "phonies" among the COs.

Shields, Sarah D. "The Treatment of Conscientious Objectors During World War I: Mennonites at Camp Funston." Student paper for History 801, University of Kansas, 1980. Pp. 26. MLA/BeC.

Showalter, John. "World War I Experiences." Paper, n.d. Pp. 4. MHL.

Showalter, Stuart W. "Coverage of Conscientious Objectors to the Vietnam War: An Analysis of the Editorial Content of American Magazines, 1964-1972." PhD dissertation, Univ. of Texas at Austin, 1975. Pp. 163. MSHL. Study finds that the nation's most widely read and respected popular magazines took seriously their responsibility to defend individual rights because they portrayed COs, certainly an ideological minority during the Vietnam War, positively most of the time.

Showalter, Stuart W. "Six Opinion Magazines' Coverage of Conscientious Objectors to the Vietnam War." Paper presented to the Association for Education in Journalism, San Diego State University. Aug. 18-21, 1974. Pp. 22. MHL.

Sibley, Mulford Q. and Jacob, Philip E. *Conscription of Conscience: The American State and the Conscientious Objector, 1940-1947.* Ithaca, NY: Cornell University Press, 1952. Pp. 580. MHL. Comprehensive treatment of subject with substantive reference to the Mennonite experience as well as that of the other historic peace churches.

Smoker, Art. "Christ's Peacemaking Way." *GH* 64 (Aug. 17, 1971), 678-80. Writer finds the basis for his conscientious objection in the lordship of Jesus Christ, but he distinguishes nonparticipation in war, which includes active reconciling, and witness to the state from total nonresistance.

Smucker, Donovan E. "Who Are the CO's?" *Fellowship* 7 (Feb., 1941), 22-24. Discusses the variety of patterns of conscientious objection in America: historic peace churches, protestant CO's, Roman Catholic pacifism, Jewish objectors, unusual sects, political objection, humanitarian war resisters, and cultural-racial objectors.

Souder, Elvin. "Problems of a Conscientious Objector in the Legal Practice." *PCMCP Seventh,* 101-12. North Newton, Kansas: The Mennonite Press. Held at Tabor College, Hillsboro, Kansas, June 16-17, 1949. A conscientious objector faces no greater problems of an ethical nature in legal practice than those one might encounter in business. Speaks to questions of law enforcement and the relationship of church and state encountered in legal practice.

Springer, Nelson S. "Making Yellow White." *ChrMon* 30 (July, 1938), 202-3. In defense of conscientious objection to war.

Sprunger, Keith L.; Juhnke, James C.; Waltner, John D. *Voices Against War: A Guide to the Schowalter Oral History Collection on World War I Conscientious Objection.* North Newton: Bethel College, 1973. Pp. 190. Alphabetical listing of 273 taped interviews with Mennonite men from the World War I era in 15 states and 4 provinces. Book includes 6 indices plus a selected bibliography on Mennonites and other pacifists during World War I.

Stauffer, Daniel. Letter to the Editor. *Fellowship* 25 (Mar., 1959), 35. Writing from prison, this CO expresses gratitude for all the Christmas cards

and messages of good will and encouragement he received from all over the world.

Steffen, Dorcas. "The Civil War and Wayne County Mennonites." *MHB* 26 (July, 1965), 1-3. Outlines provisions made by the North for conscientious objectors, then relates anecdotes from the war years concerning young men who did and did not fight, and the effects of the war on congregational life.

Stoltzfus, Grant M. "Conscientious Objection During the Civil War: Mennonites." *RepConsS* 19 (June, 1962), 3, 7. See also special issue devoted to same topic, by Stoltzfus. Describes Mennonite CO experience during the Civil War in its context—an emerging central government which had not completely established its primacy over the state governments.

Stoltzfus, Grant M. "Conscientious Objectors in the Civil War." *GH* 55 (Jan. 23, 1962), 81. Civil War CO's found more understanding with President Lincoln than in the Confederacy.

Stoltzfus, Grant M. "When the Flag Goes By." *ChrLiv* 18 (Oct., 1971), 3-9. Review of national and state policies regarding flag display and salute, with the accompanying dissent from conscientious objectors.

Stoltzfus, Victor. "You Make Beggars, Prostitutes, and Communists." *CanMenn* 14 (Apr. 19, 1966), 7, 10. A paper presented at the Faculty Forum of the Social Science Club, Youngstown University on Mar. 25. Stoltzfus, a conscientious objector to war in any form, discusses three categories of objectors to the war in Vietnam: just war theorists; secular humanists; and military personnel who have turned against this war.

Stone, Oliver. "Draft Classifications." *YCC* 30 (Jan. 30, 1949), 453. There seems to be some confusion about draft classifications. The conscientious objector should assert his CO claim and should take whatever appeal may be necessary to secure his IV-E classification.

Stoner, John K. "Conscientious Objection to Nuclear Deterrence." *GH* 72 (Oct. 2, 1979), 782. A call to Mennonites to become conscientious objectors to the concept and practice of nuclear deterrence.

Sutter, Sam and Mabel. Letter to the Editor. *Menn* 88 (Feb. 27, 1973), 151. Writers submit to *The Mennonite* a copy of the letter they sent with their Internal Revenue Service return, protesting their payment of war taxes and explaining the conscientious objector position of the Mennonite church.

Swalm, E. J. "Memories of an Old War." *ChrLiv* 16

(Dec., 1969), 7-10. From *My Beloved Brethren* by Ernest John Swalm, Evangel Press, 1969. Brethren in Christ minister tells of his experiences as a conscientious objector during World War I.

Swalm, E. J. *Nonresistance Under Test.* Nappanee, Ind.: E.V. Publishing House, 1938. Pp. 55. An account of the experiences of conscientious objectors during World War I.

Swalm, E. J. "Memories of an Old War." *ChrLiv* 16 (Dec., 1969), 7-10. From *My Beloved Brethren* by Ernest John Swalm, Evangel Press, 1969. Brethren in Christ minister tells of his experiences as a conscientious objector during World War I.

Swartzentruber, Anita. "The Argentine Mennonite Church, the State, and Military Service." Paper presented to Mennonite History class, English Clinic, Jan. 16, 1954. Pp. 7. MHL.

"Three Mennonites in Prison." *CanMenn* 2 (June 25, 1954), 2. Elmer Neufeld of NSBRO relates the story of three Mennonites who refused induction upon government's denial of CO status.

"To Publish Thesis on World War CO's." *CanMenn* 7 (Jan. 16, 1959), 1. The Canadian Mennonite Brethren Conference decides to publish J. A. Toews' master's thesis.

Teichroew, Allan, ed. "Military Surveillance of Mennonites in World War I." *MQR* 53 (Apr., 1979), 95-127. Publishes a report from the Military Intelligence Division of the War Department documenting government surveillance of Mennonites, Amish, and Hutterites between Mar., 1918 and Feb., 1919 and government pressure on them as conscientious objectors in World War I. The report concludes that their actions qualified as "treason."

The Reporter, extracted. "Russian CO Reports Alternate Service Still Possible in USSR." *ChrLiv* 3 (Sept., 1956), 11. Review of the status of alternate service in USSR since late 1800s.

Toews, John A. *Alternative Service in Canada During World War II.* Winnipeg: Publishing Committee of the Canadian Conference of the MB Church, 1959. Pp. 127. A study of the legal status and actual experiences of all conscientious objectors, including Mennonites, in Canada.

Toews, John A. (Review). *Broken Promises: A History of Conscription in Canada,* by J. L. Granatstein and J. M. Hitsman. Toronto: Oxford Univ. Press, 1977. Pp. 281. *MQR* 53 (Oct., 1979), 333. Based on extensive research, the authors cite conscription as the single issue which has "done more to destroy the unity of the nation."

Reviewer expresses disappointment that Mennonites and other conscientious objectors are mentioned only in passing.

"US Supreme Court Denies Veterans Benefits for CO's." *Forum* A (Apr., 1974), 9. In a recent decision, the US Supreme Court ruled that a conscientious objector who served two years of alternate service is not eligible for veterans' educational benefits.

"US Volunteer Army 'Succeeding' As Pentagon Juggles Figures." *Forum* (Mar., 1974), 14. The controversy over the adequacy of a volunteer army is presented and the conscientious objector is warned to watch carefully and weigh thoughtfully this allegiance.

Umble, Roy H. (Review). *Clash by Night,* by Wallace Hamilton. Pendle Hill Pamphlet No. 23. Wallingford, PA: Pendle Hill Publications, 1945. Pp. 58. *CPS Bull* 4 (Aug. 8, 1945), 3. Recommends the pamphlet and encourages conscientious objectors to direct educational efforts to the public to explain their peace position.

Unzicker, Arleta. "His Own Household." *Swords into Plowshares: A Collection of Plays About Peace and Social Justice.* Ed. Ingrid Rogers. Elgin: The Brethren Press, 1983, 228-35. One-act play portraying how one family deals with the fact that the son raised with both Christian and nationalistic ideals decides on his 18th birthday to apply for CO status.

van de Meusbrugghe, Andre. "A Letter to a Lawyer." *YCC* 36 (Feb. 13, 1955), 51-52, 55. A personal letter stating the biblical basis for the conviction to be a conscientious objector.

Vogt, Roy. "Strikes Symbolize Union Power But You Wield Power Too." *MennMirror* 4 (May, 1975), 7-8. While sympathetic to view of Henry Funk, who is fighting a legal battle over his refusal to join a union on the grounds of conscientious objection to violent union tactics, Vogt urges Christians to think critically and analytically about the way we ourselves are involved with the uses of power. We must then exercise this power with care and responsibility to Christian ethics of nonviolence, etc., rather than withdrawing from situations simply because there is use of power.

Vogt, Roy. "The Funk Case Represents a Rare Triumph of Individual Rights." *MennMirror* 5 (Jan. Feb., 1976), 21, 22. Examines some of the issues raised for conscientious objectors in the decision of the Manitoba Court of Appeals to exempt Henry Funk from labor union membership on the basis of his religious beliefs, rather than adherence to an official set of church doctrines. See also an earlier article: *MennMirror* 4 (Nov., 1974), 11, 12.

Von Wijk, Hein. "French Conscientious Objectors Under Military Jurisdiction." *CanMenn* 14 (Jan. 4, 1966), 3. A report on French CO's and their plight in camps under military jurisdiction. French law of July 9, 1965, introduced four kinds of service: the armed services; civil defense; technical aid (in overseas territories); and cooperation (in underdeveloped foreign countries). The last two (non-military) types of service are closed to CO's.

"When You Fill Out Form 150." *With* 2 (Mar., 1969), 28. Because the decision of the local draft board depends on the information given on the Form 150, one should avoid oversimplified answers.

Waltner, Edward J. B. "A CO in the First World War." Paper, Marion, SD, 1942. Pp. 39. MHL.

Waltner, Emil J. "The Conscientious Objector in History and Now." *Menn* 57 (Mar. 31, 1942), 4-6. A brief review of nonresistance from the time of the Roman Empire to the present.

Warkentine, Kendal. "Military Justice in World War I: Court Martial Trials of Mennonite Conscientious Objectors." Social Science Seminar, Feb., 1983. Pp. 127. MLA/BeC.

Webb, Jon. "Why I Choose Canada." *With* 4 (Mar., 1971), 10. The story of one man's experience in military prison. When he was unable to get a CO classification, he again went AWOL to Canada.

Wenger, C. D. "Why I Am a CO: In Two Parts." Harrisonburg, VA: By the Author, Box 182, 1947. Pp. [6]. MHL. Two lists of scriptures—one supporting the CO position, the other supporting the authority of scripture.

Wenger, Martha. "Between Two Fires: A Study of War Department Policy Toward Conscientious Objectors in World War I." Paper presented to Seminar on World War I, [Bethel College, North Newton, Ks.], Dec. 14, 1975. Pp. 22. MHL, MLA/BeC.

Wenger, Warren M. "Peace—The Vine or the Grape?" *GH* 63 (Jan. 20, 1970), 60-62. While the question of how Mennonites with a peace position rooted in love for the enemy should relate to the popular peace movement is an important one, Mennonites should be giving greater attention to providing adequate structures for conscientious objectors in I-W service.

Wert, Jim and Epp, Leonard. " . . . Some Churches and Their Leaders Are Calling for Help." *I Would Like to Dodge the Draft-dodgers But . . .* Ed. Frank H. Epp. Waterloo and Winnipeg: Conrad Press, 1970, 69-75. Pp. 95. In this two-part treatment, Wert describes the Canadian Council of Churches' involvement with the US draft dodgers and Epp describes the estimated 60,000 young Americans in Canada for reasons of conscientious objection and makes some suggestions as to how the church leadership might deal constructively with this phenomenon.

Wherry, Neal M. *Conscientious Objection.* Washington, D.C.: Government Printing Office, 1950. Vol. I, pp. 364. Vol. II, pp. 288. MHL. Chronicles World War II conscientious objection from the government's point of view. Mennonite documents and summaries of Mennonite practices and teachings are found in chapters entitled: "Church Backgrounds of CO's," "Conscientious Objection in American History," "Legislative Provisions on Conscientious Objection." Other chapters offer extensive information about the CPS program—history, assignments, administration, discipline, statistics, etc.

Widmer, Gladys. "Why I Am a Conscientious Objector." *GH* 45 (Sept. 16, 1952), 921. Widmer tells of her contacts with Mennonites and the ensuing conviction that it is biblically correct to be nonresistant.

Wiebe, Dwight. "How the Army Feels About the Conscientious Objector." *YCC* 43 (Feb. 25, 1962), 2. An exchange of correspondence showing that even in the chaplain's office the conscientious objector who thinks he or she can have a stronger Christian testimony in the military is not welcomed.

World Conference on Religion and Peace. "The Rights of Conscientious Objectors." *EV* 87 (Oct. 25, 1974), 12. A brief statement from the World Conference on Religion and Peace in Kyoto, Japan, Oct. 16-21, 1970, stating that each person should have the right, on the grounds of conscience or profound conviction, to refuse military service.

World War I. 302 interviews: over half are transcribed. Emphasis is on CO's from many Mennonite branches and other churches. Also includes several regulars and civilians (women, pastors). Some very dramatic stories of abuse in army camps, courts-martial, prison, personal testimonies about nonresistant stances, moving to Canada to escape conscription, community war fervor. Guide to interviews published as Sprunger, *et al., Voices Against War,* 1973. MLA/BeC.

World War II. 134 interviews, some transcribed. Emphasis on Mennonite CO's who did CPS work. ALso includes some civilians (women, pastors) and regulars.MLA/BeC.

Wright, Edward Needles. *Conscientious Objectors in the Civil War.* Philadelphia: University of

Pennsylvania Press, 1931. Pp. 274. While this discussion is focused more generally on CO's as a whole, there are numerous references to Mennonites. Topics include peace principles of the Mennonites, Mennonite experiences with both the North and the South, petitions and appeals, etc. Early standard work on conscientious objection in the Civil War.

Yake, C. F. "CO Facts." *YCC* 32 (Mar. 18, 1951), 508. Survey of the status of the CO positions in Europe as reported by Guy F. Hershberger.

Yake, J. Stanley. "Treatment of Mennonite Conscientious Objectors in World War I Army Camps." Paper presented to History Seminary, Goshen College, Goshen, Ind., May 30, 1957. Pp. 43. MHL.

Yoder, Edward. "You Want Another to Do Your Fighting?" *GH Supplement* 37 (Oct., 1944), 591. The CO does not want or ask anyone else to fight for him or her.

Yoder, Edward (Review). *Pacifist Handbook—Questions and Answers Concerning the Pacifist in Wartime, Prepared as a Basis for Study and Discussion, "by a number of peace societies," n.d. ChrMon* 32 (Oct., 1940), 305. Observes that the book stimulates conscientious objectors to war to consider the fuller implications of nonresistance.

Yoder, John. "Peace Is Our Business." *Intercom* 10 (Mar.-Apr., 1970), 1. VS worker in Atlanta describes his job as a draft counselor, especially his work with conscientious objectors from non-pacifist backgrounds.

Yoder, John H. "Conscientious Objection in France." *GH* 53 (Apr. 19, 1960), 345. At the moment there is no provision for the legal recognition of CO's in France. However, there is reason to believe that there is a shift there towards recognizing the CO claim.

Yoder, John H. "Nonconformity and the Nation." *ChrLiv* 2 (Feb., 1955), 8-9, 25, 33. The deeper issue behind conscientious objection to military service is the question of loyalty to the nation or to the Kingdom of God.

Yoder, John H. "The Peace Testimony and Conscientious Objection." *GH* 51 (Jan. 21, 1958), 57. "The church living in true discipleship, devoted to her Lord in service and witness, love and suffering for both neighbors and strangers, be they friend or foe, will find no time for carnal warfare."

Yoder, John H. (Review). *In Solitary Witness*, by Gordon Zahn. Holt, Rinehart, and Winston, 1965. Pp. 278. *ChrLiv* 12 (Nov., 1965), 35-36. Recommends the book as the narrative of a Catholic conscientious objector beheaded under Nazism.

Yoder, John H. (Review). *In Solitary Witness: The Life and Death of Franz Ja¹gersta¹tter*, by Gordon Zahn. Holt, Rinehart, and Winston, 1964. Pp. 278. *ChrLiv* 13 (June, 1966), 32-33. Recommends this narrative of a Catholic layperson beheaded under Nazism for conscientious objection to war.

Zehr, Albert. "US Deserter Preaches." *GH* 63 (June 2, 1970), 489. Summary of the personal story told by a US Army deserter about his coming to conscientious objector convictions and the treatment given him in military prison after going AWOL.

Ziegler, Donald. "CO's Strengthen Faith at House of Friendship." *MBH* 12 (Aug. 24, 1973), 5. Describes the work of two conscientious objectors from widely different non-Anabaptist backgrounds who have volunteered their services through MCC to work at the House of Friendship in Kitchener, Ont.

Ziegler, Donald. "MCC Examines Self and Issues." *EV* 86 (Mar. 10, 1973), 5, 6. MCC met for its annual meeting in Leamington, Ont., to discuss the progress of the MCC self-study, to adopt guidelines on the use of government funds, to resolve interest in reconstruction in Indochina, to consider a working draft statement on universal amnesty for conscientious objectors, and to recognize four dynamic leaders of past inter-Mennonite activites.

Zook, Mervin D. "Measurement of Attitudes Toward Religious Conscientious Objectors in Selected Magazines of World War II Years by Evaluative Assertion." MA in Journalism thesis, Indiana University, May, 1969. Pp. 114. BfC., MHL. Concludes that religious magazines treated COs slightly more favorably than nonreligious ones; letters to the editor tended to disagree with favorable view of COs presented in secular magazines but in the religious magazines, which also presented a favorable view of COs, the letters to the editor tended to be supportive; generally the COs choosing noncombatant service were rated higher than those choosing alternative service.

# 8

# International Relations

"A Letter of Concern." *ChrLead* 28 (July 6, 1965), 5. Letter from Reba Place Fellowship connects recent natural disasters in Mississippi and Indiana to US national sin in Vietnam and the Dominican Republic. Calls for national repentance.

"America and the War in the East." *Menn* 52 (Sept. 21, 1937), 6-7. Exhorts Mennonites as Christian citizens to do all they can to support strict enforcement of the US neutrality law. The article explains the law as a deterrent to war; arguments for and against its full application are cited.

"Associated Seminaries Hold Study Day on Conflict Between US and Iran." *GH* 72 (Dec. 25, 1979), 1032. A special meeting, "Iran Day," held at the Associated Mennonite Biblical Seminaries to bring about a better understanding and a response in prayer to the current Iranian-US conflict.

Akar, John T. "An African Views America." *MennLife* 22 (Jan., 1967), 19-23. Fundamental conflicts and opposing ideologies between Americans and Africans are dealt with from the perspective of an objective and dispassionate nationalist.

Bauman, Clarence; Dyck, Peter; and Harms, Doreen. "Communist Youth Festival." *Menn* 74 (Sept. 15, 1959), 564-65; *GH* 52 (Nov. 17, 1959), 985. Report on the Seventh World Festival (communist) of Youth and Students in Vienna attended by Mennonites whose purpose was "to learn and to witness." Summarizes the presentations at the "International Meeting of Young Christians" on the subject "Religion and Peace."

Beck, Carl. "A Church of Peacemakers Is a Church in Mission." *CanMenn* 13 (May 18, 1965), 3, 11. A report on the 1965 Tokyo Christian Student Peace Seminar entitled "Reconciliation in East Asia" which included much discussion of Japanese-Korean relationships.

Beck, Carl. "Japanese and Korean Students Find Each Other in Fellowship." *CanMenn* 13 (Sept. 28, 1965), 3. Report on a Korean-Japanese reconciliation work camp at the Mennonite Vocational School near Taegu, Korea, July 23-Aug. 2, 1965.

Beck, Carl. "Korea Church Leaders Ponder Peace." *CanMenn* 14 (Feb. 22, 1966), 1, 2. Report on first Korean Reconciliation Seminar held in Taegu, South Korea, in Oct., 1965, involving 34 pastors, seminary and university professors, elders, and lay leaders. The seminar discussed the history of Korean-Japanese hatred, industrial relations, and reconciliation as the object of Christian faith.

Beck, Carl. "Reconciliation Progress Surprises Workcampers." *CanMenn* 16 (Sept. 12, 1967), 1, 5. Report on the third MCC-sponsored Reconciliation Work Camp held in Taegu, Korea July 21 to Aug. 1 and involving thirteen young people from Japan as guests of Korean young people.

Beyler, Betsy. "Candidates for President: a Comparison." *Forum* 10 (Oct., 1976), 2-5; *MCC PS Wash. Memo* 7 (July-Aug., 1976), 1-7. A comparative analysis of Gerald Ford and Jimmy Carter focusing on their stand on some of the crucial issues: military spending, amnesty, foreign arms sales, nuclear disarmament, nuclear power, and foreign policy.

Bowman, Rufus. "The Historic Peace Churches Face the Future." In "Kansas Institute of International Relations 1938 Lecture Notes," ed. Agnes Wiens and Pauline Schmidt. Kansas Institute of International Relations, Bethel College, North Newton, Kan., 1938, 34-35. Pp. 81. MHL.

Clemens, Steve. "A Post-Indochina Foreign Policy?" *MCC PS Wash. Memo* 7 (May-June, 1975), 1-2. Congressional action since the defeat in Vietnam shows the US will continue to base its foreign policy on military might rather than humanitarian concern.

Cressman, Dave and Anita. "Especially Question the Rhetoric." *Forum* (Mar., 1971), A-4. North American judments about the affairs of other societies need to be questioned, and more particularly, the proposed boycott of Brazil by the Mennonite World Conference in an attempt to affect government policies needs to be re-examined.

Drescher, John M. "Cuba and Christian Concern." *GH* 55 (Nov. 13, 1962), 995. Some concerns arising out of the Cuban crisis are expressed. It is time to declare and believe that Christ is the Prince of Peace, and to confess that the church has not cared enough about the oppressed people of the world. This unconcern has helped give rise to communism.

Driedger, Leo. "Peacemakers in Africa." *CanMenn* 10 (Nov. 9, 1962), 6. Africa is a continent in turmoil. The need for concerned and praying Christian peacemakers is paramount.

Dyck, Ernie. "The Border That Divides." *With* 4 (July, 1971), 30. Views on the problems of American influence and Canadian nationalism.

Dyck, Peter J. "A New Wind Blowing?" *GfT* 8 (Sept.-Oct., 1973), 7, 17, 19. Comment on the Nixon-Breshnev talks and the possibility, if not of friendship, at least of cooperation and the end of the Cold War.

Dyck, Peter J. "Politics of Small Steps—Will Trust Come?" *Menn* 88 (Aug. 7, 1973), 464-5 Reflects on increased US-Soviet cooperation following Brezhnev's visit to the US, and offers suggestions for "small steps" toward superpowers reconciliation that can be implemented by individuals.

"EMC Sponsors Mid-East Teach-In." *CanMenn* 17 (Apr. 22, 1969), 3. Report on an April 11 teach-in at EMC involving Rabbi Krinsky of the U. of Virginia, Fayez A. Sayegh, as a representative of Arab interests, and Frank Epp. Epp said Palestine does not belong to the Jews if it does not also belong to the Arabs and it does not belong to the Arabs if it does not also belong to the Jews.

Epp, Frank H. "The Palestine Problem in Historical Perspective." *GH* 62 (June 10, 1969), 510-11; *CanMenn* 17 (June 6, 1969), 1, 2. Reviews Arab and Jewish historical claims to Palestinian soil, then describes the history of the conflict in this century, the role of the United Nations, the Arab perspective, and the wars following partitioning.

Ewert, Ethel G. "The Contributions of Dr. Emmet L. Harshbarger." Student paper for Constructive English, Feb. 12, 1943. Pp. 24. MLA/BeC.

Fast, Erna J. "Christian Students Face the Iron Curtain." *MennLife* 8 (July, 1953), 111-12, 143. Thoughts on international political divisions in Christian perspective. Christ provides a unity that goes beyond political divisions.

Fransen, Harold. "The Iranian Revolution." *Menn* 94 (Apr. 10, 1979), 269. The fall of the Shah's government in Iran is seen as a setback by the US.

Franz, Delton. "Chileans Try a Second Way." *Menn* 88 (Mar. 13, 1973), 174-75. Describes the peacefully-elected socialist government of Salvador Allende in Chile, explaining that the expropriation of American firms was due to the corporations' exploiting of Chilean resources.

Franz, Delton. "Foreign Aid at the Crossroads." *MCC PS Wash. Memo* 3 (Nov.-Dec., 1971), 3-5. US foreign aid needs to be restructured to cut back on military assistance and to focus aid toward people, not governments.

Franz, Delton. "Issues to Ponder in an Election Year." *MCC PS Wash. Memo* 7 (May-June, 1976), 1-2. Denounces high military spending at the expense of social programs and continuing military orientation of foreign policy.

Franz, Delton. "The Carter Doctrine: A Blatant Gamble with 'Limited' Nuclear War." *MCC PS Wash. Memo* 12 (May-June, 1980), 1-4. Compares Carter's stance of military aggressiveness toward the Persian Gulf region with the more rational approach of trying to understand the grievances of adversaries in the region.

Franz, Delton. "The Politics of Hostility and the Politics of Healing." *MCC PS Wash. Memo* 11 (Nov.-Dec., 1979), 1-2, 5. Cuba, Angola, and Vietnam might not have been driven into the Soviet camp if the US had not insisted on "cold war" foreign policy.

Franz, Delton. "Washington Report: Two Days with Bishop Kivengere of Uganda." *MennRep* 7 (Oct. 3, 1977), 6. Describes Ugandan Bishop Festo Kivengere's testimony before Congressional committees on the situation in Uganda, and his profound testimony to nonviolent love in the face of cruel dictatorship.

Franz, Delton (Review). *The Price of Power: Kissinger in the Nixon Whitehouse,* by Seymour M. Hersh. NY: Summit Books, 1983. Pp. 698. *CGR* 2 (Winter, 1984), 69-71. Hersh's book, outlining the subversion of legislative constraints by White House officials (such as Kissinger's presiding over the secret bombing of Cambodia in 1969-70 without the consent of Congress), provides an important perspective for Mennonite Christians concerned about the use of military power in implementing foreign policy.

Friesen, Duane K. *Christian Peacemaking and International Conflict: A Realistic Pacifist Perspective.* Scottdale: Herald Press, 1986. A major contribution which seeks to show that the biblical tradition stands in the service of peace with justice without violence. The church's task is to engage in sound action that befits the nature and calling of the church and thus influence and change systems of relationships, politically and internationally. The final chapter focuses on "Spiritual Resources for Empowerment."

Funk, Jacob. *War Versus Peace: A Short Treatise on War, Its Causes, Horrors, and Cost and Peace, Its History and Means of Advancement.* Elgin, Ill.: Brethren Publishing House, 1910. Pp. 175. Argues for the development of a universal court of arbitration, contending that the existing difficulties in such a proposition are outweighed by the potential savings, in money and morals, which will result.

Gerig, Benjamin. "World Organization for Peace." "Kansas Institute of International Relations 1940 Lecture Notes," ed. Margaret Ebersole and others. Kansas Institute of International Relations, Bethel College, North Newton, Kan., 1940, 11-18. Pp. 63. MHL. Notes of speaker approved by speaker.

Gibble, H. Lamar. "Search for a New China Policy." *Menn* 84 (July 1, 1969), 437-39. An assessment of the situation in China today and the present China policy of the USA. Suggests directions the USA might take in future relations with China.

Gingerich, Melvin. "Keeping Informed on World Affairs." *GH* 51 (Apr. 15, 1958), 349, 359. Argues that the nonresistant Christian who ventures to speak about world affairs should be well informed about differing interpretations of events. Suggested high quality publications are listed and described.

"Harder Reflects on His Task in the External Affairs Department." *MennRep* 9 (Nov. 26, 1979), 10. In an interview, Peter Harder, special assistant to Flora MacDonald, Canadian Minister for External Affairs, responds to questions on foreign policy, international peace, and more specifically, the Canadian response to Southeast Asia.

Habegger, Luann. "Exporting Men, Money, and Arms." *MCC PS Wash. Memo* 6 (July-Aug., 1974), 1-3. Statistics and comment on US foreign military aid to train military and police forces in policies favoring the US government.

Hamm, Ray. "Canada: Is Independence Possible?" *Menn* 88 (Mar. 13, 1973), 180-81. Hamm expresses the desire that Canada be freed from the intimate US presence there because of,

among other reasons, US domination of other peoples through multinational corporations and because the US profiteered on the war in Vietnam.

Headings, Verle E. "Conflict Evoking Images in International Exchange." Pp. 6. BfC.

Hershberger, Guy F., ed. "The Peace Committee Circular." Bibliography compiled by Peace Committee, Goshen College, Goshen, Ind., Jan., 1931. Pp. 6. MHL. Designed to assist Goshen College graduates teaching in the public schools counteract a "false patriotism: detrimental to international relations.

Hiebert, Linda Gibson and Hiebert, Murray. "What Is MCC Saying in Laos?" *Peace Section Newsletter* 8 (Feb., 1977), 1-2. The Mennonite tradition of offering aid to war victims makes it important that MCC assist the people of Laos in their time of rebuilding. Urges also that the US government become involved in in reconstruction assistance.

"International Meeting for Peace Called for Labor Day, September 5." *CanMenn* 14 (Aug. 9, 1966), 1, 10. Announcement of a proposed mass meeting of Canadians and Americans at the International Peace Gardens on the North Dakota-Manitoba border, to be addressed by A. J. Muste.

Isaac, Ron (Review). *The Star Spangled Beaver,* ed. John H. Redekop. Peter Martin Associates, Ltd., 1971. Pp. 263. *Forum* (Feb., 1973), 8. Relates excerpts from the book to illustrate the main theme of the underdog position of Canada in relation to the US. The volume contains the opinions and writings of 24 Canadians on the subject of Canadian-US relations, but Isaac criticizes the book for not including contributions from French Canadians and women, although he states the book is helpful in the search for a Canadian identity.

Jacobs, Donald R. "Race, an International Problem." *MennLife* 22 (Jan., 1967), 23-25. Blacks today "understand the intricate machinery of the power structures and see these structures almost hopelessly rigged against them. The important fact is that they now feel they know the facts earlier denied them."

Janzen, David. "A Program for the Mennonite Church." *CanMenn* 5 (Mar. 15, 1957), 2. Sets forth fifteen points toward an understanding of Christianity's encounter with communism. Also considers the role of pecifism in this encounter.

Janzen, David. "Mennonites and the East-West Conflict." *Christians Between East and West.* Winnipeg: Board of Christian Service,

Conference of Mennonites in Canada, [ca. 1965], 40-53. Links the rise of Communism with rejection of a false Christianity identifying with the exploiting class. Calls Mennonites to reject anticommunist propaganda as well as trust in nuclear weapons, in order to engage in deeper dialogue with communist people. Paper presented at the Canadian Conference Sessions, Altona, Man., July 20, 1963. Pp. 11. AMBS, MLA/BeC.

Janzen, William. "Ottawa Report: The Angolan Conflict." *MennRep* 6 (Jan. 12, 1976), 7. Relates the bloody history of Portuguese involvement in Angola and reflects on the possibility for peaceful coexistence of western and African people without the domination and military enforcement of the past.

Kehler, Peter. "Southeast Asia Work Camp Builds Roads to Assist Refugees from Mainland China." *CanMenn* 16 (Sept. 17, 1968), 3. Report on the Fourth South East Asia Reconciliation Work Camp held in Taipei involving eleven participants from Japan (including two US citizens), one from Indonesia, one PAXperson from Korea, and twenty-two from Taiwan. Korean and Indian delegates could not attend due to government restriction.

Keim, Albert N. "John Foster Dulles and the Protestant World Order Movement on the Eve of World War II." *Journal of Church and State* 21 (Winter, 1979), 73-89. Documents Dulles's involvement—active between 1937 and 1949—in the ecumenical church movement to promote world order and his role as mediator in the disagreement on intervention in European affairs. Roots his later Cold War belligerency to the convictions formed in this period of ecumenical involvement.

Klassen, John. "Viet Cong Student Urges Church to Help Stop War." *CanMenn* 15 (Oct. 17, 1967), 1. Report on a visit to Canada by three NLF students. One of the students suggested that Canada should cease selling weapons to the US and that Canada, as a member of the International Control Commission, should see to it that the Geneva agreements are enforced.

Klassen, William. "Blessed Are the Peacemakers." *CanMenn* 3 (Oct. 14, 1955), 6. Discusses the place of the Christian church in this world of international tension.

Koontz, Ted. "Foreign Policy Issues in the US Presidential Election." *Menn* 95 (Oct. 21, 1980), 608. Evaluation of the three major candidates' positions on international affairs includes discussion of their military policies.

Koontz, Ted. "Has SALT II Lost Its Savor?" *Menn* 94 (Dec. 4, 1979), 733; "SALT II Better Than No Salt." *GH* 72 (Sept. 25, 1979), 757. The writer

presents a brief argument for the case of SALT II. Although SALT II involves a choice between relative good and evil, we do not need to give up our vision of a world without nuclear catastrophe in order to support SALT II.

Koontz, Ted. "On Hostages, Diplomacy, and Rescue Raids." *Menn* 95 (May 27, 1980), 352. Analyzes the legalities of the rescue attempt for American hostages in Iran and urges American Mennonites to explore doing justice to the Iranians.

Koontz, Ted. "US-Soviet Relations After Afghanistan—1." *Menn* 95 (Aug. 19, 1980), 418. Interprets Soviet military intervention in Afghanistan as a great power saving face and protecting national strength.

Koontz, Ted. "US-Soviet Relations After Afghanistan—2." *Menn* 95 (Sept. 9, 1980), 512. In response to Soviet military intervention in Afghanistan, the US is preparing further military buildup, instead of strengthening the governments of the region and providing incentives for improved Soviet behavior.

Koontz, Ted. "US-Soviet Relations After Afghanistan—3." *Menn* 95 (Oct. 14, 1980), 592. Describes several varieties of peace witnessing that can be done without challenging the basic assumptions and commitments of the American audience.

Kraus, C. Norman. "Faint Not; Fight On." *GH* 39 (July 2, 1946), 289-90. The US fear of Russia, and the white attitude toward the blacks, are examples of attempts to overcome guilt through self-justification. Before reconciliation can take place one must admit his or her guilt and inability to solve the problem alone.

Kreider, Carl. "American Policy in the Formosa Straits." *ChrLiv* 2 (April, 1955), 22, 43. Discussion of American interests in Formosa (Taiwan) and the possibility of military intervention there.

Kreider, Carl. "Anti-Americanism." *ChrLiv* 4 (Aug., 1957), 18, 33. One of the contributing factors to anti-American sentiment abroad is the stationing of American troops on foreign soil.

Kreider, Carl. "Cuba: Revolt that Failed." *ChrLiv* 8 (July, 1961), 18, 35. The US-backed revolt in Cuba is a deplorable symbol of Cold War politics.

Kreider, Carl. "Eisenhower's Trip." *ChrLiv* 7 (Mar., 1960), 19, 37, 40. Dimming the success of the president's goodwill trip abroad is the fact that the amount of US defense spending limits the money available for foreign aid.

Kreider, Carl. "Failure at the Summit." *ChrLiv* 7

(Aug., 1960), 18, 40. Recent summit conference was doomed to failure because of the shooting down of a US spy plane deep within Russian territory.

Kreider, Carl. "H Bomb Foreign Policy." *ChrLiv* 1 (July, 1954), 35-36. The US atomic bomb test on Bikini Atoll which injured Japanese fishermen raises new fears about US military policy.

Kreider, Carl. "India and China." *ChrLiv* 6 (Nov., 1959), 18, 37. Description and analysis of the economic and military tensions between India and China.

Kreider, Carl. "Mistakes in the Middle East." *ChrLiv* 4 (Mar., 1957), 18, 34. Mistakes of the world powers in Middle East affairs include miscalculated military moves.

Kreider, Carl. "Quemoy and Matsu." *ChrLiv* 5 (Dec., 1958), 18, 37, 39. Two small islands between China and Taiwan serve as pawns in the military tensions between US and China.

Kreider, Carl. "Revolution in Cuba." *ChrLiv* 6 (Apr., 1959), 19, 39. The anti-American sentiment of the Castro government is inspired in part by US military aid to the brutal dictator Batista.

Kreider, Carl. "Russia vs. China." *ChrLiv* 9 (Feb., 1962), 18, 39. The breach between Russia and China is a reminder that the US need not arm all its allies against the threat of a combined Eastern bloc.

Kreider, Carl. "Signs of Hope." *ChrLiv* 2 (Oct., 1955), 22, 41-42. Relaxing military tensions at home and abroad are signs of improved US status in world affairs.

Kreider, Carl. "Sputnik." *ChrLiv* 5 (Jan., 1958), 18, 39. The Russian Sputnik satellite launching will affect American military strategy and spending.

Kreider, Carl. "Strife in Cyprus." *ChrLiv* 11 (Aug., 1964), 18-19. Search for a peaceful solution to the Turkish-Greek strife on Cyprus.

Kreider, Carl. "The Changing Pattern of International Relations." *ChrLiv* 3 (July, 1956), 22, 32-33. Post-World War II assumptions about American policy and military strategy are being called into question by recent international developments.

Kreider, Carl. "The Election of General Eisenhower." *Menn Comm* 7 (Jan., 1953), 31-33. Foreign policy promoting world peace is one agenda item for the new administration.

Kreider, Carl. "The Mutual Security Treaty with Japan." *ChrLiv* 7 (Sept., 1960), 19, 37. Recent political troubles with Japan over the ratification of the newest defense treaty could lead to war.

Kreider, Carl. "The United Nations Completes Its Ninth Year." *ChrLiv* 2 (Mar., 1955), 22, 45-46. Discussion of the UN peacekeeping mandate and the possibility of communist China membership.

Kreider, Carl. "The War in Indo-China." *ChrLiv* 1 (May, 1954), 35-36. Indo-China conflict is another example of the ineffectiveness of Western military intervention in dealing with communism.

Kreider, Carl. "Troubles Between Allies." *ChrLiv* 11 (May, 1964), 18-19. The Cold War lines are less clearly drawn in the face of disputes between allies.

Kreider, Carl. "US Marines in Lebanon." *ChrLiv* 5 (Oct., 1958), 19, 33. Sending Marines to the Mid-east to quell rising tensions is a serious mistake.

Kreider, Carl. "War and Revolution." *ChrLiv* 4 (Jan., 1957), 18, 39-40. Description of and comment upon British and French military intervention in Egypt, and the revolution in Hungary.

Kroeker, Marvin (Review). *Between the Eagle and the Dove: The Christian and American Foreign Policy,* by Ronald Kirkemo. Downers Grove: InterVarsity, 1976. Pp. 215. *ChrLeader* 40 (Oct. 11, 1977), 11. This "Christian perspective" on such issues as war, nuclear armaments, and international relations is not distinguishable from a "strictly secular" perspective. Therefore the book is neither newly insightful nor compatible with an Anabaptist-Mennonite view.

"Letter to Members of Congress." *Menn* 54 (Oct. 3, 1939), 3. Peace Committee of the Western District (GCM) says our nation should endeavor to adjust all international tensions by negotiation rather than by force of arms.

Lapp, John A. "A New Equation in the Middle East." *ChrLiv* 25 (Feb., 1978), 12-13. Comment on peace negotiations between Egypt and Israel, spurred by Sadat's visit to Israel.

Lapp, John A. "Camp David: The View from Jerusalem." *ChrLiv* 25 (Dec., 1978), 15, 31. Description of Camp David accords, with Israeli and Palestinian reactions.

Lapp, John A. "Getting Beyond Carter and Cuba in Africa." *ChrLiv* 25 (Aug., 1978), 15, 28. Comment on US policy toward the independence rebellion in Zaire.

Lapp, John A. "Is the UN Still Necessary?" *ChrLiv* 20 (Nov., 1973), 15, 24-25. An effective peacekeeper in the past, the UN now needs greater prestige and trust from member nations, including the US.

Lapp, John A. "Lifeboat or Luxury Liner?" *ChrLiv* 22 (Apr., 1975), 15, 34. US food politics includes threatening Arab oil countries with military action.

Lapp, John A. "The Foreign Policy Debate of 1964." *ChrLiv* 11 (Nov., 1964), 18-19. Contrasting Goldwater's militaristic goals with Fulbright's ideas of international cooperation and arms limitations.

Lapp, John A. "What the Canal Debate is All About." *ChrLiv* 24 (Nov., 1977), 19-20. The real issue for the US in the canal debate is the question of peaceful transition of authority or continued domination and imperialism.

Lapp, John A. (Review). *Anatomy of Anti-Communism,* by Peace Education Committee of Friends Service Committee. Hill and Wang, 1969. Pp. 138. *GH* 63 (Dec. 29, 1970), 1075. Highly recommends the book for its analysis of the national ideology of Cold War and its effect on American life and foreign policy.

Lapp, John A. (Review). *The Concept of Peace,* by John Macquarrie. Harper and Row, 1973. Pp. 82. *GH* 67 (June 11, 1974), 495. Although not a pacifist, Macquarrie presents a biblical vision of peace as healing in both interpersonal and international relations.

Lind, Loren. "Second Thoughts About China." *YCC* 47 (May 22, 1966), 8. Inquiry into the attitudes and policies underlying the relationship between the US and China.

Loewen, Theodore W. "Mennonite Pacifism: The Kansas Institute of International Relations." Social Science Seminar paper, Apr., 1971. Pp. 33. MLA/BeC.

Lord, Beverly Bowen and Lord, Charles R. Letter to the Editor. *ChrLead* 39 (Nov. 23, 1976), 14. Raises questions about the relationship of US foreign policy and the resulting stability in those countries with known human rights violations in terms of a hospitable environment for mission effort.

McCullum, Hugh. "In Bed with an Elephant." *Menn* 87 (May 30, 1972), 358-60. Events that have led to a falling out between Canada and the US are affecting Mennonites in Canada; what can be done to prevent a split in the international relationship?

Mennonite General Conference. "A Letter to the President." *GH* 54 (Sept. 19, 1961), 825. General Conference (MC) relates to President Kennedy Mennonite prayer support and petitions him to work for peace by easing the tensions contributing to the cold war.

Neal, Fred Warner. "War and Peace and the Problem of Berlin." 1961. Pp. 10. BfC.

Nickel, E. H. "World Peace Through World Law— Our Present Need." *CanMenn* 14 (Feb. 15, 1966), 7. Written by the secretary of World Federalists of Canada, article presents three alternatives to the destruction of civilization: massive nuclear deterrence; a transformation of human nature; rule of law. Advocates another option, system of international law, on the grounds that the first option is too volatile and the second unrealistic.

"Peace Section (US) Calls for Restraint in Iran Crisis, Supports SALT Amendment." *GH* 72 (Dec. 25, 1979), 1032, 1037. Meeting of MCC Peace Section (US) passed resolutions concerning the US-Iranian crisis, SALT II, and the proposed World Peace Tax Fund on Nov. 30-Dec. 1.

Pakraven, Parviz. "The Iran-Iraq War." *Menn* 95 (Dec. 16, 1980), 735. The world community should embrace humanitarian concern and call on Iraq to halt its aggression toward Iran in the war that will mean further destruction of already-depleted economies.

Peachey, Paul L. "Agape in Tokyo." *Fellowship* 26 (Nov., 1960), 10. Describes the riots in Tokyo as a symptom of a profound spiritual crisis in Japan of which American foreign policy is a principal cause.

Peachey, Paul L. "Interreligious Conference on Peace." *ChrCent* 83 (Apr. 13, 1966), 476-78. Author reflects on the interfaith dialogue at the conference on such issues as US military involvement in Vietnam, and a model for religious peace witness to a pluralistic society in which the religious community's primary role is to produce a moral climate in society conducive to peacemaking.

Peachey, Paul L. "Peacemakers in the Pacific." *GH* 52 (Feb. 17, 1959), 153. Peachey pays tribute to Reiji Oyama, a Japanese evangelist working to alleviate Japanese-Filipino conflict.

Peachey, Paul L. "Socialist and Pluralist Societies: The Anatomy of Encounter." Paper, [1975]. Pp. 20. MHL.

Peachey, Urbane. "Perspective for Contacts in the Soviet Union." *MCC PS Newsletter* 10 (July-Aug., 1980), 1-2. Suggestions for beginning steps of peacemaking between the people of the Soviet Union and the people of North America.

Ramseyer, Lloyd L. "Christian Love and Iron Curtains." *Menn* 71 (Sept. 25, 1956), 608-609.

Based on his own visit to Russia, the author urges further interchange between the Christians of both the United States and Russia to express love and peoplehood.

Raskcr, A. J. "The German Question and the Quest for Peace." MennLife 20 (July, 1965), 122, 123." . . . The basic Christian views of repentance and willingness to be reconciled are not only essential to a personal Christian life, but are also relevant in the realm of the political life."

Redekop, John H. "Christianity and Political Neutralism." CanMenn 4 (Aug. 10, 1956), 3, 15. The question is raised as to whether or not Christians can remain neutral in light of the oppression and suffering in the world.

Redekop, John H. "Christians in a World of International Confrontation." Menn 89 (July 9, 1974), 433-35. Describes international exploitation by firms based in North America, and the rise of nationalism which counters this colonialism. Concludes that the present nation-state system produces injustice and inequality, against which Christians must speak out.

Redekop, John H. "Race Consciousness Generates World Tension." CanMenn 3 (Mar. 4, 1955), 2. "One of the best ways to prevent communism or any other despicable 'ism' from exploiting anti-West, anti-Christian attitudes is to eliminate and eradicate the factors which give rise to those attitudes."

Redekop, John H., ed. The Star-Spangled Beaver. Toronto: Peter Martin Assoc. Ltd., 1971. Pp. 253. Includes: Brewin, Andrew, "American Foreign Policy," 99-105; Camp, Dalton, "United We Fall," 223-33; Diefenbaker, John G., "Across the Border," 36-45; Holmes, John W., "Lines Written for a Canadian-American Conference," 89-98; Keenleyside, Hugh, "Letter to an American Friend," 6-23; Manor, F. S., "Are They the New Romans," 106-113; Pickersgill, J. W., "The Americans Are Not Romans," 114-17; Thompson, Robert N., "The Foreign Policy of the United States of America," 238-53. Essays dealing with war and peace are annotated separately under author. Prominent Canadian leaders discuss Canadian-US political and military policies and interrelationships, especially Canada's involvement in US foreign policy.

Regehr, Ernie. "Ottawa Report: Canada Sides with Oppressor in Angola." MennRep 3 (Apr. 2, 1973), 7. Canada is implicated in the Angolan War because it provides the colonialist Portugal with export earnings which help finance the war, and because Canadian government policies toward Portugal differ from its words.

Regehr, Ernie. "The Days of Wine and Fighter Aircraft." MennRep 10 (Apr. 28, 1980), 7. Analysis of the detrimental effects the Canadian government's decision to buy new F-18A fighter aircraft will have on the Canadian economy and international relations.

Rempel, Peter H. and Miller, Larry. "Church Life in Russia: Two Impressions by North Americans." MennRep 9 (Dec. 10, 1979), 5. These reports from a study tour to Russia include concern over the arms race and the need for sincere peace initiatives by the United States.

Roth, Willard E. "Ireland and Mennonites." GH 71 (June 13, 1978), 470-71. Visitor to Ireland reviews the complexity of the Irish conflict, searching for ways Mennonites might contribute to peacemaking there.

Schmidt, Linda. "Perpetuating Repression: US Training of Foreign Military and Police." Peace Section Newsletter 9 (Jan.-Feb., 1978), 4-8. The training of foreign military and police has been an integral part of the US foreign policy over the past twenty-five years. The countries which have received large amounts of military and economic aid are the same countries which have been cited most often for human rights violations.

Schrag, Robert M. "Peace Fellowship Hears Reappraisal of China." CanMenn 14 (Apr. 12, 1966), 3; YCC 47 (May 22, 1966), 5. Report on the March 17-19 IPF conference at Bethel College under the theme "China and Christian Concern." S. F. Pannabecker spoke at the conference as did George Beckmann of KU. Participants saw a US State Department film on China and a color documentary by Felix Greene, a British producer.

Schroeder, Richard J. "The Cutting Edge." ChrLead 36 (Dec. 11, 1973), 25. Analysis of the Arab-Israeli conflict. US consumption of energy is seemingly directing a more open foreign policy toward the Arab side while lessening the support of Israel.

Schroeder, Richard J. "The Cutting Edge." ChrLead 38 (May 13, 1975), 17. Analysis of US foreign policy and international commitments.

Shenk, Wilbert R. "The Perils of Propaganda." CanMenn 18 (Aug. 28, 1970), 7. Analyzes the ambiguities and pitfalls of the perceived and real relationships between American missionaries and American intelligence gathering. Provides some guidelines for missionaries reporting from and about the countries where they are guests and, therefore, "obliged to be a model of sensitivity and good manners."

Shetler, Sanford G. "America Criticized in Washington Peace Conference." ST 44 (June,

1976), 9-11. Briefly summarizes conference proceedings and criticizes the Anti-American rhetoric and political activism of speakers and participants alike.

Shetler, Sanford G. "'Americans Are Stupid Diplomats.'" *GfT* 6 (Mar.-Apr., 1971), 18. American concessions to communist countries since World War II show that Christians cannot place their hopes for peace in diplomacy or "peace schemes."

Shetler, Sanford G. "Just What Is Social Justice?" *GfT* 15 (May-June, 1980), 14-15. Church people should be concerned first with the inequities of the local setting, instead of attempting the impossible task of establishing international justice.

Thomson, Murray and Regehr, Ernie. "Canadian Military Sales." *PlMon* 1 (July, 1977), 5. Documents Canadian arms sales to the Third World and comments on Canada's role in the militarization of the Third World.

Voth, David L. "An Examination of Three Mennonite Theological Alternatives with Special Note of their Views Toward Participation in Foreign Policy." MA in Peace Studies thesis, AMBS, 1982. Pp. 117. Compares the views of John H. Yoder, Gordon D. Kaufman, and Duane K. Friesen on discipleship, the believers' church, and nonresistance in an effort to determine whether Mennonite participation in the foreign policy arm of the government is theologically consistent with Mennonite faith.

Wasser, Myrtle. "The Evils of Wars and the Methods of Preventing Future Wars." *Menn* 60 (Sept. 18, 1945), 9-11. Stresses the need for international cooperation in the task of peacemaking.

Weaver, Carol Ann. "The Philippines—and US." *Forum* (Mar., 1972), 7-8. The US is considered one of the chief offenders perpetuating the deep-seated political, religious, economic, and educational problems in the Philippines.

# 9
# Justice

## A. General

"Alternatives to Violence." *RepConsS* 38 [*sic,* 35] (Jan., 1978), 2. Brief report of a peace seminar sponsored by the Mennonite Committee of Swaziland which was held Oct. 15, 1977 at Mbabane.

"Augsburger Predicts Increasing Violence in Society." *MennRep* 9 (June 25, 1979), 9. At a press luncheon, Myron Augsburger predicted that interpersonal violence in our crowded urban areas will be a greater threat than war.

Alderfer, Helen. "Family News and Trends." *ChrLiv* 12 (June, 1965), 41-42. Comments on American manufacture of toys emphasizing war and violence.

Alexander, John F. "Politics, Repentance, and Vision." *GH* 67 (July 23, 1974), 564-66. Reprinted from *The Other Side.* What American society needs is not a political program for social reform—since political gains are grossly inadequate—but a program of repentance to change people's priorities from material comforts to justice, peace, and healing.

Anderson, John B. and Penner, Archie. "Get Active Politically: Two Views." *Christianity Today* 20 (March 26, 1976), 10-12. Anderson urges evangelical Christians to become politically involved with the issues of economic injustice while Penner insists that any such involvement must find expression within the limits imposed by the concept of agape love exemplified by Christ.

Arndt, Bill. Letter to the Editor. *ChrLead* 36 (Jan. 23, 1973), 17. Encouragement for Mennonites to express outrage at the violence in Southeast Asia, especially if the church is going to take stands on issues like abortion.

Augsburger, David W. "What Answer to Violence?" *GH* 63 (Nov. 17, 1970), 970-71. Origin and character of violence and the Christian answer to its expression.

Augsburger, David W. "Who Is Bringing Communism?" *MBH* 13 (Apr. 19, 1974), 2-3.

Any society that preserves the status quo at any cost and sacrifices justice is ripe for communism.

Aukerman, Dale. "God's Rogue." *ChrLiv* 10 (Dec., 1963), 3-5. Reprinted from *Gospel Messenger.* Sir George MacLeod, former moderator of the Church of Scotland, speaks out eloquently against war and injustice.

"Bombers and Arsonists Are Hastening Integration and Freedom in the South." *CanMenn* 13 (Mar. 30, 1965), 3, 10. Points out that the very violence of those resisting integration is defeating their cause, as the church is roused from apathy to sympathy for the victims of the violence.

"Brazil Volunteers Imprisoned Without Charge." *EV* 90 (July 10, 1977), 8. MCC volunteer, Thomas Capuano of Altamont, NY and Father Lawrence Rosenbaugh, an American Catholic priest, were arrested without charge in Recife, Brazil, and held for four days until the American consulate was able to arrange for their release.

Barrett, Lois [Janzen]. "Delegation Sees Continuation of Vietnam War." *Menn* 90 (Mar. 25, 1975), 190-91; also "Torture and Harrassment Keeps Thieu in Power," *MennRep* 5 (Mar. 31, 1975), 2. Gene Stoltzfus, former service worker in Vietnam, reports on the continued war and repression of South Vietnamese people, as he witnessed it during a recent visit.

Barrett, Lois, comp. "Patricia Erb: Torture and Testimony." *Menn* 92 (Sept. 13, 1977), 518-19; *ChrLead* 40 (Oct. 11, 1977), 2. Patricia Erb, missionary daughter in Argentina, tells her story of imprisonment and torture at the hands of Argentine police, trained by the US military, for her nonviolent work with the poor.

Barrett, Lois, comp. "Tools of Torture: 'Made in USA.' The War Is Not Yet Over." *MennRep* 4 (Mar. 4, 1974), 7. Relates story of a young Vietnamese woman beaten and tortured by

South Vietnamese police using US-made instruments. Same story related in *Menn* 89 (Jan. 15, 1974), 48.

Barrett, Lois [Janzen]. "When They Draft Women." *Menn* 87 (May 9, 1972), 324. If and when women are drafted, there may be some benefits. Women will need to deal more directly with the issues of war and violence and with the formulation of clear positions on these issues.

Bartel, Peter. "Revolution, Mennonite Style." Paper for War, Peace, and Revolution class, AMBS, Elkhart, Ind. n.d. Pp. 3. AMBS.

Beck, Carl. "Justice Shall Roll Down." Sermon preached at College Mennonite Church, Goshen, Ind., Jan. 30, 1955. Pp. 9. MHL.

Bender, John M. "Youth Attacked Twice in Subway Mercy Mission." *MennRep* 9 (Apr. 30, 1979), 10. A new volunteer around-the-clock patrol along a New York subway line is meeting violence with nonviolence.

Bender, Titus. "Peacemaking." *GH* 60 (June 6, 1967), 308-309. Peace is more than the absence of violence. It is actively relating to persons, especially to those oppressed by any form of injustice in the congregation, community, or world.

Bergen, Henry. Letter to the Editor. *MBH* 18 (Dec. 21, 1979), 10. MCC in southern Africa should stand for peace and justice for the displaced on both sides of the Zimbabwe/Rhodesia political fence, rather than favoring the Patriotic Front.

Beyler, Betsy. "Continued Suffering in Kampuchea?" *MCC PS Wash. Memo* 12 (July-Aug., 1980), 1-2, 10. The US vote to seat the Pol Pot regime in the UN is a vote for continued war and repression in Kampuchea.

Beyler, Betsy. "Human Rights Criteria for US Foreign Aid." *MCC PS Wash. Memo* 9 (Mar.-Apr., 1977), 4-5. In spite of Congressional authority to cut off military and economic aid to countries which violate human rights, a large percentage of US aid is not covered by these provisions.

Bicksler, Harriet S. (Review). *Christ and Violence,* by Ronald J. Sider. Scottdale and Kitchener: Herald Press, 1979. *EV* 92, Part 1, (Dec. 25, 1979), 10, 11; Part 2, (Jan. 10, 1980), 8. Contains essays originally presented at the New Call to Peacemaking conferences in Lancaster, Pa., and Green Lake, Wis. Essays look at Jesus' life and teachings as a model for our approach to violence. Part 2 of the review, focusing on chapters 3 and 4, highlights Sider's emphasis on the centrality of the cross and resurrection as a basis for nonviolence.

Bliss, Betsy. "American Prisons: a Crime." *GH* 65, Part 1, (Jan. 4, 1972), 6-8; Part 2, (Jan. 11, 1972), 30-32. Reprinted from *US Catholic/Jubilee* (May, 1971). Documents examples of the violence, torture, and neglect characteristic of prison life, and asserts that prisons produce crime. Maintains that the American correctional system is based, not on the goal of rehabilitation, but on public vengeance.

Block, Wendell (Review). *Christian Mission and Social Justice,* by Samuel Escobar and John Driver. Scottdale: Herald Press, 1978. Pp. 112. *MBH* 17 (Sept. 1, 1978), 37. Reviewer observes that the book's thesis is that the church in the post-colonial era must identify with the oppressed and live as a messianic community of liberation and justice.

Boers, Arthur Paul. "A Spirituality Primer for Activists." MA in Peace Studies thesis, AMBS, 1983. Pp. 93. An introduction to spirituality directed toward Christians who are concretely seeking to bring about God's Kingdom of peace and justice. The first perspective explored is the political nature of spirituality. The finding is that prayer without justice is false prayer; God rejects rites of spirituality that take place in contexts of oppression and injustice. The second perspective explored has to do with the metaphors of spirituality and how these dimensions affect the activist. The finding is that while prayer enriches us, prayer also offers no guarantees of effective activism.

Boers, Arthur Paul. "Speaking for the Imprisoned." *MBH* 18 (Apr. 27, 1979), 18-19. Part of Amnesty International's concern for those unjustly imprisoned includes a special concern for conscientious objectors to war.

Bonpane, Blase, A., Fr. "The Role of the Christian in Violent Change." Address delivered at Goshen College All School Study Day, Feb. 21, 1969. Pp. 11. MHL, MLA/BeC.

Bontrager, Herman. "Relief, Development, and Justice: Synthesis or Tension?" *Peace Section Newsletter* 9 (Aug.-Sept., 1979), 4-8. Notes that the expressed concern to make MCC programs more sensitive to justice problems has revealed the important need for MCC staff to develop a self-consciousness as workers for justice. Lists some of the MCC projects for justice.

Born, Daniel (Review). *Christian Mission and Social Justice,* by Samuel Escobar and John Driver. Scottdale: Herald Press, 1978. In *ChrLead* 41 (Aug. 15, 1978), 16. The authors explore the range of theological attitudes toward social justice in Latin America.

Bowman, Jim. "No Papayas for the Poor." *Sojourners* 8 (June, 1979), 12. Experience in Indonesia supports the view that there are enough resources in the world for everyone. When the rich gain concentrated control, however, the poor lose access to these resources.

Boyer, C. W. "Look on These Things." *EV* 90 (June 10, 1977), 12, 13. Careful discerning needs to be practiced in the selection of television programs because objectionable material, such as crime and violence, are presented.

Brandt, Diana. Letter to the Editor. *Menn* 91 (Mar. 30, 1976), 226-27. Maintains that social violence cannot be uncritically linked to violence in the media. Cites news programs as more conducive to viewer violence than fictitious narratives which give violence an understandable context.

Brandt, Laurie. "Right Wing Seeks to End US Compliance with UN Sanctions Against Rhodesia." *MCC PS Wash. Memo* 11 (Jan.-Feb., 1979), 3, 7. Discusses the injustices of the white minority rule in Rhodesia and the resulting bloodshed and violence.

Brandt, Laurie. "South African Crisis Stirs Action in United Nations and Congress." *MCC PS Wash. Memo* 9 (Nov.-Dec., 1977), 4, 9. The UN arms embargo to South Africa is insufficient protest against the apartheid system.

Bressler, John F. "God Requires Social Justice." *ChrMon* 29 (Aug., 1937), 248. Sunday School lesson from Leviticus focuses on justice and equality.

Brown, Robert McAfee. "We Must Love One Another or Die." *GH* 66 (Dec. 25, 1973), 957-58. Reprinted from *California Living* (Dec. 24, 1967). Behind the manger lies the shadow of the cross, the brutal end of life for one who translated love into justice and refused to believe peace was only an ideal.

Brubaker, Paul. "Del Monte's Martial Law Pineapples." *Sojourners* 8 (Oct., 1978), 16. Describes how a company like Del Monte in the Philippines, a country of rampant unemployment, practices a capital-intensive agriculture. This practice displaces more people than it employs.

Brubaker, Paul. "Signs of Hope in the Cities." *Sojourners* 8 (Nov., 1978), 20. A description of six groups working in inner-city neighborhoods to enable poor people to obtain decent, affordable housing.

Brunk, Conrad G. "'Active' Nonresistance." *GH* 63 (Oct. 27, 1970), 902-904. Part three of a college baccalaureate address calls nonresistant Christians to witness against the violence of dissenter and patriot and to embrace a pacifism that strikes at the roots of violence and hate.

Burkholder, J. Lawrence. "Justice: The Arithmetic of Love." *ChrLiv* 8 (Apr., 1961), 24-26. Justice is the organizational form of love, and it needs the creativity of the personal encounter to lend warmth.

Burkholder, J. Lawrence. "The Mennonite Concept of the Church." *ChrLiv* 5, Part 1, "The Church," (Feb., 1958), 22-23, 40; Part 2, "The Community," (Mar., 1958), 22-23, 39. Rather than being known for its ethnic ties, the church should be known for its witness to peace and justice.

Burkholder, J. Richard. "A Perspective on Mennonite Ethics." *Kingdom, Cross, and Community.* Ed. John R. Burkholder and Calvin Redekop. Scottdale: Herald Press, 1976. 151-66. Christian responsibility in the social order does not mean "top down" responsibility utilizing the means and accepting the norms of the social order, but rather a messianic community nonviolently serving needs and working for justice. Burkholder's conclusions are drawn after careful analysis of and conversation with Mennonite writers on nonresistance and responsibility: Gordon Kaufman, John H. Yoder, Guy F. Hershberger.

Burkholder, J. Richard. *Continuity and Change: A Search for a Mennonite Social Ethic.* Akron, Pa.: MCC Peace Section, 1977. Pp. 31. MHL. Explores, in dialogue with Yoder's *Politics of Jesus,* the adequacy of the central principle of nonresistance as a foundation for ethical thinking. Concludes that justice is the goal of the kingdom order and the love ethic of the Sermon on the Mount the means to the goal.

Burkholder, J. Richard. "Witness to the State: A Mennonite Perspective." *GH* 69 (Aug. 17, 1976), 621-24. A sectarian version of witnessing to the state is to speak the truth about oppression, injustice, and evil, without succumbing to the temptation to impose one's faith on others.

Burnett, [Kris]Tina Mast and Kroeker, Wally. "Affluent People Who Neglect the Poor Are Not the People of God." *Menn* 94 (Feb. 20, 1979), 128-29. MCC (International) annual meeting discussed issues of justice and human rights, aid to Vietnam, native American outreach, hunger concerns, and militarism.

Burrell, Curtis E., Jr. "A Primer on the Urban Rebellion." *Menn* 83 (June 18, 1968), 418-20; *ChrLead* 31 (June 18, 1968), 4-6; *GH* 61 (June 18, 1968), 534-36; *EV* 81 (June 17, 1968), 5, 13-14. The judgment of God which cries "let my people go" is at the heart of the current urban "riots." Years of injustice and white racism are the cause of the cities' upheavals. White Christians must repent of their racism and follow new black leadership if America is to be reformed.

Burrell, Curtis E., Jr. "Our Mennonite Oppressors." *GH* 58 (Sept. 7, 1965), 783-84. Asking the weak and powerless to accept—not resist—intolerable living conditions is a subtle but real form of oppression exercised by Mennonite people.

Byl, Jürgen. "Jan van Leiden: Violence and Grace." *MennLife* 26 (July, 1971), 103-105. Comments on literary productions about the militant leader who is of historical interest to Mennonites, Jan van Leiden of Münster.

"College Students Focus on Christianity and Socialism." *MennRep* 9 (Dec. 10, 1979), 3. "Christianity and Socialism" was the topic of discussion at the 1979 Intercollegiate Peace Fellowship Assembly where such issues as liberation theology, various forms of socialism, and oppression were addressed.

Capuano, Thomas M. "Scenes and Echoes of Torture in Brazil." *New York Times* (Sept. 1, 1977), 31. MHL. Former Mennonite missionary to Recife, Brazil, recounts the mistreatment of Brazilian prisoners observed during four-day imprisonment.

Charles, Bob, and Suderman, Dale. Letter to the Editor. *Menn* 89 (Apr. 23, 1974), 278. Peacemakers must decry the false peace of detente, which is bought at the price of oppression for small anad powerless nations.

Charles, Howard H. "The Conquest and the Problem of Violence." *Builder* 32 (Nov., 1982), 35-39. Summarizes the Old Testament conquest theme and some representative approaches taken to the moral problem raised by the theme before suggesting that Millard Lind has provided some useful guidelines with which to think about the issues in *Yahweh Is a Warrior* (Herald Press, 1980).

Chauvin, Jacques. "Peace and the Christian Church." *Menn* 93 (June 27, 1978), 420-21. Peace is inseparable from the struggle for justice. The church, in accumulating wealth, fails to live "shalom," because it separates itself from the struggle for justice.

Cleveland, Harlan. "Trials and Tests at the UN." *ChrLiv* 12 (Aug., 1965), 14-15, 28-29. The issues of nuclear weapons, unsolicited foreign intervention, human rights, and equality threaten the UN's peacekeeping ability.

Curry, Jan. "A History of the Houma Indians and the Story of Federal Nonrecognition." *American Indian Journal of the Institute for the Development of Indian Law* 5 (Feb., 1979), 8-28. The government's failure to recognize the Houma Indians of Louisiana as an Indian tribe has resulted in many injustices, such as the loss of land, hunting and fishing rights, etc. MCCer Jan

Curry has researched and written this history in order to help the Houmas establish their claim to tribal status.

DeFehr, Arthur. "Is God for the Poor and Homeless?" *MBH* 19 (Oct. 10, 1980), 2-5. A volunteer who helped set up a relief project in Southeast Asia in the middle of three competing armies reflects on response to human need.

Derstine, C. F. "The Black Blotch on American Civilization." *ChrMon* 23 (Mar., 1931), 92. The mob violence and lynchings of blacks and other foreigners is a terrible injustice.

Derstine, C. F. "The Disturbed Waters of the Political and Economic Sea." *ChrMon* 25 (Nov., 1933), 350-51. None of the three prevailing social systems—capitalism, socialism, communism—will attain social justice.

Derstine, C. F. "What the World Ought to Do." *ChrMon* 32 (Oct., 1940), 318-19. Belief in the Son of God and the practice of social justice and stewardship are biblical prescriptions for a war-torn world.

Dick, Ernie (Review). *A Strategy for Peace*, by Frank H. Epp. Grand Rapids: Eerdmans, 1973. Pp. 128. "Essays 'Point Finger' at Exploitation and Injustice." *MennRep* 4 (Apr. 1, 1974), 8. Although the essays were delivered as addresses in the late 1960s and early 1970s, their message of striving after peace remains timely. Most helpful essays deal with themes of nationalism, dialogue between pacifists and nonpacifists, arms buildup, complicity of the Christian church in making war.

Dirks, Sylvester (Review). *Mission and the Peace Witness*, by Robert L. Ramseyer. Kitchener: Herald Press, 1979. Pp. 134. *MBH* 19 (Feb. 1, 1980), 29. Reviewer criticizes the perceived tendency of Mennonite missiologists to accept tenets of liberation theology.

Dirrim, Allen W. "Political Implications of Sixteenth Century Hessian Anabaptism." *MennLife* 19 (Oct., 1964), 179-83. The Anabaptists' striving for a free and separate church and their absolute New Testament ethic, plus real and alleged connections with the Peasants' Revolt in 1525, are reasons why they were not accepted by their contemporaries.

Drescher, John M. "Kill Toys Teach the 'Game' of Killing." *MBH* 7 (Nov. 29, 1968), 4-5; *Menn* 83 (Dec. 3, 1968), 746-47. Since replicas of the "machines of violence" contradict the spirit of Jesus, Christians should boycott and protest vigorously against "war toys."

Drescher, John M. (Editorial). "Atrocities on

Trial." *GH* 63 (Jan. 13, 1970), 29. In light of the fact that the essence of war is violence and the denial of all that is sacred in life, questions the sense of trying soldiers for committing "atrocities."

Drescher, John M. (Editorial). "Will We Awake?" *GH* 61 (Apr. 30, 1968), 385. Editorial reflects on the violence and hate bred into American society and its effects on a person of nonviolence such as Martin Luther King.

Driedger, Leo, *et. al.* "War and Rumors of War." *Menn* 78 (Nov. 5, 1963), 664-66. A symposium on war and its meaning for peacemakers. Subjects include children and the bomb, fallout shelters, disarmament, peace witness in service and evangelism, and alternatives to violence.

Dueck, Abe (Review). *No King But Caesar? A Catholic Lawyer Looks at Christian Violence,* by William R. Durland. Scottdale: Herald Press, 1975. Pp. 182. *MBH* 15 (Nov. 12, 1976), 34-35. Recommends this book for its biblical exegesis on violence, its examination of the just war theory, and its review of the types of violence found in contemporary movements.

Dueck, Abe (Review). *The Ethics of Revolution,* by Martin H. Scharlemann. St. Louis: Concordia, 1971. In *Direction* 1 (July, 1972), 102. An evaluation of the contemporary situation in terms of the revolutionary forces that are at work in society.

Durland, William R. *No King But Caesar?* Scottdale: Herald Press, 1975. Pp. 182. Catholic lawyer urges Christians to assume the risk of nonviolence through faith and hope. Argument proceeds in three sections: an examination of the pacifist and nonresistant ethic of the biblical materials, especially the Sermon on the Mount and Isaiah; an historical overview of Christian responses to state violence, from the apostolic peace gospel and the pacifism of the early church, through the Constantinian synthesis to the contemporary confusion; an analysis of that contemporary confusion concerning the demands of God and Caesar, particularly in the context of the Roman Catholic church.

Ediger, Max. "Justice—for All God's People." *Menn* 95 (July 22, 1980), 440-41. Justice is done when the rich do not merely share of their wealth with the poor but establish right relationships with them by sharing of their lives.

Ediger, Max. "Justice Is Not Just Us." *Intercom* 24 (Jan., 1980), 6-7. Describes the difference between community development and community organization and urges MCC to work at organization in order to further justice.

Ediger, Peter J. *The Prophet's Report on Religion in North America.* Faith and Life Press, 1971.

Excerpts reprinted in *Post-American* 1 (Spring, 1972), 2-3. Decries the injustice and violence in American life and the militaristic foreign policy.

Elias, Jacob W. "Games Christians Watch." *Menn* 88 (Nov. 20, 1973), 666-68. Links the "sports philosophy" of winning at any cost, even violence, to the realms of life: competition in the business world; political tactics of Watergate; Cambodian bombing.

Elias, Jacob W. "Last Night's Game." *MBH* 13 (Sept. 6, 1974), 26-29. Questions the philosophy of violence and competition promoted by spectator sports.

Engle, Albert H. "The Violence of God." *EV* 86 (Apr. 10, 1973), 6. The violence of God is motivated by love and so must our lives be motivated by God's love in Christ.

Epp, Edgar W. "The Church and Criminal Justice: Key Issues." Address given at Offender Ministries Conference, Chicago, Ill., Sept. 18-20, 1980. Pp. 11. AMBS.

Epp, Frank H. "The American Revolution and the Canadian Evolution." *GH* (Oct. 28, 1975), 771-72; *MennRep* 5 (Nov. 10, 1975), 8. Christian nonresistants in both the US and Canada need to reflect soberly on their national histories. While American revolutionary spirit has sought a violent solution to every problem, Canadian gradualism has meant being sucked into the military strategies of Britain and the US.

Epp, Frank H. "The Canadian Crisis: There Must Be a Better Way." *World Federalist* Canadian Section (Nov./Dec., 1970), C1-C2. Criticizes the extreme measures of the Quebec Liberation Front's bombings, kidnappings, and assassinations, and the Canadian government's equally extreme invocation of the War Measures Act. Argues that in a truly democratic society, other options for resolving conflict are always available.

Epp, Frank H. "The Palestinians: A Hi-jacked People." *World Federalist,* Canadian Edition (Nov./Dec., 1970), 6-7, 9. Reviews the plight of Palestinian Arabs driven from their lands and treated as non-citizens in their homeland. Analyzes recent Palestinian acts of violence as an attempt to focus world attention on their plight, since peaceful communication has been ineffective.

Epp, Frank H. (Editorial). "Evangelism and Revolution." *CanMenn* 14 (Sept. 13, 1966), 5. A call to "spearhead a world revolution" in which a rich society is called to adopt the way of the cross.

Epp, Frank H. (Review). *A Russian Dance of Death:*

*Revolution and Civil War in the Ukraine,* by Dietrich Neufeld. Winnipeg: Hyperion Press, 1977. Pp. 142. "A Russian Dance Should be Read by All Under 50." *MennMirror* 7 (Jan., 1978), 15. Summarizes the contents of this book which is a personal narrative arising out of the author's experience during the civil war in the Ukraine and the terror inflicted by anarchist Nestor Makhno. Describes the book as valuable because of the author's personalized account and critical assessment of the events and tragedies that befell the Mennonites.

Epp, Jacob. P. "The Mennonite Selbstschutz in the Ukraine: an Eyewitness Account." *MennLife* 26 (July, 1971), 138-42. A report on the emergence of the Selbstschutz (self-protection), its involvement as a protective force, and its disbanding.

Erb, Alta Mae (Review). *Prudence Crandall, Woman of Courage,* by Elizabeth Yates. Aladdin Books, 1955. *ChrLiv* 3 (Feb., 1956), 33. Recommends this story of a nineteenth-century woman who worked for justice for blacks, especially in education.

Erb, Paul. "World War III." *GH* 41 (Apr. 20, 1948), 363. It is not Christian to oppose communism by military pressure even though communism is anti-Christian. The Christian must remember that there is no righteous side in power politics.

Escobar, Samuel. "The Social Responsibility of the Church." *ChrLiv* 17 (Oct., 1970), 23-27. Church's mission must embrace social justice as well as evangelism.

Escobar, Samuel and Driver, John. *Christian Mission and Social Justice.* Institute of Mennonite Studies, Missionary Studies No. 5. Scottdale: Herald Press, 1978. Pp. 112. Four essays bring to bear biblical perspectives and a historical critique derived from a reappraisal of the distinctive Anabaptist experience in the Reformation on the issues of mission and justice today. The application of these perspectives results in seeing missions and justice as necessary complements rather than a polarity. Essays are: "The Need for Historical Awareness;" "The Gospel and the Poor;" "Reform, Revolution, and Missions;" "The Anabaptist Vision and Social Justice."

Evangelicals for Social Action. "Can My Vote Be Biblical?" *ChrLead* 43 (Oct. 21, 1980), 2-5. Guidelines for making Christ lord of our politics include emphasis on peacemaking and justice for the poor.

Ewert, Alden H. "Why Alternate Service." *ChrLead* 17 (Aug. 1, 1953), 4. Love of neighbors and enemies necessitates total rejection of participation in violence and suggests instead constructive service, e.g., in mental health services or in ministry to war-torn Korea.

"Firearms Placed on Altar." *GH* 65 (July 18, 1972), 582. United Methodist hand gun owner relinquishes his weapons as "a witness for domestic disarmament in a land of escalating violence."

Fast, Henry A. "Mennonite Response to the Russian Revolution." *JChSoc* 6 (Fall, 1970), 8. An evaluation of the Russian Mennonite response, which was largely ethnic, cultural, and narrowly religious, to the Russian Revolution of 1917.

Finger, Reta (Review). *Peace Be with You,* by Cornelia Lehn. Faith and Life Press, 1980. Pp. 126. *Daughters of Sarah* 7 (Nov.-Dec., 1981), 20-21. Praises Lehn's collection of peacemaking stories as a vivid portrayal of the power of forgiveness and active gentleness in the midst of suffering and violence.

Ford, Leighton. "The Church and Evangelism in a Day of Revolution." *GH* 62, Part 1, (Dec. 9, 1969), 1046-48; Part 2, (Dec. 16, 1969), 1076-78. Contemporary revolutions issue a crucial call to change, but only the Christian message will cause effective, lasting change, because revolutions must grapple with sin. The gospel deals with sin, but one must follow conversion with commitment to social change.

Ford, Leighton. "Violence." *GH* 64 (July 6, 1971), 601. With confession of sin, peace begins within and moves outward in forgiveness, rejecting the violence and hatred of both extreme positions in conflict.

Foth, Margaret. "Abused—and Nowhere to Go." *Menn* 94 (Nov. 20, 1979), 701. Family violence is a concern of society, and communities need to respond to the victims.

Fransen, David Warren (Review). *Canada's Refugee Policy: Indifference or Opportunism,* by Gerald Dirks. McGill-Queen's Univ. Press, 1977. "Immigration Policies Based on Economic and Political Concerns." *MennRep* 9 (Dec. 10, 1979), 8. Canadian immigration policies are based on economic and political concerns rather than human need.

Franz, Delton. "A Witness on Behalf of the Powerless. *MCC PS Wash. Memo* 9 (July-Aug., 1977), 3-4. Patty Erb's meeting with members of Congress alerted them to injustice being done to the poor and prisoners in a country supported by US military aid. Franz, Delton. "A Witness on Behalf of the Powerless. *MCC PS Wash. Memo* 9 (July-Aug., 1977), 3-4. Patty Erb's meeting with members of Congress alerted them to injustice being done to the poor and prisoners in a country supported by US military aid.

Franz, Delton. "After the First Year: A Report Card on Carter's Human Rights Course." *Peace Section Newsletter* 9 (Jan.-Feb., 1978), 1-3. Looks at the status of financial aid to oppressive regimes as one of the ways to evaluate Carter's human rights program. Concludes that the Congress deserves "B-" grade for its persistent monitoring and a "C" grace for its candor.

Franz, Delton. "Against the Wall in Latin America." *GH* 67 (Nov. 5, 1974), 846-47; "Washington Report: Latin America: A Look at North/South Relations." *MennRep* 4 (Sept. 30, 1974), 7. Multinational corporations in Latin America promote the increasing gap between rich and poor, while US military and torture procedures oppress those who work for change.

Franz, Delton. "Brazilian Bishop Works for Peace with Justice." *Menn* 89 (Dec. 17, 1974), 745; "Brazilian Bishop Helps the Poor." *MBH* 13 (Dec. 13, 1974), 21-22. Describes the work of Dom Helder Camara for peace and justice for the poor of Brazil.

Franz, Delton. "From 1776 to 1976—the Changing Style of Oppression." *MBH* 15 (July 9, 1976), 14-15; *MennRep* 6 (June 28, 1976), 7. US economic policy contributes to the invisible violence of starvation, torture, and exploitation, while seeking to avoid the visible violence of war and revolution.

Franz, Delton. "Missiles in the Pasture." *Menn* 84 (June 24, 1969), 423, 424. An analysis of the staggering costs of equipping the nation with ABM's, the failure of the nation to meet its own needs in areas of poverty and injustice, and what the church's responsibility in this situation.

Franz, Delton. "Nicaragua: A Test Case for American Policy in Latin America." *MCC PS Wash. Memo* 10 (Sept.-Oct., 1978), 1-2. The Nicaraguan war can be attributed to the wealth and abuse of power by the ruling Somoza regime.

Franz, Delton. "North-South Trade: The New Frontier for Justice." *MCC PS Wash. Memo* 9 (May-June, 1977), 1-2, 9. The US must establish freer trade laws if economic justice is to be secured with poorer countries.

Franz, Delton. "Panama Canal Treaties: The Moral Questions for American Christians." *MCC PS Wash. Memo* 10 (Jan.-Feb., 1978), 7-8. Discusses the treaties in light of the question of justice for the Panamanians.

Franz, Delton. "The Bitter Fruit of Aiding Military Dictatorships." *MCC PS Wash. Memo* 8 (Sept.-Oct., 1976), 1-2. Denounces US military aid to Third World military dictatorships, linking US aid to right-wing terrorist activity in those countries.

Franz, Delton. "Update on US Food and Development Aid." *MCC PS Wash. Memo* 9 (Sept.-Oct., 1977), 3-5. Evaluates recent US development aid legislation in light of its contribution to justice toward the poor.

Franz, Delton. "US Weapons Sales . . . The Torture Connection." *MCC PS Wash. Memo* 10 (May-June, 1978), 1-2. Encourages support of Congressional efforts to monitor the extensive sales of weapons and instruments of torture to Third World countries by American businesses.

Franz, Delton. "Washington Report: A Watershed in the Corruption of Power." *MennRep* 3 (June 11, 1973), 6-7. Corruption and deceit revealed by the Watergate scandal reminds American Christians that ultimate loyalty must be given to God, not the national leader.

Franz, Delton, ed. "'Third World' Concerns Focused with Plans for Mennonite World Conference in Brazil," *MCC PS Wash. Memo* 2 (Sept.-Oct., 1970), 1-4. Focuses on the economic injustice existing between the US and Latin American countries and raises the possibility of addressing this issue at the Mennonite World Conference in 1972.

Franz, Marian Claassen. "Bucking Sexism in Sunday School." *Daughters of Sarah* (Nov.-Dec., 1980), 5-6. Guidelines on how to avoid the violence of stereotyping and cataloguing persons in Christian education.

Franz, Marian Claassen. "Central America." *Menn* 94 (Sept. 18, 1979), 552-53. Conditions are so bad in Central America that the people would rather die fighting for change than continue to live with the economic and political injustices done to them.

Frazer, Heather T. and O'Sullivan, John. "Forgotten Women of World War II: Wives of Conscientious Objectors in Civilian Public Service." *Peace and Change* 5 (Fall, 1978), 46-51. Documents the injustice of the CPS system in the absence of government pay or benefits granted to other enlisted men. Focuses especially on the economic and emotional plight of wives of CPS workers.

Freed, Sara Ann. "Violence: A Way into the Inner City." *With* 2 (Oct., 1969), 17. The discussion of two experiences that answer the question, "What happens when Mennonites are exposed to the violence and aggression of city living?"

Friesen, Alida. Letter to the Editor. *MennMirror* 8 (Oct., 1978), 21. The writer, a former Argentinian, expresses disappointment in the Canadian attitude of indifference towards injustices, particularly in Latin America, and pleads for a response against injustices and violations of human rights.

Friesen, Dorothy. "God Loves the Poor: An Exegetical Analysis of Deuteronomy 15:1-18." Paper for Hebrew Exegesis class, AMBS, Elkhart, Ind., May 16, 1975. Pp. 21. AMBS.

Friesen, Dorothy. "In Naboth's Vinyard." *Swords into Plowshares: A Collection of Plays About Peace and Social Justice*, ed. Ingrid Rogers. Elgin: The Brethren Press, 1983, 255-59. One-act play which draws an analogy between the story of Naboth's vinyard in 1 Kings 21 and the injustices being enacted in the Philippines.

Friesen, Dorothy. "Justice and the New Community." *GH* 69 (Apr. 13, 1976), 305. Describes the new community and new views of power which are developed when people embrace Jesus' vision of peace and justice.

Friesen, Dorothy. "Meditation on the Despicable and Unimportant." *Sojourners* 7 (Feb., 1978), 22. The people from whom church workers get their information on the environment in which they want to work is reflective of who they think God is and how he works in the world.

Friesen, Dorothy. "Pineapples and Social Justice." *MCC Contact* 2 (July-Aug., 1978), 1-3. Describes the exploitation of Philippine workers by the Castle and Cook Corporation, parent company of Dole, and urges North Americans to become informed about multinational corporations.

Friesen, Dorothy (Review). *Food First: Beyond the Myth of Scarcity*, by Francis Moore Lappe and Joseph Collins. Houghton Mifflin, 1977. *Sojourners* 8 (July, 1978), 35. The underlying assertion is that every country in the world has the resources necessary for its people to free themselves from hunger. The root cause of hunger is the insecurity and poverty of the majority which results from the control over the basic national resources by a few.

Friesen, Dorothy (Review). *The Stones Will Cry Out: Grassroots Pastorals*, by Bishop Francisco F. Claver, S.J. Maryknoll: Orbis Books, 1978. "Philippino Bishop Moves the Church to Action." *MennRep* 9 (Aug. 20, 1979), 20; *Sojourners* 8 (Aug., 1979), 28. A collection of pastoral letters and speeches from 1975 to the present, arising from the oppressive conditions of the Philippines.

Friesen, Dorothy and Stoltzfus, Gene. "Human Rights: Argument and Action." *Intercom* 17 (Apr., 1977), 6. Presents responses to some of the objections of church people and coworkers against confronting injustice.

Friesen, Dorothy, and Stoltzfus, Gene. "The

Church in New China." *EV* 91 (Dec. 10, 1978), 16. In China, there is a determined policy of religious repression, but institutionless Christianity is showing strength; the church that allied itself with power has not been particularly successful.

Friesen, Eric. "David Epp Describes His Tragedy: For Those Involved It Can Never Be Just Another Crime . . ." *MennMirror* 6 (Nov., 1976), 7, 8. David Epp recalls the tragic occasion when his son-in-law shot Epp and his daughter while Epp's wife and grandchildren watched. Epp was paralyzed and his daughter was killed.

Friesen, John R. "Last of a Kind? Thoughts After the Wichita Conference." *MennMirror* 8 (Aug.-Sept., 1978), 14. The expressed purpose of the Mennonite World Conference was fellowship, but the diversity of the participants and some burning issues such as armaments, war, and justice indicate that different levels of working together will be necessary for the future.

Friesen, LeRoy. "The Church and the Middle East (3): Palestinian Christians—People with an Uncertain Future." *MennRep* 6 (May 17, 1976), 7. Explores Palestinian Christian response to Palestinian nationalism and Jewish occupation, and the question of using violence.

Friesen, Richard. "Attitudes Toward the Status of Women in the History of the Mennonites. Paper prepared for Mennonite history class, Mennonite Biblical Seminary, Elkhart, Ind., Dec., 1972. Pp. 35. MHL.

Friesen, Ronald. "A Christian Witness in a World of Economic Disparity." *Forum* 10 (Jan., 1977), 1-3. Conveys the strong negative attitudes of the disadvantaged toward the more wealthy, and presents a rationale for and possible ways of minimizing these economic disparities.

Froese, Jacob A. "An Emphasis on Love, Peace, and Justice." *ChrLead* 40 (July 5, 1977), 5. Report on the role of the Contemporary Concerns Committee in the Mennonite Brethren Church.

Funk, John F. "A Terrible Massacre." *GH* 69 (June 22, 1976), 515. Reprint from the *Herald of Truth* of 1876 views the massacre of Custer's army as the fruit of deception and injustice done by the white people. Asserts the relations with Native Americans would have been different if whites had followed Jesus' way of peace.

Garber, Robert Bates. "Peace Churches Emphasize Peacemaking." *Forum* 12 (Nov., 1978), 14-15. The New Call to Peacemaking conference held in Oct., 1978, at Green Lake, Wis., issued the challenge that the historic peace churches should play a more active role in working for peace and justice. Such participation would mean a loss of some of the religio-ethnic distinctiveness of Mennonites which, the writer states, is a small price to pay in helping promote peace and social justice.

Geissinger, Marjorie. "TV—Is Your Family Turned On?" *Menn* 91 (Feb. 10, 1976), 92-93. Examines the prevalence of violence on television, especially during children's shows, and urges nonresistant parents to carefully monitor TV use.

General Conference Mennonite Church. *A Christian Declaration on the Way of Peace.* Newton: Commission on Home Ministries, General Conference Mennonite Church, 1971. Pp. 20. Position statement maintains that peace is grounded in biblical perspectives of love, evangelism, and justice, and it applies to use of resources, views of citizenship and military service, and involvement in social change.

Gingerich, Melvin. "Four Great Political and Social Revolutions." *GH* 62 (Mar. 18, 1969), 246-47. Discusses the American, French, Russian, and Chinese revolutions as situations where the powerful ruling class refused to address the wrongs suffered by the masses, so that bloody revolution ensued. Author considers it a tragedy that the church has so often identified with the conservative privileged few against the cause of injustice.

Gingerich, Melvin. "Reactions to Revolutions." *GH* 62 (Apr. 8, 1969), 314-15. Outlines three positions commonly taken in response to revolution: 1) advocating violent overthrow of the existing order; 2) conservative reaction which may turn to propaganda of fear; 3) acceptance of change and openness to facts. Advocates the last option for nonresistant Christians.

Gingerich, Melvin. *The Christian and Revolution.* Scottdale: Herald Press, 1968. Pp. 229. The Conrad Grebel lectures for 1967. An analysis of some modern revolutionary movements and appropriate Christian responses to them.

Gingerich, Melvin. "The Gospel and Revolution." *GH* 62 (Apr. 15, 1969), 338-39. Jesus' message was revolutionary in challenging human institutions of power and prestige. The church must not continue to side with those who defend the status quo through military and economic power; the church must identify with salvation, forgiveness, and justice.

Gingerich, Melvin. "The Race Revolution in America." *GH* 62 (Apr. 1, 1969), 292-93. Links the civil rights movement to the growing worldwide consciousness among people of color that they need not be second-class citizens. Urges nonresistant people to work at the injustice of racial discrimination in order to become reconcilers.

Gingerich, Melvin (Archival). Box 62—"The Christian and Revolution;" church-state relations; communism. Box 64—"Nonresistance and Social Justice." Goshen, Ind., AMC Hist. Mss. 1-129.

Gingerich, Ray C. "Can Man Transcend Violence?" *Religion in Life* 43 (Summer, 1974), 161-74. Author discusses violence as an effort to become human—to escape the passivity of oppression—but he contends that violence is self-perpetuating. He then introduces suffering as the transcendant alternative to violence, using Jesus as a model, because Jesus actively identified with the oppressed and yet broke the cycle of violence as a Suffering Servant.

Gish, Arthur G. *Beyond the Rat Race.* Scottdale: Herald Press, 1973. Pp. 192. Handbook on simple living includes discussion of the connection between wealth and violence; the American standard of living is a basic cause of violence because it is based on imperialism and exploitation.

Gish, Arthur G. *Living in Christian Community: A Personal Manifesto.* Scottdale: Herald Press, 1979. Pp. 375. Concluding chapters in this handbook for Christian communities are entitled "The Nonconforming Community" and "The Witnessing Community." Topics discussed in these chapters include the church and state, the church and economics, and the "Lamb's War" as the struggle against all that is outside God's intentions for the world, such as militarism, injustice, and oppression.

Goertz, Hans-Jürgen. "The Mystic with the Hammer: Thomas Müntzer's Theological Basis for Revolution." *MQR* 50 (Apr., 1976), 83-113. Attempting to correct both Western theological interpretations of Müntzer, which considered his revolutionism irrational, and Marxist historiography, which ignored his theology, Goertz argues that Müntzer's theology, drawn from medieval practical mysticism, formed the basis for his revolutionary activity.

Goertzen, Arlean L. "Study of Violence Draws New Attention." *Menn* 84 (May 6, 1969), 301. Examines opposing views on the application of violence in order to bring about justice in the US racial situation.

Graber, J. D. "Christian Revolution." *GH* 32 (Apr. 20, 1939), 68. Jesus may have been a religious revolutionary but he did not sanction political and economic revolution among the unregenerate. The "new birth" is a revolutionary change in the believer which does not force on others new ideals, economic or otherwise.

Grimsrud, Theodore G. "Foundations for Christian Social Responsibility: Creation, Love, and

Justice." MA in Peace Studies thesis, AMBS, 1983. Pp. 135. In the context of the contemporary debate on the subjects of social responsibility and biblical authority, develops three theological themes as a basis for proper Christian participation in society's structures.

Guenther, Allen R. "God's Word to His Unjust People." *MBH* 14 (Feb.. 7, 1975), 6-7. "God's Word to Unjust Societies." *MBH* 14 (Jan. 24, 1975), 8, 29. "The Meaning of Justice." *MBH* 14 (Feb. 21, 1975), 6-7. Book study in Amos focuses on God's judgment of the injustice practiced by Israel and Judah; God's judgment upon the nations practicing injustice; justice and righteousness in their relationship to the oppressed.

"Human Rights in Our World." *Menn* 94 (June 5, 1979), 386-87. Table listing by country the number of prisoners of conscience identified by Amnesty International.

Habegger, Howard J. "Toward Doing Justice in Christian Missions." *MissFoc* 8 (Mar., 1980), 1-9. Commitment to Christian mission must also mean commitment to justice, carried out through nonviolent activity. Paper includes general suggestions and cautions regarding procedure.

Habegger, Luann. "Report from the Peace Section Task Force on Women in Church and Society." *MCC PS TF on Women in Ch. and Soc. Report* 1 (Aug., 1973), 1-5. Essay introduces the topic of women's concerns for peace and justice and outlines a brief history of men's and women's roles in the church.

Haddad, Anis Charles. "Conflict in the Land of Peace." *ChrMon* 29 (Feb., 1937), 53. Describes attitudes of Arabs and Jews in Palestine and the recurring outbreaks of violence.

Hamm, Ray. "A Picture Demanding Wisdom." *IPF Notes* 22 (Apr.-May, 1975), 1-3. Describing some of the glaring injustices in the world economy, the author calls Christians to spread seeds of peace and justice.

Hampton, Peter J. "They Paid the Highest Price." *MennMirror* 6 (June, 1977), 25, 26. Describes how, during the Russian Revolution, his grandfather and uncle were killed by Russian bandits while they were on a mission of mercy.

Harder, Ernst. "To Hell with Good Intentions." *Forum* (Mar., 1972), 1-2. More than good intentions, service in Latin America requires sympathetic understanding of the cultural and political situation and identification with a people struggling to establish their own liberation.

Harder, Gary, and Rempel, Ron. "Reflections on the Life and Death of Martin Luther King, Jr." *CanMenn* 16 (Apr. 30, 1968), 4. Students from Mennonite colleges and seminaries identify with blacks, deplore white racist attitudes, and honor Martin Luther King's stand for justice on a nonviolent basis after attending his funeral in Atlanta.

Harder, Kurt. "A Concrete Commitment." *Forum* 12 (Dec., 1978), 6-7. Writer supports and discusses the proposal of a National Peace Academy as a viable and concrete alternative to violence as a means of resolving conflict.

Harder, Leland. "Zwingli's Reaction to the Schleitheim Confession of Faith of the Anabaptists." *Sixteenth Century Journal* 11 (Winter, 1980), 51-66. Discussion on Zwingli's objections to article six concludes that Zwingli did not adequately appreciate the legitimacy assigned to the sword "outside the perfection of Christ;" he did not fully believe the Anabaptist claim of nonresistance because he thought they had used violence, at times, for their own ends; he considered the rejection of political power *not* to be the issue in the biblical passages cited by the Confession.

Harding, Rosemarie. "Sing a Song for Freedom." *ChrLiv* 11 (Aug., 1964), 22-24. Comment on the songs coming out of the civil rights movement and the struggle for justice.

Harding, Vincent G. "The Peace Witness and Revolutionary Movements." *CanMenn* 15 (Aug. 15, 1967), 7, 11, 12; *MennLife* 22 (Oct., 1967), 161-65. Also in *The Witness of the Holy Spirit*. Ed. Cornelius J. Dyck. Elkhart: MWC, 1967, 337-44. Asks whether we can "recommend the way of powerlessness while we dwell comfortably among the powerful" and proposes dialogue with revolutionaries in order to learn the meaning of nonresistance in situations where people have been pressed by oppression into violent resistance. A peace witness has integrity only when its messengers participate in the quest for social justice also.

Harding, Vincent G. "The Revolution that Happened; The Revolution that Didn't Happen; The Revolution that Has to Happen." Paper presented at the American History and Christian Perspective Seminar, North Newton, Kansas, Jan. 23-24, 1976. Pp. 12. MHL.

Harding, Vincent G. "Voices of Revolution." *Menn* 82 (Oct. 3, 1967), 590-93; *YCC* 49 (May 19, 1968), 12. How should the peace witness address the movement for black liberation? Who commits the greatest sin—the desperate person or the complacent person?

Harding, Vincent G. (Review). *The American Revolution*, by James Boggs. Monthly Review Press, 1963. *ChrLiv* 12 (Oct., 1965), 32-33. The book demonstrates that the secular nonconformity movement critiques American middle-class values and searches for justice.

Harmon, Jan. "Advocating for 'Supreme Law of the Land'." *EV* 92 (Sept. 25, 1979), 10. Because the government has violated many Indian rights, the Friends Committee on National Legislation and MCC are attempting to raise the consciousness of the religious community and to respond to this human rights issue in our own country.

Harms, Orlando. "In Christ There Is No Black or White." *ChrLead* 33 (Sept. 22, 1970), 24. Outlines what the Mennonite Brethren Church can do "to see the issue of race in the right perspective and to help bring justice" to the blacks.

Harms, Orlando. "What I Learned in California." *ChrLead* 39 (May 25, 1976), 2. Report on a trip made to California to investigate the practices of Mennonite Brethren and others regarding legal and illegal immigrants.

Harshbarger, Emmett L. "Are Peace Workers Communists?" *Menn* 54 (Apr. 4, 1939), 4-5. The communists are now calling for violence. Therefore the peace worker can no longer be stigmatized as a communist.

Hatfield, Mark O. "Leadership, Power, and the Purpose of Life." *Menn* 88 (July 24, 1973), 442-44. The Watergate scandal inspires reflection on abuse of power brought on in part by the national idolatry of the presidency, instead of allegiance to God and the biblical vision of God's justice and peace.

Hatfield, Mark O. "Misplaced Allegiance." *Menn* 88 (Mar. 27, 1973), 216. Statement given by the Senator at the National Prayer Breakfast in Washington, D.C., calls Americans to distinguish between the god of American civil religion and the God revealed in Scriptures and in Jesus Christ who commands justice and peace.

Hein, Marvin. "Peter and Violence." *ChrLead* 36 (Oct. 30, 1973), 2. Examination of the reasons, accomplishments, and effects of violence on people. Explores alternatives to violence.

Heisey, Marion J. "Whose Teeth Are Set on Edge?" *EV* 88 (June 25, 1975), 5. Violence and injustice have been done to the traditionally peaceful Navajo tribe and have implications for continuing ministries to the Navajo people.

Henry, Carl F. H. "The Theology of Revolution." *GfT* 6 (Mar.-Apr., 1971), 11, 16, 19. While pacifist theology oversimplifies the complexity of social problems, revolutionary theology disregards the divinely appointed civil government as the instrument of justice.

Hernandez, Armando. "Justice Versus Injustice." *GH* 67 (May 14, 1974), 303-95. In a world full of injustices ranging from high prices to war, Christians should call people to repentance and speak out against war and violence of every kind.

Herr, Edwin. "The Christian and Politics: A Query." *GH* 69 (Oct. 26, 1976), 815-16. When Mennonites believe the tasks of the church are reconciliation, redemption, and mercy, while the state's purpose is to administer justice by force, to what extent can Mennonites participate in the state?

Hershberger, Guy F. "Can the American Revolution Be Justified?" *YCC* 17 (Oct. 4, 1936), 320. History books do not always teach all the sides of the arguments in a war situation. The American Revolution is a good example of a war that is only seen as a response on the part of the Americans to the British.

Hershberger, Guy F. "Love and Justice in Economic Relations." *ChrLiv* 2 (Oct., 1955), 26. The principles of love and non-retaliation go beyond the demands of justice.

Hershberger, Guy F. "Mennonite Principles: A Re-Examination." *MennComm* 5 (Dec., 1951), 17-19, 33. Mennonite adherence to nonconformity speaks also to the issue of social justice.

Hershberger, Guy F. "Nonresistance and Industrial Conflict." *MQR* 13 (Apr., 1939), 135-54. The industrial conflict is a fight for power with which to achieve social justice, whereas biblical nonresistance enjoins submission even to injustice rather than engage in conflict.

Hershberger, Guy F. "Protest Against Evil." *GH* 61 (Jan. 30, 1968), 104. [No. 22] Asserts that protest against social evils goes hand in hand with preaching the gospel, citing prophetic witness and demonstrations by early Anabaptists.

Hershberger, Guy F. "The Modern Social Gospel and the Way of the Cross." *MQR* 30 (Apr., 1956), 83-103. A major analysis and critique of the Social Gospel. While Rauschenbusch's theology and "the way of the Cross" are similar in many respects, the Social Gospel emphasizes "demanding justice" more than doing justice or suffering injustice.

Hershberger, Guy F. "The Tragedy of the Empty House." *GH* 54 (1961), 733-35. Using Matt. 12:43-45, Hershberger identifies demons worse than communism which threaten the US because of the lack of dependence on God and growing dependence on wealth and power.

Hershberger, Guy F. *The Way of the Cross in Human Relations.* Scottdale: Herald Press, 1958. Pp. 424.

Having been crucified with Christ, Christians follow Jesus in the way of the cross: they love with a self-giving love. After examining many theological traditions, Hershberger concludes that the Anabaptists most closely approximated this ideal. He then analyzes the organizations that structure modern society, proposes conditions under which Christians can become involved in them, and advocates a role for the church as society's conscience. Yet, because Christians look forward to Christ's consummation of history to establish justice, they depend not upon human efforts.

Hershberger, Guy F. "You Are the Salt of the Earth." *GH* 62 (Jan. 7, 1969), 6-9. Calls Christians to act as society's salt in witnessing against idolatry of the state and against the US climate of violence.

Hershberger, Guy F. (Review). *Conscription of Conscience: The American State and the Conscientious Objector, 1940-1947,* by Melford Q. Sibley and Philip E. Jacob. Ithaca: Cornell University Press, 1952. Pp. 580. *MQR* 27 (1953), 351-55. Summarizes the book's story of conscription and the CO in World War II as seen through the eyes of authors whose primary interest is in civil liberties rather than the New Testament way of nonresistant love. Harshberger raises the question of whether the two causes of social justice and nonresistant love can be served best by the more militant type of pacifist or the way of MCC. Considers this book helpful in raising this issue into sharp focus.

Hershberger, Guy F. (Review). *For Peace and Justice: Pacifism in America, 1914-1941,* by Charles Chatfield. Knoxville: Univ. of Tennessee Press, 1971. In *CH* 41 (1972), 418-19. This is the story of the new Christian (social gospel) pacifism which emerged during World War I and its encounter both with the older (non-pacifist) peace movement and with secular forces working for social justice as all labored together in a kind of unofficial grand alliance for the abolition of war.

Hershey, Lynford. "Does Silence Mean Consent for Violence?" *GH* 65 (Jan. 11, 1972), 28. Offers evidence that the church has not really been loving toward the minorities.

Hertzler, Daniel. "A Little Learning at the Feet of Pew." *ChrLiv* 13 (Aug., 1966), 2. Editorial encourages the church to become involved in social concerns for justice.

Hertzler, Daniel. "Gracious Living." *ChrLiv* 19 (Mar., 1972), 40. Editorial redefines "gracious": from modern connotations of elegance to Old Testament meaning of concern for justice.

Hertzler, Daniel. "Is Peace Naive?" *GH* 71 (Oct. 10, 1978), 788. In a society filled with war and violence, peacemaking appears naive, but it is the simple-mindedness of Jesus which set the example.

Hertzler, Daniel. "To Be a Peacemaker." *GH* 73 (June 17, 1980), 504. Reflects on instances of peacemaking that go beyond merely establishing justice or staying out of trouble.

Hertzler, Daniel. "To Henry W. Pierce." *GH* 68 (June 10, 1975), 444. Comments on a local newspaper column linking violence to deprivation of affection during childhood and advocating free sex and less modesty. Cites Jesus as a pioneer in love without violence, and the historic peace churches as upholders of love and monogomy.

Hertzler, Daniel. "Violence and Deception." *GH* 66 (Dec. 11, 1973), 940. Violence and deception go hand in hand, and have become accepted parts of life, as both Watergate and children's cartoons show.

Hertzler, Daniel. "We Commend . . ." *ChrLiv* 19 (Apr., 1972), 40. Salute to good news-makers includes a Lockheed manager who developed a conscience for social justice, and a tax firm studying the question of war tax objection.

Hertzler, Daniel (Editorial). "Sex and Violence." *GH* 70 (Sept. 20, 1977), 712. Comments on the prevalence of sex and violence in the mass media, especially television, and offers suggestions for action by concerned people.

Hertzler, Daniel (Editorial). "The World Upside Down." *GH* 69 (Aug. 17, 1976), 636. Urges Mennonites to make their voices heard for justice in those areas where the world's priorities are upside down, such as spending inordinate amounts for military purposes while people are hungry.

Hertzler, James R. "The American Revolution in British Eyes." *GH* 69 (Jan. 27, 1976), 68-69. Examines the various opinions of British preachers and writers on the rebellion of the American colonies, and draws parallels between that conflict and the recent one in Vietnam.

Hiebert, Clarence. "What About Vietnam?" *ChrLead* 29 (Mar. 15, 1966), 14-15. Since God wills peace, reconciliation, justice, and redemption, God's people will also share this attitude and will work for justice, peace, and love in our present world.

Hiebert, Linda Gibson and Hiebert, Murray. "Lamentations from Thailand." *Sojourners* 6 (Mar., 1977), 7. Description of the human rights violations in Thailand since the military coup in Oct., 1976.

Hiebert, Linda Gibson and Hiebert, Murray. "Why Do You Use Guns?" *MBH* 14 (Oct. 3, 1975), 17: *GH* 68 (Aug. 26, 1975), 599-600; *RepConsS* 23 (Sept., 1975), 2; *Menn* 90 (Sept. 16, 1975), 510. A 13-year-old Vietnamese boy, paralyzed by a grenade, asks this question of soldiers.

Hiebert, Murray and Hiebert, Linda Gibson. "A Response." *Sojourners* 8 (Nov., 1978), 38. A response to "Letters to the Editor" by Dan Berrigan and Jim Forest on a highly-polarized, two-year-old debate on human rights in Vietnam.

Hiebert, Paul. "Peace, Today's Problem." *ChrLead* 24 (Oct. 31, 1961), 5. Christian peace is a gift of God, intended to permeate our total life-style, replacing force, violence, and hostility with reconciling, suffering love.

Hilborn, Jean A. "Positive Protest Through Involovement." *YCC* 49 (June 16, 1968), 2; *CanMenn* 16 (Mar. 5, 1968), 1. Text of the speech by Jean Hilborn which won the national peace oratorical contest in Canada. A challenge to protest: its positive function arises from involvement in social justice issues. To work for peace is to understand the roots of war.

Hofer, Joy. "When Violence Becomes Real." *ChrLead* 43 (Nov. 4, 1980), 10. The plight of a refugee family in Guatemala illustrates the suffering caused by violence in Central America.

Holm, Jim. "Social Implications of the Gospel." *ChrLead* 41 (Dec. 5, 1978), 4. Since the gospel is for the whole person and the whole society, the church should consider its response to and involvement in social issues.

Hoover, Donald J. "The Politics of Jahweh: On the Relationship Between Justice and War Acts." Paper for Warfare in the Old Testament class, AMBS, Elkhart, Ind., Dec. 17, 1977. Pp. 25.

Horsch, John. "The Mennonites of Russia, Part IV." *ChrMon* 28 (Sept., 1936), 262-63. Experiences of the colonists during the Russian Revolution, when Mennonites formed armed self-defense units

Horst, Sylvia. "Awakening to Suffering." *Forum* 13 (Dec., 1979), 10. Writer describes her concern for the oppressed in Argentina which led to her involvement with the Organization for Christian Action in Argentina (OCAA), an organization which raises awareness and initiates action responding to human rights situations in Argentina.

Hostetter, B. Charles. "Christian Love Forgives." *ChrLiv* 2 (Feb., 1955), 32-33. Christian love means forgiveness and mercy, not justice or vengeance.

Hostetter, B. Charles. "Golden Rule: Foundations for Human Relations." *YCC* 45 (June 28, 1964), 2. Racial prejudice, discrimination, and injustice are sin.

Hostetler, Marian. *African Adventure.* Scottdale: Herald Press, 1976. Pp. 124. Fiction, ages 10-14. In the course of an MCC-type assignment to Chad, 12-year-old Denise and her family begin to experience and understand the problems of hunger and violence in their relatedness. The story depicts a variety of ways church agencies work at the tasks of relief and mission.

Hostetter, Douglas. "Faith, Works, and the Revolution." *Sojourners* 6 (Jan., 1977), 10. With the social changes brought by the Cuban Revolution, the dilemma of faith and works is still at the center of much of the debate in the Cuban church today.

Houston, Stephen (Review). *Perceptions of Apartheid,* by Ernie Regehr. No publisher, n.d. *Intercom* 24 (Apr., 1980), 3, 12. Discusses the issues of the injustice and violence of apartheid raised by the book.

Howard, Walden. "Pay Them Back with Good." *ChrLiv* 18 (Sept., 1971), 14-17. Feedmill owner's business nearly destroyed for supporting justice in the form of school integration.

Hübner, Harry. "Television and Violence." *Menn* 94 (Mar. 20, 1979), 224. Television is doing violence to our personhood and to Christianity. We must recognize that it is deceiving us in many areas.

Hübner, Harry (Review). *King Jesus' Manual of Arms for the 'Armless,* by Vernard Eller. Nashville: Abingdon Press, 1973. Pp. 205. Also, *Liberation Ethics,* by John M. Swomley. New York: Macmillan, 1972. Pp. 238. *Menn* 88 (Oct. 30, 1973), 628-29. While Eller considers peace activism an unfaithful siezing of the reins of history, a prerogative belonging only to God, Swomley advocates nonviolent revolution as the strategy for liberation. The reviewer believes that Christian faithfulness will include political activism, but that activism will not bring the Kingdom, which is a gift of God.

Hull, Robert. *Leader's Guide: "Justice and the Christian Witness."* Newton: Faith and Life Press; Scottdale: Herald Press, 1982. Pp. 66. Companion volume to the study report provides suggestions for group activities, lesson plans, a significant number (19) of case studies, and class projects.

"Intercollegiate Peace Fellowship Almost Loses Sight of Its Theme." *CanMenn* 17 (Apr. 1, 1969), 1, 2. Report on IPF meeting March 19-22 in Washington, DC, discussing the peacemaker in revolution. Speakers with a wide range of views addressed the meetings. One was a member of SDS, another a former editor of the underground *Washington Free Press,* another was facing trial for refusing conscription. Myron Augsburger said that violent revolution is the old "just war" doctrine in a new garment. Norman Kraus said nonresistance as it is practiced will not see us through the next few decades and it is not biblical. There is no social revolution without conflict, and we must find our place in it.

"Items and Comments." *GH* 63 (Aug. 18, 1970), 685. Documents brutal torture accorded Vietnamese student peace protesters by the Saigon government and the international attempts to stop the repression.

Jackson, Dave. *Dial 911: Peaceful Christians and Urban Violence.* Scottdale: Herald Press, 1981. Pp. 150. Recounts experiences that Reba Place Fellowship members have had with different sorts of violent crime in their Evanston neighborhood. These stories are interspersed with reflections upon different aspects of a Christian response to urban violence such as making distinctions between different kinds of crimes, deterrents to crime, attitudes toward persons who commit crimes, and what the scriptures have to say to the issue.

Jackson, Dave. *Dial 911: Peaceful Christians and Urban Violence, A Leader's Guide for Group Study.* Scottdale: Mennonite Publishing House, 1982. Pp. 47. Provides plans for four sessions with the book, *Dial 911.* Resources include worship suggestions, discussion guides, group activities, and worksheets.

Jacobs, Donald R. *The Christian Stance in a Revolutionary Age.* Scottdale: Herald Press, Focal Pamphlet No. 14, 1968. Pp. 32. Describes the factors influencing social change in the developing nations and the issues, such as tribalism, racism, and nationalism, which confront the church in these areas. Then, in this context, Jacobs contends that peace and development are two parts of the same issue— that any peace theology must necessarily speak to the issues of distributive justice.

Jantz, Harold. "A Witness on Behalf of the Powerless." *MBH* 16 (Sept. 30, 1977), 16-17. Patty Erb and Thomas Capuano tell of their imprisonments and torture for their work among the poor in Latin American countries supported by US military aid.

Jantz, Harold. "God's Kingdom in the Twentieth Century." *MBH* 17 (Sept. 1, 1978), 2-3. Speakers at Mennonite World Conference in Wichita centered their talks around the theme of the peaceable kingdom's response to militarism, oppression, and racism.

Jantz, Harold. "Love Your Enemies." *MBH* 5 (Mar. 18, 1965), 3. Christians confess that evil will be overcome by good rather than through further violence.

Jantz, Harold. "Origins of West Bank Tensions." *MBH* 15 (Aug. 6, 1976), 15-16. Illegal Israeli settlements in the West Bank contribute to tensions and outbreaks of violence with Palestinians.

Jantz, Harold. "Ugandan Bishop Pleads for His People." *MBH* 16 (Nov. 11, 1977), 12-13. The suffering church in Uganda is an example of contemporary non-resistant Christianity.

Jantz, Harold (Editorial). "Mennonites in Politics." *MBH* 16 (Oct. 28, 1977), 11. Suggests that Mennonite political interest is more concerned with protecting privilege than justice.

Janzen, A. E. "Patriotism, Peace, and War." *ChrLead* 13 (July 1, 1949), 3-4. Christians are devoted to the welfare of all people; because they believe peace is the will of God, they renounce the use of force and violence.

Janzen, Waldemar. "War in the Old Testament." *MQR* 46 (Apr., 1972), 155-66. Outlines Old Testament views of war as a human reality, a result of sin; of God as a Warrior who establishes justice; and of peace as a full reality in the future of God's kingdom.

Janzen, William. "Letter to the Editor: Capital Punishment." *MBH* 15 (Apr. 2, 1976), 10-11. The question of respect for human life extends to other social issues, such as war or assistance to developing countries.

Jenks, Philip E. "Holocaust." *GH* 71 (July 4, 1978), 540. Reprinted from *The American Baptist.* While the specter of the Nazi extermination of Jews troubles pacifist convictions, it should to a greater degree trouble the church that allows evildoers to feel they are justified in their actions until it is too late to stop them except through violence.

Jeschke, Marlin. "Scapegoats for Our Hate." *CanMenn* 5 (Jan. 4, 1957), 2. The gospel is at work in all lands with all people. We must not be led to think that Christian equals American. To fall prey to the hate campaign spirit is to misunderstand the universal nature of sin, the love of God, and the divine power working in history.

Johnsson, William G. "Jesus—A Revolutionary?" *Menn* 93 (Jan. 31, 1978), 65-67. Traces contours of Jesus' life and ministry, including his nonviolent approach to revolution.

Jordan, Clarence. "A Parable of No Violence, Some Violence, and Great Violence." *ChrLiv* 13

(Feb., 1966), 35; "A Parable of Violence and No Violence." *CanMenn* 13 (Oct. 26, 1965), 14. Reprinted from *Town and Country Church*. Allegory depicting the plight of the oppressed and the struggle for justice.

Jost, Connie. Letter to the Editor. *ChrLead* 42 (Oct. 23, 1979), 11. Sees two groups in the Mennonite Brethren constituency: one group that embraces socialism, liberalism, and liberation theology and the other group that believes the Bible as God's Word.

Jost, Dean. "The Christian and Campus Ferment." *GH* 63 (July 14, 1970), 598-99. Given the division in American society between "establishment" and "radical" cultures, the church must act as a reconciler and as a prophet witnessing against the violence of both cultures: the sexism, racism, and militarism of the establishment, and the drugs, sexual mores, and individualism of the radicals.

Juhnke, James C. "Freedom and the American Revolution." *Menn* 91 (June 22, 1976), 417-18. Bicentennial celebrations reinforce the idea that freedom is a military achievement, when in fact revolution may not have been the only alternative in 1775; similarly, political independence later became a license to oppress blacks and Native Americans.

Juhnke, James C. "Freedom and the American Revolution." Paper, Feb., 1976. Pp. 4. MHL.

Juhnke, James C. "Mob Violence and Kansas Mennonites in 1918." *Kansas Historical Quarterly* 43 (Autumn, 1977), 334-50. Juhnke relates stories of local mob violence—tar and feathering, near lynching, and other coercion— toward war-resistant, German-American Mennonites of Kansas during World War I. Examines these incidents in light of the larger question of the history of American domestic violence. MLA/BeC.

Juhnke, James C. "Race Relations—A Voice from the Past." *Menn* 84 (Apr. 15, 1969), 254. A Mennonite editor in 1900 foresees race riots and an ever developing race hatred because of the injustices done to blacks.

*Justice and the Christian Witness: A Study Report and Study Guide*. Newton: Faith and Life Press; Scottdale: Mennonite Publishing House, 1982. Pp. 66. Discusses why and what issues of justice face the church, the character of biblical justice and how the Christian peace witness guides the church's efforts to speak to these issues.

"Korea: Victim of Repression and World Politics." *MennRep* 9 (Sept. 17, 1979), 2. Yoon Goo Lee, formerly of Korea, speaks to the Akron MCC staff about the situation in Korea, stressing that the main problem is the infringement of human rights in South Korea.

Kauffman, Beulah. "Family Life Education." *Builder* 31 (Jan., 1981), 24-25. Column focuses on topics such as peace for families in distress, parenting for peace and justice, nonviolence and children, etc.

Kauffman, Ellen B. "Violence in America." *GfT* 12 (Mar.-Apr., 1977), 12. Spreading the gospel of Christ is the only answer to rampant violence.

Kauffman, Ivan. "Are We the Problem?" *GH* 61 (June 18, 1968), 545-47; *ChrLead* 31 (June 18, 1968), 9-11. Summarizes the US Riot Commission Report which attributed most of the violence and riots in American cities to white racism.

Kauffman, J. Howard. "Christian Ethics and National Agriculture Policy." Paper, [Goshen, Ind., 1956]. Pp. 16. MHL.

Kauffman, Milo. "Blessings of Christian Stewardship." *ChrLiv* 1 (Sept., 1954), 29-30, 38, 44-45. While covetousness drives people to war and violence, stewardship promotes joy and helps resolve human conflict.

Kauffman, Nancy L. "Justice in the Book of Habakkuk." Paper presented to Theology of Warfare in the Old Testament class, AMBS, Elkhart, Ind., May 26, 1981. Pp. 21. AMBS.

Kauffman, Richard A.; Hostetler, David E.; and Barrett, Lois. "The Patty Erb Story—One Year Later." *GH* 70 (Sept. 27, 1977), 726-27. Relates Patty Erb's story of imprisonment and torture for her work with the poor in Argentina, a country whose police have been trained by the American military in methods of torture.

Kaufman, Gordon D. "The Christian in a World of Power." *MennLife* 21 (Apr., 1966), 65-67. Christ is central to the Christian understanding of humanity and history. The cross leads us to live lives of nonresistant love that only make sense in terms of God's Kingdom.

Kaufman, Gordon D. (Review). *The Non-Violent Cross: A Theology of Revolution and Peace*, by James W. Douglas. Macmillan, 1966. Pp. 301. *Harvard Divinity Bulletin*, New Series 2 (Winter, 1969), 12, 13. Commends this effort to develop a theology of revolution and peace as biblical and moving but regrets that the author fails to analyze the political and social realities.

Keeney, William E. "Calling the World Council of Churches to a Nonviolent Position." *MennRep* 4 (Jan. 7, 1974), 7. Examines Mennonite interaction with the WCC on peace issues, especially WCC's study on violence and nonviolence.

Keeney, William E. "The Quiet Revolution: Menno Simons." *MennLife* 25 (Jan., 1970), 15-20. In contrast to the Münsterites, Menno Simons is depicted as the "quiet revolutionary." The principles which dictated his revolutionary strategy are discussed.

Keeney, William E. "WCC Called to Nonviolent Position." *Menn* 89 (Jan. 1, 1974), 11. Summarizes the statement, "Violence, Nonviolence, and the Struggle for Social Justice," prepared by the historic peace church representatives for the World Council of Churches discussion. Reviews the history of peace church-WCC discussions on the issue of war, and alludes to the broader issues which it touches: christology, biblical interpretation, the relationship of church and state.

Keeney, William E. (Review). *The Captain America Complex: The Dilemma of Zealous Nationalism,* by Robert Jewett. Philadelphia: Westminster Press, 1973. Pp. 286. *Menn* 89 (Oct. 29, 1974), 637. Summarizes the contents of this book, centered around the thesis that American people misread the realities of history and adopt means to save the world which result in destruction and defeat. Reviewer pays special attention to the author's view of the use and results of violence.

Kehler, Larry. "Arms Sales and Canadian Violence." *CanMenn* 18 (Oct. 2, 1970), 5. Statistical information on Canadian attitudes to violence and the promotion of violence. Asks what the church should do about it.

Kehler, Larry. "Beauty and the Beast." *GH* 70 (Jan. 4, 1977), 4-5; *Menn* 92) (Jan. 18, 1977), 45-46; "Beauty and the Beast (Violence and the Children)." *ChrLead* 40 (Feb. 1, 1977), 4; "Violence and the Children—Beauty and the Beast." *EV* 90 (Feb. 25, 1977), 6. Examines the effects of the violence portrayed in children's TV programs and lists five safeguards for children's use of television.

Kehler, Larry. "Vietnamese Vignettes." *GH* 69 (Sept. 14, 1976), 685-91; *Menn* 91 (July 20, 1976), 446-47. MCC visitor to Vietnam describes the effects of war on the survivors and reports on the shape of Vietnamese society since liberation.

Kehler, Peter. "The Mennonite Church in Peace and War." *CanMenn* 6 (Jan. 24, 1958), 2, 3. An argument based on following the God of love rather than the God of righteousness and justice. Kehler believes that God's greatest attribute is love. Stresses the need for the church to accept its responsibility to God and the Word both in peace and war.

Keidel, Levi O. *Caught in the Crossfire.* Scottdale and Kitchener: Herald Press, 1979. Pp. 229. Account of the early years of Zaire's political independence, a period characterized by revolution and tribal warfare, and the ethical dilemmas the church had to face in regard to participation in violence or conscientious objection to it.

Keidel, Levi O. "The Shaping Effects of Violence." *GH* 63 (Nov. 17, 1970), 968-69. Outbreaks of violence and revolution reveal what kind of person one really is and mold one further in that direction. Author relates a story of a conflict situation and the reactions of the people involved to back up his conclusion.

Keidel, Levi O. "The Trap." *GH* 62 (Jan. 21, 1969), 50-51. Describes an imaginary dream in which a young Congolese boy searches for an escape from poverty and injustice first through education, then through guerilla warfare aimed at the overthrow of the corrupt government.

Kenagy, U. E. "The Sword of the Lord." *GH* 30 (Aug. 19, 1937), 451. Some are called to use the sword to execute the wrath of God. To these persons the saved person can only say, "Be purged in the name of Christ."

Klaassen, Walter. "Anabaptism: So What?" *GH* 67 (Feb. 12, 1974), 129-33. Among the contemporary issues to which the sixteenth-century Anabaptist movement speaks are the issues of revolutionary change and the use of violence in working toward justice.

Klaassen, Walter. "The Meaning of Anabaptism." *MBH* 14 (Jan. 24, 1975), 6-7. Giving ultimate loyalty to God over social and political powers exercising violence was one of the marks of 16th-century Anabaptists.

Klaassen, Walter. "The Peace Churches and Social Revolution." *MennRep* 2 (May 29, 1972), 11. World Council of Churches representative and peace churches dialogue on the meaning of peace emphases, thoretical and practical, and alternatives to peace, the just revolution.

Klaassen, Walter (Review). *The Non-Violent Cross: A Theology of Revolution and Peace,* by James W. Douglass. Macmillan, 1968. Pp. 301. *Faith and Violence: Christian Teaching and Christian Practice,* by Thomas Merton. South Bend: University of Notre Dame, 1968. Pp. 291. "Faith and Violence; Revolution and Peace." *CanMenn* 17 (Sept. 12, 1969), 4. Douglass' book is "an able articulation of a theology of peace" and Merton's book contains "a theology of resistance."

Klassen, Alice. "Troubled Parents, Battered Children: Support & Intervention." *MCC PS TF on Women in Ch. and Soc. Report* 24 (Jan., 1979), 1-

3. Focuses on domestic violence directed toward children.

Klassen, Bernard R. "Small Nations Are Pawns in Game of Political Chess." *CanMenn* 15 (Oct. 3, 1967), 1, 7. All through history the most advanced nations have felt that it was their prerogative to superimpose their "superior" culture on "less civilized peoples." To be a peacemaker, the Christian must condemn injustice, strive for the triumph of justice, and in the meantime show human compassion and understanding to all people, whether they are right or wrong.

Klassen, J. M. "MCC Work in Areas of Conflict Explained." *MBH* 16 (Oct. 14, 1977), 11. MCC (Canada) Executive Secretary responds to the concern that MCC personnel may be supporting terrorist activity.

Klassen, Peter J. "Evangelicals and the Vietnam War" and "The Silence of Billy Graham." *MBH* 12 (Feb. 23, 1973), 11. With the end of the Vietnam war at hand, the editor reflects and comments that it has brought home to humankind the utter futility of trying to solve serious questions through violence. He also comments on the tacit approval Billy Graham gave to the president's actions in the war.

Klassen, Peter J. "Ironic Developments." *MBH* 12 (Mar. 23, 1973), 11. Using the situation at Wounded Knee to illustrate, the author suggests that Christians in Canada and the US demonstrate to the government with deeds of justice and mercy in holding to the promises that have been made with the Indians.

Klassen, William. "Five Men Who Intervened." *Menn* 84 (July 1, 1969), 434-36. The wrath of God can be stayed and the vicious cycle of violence and injustice can be broken when a person intervenes redemptively.

Klassen, William. "Where We're at. . . on Violence and Revolution." *CanMenn* 19 (Feb. 19, 1971), 10, 30. Critical analysis of the institutional church as it relates to communication between those of the Mennonite faith.

Klassen, William (Review). *On Violence,* by Hannah Arendt. Harcourt, Brace, and World, 1970. Pp. 106. *GH* 64 (Apr. 20, 1971), 362. Recommends the book for its careful analysis of the distinction and relation between power and violence, the utility of violence when used to dramatize grievances, and the power of nonviolence in building a new order.

Klaus, Marilyn. "Rape as a Political Crime." *Daughters of Sarah* 4 (Mar.-Apr., 1978), 9-10. Rape is "the one undeniable symptom that in one group is lodged power and headship over

another group" and the guilt of rape must be shared by all those who, contrary to the interdependence espoused by Jesus, cooperate in a system that perpetuates male dominance.

Klaus, Marilyn. "The Draft and Women." *MCC PS TF on Women in Ch. and Soc. Report* 35 (Jan.-Feb., 1981), 5-6. While reasons for excluding women from registration are sexist, a greater evil is involving men in a system committed to violence and war.

Kliewer, Marion W. "Delegates Study Meaning of Christian Love." *CanMenn* 2 (July 30, 1954), 1, 8. Reports historic peace church meeting at Bluffton College, July 15-18, 1954, where a large gathering studied commitment, love and justice.

Kliewer, Warren. "War and Rumors of War." *MennLife* 17 (Jan., 1962), 39-43. Death of a friend who was a soldier in Korea raises the issue of how we all share in violence.

Klippenstein, La Verna (Review). *Days of Terror,* by Barbara Claassen Smucker. Toronto: Clark, Irwin and Co., 1979. Pp. 156. *MennLife* 34 (Dec., 1979), 31. Summarizes this story which relates the experience of the Neufeld family during and after the Russian Revolution. Recommends this book especially for church librarians.

Kolb, Noah. "Exegesis of Luke 22:35-38 with Reference to 49-51." Paper for War, Peace, and Revolution class, AMBS, Elkhart, Ind., Apr. 10, 1969. Pp. 3. AMBS.

Koontz, Gayle Gerber. "Palestinians Gain Confidence, Protest Israeli Occupation Policies." *MennRep* 6 (July 27, 1976), 2. Examines causes of recent outbreaks of Israeli-Palestinian violence, centering on Israel's occupation of the West Bank and expropriation of Palestinian property.

Koontz, Ted. "US-Soviet Relations After Afghanistan—1." *Menn* 95 (Aug. 19, 1980), 418. Interprets Soviet military intervention in Afghanistan as a great power saving face and protecting national strength.

Krahn, Cornelius. "Crossroads at Amsterdam." *MennLife* 22 (Oct., 1967), 153-56. A report on the Eighth Mennonite World Conference with an emphasis on Anabaptism, revolution, and radicalism.

Kraus, C. Norman. "A Christian Perspective on Revolution." *GH* 63 (July 21, 1970), 618-19. Calls Christianity which has set itself up as a defender of the status quo to return to the future-oriented perspective of the New Testament in order to faithfully understand and critique both the existing order and social revolutions.

Kraus, C. Norman. "Christian Perspectives on Nationalism, Racism, and Poverty in American Life." *Peacemakers in a Broken World.* Ed. John A. Lapp. Scottdale: Herald Press, 1969, 30-42. Calls Christians to disassociate themselves from national selfishness and a "might makes right" mind set to understand the black power movement and to work for fair employment and aid policies.

Kraus, C. Norman. "Confronting Revolutionary Change." *GH* 63 (June 23, 1970), 566-67. Defining "revolution" as "profound, irrevsersible change" of either a violent or nonviolent sort, the author cites Jesus and the Anabaptists as revolutionary and challenges Christians not to be threatened by those who call for change in the social structures.

Kraus, C. Norman. "Some Reflections of a Theological Nature on the Question of Freedom and Responsibility." *PCMCP Fifteenth,* 9-19. North Newton, Kansas: The Mennonite Press. Held at Bluffton College, Bluffton, Ohio, June 10-11, 1965. The concern for freedom in the academic community and the political community traces back to certain assumptions about the nature and value of human life. From the biblical perspective, human individuality and freedom find their fruition and fulfillment in the community of love.

Kraus, C. Norman. "The Nature and Causes of Revolution." *GH* 63 (June 30, 1970), 582-83. Probes into the causes of present worldwide revolution and asks how pacifist Christians relate to the violence and turmoil which accompany revolutions.

Kraus, C. Norman. "Why Political Revolution?" *GH* 63 (July 14, 1970), 602-3. Describes the self-perpetuating and sacralizing processes of human institutions which become oppressive and necessitate social revolution. Challenges Christians to follow Jesus' example in rejecting violence as a means of establishing a new order.

Kraus, C. Norman (Review). *Jesus and the Nonviolent Revolution,* by Andre Trocme. Trans. by Michael H. Shank and Marlin Miller. Scottdale: Herald Press, 1973. Pp. 211. *MQR* 51 (Jan., 1977), 85-86. Trocme presents a convincing thesis that Jesus the Messiah was a nonviolent revolutionary prophet who used the principle of the Jubilee Year and its restoration as the focal point for his ministry. Reviewer observes that while it is a helpful thesis, the author perhaps presses this framework onto too many New Testament texts.

Kreider, Alan. "The Way of Christ." *Is Revolution Change?* ed. Brian Griffiths. London: Inter-Varsity Press, 1972, 46-69. Both Jesus' rejection of violence as an option and the history of the church and state relationship point to suffering love, embodied by the (minority) church as the method of the true revolution.

Kreider, Alan. "Why the Christian Church Must Be Pacifist." *Ireland and the Threat of Nuclear War,* ed. Bill McSweeney. Dublin: Dominican Publications, 1985. Pp. 83-103. Pacifism is now growing in the Church for several reasons: people have seen the futility of military violence in attaining its objectives; new biblical and theological insights undermine former justifications for violence; because attempts to control modern events have had unanticipated results, Christians are abandoning consequential ethics for principled, prophetic nonconformity; and Christians have discovered that violence does not exhaust the possibilities for relevant involvement in the world.

Kreider, Carl. "International Economic Justice." Paper presented at MCC Justice Task Force Consultation, Goshen College, Goshen, Ind., May 22-23, 1978. Pp. 7. MHL.

Kreider, Carl. "Trouble in the Congo." *ChrLiv* 7 (Nov., 1960), 18, 35. Analysis of the violence and military conflict in the Congo following its independence from Belgium.

Kreider, Carl. "War and Revolution." *ChrLiv* 4 (Jan., 1957), 18, 39-40. Description of and comment upon British and French military intervention in Egypt, and the revolution in Hungary.

Kreider, Carl (Review). *The Church and Social Responsibility,* by J. Richard Spann. Abingdon-Cokesbury, 1953. Pp. 272. *ChrLiv* 1 (Nov., 1954), 31. Recommends this collection of essays on social problems such as war, church and state, crime, civil rights, etc.

Kreider, Evelyn B. "Shalom: God's Plan." *WMSC Voice* 54 (Dec., 1980), 3-4. Reprinted from *Lifework.* Commitment to Christ and peacemaking is a way of life that means working for peace and justice for all people and all social structures.

Kreider, Robert S. "A Litany of Violence and Reconciliation." *GH* 61 (Apr. 16, 1968), 346-47; *CanMenn* 16 (Aug. 13, 1968), 13; *MBH* 7 (Mar. 29, 1968), 4-5; *ChrLead* 31 (Mar. 26, 1968), 5, 12. Offsets scripture passages on hope and reconciliation against vignettes of the problems of war, violence, poverty, racial tensions.

Kreider, Robert S. "The Mennonite Vision for and in the World." *ChrMon* 39 (Sept., 1947), 266-67. Calls for greater ethical sensitivity to need and injustice in the world.

Kroeker, David. "Torture, Prison, Rats, and Hunger." *MennRep* 9 (Jan. 22, 1979), 6. Relating numerous incidents of persons maltreated for political and/or religious beliefs, the writer urges the reader to contact Amnesty International and become involved in the campaign to free those unjustly treated.

Kroeker, Walter.. "Justice and Relief Must Stay Together." *MBH* 18 (Feb. 16, 1979), 16-18. Papers were presented at the MCC annual meeting on the relation of peace and reconciliation to Native American outreach, hunger concerns, and militarism.

Kroeker, Walter. "Justice and Rights Issues Occupy MCC Members in Reedley." *MennRep* 9 (Feb. 19, 1979), 1. Among the issues discussed at the MCC annual meeting was aid to Vietnam, justice and human rights overseas, and a paper on militarism calling the church to renounce the development of nuclear weapons and military exports.

Kroeker, Walter. "MCC—Wide-Ranging Agenda." *EV* 92 (Mar. 25, 1979), 8-9. At the MCC annual meeting, issues of justice, aid to Vietnam, the world food crisis, and militarism were addressed and a paper on militarism by Urbane Peachey was accepted.

Kroeker, Walter. (Review). *Let Justice Roll Down*, by John Perkins. Glendale: Regal Books, 1976. In *ChrLead* 40 (Apr. 26, 1977), 18. The story of John Perkins and the founding of Voice of Calvary ministries in Mississippi.

Kuhns, Dennis R. "In Response to Violence." *GH* 68 (Apr. 8, 1975), 266-67. The best way to deal with the destructive cycle of violence is for people to take individual responsibility in rejecting violence and following Jesus' way.

Kunjam, Shantkumar S. "An Exploratory Examination of the Ethics of Gandhiji in the Light of Biblical Teachings." MA in Peace Studies thesis, AMBS, 1982. Pp. 94. A critical discussion of the theological and moral bases that guided Gandhi's effort to ease class conflicts and win liberation for the Indian people by nonviolent means. Includes statement of what Christians may learn from Gandhi.

"Lack of Concern for Rules of War." *Menn* 86 (Jan. 19, 1971), 36-38. Relief workers express their disapproval of the foreign military involvement in Vietnam and quote numerous articles from, for instance, the Nuremberg Tribunal, the Hague Convention, the Geneva Convention, and others, to point out the injustice of the USA.

"Lack of Security and Justice Key Issues of Mid-East Deadlock." *CanMenn* 20 (Sept. 11, 1970), 3. Observations gleaned from members of MCC Peace Section tour of the Middle East countries on Arab-Jewish relations.

La Roque, Emma. *Defeathering the Indian*. Agincourt, Canada: The Book Society of Canada Limited, 1975. Pp. 82. A handbook for educators on Native Studies which deals with the ways cultures clash and offers suggestions for peacemakers on how to reverse such forces of psychological violence as stereotyping, denigrating language, and selective history.

Landis, Carl. "Fighting Crime—Peacefully." *With* 10 (Jan., 1977), 13. A bail bondsman who works to give poor persons who need bond service the same opportunity that wealthier individuals have.

Lapp, Alice W. (Review). *A Russian Dance of Death: Revolution and Civil War in the Ukraine*, by Dietrich Neufeld. Ed. and Trans., Al Reimer. Winnipeg: Hyperion Press, 1977. Pp. 142. *FQ* 5 (May, June, July, 1978), 13. Chronicles the misery of war and anarchy experienced by Russian Mennonites in the Ukraine during the early part of the century.

Lapp, John A. "Bicentennial Choices." *ChrLiv* 23 (May, 1976), 17-18. Adapted from *A Dream for America*, John Lapp, Herald Press, 1976. American society today includes forces moving toward both revolution and counterrevolution.

Lapp, John A. "Can the Church Rejoin Her Revolution?" *CanMenn* 17 (Nov. 14, 1969), 4, and (Nov. 21, 1969), 4, 14. The renewed church is revolutionary because it has orders to make things new. Both the church and revolution are part of God's scheme of history.

Lapp, John A. "China in Turmoil." *ChrLiv* 14 (Apr., 1967), 18-19. The "Proletarian Cultural Revolution" with its purges, trials, and killings, is Mao Tse-tung's effort to keep the Chinese revolution alive.

Lapp, John A. "Civil War in Angola." *ChrLiv* 23 (Feb., 1976), 15-16. Review of Angolan politics, including conflict among three liberation movements.

Lapp, John A. "Fifty Years of Russian Revolution." *ChrLiv* 15 (January, 1968), 18-19. Review of 50 years of Russian life, beginning with the Revolution in 1917.

Lapp, John A. "From Rhodesia to Zimbabwe." *ChrLiv* 25 (June, 1978), 15, 32. Comment on the transitional government leading to black majority rule and the conflict leading to it.

Lapp, John A. "Gun Control in a Shoot-'Em-Up Society." *ChrLiv* 22 (July, 1975), 9, 33; *ChrLead* 38 (Sept. 30, 1975), 5. Statistics related to violence perpetrated by handguns.

Lapp, John A. "Henry Kissinger." *ChrLiv* 22 (Feb., 1975), 15, 35. Kissinger policy is based on politics of power and personality, as his negotiating of the Vietnamese cease-fire shows.

Lapp, John A. "Newark, Detroit, and _____?" *ChrLiv* 14 (Oct., 1967), 18-19. Urban riots are the ghetto-dwellers' pleas for justice.

Lapp, John A. "'Openien, You Should Have Died Long Ago.' " *ChrLiv* 20 (Feb., 1973), 15, 25, 27. Unequal distribution of land and wealth and the imposition of martial law have created a setting of violence in the Philippines.

Lapp, John A. "The Argentine Nightmare." *ChrLiv* 24 (Feb., 1977), 15-16. Review of Argentine politics, including paramilitary assassinations and armed groups preparing for guerilla warfare.

Lapp, John A. "The Coming of Black Power." *ChrLiv* 13 (Oct., 1966),.18-19. Description of the goals of the Black Power movement in the search for justice and racial equality.

Lapp, John A. "The Diplomacy of Human Rights." *ChrLiv* 24 (June, 1977), 15-16. Discussion of the Carter administration's concern for human rights; the varying interpretations of the concept among Eastern, Western, and Third World countries.

Lapp, John A. "The Hope of Zimbabwe." *ChrLiv* 27 (May, 1980), 13, 34. Birth of independent Zimbabwe ended eight years of civil war.

Lapp, John A. "The Negro Revolution: Year Two." *ChrLiv* 12 (Feb., 1965), 18-19. Comment on the search for justice in race relations in 1964.

Lapp, John A. "The Orange and the Green: 1969 Edition." *ChrLiv* 16 (Nov., 1969), 18-19. Background and discussion of current Protestant-Catholic tension and violence in Northern Ireland.

Lapp, John A. "The Politics of Terror." *ChrLiv* 21 (Aug., 1974), 15, 27. Torture as a means of political and military intimidation is used by both left-wing and right-wing governments.

Lapp, John A. "Violence in America." *ChrLiv* 15 (Aug., 1968), 18-19. Traces the prevalence of violence in American history and social change.

Lapp, John A. "Why Didn't Mennonites Join the Revolution?" *GH* 69 (Aug. 3, 1976), 594-95. Mennonites objected to the Revolutionary War for three philosophical reasons: 1) The Mennonites were already a community, which the Revolution claimed to bring about; 2) The fall of the church was represented by the dominant churches' support of the war; 3) The revolution distorted good politics.

Lapp, John A. (Review). *Christianity and*

Communism, by Russell L. Mast. Newton: Faith and Life Press, 1962. Pp. 32. *ChrLiv* 10 (Apr., 1963), 33. Recommends the book as a pacifist Christian approach to communism which calls the church to a greater concern for justice.

Lapp, John A. (Review). *For Peace and Justice: Pacifism in America, 1914-1941*, by Charles Chatfield. Knoxville: The University of Tennessee Press, 1971. Pp. 447. *MQR* 47 (Jan., 1973), 73-75. Reviewer considers the book a "masterful account" of the American peace movement in the early part of this century, emphasizing liberal Protestant pacifists and treating too lightly the impacts of the "Red Scare" and Reinhold Niebuhr on the pacifist community.

Lapp, John A. (Review). *No King But Caesar? A Catholic Lawyer Looks at Christian Violence*, by William R. Durland. Scottdale: Herald Press, 1975. *FQ* 2 (Winter, 1975), 14. Lapp observes the book's strength lies in Durland's sincere wrestling with the violence of the church through the centuries. Calls the Christian church to lay down its weapons of war.

Lapp, John A. (Review). *Violence: Reflections from a Christian Perspective*, by Jacques Ellul, Seabury Press, 1969. Pp. 179. *ChrLiv* 17 (Dec., 1970), 37. Supports Ellul's appeal for a Christian ethic that represents the rights of the poor and oppressed without resorting to violence.

Lapp, John E. "Why I Am Moved to Witness to the State." *GH* 59 (July 19, 1966), 639-41. An Anabaptist-Mennonite Christian witnesses to the state about the righteousness and justice expected of rulers, and about the supreme lordship of Jesus Christ.

Lapp, John E. "My Kingdom Is Not of This World." *GH* 68 (Nov. 25, 1975), 846-48. To live according to God's Kingdom is to be nonresistant to existing powers, to overcome evil with good, to raise a prophetic voice on social issues, in faithfulness to a New Testament ethic.

Leatherman, Paul. "Vietnams in the US." *GH* 63 (Feb. 3, 1970), 97-98. Uses the image of violence and injustice in Vietnam as a metaphor for injustice toward poor and blacks in the US.

Lee, Nancy (Review). *The Waiting People*, by Peggy Billings. Friendship Press, 1965. Pp. 127. *ChrLiv* 11 (Apr., 1964), 33. Reviewer observes that stories of people in East Asia address questions such as the meaning of nonresistance, suffering, and violence.

Lefever, Harry G. "The Articulate Conscience." *GH* 48 (Apr. 19, 1955), 369. The articulate conscience, obeying the absolute love ethic of Christ, is the salt of the world as it articulates the demands of love and speaks out against social injustice.

Lehman, Emmett R. "Martin Luther King and Civil Disobedience." *GfT* Series 2, Vol. 3 (Apr.-June, 1968), 5-6. King's nonviolent resistance takes obedience to civil authorities too lightly, and thus cannot bring about justice, since order is a prerequisite of justice.

Lehman, Emmett R. "Positive Dissent." *GfT* Series 2, Vol. 3 (Feb., 1968), 5-6. Reprinted also in *GfT* 6 (Sept.-Oct., 1971), 12. All witness to the priority of divine law over human must avoid violence and civil disobedience, since violent dissent cannot bring about justice.

Lehman, Glenn. "A Conversation." *Intercom* 9 (May-June, 1969), 1, 4. Dialogue between MCC teacher and a student guerrilla in the Congo about violence and revolutionary ideology.

Lehman, Melvin L. "Jury Duty." *GH* 73 (July 8, 1980), 540-42. Discusses his experience in being called for jury duty against the backdrop of his commitment to nonviolence and justice.

Lehman, Melvin L. (Review). *Who Burned the Barn Down?,* drama by I. Merle Good. *ChrLiv* 18 (May, 1971), 36-37. Reviewer observes the play explores the problem of peacemaking in the context of pacifism in personal relations. Lind, Loren. "One Thing to Do About It." *ChrLiv* 11 (Apr., 1964). Editorial suggests books on war, nonviolent racial revolution, nuclear arms, cold war, and poverty, in order to help our minds keep pace with our bodies living in a modern world.

Leichty, Daniel. "Grace and the Peace Question." *GH* 72 (Sept. 25, 1979), 754-55. The peace issue is central to Mennonite faith and must be kept at the center of discussion with other Christians because the gospel cannot be communicated through coercion and violence.

Leis, Vernon. "The Church and Revolution." *CanMenn* 14 (Aug. 23, 1966), 5. The church is urged to become contemporary.

Liau, Timothy Y. S. "Christian Responsibility to the Future of Taiwan." MA in Peace Studies thesis, AMBS, 1979. Pp. 133. Analyzes the role of the Taiwanese Christians in the contemporary struggle for justice in Taiwan from the perspectives of both the biblical attitude toward the principalities and powers and the classic peace tradition of nonviolence.

Lind, Loren. "The Poor Among Us." *YCC* 47 (Mar. 13, 1966), 13. The few programs that the government has to assist the poor do not begin to take care of all the problems. The rich have the poor to thank, the poor the rich to curse, for their condition.

Lind, Loren. "Violence on the Left." *YCC* 48 (June 11, 1967), 9. Violence in history has proved itself bankrupt, seldom able even to erase the wrongs it seeks to destroy.

Lind, Marcus. "From Carnal Sword to Peaceful Rod." *ST* 48 (May, 1980), 11-14. Moses led the children of Israel, not with a sword of violence, but with the more peaceful symbol of authority, a shepherd's rod.

Lind, Marcus. "How God Dispenses Justice with His Love." *ST* 46 (May, 1978), 17. A Bible study on Romans 9:15-23.

Lind, Marcus. "Learning from the Bible's First War." *ST* 47 (Jan., 1979), 19-22. Abram's acceptance of Melchizedek's bread and wine instead of Bera's war spoils marked his choice of servanthood rather than violence.

Lind, Marcus. "What Made Joe Stalin Tick?" *ST* 34 (2nd Qtr., 1966), 28. Examines the home influence, schooling, social status, culture, and general environment that made Joe Stalin an inhumane brute once he came to a position of supreme power.

Lind, Millard C. "Monotheism, Power and Justice: A Study in Isaiah 40-55." *CBQ* 46 (July, 1984), 432-46. By a careful comparison of the trial speeches, the Cyrus poems, and the servant poems, Lind shows that while all three testify to Yahweh's historical and cosmic sovereignty, only the servant poems embody the divine purpose to bring justice to the nations. The servant's work, rooted in Torah-justice, discloses a distinctive understanding of politics and, specifically, the moral quality of Yahweh's rule.

Lind, Millard C. "Politics of the Spirit." *GH* 65 (Feb. 22, 1972), 169-71. If a theology of personal integrity and a theology of politics are combined according to the Bible, a politics of power, characterized by self-interest, hypocrisy, and death must come to an end.

Lind, Millard C. "The Concept of Political Power in Ancient Israel." *Annual of the Swedish Theological Institute.* Ed. Hans Kosmala. Leiden: E. J. Brill, 1970, Vol. 7, 4-24. The ancient office of kingship is swept aside by the Mosaic covenant and "the functions of this office are taken over by the immediate rule of Yahweh," who was the political leader of Israel.

Lind, Millard C. "Transformation of Justice: From Moses to Jesus." Paper presented to Lawbreaking and Peacemaking Workshop, Camp Assiniboia, Man., May 3, 1980. Pub. by MCC U.S. Office of Criminal Justice (Akron, Pa.) and MCC Canada Victim Offender Ministries (Winnipeg), 1986. Pp. 23. Part I shows the interrelationship of justice to covenant and law in the various sections of Israel's Scripture. Part II describes four strategies of response: withdrawal as unfaithfulness; constantinian as capitulation; enlightenment as denial; and the pressure and witness of Christian community as faithfulness.

Lind, Millard C. "What About our Luxuries?" *ChrLiv* 1 (Sept., 1954), 3. There is a direct connection between luxury and oppression and war.

Lind, Millard C. *Yahweh Is a Warrior: The Theology of Warfare in Ancient Israel*. Scottdale, Pa.: Herald Press, 1980. Pp. 232; Consists of an exegetical and descriptive analysis of Hebrew warfare in the Primary History (the materials from Genesis through 2 Kings, minus Ruth). The argument has three major emphases: Yahweh delivered the people of Israel through a prophet rather than a warrior, with Yahweh's intervention in the form of a nature miracle rather than human strategy and battle; the exodus became the basis for a distinctive social order that was prophetic in nature, an order which rejected concepts of kingship based on violent force as representative of divinity; as Israel drifted toward the Ancient Near Eastern standard of kingship grounded in violence, Yahweh's war became directed against Israel itself.

Lind, Millard C. (Review). *The Way to Peace*, by L. John Topel, S.J. Maryknoll: Orbis Books, 1979. Pp. 199. *MissFoc* 8 (Mar., 1980), 19-20. Reviewer discusses Topel's biblical theology and pacifism in his approach to liberation theology.

Lind, Tim C. Letter to the Editor. *Intercom* 23 (Jan., 1979), 2. The lack of knowledge of Yahweh in China is evidenced not in the absence of Christians but in the violence present in China's creation and the violence of dictated conformity.

Lohrenz, Gerhard. "Nonresistance Tested." *MennLife* 17 (Apr., 1962), 66-68. The story of Nester Makhno, who after the Russian Revolution in 1917 roamed the countryside with his band, plundering, murdering, and raping the populace, including many Mennonites.

Lohrenz, Gerhard (Review). *A Russian Dance of Death: Revolution and Civil War in the Ukraine*, by Dietrich Neufeld, trans. Al Reimer. Winnipeg, Man.: Hyperion Press and Scottdale, Pa.: Herald Press, 1977. Pp. 137. *MQR* 53 (Jan., 1979), 85-86. A personal account of the situation in the Ukraine during the stormy years of 1919-21.

Lohrenz, Gerhard (Review). *Nestor Makhno: The Life of an Anarchist*, by Victor Peters. Winnipeg: Echo Books, n.d. "Anarchist: Nestor Makhno."

*MennMirror* 1 (Oct., 1971), 13. Recommends this readable and well-documented biography of the Russian "bandit" who plundered Mennonites and others during the 1917 revolution.

Longacre, Paul (Review). *Bread and Justice: Toward a New International Economic Order*, by James B. McGinnis. Paulist Press, 1979. *MBH* 19 (Aug. 8, 1980), 28-29. Recommends this examination of some of the root causes of world hunger.

Longacre, Paul (Review). *Hunger for Justice: The Politics of Food and Faith*, by Jack Nelson. Maryknoll: Orbis, 1980. *MBH* 19 (Aug. 8, 1980), 28-29. Recommends this analysis of some of the economic and political causes of world hunger, with reference to biblical material on hunger and justice.

Lord, Beverly Bowen and Lord, Charles R. Letter to the Editor. *ChrLead* 39 (Nov. 23, 1976), 14. Raises questions about the relationship of US foreign policy and the resulting stability in those countries with known human rights violations in terms of a hospitable environment for mission effort.

Lord, Charles R. "The Response of the Historic Peace Churches to the Internment of the Japanese Americans During World War II." MA in Peace Studies thesis, AMBS, 1981. Pp. 115. Describes and assesses Quaker, Church of the Brethren, and Mennonite responses to the evacuation, relocation, and resettlement of Japanese Americans during World War II. The conclusion drawn from news stories, denominational minutes, as well as personal interviews and letters is that while Mennonites failed to raise a voice of protest in defense of the Japanese Americans who were being treated unjustly, the Friends and the Church of the Brethren responded with greater concern and advocacy.

Lugibihl, Jan. "How Fair Is Welfare?" *Daughters of Sarah* 2 (Jan., 1976), 4-6. Calls feminist Christians to work for justice in a welfare system that denigrates and discriminates against women.

"Message from the Detroit Peace Conference." *Menn* 69 (Feb. 16, 1954), 105, 110. A call to reject nationalism, violence, and war as inconsistent with the missionary and universal character of the church.

"Most Militant Form of Violence." *GH* 65 (Nov. 21, 1972), 975. The form referred to is "Babel" as adopted by the US governing elements, an opinion held by W. Stringfellow, an Episcopal lay theologian who further quotes the Soviet novelist A. Solzhenitsyn: "Any man who has once acclaimed violence as his method must inexorably choose falsehood as his principle."

"Muggers Express Victim Recovers from Assault." *GH* 72 (Apr. 3, 1979), 272. Report of the assault and recovery of Carl Smucker, young Mennonite director of operations for a new volunteer auxiliary patrol along a New York City subway line which tries to stop violence in a nonresistant manner.

MacMaster, Richard K. *Christian Obedience in Revolutionary Times: The Peace Churches and the American Revolution.* Akron, Pa.: MCC (US) Peace Section, 1976. Pp. 26. MHL. Demonstrates that Mennonites and other Christians committed to peace during the Revolutionary War times conflicted with the government on issues of military service, war taxes, and oaths of allegiance. Discusses their stance and resulting persecution within the context of differing concepts of religious liberty; the sectarian concept of discipleship as a separate and distinct way of life was not understood by a government to whom religious freedom meant the freedom to worship according to the dictates of conscience, not the freedom to live by conscience.

Martens, Bob. Letter to the Editor. *MBH* 13 (Sept. 6, 1974), 9. Not only does the church owe a greater allegiance to God than to the state, the church must also avoid any allegiance with the power of the state.

Martens, Elmer A. (Review). *No Place to Stop Killing,* by Norman Wingert. Moody Press, 1974. Pp. 125. In *ChrLead* 37 (Apr. 30, 1974), 24; *MBH* 13 (Sept. 20, 1974), 26. The story is about Hutu people in Burundi and Rwanda who attempted in the early 1960s and again in the early 1970s to dislodge the racially different minority group, the Tutsi.

Martin, Allen G. "One Man's Answer to Revolution." *ChrLiv* 10 (June, 1963), 16-17. Mennonite plantation owner in Brazil treats his workers with dignity and human concern.

Martin, Earl S. and Martin, Patricia Hostetter. "A Letter to Americans on Vietnam." *The Other Side* 15 (Mar., 1979), 27-36. A discussion about the debate between those calling for reconciliation and those calling for human rights in the new Vietnam.

Martin, Earl S. and Martin, Patricia Hostetter. "Interview: A Family's Account of Revolution and the Church in Post War Vietnam." *Sojourners* 5 (Jan., 1976), 29. Evaluation of the Revolution in Vietnam both before and after the change of government. Predicts that the church will grow smaller as government does a better job meeting the physical needs of the people.

Martin, Harold S. "Fallacies of Liberation Theology." *ST* 48 (Apr., 1980), 1-5. Its use of

violence and its equation of social justice with salvation are two severe weaknesses of liberation theology.

Martin, Luke S. "Vietnam Undergoing a Revolution." *Menn* 93 (Sept. 12, 1978), 520. Describes political changes in post-war Vietnam under communist government.

Mast Burnett, Kristina. "Canada-US Relations, Vietnam, Issues at Reedley Meetings." *GH* 72 (Feb. 13, 1979), 128. MCC's annual meeting in Reedley, Jan. 25-27, addressed such issues as Canada-US relations, aid to Vietnam, justice and human rights overseas, Native American outreach, hunger concerns, and militarism.

Mast, Russell L. "Barabbas, the Apostle of Violence." *Menn* 66 (May 8, 1951), 298-99. Uses the Barabbas narrative as a starting point for discussing the ethical issues of means and ends in relation to violence.

McGinnis, James and Kathy. "Parenting for Peace and Justice." *ChrLiv* 27 (Dec., 1980), 10-11. Used by permission from *The Other Side.* Suggestions for helping children value peace and avoid violence.

McPhee, Arthur G. "Jesus and the Whip." *GfT* 6 (Sept.-Oct., 1971), 3, 5; (Nov.-Dec., 1971), 19. Jesus' chasing the animals out of the temple was a demonstration of his authority, not a sanctioning of violence or war; since Jesus whipped animals, not people, in the temple, the passage cannot be used to justify the use of physical violence.

Mennonite Central Committee News. "Snow Falls on MCC Agenda." *EV* 90 (Feb. 25, 1977), 7. Among the issues and concerns discussed at the MCC annual meeting in Metamora, Ill., members discussed how MCC should relate to authoritarian governments that deny justice and religious or political freedom to their citizens.

Mennonite Church General Assembly. "Letters to the US and Canadian Governments." *GH* 70 (July 12, 1977), 542-43. Letters drafted at the Mennonite Church General Assembly in 1977 call the national leaders to pursue peace and human rights.

Mennonite General Conference. "Resolutions of General Conference IV-VII." *GH* 60 (Sept. 19, 1967), 845. Describes General Conference (MC) resolutions which deal with witness against war, the relation of personal and social concerns to Christian faith, and urban riots.

Mennonite World Conference. "The Conference Message." *The Witness of the Holy Spirit.* Ed. Cornelius J. Dyck. Elkhart: MWC, 1967, xiii-xiv. Reflects a particular concern to be reconcilers in a broken world; appeals "to all governments and power structures to seek by peaceful means to bring freedom and justice" to all people."

Metzler, Edgar. "Guessing About the Next Four Years." *MCC PS Wash. Memo* 12 (Nov.-Dec., 1980), 1-2, 6, 9-10. Implications of the Reagan election for peace and justice issues.

Metzler, James E. "A Shalom Focus for Christian Education." *Builder* 29 (Nov., 1979), 2-11. Suggests that the theme of Shalom, the colorful "language of God's dreams," could appropriately focus the educational mission of the church because it combines joyful celebration of God's family with a prophetic witness for justice in God's world.

Metzler, James E. "Menno Speaks to Me." *GH* 67 (Mar. 26, 1974), 257-58. The Anabaptist vision of peace, equality, and justice still calls contemporary Mennonites to discipleship.

Meyers, Rosalyn J. "Racial Minorities: Room at the Top?" *ChrLead* 41 (Sept. 12, 1978), 24. Equal employment opportunity is a matter of justice. Does the church sit back comfortably until it is forced to change or does it go the second mile even before it is required to do so by secular authorities?

Miller, Bernice and Berdella. "Justice Shall Roll Down." *Builder* 15 (July, 1965), 10-13. A choral reading arranged from a sermon by Carl Beck that relates the message of Amos to the situation in war-torn Asia.

Miller, Ernest E. "World Revolution and the Christian." *MennLife* 11 (Apr., 1956), 51-52, 79. A plea for Christians to answer the call to service in the face of worldwide revolution.

Miller, Ernest E. "World Revolution and the Role of the Christian." *ChrLiv* 3 (Dec., 1956), 8-9. Christianity, responsible in a large part for the awakening of nations to long injustice, should now provide volunteers to do the needed relief work.

Miller, Eunice L. "The Poor Are Oppressed." *Builder* 29 (May, 1979), 6-7. A song emerging from the worship life of Timbués Mennonite Felowship in Montevideo, Uruguay. The theme is God's intervention in violence and oppression. Printed in both English and Spanish.

Miller, Helen (Review). *Alternatives to Violence,* by Saul Bernstein. Association Press, 1967. Pp. 192. *ChrLiv* 15 (Jan., 1968), 33. Recommends this analysis of poverty and the violence which stems from it.

Miller, Joseph M. S. "Change and South Africa." MA in Peace Studies thesis, AMBS, 1978. Pp.

110. Examines the roots of racial conflict in South Africa from a variety of perspectives such as political history, language, culture, economics, and religion. Also describes the contemporary situation there and assesses the barriers to positive change as well as its possibilities.

Miller, Levi (Review). *Dwell in Peace: Apply Nonviolence to Everyday Relationships,* by Ronald Arnett. Elgin: The Brethren Press, 1980. Pp. 156. *Builder* 31 (Feb., 1981), 3. Commends the book for the critique of the self-realization movement expressed in the thesis that the nonviolent peacemaker does not seek self-realization above the importance of human peace and justice.

Miller, Marlin E. "Degrees of Glory." *GH* 73 (Feb. 12, 1980), 129-32. Funeral sermon for Doris Janzen Longacre focuses in part on her concern for the false power of nationalism and military violence.

Miller, Marlin E. "Why Urbana?" *Forum* 10 (Feb., 1977), 6-7. Several reasons for Mennonite involvement and participation in Urbana are given, one of which is the growing social justice and peace concerns from which Mennonites can learn and to which they can contribute.

Miller, Mary Alene Cender. "The Concept of Political Power in Israel and in Japan." Paper presented to War in the Old and New Testaments class, AMBS, Elkhart, Ind., Nov. 28, 1981. Pp. 17. AMBS.

Miller, Paul M. "21 Ways to Oppose the Soft Violence of Apartheid." *GH* 70 (Aug. 23, 1977), 638-39. Calls nonresistant Christians to greater awareness of "soft" violence—structural violence sanctioned by law and order—by suggesting 21 ways for nonresistant Christians to witness against apartheid.

Miller, Paul M. "Reverencing God's Image." *Mission-Focus* 6 (Sept., 1978), 11-14. Discusses the meaning and nature of development as it relates to God's commission to "fill and subdue the earth" (Gen. 1:28). "Reverencing God's image" is to be the guiding factor, which is contrasted with the increased violence generally accompanying development.

Miller, Steve. Letter to the Editor. *ChrLead* 40 (Dec. 6, 1977), 15. Clarification of Orlando Costas' relationship to "liberation theology" (*Leader,* Oct. 25, 1977). Costas may have been influenced by "liberation" thinking, but he cannot be considered an exponent of liberation theology.

Miller, Vern. "The Peace Churches and Racial Justice." *CanMenn* 13 (Mar. 9, 1965), 1, 2. Friends, Mennonites, and Brethren met in

Elgin, Ill., Feb. 15-17 to reexamine historic peace church role in bringing about racial justice. Article points to absence of Mennonite funds to help blacks to help themselves.

Miller, Vern (Review). *The Long Freedom Road,* by Janet Harris. McGraw Hill, 1967. Pp. 150. *ChrLiv* 15 (Jan., 1968), 35. Reviewer considers this book a historical and readable account of the struggle for justice during the 1960s civil rights movement.

Minnich, R. Herbert. "Hunger, Revolution, and the Church." *Peacemakers in a Broken World.* Ed. John A. Lapp. Scottdale: Herald Press, 1969, 43-53. Minnich predicts revolution in Latin America as poor and oppressed people begin to demand justice. Calls Christians to work nonviolently for greater socioeconomic equality.

Mooneyham, W. Stanley. "Dialogue: Hard Questions and Harder Answers." *ChrLead* 38 (Oct. 28, 1975), 7. A dialogue between an all too typical resident of the affluent world and a person who represents the hungry, the always sick, the always tired, the always powerless.

Moore, John V. "How Did Your Children Become Involved in People's Temple?" *ChrLiv* 26 (Nov., 1979), 12-14. Methodist minister describes his children's sharing in concern for peace and social justice.

Moyal, Maurice. "Shovel, Trowel, Pick, and Pen." *ChrLiv* 6 (Mar., 1959), 28-29, 39. People's reformer in Sicily is committed to a nonviolent struggle against poverty and injustice.

Mpanya, Mutombo. "African Odyssey: from Colonialism to Identity." MA in Peace Studies thesis, AMBS, 1977. The literary work of 3 major contemporary African writers provides insight into the structural violence resulting from colonialism and maps the difficult course toward peace and wholeness via the rediscovery of an African identity.

Mpanya, Mutombo. "Apartheid in South Africa." *Forum* 11 (Oct., 1977), 2-3. Discusses aspects of apartheid exploitation and urges Western churches to seek justice by refusing to identify with apartheid systems.

Mueller, Patty Erb and Leichty, Bruce. "Different Countries, Different Realities." *Forum* 13 (Dec., 1979), 8-9. An interview with Patty Erb Mueller, who was forced to take up residence in the US after being expelled from Argentina in 1976, in which she discusses Christian responsibility towards the poor.

Mullet, Steven L. "Nonviolent Latin American Liberation Theology: A Challenge to Modern-day Pacifists." Research paper for Biblical and Christian Perspectives on War and Peace class. Pp. 15. BfC.

Mumaw, David K. Letter to the Editor. *GH* 65 (Dec. 12, 1972), 1020-21. Argues that gun ownership can be consistent with a profession of nonviolence if the gun is used only on animals, not people. Disagrees with the idea that guns breed violence.

Mumaw, John R. (Review). *Rising Above Color,* ed. Henry Lantz. Association Press, 1943. Pp. 112. *ChrMon* 36 (May, 1944), 147. Reviewer observes that the book presents the life stories of 13 outstanding blacks appealing for justice and racial equality.

Mumford, Stan. "Listen to the Poor." *ChrLiv* 11 (Jan., 1964), 8-9. Reprinted from *Faith at Work* magazine. The poor see humankind as an interdependent community, with the rich sharing the responsibility for poverty and social justice.

Murcia, Edilberto. "The University and the Individual." *Forum* 9 (Oct., 1975), 6-7. Expresses the need for a unified Christian community to assist and support those university students who are faced with situations where the only response seems to be violence, as in Colombia.

"NIBSCO Council Members Respond." *RepConsS* 31 (Oct., 1974), 3. Peace and Social Concerns Committees of the General Conference Mennonite Church and the Mennonite Church offer five suggestions as to how congregations can respond to the government's program of earned reentry.

Neube, T. L. "The Church and the Rhodesia Question." *EV* 89 (Feb. 25, 1976), 6, 7. T. L. Neube, a teacher at Wanezi Mission, outlines his understanding of the historical setting and the current attitude of the church toward the political situation in Rhodesia, noting as well the effect of the church's position on African youth.

Neufeld, Elmer *et al.* "A Christian Pacifist Witness Is Needed." *Menn* 74 (Dec. 1, 1959), 746-47. Mennonites must work aggressively for social justice within the Anabaptist framework, i.e., the way of the cross. This way grows out of faith in Christ.

Neufeld, Tom (Review). *Beyond the Rat Race,* by Arthur G. Gish. Scottdale: Herald Press, 1973. Pp. 192. *Direction* 3 (Apr., 1974), 179-80. While the book contains some profound insights (along with some "hopelessly trite suggestions for simple living"), simplicity as "the central category of value and criticism" is not an adequate approach toward the problems of poverty, violence, and technology to which Gish applies it.

Neufeld, Vernon. "Violence: Call for Study and Research." *CanMenn* 17 (Mar. 25, 1969), 4; "Questions About Violence: A Call for New Studies." *Menn* 84 (May 6, 1969), 302-304. A study of the nature, causes of, and solution to violence is proposed, with guidelines to indicate the direction the study should take.

Nisley, Weldon D. "An Analysis of Liberation Theology as a New Way of Doing Theology." MA in Peace Studies thesis, AMBS, 1977. Pp. 55. Summarizes the major themes and defines the methodological procedures of liberation theology. Also enters into some critical debate with the discipline.

Nisley, Weldon D. "Nuclear Power and Sin." *Menn* 92 (Oct. 11, 1977), 580-81. Using "nuclear power" to mean the power accompanying possession and use of nuclear weapons, Nisly discusses the morality of nuclear weapons when compared with Jesus' teachings on peacemaking.

Nord, Randy. Letter to the Editor. *ChrLead* 40 (Dec. 20, 1977), 14. Concerned about Mennonite Brethren's lack of concern for social problems, including peace and justice.

Nyoka, Justin. "Rhodesian Elections 'Programmed'." *Menn* 94 (June 5, 1979), 393. The Rhodesian elections were programmed and computerized by the Smith administration; power will consequently continue to be held by the white minority.

"On TV Violence." *EV* 90 (Feb. 10, 1977), 16. Reprinted from *Release*. Television violence has increased and encourages behavior and solutions that run contrary to the Christian caling to be peacemakers.

Oliver, Kay. "TV's Surprising Challenger: You, the Viewer." *MBH* 17 (Sept. 15, 1978), 2-5. Violence as an acceptable solution to problems is one of the objectionable elements of TV programing, say concerned consumer's groups.

Ollenburger, Ben C. (Review). *Christians and Marxists: The Mutual Challenge to Revolution,* byJose Miguez Bonino. Grand Rapids: Eerdmans, 1976. In *ChrLead* 40 (Mar. 15, 1977), 18. Bonino's thesis is that both Christianity and Marxism provide challenges to the kind of revolution which may be necessary for the "correction" of injustice and oppression in Latin America.

"Peacemaker in Revolution." *CanMenn* 17 (Apr. 1, 1969), 1. Norman Kraus addresses the Intercollegiate Peace Fellowship conference in Washington: "Although Jesus operated with agape love, God is not a pacifist. According to Revelation, the lamb that was slaughtered was the one who poured out vengeance and judgment. Revolution may be God's way of judging our sin.

"Preparing for Revolution." *MHB* 35 (July, 1974), 2-7. Series of documents traces the tension caused in Lancaster County when nonresistant Mennonites refused to serve in military units being established in preparation for the Revolutionary War.

Pauls, Alvin N. Letter to the Editor. *ChrLead* 38 (Nov. 11, 1975), 15. People, not guns, are instruments of all violence.

Peachey, Dean E. "What Do You Think of Justice?" *GH* 72 (Dec. 25, 1979), 1025-26. Three distinct criteria for deciding whether or not a given distribution of resources is just—equality, merits, and needs. Our understanding of justice affects and influences much of our lives.

Peachey, J. Lorne. "Army Men and Dart Guns." *ChrLiv* 22 (Apr., 1975), 39. Editorial recounts family search for a policy toward toys of war and violence.

Peachey, J. Lorne. "Atrocities—1966 Style." *ChrLiv* 13 (June, 1966), 11, 37. Reprinting of a press release from the Council of the Society for the Psychological Study of Social Issues condemning American torture of prisoners of war in Vietnam.

Peachey, J. Lorne. "Community News and Trends." *ChrLiv* 15 (Aug., 1968), 11. Mennonites in Iowa City and Ottawa respond to war and violence through a public letter and through assisting draft evaders.

Peachey, J. Lorne. "Community News and Trends." *ChrLiv* 16 (Feb., 1969), 11. Two subjects highlighted: a Mennonite family responds to armed intruders; violence portrayed on TV.

Peachey, J. Lorne. *How to Teach Peace to Children.* Scottdale and Kitchener: Herald Press, 1981. Pp. 32. MHL. Surveys historic peace church writing since World War II on peace education and condenses this wisdom into 20 suggestions for parents and other caretakers. Addresses such issues as war toys, entertainment glorifying violence, competitive vs. cooperative play, international experience, peace projects, etc. Other resources included in the book are a discussion guide and reading list.

Peachey, Paul L. "Agape in Tokyo." *Fellowship* 26 (Nov., 1960), 10. Describes the riots in Tokyo as a symptom of a profound spiritual crisis in Japan of which American foreign policy is a principal cause.

Peachey, Paul L. "Love, Justice, and Peace." *GH* 49, Part 1, (Feb. 21, 1956), 177, 189; Part 2, (Mar. 20, 1956), 273, 287; Part 3, (Apr. 17, 1956), 369;

Part 4, (May 15, 1956), 465; Part 5, (July 17, 1956), 680. Love is interpersonal, relational. It cannot be a principle on which to build society. Mennonites have seriously compromised the love community they profess.

Peachey, Paul L. "Peace or Revolution: The Coming Struggle." *MennLife* 20 (July, 1965), 99-101. Change, not peace, is the task at hand; the question of how change occurs is of importance—is it by evolution or revolution? The answer lies in the healing of the broken community of faith—the church.

Peachey, Urbane. "Human Rights in South Korea." *Peace Section Newsletter* 8 (June, 1977), 4-5. Examines the involvement of the many American Christian enterprises in South Korea. Notes that there seems to be a contradiction between the presence of so many Christians and the very repressive environment.

Peachey, Urbane, comp. "Mennonite Peace Theology Colloquium II: Theology of Justice, Bethel Mennonite Church, North Newton, Ks., Nov. 15-18, 1978, [Papers]." Akron, Pa.: MCC Peace Section, 1979. MHL. Includes: Brubacher, Ray, "Case Study of Southern Africa," pp. 9; Keeney, William, "Reactions to Case Study of Southern Africa," pp. 3; Friesen, LeRoy, "A Brief on the Southern Africa Case Study," pp. 3; Lind, Millard, "Programmatic Decision/Action in Southern Africa: Implications of the Decision from the Viewpoint of Biblical Theology," pp. 4; Rempel, Henry, "Response to the South Africa Case Study," pp. 4; Wiebe, Menno, "Canadian Northern Development, An Account of the Churchill-Nelson River Diversion Project," pp. 18; Schroeder, David, "Case Study: Native Concerns, The Frame of Reference from the Standpoint of Biblical Theology," pp. 2; LaRogne, Emma, "Response to Menno Wiebe," pp. 3; Klassen, A. J., "Response to Northern Development Case Study," pp. 2; Vogt, Roy, "Response to Menno Wiebe's Case Study of Canadian Northern Development," pp. 4; Defehr, Art, "Northern Development and Justice: The Business Perspective," pp. 3; Kraus, C. Norman, "Toward a Biblical Perspective on Justice," pp. 17; Stoltzfus, Edward, "Response to Study Paper 'Toward a Biblical Perspective on Justice' by C. Norman Krause," pp. 3; Gajardo, Joel V., "The Latin American Situation: The Challenge of Liberation Theology," pp. 12; Lind, Millard, review, *Marx and the Bible* by José Miranda (Maryknoll, NY: Orbis, 1974. Pp. 338), pp. 9.

Peachey, Urbane. "The Violence of Complicity." *Peace Section Newsletter* 8 (Feb., 1977), 5-6. Even though the United States government is increasingly concerned about the proliferation of weapons technology in various parts of the world, United States firms are participating in a diversity of multinational arms schemes.

Peachey, Urbane. "What Is a Military Occupation?" *Peace Section Newsletter* 8 (Aug., 1977), 6-7. Describes the treatment of West Bank inhabitants as military in every respect—labor exploitation, collective punishment, expulsion of leadership, land expropriation, arbitrary arrests, restrictions on place of residence, and restrictions on assembly and right of expression.

Peachey, Urbane (Review). *Christ and Violence,* by Ronald J. Sider. Scottdale: Herald Press, 1979. Pp. 108. *MissFoc* 8 (June, 1980), 40. Reviewer considers the book's strength its direct connection between commitment to biblical nonviolence and life within modern society dominated by violent structures.

Peters, Frank C. "The Christian in a World of Violence." *ChrLead* 22 (Feb. 10, 1959), 4-5, 16. Jesus did not intend truth to be defended with coercion and violence, but with the strength of the Spirit and love of God.

Peters, Frank C. "The Scriptural Basis for Nonresistance." *ChrLead* 22 (Oct. 20, 1959), 4-5, 18. While Israel was, in a sense, the carrier and promoter of divine justice, the church is clearly the carrier of divine grace and redemptive love.

Peters, Peter H. (Review). *Christ and Violence,* by Ron Sider. Herald Press, 1979. Pp. 105. *MennRep* 10 (Aug. 18, 1980), 8. The book locates Christ's love and suffering for enemies at the heart of the gospel and examines the relationship of subjection to government and nonviolent resistance to governmental injustice.

Peters, Robert V. "In the Big Apple." *Menn* 94 (July 10, 1979), 461. Two current movements struggling to promote life and justice are the Catholic Worker Movement and Mobilization for Survival. The writer participates in both.

Peters, Robert V. Letter to the Editor. *Menn* 91 (July 6, 1976), 440. Justice for all is the precursor of peace, made possible through discipleship, not through accepting instant salvation.

Peters, Robert V. "Speaking Out." *Menn* 94 (Mar. 27, 1979), 237. Mennonite involvement in the take-over of native American lands in Kansas and Manitoba calls us to repentance, to side with the poor, and to speak out against injustice.

Peters, Robert V. "The Singing Prophet." *Menn* 94 (June 19, 1979), 429. Pete Seeger, an American folksinger, is one of the most significant voices for freedom and justice throughout the world.

Peters, Robert V. "Weeping Over Winnipeg." *Menn* 94 (Mar. 13, 1979), 205. While the Mennonites have become powerful in

Winnipeg, the large native population has become more powerless. Writer fears we are moving close to the brink of apostasy by being indifferent to these injustices.

Pinnock, Clark. "A Statement for Disciples in Society." *MBH* 15 (Feb. 20, 1976), 2-3, 29. Evangelical Christians need a systematic theology dealing with Christian concern for injustice, racism, and militarism.

Powell, Donald E. Letter to the Editor. *GH* 65 (Nov. 21, 1972), 973. Labels as communist propaganda the idea that guns cause violence. Asserts his intention to use his hunting weapons on criminal intruders if necessary, since God does not intend people to die at the hand of "senseless criminals," but rather to die for Christ's sake.

Preheim, Marion Keeney. "Do the Rich Make Indonesians Poor?" *MBH* 19 (Jan. 18, 1980), 19-20. Unjust structures such as economic inequity and North American military support for dictatorships help keep people poor.

Prieb, Wesley. "A Triple Revolution Changes the Church." *CanMenn* 13 (Mar. 16, 1965), 7. Cybernation, weaponry, and human rights were points of discussion at the Elgin, Ill., historic peace churches meeting.

(Review). *Shall We Overcome?* by Howard O. Jones. Fleming H. Revell Co., Westwood, NJ, 1966. Pp. 146. *GfT* Series 2, 3 (Dec., 1968), 16. Commends the book for its view that violence and racism will be answered only by a spiritual revival among all Christians.

Rahmeier, Paul. "Where You Fit In." *YCC* 49 (June 23, 1968), 12. Discusses ways in which a young Christian might respond to the call of conscience with regard to the problem of poverty in the United States.

Raid, Howard. "Death on the Road." *Menn* 87 (May 30, 1972), 372. Mennonite concerns about violence should lead to Mennonite action on the issues of the incidence of highway accidents which maim and kill.

Ratzlaff, Erich L. "Another Point of View on Brazil." *Menn* 85 (Dec. 1, 1970), 743. There is a paradox in being sympathetic to revolutionary leftist movements while supporting MCC, which was begun to rescue people from revolutionary violence.

Ratzlaff, Vernon. "The Church and Changing Culture." *Direction* 1 (July, 1972), 85-91. There are several responses to the rapidly changing society the church can develop in the areas of rejecting violence, accepting pluralism, developing a consistent Christian theistic world view, appreciating Christian community, and changing the patterns of decision-making in the Christian community.

Ratzlaff, Vernon (Review). *Is Revolution Change?* ed. Brian Griffiths. London: InterVarsity Press, 1972. In *Direction* 2 (Jan., 1973), 30. Book contains brief essays that cogently point up the need for biblical evaluation of the church's role within a violence-torn society.

Ratzlaff, Vernon (Review). *The Struggle for Humanity,* by Marjorie Hope and James Young. Maryknoll: Orbis Books, 1977. Pp. 305. *MBH* 17 (Dec. 22, 1978), 31. Recommends this collection of the stories of seven people working nonviolently for reconciliation and justice.

Raud, Elsa. "Jesus Was Not a Revolutionary." *ST* 37 (Sept., 1969), 19. In all his teaching Jesus stressed faith in God as a basic element of human life. Not revolution to overthrow the economic, or the political, or the religious establishment, but faith was the path he appointed for his followers.

Redekop, Calvin W. "Institutions, Power, and the Gospel." *Kingdom, Cross, and Community.* Ed. John R. Burkholder and Calvin Redekop. Scottdale: Herald Press, 1976, 138-50. Religious movements use power and create institutions, thus emphasizing the goal-oriented or "doing" side of life rather than the relationship-oriented, or "being" side. Institutional power in itself is a neutral entity, but it becomes contrary to the gospel when it is used to solidify status differences and domination. Nonresistant or "free" churches have tended to ignore rather than analyze their use of power.

Redekop, Calvin W. "Why a True-Blue Nonresistant Christian Won't Waste Natural Resources." *FQ* 4 (Aug., Sept., Oct., 1977), 14-15. Christian nonresistance means refusing to do violence to life—human, animal, or natural environment.

Redekop, John H. "A Call to Consistency." *MBH* 16 (Aug. 5, 1977), 10. Concerned about MCC personnel identification with black resistance movements in Africa, author cannot reconcile pacifism with terrorism.

Redekop, John H. "A Christian Pacifist Looks at the Expression of Our Peace Witness." *MBH* 7 (Nov. 1, 1968), 7-10. Mennonites have been too hesitant to engage in lobbying or demonstrating for peace; they have not seen peace as integrally related to love and justice.

Redekop, John H. "Christianity and Political Neutralism." *CanMenn* 4 (Aug. 10, 1956), 3, 15. The question is raised as to whether or not Christians can remain neutral in light of the oppression and suffering in the world.

Redekop, John H. "Christians in a World of International Confrontation." *Menn* 89 (July 9, 1974), 433-35. Describes international exploitation by firms based in North America, and the rise of nationalism which counters this colonialism. Concludes that the present nation-state system produces injustice and inequality, against which Christians must speak out.

Redekop, John H. "Varieties of Violence." *MBH* 13 (Oct. 18, 1974), 8. White oppression of native Canadians lies behind present Indian violence.

Redekop, John H. (Review). *Government Is for Your Good,* by Ben Vandezande. St. Catharines: Outreach Niagara, 1979. Pp. 40. *MBH* 19 (Sept. 26, 1980), 27. Limited recommendation for this introductory study of justice as the political expression of love.

Redekopp, Orlando. "Rhodesia/Zimbabwe Elections: The Future Is Not Bright." *MennRep* 9 (Apr. 16, 1979), 7. Although an election is possible, it is not known what form it will take. Churches in Zimbabwe have been only minimally involved and are not unified on issues of racism, violence, rich and poor relations, or minority domination.

Redekopp, Orlando (Review). *Between a Rock and a Hard Place,* by Mark Hatfield. Waco: Word, 1976. *MBH* 15 (Dec. 10, 1976), 30-31. Reviewer observes that Hatfield critiques both a Christian apologist, who condones violence by splitting ethics into personal and private spheres, and a purist, who refuses all violence and withdraws from the political world.

Redekopp, Orlando (Review). *Biko,* by Donald Woods. New York and London: Paddington Press, 1978. Pp. 288. And *Steve Biko,* by Hilda Bernstein. London: International Defense and Aid Fund for Southern Africa, 1978. Pp. 147. *MennRep* 9 (Feb. 5, 1979), 11. Both books recount the life and death of Steve Biko, a founder and respected leader in the South African Black consciousness movement. They reveal a world where the ideology of apartheid cruelly crushes eighty percent of South Africa's population.

Redekopp, Orlando (Review). *Perceptions of Apartheid: The Churches and Political Change in South Africa,* by Ernie Regehr. Toronto: Between the Lines, 1979. Pp. 280. *MBH* 19 (Feb. 15, 1980), 32. Book's theme is the role of the churches in creating and maintaining apartheid in South Africa. Reviewer considers it "indispensable to any Christian concerned with justice and peace."

Reed, Watford. "How to Cool a Hot Summer." *ChrLiv* 19 (May, 1972), 2-7. How the city of Portland avoided violence and rioting during demonstrations in the summer of 1970.

Reedy, Janet Umble. "Sexual Equality and Peace." *MCC PS TF on Women in Ch. and Soc. Report* 35 (Jan.-Feb., 1981), 1-3. Analysis of the polarization of men's and women's roles into dominance and passivity, leading to violence and militarism.

Reese, Boyd (Review). *Beyond the Rat Race,* by Art Gish. Herald Press, 1973. Pp. 190. *Post-American* 3 (Feb.-Mar., 1974), 7. Recommends the book for its critique of the inherent injustice of a consumer, capitalist economy.

Regehr, Ernie. "African Anabaptists: Confronting a Continent at War." *MennRep* 10 (July 21, 1980), 7. African Mennonites and Brethren in Christ grapple with the peace tradition in countries embroiled in struggles against repressive political and economic structures.

Regehr, Ernie. "Civil War in El Salvador: North America Supports a Repressive Regime." *MennRep* 10 (Dec. 8, 1980), 8. Reports on North American military support of the violently repressive Salvadorian government, and calls for the right to self-rule by the people of El Salvador and an end to foreign arms shipments.

Regehr, Ernie. "Conscientious Objection in South Africa." *GH* 68 (Dec. 9, 1975), 872-73; *MennRep* 5 (May 12, 1975), A7. Examines a resolution by the South African Council of Churches to consider conscientious objection as a means of refusing to support apartheid. Considers the resolution a "modest beginning," since it denounces violence only when supporting an unjust cause.

Regehr, Ernie. "Mennonites and Iran: Confession Is Good for the Soul." *MennRep* 10 (June 23, 1980), 7. Author documents Canadian complicity in the military dictatorship of the Shah of Iran and calls for Canadian Mennonites to join with American Mennonites in a confession of corporate guilt.

Regehr, Ernie. *Perceptions of Apartheid: The Churches and Political Change in South Africa.* Scottdale: Herald Press; Kitchener: Between the Lines, 1979. Pp. 309. Detailed analysis of racial violence in South Africa. Includes extensive discussion of the church and state relationship in that context as well as a final chapter entitled "Violence/Nonviolence and the Dilemma of the Churches" in which the issues of conscientious objection, as well as other issues of war and peace, are raised.

Reimer, Al. "Questions Raised by the Death of a Mennonite Terrorist." *MennMirror* 9 (Sept., 1979), 22. Two German articles on the death of Elizabeth von Dyck, a young Mennonite terrorist who was gunned down by police in West Germany in May, 1979, are included in this issue. The editor looks at some of the questions they raise about Christian responsibility towards such people and their destructive acts.

Reimer, Jim (Review). *The Odyssey of the Bergen Family,* by Gerhard Lohrenz. Winnipeg: Gerhard Lohrenz, 1978. *Thy Kingdom Come: The Diary of Johann J. Nickel,* ed. John P. Nickel. Saskatoon: John P. Nickel, 1978. "Two Books Focus on Revolutionary Russia," *MennRep* 9 (Mar. 5, 1979), 8. These two books attempt to tell the Mennonite story of what happened in revolutionary and post-revolutionary Russia, depicting both the glory and the shame which the reviewer suggests is as much a part of the essence of "Mennonitism" as is "ideal Anabaptism."

Reimer, Luetta. "The Christian Response to the Women's Liberation Movement." *ChrLead* 37 (Oct. 29, 1974), 4. The general spirit of equality, justice, and personal dignity promoted by the movement is clearly compatible with Christ's teachings on human relationships.

Reimer, Vic. "The Gospel, Marxism, and Christian Mission: A View from Latin America." *Menn* 92 (Oct. 11, 1977), 584-85. Interview with Orlando Costas, Latin American theologian, discussing evangelization and challenging Mennonites to place their peace witness behind ratification of the Panama Canal treaty and other Latin American human rights issues, as they did in the struggle against the Vietnam War.

Reitz, Herman R. "On Advocating Social Justice." *ST* 46 (Feb., 1978), 12-17. Lists the various ways of dealing with injustice, from conservative to liberal, and calls for Christians to be more active in the struggle for justice.

Rempel, David G. "A Response to the 'Lost Fatherland' Review." *CanMenn* 16 (Aug. 13, 1968), 7. An interpretation of the Mennonite involvement in the Russian famine and revolution during and after World War I.

Rempel, John (Review). *The Peacemaker,* by Levi Miller. Faith and Life Press/Mennonite Publishing House, 1972. "Booklet on Nonresistance: What About Power?" *MennRep* 4 (Feb. 18, 1974), 8. Study guide on the characteristics of a peacemaking life is adequate as a study guide, but it fails to plow new ground on issues of power or definition of nonresistance.

Rempel, Ruth Yoder (Review). *Against Our Will: Men, Women, and Rape,* by Susan Brownmiller. Simon & Schuster, 1975. Pp. 480. *MCC PS TF on Women in Ch. and Soc. Report* 10 (Mar.-Apr., 1976), 5-7. Reviewer observes that one-half of the book is devoted to documenting the use of rape during war to prove dominance and power.

Rich, Ronald. Letter to the Editor. *Menn* 92 (Jan. 11, 1977), 29-30. Quotes Andrei Sakharov and two persecuted Russian Christians to call attention to the responsibility of peacemakers to speak for prisoners of conscience in the Soviet Union.

Rich, Ronald. Letter to the Editor. *Menn* 92 (Apr. 26, 1977), 285-86. Marxism is the political movement showing the most blatant militarism in its march toward world power and its repression of its own citizens.

Rich, Ronald. Letter to the Editor. *Menn* 93 (Apr. 4, 1978), 237. Calls peacemakers not to use editorial power to cover up reports of violence and repression in communist countries, while exposing such violations of human rights in fascist countries.

Riddick, Ed. "An Anabaptist View of Social Protest." Paper presented to the Mennonite Graduate Fellowship, Waterloo, Ont., Dec., 1962. Pp. 6. MHL, MLA/BeC.

Robinson, James H. "The Revolution of Communism." *ChrLiv* 3 (July, 1956), 18-20, 41-42. Reprinted from *Tomorrow Is Today,* by James H. Robinson. Christian Education Press, 1954. Poverty and injustice alone do not motivate people to accept communism, as shown by the overwhelming rejection of communism by black Americans.

Rogers, Ingrid, ed. *Swords into Plowshares: A Collection of Plays About Peace and Social Justice.* Elgin: The Brethren Press, 1983. Pp. 281. Plays by Mennonite authors annotated separately.

Ruth, John L. *'Twas Seeding Time: A Mennonite View of the American Revolution.* Scottdale and Kitchener: Herald Press, 1976. Pp. 224. An informal history of Mennonites in Pennsylvania during the Revolutionary War, focusing on the personalities and problems of the Mennonites of this period.

Rutschmann, LaVerne. "Anabaptism and Liberation Theology." *MQR* 55 (July, 1981), 255-70. Defines liberation theology in terms of its ideological emphases, its self-conscious task of liberation, and the tools it uses to accomplish this task. Author then discusses the possible interaction of liberation theology with Anabaptism based on their similarities and differences.

"Students 252-54. Differing theologies and political theories are presented in order to find an answer to the problems of our time: injustice, war, poverty, inequality, conscription, and violence.

Samuel, Dorothy T. "Love Is a Self-Feeding Explosion." *Menn* 91 (Sept. 28, 1976), 561. Reprinted from *Safe Passages on City Streets*, by Dorothy T. Samuel (1975). Relates the story of two women accosted at night who responded with dignity and understanding love, transforming the scene of potential violence into a genuine human meeting.

Sawatsky, Walter W. "Power in Church-State Relations in Eastern Europe." *MQR* 55 (July, 1981), 214-17. Testing a thesis formulated by the Lutheran World Federation that the state's power is the primary variable shaping encounters between church and state in Marxist countries, the author reflects on particular meetings of Mennonites with state officials of Yugoslavia, East Germany, and the Soviet Union.

Sawatzky, Sharon R. "Rape: Keeping Women in Their Place." *Menn* 91 (Sept. 28, 1976), 558-60. Just as the church works against war, it must work against other violence such as rape, which demeans women. Limited resistance to an attacker is a response in line with Jesus' perfect love.

Schmidt, Linda. "Perpetuating Repression: US Training of Foreign Military and Police." *Peace Section Newsletter* 9 (Jan.-Feb., 1978), 4-8. The training of foreign military and police has been an integral part of the US foreign policy over the past twenty-five years. The countries which have received large amounts of military and economic aid are the same countries which have been cited most often for human rights violations.

Schrag, Martin H. "Mars Rides Again." *GH* 62 (Apr. 15, 1969), 340-44. Relates statistics concerning burgeoning American military spending and production and its relation to domestic violence, and challenges Christians to bring Christian insights of internationality, forgiveness, and love to bear on this problem.

Schrag, Robert M. "Revolution in World Society." *Menn* 73 (Sept. 30, 1958), 601-602. The Christian task is to be expendable, to suffer, and to sacrifice in the context of present social revolution.

Schrock, Paul M. "Peace and War: Atomic Love." *GH* 47 (July 20, 1954), 681. The greatest power in the universe is nonresistant love. It is required of the New Testament believer in all aspects of life.

Schroeder, Ardith. "Nonviolence Begins at Home." Paper speaks against domestic violence. Entry in C. Henry Smith Peace Contest, Bethel College, North Newton, Ks., May 19, 1977. Pp. 5. MHL.

Schroeder, David. "The Church Representing the Kingdom." *MBH* 17 (Sept. 29, 1978), 4-6. The church is a sign of the kingdom when it speaks against injustice and manifests in its life the liberating action of God.

Schultz, Harold J. (Review). *The Church Struggle in South Africa*, by John W. De Gruchy. Grand Rapids: William B. Eerdmans, 1979. Pp. 237. *MennLife* 34 (Sept., 1979), 28. Describes this book as a perceptive and sensitive account of the moral and political dilemmas facing South African Christians and also as providing an analysis of the need for the worldwide church to break the circle of cumulative violence.

Schwartzentruber, Hubert. "A Foundation for the Urban Church." *GH* 72 (Jan. 30, 1979), 76-77. Proposes some essential elements that belong to a biblical foundation for urban and social justice concerns identified at Estes '77.

Schwartzentruber, Hubert. "Mennonites and the City." *Peace Section Newsletter* 9 (Mar.-Apr., 1978), 1-3. The Mennonite must continue to support a redemptive mission in urban communities with a renewed commitment to justice and shalom.

Schwartzentruber, Hubert. "'Schleitheim,' a Peace Document." *MHB* 38 (Apr., 1977), 7. Author takes inspiration from 16th-century Anabaptists who risked death to counter the principalities and powers, and he calls for a similar commitment to justice and righteousness through nonviolence among Mennonites today.

Schwartzentruber, Hubert. "The Brokenness of the City." *Peacemakers in a Broken World*. Ed. John A. Lapp. Scottdale: Herald Press, 1969, 20-29. Also in "The Broken People of the City." *ChrLiv* 17 (Dec., 1970), 30-33. Outlines problems of poverty, unemployment, depression, racism, violence in city ghettos and rural areas, and calls Christians to help relieve these conditions as part of spreading the gospel.

Scott, W. Herbert. "The Christian's Position— Above or Beside the Needy?" *ChrLead* 38 (Oct. 28, 1975), 2. To suggest that the spiritual features of love, justice, mercy, and compassion are to be exclusively applied in the Christian community and denied to the unreached, non-Christian world, contradicts both the teaching and example of Jesus.

Seitz, Blair. "Putting Words into Actions." *ChrLiv* 25 (Mar., 1978), 16-19. Working toward a simpler lifestyle in the concern for global justice.

Seitz, Ruth. "Agony and Ecstacy in Uganda." *Menn* 92 (Oct. 11, 1977), 589-90. Bishop Festo Kivengere of Uganda discusses Archbishop Luwum's martyrdom for speaking out for human rights and challenges Mennonites to bring their peace witness to bear actively on situations of oppression in the world.

Seitz, Ruth. "Growing Inside." *With* 12 (Mar., 1979), 22. The story of Amado Galzim and the political prisoner situation in the Philippines under the Marcos regime.

Shank, J. Ward. "Age of Violence." *ST* 36 (Aug., 1968), 13. A survey of the present violent times is strikingly in accord with the biblical description of conditions in the latter days. The church should respond by preaching the gospel of salvation through the blood of Christ with the greater zeal.

Shank, J. Ward. "Focus on Revolution." *ST* 38 (Sept., 1970), 10. Report on a seminar on "Peacemaking in a World of Revolution" at Eastern Mennonite College, June 15-26, 1970.

Shank, J. Ward. "In Time of Revolution." *ST* 38 (July, 1970), 6. Suggests ways to respond to a revolutionary climate.

Shank, J. Ward. "The Pursuit of Justice." *ST* 47 (Apr., 1979), 8-10. The former Mennonite emphasis on love and nonresistance is changing to emphasis on peace and justice through social programs and reform.

Shank, J. Ward (Editorial). "Preaching the Gospel to the Poor." *ST* 47 (Mar., 1979), 5. Although there is an emphasis on the poor as special recipients of the gospel in the Bible, God does not side with the poor over and against the rich.

Shank, J. Ward (Editorial). "The Pursuit of Justice." *ST* 47 (Spr., 1979), 8. Notes the growing emphasis on justice along with peace. Examines biblical justice and concludes that the common usage is more in line with the concepts and techniques of social action.

Shank, J. Ward (Editorial). "The Revolutionary Idea." *ST* 37 (Sept., 1969), 1. With so much emphasis on the "revolution" or radical social change, the church must keep its eyes on spiritual strength and foundational beliefs.

Shank, J. Ward (Review). *A Russian Dance of Death,* by Dietrich Neufeld. Translated and edited by Al Reimer. Hyperion Press and Herald Press, 1977. Pp. 142. *ST* 46 (Nov., 1978), 22-24. Recommends this firsthand account of the violence and hardship experienced by Mennonite colonists during the Russian Revolution.

Shank, J. Ward (Review). *Agenda for Biblical People,* by Jim Wallis. Harper and Row, n.d. Pp. 145. *ST* 45 (Nov., 1977), 26-27. Reviewer notes the book's thesis is that the church must work toward liberation and justice for the poor and oppressed.

Shank, J. Ward (Review). *Christ and Violence,* by Ronald J. Sider. Scottdale: Herald Press, 1979. Pp. 108. *ST* 48 (July, 1980), 28-29. Reviewer observes that rather than serving as a study of Jesus' teachings on war and violence, the book advocates Christian social reform.

Shank, J. Ward (Review). *Let Justice Roll Down,* by John Perkins. Regal Publications, n.d. Pp. 223. *ST* 45 (Apr., 1977), 32-33. While reviewer appreciates Perkins' emphasis on spiritual conversion in combating racism, he raises questions about Perkins' involvement in forms of active resistance such as boycotts.

Shank, J. Ward (Review). *Rich Christians in an Age of Hunger,* by Ronald J. Sider. Downers Grove: Intervarsity Press, n.d. Pp. 249. *ST* 48 (Jan., 1980), 24-25. The book is a mild form of liberation theology in its advocacy of social justice, says the reviewer.

Shank, J. Ward (Review). *The Christian and Revolution,* by Melvin Gingerich. Herald Press, 1968. *ST* 37 (Sept., 1969), 18. Offers a helpful analysis of the revolutionary movements sweeping over the world; includes some suggestions to Christians regarding their attitude toward these movements.

Shearer, Jon (Review). *Jesus and the Nonviolent Revolution,* by André Trocmé. Scottdale: Herald Press, 1971. Pp. 173. "The Ministry of Jesus: Justice and Redemption Inseparable." *MennRep* 4 (Apr. 29, 1974), Section A, 8. Book focuses on Jesus' ministry of active nonviolence rooted in his inauguration of the Year of Jubilee. Shearer observes it is foundational work for John H. Yoder's *Politics of Jesus.*

Shelly, Maynard. "A Message for Revolutionists." *Menn* 65 (May 9, 1950), 327. "Quench not the Spirit" is the word to the church which has failed to live the revolution of suffering love. Shelly, Maynard. "Conversation with Erna." *GH* 62 (Dec. 9, 1969), 1049-51. Thoughtfully probes the perspectives of right wing extremists who oppose social justice on grounds of communist conspiracy, and challenges Mennonites not to accept these fears in place of trust in God.

Shelly, Maynard. "Liberation in Bangladesh a Tough Miracle." *MBH* 13 (Mar. 22, 1974), 13-14. Not military strength, but massive migrations of people out of the country broke the power of East Pakistan's military government and won independence for Bangladesh.

Shelly, Maynard. "Palestinian Arabs Tap Antiwar Activists." *Menn* 94 (June 19, 1979), 422-23. A national conference on human rights and the Palestinian-Israeli conflict discussed efforts to work for Palestinian freedom.

Shelly, Maynard. "Prague Fails to Get Down to Business." *CanMenn* 16, Part 2, (Apr. 23, 1968), 1, 4. Reports on the Christian Peace Conference held in Prague. The conference showed that it is easy enough to condemn the other person's war but difficult to condemn one's own. Shelly feels that this difference may begin to change because the Czech theologian Josef Smolik called for a study of the abuses of power by countries of both the East and West and the proposal was passed by the conference.

Shelly, Maynard. "The Uniqueness and Anguish of Bangla Desh." *Fellowship* 38 (Oct., 1972), 4. The poetry of Kazi Nagrul Islam, Bengal's greatest living poet, reflects the anger of oppression and the hope for something better which helped Bangladesh to win its independence.

Shelly, Maynard. "World Conference Site Being Questioned," *Menn* 85 (Sept. 15, 1970), 556, 558; "Militarism Blocks Social Reform in Brazil." *Menn* 85 (Oct. 6, 1970), 604, 605; "Church Can Shape Revolution in Brazil." *Menn* 85 (Oct. 13, 1970), 620. North Americans comment on the situation in Brazil and how the church ought to witness to it for change and peace.

Shelly, Maynard. "50-450." Convocation address, 1967. Pp. 8. Revolution, nonviolence, response to Communism. MLA/BeC.

Shenk, Lois Landis. "A House for David." *Swords into Plowshares: A Collection of Plays About Peace and Social Justice.* Ed. Ingrid Rogers. Elgin: The Brethren Press, 1983, 19-27. Dramatization of the temptation of Jesus in the wilderness explores the reasons Jesus rejected all Satan's "solutions" to the injustice and unfaithfulness Jesus had encountered in his world.

Shenk, Phil M. "A Sculptor of Justice and Peace." *Sojourners* 9 (Dec., 1980), 10-11. Describes the vision and work of Adolfo Perez Esquivel, human rights worker in Argentina and winner of the 1980 Nobel Peace Prize.

Shenk, Phil M. "Hope, Faith, and Love." *GH* 70 (May 17, 1977), 401-402. Participant in a "Christians Against Torture" demonstration reflects on the Christian call to witness and hope for national repentance for supporting repressive governments through economic and military aid.

Shenk, Phil M. "Washington for Jesus." *Sojourners* 9 (June, 1980), 10-11. The religious rally in Washington focused on issues such as waning US military power and ignored problems of the arms race and proliferating violence.

Shenk, Phil M. (Review). *The Chant of Jimmie Blacksmith.* Directed and produced by Fred Schepisi. Released by New Yorker Films. *Sojourners* 9 (Dec., 1980), 34-35. Observes that violence in the film does not serve the cause of "good;" rather, violence is the enemy and humanity the hero.

Shenk, Wilbert R. (Review). *The Original Revolution,* by John H. Yoder. Scottdale: Herald Press, 1972. Pp. 189. *GH* 66 (Jan. 2, 1973), 13. Comments primarily on the title essay, in which Yoder sets forth the model of the "messianic community"—a community of committed believers living out the ethics of Jesus, including pacifism.

Sherk, J. Harold. "Reflections." *RepConsS* 25 (June, 1968), 1, 2. The assassination of Robert Kennedy reminds us of the pervasiveness of evil and calls us to a renewed commitment to the way of peace.

Sherk, J. Harold (Editorial). "From Where I Sit." *RepConsS* 21 (Jan., 1964), 1, 2. Deplores the violence that felled John F. Kennedy and Lee Oswald. Sherk calls for a renewed commitment to peacemaking.

Shetler, Jan Bender. "Editorial." *IPF Notes* 24 (Nov., 1977), 2-3. Human rights issue in light of the church-state relationship.

Shetler, Sanford G., ed. "Churchmen Continue to Support Militant Chavez." (Article unsigned) *GfT* 8 (Nov.-Dec., 1973), 6. Chavez's methods of boycotting and picketing do not correspond to Mennonite concern for love and goodwill among all sides.

Shetler, Sanford G. "Just What Is Social Justice?" *GfT* 15 (May-June, 1980), 14-15. Church people should be concerned first with the inequities of the local setting, instead of attempting the impossible task of establishing international justice.

Shetler, Sanford G. "More on Social Justice." *GfT* 15 (Nov.-Dec., 1980), 14-15. Christians should focus attention on stewardship and sharing in the local context instead of fighting international injustice through liberation theology.

Shetler, Sanford G. "'The Revolution.'" *GfT* Series 2, 5 (Sept.-Oct., 1970), 4-5. The peaceful revolution initiated by Christ is very different from the Marxist revolution of violent social change.

Shetler, Sanford G. "What Is Social Justice?" *ST* 48 (Aug., 1980), 1-3. Social justice is an agenda borrowed from other traditions, and peace churches should re-examine the biblical basis for peace.

Shetler, Sanford G. "Youth in an Age of Revolution." *ST* 35 (June, 1967), 10. In a world of revolution, the youth are both the target of the revolution and a part of the revolution. Suggests some criteria that can be used to evaluate programs and innovations for the youth.

Showalter, Stuart W., ed. "Peacemaking in a World of Revolution." Seminar lectures delivered at EMC, Harrisonburg, VA, June 15-26, 1970. Pp. 88. MSHL. Includes: Lapp, John A., "Revolution as a Political Event," 1-8; Yutsy, Daniel, "Revolution in the Economic Struggle," 9-15; Epp, Frank, "Revolution in the Middle East," 16-23; Skinner, Tom, "Revolution in Racial Relationships," 24-36; Jacobs, Donald R., "Revolution Amid Social Change," 37-42; Augsburger, Myron, "Revolution in the Church," 43-52; Yoder, John H., "Peacemaking Amid Political Revolution," 53-60; Miller, John W., "Steps Toward Peace in a World of Economic Conflict," 61-71; Haynes, Michael, "Peacemaking in Race Relations," 72-82; Trueblood, Elton, "Peacemaking Through the Church," 83-88.

Shutt, Joyce M. (Review). *The Velvet Covered Brick,* by Howard Butt. Harper and Row, n.d. Pp. 186. *Soul on Fire,* by Eldridge Cleaver. Waco: Word Books. Pp. 240. *Theology in a New Key: Responding to Liberation Themes,* by Robert McAffee Brown. Westminster Press, n.d. Pp. 212. "On Authority, Justice, and Discipleship." *GH* 72 (Apr. 24, 1979), 342. Briefly describes the main theme of each book and its usefulness to the Mennonite reader. Authority and power in leadership, social injustices, and the basic theological and human issues of liberation theology are the respective themes drawn from these books.

Sider, Ronald J. "An Evangelical Theology of Liberation." *Perspectives on Evangelical Theology,* ed. Kenneth S. Kantzer and Stanley N. Gundry. Grand Rapids: Baker Book House, 1979, 117-33. Claims evangelical theology's failure to take seriously the biblical teaching that God identifies with the poor is evidence that evangelicals have fallen into the heresies of theological liberalism.

Sider, Ronald J. "Christ and Power." *International Review of Mission* 69 (Jan., 1980), 8-20. Author appeals to New Testament passages to support his thesis that power is not inherently evil but becomes compatible with the way of the cross when it is exercised for the other's good. Calls the church to actively witness to and resist the evil in government.

Sider, Ronald J. *Christ and Violence.* Scottdale: Herald Press, 1979. Pp. 108. Four essays which speak both exegetically and practically to the thesis that the concept of active nonviolence is a more adequate expression of the way of Jesus than the concept of nonresistance.

Sider, Ronald J., ed. *Cry Justice: The Bible Speaks on Hunger and Poverty.* New York: Paulist Press, 1980. A collection of biblical passages on justice issues accompanied by brief commentary, tables containing information on such topics as the infant mortality rate in different countries, and study questions designed for use by individuals and/or groups.

Sider, Ronald J. "Evangelical Influence Felt." *EV* 89 (Apr. 25, 1976), 5-6. A report on the Fifth Assembly of the World Council of Churches which met in Nairobi, Kenya, Nov. 23-Dec. 10, 1975, where, among other concerns, peace, justice, and human rights were discussed.

Sider, Ronald J., ed. *Evangelicals and Development: Toward a Theology of Social Change.* Philadelphia: Westminster Press, 1981. A collection of articles addressing the ethical issues of justice and social change from an evangelical Christian point of view.

Sider, Ronald J. "Evangelism or Social Justice: Eliminating the Options." *Christianity Today* 21 (Oct. 8, 1976), 26-29. Explores the interrelationship of evangelism and social justice by noting the biblical basis for the connection and by naming social injustice sin.

Sider, Ronald J. "Evangelism, Salvation and Social Justice." *International Review of Mission* 64 (July, 1975), 251-67; reprint ed., Bramcote Notts: Grove Books, 1977. Evangelism and social action are distinct but inseparable aspects of the church's mission. Not only does evangelism often lead to greater social justice, and vice versa, but those who follow Jesus' example must seek liberty for the oppressed as well as announce the good news.

Sider, Ronald J. "Jesus' Resurrection and the Search for Peace and Justice." *Christian Century* 99 (Nov. 3, 1982), 1103-1108. Develops four theses explaining why the bodily resurrection of Jesus is important to the issues of nuclear war: 1) As the foundation for understanding the lordship of Jesus, 2) as source of strength for the struggle for justice, 3) as the clue to the relationship between our work for justice and the shalom of the second coming, and 4) as the base from which to confront the powers.

Sider, Ronald J. "Mischief By Statute: How We Oppress the Poor." *Christianity Today* 20 (July 16, 1976), 14-19. Traces causes and effects of several specific economic oppressions and calls biblical

Christians to acknowledge their participation in these oppressions with repentance.

Sider, Ronald J. "Resurrection and Liberation: An Evangelical Approach to Social Justice." *The Recovery of Spirit in Higher Education,* ed. Robert Rankin. New York: Seabury Press, 1980, 154-77. Develops three biblical themes as central to the pursuit of justice: the prophetic model, God's identification with the poor, and the bodily resurrection of Jesus of Nazareth as the foundation of hope.

Sider, Ronald J. *Rich Christians in an Age of Hunger: A Biblical Study.* Intervarsity and Paulist Press, 1977. Warns that the critical problem of world hunger could lead to wars of redistribution and outlines ways North American Christians can respond to this tragic situation with compassion.

Sider, Ronald J. "Sharing the Wealth: The Church as Biblical Model for Public Policy." *Christian Century* 94 (June 8-15, 1977), 560-65. Contends that the church must demonstrate the biblical model of economic sharing if its demand for social change is to have integrity and impact.

Sider, Ronald J. "Spirituality and Social Concern." *The Other Side* 9 (Sept.-Oct., 1973), 8-11, 38-41; *GH* 67 (Apr. 23, 1974), 337-40. Spirituality and social concern are a unity—regeneration involves changed attitudes toward poverty, racism, and war; the disciplines of the spirit are essential to social change.

Sider, Ronald J. "To See the Cross, To Find the Tomb." *The Other Side* 13 (Feb., 1977), 16-23. Drawing on Christ's death and resurrection, the author calls for a new movement of nonviolent direct action against economic injustice.

Sider, Ronald J. "Watching Over One Another . . . in Love." *The Other Side* 11 (May-June, 1975), 13-19, 58-60. Discusses church discipline as a component of proclaiming the gospel, a component necessitated by the nature of the church as a body called out of a greedy, materialistic, adulterous, warmongering society.

Sider, Ronald J. "What If Ten Thousand . . . " *The Other Side* 15 (Nov., 1979), 14-15. Report on the South African Christian Leadership Assembly (SACLA) which has prompted hundreds of South African Christians to ask in a new and urgent way what biblical faith demands of them.

Sider, Ronald J. "Words and Deeds." *Journal of Theology for South Africa* 29 (Dec., 1979), 31-50. Discusses the biblical basis for both evangelism and social justice as well as the interrelationship between the two in formulating a vision for the church today.

Sider, Ronald J. and Taylor, Richard K. "Fighting Fire with Water." *Sojourners* 12 (Apr., 1983), 14-17. Addresses the issue of Christian responsibility to resist evil, injustice, and oppression by suggesting that nonviolent resistance to aggression has potential as a system of national defense.

Sider, Ronald J. and Taylor, Richard K. "International Aggression and Nonmilitary Defense." *Christian Century* 100 (July 6-13, 1983), 643-47. Military power is not the only way for nations to defend their independence and values. Asymetric strategy, a technique of pitting nonmilitary means against an opponent's military forces, has had some historical success and should be considered in the nuclear age.

Siebert, Allan J. "Mennonites and Political Power: Yoder Gives Lectures in Winnipeg." *MennRep* 9 (Oct. 1, 1979), 13. John Howard Yoder gave a series of three lectures at the Univ. of Winnipeg, each centering around political themes: "An Anabaptist View of Political Power;" "Mennonite Political Conservatism: Paradox or Contradiction;" and "An Anabaptist View of Liberation Theology."

Siebert, John. "New Call to Peacemaking." *MBH* 17 (Oct. 27, 1978), 18-19. Consensus from the New Call to Peacemaking conference includes commitments to local peace education, peacemaking lifestyle, confronting militarism, and continued witness to peace and justice.

Smith, Allan W. (Review). *The Crucifixion of the Jews,* by Franklin H. Littell. New York: Harper and Row, 1975. "How Do Christians Respond to the Holocaust?" *MennRep* 9 (Aug. 20, 1979), 20. A work directed at Christians gives the historical development of antisemitism and prompts the question of how one could respond to the holocaust in a time of antisemitic persecution.

Smucker, Barbara Claassen. *Days of Terror.* Scottdale: Herald Press, 1979. Pp. 152. Young Peter Neufeld and his family are Mennonites in Russia during the internal and external turbulence experienced by the Russian nation during the World War I era. A strong theme of this moving juvenile novel is the theme of how people of faith, people who have practiced nonresistance for four hundred years, respond to acts of violence committed against their persons and their possessions in their own homes and barnyards. Both the Mennonite Self-Defense movement and the connections between the economic and cultural distance maintained by the Mennonites and the violence inflicted upon them are sensitively portrayed. For ages 8-12 and up.

Smucker, Donovan E. "Deep, Dark Memories of

Capital Punishment." *Menn* 94 (Apr. 17, 1979), 274-75. An argument against capital punishment, which is seen as an instrument of repression, not a scale for justice.

Smucker, Donovan E. Letter to the Editor. *Menn* 94 (May 1, 1979), 316-17. Comments on the growing violence in professional hockey.

Smucker, Donovan E. "What I Saw in CPS." *GH* 37 (June 2, 1944), 156-57. CPS is a real witness to love over justice in spite of some spiritual shortcomings.

Snider, Marie. "Battered Wives and the Comic Strips." *MCC PS TF on Women in Ch. and Soc. Report* 23 (Dec., 1978), 6-8. In spite of the fact that cases of wife-beating outnumber husband-beatings 16 to 1, comics portray violence directed from females to males but seldom vice versa.

Snyder, C. Arnold. "The Relevance of Anabaptist Nonviolence for Nicaragua Today." *CGR* 2 (Spring, 1984), 123-37. In comparing the Peasants' War of 1525 and the Nicaraguan Revolution of 1979, one notes that both produced theologies of social justice allowing for armed resistance. However, in response to the 16th century peasant revellion, the Anabaptists (Schleitheim, 1527) specifically rejected armed resistance as a response to injustice. Is this sort of response relevant to the situation in Central America? Concludes that the Anabaptists not only rejected violence but reinterpreted and preserved a vision of justice in their ecclesiology. Concludes that this reinterpreted vision of justice can be relevant to Nicaragua if we abandon the strict dichotomy between church and world and try to be the church in the middle of the world, acting for justice. Also "The Relevance of Anabaptist Nonviolence for Nicaragua Today." Pp. 21. BfC.

Sperling, Ken (Review). *Christ and Violence,* by Ronald J. Sider. Kitchener: Herald Press, 1979. Pp. 102. *MBH* 19 (Jan. 18, 1980), 28. Recommends the book for its presentation of a biblical basis for nonviolence, plus suggestions for active peacemaking.

Sprunger, Keith L. "Learning the Wrong Lessons." *MennLife* 23 (Apr., 1968), 64-68. An analysis of the psychology and history leading to Vietnam in an attempt to find a clearer understanding of revolution in our world.

Stayer, James M. *Anabaptists and the Sword.* Lawrence, Ks.: Coronado Press, 1972; reprint edition including "Reflections and Retractions," Lawrence, Ks., 1976. Pp. 375. The larger Reformation developments, within which Anabaptist discussions took place regarding the legitimacy and limits of coercive force as a means for preserving society, provided three

options: moderate apoliticism, represented by Luther; realpoliticism, represented by Zwingli; the crusade, represented by Müntzer. Stayer reviews the histories of the Swiss Brethren, the Upper German sects, and the Melchiorites in light of the three options and concludes that the Anabaptists pursued all three of these options and developed a position of nonresistant apoliticism only over a period of time.

Stayer, James M. "Anabaptists and the Sword." *MQR* 44 (Oct., 1970), 371-75. Argues that Anabaptist nonresistance originated because "sects without a real possibility of revolution, and with a very real experience of the misuse of power, arrived with compelling historical and religious logic at this most radical form of apolitical thought."

Stayer, James M. "The Doctrine of the Sword in the First Decade of Anabaptism." *MQR* 41 (Apr., 1967), 165-66. Abstract of dissertation which argues that an absolute renunciation of violence and coercion was regarded by the majority of the Anabaptists of this period as an essential of the Christian life.

Steele, Richard. "Rape—Male Violence: A Personal and Political Perspective." Paper presented to Women and Men: History and Vision, and War, Peace, and Revolution classes, AMBS, Elkhart, Ind., Dec., 1982. Pp. 73. AMBS.

Steiner, Susan Clemmer. *Joining the Army that Sheds No Blood.* Scottdale: Herald Press, 1982. Pp. 155. Written to help youth make responsible and informed decisions about peacemaking, the book explores such questions as why wars and other kinds of violence exist, what Jesus' response to violence was and how followers of Jesus can live as peacemakers. Other issues addressed are the classic arguments against pacifism and some practical ways people can become involved in the creation of peace.

Steinmetz, Rollin C. *Loyalists Pacifists and Prisoners.* Lititz, Pa.: Lancaster County Historical Society, 1976. Pp. 80. MHL. Discusses the circumstances and actions of Lancaster County's pacifists during the Revolutionary War in the context of the "underside" of the Revolution.

Stobbe, Leslie H. "Anabaptist Distinctives." *MBH* 1 (Dec. 14, 1962), 6-7. Anabaptists responded nonviolently to persecution, yet vigorously opposed capital punishment and participation in any form of violence.

Stoltzfus, Edward. "Where 'On the Way' Is the Mennonite Church?" *GH* 70 (July 12, 1977), 522-25. Mennonite Church moderator urges Mennonites to use power nonviolently to confront evil in the world instead of advocating absolute nonresistance and cultural separation from the world.

Stoltzfus, Eldon Roy. "Power and Intervention: Reflections on the Ethics of Power in Development." MA in Peace Studies thesis, AMBS, 1982. Pp. 63. Suggests that power, as the ability to influence behavior, is an entity in and of itself—and can be either disintegrative or integrative. Further suggests that the character and quality of the power identified from within the story of the people of God, the power most concretely expressed in Jesus, is unique and can be integrated toward creative participation in the church and in the world.

Stoltzfus, Gene. "The Philippines: Nuclear Power Versus People." MennRep 9 (Apr. 16, 1979), 2; "Philippines Town Fears Nuclear Development, Government Authority." Menn 94 (Apr. 24, 1979), 294. Development of a nuclear power plant worries Barrio people in Morong but attempts to discuss and question this are seen as subversive activity by the government.

Stoltzfus, Gene. "Westinghouse the Helpful Neighbor." Sojourners 8 (Mar., 1979), 10. Description of what happens to a local community when Westinghouse decides to build a nuclear power plant in the Philippines.

Stoltzfus, Gene and [Janzen], Lois Barrett. "Vietnam Revisited." Post-American 4 (Apr., 1975), 18-23. Documents the harrassment and torture inflicted on opponents of the corrupt Thieu regime in South Vietnam who are not pro-Communist.

Stoltzfus, Gene and Friesen, Dorothy. Letter to the Editor. The Other Side 13 (Dec., 1977), 7. In a time when violent revolutionary change threatens to replace the violence of military dictatorships, Christians must be clear about their biblical foundation and responsibility.

Stoltzfus, Gene and Friesen, Dorothy. "Working for Human Rights." Peace Section Newsletter 8 (June, 1977), 1-3. Biblical words on justice are firm and consistent throughout the Old and New Testament. People who work for justice are sometimes the object of much criticism. Lists common objections voiced during the Vietnam era that continue to surface.

Stoltzfus, Ruth Ann (Review). Conjugal Crime, by Terry Davidson. Cambridge: Hawthorn, 1978; The Battered Woman, by Lenore Walker. New York: Harper & Row, 1979. Sojourners 9 (Nov., 1980), 30. Compares these two treatments of the problem of wife abuse and its components of sexism, violence, and intimacy.

Stoltzfus, Ruth Carol. "Domestic Violence and the Legal System." MCC PS TF on Women in Ch. and Soc. Report 23 (Dec., 1978), 3-6. Legal Aid attorney documents cases of women victims of domestic violence and the limitations of legal settlements.

Stoltzfus, Victor (Review). Christ and Your Job, by Alfred P. Klausler. Concordia, 1956. Pp. 145. The Christian Calling, by Virgil Vogt. Scottdale: Herald Press, 1961. Pamphlet. ChrLiv 9 (Jan., 1962), 33. Reviewer compares and contrasts Lutheran and Mennonite views on the definition of vocational calling and its relation to social concerns and justice.

Stoner, John K. "Jesus, Are You Really Serious?" Lifework 2 (1979), 3-5. Places Jesus' ministry in the context of national oppression by Rome, emphasizing Jesus' nonviolence as seen through eyes of Peter who hoped for a national revolution.

Stoner, John K. "Meditation on Worship and Justice." MBH 15 (Oct. 29, 1976), 5-6, 31. To draw closer to God means to participate in the struggle for interhuman justice.

Stoner, John K. "Shalom Means 'The Extra Thing'." CanMenn 18 (Dec., 11, 1970), 6. An interpretation of "the extra thing," taken from the Sermon on the Mount, as that which "moves Christian ethics beyond legalistic justice toward positive reconciliation."

Stoner, John K. "The West Is Losing Ground." Menn 93 (Aug. 8, 1978), 480. Truth and justice, not bombs and weapons delivery systems, are the only adequate weapons against communism. Stoner, John K. "Where Are the Prophets?" EV 90 (Nov. 25, 1977), 4. Recognizing the diabolical advance in the technology of violence, the writer asks "where are the preachers who will condemn the sin of violence, in the tradition of the prophets and the apostles."

Stoner, John K. (Review). Between a Rock and a Hard Place, by Mark Hatfield. Waco, Tex.: Word Books, 1976. Pp. 224. Menn 91 (Oct. 26, 1976), 633; ChrLead 39 (Aug. 17, 1976), 14. Hatfield prods the church to separate its vision from the destiny of America, examining questions of nuclear war, violence, and patriotism.

Studer, Gerald C. "Will a Christian Be Patriotic?" ChrLead 39 (Jan. 20, 1976), 5. Christian patriotism notes that it is righteousness not military might that exalts a nation, that it is justice for all, tempered with mercy that gives strength to a nation. A Christian must first give loyalty to Christ.

Suderman, Jacob. "The Climber." ChrLiv 2 (Jan., 1955), 4-5, 42-45; (Feb., 1955), 6-7, 41-45; (Mar., 1955), 8-9, 41-44; (Apr., 1955), 12-13, 34-35, 44-46; (May, 1955), 32-33, 41-45; (June, 1955), 28-29, 41-43. Six-part fictional serial about

Zacchaeus focuses on the justice and reconciliation brought about by the coming of God's kingdom in Jesus.

Summer, Bob. "War Is Inevitable." *YCC* 47 (July 10, 1966), 8. The conclusion that war is inevitable is based on the human greed for power, opposition of communism, and lack of international power to control actions of modern societies.

Swarr, John. "Passivism or Pacifism?" *GH* 65 (Sept. 5, 1972), 697. Calls Mennonites to active peacemaking, overcoming evil with good, instead of passivism, giving silent consent to injustice.

"The Dilemma of Christian Involvement." *ChrLead* 28 (Nov. 9, 1965), 14-15. MCC relief operations, as a part of the Mennonite peace witness, must be expanded in spite of the danger of being identified with American military violence.

"Theologian Advocates Mennonite Power." *CanMenn* 17 (Mar. 11, 1969), 1. J. Lawrence Burkholder speaks on "Nonresistance and Nonviolence" on a lecture tour in Canada. After distinguishing the major differences between the two and advocating the second, he points out some of the limits and dangers of this response.

"Trudeau on Violence." *CanMenn* 18 (Apr. 10, 1970), 1. The prime minister's positive attitude to nonviolence and the draft dodgers is cited.

Task Force on Violence in the Mass Media and Pornography. "Quiet Violence." *MCC PS TF on Women in Ch. and Soc. Report* 14 (May, 1977), 2-5. Excerpts from the study by the Western Ontario Mennonite Conference Task Force; highlights references to forms of nonphysical violence.

*The Christian and War: A Theological Discussion of Justice, Peace, and Love.* Amsterdam: Historical Peace Churches and Fellowship of Reconciliation, 1958. Pp. 47. MHL. Sequel to *Peace Is the Will of God* makes a greater effort to take seriously the nonpacifist position by including chapter entitled "God Wills Both Peace and Justice," written by Angus Dun and Reinhold Niebuhr at the invitation of the historic peace churches and FOR. Grapples with the questions of pacifism and social responsibility in the context of this dialogue.

Teichroew, Lowell (Review). "The Christian and War: A Theological Discussion of Justice, Peace, and Love." Historic peace churches and the FOR, 1958, *CanMenn* 7 (Aug. 21, 1959), 2. Peace dialogue bewtween the historic peace churches and the World Council of Churches.

Thomas, Kobangu. "I Preach with Happiness and Power Because I Did Not Use My Gun." *CanMenn* 12 (Jan. 7, 1964), 8. Testimony of African pastor who takes pacifist position amidst the terrors and pressures of tribal warfare.

Thomson, Murray and Regehr, Ernie. "Militarism and Human Rights." *PlMon* 2 (Dec., 1978), 3-4. Analyzes the relationship between human rights violations and the presence of externally supplied and trained armed forces.

Thut, John. "The World System." *ChrMon* 26 (Feb., 1934), 42-43. The present world system, like that of the prophet Habakkuk, is full of endless conflict and violence.

Tiessen, Daniel. "Yoder Says Mennonite View of Power Faulty." *Menn* 94 (Oct. 30, 1979), 649. John Howard Yoder presented a series of lectures around the theme "The Christian Use of Political Power" in Winnipeg, Manitoba.

Tinbergen, Jan. "1982." *PlMon* 1 (May, 1978), 2-4. Forward to the book *1982* by researchers at the Canadian Peace Research Institute discusses the conditions of violence and illustrates models of international violence in the past and projected models of the future.

Toews, David. "In Washington Love Was Realistic." *CanMenn* 17 (Nov. 28, 1969), 5. Notes ironically that Washington officials are dismayed by the violence of fringe groups in the March Against Death, which is hardly to be compared with the violence being done by American forces in Vietnam.

Toews, John A. "Christ's Example and Social Involvement." *MBH* 4 (May 14, 1965), 7, 19. The disciple, like the Master, should engage in a teaching, healing, and relief ministry of rehabilitation and restoration which avoid coercion or violence.

Toews, John B. "On Revolution—Past and Present." *JChSoc* 6 (Fall, 1970), 2. Whether Christian or not, today we have little choice but to become engaged in revolution. The Jesus Revolution needs Jesus People with lofty visions and great dreams about great and just societies.

Toews, John B. "The Halbstadt Volost 1918-1922: A Case Study of the Mennonite Encounter with Early Bolshevism." *MQR* 48 (Oct., 1974), 489-514. Documents Mennonite experience with the violence and terror of the early days of Red Army and anarchist rule in southern Russia. The ensuing disillusionment among Mennonites regarding future life in the Soviet Union led by 1922 to applications for mass exodus.

Toews, John B. "The Origin and Activities of the

Mennonite *Selbstschutz* in the Ukraine (1918-1919)." *MQR* 46 (Jan., 1972), 5-40. Describes the rise and consequences of Russian Mennonite self-defense units (Selbstschutz) armed against the violence of Bolshevik and bandit forces, their strategies, and ensuing revenge. Traces the rise of such units to the credal, separatist, and largely untested pacifism of the Mennonite settlers, and to the threat of violence against Mennonite women, more than the threat of property loss.

Toews, Leann. "Mennonite Theology and Spankings." *Menn* 93 (Apr. 4, 1978), 239. A parent refrains from using spanking as a disciplinary measure because of its message of violence to the child.

Toews, Paul (Review). *The Original Revolution*, by John Howard Yoder. Scottdale: Herald Press, 1971. Pp. 188. *Direction* 1 (Oct., 1972), 134-35. Finds Yoder's analysis of such issues as the questions of "Christ and culture," the relationship between the Old Testament and New Testament on violence, the pacifist options for personal ethics and public policy, etc., to be a significant and helpful treatment.

Trocmé, André. *Jesus and the Nonviolent Revolution.* Trans. Michael H. Shank and Marlin E. Miller. Introduction by Marlin E. Miller. Scottdale: Herald Press, 1973. Pp. 211. Develops the thesis that the social, economic, and political revolution based upon the jubilary law of Moses was central to Jesus' vision and led to the conflict which ended on the cross. The second part of the book surveys the history of violence and nonviolence from Elijah to Herod and identifies a prophetic concept of nonviolent resistance within the broader stream of nationalism and messianism. The last section traces Jesus' expansion of contemporary religious thought by transforming messianic expectations through the choice of nonviolent resistance as his kingdom method.

"Use of Power and Conflict." *Menn* 82 (May 16, 1967), 330-31. The GCMC Peace and Social Concerns Committee suggests that power and conflict need not be totally negative; they can be used to liberate the oppressed and protect the persecuted.

Ulle, Robert F. "Neither Compulsion Nor Blindness." *Forum* 11 (Jan., 1978), 2. Christian conviction demands support of affirmative action as redress for injustice toward minority races.

Ulle, Robert F. "The Approaching Revolution." *GH* 69 (Apr. 20, 1976), 329. Ulle examines the responses of Pennsylvania Mennonites to the rise of local colonial militia in the early 1770s.

Unrau, Harlan D. "Institutional Racism and the Military-Industrial Complex." *Forum* (Mar., 1972), 5. The military-industrial complex which has direct bearing on the welfare of the minority worker is a form of racism that is no less destructive of human values than physical violence.

Unruh, John D. and Loewen, Esko. "Is This Our Revolution?" *Menn* 78 (Sept. 10, 1963), 534-36. Mennonites need to give a clearer peace witness to government in the context of struggle for constructive action and change at the grass roots.

Unruh, Pamela J. Letter to the Editor. *Menn* 92 (Feb. 22, 1977), 142. The World Peace Tax Fund is an extension of liberal politics which, however well-intentioned, does not remove warmakers from power or curb excessive government spending.

Unsigned. "Maione Makes Plea for Justice." *Intercom* 22 (Mar., 1978), 4. CIDA coordinator speaks on justice and development and Christian responsibility.

Vogt, Esther L. "Urban Encounter." *ChrLead* 39 (Aug. 17, 1976), 2. Description of the activities of World Impact in Wichita's ghetto.

Vogt, Roy. "Our Word: Questions Raised by the Death of a Mennonite Terrorist." *MennMirror* 9 (Sept., 1979), 22. Elizabeth von Dyck's death during a bank robbery in West Germany raises questions of the church's relationship both to an unjust society and to its youth.

Vogt, Roy. "Strikes Symbolize Union Power But You Wield Power Too." *MennMirror* 4 (May, 1975), 7-8. While sympathetic to view of Henry Funk, who is fighting a legal battle over his refusal to join a union on the grounds of conscientious objection to violent union tactics, Vogt urges Christians to think critically and analytically about the way we ourselves are involved with the uses of power. We must then exercise this power with care and responsibility to Christian ethics of nonviolence, etc., rather than withdrawing from situations simply because there is use of power.

Vogt, Roy (Editorial). "Conscientious Objections Irk Manitoba Government, So It Changes the Labor Law and Thereby Subverts a Right." *MennMirror* 5 (Summer, 1976), 22. Several months after the court decision in the Funk case (*MennMirror* 5, [Feb., 1976]) to support the right of an individual to refuse, on grounds of conscience, to pay labor union dues, the Manitoba government has changed the labor law, making it virtually impossible to exercise this right. This is viewed as a tragic step backwards for human rights.

Vogt, Roy (Review). *A Russian Dance of Death: Revolution and Civil War in the Ukraine,* by Dietrich Neufeld. Winnipeg: Hyperion Press, 1977. Pp. 138. "Mennonite's Journal Captures Gripping Detail of Russian Revolution." *MennMir* 7 (Dec., 1977), 15. Describes the history and summarizes the contents of this book, which is an annotated and edited journal of Dietrich Neufeld's experiences in the Russian Revolution and Civil War.

Vogt, Roy (Review). *Storm Tossed,* by Gerhard J. Lohrenz. Winnipeg: The Christian Press, 1976. Pp. 204. "Lohrenz Writes of His Life in Russia." *MennMirror* 5 (Apr., 1976), 12. Briefly summarizes this personal narrative in which Lohrenz describes the tragic impact of the Russian Revolution on some of the Russian Mennonites through the telling of his own life story. Concludes that it is a valuable contribution to our understanding of past and present events.

Voolstra, Sjouke. "The Search for a Biblical Peace Testimony." *Mission and the Peace Witness.* Ed. Robert L. Ramseyer. Scottdale and Kitchener: Herald Press, 1979, 24-35. An adequate peace theology will interpret the Bible in its social and political context, paying special attention to Old Testament visions of shalom and justice. An authentic peace witness must be active (not merely nonresistant) and community-oriented. Also available as paper, 1977. Pp. 6. MLA/BeC.

"Why Glamorize War?" *CanMenn* 16 (June 25, 1968), 1. Bergtaler Mennonite Church sends a note of dissatisfaction to the Canadian Broadcasting Corporation: "We the undersigned urge you as those responsible for our public communication media, to use our common resources to promote not the causes of war and violence, but rather those of peace and internationalism."

"Worker Seeks to Identify with Thai Slum Dwellers." *GH* 72 (Nov. 13, 1979), 891. Max Ediger feels that to effect change for the oppressed, one must identify with them and work for change before violence breaks out. He wishes to do this in Bangkok, Thailand.

"World Conference Message." *GH* 65 (Oct. 24, 1972), 860-61. Statement adopted at the conclusion of the Ninth Mennonite World Conference focuses on reconciliation as the primary task of the church—reconciliation in situations of war, violent repression, racism, economic oppression.

Wagler, Harley. "The Peace Churches in Nicaragua (2): Mixed Reaction to Revolution." *MennRep* 10 (Oct. 13, 1980), 6-7. Review of the Catholic, evangelical, and Mennonite church responses to the Sandinista revolution and attitudes toward the new government.

Wallis, Jim. "Where Are the Christians?" *ChrLead* 39 (Aug. 17, 1976), 4. *Leader* interview with Al Ewert, a Mennonite Brethren worker with the World Impact ministry; focuses on issues of social justice.

Warkentine, Kendal. "Military Justice in World War I: Court Martial Trials of Mennonite Conscientious Objectors." Social Science Seminar, Feb., 1983. Pp. 127. MLA/BeC.

Weaver, J. Denny. "Cut and Run or Do It All?" *GH* 73 (Sept. 30, 1980), 772-73. Although evil will not be fully conquered until Jesus returns, Christians have the responsibility to work for justice in the present.

Wenger, J. C. "Nonresistant and Nonpolitical." *GH* 59 (Mar. 15, 1966), 229. The nonresistant Christian will not become involved in political functions or offices that employ coercion. However we must speak out against injustice.

Wenger, J. C. "Revolutionaries or Reconcilers?" *GH* 64 (Mar. 9, 1971), 217. Reprinted from *Sword and Trumpet.* Cites the contrasting examples from the 16th century of Jan Matthijs, who espoused a revolutionary theocracy, and Obbe Philips, committed to nonresistance, to show the error of setting up the rule of God through violent coercion.

Wenger, J. C. "Theologies of Revolution." *GH* 64 (Nov. 2, 1971), 902-904. The Christian's central task is proclamation of the gospel, not social justice. While Christians are to be concerned for the total person, true peace and justice will be created only by the second coming of Christ.

Wenger, Martha. "The Potential to Respond." *Forum* 11 (Dec., 1977), 4-5. Mennonite student enrolled in Palestinian Arab university on the West Bank reflects on the conflict and violence present in the Israeli-occupied West Bank.

Wengerd, Carolyn. "Nonresistance of the Mennonites in Pennsylvania During the Revolution." Research paper for American Colonial and Revolutionary History class. 1970. Pp. 23. BfC.

Wentland, Theodore. Letter to the Editor. *GH* 61 (Mar. 19, 1968), 262-63. Calls attention to Mennonite acts of violence toward one another in conflict situations and schisms, and calls for a spirit of forgiveness and peacemaking in congregations.

Wesselhoeft, Carl. Letter to the Editor. *GH* 63 (Oct. 13, 1970), 870-71. Cautions against identifying God as our contemporary working in revolutionary movements, on the premise that if we condemn the violence of institutions, we cannot then condone revolutionary violence.

West, Jessamyn. "The True Meaning of Violence." *ChrLiv* 17 (Dec., 1970), 22-24. Reprinted from *Redbook* magazine, Jan., 1963. Violence portrayed in the media dulls the imagination, making it unable to feel the suffering of the victim.

Wiebe, Christine (Review). *Agenda for Biblical People,* by Jim Wallis. New York: Harper and Row, 1976. Pp. 145. *ChrLeader* 40 (Jan. 18, 1977), 13-14. Applauds Wallis' challenge to the established church on such issues as money, power, violence, etc., while lamenting that the book is too abstract and "intellectual" for the average reader.

Wiebe, Franz. "A Look at John 2:15." Paper for War, Peace, and Revolution class, AMBS, Elkhart, Ind., n.d. Pp. 2. AMBS.

Wiebe, Katie Funk. "A Conversion to Violence." *MBH* 15 (Feb. 6, 1976), 4; *Menn* 90 (Oct. 28, 1975), 605; *GH* 68 (Nov. 25, 1975), 849; *ChrLead* 38 (Oct. 14, 1975), 19. The acceptance of violence as a way of life may take place in different ways: a Charles Manson follower experienced a conversion, while the American society as a whole slowly drifts toward it.

Wiebe, Katie Funk. "Education for Violence." *CanMenn* 18 (July 31, 1970), 7; *GH* 63 (Nov. 17, 1970), 973. Analyzes the way our culture socializes us to accept violence as a lifestyle. Asks the church for more help in distinguishing spiritual values from those acquired torough the media.

Wiebe, Katie Funk. "Making Peace with Violence." *ChrLead* 40 (Jan. 18, 1977), 17; *GH* 70 (Feb. 8, 1977), 114; *MBH* 16 (Apr. 15, 1977), 32. While American Mennonites reject the violence of war, their rejection of other forms of violence in American society—TV, structural violence, etc.—is not so clear.

Wiebe, Katie Funk. "Power and the Gospel." *GH* 73 (Dec. 30, 1980), 1045. On the dangers of identifying the Christian gospel with political power and force.

Wiebe, Katie Funk. "While Making Gravy." *ChrLead* 37 (July 23, 1974), 19. Thoughts on the role of an "advocate" and social action. Advocates are people who speak and act on Christ's behalf for the person who has no courage or power to keep going.

Wiebe, Menno. "Red and Yellow, Black and White, All Can Be Equally Mennonite." *MennMirror* 8 (Aug.-Sept., 1978), 11, 14. Reflections on the Mennonite World Conference in Wichita, Kans., with particular attention to our response to violence and injustice as a people of peace.

Wiebe, Michael. Letter to the Editor. *MBH* 13 (May 3, 1974), 11, 31. One form of the American government's oppression of poor countries is US military aid to corrupt governments.

Wingert, Norman. "Wounded Knee: Symbol of the Indian Problem." *MBH* 14 (Oct. 17, 1975), 19-20. Recounts the confusion and violence of the two-month-long occupation of Wounded Knee in 1973 and the continuing conflict between Native Americans and white officials.

Winsor, Richard J. "The Automobile: Unguided Missile." *GH* 64 (June 29, 1971), 586-88. Traffic safety is a religious concern, since there is more highway violence than in Vietnam, ghettos, or on university campuses.

Wittlinger, Carlton O. (Review). *Twas Seeding Time: A Mennonite View of the American Revolution,* by John L. Ruth. Scottdale, Pa. and Kitchener, Ont.: Herald Press, 1976. Pp. 224. *MQR* 52 (July, 1978), 271-72. Reviewer considers this book of stories of Mennonite noncooperation in the Revolution a good, and informal, contribution to the subject of Mennonite history during the Revolution.

Woelk, Harry. Letter to the Editor. *MBH* 12 (Apr. 20, 1973), 11. Reader writes concerning gun laws and violence, commenting that we are much more cruel to cattle or pigs which we slaughter for consumption than we are when hunting deer.

Wollmann, Naomi. "Violence in the United States." *ChrLead* 39 (Oct. 26, 1976), 24. Surveys the growth of violence in our society. Encourages Christians to work against what is destroying society and to promote healing and dignity.

Yoder, Bruce (Review). *Christ and Violence,* by Ronald Sider. Scottdale: Herald Press, 1979. Pp. 104. *FQ* 6 (Nov., Dec., 1979, Jan., 1980), 9. Filled with unanswered questions, Sider's book sensitizes readers to violent social structures, calling for activist nonviolence based in God's work in Christ on the cross.

Yoder, Edward. "Are Nonresistant Christians Parasites? Peace Principles from a Scriptural Viewpoint" Part 15. *GH* 31 (Apr. 21, 1938), 78-79. While nonresistant Christians may not contribute directly to social justice, they are not parasites on society if living and preaching the gospel of Christ.

Yoder, Edward. *Compromise with War.* Akron: MCC, 1943. Pp. 15. A critique of liberalism's capitulation to nationalism and violence, focusing particularly on the writings of Charles C. Morrison, editor of *The Christian Century.*

---

*For additional listing, see Supplement, pp. 717-719.

Yoder, Edward. "Note on John 2:13-17." *GH* 29 (Jan. 21, 1937), 927. This passage is an argument against, rather than for, the use of violence.

Yoder, Edward. "The Power of Love—A Notable Testimony: Peace Principles from a Scriptural Viewpoint." Part 2. *GH* 28 (Apr. 18, 1935), 78-79. The nonresistant love ethic can successfully deal with the threat of danger or violence. Examples are given.

Yoder, Edward. "The Power of Love: Peace Principles from a Scriptural Viewpoint." Part 9. *GH* 29 (Apr. 16, 1937), 78-79. Christian is a "permanent heart set" which does no harm to the neighbor and drives out all fears.

Yoder, Henry P. and Yoder, Allan. "Possession of Guns and Peace." *GH* 65 (Oct. 31, 1972), 883-84. Mennonites committed to peace and nonviolence should not own guns, since owning such instruments of violence is not consistent with belief in peace, and it hampers a consistent peace witness.

Yoder, Howard. "Reflections on Riots." *GH* 60 (Oct. 3, 1967), 894-95. Riots are the harvest of violence whites have been sowing for years. Christians must comdemn all violence, recognize our part in it, and stand with the poor and the oppressed.

Yoder, John H. "Anabaptist Vision and Mennonite Reality." *Consultation on Anabaptist-Mennonite Theology.* Ed. by A. J. Klassen. Fresno: Council of Mennonite Seminaries, 1970, 1-46. Pp. 147. The way of the cross, components of which are the renunciation of power and refusal of war, is one of the criteria Yoder uses to analyze and describe the history of Mennonitism in the last century.

Yoder, John H. "Exodus: Probing the Meaning of Liberation." *Sojourners* 5 (Sept., 1976), 26. Contrasts the form, content, and means of liberation in the Bible with liberation theology.

Yoder, John H. "Our Witness to the State." *Menn* 81 (Jan.25, 1966), 58-59. We witness to the lordship of Jesus; God is on the side of humanity, especially the poor; the state cannot be trusted to be its own judge; violence is no basis for social peace.

Yoder, John H. "Power and the Powerless." *Covenant Quarterly* 36 (Nov., 1978), 29-35. If, as the Bible says, God is on the side of the oppressed and if we want to be on God's side, the answer is not to spiritualize or universalize oppression so that we might be included but to begin dealing with the real ways in which we oppress others.

Yoder, John H. "Radical Reformation Ethics in Ecumenical Perspective." *Journal of Ecumenical Studies* 15 (Fall, 1978), 647-61. The constitution of the church as voluntary determines the shape of the Christian community and, thus, the structure of Christian ethical reasoning. Moreover, since this voluntary nature disengages the church from alliances with the sword, wealth, and hierarchy, the substance of a believers' church ethic becomes the rejection of violence.

Yoder, John H. "The Anabaptist Dissent—The Logic of the Place of the Disciple in Society." *Concern* 1 (June, 1954), 45-68. An elaboration of a doctrine of social responsiility logically consistent with the concept of discipleship as understood and interpreted within the Anabaptist-Mennonite tradition. Issues relating to violence and war are discussed.

Yoder, John H. "The Biblical Mandate." *Post-American* 3 (Apr., 1974), 21-25. (Address given at the Evangelical and Social Concern Workshop, Chicago, Ill., Nov. 23, 1973. Pp. 14. AMBS.) Discusses many strands of Christian faith that call for Christian responsibility for love and justice in the social order.

Yoder, John H. "The Lordship of Christ and the Power Struggle." *The Lordship of Christ (Proceedings of the Seventh Mennonite World Conference).* Ed. Cornelius J. Dyck. Elkhart: MWC, 1962, 507-512. As a servant people, refusing to participate in the power struggle, we are called to share with our Servant-Lord "in that servanthood which shall reign forever and ever."

Yoder, John H. "The Original Revolution." *Forum* (Mar., 1971), A-2. God's original revolution involves the creation of a new, distinct community with its own deviant set of values and way of life, which rejects our classical revolutionary strategies.

Yoder, John H. *The Original Revolution.* Scottdale: Herald Press, 1971. Pp. 129. Excerpts printed in *Post-American* 2 (Sept.-Oct., 1973), 4-5, 14. Excerpts from the book center on the Christian community witnessing without violence to the kingdom of God.

Yoder, John H. "The War in Algeria." *GH* 51 (Mar. 18, 1958), 254-56. Reviews the Algerian war and considers how a nonresistant Christian may respond to it. Concludes the nonresistant Christian will witness against injustice and oppression on both sides of the conflict.

Yoder, John H. *What Would You Do?* Scottdale: Herald Press, 1983. Pp. 119. Takes seriously the question frequently asked pacifists of what action is right should a violent person threaten to harm a loved one. Considers the assumptions behind the question, how this hypothetical situation differs from the questions of war, and what the options for response to the situation might be. Subsequent sections of the book excerpt thinking other pacifists have done on the topic and offer examples of how nonviolent responses to threatening situations have functioned to defuse the violence.

Zehr, Daniel. "Teach-In Looks at Religion and International Affairs." *CanMenn* 15 (Oct. 31, 1967), 1, 10. Reflections of attitudes on revolution, war, and the church by prominent leaders in theology, education, and the church from South America, North America, and Africa.

Zehr, Howard. "The Case of the Wilmington 10." *GH* 70 (Nov. 1, 1977), 814-15. Summarizes events leading to the conviction of the "Wilmington 10," and appeals to Mennonites as a peacemaking people to become aware of the miscarriage of justice in this racial issue, and to play a reconciling role.

Zehr, Howard. "The Injustice of Criminal Justice in America." *Peace Section Newsletter* 8 (Nov.-Dec., 1977), 1-4. Examines the underlying assumptions for the belief that the criminal justice system is a kind of automatic machine governed by laws and regulations, which administers an apolitical justice and maintains a neutral order.

Zercher, John A. "The Need for Discernment." *EV* 88 (Oct. 10, 1975), 3. Recognizing that the history of the US entails much violence and destruction, our observances of the nation's bicentennial will call for discernment.

Zercher, John E. "The Other Commandment." *EV* 90 (Nov. 10, 1977), 3. We need to be aware of the sex, violence, and covetousness portrayed on TV and its subtle influences on our minds and lives.

Zercher, John E. "Violence." *EV* 85 (Mar. 10, 1972), 3. An examination of the significance of the cross against the dark background of violence.

Zercher, John E. (Review). *No Place to Stop Killing,* by Norman A. Wingert. Chicago: Moody Press, n.d. Pp. 126. "Violence Compounded," *EV* 88 (Mar. 10, 1975), 5. Realizing that when violence is the response to violence there is no stopping point, the Christian church in Burundi engages in a suffering ministry and testimony.

Zochert, Donald (Review). *Thaddeus Stevens and the Fight for Negro Rights,* by Milton Metzler. Thomas Y. Crowell Co., 1967. Pp. 231. *ChrLiv* 15 (Feb., 1968), 36-37. Reviewer observes the book's thesis is that while Stevens worked for justice in promoting the 13th, 14th, and 15th amendments to the Constitution, he was politically a contradictory figure.

Zook, J. K. *War. Its Evils and Its Blessings: The Parable of the Tares.* N.p., [1895]. Pp. 30. MHL. Protests that war is not criminal but the tool of God's judgment; while saints living under the new covenant seek no vengeance, those same saints should be content to allow the "ordained powers" to execute God's justice. In this age, after all, the wheat and the tares coexist.

# B. Abortion

Arndt, Bill. Letter to the Editor. *ChrLead* 36 (Jan. 23, 1973), 17. Encouragement for Mennonites to express outrage at the violence in Southeast Asia, especially if the church is going to take stands on issues like abortion.

Beachy, Marcia Froese. Letter to the Editor. *Forum* (Apr., 1973), 7. In response to an earlier article and letter on the abortion issue, this letter presents an argument in favor of abortion.

Bender, Ross T. "The Religious Perspective on Abortion." *Life and Values,* ed. Edwin and Helen Alderfer. Scottdale: Mennonite Publishing House, 1974, 25-33. Pp. 124. Considers, among other questions pertaining to the issue, the question of whether abortion is the moral equivalent of homicide or killing in war. Concludes there are significant differences in the cases; to label abortion an act of violence is a distortion because the elements of conflict and hostility between equal, contending parties are absent.

Bergen, J. "Let Caesar Be Caesar." *MBH* 12 (Apr. 20, 1973), 25. Believes that to interfere with the work of the police force and judges is an error and should not be done, even as it relates to questions of capital punishment and abortion.

Birky, Luke. "When Is Life?" *GH* 61 (Jan. 30, 1968), 98-99. Raises complex questions related to abortion and euthanasia in the context of Mennonite belief in the sacredness of life, seen in the practice of nonresistance.

Brenneman, George. "Abortion: Review of Mennonite Literature, 1970-1977." *MQR* 53 (Apr., 1979), 160-72. Written to challenge Mennonites to continue the abortion dialogue, this article summarizes what has been written on the issue in Mennonite literature. One of the nine questions addressed regarding abortion calls attention to the relationship of the issue of abortion to a "peace church" stance.

Brubaker, Samuel M. "Life and Human Values. The Problem of Abortion." *EV* 87 (Jan. 25,

1974), 5. A Conference on Life and Human Values sponsored by the Mennonite Medical Association studied the abortion issue from ethical, religious, personal, social, and institutional perspectives and discussed church involvement with the issue.

"Conference on Life and Human Values." Proceedings of Mennonite Medical Association Conference on Abortion. Chicago, Ill, Oct. 5-6, 1973. Pp. 114. MHL. Similarities and dissimilarities between abortion and killing are minor points in some of the discussions. Major addresses include: Bender, Ross T., "The Religious Perspectives," 16-31; Alderfer, Helen, "The Personal Aspects," 40-45; Koontz, Ted, "Social Implications," 55-80; Ewert, Marvin, "Institutional Responsibilities," 86-94; Erb, Paul, "Church Involvement," 104-109.

Cunningham, Jim. "Putting Waste in Its Proper Perspective." *MBH* 16 (May 13, 1977), 32. The problem of household waste compared with national waste of war, abortion, drunk driving.

Dueck, H. M. R. "Abortion: An Easy Way Out?" *MennMirror* 10 (Sept., 1980), 11-12. Mennonite mother of infant with "congenital defects" reassesses (and reaffirms) her anti-abortion convictions in light of her experience and her upbringing in the Mennonite peace tradition.

Enns, Elizabeth. Letter to the Editor. *MennRep* 10 (Mar. 31, 1980), 6. Registered nurse relates conscientious objection to the taking of fetal life to protesting war, nuclear weapons, and capital punishment.

Erb, Paul. "What About Easier Abortion Laws?" *ChrLiv* 19 (July, 1972), 2-5. Discussion of the morality of abortion is related to convictions regarding war and capital punishment.

Fast, Rebecca; Kraus, C. Norman; and Alderfer, Helen. "More Discussion . . ." *Forum* (Dec., 1971), 6. Three persons respond to Gayle and Ted Koontz's article on abortion (also Dec., 1971, *Forum*), each presenting their particular concern: respectively, that it be an option only in the early months of pregnancy, questioning where the responsibility for the decision lies, and expressing bewilderment and the hope that the church will help think through the issue.

Friesen, Duane K. *Moral Issues in the Control of Birth.* Newton: Faith and Life Press, 1974. Pp. 69. Addresses, in the final chapter, whether abortion and war are comparable moral issues. Concludes that while these issues have one very important principle in common, the sanctity of human life, a number of significant differences would likely lead us to quite different judgments on each of these moral issues.

Friesen, Duane K; Friesen, Henry and Marilyn; and Hurst, Ken and Janice. "The Moral Dilemma." *Forum* (Nov., 1973), 6. Duane Friesen presents a case in which legal abortion presents a moral dilemma. Two different responses are given to this case study.

Froese, G. J. Letter to the Editor. *MBH* 12 (Apr. 20, 1973), 10-11. This letter and editorial response deal with issues of war and abortion and the position of the Mennonite Brethren Church in taking life.

Gerber, Judith Schmell. Letter to the Editor. *Forum* (Mar., 1973), 10. Responding to Vern Ratzlaff's article on abortion (*Forum*, [Jan., 1973]), this letter defends the need for abortion.

Hertzler, Daniel. "Going to Church . . ." *GH* 70 (May 10, 1977), 400. Beginning from a medical report stating that church attendance is good for your health, editor comments on medical ethics for the unborn, linking nonresistance to protecting fetal life.

Hurd, Menno B. "Menno's Opinion." *GH* 69 (Feb. 3, 1976), 86. Encourages Mennonites to see the relationship between nonresistance and the abortion issue, and to be consistent in respecting human life.

Janzen, David. "The Abortion Dialogue." *MennRep* 2 (Aug. 7, 1972), 6, 7. Issues involved in practicing abortion when pregnancies and children are unwanted, including biblical and theological ones.

Janzen, David. "Two Helpful Books on Abortion." *MennRep* 2 (Sept. 4, 1972), 8. Two reviews of books which emphasize an honest look at the issues involved in abortion, e.g., medical, social, and spiritual issues.

Koontz, Gayle Gerber and Koontz, Ted. "The Abortion Issue." *Forum* (Dec., 1971), 1-2. After presenting and examining six arguments in the abortion debate, the authors conclude that sometimes abortion may be the best realistic alternative and that the development and distribution of contraceptives needs to be supported.

Koontz, Ted, comp. "Abortion: Resources for Study and Discussion." *Persons Becoming: Project of MCC Peace Section Task Force on Women.* Ed. Dorothy Yoder Nyce. Akron, Pa.: MCC Peace Section, 1974. Pp. 2.

Koontz, Ted. "Abortion: Some Social Considerations." Paper presented to Mennonite Medical Association Conference on Life and Human Values, O'Hare Concord Motor Inn, Des Plaines, IL, Oct. 5-6, 1973. Pp. 25. MLA/ BeC.

Koontz, Ted. "Hard Choices: Abortion and War."
*Menn* 93 (Feb. 28, 1978), 132-34. Analyzes the
inconsistency of Mennonite prohibition of
killing in war, without a corresponding
prohibition on abortion. Concludes that
rethinking both issues will lead to a less
simplistic formulation of Mennonite pacifism.

Lapp, John E. "Social Issues the Church Can Not
Ignore." *Builder* 21 (Oct., 1971), 10-12. Some
issues demanding the attention of the church
are: communism, war, poverty, racism,
Zionism, drugs, sex, abortion, wealth and
popularity.

Mast, Wesley. Letter to the Editor. *Forum* (Apr.,
1973), 6. Speaks out against abortion and
expresses concern that as Mennonites we take
our stance, whether it be on abortion, war, or
another issue, according to the mood or spirit of
the times.

Matty, Maria. "Sanctity of Life Is Theme for Eben-
Ezer Education Week." *MennRep* 9 (Dec. 24,
1979), 5. Education week at the Eben-Ezer
Mennonite Church of Abbotsford, BC resulted
in resolutions on capital punishment,
militarism, and abortion.

Ratzlaff, Vernon. "A Christian Perspective of
Abortion." *ChrLead* (Nov. 2, 1971), 2-7.
Mennonite Brethren look at the abortion issue
from the statistical information available, from
the standpoint of ethicists, medicine, theology,
and society.

Ratzlaff, Vernon. "Issues of Life and Death—
Abortion: Some Comments." *Forum* (Jan.,
1973), 1-4. Looks at the various aspects of
abortion and arguments used in the issue, and
concludes that where abortion is seen as the
solution to problems of quite unrelated areas,
the Christian community needs to voice its
concern and moral convictions.

Ratzlaff, Vernon. "Why I'm Against Abortion." *Life
and Values.* Ed. Edwin and Helen Alderfer.
Scottdale: Mennonite Publishing House, 1974,
58-66. Pp. 124. Believes the word "abortion" is
a euphemism for willful and deliberate
homicide. Therefore the issues of abortion and
war are comparable moral cases and should
both be absolutely rejected.

Regier, Harold R. "Questions of Life and Death."
*Menn* 87 (Apr. 18, 1972), 274. Although
Mennonites have always been clear that taking
life is immoral, the abortion issue raises new
questions about the definition and meaning of
life.

Reimer, Margaret Loewen. "Abortion: The
Church Must Face the Issue More Seriously."
*MennRep* 2 (Sept. 4, 1972), 7. An appeal to love
and to deal realistically with the abortion issue,
taking a pro-abortion stand.

"Statement of Position from Mennonite MP."
*MennRep* 9 (Nov. 12, 1979), 7, 8. John Reimer,
MP for Kitchener, Ont., responds to a list of
questions from the *Mennonite Reporter,* setting
forth his position on various issues including
arms sales, abortion, and capital punishment.

Scholl, Otto. Letter to the Editor. *ChrLead* 36 (Aug.
21, 1973), 12. Looks at the issue of abortion.
Both war and abortion take lives, thus
Christians cannot support either one.

"Western District Accents Quality of Life Issues."
*Menn* 94 (Nov. 13, 1979), 681-82. The 88th
Western District conference in Hutchinson,
Kansas, dealt with quality of life issues related
to euthanasia, abortion, prolongation of life as
well as personal life styles and community
justice.

"Where Do We Stand on Abortion?" *ChrLeader* 38
(Oct. 14, 1975), 3-5. Statement by the
Mennonite Brethren Board of Reference and
Counsel contends that the issue of abortion
should be viewed in the context of other life
and death issues such as capital punishment,
war, some forms of contraception, euthanasia,
etc. Concludes that decisions in these areas are
properly made in the church "via personal and
pastoral counsel."

Wiebe, Bernie. "Abortion and War." *Menn* 92 (Oct.
4, 1977), 576. Mennonites lack unanimity on
the question of abortion as on participation in
war. A key to both questions is respect for life
in God's image which motivates people to seek
the best for one another.

# C. Labor Unions

"A Statement of Concerns: Adopted at a Study
Conference on Christian Community
Relations." *GH* 44 (Aug. 14, 1951), 780-81.
Contains sections on: 1) Doctrine and practice;
2) Nonresistance in daily life; 3) Christian ethics
in business and prpfessions; 4) Organized labor;
5) Race and minority group relations; and 6)
other related concerns.

Barrett, Lois. "Make Your Labor Christian." *The
Other Side* 12 (Mar.-Apr., 1976), 52-57. Explores
how the Church can respond to the fact that
many people in industrial societies find work to
be distasteful, often boring, and frequently
requiring a compromise of one's principles.

Burkholder, Oscar. "Why Christians Should Not

Belong to Labor Organizations." *ST* 15 (3rd Qtr., 1947), 6. Christians should not belong to labor unions because such unions violate the scriptures, disregard the church, violate conscience, and exhibit many inconsistancies.

"Church and Society Conference." Paper, reports, minutes, etc., of General Conference Mennonite Church conference, Chicago, Ill., Oct. 31-Nov. 3, 1961. Two volumes. MHL. Some pertinent commission papers include: "The Christian Church and Civil Defense;" "Christian Labor and Management Relations;" "The Christian in Race Relations;" "The Christian Church and the State;" "The Church, the State, and the Offender."

Ebersol, Carmen. "Ethics and the Problems of Management and Labor." Paper presented to Commerce Seminar, Goshen College, Goshen, Ind., June 3, 1955. Pp. 47. MHL.

Fretz, J. Winfield. "The Church's Attitude Toward Organized Labor." *Menn* 61 (June 18, 1946), 5-6. The church must be concerned to break down class warfare; it must teach ethical sensitivity regarding exploitation and adhere to love and nonviolence in the midst of "industrial warfare."

Froese, David. Letter to the Editor. *MBH* 12 (Oct. 5, 1973), 9. In the area of labor relations, writer suggests legislation to make arbitration compulsory with no strike or picket line permitted during arbitration, so as not to affect a third mediating party.

Hager, Albert. "Should Christians Join Labor Unions?" *ChrMon* 40 (July, 1948), 203-4. Christians should not participate in labor union methods because they are not consistent with Jesus' teachings on suffering injustice.

Hershberger, Guy F. "Alert to the Question of Labor Union Relations." *ChrLiv* 2 (Jan., 1955), 26, 25. Guidelines for union membership that does not violate nonresistant principles.

Hershberger, Guy F. "Christian Labor Relations." Mimeographed, 1955. Goshen College, Good Library. The biblical faith and nonresistant way of life are sources of power to deal with labor-management issues.

Hershberger, Guy F. "Christian Nonresistance: Its Foundation and its Outreach." *MQR* 24 (Apr., 1950), 156-62; *GH* 44 (Oct. 16, 1951), 1002-1003, 1013. The doctrine of love and nonresistance is an integral part of the Gospel. It has consequences for all areas of life including race, labor, family, community, and nation. If Mennonites are to recover the dynamic of sixteenth century Anabaptism it will be on this biblical basis.

Hershberger, Guy F. "Committee on Economic and Social Relations." *ME* I (1955), 650-51. Major task of this committee has been to assist Mennonite labor employees to maintain the stand of the church (on grounds of nonresistance) against joining labor unions.

Hershberger, Guy F. "Continued Study on Labor Union Relations." *ChrLiv* 2 (Feb., 1955), 26. Resolutions regarding labor union involvement that is in harmony with nonresistant love.

Hershberger, Guy F. "Labor Union Relations: The Basis of Understanding." *ChrLiv* 2 (Mar., 1955), 26. Copy of the alternative union card expressing the Basis of Understanding bewtween Mennonite and Brethren in Chrsit churches and any given labor union on the question of conscientious objector employees.

Hershberger, Guy F. "Labor Unions." *ME* III (1957), 266-67. Surveys the Mennonite Church position toward labor unions. The Christian may cooperate with the union as long as the relationship does not conflict with his or her Christian testimony.

Hershberger, Guy F. "Nonresistance and Industrial Conflict." *MQR* 13 (Apr., 1939), 135-54. The industrial conflict is a fight for power with which to achieve social justice, whereas biblical nonresistance enjoins submission even to injustice rather than engage in conflict.

Hershberger, Guy F. "Promoting Christian Employer-Employee Relations." *ChrLiv* 3 (Oct., 1956), 22. Christian employer-employee relations can be maintained and promoted in an industrial world—which for the most part does not follow the way of love and the cross—only through the mutual resolution of the common problems of management and labor.

Hershberger, Guy F. "Relations with Labor Organizations." *ChrLiv* 1 (Dec., 1954), 36. Survey of provisions possible for conscientious objectors to labor unions.

Hershberger, Guy F. "The Christian Attitude Toward Labor Unions." *ChrLiv* 3 (Aug., 1956), 26. Motives and practices which a nonresistant Christian can and cannot support. Labor union is compared with the state.

Hershberger, Guy F. "The Christian's Accomodation to the Organized Industrial Order." *ChrLiv* 3 (Dec., 1956), 22, 32. Summary of guidelines for nonresistant Christian presence in industry.

Hershberger, Guy F. "The Committee on Economic and Social Relations Is Important Too." *GH* 56 (1963), 384, 394. A report outlining the contributions of the Committee on Economic and Social Relations. It was started in 1939 by the MC General Conference to work primarily with ethical questions involved in labor union relationship, but its scope has become much broader.

Hershberger, Guy F. "The Nonresistant Christian Betwixt Management and Union." *ChrLiv* 3 (Sept., 1956), 26, 45. Guidelines for remaining neutral and working toward justice with love.

Hershberger, Guy F. (Archival). Boxes 10-19—writings: church history; labor. Goshen, Ind. AMC. Hist. Mss. 1-171.

Hess, J. Daniel. *Ethics in Business and Labor.* Scottdale, Pa.: Herald Press, 1977. Pp. 85. A study book for small groups which approach the ethical questions of business from both viewpoints—management and labor—advocating the Christian imperative as the basis for action.

Indiana-Michigan Mennonite Conference—Peace and Social Concerns Committee. (Archival). II-5-6, Box 4. Material on various peace and social concerns, including labor relations. Goshen, Ind. AMC.

Irvin, Maurice R. "The Christian and Labor." *ST* 40 (Apr., 1972), 26. Discussion of the biblical understanding about labor and the Christian's attitude toward it.

Jantz, Harold. "Conscience Doesn't Count, Says Labor Board." *MBH* 13 (May 31, 1974), 16-17; *MennMirror* 3 (Summer, 1974), 22. Two nurses in Manitoba who requested exemption from membership and dues in the Nurses' Association on the basis of conscientious objection were turned down by the Labor Board. Includes a letter written by the editor to the Premier of Manitoba requesting him to investigate this decision.

Jantz, Harold. "Court Recognizes Funk's Beliefs on Union." *GH* 69 (Jan. 27, 1976), 70; *MBH* 15 (Jan. 23, 1976), 12. Reports on the case of Henry Funk of Manitoba, who opposed union membership on grounds of conscientious objection, and who won his case in the Manitoba Court of Appeals.

Jantz, Harold. "Labour Board Rejects Conscientious Objector." *Menn* 89 (Nov. 5, 1974), 649; *MennMirror* 4 (Nov., 1974), 11, 12; *MBH* 13 (Oct. 18, 1974), 10. Relates the case of Henry Funk of Nivervills, Man., who refused to sign a union membership application for reasons of conscience and was consequently fired from his place of work.

Jantz, Harold. "Mennonites Struggle with Union Membership." *MBH* 14 (Dec. 12, 1975), 13-15. In a paper presented to MCC (Manitoba) annual meeting, Harold Jantz urged

congregations to support conscientious objectors to union membership.

Juhnke, James C. "New Black Consciousness in South Africa." *Menn* 87 (Nov. 28, 1972), 700, 701. The black separatism movement still is in its infancy; however, it is showing remarkable vigor in its quest for political power, in its anticipated organization of an African workers' union, and in the emergence of a "black theology" movement.

Julian, Cheyne. Letter to the Editor. *ChrLead* 42 (June 19, 1979), 13. Questions an article on peacemaking on the job (*ChrLead*, Mar. 27, 1979) for it seems to put the burden of peacemaking on the employee rather than on the shareholders, company directors, etc.

Kauffman, Daniel. "Labor Unionism: Scriptural Reasons Why." (Part 4). *GH* 30 (July 1, 1937), 289-90. Mennonites should not hold membership in labor unions because it is a form of conflict between unions and management.

Kauffman, Daniel. "Principles Involved in the Present Struggle Between Labor and Capital." *GH* 29 (Feb. 11, 1937), 977-78. An analysis of the labor struggle which concludes that the nonresistant Christian can have no part in labor unions.

Kauffman, J. Howard. "Christian Ethics and Organized Labor." Paper, n.d. Pp. 11. MHL.

Kauffman, J. Howard. "The Christian and Labor Unions." *ChrLiv* 1 (Jan., 1954), 38. Mennonites view the methods used by labor unions—striking, picketing, and boycotting—as incompatible with nonresistant love.

Klassen, William. "Mennonite Witness on the Line: An Attempt at Clarifying the Issues." *MennRep* 6 (Aug. 23, 1976), 7. Criticizes Mennonite Brethren Member of Parliament Jake Epp for his stance favoring capital punishment, observing that it is not consistent with Mennonite conscientious objection to violence in other forms, such as labor union strikes.

Koontz, Ted. "The Farm Labor Conflict in California." *GH* 67 (June 25, 1974), 516-17. Reports on the complexity of the farm labor conflict as seen by Mennonite church and peace representatives in conversations with both Mennonite growers and farm laborers.

Kreider, Carl. "Merger of AFL and CIO Unions." *ChrLiv* 2 (May, 1955), 22, 40. Discussion of the merger, giving some history of the two unions, with implications for nonresistant Christians.

Kreider, Robert S. "The Ethics of Nonviolence in

American Trade Unionism." MA Thesis, Divinity School, Univ. of Chicago, Chicago, Ill., Aug., 1941. Pp. 98. MHL. Examines the ethics of the ends sought and the means employed by different types of American unionism. Includes a chapter on nonviolent unionism, analyzing such examples of peaceful arbitration as the Quaker-led effort at the Berkshire Knitting Mills, Pa., and the Oklahoma coal miners who simply prayed, audibly, fervently, and by name, for their employers and the strike-breakers who violated the picket lines until negotiations were concluded. Concludes, in light of this examination, that the church ought to establish relationships with such social movements as unionism and then pursue its historic role of being prophetically critical and ethically constructive in social change.

Kroeker, Walter. (Review). *Labor Problems in Christian Perspective,* by John H. Redekop. Grand Rapids: Eerdman's, 1972. Pp. 364. *MBH* 12 (Feb. 23, 1973), 22. Describes the contents of this book which is a compilation of 26 essays expressing views on the Christian ethic as it relates to labor problems. Points out several shortcomings, but identifies it as a major contribution deserving praise.

Lapp, John A. (Review). *The Military Industrial Complex,* by Sidney Lens. Pilgrim Press/National Catholic Reporter, 1970. Pp. 183. *GH* 64 (Oct. 19, 1971), 875. Regards book as "comprehensive," "well-written," and "imbued with moral sensitivity," in its analysis of the military's impact on the economy, political processes, the labor movement, and college campuses.

Lind, Ivan Reuben. "The Attitude of the (Old) Mennonite Church Toward Labor Unions." *PCMCP Third,* 89-97. North Newton, Kansas: n.p. Held at North Newton, Kansas, Aug. 18-19, 1944. Scriptural bases for the nonresistant position in war can also be applied to the labor situation. Exploration of the attitudes which the Mennonites have taken through the years toward labor organizations.

Lind, Ivan Reuben. *The Labor Union Movement in the Light of Nonresistance as Held by the Mennonite Church.* Unpublished MA thesis, Dept. of Commerce, the State Univ. of Iowa, 1941. Pp. 69. Mennonites see unions as power groups organized for coercion in which nonresistant Christians cannot participate. Compromises are being made, however, as well as new attempts to find alternate solutions, including migration to rural areas.

Lutz, Clarence E. "Our Nonresistant Attitude Toward Labor Unions." *GH* 32 (Dec. 28, 1939), 819-20. Unions use some forms of coercion and therefore nonresistant Christians cannot join them.

"MCC (Manitoba) Asks for Stronger CO Provisions in Labor Act." *RepConsS* 32 (Mar., 1975), 5. Request prompted by Labor Board's denial of eight recent applications for exemption from union membership for reasons of conscientious objection.

Martin, Lewis. "Nonresistance: In Industrial Problems." *The Eastern Mennonite School Journal* 18 (Apr., 1940), 71-75. Christians involved in labor problems should remember: Christians have a place in the world; they have a testimony in the world; they should be steadfast in suffering wrong rather than doing wrong.

Mennonite Church General Conference Statements (Archival). Goshen, IN. AMC. 1-1-1, Box 5. File 5/4: Mennonites and industrial organizations, 1937.

Mennonite General Conference. "Mennonites and Industrial Organizations." *GH* 30 (Feb. 10, 1938), 989-90. General Conference (MC) statement that Mennonites of the nonresistant faith cannot participate in unions. Further, Mennonites should work for peace between the factions and protect the rights of all

"New Labour Code No Help." *MBH* 12 (Nov. 16, 1973), 12. Chris Nan Der Nagel, employed by Dominion Bridge in Winnipeg, has refused to pay union dues by reason of his religious beliefs, but his efforts to gain this right were turned down by the Labor Relations Board.

"Peace, War, and Social Issues: A Statement of the Position of the Amish Mennonite Churches." Officially adopted by the ministerial body of the Beachy Amish Mennonite constituency . . . at Wellesley, Ont., Apr. 18-19, 1968. [n.p., 1968]. Pp. 16. MSHL. Topics include the role of government, military service, civil defense, the Christian's role in race relations, unions, etc.

Peters, Gerald (Review). *No Strangers in Exile,* by Hans Harder, trans. Al Reimer. Winnipeg, 1979. Pp. 123. *MennLife* 34 (Dec., 1979), 27. Provides a literary critique of this book which is a fictional account of life in forced labor camps in northern Russia and the struggle to survive under impossible conditions. Finds it worthwhile in terms of its intent to preserve the fate and labors of the Russian Mennonites during the 1930's.

Redekop, John H. "Labor Strife and the Church." *ChrLead* 39 (Mar. 2, 1976), 4. Notes some of the major trends in organized labor. Explores the Christian response and suggests some practical options for involvement.

Redekop, John H. "The New Conscientious Objectors." *MBH* 14 (Mar. 21, 1975), 8. Although Canadian youths do not face the draft, other forms of conscientious objection are being practiced, such as noncooperation with unions or forced tax evasion.

Regehr, Ernie. "The CLAC and the Union Giants." *MBH* 12 (Jan. 26, 1973), 32. Discusses the philosophy behind the Christian Labour Association of Canada (CLAC) and the reasons it raises the rancor of the union giants, even though numerically it is only a small fraction of the labor movement.

Regier, Kenneth P. Letter to the Editor. *MennMirror* 6 (Oct., 1976), 23. The lawyer who defended Funk in his objection to paying labor union dues speaks out against the recent amendment to the Labour Relations Act. (See editorial *MennMirror* 5 (Summer, 1976).

"Statement of Concerns." *MennComm* 5 (Nov., 1951), 17-19. Statement resulting from Study Conference on Christian Community Relations links the doctrine of nonresistance to war to issues of business ethics, organized labor, race and minority relations, and standard of living.

Schulz, Herb. Letter to the Editor. *MennMirror* 6 (Oct., 1976), 22, 23. Schulz, assistant to the Premier of Manitoba, responds to the Summer, 1976, editorial on the Henry Funk vs. labor union case, presenting the government's view and explanation for amending the Labour Code.

Shank, J. Ward (Editorial). "America! America!" *ST* 42 (May, 1974), 7. As nonresistant Christians, we live in unique relationship to our country—as neither patriots in the ordinary sense nor as radical revolutionaries. We owe our nation a deep loyalty, expressed in productive labor, service to others, and preeminently as stewards of the gospel.

Shetler, Sanford G., ed. "Churchmen Continue to Support Militant Chavez." (Article unsigned) *GfT* 8 (Nov.-Dec., 1973), 6. Chavez's methods of boycotting and picketing do not correspond to Mennonite concern for love and goodwill among all sides.

Stoltzfus, Grant M. "The Christian Church and Social Justice." *GH* 39 (June 18, 1946), 244-45. An address given at the Conference on Industrial Relations, Scottdale, Pa., Mar. 29, 1946. The nonresistant Christian is always opposed to the concentration of wealth but will not belong to a union.

Vogt, Roy. "Mennonites and the Strike." *MennMirror* 9 (June, 1980), 42. Suggests that traditional Mennonite nonparticipation in unions is less redemptive than a potential Mennonite participation characterized by witness against militancy and for constructive processes of reconciliation.

Vogt, Roy. "Strikes Symbolize Union Power But You Wield Power Too." *MennMirror* 4 (May, 1975), 7-8. While sympathetic to view of Henry Funk, who is fighting a legal battle over his refusal to join a union on the grounds of conscientious objection to violent union tactics, Vogt urges Christians to think critically and analytically about the way we ourselves are involved with the uses of power. We must then exercise this power with care and responsibility to Christian ethics of nonviolence, etc., rather than withdrawing from situations simply because there is use of power.

Vogt, Roy. "The Funk Case Represents a Rare Triumph of Individual Rights." *MennMirror* 5 (Jan.-Feb., 1976), 21, 22. Examines some of the issues raised for conscientious objectors in the decision of the Manitoba Court of Appeals to exempt Henry Funk from labor union membership on the basis of his religious beliefs, rather than adherence to an official set of church doctrines. See also an earlier article: *MennMirror* 4 (Nov., 1974), 11, 12.

Vogt, Roy (Editorial). "Conscientious Objections Irk Manitoba Government, So It Changes the Labor Law and Thereby Subverts a Right." *MennMirror* 5 (Summer, 1976), 22. Several months after the court decision in the Funk case (*MennMirror* 5, [Feb., 1976]) to support the right of an individual to refuse, on grounds of conscience, to pay labor union dues, the Manitoba government has changed the labor law, making it virtually impossible to exercise this right. This is viewed as a tragic step backwards for human rights.

Weaver, Miriam. "Compulsory Union Membership and the Conscience Clause Amendment." *MCC PS Wash. Memo* 9 (July-Aug., 1977), 5-6. Discussion of the amendment to the National Labor Relations Act which would exempt members of historic peace churches from compulsory union membership.

# D. Law and Litigation*

"America and the War in the East." *Menn* 52 (Sept. 21, 1937), 6-7. Exhorts Mennonites as Christian citizens to do all they can to support strict enforcement of the US neutrality law. The article explains the law as a deterrent to war; arguments for and against its full application are cited.

"Applied Nonresistance." Papers read at the Mennonite Conference on Applied Nonresistance, Goshen, Indiana, Apr., 1939. Reprinted from *MQR* 13 (Apr., 1939), 75-154. MHL. Published by Peace Problems Committee, Mennonite General Conference, Scottdale, 1939. Includes Erb, Paul, "Nonresistance and Litigation," 75-82; Hershberger, Guy F. "Nonresistance and Industrial Conflict," 135-54.

*Arthur Jost, Petitioner v. United States of America.* Petition [to the Supreme Court of the United States, October Term, 1953] for a Writ of Certiorari to the District Court of Appeal for the Fourth Appellate District of California. By Dean Acheson and others, attorneys for the petitioner, Covington and Burling, of Counsel. [Washington, DC: Supreme Court, 1953.] Pp. 39. MHL. This petition, to review the denial of naturalization to Arthur Jost on grounds that his request to take the conscientious objector's oath was unconvincing, includes summary of Mennonite teachings on nonresistance as well as the questions, perceptions, and arguments emerging from the opposition in a legal context.

Brubaker, Paul. "Del Monte's Martial Law Pineapples." *Sojourners* 8 (Oct., 1978), 16. Describes how a company like Del Monte in the Philippines, a country of rampant unemployment, practices a capital-intensive agriculture. This practice displaces more people than it employs.

Brunk, Conrad G. "Law and Morality: Tensions and Perspectives." In *The Bible and Law*, ed. Willard M. Swartley, 107-138. *Occasional Papers* No. 3. Elkhart: Institute of Mennonite Studies, 1982. An earlier version of Brunk's article in the *Conrad Grebel Review*; see below.

Brunk, Conrad G. "Reflections on the Anabaptist View of Law and Morality." *CGR* 1 (Spring, 1983), 1-20. Law is never amoral; only within the church can law really reflect Christian justice and Christian love. While the church's ethic cannot truly be put into effect in the state, the ethic should, nevertheless, guide the law of the state because Christians live in both kingdoms and both are orders of law and morality.

"CO's in Spain Seek New Law." *MennRep* 9 (Dec. 10, 1979), 2. International support is necessary for a law which would meet some of the demands of Spanish conscientious objectors.

"Consultation on Litigation Problems." Papers from consultation held at Goshen, Ind., 1961. Pp. 57. MHL. Wenger, S. S., "Classification of Types of Legal Procedures," 3-11; Beyler, Clayton, "Scriptural Principles Bearing on Our Litigation Problems and Our Mennonite Practices," 12-22; Kreider, Carl, "Legal Principles Which Are Compatible with Scriptural Principles and Those Which Are Incompatible," 24-35; Yoder, John H., "Possible New Procedures," 37-47.

Curry, Jan. "A History of the Houma Indians and the Story of Federal Nonrecognition." *American Indian Journal of the Institute for the Development of Indian Law* 5 (Feb., 1979), 8-28. The government's failure to recognize the Houma Indians of Louisiana as an Indian tribe has resulted in many injustices, such as the loss of land, hunting and fishing rights, etc. MCCer Jan Curry has researched and written this history in order to help the Houmas establish their claim to tribal status.

Dyck, John H. A. "Response to Conrad Brunk, 'Reflections on the Anabaptist View of Law and Morality,' and to Duane K. Friesen, 'A Moral Justification for War Tax Resistance,' *CGR* 1 (Spring, 1983), 1-28." *CGR* 2 (Winter, 1984), 51-56. Questions whether reality supports the assumption by Brunk and Friesen of a common moral norm.

Ediger, Peter J. "The Alpha and the Omega." Dramatic reading presented to the Conference on Conscience, Religion, and Resistance: Civil Disobedience and the Law in the Nuclear Crisis, sponsored by Center on Law and Pacifism, Philadelphia, Pa., n.d. Pp. 7. MHL.

Erb, Paul. "Nonresistance and Litigation." *MQR* 13 (Apr., 1939), 75-82. Nonresistance is to be integrated into the Christian's total life-style; going through law courts to settle conflicts is foreign to the spirit of the loving fellowship.

Finger, Thomas N. "The Problem of Law During the Protestant Reformation." In *The Bible and Law*, ed. Willard M. Swartley, 65-93. *Occasional Papers* No. 3. Elkhart: Institute of Mennonite Studies, 1982. Compares and contrasts the Lutheran, Calvinist and anabaptist views of law during the Reformation era. Fransen, Harold. "Reflections on Minneapolis: Is the Law of the Land Higher Than God's Law?" *MennRep* 9

---

*Does not include references to draft laws. See 11B, Conscription.

(Feb. 19, 1979), 7. Writer reflects on the mood and the process of the General Conference midtriennium which dealt with the question of war taxes.

Friesen, Dorothy (Review). *Letters from South Korea.* T. K. Idoc/North America. *Sojourners* 6 (July, 1977, 35. A collection of anonymous letters sparked by a declaration of martial law by Korea's President Park in late 1972.

"Government Changes Citizenship Law." *RepConsS* 34 (Mar., 1977), 2. MCC (Canada) influential in eliminating conscientious objection as a barrier to Canadian citizenship.

Gingerich, Melvin. "Christian Youth and Law Observance; Christian Youth and the State." *YCC* 21, Part 3, (Dec. 29, 1940), 410. The observance of even "minor" laws during peacetime gives more credibility to our saying no, if asked, to laws that are a part of supporting war or war psychology.

Harmon, Jan. "Advocating for 'Supreme Law of the Land'." *EV* 92 (Sept. 25, 1979), 10. Because the government has violated many Indian rights, the Friends Committee on National Legislation and MCC are attempting to raise the consciousness of the religious community and to respond to this human rights issue in our own country.

Hawk, William J. "On the History of Law and its Influence in Western Society." In *The Bible and Law,* ed. Willard M. Swartley, 95-105. *Occasional Papers* No. 3. Elkhart: Institute of Mennonite Studies, 1982. Critically evaluates Harold J. Berman's thesis regarding the crisis of law in the twentieth century and makes alternative proposals showing that the disjunction between law and morality has earlier roots, based upon the autonomy of legal theory, both from reason and religion.

Hershberger, Guy F. "Litigation." *ME* III (1957), 375-77. Surveys the historic view on litigation and the biblical roots for this position.

Hershberger, Guy F. "Litigation in Mennnonite History." Paper presented at the Laurelville, Pa., conference on "Nonresistance and Political Responsibility," 1956. N.p.: Peace Problems Committee, 1956, 32-35. MHL. Those Mennonites who have been most consistent in rejecting military service have also been most consistent in their refusal to seek legal redress.

Hershberger, Guy F. "What About the Outlawry of War?" *MQR* 2 (July, 1928), 159-75. Outlines Dr. C. C. Morrison's thesis that war as an institution must be rejected and avoided by means of an international law code. Nonresistant Christians should support such anti-war movements.

Johnson, Steven. "Where Is a Christian's First Allegiance?" *With* 2 (Mar., 1969), 16. For many Christians, one's obedience to the law is always conditional.

Kauffman, Daniel. "The European War Situation." *GH* 31 (Oct. 13, 1938), 601-602. In war time the Christian must live according to civil law until the point he or she is forced to disobey it in order to obey God, love the enemy, and pray for the authorities.

Kauffman, Daniel. "Thoughts on the Recent Election." *GH* 29 (Nov. 12, 1936), 705-706. Politics is not a realm for Christian people but one must be thankful if he or she lives in a land of law and order.

Kreider, Carl. "The Use of the Law." *GH* 72 (July 3, 1979), 532-33. One of the issues before the 1979 General Assembly will be litigation, and a statement has been prepared for consideration.

Landis, Maurice W. "The Secularization of the Church and Civil Religion, Part 2." *GfT* 8 (Nov.-Dec., 1973), 10-11, 15. By advocating amnesty for those who broke the Selective Service law, the church is violating the principle of separation of church and state and becoming an instrument of lawlessness.

Lapp, John A. "'Openien, You Should Have Died Long Ago.' " *ChrLiv* 20 (Feb., 1973), 20, 25, 27. Unequal distribution of land and wealth and the imposition of martial law have created a setting of violence in the Philippines.

Lapp, John A. (Review). *Democracy, Dissent, and Disorder: The Issues and the Law,* by Robert F. Drinan. Seabury Press, 1969. Pp. 152. *GH* 63 (June 9, 1970), 524. Recommends the book for its insights into legal dimensions of current social protest, including conscientious objection and opposition to the Vietnam war.

Lasserre, Jean. *War and the Gospel.* Scottdale: Herald Press, 1962. Pp. 243. Determines, through exegetical and theological analysis, that the Decalogue is the link between the gospel and public morality, the criterion of good by which Christians can judge the actions and commands of the state. Having reached this conclusion, Lasserre then applies the criterion of the sixth commandment to an evaluation of the police and military functions of the state. He concludes that while both law enforcement and defense are legitimate state functions, the death penalty and war are illegitimate ways to perform these functions.

Lehman, Emmett R. "Positive Dissent." *GfT* Series 2, Vol. 3 (Feb., 1968), 5-6. Reprinted also in *GfT* 6 (Sept.-Oct., 1971), 12. All witness to the priority of divine law over human must avoid violence and civil disobedience, since violent dissent cannot bring about justice.

Lehman, Emmett R. "The Rule of Law." *GfT* Series 2, 4 (Nov.-Dec., 1969), 16-17. Civil disobedience for any reason less worthy than preservation of the spiritual life shows disregard of God's command to obey the civil authorities.

Lind, Millard C. "Law in the Old Testament." In *The Bible and Law*, ed. Willard M. Swartley, 9-41. *Occasional Papers* No. 3. Elkhart: Institute of Mennonite Studies, 1982. Examines different types of law in the Old Testament and argues for a major distinction between biblical law and state law.

Matsuo, Hilda. "No-Fault Divorce Proposed." *MennMirror* 6 (Dec., 1976), 13. Looks at some of the injustices of family law and the need for reform to create greater equity.

Miller, D. D. "Nonresistance: In Litigation Provocations." *The Eastern Mennonite School Journal* 18 (Apr., 1940), 67-75. Describes policies and experiences of the Elkhart Mission Board in regards to various kinds of legal procedures.

Miller, D. D. "The Christian Attitude Toward the Government in Peace and War." *The Eastern Mennonite Journal* 18 (Apr., 1940), 59-63; *GH* 33 (May 23, 1940), 163-64. We ought to submit to every law and every regulation as long as such obedience does not conflict with the Law of God.

Miller, Ellene. Letter to the Editor. *Menn* 94 (May 1, 1979), 316. The Minneapolis midtriennium conference placed a great deal of emphasis on law, but the church must deal with a "higher law" of compassion, justice, and mercy in responding to all the victims of the arms race and nuclear proliferation.

Nickel, E. H. "World Peace Through World Law— Our Present Need." *CanMenn* 14 (Feb. 15, 1966), 7. Written by the secretary of World Federalists of Canada, article presents three alternatives to the destruction of civilization: massive nuclear deterrence; a transformation of human nature; rule of law. Advocates another option, system of international law, on the grounds that the first option is too volatile and the second unrealistic.

Redekop, John H. "Above the Law." *MBH* 14 (June 13, 1975), 8. Militant Canadian postal strikers typify an "above the law" stance motivated by self-interest, while nonviolent figures such as Jesus stand above the law because of a higher moral commitment.

Regehr, John. "Christians and the Courts." *MBH* 15; Part I (May 28, 1976), 6-7, 26; Part II (June 11, 1976), 4-5, 8-9. Conflict resolution between Christians should be through other means than litigation; guidelines for Christians in the use of legal processes for resolving conflict.

Shank, J. Ward. "Due Regard for Civil Law." *ST* 20 (2nd Qtr., 1952), 10. The true child of God will yield obedience where God has required it, whether to the institutions of the home, the church, or the state.

Souder, Elvin. "Problems of a Conscientious Objector in the Legal Practice." *PCMCP Seventh*, 101-12. North Newton, Kansas: The Mennonite Press. Held at Tabor College, Hillsboro, Kansas, June 16-17, 1949. A conscientious objector faces no greater problems of an ethical nature in legal practice than those one might encounter in business. Speaks to questions of law enforcement and the relationship of church and state encountered in legal practice.

Stauffer, John L. "Should a Christian Sue at Law." *ST* 15 (3rd Qtr., 1947), 15. Explains how lawsuits are contrary to the gospel and the spirit of Christ with a review of several passages of scripture.

Stoltzfus, Gene and Friesen, Dorothy. "A Shaky Triumph for Injustice." *Sojourners* 7 (Feb., 1978), 20. Description of the sixth year of Philippine martial law.

Stoner, John K. "Loving Confrontation in the Life of Jesus." *Affirm Life: Pay for Peace*. Ed. Maynard Shelly and Ron Flickinger. Newton: Historic Peace Church Task Force on Taxes, 1981, 11-12. Pp. [87]. MHL. The instances in which Jesus confronted the political, religious, and satanic powers of his day reveal that Jesus: did not compromise truth for tranquility; was clear that evil had both cosmic and human dimensions; regarded the law highly but right more highly; took initiative in confronting evil.

Stoner, Mary Beth. Letter to the Editor. *EV* 92 (July 10, 1979), 5. The recent execution of John Spenkelink and the approval Brethren in Christ ministers and members have seemingly given capital punishment prompts this letter, which states that Jesus followed the difficult, unsafe way and not the "law and order method of the Roman system."

"The Draft Law and Your Choices." *With* 2 (Mar., 1969), 4. Explanation of four responses, three of which are recognized as legitimate by Selective Service, that can be made to the draft law.

Toews, John E. "Some Theses Toward a Theology of Law in the New Testament." In *The Bible and Law*, ed. Willard M. Swartley, 43-64. *Occasional Papers* No. 3. Elkhart: Institute of Mennonite Studies, 1982. In eleven separate theses proposes that the New Testament writings affirm the validity and continuity of Old

Testament law for the people of God as maintenance, but not entrance, to life in Christ.

Vogt, Roy. "The RCMP—Does It Matter How They Get Their Man?" *MennMirror* 7 (Feb., 1978), 26. The RCMP, as enforcers of law and order, deserve respect but are no more immune from criticism and prosecution than any other citizen who violates the law.

"War Tax Packet." [Akron, Pa.]: MCC, Feb., 1976. MHL. Includes: Stoltzfus, Ruth C., "War Tax Research Report: Challenging Withholding Law on First Amendment Grounds," pp. 9.

Wellcome, I. C. *Should Christians Fight?* Scottdale, Pa.: Mennonite Publishing House, 1951. Pp. 53. MHL. Format is a debate between "Demi," representative of those "half-christianized by the Gospel," and "Christian," representative of those to whom Christ's law is supreme—and, who, consequently, believe in nonresistance. Topics discussed within this polemic are Christ's teaching on warfare, obedience to civil law, Old Testament warfare, the standards of the early church, etc.

Wenger, J. C. "Nonresistants and the Courts." *GH* 50 (Nov. 12, 1957), 964. One should not take someone to court in an "ordinary lawsuit" but it is generally acceptable to allow the court to act on "friendly lawsuits."

Wenger, Samuel S. "Mennonites and Litigation." Paper presented at the Laurelville, Pa., conference on "Nonresistance and Political Responsibility," 1956. N.p.: Peace Problems Committee, 1956, 35-39. MHL. A Mennonite lawyer's perspective. Wenger would not, for example, consider presenting a claim in Orphan's Court as "going to law."

Wenger, Samuel S. "Mennonites and the Law." *ChrLiv* 5 (Feb., 1958), 6-8, 33. Guidelines regarding nonresistance and litigation.

Yoder, Edward. "A Peace Meditation." *GH Supplement* 36 (Apr., 1943), 78. Those who live against the law of God have no peace.

Yoder, John H. with Miller, Donald E. "Does Natural Law Provide a Basis for a Christian Witness to the State? (A Symposium)." *Brethren Life and Thought* 7 (Winter, 1962), 8-22. In this Brethren-Mennonite dialogue, Yoder takes issue with Miller's delineation of natural law tendencies as a basis for Christian witness to the state and suggests, as an alternative, that we seek moral constants in the themes of covenant and incarnation, and, then, base moral dialogue with the state on the assumption that both the realm of unbelief and the church have, by the work of Christ, been subjugated to his lordship.

# E. Corrections

"Amishman Released from Prison After Mental Breakdown." *RepConsS* 15 (July, 1958), 3. Judge grants parents' request for release of son who suffered mental illness while serving sentence for conscientious objection.

"Authority Says Death Penalty Neither Moral Nor Useful." *CanMenn* 13 (Feb. 23, 1965), 1, 12. Report on a Toronto lecture on capital punishment by Thorstein Sellin, professor at U. of Penn. Sellin argued against capital punishment on both moral and utilitarian grounds.

Abbot, Jack Henry. "In Prison." *MCC Offender Ministries Network Newsletter* (Sept.-Oct., 1980), 6-9. Reprinted from *The New York Review* (June 26, 1980). Prison inmate describes the violence of prison life.

"Bars and Stripes Forever." *Menn* 94 (May 8, 1979), 328-29. Reports views of columnist Sydney Harris, who questions the need for the new Olympic prison near Lake Placid, NY, and suggests some alternatives to incarceration.

Baerg, Henry R. "Viewpoints on Capital Punishment and on Tobacco Smoking." *CanMenn* 12 (Apr. 28, 1964), 5-6. A letter to the editor supporting capital punishment as the duty of the state.

Baerg, Henry R. Letter to the Editor. *MBH* 15 (Feb. 20, 1976), 9, 28-29. Supporter of capital punishment builds his case from biblical passages and criticizes contemporary understandings of nonresistance that would tend to prohibit the use of the death penalty.

Baerg, Henry R.; Noth, H. H.; and Klassen, J. M. "Capital Punishment: Christian Leaders Give Their Views." *MBH* 12 (Nov. 21, 1973), 21-23. Two Manitoba Mennonite leaders present arguments for capital punishment; one argues against it.

Beachy, Alvin J. "You Shall Not Kill." *Menn* 94 (Aug. 7, 1979), 493. A study of the sixth commandment with emphasis on the sacredness of human life.

Bergen, J. "Let Caesar Be Caesar." *MBH* 12 (Apr. 20, 1973), 25. Believes that to interfere with the work of the police force and judges is an error and should not be done, even as it relates to questions of capital punishment and abortion.

Bliss, Betsy. "American Prisons: a Crime." *GH* 65, Part 1, (Jan. 4, 1972), 6-8; Part 2, (Jan. 11, 1972), 30-32. Reprinted from *US Catholic/Jubilee* (May, 1971). Documents examples of the violence, torture, and neglect characteristic of prison life, and asserts that prisons produce crime. Maintains that the American correctional system is based, not on the goal of rehabilitation, but on public vengeance.

Brubacher, S. C. Letter in "Our Readers Say." *GH* 53 (May 17, 1960), 442, 461. Capital punishment is a legitimate duty of the state according to biblical teachings. The Christian's duty is not to work for the abolition of capital punishment but rather to preach the Gospel so that people might be saved.

Burkholder, J. Richard. "What About Capital Punishment?" *Menn* 74 (Oct. 20, 1959), 646. An argument against capital punishment on the grounds that the gospel of forgiveness has superseded the Old Testament principle of "an eye for an eye."

"Capital Punishment 'Contrary to the Laws of God.' " *CanMenn* 10 (Feb. 16, 1962), 9. Members of the Department of Pastoral Services of the National Council of Churches call for the abolition of capital punishment.

"Capital Punishment Opposed by Overshelming Majority." *CanMenn* 13 (July 20, 1965), 1. Report on the GCMC Estes Park rejection of capital punishment as unbiblical and ineffective.

"Conference for Workers with Men in Prisons." Sponsored by Mennonite Board of Missions and Charities and Goshen Biblical Seminary at Goshen College, Goshen, Ind., Feb. 15-16, 1957. Pp. 33. MHL. Glick, Lester, "Prevailing Mental Patterns of Men in Conflict with the Law," 1-5; Wall, James, "Effects of Incarceration upon the Individual," 5-9; King, Louis R., "Qualifications for Workers with Men in Conflict with the Law," 9-12; Weaver, Clyde, "Self-Understanding—the Key to Helping People in Trouble," 19-24; King, Louis R., "Principles of Cooperation with Chaplains and Prison Officials," 29-33.

"COs Forced to Stay in Barracks Without Food." *RepConsS* 13 (June-July, 1956), 1, 3. Five Amish men serving prison sentences as a result of conscientious objection are punished for refusing to wear clothing prohibited by their church.

Chase, Mary T. "The Church and the Offender." *ChrLead* 39 (June 8, 1976), 2. Statement on offender ministries presented by the Mennonite Brethren Board of Reference and Counsel at the general conference sessions in Winnipeg in 1975.

*Christian Responsibility to Society.* Newton: Faith and Life Press, Church and Society Series No. 2, 1963. Because Jesus is Lord not only of the church but also of the world, some social ills may be partially corrected. Therefore we are mandated to labor toward the eradication of racial discrimination, capital punishment, war, etc.

Craighead, Shirley S. Letter to the Editor. *EV* 92 (Dec. 25, 1979), 2. Responding to an earlier letter opposing capital punishment, this letter argues that capital punishment is "part of the answer to our society's dilemma" and that the church should be more actively involved in prison ministry.

"Decisions on the Death Penalty." *CanMenn* 4 (July 6, 1956), 2. The Canadian Joint Senate-Commons Committee on Capital Punishment should revise its recommendations in light of Britain's abolition of the death penalty.

Derstine, C. F. "Kidnaping [*sic*]—The Hauptmann Trial—Capital Punishment." *ChrMon* 27 (Mar., 1935), 94-95. Discusses the attitudes of the church and state toward evildoers.

Drescher, James M. *Family Guide to the Juvenile Justice System: Questions and Answers About . . .* Lancaster: By the Author, 1979. Pp. 24. MHL. Answers basic questions about such matters as juvenile probation, detention, placement facilities, rights, etc.

Drescher, John M. (Editorial). "Remember the Prisoners . . . ." *GH* 65 (Jan. 11, 1972), 29. Editorial which considers the historical correlation between spiritual renewal and prison reform in this call for social action.

Driedger, Leo (Review). *Das Problem der Todes Strafe,* by Hans-Peter Alt. München: Christian-Kaiser-Verlag, n.d. Pp. 168. "Capital Punishment." *CanMenn* 9 (Aug. 25, 1961), 2. The strength of the book is its systematic interpretation of the Scriptures' view of capital punishment.

Dueck, H. M. R. "A Christian Response to Crime and Punishment." *MennMirror* 9, Part 1, (Feb., 1980), 8-9. Raises issues such as the disproportionate number of poor, young, and ethnic minorities punished by the penal system and the moral confusion resulting from society's reliance on violence to solve conflict while punishing violence in others.

Dueck, H. M. R. "Christians Haven't Made Much of an Impact in the 'Corrections' Field Where Their Compassion is Badly Needed." Part 2, *MennMirror* 9 (Mar., 1980), 11-13. Addresses the problem of the feeling that little or nothing can be done about the penal system and suggests actions Christians might take toward resolution of the injustices inherent in that system.

Dueck, Henry. "Grosvenor Place—An Alternative to Jail." *Menn* 87 (Nov. 14, 1972), 668. Grosvenor Place is a probation hostel for seven eighteen- to twenty-five-year-old men accused of minor crime. It seeks to rehabilitate the men by setting up stable living conditions, helping them acquire jobs, and providing group activities.

Dueck, Len. "Capital Punishment." *CanMenn* 5 (July 12, 1957), 2. A letter to the editor disagreeing with his views regarding capital punishment. The desire to abolish capital punishment comes from the spirit of lawlessness rather than the Spirit of God.

E. P. A. Release. "The Contemporary Scene—Future of Capital Punishment Uncertain." *EV* 86 (Sept. 25, 1973), 16. Although the US Supreme Court officially eliminated capital punishment from the US, many are working for its reinstatement.

Ediger, Max, comp. and Longacre, Doris, ed. *Release Us from Bondage: Six Days in a Vietnam Prison.* Akron, Pa.: MCC Peace Section, 1974. Pp. 28. MHL. Materials for group use in six sessions include information about conditions in Vietnam prisons, poetry and art work done by some of the prisoners, Bible readings, and suggestions for action.

Enns, Elizabeth. Letter to the Editor. *MennRep* 10 (Mar. 31, 1980), 6. Registered nurse relates conscientious objection to the taking of fetal life to protesting war, nuclear weapons, and capital punishment.

Epp, Clarence. "Capital Punishment: Vital Current Issue." *CanMenn* 13 (May 11, 1965), 7. An appeal to Christians to speak clearly for the abolition of capital punishment in Canada.

Epp, Edgar W. "Death of the Gallows." *With* 10 (Jan., 1977), 8. Part of the conflict inherent in being a prison superintendent and a Christian is resolved with the destruction of the gallows.

Epp, Edgar W. "Dismantling the Gallows." *GH* 70 (Feb. 1, 1977), 94-95; "A Christian in 'the System:' No Such Thing as Non-involvement."

*MennRep* 6 (Oct. 18, 1976), 7. Christian responsibility called this superintendent of a correctional center to destroy the gallows and thus protest the system of taking human life.

Epp, Edgar W. "The Church and the Offender." *MBH* 11 (Feb. 11, 1972), 3-5. Analyzes various methods of dealing with offenders and considers what might be the outcome if practices of nonresistant love were applied to the system of corrections.

Epp, Frank H. "Abolish the Death Penalty." *CanMenn* 5 (Dec. 20, 1957), 2. Supports a bill in the House of Commons to abolish the death penalty. The redemptive rather than the retaliatory approach to the criminal is not only the obligation of the church, but also of the government.

Epp, Frank H. "Britain Suspends Capital Punishment." *CanMenn* 4 (Feb. 24, 1956), 2. North America should take note of Britain's enlightened approach to criminals in voting to abolish capital punishment.

Epp, Frank H. "Canada Is Cruel to Criminals." *CanMenn* 4 (Nov. 9, 1956), 2. Denounces the cruelty and injustice of Canada's Criminal Code. "In a civilized society capital punishment is not a strength, but a weakness."

Epp, Frank H. "Capital Punishment." *CanMenn* 2 (Jan. 29, 1954), 2. We have a responsibility to train our and society's children in the fundamentals of God's moral law as exemplified in Christ. On this basis we will restore persons rather than condemn them.

Epp, Frank H. "Capital Punishment." *CanMenn* 3 (Nov. 25, 1955), 2. God, not humans, must decide life and death. The supreme challenge of the Christian life is to restore, rather than punish, sinners.

Epp, Frank H. "Convicts Have Feelings." *CanMenn* 4 (June 29, 1956), 2. Convicts not only have feelings, they have immortal souls. Capital punishment reveals a glaring weakness in our society.

Epp, Frank H. "Criminals and Their Punishment." *CanMenn* 2 (Sept. 10, 1954), 2. Speaks to the question of capital punishment. "We have not done our duty until we have done everything possible to save these men [sic] for the life here and the life hereafter."

Epp, Frank H. "Death Penalty Will Go." *CanMenn* 13 (Jan. 12, 1965), 5. A prediction that capital punishment in Canada will end before long and a hope that Mennonites will support this change.

Epp, Frank H. "In Bad Taste?" *CanMenn* 10 (Dec.

14, 1962), 6. The CBC is criticized for postponing a radio broadcast opposing capital punishment because it would be in "bad taste" in view of the scheduled hanging of two men about 30 hours later.

Epp, Frank H. "Notes on Capital Punishment." *CanMenn* 5 (Mar. 22, 19570, 2. The effort of leading world figures to abolish the primitive law of capital punishment is hailed as a positive step to the civilization of humankind. Christians should support this campaign.

Epp, Frank H. "The Death Penalty." *Menn* 75 (Mar. 22, 1960), 184. Explains Mennonite opposition to capital punishment and urges Mennonites to join the movement to abolish it in Canada.

Epp, Frank H. "The Last Man to Hang." *CanMenn* 7 (Apr. 17, 1959), 6. Examines the biblical and historical evidence for and against capital punishment and argues that to "kill a man for his sins is human, to forgive and restore him is divine."

Erb, Paul. "What About Easier Abortion Laws?" *ChrLiv* 19 (July, 1972), 2-5. Discussion of the morality of abortion is related to convictions regarding war and capital punishment.

Esau, Alvin (Review). *Christian Faith and Criminal Justice*, by Gerald Austin McHugh. Paulist Press, 1978. Pp. 234. *MBH* 18 (Sept. 14, 1979), 26-27. Reviewer observes that the book's thesis states that a Christian approach to the penal system must be based on love of enemies, forgiveness, and reconciliation.

Ewert, Mrs. D. P. "What Should We Be Doing for Peace?" *Menn* 85 (Jan. 20, 1970), 42, 43. Suggests areas in which peacemaking is urgently needed: the search for true and reliable information; the chasm between youth and adult; poverty areas, race relations, and corrections.

Fast, Victor. "Diary: Law-Abiding Mennonites Study the Criminal Justice System." *MennRep* 9 (June 11, 1979), 6, 7. Summarizes the topics of the 23-session study of the Canadian criminal justice system presented in Valleyview Mennonite Church, London, Ont.

Franz, Marian Claassen. "Justice and Capital Punishment." Student paper for Basic Christian Ethics, Bethany Biblical Seminary, Chicago, 1956. Pp. 33. MLA/BeC.

Gooding, Lorie C. Letter in "Our Readers Say." *GH* 53 (July 19, 1960), 618, 636. A letter commenting at length on the capital punishment debate, giving both affirmative and negative arguments.

Harms, Orlando. "Ignorance Is No Excuse."

*ChrLead* 35 (Jan. 11, 1972), 24. Summarizes what Mennonites can do to dispel the ignorance which prevents us from loving the offender.

Harms, Peter G. "Capital Punishment." *CanMenn* 4 (Mar. 9, 1956), 2, 5. A letter disagreeing with an earlier editorial lauding Britain's new legislation abolishing capital punishment. The state has been given the right to bear the sword to execute justice.

Hartz, Ira. Letter in "Our Readers Say." *GH* 53 (June 7, 1960), 525. A response to *GH* articles on capital punishment; God intended a murderer to be executed according to Old Testament law and nothing has taken place to change this concept.

Hawbaker, John. "Remember Those in Prison . . ." *EV* 86 (July 25, 1973), 4-6. An article addressing the need and problems of the prison system and suggesting various ways in which a Christian can respond.

Hershberger, Bernie; Bender, Brent; Kauffman, Duane; Yoder, Steve; and Nafziger, Beverly. "A Four-College Comparison of Ethical Ideologies in Relation to Current Moral Issues." *Journal of Psychology and Christianity* 1 (Fall, 1982), 32-39. A study of 207 General Psychology students explores the influence of ideology on responses to specific ethical issues, including such items as the death penalty, the military draft, and nuclear weapons.

Hershberger, Guy F. "Can Christians Condone the Death Penalty as a Means of Justice? Questions of Social Concern for Christians," (Part 3). *GH* 53 (Apr. 5, 1960), 292. No, because they live in a new order which does not operate on the basis of "an eye for an eye."

Hershberger, Guy F. "Capital Punishment." *GH* 58 (1965), 339. The August 1965 session of the General Conference will consider a resolution witnessing against capital punishment. This article includes a preparatory statement by Vern Preheim, Committee on Peace and Social Concerns.

Hershberger, Guy F. "Conscientious Objectors in Prison." *GH Supplement* 39 (Aug., 1946), 460. There is growing support for the policy of granting amnesty to the war objectors still in prison. Many of these persons have been imprisoned unjustly.

Hershberger, Guy F. "French Conscientious Objectors: Henri Roser." *YCC* 21 (Oct. 13, 1940), 328. The French military laws have made no provision for exemption of conscientious objectors. Roser served four years in prison for being a CO.

Hershberger, Guy F. "Have Modern Mennonites Had Any Experience with the Death Penalty? Questions of Social Concern for Christians," (Part 6). *GH* 53 (Apr. 26, 1960), 364. Yes, the Amish of Holmes County intervened on behalf of a man who had killed one of their members.

Hershberger, Guy F. "Is the Death Penalty a Protection to Society? Questions of Social Concern for Christians," (Part 2). *GH* 53 (Mar. 29, 1960), 276. Reasons are given to explain why the death penalty is not effective as a crime deterrent.

Hershberger, Guy F. "Is This the Time for the Church to Speak Out on the Issue of Capital Punishment? Questions of Social Concern for Christians," (Part 9). *GH* 53 (May 17, 1960), 444. It is time that Mennonites speak out as part of their peace witness.

Hershberger, Guy F. "Ministry to the Offender." *GH* 58 (1965), 633. In addition to the proposed General Conference statement on capital punishment, Hershberger expresses the need to develop a ministry to the delinquent as well.

Hershberger, Guy F. "Reflection on Capital Punishment Resolution." *GH* 59 (Feb. 1, 1966), 107-108. A historical sketch of the Mennonite Church's position on capital punishment. The congregations must prepare to witness to the state against capital punishment.

Hershberger, Guy F. "What About the Death Penalty? Questions of Social Concern for Christians." (Part 1). *GH* 53 (Mar. 22, 1960), 252. A review of the use of the death penalty. Many countries are discontinuing its use but America continues this practice.

Hershberger, Guy F. "What Are Some Arguments Used by Those Who Think Christians Should Endorse Capital Punishment? Questions of Social Concern for Christians." (Part 4). *GH* 53 (Apr. 12, 1960), 316. Since the death penalty was used in the Old Testament, some Christians say it should be approved of today.

Hershberger, Guy F. "What Did the Anabaptists Say About the Death Penalty? Questions of Social Concern for Christians," (Part 5). *GH* 53 (Apr. 19, 1960), 340. Menno Simons and Felix Manz rejected capital punishment.

Hershberger, Guy F. "What Should Christians Say to the State About the Death Penalty? Questions of Social Concern for Christians." (Part 8). *GH* 53 (May 10, 1960), 420. The death penalty should be abolished; reasons for this this should be presented to the state.

Hershberger, Guy F., Metzler, Edgar, and Meyer, Albert J. "Theses on the Christian Witness to the State." Sub-committee report to the Peace Problems Committee of the Mennonite Church, June 22, 1960. Pp. 32. MHL. Includes statements on corrections and capital punishment.

Hildebrand, Jake. "Capital Punishment? Yes or No? *CanMenn* 13 (June 8, 1965), 4. St. Catharines, Ontario, Mennonite lawyer argues against capital punishment on the basis of religious and juridical conviction.

Hooley, E. M. *The 1918 Christmas Eve Man of the Hour at Leavenworth: Written by a Mennonite Who Was Entrapped in that Riot.* n.p., [1960]. Pp. 13. MHL. World War I conscientious objector sentenced to 10 years at Leavenworth relates, with considerable awe, the story of how Col. Sedgwick Rice quelled a prison riot using no force other than the strength of his presence and the respect he had acquired among the prisoners.

Howland, Larry O. "Capital Punishment." *GH* 72 (May 8, 1979), 377-78. An ex-con tells about the change he has experienced in his life and how Christ's message of eternal hope and reconciliation is incompatible with capital punishment.

"I Was in Prison and You Visited Me—Jesus." *EV* 88 (Jan. 25, 1975), 16. Opportunities for involvement with offenders are increasing for Mennonite Central Committee volunteers in North America.

"In Facing the Offender Church Turns Other Cheek." *CanMenn* 13 (Nov. 30, 1965), 1, 16. Report on a talk by Chaplain S. G. West, president of the Canadian Correctional Chaplains Association and director of the Anglican Correctional Chaplaincy, Diocese of Toronto, to an inter-Mennonite meeting in Toronto. West takes literally the words of Christ to "turn the other cheek" and appeals to the church to become informed about the prison system and the offender.

Indiana-Michigan Mennonite Conference—Peace and Social Concerns Committee. (Archival). II-5-6, Box 4. Material on various peace and social concerns: labor relations; draft; capital punishment; witness to the state. Goshen, Ind. AMC.

Jackson, Dave. *Dial 911: Peaceful Christians and Urban Violence.* Scottdale: Herald Press, 1981. Pp. 150. Recounts experiences that Reba Place Fellowship members have had with different sorts of violent crime in their Evanston neighborhood. These stories are interspersed with reflections upon different aspects of a Christian response to urban violence such as making distinctions between different kinds of crimes, deterrents to crime, attitudes toward persons wno commit crimes, and what the scriptures have to say to the issue.

James, J. T. L. "Is Society Responsible for Crime?" *CanMenn* 18 (Mar. 13, 1970), 4, 10. The concern of this article is to consider whether society is acting responsibly towards the criminal, thus dealing with questions: innocent or guilty?; changing the criminal; respectable punishment; and security and education in a prison cell.

James, Kathleen Lehigh. ". . . and You Visited Me." *Daughters of Sarah* 2 (Sept., 1976), 8-9. Describes the needs of young women in prison for successful relationships with adults and offers advice on how to go about establishing these relationships.

Janzen, Arthur. "Student Opposes MPs' Support of the Death Sentence." *MennRep* 10 (Mar. 3, 1980), 11. Letter to former Members of Parliament explains why the writer cannot consider capital punishment a just and effective disciplinary system.

Janzen, David. "'Corrections' as Christian Witness." *Fellowship* 38 (Sept., 1972), 3-4. A response to Christians seeking personal involvement in corrections in a way that will express solidarity with the offender rather than being extensions of the state.

Janzen, David. "Jesus and the Offender." *Menn* 86 (Nov. 16, 1971), 678-81. Information on the state of prisons and prisoners, the church's neglect and what communities, churches, and individuals can do to change the situation.

Janzen, David. "Toward a Theology of Involvement in Corrections." *Menn* 92 (May 31, 1977), 354-55. Disciples of Jesus must reject coercive force when exercised either internationally or internally toward national citizens, such as prisoners, because violence breeds counterviolence.

Janzen, William. "A Dialogue on Capital Punishment." *MennRep* 10 (Feb. 4, 1980), 7; *MBH* 19 (May 9, 1980), 26. Mennonite representatives dialogue with their Member of Parliament on the right of the state to exercise capital punishment.

Janzen, William. "Capital Punishment and the Possibilities of Life." *Menn* 91 (Apr. 13, 1976), 252-53. Outlines issues surrounding the capital punishment debate, concluding that the highest law in human life must not be repaying good for good and evil for evil, but rather the fullest development of the human person.

Janzen, William. "Letter to the Editor: Capital Punishment." *MBH* 15 (Apr. 2, 1976), 10-11. The question of respect for human life extends to other social issues, such as war or assistance to developing countries.

Jeschke, Marlin. "Rehabilitating Offenders—a Challenge to the Church." *CMR* 1 (Dec. 27, 1971), 7, 8. Applauds new efforts to help offenders to function positively within their communities rather than to reinforce anti-social behavior via the prisoner system.

Jeschke, Marlin. "Rehabilitation of Offenders." *ChrLead* 35 (Jan. 11, 1972), 2-4. Speaks to the need for reform in the treatment of prisoners, the place of the church in this program and what Mennonites, specifically, can do to assist in the rehabilitation of the offender.

Jeschke, Marlin. "Retribution or Restitution?" *United Evangelical Action* 41 (Fall, 1982), 21-23. Points out that the American justice system is based neither upon the authority of Scripture nor the Protestant concept of justification by faith. To apply these concepts to the judicial system in a program that emphasizes restitution and reconciliation, such as the Mennonite Victim-Offender Reconciliation Program, would not only be more compatible with Christian love and nonviolence but more practical, more economical, and afford society more real security than the present system.

Jeschke, Marlin. "Toward a Christian Approach to Criminal Justice." Paper presented at the Church and Criminal Justice Conference, Evanston, Ill., Sept. 18-20, 1980. Pp. 12. AMBS.

"Korean Protestant Leaders Speak Against Death Penalty." *CanMenn* 10 (Feb. 9, 1962), 9. Report of an appeal to the Korean government against the use of the death penalty for political prisoners.

Kaiser, Ward L. "A Matter of Life or Death." *YCC* 47 (Mar. 6, 1966), 3. A call to Christians to work to abolish capital punishment.

Kauffman, J. Howard and Harder, Leland. *Anabaptists Four Centuries Later: A Profile of Five Mennonite and Brethren in Christ Denominations.* Scottdale: Herald Press, 1975. Pp. 399. Reports a survey of 3,591 church members. Chapter 8, entitled "Social Ethics," probes participants' adherence to a nonresistant ethic in relation to a variety of issues such as war, race relations, labor-management relations, concern for the poor, capital punishment, etc.

Kehler, Larry. "Capital Punishment: A Contemporary Political Issue." Student paper for Contemporary Political Issues, Nov., 1960. Pp. 31. MLA/BeC.

Klassen, Aaron. "Alternative to Capital Punishment." *CanMenn* 8 (Feb. 26, 1960), 2. It is clear that society needs protection from the murderer and that the criminal needs redemption. Therefore no person should be released from care so long as his or her retention is essential to the well-being of society and to his or her reformation.

Klassen, Aaron. "On Capital Punishment." *CanMenn* 7 (Sept. 25, 1959), 2. "Christians are often the last to advocate the abolition of capital punishment when they ought to be among the first."

Klassen, Aaron. "The Death Penalty." *CanMenn* 9 (May 26, 1961), 2. The Canadian government is praised for its forthcoming legislation that will all but abolish the death penalty. Christians should welcome this retreat from brutal retaliation as a step in the direction of complete abolition.

Klassen, F. V. Letter to the Editor. *MBH* 15 (Apr. 2, 1976), 10. A stand in favor of capital punishment cannot be reconciled with conscientious objection.

Klassen, Isaac I. Letter to the Editor. *MBH* 13 (Jan. 25, 1974), 10. Maintains that the death penalty is a deterrent to crime, but that Christians should prevent crime by spreading Jesus' way of life, not by resorting to this violent form of punishment.

Klassen, Isaac I. "Letter to the Editor: Capital Punishment." *MBH* 13 (Apr. 19, 1974), 31. The death penalty should not be accepted as part of the Kingdom of God, but as a method of punishment inherent in a nonpacifist society.

Klassen, James R. "Justice? Don't Bank on It." *Sojourners* 7 (Dec., 1977), 26. Reflection on the justice system from a Wichita, Kans., courtroom.

Klassen, William. "Mennonite Witness on the Line: An Attempt at Clarifying the Issues." *MennRep* 6 (Aug. 23, 1976), 7. Criticizes Mennonite Brethren Member of Parliament Jake Epp for his stance favoring capital punishment, observing that it is not consistent with Mennonite conscientious objection to violence in other forms, such as labor union strikes.

Klassen, William. *Release to Those in Prison.* Scottdale: Herald Press, 1977. Pp. 41. Describes briefly the biblical patterns of response to offenses committed against the human community and concludes that, in light of that biblical vision, the church should take leadership in finding better ways to deal with offenders than imprisonment.

Kniss, Lloy A. "The Sacredness of Human Life." *ST* 39 (Jan., 1971), 1. Examines the responsibility of Christians regarding the sacredness of human life, the responsibility of the non-Christian, and government regarding the same concern.

Koehn, Dennis. "Draft Resistance: A Christian Response." *Lifework* 4 (1979), 3-6. Draft resister who spent 18 months in prison in the early 1970s relates the story of his decision, arrest, trial, sentencing, and reorientation to society after being released.

Kroeker, David. "An 'Upbeat' Conference in Canada's Oil Capital." *MennRep* 9 (July 23, 1979), 1. Among the decisions made at the 77th annual Canadian General Conference session were decisions to make capital punishment an issue for study in preparation for 1980, and to study a joint MCC-Mennonite World Conference statement on militarism and development.

Kroeker, David. "Torture, Prison, Rats, and Hunger." *MennRep* 9 (Jan. 22, 1979), 6. Relating numerous incidents of persons maltreated for political and/or religious beliefs, the writer urges the reader to contact Amnesty International and become involved in the campaign to free those unjustly treated.

Kvaraceus, William C. "Tackling Juvenile Delinquency." *YCC* 46 (May 16, 1965), 8. Education, home life, and employment are some of the areas that are crucial in finding answers to juvenile delinquency.

Kvaraceus, William C. "What Is a Juvenile Delinquent?" *YCC* 46 (May 2, 1965), 6. Who is a delinquent? The differences from country to country indicate how divided the world is on who is a delinquent.

Kvaraceus, William C. "Why Juvenile Delinquency?" *YCC* 46 (May 9, 1965), 5. To understand delinquent behavior, one must understand the offender and his or her environment.

Landis, Carl. "Fighting Crime—Peacefully." *With* 10 (Jan., 1977), 13. A bail bondsman who works to give poor persons who need bond service the same opportunity that wealthier individuals have.

Lapp, John A. "Capital Punishment Again." *ChrLiv* 23 (Nov., 1976), 19-20. The Canadian abolishing of the death penalty and the US reinstatement of it provide occasion to comment on the injustice and violence of that form of punishment.

Lapp, John A. (Review). *Letters of a CO from Prison,* by Timothy W. L. Zimmer. The Judson Press, 1969. *GH* 63 (May 19, 1970), 460. Earlham College student imprisoned for refusing induction into the army or alternative service reflects on the topics of government, faith, revolution, protest, love. Recommended for its insight into the thinking of young American idealists.

Leatherman, Noah H. *Diary Kept by Noah H. Leatherman While in Camp During World War I.* Linden, Alberta: Aaron L. Toews, 1951. Pp. 86. MHL. A day to day account gives a detailed portrait of life as a World War I CO including prison experience at Fort Leavenworth. Materials include journal reflections, menus, schedules, letters, and essays.

Linehan, Kevin. Letter to the Editor. *Forum* 10 (Mar., 1977), 12. Responding to Maynard Shelly's article, "Alternatives to Prison," Linehan questions whether prisons are not necessary for confinement and discipline, not punishment, and that the only rehabilitation is in Christ.

Loewen, H. Harry, Jr. Letter to the Editor. *MBH* 13 (Mar. 8, 1974), 13, 38-39. Capital punishment is a violent, inhumane form of retaliation against an offender, not an instrument of justice.

Lubosch, Lore. "Put in a Good Word for Me." *MennMirror* 2 (Feb., 1973), 4-7. Grosvenor Place is an alternative to prison for several adult men. It operates as a program under MCC, Peace and Social Concerns Committee in Winnipeg, Man.

"MCC (Canada) Annual Meeting." *MBH* 12 (Jan. 26, 1973), 8-9. Among other agenda items, the MCC Canada board discussed capital punishment, amnesty for US war resisters, and ecumenical relations at its annual meeting.

Mackey, Lloyd. "M-2 Matches Christian Men with Prison Inmates." *MBH* 10 (July 9, 1971), 10. Some Mennonite Brethren are "going to jail" to become involved with prisoners to provide friendship and job opportunities.

Mackey, Lloyd. "Mennonite Men Go to Jail." *CanMenn* 18 (May 15, 1970), 4, 12. Persons from Mennonite and other churches in the Fraser Valley, British Columbia make monthly visits to friends in prison. On a one to one basis, they seek to identify with the prisoners and share feelings of love with them.

Mast, C. Z. "Imprisonment of Amish in the Revolutionary War." *ChrMon* 44 (May, 1952), 131, *MHB* 13 (Jan., 1952), 6-7. Relates the story of several nonresistant Amish men imprisoned in Reading, Pa. during the Revolutionary War, who were saved from execution by the intervention of a local minister of the German Reformed Church.

Matsuo, Hilda. "Siberian Camps Kept This Family Scattered." *MennMirror* 8 (Nov., 1978), 7-8. An elderly couple relates their experiences of being separated and sent to different prison camps in Siberia and their eventual move to Canada in 1963.

Matty, Maria. "Sanctity of Life Is Theme for Eben-Ezer Education Week." *MennRep* 9 (Dec. 24, 1979), 5. Education week at the Eben-Ezer Mennonite Church of Abbotsford, BC resulted in resolutions on capital punishment, militarism, and abortion.

Melchert, Mary Ann. Letter in "Our Readers Say." *GH* 53 (Aug. 9, 1960), 682. In view of the unjust application of the death sentence in the US, Christians should speak out against capital punishment.

Mennonite Central Committee (Canada) Release. "Restitution and Reconciliation." *EV* 89 (Jan. 10, 1976), 16. A MCC (Canada) program which attempts to bring offenders and victims together to effect reconciliation has received a grant from the Canadian federal government.

Miller, Ernest H. "I Tried to Be Reasonable." *GH* 67 (Jan. 22, 1974), 72-74. Conscientious objector in World War I relates his experiences in Camp Funston, Kansas, and a short time in Leavenworth Prison.

Miller, William Robert. "An Epitaph for Adolf Eichmann." *ChrLiv* 9 (Aug., 1962), 26-28. Used by permission of the *United Church Herald.* Adolf Eichmann's sin is shared by all, and his death represents a lost opportunity for reconciliation.

Myers, Rosalyn. "Will Congress Reinstate the Death Penalty?" *MCC PS Wash. Memo* 10 (Jan.-Feb., 1978), 3-4. Discusses the death penalty in light of Mennonite commitment to peace and justice.

"News from the Peace Front." *Fellowship* 24 (June 1, 1958), 4. News statement reporting that Benjamin Kauffman, a 23-year-old Amish farmer, has been sentenced to eighteen months in prison for refusing to accept a civilian work assignment as a CO in an institution using modern conveniences.

National Council of Churches of Christ in the United States. "Statement of Concern." *MCC Offender Ministries Network Newsletter* 1 (Jan., 1980), 5-7. Reprinted from *Criminal Justice Newsletter* (Dec. 3, 1979). Excerpts from the denominational statement on the injustice of the criminal justice system, including agenda for Christians to pursue.

Neufeld, Elmer. "Three Mennonites in Prison." *CanMenn* 2 (June 25, 1954), 2. The testimony of three men who refused induction into the US armed forces.

Neufeld, John H. "Thoughts on Capital Punishment." *CanMenn* 7 (Dec. 18, 1959), 2. A letter to the editor raises some questions about the interpretation of difficult Scripture passages.

Nigh, Harry. "After Prison." *EV* 92 (Aug. 10, 1979), 8, 9. Reflecting on the problems of a released prisoner, the writer relates his particular involvement with an ex-convict and, more generally, how we can minister to those who are leaving prison.

"Ontario Committee Intensifies Protest on Capital Punishment." *CanMenn* 11 (Dec. 31, 1963), 1-2. The Peace, Social, and Economic Relations Committee issues a statement protesting capital punishment.

"Peace Section Testifies on Capital Punishment." *ChrLead* 41 (Aug. 29, 1978), 18. Report on a statement presented by D. Franz, MCC Washington Peace Section office director, to the House of Representatives Judiciary Committee on the death penalty.

"Prison Brutality Bared in Amish CO's Ordeal." *Fellowship* 22 (Sept., 1956), 25. This news release states that what was first reported as a "hunger strike" by five Amish CO's at a W. Va. prison camp has been exposed as an act of prison brutality.

"Prison Is No Picnic." *With* 2 (Mar., 1969), 14. A look at some of the men and their reasons of conscience serving time in a United States federal prison.

"Proposed Statement on Capital Punishment." *GH* 58 (July 20, 1965), 632-34. Contains a statement requesting the governments of Canada and the USA to discontinue the use of the death penalty and to set rehabilitation as the ultimate goal, which will be presented at the Aug., 1965, General Conference session.

Penner, Lydia. "The Inside and the Outside." *ChrLead* 39 (June 8, 1976), 4. Reflections on first hand exposure to the corrections system.

Peters, Frank C. "Capital Punishment." *MBH* 15 (Jan. 23, 1976), 17. Nonresistant position leads author to favor abolishing the death penalty.

Preheim, Marion Keeney. "Wrongly Imprisoned: Riding It Out with a Purpose." *GH* 72 (Oct. 23, 1979), 825-26. Opher Hinton, a black Mennonite from Philadelphia, was wrongly accused of a crime in July 1975 but has been serving his prison sentence believing that "the Lord had a reason for me to be in prison."

Quenzer, Kenneth. "The Church's Ministry to the Offender." Paper presented to Congregational and Denominational Ministries class, AMBS, Elkhart, Ind., Dec. 14, 1967. Pp. [7]. AMBS.

"Resolutions on Capital Punishment Read into House of Commons Record." *CanMenn* 14 (Apr. 15, 1966), 3. Excerpts from a speech in the Canadian House of Commons by the Honorable Howard Johnston, MP, on Mar. 23 which refers to the Mennonite Church's position on capital punishment.

(Review). "The Christian and Capital Punishment," by John Howard Yoder. Newton: Faith and Life Press. Pp. 24. *Fellowship* 27 (July, 1961), 34. Along with a summary of "Capital Punishment," by R. M. Werkheiser and A. C. Barnhart, this review gives a brief summary statement of Yoder's biblical and Christ-centered approach to the study of the death penalty. Reviewer states it "may qualify as the sturdiest indictment of the death penalty that has yet been produced by a theologian."

Ratzlaff, Vernon. "Capital Punishment Needs More Study." *MBH* 12 (Dec. 14, 1973), 31. Provides several biblically-based arguments against capital punishment.

Redekop, John H. "Getting Through." *MBH* 12 (Apr. 20, 1973), 10. Writer expresses his concern about the pressure evangelical churches are placing on government to vote for capital punishment.

Redekop, John H. "On Capital Punishment." *MBH* 5 (Jan. 7, 1966), 2. To advocate capital punishment while also endorsing biblical nonresistance is fundamentally inconsistent.

Reed, Kenneth. *Mennonite Soldier.* Scottdale, Pa.: Herald Press, 1974. Pp. 518. Novel uses the prodigal son motif to order this story of two brothers, Ira and Mastie Stoltzfus, and their different responses to the moral dilemmas posed for them by World War I. Ira, the older brother, remains true to the Mennonite Church position and endures camp life and a prison term as a CO. Mastie joins the army and is sent to fight on the French front. In addition to following these two stories, the novel also portrays the divisive effects of the war upon the Pennsylvania community that is home to the Stoltzfuses.

Regehr, Ernie. "Capital Punishment a Handy Escape." *MBH* 12 (Oct. 19, 1973), 12-13. Bill C-2, the bill which would extend the partial ban on capital punishment another five years in Canada, has been a convenient tool for the Liberal minority government but should finally see resolution when the House of Commons resumes.

Regehr, Ernie. "Edgar Epp's Prison Riot." *ChrLiv* 19 (Apr., 1972), 20-23. Mennonite warden opposed to capital punishment disarmed the prison and dealt effectively with a subsequent riot.

Regehr, Ernie. "The State, the Church, and the Penal System." *CMR* 1 (Dec. 27, 1971), 7. The responsibility of the Christian community toward the penal system is to influence the government toward granting more concessions and to be the kind of community in which the offender experiences love and forgiveness.

Reimer, Jacob J. Letter to the Editor. *MBH* 13 (Feb. 22, 1974), 31. Capital punishment, rather than being outlawed for its violent nature, should be viewed as an instrument of human authority under God.

Reimer, Paul. "Conscientious Objectors at Fort Leavenworth Prison During World War I: A Mennonite Perspective." Social Science Seminar paper, Apr., 1973. Pp. 41. MLA/BeC.

"Saskatoon YP Hear Debate on Capital Punishment." *CanMenn* 8 (Mar. 4, 1960), 3, 10. A joint Saskatoon Mayfair First Mennonite Youth Fellowship focuses on the current national issue.

"Statement of Position from Mennonite MP." *MennRep* 9 (Nov. 12, 1979), 7, 8. John Reimer, MP for Kitchener, Ont., responds to a list of questions from the *Mennonite Reporter*, setting forth his position on various issues including arms sales, abortion, and capital punishment.

"Statement of Position from Niagara MP." *MennRep* 9 (Nov. 26, 1979), 10. Jake Froese, MP from the Niagara Falls riding, responds to questions regarding his views and positions on such issues as increasing military expenditures and capital punishment.

"Statement on Capital Punishment Adopted by MCC (Canada)." *MennRep* 3 (Jan. 22, 1973), 10. MCC (Canada) resolution of opposition to capital punishment is based on sociological studies, biblical guidelines, and historical precedent, including the Mennonite history of opposition to the taking of life.

"Supporting Capital Punishment." *GH* 65 (May 23, 1972), 468. The NAE passed a resolution supporting capital punishment emphasizing "if capital punishment is eliminated, the value of human life is reduced and the respect for life is correspondingly eroded.

Sauder, Menno. "Capital Punishment." *CanMenn* 13 (July 27, 1965), 4, 6. Letter to the Editor arguing against capital punishment on religious grounds.

Sauder, Menno. "Capital Punishment." *CanMenn* 2 (Nov. 19, 1954), 3. A statement from Menno Simons on capital punishment and a note by the author.

Sauder, Menno. "Capital Punishment and Colleges." *CanMenn* 12 (Apr. 28, 1964), 6. A letter to the editor claiming clarification of the issues at hand.

Schrader, Don. Letter to the Editor. *GH* 70 (May 24, 1977), 429-30. Call for Christian conscientious objectors to take a stand against capital punishment as an extension of their nonresistant convictions, and to attack the causes of social violence.

Shafer, R. Don. "Thoughts on Capital Punishment—The Decision to Take Life." *EV* 90 (Mar. 10, 1977), 7. The writer, who does not favor the death penalty, offers some thoughts and questions to encourage the reader to seriously think through the issue of capital punishment.

*

Shank, J. M. "'A Time to Kill and a Time to Heal.'" *ChrMon* 35, Part 1, (July, 1943), 201-3; Part 2, (Aug., 1943), 235-36, 255-56. Comment on Old Testament passages regarding war and killing concludes that war was sometimes the instrument of God's justice. While God commanded Israel to go to war and exercise capital punishment, God has forbidden both for the Christian church.

Shank, J. M. *"A Time to Kill and a Time to Heal:"* A Treatise on the Sanctity of Human Life, War and Human Government, and Nonresistance. N.p.: Mennonite Messianic Mission, 1967. Pp. 24. Citing examples and stories from Genesis to Samuel, the author contends that God in the Old Testament commanded war and capital punishment. As a new dispensation, however, the New Testament forbids both, commanding instead love and nonresistance.

Shank, J. Ward. "The Debate on Capital Punishment." *ST* 28 (1st Qtr., 1960), 4. Civil government has the right, and even the responsibility, given it by God, to use capital punishment when it becomes necessary to use it as a restraining force and as an instrument of justice in a corrupt society.

Shank, J. Ward (Editorial). "Position on Capital Punishment." *ST* 33 (2nd Qtr., 1965), 3. We should not have an official position on capital punishment; it is an affair of the state. We have no right to deny to the state the right to the use of capital punishment as a civic order that the common welfare might demand.

Shelly, Maynard. "Alternatives to Prisons." *Forum* 10 (Jan., 1977), 12; *IPF Notes* 23 (Mar., 1977), 2-3. Reports on a conference at Bethel College in North Newton, Kans., at which the American prison system came under heavy criticism for failing to provide treatment or rehabilitation and for being costly and brutal. Vengeance, not reconciliation, is the motive behind the prison

---

system. A better objective of reconciliation between victim and offender was proposed.

Shelly, Maynard. "The Church Witness in Society." *CanMenn* 9 (Nov. 24, 1961), 34. Regarding capital punishment, there is no reason to demand the death penalty on any moral, religious, or empirical grounds.

Shelly, Tom. "Crammed Off in a Cell." *CanMenn* 18 (Mar. 13, 1970), 4. An inmate of the Minneapolis Workhouse, a one-year maximum term institution, reflects on the negative feelings he is developing in a prison cell.

Shenk, Coffman S. "Another Look at Capital Punishment." *GH* 60 (Aug. 8, 1967), 712-13. Capital punishment is biblical.

Smucker, Donovan E. "Deep, Dark Memories of Capital Punishment." *Menn* 94 (Apr. 17, 1979), 274-75. An argument against capital punishment, which is seen as an instrument of repression, not a scale for justice.

Stauffer, Daniel. Letter to the Editor. *Fellowship* 25 (Mar., 1959), 35. Writing from prison, this CO expresses gratitude for all the Christmas cards and messages of good will and encouragement he received from all over the world.

Stobbe, Leslie H. "Anabaptist Distinctives." *MBH* 1 (Dec. 14, 1962), 6-7. Anabaptists responded nonviolently to persecution, yet vigorously opposed capital punishment and participation in any form of violence.

Stoneback, G[eorge] S[tauffer]. "When Society Plays God: Meditations on Crime and Punishment, Especially Capital Punishment." Sermon preached at Lorraine Ave. Mennonite Church, Wichita, KS, 1959. Pp. 9. MLA/BeC.

Stoner, Mary Beth. Letter to the Editor. *EV* 92 (July 10, 1979), 5. The recent execution of John Spenkelink and the approval Brethren in Christ ministers and members have seemingly given capital punishment prompts this letter, which states that Jesus followed the difficult, unsafe way and not the "law and order method of the Roman system."

Studer, Gerald C. (Review). *Death Row Chaplain*, by Byron Eshelman with Frank Riley. Prentice Hall, 1962. Pp. 252. *ChrLiv* 19 (Mar., 1963), 33. Recommends the book as a probing discussion of prison life, capital punishment, and nonresistance.

"The Taking of Human Life Is Always Wrong." *CanMenn* 12 (Mar. 24, 1964), 6. The Inter-Mennonite Ontario Peace and Social Concerns Committee issues a statement on capital punishment giving the arguments against it.

"Three Mennonites in Prison." *CanMenn* 2 (June 25, 1954), 2. Elmer Neufeld of NSBRO relates the story of three Mennonites who refused induction upon government's denial of CO status.

"Two Draft Resisters—Where Are They Now?" *Menn* 88 (Apr. 17, 1973), 254-55. Dennis Koehn and David Rensberger, Mennonite draft resisters sentenced to prison, reflect on their decisions not to cooperate with Selective Service and their experiences in prison.

*The Church, the State, and the Offender.* Newton: Faith and Life Press, Church and Society Series No. 3, 1963. Pp. 24. Explores the biblical and theological premises which bear on the issues of criminal and capital punishment and makes some suggestions as to what might be some Christian responses to the laws, to crime prevention, and to offenders. Prepared by the Peace and Social Concerns Committee of the General Conference Mennonite Church and approved at a study conference in 1961.

Toews, Ron. "Capital Punishment and Vietnam." *CanMenn* 14 (May 3, 1966), 5. Letter to the Editor against the abolition of capital punishment in Canada and against peace marches.

Umble, Diane Z. *Choices for Human Justice: How to Care About the Poor, Disabled, Abused, Oppressed.* Harrisonburg, Va.: Choice Books, 1978. Pp. 111. A collection of articles, reprinted from a variety of sources such as *Sojourners*, the *Gospel Herald*, and *The Mennonite*, which focus various justice issues such as the exploitation of native Americans, the penal system, racism, rape and the battering of women, and the arms race.

Unger, George. "Executions: Let's Be Consistent." *CanMenn* 13 (Feb. 23, 1965), 5. Letter to the Editor concerning capital punishment. Everyone should believe as his or her conscience dictates and everyone should be consistent in her or his thinking. Concludes with appeal to those opposed to capital punishment to begin at home by not buying war toys at Christmas and not mixing alcohol and gasoline.

Unruh, Vic, Jr. Letter to the Editor. *MBH* 15 (Mar. 5, 1976), 10. Maintains that capital punishment is inconsistent with Jesus' way of love and peace.

Vogt, Roy. "What Should We Do with Murderers?" *MennMirror* 4 (Oct., 1975), 22. Discusses a Christian response to murder, recognizing the necessity for protection from criminal behavior but noting that the message of Christ is one of forgiveness and not revenge and retribution in the form of capital punishment.

Vogt, Ruth. "A Hard-Nosed, No-Nonsense Bleeding Heart." *MennMirror* 7 (Feb., 1978), 7, 8. On the occasion of his retirement, this article describes David Rempel's long involvement in the field of corrections and some of the changes in the field of which he has been a part.

"Where Do We Stand on Abortion?" *ChrLeader* 38 (Oct. 14, 1975), 3-5. Statement by the Mennonite Brethren Board of Reference and Counsel contends that the issue of abortion should be viewed in the context of other life and death issues such as capital punishment, war, some forms of contraception, euthanasia, etc. Concludes that decisions in these areas are properly made in the church "via personal and pastoral counsel."

Webb, Jon. "Why I Choose Canada." *With* 4 (Mar., 1971), 10. The story of one man's experience in military prison. When he was unable to get a CO classification, he again went AWOL to Canada.

Willms, Abe M. "Capital Punishment: The Argument." *CanMenn* 13 (July 6, 1965), 4. Presents analysis of three main arguments for capital punishment and three main arguments for abolition of capital punishment by a Carleton U. associate professor of political science.

World War I. 302 interviews: over half are transcribed. Emphasis is on CO's from many Mennonite branches and other churches. Also includes several regulars and civilians (women, pastors). Some very dramatic stories of abuse in army camps, courts-martial, prison, personal testimonies about nonresistant stances, moving to Canada to escape conscription, community war fervor. Guide to interviews published as Sprunger, *et al., Voices Against War,* 1973. MLA/ BeC.

Yoder, Bruce. "A Night in Cell Block 9." *MBH* 12 (Aug. 24, 1973), 20-21. Writes about his observations and conversations with prisoners while participating as a citizen observer at the Walpole State Prison in Massachusetts. Comments on the loss of human dignity under prison conditions.

Yoder, Edward. "Mennonites on Capital Punishment." *GH Supplement* 36 (Oct., 1943), 639. Lists quotations against capital punishment from three Mennonite sources including Menno Simons.

Yoder, Edward. "Notes on Genesis 9:3-6: Peace Principles from a Scriptural Viewpoint." Part 37. *GH* 33 (Oct. 17, 1940), 637-38. An argument against the position that this passage sanctions capital punishment and/or retaliation.

Yoder, John H. "Capital Punishment and Our Witness to Government." *Menn* 78 (June 11, 1963), 390-94. A discussion of the Christian's relation to the state, using capital punishment as a case study.

Yoder, John H. *The Christian and Capital Punishment.* (Institute of Mennonite Studies, No. 1.) Faith and Life Press, 1961. Pp. 24. MHL. Both biblical reasons, such as that to deprive persons of their lives denies them the possibility of reconciliation with God and others, and logical reasons, such as the lack of correlation between the crime rate and the death penalty, indicate that Christians should support efforts to abolish the death penalty as a legal way to deal with offenders.

Yoder, John H. "The Churches' Concern: The Death Penalty." Part 1. *CanMenn* 7 (Oct. 2, 1959), 2. Recounts Holmes Co. Amish community's intervention on behalf of the prisoner who had murdered one of their members. As a result of this intervention, the prisoner's death sentence was commuted.

Yoder, John H. "The Cross of Christ and the Death Penalty." Part 3. *CanMenn* 7 (Oct. 9, 1959), 2. Relates the question of capital punishment to New Testament materials.

Yoder, John H. "The Cross of Christ and the Death Penalty." Part 4. *CanMenn* 7 (Oct. 16, 1959), 2. Gives overview of the American history of capital punishment.

Yoder, John H. "The Cross of Christ and the Death Penalty." Part 5. *CanMenn* 7 (Oct. 23, 1959), 2. Analyzes the current status of the death penalty in America.

Yoder, John H. "The Cross of Christ and the Death Penalty." Part 6. *CanMenn* 7 (Oct. 30, 1959), 2. Suggests Christian responses to the issues of capital punishment.

Yoder, John H. "The Death Penalty." *Menn* 74 (Nov. 24, 1959), 724-25. It is right for Christians to ask mercy for particular Christians (e.g., Cleo Eugene Peters) and they should support efforts to abolish the death penalty.

Yoder, John H. "The Moral Order and the Death Penalty." Part 2. *CanMenn* 7 (Oct. 2, 1959), 2. Relates the question of capital punishment to Old Testament materials.

Yoder, John H. "What Do You Think of Capital Punishment?" *ChrLiv* 11 (Sept., 1964), 22-26. Relating nonresistance to the role of government and capital punishment.

Zehr, Albert. "US Deserter Preaches." *GH* 63 (June 2, 1970), 489. Summary of the personal story told by a US Army deserter about his coming to conscientious objector convictions and the treatment given him in military prison after going AWOL.

Zehr, Howard. *Crime and the Development of Modern Society: Patterns of Criminality in Nineteenth Century Germany and France.* Totawa: Rowman and Littlefield, 1976. Pp. 188. Extensive descriptive analysis yields conclusion that crime, contrary to popular belief, is rational—the result of a decision—and often functional and inherently political. Thus, the entire responsibility for crime rests neither with the individual nor the society.

Zehr, Howard. "Maintaining Order in an Unredeemed World." *Sojourners* 8 (Oct., 1978), 20. Examines the belief that many cases which seem to demonstrate gross irregularities and misuses of the criminal justice system are, in fact, indicative of the everyday workings of criminal justice in America.

Zehr, Howard. "Offenders and Victims: Righting Relationships." *MCC Offender Ministries Network Newsletter* 1 (Oct., 1979), 7-8. Biblical justice involves healing the relationships ruptured by crime, not merely giving the state a mandate to carry out punishment.

Zehr, Howard. "Victims and Offenders Meet in Reconciliation Program." *MennRep* 9 (Oct. 1, 1979), 4. The Victim Offender Reconciliation Program (VORP) operates with the recognition that crime involves conflict between people which ruptures right relationships within the community; VORP, therefore, works for reconciliation between the victim and offender.

Zercher, John E. "Editorial—A Mission Field." *EV* 86 (July 25, 1973), 3. The church has an opportunity to merge its social and evangelistic concerns in a redemptive ministry by becoming involved in social service and criminal justice.

# F. Conflict and Conciliation

"Associated Seminaries Hold Study Day on Conflict Between US and Iran." *GH* 72 (Dec. 25, 1979), 1032. A special meeting, "Iran Day," held at the Associated Mennonite Biblical Seminaries to bring about a better understanding and a response in prayer to the current Iranian-US conflict.

Arnett, Ronald D. "Conflict from the Peace Tradition, by Ronald C. Arnett." Dept. of Interpersonal Communication, Ohio Univ., Fall, 1976. Pp. 33. MLA/BeC.

Augsburger, David W. *The Love-Fight.* Scottdale: Herald Press, 1973. Pp. 128. Handbook on interpersonal conflict resolution. Includes chapter relating conflict resolution to biblical peacemaking.

Aukerman, Dale. "Jesus at Blast Center." *ChrLiv* 10 (Sept., 1963), 36-37. Jesus stands in the center of human war and conflict, suffering injury and death with the wounded.

Beck, Carl. "Japanese and Korean Students Find Each Other in Fellowship." *CanMenn* 13 (Sept. 28, 1965), 3. Report on a Korean-Japanese reconciliation work camp at the Mennonite Vocational School near Taegu, Korea, July 23-Aug. 2, 1965.

Beck, Carl. "Peace Witness Is Mission." *GH* 58 (June 1, 1965), 477-78. Report of the proceedings of the 1965 Tokyo Christian Student Peace Seminar, focusing on the resolution of conflict in Japanese-Korean relationships and in other tension spots of East Asia.

Bender, Ross T. "The Religious Perspective on Abortion." *Life and Values,* ed. Edwin and Helen Alderfer. Scottdale: Mennonite Publishing House, 1974, 25-33. Pp. 124. Considers, among other questions pertaining to the issue, the question of whether abortion is the moral equivalent of homicide or killing in war. Concludes there are significant differences in the cases; to label abortion an act of violence is a distortion because the elements of conflict and hostility between equal, contending parties are absent.

Bergmann, Frank. "Talking About Peace." *MBH* 14 (Jan. 10, 1975), 12-13. MCC (BC) Peace and Service Committee consulted on such topics as peace education, conflict resolution, distribution of wealth, and family ties as compared with Christian fellowship ties.

Bohn, E. Stanley. "A Hard Look in the Vietnam Mirror." *Menn* 81 (Nov. 1, 1966), 658-61. Most Mennonite congregations have no way of coping with social issues, are not accustomed to the protagonist role, and are too afraid of conflict to engage in a clear peace witness.

Bohn, E. Stanley. "Toward a New Understanding of Nonresistance." *Peacemakers in a Broken World.* Ed. John A. Lapp. Scottdale: Herald Press, 1969, 103-110. Reprinted from *MennLife* (Jan., 1967). Nonresistance is possible only for those who take sides in a conflict, not for those who act only as "go-betweens" or "umpires." Based on the incarnation, it means siding with the oppressed. Bohn describes his experience as a reconciler amid racial tensions.

Bontreger, Eli J. "Nonresistance." *GH* 41 (Jan. 6, 1948), 5. The Christian does not participate in carnal conflict because he or she is under the new dispensation.

Brenneman, Sheryl. "It Was Difficult to Practice What We Preached." *Menn* 91 (Nov. 9, 1976), 664-65. Reflects on difficulty encountered by the 7-member summer voluntary service peace team in managing interpersonal conflict.

Brenneman, Virgil J. "Christ, Israel, and Palestine." *GH* 63 (Oct. 6, 1970), 832-34. Maintains that God's ethical and salvific requirements for Israel are not unique. Therefore, Christians cannot take sides in the present conflict, but should instead support reconciliation and justice for all involved.

Brubacher, Donald L. "Nonresistance and Industrial Conflict." *YCC* 40 (April 5, 1959), 218. With more Mennonites moving to urban industrial areas, the application of nonresistance to the concerns associated with this type of work are needed. Prize-winning essay.

Brusewitz, C. F., *et al.* "A Dutch Peace Testimony." *Menn* 72 (Jan. 15, 1957), 37. In the context of military conflict in Egypt and Hungary, the Dutch Mennonite Peace Group issues a call to the total church to live in the Spirit of Jesus and to pray for peace.

Buckwalter, Ralph. "That They May Be One . . ." *GH* 54 (Oct. 3, 1961), 865, 878-79. A recounting of peace ventures in Japan, particularly the 1961 seminar on "the Ministry of Reconciliation in a World of Conflict" which brought together representatives of seven denominations active in Japan.

Burkholder, J. Lawrence. "Conflict in the Churches?" *Harvard Divinity Bulletin,* New Series, 2 (Winter, 1969), 14-20. Differentiates constructive conflict from destructive conflict and establishes some guidelines for creative management of conflict in the congregations. The goal of the church is conflict resolution, which can be a profound expression of worship in the congregational meeting.

Buzzard, Lynn and Kraybill, Ron, eds. *Mediation: A Reader.* Oak Park, Ill.: Christian Legal Society, 1980. Pp. various. MHL. Mennonite contributions include: Kraybill, "An Outline of the Biblical Basis for a Ministry of Reconciliation;" Kraybill, "Institutionalizing Mediations as an Alternative Dispute Mechanism: An Ethical Critique;" Kraybill, "The Mennonite Conciliation Service."

"Conciliation Service Tries to Mediate Dispute Between Mohawk Groups in New York State." *GH* 72 (Nov. 27, 1979), 928. Ron Kraybill, Mennonite Conciliation Service director, traveled to St. Regis, NY, to help mediate a dispute between traditionalists and elected officials of the Mohawk Indian tribe.

Charles, Howard H. "The Christian Warfare." *Builder* X [sic, 1] (Nov., 1960), 20, 21. The New Testament clearly teaches that conflict is the life pattern for the followers of Jesus. In this conflict, we must remember both that the decisive victory is already won and that the complete victory over evil awaits the second coming.

Charles, Howard H. "The Kingdom Beyond Caste." *Builder* 14 (Feb., 1964), 17-18. What the Bible teaches about the way of the cross in group relations can and should be applied to the issues of racial conflict: the church "must reach agressively across all barriers with the call of the Gospel."

Cutrell, Ben (Review). *Barriers and Bridges to Brotherhood,* by Haskell M. Miller. Abingdon, 1962. Pp. 192. *ChrLiv* 11 (Feb., 1964), 34. Recommends the book as a manual for intergroup relations and techniques for solving intergroup conflict.

Derksen, John (Review). *Conflict and Christianity in Northern Ireland,* by Ronald A. Wels and Brian S. Mawhinney. Grand Rapids: Eerdmans, 1975. Pp. 126. *MBH* 16 (Jan. 21, 1977), 29-30. Recommends the book's overview of the complexity of the Irish conflict, but notes that the author separates the mandates to preach the gospel and to work for social justice.

Derstine, C. F., "Eight Point Principle for a Better World." *ChrMon* 33 (Oct., 1941), 318-19. Settlement for the present world conflict will be found not in political documents but in individuals being reconciled to God.

Derstine, C. F. "Things As They Are in Spain." *ChrMon* 30 (Sept., 1938), 290-91. Anonymous eyewitness account of the conflict in the Spanish civil war.

Drescher, John M. (Editorial). "What Peace Testimony?" *GH* 61 (Feb. 27, 1968), 165; *CanMenn* 16 (July 2, 1968), 4. Contrasts a Mennonite witness to peace with the disharmony found in many congregations, and suggests that young people will more readily commit themselves to nonresistance when they see it practiced in situations of conflict.

Dueck, Allan. "Education for Justice." *Direction* 6 (Jan., 1977), 12-20. Christian education includes education for awareness of injustice and the encouragement of Christians to involve themselves in social conflict.

Duerksen, Tony. "White Horse Plains Dominion Day Confrontation." *MennMirror* 3 (Jan.-Feb., 1974), 25, 26. Relates an incident in which

Mennonites who were scouting out land in Manitoba in 1873 encountered a group of Metis in a confrontation and how the government and media handled the situation.

Early, Richard K. "The Origin of Conflict." *GH* 73 (July 8, 1980), 539. Also in *The Menn* 95 (Oct. 14, 1980), 582-83. No one who believes Jesus destroyed Satan's power through the cross can justify the use of conflict as a method of peacemaking.

Eby, Omar. "Vietnam: Compassion Provokes Conflict." *CanMenn* 15 (Dec. 5, 1967), 1, 2. Reports that Vietnam service worker Doug Hostetter felt he could not form any close associations with American AID officials or the US Armed Forces in Vietnam. Instead, he identified closely with the Vietnamese people in order to communicate Christian love and to understand Vietnamese feelings.

Eby, Omar. "White Skin Worth More on World Market than Black Skin." *CanMenn* 16 (May 7, 1968), 1, 7. Rejects the idea that the civil war in Nigeria can be ignored because the struggle pits blacks against blacks and appeal to Mennonites to respond generously to the call, when it comes, to give relief for Nigerian war victims. Gives historical background to the Nigeria-Biafra conflict.

Ellis, Marion Art. "Conflict in Marriage." *EV* 86 (July 25, 1973), 12, 13. Healthy, creative ways to deal with conflict in a marriage relationship are discussed.

Epp, Frank H. "The Canadian Crisis: There Must Be a Better Way." *World Federalist* Canadian Section (Nov./Dec., 1970), C1-C2. Criticizes the extreme measures of the Quebec Liberation Front's bombings, kidnappings, and assassinations, and the Canadian government's equally extreme invocation of the War Measures Act. Argues that in a truly democratic society, other options for resolving conflict are always available.

Epp, Frank H. "The Conflict and the Church." *CanMenn* 9 (Sept. 29, 1961), 6. The Christian response to the communist advance must bypass militarism and go beyond nationalism and Phariseeism. The church is not contending against political systems but against the spiritual powers of darkness.

Epp, Frank H. "The Mennonite Presence in the Middle East." *GH* 64 (Apr. 27, 1971), 378-80. Advances the thesis that since the root of the Mideast conflict is a religious/ideological conflict, Mennonite presence should incarnate the Word of peace found through Jesus the Messiah.

Epp, Frank H. "The Palestine Problem in Historical Perspective." *GH* 62 (June 10, 1969), 510-11; *CanMenn* 17 (June 6, 1969), 1, 2. Reviews Arab and Jewish historical claims to Palestinian soil, then describes the history of the conflict in this century, the role of the United Nations, the Arab perspective, and the wars following partitioning.

Epp, Frank H. and Goddard, John. *The Israelis: Portrait of a People in Conflict.* Scottdale: Herald Press, 1980. Pp. 205. Excerpts from interviews with ninety-six Israelis attempt to present their stories and feelings in the long conflict with Arabs.

Epp, Frank H. and Goddard, John. *The Palestinians: Portrait of a People in Conflict.* Toronto: McClelland and Stewart, 1976. Pp. 240. Based on interviews with 172 Palestinians in 1971 and 1974, the book attempts to make known the stories and feelings of Palestinian people caught in the longstanding conflict between Israelis and Arabs.

Erb, Paul. "A Call to Prayer." *GH* 43 (Aug. 29, 1950), 851. Comments on plans for a day of prayer for peace. Calls for prayer that people will realize that faults lie on both sides of the Korean conflict, and that Mennonites will have the courage to preach and live nonresistance.

"Five Peace Ambassadors to Speak for Church." *CanMenn* 12 (Jan. 28, 1964), 3. A report on the MCC Peace Section's annual meeting, focusing on race relations. Summary of a panel discussion on racial conflict.

"From the Files of NSBRO." *GH* 45 (Nov. 18, 1952), 1129. Statements revealing the intense conflict experienced by Christian youth in the Armed Services.

Fast, Henry A. *Jesus and Human Conflict.* Scottdale: Herald Press, 1959. Pp. 209. An exegetical and theological study of the words of Jesus on peace and nonresistant love.

Ford, Leighton. "Violence." *GH* 64 (July 6, 1971), 601. With confession of sin, peace begins within and moves outward in forgiveness, rejecting the violence and hatred of both extreme positions in conflict.

Friesen, Duane K. "Ethical Dimensions of Conflict Resolution." Paper delivered at the International Workshop on Conflict Resolution, Univ. of Haifa, Israel, June 20, 1978. Pp. 12. MLA/BeC.

Friesen, Orly. Letter to the Editor. *MennMirror* 7 (Mar., 1978), 25. The "Quebec problem" calls for love and reconciliation rather than the prejudice and animosity with which we view the French-Canadians.

Friesen, Rudy. "CMBC Prof Calls for Creative Ways of Solving Human Conflict." *CanMenn* 18 (Feb. 27, 1970), 1, 2. During a one-day teach-in on "War and Peace" at the Univ. of Saskatchewan, David Schroeder outlines reasons why war is unrealistic as a problem-solving institution to an audience that challenges his point of view.

Garde, Michael. "Irish Theology." *Mission-Focus* 6 (Sept., 1977), 5-9. Examines the conflict in Ireland between Protestant and Catholic in terms of Irish theology, its difficulties and the possibilities it holds for transcending the "sectarian divide."

George, Elias. "Ten Things I Wish I North American Mennonites Knew About My People." *FQ* 6 (Nov., Dec., 1979, Jan., 1980), 15. Arab Mennonite social studies teacher clarifies misconceptions about Arabs and offers his perspective on the Arab-Israeli conflict and prospects for peace.

Haddad, Anis Charles. "Conflict in the Land of Peace." *ChrMon* 29 (Feb., 1937), 53. Describes attitudes of Arabs and Jews in Palestine and the recurring outbreaks of violence.

Harder, Kurt. "A Concrete Commitment." *Forum* 12 (Dec., 1978), 6-7. Writer supports and discusses the proposal of a National Peace Academy as a viable and concrete alternative to violence as a means of resolving conflict.

Harding, Vincent G. "Build on Christ in the City." *Menn* 74 (Oct. 20, 1959), 644-45, 655. A call to break down the walls of fear and hostility which prevent Christian ministry in the urban situation.

Hartman, Wilmer J. "Living Peaceably with Others." *Builder* 20 (Sept., 1970), 21-25. An adult Sunday school lesson utilizing the story of Isaac's conflict with the Philistine herders over a well (Gen. 26) to focus discussion of peacemaking.

Headings, Verle E. "Conflict Evoking Images in International Exchange." Pp. 6. BfC.

Headings, Verle E. "How Shall We Prepare Ourselves for Conflict and Conflict Resolution?" Dec. 29, 1969. Pp. 8. MLA/BeC., BfC.

Heisi, Evan. "Saskatchewan Peace Talk Attracts 200 Participants. *Menn* 94 (Mar. 20, 1979), 214. "Peace is not the absence of conflict, but the presence of the Creator," was the theme of the native and Mennonite "peace talk" held Feb. 23-24 at Tiefengrund Mennonite Church.

Hershberger, Guy F. "Nonresistance and Industrial Conflict." *MQR* 13 (Apr., 1939), 135-54. The industrial conflict is a fight for power with which to achieve social justice, whereas biblical nonresistance enjoins submission even to injustice rather than engage in conflict.

Hiebert, Robert. "The Middle East: A Moral Conflict." *MBH* 14 (Dec. 26, 1975), 2-3, 27. While Israel is concerned with maintaining its God-given right to the land, some Arabs have escalated the conflict to the level of a "holy war," determined to destroy all Jews.

Hiebert, Robert (Review). *The Palestinians: Portrait of a People in Conflict,* by Frank H. Epp. McClelland and Stewart, 1976. Pp. 240. *MBH* 15 (Nov. 12, 1976), 35. Reviewer maintains that the author paints too rosy a picture of the Palestinians, a perspective which will not further the cause of peace in the Mideast.

Hochstedler, Eli. "What's So Good About Conflict?" N.d. Pp. 11. Positive aspects of conflict. MLA/BeC.

Holderman, George. "A Sure Foundation for Peace." *ChrMon* 27 (June, 1935), 171-72. Cites examples of conflict settled through trust and goodwill to show that New Testament principles do work.

Horsch, John. "The Swiss Brethren in Canton Berne." *ChrMon* 31, Part 1, (Nov., 1939), 325-26, 340; Part 2, (Dec., 1939), 357-58, 379; *ChrMon* 32, Part 3, (Jan., 1939), 5-6, 23. Reviews the conflict of the Swiss Brethren with the state church in Berne over the separation of church and state.

Hostetler, John Andrew. "The Amish and the Public School." *ChrLiv* 3 (Sept., 1956), 4-6, 41-43. Amish conflict with public school systems over their religious right not to send children to school beyond the eighth grade.

Hostetler, Nancy Gingrich. "War of Words Destroying Peace." *ChrMon* 23 (Sept., 1931), 268. Verbal conflict destroys peace as surely as armed conflict.

Hostetter, Robert D. "Conflict, Celebration, Creation." N.d. Pp. 12. MLA/BeC. BfC.

Huebert, Norman. Letter to the Editor. *ChrLead* 41 (July 18, 1978), 15. Mennonites are progressively entering into the arena of political and social conflict as is evident from the articles and readers' responses in the *Christian Leader* and other Mennonite periodicals.

Jantz, Harold. "Mediation—A Way to Settle Disputes." *MBH* 19 (Nov. 7, 1980), 5. Description of the process used by mediation centers to settle local conflicts.

Jantz, Sylvia. "Peace Is . . . " *GH* 65 (Mar. 21,

1972), 266. Vignettes of inner turmoil and conflict with neighbors and friends present images of the meaning of peace and peacemaking in the local setting.

Janzen, Rudy H. P. "Can Mennonite Brethren with Anabaptist Peace Emphases and Fundamentalist Leanings Constructively Utilize Inherent Hostility." Thesis (MTS), Waterloo Lutheran Seminary, 1981. Pp. 55. MBBS.

Kauffman, Daniel. "The Destructiveness of Carnal Strife." *GH* 29 (Apr. 30, 1936), 113-14. That strife is unbiblical and destructive is as true in the church as in the world.

Kauffman, Daniel. "The Struggle in Spain." *GH* 30 (July 29, 1937), 385-86. The Christian cannot support either side of this conflict but should attempt to give life to body and soul everywhere.

Kauffman, Ivan. "Practicing the Peace We Preach." *GH* 73 (Dec. 2, 1980), 966. Suggestions for peacemaking and conflict resolution within the congregation.

Kauffman, Ivan and Francis, Dale. "A Mennonite and a Catholic in Dialogue." *CanMenn* 15 (Feb. 21, 1967). Exchange of letters discussing pacifism. Francis, editor of the *Operation Understanding* edition of *Our Sunday Visitor* asks how Mennonites acquit themselves of responsibility for others; Kauffman argues that Mennonite pacifism is theologically, not politically, motivated and points out the conflict between service under Christ and service under the state involved in war.

Kauffman, Milo. "Blessings of Christian Stewardship." *ChrLiv* 1 (Sept., 1954), 29-30, 38, 44-45. While covetousness drives people to war and violence, stewardship promotes joy and helps resolve human conflict.

Kaufman, Maynard. "Where Peace Begins." *MennLife* 7 (Oct., 1952), 147-48. In regeneration, faith ought to displace anxiety, which is one of the causes for social conflict. Because regeneration does not achieve complete cessation of conflict, the realization of world peace comes through practicing Christian love.

Keeney, William E. (Review). *Quaker Experiences in International Conciliation,* by C. N. Mike Yarrow. New Haven: Yale University Press, 1978. *MennLife* 34 (Mar., 1979), 29-30. Briefly summarizes the book which studies three cases of Quaker efforts at conciliation and asses their outcomes in an effort to learn what might contribute to the knowledge of the conciliation process in general. Notes various other efforts being made to understand the nature of conflicts and the peacemaking processes, and

points out the need for a major synthesis of these efforts.

Kehler, Larry. "Peacemaking Efforts Fall Behind for Lack of Greater Financial Support." *CanMenn* 15 (Feb. 14, 1967), 1, 2. Expresses convictions on the urgency of the work of the MCC Peace Section and reports discussion "regarding the direction which its concern in the area of international conflict should take."

Kehler, Larry. "People Without a Homeland." *GH* 67 (Aug. 27, 1974), 644-45; *MennRep* 4 (Aug. 5, 1974), 6; *Menn* 89 (July 23, 1974), 454-55. Describes the plight of the Palestinians as a politically naive peasant people used as pawns in an international conflict.

Keidel, Levi O. "The Shaping Effects of Violence." *GH* 63 (Nov. 17, 1970), 968-69. Outbreaks of violence and revolution reveal what kind of person one really is and mold one further in that direction. Author relates a story of a conflict situation and the reactions of the people involved to back up his conclusion.

Klassen, J. M. "MCC Work in Areas of Conflict Explained." *MBH* 16 (Oct. 14, 1977), 11. MCC (Canada) Executive Secretary responds to the concern that MCC personnel may be supporting terrorist activity.

Klassen, Peter J. (Editorial). "On Being a Brotherhood." *MBH* 12 (Jan. 26, 1973), 11. Offers suggestions for ways of working at conflict within the Mennonite Brethren Church and also with other Mennonite denominations.

Klassen, William. "Where We're at. . . on Violence and Revolution." *CanMenn* 19 (Feb. 19, 1971), 10, 30. Critical analysis of the institutional church as it relates to communication between those of the Mennonite faith.

Klassen, William (Review). *The View from East Jerusalem,* by John A. Lapp. Herald Press, 1980. Pp. 124. *MennRep* 10 (Nov. 10, 1980), 9. Reviewer observes that the book presents the complexity of the Mideast conflict, giving special attention to the Palestinian perspective.

Kossen, Henk B. "The Peace Church in a World of Conflict." *CGR* 2 (Winter, 1984), 1-9. Reflects upon the church's mission in a society organized around economic, a political, and ideological conflict. Concludes that the church is true to its mission to the degree it follows the example of Jesus, the Liberator, in identifying and repelling the powers operating within society.

Kraybill, Donald B. "The Master Welder." *GH* 63 (Nov. 17, 1970), 962-64. Reconciliation with God and one another is the core of the gospel, and it must be worked out by people acting as ministers of reconciliation in all situations of conflict.

Kraybill, Ron S. "Healing Conflicts in Today's World." *ChrLead* 43 (Sept. 23, 1980), 8-9. Mennonite Conciliation Service helps bring community conflicts to peaceful conclusions.

Kraybill, Ron S. "Introducing Mennonite Conciliation Service." *Peace Section Newsletter* 9 (Dec., 1979), 9. Goal of this service is greater faithfulness to the biblical call to peacemaking through ministries in community conflicts. MSC aims to equip locally-based Mennonites for relating to disputes of various kinds in their surrounding communities.

Kraybill, Ron S. "Making Peace Out of Local Tensions." *MBH* 19 (Aug. 8, 1980), 16-17. Mennonite Conciliation Service works at peacemaking in local situations of conflict.

Kraybill, Ron S. *Repairing the Breach: Ministering in Community Conflict.* Scottdale, Pa.: Herald Press, 1980. Pp. 95. A manual providing suggestions and guidance for the art of Christian peacemaking based on the biblical emphasis of shalom. Reconciliation processes between groups, between individuals and within groups are discussed and illustrated by examples.

Kraybill, Ron S. "Report on the Mennonite Conciliation Service" [Akron: MCC Peace Section], 1980. Pp. 4. MHL.

Kreider, Alan. "The Arms Race: The Defense Debate—Nuclear Weaponry and Pacifism." *The Year 2000*, ed. John R. W. Stott. Downers Grove: InterVarsity Press, 1983, 27-55. Pp. 179. Since the security afforded by deterrence policy is neither adequate nor real, and since pacifists and just war theorists agree that nuclear war is indefensible, we ought to unite, despite other differences, in order to search for viable alternatives for conflict resolution.

Kreider, Carl. "Ferment in Africa." *ChrLiv* 6 (June, 1959), 18, 34. Rising nationalist tendencies and white racism contribute to sometimes violent ferment across the continent.

Kreider, Carl. "India and China at War." *ChrLiv* 10 (Feb., 1963), 19, 38. Analysis of the border conflict.

Kreider, Carl. "Trouble in the Congo." *ChrLiv* 7 (Nov., 1960), 18, 35. Analysis of the violence and military conflict in the Congo following its independence from Belgium.

"Letter to Members of Congress." *Menn* 54 (Oct. 3, 1939), 3. Peace Committee of the Western District (GCM) says our nation should endeavor to adjust all international tensions by negotiation rather than by force of arms.

"'Love Works in Conflicts' Says Hostetter." *MBH* 10 (May 28, 1971), 18-19. Former MCC worker Doug Hostetter speaks of the effects of propaganda and the American military presence in war-torn Vietnam. Also speaks of the power of love at work in his relationships with the Vietnamese people.

Lapp, John A. *A Dream for America.* Scottdale, Pa.: Herald Press, 1976. Pp. 128. Bicentennial reflection calls the nation to attend to the issues of the moment—issues such as racial equality, disproportionate distribution of global resources, learnings from the Vietnam War, conflict resolution, honest government, civil religion, etc.—and decide to implement in our time the worthy goals of the Declaration of Independence.

Lapp, John A. "An Independent Bangladesh." *ChrLiv* 19 (Feb., 1972), 18-19. Political and military conflict leading to the birth of a nation, and the problems it faces.

Lapp, John A. "'Chaos' in the Middle East.'" *ChrLiv* 16 (Mar., 1969), 18-19. Background of and comment upon the escalating Arab-Israeli military conflict.

Lapp, John A. "Civil War in Angola." *ChrLiv* 23 (Feb., 1976), 15-16. Review of Angolan politics, including conflict among three liberation movements.

Lapp, John A. "From Rhodesia to Zimbabwe." *ChrLiv* 25 (June, 1978), 15, 32. Comment on the transitional government leading to black majority rule and the conflict leading to it.

Lapp, John A. "Lebanon's Self-Destruction." *ChrLiv* 23 (Mar., 1976), 15-16. Description of the many-sided conflict in Lebanon.

Lapp, John A. "On the Spot in the Middle East." *ChrLiv* 16 (Sept., 1969), 18-19. Analysis of the demands of both sides in the Arab-Israeli political and military conflict.

Lapp, John A. "Round Four: The Arab-Israeli War." *ChrLiv* 21 (Feb., 1974), 15, 35. Review of the October, 1973, round of the war and the world-wide involvement in the conflict.

Lapp, John A. "Seminary Letter Precipitates Intense Brotherly Discourse." *CanMenn* 18 (Mar. 13, 1970), 1, 11. Describes tensions aroused between MCC and the AMBS community over a letter sent to the seminary sent to President Nixon. Also describes the efforts to resolve the conflict and the very solid discussion of the issues of church and state which resulted from the tensions.

Lapp, John A. "The Birth of Bangla Desh." *ChrLiv* 18 (June, 1971), 18-19. Description of the conflict leading to civil war between East and West Pakistan.

Lapp, John A. "The Lull in Ireland." *ChrLiv* 22 (Oct., 1975), 10-11. Review and analysis of the circumstances leading to the Irish civil conflict.

Lapp, John A. (Review). *The Israelis: Portrait of a People in Conflict*, by Frank H. Epp. McClelland and Stewart and Herald Press, 1980. Pp. 208. *FQ* 7 (Feb., Mar., Apr., 1980), 10. Sequel to Epp's *The Palestinians: Portrait of a People in Conflict* contains a range of political opinion on war and peace through interviews with 99 people.

Lind, Marcus. "A Prophet of Grace and Peace." *ST* 47 (June, 1979), 10-13. Elisha's overcoming of evil with good in II Kings 6:23 is a paradigm for present day conflict.

Lind, Millard C. "Is It Worth a Quarrel?" *ChrLiv* (Mar., 1959), 2. Controversy is nearly always an earmark of true religion, but we must make sure the controversies have substance.

"Minneapolis Consultation on Faithfulness to Christ in Situations of International Conflict." *GH* 60 (Jan. 17, 1967), 67-68. The statement is an outline for Mennonite response to Vietnam and other conflict situations. The Christian obligation to call people to repentance and reconciliation includes an obligation to witness to the state.

Martens, Larry. Letter to the Editor." *ChrLead* 42 (Nov. 20, 1979), 14. Sees the conflict over recent articles on Amway, materialism, peace, taxes as beneficial to the integrity of the church.

Martin, Warren B. "Weak Christian: Strong President." *ChrLiv* 8 (Jan., 1961), 28-29. Reprinted from *Christian Century*. Conflict between Christian conscience and political goals.

Mast, Russell L. "How Much Is Seventy Times Seven?" *Menn* 69 (Nov. 9, 1954), 692-93. The forgiving community seeks to overcome hostilities and resentments and seeks restoration among brothers and sisters.

Matsuo, Hilda. "No-Fault Divorce Proposed." *MennMirror* 6 (Dec., 1976), 13. Looks at some of the injustices of family law and the need for reform to create greater equity.

Menninger, William C. "Controlling Hostile Feelings." *YCC* 43 (Mar. 18, 1962), 5. The person who is emotionally mature has learned to turn the energy derived from hostile feelings into creative and constructive outlets.

Menninger, William C. "Handling Tension and Anxiety." *YCC* 43 (Feb. 18, 1962), 8. The ability to handle problems has to be learned.

Menninger, William C. "Understanding Defense Mechanisms." *YCC* 43 (Feb. 25, 1962), 5. Discussion of a variety of defense mechanisms that are used to deal with problems either within ourselves or with others.

Mennonite student in Yugoslavia. "My Concern for Yugoslav Christians." *MBH* 18 (Sept. 28, 1979), 36. Christians in Yugoslavia have to deal with the history of religious conflict, "the church at war with itself."

Metzler, Edgar. "Breaking the Cycle." *YCC* 32 (July 29, 1951), 660, 664. The vicious cycle of wars will cease when enough people believe, live, and practice the answer of Christ which is the triumph over conflict by love.

Metzler, Edgar (Review). *At the Heart of the Whirlwind*, by John P. Adams. Harper & Row, 1976. Pp. 160. *MennRep* 7 (Oct. 3, 1977), 8. Adams' reference to Mennonite Disaster Service work following the 1973 Wounded Knee conflict accurately depicts the Mennonite contribution as "post-peace patching" rather than peacemaking in the center of conflict.

Miller, Levi. "A Conversation on Nurturing Peacemakers." *Builder* 26 (Feb., 1976), 1-4. An interview with Atlee Beechy in which he says that church people need to begin regarding conflict as having potential for growth and to teach Sunday School children to deal with conflict creatively in order to prepare them for discipleship in our competitive, violent world.

Miller, Melissa and Shenk, Phil M. *The Path of Most Resistance*. Scottdale: Herald Press, 1982. Pp. 239. Accounts of ten young people who, during the turbulent Vietnam years, resisted cooperating with the draft. The stories relate not only the conflict with the government concerning these illegal actions, but also the conflicts in the church as the generations struggled to understand the demands of faithfulness for their concrete situations.

Newberry, Loren. "Areas of Co-operation and Conflict Between the Communities of Newton and North Newton." Social Science Seminar paper, May, 1962. Pp. 11. Includes nonresistance as cause for conflict. MLA/BeC.

"Peace in Vietnam Calls for Escalation of Compassion, Not of Conflict and War." *CanMenn* 13 (June 8, 1965), 1. Text of a letter from the MCC Executive Committee to President Lyndon B. Johnson urging him to escalate compassion in Vietnam rather than conflict.

Peachey, Paul L. "Peacemakers in the Pacific." *GH*

52 (Feb. 17, 1959), 153. Peachey pays tribute to Reiji Oyama, a Japanese evangelist working to alleviate Japanese-Filipino conflict.

Peachey, Paul L. "Socialist and Pluralist Societies: The Anatomy of Encounter." Paper, [1975]. Pp. 20. MHL.

Peachey, Paul L. *Your Church and Your Nation: An Appeal to American Churchmen.* Washington, DC: The Church Peace Mission, [1963]. Pp. 22. MHL. Contends that to construct a theological sanction of war just because conflict is inevitable in a fallen world is no more justifiable than to construct a theology of segregation because we have not achieved human equality.

Peachey, Urbane. "Lebanon: The Roots of Conflict Are Complex." *MennRep* 6 (Jan. 26, 1976), 7. Reviews social history of Lebanese people, asserting that the civil war cannot be boiled down into a Moslem-Christian conflict.

Peachey, Urbane. "Refugees Flee Israeli Forces." *Intercom* 22 (May, 1978), 1, 4. Describes the plight of refugees from Israel's invasion of Lebanon and outlines the issues involved in the conflict.

Peachey, Urbane. "The Middle East Cauldron and Mennonite Involvement." *MennRep* 3 (Sept. 3, 1973), 7. Discusses Mideast conflict factors shaping MCC work in Jordan, and describes MCC projects there.

Peachey, Urbane (Review). *At the Heart of the Whirlwind,* by John P. Adams. New York: Harper and Row, 1976. "Making Peace in Turmoil." *EV* 90 (Dec. 25, 1977), 10; *Peace Section Newsletter* 8 (June, 1977), 8-9. Various nationally known conflicts are examined, offering insights into the kind of energies and strategies that went into crisis intervention and resolution.

Peters, Frank C. "Two Worlds." *The Voice* 20 (July, 1971), 17. Explores the "possibilities of confrontation" that exist between various individuals and groups, both in the world and in the Christian setting.

(Review). *The Israelis: Portrait of a People in Conflict,* by Frank Epp. Herald Press and McClelland & Stewart, 1980. *MCC PS Newsletter* 10 (Mar.-Apr., 19800, 11. Recommends the book as a portrayal of the Israeli point of view, and as a companion volume to the author's earlier work on the Palestinian people.

Redekop, John H. "The Essence of the Gospel." *MBH* 18 (Oct. 26, 1979), 12. Relief work and conflict resolution in the question of militarism are both applications of the gospel, but not its essence.

Regehr, John. "Christians and the Courts." *MBH* 15; Part I (May 28, 1976), 6-7, 26; Part II (June 11, 1976), 4-5, 8-9. Conflict resolution between Christians should be through other means than litigation; guidelines for Christians in the use of legal processes for resolving conflict.

Regier, Dwight. "Resolution of Conflict in First Mennonite Church." Student paper for Capstone, Feb. 23, 1979. Pp. 13. MLA/BeC.

Reimer, Al. "The War Brings Its Own Conflict to Steinbach." Part 1. *MennMirror* 3 (June, 1974), 15, 16. The writer reflects on his emergence into the difficult years of adolescence, which coincided with the onset of the grim years of World War II.

Roth, Willard E. "Ireland and Mennonites." *GH* 71 (June 13, 1978), 470-71. Visitor to Ireland reviews the complexity of the Irish conflict, searching for ways Mennonites might contribute to peacemaking there.

Ruth, Janet. "National Peace Academy." *MCC PS Wash. Memo* 12 (Nov.-Dec., 1980), 7-8. Description, background of, and possible problems with the establishment of a National Academy of Peace and Conflict Resolution.

Rutt, Clarence. "Peace, Peace, When There Is No Peace." *GH* 44 (Aug. 28, 1951), 829-31. The only solution to conflict is the spirit of Jesus. Mennonites have been negligent in teaching this principle.

Sanchez, George. "Growing Through Conflict." *ChrLead* 42 (Mar. 27, 1979), 6. By applying biblical principles, interpersonal conflicts can help us become strong and flexible Christians.

Sawatsky, Rodney J. (Review). *A People of Two Kingdoms: The Political Acculturation of the Kansas Mennonites,* by James C. Juhnke. North Newton, Kansas: Faith and Life Press, 1975. Pp. 215. *MQR* 50 (Jan., 1976), 72-73. Juhnke defines the dualism of the title as "conflict between the ethic of modern nationalism and the ethic of traditional Mennonitism" characterized by pacifism, apoliticism, and German ethnic identity.

Sawatzky, H. L. "Student Participation with Vengeance." *MennMirror* 2 (Jan., 1973), 5, 6. Discusses the tactics used by student radicals at German universities today.

Schmitt, Abraham and Dorothy. "Conflict and Ecstasy: A Model for a Maturing Marriage." *EV* 90 (Apr. 10, 1977), 12-14. The authors, marriage counsellors, share their insights on the "two shall become one" process that can emerge out of the conflict and ecstasy of a marriage union.

Schoenhals, G. Roger. "Coping with Conflict."

*Menn* 94 (Feb. 6, 1979), 82-83. Conflicts exist at every level of society and require love, listening, and working together for peace. We must leave the final resolution of conflict with God.

Schrag, Don. "On the Serious Side: A Study of the Templin Incident and a College Under Pressure." Social Science Seminar paper, Apr., 1971. Pp. 18. Bethel College and community relations in World War II—issue of registration. MLA/BeC., BfC.

Schultz, Harold J. "A Christian College: Vision for Peacemaking." *Menn* 88 (Apr. 24, 1973), 266-67. The central focus of a small, Mennonite, liberal arts college on peacemaking and conflict resolution can inform its other commitments: reconciling a fractured Christianity; genuine community with the campus; a philosophy of continuing education.

Shank, Duane. "Hearings on Peace Academy." *RepConsS* 32 [sic33] (May, 1976), 6, 5. Reports on Senate hearings in relation to a bill proposing to establish a "George Washington Peace Academy" where the issues of nonviolent conflict resolution could be studied.

Shelly, Maynard. "Becoming Reconciled." *Builder* 25 (Nov., 1975), 98-103. A Sunday school lesson for adult students which uses the conflict between Joseph and his brothers, Genesis 45-50, to focus contemporary peacemaking concerns.

Shenk, David W. *Peace and Reconciliation in Africa.* Nairobi, Kenya: Uzima Press Limited, 1983. Pp. 180. The first part of the book provides background on peace themes and conflict resolution in traditional African religion. The 2nd part of the book comments on the ways African Christianity has interacted with these traditional concepts and, in that process, created a unique contribution to the whole of Christianity.

Shetler, Sanford G., ed. "Churchmen Continue to Support Militant Chavez." (Article unsigned) *GfT* 8 (Nov.-Dec., 1973), 6. Chavez's methods of boycotting and picketing do not correspond to Mennonite concern for love and goodwill among all sides.

Smucker, Donovan E., ed. *The Sociology of Canadian Mennonites, Hutterites and Amish: A Bibliography with Annotations.* Waterloo, Ont.: Wilfried Laurier University Press, 1977. Pp. 232. Subject index includes: alternative service, church and state, conflict, draft-conscription, government, National Socialism, peace, race, war.

Smucker, Joseph. "Mennonites and Confrontation." *MennLife* 25 (Jan., 1970), 38-40. Describes various ways Mennonites respond when confronted with political issues and suggests ways Mennonites might confront others more effectively.

Sokoloff, B. (Review). *The Israelis; Portrait of a People in Conflict,* by Frank H. Epp. Toronto: McClelland and Stewart, 1980. Pp. 205. "Jewish Reviewer Finds Epp's Book Worthwhile." *MennMirror* 10 (Nov., 1980), 18. Appreciates Epp's sensitivity to the issue of Jewish suffering as well as Palestinian suffering in the Mideast conflict entangling these peoples, but regrets that too many of those interviewed by Epp for the book "are simply not knowledgeable and speak purely out of emotion and unsupported opinion."

Sommer, Don. "The Economic Teachings of Menno Simons and Peter Rideman as Representative of Sixteenth Century Anabaptists." Paper presented to economics seminar, Goshen College, Goshen, Ind., May 2, 1952. Pp. 66. MHL.

Stoltzfus, Victor. "Nonresistance Without Christ." *ChrLiv* 9 (July, 1962), 2. Withdrawing from conflict meets the criteria of nonresistance, but neglects reconciliation.

"The Conflict and the Church." *CanMenn* 9 (Sept. 29, 1961), 6. A biblical basis for "bypassing militarism."

Taves, Harvey. "The Church Makes Peace in a World at War." *GH* 58 (Aug. 17, 1965), 714-17. The Mennonite church needs to be a more aggressive and prophetic voice and actor for peace. We need to move into actual conflict areas.

Thut, John. "The World System." *ChrMon* 26 (Feb., 1934), 42-43. The present world system, like that of the prophet Habakkuk, is full of endless conflict and violence.

Toews, John A. *Our Ministry of Reconciliation in a Broken World.* Mennonite Brethren Church Board of Reference and Counsel, [1975]. Pp. 9 (pamphlet). Attached to *ChrLead* 38 (Oct. 28, 1975), 15. Position statement on peace outlines a biblical basis for peacemaking, then discusses its contemporary application in areas of international, national, industrial, racial, and economic conflict. Contends that a Christian attitude toward evil is not an attitude of passive acquiescence but one of positive and effective counteraction expressed in ways consistent with Scriptural principles of limitless love. MHL.

"US Missionaries in Japan Protest Vietnam Policy." *CanMenn* 15 (Nov. 7, 1967), 1, 11. Text of a letter addressed to the "Reader's Forum" of Japan's *The Mainichi Daily News* by 11 American missionaries (including Carl Beck). The letter calls for an American expression of contrition for mistakes in the past and a willingness to take greater risks in the quest for peace by negotiation in the future.

"Use of Power and Conflict." *Menn* 82 (May 16, 1967), 330-31. The GCMC Peace and Social Concerns Committee suggests that power and conflict need not be totally negative; they can be used to liberate the oppressed and protect the persecuted.

Vogt, Roy. "Response to Henk B. Kossen, 'The Peace Church in a World of Conflict,' *Conrad Grebel Review* 2 (Winter, 1984), 1-9." *CGR* 2 (Spring, 1984), 149-51. Agrees with Kossen's basic assumptions that the church must simultaneously identify with society and distinguish itself from society but criticizes Kossen's hyperbolic reasoning for producing simplistic and misleading conclusions about the capitalist system.

Vogt, Virgil. "The Implications of Christian Ethics for Modern Business." Paper reflects class conflict, presented to social science seminar, Goshen College, Goshen, Ind., 1953-54. Pp. 66. MHL.

Wenger, J. C. "The Minister as a Mediator." *Builder* 20 (Apr., 1970), 2-3. Summarizes both a general approach and some specific measures a pastor might take in resolving conflict within her or his congregation.

Wenger, Linden M. "Trends in Peace Education." *ST* 43 (July, 1975), 1-6. Review of Mennonite peace emphases in this century calls for a greater focus on the biblical basis for peace and less attention to the strategy of conflict resolution.

Wenger, Martha, *et al.* "Wounded Knee: Four Papers by Bethel College Students in Interterm Class on Causes of Human Conflict, January, 1974." Pp. 75 total. MLA/BeC.

Wentland, Theodore. Letter to the Editor. *GH* 61 (Mar. 19, 1968), 262-63. Calls attention to Mennonite acts of violence toward one another in conflict situations and schisms, and calls for a spirit of forgiveness and peacemaking in congregations.

Wiebe, Katie Funk. "The Conflict of Peace." *ChrLead* 35 (June 27, 1972), 19. Assesses what it means to be violent and to resolve conflict, how women can relate to peacemaking, and what it means for the proclamation of the gospel to believe in peace and reconciliation.

Wingert, Norman. "Wounded Knee: Symbol of the Indian Problem." *MBH* 14 (Oct. 17, 1975), 19-20. Recounts the confusion and violence of the two-month-long occupation of Wounded Knee in 1973 and the continuing conflict between Native Americans and white officials.

Yoder, Edward. "Is the World Too Small? Peace Principles from a Scriptural Viewpoint." Part 13. *GH* 30 (Jan. 20, 1938), 926-27. New birth in Jesus Christ is the only solution for individuals in a world too small to tolerate selfishness, greed, and conflict.

Yoder, Edward. "On Overcoming Class Enmity and Hatred: Peace Principles from a Scriptural Viewpoint." Part 22. *GH* 31 (Jan. 19, 1939), 917-19. The way to overcome race and class conflict is to unite persons on the higher level of Christian society.

Yoder, Edward. "The Mind to War: Peace Principles from a Scriptural Viewpoint." Part 5. *GH* 28 (Jan. 16, 1936), 910-11. Modern war is essentially conflict between whole populations. Governments employ propaganda techniques to arouse a populace against the enemy. The Christian must be alert to this.

Yoder, John H. "The Imperative of Christian Unity." Resume of a lecture presented to Church and Ministry courses, AMBS, Elkhart, Ind., Nov., 1983. Pp. 8. AMBS.

Zehr, Howard. "Victims and Offenders Meet in Reconciliation Program." *MennRep* 9 (Oct. 1, 1979), 4. The Victim Offender Reconciliation Program (VORP) operates with the recognition that crime involves conflict between people which ruptures right relationships within the community; VORP, therefore, works for reconciliation between the victim and offender.

Zerger, Sandra. "Martha Wenger: Go-Between." *Menn* 92 (Apr. 12, 1977), 246-47. Bethel College senior and peace intern reflects on her year of study in Israel and the occupied territories and the complexity of the Mideast conflict.

Ziegler, Donald (Review). *Whose Land Is Palestine?*, by Frank H. Epp. Grand Rapids: Wm. B. Eerdmans, n.d. *GH* 63 (Nov. 10, 1970), 950. Reviewer quotes extensively from the book's description of the meeting of a Palestinian man and a Jewish man, an event symbolizing the author's thesis that a Christian contribution toward Mideast peace means understanding both sides of the conflict.

# 10

# Mennonite Central Committee

## A. General

"A Good Year for MCC Manitoba." *MennMirror* 1 (Mar., 1972), 12. Among other agenda, the MCC (Manitoba) annual meeting featured John A. Lapp as the keynote speaker who spoke of peacemaking as a Christian discipline.

"A Message from Participants of the 1969 MCC Peace Section Middle East Study Tour." *CanMenn* 17 (July 18, 1969), 4. Statement approved by study tour participants summarizing impressions received in the Middle East and urging others to become versed in the human struggle going on there.

"A Message from the Consultation on Conscience and Conscription." *GH* 63 (Jan. 6, 1970), 12-13. Outlines concerns, affirmations, objections, and appeals to obedience in relationship to war and peace drawn up by the Peace Assembly of the MCC Peace Section. Statement affirms both alternative service and noncooperation as valid Christian responses to the draft and encourages the government to grant exemption from military service to selective objectors to war.

"A Statement of Concern to the Committee on Armed Services of the United States House of Representatives on H.R. 3005 Amending the Universal Military Service and Training Act." *CanMenn* 3 (Feb. 25, 1955), 2. Statement presented on behalf of MCC by C. N. Hostetter on Feb. 2, 1955.

"After Decades a Voice Still Remembers MCC in China." *MennMirror* 8 (May, 1979), 17, 18. Outlines the past involvements of MCC in China and shares excerpts from a letter recently written to MCC from a Chinese citizen who still remembers some of these involvements after many years of closed relations between the two countries.

"Automatic Registration a Live Possibility." *GH* 72 (June 12, 1979), 472. Summarizes a testimony on the draft to the Senate Armed Services Committee by K. B. Hoover, a Brethren in Christ representative to MCC.

*A Civilian Public Service in the Caribbean.* Elgin:

Brethren Service Committee, [1945]. Pp. 15. MHL. Includes description of La Plata project sponsored by MCC in Puerto Rico.

"Bishop Appears Before US Committee to Testify on Military Draft Laws." *CanMenn* 15 (May 23, 1967), 1, 5. Text of a statement made by John E. Lapp, MCC Peace Section resentative, before the Armed Services Committee of the US House of Representatives on May 3, 1967. Lapp's requests included: equal liberties for COs of all denominations; equal liberties for all COs of sincere religious convictions; freedom for all sincerely troubled by ethical problems of militarism; abolition of universal military training.

"Brazil Volunteers Imprisoned Without Charge." *EV* 90 (July 10, 1977), 8. MCC volunteer, Thomas Capuano of Altamont, NY and Father Lawrence Rosenbaugh, an American Catholic priest, were arrested without charge in Recife, Brazil, and held for four days until the American consulate was able to arrange for their release.

"But I Say Unto You, 'Love Your Enemies' Jesus." *EV* 90 (Nov. 25, 1977), 11. Christians are experienceing much suffering in Uganda; MCC and the Mennonite mission boards are working on the problems which refugees from Uganda and several other African states face.

Barrett, Lois [Janzen]. "After Getting Out of Vietnam." *Menn* 89 (Jan. 15, 1974), 48. Prints a letter from an MCC worker in Vietnam detailing the plight of a civilian prisoner tortured by South Vietnamese police trained in America.

Barrett, Lois [Janzen]. "Peace Assembly Looks at Male-Female Stereotypes." *Forum* (Dec., 1973), 12-13. The MCC Peace Section Assembly dealt with the theme of "the interdependence of men and women," noting that biblical peace is not only "the absence of war" but total well-being and the reconciliation of those who are separated from one another.

Bartel, R. F. "Prepare Statement on Draft-Dodgers, Protests." *CanMenn* 16 (July 2, 1968), 1, 2. A report on the 37th convention of the Ontario MB Conference held in Kitchener July 14-16 which includes the text of a statement of non-support for US draft-dodgers in Canada and rejection of all MCC involvement in marches and protests.

Beck, Carl. "Students in Japan Talk Peace." *CanMenn* 13 (Aug. 24, 1965), 3. Report on first Student Christian Peace Seminar, held in Osaka, Japan. Seminar sponsored by MCC Peace Section, Japan.

Beck, Carl C. "Japanese-Korean Encounter Brings Pleas for Reconciliation." *CanMenn* 14 (July 19, 1966), 1, 6. A report on the fifth MCC Peace Section-sponsored annual Christian Youth Peace Seminar held in Tokyo, May 13-15. Fifty-one participants (including eight Koreans) listened to Prof. Saburo Takahashi of Tokyo University and Prof. Kidong Chang of the graduate school of Taegu University. It was decided to invite Koreans into leadership positions of the seminar.

Beechy, Atlee. "Courteous Reception by NLF, DRVN Representatives." *CanMenn* 16 (Oct. 8, 1968), 1, 2; (Oct. 15, 1968), 4. After a visit to North Vietnam, Beechy outlines his preparations for the contact with communist leaders, describes his contacts with North Vietnam government officials in various countries of Asia, Africa, and Europe, and cites his impressions of the mission sponsored by MCC. Part 1 deals with the translated Mennonite documents given to all the representatives and the courteous reception given to Beechy.

Beechy, Atlee. "Impressions on Vietnam." *CanMenn* 16, Part 2, (Oct. 15, 1968), 4, 5. Continuation of a report following Beechy's month-long trip to talk with NLF and DRVN representatives. Includes interpretation of MCC purposes and program to DRVN and NLF representatives as well as to the US and Saigon governments.

Beechy, Atlee. "In Hanoi: The Wounds of War." *GH* 67 (Mar. 26, 1974), 262-63; "Journey to Hanoi: How Do We Heal the Wounds of War?" *MennRep* 4 (Mar. 4, 1974), 7; "HanoiWounds of War," *MBH* 13 (Mar. 8, 1974), 18-19. MCC representative visiting Hanoi to assess the effects of the war reports on the destruction and continued suffering of the Vietnamese people, as well as their friendliness and determination to rebuild the country.

Beechy, Atlee. "MCC Contacts Affirm Peace Witness." *ChrLiv* 16 (Jan., 1969), 11, 34-35. MCC assistant secretary reports on his talks with the National Liberation Front of South Vietnam and the Democratic Republic of [North] Vietnam.

Beechy, Atlee. "To Aid or Not to Aid? Some Reflections on Voluntary Agencies and Vietnam." Paper presented at Pendle Hill, Pa., Aug. 14, 1975. Pp. 18. MHL.

Beechy, Atlee (Review). *In the Name of Christ: A History of the Mennonite Central Committee and Its Service 1920-1951*, by John D. Unruh. Scottdale: Herald Press, 1952. Pp. 404. *MHB* 14 (Jan., 1953), 8. Recommends the book as a useful and factual account of MCC relief and service work.

Bender, Harold S. "A Historical Review of the Anabaptist-Mennonite Position and Practice from 1525 to the Present." Paper presented at the MCC Peace Section Study Conference, Chicago, 1958. Pp. 11. MHL, BfC.

Bender, Harold S. "Hearing Before the Preparedness Subcommittee of the Committee on Armed Services United States Senate, Eighty second Congress." Washington: US Printing Office, 1951. Opposes peacetime conscription on grounds that such action is first step toward national and international policy characterized primarily by militarism. Transcript includes copy of MCC statement submitted to House Armed Services Committee on April 17, 1948.

Bender, Harold S. "Mennonites Testify at Hearings on Post-War Military Policy." *Menn* 60 (July 10, 1945), 5-6. The MCC statement made at the hearings of the House Select Committee on Post-War Military Policy. The statement recounts the history of the Mennonite peace witness, and witnesses against permanent peacetime conscription.

Bender, Harold S. "Peace Section" (of MCC). *The Mennonite Encyclopedia* IV:131, Scottdale-Newton-Hillsboro Mennonite Publishing Offices, 1959. Describes origin and function of MCC's Peace Section.

Bender, Urie A. "Earl Martin: PAXman with an Impulse to Kick." *With* 2 (Apr., 1969), 28. Martin is a PAXman working with others on the Mennonite Central Committee team under Vietnam Christian Service.

Benner, Norman. "Our Civilian Public Service CampsThe Camp on the Skyline Drive." *YCC* 24 (June 20, 1943), 615. Description of CPS Camp No. 45 at Luray, Va. One of the largest and most commodious of the camps administered by Mennonite Central Committee.

Berg, Ford. "Peace Study Conference at Winona Lake." *GH* 44 (Jan. 16, 1951), 59. A report of the MCC peace conference of Nov., 1950; summarizes the study papers dealing with "the problems of nonresistance in its implications with the world."

Berg, Ford. "The Status of Conscientious Objectors in Europe." *GH* 45 (Jan. 15, 1952), 56-57. A brief survey of nine European countries based on a report by Guy F. Hershberger for the Mennonite Central Committee Peace Section.

Bergen, Henry. Letter to the Editor. *MBH* 18 (Dec. 21, 1979), 10. MCC in southern Africa should stand for peace and justice for the displaced on both sides of the Zimbabwe/Rhodesia political fence, rather than favoring the Patriotic Front.

Bergman, Gene. "An Evaluation of Foreign Service Experience." *PCMCP Sixteenth*, 40-49. N.p. Held at Hesston College, Hesston, Kansas, June 8-9, 1967. A personal experience of being in MCC with the PAX program raised serious questions about the inadequate training and preparation offered before assuming the assignment.

Bergmann, Frank. "Talking About Peace." *MBH* 14 (Jan. 10, 1975), 12-13. MCC (BC) Peace and Service Committee consulted on such topics as peace education, conflict resolution, distribution of wealth, and family ties as compared with Christian fellowship ties.

Bontrager, Herman. "Relief, Development, and Justice: Synthesis or Tension?" *Peace Section Newsletter* 9 (Aug.-Sept., 1979), 4-8. Notes that the expressed concern to make MCC programs more sensitive to justice problems has revealed the important need for MCC staff to develop a self-consciousness as workers for justice. Lists some of the MCC projects for justice.

Brademas, John. "'They Cannot Stand Alone'The Work of the Mennonite Central Committee." *Cong. Record* (Apr. 23, 1964), 1-2. Reprint of an article appearing in the 1963 MCC Annual Report describing case studies in MCC's relief, service, and peace efforts. Brademas, representing northern Indiana, inserts commendatory remarks.

Brubaker, Ray. "MCC Enters the Transkei." *Peace Section Newsletter* 9 (Feb.-Mar., 1979), 1-5. Explains the reasons why MCC is entering the Transkei. Notes that a major task of MCC within the oppressive context of South Africa is to identify with persons, institutions, or movements which are being prophetic and leading the struggle for liberation in ways consistent with biblical teachings of love and nonviolence, that is, overcoming evil with good.

Brunk, Emily. *Espelkamp: The MCC Shares in Community Building in a New Settlement for German Refugees*. Frankfurt, Germany: MCC, 1951. Pp. 42. MHL. Relates the story of Espelkamp, an initial experiment in resettlement of the refugees of World War II in which both American and European Mennonite youth participated on a Voluntary Service basis.

Brunk, Ivan, ed. *Dear Alice: The Tribulations and Adventures of J. E. Brunk, a Mennonite Relief Worker in Turkey in 1920-21, as Depicted in Letters to His Wife*. Goshen, Ind.: Historical Committee of the Mennonite Church, 1978. Pp. 187. MHL. Voluminous and sensitive letters describe and interpret one of the first efforts of the newly-organized Mennonite Central Committee to respond to human suffering.

Burnett, Kristina Mast. "Amidst Injustice Palestinian Teaches Resistance Based on Love." *Menn* 94 (Oct. 9, 1979), 600. Bishara Awad, headmaster of a school established by MCC in the West Bank, advocates a resistance based on love and reports that Palestinian Christian pacifists are looking for peaceful, nonviolent methods of protest.

Burnett, [Kris]Tina Mast and Kroeker, Wally. "Affluent People Who Neglect the Poor Are Not the People of God." *Menn* 94 (Feb. 20, 1979), 128-29. MCC (International) annual meeting discussed issues of justice and human rights, aid to Vietnam, native American outreach, hunger concerns, and militarism.

Burnett, Kristina Mast and Rennei, Amy. "The 'Boat People'Why They Are Leaving and How to Be a Sponsor." *Menn* 94 (Jan. 16, 1979), 40-41. MCC gives an explanation for why people are leaving Vietnam and how to sponsor the refugees for resettlement.

Byrne, Kevin. "Significantly Involved." *GH* 64 (Jan. 12, 1971), 32-33. MCC volunteer in Vietnam writes a letter to his parents describing the suffering and destruction in which the US is very significantly involved.

"Christian Nonresistance Only Alternative to Communism." *CanMenn* 7 (Oct. 16, 1959), 1, 10. André Trocmé addresses MCC personnel in Akron, Pennsylvania, stressing the church's responsibility for the Christian peace witness.

"Christian Obedience in a Divided World: An East-West Student Encounter Between Mennonites and Persons from Czechoslovakia, Hungary, and the GDR." MCC Peace Section, June, 1965. Various pagings. MHL. Includes: Janz, Hugo. "The Eastern Setting of Christian Encounter." Pp. 8. Keeney, William. "Report of the Advisory Committee of the Christian Peace Conference, Prague, Czechoslovakia, June 4-8, 1963." Pp. 3. Miller, Marlin E. "An East-West Encounter." Pp. 8. Miller, Marlin E. "Interview on East-West Student Encounter." (Interview of John Howard Yoder.) Pp. 7.

"Christians to be Lambs, Not Hawks or Doves."
*CanMenn* 14 (Dec. 13, 1966), 1, 8, 9. Report on
an inter-Mennonite consultation in
Minneapolis Dec. 2-4 called by MCC Peace
Section to discuss the nature of the Mennonite
witness to government.

"Christmas Gifts for Peace." *CanMenn* 10 (Nov. 23,
1962), 12. The MCC Peace Section staff offers an
opportunity to give to the peace witness of
MCC in lieu of giving Christmas gifts.

"Civil Defense and Christian Responsibility." *Menn*
77 (Mar. 20, 1962), 178-180. The MCC Peace
Section's position statement on civil defense
and preparation for nuclear war stresses the
call to be a community of faith rather than of
fear, one which witnesses against the false
securities of preparation for war.

"Conscription Moves Accelerate." *GH* 72 (Mar. 27,
1979), 256. Three principal legislative
approaches are being introduced in the
Congress to reinstate military conscription;
MCC has responded, speaking against the
development.

"Consumerism and Fear Cited as Reasons for
Arms Race." *Menn* 94 (Jan. 2, 1979), 9. MCC
Peace Section (US) adopted a resolution on the
world arms race. The resolution identifies trust
in nuclear weapons as a form of idolatry and
calls on people to put their trust in Jesus Christ.

"Continued Ties with Vietnam Urged by
Delegation." *MennRep* 9 (July 9, 1979), 3. Despite
difficulties with the Vietnamese government,
the Canadian delegation urged that MCC
continue to relate in creative ways to the
Vietnamese people.

Capuano, Thomas M. "The Nightmare." *With* 11
(Feb., 1978), 16. Because of his efforts in
working with the poor as a Mennonite Central
Committee volunteer, Capuano was
imprisoned.

Charles, Howard H. "A Presentation and
Evaluation of MCC Draft Status Census."
*PCMCP Fourth*, 83-106. North Newton: Bethel
College, 1945. Held at Bluffton, Ohio, Aug. 24-
25, 1945. The purpose of the draft status census
was to ascertain the number of men who had
gone into military service and to learn why
they did. Factual data revealed a variety of
factors which influenced these decisions.

Climenhaga, Arthur M. "The Role of Foreign
Service and Foreign Study in Education for
World Mission." *PCMCP Fourteenth*, 33-46. N.p.
Held at Eastern Mennonite College,
Harrisonburg, Virginia, June 6-7, 1963. The
church must approach overseas preparation,
some of which should take place in college, as
one of its many tasks. It will pursue the Great

Commission most effectively through ministries
like the Teachers Abroad program of MCC.

"Daniel Gerber Never Returned from His MCC
Assignment." *MennMirror* 8 (Nov., 1978), 24.
Gerber, captured in May, 1962, while on an
MCC assignment in Vietnam and never again
heard from, is a reminder that to follow Christ
demands a willingness to sacrifice oneself.

"Demobilization." *RepConsS* 3 (Dec 1, 1944), 1, 2;
(Jan. 15, 1945), 7, 8. Describes MCC plans to
offer CPS personnel educational, vocational,
and financial counseling as part of the
demobilization process.

DeFehr, Arthur. "A Proposal for an MCC Food
Bank." *MennMirror* 4 (June, 1975), 7-8. Suggests
ways MCC might become involved in an effort
to stockpile a designated supply of food for
humanitarian purposes.

Derstine, C. F. "Mennonite Ex-CPS Men Serve in
Sixteen Nations." *ChrMon* 39 (Aug., 1947), 255-
56. The MCC post-war relief programs have
their roots in the Civilian Public Service
program.

Dettwiler, Alma W. "'In the Name of Christ.'"
*ChrLiv* 15 (Aug., 1968), 22-23. Explanation of
the MCC label illustrating peace and worldwide
friendship.

Detweiler, Henry S. "Laying Bricks and Sawing
Boards in the Name of Christ." *MCC WSRB* 2
(Sept., 1946), 1-3, 4. Describes the work of the
MCC Reconstruction unit established in post-
war Holland.

Devadoss, M. B. "A Talk with Little Lien." *GH* 63
(Oct. 6, 1970), 837. MCC worker in Vietnam
describes his short friendship with a seven-year-
old girl orphaned by the war.

Dourte, Eber. "To Serve the Present Age." *EV* 92
(Jan. 25, 1979), 9. At the semi-annual meeting
of the MCC Peace Section, the agenda included
reports and discussion on the New Call to
Peacemaking, peace education, the World
Arms Race and our peace witness, and the
possibility of draft for military service.

Dyck, Cornelius J. *The Mennonite Central Committee
Story*. Vol. 1: *From the Files of MCC, 1980*; Vol. 2:
*Responding to Worldwide Needs*, 1980; Vol. 3:
*Witness and Service in North America*, 1980; Vol. 4:
*Something Meaningful for God*, 1981. Scottdale and
Kitchener: Herald Press. Volume 1 tells the
beginning of the MCC story, highlighting the
relief and refugee work in Russia and South
America. It includes also the origin of MCC
Canada. Volume 2 documents MCC's response
to world wide needs in Europe, the Middle East
and Asia, mostly during the post-WW II years
through the seventies. It presents also MCC's

peace and service philosophy, "In the Name of Christ." Volume 3 focuses on MCC's North American work in Mental Health, Voluntary Service, and Mennonite Disaster Service. Volume 4 describes MCC's work through the stories of fifteen testimonies of individuals and couples who participated extensively in MCC service.

Dyck, Peter J. "A Twentieth Century Miracle." *ChrMon* 39 (Oct., 1947), 305-7. Relates the story of MCC efforts to bring Russian Mennonite refugees out of Berlin.

Dyck, Peter J. "'The Woodlands': A Symbol of Love and Service to Aged War Sufferers." *ChrMon* 34 (July, 1942), 209-10. Description of the MCC home in England for elderly people evacuated from war zones.

"Earned Reentry Has Many Weaknesses." *Forum* 8 (Oct., 1974), 3. Reaction to President Ford's earned reentry program has been mixed and many are determined to refuse anything less than full amnesty which an MCC Peace Section statement supports.

"Eight Conferences, 100 Delegates Attended Race Conference." *CanMenn* 12 (Mar. 17, 1964), 3, 11. "It is a sin to prevent a Christian brother, whatever his color, from worshipping with us." This theme was emphasized at an MCC Peace Section conference on race relations.

"Elmer Neufeld Begins As Peace Section Exec.-Sec." *CanMenn* 7 (Sept. 18, 1959), 5. The appointment of Elmer Neufeld as full-time executive secretary of MCC Peace Section will make possible intensified witness in the areas of militarism and race relations.

"Escalation of Compassion for Vietnam." *Menn* 80 (June 22, 1965), 420. Text of a letter sent to President Johnson by the Mennonite Central Committee. MCC urges the president to turn from the military solution to the way of compassion and peace.

Ebersole, Myron. "A History of Mennonite Central Committee Voluntary Service, 1944-1949." Paper presented to Mennonite History Class, n.d. Pp. 38. MHL.

Eby, Sarah Ann. "Following Christ in a Cauldron of Tragedy." *ChrLead* 39 (Sept. 28, 1976), 18. Description of the work of LeRoy and Carol Friesen as a listening, mediating presence in the Middle East with MCC.

Edgar, Max. "April 30, 1975." *RepConsS* 32 (July, 1975), 2. Poem reflecting the jubilation of an MCC worker in Vietnam at war's end.

Ediger, Max. *A Vietnamese Pilgrimage.* Newton, Ks.: Faith and Life Press, 1978. Pp. 79. Poems,

essays, biographical comments, short stories written by an MCC worker in Vietnam for five years of the Vietnam war. Also included are the art work of a Vietnamese prisoner and poems written by Vietnamese people.

Ediger, Max. "Handles for Lending a Hand." *Menn* 88 (July 10, 1973), 440. Outlines tasks in which MCC could participate in reconstructing Vietnam after the ceasefire, such as encouraging refugees to move back to their lands, helping to clear the land of unexploded ordnance, continuing with missions and medical programs.

Ediger, Max. "Justice Is Not Just Us." *Intercom* 24 (Jan., 1980), 6-7. Describes the difference between community development and community organization and urges MCC to work at organization in order to further justice.

Ediger, Max. "Profile of a Vietnam Mennonite." *GH* 67 (Oct. 1, 1974), 739; also in *Menn* 89 (Oct. 1, 1974), 268. Describes a young male Vietnamese Mennonite employed by MCC, whose future is threatened by the continuation of the war.

Ediger, Max, comp. and Longacre, Doris, ed. *Release Us from Bondage: Six Days in a Vietnam Prison.* Akron, Pa.: MCC Peace Section, 1974. Pp. 28. MHL. Materials for group use in six sessions include information about conditions in Vietnam prisons, poetry and art work done by some of the prisoners, Bible readings, and suggestions for action.

Ediger, Peter J. "Encounters at Explo." *Forum* (Oct., 1972), 4-5. The People's Christian Coalition and Mennonite Central Committee were represented at Explo, a Campus Crusade for Christ event, to witness for peace in the midst of Americanized civil religion.

Enns, Mary M. "Christians on Both Sides of the Iron Curtain Need Each Other." *MennMirror* 6 (Mar., 1977), 7, 8. Dr. Henry D. Wiebe, as part of an MCC delegation to Russia, shares his perceptions of the visit which sought to strengthen previous contacts with believers and to learn from them.

Enns, Mary M. "Keeping the Faith Alive Behind the Iron Curtain." *MennMirror* 5 (Mar., 1976), 9, 10. A report on the research Walter Sawatsky is doing under MCC in Russia and East European countries with particular attention to the current religious situation.

Enns, Mary M. "MCC: Honey and Money Help to Meet Human Needs." *MennMirror* 4 (June, 1975), 7-9. Spending a working day with Arthur Driedger, executive director of MCC (Manitoba), gives author a sense of the variety of activities with which MCC is involved.

Enns, Mary M. "Meet Harold of the Herald." *MennMirror* 6 (May, 1977), 7-10. An interview with Harold Jantz, editor of the *Mennonite Brethren Herald,* in which he discusses and shares, among other things, his perceptions after a visit to Vietnam as part of an MCC delegation.

Epp, Frank H. "Communism, Anti-Communism, and the Mennonite Christian." Paper presented to MCC Peace Section Annual Meeting, Jan. 18, 1962. Pp. 9. MHL.

Epp, Frank H. "Frontiers for Peace." *CanMenn* 11 (Nov. 5, 1963), 5. The MCC Peace Section lists frontiers on which it is working to advance Christ's gospel of peace.

Epp, Frank H. "Guidance Concerning Civil Defense." *CanMenn* 4 (May 4, 1956), 2. Support is expressed for the statement drafted by MCC Peace Section concerning Mennonite participation in Civil Defense. We must be ready to minister to human needs at all times, yet look first to our Lord for protection in any emergency.

Epp, Frank H. "MCC Group Studies Christian Responsibility to the State." *CanMenn* 5 (Nov. 22, 1957), 5-6. An indepth report of the study of the questions and implications connected with the pacifist position. The study conference called by MCC Peace Section brought together 59 persons from various Mennonite groups in Canada and the US to work at the difficult questions of the Christian's involvement in politics. Participants included: H. S. Bender, J. Harold Sherk, John Howard Yoder, J. A. Toews, Elmer Neufeld, J. Winfield Fretz, John E. Lapp, and Edgar Metzler.

Epp, Frank H. "Peace Mission in Orient Should Be Escalated." *CanMenn* 14 (Apr. 5, 1966), 3. A report on the peace activity, history and present needs of the MCC peace section in Japan. Based on Mar. 1-Apr. 5 tour to Asia, Epp argues that with nationalism's threat to the church in Asia, MCC Peace Section should support more peace education activity in the Far East.

Epp, Frank H. "Peace Witness as Evangelism." *Probe.* Ed. James Fairfield. Scottdale: Herald Press, 1972, 27-41. Also "Which Call?" *Evangelism: Good News or Bad.* Pamphlet of MCC Peace Section and MCC (Canada), n.d. [1973?], 1-9. Epp supports his thesis that evangelism and peace must go together by looking at the person of Christ, the human social condition, and effective communication.

Epp, Frank H. "Socialism in Southeast Asia Is Traditional and Practical Way." *CanMenn* 13 (Sept. 21, 1965), 6. Concludes on basis of interview with Peter Fast, who recently returned from a 3-year theological teaching

assignment with MCC in Indonesia, that Indonesia has a tribal tradition of mutual aid which is in agreement with socialism.

Epp, Frank H. "The East-West Assignment." *CanMenn* 5 (July 5, 1957), 2. "The very essence of the Mennonite faith and principles will be put to the test" for all Mennonites as Elfrieda and Peter J. Dyck undertake a three-year MCC assignment in Europe. This assignment will focus on East-West relations and communication.

Epp, Merle L. "MCC Voluntary Service, 1946-1955." Paper for Mennonite Missions class, MBS, [Chicago, Ill.], May 9, 1956. Pp. 15 plus charts. AMBS.

"Five Peace Ambassadors to Speak for Church." *CanMenn* 12 (Jan. 28, 1964), 3. A report on the MCC Peace Section's annual meeting, focusing on race relations. Summary of a panel discussion on racial conflict.

"Food and Peace Traveler Visits Campuses." *Forum* 8 (Apr., 1975), 8. Ray Hamm has joined the MCC Peace Section as campus food and peace traveler, which will involve visiting various Mennonite, Brethren in Christ, evangelical colleges, and universities to share food crisis and peace concerns, to facilitate activities related to food crises and to make resource materials available.

"Food for Peace." *CanMenn* 7 (July 31, 1959), 15. Describes the government's Food for Peace program. MCC, as a voluntary agency, has given over $1.5 million worth of US government surplus to eleven foreign countries.

Fast, Margaret. "A Doctor in Vietnam." *MennMirror* 3 (Nov., 1973), 9, 10. Dr. Margaret Fast reports on her experiences during the two years she practiced medicine under the auspices of MCC in a Vietnam hospital.

Franz, Delton. "The Middle East: Concern for Palestinians Is Seldom Heard." *MennRep* 6 (Oct. 18, 1976), 7. Describes MCC efforts to encourage policymakers in Washington to hear Palestinian grievances and recognize their right to a homeland as well as Israeli rights.

Franz, Delton, ed. "A Week of Witnesses on the War." *MCC PS Wash. Memo* 3 (May-June, 1971), 1-2. Returned MCC worker and Vietnam veteran both testify to the anguish of the Indochina war.

Fretz, J. Winfield. "Postwar Needs of Civilian Public Service Men." *ChrMon* 36 (June, 1944), 179-80. Findings of an MCC survey of CPS personnel deals largely with financial needs.

Friesen, Leonard. "The Option of Nonviolent

Activism in Latin America's Struggle for Liberation." MCC Canada Peace Scholarship paper, Oct. 18, 1977. Pp. 42. CGCL.

"Gift of Love Is Theme of Palestinian Worker." *GH* 72 (Oct. 9, 1979), 802. A Palestinian who is working as an MCC volunteer on the West Bank speaks of the suffering of the Palestinian people.

"Government Changes Citizenship Law." *RepConsS* 34 (Mar., 1977), 2. MCC (Canada) influential in eliminating conscientious objection as a barrier to Canadian citizenship.

"Graduates Ask, What Is Nonviolence." *Menn* 87 (Jan. 18, 1972), 40. Mennonite graduate students conference on nonviolence includes such topics as: testing a fifth-grade history curriculum; applying nonviolent problem solving models to government and organizations; and critical analyses of MCC involvement in the Middle East.

"Guiding Principles in Special Emergencies." *Menn* 71 (June 19, 1956), 396, 398. At a time when nationwide preparation for war emergencies is at a height, MCC and MDS urge clear distinction between relief ministries and activities of Civil Defense which "support the war effort."

Gerlach, Horst. "Through Darkness to Light." *ChrLiv* 3 (Aug., 1956), 6-9, 40-41; 3 (Sept., 1956), 12-15, 40; 3 (Oct., 1956), 14-17, 19, 34, 36; 3 (Nov., 1956), 19-22, 24, 34, 35-37; 3 (Dec., 1956), 24-29, 36; 4 (Jan., 1957), 24-29; 4 (Feb., 1957), 24-29. Life story of a young German man growing up in a pro-Nazi family during the Hitler and World War II era. Enemy occupation of home town; prisoner of war in northern Russia as slave laborer; conversion to Christianity from trust in military force while an MCC trainee serving in the US.

Gingerich, Melvin. "A Peace Witness." *Menn* 74 (Mar. 31, 1959), 197-98; "Concerning Military Conscription," *GH* 52 (Apr. 21, 1959), 369, 381. A statement presented to the Senate Armed Services Committee in behalf of the MCC Peace Section, protesting conscription and America's preoccupation with military superiority. Proposals are given for various programs of peace and goodwill.

Gingerich, Melvin. "Mennonite Central Committee Assignment in Japan, 1955-57." Reports of MCC Peace Section representative, Goshen, Ind., 1962. Pp. 57. MHL. Sixfold mission included working with Mennonite and Brethren missionaries to correlate the peace message with the Gospel; making contact with the Japanese Christian peace movement; production of peace literature; building a peace library; studying the problem of legal

recognition for the CO position in Japan; and visiting Formosa and Korea to evaluate potential for similar peace-oriented work there.

Gingerich, Melvin. "Statement of Melvin Gingerich." *Extension of the Draft and Related Authorities*. Hearings before the Committee on Armed Services United States Senate . . . H.R. 2260. Washington, DC: Government Printing Office, 1959, 49-54. A statement on behalf of the MCC Peace Section protesting conscription and proposing various programs of peace and goodwill.

Gingerich, Melvin (Archival). Box 18Peace Committees: General Conference Mennonite, 1935-48; MCC, 1944-48; CPS history, 1938-49. Box 20Peace Deputation trips. Box 39Draft; Committee on Armed Service hearing, 1959. Box 91Service for Peace; CPS history and correspondence. Goshen, Ind., AMC Hist. Mss. 1-129.

Hackman, Walton. "Out of Sight, Out of Mind in Vietnam." *MBH* 12 (Sept. 7, 1973), 32. MCC Peace Section is urging Mennonite congregations to make Sept. 23 a special concern because it is being declared an International Day of Concern and Action for the thousands of civilians imprisoned in South Vietnam.

Hackman, Walton. "Peace Seminar Encounters Communism in Eastern Europe." *CanMenn* 15 (Nov. 7, 1967), 7, 8. Report on MCC Peace Section study tour of Eastern Europe to speak with both Christians and Marxists in order to transcend some of the barriers which have divided for so long.

Hackman, Walton. "The Issue Now Is Amnesty." *GH* 65 (Jan. 4, 1972), 9-10. Reprinted from MCC Peace Section *Newsletter*. After World War II, only 10 percent of Selective Service violators were pardoned. Writer wonders whether present society has enough latitude to respect and accept the estimated 100,000 Vietnam War resisters.

Hackman, Walton. "The Right of Appeal: A Time for Testing." *CanMenn* 18 (May 22, 1970), 9, 12. Court action on Jerry Penner's refusal to accept induction into the armed forces is summarized. The MCC executive committee supports the role of the Peace Section in helping Penner file his request for a US Supreme Court review of the case.

*Handbook with Draft Manual.* Akron, Pa.: MCC Peace Section, [1943]. Pp. 31. MHL.

Harmon, Jan. "Advocating for 'Supreme Law of the Land'." *EV* 92 (Sept. 25, 1979), 10. Because the government has violated many Indian rights, the Friends Committee on National

Legislation and MCC are attempting to raise the consciousness of the religious community and to respond to this human rights issue in our own country.

Hershberger, Guy F. "A Plan of Action: Suggestions for Mennonite Young Men of Draft Age in Case of War." *YCC* 21 (June 9, 1940), 178-79. A proposed plan of action formulated by Mennonite Central Committee Peace Section that encourages the church to follow a course which will separate its members as completely as possible from the war machinery is outlined.

Hershberger, Guy F. "A Study of Church-State Relations." *GH* 57 (Oct. 13, 1964), 889-90. An announcement of a program to study issues related to church-state theory; includes the MCC Peace Section statement which proposes an outline for this study.

Hershberger, Guy F. *Conscientious Objectors in Europe.* Washington, DC: National Service Board for Religious Objectors, 1952. Excerpts from "Report on My Term of Service for the Peace Section of the Mennonite Central Committee, June 10, 1949 to Aug. 21, 1950."

Hershberger, Guy F. "Historical Background to the Formation of the Mennonite Central Committee." *MQR* 44 (1970), 213-44. Hershberger traces the events that led to the birth of MCC beginning with Menno Simons up to its formation in 1920.

Hershberger, Guy F. "How Important Is the Peace Problems Committee?" *GH* 56 (Apr. 23, 1963), 346-47. An historical sketch of the PPC, giving witness to its importance and attempting to raise funds for this program as well as General Conference (MC) involvement in other projects such as PAX, I-W, MCC, etc.

Hershberger, Guy F. "Mennonites and Government: A Historical Perspective." In *Our National Government and the Christian Witness: Seminar Report,* pp. 11-16. Sponsored by Mennonite Central Committee Peace Section, Akron, Pa., held at Washington, DC, Apr. 27-29, 1961. While it is clear that participation in public office has serious questions for the nonresistant Christian, it is equally clear that complete aloofness from all concern for the state is not the answer either.

Hershberger, Guy F. "Report on My Term of Service for the Peace Section of the Mennonite Central Committee, June 10, 1949, to Aug. 21, 1950." Mimeographed. Goshen: MHL. Study of pacifism in Europe, the peace attitudes of European Mennonites and the legal status of conscientious objectors in Europe.

Hershberger, Guy F. "Why Does the MCC Peace Section Plan to Establish an Office in Washington? Our Peace WitnessIn the Wake of May 18." (Part 25). *GH* 61 (Feb. 27, 1968), 186. Such an office would greatly enhance our peace witness.

Hiebert, Linda Gibson. "The Indochina Project." *MCC PS Newsletter* 9 (June-July, 1979), 3-5. The Indochina Project began in mid-1978 as a cooperative effort between the Mennonite Central Committee and the American Friends Service Committee, with the Center for International Policy joining later. Explains the role and concerns of the project.

Hiebert, Linda Gibson and Hiebert, Murray. "MCC Volunteer Describes Life in Vietnam." *Menn* 92 (Jan. 25, 1977), 55. Yoshihiro Ichakawa, MCC volunteer in Vietnam, describes post-war life in Saigon since the change in government, reporting on changes in local administration, land reform, reeducation centers, attitudes of church people.

Hiebert, Linda Gibson and Hiebert, Murray. "Philippines: The Next Indochina?" *Menn* 90 (Apr. 22, 1975), 256-57. MCC workers in the Philippines trace political history which approximates that of Vietnam and could lead to similar military confrontation.

Hiebert, Linda Gibson and Hiebert, Murray. "What Is MCC Saying in Laos?" *MCC PS Newsletter* 8 (Feb., 1977), 1-2. The Mennonite tradition of offering aid to war victims makes it important that MCC assist the people of Laos in their time of rebuilding. Urges also that the US government become involved in in reconstruction assistance.

Hiebert, Murray and Hiebert, Linda Gibson. "Laos Invites the World to View Damage Caused by War." *MennRep* 8 (Jan. 23, 1978), 2. MCC representatives describe destruction in Laos caused by bombing.

Hofer, Rodney. "Sour Grapes, the Modest Mind, and the Idealist." *Intercom* 10 (July-Aug., 1970), 1-2. MCC worker in Yugoslavia reflects on the idealism of not participating in war.

Hoover, Jesse W. "'Inasmuch': A Story of Relief Work in France." *ChrMon* 34 (Feb., 1942), 45, 63. Description of a convalescent colony run by MCC, operated for children displaced by the war.

Hoover, Jesse W. and Orie O. Miller. "The Civilian Bond Purchase Plan." *Menn* 57 (July 21, 1942), 1-4. A description of efforts on the part of MCC, NSBRO, the Friends, and the Brethren to work with the US Treasury Department to provide an alternative to war bonds for conscientious objectors.

Hope, Sam R. "Personal Reflections on Our Experience in Vietnam." *GH* 62 (Apr. 8, 1969), 320-22; "Personal Reflection on Vietnamese Experience." *CanMenn* 17 (Mar. 4, 1969), 4. Text of a speech by a former director of personnel for Vietnam Christian Service to MCC annual meeting in Chicago on Jan. 24. Reflects on his deepened faith and anti-war convictions because of his work in war-torn Vietnam.

Hostetler, David E. "Responses to a Possible Draft Registration." *GH* 73 (Feb. 12, 1980), 144. Cites voices of opposition in American society to draft registration and urges all Mennonites to file their position with MCC on the Christian Peacemaker Registration form.

Hostetler, John Andrew. "Its Affiliation with the MCC Ministry in Europe: Current Work of the Peace Problems Committee." (Part 2). *GH* 42 (July 12, 1949), 660. In supporting the work of MCC Peace Section, the Peace Problems Committee is in full agreement with the desire of Peace Section workers to establish a spiritual contact with European Mennonite churches in order to reawaken a nonresistant faith.

Hostetter, C. N., Jr. "A Statement of Concern to the Committee on Armed Services of the United States House of Representatives on H.R. 3005 Amending the Universal Military Service and Training Act." *CanMenn* 3 (Feb. 2, 1955), 2. An MCC statement urging the House not to extend the draft.

Hostetter, Douglas. "In Search of Peace for Vietnam." *With* 4 (July, 1971), 15. A former Mennonite Central Committee worker was asked by the National Student Association to return to Vietnam to help draw up a peace treaty.

"I Was in Prison and You Visited Me.Jesus." *EV* 88 (Jan. 25, 1975), 16. Opportunities for involvement with offenders are increasing for Mennonite Central Committee volunteers in North America.

"Japan Christians Ask Abolition of Nuclear Weapons." *CanMenn* 10 (July 6, 1962), 8. A group of Christians in Japan form the Miyazaki Council of Christians for the Abolition of Nuclear Weapons. Their statement was made available to MCC Peace Section by Ferd Ediger.

Jantz, Harold. "Aid to Vietnam/ese Major Agenda Item in Calgary." *MennRep* 9 (Feb. 5, 1979), 1. At an MCC (Canada) meeting in Jan., considerable discussion revolved around aid to Vietnam and the Vietnamese boat refugees. Among other decisions, it also supported the intention of the Peace and Social Concerns Committee to issue a statement on militarism in Canada.

Jantz, Harold. "Depoliticizing Our Aid." *MBH* 18

(Dec. 7, 1979), 10. Editorial expresses the opinion that MCC workers, especially in Southeast Asia, should refrain from becoming involved in political activity.

Jantz, Harold. "Workers Caution About Babylift." *MBH* 14 (May 2, 1975), 16. MCC and Mission Board personnel are concerned that many children being evacuated from Vietnam may not be true orphans.

Jantz, Hugo W. "Our Encounter in the East." *CanMenn* 13 (Aug. 3, 1965), 5. Report of 1965 Christian Peace Conference and MCC Peace Section talks in East Germany and Czechoslovakia.

Janzen, David. Letter to the Editor. *MennRep* 7 (Jan. 10, 1977), 6. Maintains that MCC should not help the Jehovah's Witnesses family, Jensens, gain Canadian citizenship thus far denied on grounds of their conscientious objection to war, since to help JW's become members of an institution the denomination regards as Satanic would be morally wrong, and because conscientious objection is a special, not general, right, granted by the Canadian government only to members of peace churches.

Janzen, William. "Can Conscientious Objectors Be Citizens?" *Menn* 92 (Jan. 4, 1977), 9. Jehovah's Witness conscientious objector relates his views on Christians, war, and politics to an MCC representative assisting him in appealing his Canadian court decision not to grant citizenship because of conscientious objection.

Janzen, William. Letter to the Editor. *MennRep* 7 (Feb. 21, 1977), 6. Defends and explains MCC intervention in the Jensen case, conscientious objectors who were denied Canadian citizenship for reasons of conscientious objection to war.

Janzen, William. "MCC's Ottawa Listening Post." *MBH* 14 (Oct. 31, 1975), 9. Describes the MCC (Canada) Ottawa office as a "listening post" because it is an attempt by the church to neither dominate nor withdraw from the state.

Jost, Arthur. "Mennonite Ex-CPS Men Serve in Sixteen Nations." *RepConsS* 5 (Mar., 1947), 1, 4, 5. One-third of current MCC relief workers have experience with CPS.

Juhnke, James C. "Mennonites and Military Conscription in the Twentieth Century." Paper presented to the MCC US Assembly on the Draft and National Service, Goshen, Ind., Mar. 27-29, 1980. Pp. 12. MHL.

Jutzi, Bruce. "Friends Peace Caravan Visits Kitchener-Waterloo Community." *CanMenn* 14 (July 12, 1966), 4. Report of a visit by a Quaker peace caravan to the Kitchener-Waterloo area June 15-22. The caravaners met daily at the offices of MCC (Ontario) for worship and planning and had several exchanges with Dan Zehr of MCC. They visited several Mennonite churches during their stay in the area and had other contacts as well.

Jutzi, Bruce. "Ten Thousand Gave Serious Consideration to Peace Message." *CanMenn* 14 (Nov. 22, 1966), 1, 3. Report on MCC (Canada) Peace Booth at the Toronto Exhibition with theme "Peace on Earth . . . Peace in Vietnam." While it is difficult to determine the success or failure of such a witness, the booth was an opportunity to take a necessary and unpopular position and defend its validity to a cross-section of society.

"King Hussein Lauds Mennonite Work in Jordan." *RepConsS* 17 (Oct., 1960), 1, 3. King Hussein expresses appreciation for MCC aid to 63,000 Jordanian refugees.

"Korea: Victim of Repression and World Politics." *MennRep* 9 (Sept. 17, 1979), 2. Yoon Goo Lee, formerly of Korea, speaks to the Akron MCC staff about the situation in Korea, stressing that the main problem is the infringement of human rights in South Korea.

"Krauses Stress Peace in Asia Teaching Mission." *GH* 72 (Jan. 30, 1979), 80. Norman and Ruth Kraus report on their biblical peace teaching mission to India and Indonesia under the sponsorship of MCC Peace Section and overseas services. They conclude that leadership in peace education must come from within Asia.

Kauffman, Ivan. "Congress Decision on CO Provisions Influenced by Peace Section Testimony." *CanMenn* 15 (June 6, 1967), 2. A proposed bill, which would have been a return to the provisions for CO's that were in effect in World War I, was changed to one with little difference from the present law. The change was due to MCC Peace Section testimony.

Kauffman, Ivan. "Peace Movement Completes 25 Years of Service." *CanMenn* 15 (Jan. 3, 1967), 1, 7. Historical summary of MCC Peace Section since Jan., 1942, when it assumed the responsibilities, records, and assets of its predecessor, the Mennonite Central Peace Committee founded in 1939.

Kauffman, Ivan. "War: A Necessary Evil and a Time for Tears." *CanMenn* 15 (Nov. 21, 1967), 3, 11. On Nov. 2, five MCC persons spoke with two members of President Johnson's staff about Vietnam. While there was agreement that war is evil, the Johnson people saw this evil as necessary to preserve the American way of life. Therefore the government officials asked for alternatives but quickly rejected those and were interested only in those alternatives capable of achieving the aims of the present war but without violence. Since the MCC personnel argued from totally different assumptions, there was little agreement beyond the basic affirmation that war is evil.

Kauffman, Richard A. "Draft Consultation Calls for Peace Education." *ChrLead* 40 (Dec. 20, 1977), 18. Reports on the Consultation on the Draft at Kansas City sponsored by MCC Peace Section (US).

Keeney, William E. "A Strategy for Waging a Battle for Peace." *CanMenn* 12 (Feb. 18, 1964), 6, 7. Address at MCC Peace Section Annual Meeting, 1964 which describes the motivation and task of the Peace Section.

Kehler, Larry. "America, Israel, and the Arabs." *GH* 67 (Aug. 20, 1974), 625-27; *Menn* 89 (July 9, 1974), 436-37; *MennRep* 4 (July 22, 1974), 6. MCC representative visiting the Mideast reports perspectives of both Arabs and Israelis and assesses the US role in the conflict.

Kehler, Larry. "Blossoms Amidst the Bursting Bombs." *Menn* 89 (June 25, 1974), 413-14; *MennRep* 4 (July 8, 1974), 7. Initial impressions of conflict-ridden Middle East by member of MCC delegation visiting there.

Kehler, Larry. "David and Goliath." *Menn* 89 (June 25, 1974), 424. MCC representative reflects on a recent trip to the Mideast, concluding that while the area is highly polarized, voices of moderation and reconciliation are beginning to be heard from both sides.

Kehler, Larry. "Peace Section of MCC Extends Witness into East Asia in 1963." *CanMenn* 11 (Jan. 25, 1963), 3. Roy Just plans to leave for a two-year assignment in East Asia as part of the Peace Section witness.

Kehler, Larry. "Peacemaking Efforts Fall Behind for Lack of Greater Financial Support." *CanMenn* 15 (Feb. 14, 1967), 1, 2. Expresses convictions on the urgency of the work of the MCC Peace Section and reports discussion "regarding the direction which its concern in the area of international conflict should take."

Kehler, Larry. "Structures and Nationalism Looms [sic] Large at MCC Meeting." *MBH* 14 (Feb. 7, 1975), 10-12. At the annual meeting, the committee passed a resolution on world hunger calling for reduced military expenditure and increased food development.

Kehler, Larry. "Sympathetic Ear Needed for Community Development Work." *CanMenn* 16 (Jan. 16, 1968), 6. A report on a MCC community development project on the Beardy Indian Reserve near Rosthern, Saskatchewan.

The project headed by Bill Siemens involves listening to the people, teaching leathercraft to a paraplegic, and attending meetings in an effort to relate meaningfully in a non-governmental manner to the native American population.

Kehler, Larry. "The Challenge of Peace Witness Is Very Close to Home." *CanMenn* 13 (Feb. 9, 1965), 3. Report on MCC Peace Section's annual meeting in Chicago on Jan. 14. Crucial issue for 1965 is the local church's involvement in peacemaking. Continuation of participation in Prague Peace Conference was proposed and a major study conference on church-state relations, in which MCC Peace Section would be involved, was discussed.

Kehler, Larry. "Vietnamese Vignettes." *GH* 69 (Sept. 14, 1976), 685-91; *Menn* 91 (July 20, 1976), 446-47. MCC visitor to Vietnam describes the effects of war on the survivors and reports on the shape of Vietnamese society since liberation.

Klassen, J. M. "MCC Work in Areas of Conflict Explained." *MBH* 16 (Oct. 14, 1977), 11. MCC (Canada) Executive Secretary responds to the concern that MCC personnel may be supporting terrorist activity.

Klassen, James R. "To Push or Not to Push." *With* 10 (June, 1977), 32. A Mennonite Central Committee worker in Vietnam reflects on working for peace in that country.

Koontz, Gayle Gerber. "Mennonite Peace in the Middle East Puzzle." *MBH* 13 (Aug. 23, 1974), 16-17. People-oriented MCC efforts, cooperation with Middle Eastern churches, and food and development programs will continue to receive Mennonite attention in the Mideast conflict.

Koontz, Gayle Gerber. "Vietnam Churches See Challenges, Pressures." *Menn* 90 (Sept. 16, 1975), 511. MCC volunteer returned from Vietnam discusses the change of government there and the challenges facing the church in helping to rebuild the country after the war.

Koontz, Ted. "Urbana 73 Stresses Hope, CommitmentReactions." *Forum* (Feb., 1974), 6. MCC Peace Section experienced many favorable responses to their peace witness at Urbana 73.

Koop, Robert. "Ottawa Report: Government Consults MCC on Mid-East Policy." *MennRep* 9 (Sept. 3, 1979), 7. Representatives from MCC and Robert Stanfield, the Canadian government's special representative to study Canada's relationship with the Middle East, met to discuss the vital role Canada could play in the future of Middle East peace negotiations.

Kreider, Carl. "International Economic Justice." Paper presented at MCC Justice Task Force Consultation, Goshen College, Goshen, Ind., May 22-23, 1978. Pp. 7. MHL.

Kreider, Carl. "The Mennonite Central Committee Relief Training School Held at Goshen College." *ChrMon* 35 (Nov., 1943), 336-37. Development of the training program, negotiation with the Selective Service system, and final cancellation by Congress.

Kreider, Robert S. "A Statement of Concern." *Menn* 70 (July 12, 1955), 425. MCC opposes the extension of the draft act and urges the complete cessation of universal military conscription.

Kreider, Robert S. "Mennonite Refugees in Germany." *MCC WSRB* 2 (July, 1946), 4. Describes MCC efforts to make possible the migration of Russian Mennonite refugees in Berlin.

Kreider, Robert S. "Mennonites Around the Rim of the Mediterranean." *Menn* 86 (Mar. 23, 1971), 186-89. The vice-chairman of MCC reports on the Mennonite witness for peace through projects around the Mediterranean.

Kroeker, David. "Delegates Vote for College Expansion; Adopt Peace Witness Policy Statement." *CanMenn* 17 (July 11, 1969), 1. At the annual Canadian MB conference delegates adopt a critical position toward MCC and specifically to the MCC peace section.

Kroeker, Walter. "Justice and Rights Issues Occupy MCC Members in Reedley." *MennRep* 9 (Feb. 19, 1979), 1. Among the issues discussed at the MCC annual meeting was aid to Vietnam, justice and human rights overseas, and a paper on militarism calling the church to renounce the development of nuclear weapons and military exports.

Kroeker, Walter. "MCCWide-Ranging Agenda." *EV* 92 (Mar. 25, 1979), 8-9. At the MCC annual meeting, issues of justice, aid to Vietnam, the world food crisis, and militarism were addressed and a paper on militarism by Urbane Peachey was accepted.

"Lack of Security and Justice Key Issues of Mid-East Deadlock." *CanMenn* 20 (Sept. 11, 1970), 3. Observations gleaned from members of MCC Peace Section tour of the Middle East countries on Arab-Jewish relations.

"'Love Works in Conflicts' Says Hostetter." *MBH* 10 (May 28, 1971), 18-19. Former MCC worker Doug Hostetter speaks of the effects of propaganda and the American military presence in war-torn Vietnam. Also speaks of the power of love at work in his relationships with the Vietnamese people.

Lapp, John A. "Peace Section Not Political." *CanMenn* 19 (Feb. 2, 1971), 2. A concern that the MCC Peace Section not be a political unit but inspire to a life of peace that has political dimensions.

Lapp, John A. "Seminary Letter Precipitates Intense Brotherly Discourse." *CanMenn* 18 (Mar. 13, 1970), 1, 11. Describes tensions aroused between MCC and the AMBS community over a letter the seminary sent to President Nixon. Also describes the efforts to resolve the conflict and the very solid discussion of the issues of church and state which resulted from the tensions.

Lapp, John E. "Testimony to US Armed Services Committee." *MBH* 6 (May 26, 1967), 7, 18-19. MCC believes reliance on military strength to be both futile and wrong, and urges an end to conscription and war.

Leatherman, Loretta and Paul. "Our Case for Tax Resistance." *GH* 73 (Apr. 29, 1980), 350-52. In an interview with the MCC Peace Section, the Leathermans describe their reasons for not paying war taxes and their experiences with this practice.

Lehman, Glenn. "A Conversation." *Intercom* 9 (May-June, 1969), 1, 4. Dialogue between MCC teacher and a student guerrilla in the Congo about violence and revolutionary ideology.

Lehman, John P. "The Mennonite Central Committee Peace Section." Paper presented to Mennonite History class, AMBS, Elkhart, Ind., Dec. 3, 1973. Pp. 14. MHL.

Lehman, M[artin] C[lifford]. *The History and Principles of Mennonite Relief Work*An Introduction. Akron: MCC, 1945. Pp. 67. A statement of the theological and historical basis of Mennonite relief work, including an annotated bibliography of 145 items on the subject.

Lehman, M[artin] C[lifford]. "The Program of the Mennonite Central Committee to Train Relief Workers." *ChrMon* 36 (Feb., 1944), 43. Removal of the training program from Goshen College to mental hospitals, where trainees could continue the CPS work into which they were drafted.

Leis, Vernon. "Mennonites Fearful of War-Resisters." *CanMenn* 18 (May 22, 1970), 8. MCC (Ontario) sponsors a seminar at which the concerns of the churches about involvement with draft-dodgers are set forth and at which five recommendations for sympathetic action are made on behalf of them.

Lind, Suzanne. "Mennonites Help Pay Fines." *Menn* 94 (Mar. 20, 1979), 215. MCC has provided funds to help pay fines to secure the release of imprisoned squatters in East London, South Africa.

Linscheid, Ruth. "THe MCC in South Vietnam." Student paper for Anabaptist-Mennonite Seminar, May, 1967. Pp. 33. MLA/BeC.

Loewen, Esko. "Better than Military Conscription." *Menn* 74 (Feb. 24, 1959), 115. The MCC statement to the Congressional Committee on Armed Services which implores national leaders to "beat their swords into plowshares."

Loewen, Esko. "MCC in Europe Today." *Menn* 70 (Nov. 22, 1955), 728. MCC continues the peace witness via PAX, the Heerewegen Conference Center, the Puidoux conferences, and voluntary service projects.

Longacre, Doris Janzen. *More-with-Less Cookbook.* Scottdale: Herald Press, 1976. Pp. 328. A cookbook which emphasizes the global perspective of MCC by offering recipes, based on economy of money, time, and energy, which express the spirit of a people "looking for ways to live more simply and joyfully, ways that grow out of our tradition but take their shape from living faith and the demands of our hungry world."

Longacre, Paul. "No Peace for the Vietnamese." *MBH* 12 (Apr. 6, 1973), 32; "Peace Not Yet at Hand for Vietnamese." *Menn* 88 (Apr. 3, 1973), 225. MCC representative visiting Vietnam after the ceasefire reports on the continuing struggle for control of contested areas and the likely continued military activity after the reduction of US forces.

Longacre, Paul. "Vietnam: The Church's Dilemma." *GH* 60 (Oct. 17, 1967), 939-40. MCC workers in Vietnam are not really free to speak out against the war; the church at home must do it for them.

Lubosch, Lore. "Put in a Good Word for Me." *MennMirror* 2 (Feb., 1973), 4-7. Grosvenor Place is an alternative to prison for several adult men. It operates as a program under MCC, Peace and Social Concerns Committee in Winnipeg, Man.

Luft, Murray. "'God Sides with the Poor' Says Seminar Leader in Calgary." *MennRep* 9 (Sept. 17, 1979), 4. Ron Sider, speaker at the MCC (Alberta)-sponsored seminar, presented two lectures calling the church to Christ's ongoing work of reconciliation in a suffering world.

"MCC." *RepConsS* 23 (Aug., 1966), 3, 4. Summarizes the work of MCCfocusing on PAX, Voluntary Service, and Teachers Abroad Program.

"MCC, Peace Conference Topics for Rev. G.

Rempel." *CanMenn* 2 (Jan. 22, 1954), 8. Rempel reports on the Detroit Peace Conference and the annual meeting of the Mennonite Central Committee, encouraging the churches to continue their relief programs and peace witness. Strong statements on biblical nonresistance are reported. The problem of the fundamentalists and the peace witness is brought out in an example of the Old Fashioned Revival Hour refusing donations from Mennonite COs.

"MCC Asks Unconditional Outlaw of All Nuclear Weapons." *CanMenn* 6 (May 23, 1958), 1. A joint statement against nuclear weapons is made by Mennonites, Brethren, and Friends.

"MCC (Canada) Annual Meeting." *MBH* 12 (Jan. 26, 1973), 8-9. Among other agenda items, the MCC Canada board discussed capital punishment, amnesty for US war resisters, and ecumenical relations at its annual meeting.

"MCC (Canada) Answers Queries re Draft Evaders." *CanMenn* 18 (Apr. 17, 1970), 1, 2. Six of the most frequently asked questions about the draft refugee situation are clarified.

"MCC (Canada) Endorses Resolution on Amnesty." *MennRep* 3 (Jan. 22, 1973), 11. Publishes the working draft of the MCC Peace Section statement on the necessity of amnesty for US war resisters.

"MCC Gives a Voice for the Voiceless." *EV* 91 (Oct. 10, 1978), 10. MCC volunteer, Jan Curry, is completing the history of the Houma Indians in Dulac, Louisiana, which will enable the now "unrecognized" tribe to begin the process for official recognition by the US government.

"MCC (Manitoba) Asks for Stronger CO Provisions in Labor Act." *RepConsS* 32 (Mar., 1975), 5. Request prompted by Labor Board's denial of eight recent applications for exemption from union membership for reasons of conscientious objection.

"MCC Makes Plea to Unite Families." *MennMirror* 1 (Nov., 1971), 22. Mitchell Sharp, Canada's Minister of External Affairs, was urged by the Mennonite Central Committee to impress on Premier Alexei Kosygin the urgency of allowing separated families in the Soviet Union and Canada to be reunited.

"MCC Opens Contacts with North Vietnam." *EV* 87 (Feb. 25, 1974), 16. Atlee Beechy, a member of the MCC executive committee returning from a visit to North Vietnam, reports that although MCC personnel will not be able to accompany material aid into North Vietnam, there is still possibility for a Christian peace witness there.

"MCC Plans for 1978." *EV* 91 (Mar. 10, 1978), 5. MCC's annual meeting held in Kitchener, Ont., included in its agenda discussion on MCC's response to need in Vietnam.

"MCC Postwar Planning." *RepConsS* 2 (May 1, 1944), 3. A survey of CPS camps operated by MCC and Mennonites in other camps indicates that CPS has created interest in further education, that 60 percent of those surveyed plan to farm after CPS, etc.

"MCC Questionnaire." *RepConsS* 4 (June 21, 1946), 3. Progress report on CPS evaluation questionnaires sent to assignees in MCC camps and units.

"MCC Resolution on World Food Crisis." *EV* 87 (July 10, 1974), 3. MCC has resolved to give priority to the world food crisis in the next five to ten years, recognizing that world peace may depend on the solution to the hunger problem in developing countries.

"MCC Seeks Channel to Aid Kampuchea." *Menn* 94 (Oct. 30, 1979), 647. Famine follows years of wars and internal upheavals in Kampuchea, and MCC is working through various channels to send aid and to urge the US to normalize relations with Indochinese countries.

"MCC to Establish Washington Office." *CanMenn* 16 (Feb. 13, 1968), 1. The "office in Washington is not for lobbying. It shall serve as an *observer*, particularly with reference to developments in the federal government, but also in liaison with other church, welfare, and professional agencies. It would analyze and interpret trends which may affect peace, religious liberty, social welfare, education, and related fields."

"MCC to Send Aid to Vietnam." *RepConsS* 33 (Feb., 1976), 3. In annual meeting, MCC approves million-dollar shipment of material aid and reconstruction supplies to Vietnam.

"MCC Workers Remain in Quang Ngai." *EV* 88 (Apr. 25, 1975), 15. Four of the MCC Vietnam volunteers have chosen to stay in Quang Ngai, which is being held by the Provisional Revolutionary Government.

"Mennonite Witness in Race Crisis." *CanMenn* 12 (July 14; 1964), 3, 10. A cooperative witness in the racial crisis in the South is announced by the MCC Peace Section and the Board of Christian Service of the General Conference Mennonite Church.

"Mennonites Expand Voluntary Service." *RepConsS* 6 (Nov., 1948), 1, 2. Reports MCC intentions to expand number and kinds of service projects as extension of belief in applied Christian love.

"Mennonites Open Forestry Project." *RepConsS* 16

(Dec., 1959), 1. MCC has begun a project near Reedley, Calif., that involves soil conservation, forest preservation, and fighting forest fires.

"Mennonites Stay In." *RepConsS* 4 (Jan. 15, 1946), 1, 3. MCC decides to continue administrating CPS until all persons are released.

"Minority Job Program Ready." *RepConsS* 32 (Dec., 1975), 4. An advisory committee appointed by MCC US Ministries is planning a job training program for Mennonite minority youth being pressured toward the military by the economic situation.

"More Questions Than Answers on Middle East Situation." *CanMenn* 17 (Feb. 4, 1969), 1, 2. Reports on the MCC Peace Section annual meeting in Chicago on Jan. 23 where Frank Epp presented a 40-page paper entitled "Whose Land Is Palestine?" Respondents were Wilbert Shenk, Waldemar Janzen, and Elmer A. Martens. Theological and other issues stand at the root of a solution for the crisis in the Middle East and also affect the promotion of peace by MCC workers in the area.

Martin, Earl S. *Reaching the Other Side: The Journal of an American Who Stayed to Witness Vietnam's Post-War Transition.* New York: Crown Publishers, Inc., 1978. Pp. 281. Journal records actions and observations of an MCCer during the six-week period between the time the Provisional Revolutionary Government (Viet Cong) stages a peaceful takeover of Quang Ngai City and the fall of Saigon. An intimate view of the day to day ramifications of trying to live out the MCC philosophy of ministering beyond the boundaries of nationality and political ideology.

Martin, Earl S. "Tough Enough for Peace." *Lifework* 5 (1981), 7-9. MCC worker in Vietnam describes peacemaking work as requiring as much, if not more, strength and courage than military work.

Martin, Luke S. Letter to the Editor. *Menn* 90 (Feb. 4, 1975), 75. MCC director in Vietnam reports recent events there: upsurge in fighting; public opposition to the policies and corruption of the South Vietnamese government; popular call for peace.

Martin, Patricia Hostetter. "Sometimes Family Has to Go." *ChrLiv* 22 (Aug., 1975), 4-7. As the Vietnam war progresses, MCC volunteers Earl and Pat Martin decide to separate as a family.

Matsuo, Hilda. "Can We Handle All Those Boat People?" *MennMirror* 9 (Sept., 1979), 10. The writer looks at the varying attitudes of Canadians towards Indochinese refugees and points out what two MCC employees have advisedthat Canadians should act as peacemakers rather than continuing the more popular route of polarizing the situation in Southeast Asia.

*MCC Draft Counselor's Manual.* Akron, Pa.: MCC [Peace Section, 1980]. MHL.

Mennonite Central Committee. "A Letter to the President." *GH* 58 (June 29, 1965), 567. The text of a letter sent to President Johnson. MCC describes relief work in Vietnam and calls the president to an escalation of compassion rather than an escalation of conflict.

Mennonite Central Committee. "Civil Defense." *GH* 49 (June 12, 1956), 558-59. A statement made by MCC and MDS suggests that Mennonites should not become integrally involved in Civilian Defense.

Mennonite Central Committee. "Civil Defense: A Statement of Guiding Principles," *GH* 52 (Aug. 11, 1959), 695. Mennonites should refrain from membership in Civil Defense organizations.

Mennonite Central Committee. "Civil Defense and Disaster Services," *GH* 55 (Feb. 20, 1962), 169. A position statement indicates that Mennonites will support those efforts which make war less likely and avoid a hysterical war spirit.

Mennonite Central Committee. *Conscience and Conscription.* Akron: MCC Peace Section, 1970. Pp. 48. Papers of the Chicago peace assembly, Nov., 1969. Includes: Burkholder, J. R., "Christ, Conscience, Church, and Conscription: Toward an Ethical Analysis of Mennonite Draft Resistance;" Juhnke, James, "Conflicts and Compromises of Mennonites and the Draft: An Interpretative Essay;" Keeney, William, "The National Debate Over the Draft;" a message from the consultation participants.

Mennonite Central Committee. *Handbook of the Mennonite Central Committee.* 6th edn. Akron: Mennonite Central Committee, 1969. Pp. 72. A summary statement of Mennonite history and faith, together with explanation of the operation and work of MCC, including the Peace Section.

Mennonite Central Committee. "MCC Peace Commissioner Visits India and Vietnam," *GH* 53 (May 17, 1960), 449. A report on the churches in these countries and their successes and problems.

Mennonite Central Committee. "MCC Presents Testimony Opposing Draft Extension," *Menn* 70 (Feb. 15, 1955), 110. The MCC Peace Section's statement of concern opposes the extension of the draft, while recognizing that this testimony may not be heeded.

Mennonite Central Committee. "MCC Presents

Vietnam Letter," *GH* 60 (Nov. 21, 1967), 1069-70. The letter, presented to President Johnson, questions US activities in Vietnam.

Mennonite Central Committee. "Mennonites Testify at Hearings on Post-War Military Policy," *Menn* 60 (July 10, 1945), 5-6; "A Statement of Position on Permanent Peacetime Conscription and the Christian Conscience Against War," *GH* 38 (July 20, 1945), 297-98. A statement presented to the House Select Committee on Postwar Military Policy opposes conscription from the perspective of biblical understandings, the nonresistant tradition, and a concern for freedom of conscience.

Mennonite Central Committee. *Report: A New Look at the Church and State Issue.* Akron: Mennonite Central Committee, 1966. Pp. 35. Three documents from the MCC Peace Section study conference held in Chicago, Oct., 1965: Metzler, Edgar, "Why Another Look at Church-State Relations?;" Littell, Franklin H., "The New Shape of the Church-State Issue;" and a findings statement from the conference.

Mennonite Central Committee. "Statement on Conscription for Military Training, and Provisions for Conscientious Objectors," *GH* 38 (Dec. 21, 1945), 733-34. A statement submitted to the House Military Affairs Committee. Expresses opposition to any program of compulsory military training, and support for provisions for conscientious objectors in case such legislation is passed.

Mennonite Central Committee. "Telegram Commends President's Efforts," *GH* 61 (Apr. 23, 1968), 375-76. A telegram commending President Johnson for stopping the bombing of North Vietnam.

Mennonite Central Committee. "The Civilian Bond Purchase Plan," *GH* 35 (July 16, 1942), 346-47. A description of the plan includes copies of the correspondence which brought about the Civilian Bond Purchase Plan and explains how to use the plan.

Mennonite Central Committee. *The Evangelical Christian and Modern War.* A seminar at Winona Lake, Ind., Aug., 1963. Akron: MCC Peace Section, 1963. Includes seven study papers: Ladd, George E., "The Evangelical Christian and the State;" Backer, Glenn W., "A New Testament Perspective;" Klassen, William, "Biblical Faith and War;" Peachey, Paul, "War and the Christian Witness;" Reid, W. Stanford, "The Christian and Modern War: The Reformed Perspective;" Yoder, John H., "The Christian and War in the Perspective of Historical and Systematic Theology."

Mennonite Central Committee. "The War Bond Campaign," *GH* 36 (Sept. 23, 1943), 538. Those

who want to invest should do so in the Civilian Bond Program through MCC as a witness against war.

Mennonite Central Committee. *Twenty-Five Years. The Story of the MCC, 1920-1945.* Akron: MCC, 1945. Pp. 24. An interpretive history of North American Mennonite relief and service activities, including CPS and direct peace activities.

Mennonite Central Committee. "Vietnam Study: Relief Often Tied to Politics, Military." *MennRep* 2 (Oct. 2, 1972), 1. Relief agencies enjoy the benevolences of a government because the latter recognizes a potential in the former to realize its political and military ends.

Mennonite Central Committee. "White House Hears Mennonite Concern on War." *Menn* 82 (Nov. 21, 1967), 704-705. MCC message to the president deplores the present US policy in Vietnam and calls for a radical reversal of military policy.

Mennonite Central Committee (Archival). Papers related to peace and social concerns, 1920 to present. Goshen, IN. AMC. MCC Peace Section Materials IX.

Mennonite Central Committee (Canada) Release. "Alternative to PrisonIs There a Christian Response?" *EV* 89 (May 10, 1976), 16. At a Canadian MCC seminar on the Christian response in a ministry to the offender, more personal, humane, and just alternatives to imprisonment were discussed.

Mennonite Central Committee (Canada) Release. "Restitution and Reconciliation." *EV* 89 (Jan. 10, 1976), 16. A MCC (Canada) program which attempts to bring offenders and victims together to effect reconciliation has received a grant from the Canadian federal government.

Mennonite Central Committee (US). "Statement on World Tensions and the Draft." Adopted Jan. 24, 1980. P. 1. (Located in MCC Peace Section Official Statements folder in MHL.) Urges young Mennonite men and women to register their conscientious objector convictions with the Peacemaker Registration Program in response to proposed military conscription.

Mennonite Central Committee Annual Meeting. "Christian Love and Faith Transform Problems into Opportunities." *EV* 89 (Mar. 10, 1976), 5. MCC ministries in 1976 will include responses to victims of war and political tensions.

Mennonite Central Committee Canada News Service (Review). *Making a Killing: The Truth About the Canadian Arms Industry,* by Ernie Regehr. N.p., n.d. *Forum* 9 (Feb., 1976), 6-7. Summarizes the main thesis of this book:

Canada's diplomatic stance as a nation favoring nonviolent solutions is inconsistent with its promotion of Canadian-made arms abroad.

Mennonite Central Committee Information Services. "Palestinian MCCer Discusses Middle East." *EV* 92 (Oct. 10, 1979), 16. Palestinian Bishara Awad, an MCC volunteer working as headmaster of a school established by MCC in the West Bank, is involved in a ministry of love in the Middle East conflict.

Mennonite Central Committee News. "Snow Falls on MCC Agenda." *EV* 90 (Feb. 25, 1977), 7. Among the issues and concerns discussed at the MCC annual meeting in Metamora, Ill., members discussed how MCC should relate to authoritarian governments that deny justice and religious or political freedom to their citizens.

Mennonite Central Committee News Release. "Nicaragua Struggles to Recover." *EV* 92 (Sept. 25, 1979), 8-9. MCC cooperates with other Mennonite organizations in assessing needs and arranging for food shipments to Nicaragua in an effort to help the country recover from the pain and destruction of war.

Mennonite Central Committee News Service. "Church Still Active in Vietnam." *ChrLead* 38 (Sept. 30, 1975), 18. Earl Martin, MCC volunteer returning from Vietnam, reports that there are signs of hope amid the upheaval for the church in Vietnam.

Mennonite Central Committee News Service. "Dateline: Veintiane, Laos-Vietnam Delegation Receives Aid Report." *EV* 89 (Feb. 25, 1976), 10, 11. The aid that MCC gives to Vietnam is an important contribution in healing the wounds of war and demonstrating the desire to reconcile and share resources despite the US policy of continuing hostility.

Mennonite Central Committee News Service. "Mennonites Report No Bloodbath in Vietnam." *ChrLead* 38 (July 8, 1975), 14. Letters from Mennonite Central Committee workers indicate no apparent slaughter took place when the Provisional Revolutionary Government took control of Saigon.

Mennonite Central Committee Peace Section. "A Guide to Peace Resources." 1977 pamphlet. Pp. 3. (Located in MCC Peace Section Official Statements folder in MHL.) Bibliography of books, study guides, periodicals, church statements, and visual aids on peace and war. (Located in MCC Peace Section Official Statements folder in MHL.)

Mennonite Central Committee Peace Section. "A Plea to Resist the Nuclear Arms Race." Adopted Nov. 20, 1981. P. 1. (Located in MCC Peace Section Official Statements folder in MHL.) Urges Mennonite and Brethren in Christ churches to witness against the momentum of the nuclear arms race.

Mennonite Central Committee Peace Section. "A Christian Declaration on Amnesty." *GH* 66 (May 15, 1973), 413-14; *Menn* 88 (Apr. 24, 1973), 268-69. Based on the belief that peace and reconciliation are at the heart of the gospel, the Peace Section urges adopting a "general amnesty" to cover all types of conscientious objectors, an action that would help to bind up the wounds of the Vietnam war.

Mennonite Central Committee Peace Section. "Christians and the Bicentennial: Facing the Ambiguities." *Menn* 90 (July 8, 1975), 412-13. Statement for reflection focuses on distinguishing loyalty to the nation from loyalty to God.

Mennonite Central Committee Peace Section. "Testimony Given on Draft." *GH* 64 (Mar. 2, 1971), 201-202. Reprint of the testimony given to the Senate Armed Services Committee calling for the draft to be abolished. Argues for the end of the draft on the bases of opposition to military activities and the inequities of the system.

Mennonite Central Committee Peace Section. "The Contemporary Scene. Amnesty: A Christian Declaration." *EV* 86 (July 25, 1973), 16. This statement represents the consensus of the MCC Peace Section which has attempted to state with clarity and precision the position which it feels reflects the Mennonite theology of peacemaking and reconciliation.

Mennonite Central Committee Peace Section. "World Peace Tax Fund . . . Congressional Hearings?" *God and Caesar* 1 (June, 1975), 8. *Washington Memo* (July-Aug., 1975). Supporters of the World Peace Tax Fund Act should be indicating their Interest in order for the World Peace Tax Fund witnesses to be able to testify at the Congressional tax reform hearings.

Mennonite Central Committee Peace Section Consultation on Conscience and Conscription, Chicago, Nov. 22, 1969. "Christian Obedience and Selective Service," *Menn* 84 (Dec. 16, 1969), 759-60. Christian vocation is the context for our response to militarism and conscription, and results in various forms of obedience to Christ, including noncooperation with the draft.

*Mennonites and Conscientious Objection in 1980*. Akron, Pa.: MCC US Peace Section, 1980. Pp. 95. MHL. Papers presented at the MCC US Peace Section Assembly on the Draft and National Service, Mar. 27-29, 1980, at Goshen, Ind. Includes: Blosser, Don, "Biblical Principles and Government Conscription: The Mennonite

Dilemma;" Juhnke, James, "The Response of Christians to Conscription in United States History;" Franz, Delton, "Current Legislative Proposals and Their Implications for Conscientious Objectors;" Beals, J. Duane, "The Case for Selective Participation in Military Service;" Martin, Charles D., "The Case for Noncombatant Military Service;" Beechy, Winifred, "The Case for Alternative Service;" Koehn, Dennis, "A Call to Conscientious Resistance;" Graff, Tom, "The Case for Emigration;" Neufeld, Elmer, "Mennonite Response to Conscription: A Majority Response and Variations from It;" Klassen, Mike, "Implementing a Congregational Dialogue on the Draft and National Service."

Metzler, Edgar. "Christians Open to Peace Witness, Says Physics Professor." *CanMenn* 8 (Feb. 12, 1960), 7. Albert Meyer presents the needs and challenges of a world-wide peace witness to the MCC Peace Section meeting at Chicago.

Metzler, Edgar. "Selective Conscientious Objectors." *GH* 60 (Mar. 14, 1967), 233. NSBRO and MCC Peace Section support the concern for the civil rights of religious selective objectors. This support was declared on Nov. 19-20, 1965.

Metzler, Edgar. "Six Questions About Peace." *GH* 59 (Mar. 23, 1965), 249; "Students and Leaders in India Ask Six Questions About Peace." *CanMenn* 12 (Dec. 29, 1964), 7. Report by the MCC Peace Missioner to India about the growing interest in nonresistance in India. Outlines six questions frequently asked there about nonresistance.

Miller, Levi (Review). *Mennonites and Conscientious Objection in 1980,* Mennonite Central Committee, 1980. Pp. 95. *FQ* 7 (Nov., Dec., 1980, Jan., 1981), 9. Publishes papers presented at the MCC Peace Section Assembly on the Draft and National Service, 1980, in Goshen, Ind. Reviewer assesses its main purpose as informing interested persons of Mennonite thinking, since the book bears typewritten copy and no particular editing to draw it into a volume.

Miller, Marlin E. "Christian Obedience in a Divided World to be Subject of East-West Encounter." *CanMenn* 13 (Apr. 13, 1965), 1, 2. Preliminary report of 1965 Christian Peace Conference and MCC Peace Section talks with East German and Czechoslovakian theology students.

Miller, Orie O. (Archival). Boxes 1-80; collection contains MCC and various peace related materials; Committee on Economic and Social Relations; Mennonite Relief Commission on War Sufferers; Peace Problems Committee. Goshen, IN. AMC. Hist. Mss. 1-45.

Miller, Robert W. "What Is MCC Doing in Vietnam?" *ChrLead* 36 (July 10, 1973), 6; *MBH* 12 (Aug. 24, 1973), 17; "What Is Mennonite Central Committee Doing in Vietnam?" *GH* 66 (July 3, 1973), 538; *MennRep* 3 (July 9, 1973), 9.. From 1966-72, MCC was part of Vietnam Christian Service (VNCS), a joint effort of Church World Service, Lutheran World Relief, and MCC, but since Jan., 1973, MCC has been operating its own programs in cooperation with the national church and VNCS. These programs are described in this article.

"Native Concerns Are Significant." *EV* 92 (July 25, 1979), 8, 9. MCC US Ministries is seeking to support Indian rights and trying to build an understanding between immigrant Americans and native Americans.

"New Project in Salzburg." *RepConsS* 18 (July, 1961), 2. MCC will assist Nazarene refugees, who have been living in wooden barracks for fifteen years, with new housing construction.

"Non-Resistance Relief Organization." *CanMenn* 7 (Nov. 6, 1959), 8. A short history of this Ontario organization whose purpose is to actively express the principles of non-resistance through relief. The NRRO has cooperated in the past with other Mennonite relief agencies and is now a member of MCC.

"Nuclear Energy, Hot Topic at Peace Section Meeting." *GH* 72 (June 19, 1979), 504-505. Agenda items at the annual MCC Peace Section Meeting in Washington, DC, June 1-2, included proposed draft registration legislation, various peace education projects, and nuclear energy.

Neufeld, David (Review). *Reaching the Other Side,* by Earl S. Martin. New York: Crown Publishers, Inc., 1978. Pp. 282. *MennRep* 9 (Sept. 17, 1979), 8. A journal written by an American working for MCC in Vietnam depicting the situation and people of Vietnam during the post-war transition.

Neufeld, Elmer. "PEACE the Way of the Cross." *Menn* 74 (June 16, 1959), 374-75. From an address to the MCC annual meeting; calls for consistent witness regarding the way of suffering love.

Nisimura, Umeno. "MCC Peace Section in Japan." Paper presented to Mennonite History class, AMBS, Elkhart, Ind., May, 1963. Pp. 8. MHL.

"Office Restructured, Clearer Witness Urged at Peace Section Meeting." *GH* 72 (Jan. 2, 1979), 8-9. Report from the annual MCC Peace Section (International) meeting at Hesston, Kansas, in Dec., 1978, where a statement was accepted calling North American Mennonites to give clearer witness to government and other bodies against militarism and the arms race.

"Palestinian Teacher Shares Agony of His People." *MennRep* 9 (Oct. 1, 1979), 13. Bishara E. Awad, an MCC volunteer as headmaster of a school in the West Bank, shares his concern and agony for the plight of the Palestinian people.

"Peace and Social Concerns." *CanMenn* 13 (June 22, 1965), 3. Report on meeting in Chicago of MCC Peace Section, which consists of two MC peace committees and one GC peace committee. Enthusiasm was expressed at the meeting for coordinated effort between these committees.

"Peace Church Officials Contact State Directors." *RepConsS* 9 (Mar.-Apr., 1952), 6. MCC finds both receptive and punitive attitudes toward COs among contacted state directors of Selective Service.

"Peace Groups Affirm SALT, Caution President." *Menn* 94 (June 19, 1979), 424. Thirty national organizations, including MCC Peace Section and individuals, urge President Carter not to use promises of new weapons to win Senate votes for the approval of the SALT II Treaty.

"Peace in the Middle East, Assembly Concern." *MBH* 12 (Dec. 28, 1973), 18. The MCC Peace Section semi-annual meeting discussed the current Middle East situation and the need to help reconcile not only Israel and the Arab states but also North Americans who have become polarized over the situation.

"Peace in Vietnam Calls for Escalation of Compassion, Not of Conflict and War." *CanMenn* 13 (June 8, 1965), 1. Text of a letter from the MCC Executive Committee to President Lyndon B. Johnson urging him to escalate compassion in Vietnam rather than conflict.

"Peace Section (US) Calls for Restraint in Iran Crisis, Supports SALT Amendment." *GH* 72 (Dec. 25, 1979), 1032, 1037. Meeting of MCC Peace Section (US) passed resolutions concerning the US-Iranian crisis, SALT II, and the proposed World Peace Tax Fund on Nov. 30-Dec. 1.

"Peace Section Opens Washington Office." *CanMenn* 16 (Sept. 3, 1968), 3. MCC Peace Section's Washington office opened July 1, 1968. The purpose of the office is: to give Mennonites current and accurate information on governmental developments in areas affecting the life and work of Mennonite and Brethren in Christ churches; to equip and assist constituent groups when they want to make statements to the government; and to serve as a source of knowledge on peace and social issues related to government.

"Peace Section Testifies on Capital Punishment."

*ChrLead* 41 (Aug. 29, 1978), 18. Report on a statement presented by D. Franz, MCC Washington Peace Section office director, to the House of Representatives Judiciary Committee on the death penalty.

"Peacemaking Should not Wait till Hostilities Begin." *CanMenn* 15 (Nov. 14, 1967), 1, 11. On Nov. 11 there was a one-day peace conference at the Portage Avenue MB Church in Winnipeg sponsored by MCC. John Howard Yoder was the guest speaker. He said that the Christian life is the normal life and we misunderstand the gospel if we think it is a call to a difficult life. Definitions of the life of peace in Christ, the meaning of bearing the cross, and the meaning of rediscovering discipleship.

"Protest Simmers in Vietnam." *Forum* 8 (Dec., 1974), 3. MCC volunteers in Vietnam report that political movements are mushrooming and there is dissatisfaction with the leadership of Nguyen Nan Thieu and his government's corruption.

Pacifism (since 1945). 12 interviews. Includes Historic Peace Churches Consultation (1975), MCC involvement, National Service Board for Religious Objectors, and draft counselling. MLA/BeC.

Peachey, J. Lorne. "Aid to the 'Enemy'?" *ChrLiv* 14 (Dec., 1967), 11. MCC workers in Vietnam face the dilemma of trying to remain neutral in a country at war.

Peachey, J. Lorne. "North Vietnam Not Our Enemy." *ChrLiv* 15 (Apr., 1968), 11. MCC shipments of aid to North Vietnamese war victims illustrates the view that aid given in the name of Christ should not be limited on the basis of political affiliation.

Peachey, Paul L. "Rehabilitation in the Name of Christ." *ChrMon* 40 (Jan., 1948), 16-17. Outlines the plight of Belgian collaborators with the enemy and MCC efforts to provide help to their families.

Peachey, Paul L. "The Relevancy of the Peace Witness of the Prophetic Christian Community." Paper presented at Church Peace Mission Consulation on the Relevance of Christian Pacifism, New Windsor, Md., Sept. 23-24, 1954. Pp. 5. MHL. Published Akron: MCC, 1953. Pp. 5. MHL, MLA/BeC.

Peachey, Urbane, comp. "Mennonite Peace Theology Colloquium II: Theology of Justice, Bethel Mennonite Church, North Newton, Ks., Nov. 15-18, 1978, [Papers]." Akron, Pa.: MCC Peace Section, 1979. MHL. Includes: Brubacher, Ray, "Case Study of Southern Africa," pp. 9; Keeney, William, "Reactions to Case Study of Southern Africa," pp. 3; Friesen, LeRoy, "A

Brief on the Southern Africa Case Study," pp. 3; Lind, Millard, "Programmatic Decision/Action in Southern Africa: Implications of the Decision from the Viewpoint of Biblical Theology," pp. 4; Rempel, Henry, "Response to the South Africa Case Study," pp. 4; Wiebe, Menno, "Canadian Northern Development, An Account of the Churchill-Nelson River Diversion Project," pp. 18; Schroeder, David, "Case Study: Native Concerns, The Frame of Reference from the Standpoint of Biblical Theology," pp. 2; LaRogne, Emma, "Response to Menno Wiebe," pp. 3; Klassen, A. J., "Response to Northern Development Case Study," pp. 2; Vogt, Roy, "Response to Menno Wiebe's Case Study of Canadian Northern Development," pp. 4; Defehr, Art, "Northern Development and Justice: The Business Perspective," pp. 3; Kraus, C. Norman, "Toward a Biblical Perspective on Justice," pp. 17; Stoltzfus, Edward, "Response to Study Paper 'Toward a Biblical Perspective on Justice' by C. Norman Krause," pp. 3; Gajardo, Joel V., "The Latin American Situation: The Challenge of Liberation Theology," pp. 12; Lind, Millard, review, *Marx and the Bible* by José Miranda (Maryknoll, NY: Orbis, 1974. Pp. 338), pp. 9.

Peachey, Urbane, ed. *Mennonite Statements on Peace and Social Concerns, 1900-1978.* Akron: Mennonite Central Committee US Peace Section, 1980. Pp. 262. Statements and actions of major Mennonite general conferences and a few district conferences, arranged topically according to conference.

Peachey, Urbane. "The Middle East Cauldron and Mennonite Involvement." *MennRep* 3 (Sept. 3, 1973), 7. Discusses Mideast conflict factors shaping MCC work in Jordan, and describes MCC projects there.

Pellman, Phyllis. "What I Heard the Arabs Say." *GH* 62 (Sept. 16, 1969), 806-807. Participant in MCC Middle East Study Tour heard Arabs calling for an end to Zionism and a homeland for Palestinians to end the present Mideast conflicts.

Penner, Helen. "Have a Heart in a World of Need." *ChrMon* 34 (Nov., 1942), 338-39. Describes MCC relief work in France and the motivating belief in nonviolence and aggressive good will.

Preheim, Marion Keeney. "A Miracle Sent by God." *EV* 92 (June 10, 1979), 14. An MCC release relating the imprisonment and release of the Russian dissident Baptist prisoner Georgi Vins.

Preheim, Vern. "MCC's Efforts in the Middle East." *GH* 62 (June 10, 1969), 517-18. Describes MCC activities, primarily in Jordan, which range from war relief and reconstruction to education and crafts projects.

Preheim, Vern. "Mennonite Churches and Returning Service Volunteers." *GH* 65 (Feb. 22, 1972), 177. Service volunteers encounter difficulty upon reentry; they can be helped and they can also make meaningful contributions for further church extension and growth.

"Race Is Major Issue at Annual Peace Meetings." *CanMenn* 12 (Jan. 14, 1964), 1. MCC Peace Section's annual meeting in Chicago discusses race as priority item.

"Reconciliation in North America and Vietnam." *Forum* 8 (Jan., 1975), 4-6. An interview with Max Ediger, assistant director of MCC programs in Vietnam, focusing on his work in Vietnam and his perceptions of his mediator role in Vietnam and now in North America.

"Relief Groups Try to Avert Mass Death in Kampuchea." *GH* 72 (Nov. 6, 1979), 872. Various relief groups including MCC have tried to avert the mass starvation in Kampuchea, but most of their efforts have met with little success.

"Religious Statements on Amnesty." *RepConsS* 30 (Apr., 1973), 3-8. Prints the MCC Peace Section statement on amnesty (Mar. 31, 1973) alongside a number of similar statements from other religions and peace groups.

"Resettlement Program Promoting Grave Injustices to South Africans." *MennRep* 9 (Oct. 15, 1979), 2. MCC is attempting to respond to the adverse conditions of several million black people who are being systematically resettled in camps by the white minority rule in South Africa.

"Responses to Amnesty." *Menn* 88 (Apr. 24, 1973), 269-71. Seven persons share their responses to "A Declaration on Amnesty," a statement by the Mennonite Central Committee Peace Section. Responses range from unconditional support of the document's call for universal amnesty for war resisters, to disagreement with the statement, to discouragement that amnesty will in fact become a reality.

(Review). *Gewaltlosigkeit im Täufertum,* by Clarence Bauman. "New Book on Nonviolence in Anabaptism Recommended." *CanMenn* 17 (Sept. 19, 1969), 3. MCC Peace Section recommends book as an investigation of the theological ethic of North German Anabaptism during the Reformation which focuses on the theology underlying the Anabaptist concern with nonviolence.

Ratzlaff, Erich L. "Another Point of View on Brazil." *Menn* 85 (Dec. 1, 1970), 743. There is a paradox in being sympathetic to revolutionary leftist movements while supporting MCC, which was begun to rescue people from revolutionary violence.

Ratzlaff, Vernon. "A Christian Thinks About His Nation: A Response to Eight Lectures in March." *MennRep* 4 (May 13, 1974), 7. Responding in part to MCC Peace Section Assembly lectures, Ratzlaff reflects on the dream of the American destiny, civil religion, and an appropriate Christian concern for the nation that does not idolize it.

Redekop, John H. "A Call to Consistency." *MBH* 16 (Aug. 5, 1977), 10. Concerned about MCC personnel identification with black resistance movements in Africa, author cannot reconcile pacifism with terrorism.

Redekop, John H. "Clarifying the Call to Consistency." *MBH* 16 (Oct. 14, 1977), 12. Continued concern that MCC policies may be compromising its pacifist, non-political stance.

Redekop, John H. "Penner vs. Beaver County Draft Board." *MBH* 9 (Aug. 21, 1970), 8. MCC assists a CO from Oklahoma to make his stand before the courts. Article discusses how one can learn from this encounter.

Redekop, John N. "Christians in a World of International Confrontation." *Citizens and Disciples: Christian Essays on Nationalism.* Akron: MCC Peace Section, [1974], 26-30. Pp. 30. MHL. Contends that nationalism is neither primarily a blessing or a curse but a fact, a dynamic which can be used for good or evil. A constructive nationalism recognizes the nation-state system as sub-Christian, checks militant nationalism without becoming a crusading universalist, and listens to prophetic criticisms.

Reimer, Vic. "MCC (US) Promoting Refugee Sponsorship." *Menn* 94 (Oct. 2, 1979), 582. Interest by US Mennonites in sponsoring refugees from Southeast Asia is increasing.

Rennir, Amy. "MCC Helping Local Churches Respond to Nicaraguan Needs." *Menn* 94 (Sept. 4, 1979), 518. MCC is responding to various needs in Nicaragua resulting from nearly a year of intense fighting between the Nicaraguan National Guard and the Sandinista rebels.

"Seventy Will Discuss Duty to the State in Chicago Meeting." *CanMenn* 5 (Sept. 27, 1957), 1. Noted Mennonite speakers address the conference planned by MCC peace section.

"Sponsorship Rises to 2,500; Over 200 Have Arrived." *MennRep* 9 (Sept. 3, 1979), 1. MCC (Canada) reports on the Canadian Mennonite churches' response to the refugees coming from Southeast Asia.

"Statement on Capital Punishment Adopted by MCC (Canada)." *MennRep* 3 (Jan. 22, 1973), 10. MCC (Canada) resolution of opposition to capital punishment is based on sociological studies, biblical guidelines, and historical precedent, including the Mennonite history of opposition to the taking of life.

"Stress in Chad Underscores Divisions." *Menn* 94 (Mar. 13, 1979), 199. MCC volunteers in Ndjamina, Chad, scene of a new outbreak of civil war, are believed to have left the city for more peaceful areas in the south.

"Supreme Court Broadens Definition of Religious Conscientious Objection." *CanMenn* 13 (Sept. 14, 1965), 2. An MCC report on a US Supreme Court ruling concerning religious conscientious objection. MCC is urging the government to recognize freedom of conscience without attempting to require a particular theological point of view.

Schmidt, Linda. "Peace Section (US) Opposes Registration; Less Clear About Nuclear Issues." *Menn* 94 (June 26, 1979), 438. MCC Peace Section (US) annual meeting agenda includes proposed draft registration legislation, discussion of various peace education projects, and debate on nuclear energy.

Schrag, Martin H. "The Cross on a Canteen." *GH* 69 (July 20, 1976), 562. Refers to the story of an MCC worker in Vietnam meeting a Christian North Vietnamese soldier with a cross on his canteen, and concludes that Christian commitment to God precludes rule by the sword.

Schroeder, David. "Nationalism and Internationalism: Ground Rules for a Discussion." *Citizens and Disciples: Christian Essays on Nationalism.* Akron: MCC Peace Section, [1974], 1-3. MHL. Also in *Menn* 89 (July 9, 1974), 426-27. Suggests that there are basic biblical principles that can help to form a frame of reference within which the questions of nationalism and internationalism can be discussed constructively. Schroeder concludes that Christians are called to be citizens of the state also, discerning carefully among national policies which work for and against justice and goodness.

Sensenig, Donald E., and Sensenig, Doris, *et al.* "Letter from Saigon." *GH* 65 (June 20, 1972), 530-31. Mennonite missionaries and MCC workers in Vietnam send letter to President Nixon describing the hopelessness of the US involvement and appealing for cessation of hostile action by all US military forces.

Shelly, Maynard. "Bangladesh: Hope, Despair, Opportunity." *EV* 87 (Mar. 10, 1974), 6. Some students in Bangladesh are resorting to political agitation, others are turning swords into plowshares. MCC is also trying to create change.

Shelly, Maynard. "Peacemakers in a Guerilla Tent?" *CanMenn* 17 (July 11, 1969), 1. During a Middle East tour, 21 American and Canadian Mennonites met an al-fateh leader in a refugee camp in Jordan. Refugees have tried nonviolent means for 20 years, he said, and no one has listened. Now they will fight to the death to regain their homeland. The tour was sponsored by the MCC peace section.

Shelly, Maynard. "Peacemakers In Spite of Ourselves." *MennRep* 8 (Oct. 16, 1978), 6. Senator Bob Dole's visit to an MCC relief sale in Kansas gave this fundraising event for peace the appearance of condoning militaristic government policies.

Shenk, Stanley C. "It Has Been Ten Years." *GH* 65 (May 30, 1972), 478-79. On the ten-year anniversary of MCC Paxman Daniel Gerber's capture in Vietnam, the author reflects on Dan's witness, the home life which prepared him for difficult experiences, and the message he might have about American involvement in Southeast Asia if he did return.

Sherk, J. Harold, comp. "Report of the MCC Peace Section Study Conference." Winona Lake, Ind., Nov. 9-12, 1950. Pp. 149. MHL. Includes: Toews, J. B., "Nonresistance and the Gospel," 45-50; Wenger, J. C., "Nonresistance and the Gospel," 51-52; Hershberger, Guy F., "The Disciple of Christ and the State," 53-58; Kreider, Robert, "The Disciple of Christ and the State," 59-65; Fretz, J. Winfield, "Nonresistance and the Social Order," 66-72; Good, Noah, "Nonresistance and the Social Order," 73-76; Gingerich, Melvin, "What About the Noncombatant Position?" 77-85; Rempel, J. G., "What About the Noncombatant Position?" 86-90; Hostetter, C. N. Jr., "Our Peace Witness to Christendom," 91-95; Peachey, Paul, "Our Peace Witness to Christendom," 96-100; Smucker, Don, "Nonresistance and Pacifism," 101-108; Fast, H. A., "CPS Past and Future," 109-112; Sherk, J. Harold, "ASW Past and Future," 113-16; Graber, J. D., "Nonresistance and Missions," 117-20; Pannabecker, S. F., "Nonresistance and Missions," 121-26; Janzen, A. E., "Nonresistance and Missions," 127-28.

Shetler, Sanford G., ed. "Is the Mennonite Central Committee Peace Section Becoming Political?" *GfT* 9 (Sept.-Oct., 1974), 15, 20. Questions whether the church should tell the government how to run its business, as the Mennonite lobby in Washington does.

Siebert, Allan J. "MCC (Manitoba): Questions on Police Force Rouse Delegates." *MennRep* 9 (Dec. 24, 1979), 3. Discussion at the MCC (Manitoba) annual meeting on the shooting and killing of a Mennonite youth by an RCMP officer led to a resolution calling MCC (Man.) to develop a study guide on Mennonite relations to the police force.

Siebert, Allan J. "Response to Refugees Criticized as 'Cautious and Restrained'." *MennRep* 9 (Dec. 10, 1979), 1, 3. MCC (Canada) refugee assistance program has encountered criticism in recent weeks over its limited response to the refugee crisis in Southeast Asia.

Smucker, Barbara Claassen. *Henry's Red Sea.* Scottdale: Herald Press, 1955. Pp. 108. Eleven-year-old Henry Bergen and his family are Mennonite refugees waiting in Berlin after having fled post-World War II Russia. Through the eyes of this family, Claassen Smucker provides a moving account of refugee experiences, the work of MCC and the dangerous trip across the Russian zone of Germany to meet the SS Volendam at Bremerhaven. For children ages 8-12.

Smucker, Donovan E. "A Statement of Position to the Armed Services Committee of the US Senate Concerning Peacetime Conscription and the Christian Conscience Against War." *Menn* 63 (May 4, 1948), 6-7. Statement made at public hearing Mar. 31, 1948, on behalf of MCC, vigorously opposing peacetime conscription and witnessing against war itself.

Snyder, William T. "The Road Ahead for MCC." *EV* 93 (Oct. 10, 1980), 5. MCC Executive Secretary outlines areas of the world marked by famine and war that will receive MCC's attention in the coming year.

Sprunger, Joseph. "'What's It Like to Live in Vietnam?' . . . Some Reflections." *Forum* (Mar., 1972), 4. A former MCC worker reflects on his experiences in Vietnam, the physical, cultural, and sociological destruction of the war, and his growing appreciation of the Vietnamese people.

Stoltzfus, Victor. "A History of the Peace Section of the Mennonite Central Committee." Paper presented to Mennonite History and Church History classes, Goshen College Biblical Seminary, Goshen, Ind., 1959. Pp. 57. MHL.

Stoltzfus, Victor. "A Talk with Vincent Harding." *ChrLiv* 9 (Oct., 1962), 11, 37-38, 40. MCC representative's views on racial injustice and peaceful resistance.

Stoner, John K. "MCC Testifies on Draft." *EV* 92 (July 10, 1979), 14. K. B. Hoover, a representative of the Brethren in Christ Church to MCC, appeared May 21 before the Senate Armed Services Subcommittee on Manpower and Personnel to testify for MCC Peace Section against the renewal of draft registration.

Studer, Gerald C. "That Controversial Peace Symbol." *GH* 63 (Aug. 11, 1970), 662-63; *CanMenn* 18 (Aug. 21, 1970), 5. Presents the findings of his research into the origins of the inverted broken cross within a circle, research which shows no demonic or communist connections. Also discusses the meanings of the MCC peace symbol.

Swartzendruber, Fred. "A Mennonite Lobby in Washington?" *Forum* 12 (Dec., 1978), 1-3. Describes the functions of the MCC Peace Section office in Washington, DC, and the difficult task of relating to a very diverse Mennonite constituency, from those offering strong resistance to a Mennonite presence in Washington to those who are strong supporters.

"The Dilemma of Christian Involvement." *ChrLead* 28 (Nov. 9, 1965), 14-15. MCC relief operations, as a part of the Mennonite peace witness, must be expanded in spite of the danger of being identified with American military violence.

"The Mennonite Civilian Service Program." *GH* 33 (Jan. 9, 1941), 867, 879. A description of the history and functioning of Civilian Service and the MCC Peace Committee.

"Thirty Evangelicals to Discuss War Attitudes." *CanMenn* 11 (July 19, 1963), 1, 9. MCC Peace Section arranges a summer seminar at Winona Lake, Ind.

Thomas, Everett. "What I Heard the Israelis Say." *GH* 62 (Sept. 16, 1969), 807-808. Participant in MCC Middle East Study Tour heard Israelis calling for the survival of the Jewish state at any military price.

Trocmé, André. "Christian Nonresistance Only Alternative to Communism." *CanMenn* 7 (Oct. 16, 1959), 1, 10. Discussion with MCC personnel at Akron, Pa.

Unruh, John D. *In the Name of Christ: A History of the Mennonite Central Committee and its Service, 1920-1951.* Scottdale, Pa.: Herald Press, 1952. Pp. 404. Detailed summary of the organization and activities of MCC in various parts of the world. The connections between peace and service, both in terms of relief work as a practical Christian response to problems created by war and in terms of theological understandings, become very clear in the MCC context.

Unsigned. "MCC Administrative Policy." *CPS Bull* 1 (May 8, 1943), 1, 3. Examines assumptions behind MCC administrative policy and describes functioning principles.

Unsigned. "The 'MCC': What Is It?" *CPS Bull Supp* 5 (Sept. 26, 1946), 1, 3-4. Describes the beginnings of Mennonite Central Committee

and its expansion into various forms of relief and peace work.

"Vietnam Workers Urge Cut in Arms Flow." *GH* 67 (July 2, 1974), 536. Reprints the text of a letter from 22 MCC and Eastern Board of Missions workers to congressional committees responsible for military funding in Vietnam. Letter calls for drastic reductions in military hardware to Vietnam.

"Volunteer to Defuse Vietnam Bombs." *MBH* 12 (Oct. 19, 1973), 15-16. MCC volunteers will be doing exploratory work in the Vietnamese countryside to find ways to help local farmers clear their land of unexploded bombs.

Vogt, Roy. "Art Defehr's Proposal for an MCC Food Bank." *MennMirror* 4 (June, 1975), 14. Urges farmers and others to support Defehr's proposal.

"War Tax Conference at Kitchener." *God and Caesar* 1 (June, 1975), 2-3. Announcement of a conference for theological and practical discernment on war tax issues sponsored by the General Conference Mennonite Church, Mennonite Church, Brethren in Christ, and the MCC Peace Section to be held in Kitchener, Ont., Oct. 30-Nov. 1.

"War Tax Packet." [Akron, Pa.]: MCC, Feb., 1976. MHL. Includes: Stoner, John K., "Suggestions for Use of Packet and for Additional Resources," pp. 2; King, Col. Edward L. (retired), "Militarism in Today's Society . . . in the United States, . . . in Canada," pp. 12; Kaufman, Donald D., "A Chronology of Wars Reflecting the 'Anabaptist' Response to War Taxes," pp. 28; Klaassen, Walter, "Anabaptism and Church/Government Issues," pp. 12; Miller, Marlin, "The Christian's Relationship to the State and Civil Authority," pp. 6; Swartley, Willard, "The Christian and Payment of War Taxes," pp. 18; Hess, James, "The Case for the Payment of All Taxes," pp. 8; Ediger, Peter J., "Christ and Caesar: A Ballad of Faith," pp. 4; Lehman, Carl M., "Tax ResistanceA Form of Protest?" pp. 2; Stoltzfus, Ruth C., "War Tax Research Report: Challenging Withholding Law on First Amendment Grounds," pp. 9; National Council for World Peace Tax Fund, *Support the World Peace Tax Fund* (brochure); National Council for World Peace Tax Fund, "Conscientious Objection for Taxpayers Too?" pp. 1; National Council for World Peace Tax Fund, "Commonly Asked Questions About the World Peace Tax Fund Act," pp. 1; Shank, Duane, "World Peace Tax Fund ActSome Unanswered Questions," pp. 2; MCC Peace Section, "Taxes for Military Purposes" (brochure); Church of the Brethren Annual Conference, "Taxation for War," pp. 6. Also includes a questionnaire on war taxes and a bibliography on war taxes.

"Witnessing to God's Will for Peace." *CanMenn* 18 (July 17, 1970), 16. Purpose, organization, and action of the MCC Peace Section are outlined. The draft, the Washington office, the Middle East, and International relationships are topics receiving special emphasis.

Wiebe, Katie Funk. "Caught in the Draft." *GH* 72 (Aug. 21, 1979), 667; *ChrLead* 42 (June 19, 1979), 19. With impending conscription, we are urged to be more prepared than we were for the World War II crisis. Peacemaker registration through MCC Peace Section is one suggestion for getting ready.

Wiebe, Katie Funk. "The Gospel and the Nation." *ChrLead* 39 (Apr. 13, 1976), 19. Reports on the MCC Peace Assembly on "Civil Religion and the American Empire" held Mar. 21-23, 1976 in Washington, DC.

Wiebe, Menno. Letter to the Editor. *God and Caesar* 1 (June, 1975), 7. In response to a previous letter regarding a question on war taxes in Canada, the writer suggests contacting the MCC (Canada) office in Ottawa and reading the book *Making a Killing* by Ernie Regehr.

Wiens, Marie K. (Review). *More-with-Less Cookbook*, ed. Doris J. Longacre. Scottdale: Herald Press, 1976. *ChrLead* 39 (Apr. 27, 1976), 16. The book, commissioned by Mennonite Central Committee in response to world food needs, starts with recognizing the shortage of food, builds on the premise that Mennonites are basically thrifty people who believe that waste is sin, and shows correlation between food habits and peaceful way of life.

Wiggers, Arverd. *History and Report of the 1-W Program of the Church of God in Christ (Mennonite): Covering Nearly Ten Years of Activity from the Fall of 1950-July 1, 1960.* Galva, Ks.: Christian Public Service, Inc., [1960?] Pp. 112. MHL. In addition to summary statement of the work of various units, the report addresses such topics as the relationship with MCC, spirituality in the units, improving our peace witness, etc.

Yoder, John H. "Why Speak to Government." *CanMenn* 14 (Dec. 13, 1966), 10; *GH* 59 (Jan. 25, 1966), 73-74. Background paper for the MCC consultation in Minneapolis. We should speak to government because: we love our neighbor; we reject idolatry; the statespersons in North America are church people; we are Christian missionaries; we live in a democracy; we are already involved. In so speaking, what do we say? That God is on the side of humanity; that human beings cannot be trusted to be their own judges; that violence is no basis for social peace.

Zehr, Daniel. "Inter-Mennonite Peace Retreat Conducted by MCC (Ontario)." *CanMenn* 13 (Sept. 28, 1965), 1, 2, 14. A synopsis of messages and talks on the teaching of peace as portrayed in the Bible and through Christ with an application to the current situation. Edgar Metzler and Frank C. Peters were the main speakers.

Zehr, Daniel. "Special Committee Advises on Peace." *CanMenn* 16 (Mar. 5, 1968), 4. Peace witness apologetic by Zehr on his appointment as MCC (Canada) peace secretary.

Ziegler, Donald. "CO's Strengthen Faith at House of Friendship." *MBH* 12 (Aug. 24, 1973), 5. Describes the work of two conscientious objectors from widely different non-Anabaptist backgrounds who have volunteered their services through MCC to work at the House of Friendship in Kitchener, Ont.

Ziegler, Donald. "Leamington Hosts MCC Annual Meeting." *MBH* 12 (Feb. 23, 1973), 2-3. Among other concerns, the MCC annual meeting adopted in principle a working draft on amnesty and a resolution on reconstruction in Indochina.

Ziegler, Donald. "MCC Examines Self and Issues." *EV* 86 (Mar. 10, 1973), 5, 6. MCC met for its annual meeting in Leamington, Ont., to discuss the progress of the MCC self-study, to adopt guidelines on the use of government funds, to resolve interest in reconstruction in Indochina, to consider a working draft statement on universal amnesty for conscientious objectors, and to recognize four dynamic leaders of past inter-Mennonite activities.

# B. Development

Atmosuwito, S. "The Desert: for Peace or War?" *ChrLiv* 8 (July, 1961), 36-37. Options for use of desert lands include development for food production or the testing of nuclear weapons.

Bauman, Clarence. "Conscientious Objection and Alternative Service." *CanMenn* (Mar. 13, 1959), 2, 11; "Conscientious Objection in Germany," *Menn* 74 (Apr. 14, 1959), 231-32. An analysis of the political and social climate of West Germany and how this relates to the pacifist. Traces recent development of legal provisions for conscientiouos objectors and describes the EIRENE program in Morocco, a joint project for the historic peace churches and FOR.

Beechy, Atlee. "To Aid or Not to Aid? Some Reflections on Voluntary Agencies and Vietnam." Paper presented at Pendle Hill, Pa., Aug. 14, 1975. Pp. 18. MHL.

Bontrager, Herman. "Is Development Possible?" *Forum* 10 (Apr., 1977), 4-5. Although the United States has attempted to promote development in Third World countries, there are more destitute people in the world today than ever before. With the knowledge we have of what does *not* work in development projects, the writer challenges us to make more concerted and more realistic development efforts.

Bontrager, Herman. "Relief, Development, and Justice: Synthesis or Tension?" *Peace Section Newsletter* 9 (Aug.-Sept., 1979), 4-8. Notes that the expressed concern to make MCC programs more sensitive to justice problems has revealed the important need for MCC staff to develop a self-consciousness as workers for justice. Lists some of the MCC projects for justice.

"Canadians Claim US Imperialism." *CanMenn* 18 (Mar. 13, 1970), 3. Fifty-three American and Canadian Mennonites join to conduct a Christian Citizenship Seminar in New York City. Focusing on each nation's problems (imperialism, poverty, native American policies, external affairs, bureaucracy), an attempt is made to pinpoint the Christian's responsibility as the member of a nation and of the world community.

DeFehr, Arthur. "Development from an Anabaptist Perspective or Which is the Other Side of the Boat?" *Direction* 5 (Oct., 1976), 12-19. Identifies the unique contribution that Mennonites can make in development.

DeFehr, Arthur. "Garden of God." *Direction* 4 (Apr., 1975), 294-302. Collectively, people must tend the garden God has given to them, rather than exploit it for their own use.

Drescher, John M. "Graham's Vietnam Visit." *GH* 60 (Feb. 1, 1967), 117. Drescher praises Graham's evangelistic work but seriously questions his identification, as an evangelist, with American nationalism and imperialism in Vietnam.

Dueck, Allan. "Implications of the Early Anabaptist View of Economics for Hutterites and Mennonites Today." Paper entered in John Horsch Essay Contest, Goshen College, Goshen, Ind., May 15, 1972. Pp. 20. MHL.

Ediger, Max. "Justice Is Not Just Us." *Intercom* 24 (Jan., 1980), 6-7. Describes the difference between community development and community organization and urges MCC to work at organization in order to further justice.

Franz, Delton. "Exported to Latin America: Safe Religion or Costly Discipleship?" *MCC PS Newsletter* 9 (Aug.-Sept., 1979), 1-4. Personal visit to Latin America raises concern about the impact of Mennonite mission and development programs in those countries. Concludes the Mennonite mission and service/development programs in Latin America have tended to take a "safe" theological and tactical posture.

Franz, Delton. "The Other Arms Race." *Menn* 84 (Oct. 21, 1969), 640. Information on US arms sales to other countries making continued warfare possible but limiting success in promoting agricultural and educational development.

Franz, Delton. "Update on US Food and Development Aid." *MCC PS Wash. Memo* 9 (Sept.-Oct., 1977), 3-5. Evaluates recent US development aid legislation in light of its contribution to justice toward the poor.

Franz, Delton. "US Senators Propose Department of Peace." *CanMenn* 16 (Dec. 31, 1968), 1, 2. The proposal is for an umbrella organization for the Agency for International Development, the Peace Corps, and the Arms Control and Disarmament Agency.

Franz, Delton. "Washington Report: Middle East War: Lessons Not Learned." *MennRep* 3 (Nov. 12, 1973), 7. The superpowers contributed to resumption of open war in the Mideast by arming Egypt and Israel. Alternatives, such as economic development aid to lessen national insecurity, are feasible, in light of de-escalation strategies that have worked in the past.

Friesen, Dorothy and Stoltzfus, Gene. "Pantabangan: Victim of Development." *The Other Side* 15 (May, 1979), 23-29. The story of how a village was destroyed in the name of Third World development on the largest island in the Philippines, Luzon.

Gish, Arthur G. *Beyond the Rat Race*. Scottdale: Herald Press, 1973. Pp. 192. Handbook on simple living includes discussion of the connection between wealth and violence; the American standard of living is a basic cause of violence because it is based on imperialism and exploitation.

Heisey, M. S. "More Than Just Crafts." *Sojourners* 8 (Oct., 1979), 25. A description of Jubilee crafts located in Philadelphia, Pa. This self-help program distributes crafts made by people from Bangladesh, the Dominican Republic, Colombia, Haiti, and the Philippines.

Hershberger, Guy F. "Christian Missions and Colonialism: The Christian Witness to the State." (Part 3). *GH* 53 (Sept. 20, 1960), 826. The identification of missions with paternalistic colonialism is an area in which a stronger witness to the state has been needed in the past. The Christian mission today must still speak out against paternalism and colonialism in word and deed.

---

*For additional listing, see Supplement, pp. 717-719.

Hershberger, Guy F. "What Is the Meaning of the War in China?" *YCC* 18 (Oct. 31, 1937), 764a. The war in China has many roots in a variety of conflicts with Japan and the western countries. China has many resources and is vulnerable because of less development in relation to the other countries.

Hertzler, Daniel. "To Henry G. Ciocca, The Nestle Co." *GH* 72 (Feb. 13, 1979), 152. A letter addressed to the above, identifying their highly developed ability in the areas of production and marketing of goods but also their need to determine whether the goods are really needed or are a hindrance to those who purchase them. Providing real help to all those in need of the basics for sustaining life is the key problem.

Jacobs, Donald R. *The Christian Stance in a Revolutionary Age*. Scottdale: Herald Press, Focal Pamphlet No. 14, 1968. Pp. 32. Describes the factors influencing social change in the developing nations and the issues, such as tribalism, racism, and nationalism, which confront the church in these areas. Then, in this context, Jacobs contends that peace and development are two parts of the same issue— that any peace theology must necessarily speak to the issues of distributive justice.

Kehler, Larry. "Structures and Nationalism Looms [sic] Large at MCC Meeting." *MBH* 14 (Feb. 7, 1975), 10-12. At the annual meeting, the committee passed a resolution on world hunger calling for reduced military expenditure and increased food development.

Kehler, Larry. "Sympathetic Ear Needed for Community Development Work." *CanMenn* 16 (Jan. 16, 1968), 6. A report on a MCC community development project on the Beardy Indian Reserve near Rosthern, Saskatchewan. The project headed by Bill Siemens involves listening to the people, teaching leathercraft to a paraplegic, and attending meetings in an effort to relate meaningfully in a non-governmental manner to the native American population.

Klassen, J. M. "Voluntary Agencies Play Unique Role in International Development." *CanMenn* 18 (June 12, 1970), 4, 8. Of 150 Canadian voluntary agencies engaged in international programs, 50 are religious in character. The author reviews why these fill an important and unique role in international development.

Koontz, Gayle Gerber. "Mennonite Peace in the Middle East Puzzle." *MBH* 13 (Aug. 23, 1974), 16-17. People-oriented MCC efforts, cooperation with Middle Eastern churches, and food and development programs will continue to receive Mennonite attention in the Mideast conflict.

Koontz, Ted. "Peace Groups Examine Development Strategies." *MBH* 12 (June 1, 1973), 14-15. Reports on the annual Intercollegiate Peace Fellowship Conference at the Church Center for the United Nations in New York which focused on "Third World Development and Exploitation."

Kreider, Alan. "The Gospel No to the Bomb." *Dropping the Bomb: The Church and the Bomb Debate*, ed. John Gladwin. London: Hodder and Stoughton, 1985. Pp. 74-95. Technological development, self-righteous rhetoric, and nuclear proliferation are undermining deterrence as a viable nuclear strategy. The values implicit within deterrence undermine it morally. As the stronger party in the nuclear stalemate, the West must take incremental, unilateral steps to reverse the arms race.

Kreider, Carl. "Trouble in the Congo." *ChrLiv* 7 (Nov., 1960), 18, 35. Analysis of the violence and military conflict in the Congo following its independence from Belgium.

Kroeker, David. "An 'Upbeat' Conference in Canada's Oil Capital." *MennRep* 9 (July 23, 1979), 1. Among the decisions made at the 77th annual Canadian General Conference session were decisions to make capital punishment an issue for study in preparation for 1980, and to study a joint MCC-Mennonite World Conference statement on militarism and development.

La Roque, Emma. "Did the Devil Make You Do It?" *The Other Side* 13 (May, 1977), 73-74. Examines how Christianity and imperialism have affected the native American world.

Lapp, John A. "Congo Civil War." *ChrLiv* 12 (Mar., 1965), 18, 35. Analysis of the problems faced by the Congo in attempting to create a stable nation-state.

Lapp, John A. "What the Canal Debate is All About." *ChrLiv* 24 (Nov., 1977), 19-20. The real issue for the US in the canal debate is the question of peaceful transition of authority or continued domination and imperialism.

"Mennonites Plan for Minority Youth." *RepConsS* 34 (Mar., 1977), 4. Mennonite Economic Development Associates to consider proposal to provide job opportunities for Mennonite minority youth for whom the military is often the most viable employment option.

Martin, Earl S. and Martin, Patricia Hostetter. "Who Are You Kidding, Brother?" *GH* 62 (Oct. 28, 1969), 938. Community development workers with Vietnam Christian Service reflect on giving aid to the Vietnamese when they resent the American military and economic presence.

Metzler, Edgar. "New Name for Peace Is World Development." *CanMenn* 15 (Apr. 18, 1967), 1, 11. Pope John encyclical "Peace on Earth" is reviewed with implications for our own churches: service ministries must be integral part of total mission and witness of the church; the churches should make sacrifices to provide for greatly increased service opportunities.

Metzler, James E. "Vietnam, American Tragedy." *GH* (May 2, 1967), 393. The identification of Christianity with Americanism (i.e., western ideologies, colonialism, war, anti-communism, white racism) has alienated much of the nonwestern world from the Christian message. Vietnam is our symbol of failure and a call to repentance.

Miller, Mary Alene Cender. "The Yin/Yang Potential for Discipleship: Can Yin/Yang Be Normative for Peacemaking/Mission?" MA in Peace Studies thesis, AMBS, May 10, 1983. Pp. 87. This interpretation and critique of Yin/Yang philosophy in light of its peacemaking potential begins by noting that the Christian mission has often taken an oppressive yang position in relation to Oriental culture and that fact requires repentance. Next, the socio-historical development is explored with particular attention to the way gender has been assigned to yin/yang and other applications of the philosophy to the social structure. Finally, consideration is given to some specific theological dimensions of yin/yang such as God, Creator and creature, and Jesus. Concludes that while yin/yang symbol is not adequate according to the logic of systematic theological formulations, the yin/yang concept of wholeness—harmony, balance, peace, and rest—is a profound comment on Western materialistic perspectives.

Miller, Paul M. "Reverencing God's Image." *Mission-Focus* 6 (Sept., 1978), 11-14. Discusses the meaning and nature of development as it relates to God's commission to "fill and subdue the earth" (Gen. 1:28). "Reverencing God's image" is to be the guiding factor, which is contrasted with the increased violence generally accompanying development.

Mpanya, Mutombo. "African Odyssey: from Colonialism to Identity." MA in Peace Studies thesis, AMBS, 1977. The literary work of 3 major contemporary African writers provides insight into the structural violence resulting from colonialism and maps the difficult course toward peace and wholeness via the rediscovery of an African identity.

Mumaw, Adam H. "Second Company Development Battallion." Paper. Pp. 11. MSHLA.

Peachey, Urbane, comp. "Mennonite Peace Theology Colloquium II: Theology of Justice, Bethel Mennonite Church, North Newton, Ks., Nov. 15-18, 1978, [Papers]." Akron, Pa.: MCC Peace Section, 1979. MHL. Includes: Wiebe, Menno, "Canadian Northern Development, An Account of the Churchill-Nelson River Diversion Project," pp. 18; Schroeder, David, "Case Study: Native Concerns, The Frame of Reference from the Standpoint of Biblical Theology," pp. 2; LaRogne, Emma, "Response to Menno Wiebe," pp. 3; Klassen, A. J., "Response to Northern Development Case Study," pp. 2; Vogt, Roy, "Response to Menno Wiebe's Case Study of Canadian Northern Development," pp. 4; Defehr, Art, "Northern Development and Justice: The Business Perspective," pp. 3.

Preheim, Vern. "Service Frontiers in Community Development." *PCMCP Fourteenth*, 83-91. Held at Harrisonburg, Virginia. Discusses community development as peacemaking.

Ratzlaff, Vernon (Review). *Multinationals and the Peaceable Kingdom*, by Harry Antonides. Toronto: Clarke, Irwin, and Co., 1978. Pp. 201. *MBH* 18 (Sept. 14, 1979), 27. Reviewer summarizes the book's thesis that multinational corporations monopolize available capital and drain the economic capabilities of developing countries.

Redekop, John H. "Christians in a World of International Confrontation." *Menn* 89 (July 9, 1974), 433-35. Describes international exploitation by firms based in North America, and the rise of nationalism which counters this colonialism. Concludes that the present nation-state system produces injustice and inequality, against which Christians must speak out.

Shenk, Lois Landis. "New Music to Dance To." *GH* 72 (Oct. 30, 1979), 849-51. Harold Miller, secretary of the National Christian Council of Kenya's Rural Development Services, talks about the goal of development being "well-being in community" and how the North American churches and Third World should relate for authentic development to take place.

Sider, Ronald J., ed. *Evangelicals and Development: Toward a Theology of Social Change*. Philadelphia: Westminster Press, 1981. A collection of articles addressing the ethical issues of justice and social change from an evangelical Christian point of view.

Sider, Ronald J. "God and the Poor: Toward a Theology of Development." *The Ministry of Development in Evangelical Perspective: A Symposium on the Social and Spiritual Mandate*, ed. Robert Lincoln Hancock. Pasadena: William Carey Library, 1979, 35-59. Uses biblical themes to critique an understanding of development as GNP growth and of development as structural change via revolutionary violence. Concludes by proposing that the church's contribution to development is the concept of the new community.

Snyder, Brian. "MacGuigan Links Disarmament and Development." *PlMon* 3 (Dec., 1980), 1-2. Reprinted from University of Waterloo *Imprint*. Summarizes a speech given by Canadian External Affairs Minister Mark MacGuigan, and includes an interview with him on Canadian policy on arms sales.

Stoltzfus, Eldon Roy. "Power and Intervention: Reflections on the Ethics of Power in Development." MA in Peace Studies thesis, AMBS, 1982. Pp. 63. Suggests that power, as the ability to influence behavior, is an entity in and of itself—and can be either disintegrative or integrative. Further suggests that the character and quality of the power identified from within the story of the people of God, the power most concretely expressed in Jesus, is unique and can be integrated toward creative participation in the church and in the world.

Stoltzfus, Gene. "The Philippines: Nuclear Power Versus People." *MennRep* 9 (Apr. 16, 1979), 2; "Philippines Town Fears Nuclear Development, Government Authority." *Menn* 94 (Apr. 24, 1979), 294. Development of a nuclear power plant worries Barrio people in Morong but attempts to discuss and question this are seen as subversive activity by the government.

Taylor, James. "What Preparing for War Is Costing Us." *MBH* 19 (Nov. 7, 1980), 36. Statistics comparing the cost of defense spending with the cost of development and peace programs.

Thomson, Murray and Regehr, Ernie. *A Time to Disarm*. Montreal, Que.: Harvest House Ltd., 1978. Pp. 38. Speaks to such issues of disarmament as securing a comprehensive test ban treaty, preventing the spread of nuclear weapons, curbing the growth and use of conventional weapons, and linking disarmament and development.

Thomson, Murray and Regehr, Ernie. "Arms Control and Disarmament: New Initiative from the Third World." *PlMon* 1 (Oct., 1977), 1. Relates the failure of development in Third World countries to the failure of disarmament in the 1970s.

Unsigned. "Maione Makes Plea for Justice." *Intercom* 22 (Mar., 1978), 4. CIDA coordinator speaks on justice and development and Christian responsibility.

Weaver, Erma (Review). *The Politics of Food and Faith*, by Jack A. Nelson. Orbis, 1980. Pp. 230. *FStP* 5 (May, 1980), 10-11. Recommends this study of how US military and economic policies prevent self-reliance and the feeding of the poor in underdeveloped countries.

# C. Relief

"A Statement of Purpose Mennonite Disaster Service." *CanMenn* 7 (Nov. 6, 1959), 9. Part of the MDS purpose is to minister to human need in "ways that speak of peace and not for war."

Alderfer, Edwin. "The Giving of the Mennonite Church to Missions, Charities, and Relief." Term paper, Apr. 24, 1945. Pp. 18 (handwritten, includes charts). MHL.

Barnhouse, Donald. "We Are Already Fighting World War Four." *YCC* 48, Part 1, (Nov. 19, 1967), 3; Part 2, (Nov. 26, 1967), 6. World War Four is a war against hunger. We are losing this war because so few have begun to fight.

Beachy, Miriam. "Famine—An Irresistible Army." *YCC* 48 (Oct. 8, 1967), 8. Report on the famine conditions in Bihar, India.

Beechy, Atlee. "Our Relief in a Country at War (Vietnam)." *The Witness of the Holy Spirit*. Ed. Cornelius J. Dyck. Elkhart: MWC, 1967, 199-207. A discussion of Vietnam Christian Service and the place of the Mennonite Church in a country at war.

Beechy, Atlee. "To Aid or Not to Aid? Some

Reflections on Voluntary Agencies and Vietnam." Paper presented at Pendle Hill, Pa., Aug. 14, 1975. Pp. 18. MHL.

Beechy, Atlee (Review). *In the Name of Christ: A History of the Mennonite Central Committee and Its Service 1920-1951*, by John D. Unruh. Scottdale: Herald Press, 1952. Pp. 404. *MHB* 14 (Jan., 1953), 8. Recommends the book as a useful and factual account of MCC relief and service work.

Bender, Bertha Burkholder. "Youth, Church, and State." *YCC* 12, Part 1, (Jan. 4, 1931), 420-21; Part 2, (Jan. 11, 1931), 426-27; Part 3, (Jan. 18, 1931), 434-35; Part 4, (Jan. 25, 1931), 444-45; Part 5, (Feb. 1, 1931), 450, 451, 453; Part 6, (Feb. 8, 1931), 461-62; Part 7, (Feb. 15, 1931), 466-67; Part 8, (Feb. 22, 1931), 479-80; Part 9, (Mar. 1, 1931), 487, 488; Part 10, (Mar. 8, 1931), 491, 493; Part 11, (Mar. 15, 1931), 498, 499; Part 12, (Mar. 22, 1931), 505, 506; Part 13, (Mar. 29, 1931), 515, 517; Part 14, (Apr. 5, 1931), 523, 525; Part 15, (Apr. 12, 1931), 534, 535; Part 16, (Apr. 19, 1931), 539, 541; Part 17, (Apr. 26, 1931), 545-47; Part 18, (May 3, 1931), 559, 560; Part 19, (May 17, 1931), 571, 573; Part 20, (May 31, 1931), 589; Part 21, (June 7, 1931), 595; Part 22, (June 21, 1931), 610; Part 23, (July 5, 1931),

627, 629; Part 24, (July 19, 1931), 645, 646; Part 25, (July 26, 1931), 650, 651; Part 26, (Aug. 2, 1931), 657-59; Part 27, (Aug. 16, 1931), 675-77. Written in a narrative style, the progression of peace-related topics include: the biblical story, the history of the church, issues about responding to government and militarism, e.g., CO status during Civil War and World War I, and Mennonite relief work.

Bender, Harold S. "Money and War: In the Midst of War—Thoughts for Nonresistants," (Part 4). *GH* 35 (Feb. 18, 1943), 1002-1003. The nonresistant Christian should use money sacrificially and try to keep it out of the war effort by refusing to purchase war bonds and by donating excess profits to relief and mission work.

Bender, Harold S. "Russian Relief." Address to the General Conference, Aug. 24, 1933. Pp. 3. MHL.

Bender, John E., comp. "Principles and Problems of International Relief Administration: Notes on Twelve Lectures by Dr. Hertha Kraus." Summer Institute in International Relief Administration, Bryn Mawr College, Bryn Mawr, Pennsylvania, June 13-26, 1943. Pp. 117 MHL. [Also Akron, PA, May 15, 1944.]

Bishop, C. Franklin. "What We Can Do About Hunger." *YCC* 49 (May 26, 1968), 5. Surveys the current hunger problem and suggests ways that the Mennonite church can respond.

Bohn, E. Stanley. "Resources for Peacemaking." *Builder* 18 (Apr., 1968), 15-16. Listing of audio-visual resources prepared for use with series of Sunday school lessons on "Peacemakers in a Broken World." Subjects covered in this listing are: "Introduction to Peacemaking," "Relief and Service as Peacemaking," and "The Peace Witness Itself."

Bontrager, Herman. "Relief, Development, and Justice: Synthesis or Tension?" *MCC PS Newsletter* 9 (Aug.-Sept., 1979), 4-8. Notes that the expressed concern to make MCC programs more sensitive to justice problems has revealed the important need for MCC staff to develop a self-consciousness as workers for justice. Lists some of the MCC projects for justice.

Brademas, John. "'They Cannot Stand Alone'—The Work of the Mennonite Central Committee." *Cong. Record* (Apr. 23, 1964), 1-2. Reprint of an article appearing in the 1963 MCC Annual Report describing case studies in MCC's relief, service, and peace efforts. Brademas, representing northern Indiana, inserts commendatory remarks.

Brinkley, Torrey (Review). *Rich Christians in an Age of Hunger*, by Ronald J. Sider. Downers Grove, IL: Inter Varsity, 1977. In *ChrLead* 40 (Nov. 8, 1977), 11. *Rich Christians* is a bold undertaking, since it tackles one of the world's biggest socio-economic problems: Third World starvation, causes and cures.

Brunk, Ivan, ed. *Dear Alice: The Tribulations and Adventures of J. E. Brunk, a Mennonite Relief Worker in Turkey in 1920-21, as Depicted in Letters to His Wife.* Goshen, Ind.: Historical Committee of the Mennonite Church, 1978. Pp. 187. MHL. Voluminous and sensitive letters describe and interpret one of the first efforts of the newly-organized Mennonite Central Committee to respond to human suffering.

Buchanan, Roy. Letter to the Editor. *GH* 62 (July 1, 1969), 594. World War I conscientious objector describes his experience of finding a response of positive action to the war in relief work in France. Written in response to Tom Brubaker, "Don't Just Say No" (May 27, 1969).

Buckwalter, Clair. Letter to the Editor. *GH* 64 (July 6, 1971), 611. Criticizes *Gospel Herald* reporting of MDS repairing park benches at the Washington Monument because it incorrectly implies that the damage was done by peace demonstrators. Criticizes the MDS action for responding to a peace demonstration as an apparent blessing on Nixon's war policies, when it has not made similar gestures toward reconstruction after race riots.

Buller, Henry P. *The Nazis Interned Me.* Akron, Pa.: MCC, about 1944. Pp. 8. MHL. When a group of relief workers and American diplomats are interned in the "golden cage," a German resort, they spend their time in study and exercise.

Burnett, [Kris]Tina Mast and Kroeker, Wally. "Affluent People Who Neglect the Poor Are Not the People of God." *Menn* 94 (Feb. 20, 1979), 128-29. MCC (International) annual meeting discussed issues of justice and human rights, aid to Vietnam, native American outreach, hunger concerns, and militarism.

Byler, Joseph N. (Archival). Collection contains materials on Mennonite Central Committee—CPS camps and relief work. Goshen, Ind., AMC Hist. Mss. 1-354.

Castro, Emilio. "Hunger and Economic Independence." *MennLife* 20 (July, 1965), 132-35. Theological basis for a concern to meet poverty and other economic issues and the implications for the task.

Coffman, John E. "The Mennonite London Clothing Center." *ChrMon* 36 (Oct., 1944), 297, 301. Describes the program of clothing distribution to war victims.

Coffman, Margery, comp. "Extracts from the Letters of John Coffman, Relief Worker."

*ChrMon* 34 (Feb., 1942), 50-51, 60. Describes distribution of clothing to war victims in London, England.

Coffman, Margery, comp. "Extracts from the Letters of John Coffman, Relief Worker." *ChrMon* 34 (Mar., 1942), 76-77. John Coffman and Peter Dyck describe the work at "The Woodlands," a home for evacuated elderly people.

Davies, Blodwen. "From Militia Tax to Relief." *MennLife* 5 (Oct., 1950), 27-28. A Canadian government exemption for CO's could at one time be attained by paying a government imposed tax. Thomas Reesor helped form the Non-Resistant Movement of Ontario in 1918 which went beyond the government tax by raising $100 for each exempt church member for relief.

DeFehr, Arthur. "Is God for the Poor and Homeless?" *MBH* 19 (Oct. 10, 1980), 2-5. A volunteer who helped set up a relief project in Southeast Asia in the middle of three competing armies reflects on response to human need.

Derstine, C. F. "'If Goods Do Not Cross Frontiers, Armies Will!'" *ChrMon* 35 (Dec., 1943), 381. Advocates free flow of food across national borders to lessen hunger and the subsequent risk of war.

Derstine, C. F. "Interned Mennonite Relief Worker Returns from Germany to America." *ChrMon* 34 (Aug., 1942), 254. Relief worker in Germany taken prisoner when war was declared with the US describes his experiences.

Derstine, C. F. "Mennonite Ex-CPS Men Serve in Sixteen Nations." *ChrMon* 39 (Aug., 1947), 255-56. The MCC post-war relief programs have their roots in the Civilian Public Service program.

Derstine, C. F. "The War Ended, the Malady Lingering On." *ChrMon* 39 (Dec., 1947), 382-83. In the face of continued world tensions, evangelical Christians should pray, practice loving enemies, support European evangelism and relief work.

Derstine, C. F. "War, Pestilence, Famine, and Depression, the Scourges of God on a Sinful and Immoral World." *ChrMon* 23 (Mar., 1931), 93, 95. These social evils are acts of God to bring people to repentance.

Dueck, Allan. "Implications of the Early Anabaptist View of Economics for Hutterites and Mennonites Today." Paper entered in John Horsch Essay Contest, Goshen College, Goshen, Ind., May 15, 1972. Pp. 20. MHL.

Dyck, Cornelius J. *From the Files of MCC.* Vol. 1 in *The Mennonite Central Committee Story.* Scottdale and Kitchener: Herald Press, 1980. Pp. 159. The documents in this volume tell the story of MCC's beginning intertwined with relief work in Russia and refugee settlements in Paraguay. Later reports on immigrations to and settlements in Uruguay, Brazil, and Mexico are also included.

Dyck, Peter J. "South Meadow: A Service of Love 'Unto the Least of These'." *ChrMon* 34 (Oct., 1942), 309-10. Describes an MCC-sponsored children's convalescent home in North Wales as part of the war relief work.

Ebersole, Myron. "A History of Mennonite Central Committee Voluntary Service, 1944-1949." Paper presented to Mennonite History Class, n.d. Pp. 38. MHL.

Eby, Omar. "A Time to Build." *GH* 63 (Feb. 3, 1970), 105. Reviews the events leading to the Nigeria/Biafra war and describes Mennonite and Quaker relief activities during the war.

Eby, Omar. "White Skin Worth More on World Market than Black Skin." *CanMenn* 16 (May 7, 1968), 1, 7. Rejects the idea that the civil war in Nigeria can be ignored because the struggle pits blacks against blacks and appeal to Mennonites to respond generously to the call, when it comes, to give relief for Nigerian war victims. Gives historical background to the Nigeria-Biafra conflict.

Ediger, Elmer. "The Voluntary Service Program." *PCMCP Sixth,* 31-40. North Newton: The Bethel College Press. Held at Goshen College, Goshen, Indiana, Aug. 1-2, 1947. Voluntary service is motivated by Christian teachings and is expressed in a world of need and confusion, during peace as well as war time. The church must continue to develop a well-balanced voluntary service program.

Ediger, Peter J. "Hunger and Handwashing." *God and Caesar* 3 (Nov., 1977), 1. Poem concerning how we have tried to quench our hunger with bombs and bullets rather than with the "Word of the Lord."

Epp, Frank H. "Mennonite-Quaker Cooperation." *Canadian Friend* (Oct.-Nov., 1972), 8. Addressing Quakers at a consultation at Grindstone Island in Sept., 1972, Epp reviews the history of Mennonite-Quaker cooperation in petitioning government and in providing relief and service.

Epp, Merle L. "MCC Voluntary Service, 1946-1955." Paper for Mennonite Missions class, MBS, [Chicago, Ill.], May 9, 1956. Pp. 15 plus charts. AMBS.

Erb, Paul. "The Bloodiest Century in History." *GH*

43 (Oct. 10, 1950), 995. Christians must humbly confess to the part they have played in the wars of the twentieth century and pray for the opportunity to carry relief into Korea as the war there comes to an end.

Fast, Henry A. "The Spiritual Values of Contributing to Relief." *MennLife* 2 (Apr., 1947), 5-7. The author shows the positive side of nonresistance by describing Mennonite relief work as a ministry of reconciliation responding to the hate and destruction of war.

Franz, Delton. "The Moral Factor in the World Hunger Equation." *MCC PS Wash. Memo* 6 (May-June, 1974), 1-2, 6. The American Farm Bureau policy, while supporting the Food for Peace program, is based more on US self-interest than on true compassion.

Franz, Delton. "Witness in Washington." *MennLife* 26 (Dec., 1971), 158-59. As Mennonites we continue to minister to the victims of warfare, hunger, and oppression, but now we also need to be concerned with the underlying causes of suffering.

Fretz, Clarence Y. "Helping the Needy in Spain." *ChrMon* 31 (Apr., 1939), 108. Report of the relief work being done among Spanish war refugees.

Friesen, Dorothy (Review). *Food First: Beyond the Myth of Scarcity,* by Francis Moore Lappe and Joseph Collins. Houghton Mifflin, 1977. *Sojourners* 8 (July, 1978), 35. The underlying assertion is that every country in the world has the resources necessary for its people to free themselves from hunger. The root cause of hunger is the insecurity and poverty of the majority which results from the control over the basic national resources by a few.

Friesen, Paul A. "Relief Work, an Evangelical Witness." Seminary Paper, Goshen College, Goshen, Ind., 1947. Pp. 29. MHL.

"Guiding Principles in Special Emergencies." *Menn* 71 (June 19, 1956), 396, 398. At a time when nationwide preparation for war emergencies is at a height, MCC and MDS urge clear distinction between relief ministries and activities of Civil Defense which "support the war effort."

Gaeddert, Albert M. "The New Draft Legislation." *Menn* 66 (July 31, 1951), 482. Explains how present programs of relief and service can be expanded to accomodate the CO's who will now be "ordered to work" under the new draft law.

Gingerich, Melvin. "The Measure of Love; Christian Youth and the State." *YCC* 22, Part 6, (Feb. 23, 1941), 478. There are numerous ways to give our lives for fellow humans. CO's should be willing to risk everything in order to do relief work to alleviate human suffering.

Gleysteen, Jan (Review). *Transfigured Night,* by Eileen Egan and Elizabeth Reiss. Livingston Pub. Co., 1964. Pp. 186. *ChrLiv* 12 (Dec., 1965), 37. Recommends this documented account of relief work done in Germany following World War II by eighteen relief agencies, including Mennonite work.

Gratz, Delbert L., ed. "Abstracts from the Report on the Mennonite World Relief Conference, August 31 to September 3, 1930 in Danzig Which was Published by Christian Neff." Translated by Paul Schmidt. Akron, Pa., Sept. 1, 1946. Pp. 43. MHL. Includes: Göttner, Erich, "Mutual Aid in the Past," 4-6; Kühler,Wilhelm J., "Dutch Mennonite Relief Work in the Seventeenth and Eighteenth Centuries," 7-11; Klassen, Cornelius F., "The Mennonites of Russia, 1917-1918," 12-19; Gorter, S. H. N., "Relief Work of the Dutch Mennonites," 20; Neff, Christian, "Relief Work of the German Mennonites," 21-22; Fast, Gerhard, "A Supplementary Picture of Relief Work," 23-25; Unruh, Benjamin F., "The Mass Flight of German Farmers from the Soviet Union, Their Basis, The Results in Russia and Its Effects on Foreign Relief Work," 26-32; Gorter, S. H. N., "Emigration to Brazil," 33-35; Hándiges, Emil, "Experiences in Relief Work," 36-37; Kroeker, Jacob, "Relief Work in the Mission Society Light in the East," 38; Horsch, Michael, "The Mennonite Relief Organization Christian Duty," 39-41.

Gratz, Delbert L. "Peace and Our Heritage." In *Mennonite Community Sourcebook,* 25-33. Ed. Esko Loewen. Akron: MCC, 1946. Pp. 147. MHL. Bibliography of peace literature on such topics as the principles of nonresistance, the history of the peace witness, alternative service, relief work, etc.

Gunden, Lois. *At Brenner's Park Hotel.* Akron, Pa.: MCC, ca. 1945. Pp. 8. MHL. Personal narrative reflecting upon the year in which 13 relief workers, some American diplomats, Red Cross representatives, and members of the press were interned in southwestern Germany by the German army.

"Historic Peace Churches Meeting in Kitchener." *CanMenn* 2 (Oct. 29, 1954), 1. Topics include: Israel and Christianity, the power of love, relief and voluntary service.

"Hunger Packet." Akron: MCC, n.d. MHL.

Hallman, William. "Relief and Social Service as Related to Mennonite Missions." Paper presented to the Mennonite Seminar, Goshen College, Goshen, Ind., 1945. Pp. 16. MHL.

Hartzler, Jonas S. *Mennonites in the World War or Nonresistance Under Test.* Scottdale: Mennonite Publishing House, 1922. Pp. 246. MHL. Treatment of the World War I conscientious objector experience includes analysis of the issues, summaries of meetings and position papers, descriptions of camp life and life in the disciplinary barracks, congregational reaction, and relief work.

Hartzler, Levi C. "Entering New Fields in Spanish Relief." *ChrMon* 31 (Oct., 1939), 302-3. Summary of the relief work in Spain during the final year of the civil war.

Hartzler, Levi C. "Glimpses of Spain's Need." *ChrMon* 30 (Mar., 1938), 71, 96. Author visited town where war relief work is being done.

Hartzler, Levi C. "How Can We Help Save the Sufering Children of Spain?" *ChrMon* 29 (Sept., 1937), 259-60. Describes the need created by the civil war.

Hartzler, Levi C. "Our Relief Work Once Our Peace Testimony." *YCC* 22 (July 20, 1941), 641. Description of the relief work done in Spain. Relief work is a part of a positive peace testimony.

Hartzler, Levi C. "Spain and Its Present Needs for Relief of War Sufferers." *ChrMon* 29 (Aug., 1937), 227-28. Political history of Spain, description of the present civil war, and analysis of the relief work needed.

Hartzler, Levi C. "Spain Calls for Food and Clothing." *ChrMon* 29 (Oct., 1937), 294-95. Description of the progress of the Spanish civil war and directions for contributing relief items.

Hartzler, Levi C. "We Welcome Franco." *ChrMon* 31 (July, 1939), 205-6. Report of the Mennonite relief work in Spain taken over by victorious Franco.

Hatfield, Mark O. "A Time to Share." *MBH* 13 (Oct. 4, 1974), 3-4, 27. In the face of the world hunger crisis, US national budget calls for $90 billion of military spending and $1.9 billion humanitarian aid.

Hershberger, Guy F. "Mennonite Relief and Service Committee." *ME* III (1957), 635-36. Surveys the history of this committee which has maintained a policy of supporting the work of Mennonite Central Committee and has maintained relief and service projects under its own administration.

Hershberger, Guy F. "Mennonite Relief Commission for War Sufferers." *ME* III (1957), 636-37. Organized in 1917 to distribute funds and supplies for the relief of war sufferers.

Hershberger, Guy F. "Relief Work." *ME* IV (1959), 284-91. Surveys the history of relief work in the Anabaptist-Mennonite tradition.

Hershberger, Guy F. "Why Is the Mennonite Church Doing Relief Work in Spain?" *YCC* 18 (Dec. 5, 1937), 808. There are many relief needs in Spain. Nonresistance is a readiness to sacrifice and to suffer for the sake of Christ, and for the welfare of people.

Hiebert, Linda Gibson and Hiebert, Murray. "Laos: The Enemy at Home." *Sojourners* 6 (June, 1977), 35. The war in Laos continues as a war against sickness and hunger. The US has some responsibility since it spent billions of dollars financing twenty years of warfare.

Hoover, Jesse W. "'Inasmuch': A Story of Relief Work in France." *ChrMon* 34 (Feb., 1942), 45, 63. Description of a convalescent colony run by MCC, operated for children displaced by the war.

Hoover, Jesse W. "War Sufferers and Our Christian Mission." *GH Supplement* 34 (Mar., 1942), 1055, 1064. Relief work brings hope, peace, and renewed confidence in God to those ravaged by war. The purpose of such mission is to be instruments of God in bringing restoration to the victims' souls.

Horst, Irvin B. *A Ministry of Goodwill. A Short Account of Mennonite Relief, 1939-1949.* Akron: MCC, 1949. Pp. 119. An account of Mennonite relief work around the world during and following World War II.

Horst, Irvin B. "Mennonite Position on Relief and Service." *Menn* 65 (Nov. 7, 1950), 734. Social concern flows spontaneously from the life of discipleship and includes the practice of nonresistance, service, and mutual aid.

Horst, John L. "Opportunities for Relief in Belgium." *ChrMon* 38 (Jan., 1946), 19. Outlines needs present in this war-torn country.

Horst, John L. "Relief Work as a Testimony for Christ and the Church." *GH* 39 (Jan. 7, 1947), 869, 872. Address at the 1946 Mennonite General Conference. The relief of suffering is a task based on Scripture and is one way to provide a platform for giving a testimony of peace.

Hostetler, John Andrew. "Mennonite Relief in China; Problems and Needs of China." *ChrMon* 38, Part 3, (Sept., 1946), 270-71, 278. The recent war with Japan intensified many of the already-existing problems of food and shelter shortages.

Hostetler, John Andrew. *The Sociology of Mennonite Evangelism.* Scottdale, Pa.: Herald Press, 1954.

Pp. 287. MHL. Includes: "Rules and Discipline: Nonparticipation in the Affairs of Government," 28-29; "Unanticipated Evangelistic Interaction: Relief and Peace Activities," 128-30; "Religious Experience and Values Discovered: Nonresistance," 207; "Out-Group Social Attractions: Military Service," 236-37.

Hostetler, Marian. *African Adventure.* Scottdale: Herald Press, 1976. Pp. 124. Fiction, ages 10-14. In the course of an MCC-type assignment to Chad, 12-year-old Denise and her family begin to experience and understand the problems of hunger and violence in their relatedness. The story depicts a variety of ways church agencies work at the tasks of relief and mission.

Hylkema, T. O. "To the Mennonites in America a Message from the Dutch Mennonites." *ChrMon* 40 (Jan., 1948), 5-7. A leader of the peace movement among Dutch Mennonites thanks American Mennonites for their relief work during and after the war.

"In This Time of Cold War." *CanMenn* 9 (Sept. 29, 1961), 2, 11. A reaffirmation of MDS and "A Plan of Action" to be used instead of complete, unconditional cooperation with Civil Defense.

Jones, Brennon. "Paper Flowers and Stethoscope." *GH* 63 (June 2, 1970), 494-95. Describes the medical and rehabilitation work of a Vietnam Christian Service nurse, as her work is shaped by the presence of war.

Jost, Arthur. "Mennonite Ex-CPS Men Serve In Sixteen Nations." *RepConsS* 5 (Mar., 1947), 1, 4, 5. One-third of current MCC relief workers have experience with CPS.

Juhnke, James C. "Mennonite Benevolence and Civic Identity: the Post-War Compromise." *MennLife* 25 (Jan., 1970), 34-37. Examines the thesis that Mennonite relief and service efforts, historically most energetic during wartime, originate in American nationalism. Notes that these efforts may in fact grow from a Mennonite need to contribute "meaningfully and sacrificially toward national goals" in a time when others are ofering their lives to the war effort.

Kauffman, Daniel. "Our Evangelical Witness." *GH Supplement* 36 (June, 1943), 217. Bringing relief to physical suffering can open opportunities for ministering to spiritual needs.

Kaufman, Donald D. "Implications of Pax, Relief, and Voluntary Service for World Mission." Paper presented to Mennonite Misions and World Service class, MBS, Chicago, Ill., Nov. 27, 1957. Pp. 35.

Kaufman, J. N. "The Place of Relief Work in Our Church Program." *GH Supplement* 34 (Dec., 1941), 767-68. A very large portion of the Bible deals with human relationships and the need for mutual care. Therefore, relief is part of the church's mission.

Keeney, William E. "Serving a Nation in Agony." *MennLife* 23 (Apr., 1968), 54-58. Outlines the various kinds of problems the Vietnam people face in their war-torn country.

Kehler, Larry. "Structures and Nationalism Looms [sic] Large at MCC Meeting." *MBH* 14 (Feb. 7, 1975), 10-12. At the annual meeting, the committee passed a resolution on world hunger calling for reduced military expenditure and increased food development.

Kehler, Peter. "Responsibility to the World." *CanMenn* 6 (Feb. 7, 1958), 2. The Christian's responsibility to the world lies both in evangelism and in loving service to the needy.

Keidel, Levi O. *War to Be One.* Grand Rapids: Zondervan, 1977. Pp. 239. An account of the Mennonite church in the Congo, now Zaire, during the turbulent years of famine and warfare from 1930-1960. The story is one in which both the African Mennonite leaders and the US missionaries participated in the processes of survival and reconciliation.

King, Mrs. Noah and Miller, Mrs. D. D. "Conditions in War-Stricken Countries and Relief Work." Papers read at Indiana-Michigan Branch of Sisters' Sewing Circle Meeting, June, 1918. Pp. 16.

Kraus, Hertha. *International Relief in Action, 1914-1943.* Scottdale, Pa.: Herald Press, 1944. Pp. 248. MHL. Textbook for relief training schools which summarizes case records from 57 relief projects around the world sponsored by a wide variety of social and church agencies. Following each summary is a series of questions designed to help students identify and solve the problems raised by human need.

Kraybill, Donald B. "An Open Letter to American Mennonite Farmers." *YCC* 49 (June 9, 1968), 9. Because the Mennonite church has a strong rural tradition and heritage, there are many creative ways that the church can respond to world hunger.

Kreider, Carl. "Food for Peace." *ChrLiv* 6 (Dec., 1959), 18, 32. Exploring programs to disperse surplus American grain to needy people around the world.

Kreider, Carl. "How Can I Respond to World Hunger?" Chapel address given at Goshen College, Goshen, Ind., July 15, 1974. Pp. 6. MHL.

Kreider, Carl. "How Can We Respond to World Hunger?" *GH* 67 (Nov. 19, 1974), 891-94. Examines causes of hunger, from affluence to the energy crisis, and suggests seven responses, rooted in nonresistance, including cutting the defense budget.

Kreider, Carl. "International Economic Justice." Paper presented at MCC Justice Task Force Consultation, Goshen College, Goshen, Ind., May 22-23, 1978. Pp. 7. MHL.

Kreider, Carl. "Peace Thought in the Mennonite Church from the Beginning of the World War in Europe, August, 1914, to the Establishment of the War Sufferer's Relief Commission, December, 1917." Paper presented to American History class, 1936. Pp. 34. MHL.

Kreider, Carl. "The Mennonite Central Committee Relief Training School Held at Goshen College." *ChrMon* 35 (Nov., 1943), 336-37. Development of the training program, negotiation with the Selective Service system, and final cancellation by Congress.

Kreider, Lucille. *The Friendly Way: A One-Act Play in Three Scenes.* Newton: Faith and Life Press, 1961. Pp. 22. Set in 1917, the drama depicts some of the struggles experienced by a Quaker family as the son refuses to join the military and, instead, volunteers for relief work in Beirut, where his nonresistant ideals are tested.

Kreider, Robert S. "Holy Bread." *MCC WSRB* 2 (Feb., 1947), 1-2. Discusses white flour shipped to German war-sufferers as holy bread, since it was given freely in love.

Kreider, Thomas Edmund. "J. E. Brunk, Mennonite Relief Worker in Constantinople, 1920-21." Paper presented to History Seminar, Goshen College, Goshen, Ind., Jan. 6, 1979. Pp. 27. MHL.

Kroeker, David. "Torture, Prison, Rats, and Hunger." *MennRep* 9 (Jan. 22, 1979), 6. Relating numerous incidents of persons maltreated for political and/or religious beliefs, the writer urges the reader to contact Amnesty International and become involved in the campaign to free those unjustly treated.

Kroeker, Walter.. "Justice and Relief Must Stay Together." *MBH* 18 (Feb. 16, 1979), 16-18. Papers were presented at the MCC annual meeting on the relation of peace and reconciliation to Native American outreach, hunger concerns, and militarism.

"Lack of Concern for Rules of War." *Menn* 86 (Jan. 19, 1971), 36-38. Relief workers express their disapproval of the foreign military involvement in Vietnam and quote numerous articles from, for instance, the Nuremberg Tribunal, the Hague Convention, the Geneva Convention, and others, to point out the injustice of the USA.

Lapp, John A. "East Pakistan an Unthinkable Horror." *Menn* 86 (Sept. 7, 1971), 521, 522. Realizing that the only real solution to the suffering in Pakistan is a political one, there are five positive things American Christians can do to alleviate the suffering.

Lapp, John A. "The United Nations in the Middle East." *ChrLiv* 26 (Aug., 1979), 15, 25. Description of UN peacekeeping operations in the Middle East, from relief for Palestinian refugees to troops stationed in demilitarized zones.

Lehman, M[artin] C[lifford]. "An Annotated Bibliography for a Course in the History and Philosophy of Mennonite Relief Work for the 1943 Mennonite Relief Training School." Held at Goshen College, Goshen, Ind., June 12-Aug. 27, 1943. Pp. 18. MHL.

Lehman, M[artin] C[lifford]. "Relief Work in Alsace-Lorraine." *MCC WSRB* 1 (Nov., 1945), 5. Describes war relief efforts and the attitude toward military service in Switzerland.

Lehman, M[artin] C[lifford]. *The History and Principles of Mennonite Relief Work—An Introduction.* Akron: MCC, 1945. Pp. 67. A statement of the theological and historical basis of Mennonite relief work, including an annotated bibliography of 145 items on the subject.

Lehman, M[artin] C[lifford]. "The Philosophical Basis for Mennonite Relief and Non-Resistance." *PCMCP Second,* 95-105. North Newton, Kansas: The Bethel College Press. Held at Goshen, Indiana, July 22-23, 1943. There are internal factors that need to be rediscovered and defined as to theological origin, philosophical implication, and social application which can operate in encouraging cooperation among the various Mennonite groups. These factors should not be related to responding to concerns associated with war.

Lehman, M[artin] C[lifford]. "The Program of the Mennonite Central Committee to Train Relief Workers." *ChrMon* 36 (Feb., 1944), 43. Removal of the training program from Goshen College to mental hospitals, where trainees could continue the CPS work into which they were drafted.

Long, C. Warren. "Christian Service in Belgium." *ChrMon* 39 (Sept., 1947), 272. Although emergency relief in Belgium is no longer needed, rehabilitation from the effects of the war continues.

Long, C. Warren. "The Whispered Door." *ChrMon* 39 (Nov., 1947), 336-37. Describes Mennonite relief aid given to the families of people accused of collaborating with the enemy during the war.

Longacre, Doris Janzen. "Why Orphanages Aren't Vietnam's Answer." *ChrLiv* 14 (July, 1967), 26-28. Christians should be providing aid to family structures strained by war, not building institutions to house children.

Longacre, Paul. "Learning About World Hunger." *Builder* 29 (May, 1979), 1-5. An annotated list of audiovisual and print resources to help congregational educators to promote both awareness and response on the issue of world hunger.

Longacre, Paul (Review). *Bread and Justice: Toward a New International Economic Order,* by James B. McGinnis. Paulist Press, 1979. *MBH* 19 (Aug. 8, 1980), 28-29. Recommends this examination of some of the root causes of world hunger.

Longacre, Paul (Review). *Hunger for Justice: The Politics of Food and Faith,* by Jack Nelson. Maryknoll: Orbis, 1980. *MBH* 19 (Aug. 8, 1980), 28-29. Recommends this analysis of some of the economic and political causes of world hunger, with reference to biblical material on hunger and justice.

"MCC, Peace Conference Topics for Rev. G. Rempel." *CanMenn* 2 (Jan. 22, 1954), 8. Rempel reports on the Detroit Peace Conference and the annual meeting of the Mennonite Central Committee, encouraging the churches to continue their relief programs and peace witness. Strong statements on biblical nonresistance are reported. The problem of the fundamentalists and the peace witness is brought out in an example of the Old Fashioned Revival Hour refusing donations from Mennonite COs.

"MCC Resolution on World Food Crisis." *EV* 87 (July 10, 1974), 3. MCC has resolved to give priority to the world food crisis in the next five to ten years, recognizing that world peace may depend on the solution to the hunger problem in developing countries.

"MCC Seeks Channel to Aid Kampuchea." *Menn* 94 (Oct. 30, 1979), 647. Famine follows years of wars and internal upheavals in Kampuchea, and MCC is working through various channels to send aid and to urge the US to normalize relations with Indochinese countries.

"MDS Converses with Black Front Leaders." *CanMenn* 16 (Dec. 31, 1968), 1, 2. Conversation centers on possibility of MDS working with blacks to rehabilitate urban housing.

"MDS Discusses Motivation and Alternative Service." *CanMenn* 6 (Apr. 18, 1958), 1, 10. J. A. Toews, Wilbert Loewen, and Henry Poettcker

address Manitoba representatives at the Winnipeg regional meeting of the Mennonite Disaster Service, on the opportunities for alternative service and disaster service.

"'Meals of Reconciliation' at Bethel College." *CanMenn* 15 (Nov. 7, 1967), 1, 11. The BC Peace Club conducted a week of frugal meals, and sent the money saved for relief in North and South Vietnam. The purpose of the meals was: to identify with war sufferers; to search for new methods of peace witness; repentance for personal involvement in situations making for war; and commitment and rededication to search for a peaceful world.

"Mennonite Conference on War and Peace: A Report of the Conference, Including the Principal Addresses Given." Goshen College, Goshen, Ind., Feb. 15-17, 1935. Pp. 68. MHL. Includes: Hershberger, Guy F., "Is Alternative Service Desirable and Possible?" 49-59; Stoltzfus, Eli, "Experiences of a Relief Worker During the World War."

Mann, Cleo A. "Relief Work in Belgium." *ChrMon* 38 (Feb., 1946), 47. Excerpts from the diary of a relief worker describes destruction from the war.

Martens, Harry E. "Houses on Cold Amman Hills." *GH* 61 (Nov. 12, 1968), 1028. Describes the plight of Palestinian war refugees facing a cold winter with only tents, and challenges North American Christians to share out of their abundance to construct makeshift shelters.

Mast Burnett, Kristina. "Canada-US Relations, Vietnam, Issues at Reedley Meetings." *GH* 72 (Feb. 13, 1979), 128. MCC's annual meeting in Reedley, Jan. 25-27, addressed such issues as Canada-US relations, aid to Vietnam, justice and human rights overseas, Native American outreach, hunger concerns, and militarism.

Mennonite Central Committee. "A Letter to the President." *GH* 58 (June 29, 1965), 567. The text of a letter sent to President Johnson. MCC describes relief work in Vietnam and calls the president to an escalation of compassion rather than an escalation of conflict.

Mennonite Central Committee. "Civil Defense." *GH* 49 (June 12, 1956), 558-59. A statement made by MCC and MDS suggests that Mennonites should not become integrally involved in Civilian Defense.

Mennonite Central Committee. *Twenty-Five Years. The Story of the MCC, 1920-1945.* Akron: MCC, 1945. Pp. 24. An interpretive history of North American Mennonite relief and service activities, including CPS and direct peace activities.

Mennonite Central Committee. "Vietnam Study: Relief Often Tied to Politics, Military." *MennRep* 2 (Oct. 2, 1972), 1. Relief agencies enjoy the benevolences of a government because the latter recognizes a potential in the former to realize its political and military ends.

Mennonite Disaster Service. "Mennonite Disaster Service and Civilian Defense." *GH* 54 (Oct. 3, 1961), 873. In the event of nuclear war Mennonites should give service to save lives through MDS and without involvement in military aspects of Civilian Defense.

Miller, Alvin J. "The Beginning of American Mennonite Relief Work." *MennLife* 17 (Apr., 1972), 71-75. Mennonites of America heard of the need in Russia and in 1921 made contacts with the Mennonites there and provided aid for the starving.

Miller, Ernest E. "World Revolution and the Role of the Christian." *ChrLiv* 3 (Dec., 1956), 8-9. Christianity, responsible in a large part for the awakening of nations to long injustice, should now provide volunteers to do the needed relief work.

Miller, Mary. "France with the Glamor Veil Drawn." *ChrMon* 40 (Nov., 1948), 336-37, 339. Relief worker in France describes the postwar conditions there.

Miller, Orie O. "Give Ye Them to Eat." *GH* 39 (Apr. 9, 1946), 17-18. There is a direct connection between the nonresistant faith and the church's relief services.

Miller, Orie O. (Archival). Boxes 1-80: collection contains MCC and various peace related materials; Committee on Economic and Social Relations; Mennonite Relief Commission on War Sufferers; Peace Problems Committee. Goshen, IN. AMC. Hist. Mss. 1-45.

Miller, Robert W. "What Is MCC Doing in Vietnam?" *ChrLead* 36 (July 10, 1973), 6; *MBH* 12 (Aug. 24, 1973), 17; "What Is Mennonite Central Committee Doing in Vietnam?" *GH* 66 (July 3, 1973), 538; *MennRep* 3 (July 9, 1973), 9.. From 1966-72, MCC was part of Vietnam Christian Service (VNCS), a joint effort of Church World Service, Lutheran World Relief, and MCC, but since Jan., 1973, MCC has been operating its own programs in cooperation with the national church and VNCS. These programs are described in this article.

Miller, S. Paul. "Give Ye Them to Eat." *YCC* 47 (Nov. 20, 1966), 2. Report on famine conditions in India.

Minnich, R. Herbert. "Hunger, Revolution, and the Church." *Peacemakers in a Broken World.* Ed. John A. Lapp. Scottdale: Herald Press, 1969, 43-53. Minnich predicts revolution in Latin America as poor and oppressed people begin to demand justice. Calls Christians to work nonviolently for greater socioeconomic equality.

Mooneyham, W. Stanley. "The Facts of Hunger." *EV* 87 (Dec. 10, 1974), 5, 6. Compassion that leads to commitment is necessary to fight the hunger and famine that is causing millions to suffer and die.

"Non-Resistance Relief Organization." *CanMenn* 7 (Nov. 6, 1959), 8. A short history of this Ontario organization whose purpose is to actively express the principles of non-resistance through relief. The NRRO has cooperated in the past with other Mennonite relief agencies and is now a member of MCC.

Nelson, Boyd N. "How Shall They Hear? Through Relief and Service." *GH* 49 (Oct. 16, 1956), 985-86. Relief and service are being increasingly acknowledged as a genuine part of the church's total mission.

Neufeld, Elmer. "Alternative to Civil Defense." *GH* 54 (Apr. 4, 1961), 321; "MDS Meets Civil Defense." *Menn* 76 (May 23, 1961), 342, 346; "Alternative to Civil Defense." *CanMenn* 9 (Mar. 31, 1961), 5. Mennonites are encouraged to refrain from membership in Civil Defense organizations; MDS should be recognized as an alternative.

Neufeld, Elmer. "Defense: Civilian, Military, or Spiritual." Paper read to MDS meeting, Chicago, Ill., Feb. 11, 1960.

Non-Resistant Relief Organization, 1917-1964 (Archival). 2 feet. CGCL.

"People and Hunger." Papers presented to the Consultation on World Hunger and Population Pressures, Chicago, Ill., May 24-25, 1968. MHL. Sponsored by Council of Mennonite Colleges, Council of Mission Board Secretaries, Mennonite Central Committee. Includes: Klassen, William, "God's People and the Poor," pp. 9; Kreider, Carl, "Economic Factors Affecting Hunger," pp. 8; Blase, Melvin, "Programs for Economic Development in Latin America," pp. 16; Bishop, Franklin, "World Hunger: Reality and Challenge," pp. 11; Rhoades, J. Benton, "Programs of Agricultural Development in Latin America," pp. 7; Fretz, J. Winfield, "Population Pressures in Latin America: The Current Situation and Trends," pp. 9; Minnich, R. Herbert, "Hunger, Revolution, and the Church in Latin America," pp. 17; Hiebert, T. G., "Family Planning in Christian Relief Programs," pp. 7.

"Prison Brutality Bared in Amish CO's Ordeal." *Fellowship* 22 (Sept., 1956), 25. This news release states that what was first reported as a "hunger strike" by five Amish CO's at a W. Va. prison camp has been exposed as an act of prison brutality.

Peachey, J. Lorne. "To Heal the Scars of War." *ChrLiv* 15 (June, 1968), 11. Activities of Vietnam Christian Service volunteers in Southeast Asia.

Penner, Helen. "Have a Heart in a World of Need." *ChrMon* 34 (Nov., 1942), 338-39. Describes MCC relief work in France and the motivating belief in nonviolence and aggressive good will.

Preheim, Vern. "MCC's Efforts in the Middle East." *GH* 62 (June 10, 1969), 517-18. Describes MCC activities, primarily in Jordan, which range from war relief and reconstruction to education and crafts projects.

"Relief Groups Try to Avert Mass Death in Kampuchea." *GH* 72 (Nov. 6, 1979), 872. Various relief groups including MCC have tried to avert the mass starvation in Kampuchea, but most of their efforts have met with little success.

"Resign Vietnam Service Posts to Protest War." *CanMenn* 15 (Sept. 26, 1967), 1. Increased suffering on the part of the Vietnamese and the self-interest of the USA in the area are reasons given for resignation from relief agency.

"Rockway Students Fast for War Sufferers Relief." *CanMenn* 14 (Jan. 4, 1966), 1, 16. During the week of Dec. 13-17 about thirty-five students of Rockway Mennonite School fasted for the innocent sufferers of Vietnam. The students gave up their noon lunches and gave the equivalent value of the food to a relief fund for Vietnam. During the lunch periods when they did not eat, they informed themselves on the war.

(Review). *The Mennonite Church in the Second World War*, by Guy F. Hershberger. Scottdale: Mennonite Publishing House, 1951. Pp. 308. *Fellowship* 18 (Nov., 1952), 28. This book is "not only an account of the direct relation of the church to the war, but includes as well chapters on missions, education, relief, voluntary service, and intergroup relations both within and without the Mennonite family."

(Review). *Vietnam: Who Cares?*, by Atlee and Winifred Beechy. Scottdale: Herald Press, 1968. Pp. 154. *Fellowship* 36 (May, 1970), 27. Brief summary of the book which is a compilation of the reports from six months of working with the Church World Service's relief and refugee service program in Vietnam. Recommended for its detail, excellent historical outline, and bibliography.

Redekop, John H. "The Essence of the Gospel." *MBH* 18 (Oct. 26, 1979), 12. Relief work and conflict resolution in the question of militarism are both applications of the gospel, but not its essence.

Reeser, Ethel. "The Significance of Relief Work in the Program of the Mennonite Church." Paper presented to Sociology Seminar, Goshen College, Goshen, Ind., May 20, 1949. Pp. 43. MHL.

Regehr, Lydia. "War's Aftermath." *MBH* 18 (Oct. 26, 1979), 7. Short poem on famine, the only victor in war.

Regier, C. C. "A Christian Witness in War and Peace." *MennLife* 4 (Jan., 1949), 17-20. Describes the work of the historic peace churches in setting up the CPS program with Selective Service. Includes history and statistics of the Civilian Public Service program during World War II and post-war relief work.

Rempel, David G. "A Response to the 'Lost Fatherland' Review." *CanMenn* 16 (Aug. 13, 1968), 7. An interpretation of the Mennonite involvement in the Russian famine and revolution during and after World War I.

*Report of American Mennonite Relief to Holland, 1945-1947.* Druk de Bussy, Amsterdam: MCC, [1947]. Pp. 14. MHL. Text and photos recount the story of the post-war service project. Describes distribution of clothes and food, reconstruction efforts, caring for the Mennonite refugees, etc.

Ressler, Lawrence and Peachy, Dean. "A Call to Nonconformity." *GH* 72 (Nov. 6, 1979), 869-70. We need to re-examine our economic system and structures and seek alternatives if we want to seriously address problems such as poverty, hunger, urban decay, and militarism.

Root, Robert. "European Relief Needs." *ChrMon* 39 (Feb., 1947), 37. Church World Service peace correspondent outlines the needs present in war torn Europe.

Roth, Willard E., ed. *Hunger Hurts: How Shall Christians Respond?* Newton: Faith and Life Press; Scottdale: Herald Press, 1968. Pp. 63. Includes: Klassen, William, "God's People and the Poor," 9-17; Fretz, J. Winfield, "Population Pressure," 19-25; Bishop, C. Franklin, "World Hunger: Reality and Change," 27-35; Preheim, Vern, "Agricultural Development Overseas," 39-43; Beachy, Miriam, "Famine in Bihar," 45-49; Shelly, Andrew, "Agriculture in the Andes," 51-55; Hess, Mahlon M., "An Experiment in Tanzania," 57-62. Compilation of short essays designed to help individuals, families, congregations, and church agencies sharpen their awareness and sensitivity toward this issue and, most importantly, to motivate the church toward action in the crusade against hunger. Leader's guide by Paul Lederach also available.

Schrock, Paul M. "Sheets for South Vietnam Saturday." *ChrLiv* 11 (May, 1964), 20-23. One community's effort to collect sheets for medical use in South Vietnam.

Shank, J. Ward (Editorial). "On Vietnam." *ST* 34 (1st Qtr., 1966), 1. We should seriously question the obligation, or even the competency, of the church, as such, to pronounce upon matters like the Vietnam War and international policy. We should pursue avenues of relief and service as opportunities to relieve the sufferings of war.

Shank, J. Ward (Review). *Rich Christians in an Age of Hunger,* by Ronald J. Sider. Downers Grove: Intervarsity Press, n.d. Pp. 249. *ST* 48 (Jan., 1980), 24-25. The book is a mild form of liberation theology in its advocacy of social justice, says the reviewer.

Shantz, Gordon. "Postwar Plans." *YCC* 26 (Feb. 18, 1945), 447, 448. The church will have to be cautious in its postwar plans in the areas of social service and relief work.

Shelly, Maynard. "Peacemakers In Spite of Ourselves." *MennRep* 8 (Oct. 16, 1978), 6. Senator Bob Dole's visit to an MCC relief sale in Kansas gave this fundraising event for peace the appearance of condoning militaristic government policies.

Shenk, Phil M. and Bicksler, Harriet. "Blessed Are the Peacemakers." *EV* 91 (June 25, 1978), 6. Peacemakers met together in Pennsylvania, Apr. 8 and 9, to lift up hunger, militarism, and self as three issues in need of peacemaking attention by the historic peace churches.

Shetler, Sanford G. "The Future of Civilian Public Service and Relief Work." *ST* 14 (July, 1946), 561. Raises some questions and offers some suggestions about Civilian Public Service and relief.

Sider, Ronald J., ed. *Cry Justice: The Bible Speaks on Hunger and Poverty.* New York: Paulist Press, 1980. A collection of biblical passages on justice issues accompanied by brief commentary, tables containing information on such topics as the infant mortality rate in different countries, and study questions designed for use by individuals and/or groups.

Sider, Ronald J. *Rich Christians in an Age of Hunger: A Biblical Study.* Intervarsity and Paulist Press, 1977. Warns that the critical problem of world hunger could lead to wars of redistribution and outlines ways North American Christians can respond to this tragic situation with compassion.

Snyder, William T. "The Road Ahead for MCC." *EV* 93 (Oct. 10, 1980), 5. MCC Executive Secretary outlines areas of the world marked by famine and war that will receive MCC's attention in the coming year.

*

Stoltzfus, Gene and Friesen, Dorothy (Review). *Food First: Beyond the Myth of Scarcity,* by Frances Moore Lappé and Joseph Collins. Boston: Houghton Mifflin Co., 1977. *Peace Section Newsletter* 9 (Aug.-Sept., 1979), 12. Begins with the assertion that every country in the world has the resources necessary for its people to free themselves from hunger. Well-documented study of how we in North America, as well as Third World countries, are losing control over our food and food policies.

Stoner, John K. "Peace and Evangelism . . . Are They Related?" *ChrLead* 42 (June 19, 1979), 5; *MBH* 18 (Oct. 26, 1979), 8-9. An evangelistic message can speak to people's hunger for peace and freedom from the idolatry of militarism.

Studer, Gerald C. "What About Relief?" *GH* 39 (Aug. 13, 1946), 418. The Christian must not supply only physical needs but seek to meet the needs of the soul also.

"The Dilemma of Christian Involvement." *ChrLead* 28 (Nov. 9, 1965), 14-15. MCC relief operations, as a part of the Mennonite peace witness, must be expanded in spite of the danger of being identified with American military violence.

Taves, H. T. "Ontario MDS Reports 1732 St. John's Participants." *CanMenn* 7 (Dec. 4, 1959), 1, 13. The first annual meeting of the Mennonite Disaster Service organization was held in Waterloo.

Thierstein, J. R. "America's Opportunity." *Menn* 55 (Oct. 15, 1940), 1-2. America should take the lead in relief work and peace movements.

Toews, John A. "Christ's Example and Social Involvement." *MBH* 4 (May 14, 1965), 7, 19. The disciple, like the Master, should engage in a teaching, healing, and relief ministry of rehabilitation and restoration which avoid coercion or violence.

Unruh, John D. *In the Name of Christ: A History of the Mennonite Central Committee and its Service, 1920-1951.* Scottdale, Pa.: Herald Press, 1952. Pp. 404. Detailed summary of the organization and activities of MCC in various parts of the world. The connections between peace and service, both in terms of relief work as a practical Christian response to problems created by war and in terms of theological understandings, become very clear in the MCC context.

Unsigned. "Tales of French Relief Told by Brother J. N. Byler." *CPS Bull* 1 (Dec. 7, 1942), 3-4.

---

*For additional listing, see Supplement, pp. 717-719.

Describes living conditions in France during the war and includes letters of thanks from children who received help through Mennonite relief work.

Unsigned. "The 'MCC': How It Works." *CPS Bull Supp* 5 (Oct. 31, 1946), 1, 2, 4. Describes MCC's diversification into various aspects of relief and peace work.

Unsigned. "The 'MCC': What Is It?" *CPS Bull Supp* 5 (Sept. 26, 1946), 1, 3-4. Describes the beginnings of Mennonite Central Committee and its expansion into various forms of relief and peace work.

"Vietnam Study: Relief Often Tied to Politics, Military." *MennRep* 2 (Oct. 2, 1972), 1. Relief agencies enjoy the benevolences of a government because the latter recognizes a potential in the former to realize its political and military ends.

"Visit to Nicaragua Launches Assistance Programs." *MennRep* 9 (Sept. 3, 1979), 2. Eight representatives from Mennonite churches and organizations met in Nicaragua to review the current situation, renew church contacts, and discuss relief efforts.

Van Den Heuvel, Albert H. "Kyrie Eleison." *YCC* 48 (Oct. 8, 1967), 11. Reflections and comments on hunger.

Vogt, Virgil. "The Role of Well-Fed Mennonites in a Hungry World." *ChrLiv* 15 (Dec., 1968), 5-8. Comments on a Mennonite consultation on world hunger and calls Mennonites to confront wasteful militarism with greater witness against oppression and wealth.

Wagler, David and Raber, Roman, eds. *The Story of the Amish in Civilian Public Service, with Directory.* Boonsboro, Md.: CPS Camp No. 24, Unit III, 1945. Pp. 145. MHL. Essays relate experiences of various aspects of CPS camp life such as flood clean-up, forestry, fire-fighting, hospital work, human guinea pig experiments, relief work, etc. Directory provides names, addresses, induction dates, projects, etc.

Wenger, J. C. *History of the Mennonites of the Franconia Conference.* Telford: Franconia Mennonite Historical Society, 1937. Pp. 523. Includes a chapter on nonresistance and relief activities.

Widmer, Marie. "Switzerland Serves War-Swept Humanity." *YCC* 25 (Apr. 23, 1944), 129, 134-35. A description of some of the work Switzerland is doing for Europe's starving children.

Yoder, John H. "Which Ranks First?" *GH* 39 (June 11, 1946), 229. Missions and relief are both part of Christian witness.

Yoder, Orrie D. "The Awful Gravity of These Perilous Times." *GH* 42 (July 5, 1949), 634. Are the nonresistant Christians doing all they should in helping the world, spiritually and physically, to make amends for the sins of the last war?

Yoder, Samuel A. *Middle-East Sojourn.* Scottdale, Pa.: Herald Press, 1951. Pp. 310. Reminisces and reflects on travels and work undertaken on eighteen-month assignment to relief work in the Sinai Desert following World War II. Appendices offer specific information about the various efforts of this one refugee project.

# 11
# Military Service

## A. General

"A Christian Approach to Nuclear War." *Menn* 77 (Nov. 6, 1962), 707-709. Adapted from the statement by the Church Peace Mission, this article calls on American Christians to renew their hope in the way of peace and to abandon reliance on military might. Includes an urgent plea for the discontinuation of stockpiling of nuclear armaments.

"A Declaration on Peace, War, and Military Service." *Menn* 68 (Oct. 13, 1953), 632-33, 640. The official statement adopted at the 1953 conference of the GCMC. The way of peace and suffering love is rooted in the biblical witness to the gospel of Jesus. On this basis all forms of military service are disapproved.

"A Statement of the Position of the General Conference of the Mennonite Church of North America on Peace, War, Military Service, and Patriotism." *Menn* 56 (Sept. 9, 1941), 7-8. The statement approved at the 1941 meeting. "We believe that war is altogether contrary to the teaching and spirit of Christ and the gospel . . . ."

"An Urgent Appeal to the Churches." *EV* 90 (May 25, 1977), 6. With this appeal, twenty-five persons at a workshop on the church and militarism call our attention to the surprising silence of the Christian church in the face of mass starvation and nuclear stockpiling and urge the church to respond to these attrocities.

*A Christian Declaration on the Way of Peace.* Newton: Faith and Life Press, 1972. Pp. 24. MHL. Resolution adopted by the GCMC at its triennial session at Fresno, Cal., Aug., 1971. Presented in two sections. The first deals with biblical perspectives on peace; the second with issues of practical application such as the use of resources, citizenship, conscription and military service, and social change.

*A Petition.* N.p., [1919]. Pp. 141. MHL. [Printed copy of a petition against universal military training presented to the United States Congress by approximately 20,400 Mennonites of various branches in 31 states.]

Adrian, Walter. "A Thrilling Story from an Old Diary." *MennLife* 3 (July, 1948), 23-28, 39, 44. Narrative of one family's trek in the mid-1800's from Prussia into the Ukraine to settle in an area offering freedom from military service.

Anderson, Jack. "Armed Intervention Over Oil Eyed." *MCC PS Wash. Memo* 6 (Nov.-Dec., 1974), 8. Reprinted from *The Washington Post* (Nov. 8, 1974). Discusses government deliberations over using military action in the Mideast to secure US oil interests.

"Bishop Appears Before US Committee to Testify on Military Draft Laws." *CanMenn* 15 (May 23, 1967), 1, 5. Text of a statement made by John E. Lapp, MCC Peace Section resentative, before the Armed Services Committee of the US House of Representatives on May 3, 1967. Lapp's requests included: equal liberties for COs of all denominations; equal liberties for all COs of sincere religious convictions; freedom for all sincerely troubled by ethical problems of militarism; abolition of universal military training.

Baker, Robert J. "Before You Go 1-AO." *Menn* 66 (May 8, 1951), 302-303. Autobiographical sketch suggesting the incompatibility of noncombatant service with the way of love and reconciliation.

Baker, Robert J. *Is There a Middle Road?* Scottdale: Herald Press, 1956. Pp. 15. The Christian Youth and War Pamphlets, No. 6. Author recounts his experience in noncombatant service as an attempt to find a middle road between complete participation and nonparticipation in the military. Asserts that true conscientious objectors cannot in good conscience serve noncombatantly.

Barrett, Lois [Janzen]. "War Investments and Mennonites." *Menn* 87 (June 6, 1972), 378, 379. Mennonites are aware of problems other denominations have with investing stocks in military firms and are examining situations where they, too, may be involved.

Beachy, Alvin J. *The Concept of Grace in the Radical Reformation.* Nieuwkoop: De Graaf, 1977. Pp. 238. In this theological study of the Anabaptist movement, the chapter entitled "Anabaptist or Radical Ethics and the Works of Grace," 153-72, outlines the major points of the Anabaptist ethic: discipleship in conformity with the example of Christ is only possible through the power of the Holy Spirit; while the state has a legitimate place and function, it is limited by the example of Christ which precludes violence; oath-taking is one area in which Christians must disobey the state, according to the example of Christ; military duty is another area demanding disobedience to the state.

Beachy, Rosemary. "The Mennonites and the State." *MHB* 9 (Oct., 1948), 4. Focuses on separation of church and state as it has been expressed in Mennonite refusal to swear oaths and perform military duty. Reviews US government policies regarding such scruples from 1689 through the Civil War.

Beckett, W. M. "Canadian Defence Policy Today." *PlMon* 2 (Nov., 1979), 3-4. Description and rationalization of current Canadian defense policy.

Beechy, Atlee. *What Mennonites Believe About the Military.* Scottdale, Pa.: Mennonite Publishing House, 1980. Pp. 8. MHL. Also in *With* 13 (Apr., 1980), 32-36. Advises high school students to identify the gap between military recruiters' promises and the reality of military life as well as to consider seriously Christ's call to his disciples to build the kingdom of God.

Beechy, Winifred Nelson. "The Impact of Militarism on the Chinese Women's Movement." *MCC PS TF on Women in Ch. and Soc. Report* 35 (Jan.-Feb., 1981), 7-9. Traces the evolving emphases of the Chinese women's movement in this century.

Beitler, Jim. "How I Came to Be a Conscientious Objector." *With* 4 (July, 1971), 27. Personal experience in military basic training clarified the difference between being a soldier and being a conscientious objector.

Bender, Bertha Burkholder. "Youth, Church, and State." *YCC* 12, Part 1, (Jan. 4, 1931), 420-21; Part 2, (Jan. 11, 1931), 426-27; Part 3, (Jan. 18, 1931), 434-35; Part 4, (Jan. 25, 1931), 444-45; Part 5, (Feb. 1, 1931), 450, 451, 453; Part 6, (Feb. 8, 1931), 461-62; Part 7, (Feb. 15, 1931), 466-67; Part 8, (Feb. 22, 1931), 479-80; Part 9, (Mar. 1, 1931), 487, 488; Part 10, (Mar. 8, 1931), 491, 493; Part 11, (Mar. 15, 1931), 498, 499; Part 12, (Mar. 22, 1931), 505, 506; Part 13, (Mar. 29, 1931), 515, 517; Part 14, (Apr. 5, 1931), 523, 525; Part 15, (Apr. 12, 1931), 534, 535; Part 16, (Apr. 19, 1931), 539, 541; Part 17, (Apr. 26, 1931), 545-47; Part 18, (May 3, 1931), 559, 560;

Part 19, (May 17, 1931), 571, 573; Part 20, (May 31, 1931), 589; Part 21, (June 7, 1931), 595; Part 22, (June 21, 1931), 610; Part 23, (July 5, 1931), 627, 629; Part 24, (July 19, 1931), 645, 646; Part 25, (July 26, 1931), 650, 651; Part 26, (Aug. 2, 1931), 657-59; Part 27, (Aug. 16, 1931), 675-77. Written in a narrative style, the progression of peace-related topics include: the biblical story, the history of the church, issues about responding to government and militarism, e.g., CO status during Civil War and World War I, and Mennonite relief work.

Bender, Harold S. "Mennonites Testify at Hearings on Post-War Military Policy." *Menn* 60 (July 10, 1945), 5-6. The MCC statement made at the hearings of the House Select Committee on Post-War Military Policy. The statement recounts the history of the Mennonite peace witness, and witnesses against permanent peacetime conscription.

Bender, Harold S. "The Christian Nurse's Position in Time of War." *ChrMon* 43 (Mar., 1951), 87-88. Encourages absolute commitment to the way of peace by avoiding all noncombatant military service.

Bender, Paul. "Conscientious Objection to Military Service in North America, South America, and Europe: Legislation, Objection, Alternative Service, and Peace Work." Report to the Sixth Mennonite World Conference, Karlsruhe, Aug. 10-16, 1957. Pp. 10. MHL.

Berg, Ford. "The Inescapable Responsibility in Accepting Deferments." *GH* 41 (July 20, 1948), 667. Is voluntary Christian service a permanent commitment of nonresistant Mennonites, or only something prompted by the government and done in lieu of military service?

Beyler, Betsy. "Candidates for President: a Comparison." *Forum* 10 (Oct., 1976), 2-5; *MCC PS Wash. Memo* 7 (July-Aug., 1976), 1-7. A comparative analysis of Gerald Ford and Jimmy Carter focusing on their stand on some of the crucial issues: military spending, amnesty, foreign arms sales, nuclear disarmament, nuclear power, and foreign policy.

Beyler, Betsy. "Economic Conversion: Reformulating Guns vs. Butter." *MCC PS Wash. Memo* 10 (Mar.-Apr., 1978), 7-8. Supports the process of converting resources used for military production into facilities for meeting human needs.

Beyler, Betsy. "Human Rights Criteria for US Foreign Aid." *MCC PS Wash. Memo* 9 (Mar.-Apr., 1977), 4-5. In spite of Congressional authority to cut off military and economic aid to countries which violate human rights, a large percentage of US aid is not covered by these provisions.

Blosser, Don. "In Jail with the Apostle Paul." *GH* 69 (Apr. 20, 1976), 324-25; also "On Sharing a Jail Cell with Paul," *Menn* 91 (Mar. 9, 1976), 165-66. The "principalities and powers," about which Paul warned the Ephesians, express themselves today in corrupt institutions and military madness, evils which Christians are called to confront.

Bonpane, Blase, A., Fr. "The Role of the Christian in Violent Change." Address delivered at Goshen College All School Study Day, Feb. 21, 1969. Pp. 11. MHL, MLA/BeC.

Bontrager, Robert. "Missiles or Missions." *YCC* 40 (July 19, 1959), 461. Challenges the idea that security can be guaranteed with military might. Prize-winning essay.

Bontreger, Eli J. "Nonresistance in Daily Practice." *GH* 41 (June 1, 1948), 511. Many parents and other church members who oppose participation in war fail to live a truly nonresistant daily life. Consequently many young men choose military service.

Boserup, Anders and Mack, Andrew. "Nonviolence in National Defense." *PlMon* 2 (Nov., 1979), 5. Reprinted from the introduction to *War Without Weapons: Non-violence in National Defense,* by the same authors. New York: Schocken Books, 1975. Reviews military strategy since the advent of nuclear weapons to show that national security through military means in the nuclear age is a fallacy.

Brenneman, George. "Can We Have Peace and the Automobile?" *GH* 71 (Nov. 14, 1978), 893-97. Compares statistically American Mennonite monetary involvement in the auto and military industries and raises ethical questions about the dehumanizing and destructive tendencies of automobiles.

Brubacher, Glenn. "The Strange Gods in the Land." *GH* 65 (Jan. 18, 1972), 56-57. Militarism and nationalism are mentioned as false gods to whom Christians are paying homage, as well as materialism and sensuousness.

Brunk, Conrad G. "Lewis B. Hershey, A Four-Star General from Pacifist Family." *MennRep* 7 (June 13, 1977), 11. Reflects on the life of Gen. Lewis Hershey, Mennonite descendent, director of Selective Service from 1940-1970, and his contribution to forming alternative service programs.

Brunk, Conrad G. (Review). *The Rule of the Sword,* by Charlie Lord, and *The Rule of the Lamb,* by Larry Kehler. Both published by Newton: Faith and Life Press, 1978. Pp. 68 each. *MennRep* 23 (Nov. 13, 1978), 10. Study guides on militarism and taxes go beyond the Bible to study current events, history, and politics, in order to arrive at a more complete ethical response.

Buchanan, Roy. "A Personal Testimony." *GH* 63 (May 5, 1970), 408-409. World War I conscientious objector disagrees with the position of draft resisters, describing his positive experiences in obtaining cooperation from the military to perform alternative service.

Burkholder, J. Richard. "Wars and Rumors . . ." *GH* 71 (Jan. 24, 1978), 62-64. Using statistics from global military and social expenditures, Burkholder challenges Christians to speak out against the worldwide armaments buildup.

Burkholder, J. Richard. "Where Are We Going if Anywhere?" Paper presented to the Mennonite Graduate Fellowship, Earlham College, Richmond, Ind., Christmas, 1964. Pp. 13. MHL.

Burkholder, J. Richard and Bender, John. *Children of Peace.* Elgin: The Brethren Press; Nappanee: Evangel Press; Newton: Faith and Life Press; Scottdale: Mennonite Publishing House, 1982. Pp. 160. Theme of book is that peace is a way as well as a goal. The first unit explores the biblical meanings of peace in both their Old Testament and New Testament contexts. The second unit deals with the practice of peace in various areas of life, such as home, community, politics, and the military. The third unit explores the church and state relationship and includes accounts of the ways some people are effectively and creatively witnessing to peace in militaristic and totalitarian countries.

Burkholder, Marlin S. "If You Register I-A-O." *YCC* 32, Part 1, (1951), 624; Part 2, (July 1, 1951), 632; Part 3, (July 8, 1951), 636. An account of a personal experience as a person with the classification of I-A-O in the military.

Burkholder, Marlin S. "The Truth About Noncombatant Service." *YCC* 32 (Jan. 21, 1951), 441. A personal testimony to the reality that for a conscientious objector, there is absolutely no difference at all between noncombatant service and regular military service.

Burnett, [Kris]Tina Mast and Kroeker, Wally. "Affluent People Who Neglect the Poor Are Not the People of God." *Menn* 94 (Feb. 20, 1979), 128-29. MCC (International) annual meeting discussed issues of justice and human rights, aid to Vietnam, native American outreach, hunger concerns, and militarism.

Byl, Jürgen. "Jan van Leiden: Violence and Grace." *MennLife* 26 (July, 1971), 103-105. Comments on literary productions about the militant leader who is of historical interest to Mennonites, Jan van Leiden of Münster.

"Cheyenne Leader Switches from Military to

Ministry." *CanMenn* 9 (Dec. 1, 1961), 4. Laurence Hart discusses the Cheyenne and the doctrine of nonresistance.

"Christ Is Not Enough." *GH* 47 (Feb. 16, 1954), 153. Growing militarism and nationalism call people to put their trust in armies rather than in God.

Charles, Howard H. "The Christian and Military Taxes." *Builder* 29 (Nov., 1979), 26-30. Comments on Mark 12:13-17 and Romans 13:1-7 and then, in light of these Scriptures, considers the role of money in modern militarism and outlines some options for significant biblical responses to this issue.

Charles, Howard H. in collaboration with Jesse W. Hoover. *Before You Decide.* Akron: MCC, 1948. Pp. 70. Alternatives to military service for young people facing the draft discussed in biblical and historical perspective.

Clemens, Fred. "The Prussian Mennonites' Attitudes Toward the Loss of Their Military Service Exemption." Paper prepared for history seminar, Goshen College, Goshen, Ind., July 14, 1980. Pp. 33. MHL.

Clemens, Rachel. "Mennonites as the Military: The Selbstschutz Experience." 1984. Pp. 10. BfC.

Clemens, Steve. "A Post-Indochina Foreign Policy?" *MCC PS Wash. Memo* 7 (May-June, 1975), 1-2. Congressional action since the defeat in Vietnam shows the US will continue to base its foreign policy on military might rather than humanitarian concern.

Coffman, J. F. *The Sixth Commandment: "Thou Shalt Not Kill."* Scottdale, Pa.: Peace Problems Committee of the Mennonite Church, n.d. Pp. 4. MHL. Excerpts statement prepared by Mennonite General Conference, Goshen, Ind., Aug. 29, 1917, which addressed, among other matters, the reasons for nonparticipation in military service.

*Congressional Record*—Senate. "Women in the Military Will Help Recruiting Crunch." *MCC PS TF on Women in Ch. and Soc. Report* 19 (Apr.-May, 1978), 7. Reprinted entry includes *New York Times* editorial describing the Defense Department's petition to Congress lifting the ban on women being assigned to combat zones.

Conrad, Tom. "Counsel Decides Against Military Chaplaincy." *ChrLead* 39 (Mar. 30, 1976), 10. The Board of Reference and Counsel decided that the US Mennonite Brethren Conference will not try to place men in the military chaplaincy because that might harm the church's historic position on peace and conscientious objection.

Conrad, Tom. "Junior ROTC: Marching to the Beat of the Wrong Drummer." *With* 11 (Nov., 1978), 29. One of the ways the military is using to win the hearts and minds of youth is Junior ROTC, a high school military training program.

Cosby, Gordon. "Resting on Golgotha's Cross." *GH* 72 (Apr. 3, 1979), 268-69. The idolatry of our dependence on military expenditures for "national defense" negates our biblical faith and therefore we need to repent and pay the cost of repentance.

Curry, A. Stauffer. "UMT Can Still Be Deflated." *YCC* 33 (Jan. 13, 1952), 16. Encouragement to read the 123-page UMT (universal military training) report and arguments against UMT.

"Declaration of Peace." *Menn* 53 (Nov. 29, 1938), 5. Official statement adopted by the Eighth Street Mennonite Church, Goshen, Indiana, in a time of increasing national militarism. "We cannot sanction war" nor lend our support to its implementation, states the document.

"Does God Purpose His People Interfering in Earthly Government, Civil or Military?" *GH* 43 (Feb. 7, 1950), 126-28. Deals with the question of whether a believer should be a politician. Several incidents from the Gospels show that Jesus was not a politician; his disciples, then, should not be politicians, either.

Decker, LaVerne. Letter to the Editor. *ChrLead* 42 (Aug. 28, 1979), 14. To enjoy the advantages of freedom and yet to condemn those in the military, certainly does not reflect real Christian love.

Derstine, C. F. "Are the Last Days Upon Us?" *ChrMon* 29 (Dec., 1937), 381, 384. Cites the militant forces gathering in many parts of the world in opposition to the peace principles of Christ.

Derstine, C. F. "CO's in World War I and World War II." *ChrMon* 36 (May, 1944), 158-59. Comparison of Selective Service regulations and penalties for refusing to comply in World Wars I and II.

Derstine, C. F. "Compulsory Military Training for Peacetime Youth—Pro and Con." *ChrMon* 37 (July, 1945), 190-92. Cites the arguments favoring peacetime draft but sides with those against it.

Derstine, C. F. "Is Europe Marching Back to 1914?" *ChrMon* 28 (June, 1936), 191. Tabulates the armies and airplanes amassed by European countries and decries the rising militarism.

Derstine, C. F. "Mennonite Group Against Military Service in Holland." *ChrMon* 26 (Dec., 1934), 380. Includes statement of principles by the Peace Committee of Dutch Mennonites and news of war resisters there.

Derstine, C. F. "Our Testimony and a Wartorn World." *ChrMon* 28 (Aug., 1936), 254-55. Mennonites with a heritage of peace should witness publicly to the rising militarism.

Derstine, C. F. "Permanent Universal Peace." *ChrMon* 39 (Feb., 1947), 62-63. True peace will come only through turning away from false gods of military security, liberalism, and Marxism.

Derstine, C. F. "'Seven Men Went Singing into Heaven.'" *ChrMon* 32 (July, 1940), 222-23. Story of seven Bolshevik soldiers who were converted underscores the idea that the Gospel must be preached also to military personnel.

Derstine, C. F. "Zero Hour." *ChrMon* 36 (July, 1944), 222. The occasion of the Allied invasion of Europe should serve as a reminder not to trust in military might.

Derstine, Norman. "Our Tangled World." *GH* 62 (Nov. 18, 1969), 1006-1008. Part 2 of a series discussing symptoms of a sick American society focuses in part on growing militarism.

DeWolf, L. Harold, "Blind Samson or Christ?" *ChrLiv* 7 (May, 1960), 16-17. US defense policy parallels blind Samson's suicidal revenge on his enemies.

Dick, Jacob J. "America's at the Crossroad." *YCC* 33 (Feb. 24, 1952), 62. Discussion of the specifics of the Universal Military Training Bill.

Dick, Mervin. "Reservations: Taking the Military Oath: Practicing Civil Disobedience." Exploring Peace Study, March 19-20, 1980. Pp. 6. MBBS.

Dick, N. S. *The Peacemaker*. Scottdale: Herald Press and Newton: Faith and Life Press, 1972. Pp. 63. A Bible study guide on peacemaking organized into 13 lessons. Topics include the Jesus way, Old Testament wars, the relationship between poverty and militarism, patriotism, servanthood, etc. Resources include films, music, poetry, discussion questions.

Dickinson, Robert E. "What Belongs to Caesar?" *GH* 65 (Apr. 4, 1972), 319. Paying war taxes in order to protect property and job may amount to paying taxes so that others can serve in the military while I refuse to do so.

Diller, Duane A. and Diller, Esther W. "A Letter to the IRS." *GH* 67 (Apr. 30, 1974), 370. Couple informs the IRS of withholding the 30 percent of their income tax earmarked for military production and asks the IRS to honor their payment of this money to the Mennonite

Central Committee Peace Section Taxes-for-Peace Fund.

Drescher, James M. "A Letter from Freddy." *Swords into Plowshares: A Collection of Plays About Peace and Social Justice*, ed. Ingrid Rogers. Elgin: The Brethren Press, 1983, 236-41. An 18-year-old son presses his family for consistency by offering them a deal—he won't enroll in military service if they will resist paying the war tax.

Drescher, James M. "To Protest or Not to Protest: Is That the Question?" *With* 4 (Oct., 1971), 4. The question is not whether one should protest, but "when" and "how" to protest.

Drescher, John M. (Editorial). "Peacemaker Questions." *GH* 61 (July 2, 1968), 585. Interprets "separation of church and state" to mean that the church should be the conscience of society raising questions on issues of military service and payment of war taxes.

Driedger, Leo. "Doctrinal Belief: A Major Factor in the Differential Perception of Social Issues." *Sociological Quarterly* 15 (Winter, 1974), 66-80. This survey of clergy (including Mennonite clergy) to determine the correlation between doctrine and positions on social issues includes questions concerning military readiness, bombing of Vietnam, rights of communists, and racial integration.

Driediger, Ab Douglas. Letter to the Editor. *MennRep* 9 (Sept. 3, 1979), 6. In response to the third part of John Friesen's series on church-state relations (Aug. 20, 1979), the writer argues that there were many more Mennonite men who accepted full military service in World War II than is commonly believed.

Duce, Stanley J. "The Christian's Attitude Toward Military Service." *GH* 51 (Mar. 18, 1958), 249. Scriptural support for the position that the Christian should refrain from participating in military service. Refutes some arguments that the Bible sanctions participation in armies.

Dueck, Dora. "Mexico Mennonites Return to Canada." *MBH* 14 (Jan. 10, 1975), 22. Mennonites who left Canada to preserve religious and ethnic freedom (including nonparticipation in the military) are returning to Canada for the same reasons.

Dyck, Walter H. "The Mutual Responsibility of the Church and Returning Service Men." *Menn* 60 (Nov. 13, 1945), 5-7. A survey of CPS and military servicemen, and others. Centers around the problem of re-integrating servicemen into the congregations. There is a wide divergence of opinion as to the attitude of the Mennonite church toward those who chose military service.

Dymond. "The Opinions of the Primitive Christians on the Lawfulness of War." *GH* 44 (Mar. 20, 1951), 274-75, 285. Reprinted from *Herald of Truth* (Dec., 1866). Christ, the disciples, and the first Christians disavowed any part in the military. Quotations from early church sources show numerous incidences of this stand.

"Elmer Neufeld Begins As Peace Section Exec.-Sec." *CanMenn* 7 (Sept. 18, 1959), 5. The appointment of Elmer Neufeld as full-time executive secretary of MCC Peace Section will make possible intensified witness in the areas of militarism and race relations.

"Escalation of Compassion for Vietnam." *Menn* 80 (June 22, 1965), 420. Text of a letter sent to President Johnson by the Mennonite Central Committee. MCC urges the president to turn from the military solution to the way of compassion and peace.

Eby, John W. "January 27, 1973; Will Peace Last?" *GH* 66 (Mar. 20, 1973), 254. Eby's joy in the Vietnam peace agreement is tempered by realization of the moral costs of the war; such as expanded power of the military over national priorities, and neglect of the problem of poverty.

Ediger, Elmer. "Facing Civil Defense." *Menn* 70 (Dec. 6, 1955), 758, 765. Discusses the dilemma of Mennonite participation in Civil Defense, i.e., it is not purely military in purpose, but includes welfare service. Several guidelines for action are suggested.

Ediger, Elmer. "Our Colleges and the Voluntary Service Program in the Present Crisis." *PCMCP Eighth*, 54-61. Newton, Kansas: Herald Book and Printing Co., Inc. Held at Messiah Bible College, Grantham, Pennsylvania, June 14-15, 1951. Colleges and voluntary service must be seen together as part of the response to mounting military training and statism. Discusses many possibilities emerging from this relationship.

Ediger, Max. "Freedom." *GH* 67 (Oct. 29, 1974), 817-19. Contrasts the spiritual freedom of prisoners of conscience who have refused to compromise their convictions, with the bondage of those enslaved to militarism, apathy, fear, hate.

Ediger, Max. "Mennonites Urge Congressmen to End Vietnam War." *MBH* 12 (Jan 26, 1973), 2. Describes how Mennonites and Brethren in Christ spontaneously gathered with other peace advocates in Washington, DC, Jan. 3-4, 1973, to petition congresspersons to terminate funds for military operations in Vietnam, unless a negotiated peace settlement is reached by the end of January.

Ediger, Peter J. "America! America!" *GH* 69 (June 29, 1976), 527-28; "America! America! A Litany of Love and Lamentation." *MennRep* 6 (June 28, 1976), 5; *Menn* 91 (June 22, 1976), 413-16. Poem intended for use during worship on July 4 includes allusions from the Declaration of Independence, national hymns, Old Testament prophets, and Martin Luther King, woven into an outcry against American militarism and exploitation, and a prayer for peace.

Ediger, Peter J. "America Is on the Road to Hell." *GH* 62 (July 15, 1969), 609. Poem mourns American trust in militarism.

Ediger, Peter J. "Amos Visits America." *Peacemakers in a Broken World*. Ed. John A. Lapp. Scottdale: Herald Press, 1969, 8-19. Ediger rewrites passages from Amos, placing the contemporary translation parallel to original passages on facing pages, in order to illustrate God's judgment for wealthy and religious Americans who oppress the poor and trust in military protection.

Ediger, Peter J. "Summer's End." *God and Caesar* 6 (Sept., 1980), 1. Poem outlines choices Mennonites face between serving God and serving a government committed to military might.

Ediger, Peter J. "Which Gospel?" *God and Caesar* 2 (June, 1976), 1. The writer juxtaposes the Gospel of Christ with the gospel of military power.

Ehlers, Randall. Letter to the Editor. *ChrLead* 36 (Jan. 23, 1973), 17. Support for the military. The liberty and freedom in America are preserved because Americans have fought and died on foreign soil.

Ens, Robert D. Letter to the Editor. *ChrLead* 41 (Jan. 31, 1978), 16. Advocates Mennonite involvement with military personnel and Mennonite rejection of the military's purposes.

Epp, Frank H. "A Policy of Force." *CanMenn* 5 (Jan. 11, 1957), 2. "Increasing dependence on and resort to force in many areas of life are a sure sign of loss of Christian virtue and integrity." The idea of physical and political force increasingly dominates American Christianity.

Epp, Frank H. *A Strategy for Peace: Reflections of a Christian Pacifist*. Grand Rapids: Wm. B. Eerdmans, 1973. Pp. 128. Eleven essays on topics related to war and peace, such as pacifism, militarism, nationalism, social order. Includes essays previously published in other collections, for example: "The Unilateral Disarmament of the Church" (*Peacemakers in a Broken World*, 1969); "American Causes of World War III" (*The Star-Spangled Beaver*, ed.

Redekop, 1971); "Evangelism and Peace" (*Probe*, ed. Fairfield, 1972).

Epp, Frank H. "American Causes of World War III." *The Star-Spangled Beaver*. Ed. John H. Redekop. Toronto: Peter Martin Assoc. Ltd., 1971, 118-33. While causes of World War III would be complex and widespread, American causes include a shift toward economic greed and international profiteering; dependence on an oversized military machine; and belief in a national religion that paints opponents as anti-Christs.

Epp, Frank H. "An Army Is Not an Asset." *CanMenn* 3 (Sept. 2, 1955), 2. An army is eventually a liability to any nation because it wastes both manpower and public money.

Epp, Frank H. "Christianity and the Military." *CanMenn* 11 (May 31, 1963), 5. A critique of *Christianity Today*'s support of the US's vast weapons system. The magazine falls short of its mission when it supports military policy with biblical texts.

Epp, Frank H. "Christians Between East and West." *Christians Between East and West*. Christian Concerns Series No. 1. Winnipeg: Board of Christian Service, Conference of Mennonites in Canada, [ca. 1965], 7-16. Describes features of communist and anticommunist propaganda which have attracted Mennonites to both camps, then uses the image of Christ to critique the materialism, militarism, power, and propaganda of both perspectives.

Epp, Frank H. "Churchmen and the Military." *CanMenn* 12 (Aug. 25, 1964), 4. The close linkage of church people with the military is troublesome because these same persons make the claim of greatest faithfulness to the Bible and the Christian faith.

Epp, Frank H. "Civil Defense Moves." *CanMenn* 7 (Apr. 10, 1959).2. It is of paramount importance that changes in the Civil Defense structure be watched closely. A specific point of concern is whether the military or the civil authorities will assume top authority in an emergency.

Epp, Frank H. "Force Is Futile, But . . . " *CanMenn* 5 (Feb. 22, 1957), 2. A comment on the action of more than 100 members of the British Parliament who passed a motion affirming that the use of force in the modern world is futile. Still, force is being used. To reject force is the test of complete renunciation of the things of this world and complete obedience to the Spirit of God.

Epp, Frank H. Letter to the Editor, "Information on Military Experience Needed." *MennRep* 9 (Dec. 24, 1979), 6. A letter commenting on recent discussion in the *MennRep* on the subject of Mennonites in the armed forces during World War II and requesting assistance from readers in obtaining more information on military service.

Epp, Frank H. "Man and His World of War." *GH* 59 (June 28, 1966), 574; *YCC* 47 (July 17, 1966), 2. It is shocking that Christians show the same tendency to believe in military might rather than in love that non-Christians do. This tendency denies the kingdom, love, and cross of Christ.

Epp, Frank H. "Man and the Missile." *CanMenn* 5 (Aug. 30, 1957), 2. Western Christendom is as missile-minded as atheistic communism. The missile race is a test because the true members of the church of Christ will die rather than take part in such a slaughter.

Epp, Frank H. "Mass Migration from Russia to Manitoba: The Choice Wasn't Easy." *MennRep* 4 (Nov. 25, 1974), 12-16. Detailed account of circumstances leading to the decision of thousands of Russian Mennonites to migrate to Canada, including the impact of threatened compulsory military service.

Epp, Frank H. *Mennonites in Canada, 1786-1920: The History of a Separate People*, Vol. 1. Toronto: Macmillan of Canada, 1974. Pp. 480. History includes discussion of such pertinent war and peace topics as the effects of the American Revolution; the nonresistors and the militia in the War of 1812; World War I; and military exemptions. See table of contents.

Epp, Frank H. "Military Draft Presents Major Problem to USA and Peace Groups." *CanMenn* 15 (Apr. 25, 1967), 1, 2. Peace groups express three major concerns: probable extension of conscription in US; the "inequalities" of the present draft system; and the Vietnam war and military service in general.

Epp, Frank H. "Prophets Wanted." *CanMenn* 4 (Feb. 10, 1956), 2. America's greatest sins are luxury and militarism. These not only prevent the full bloom of Christianity at home, they also taint our witness abroad.

Epp, Frank H. "The American Revolution and the Canadian Evolution." *GH* (Oct. 28, 1975), 771-72; *MennRep* 5 (Nov. 10, 1975), 8. Christian nonresistants in both the US and Canada need to reflect soberly on their national histories. While American revolutionary spirit has sought a violent solution to every problem, Canadian gradualism has meant being sucked into the military strategies of Britain and the US.

Epp, Frank H. "The Conflict and the Church." *CanMenn* 9 (Sept. 29, 1961), 6. The Christian response to the communist advance must bypass militarism and go beyond nationalism and Phariseeism. The church is not contending against political systems but against the spiritual powers of darkness.

Epp, Frank H. "The Military Threat." *CanMenn* 10 (Aug. 31, 1962), 2. Analyzes the trend toward military control in American life. The church has not dealt with the military-mindedness of society.

Epp, Frank H. "The Peace Force." *CanMenn* 12 (May 5, 1964), 5. The basic problem with the Pearson peace force plan is suggested by the paradoxical name—"peace force." Yet this force may still be better than the national army.

Epp, Frank H. "War and Economy." *CanMenn* 15 (Jan. 31, 1967), 4. Describes Canada's contribution to the conflagration in Vietnam and the ever-rising costs of the military machine there.

Epp, Frank H. (Editorial). "A Policy of Force." *CanMenn* 5 (Jan. 11, 1957), 2. A warning against the philosophy of force that American Christianity supports. A call to the only ethical force—Christian love.

Epp, Frank H. (Editorial). "Force Is Futile, But . . ." *CanMenn* 5 (Feb. 22, 1957), 2. Christendom is blamed for not showing politicians that military might is totally futile. However, even though many politicians see the futility of force, they are unable to take the leap of faith into the way of love.

Epp, Frank H. (Editorial). "Prophets Wanted." *CanMenn* 4 (Feb. 10, 1956), 2. Epp decries North American materialism and militarism.

Epp, Henry H. "The Word of God in the Nuclear Age." *CanMenn* 7 (May 29, 1959), 2. An interpretation of the Church Peace Mission conference at Evanston, Ill. The military chaplaincy, civil disobedience, and nonviolence as a means of social change were among the topics discussed.

Erb, Paul. "Militarism as Social Service." *GH* 39 (July 16, 1946), 339. The evangelical fundamentalists are inconsistent when they so greatly emphasize participation in war as a Christian form of service to the world.

Erb, Paul. "Noncombatant Service." *GH* 37 (June 30, 1944), 243. One who believes war is wrong has no business in any part of the army, including noncombatant service. Such service is at best a very weak witness against war.

Erb, Paul. "Prayer for Our Government." *GH* 44 (May 8, 1951), 435-36. Even though Mennonites cannot agree with the militarism of the US, we must still pray for the leaders of the country.

Erb, Paul. "V-Day." *GH* 37 (Dec. 8, 1944), 699. Mennonites cannot help celebrate a military victory, but V-Day may be an appropriate time for prayers of thanksgiving, confession, and intercession.

Ewert, Mrs. D. P. Letter to the Editor. *Menn* 89 (Feb. 19, 1974), 126-27. The Christian church must not reduce itself to a position of nation-worship by overlooking corruption in high places or baptizing military strategies, since to be truly pro-American is to be a world citizen.

"Forces That Make for War." *Menn* 53 (Oct. 25, 1938), 10-11. A Young People's program suggested by the GCMC. Causes of war need to be dealt with if war is to cease. Some of these causes are economic rivalry, secret diplomacy, and large military establishments.

Foster, Edith. "In Pursuit of Freedom." *ChrLiv* 5, Part 1, (Jan., 1958), 14-17, 34, 39; Part 2, (Feb., 1958), 14-17, 19, 37 and (Mar., 1958), 14-47, 19, 37; Part 3, (Apr., 1958), 24-29, (May, 1958), 24-29, and (June, 1958), 24-28. Story traces the migrations of the Pannabakker family through nearly 300 years. Includes the migration of a young Dutch man to Pennsylvania to escape military service, and the troubles of a Menonite family in Canada during the 1812 war.

Fransen, Harold. "The North American Military—1." *Menn* 93 (Mar. 21, 1978), 206. Comments on the exorbitant defense budget and the high incidence of drug and alcohol use in the volunteer army. Laments the fact that the evangelical community is one of the strongest supporters of the military.

Fransen, Harold. "The North American Military—2." *Menn* 93 (Apr. 18, 1978), 268. Discusses Canadian complicity in the arms race and the burgeoning military enterprise around the world.

Franz, Arthur R. "What Should My Attitude as a Christian Be Toward War?" *MCE* 1 (Aug. 21, 1934), 2-4. The Mennonite church is not now taking an active part in the fight against war and militarism. Those who do not raise a voice of protest against the evils of war are guilty of these evils.

Franz, Delton. "A Visit to the Arms Bazaar." *ChrLiv* 41 (Nov. 21, 1978), 24; "I Went to an Arms Bazaar." *GH* 71 (Dec. 5, 1978), 945; *Menn* 94 (Jan. 23, 1979), 61. Description of the annual weapons extravaganza sponsored by the Association of the US Army which is designed to entice the US and foreigners to buy the latest, most powerful, and deadly weapons.

Franz, Delton. "A Witness on Behalf of the Powerless." *MCC PS Wash. Memo* 9 (July-Aug., 1977), 3-4. Patty Erb's meeting with members of Congress alerted them to injustice being done to the poor and prisoners in a country supported by US military aid.

Franz, Delton. "Against the Wall in Latin America." *GH* 67 (Nov. 5, 1974), 846-47; "Washington Report: Latin America: A Look at North/South Relations." *MennRep* 4 (Sept. 30, 1974), 7. Multinational corporations in Latin America promote the increasing gap between rich and poor, while US military and torture procedures oppress those who work for change.

Franz, Delton. "An Opportunity to Cut Military Waste." *MCC PS Wash. Memo* 5 (July-Aug., 1973), 4-5. Comment on the congressional amendment to decrease the size of overseas troops and thus reduce the defense budget.

Franz, Delton. "By Taking $6,480 an Hour X 2,000 Years, You Get . . ." *MCC PS Wash. Memo* 7 (Mar.-Apr., 1976), 1-2. Denounces the level of military spending in the requested budget for Fiscal Year 1977.

Franz, Delton. "CIA Reverses Policy on Relation to Missionaries." *ChrLead* 39 (July 20, 1976), 14. Reports on the new regulation issued by the CIA to restrict its agents from initiating contacts with missionaries.

Franz, Delton. "Foreign Aid at the Crossroads." *MCC PS Wash. Memo* 3 (Nov.-Dec., 1971), 3-5. US foreign aid needs to be restructured to cut back on military assistance and to focus aid toward people, not governments.

Franz, Delton. "If I Had a Hammer." *MCC PS Wash. Memo* 9 (Mar.-Apr., 1977), 1-2. Advocates support of the Transfer Amendment, which would in one step shift funds budgeted for the military into human needs programs.

Franz, Delton. "Implements of Death at a Washington Bazaar." *EV* 92 (Feb. 10, 1979), 5. Reflections on a visit to the annual weapons extravaganza sponsored by the Association of the United States Army.

Franz, Delton. "Inflation Is a Stewardship Matter." *MCC PS Wash. Memo* 6 (Nov.-Dec., 1974), 1-3. The excessive and wasteful military budget is the primary cause of the inflated economy.

Franz, Delton. "Issues to Ponder in an Election Year." *MCC PS Wash. Memo* 7 (May-June, 1976), 1-2. Denounces high military spending at the expense of social programs and continuing military orientation of foreign policy.

Franz, Delton. "June 28—First Day Your Income

Taxes Go for Non-military Purposes." *MCC PS Wash. Memo* 10 (Mar.-Apr., 1978), 1-3. Decries the percentage of the federal budget allocated for defense purposes and supports the Transfer Amendment to transfer military funds into humanitarian programs.

Franz, Delton. Letter to the Editor. *God and Caesar* 1 (Mar., 1975), 6. Writer shares the views of Congresswoman Pat Schroeder who holds a strong dove position on the military but expresses concerns about the World Peace Tax Fund in that it will divert equal energies of the Mennonite people from helping to actually curb military growth.

Franz, Delton. "Middle East a Proving Ground." *MCC PS Wash. Memo* 5 (Nov.-Dec., 1973), 1-2. The US is using Israel as testing ground for new weapons systems, thus threatening the military balance of power in the Mideast.

Franz, Delton. "Military Budget Under Scrutiny." *MCC PS Wash. Memo* 5 (Sept.-Oct., 1973), 1-3. Congressional committees are recommending cuts in the defense budget.

Franz, Delton. "Military Strike Force Planned to Safeguard Oil Supply." *MCC PS Wash. Memo* 11 (July-Aug., 1979), 1-2, 9. While publicly committed to nonintervention, the US is preparing a strike force of 110,000 to safeguard a continuous flow of oil from the Mideast.

Franz, Delton. "Missiles in the Pasture." *Menn* 84 (June 24, 1969), 423, 424. An analysis of the staggering costs of equipping the nation with ABM's, the failure of the nation to meet its own needs in areas of poverty and injustice, and what the church's responsibility in this situation.

Franz, Delton. "Panama Canal Treaty: The Test for Future Inter-American Relations." *MCC PS Wash. Memo* 9 (Sept.-Oct., 1977), 1-2, 7. Exposes injustices present in the US administration of the Canal Zone and argues with the mythology of US military security insured by the US presence there.

Franz, Delton. "Rich Nation in a Poor World: What Response?" *MCC PS Wash. Memo* 5 (July-Aug., 1973), 1-3. The quantity and quality of US foreign aid is declining, due in part to the inclusion of military aid in the same package with economic aid.

Franz, Delton. "The Bitter Fruit of Aiding Military Dictatorships." *MCC PS Wash. Memo* 8 (Sept.-Oct., 1976), 1-2. Denounces US military aid to Third World military dictatorships, linking US aid to right-wing terrorist activity in those countries.

Franz, Delton. "The Carter Doctrine: A Blatant

Gamble with 'Limited' Nuclear War." *MCC PS Wash. Memo* 12 (May-June, 1980), 1-4. Compares Carter's stance of military aggressiveness toward the Persian Gulf region with the more rational approach of trying to understand the grievances of adversaries in the region.

Franz, Delton. "Thunder on the Right: 'The Russians Are Coming!'" *MCC PS Wash. Memo* 9 (Jan.-Feb., 1977), 1-2. Comment on the outgoing Ford administration's efforts to pressure Congress into increasing military spending.

Franz, Delton. "Volunteer Army 'Succeeding' as Pentagon Juggles Figures." *RepConsS* 31 (Feb., 1974), 1, 4. Questions whether the army is attempting to undermine the success of an all-volunteer military force.

Franz, Delton. "Washington Report: Mortgaging the Future to the Military." *MennRep* 5 (Apr. 14, 1975), 7. Deplores the size of the requested military budget for 1976 and "cold war idealogue" Schlesinger's introduction of the military budget by using scripture.

Franz, Delton. "Will We Mortgage Our Future to the Military?" *MCC PS Wash. Memo* 7 (Mar.-Apr., 1975), 1-2. Outlines the hidden and future costs behind the Defense Department's budget askings.

Franz, Delton, ed. "Pending Legislation . . . Swords; Pending Legislation . . . Plowshares." *MCC PS Wash. Memo* 7 (Mar. Apr., 1975), 5-6. Compares legislation concerning foreign military aid to legislation initiating food aid.

Franz, Delton, ed. "Review of Congress in 1972." *MCC PS Wash. Memo* 4 (Nov.-Dec., 1972), 4-5. Evaluates congressional action on topics such as the Vietnam War, military spending, the draft, etc.

Franz, Delton, ed. "The American Dream: For Whom?" *MCC PS Wash. Memo* 5 (Mar.-Apr., 1973), 1-3. Federal policy and budget show misplaced priorities favoring military spending over people-oriented projects.

Franz, Delton (Review). *The Price of Power: Kissinger in the Nixon Whitehouse,* by Seymour M. Hersh. NY: Summit Books, 1983. Pp. 698. *CGR* 2 (Winter, 1984), 69-71. Hersh's book, outlining the subversion of legislative constraints by White House officials (such as Kissinger's presiding over the secret bombing of Cambodia in 1969-70 without the consent of Congress), provides an important perspective for Mennonite Christians concerned about the use of military power in implementing foreign policy.

Fretz, J. Winfield. "Our Peace Witness During World War II." *The Power of Love; A Study Manual Adopted for Sunday School Use and for Group Discussion,* pp. 58-96. Ed. Peace Committee of the General Conference Mennonite Church. Newton: Board of Publication, 1947. MHL. Discusses the history and operation of the CPS program, the point of view of those Mennonites who entered military service as chaplains, etc., and the witness of the noncombatants. Concludes that the CPS program was the choice most consistent with Mennonite belief and practice and that the program was an effective witness for peace to the nation, to the community, and to the Mennonite churches.

Fretz, J. Winfield. "Sociological Aspects of Divorce Among Mennonites." *PCMCP Eighth,* 132-38. Newton, Kansas: Herald Book and Printing Co., Inc. Held at Messiah Bible College, Grantham, Pennsylvania, June 14-15, 1951. Family tension and divorce are common problems in every Mennonite group. Divorces are related to social conservatism. The church's responses to military service and divorce are similar.

Fretz, J. Winfield. "Why Mennonite Boys Choose Military Service." (Part 2) *Menn* (July 31, 1945), 5-6. The position of drafted men generally reflects the attitudes of their pastors. The census as a whole indicates that the General Conference is losing its doctrine of biblical nonresistance.

Friedmann, Michael. Letter to the Editor. *God and Caesar* 6 (Jan., 1980), 11-12. Expresses pessimism over the possibility of legislatively decreasing the amount of money available to the military and calls for increased war tax resistance and nonviolent action at military centers.

Friesen, Jake. Letter to the Editor. *Intercom* 5 (May-June, 1965), 2-3. Calls attention to inconsistencies in the Mennonite peace witness, such as accepting protection from American military personnel while working in a foreign country.

Friesen, Mrs. Dee. Letter to the Editor. *ChrLead* 41 (Jan. 31, 1978), 16. Pacifism is a very privileged position. There are many members of the military who are just as devout and sincere Christians as the "best" Mennonites.

Friesen, Tom (Review). *Our Star-Spangled Faith,* by Donald B. Kraybill. Scottdale: Herald Press, 1976. Pp. 216. *Menn* 92 (Mar. 1, 1977), 157. Kraybill's exposure of America's "God and country" religion helps Christians distinguish the symbols of the military and government from those of Christianity.

Fundenburg, Harry C. "Military Training

Unchristian." *GH* 28 (Nov. 14, 1935), 706-707. Military training, war, and killing of any sort are not sanctioned by the New Testament. The Church of the Brethren has since its beginning opposed war and maintained the principle of nonresistance.

Funk, John F. *Warfare. Its Evils Our Duty. Addressed to the Mennonite Churches Throughout the United States, and All Others Who Sincerely Seek and Love the Truth.* Chicago: By the Author, 1863. Pp. 16. MHL. Despite the pressures of society and the lure of military glory, let us remain faithful to the example of Jesus, who lived the nonresistant life in every way.

General Conference Mennonite Church. "Resolution or Nationalism." *GH* 61 (Nov. 5, 1968), 992-93. Calls for a spirit of internationalism in the face of advocated military solutions to exaggerated national threats.

General Conference Mennonite Church. *Studies in Church Discipline*. Newton: Mennonite Publication Office, 1958. Pp. 241. Eighteen papers on the nature of the church and the meaning of church membership, together with tables on the practice of church discipline in General Conference congregations, and five appendices, including the Portland, Ore., 1953 statement of the General Conference on Peace, War, and Military Service.

Gerlach, Horst. "Through Darkness to Light." *ChrLiv* 3 (Aug., 1956), 6-9, 40-41; 3 (Sept., 1956), 12-15, 40; 3 (Oct., 1956), 14-17, 19, 34, 36; 3 (Nov., 1956), 19-22, 24, 34, 35-37; 3 (Dec., 1956), 24-29, 36; 4 (Jan., 1957), 24-29; 4 (Feb., 1957), 24-29. Life story of a young German man growing up in a pro-Nazi family during the Hitler and World War II era. Enemy occupation of home town; prisoner of war in northern Russia as slave laborer; conversion to Christianity from trust in military force while an MCC trainee serving in the US.

Gillespie, Malcolm. "Three-Year Struggle." *YCC* 47 (July 3, 1966), 5. A conscientious objector convinces the court only after a grueling three-year struggle and wins the I-O classification.

Gingerich, Melvin. "*As Others See Us.*" *ChrLiv* 5 (Oct., 1958), 7-9. One factor contributing to anti-American feeling abroad is the US trust in military and nuclear force.

Gingerich, Melvin. "Moral Standards and Military Life." *GH* 55 (July 17, 1962), 625. When persons are trained in the art of killing, other moral values no longer seem absolute or relevant. This problem will not be solved until the immorality of war itself is faced.

Gingerich, Melvin. "The Gospel and Revolution." *GH* 62 (Apr. 15, 1969), 338-39. Jesus' message was revolutionary in challenging human institutions of power and prestige. The church must not continue to side with those who defend the status quo through military and economic power; the church must identify with salvation, forgiveness, and justice.

Gingerich, Melvin. "The Need for a Peace Witness in the Orient." *MennLife* 14 (July, 1959), 99-101. Asia longs for peace. While Buddhism and communism carry the banner of peace, "Christian" America, including many of its missionaries, are identified with militarism and conquest.

Gingerich, Melvin. "What About the Noncombatant Position?" Goshen College, n.d. Pp. 9. MLA/BeC.

Gingerich, Melvin. *What of Noncombatant Service? A Study of Alternatives Facing the Conscientious Objector.* Scottdale: Herald Press, 1949. Pp. 48. MSHL. Concludes that the demands of the love ethic are such that Christians must refuse any participation in an organization, such as the military, whose purpose is to kill those for whom Christ died.

Gleysteen, Jan. Letter to the Editor. *GH* 69 (Apr. 27, 1976), 277. As a recently naturalized US citizen, Gleysteen cites realities which show that the US is not a favored Christian nation, and that its national priorities in military expenditures, etc., do not conform to Jesus' way.

Goering, Terence R. "The Mennonites in Russia and Their Relations with the Political and Military Authorities of the Russian Government." Student paper for A Decade Relived, Jan. 25, 1974. Pp. 59. MLA/BeC.

Goertzen, Don. Letter to the Editor. *ChrLead* 41 (Jan. 3, 1978), 15. Explores three basic reasons why relatively few Mennonite Brethren pastors speak on the military and Christianity.

Goertzen, Pete. Letter to the Editor. *ChrLead* 40 (Oct. 25, 1977), 10. Hard to see any of the works of Christ in the military profession.

Gross, Leonard, comp. "Alternative to War: A Story Through Documents, Part 1." *GH* 65 (Nov. 7, 1972), 899-901; Part 2, (Dec. 26, 1972), 1046-47; 66, Part 3, (Jan. 2, 1973), 10-12; Part 4 (Jan. 9, 1973), 34-36; Part 5, (Jan. 16, 1973), 52-55. Uses contemporary documents to describe the difficulties Mennonites encountered during the Civil War and World War I, as well as the Mennonite response.

Gross, Leonard, ed. "John M. Brenneman and the Civil War." *MHB* 34 (Oct., 1973), 1-3. Publishes the draft of a letter to President Lincoln written by a group of Ohio Mennonites, requesting exemption from military duty. Includes draft of a cover letter written by Brenneman.

Guest-Smith, Kathleen N. "The Militarization of Women." *Forum* 9 (Feb., 1976), 5. A growing number of women are entering the military and the Equal Rights Amendment would ensure their participation in registration and the draft. Women therefore must look critically at their role in the all-volunteer army.

Habegger, Luann. "Exporting Men, Money, and Arms." *MCC PS Wash. Memo* 6 (July-Aug., 1974), 1-3. Statistics and comment on US foreign military aid to train military and police forces in policies favoring the US government.

Hackman, Walton. "'Pursue What Makes for Peace.'" *GH* 66 (Feb. 6, 1973), 108-109. The growing civil religion in the US increasingly blesses national interests and policies, including military actions.

Handrich, Rick L. "My God, My Country, and My Fellowman." *GH* 61 (Oct. 15, 1968), 930-31. Conscientious objector serving as research subject at an army hospital explains why he decided to enter the military in a noncombatant role.

Harding, Vincent G. "Vietnam: What Shall We Do?" *Menn* 80 (Sept. 21, 1965), 582-85; "What Shall We Do About Vietnam?" *CanMenn* 13, Part 1, (Sept. 14, 1965), 6; Part 2, (Sept. 21, 1965), 6; *MBH* 4 (Sept. 17, 1965), 14 (shortened version). It is time that Mennonites' professed opposition to war be proclaimed as public dissent to American military policy. Response must begin with repentance and then seek to witness openly to the way of love and reconciliation.

Harriott, John. "The Obsession of Our Age." *Menn* 94 (Nov. 17, 1979), 708-709. The build-up of militarism is the most insidious disease and afflicts humanity beyond any other moral, political, social, economic, or personal danger.

Harshbarger, Emmett L. "A Mennonite Preparedness Program." *Menn* 53 (Dec. 20, 1938), 5-6. A peacemaking response to international strife demands a different sort of preparedness than a military response. Mennonites must prepare themselves for wartime individually, educationally, and by taking part in peace programs.

Harshbarger, Emmett L. "Out of the Czech Crisis." *Menn* 53 (Nov. 8, 1938), 2. The myth of "collective security" has been shattered, providing the church with further challenge and opportunity for peace witness. Analysis of military defense policy.

Hatfield, Mark O. "A Time to Share." *MBH* 13 (Oct. 4, 1974), 3-4, 27. In the face of the world hunger crisis, US national budget calls for $90 billion of military spending and $1.9 billion humanitarian aid.

Hatfield, Mark O. "Piety and Patriotism." *MBH* 13 (Aug. 9, 1974), 1-4. Since ultimate loyalty belongs to God, not the state, Christians must confront militarism, materialism, and racism. Cites cases of third century pacifist stances.

Hatfield, Mark O. "Senator Mark Hatfield's 'End the War' Bill." *MCC PS Wash. Memo* 2 (May-June, 1970), 1-3. Reprint of a speech by Mark Hatfield urging support of an amendment withholding funds for military expenditures in Vietnam.

Haury, David A. "The Mennonite Congregation of Boston." *MennLife* 34 (Sept., 1979), 24-27. The birth and development of the Mennonite congregation of Boston including their concerns and mission regarding nuclear weapons, the Vietnam war, military service, and war taxes.

Heatwole, Reuben Joseph. "A Civil War Story." *MHB* 9 (Jan., 1948), 3-4; *ST* 40 (Oct., 1972), 12. Relates his experiences as a seventeen-year-old migrating north from Virginia to escape military duty during the Civil War. Written in 1919.

Hershberger, Bernie; Bender, Brent; Kauffman, Duane; Yoder, Steve; and Nafziger, Beverly. "A Four-College Comparison of Ethical Ideologies in Relation to Current Moral Issues." *Journal of Psychology and Christianity* 1 (Fall, 1982), 32-39. A study of 207 General Psychology students explores the influence of ideology on responses to specific ethical issues, including such items as the death penalty, the military draft, and nuclear weapons.

Hershberger, Guy F. "Litigation in Mennonite History." Paper presented at the Laurelville, Pa., conference on "Nonresistance and Political Responsibility," 1956. N.p.: Peace Problems Committee, 1956, 32-35. MHL. Those Mennonites who have been most consistent in rejecting military service have also been most consistent in their refusal to seek legal redress.

Hershberger, Guy F. "Military Training in Schools and Colleges." *YCC* 19 (Apr. 3, 1938), 111-12. History and description of the military training efforts in US schools and colleges. Mennonite young people should receive their education in Mennonite schools.

Hershberger, Guy F. "Noncombatant Military and Noncombatant Civilian Service." *YCC* 20 (Dec. 24, 1939), 832. The Mennonite Church stands against the noncombatant military service choice. Noncombatant civilian service is wholly consistent with the nonresistant way of life.

Hershberger, Guy F. "Reflections on Armistice Day." YCC 20 (Nov. 5, 1939), 776. The growing spirit of militarism shows how short our memories are in light of the cost (human, economic, social) of the World War.

Hershberger, Guy F. "The Origin of the Peace Problems Committee." YCC 18 (Aug. 1, 1937), 664. The Peace Problems Committee, as well as the earlier Military Problems Committee, concerned itself chiefly with problems arising out of World War I. The ongoing work of the Peace Problems Committee was to encourage the efforts to strengthen the nonresistant faith and stay in touch with government.

Hershberger, Guy F. "What Happened on May 18, 1967? Our Peace Witness—In the Wake of May 18." (Part 1). GH 60 (Sept. 5, 1967), 803-804. The news report was published that Congress was considering a bill calling for the induction of CO's into the military forces.

Hershberger, Guy F. "What Shall a Christian Youth Do in Time of War?" YCC 18 (June 6, 1937), 600. From the experience in World War I, there seem to be four possible courses of action a person might follow in time of war: regular military service; noncombatant service; complete refusal to participate in the military; alternative Christian service.

Hershberger, Guy F. (Review). War Comes to Quaker Pennsylvania, 1682-1756, by Robert L. D. Davidson. New York: Columbia Univ. Press, Temple Univ. Publications, 1957. In Bulletin of Friends Historical Association 47 (1958), 113-15; also in William and Mary Quarterly 15 (1958), 532-34. A military history of colonial Pennsylvania.

Hertzler, Daniel. "The Isaiah Vision." GH 67 (July 2, 1974), 544. Isaiah's vision of God standing apart from the military victories or defeats of a people is more profound than the Exodus vision, which viewed God as a great warrior.

Hertzler, Daniel. "When Do We Get the Goodies?" GH 73 (Sept. 2, 1980), 712. Criticizes TV-peddled religion's emphasis on protecting American riches through military force instead of following the way of Christ's love.

Hertzler, Daniel (Editorial). "The World Upside Down." GH 69 (Aug. 17, 1976), 636. Urges Mennonites to make their voices heard for justice in those areas where the world's priorities are upside down, such as spending inordinate amounts for military purposes while people are hungry.

Hess, James R. "The Christian and the Bicentennial Celebrations." ST 44 (Apr., 1976),

24-26. Reprinted from Pastoral Messenger. Among the positive aspects of life in the US is the fact that nearly 5 times as much of the Gross National Product goes for social services as for military expenditures.

Hess, James R. "The Christian and the US Bicentennial." GH 69 (Apr. 13, 1976), 306-307. Government is ordained by God, but not called to operate according to the Sermon on the Mount. Christians should neither endorse militarism nor excessively criticize the government.

Hiebert, Murray. "War Scraps Forged into Plows." FStP 1 (Sept., 1976), 1-2. Foundry near Vientiane, Laos, buys military scrap metal and forges it into farm implements.

Hirsch, Charles B. "The Civilian Public Service Camp Program in Indiana." Indiana Magazine of History 46 (1950), 259-81. CPS program in Indiana, with all its inadequacies, was a distinct imporvement over World War I treatment of COs. Innovations included the recognition of COs of all faiths and an alternative program of military service.

Hirstine, Ed. "What Choice Shall I Make?" Menn 54 (Jan. 31, 1939), 9-10. Mennonites should not compromise with the military regarding a possible draft, by accepting a kind of alternative to drilling with guns. Only total nonresistance is sufficient.

Hornus, Jean-Michel. It Is Not Lawful for Me to Fight: Early Christian Attitudes Toward War, Violence, and the State, trans. Alan Kreider and Oliver Coburn. Rev. ed. Scottdale and Kitchener: Herald Press, 1980. Pp. 367. Hornus studies the social, political, and theological framework and extant writings from the first 3 centuries of Christianity to show: Christian teaching consistently opposed military participation; this position was based in commitment to nonviolence, not merely the rejection of idolatry in emperor worship; why this position was abandoned in the 4th century.

Horsch, John. "Conscientious Objectors to Military Service in European Countries." GH 29 (Feb. 18, 1937), 996-97. A summary of the most recent information on conscientious objection in Europe, including statistics about those imprisoned in a number of countries.

Horsch, John. "Menno Simons on the Principle of Nonresistance." GH 31 (Jan. 12, 1939), 874-75. A collection of Menno's writings supporting nonresistance. It is clear that no one familiar with Menno's writings could say he approved of military service.

Horsch, John. "The Mennonites of Russia, Part III." ChrMon 28 (Aug., 1936), 230, 237.

Experiences of the Rusasian Mennonites during World War I, when young men served in noncombatant posts.

Horsch, John. "The So-Called Noncombatant Military Service." *GH* 32 (June 8, 1939), 210. Noncombatant army service is off-limits for the nonresistant Christian. It is not true, however, that farmers who produce food in wartime are doing noncombatant service.

Horsch, John. "War Resisters and Conscientious Objectors in European Countries." *GH* 29 (Oct. 8, 1936), 602-603. Factual account of the existing situation in Europe, where alternative civil service is offered by some countries while others imprison CO's who refuse military service.

Horst, Samuel. *Mennonites in the Confederacy: A Study in Civil War Pacifism.* Scottdale: Herald Press, 1967. Pp. 148. Documents the variety of ways Mennonites responded to the issues raised by the crisis of the Civil War, such as reluctant cooperation with the military, desertion, flight, choosing prison, working with government officials for legal alternatives, etc. Concludes that the Mennonite witness for peace in this era was not faultless but, nevertheless, significant and sincere. Includes extensive bibliography.

Horst, Samuel L., ed. "The Journal of a Refugee." *MQR* 54 (Oct., 1980), 280-304. Journal of a young Mennonite refugee from Virginia fleeing military duty during the Civil War.

Hostetler, John Andrew. *The Sociology of Mennonite Evangelism.* Scottdale, Pa.: Herald Press, 1954. Pp. 287. MHL. Includes: "Rules and Discipline: Nonparticipation in the Affairs of Government," 28-29; "Unanticipated Evangelistic Interaction: Relief and Peace Activities," 128-30; "Religious Experience and Values Discovered: Nonresistance," 207; "Out-Group Social Attractions: Military Service," 236-37.

Hostetter, B. Charles. "Christian Love Is Needed." *CanMenn* 2 (Feb. 26, 1954), 6. Humanity's basic need is spiritual. Christian love, not military strength, is needed for human salvation.

"International 'Arms Bazaar' Hampered by Protesters." *MennRep* 9 (Apr. 2, 1979), 10. A report on the protest activities of more than 2,000 people at an international military conference and trade show in suburban Chicago.

Isaak, George P. Letter to the Editor. *ChrLead* 36 (Apr. 3, 1973), 12. The doctrinal position of the Mennonite Brethren conference on the issue of nonresistance needs a thorough reevaluation.

Desires more openness to equal time to military participation.

Jacks, Ethel Andrews. "Promote Peace Where You Are." *ChrLiv* 1 (Nov., 1954), 15. The military machine can be halted only if each person contributes something to the cause of peace where he or she is.

Jantz, Harold. "Aid to Vietnam/ese Major Agenda Item in Calgary." *MennRep* 9 (Feb. 5, 1979), 1. At an MCC (Canada) meeting in Jan., considerable discussion revolved around aid to Vietnam and the Vietnamese boat refugees. Among other decisions, it also supported the intention of the Peace and Social Concerns Committee to issue a statement on militarism in Canada.

Jantz, Harold. "God's Kingdom in the Twentieth Century." *MBH* 17 (Sept. 1, 1978), 2-3. Speakers at Mennonite World Conference in Wichita centered their talks around the theme of the peaceable kingdom's response to militarism, oppression, and racism.

Jantz, Harold. "'I Will Joy in the God of My Salvation.'" *MBH* 18 (Dec. 21, 1979), 13. Fear of the future is one response Christians have to unpleasant world events, typified in Jerry Falwell's urgent pleas for American moral and military might.

Jantz, Harold. "Protest Simmers in Vietnam." *MBH* 13 (Nov. 29, 1974), 16-17. Dissatisfaction with the leadership of Nguyen Van Thieu may lead to increased military activity.

Janzen, William. "Opposition to War No Bar to Citizenship." *MBH* 16 (Mar. 4, 1977), 12. The denial of Canadian citizenship to a Jehovah's Witnesses couple refusing military service was the basis for a court ruling guaranteeing citizenship to conscientious objectors.

Jost, Dean. "The Christian and Campus Ferment." *GH* 63 (July 14, 1970), 598-99. Given the division in American society between "establishment" and "radical" cultures, the church must act as a reconciler and as a prophet witnessing against the violence of both cultures: the sexism, racism, and militarism of the establishment, and the drugs, sexual mores, and individualism of the radicals.

Juhnke, James C. "Mennonites and a Christian America." *Citizens and Disciples: Christian Essays on Nationalism.* Akron: MCC Peace Section, [1974], 18-20. MHL. Suggests that, instead of vainly trying to escape participation in the political communities, Mennonites would do well to renew the affirmations that Jesus is Lord and that the kingdom of God takes precedence over all earthly nations, and to recover a prophetic witness to the powers more comprehensive than the refusal of military service.

Jutzi, Robin (Review). *XX Century and Peace*, ed. A. Khomenko. Soviet Peace Committee, n.d. *MennRep* 10 (Sept. 1, 1980), 8. Observes that the official magazine of the Soviet Peace Committee reveals that the Soviets have a particular horror for war but believe that peace is achieved through the presence of a strong military.

Kauffman, Daniel. "Militarism, Pacifism, Nonresistance." *GH* 35 (Oct. 22, 1942), 641-42. The militarist supports war; the pacifist opposes it because of its physical and spiritual destructiveness; the nonresistant opposes it out of obedience to Christ.

Kauffman, J. Howard. "Challenge of Our Day." *ChrLiv* 1 (Nov., 1954), 36. Included in the list of jobs questionable for a Christian are those which contribute to military activity.

Kauffman, Milo (Review). *Christ and Your Job*, by Albert P. Klausler. Concordia Publishing House, 1956. Pp. 145. *ChrLiv* 5 (Dec., 1958), 29. Reviewer observes that included in the discussion of Christian faith and vocation is the conflict between Christian conscience and such jobs as building warheads.

Kauffman, Nelson E. (Review). *Viet-Nam Witness 1953-66*, by Bernard B. Fall. Frederick A. Praeger, 1966. Pp. 363. *ChrLiv* 14 (June, 1967), 36-37. Reviewer observes that the author accuses the US of making the same mistake as France; trying to solve Vietnam's problems through military might without knowledge of the real problems of the country.

Kauffman, Ralph C. "The Implications of Military Toys and Games for Children." *Menn* 63 (Dec. 21, 1948), 12-13. Though war games need not be regarded with alarm, more constructive games and activities should be encouraged.

Kauffman, Richard A.; Hostetler, David E.; and Barrett, Lois. "The Patty Erb Story—One Year Later." *GH* 70 (Sept. 27, 1977), 726-27. Relates Patty Erb's story of imprisonment and torture for her work with the poor in Argentina, a country whose police have been trained by the American military in methods of torture.

Kaufman, Dennis. "An Analysis of the Economic Impact of Military Spending." Student paper for Mathematics/Advanced Peace Studies Seminar, Apr. 27, 1979. Pp. 71. MLA/BeC.

Kaufman, Donald D. "Boot Camp for Peace." *GH* 62 (Mar. 18, 1969), 249-50. Reports and reflects on a mock boot camp held for pre-draft young Mennonite men in order to present and discuss issues related to the draft and military service.

Kaufman, S. Roy. "Ethics for Land Use." *FStP* 4 (Jan., 1979), 8-10. Study of passages in Ezekiel shows that greed, idolatry, and trust in military might are bound up with destruction of the land.

Keeney, William E. "Not Yet Peace." *GH* 66 (July 3, 1973), 533-35; *ChrLead* 36 (July 10, 1973), 2; *Menn* 88 (July 10, 1973), 426-27. The ceasefire in Vietnam means only that American troops have withdrawn. It does not stop the Selective Service or decrease military expenditures or free South Vietnam's political prisoners or begin the immense reconstruction process. Concerns like amnesty, draft, and political prisoners need to be addressed.

Kehler, Larry. "Evangelism, Militarism, and Nationalism." *Menn* 86 (June 22, 1971), 405-408. Relating the idolatry of nationalism and of militarism to the evangelistic message is an integral part of the proclamation of the gospel to repentance.

Kehler, Larry. "Israel Faces a New Reality." *GH* 67 (Sept. 3, 1974), 664-65; *Menn* 889 (Aug. 6, 1974), 469-70; *MennRep* 4 (Aug. 19, 1974), 7; *EV* 87 (Oct. 10, 1974), 5, 6. Since Israel's military superiority over the Arabs was shaken in the 1973 Yom Kippur War, it should learn to build its security on the goodwill of its neighbors rather than on the strength of its borders.

Kehler, Larry. "Our Christian Civil Responsibility—1." *Menn* 93 (Nov. 21, 1978), 685; *MennRep* 8 (Nov. 27, 1978), 6. Urges congregations to study the war tax and militarism questions in preparation for the midtriennium conference in Feb., 1979.

Kehler, Larry. "Our Christian Civil Responsibility—3." *Menn* 93 (Dec. 5, 1978), 717; *MennRep* 8 (Dec. 25, 2978), 6. Militarism and war taxes are live issues in Canada as well as the US, needing Mennonite attention and activity, says Kehler, in preparation for the midtrienium conference discussion on these issues.

Kehler, Larry. "Starve the Military Monster." *Menn* 89 (Apr. 30, 1974), 296. Calls Christians to speak forcefully against the arms race by writing to Parliament and Congress and by supporting the April 30 national day of repentance for trusting in military security.

Kehler, Larry. "Structures and Nationalism Looms [sic] Large at MCC Meeting." *MBH* 14 (Feb. 7, 1975), 10-12. At the annual meeting, the committee passed a resolution on world hunger calling for reduced military expenditure and increased food development.

Keim, Ray; Beechy, Atlee; and Beechy, Winifred. *The Church: The Reconciling Community*. Scottdale: Mennonite Publishing House; Newton: Faith and Life Press, 1970. Pp. 92. Examines the direction set for the church by the reconciling work of Jesus and looks at such issues as militarism, nationalism, human rights, racism, poverty, crime and violence as tasks for the church which embodies that reconciliation.

King, Martin Luther, Jr. "Transformed Nonconformist." *ChrLiv* 11 (Feb., 1964), 9-10, 38. Reprinted from *Strength to Love*, by King; Harper and Row, 1963. Urges nonconformity to the world in matters of nationalism, militarism, racism, and lifestyle.

Kirkwood, Ronald. "Passive-ism or Pacifism." *Menn* 70 (Mar. 8, 1955), 150. The American government, in its very tolerance, is employing its most effective weapon against us. Our vigorous witness against militarism has become a passive witness to the way of love.

Klaassen, Walter. "What Constitutes National Security for Israel and for Canada?" *CanMenn* 15 (July 4, 1967), 1, 2. Sermon for Canada Day which defines national security in lights of the prophets and Israel's ancient and recent history. Hosea regarded the geographical boundaries and the political institutions of Israel as of secondary importance; i.e., not worth military defense. Suggests, therefore, that modern nations take the first step in breaking out of the fatal dependence on violence and military solutions. As a first step for Mennonites, Klaassen suggests meeting with a representative to discuss the discontinuance of the NORAD agreement.

Klassen, James R. "Dear Computer:" *Menn* 95 (Feb. 12, 1980), 109; *God and Caesar* 6 (Jan., 1980), 1. Poem reflecting on war tax resistance and the inhumanity of government military policy.

Klassen, Randolph. "A Matter of Conscience." *HIS* (Magazine of Inter-Varsity Christian Fellowship) 28 (June, 1968), 14-16, 21. From the examples of Christ and the Scripture, the author argues that a military profession may be consistent with God's will, that lifetaking must be without hate, and that Christians should aid the state's God-given mandate to preserve order in society. Argues that a Christian may carry a draft card and participate in military activities if that person recognizes clearly that his/her first loyalty is to the heavenly King.

Kliewer, George M. Letter to the Editor. *ChrLead* 40 (Dec. 6, 1977), 15. God is alive and is actively working on military installations around the world.

Kliewer, John D. Letter to the Editor. *ChrLead* 40 (Dec. 20, 1977), 15. If nonresistance is really the all-important goal of our church, then civilians are already ideal in life-style, and our ministry should be on military bases all over the world.

Kliewer, John W. "A Sermon on Christian After War Questions." Preached at Bethel College, Newton, Ks., Jan. 5, 1919. Pp. 12. MHL.

Kniss, Lloy A. *I Couldn't Fight: The Story of a CO in World War I*. Scottdale, Pa.: Herald Press, 1971. Pp. 47. Portrays the ridicule and hardship experienced by a World War I CO as a result of his steadfast refusal to cooperate with the military system in the military training camps into which he had been forced.

Kolb, Norman. "Nations on the Verge of Calamity." *ST* 47 (July, 1979), 24. A Bible study from which one learns that national preservation depends on national spirituality and not on national military might.

Koontz, Gayle Gerber and Koontz, Ted. "New Front in the Battle with Militarism." *Menn* 88 (June 19, 1973), 400. Calls attention to the expanding Junior Reserve Officer Training Corps (JROTC) programs in high schools, maintaining that such training produces adults who tend to advocate forceful solutions to conflicts at all levels of society.

Koontz, Ted. "Foreign Policy Issues in the US Presidential Election." *Menn* 95 (Oct. 21, 1980), 608. Evaluation of the three major candidates' positions on international affairs includes discussion of their military policies.

Koontz, Ted. "Join Now, Pay Later." *With* 7 (Sept., 1974), 12. The myths that operate behind the military recruitment efforts. Suggestions for positive peacemaking are offered.

Koontz, Ted. "Military Woos High School Counselors." *Menn* 89 (May 21, 1974), 333-34. Describes strategies used by the military to enlist the aid of high school guidance counselors in recruiting students.

Koontz, Ted. "US-Soviet Relations After Afghanistan—1."·*Menn* 95 (Aug. 19, 1980), 418. Interprets Soviet military intervention in Afghanistan as a great power saving face and protecting national strength.

Koontz, Ted. "US-Soviet Relations After Afghanistan—2." *Menn* 95 (Sept. 9, 1980), 512. In response to Soviet military intervention in Afghanistan, the US is preparing further military buildup, instead of strengthening the governments of the region and providing incentives for improved Soviet behavior.

Koop, Robert. "Canadian Military Recruitment: Coating the Bitter with the Sweet." *Lifework* 3 (1979), 14-15. Describes programs run by the Canadian government, such as the cadets, the militia, and a voluntary service program, as efforts aimed toward channeling young people into military participation by disguising the true military purpose of the programs.

Koop, Robert. "Ottawa Report: Is There Hypocrisy in Trudeau's Call for Disarmament?" *MennRep* 8 (June 26, 1978), 7. Comments on Prime Minister Trudeau's recent speech to the United Nations special session on disarmament, noting that while Canada indeed possesses no nuclear weapons, it sells uranium and military equipment freely, and makes huge domestic military expenditures.

Koop, Robert. "Ottawa Report: National Defense, Disarmament and the Neutron Bomb." *MennRep* 8 (Mar. 6, 1978), 7. Recent NATO meeting shows Canada's defense policy is changing from limited defense spending to major increases in armaments and forces.

Kratz, James D. "Mennonites and Military Service in Argentina." *GH* 66 (Oct. 16, 1973), 790-91. Relates the story of Dennis Byler, US and Argentine citizen, who was drafted in Argentina while serving in a missions assignment. His conscientious objector stance is helping to sensitize the conscience of the Argentine church.

Kraybill, J. Charles. "Conceit and Folly." *Sojourners* 9 (Apr., 1980), 8-10. Author considers present nuclear waste disposal plans foolish and dangerous. Does not distinguish between the military weapons industry and the commercial power industry in their production and disposal of nuclear wastes.

Kreider, Alan. "An International Call to Simpler Living." *MBH* 19 (Apr. 25, 1980), 20-21; *ChrLead* 43 (Apr. 22, 1980), 17; *EvVis* 93 (May 10, 1980), 16. An international gathering of evangelical leaders near London, England, makes a commitment to a simple lifestyle in recognition that wealth and militarism contribute to poverty and powerlessness.

Kreider, Alan. "Biblical Perspectives on War." *Third Way* 4 (Nov., 1980), 13-14. Brings the Old Testament prophetic insistence—that Israel rely on Yahweh rather than numerical, technological or nonrestricted military strength—to bear upon our modern quest for security in nuclear weapons.

Kreider, Alan, ed. "Thoughts from Conference Speakers." *IPF Notes* 6 (June, 1960), 3-10. Detailed summary of addresses on the topics of the Christian witness against militarism through politics, I-W program, and missions.

Kreider, Alan. "Why the Christian Church Must Be Pacifist." *Ireland and the Threat of Nuclear War,* ed. Bill McSweeney. Dublin: Dominican Publications, 1985. Pp. 83-103. Pacifism is now growing in the Church for several reasons:

people have seen the futility of military violence in attaining its objectives; new biblical and theological insights undermine former justifications for violence; because attempts to control modern events have had unanticipated results, Christians are abandoning consequential ethics for principled, prophetic nonconformity; and Christians have discovered that violence does not exhaust the possibilities for relevant involvement in the world.

Kreider, Carl. "American Involvement in South Vietnam." *ChrLiv* 9 (May, 1962), 19, 39. Background of the escalating military tension between North and South Vietnam.

Kreider, Carl. "American Leadership." *ChrLiv* 2 (July, 1955), 22, 11, 19, 46. In material possessions, political influence, and military power, America is one of the world leaders; but secular leadership is transient.

Kreider, Carl. "Crises in the Middle East." *MennComm* 5 (Dec., 1951), 26, 32. Present crises in Iran and Egypt center on economic and military concerns.

Kreider, Carl. "Current Difficulties in Foreign Relations." *MennComm* 6 (Oct., 1952), 29-31. Questionable results of American military expenditure emerge in Korea, France, and Germany.

Kreider, Carl. "Defense Against H Bomb." *ChrLiv* 1 (Jan., 1954), 39-40. Military, political, and economic defenses are discussed, as well as some practical suggestions for the Christian nonresistant.

Kreider, Carl. "Foreign Aid." *ChrLiv* 5 (July, 1958), 18, 36-37. American foreign aid since World War II has tended toward military instead of economic aid.

Kreider, Carl. "H Bomb Foreign Policy." *ChrLiv* 1 (July, 1954), 35-36. The US atomic bomb test on Bikini Atoll which injured Japanese fishermen raises new fears about US military policy.

Kreider, Carl. "President Peron vs. the Catholic Church." *ChrLiv* 2 (Sept., 1955), 22, 47. The military forces are one source of power for Peron of Argentina.

Kreider, Carl. "Revolution in Cuba." *ChrLiv* 6 (Apr., 1959), 19, 39. The anti-American sentiment of the Castro government is inspired in part by US military aid to the brutal dictator Batista.

Kreider, Carl. "Safe or Unsafe Investment?" *ChrLiv* 1 (July, 1954), 12-14, 38-39. Overview of many types of investments, raising questions when the money invested is used for military purposes.

Kreider, Carl. "Signs of Hope." *ChrLiv* 2 (Oct., 1955), 22, 41-42. Relaxing military tensions at home and abroad are signs of improved US status in world affairs.

Kreider, Carl. "Sputnik." *ChrLiv* 5 (Jan., 1958), 18, 39. The Russian Sputnik satellite launching will affect American military strategy and spending.

Kreider, Carl. "The Christian Message of Peace." *Japan Christian Quarterly* 18 (Autumn, 1952), 293-99. Both the teachings of Jesus and his own example call us to practice the way of love and peace, as an answer to those who trust in military power.

Kreider, Carl. "The Fall of the Almighty Dollar." *ChrLiv* 20 (May, 1973), 15, 25. Military spending abroad is one factor leading to a loss in US balance of payments which necessitates a devaluing of the dollar.

Kreider, Carl. "The MacArthur Dismissal." *MennComm* 5 (June, 1951), 28, 30. Analysis of disagreements between General Douglas MacArthur and President Truman over military policies in Korea.

Kreider, Carl. "The Mennonite Central Committee Relief Training School Held at Goshen College." *ChrMon* 35 (Nov., 1943), 336-37. Development of the training program, negotiation with the Selective Service system, and final cancellation by Congress.

Kreider, Carl. "The Republican Presidential Nomination." *MennComm* 6 (Sept., 1952), 29 30. Discussion includes comments on the advantages and liabilities of having a military man, Eisenhower, as the Republican Party nominee.

Kreider, Carl. "The War in Indo-China." *ChrLiv* 1 (May, 1954), 35-36. Indo-China conflict is another example of the ineffectiveness of Western military intervention in dealing with communism.

Kreider, Carl. "Trouble in the Congo." *ChrLiv* 7 (Nov., 1960), 18, 35. Analysis of the violence and military conflict in the Congo following its independence from Belgium.

Kreider, Carl. "Truce in Indo-China." *ChrLiv* 1 (Oct., 1954), 37-39. Comment on the partitioning of Vietnam and the effect of American military force in meeting communism.

Kreider, Carl. "Underdeveloped Areas." *ChrLiv* 3 (April, 1956), 22, 43-44. Much of the post-war US economic aid is being diverted into military aid.

Kreider, Carl. "Wanted—Christian Capitalism." *MennComm* 6 (Jan., 1952), 30, 32. Discusses the relationship of government regulations to militarism and Cold War mentality.

Kreider, Carl. "Will Recovery Bring Inflation?" *ChrLiv* 8 (Nov., 1961), 18, 38-39. Military spending is a factor in possible inflation.

Kreider, Carl (Review). *Our Depleted Society,* by Seymour Melman. Holt, Rinehart, and Winston, 1965. Pp. 366. *ChrLiv* 12 (Dec., 1965), 37-38. Recommends this discussion of the devastating effect of military spending on the American economy.

Kreider, Connie. "Countering Militarism in the Schools." *MCC PS TF on Women in Ch. and Soc. Report* 35 (Jan.-Feb., 1981), 6-7. Lists myths perpetuated by military recruiters, especially regarding opportunities for women, and counters them with facts.

Kreider, Lucille. *The Friendly Way: A One-Act Play in Three Scenes.* Newton: Faith and Life Press, 1961. Pp. 22. Set in 1917, the drama depicts some of the struggles experienced by a Quaker family as the son refuses to join the military and, instead, volunteers for relief work in Beirut, where his nonresistant ideals are tested.

Kroeker, David. "American Military Men in Vietnam Dedicated and Highly Motivated." *CanMenn* 15 (Jan. 10, 1967), 1, 2. Commentary on the Graham Team's view of the war in Vietnam based on the Jan. 8 radio broadcast of *The Hour of Decision,* a first-hand report of the Graham Team's 9-day visit in Vietnam. Graham and Co. praised efforts of American soldiers in Vietnam and encouraged listeners to write to the soldiers in a show of support.

Kroeker, David. "An 'Upbeat' Conference in Canada's Oil Capital." *MennRep* 9 (July 23, 1979), 1. Among the decisions made at the 77th annual Canadian General Conference session were decisions to make capital punishment an issue for study in preparation for 1980, and to study a joint MCC-Mennonite World Conference statement on militarism and development.

Kroeker, David. "Massive Increases Ahead in Canadian Military Spending." *MennRep* 9 (May 14, 1979), 3. Conrad Grebel College held a workshop on militarism with speakers addressing the biblical basis for peacemaking as well as the military realities in Canada.

Kroeker, Walter.. "Justice and Relief Must Stay Together." *MBH* 18 (Feb. 16, 1979), 16-18. Papers were presented at the MCC annual meeting on the relation of peace and reconciliation to Native American outreach, hunger concerns, and militarism.

Kroeker, Walter. "Justice and Rights Issues Occupy MCC Members in Reedley." *MennRep* 9 (Feb. 19, 1979), 1. Among the issues discussed at the MCC annual meeting was aid to Vietnam, justice and human rights overseas, and a paper on militarism calling the church to renounce the development of nuclear weapons and military exports.

Kroeker, Walter. "MCC—Wide-Ranging Agenda." *EV* 92 (Mar. 25, 1979), 8-9. At the MCC annual meeting, issues of justice, aid to Vietnam, the world food crisis, and militarism were addressed and a paper on militarism by Urbane Peachey was accepted.

"Lack of Concern for Rules of War." *Menn* 86 (Jan. 19, 1971), 36-38. Relief workers express their disapproval of the foreign military involvement in Vietnam and quote numerous articles from, for instance, the Nuremberg Tribunal, the Hague Convention, the Geneva Convention, and others, to point out the injustice of the USA.

Landes, Carl J. "Why I Cannot Accept Non-Combatant Service." *Menn* 56 (Mar. 4, 1941), 9. Essential reason for refusing noncombatant service is that there is no *basic* difference between combatant and noncombatant service.

Lapp, John A. "Conference Table or World War?" *ChrLiv* 12 (May, 1965), 18-19, 32-33. Background of the Vietnam conflict and the recent escalation of American military involvement there.

Lapp, John A. "Educators Protest Actions of Israel on West Bank." *GH* 72 (Jan. 9, 1979), 24. Report of harassment by Israeli military authorities at Bir Zeit University on the Israeli-occupied West Bank.

Lapp, John A. "Laos: Domino or Diversion?" *ChrLiv* 17 (May, 1970), 18-19. Military activity previously in Vietnam has been transferred to neighboring Laos.

Lapp, John A. "The Church and the Social Question." *GH* 66 (July 17, 1973), 553-55. The church as a re-created community extends the message of reconciliation by rooting out racism and militarism within itself and thus becoming able to address these structures in society.

Lapp, John A. "The CIA Surfaces Again." *ChrLiv* 21 (Nov., 1974), 15, 32. Discussion of CIA involvement in Chile and Greece, subverting moderate governments and supporting military ones.

Lapp, John A. (Review). *The Military Industrial Complex,* by Sidney Lens. Pilgrim Press/National Catholic Reporter, 1970. Pp. 183. *GH* 64 (Oct. 19, 1971), 875. Regards book as "comprehensive," "well-written," and "imbued with moral sensitivity," in its analysis of the military's impact on the economy, political processes, the labor movement, and college campuses.

Lapp, John E. "Testimony to US Armed Services Committee." *MBH* 6 (May 26, 1967), 7, 18-19. MCC believes reliance on military strength to be both futile and wrong, and urges an end to conscription and war.

Lawson, Mark S. Letter to the Editor. *Menn* 95 (Jan. 22, 1980), 62. Benefits granted by the US government are overshadowed by the same government's commitment to rampant militarism.

Leatherman, Loretta. "Taking a Stand." *WMSC Voice* 54 (Dec., 1980), 7. Encourages some form of war tax resistance to protest the dollars being used to finance American military endeavors.

Lehman, Carl M. "Tax Resistance—A Form of Protest?" *Menn* 90 (Oct. 14, 1975), 573-74. While tax resistance may be acceptable for activists and absolutists, the focus of Christian opposition to paying for war should be pressure on Congress to keep military spending down.

Lehman, Emmett R. "Wyzanski Decision Is Significant." *GH* 62 (May 20, 1969), 461. Reports and discusses this District Court judge's ruling that conscientious objectors outside of religious traditions may be eligible for exemption from military duty.

Lehman, J. Irvin. "Shall We Have Another CPS?" *ST* 16 (2nd Qtr., 1948), 4. Concerned that many of the Mennonite leaders representing Mennonites before the government on issues of military legislation represent Mennonite groups who have largely lost the doctrine of nonresistance.

Lehman, James O. "Conflicting Loyalties of the Christian Citizen: Lancaster Mennonites and the Early Civil War Era." *Pennsylvania Mennonite Heritage* 7 (Apr., 1984), 2-15. In the face of a growing war hysteria and the threat of the draft, the Lancaster Mennonites were not always clear on what position to take in that early period of the war. While most Mennonites tried to avoid entering military service, they also wanted to make clear their loyalty to the Union cause.

Lehman, M[artin] C[lifford]. "Relief Work in Alsace-Lorraine." *MCC WSRB* 1 (Nov., 1945), 5. Describes war relief efforts and the attitude toward military service in Switzerland.

Liechty, C. Daniel. "War in the Old Testament: Three Views." *GH* 71 (May 23, 1978), 408-409;

*Menn* 94 (Nov. 6, 1979), 658-59. Examines three types of Mennonite writers on the subject of war in the Old Testament: 1)Those who posit discontinuity between the Old and New Testaments; 2) those who find nonresistance as an ideal presesnt in the Old as well as New Testaments; 3) those who see Israel's trust in a warrior-God instead of a warrior-king as a challenge to military action.

Lind, Loren. "War or Peace?" *YCC* 43 (Mar. 18, 1962), 2. An examination of the real meaning of words used to describe the function of the military, e.g., civil defense, peace, strength.

Loewen, Esko. "Better than Military Conscription." *Menn* 74 (Feb. 24, 1959), 115. The MCC statement to the Congressional Committee on Armed Services which implores national leaders to "beat their swords into plowshares."

Longacre, Paul. "No Peace for the Vietnamese." *MBH* 12 (Apr. 6, 1973), 32; "Peace Not Yet at Hand for Vietnamese." *Menn* 88 (Apr. 3, 1973), 225. MCC representative visiting Vietnam after the ceasefire reports on the continuing struggle for control of contested areas and the likely continued military activity after the reduction of US forces.

Lord, Beverly Bowen. "Women and the Social Costs of Militarism." *MCC PS TF on Women in Ch. and Soc. Report* 35 (Jan.-Feb., 1981), 3-4. Compares national defense budget to social spending, especially those programs assisting women.

Lord, Charles R. *The Rule of the Sword: A Study Guide on Technological Militarism.* Newton, Ks.: Faith and Life Press, 1978. Pp. 72. Lessons designed to clarify the issues and show how these issues relate to us. Another goal of the guide is to help students develop a background helpful for examination of the questions of civil responsibility and war taxes.

"Meeting Shows Diversity of Views on Militarism." *GH* 72 (Feb. 20, 1979), 167. Report of a meeting of the General Conference Mennonite Church on Feb. 9-10, 1979, in Minneapolis where war tax resistance was discussed.

"Mennonites on Military Service: Statement of Our Position on Military Service as Adopted by the Mennonite General Conference, Aug. 29, 1917." Pp. 4. MHL.

"Mennonites Plan for Minority Youth." *RepConsS* 34 (Mar., 1977), 4. Mennonite Economic Development Associates to consider proposal to provide job opportunities for Mennonite minority youth for whom the military is often the most viable employment option.

"Military Only Choice for Minority Mennonites." *RepConsS* 32 (June, 1975), 6. A thirty percent unemployment rate and family responsibilities pressure Mennonite urban minority youth to choose the military.

"Minority Job Program Ready." *RepConsS* 32 (Dec., 1975), 4. An advisory committee appointed by MCC US Ministries is planning a job training program for Mennonite minority youth being pressured toward the military by the economic situation.

MacMaster, Richard K. *Christian Obedience in Revolutionary Times: The Peace Churches and the American Revolution.* Akron, Pa.: MCC (US) Peace Section, 1976. Pp. 26. MHL. Demonstrates that Mennonites and other Christians committed to peace during the Revolutionary War times conflicted with the government on issues of military service, war taxes, and oaths of allegiance. Discusses their stance and resulting persecution within the context of differing concepts of religious liberty; the sectarian concept of discipleship as a separate and distinct way of life was not understood by a government to whom religious freedom meant the freedom to worship according to the dictates of conscience, not the freedom to live by conscience.

Maddrey, Kenneth D. Letter to the Editor. *ChrLead* 41 (Jan. 3, 1978), 15. Calls for Mennonite Brethren not to ignore the military personnel and their families.

Martin, E. K. *The Mennonites.* Philadelphia: Everts and Peck, 1883. Pp. 17. MHL. A history which discusses at some length the struggles of the Mennonites and other peace sects to maintain a nonresistant stance in relation to the conflicts between the colonists and native Americans as well as in relation to the government's demands for support for the military in the pre-Revolutionary and Revolutionary War periods.

Martin, Luke S. "The War and Our Witness." *GH* 66 (July 3, 1973), 536; "The Gospel—Down But Not Out." *Menn* 88 (July 10, 1973), 430; "What the War Has Done to the Faith Witness." *MennRep* 3 (July 9, 1973), 5; "Vietnam War Makes Witness Hard." *MBH* 12 (Nov. 2, 1973), 14; "What War Has Done to Our Witness." *ChrLead* 36 (July 10, 1973), 4. Former missionary in Vietnam says that Christianity's entanglement with political and military power in that country has damaged the Christian witness, but the gospel must continue to be presented there in spite of past mistakes.

Mast Burnett, Kristina. "Canada-US Relations, Vietnam, Issues at Reedley Meetings." *GH* 72 (Feb. 13, 1979), 128. MCC's annual meeting in Reedley, Jan. 25-27, addressed such issues as Canada-US relations, aid to Vietnam, justice and human rights overseas, Native American outreach, hunger concerns, and militarism.

Matty, Maria. "Sanctity of Life Is Theme for Eben-Ezer Education Week." *MennRep* 9 (Dec. 24, 1979), 5. Education week at the Eben-Ezer Mennonite Church of Abbotsford, BC resulted in resolutions on capital punishment, militarism, and abortion.

Meier, Hans. "The Dissolution of the Rhön Bruderhof in Germany." *MHB* 41 (July, 1980), 1-7. Account of the German Rhön Bruderhof's ordeal under Hitler focuses also on their refusal to comply with military service regulations.

Mennonite Brethren Church. "Report to the Committee of Reference and Counsel . . . in Relation to the Question of Non-combatant Service." *Yearbook of the 46th General Conference of the Mennonite Brethren Church of North America.* Hillsboro: M.B. Publishing House, 1954, 115-21. A report of intensive study of the issues and conversation with government authorities in Washington. Noncombatant service is to be rejected in favor of alternative service. The report was adopted.

Mennonite Central Committee. "Vietnam Study: Relief Often Tied to Politics, Military." *MennRep* 2 (Oct. 2, 1972), 1. Relief agencies enjoy the benevolences of a government because the latter recognizes a potential in the former to realize its political and military ends.

Mennonite Central Committee. "White House Hears Mennonite Concern on War." *Menn* 82 (Nov. 21, 1967), 704-705. MCC message to the president deplores the present US policy in Vietnam and calls for a radical reversal of military policy.

Mennonite Central Committee (US). "Statement on World Tensions and the Draft." Adopted Jan. 24, 1980. P. 1. (Located in MCC Peace Section Official Statements folder in MHL.) Urges young Mennonite men and women to register their conscientious objector convictions with the Peacemaker Registration Program in response to proposed military conscription.

Mennonite Church General Conference Statements (Archival). Goshen, IN. AMC. 1-1-1, Box 5. File 5/5: Peace, war, and military service, 1937.

Mennonite General Conference. "Letter to Selective Service, Aug. 26, 1941." *GH* 34 (Nov. 13, 1941), 707. General Conference (MC) expresses gratitude and hopes for continued cooperation.

Mennonite General Conference. "Telegram to the President." *GH* 58 (Sept. 14, 1965), 813. General Conference (MC) calls upon the president to reverse the trend of increasing militarism and war policies.

*Mennonites and Conscientious Objection in 1980.* Akron, Pa.: MCC US Peace Section, 1980. Pp. 95. MHL. See Topic 9.

Metzler, Edgar. "More Money, More Weapons, More Men: The Military Mania Marches On." *MCC PS Wash. Memo* 12 (Sept.-Oct., 1980), 1-2, 5-6. Discusses reinstated draft registration, nerve gas manufacturing, and an enlarged military budget as signs of renewed military preparedness.

Metzler, Edgar. "Selective Service Act." *GH* 57 (Mar. 17, 1964), 225. Reviews the act and then states that the youth and elders of the church ought to be ready to support VS without the prodding of Uncle Sam.

Meyer, Ron. "Reflections on Paying War Taxes." *GH* 65 (May 23, 1972), 465-66. Since 60 to 75 percent of income tax is used as revenue for warfare, the writer outlines various approaches to tax resistance aimed at witnessing against this use of money for military purposes.

Meyers, Willie. "Why I Left Vietnam." *ChrLiv* 15 (Aug., 1968), 6-7. International Voluntary Service worker left Vietnam in order to disassociate himself from the American military presence there.

Military Problems Committee (Archival). 5 feet. CGCL.

Miller, Ernest E. "Training Young People to Give a Christian Witness in the Face of World Ideologues." *ChrMon* 44 (Aug., 1952), 242-44. Addresses, among others, the issue of militarism.

Miller, Marlin E. "Degrees of Glory." *GH* 73 (Feb. 12, 1980), 129-32. Funeral sermon for Doris Janzen Longacre focuses in part on her concern for the false power of nationalism and military violence.

Miller, Orrie L. "Mennonites of the Chaco." *Fellowship* 2 (Apr., 1936), 8-9. Reviews the German Mennonite trek to Russia for exemption from military service, then describes their migration to and settlement in the Argentine Chaco following the 1918 revolution.

Morrow, Brent. Letter to the Editor. *ChrLead* 43 (June 3, 1980), 14-15. Contends that the I-A-O noncombatant position is a viable option for conscientious objectors.

Mosemann, John H. "The March of Militarism." *GH* 33 (July 11, 1940), 322. The Christian must guard against allowing his or her attitudes to be shaped by the worldwide spirit of militarism.

"New Call to Peacemaking." *EV* 91 (Nov. 10, 1978), 16. The New Call to Peacemaking, a coalition of the historic peace churches, agreed to carry its concern about military spending, nuclear weapons, arms sales, and related matters to President Carter.

Nestor, Bob A. Letter to the Editor. *ChrLead* 36 (May 29, 1973), 13. To say the Christian cannot participate in the military is certainly without scriptural basis.

Neufeld, Elmer. "Defense: Civilian, Military, or Spiritual." Paper read to MDS meeting, Chicago, Ill., Feb. 11, 1960.

Neufeld, Elmer. "Peace—the Way of the Cross." *ChrLiv* 7 (Jan., 1960), 6-7, 34. Prose poem relating peace to issues of militarism, nationalism, and racism.

Nisley, Weldon D. "The Case of David Gracie." *God and Caesar* 1 (Mar., 1975), 7. The Episcopal Diocese has developed and maintained their defense against IRS in support of one of their employees, Rev. David M. Gracie of Philadelphia, who has refused to pay 50 percent of his income tax as that amount which approximates the percentage used for military expenditures.

Nolt, Philip. "For Christ and the Country?" *GH* 67 (May 28, 1974), 447. Writer describes a county fair parade in which churches entered patriotic floats symbolizing the message that since wars will always abound, Christians must support their country and its military.

"Office Restructured, Clearer Witness Urged at Peace Section Meeting." *GH* 72 (Jan. 2, 1979), 8-9. Report from the annual MCC Peace Section (International) meeting at Hesston, Kansas, in Dec., 1978, where a statement was accepted calling North American Mennonites to give clearer witness to government and other bodies against militarism and the arms race.

Olson, Ted. "An Alternative Defense Strategy for Canada." *PlMon* 2 (Nov., 1979), 4-5. Suggests Canada look seriously at non-military methods of civilian resistance in order to lessen dependence on American military protection.

Omura, Isamu. "A Letter from Japanese Christians Concerning Vietnam." *CanMenn* 13 (Sept. 14, 1965), 6. The letter serves as an introduction of a peace mission to American Christians, focusing on the folly of military involvement on the part of the USA in Vietnam.

"Peace, War, and Social Issues: A Statement of the Position of the Amish Mennonite Churches." Officialy adopted by the ministerial body of the Beachy Amish Mennonite constituency . . . at Wellesley, Ont., Apr. 18-19, 1968. [n.p., 1968]. Pp. 16. MSHL. Topics include the role of government, military service, civil defense, the Christian's role in race relations, unions, etc.

"Peace Assembly Considers Money, Military." *Menn* 87 (Dec. 5, 1972), 714. Since the North American economy is a cancerous tumor on the rest of the world, which eventually may destroy it, we need to consider alternatives to the affluent way of life which needs the military to protect it.

"Preparing for Revolution." *MHB* 35 (July, 1974), 2-7. Series of documents traces the tension caused in Lancaster County when nonresistant Mennonites refused to serve in military units being established in preparation for the Revolutionary War.

"Probe Military Recruitment in High Schools." *Forum* 13 (Oct., 1979), 11. As a result of a survey of military recruitment practices which included eight Mennonite students in Indianapolis, the local New Call to Peacemaking group recommends, among other things, elimination of military recruitment on school grounds or equal time for peacemaking recruitment.

Peachey, Paul L. "Billy Graham on Nonresistance." *GH* 50 (Oct. 22, 1957), 896-97. Billy Graham's acceptance of war and the military is inconsistent with the Gospel. The writer urges him to seriously study this topic.

Peachey, Paul L. "Interreligious Conference on Peace." *ChrCent* 83 (Apr. 13, 1966), 476-78. Author reflects on the interfaith dialogue at the conference on such issues as US military involvement in Vietnam, and a model for religious peace witness to a pluralistic society in which the religious community's primary role is to produce a moral climate in society conducive to peacemaking.

Peachey, Paul L. "The Christian Peace Conference and the Czech Crisis." *GH* 61 (Dec. 31, 1968), 1147-48; *CanMenn* 16 (Dec. 31, 1968), 5. Describes the process followed by the ecumenical Christian Peace Conference in responding to the Soviet movement into Czechoslovakia. Asserts that the same "demons of war and hate" are behind the Soviet action and American military activities in Vietnam.

Peachey, Shem. "The Scriptural Alternative to War." *GH* 43 (Oct. 24, 1950), 1044. Mennonites should give their peace testimony "in the name of Christ" via church organizations and not first of all through CPS camps as an alternative to military service.

Peachey, Urbane. "Militarism and the Christian Disciple." *GH* 69 (Aug. 24, 1976), 640-42.

Christians are called to be deeply aware of the world idolatry of militarism, and to make their voices heard against this system.

Peachey, Urbane. "What Is a Military Occupation?" MCC PS Newsletter 8 (Aug., 1977), 6-7. Describes the treatment of West Bank inhabitants as military in every respect— labor exploitation, collective punishment, expulsion of leadership, land expropriation, arbitrary arrests, restrictions on place of residence, and restrictions on assembly and right of expression.

Pennell, Christine Hamilton. "Women and Militarism." Daughters of Sarah 7 (Nov.-Dec., 1981), 3-10. Recognizing that the systematic dehumanization of males, which is an essential part of military training, has sinister implications for women as well. A growing number of feminist women are protesting militarism by becoming involved in the nonviolent struggle for a just world.

Pierce, Glen. "Personal Reflections on the NAE Convention." EV 89 (June 10, 1976), 6. The National Association of Evangelicals convention in Washington, DC, showed a strong flavor or nationalism, even promoting militarism.

Pinnock, Clark. "A Statement for Disciples in Society." MBH 15 (Feb. 20, 1976), 2-3, 29. Evangelical Christians need a systematic theology dealing with Christian concern for injustice, racism, and militarism.

Preheim, Marion Keeney. "Do the Rich Make Indonesians Poor?" MBH 19 (Jan. 18, 1980), 19-20. Unjust structures such as economic inequity and North American military support for dictatorships help keep people poor.

Preheim, Marion Keeney. "Lawrence Hart: Indian Chief in a Tradition of Peace." MennRep 10 (Nov. 24, 1980), 10. Reviews the pilgrimage of a native American from military service to affirming both Cheyenne and Christian commitments to peace.

Purves, John H. "My Decision on Militarism." Menn 67 (Jan. 1, 1952), 11-12. An account of a pilgrimage from the militaristic point of view to persuasion that nonresistance is God's will and way.

Q[Anonymous]. "Letter from a I-A-O." MCC Bull 3 (Oct. 8, 1944), 5-6. This letter, written to CPS and AFSC, describes the hateful attitudes and military environment which he (Q) experienced in noncombatant service. Because of his resistance to these attitudes, his colonel rightly decided he belonged in CPS.

Ratzlaff, Don. "Our Deafening Silence." ChrLead 42

(Apr. 24, 1979), 24. Raises question about Mennonite Brethren silence on taxes used for the military.

Ray Crichton, Jim. "The Military: A View from the Inside." Lifework 5 (1981), 3-5. Former Coast Guard draftee describes his reactions to basic training and navy policies and his decision not to participate in the military, based on Chrsitian convictions.

Redekop, John H. "Billions for Defense, Atomic Research, Industry." CanMenn 4 (Jan. 27, 1956), 3. Our governments continue to spend billions on defense while ignoring pressing social needs. Christians must press on in the task of evangelization before it is too late.

Redekop, John H. "Reunion at San Francisco." CanMenn 3 (July 15, 1955), 2. "The wicked shall be cast into hell and all the nations that forget God." Satiric piece pointing out the absurdity of enormous expenditures for military defense.

Redekop, John H. "Should a Christian Join a Political Party?" CanMenn 5 (Nov. 22, 1957), 7. Discusses whether, in the terms of nonresistant Christianity, pacifists can participate in those higher governmental politics that deal in military matters?

Redekop, John H. "The Essence of the Gospel." MBH 18 (Oct. 26, 1979), 12. Relief work and conflict resolution in the question of militarism are both applications of the gospel, but not its essence.

Reedy, Janet Umble. "Sexual Equality and Peace." MCC PS TF on Women in Ch. and Soc. Report 35 (Jan.-Feb., 1981), 1-3. Analysis of the polarization of men's and women's roles into dominance and passivity, leading to violence and militarism.

Regehr, Ernie. "Civil War in El Salvador: North America Supports a Repressive Regime." MennRep 10 (Dec. 8, 1980), 8. Reports on North American military support of the violently repressive Salvadorian government, and calls for the right to self-rule by the people of El Salvador and an end to foreign arms shipments.

Regehr, Ernie. "Conscientious Objection: Escape from or Challenge to Militarism?" MennRep 10 (Mar. 3, 1980), 8. Reprinted from MCC PS Newsletter 10 (Mar.-Apr., 1980), 8-9. Author contends that conscientious objection can be used to combat social evil, and cites the South African Council of Churches' resolution on conscientious objection as an example.

Regehr, Ernie. "Defense Production in Canada." Pp. 85. BfC.

Regehr, Ernie. "Mennonites and Iran: Confession Is Good for the Soul." *MennRep* 10 (June 23, 1980), 7. Author documents Canadian complicity in the military dictatorship of the Shah of Iran and calls for Canadian Mennonites to join with American Mennonites in a confession of corporate guilt.

Regehr, Ernie. *Militarism and the World Military Order: A Study Guide for Churches.* Geneva, Switzerland: Commission of the Churches on International Affairs of the World Council of Churches, 1980. Pp. 69. Discussion in 4 parts: "The Dynamics of Militarism," which deals with such issues as the nuclear arms race, international trade, and the United Nations; "The Fruits of Militarism," which discusses the security question and the social/economic consequences of militarism; "The Roots of Militarism," including external and internal factors; "Militarism and the Response of the Church."

Regehr, Ernie. *What Is Militarism?* Akron: Mennonite Central Committee, 1977. Pp. 18. Distinguishes between "the military way," which is the pursuit of specific, limited military objectives, and "militarism," which claims transcendent purposes. Maintains that militarism threatens military efficiency, and that its primary source is corporate interest, not the Pentagon.

Regier, P. K. "When the Boys Come Home." *Menn* 60 (Dec. 11, 1945), 4, 14. Pleads for understanding and tolerance toward "the boys" who return from military service. Asks the church to minister to their spiritual needs.

Reichart, Elmer C. Letter to the Editor. *Menn* 88 (Sept. 4, 1973), 502-503. Response to the TV documentary, "The Sins of Our Fathers," which depicted US soldiers in Vietnam deserting their offspring and the children's mothers. The writer pleads for the blame to be placed with the US military, which drafted the young men, taught them to kill, and separated them from their loved ones by sending them overseas.

Reimer, Helene. "The Christian and Militarism." *Forum* 10 (Feb., 1977), 11. In response to Fred Swartzendruber's report on the Intercollegiate Peace Fellowship conference at Tabor College (*Forum* [Dec., 1976]), a Canadian student offers a different view of the conference, arguing that the focus "was not American elections, but militarism and Christianity in North America."

Reimer, Margaret Loewen. "Militarism in Canada: Are We Willing to Face the Issue?" *MennRep* 8 (Nov. 13, 1978), 8. Maintains that Canadian Mennonites live under the illusion that Canada's military establishment is inconsequential and that Mennonites are not part of the national mainstream. Urges support

for recent efforts to publicize the extent of Canadian militarism and educate Mennonites on this issue.

Reimer, Vic. "Church Should Not Be a Tax Collector." *MBH* 18 (Mar. 2, 1979), 19. As a response to militarism, the General Conference church voted to pursue exemption for the church from withholding taxes from employees.

Reimer, Vic. "Is Military Spending Good or Bad for the Economy?" *Menn* 93 (May 23, 1978), 344. Military spending is inflationary and destroys jobs, says Lloyd Dumas of Columbia University, NY.

Ressler, Lawrence and Peachy, Dean. "A Call to Nonconformity." *GH* 72 (Nov. 6, 1979), 869-70. We need to re-examine our economic system and structures and seek alternatives if we want to seriously address problems such as poverty, hunger, urban decay, and militarism.

Rich, Ronald. Letter to the Editor. *Menn* 92 (Apr. 26, 1977), 285-86. Marxism is the political movement showing the most blatant militarism in its march toward world power and its repression of its own citizens.

Richert, P. H. "Our Post-War Youth Problem." *Menn* 58 (Aug. 10, 1943), 6-7. Those who participated in the military voluntarily should receive some disciplining action when they return. Yet the church must find a way to deal with the individual conscience.

Roberts, Marge. "Advent at the Air Force Academy." *Menn* 95 (Dec. 2, 1980), 696-97. Describes the symbolism evident in the Air Force Academy chapel and its dedication to the god of military might and destruction.

Robinson, James H. "The Changed World." *ChrLiv* 3 (Aug., 1956), 18-20, 42-43. Reprinted from *Tomorrow Is Today,* by James H. Robinson. Christian Education Press, 1954. One element in the present world crisis is the fear felt by the US and its resulting trust in military force.

Rosenberger, A. S. "Conference on Historic Peace Churches." *Menn* 54 (Feb. 25, 1936), 2-3. A report of the procedings which includes the conference statement against militarism.

Roth, Willard E., ed. *Is There a Middle Road?* Scottdale: Herald Press, 1964. Pp. 15. Peacemaker Pamphlet No. 5. Bob Baker describes his experience in noncombatant service during World War II to show that such service is not an acceptable alternative to either military duty or a rejection of military duty if one wants to follow Christ's way of love.

Rutschman, Tom. "Repentance in a Year of

Revelry." *GH* 69 (June 29, 1976), 528-29. A call for a fresh analysis of US history and a repentance from military policies and injustices born of mythologizing national history.

"Speakers Say: Peace Witness Goes Beyond Secular Pacifism and 'Christian Militarism.' " *CanMenn* 9 (Oct. 20, 1961), 1, 10. Elmer Neufeld and Paul Peachey speak to peace conferences in Manitoba.

"Statement of Position from Niagara MP." *MennRep* 9 (Nov. 26, 1979), 10. Jake Froese, MP from the Niagara Falls riding, responds to questions regarding his views and positions on such issues as increasing military expenditures and capital punishment.

"Swiss Mennonite Refuses to Do Military Service." *RepConsS* 27 (Mar., 1970), 4. Michael Gerber, in refusing to serve in the army medical corps, has become the first Swiss Mennonite in many years to take a CO position.

Sartin, Nancy E. "High Stakes." *YCC* 49 (June 16, 1968), 12. Military struggles not only create much larger forces than necessary but divert billions of dollars yearly from essential programs. There are signs of hope that some of this may change.

Sauder, Menno. *Christian Methods: Are Superior to Compulsory Social Legislation, Militarism, and War.* Elmira, Ont.: by the author, 1967. Pp. 8. MHL. A variety of comments, on these subjects as well as sundry others, interspersed with quotations from the Dordrecht confession and John Horsch's *Mennonites in Europe*, a summary of Jean Laserre's *War and the Gospel*, etc.

Savage, Regan. "The Military is Not All It's Cracked Up to Be." *With* 11 (Nov., 1978), 4. Savage received a conscientious objector's discharge after six years as a tank commander in the United States Army.

Sawatsky, H. L. "A Look at the Mexican Situation: Mennonite Exodus from Mexico to Canada?" *MennMirror* 4 (Dec., 1974), 11-13. Discusses the land situation of the Mennonites in Mexico which has resulted from their refusal to become full citizens because of the requirement of military service.

Sawatzky, P. J. Letter to the Editor. *MennRep* 9 (July 9, 1979), 6; "The Question of War Taxes." *GfT* 14 (Sept./-Oct., 1979), 17-1. In response to the decision on war taxes made at the General Conference midtriennium, this writer stresses the need for military protection against communism and the biblical teachings to support the government and pay taxes.

Schlabach, Dan. "The Military Question." *GH* 40 (June 10, 1947), 229. Mennonite youth should

not participate in the military even in peace time.

Schmidt, Linda. "Perpetuating Repression: US Training of Foreign Military and Police." *MCC PS Newsletter* 9 (Jan.-Feb., 1978), 4-8. The training of foreign military and police has been an integral part of the US foreign policy over the past twenty-five years. The countries which have received large amounts of military and economic aid are the same countries which have been cited most often for human rights violations.

Schmidt, Steven G. Letter to the Editor. *ChrLiv* 20 (Mar., 1973), 28. Speaks out against US military destruction in Vietnam; suggests that opposers of war refuse payment of war taxes.

Schrag, Martin H. "Mars Rides Again." *GH* 62 (Apr. 15, 1969), 340-44. Relates statistics concerning burgeoning American military spending and production and its relation to domestic violence, and challenges Christians to bring Christian insights of internationality, forgiveness, and love to bear on this problem.

Schrag, Martin (Editorial). "United States and Militarism." *GH* 65 (Sept. 19, 1972), 772. Summarizes the dollar amounts spent by the American military establishment, home and foreign.

Schrag, Myron. "Dear Jerry Falwell:" *Menn* 95 (Nov. 4, 1980), 642. Questions Falwell's stance on a strong American military and challenges him to preach a gospel of peace.

Schrock, Beulah. "Military Training in Our Schools." *GH* 38 (Sept. 7, 1945), 426. Military training of young people is directly contrary to Christian principles.

Schroeder, Richard J. "The Cutting Edge." *ChrLead* 37 (Jan. 22, 1974), 17. A military coup in Washington, DC is very unlikely because of the nature of the American government.

Shank, Duane, ed. "Conscience and Militarism." *RepConsS* 32 (June, 1975), 2. Editorial policy of this publication will begin to reflect the growing awareness that the religious community must deal with the causes of militarism, such as economic injustice, as well as the effects.

Shank, Duane (Editorial). "Now That the Draft Is Over . . . ?" *RepConsS* 32 [*sic,* 33] (Mar., 1976), 2. The draft over, NISBCO will work on such issues as military recruitment for the all-volunteer force and war taxes.

Shank, Duane (Editorial). "The National Service Debate." *RepConsS* 33 [*sic,* 32] (July, 1976), 2. Exposes the rationale, including militarism, supporting the idea of national youth service.

Shank, J. Ward. "Aftermath of the Vietnam War." *ST* 48 (Jan., 1980), 6-7. Comment on and questions about the American military involvement in Vietnam.

Shank, J. Ward. "Question of the Surtax." *ST* 36 (Mar., 1968), 23. Examines the issue of tax monies that are collected by the government to pay for military and war expenditures.

Shank, J. Ward (Editorial). "Which Way to Peace." *ST* 38 (Aug., 1970), 5. The Christian makes his most fundamental contribution to peace neither in conjunction with the military nor in fighting against it.

Shank, Lester. "Can We Accept Noncombatant Service." *YCC* 23 (May 3, 1942), 140, 144. The person in noncombatant service shares the responsibility for taking human life. The Mennonite church supports civilian service.

Shelly, Maynard. "Decrees from Caesar Still Shape the World." *MennRep* 6 (Nov. 29, 1976), 6. Modern emperor worship is the cult of materialism which robs the poor in order to finance luxury and militarism.

Shelly, Maynard. "Liberation in Bangladesh a Tough Miracle." *MBH* 13 (Mar. 22, 1974), 13-14. Not military strength, but massive migrations of people out of the country broke the power of East Pakistan's military government and won independence for Bangladesh.

Shenk, Coffman S. "Mennonite Youth and Nonresistance." *GH* 38 (Sept. 28, 1945), 489-90. When approximately fifty percent of drafted Mennonite youth enter the military, the fact that Mennonites have been too unconcerned with spiritual matters is exposed.

Shenk, Phil M. "Hope, Faith, and Love." *GH* 70 (May 17, 1977), 401-402. Participant in a "Christians Against Torture" demonstration reflects on the Christian call to witness and hope for national repentance for supporting repressive governments through economic and military aid.

Shenk, Phil M. "Washington for Jesus." *Sojourners* 9 (June, 1980), 10-11. The religious rally in Washington focused on issues such as waning US military power and ignored problems of the arms race and proliferating violence.

Shenk, Phil M. and Bicksler, Harriet. "Blessed Are the Peacemakers." *EV* 91 (June 25, 1978), 6. Peacemakers met together in Pennsylvania, Apr. 8 and 9, to lift up hunger, militarism, and self as three issues in need of peacemaking attention by the historic peace churches.

Shenk, Stanley C. "Peace and War: Why Not Noncombatant Service?" *GH* 44 (May 8, 1951), 440-41. The noncombatant is essentially a part of the military and serving in this position is thus a compromise of the nonresistant stance.

Shetler, Sanford G., ed. "Churchmen Continue to Support Militant Chavez." (Article unsigned) *GfT* 8 (Nov.-Dec., 1973), 6. Chavez's methods of boycotting and picketing do not correspond to Mennonite concern for love and goodwill among all sides.

Showalter, Dennis. "References to Nonresistance and Militarism in the Virginia Mennonite Conference Minutes (1835-1966)." Term paper for Menonite History and Thought course, Feb. 14, 1973. Pp. 20. MSHL.

Sider, Ronald J. "Aside: Where Have All the Liberals Gone?" *The Other Side* 12 (May-June, 1976), 42-44. The essence of liberal theology can be described as when the current culture supplies the operational norms and values for a significant number of evangelicals and mainline church people. Concerns like racism, militarism, civil religion, and unjust economic structures are not spoken of because of the liberal context.

Sider, Ronald J. "Is Racism as Sinful as Adultery?" *GH* 65 (Apr. 4, 1972), 315; *EV* 84 (Sept. 25, 1971), 5, 6. Calls evangelicals to concern over social evils of racism and militarism equal to concern about personal evils such as adultery.

Sider, Ronald J. and Taylor, Richard K. "International Aggression and Nonmilitary Defense." *Christian Century* 100 (July 6-13, 1983), 643-47. Military power is not the only way for nations to defend their independence and values. Asymetric strategy, a technique of pitting nonmilitary means against an opponent's military forces, has had some historical success and should be considered in the nuclear age.

Siebert, John. "New Call to Peacemaking." *MBH* 17 (Oct. 27, 1978), 18-19. Consensus from the New Call to Peacemaking conference includes commitments to local peace education, peacemaking lifestyle, confronting militarism, and continued witness to peace and justice.

Smith, Willard H. (Review). *The Military Establishment*, by John M. Swomley, Jr. Boston: Beacon Press, 1964. Pp. 266. *MHB* 26 (July, 1956), 8. Recommends the book for its disturbing but accurate thesis that US policy is being increasingly controlled by the Pentagon, disregarding all historical safeguards to prevent such a situation.

Smucker, Brian. "Uncle Sam Wants You!" *With* 6 (Nov., 1973), 10. Intense military recruitment drives include Junior ROTC in the high schools.

Smucker, Donovan E. "Protestantism Faces the Peace." *Menn* 60 (Mar. 6, 1945), 6-7. The Protestant churches have come a long way towards Christian principles since the militarism of World War I but are still committed to a policy of willful compromise on the question of peace.

Smucker, Donovan E. "The Position of the Christian Soldier." *Menn* 62 (Jan. 21, 1947), 3. Most military personnel hate war and think it is evil but, at times, necessary.

Stauffer, J. L. "Ten Violations Through Military Service." *GH Supplement* 40 (Apr., 1947), 86. "For these reasons the Mennonite Church requires an acknowledgement of repentance from former members who were in the army before they can again become communicant members."

Stoesz, Edgar. "Holy Living and Structural Evil." *EV* 89, Part 1, (Aug. 25, 1976), 5-6; Part 2, (Sept. 10, 1976), 6. America's dependence on military might, international trade policies, national indifference to the poor, and disproportionate consumption of the world's resources embody structural evil, but the responsible Christian can respond through alternative structures.

Stoltzfus, Edward. "A Statement Relating to the Local Ground Observers Corps." *GH* 48 (Nov. 15, 1955), 1089. Since GOC is basically part of the military program, nonresistant Christians should not participate in it. Alternate proposals are outlined.

Stoltzfus, Luke G. (Review). *A Strategy for Peace,* by Frank Epp. Grand Rapids: Wm. B. Eerdmans, 1973. *GH* 67 (Oct. 1, 1974), 758. Recommends the book for its fresh approach to issues of nationalism, North American militarism, separation of church and state, a biblical response to communism, evangelism and peace witness.

Stoner, John K. Letter to the Editor. *EV* 92 (Feb. 10, 1979), 6. In our emphasis on human depravity we consider people more capable of believing lies about our national security based on military strength than the truth about the real basis of security.

Stoner, John K. "Peace and Evangelism . . . Are They Related?" *ChrLead* 42 (June 19, 1979), 5; *MBH* 18 (Oct. 26, 1979), 8-9. An evangelistic message can speak to people's hunger for peace and freedom from the idolatry of militarism.

Stoner, John K. "The Military Wants to Train Your Child." *ChrLiv* 25 (July, 1978), 20-23. Statistics and comment on public school

recruiting by the US armed forces, as well as suggestions for a Christian response.

Stucky, Harley J. "Report on Trip to Washington." *Menn* 70 (Jan. 22, 1955), 181, 192. Representatives of the Peace and Education Committees of the Western District (GCMC) expressed concern to congresspersons concerning the growing militarization of America, especially with respect to Universal Military Training.

Stucky, Vernon. Letter to the Editor. *Menn* 90 (Feb. 11, 1975), 92. In "How to Live with Inflation" (Jan. 7, 1975), Leighton Ford's failure to mention the outrageous military budget as a source of inflation reveals a superficial understanding of the economy and of commitment to Christ.

Studer, Gerald C. "Will a Christian Be Patriotic?" *ChrLead* 39 (Jan. 20, 1976), 5. Christian patriotism notes that it is righteousness not military might that exalts a nation, that it is justice for all, tempered with mercy that gives strength to a nation. A Christian must first give loyalty to Christ.

Swartzendruber, Fred. "The Christian, Militarism, and the State." *Forum* 10 (Dec., 1976), 6-7. A report on the Intercollegiate Peace Fellowship conference at Tabor College, Hillsboro, Kans., Oct. 28-30, 1976, which focused on militarism and the Christian response.

Swartzentruber, Anita. "The Argentine Mennonite Church, the State, and Military Service." Paper presented to Mennonite History class, English Clinic, Jan. 16, 1954. Pp. 7. MHL.

Swift, Richard and Regehr, Ernie. "Dubious Sentinel: Canada and the World Military Order." Waterloo, Ont.: "Project Plowshares," Institute for Peace and Conflict Studies, Conrad Grebel College, [1979]. Pp. [40]. MHL. Education kit. Table of Contents: I The World Military Order; II Canadian Military Spending and Waste; III The Arms Trade and the Third World; IV Spheres of Influence; V State of Siege; VI Guide to Action; VII Christian Perspectives on Militarism.

"Tent Dwellers Witness at Arms Show." *EV* 92 (Apr. 10, 1979), 13. A group protests "Defense Technology '79," an international military conference and trade show, in Rosemont, Ill., and one member of this group, Doug Wiebe, contributes a poem, "The Second Nativity," which expresses his reflections on nuclear weapons.

"The Churchman and the Military." *CanMenn* 12 (Aug. 25, 1964), 4. Statement questioning Mennonites who are exchanging the nonresistant Christ for a national flag.

"The Conflict and the Church." *CanMenn* 9 (Sept. 29, 1961), 6. A biblical basis for "bypassing militarism."

"The Position of the Mennonite Church of North America on Peace, War, Military Service, and Patriotism." *Menn* 63 (Oct. 12, 1948), 5-6. The official statement of the GCMC on this subject. Appeals to the biblical basis for love and nonviolence. While refusing military service, Mennonites have shown genuine willingness to render service of national importance in alternative programs.

"To Place 'Peace Person' with World Council of Churches." *MennRep* 9 (Jan. 8, 1979), 2. Mennonites of the Netherlands are ready to finance the salary of one staff worker in the World Council of Churches program to combat militarism.

Taber, Charles R. "No More 'Crusades.'" *MBH* 17 (Sept. 29, 1978), 7. The despicable militarism of the Crusades has resulted in fierce rejection of Christianity by Muslims.

Tarasoff, Koozma J. "Doukhobors and Mennonites—A Comparative Study of Ideological Persistence in Response to the Institution of Militarism." Term paper for Tutorial on the Nature and Dynamics of Plural Societies (Carleton Univ., Ottawa), June, 1975. Pp. 66. CGCL.

Teichroew, Allan, ed. "Military Surveillance of Mennonites in World War I." *MQR* 53 (Apr., 1979), 95-127. Publishes a report from the Military Intelligence Division of the War Department documenting government surveillance of Mennonites, Amish, and Hutterites between Mar., 1918 and Feb., 1919 and government pressure on them as conscientious objectors in World War I. The report concludes that their actions qualified as "treason."

Thiessen, Linda Dyck. "Mennonites and Military Exemption in Canada During World War I." Term paper, Feb. 21, 1978. Box 10-C-4. CMBS/ Win.

Thomas, Everett. "What I Heard the Israelis Say." *GH* 62 (Sept. 16, 1969), 807-808. Participant in MCC Middle East Study Tour heard Israelis calling for the survival of the Jewish state at any military price.

Thomson, Murray and Regehr, Ernie. "Canadian Military Sales." *PlMon* 1 (July, 1977), 5. Documents Canadian arms sales to the Third World and comments on Canada's role in the militarization of the Third World.

Thomson, Murray and Regehr, Ernie. "Conversion." *PlMon* 1 (Feb., 1978), 3-5. Statistics and information support the thesis that industrial conversion from military to socially useful production is possible and practical.

Thomson, Murray and Regehr, Ernie. "Counting the Costs." *PlMon* 1 (Apr., 1977), 4-5. Comment on the economic effects of Canada's proposed increase in military spending.

Thomson, Murray and Regehr, Ernie. "Global Militarism." *PlMon* 2 (Apr.-May, 1979), 3-4. Statistics on world militarization reveal global priorities focused on destruction, not on eliminating suffering or reducing economic disparities.

Thomson, Murray and Regehr, Ernie. "Militarism and Human Rights." *PlMon* 2 (Dec., 1978), 3-4. Analyzes the relationship between human rights violations and the presence of externally supplied and trained armed forces.

Thomson, Murray and Regehr, Ernie. "The Election and Canadian Military Policy." *PlMon* 2 (Apr.-May, 1979), 1-2. Challenges the direction of Canadian military policy toward greater spending for military purpose and increased export of armaments.

Tochterman, Frank. "Military Chaplaincy and its Implications." Paper for War, Peace, and Revolution class, AMBS, Elkhart, Ind., May 1, 1969. Pp. 3. AMBS.

Toews, John A. "Confronting Communism with Love." *MBH* 16 (May 27, 1977), 17. Two-thirds of Mennonite Brethren support resisting communism by military force, while the church should be a messenger of peace.

Toews, John A. "The Christian and Armed Combat." *The Voice* 9 (May-June, 1960), 9. Central thesis is that those who submit unconditionally to the Lordship of Jesus Christ in faith and life cannot participate in armed combat or war.

Toews, John B. "The Russian Mennonite Migrations of the 1870s and 1880s—Some Background Aspects." *ChrLead* 37 (Apr. 2, 1974), 4. A czarist decree intorduced universal military conscription in 1870s with no provisions for exempting the Mennonites. The question of their historic pacifism became a watershed in the history of the Russian Mennonites.

Toews, John B. "The Russian Mennonites and the Military Question (1921-1927)." N.d. Pp. 28. MLA/BeC.

Troutt, Margaret. "Army of Salvation." *ChrLiv* 7 (Apr., 1960), 20-23. Introductory sketch of the Salvation Army, the military system that wars against evil.

Trueblood, Elton. "The Call to Enlistment." *ChrLiv* 9 (July, 1962), 23-26. Condensed from chapter 2 of *Company of the Committed* by Trueblood, Harper and Brothers, Publishers. The arduous discipline of the early Christian community resembled a military band.

Unrau, Ed (Review). *The Mennonite Brotherhood in Russia,* by P. M. Friesen. Mennonite Brethren, 1978. "Russian Mennonites Created a Brotherhood in Name Only," *MennMirror* 8 (Nov., 1978), 9, 10. Provides a summary of this book, which is a detailed and critical summary of the Mennonites of Russia, and gives a brief statement of the author's view on military service and nonresistance. Describes the book as "overwhelming in its scope and shattering in its impact."

Unruh, Elmer. Letter to the Editor. *ChrLead* 40 (Feb. 1, 1977), 13. Weary of those people who show little or no respect for the many Christian military personnel who feel it is God's will for them to serve.

Unruh, John D. "Peace and War: Peace Conferences Transcend Political Barriers." *GH* 53 (Jan. 19, 1960), 57. Christians from all over the world are coming together to think about militarism and peace. Mennonites should be thankful and live lives that present a clear peace testimony.

"Vietnam Study: Relief Often Tied to Politics, Military." *MennRep* 2 (Oct. 2, 1972), 1. Relief agencies enjoy the benevolences of a government because the latter recognizes a potential in the former to realize its political and military ends.

"Vietnam Workers Urge Cut in Arms Flow." *GH* 67 (July 2, 1974), 536. Reprints the text of a letter from 22 MCC and Eastern Board of Missions workers to congressional committees responsible for military funding in Vietnam. Letter calls for drastic reductions in military hardware to Vietnam.

"Visitors Cite Pervasive Militarism in South Africa." *Menn* 94 (Dec. 18, 1979), 762. Three South African members of the Africa National Congress visited the MCC-Canada office to give information about the conditions in South Africa and to ask for discontinuation of financial investment in their country and of sale of arms.

Van Houten, Diether H. Letter to the Editor. *ChrLead* 41 (Jan. 31, 1978), 16. There are "born-again" Christians in the military services and many are members of Officers' Christian Fellowship, an internationally affiliated organization with the purpose of witnessing for Christ to the military officer.

Vogt, Roy. "Ideology Is Sometimes Only Skin Deep . . . Behind the Stone Faces Are Sensitive Hearts and Minds." Part 4. *MennMirror* 6 (Apr., 1977), 6-8. Writer describes two different encounters he has had with military personnel in East Germany when he has been able to penetrate their military mask and learn something about their personal experience in the military.

Vogt, Roy. "What Shall We Do With Our Prophets?" *MennMirror* 8 (Apr., 1979), 22. There are prophets in our midst who are voicing concern over the growing militarism, but the Minneapolis conference did not elect to support them.

Vogt, Virgil. "A Nonresistant Christian Looks at Civil Defense." *ChrLiv* 2 (Dec., 1955), 4-5, 38-39. The Civil Defense system is intimately linked to the military in both its motivation and its tasks.

Vogt, Virgil. "The Role of Well-Fed Mennonites in a Hungry World." *ChrLiv* 15 (Dec., 1968), 5-8. Comments on a Mennonite consultation on world hunger and calls Mennonites to confront wasteful militarism with greater witness against oppression and wealth.

Von Wijk, Hein. "French Conscientious Objectors Under Military Jurisdiction." *CanMenn* 14 (Jan. 4, 1966), 3. A report on French CO's and their plight in camps under military jurisdiction. French law of July 9, 1965, introduced four kinds of service: the armed services; civil defense; technical aid (in overseas territories); and cooperation (in underdeveloped foreign countries). The last two (non-military) types of service are closed to CO's.

Voth, Debra. "Junior Reserve Officers Training Corps." *IPF Notes* 23 (Nov., 1976), 5-7. Junior ROTC is not a leadership training program but a course in militarism.

Waltner, Emil J. "Difficulties in Applying Non-Conformity in Modern Life." *PCMCP Third,* 53-67. North Newton, Kansas: n.p. Held at North Newton, Kansas, Aug. 18-19, 1944. As people attempt to live a life of nonconformity in modern times, the issue of post-war military training is one of the most challenging.

Warkentin, Bernard. Letter to the Editor. *MennRep* 8 (Aug. 7, 1978), 7. Relates personal experience of noncombatant duty in World War I, concluding that noninvolvement in war is an impossible dream given the interconnectedness of people and institutions in a society.

Warkentine, Kendal. "Military Justice in World War I: Court Martial Trials of Mennonite Conscientious Objectors." Social Science Seminar, Feb., 1983. Pp. 127. MLA/BeC.

Weaver, Erma (Review). *The Politics of Food and Faith,* by Jack A. Nelson. Orbis, 1980. Pp. 230. *FStP* 5 (May, 1980), 10-11. Recommends this study of how US military and economic policies prevent self-reliance and the feeding of the poor in underdeveloped countries.

Weaver, John W. "Presidents, Prayers, and Breakfasts." *GH* 64 (June 1, 1971), 492-93. Criticizes presidential prayer breakfasts for reinforcing values of militarism and oppressive economic policies, and calls Mennonites to greater courage in "speaking truth to power."

Weaver, Robert. "Comments on War." *Menn* 55 (July 30, 1940), 13-14. Love and kindness will break down a Hitler quicker than military means.

Webb, Jon. "Why I Choose Canada." *With* 4 (Mar., 1971), 10. The story of one man's experience in military prison. When he was unable to get a CO classification, he again went AWOL to Canada.

Wenger, J. C. *Separated unto God.* Scottdale: Mennonite Publishing House, 1951. Pp. 350. A plea for Christian simplicity of life and for a scriptural nonconformity to the world. Nonconformity functions as the context for separation from the worldly military nature of political rule, and for nonresistance specifically church and state.

Widmer, Pierre. "From Military Service to Christian Nonresistance: the Testimony of a Former French Army Officer." *MQR* 23 (Oct., 1949), 245-56. The history of French Mennonite attitudes toward nonresistance, together with an autobiographical account of renewed peace concern.

Wiebe, Arns. "The Principle of Love." *ChrLead* 31 (Oct. 22, 1968), 6, 7, 12. Love is to be exercised toward God, brothers and sisters, and the enemy. When that love becomes militant and political, however, it has lost its base in the experience of the love of God in our hearts.

Wiebe, Bernie. "Uneasy About Canada." *Menn* 93 (Jan. 10, 1978), 32. In light of Canadian Mennonite denunciation of Pentagon strategies, Wiebe challenges Mennonites of Canada to examine militarism also in their country.

Wiebe, Don (Review). *Agenda for a Biblical People,* by Jim Wallis. Harper and Row, 1976. Pp. 145. *MBH* 15 (Dec. 24, 1976), 21. Wallis attacks the peace between the Christian church and present economic and military goals of Western capitalism, but reviewer labels his ethics "utopian."

Wiebe, Dwight. "How the Army Feels About the Conscientious Objector." *YCC* 43 (Feb. 25, 1962), 2. An exchange of correspondence showing that even in the chaplain's office the conscientious objector who thinks he or she can have a stronger Christian testimony in the military is not welcomed.

Wiebe, Dwight. "What Manner of Men Are We?" *Peace Orations: Winners in National Speech Contests.* Hillsboro: Tabor College Bulletin, Mar., 1950, 1-6. Pp. 15. MHL. The contemporary situation of militarism is evidence that our technology has far outstripped our morality—"ours is a world of nuclear giants and ethical infants."

Wiebe, Katie Funk. "No-sweat Christianity." *ChrLead* 40 (Oct. 25, 1977), 17; *MBH* 16 (Oct. 28, 1977), 5. Reflections on hearing a Latin American evangelist challenge the church to break its ties to the state and the military.

Wiebe, Katie Funk. "The Militarization of Women." *ChrLead* 41 (Apr. 25, 1978), 10; *GH* 71 (June 6, 1978), 451. ERA discussion is shattering the idea that nonresistance and nonviolence is a doctrine mainly for men. Just as many women are joining the military, so women of the historic peace churches should share with men in the commitment to nonviolence and peacemaking.

Wiebe, Michael. Letter to the Editor. *MBH* 13 (May 3, 1974), 11, 31. One form of the American government's oppression of poor countries is US military aid to corrupt governments.

Wilson, William Jerome. "A Letter from a Noncombatant." *GH* 38 (Aug. 31, 1945), 419-20. Expresses deep regret at having left CPS to become a noncombatant.

World Conference on Religion and Peace. "The Rights of Conscientious Objectors." *EV* 87 (Oct. 25, 1974), 12. A brief statement from the World Conference on Religion and Peace in Kyoto, Japan, Oct. 16-21, 1970, stating that each person should have the right, on the grounds of conscience or profound conviction, to refuse military service.

Yake, C. F. "On the Spot." *YCC* 35 (Nov. 28, 1954), 380. Freedom of religion to worship God according to the dictates of conscience is tested when it interferes with the United States military.

Yake, C. F. "'Peace, Peace' When There Is No Peace." *YCC* 12, Part 1, (June 21, 1931), 612; Part 2, (June 28, 1931), 620. Encouragement for youth to keep guard in the interest of true peace and the biblical principle of nonresistance. Reports on the current promotion of militarism in the United States.

Also the forces opposing this militarism and promoting peace are mentioned.

Yake, C. F. "Soldiers Must Be Killers." *YCC* 34 (Nov. 29, 1953), 796. The purpose of all military training and the method used to accomplish the objective to make our boys "the best killers in the world."

Yake, C. F. "Universal Military Training." *YCC* 29 (May 23, 1948), 164. Discussion of peacetime conscription in the form of universal military training. Caution about fundamentalists who teach it is the Christian's duty to fight.

Yoder, Edward. "Luke 3:14: Peace Principles from a Scriptural Viewpoint." Part 33. *GH* 32 (Jan. 18, 1940), 912. An appeal to this reference cannot justify military life for a Christian.

Yoder, Edward. "Military Figures in the New Testament: Peace Principles from a Scriptural Viewpoint." Part 39. *GH Supplement* 34 (Apr., 1941), 78. Paul did not mean to sanction the military by his repeated use of military metaphors.

Yoder, Edward. "The Christian's Attitude Toward Participation in War Activities." *MQR* 9 (Jan., 1935), 5-19. Mennonites have consistently chosen a moderate position between total noncooperation with the military and a willingness to engage in noncombatant duty in their witness against war.

Yoder, John H. "A Historic Free Church View." *Church Unity in North America: A Symposium.* Ed. J. Robert Nelson. St. Louis: The Bethany Press, 1958, 89-97. Pp. 208. Within a broader discussion of ecumenism, holds that one of the most formidable obstacles to Christian unity is the churches' "unhesitating consent to nationalism in its demonic military form."

Yoder, John H. "Clarifying the Gospel." *Builder* 23 (Aug., 1973), 1-2. Faithfulness to the Jesus of the gospel demands disavowal of the Jesus in whose name Christians have sanctioned colonialism, racism, militarism, and anti-communism.

Yoder, John H. "Love Seeketh Not Its Own." *ChrLiv* 3 (Jan., 1956), 26-28. Mennonite nonconformity, historically directed toward baptism, oath, and military service, should now be directed toward economics and our use of money.

Yoder, John H. "Nonconformity and the Nation." *ChrLiv* 2 (Feb., 1955), 8-9, 25, 33. The deeper issue behind conscientious objection to military service is the question of loyalty to the nation or to the Kingdom of God.

Yoder, Mervin. "A Study of the Church Status of Mennonites Who Accepted Military Service." Paper prepared for Mennonite Seminar, [1949]. Pp. 22, plus charts. MHL.

Zehr, Albert. "US Deserter Preaches." *GH* 63 (June 2, 1970), 489. Summary of the personal story told by a US Army deserter about his coming to conscientious objector convictions and the treatment given him in military prison after going AWOL.

Zehr, Daniel. "Christian Perspectives on Militarism." *MCC PS Newsletter* 9 (Dec., 1979), 5-7. Notes the distortions of the words and deeds of Jesus Christ when they are drawn upon to provide moral support for warmaking or preparations for warmaking.

# B. Conscription

"A Manual of Draft Information for Ministers and Other Counsellors." Akron: MCC Peace Section, 1951. Pp. 31. MHL.

"A Message from the Consultation on Conscience and Conscription." *GH* 63 (Jan. 6, 1970), 12-13. Outlines concerns, affirmations, objections, and appeals to obedience in relationship to war and peace drawn up by the Peace Assembly of the MCC Peace Section. Statement affirms both alternative service and noncooperation as valid Christian responses to the draft and encourages the government to grant exemption from military service to selective objectors to war.

"A Statement of Concern to the Committee on Armed Services of the United States House of Representatives on H.R. 3005 Amending the Universal Military Service and Training Act." *CanMenn* 3 (Feb. 25, 1955), 2. Statement presented on behalf of MCC by C. N. Hostetter on Feb. 2, 1955.

"An Announcement by the Peace Problems Committee." *GH* 33 (Nov. 21, 1940), 730-31. Announces the financial needs of the civilian service program, the establishment of NSBRO, and a plan to keep the church informed of matters relating to the draft.

"Analysis of Draft Census of Five Mennonite Conferences." *GH* 49 (Nov. 20, 1956), 1105. Mennonite Research Foundation reports the CO record of the Mennonite Church in 1952-56 was better than it was in World War II.

"Automatic Registration a Live Possibility." *GH* 72 (June 12, 1979), 472. Summarizes a testimony on the draft to the Senate Armed Services

Committee by K. B. Hoover, a Brethren in Christ representative to MCC.

*A Manual of Draft Information for Conscientious Objectors.* Akron, Pa.: MCC Peace Section, 1968. Pp. 206. MHL.

*A Manual of Draft Information for Ministers and Other Counsellors.* Akron, Pa.: MCC Peace Section, 1951. MHL. Revisions and additions: Feb., 1952; Mar., 1952; July, 1952; Dec., 1952; June, 1953; July, 1954; Oct., 1955.

Ames, Winslow. "Thoughts of an Outsider on Mennonite Civilian Public Service." *MennLife* 3 (Apr., 1948), 41-42. Non-Mennonite CPS worker comments on aspects of Mennonite culture seen in camp and criticizes peace churches for aiding in conscription through administering CPS.

Assembly on the Draft. "Findings Committee Report." *MCC PS Newsletter* 10 (Mar.-Apr., 1980), 7-8. Statement from the Mar., 1980, Assembly deals with proposals for active witness against conscription, calls for congregational support for those affected by the draft, and suggestions for congregational study and witness

"Bishop Appears Before US Committee to Testify on Military Draft Laws." *CanMenn* 15 (May 23, 1967), 1, 5. Text of a statement made by John E. Lapp, MCC Peace Section resentative, before the Armed Services Committee of the US House of Representatives on May 3, 1967. Lapp's requests included: equal liberties for COs of all denominations; equal liberties for all COs of sincere religious convictions; freedom for all sincerely troubled by ethical problems of militarism; abolition of universal military training.

"Board Addresses President's Task Force." *RepConsS* 35 (July, 1978), 2. Statement opposing conscription delivered by John Stoner, Vice-Chairperson of NISBCO, to Selective Service Task Force on May 19, 1978.

Baker, Robert J. "And Now, A Few Words from the Establishment." *With* 3 (Jan., 1970), 4; "A Few Words from the Establishment," *GH* 63 (Jan. 13, 1970), 30-31. A letter from a father to a son concerning the son's position of noncooperation with the Selective Service System of the United States.

Bargen, Ralph. "This Is the Sorrow." *Fellowship* 15 (May, 1949), 7-9. Statement which a young Mennonite nonregistrant presented to the FBI at the time of his arrest; statement outlines the convictions which have led him to a stance of nonresistance.

Barrett, Lois [Janzen]. "When They Draft Women." *Menn* 87 (May 9, 1972), 324. If and when women are drafted, there may be some benefits. Women will need to deal more directly with the issues of war and violence and with the formulation of clear positions on these issues.

Bauman, Clarence. "Conscientious Objection and the German Draft Law." Paper presented at the Historic Peace Churches and IFOR Conference, Beatrice Webb House, England, Sept. 11-14, 1956. Pp. 12. MHL.

Beachy, Alvin J. "Conscription: The Pacifist View." *ChrCent* 73 (Sept. 26, 1956), 1097-98. Responds to a previous writer's assertion that military service is not incompatible with discipleship by recommending Christian pacifism and its commitment to the lordship of Christ and the call to make disciples in all nations.

Becker, Mark. "Mennonite Resistance to Draft Registration in the 1980's." Social Science Seminar paper, Apr., 1985. Pp. 85. MLA/BeC.

Beechy, Atlee. "Implications of the Draft for Our Young People." *GH* 43 (Nov. 21, 1950), 1140-42. An explanation of the draft, deferments, and service opportunities.

Bender, Harold S. "Hearing Before the Preparedness Subcommittee of the Committee on Armed Services United States Senate, Eighty-second Congress." Washington: US Printing Office, 1951. Opposes peacetime conscription on grounds that such action is first step toward national and international policy characterized primarily by militarism. Transcript includes copy of MCC statement submitted to House Armed Services Committee on April 17, 1948.

Bender, Harold S. "When May Christians Disobey the Government?" *GH* 53 (Jan. 12, 1960), 25-26, 44; *GfT* Series 2, 5 (Mar.-Apr., 1970), 16-17. Maintains that draft legislation is a civil, not a military act, and as such, Christians should obey the law and register. The Christian may disobey the government only when the content of an act required by the state is an evil in itself since "the desire to witness to the truth or against an evil cannot be a ground to disobey the requirements of the state which in themselves are not wrong."

Bender, John M. "The Draft: a Personal Statement." *GH* 64 (Apr. 13, 1971), 338. Even after registering with the Selective Service System and taking a CO stand, there are many questions as to what it means to live a nonresistant life. The writer, a Canadian resident in the US, reviews his dilemma of considering nonregistration for the draft in order to refuse cooperation with the war industry.

Bergen, Lois. "Youth Education: Peace Education Is Lifelong Growth." *Builder* 31 (Jan., 1981), 28-29. Lists resources and makes suggestions for helping youth think through their positions on militarism, registration, conscientious objection, biblical peacemaking, etc.

Bethel College Peace Activities. About 65 interviews. Emphasis is on the 1960's and 1970's, including news reports on Bethel's Moratorium Day protest, nonregistration, bellringing, student attitudes, and Women's International League for Peace and Freedom. MLA/BeC.

Beyler, Betsy, and Franz, Delton. "After Afghanistan—The Fallout." *MCC PS Wash. Memo* 12 (Jan.-Feb., 1980), 5-6, 8. Calculates the effect of the Soviet invasion of Afghanistan on the SALT II agreements, the arms race, the draft, etc.

Blosser, Richard (Review). *In Solitary Witness,* by Gordon Zahn. Collegeville, Minn.: Liturgical Press, 1964. Pp. 278. "Solitary Witness." *Menn* 94 (Nov. 6, 1979), 668. Briefly describes the book which gives an in-depth study of the life and witness of an Austrian peasant whose religious convictions led him to reject the Nazi movement as anti-Christian and to refuse service in the wars in the 1940's. Point out the book's relevance for North American Christians facing issues of the nuclear arms race and peacetime draft.

Born, Daniel. "Obeying God Over Caesar." *ChrLead* 43 (Nov. 4, 1980), 12. Encourages readers to consider nonregistration for the draft as a valid Christian response by relating it to other historical circumstances where Christian commitment called for civil disobedience.

Brenneman, Don. Letter to the Editor. *GH* 63 (Feb. 24, 1970), 190. Response to Robert J. Baker's letter to his draft resisting son (Jan. 13, 1970, 30-31) expressing support for the position of noncooperation with the draft, since the registration process contributes to the war effort.

Brown, Roland. "The Implications of Registering for War and the Alternatives." *Menn* 63 (Oct. 12, 1948), 13-14. Since war is evil and conscription serves war, registration for conscription is a compromise with war. Such a compromise dulls the pointed witness against war which Christian obedience demands.

Brubacher, Dwight. "Mennonite Nonresistance in Ontario, World War I: The Persecution of a Separate People." Paper presented to Social Science Seminar, Goshen College, Goshen, Ind., May 13, 1976. Pp. 23. MHL.

Brubaker, Dean M. "To Resist or Not to Resist, That Is the Question." *GH* 63 (Dec. 8, 1970), 1012-14. Discusses biblical passages related to the subject of Christian obedience to government, and questions whether draft registration is really part of the military system. Opposes nonviolent resistance because he considers it foreign to biblical nonresistance.

Brunk, Conrad G. "Another Side of the 'New' Selective Service System." *RepConsS* 28 (Jan., 1971), 2. Protests that Draft Director Curtis Tarr's image as a liberal reformer of an outdated draft system conceals his primary concern—the efficiency of the drafting machine.

Brunk, Conrad G. *Conscientious Objectors and the Draft.* Washington, DC: National Interreligious Service Board for Conscientious Objectors, 1972. Pp. 48. MHL. Information pamphlet covering such topics as the tradition of conscientious objection to war, the various alternatives open for those confronted with the draft and some of the moral implications of these alternatives.

Burkholder, J. Lawrence. "Other Kinds of Conscientious Objectors." *GH* 60 (Feb. 21, 1967), 148, 154; *Menn* 82 (Mar. 28, 1967), 213-15. Says Mennonites need to support, in various ways, nonreligious and selective objectors to war. Urges Mennonites to work for draft legislation recognizing such objectors as CO's.

Byler, Dennis. "Letter to Draft Board." *GH* 63 (June 30, 1970), 586-87. Conscientious objector who chose noncooperation with the draft explains his reasons for opposing participation in war or any of its accompanying machinery.

Byler, Frank. "A History of the Nonresistant People of Logan and Champaign Counties, 1917-1918." Paper presented to Social Science Seminar, Goshen College, Goshen, Ind., n.d. Pp. 32. MHL.

"Chicago Area Draft Resisters." *GH* 62 (Oct. 14, 1969), 904. Statistical report on number of draft resisters, participants in alternative service, etc., in 125 churches as reported by the Selective Service system.

"Conference Response to Conscription and Militarism." *GH* 62 (Oct. 7, 1969), 869. An appeal to nonresistant faith, service and alternate service, and noncooperation as the situation may require.

"Conscription and Militarism Is Always a Disastrous Policy." *CanMenn* 7 (Feb. 6, 1959), 1, 4. Statement made by Esko Loewen for the Mennonite churches of the US to the US House of Representatives committee on armed services is a strong appeal to abolish conscription.

"Conscription Bills Seen as Trial Balloons." *Menn* 94 (Mar. 27, 1979), 231. A plea to send letters to senators and representatives in response to the growing number of bills that have been introduced in the House and Senate seeking to reinstate military conscription.

"Conscription Moves Accelerate." *GH* 72 (Mar. 27, 1979), 256. Three principal legislative approaches are being introduced in the Congress to reinstate military conscription; MCC has responded, speaking against the development.

"Counsel to Mennonite Young Men Regarding the Selective Training and Service Act of 1940 as it Applies to Conscientious Objectors." *GH* 33 (Oct. 10, 1940), 603-604. PPC summarizes certain aspects of the act and adds a personal message to the youth who will be facing conscription.

Catton, Bruce. "Draft More Liberal Than in 1917 Toward Conscientious Objectors." *Goshen News* n.d., 16. Describes the Selective Service registration process for conscientious objectors (during World War II). Includes photo of a Mennonite from Pa. registering.

Charles, Howard H. "A Presentation and Evaluation of MCC Draft Status Census." *PCMCP Fourth*, 83-106. North Newton: Bethel College, 1945. Held at Bluffton, Ohio, Aug. 24-25, 1945. The purpose of the draft status census was to ascertain the number of men who had gone into military service and to learn why they did. Factual data revealed a variety of factors which influenced these decisions.

Conrad, Tom. "Do You Feel the Draft?" *ChrLead* 42 (Apr. 10, 1979), 8; *With* 12 (Mar., 1979), 18. Examines a variety of responses people have had to the threat of conscription.

"Deserters for Conscience' Sake." *GH* 62 (May 13, 1969), 429. Reprinted from *The Reporter* (Feb., 1969), pub. by National Service Board for Religious Objectors. Reviews the unstable plight of army deserters for reasons of conscience and the policies of Canadian and Swedish governments toward them.

"Doubt that the Draft Can Ever Be Fair and Just." *Menn* 86 (June 8, 1971), 378. A dozen Bethel College students conduct a 140-mile, eight-day walk to convey to US Senator James Pearson their belief that the Selective Service System ought to be abolished.

"Draft Resisters in Israel." *GH* 64 (Sept. 28, 1971), 806. Political reasons for sending draft notices back to the Minister of Defense.

D. A. S. "The Christian Witness and Conscription." *CPS Bull Supp* 5 (May 16, 1946), 9. Since

peacetime conscription would increase militarism and limit freedom of conscience, the church should make its convictions on this issue known to the government.

Derstine, C. F. "Conscription and Conscientious Objectors." *ChrMon* 32 (May, 1940), 158-59. Reviews the government attitude toward conscientious objection during World War I and strongly advocates the position to youth in World War II.

Dourte, Eber. "To Serve the Present Age." *EV* 92 (Jan. 25, 1979), 9. At the semi-annual meeting of the MCC Peace Section, the agenda included reports and discussion on the New Call to Peacemaking, peace education, the World Arms Race and our peace witness, and the possibility of draft for military service.

Drescher, James M. "Clergy and the Draft." *GH* 73 (Sept. 2, 1980), 697. Discusses five reasons why Mennonite clergy should not seek exemption from the draft.

Drescher, James M. "Oh Yes—I Guess." *Swords into Plowshares: A Collection of Plays About Peace and Social Justice*, ed. Ingrid Rogers. Elgin: The Brethren Press, 1983, 221-27. A satiric drama in which a draft board questions a young man and finds him unsuitable for the active duty classification he has requested because he possesses too many human and religious values.

Drescher, John M. (Editorial). "Draft Resisters at General Conference." *GH* 62 (Oct. 7, 1969), 865. Outlines the resolution adopted by the Mennonite General Conference in support of the draft resisters and comments on the difficulty Mennonites had in showing love toward the resisters who presented their position.

Dueck, Dora (Review). *Mennonite Soldier*, by Kenneth Reed. Scottdale: Herald Press, 1974. Pp. 518. *MBH* 14 (Mar. 7, 1975), 27. Recommends this novel about two Mennonite brothers' responses to the draft: one joins the army; the other takes a conscientious objector stance.

Dyck, Peter J. "Our Peace Witness in Relation to Government." Revised from an address given at a Peace Conference, Eden Church, Moundridge, Kansas, June 17, 1956. Pp. 8. MLA/BeC., MHL.

"FMC Student Arrested for Not Registering with Draft Board." *CanMenn* 18 (July 3, 1970), 1, 2. Anticipating court action and imprisonment, 18-year-old Duane Shank writes about prosecution and arrest for nonregistration with the Selective Service System of the USA.

Eby, John W. "In Case of Conscription: a 5-Point Proposal." *GH* 72 (Aug. 14, 1979), 642-43. Five proposals for the Mennonite Church to consider in responding to conscription and in giving a clear testimony to a biblical place and mission position.

Eby, Omar. "Consultation on Conscience and Conscription: A Personal Impression." *GH* 63 (Jan. 13, 1970), 34-35. Author reflects on the generous support for the position of noncooperation with the draft shown at the recent Chicago Peace Assembly. He affirms resisters, but expresses concern that they not become as tyrannical on this issue as past church leaders on other issues of nonconformity.

Eby, Omar and Shetler, Sanford G. "Chicago Consultation on Conscience and Conscription." *GfT* Series 2, 5 (Jan.-Feb., 1970), 3-9. Personal reflections on the question of compliance with or resistance to the draft.

Ediger, Elmer. "Voluntary Service and the Draft." *Menn* 66 (Jan. 23, 1951), 58. Urges CO's to enter the VS grogram now, rather than waiting for the prodding of conscription. The VS program offers much greater opportunities for witness and service than the CPS program did.

Ens, Robert D. "If Uncle Sam Comes Calling Again." *With* 10 (July-Aug., 1977), 48. Renewed debate over the All-Volunteer Army raises concern about a possible reinstatement of a new draft.

Ens, Robert D. Letter to the Editor. *ChrLead* 42 (May 8, 1979), 16. Mennonites should be preparing young people to refuse to register for any military draft.

Epp, Arnold A. "Draft Status of Mennonite Men in American Wars from the French and Indian War to World War II." Student paper for Mennonite History course, May 24, 1949. Pp. 31. MLA/BeC.

Epp, Frank H. "American Draft-Resisters and Canadian Mennonites." *CanMenn* 16 (Apr. 30, 1968), 1, 2. Appeals to Canadian Mennonites to be sympathetic to Americans fleeing to Canada to avoid going to Vietnam because of the parallel between American draft resisters who leave their country and Mennonites who also migrated for reasons of conscience.

Epp, Frank H. "I Would Like to Dodge the Draft Dodgers, But History Won't Let Me." *ChrLiv* 17 (Nov., 1970), 24-29. Draft dodger counselor reviews fifty years of Canadian policy toward American war resisters.

Epp, Frank H. "Military Draft Presents Major Problem to USA and Peace Groups." *CanMenn* 15 (Apr. 25, 1967), 1, 2. Peace groups express three major concerns: probable extension of

conscription in US; the "inequalities" of the present draft system; and the Vietnam war and military service in general.

Epp, Frank H. "Witness in Washington." *CanMenn* 3 (Feb. 25, 1955), 2. Challenges Canadian Mennonites to observe the example of American Mennonites' witness against conscription in order to be ready to make a similar witness.

Epp, Frank H. (Editorial). "Conscription in Canada." *CanMenn* 2 (Nov. 19, 1954), 2. Counters the Canadian Legion's argument that Canada should have compulsory military service. "Peace through strength" for the Christian means belief in the power of the God of love and peace.

Epp, Leonard. "Canada: Refuge from Militarism?" *CanMenn* 18 (May 22, 1970), 1, 2. Draft refugees coming to Canada from the United States are often denigrated. In describing a number of cases, the author describes them as draft resisters, deserters, frustrated and confused, of extraordinary caliber, and less politically and mre religiously inclined.

Erb, Paul. "Alternative Service." *GH* 41 (Apr. 13, 1948), 339-40. If universal peacetime conscription is adopted, Mennonites must have creative alternative programs ready to be initiated.

Erb, Paul. "Looking Forward in CPS." *GH* 39 (Sept. 3, 1946), 483. If there is a peacetime draft, Mennonites should continue to operate CPS camps. The camps should be structured to protect the participants from worldly influences and to offer maximum opportunities to witness to the Christian way.

Erb, Paul. "The Draft." *GH* 41 (July 27, 1948), 683. Because nonresistant Christians have been granted deferments there needs to be a great emphasis on voluntary service to show both our neighbors and our government that such privileges are deserved.

Erb, Paul. "The War Is Not Over." *GH* 38 (Aug. 31, 1945), 411. The war seems to be over but the evils which it was to cure still exist. The Atomic bomb, enormous national debts, and continued conscription are part of the legacy of this war.

"Five Mennonite COs Convicted of Draft Violation." *RepConsS* 13 (Dec., 1956), 1, 3. Expressing personal distress, Philadelphia judge sentences five Lancaster County men for various types of conscientious objection.

Faculty of the Mennonite Brethren Biblical Seminary. "Seminary Faculty Gives Draft Position." *ChrLead* 43 (July 29, 1980), 12-13. Consensus statement recommends alternative service to military duty but supports positions of noncombatant service and noncooperation as well.

Farrar, Peter. "My Response to Registration." *Menn* 95 (Oct. 7, 1980), 576. Writer in letter to his Senator announces his intentions to promote nonregistration for the draft and to withdraw participation in the benefits of the federal government upon prosecution of nonregistrants.

Fast, Darrell. "SSS or Christ." *Menn* 84 (Sept. 9, 1969), 544. Mennonite youth are raising questions about their relationship to conscription. The vitality of the Mennonite peace position should be a response to the command of Christ rather than that of the Selective Service System.

Fast, Peter G. "The Russian Mennonites and the State." Paper presented to the Social Science Seminar, Goshen College, Goshen, Ind., May 31, 1949. Pp. 39. MHL.

*Forum* staff. "A Random Sampling on Registration." *Forum* 13 (Apr., 1980), 3-5. Five undergraduates respond to questions on the appropriateness of the draft registration, military service, and the registering of women.

Franz, Delton. "Peace Section Testifies at Senate's Hearings." *CanMenn* 19 (Feb. 19, 1971), 23. Peace witness before government expresses hope that the US will discontinue conscription. Includes short dialogue between Senator Goldwater and William Keeney.

Franz, Delton. "A Return to Draft Registration?" *MCC PS Wash. Memo* 11 (Jan.-Feb., 1979), 4, 10. Describes the pending legislation for resumption of draft registration.

Franz, Delton. "Congress Defeats Draft Registration . . . for Now." *GH* 72 (Oct. 9, 1979), 800; *ChrLead* 42 (Oct. 9, 1979), 16. Although the draft registration bill was defeated, various members of Congress can be expected to keep the issue alive.

Franz, Delton. "Congress Threatens to Reactivate Registration of Draft-Age Youth." *GH* 72 (Mar. 6, 1979), 200. Legislation to reactivate registration of draft-age youth has been introduced in both the House and Senate which would provide for peacetime military registration to commence not later than Oct, 1979.

Franz, Delton. "Conscription Not Upon Us, But the Arms Race Is." *MCC PS Wash. Memo* 10 (Sept.-Oct., 1978), 3-4. Disagrees with news releases implying that military conscription is near; urges people to focus their energies on working to halt the arms race.

Franz, Delton. "Draft Debate in Washington: Repeal vs. Reform." *GH* 63 (Apr. 28, 1970), 391. Comments on the recommendation of "The President's Commission on an All-Volunteer Armed Force" to end conscription, and the reactions to this proposal by Congress.

Franz, Delton. "Legislation Seeks Registration of Draft-Age Youth." *Menn* 94 (Mar. 6, 1979), 185. Legislation to reactivate Selective Service registration of draft-age youth has been introduced in the House and Senate.

Franz, Delton. "Pro-Draft Groups Expected to Keep Issue Alive and Kicking." *Menn* 94 (Oct. 9, 1979), 598. Although the House voted against reactivating compulsory draft registration of all 18-year-old males, pro-draft members of Congress are expected to keep the issue alive in the coming months.

Franz, Delton. "The Pentagon's Strategy: More Regimentation." *Menn* 89 (Jan. 29, 1974), 80. Presents statistics indicating the military is trying to undermine the success of a volunteer army, in order to reinstate the draft.

Franz, Delton. "Washington Report: An Army of Taxpayers." *MennRep* 3 (Jan. 22, 1973), 7. Discusses the proposed end of military conscription and the conditions under which it might be reinstated.

Franz, Delton. "Washington Report: Conscription May Return Within the Year." *MennRep* 4 (Jan. 21, 1974), 7. Speculates on the possibility of resumed military conscription, based on the shaky state of the volunteer army.

Franz, Delton. "Washington Report: Draft-Age Registration May Be Near." *MennRep* 9 (Mar. 19, 1979), 7. An interpretation of the implications of a bill, which has been introduced in the House and Senate, providing for peacetime military registration.

Franz, Delton. "Where the Draft Is . . . and Why." *ChrLead* 42 (Aug. 28, 1979), 20. Report on the status of the draft registration bill.

Franz, Delton. "Youth, Conscription, and the Congress." *Lifework* 3 (1979), 12-14. Outlines reasons young people should evaluate their positions on military service in light of pending draft registration, and reprints part of the Congressional debate on the reinstatement of draft registration.

Franz, Delton, ed. "Nixon, McGovern Compared on Key Issues." *MCC PS Wash. Memo* 4 (Sept.-Oct., 1972), 1-4. Comparative analysis of the two presidential candidates on the draft and military spending as well as other social issues.

Franz, Delton, ed. "Review of Congress in 1972."

MCC PS Wash. Memo 4 (Nov.-Dec., 1972), 4-5. Evaluates congressional action on topics such as the Vietnam War, military spending, the draft, etc.

Fretz, J. Winfield. "Do You Want Conscription?" MennLife 3 (Jan., 1948), 29, 37. A strong statement opposing the National Security Training Act of 1947. Cites some results to be expected from conscription.

Fretz, J. Winfield. "Mennonite Ministers and Special Privilege." Menn 56 (Jan. 28, 1941), 6. Ministers' exemption from conscription is an ethical/religious problem for Mennonties who traditionally believe the minister to be on the same level as the layperson. Perhaps the ministers should renounce this special privilege.

Fretz, J. Winfield. "The Draft Status of General Conference Men in World War II." (Part 1) Menn 60 (July 24, 1945), 1-2. A summary, with tables, of the Peace Committee's census of draft-age men. Of the drafted men about 27 percent were CO's, 18 percent had I-A0 status, and 55 percent enlisted as 1-A's.

Friends Committee on National Legislation. "Questions Answered on the Draft." GH 64 (Mar. 16, 1971), 249. Questions and answers on the subject of the draft center on the issues of draft repeal and the makeup of an all-volunteer army.

Friesen, Bert. Where We Stand: An Index of Peace and Social Concern Statements by Mennonites and Brethren in Christ in Canada, 1787-1982. Winnipeg: MCC Canada and Akron, PA: MCC U.S., 1986. Pp. 300. Distributed by Mennonite Heritage Center, 600 Shaftesbury Blvd., Winnipeg. This publication lists and indexes approximately 2000 statements by church conference (GCMC, MC, MB, BIC) and by general topic. The topics include peace and war, military service, conscription, relief, immigration and emigration, and church and social problems. The texts of these statements are available on microfilm from the MCC Canada office.

Gaeddert, Albert M. "An Important Peace Meeting." Menn 66 (July 10, 1951), 424. Church agencies affiliated with NSBRO state their concerns to Washington officials and propose a list of the kinds of work they would be willing to do under the new conscription law.

Gaeddert, Albert M. "Should I Register Under the Draft Act?" Menn 63 (July 27, 1948), 3. Accepts the Voluntary Service Program as an appropriate way to serve within the "system" while also recognizing the validity of non-registration for the draft.

Gaeddert, Albert M. "The New Draft Legislation." Menn 66 (July 31, 1951), 482. Explains how present programs of relief and service can be expanded to accomodate the CO's who will now be "ordered to work" under the new draft law.

Gaeddert, Albert M. and Dyck, Walter H. "General Conference Position in Regard to UMT." Menn 63 (Feb. 10, 1948), 1, 9. A statement sent to officials in Washington strongly opposing any Universal Military Training program. Points out three danger areas in the adoption of UMT.

Gaeddert, Donald. Letter to the Editor. Menn 95 (Aug. 19, 1980), 482. Describes actions taken by a group of Colorado Mennonites in response to the reinstated draft registration.

General Board of the Mennonite Church. "GB Response to Selective Service Registration." GH 73 (Feb. 26, 1980), 184. Statement urges Mennonites into active witnessing for peace and seeking legal alternatives to registration.

Gerlach, Horst. "Before the German Draft Board." YCC 42 (Sept. 24, 1961), 613. A man's testimony on his CO position befor the German draft board.

Gibble, Kenneth L. "Ethics in War and Peace." Builder 18 (June, 1968), 15-16. Explores some of the basic ethical issues facing young men of draft age and suggests ways these youths might be assisted in their process of thinking through these issues for themselves.

Gingerich, Andre. Letter to the Editor. Menn 95 (Sept. 16, 1980), 530. Defends nonregistration for the draft on the grounds of refusing to cooperate with the military machinery.

Gingerich, Melvin. "A Peace Witness." Menn 74 (Mar. 31, 1959), 197-98; "Concerning Military Conscription," GH 52 (Apr. 21, 1959), 369, 381. A statement presented to the Senate Armed Services Committee in behalf of the MCC Peace Section, protesting conscription and America's preoccupation with military superiority. Proposals are given for various programs of peace and goodwill.

Gingerich, Melvin. "American Youth and the Draft." GH 51 (Nov. 18, 1958), 1093, 1105. There is an increasing outcry against universal conscription and a correspondingly increasing advocacy of volunteer armed services. As the pressure grows to volunteer we need to help our youth sort through this problem.

Gingerich, Melvin. "Statement of Melvin Gingerich." Extension of the Draft and Related Authorities. Hearings before the Committee on Armed Services United States Senate . . . H.R. 2260. Washington, DC: Government Printing Office, 1959, 49-54. A statement on behalf of the MCC Peace Section protesting conscription and proposing various programs of peace and goodwill.

Gingerich, Melvin. "The Military Draft During the American Civil War." *MHB* 12 (July, 1951), 3. Publishes official documents pertaining to the drafting of Samuel D. Guengerich of Pennsylvania in 1865 and the process he followed to be exempted from military duty.

Gingerich, Melvin (Archival). Box 39—Draft; Committee on Armed Service hearing, 1959. Box 51—Congressional Record (debate on universal military training), Feb. 5, 1959. Goshen, Ind., AMC Hist. Mss. 1-129.

Gingerich, Ray C. "Shalom for the '80s." *Builder* 31 (Jan., 1981), 4-9. The challenge for each congregation is to be a model of shalom and congregations need to begin thinking about the implications of this vision for daily life. Also suggests the issues of draft registration and war taxes as appropriate agenda items for this process of reflection.

Glassburn, Lorene. "Our Sisters' Part in the Present World Crisis." *GH* 34 (July 10, 1941), 318. While the nonresistant witness falls most directly to young men, there are numerous ways that women can give their full cooperation and support. Moreover, it is not impossible that women will need to face the issue of conscription in the future as the men do now.

*
Goering, Paul L. "Proposed Registration Act Endangers CO's." *Menn* 65 (Mar. 14, 1950), 178-79. An analysis of the Manpower Registration Act. Mennonites are urged to write Congress protesting the proposed elimination of certain provisions for CO's.

Goering, Paul L. "Senate Armed Services Committee Concludes Hearings." *Menn* 63 (Apr. 20, 1948), 3-4. A report on the proceedings of the final hearings on Universal Military Training, including the testimony of Mennonites and several other groups against UMT and Selective Service.

Goering, Paul L. "Should We Make Registration the Issue?" *Menn* 63 (June 22, 1948), 3. In contrast to Gordon Kaufman's stance (*Menn,* June 8, 1948), Goering argues that Mennonites could present a more effective witness against war by entering alternative service than by refusing to register.

Graber, Eldon W. "Some Questions Concerning Peacetime Conscription." *Menn* 60 (June 3, 1945), 13. Argues that peacetime conscription would not improve the health of the nation. It would neither contribute to discipline or character education nor would it produce the

right kind of leaders or technical institutions for peacetime.

Graber, Richard D. "The Evolution of the Treatment of the Conscientious Objectors by the War Department During the First World War." Paper presented to the Social Science Seminar, Goshen College, Goshen, Ind., June, 1957.

Graybill, Dave. "Participants Focus on Acts, Churchwide Issues at Waterloo." *GH* 72 (Aug. 28, 1979), 688-90. Conference decisions at Waterloo Assembly '79 included accepting an amended resolution extending the Mennonite Church's emphasis on urban concerns for the next two years, approving with minor amendments a statement on militarism and conscription, and calling for further study on a proposed statement on leadership and authority in the church.

Groff, Weyburn W. "Report of the Draft Census of the Mennonite Church: Observations, Generalizations and Conclusions." Paper presented to Mennonite seminar, Goshen College, Goshen, Ind., May, 1945. Pp. 12. MHL.

Groves, Esther. "Why I Resisted the Draft and What Happened When I Did." *With* 5 (June, 1972), 25. A personal account of noncooperation with the draft.

Gundy, Lloyd. "Message to the Churches from Our District Peace Committees." *Menn* 67 (Jan. 1, 1952), 14. An urgent plea for Mennonites to witness against the proposed Universal Military Training program. Outlines the provisions of the program and its possible harmful effects.

"House Passes Bill and Revises Alternate Service." *GH* 64 (Apr. 20, 1971), 365. Describes significance of the vote to extend the military draft till June, 1973 for the CO.

Hackman, Walton. "No Drafting of Young Men, But." *EV* 86 (Mar. 25, 1973), 9. Although the draft has ended, the machinery of the Selective Service System remains in operation.

Hackman, Walton. "The Draft Lottery: An Explanation of a Stopgap Move." *GH* 63 (Jan. 6, 1970), 14-15. Explains the procedures followed in the draft lottery system and contends that, instead of removing the draft's inequities, the changes represent a stopgap move to quiet protest against the draft and war.

*Handbook with Draft Manual.* Akron, Pa.: MCC Peace Section, [1943]. Pp. 31. MHL.

Harley, Isaiah Buckwalter. "Goshen's Attitude Toward Conscientious Objectors as Reflected in the News and Editorial Columns of the *Goshen Daily News Times,* Apr. 1, 1917-Nov. 11, 1918."

*For additional listing, see Supplement, pp. 717-719.

Paper presented to the Peace and War Seminar, Goshen College, Goshen, Ind., n.d. Pp. 15. MHL.

Hartman, O. E. "An Original Draft Resister." *ST* 42 (June, 1974), 24. Taped interview of a personal account of someone who, when subject to the draft as a young man during World War I, solved his problem of conscientious objection to the war by living in the woods.

Hartzler, Levi C. "Our Voluntary Service Program, Principles and Practices, and Relation to our Peace Testimony." *ChrMon* 41 (May, 1949), 142-44. While the Civilian Public Service program served as a model, the peacetime draft law provided the impetus for continued alternative service on a volunteer basis.

Hartzler, R. L. "A Covenant Movement for Peace." *Menn* 86 (Sept. 28, 1971), 577-78. The issues of conscription and the payment of war taxes are secondary; the basic issue is, militarism as a long established, deeply engrained element in national policy.

Hartzler, Robert. "Post Office Drama." *God and Caesar* 6 (Sept., 1980), 9; "From Iowa Post Office Steps—July, 1980." *Menn* 95 (Oct. 7, 1980), 578. Poem on watching young men register for Selective Service.

Hartzler, Robert W. "Witnessing in Washington." *Menn* 67 (Feb. 19, 1952), 117-18. Report of a GCMC delegation to Washington, DC, to protest Universal Military Training; letters to Congressmen have also had a great impact.

Hatfield, Mark O. "The Draft Is Obsolete." Address to the American Society of Newspaper Editors. 1967. Pp. 21. BfC.

Heinrichs, Alfred. "Helping the Resisters." *CanMenn* 16 (June 4, 1968), 4, 5. Letter to the Editor championing the cause of the war resisters coming to Canada.

Heisey, J. Wilmer. "Conscription: Its Effect on You." *EV* 82 (Dec. 29, 1969), 5, 11. Issues that face a Christian whether of draft age or older.

Heisey, J. Wilmer. "If the Draft Dies—What About Voluntary Service?" *EV* 86 (Jan. 10, 1973), 13. Hope is expressed for volunteerism to come into a new and truer perspective rather than die out when the draft expires in 1973.

Heisey, J. Wilmer. "The Military Draft Alive and Functioning." *EV* 85 (Feb. 25, 1972), 10, 11. Information regarding the new US draft law of Sept. 28, 1971.

Hershberger, Guy F. "A Plan of Action: Suggestions for Mennonite Young Men of Draft Age in Case of War." *YCC* 21 (June 9, 1940),

178-79. A proposed plan of action formulated by Mennonite Central Committee Peace Section that encourages the church to follow a course which will separate its members as completely as possible from the war machinery is outlined.

Hershberger, Guy F. "Is There Hope that Conscription Can Come to an End in the United States in the Foreseeable Future? Our Peace Witness—In the Wake of May 18." (Part 26). *GH* 61 (Mar. 5, 1968), 203-204. There are signs that opposition to conscription is growing. Mennonites should therefore take courage and persist in their peace testimony.

Hershberger, Guy F. "Mennonites and Conscription in the World War." Prepared for use by Peace Problems Committee in view of approaching conscription (Burke-Wadsworth Bill). Typescript, 1940. Goshen: MHL. The Mennonite church is an historic peace church, having maintained a consistent testimony against war and military service throughout its entire history. Surveys the experience of Mennonites under conscription and the effect of the war experience upon the Mennonite church.

Hershberger, Guy F. "Mennonites in the Civil War." *MQR* 18 (July, 1944), 131-44. Although Mennonites of the Civil War era were rooted deeply enough in their nonresistant faith to refuse conscription to combat duty, many either hired substitutes, paid a commutation fee which benefited the sick and wounded soldiers, or served in noncombatant roles.

Hershberger, Guy F. "Military Conscription and the Conscientious Objector." *YCC* 20 (Dec. 10, 1939), 809-10. Description of the Selective Service plan for conscription. The official committees of the church can only do so much. The individual must decide on the hard questions about being a CO.

Hershberger, Guy F. *Military Conscription and the Conscientious Objector: A World-Wide Survey.* Akron: Mennonite Central Committee Peace Section, 1962. A survey country by country outlining the status of military conscription and the conscientious objector in each.

Hershberger, Guy F. "Military Conscription and the Conscientious Objector: A World-Wide Survey, with Special Reference to Mennonites." Paper presented at the Seventh Mennonite World Conference, Kitchener, Ont., Aug. 7, 1962. Mimeographed. Goshen: MHL. Pp. 38. Reports on draft laws in the worldwide Mennonite experience. Concluding comments focus on the status of the nonresistant teaching on the mission field.

Hershberger, Guy F. "Our Peace Witness—In the

Wake of May 18." *GH* 61 (Jan. 2, 1968), 7. [No. 18] Discusses "unjust war objectors," persons who may be opposed to some but not all wars, and raises the question whether draft boards should recognize such persons as conscientious objectors.

Hershberger, Guy F. "Questions for Nonresistant Christians." *GH* 33, Parts 1-3, (July 18, 1940), 338; Part 4, (July 25, 1940), 371; Parts 5-7, (Aug. 1, 1940), 386; Parts 8-9, (Aug. 8, 1940), 418; Parts 10-11, (Aug. 15, 1940), 435; Part 12, (Aug. 22, 1940), 450; Part 13, (Aug. 29, 1940), 466-67; Part 14, (Sept. 12, 1940), 514; Part 15-16, (Sept. 19, 1940), 530; Part 17, (Oct. 3, 1940), 562; Part 19-22, (Oct. 31, 1940), 658-59; Part 23, (Nov. 7, 1940), 675; Part 24, (Nov. 28, 1940), 738; Part 25, (Dec. 5, 1940), 754. Series includes such topics as war propaganda, conscription, alternative service, conscientious objection, registration, noncombatant service, etc.

Hershberger, Guy F. "The Christian and the Draft." Address given at Campus Church, July, 1969, at Goshen College, Goshen, Ind. Typescript. Goshen: AMC Hist. MSS 1-171 Box 10. War is sin. There will be differences of opinion in the church on how to faithfully respond to it.

Hershberger, Guy F. "The Methodist Church and the Conscientious Objector." *YCC* 21 (Sept. 15, 1940), 296. The Methodist Church is one of the many groups who are giving attention to and support for the CO position. The US government has taken into account the nonresistant stand of these churches not among the historic peace churches in the Bukke-Wadsworth military conscription bill.

Hershberger, Guy F. "What Changes Does the New Draft Law Actually Make With Respect to Conscientious Objectors? Our Peace Witness— In the Wake of May 18." (Part 3). *GH* 60 (Sept. 19, 1967), 847. The definition of a CO and the appeal procedure were changed.

Hershberger, Guy F. "Why Does the New Draft Law (1967) Change the Definition of a Conscientious Objector? Our Peace Witness— In the Wake of May 18." (Part 5). *GH* 60 (Sept. 26, 1967), 874. Congress sought to narrow the definition of conscientious objector but actually broadened it.

Hershberger, Guy F. "Why Does the New Draft Law (1967) Change the Appeal Procedure for Conscientious Objectors? Our Peace Witness— In the Wake of May 18." (Part 6). *GH* 60 (Oct. 3, 1967), 889. It is believed that the new procedure will save time.

Hershberger, Guy F. "Will Conscription End?" *GH* 61 (Mar. 5, 1968), 203-204. [No. 26] Cites speeches from the 1967 House of

Representatives debate on the draft favoring the end of conscription.

Hershberger, Guy F. "World Wide Report on Military Draft and CO's." In *The Lordship of Christ: Proceedings of the Seventh Mennonite World Conference*, ed. C. J. Dyck, pp. 544-48. Scottdale: Mennonite Publishing House, 1962. Held at Kitchener, Ont., Aug. 1-7, 1962. Surveys the status of the military draft and conscientious objector's position in countries where Mennonites reside.

Hershberger, Guy F. (Archival). Boxes 23-33— includes Draft Law 1967. Goshen, Ind. AMC. Hist. Mss. 1-171.

Hershberger, Guy F. (Review). *Conscription of Conscience: The American State and the Conscientious Objector, 1940-1947*, by Melford Q. Sibley and Philip E. Jacob. Ithaca: Cornell University Press, 1952. Pp. 580. *MQR* 27 (1953), 351-55. Summarizes the book's story of conscription and the CO in World War II as seen through the eyes of authors whose primary interest is in civil liberties rather than the New Testament way of nonresistant love. Harshberger raises the question of whether the two causes of social justice and nonresistant love can be served best by the more militant type of pacifist or the way of MCC. Considers this book helpful in raising this issue into sharp focus.

Hertzler, Daniel. "The Legacy of Timothy Lee Yoder." *GH* 69 (Aug. 24, 1976), 642. Reprints the letter written to the draft board requesting a conscientious objection classification by a Mennonite high school senior later killed in a car accident.

Hess, James R. "Church and State Ordained for Separate Functions." *ST* 45 (Jan., 1977), 10-13. Draft registration and war tax payment are examples of proper responses of the Christian toward government.

Hoover, Warren. [Ending the Draft.] *IPF Notes* 17 (Feb., 1971), 1-2. Information on participating in the movement to abolish the draft through supporting a congressional draft repeal.

Horsch, John. "Nonresistance Under Difficulties." *GH* 28 (Oct. 24, 1935), 650. The Hutterite Brethren of Germany have settled in Liechtenstein to avoid military conscription but their colonies have encountered financial difficulties. They have, nevertheless, remained faithful to the principle of nonresistance.

Horst, John L. "Concerning the New Draft Law." *ChrMon* 43 (July, 1951), 200. Reprints section of the draft law pertaining to conscientious objectors and comments on the possible changes in voluntary service programs.

Horst, John L. "Peacetime Conscription and Military Training." *ChrMon* 38 (Feb., 1946), 40-41. Questions for nonresistant Christians to consider in light of the possibility of peacetime military conscription.

Horst, John L. "Selective Service Act of 1948." *GH* 41 (Aug. 10, 1948), 732. A review of the Selective Service Act which inaugurated the draft in 1948. Outlines the provisions made for the deferment of conscientious objectors.

Horst, John L. "The Draft Law and Voluntary Service." *GH* 41 (Oct. 26, 1948), 1003-1004. Because Mennonite youth have so generously been exempted from the draft, they should make a special effort to enlist in VS programs.

Horst, John L. (Editorial). "Selective Service Act of 1948." *ChrMon* 40 (Aug., 1948), 233. Comments on the passage of the peacetime draft law.

Horst, John L. (Editorial). "The Test of our Nonresistance." *ChrMon* 41 (Feb., 1949), 41. Provides suggestions for maintaining a peace witness in the face of the peacetime draft law.

Horst, Samuel L. "Mennonites in the Confederacy." *PCMCP Fifteenth*, 47-61. North Newton, Kansas: The Mennonite Press. Held at Bluffton College, Bluffton, Ohio, June 10-11, 1965. The Mennonites living in the Confederacy provide an impressive historical model of religiously-based opposition to war and conscription.

Hostetler, David E. "Responses to a Possible Draft Registration." *GH* 73 (Feb. 12, 1980), 144. Cites voices of opposition in American society to draft registration and urges all Mennonites to file their position with MCC on the Christian Peacemaker Registration form.

Hostetler, Hugh. "The Challenges of Exemption." *Menn* 63 (Sept. 7, 1948), 11-12. Rather than simply "sitting tight" through exemption, Mennonites could well (1) refuse to register, (2) fight for the repeal of the draft law, and/or (3) expand voluntary service programs.

Hostetler, Virginia A. "It's a Matter of Conscience." *With* 13 (Dec., 1980), 1D-1H. Luke Horst and Andre Gingerich explain their decisions not to cooperate with draft registration.

Hostetter, C. N., Jr. "A Statement of Concern to the Committee on Armed Services of the United States House of Representatives on H.R. 3005 Amending the Universal Military Service and Training Act." *CanMenn* 3 (Feb. 2, 1955), 2. An MCC statement urging the House not to extend the draft.

Hostetter, Douglas. "Joe." *Menn* 89 (Apr. 16, 1974),

264. Hostetter relates the story of his involvement with one draft resister, whose dilemma symbolizes that of thousands of Vietnam War objectors who need the support of church and government.

Houser, Gordon. "Mid-America New Call Views Conscription, Taxes." *GH* 72 (Dec. 11, 1979), 997. Reports on the fourth New Call to Peacemaking conference held at Hesston College Mennonite Church, Nov. 16-17, with the theme "Conscription of Youth and Wealth."

Houser, Gordon. "Peacemakers Declare War on All Conscription." *Menn* 94 (Dec. 4, 1979), 726. Report on the 4th Mid-America New Call to Peacemaking Conference, which had as its theme "conscription of Youth and Wealth."

Hull, Robert. "How Should We Respond?" *Menn* 95 (Feb. 19, 1980), 125. Until Selective Service registration plans are finalized, Mennonites can pray, register their peace stance with the church, witness to lawmakers, and apply for volunteer service.

"I Have to Follow My Conscience." *CanMenn* 18 (May 22, 1970), 6, 7. Following the conscience regardless of consequences, breaking with the Selective Service System, and becoming a draft dodger are issues for discussion in correspondence between brothers Jim and Elias Hochstedler.

"Intercollegiate Peace Fellowship Almost Loses Sight of Its Theme." *CanMenn* 17 (Apr. 1, 1969), 1, 2. Report on IPF meeting March 19-22 in Washington, DC, discussing the peacemaker in revolution. Speakers with a wide range of views addressed the meetings. One was a member of SDS, another a former editor of the underground *Washington Free Press*, another was facing trial for refusing conscription. Myron Augsburger said that violent revolution is the old "just war" doctrine in a new garment. Norman Kraus said nonresistance as it is practiced will not see us through the next few decades and it is not biblical. There is no social revolution without conflict, and we must find our place in it.

Indiana-Michigan Mennonite Conference—Peace and Social Concerns Committee. (Archival). II-5-6, Box 4. Material on various peace and social concerns: labor relations; draft; capital punishment; witness to the state. Goshen, Ind. AMC.

Iutzi, Donna. "Ontario Youth Go 'Beyond Words'" *CanMenn* 16 (Oct. 22, 1968), 1, 2. Report on a peace action retreat at Chesley Lake, Oct. 4-6. The retreat dealt with welfare, drugs, the draft, and the native American.

Janzen, William. Letter to the Editor. *MennRep* 10

(May 26, 1980), 6. Clarification of possible American draft dodgers' status in Canada.

Juhnke, James C. "Bibles and Bullets; Military Conscription in South Africa." *MennRep* 2 (May 1, 1972), 2. Draft ruling in South Africa includes whites and excludes blacks, but what of the conscientious objectors?

Juhnke, James C. "Conflicts and Compromises of Mennonites and the Draft: An Interpretive Essay," 1969. Pp. 20. MHL.

Juhnke, James C. "Mennonites and Military Conscription in the Twentieth Century." Paper presented to the MCC US Assembly on the Draft and National Service, Goshen, Ind., Mar. 27-29, 1980. Pp. 12. MHL.

Juhnke, James C. "Our Almost Unused Political Power." *GH* 61 (Jan. 9, 1968), 38-39. Reflects on Mennonite use of political power to defeat proposed changes in the draft laws that would have been unfavorable to conscientious objectors, and urges Mennonites to use this power to influence foreign policy toward de-escalation in Vietnam.

Kauffman, Milo. "Christian Alternatives to Conscription." *GH* 39 (Jan. 21, 1947), 333. Address given at the 1946 General Conference (MC). Christian alternative service programs should not appear to defy the government. Various forms of service are suggested.

Kauffman, Richard A. "Draft Consultation Calls for Peace Education." *ChrLead* 40 (Dec. 20, 1977), 18. Reports on the Consultation on the Draft at Kansas City sponsored by MCC Peace Section (US).

Kaufman, Gordon D. "Should Mennonites Register for the Draft?" *Menn* 63 (Jun3 8, 1948), 4-5. Since the purpose of registration and conscription is to change persons into an army of automatons, threatening world peace, Mennonites should not register.

Kaufman, Maynard. *Here I Stand: A Human Drama in Three Acts.* By the author, 1953. Pp. 39. Available at AMBS library. James Dean, a 23-year-old college student, faces the draft. This short play portrays his thought processes and struggles as he moves toward a pacifist position. Set in post-World War II Midwest.

Kaufman, S. Roy, and Roger Kaufman "Two Views on Draft Resistance." *Menn* 83 (May 14, 1968), 344-45. Two points of view are presented: a) The primary arena of Christian activity should be within the legal alternatives. b) Non-cooperation is necessary when service "in the national interest" perpetuates massive suffering and exploitation.

Keeney, William E. "Mennonite Cooperation with Government Agencies and Programs." *PCMCP Fifteenth,* 62-74. North Newton, Kansas: The Mennonite Press. Held at Bluffton College, Bluffton, Ohio, June 10-11, 1965. In its relationship to a benevolent state, the church must learn to critically distinguish between the areas in which there can be cooperation and the areas in which noncooperation is appropriate. To preserve the prophetic stance of the church, a sense of tension needs to be maintained with the state.

Keim, Albert N. "Service or Resistance? The Mennonite Response to Conscription in World War II." *MQR* 52 (Apr., 1978), 141-55. Describes the development of an alternative service program during World War II, and stresses the degree to which such a plan was satisfactory to both nonresistant Mennonites and the Selective Service.

Keim, Albert N. "The Legacy of Civilian Public Service." *GH* 72 (Aug. 7, 1979), 612-13. With the possibility of military conscription emerging again, the CPS program is presented as a frame of reference for developing a Mennonite response to the present issue.

Klaassen, Walter. "Why Should We Care About Draft Resisters?" *CanMenn* 18 (May 22, 1970), 5. Analyzes the dynamics of Mennonite attitudes to the draft refugee and suggests a positive response to the resisters on the basis of Mennonite history.

Klassen, Mike. "Implementing a Congregational Dialogue on the Draft and National Service." *MCC PS Newsletter* 10 (Mar.-Apr., 1980), 1-5. Paper presented at the Mar., 1980, Assembly on the Draft and National Service suggests methods for effective conscientious objection education in the congregation. Includes extensive bibliography.

Klassen, Mike. "The Draft as a Chance for Witness." *Forum* 13 (Apr., 1980), 1-3. Pastor of the Mennonite fellowship in Manhattan, Kansas, describes how potentially resumed draft registration became the vehicle for peace witnessing.

Klaus, Marilyn. "The Draft and Women." *MCC PS TF on Women in Ch. and Soc. Report* 35 (Jan.-Feb., 1981), 5-6. While reasons for excluding women from registration are sexist, a greater evil is involving men in a system committed to violence and war.

Koehn, Dennis. "Draft Resistance: A Christian Response." *Lifework* 4 (1979), 3-6. Draft resister who spent 18 months in prison in the early 1970s relates the story of his decision, arrest, trial, sentencing, and reorientation to society after being released.

Koontz, Ted. "Call to Draft Marks End of a Peculiar Era." *Menn* 95 (Mar. 11, 1980), 176. Resumed draft registration confronts Mennonites with the choice of continuing to focus peace concern on the broader question of government policy, or retaining pacifism merely as a personal response to military service.

Koontz, Ted. "Commission Recommends Registration." *RepConsS* 32 [sic, 33] (Apr., 1976), 1, 3, 5. Evaluates the report of the Defense Manpower Commission mandated by the 1973 Congress to study the military's personnel needs for the following decade.

Koontz, Ted. "Compulsory National Service or Voluntary Christian Service?" *Menn* 91 (May 18, 1976), 345-46. With the cancellation of proposed draft registration, Koontz analyzes the military's options for securing personnel, focusing on mandatory national service as more unjust than a volunteer army or a return to conscription.

Koontz, Ted. "Few Benefit from Earned Reentry." *Menn* 89 (Oct. 22, 1974), 612. Lists the vast differences between President Ford's clemency program and universal amnesty for draft resisters, which include assuming moral and legal guilt on the part of resisters, and overlooking all who received less than honorable military discharges for protesting the war.

Koontz, Ted. "No Opportunity to Be Given for CO Registration." *Menn* 90 (Dec. 9, 1975), 705. Describes pending Selective Service plans for draft registration, which at the inital stage include no place for registering conscientious objection.

Koontz, Ted. "Peace Section (US) Plans Response to Selective Service Registration Drive." *IPF Notes* 22 (Nov., 1975), 8-11. Comment on Selective Service plans for registration and Peace Section response; includes suggestions for other concerned Christians.

Koontz, Ted. "Peace Section Protests Selective Service Drive." *ChrLead* 38 (Dec. 9, 1975), 7. Peace Section views the registration and draft as inherently evil and as an essential element in the militarization of American society.

Koontz, Ted. "The Logic of Noncooperation." *Menn* 95 (July 8, 1980), 432. Cautions Mennonites who contemplate not registering for Selective Service to do so from authentic pacifist motivations and not because of a selective just war theory.

Kraus, C. Norman. *Christians and the State.* Ed. Paul Peachey, n.p.: Mennonite General Conference. Peace Problems Committee, 1956. Pp. 13. The Christian Youth and War Pamphlets No. 4. Directed to young men approaching draft age, pamphlet encourages them to obey the government but give primary allegiance to God, not the country.

Krehbiel, Leona. "Peacetime Military Conscription." *Menn* 60 (Apr. 17, 1945), 1-2. The bills to establish peacetime conscription rest on the assumption that the individual exists for the state. That is contrary to both the founding principles of America and to Christ's teachings.

Kreider, Karen, et al. Letter to the Editor. *Menn* 90 (Mar. 25, 1975), 196. Reprints a letter from several Goshen College students to President Ford, offering themselves as substitutes for draft resisters ordered to give a term of work as part of their earned reentry. The students respond to a Mennonite Church resolution suggesting this course of action.

Kreider, Robert S. "A Statement of Concern." *Menn* 70 (July 12, 1955), 425. MCC opposes the extension of the draft act and urges the complete cessation of universal military conscription.

Kreider, Robert S. Letter to the Editor. *Menn* 93 (Jan. 10, 1978), 30. Maintains that Mennonite organizations such as Voluntary Service and Teachers Abroad Program were rooted in Mennonite theology of service, not in reaction to the military draft.

Kreider, Robert S. "The Environmental Influences Affecting the Decisions of Mennonite Boys of Draft Age." *PCMCP First,* 75-88. North Newton, Kansas: The Bethel College Press. Held at Winona Lake, Indiana, Aug. 7-8, 1942. Based on the assumption that the behavior of an individual is profoundly affected by environmental factors, e.g., church, home, community, education, and personal associations.

Kroeker, David. "Conscription? Now, Really, Barney . . ." *MennRep* 7 (Oct. 3, 1977), 6. Responds with skepticism and opposition toward the Canadian Defense Minister's advocating compulsory conscription to strengthen Canadian armed forces.

Kroeker, David (Review). *I Would Like to Dodge the Draft-Dodgers But . . .,* ed. Frank H. Epp. Winnipeg and Waterloo: Conrad Press, 1970. Pp. 95. *MQR* 46 (Jan., 1972), 92-93. Selected essays on the peace position, conscientious objection, treatment of war deserters, and biblical foundations call Canadian churches and Mennonites in particular to assist American draft resisters in Canada.

"Leaders Oppose Draft Extension." *CanMenn* 11 (Mar. 22, 1963), 1, 12. Statements on the draft and conscription before House and Senate Armed Services Committees by Ed Metzler and Alvin Beachy, who represented the Mennonite Church.

Lapp, John A. "The Draft: Reform or Repeal?" *ChrLiv* 16 (Oct., 1969), 12-13. Issues at stake in the national debate over the draft system.

Lapp, John A. ". . . The New Militarism Makes Its Harsh Demands." *I Would Like to Dodge the Draft-Dodgers But . . . .* Ed. Frank H. Epp. Waterloo and Winnipeg: Conrad Press, 1070, 21-26. Pp. 95. Assesses the contemporary conscription process, outlines the options available to conscientious objectors and the varieties of positions labeled CO, and discusses reform of the draft laws.

Lapp, John A. (Review). *The Draft?* by the Peace Education Committee of the American Friends Service Committee. Hill and Wang, 1968. Pp. 112. *ChrLiv* 16 (Feb., 1969), 36. Reviewer notes that the author opposes national service, whether civilian or military, and makes a case for the "selective objector."

Lapp, John A. (Review). *Why the Draft? The Case for the Volunteer Army,* ed. James C. Miller, III. Penguin, 1968. Pp. 197. *ChrLiv* 16 (Mar., 1969), 36-37. Recommends this analysis of the inequities and inconsistencies of the draft and presentation of the case for a volunteer army.

Leatherman, Daniel R. Letter to the Editor. *GH* 61 (Jan. 23, 1968), 94. Disagrees with Jim Juhnke's conclusion (Jan. 9, 1968, 38-39) that the threat of widespread Mennonite civil disobedience influenced Congress to enact more favorable Selective Service laws. Supports political mobilization on issues such as draft laws, even though such action can be misconstrued as "self-interest."

Lederach, James S. "A Case for Mandatory Public Service for Conscientious Objectors." *CGR* 2 (Spring, 1984), 139-48. Argues that nonregistration for the draft is not superior to registration and alternative service as a means to Christian obedience because nonregistration provides the state the same information as does registration—in fact, anything short of subversion similarly serves the state; and the rights that nonregistrants forfeit limit their capacity both to proclaim and to serve. Suggests a program involving longer terms and less pay for COs than military inductees for all persons of draft age; this would have the kind of moral force that nonregistration has as well as expand the benefits of traditional alternative service.

Leis, Vernon. "Mennonites Fearful of War-Resisters." *CanMenn* 18 (May 22, 1970), 8. MCC (Ontario) sponsors a seminar at which the concerns of the churches about involvement with draft-dodgers are set forth and at which five recommendations for sympathetic action are made on behalf of them.

Lind, Loren. "Fit Not to Be Drafted." *YCC* 47 (Nov. 13, 1966), 5. There are many similarities between slavery and conscription.

Lind, Loren. "The Evil Called Conscription." *Menn* 82 (Mar. 28, 1967), 222-23. Exposes the evils of "involuntary servitude" and other inequities of the present draft system.

Lind, Millard C. *Christ and War.* Ed. Paul Peachey, n.p.: Mennonite General Conference Peace Problems Committee, 1956. Pp. 19. The Christian Youth and War Pamphlets No. 3. Pamphlet directed to young men approaching draft age enjoins them to follow Christ by following the way of nonresistant love, even toward national enemies.

Lott, John C. "The Christian, His Country, His Conscience, an Apology for Noncooperation." *CanMenn* 17 (Oct. 24, 1969), 6, 8. An American army deserter preaches a sermon in the Ottawa Mennonite Church. Besides sharing his pilgrimage, he says: war cannot be Christianized; a Christian cannot be a murderer; the highest allegiance is to God; a CO cannot be a soldier, etc.

Löwen, Kenneth. "The Draft Counselor System." *MennLife* 13 (July, 1958), 114-15. The Draft Counselor System "of providing information, counsel, and representation for I-O registrants has contributed immeasurably to the I-W service program."

Lowry, Steve. Letter to the Editor. *GH* 64 (June 29, 1971), 594-95. Supports draft resistance when inspired by Christian motives, because it is a good witness that Christian people are not afraid to threaten their position in society by obeying God rather than human authorities.

Lubosch, Lore. "The Mennonites in Brazil—'They Did It Almost Without Help . . . ' " *MennMirror* 1 (Jan., 1972), 10-14. Dr. Boruszenko, economic historian in Curitiba, Brazil, gives a detailed report on the history of Brazil's Mennonites from the emigration from Russia in 1929 to the present, including such aspects as education, economics, and conscription.

"MCC (Canada) Answers Queries re Draft Evaders." *CanMenn* 18 (Apr. 17, 1970), 1, 2. Six of the most frequently asked questions about the draft refugee situation are clarified.

"MCC (Canada) Endorses Resolution on Amnesty." *MennRep* 3 (Jan. 22, 1973), 11. Publishes the working draft of the MCC Peace Section statement on the necessity of amnesty for US war resisters.

"Mennonites Discuss Alternative Service, Nonregistration." *RepConsS* 37 (June, 1980), 2, 4. Two-day conference results in statement asking the Mennonite Church to fully support both registration and nonregistration or noncooperation within its understanding of conscientious objection.

"Mennonites Discuss Conscription." *RepConsS* 38 [*sic,* 35] (Jan., 1978), 3. Brief report of a nationwide Mennonite consultation on draft issues held in Kansas City, Oct. 11-12, 1977.

"Mennonites Lead in Alternate Service." *Fellowship* 30 (Nov., 1964), 12. According to a survey completed by the National Service Board of Religious Objectors, Mennonites had the largest total of men in draft age in alternative service of all major US denominations since 1951.

"Mennonites on Militarism and Conscription." *RepConsS* 36 (Nov., 1979), 2. Reports discussion on war and peace topics at the 1979 MC General Assembly held at Waterloo, Ont., Aug. 11-16.

Mast, Russell L. "The Church and Conscription." *Menn* 67 (Mar. 11, 1952), 164-65. The church has a vital stake in the proposed universal military training bill because the bill would jeopardize the spiritual influence of the home, would militarize America, and would block any adequate peace efforts.

Mast, Wesley. Letter to the Editor. *GH* 63 (July 28, 1970), 643. Commends Dennis Byler ("Letter to the Draft Board," June 30) for refusing to cooperate with the draft, since it signifies saying "no" to national boundaries and militarism.

*MCC Draft Counselor's Manual.* Akron, Pa.: MCC [Peace Section, 1980]. MHL.

Mennonite Central Committee. *Conscience and Conscription.* Akron: MCC Peace Section, 1970. Pp. 48. Papers of the Chicago peace assembly, Nov., 1969. Includes: Burkholder, J. R., "Christ, Conscience, Church, and Conscription: Toward an Ethical Analysis of Mennonite Draft Resistance;" Juhnke, James, "Conflicts and Compromises of Mennonites and the Draft: An Interpretative Essay;" Keeney, William, "The National Debate Over the Draft;" a message from the consultation participants.

Mennonite Central Committee. "MCC Presents Testimony Opposing Draft Extension," *Menn* 70 (Feb. 15, 1955), 110. The MCC Peace Section's statement of concern opposes the extension of the draft, while recognizing that this testimony may not be heeded.

Mennonite Central Committee. "Mennonites Testify at Hearings on Post-War Military Policy," *Menn* 60 (July 10, 1945), 5-6; "A Statement of Position on Permanent Peacetime Conscription and the Christian Conscience Against War," *GH* 38 (July 20, 1945), 297-98. A statement presented to the House Select Committee on Postwar Military Policy opposes conscription from the perspective of biblical understandings, the nonresistant tradition, and a concern for freedom of conscience.

Mennonite Central Committee. "Statement on Conscription for Military Training, and Provisions for Conscientious Objectors," *GH* 38 (Dec. 21, 1945), 733-34. A statement submitted to the House Military Affairs Committee. Expresses opposition to any program of compulsory military training, and support for provisions for conscientious objectors in case such legislation is passed.

Mennonite Central Committee (US). "Statement on World Tensions and the Draft." Adopted Jan. 24, 1980. P. 1. (Located in MCC Peace Section Official Statements folder in MHL.) Urges young Mennonite men and women to register their conscientious objector convictions with the Peacemaker Registration Program in response to proposed military conscription.

Mennonite Central Committee Peace Section. "Testimony Given on Draft." *GH* 64 (Mar. 2, 1971), 201-202. Reprint of the testimony given to the Senate Armed Services Committee calling for the draft to be abolished. Argues for the end of the draft on the bases of opposition to military activities and the inequities of the system.

Mennonite Central Committee Peace Section Consultation on Conscience and Conscription, Chicago, Nov. 22, 1969. "Christian Obedience and Selective Service," *Menn* 84 (Dec. 16, 1969), 759-60. Christian vocation is the context for our response to militarism and conscription, and results in various forms of obedience to Christ, including noncooperation with the draft.

Mennonite Resistance to Draft Registration from 1980-84. 57 interviews by Mark Becker, 1984. Interviews of Mennonite conscientious resisters: registrants, nonregistrants, women, conference workers. Includes personal experiences, delegations to Selective Service, conferences, and persecutions. MLA/BeC.

Metz, Floyd. "Analysis of the Draft Census of the Franconia, Illinois, Indiana-Michigan, Ohio, South Central, and Pacific Conferences, Jan. 1, 1952-April, 1956." Paper presented to Sociology Seminar, Goshen College, Goshen, Ind., June 1, 1956. Pp. 23. MHL.

Metzler, Edgar. "Another Alternative for Draft-Age Youth." *GH* 52 (Nov. 17, 1959), 977-78. Metzler offers the alternative of noncooperation with the Selective Service system as a clear and compelling witness of conscientious objection against a militaristic society.

Metzler, Edgar. "Conscription—Is the End in Sight?" *Menn* 79 (May 26, 1964), 342-44. In the context of growing pressures to end the draft, the church must expand its service program.

Metzler, Edgar. "How Recent Draft Changes Affect the CO." *CanMenn* 13 (Sept. 28, 1965), 3, 16. No change in status of conscientious objectors is expected. Increased draft calls will have same consequences for CO's as for non-CO's.

Metzler, Edgar. Letter to the Editor. *GH* 48 (Dec. 6, 1955), 1154. "Now that our position as conscientious objectors to the draft is generally recognized, has the time come to extend our witness to a more positive conscientious objection to militarism in general?"

Metzler, Edgar. "Washington Report: Gearing Up for Return of Draft." *MennRep* 10 (Oct. 27, 1980), 7. As plans for draft resumption unfold in Washington, Mennonites must witness to a faith that does not depend on arms for security.

Metzler, Gretchen. "A Student Reflects on the Draft Assembly." *MCC PS Newsletter* 19 (Mar.-Apr., 1980), 6, 12. Writer reflects on feelings and questions surfacing as a result of discussing the draft and alternatives to it.

Miller, Albert. Letter to the Editor. *ChrLead* 41 (June 6, 1978), 10. Raising the concern that a "reemphasis" of biblical nonviolence falls short if it is only a response to a draft.

Miller, Levi. "The Nuclear Threat." *Builder* 32 (Jan., 1982), 2-3. Although the historic peace churches have a long history of dealing with such war and peace issues as conscription, the issues of nuclear war are relatively new and require study and action.

Miller, Melissa and Shenk, Phil M. *The Path of Most Resistance*. Scottdale: Herald Press, 1982. Pp. 239. Accounts of ten young people who, during the turbulent Vietnam years, resisted cooperating with the draft. The stories relate not only the conflict with the government concerning these illegal actions, but also the conflicts in the church as the generations struggled to understand the demands of faithfulness for their concrete situations.

Miller, Orie O. "Further Word on Conscription Act Procedure." *GH* 33 (Oct. 3, 1940), 570. A non-evaluative summary of certain provisions of the Conscription Act.

Moyer, Jacob M. "The Old Order Changes." *ChrLiv* 1 (May, 1954), 12-13, 36. World wars and draft were two factors contributing to greater mobility and changed lifestyle for Mennonites.

Moyer, John. "Upholding the Spiritual Revolution." *Forum* 13 (Oct., 1979), 12-13. Among the issues addressed at the Waterloo 1979 Assembly of the Mennonite Church was that of peace. The Assembly accepted a statement on "Militarism and Conscription," addressing the topics of peace and obedience, Christian service and conscription, and militarism and taxation.

Musser, Daniel. *Nonresistance Asserted: Or the Kingdom of Christ and the Kingdom of This World Separated, and No Concord Between Christ and Belial.* Lancaster: Elias Barr and Co., 1864. Pp. 74. MHL. Argues the biblical basis of nonresistance and contends, in regard to the pending draft, that to pay another person to go to war in one's place is just as wrong as actually going to war one's self.

"National Service Study Underway." *RepConsS* 32 [*sic*, 33] (Mar., 1976), 3. With Schowalter Foundation funding, NISBCO has hired Luann Habegger Martin to update 1971 study on national service.

"Negro Youth Resist the Draft." *GH* 64 (Nov. 25, 1969), 1034. Reasons given for an appeal to blacks to resist the draft.

"Nonresistant Nurses and the Draft." *GH* 37 (Feb. 9, 1945), 901. The nonresistant nurse could not cooperate with the government proposal to draft nurses into the army, says PPC.

"Nuclear Energy, Hot Topic at Peace Section Meeting." *GH* 72 (June 19, 1979), 504-505. Agenda items at the annual MCC Peace Section Meeting in Washington, DC, June 1-2, included proposed draft registration legislation, various peace education projects, and nuclear energy.

Nelson, Boyd N. "The Responsibility of Pre-Draft Preparation." *MennLead* 13 (July, 1958), 110-13. Encourages individuals and congregations to help prepare Mennonite youth more adequately for the draft and I-W service.

Neufeld, Elmer and Habegger, David. "Mission to Washington, DC." *Menn* 70 (Aug. 9, 1955), 486-87. Report of peace committee representatives concerning their witness against the reserve bill, which seems to be a preliminary step toward UMT

"Peace Churches Challenge Conscription by New Government in Nicaragua." *GH* 72 (Sept. 11, 1979), 728. The peace churches in Nicaragua are assuming a positive peace witness by challenging the government's decree for conscription.

"Peace-Time Conscription." *Menn* 60 (Jan. 2, 1945), 4. Letter from GCMC to President Roosevelt and members of Congress stating several reasons for the conference's opposition to peace-time conscription. Chief among them is that it is contrary to the spirit of Jesus' life, teachings, and gospel.

"Please Read the Following and Act." *Menn* 52 (May 4, 1937), 5. Statements *against* conscription, *in favor of* a popular referendum regarding the declaration of war, and *for* a senatorial investigation of defense spending.

"Pre-Draft Census Conducted by Service Board." *CanMenn* 3 (Nov. 11, 1955), 7. A census is being conducted to facilitate peace and service literature mailings to draft age youth.

"Prepare Draft, Peace Materials for Spanish Speaking." *GH* 65 (Sept. 26, 1972), 787. Puerto Rican Mennonites are requesting materials in the Spanish language because of an admitted passive and dormant peace witness.

Pacifism (since 1945). 12 interviews. Includes Historic Peace Churches Consultation (1975), MCC involvement, National Service Board for Religious Objectors, and draft counselling. MLA/BeC.

Peachey, J. Lorne. "Community News and Trends." *ChrLiv* 15 (Aug., 1968), 11. Mennonites in Iowa City and Ottawa respond to war and violence through a public letter and through assisting draft evaders.

Peachey, Paul L. *The Churches and War.* N.p.: Mennonite General Conference Peace Problems Committee, 1956. 19 pages. The Christian Youth and War Pamphlets No. 5. Directed toward young men approaching draft age, pamphlet traces the attitudes of the Christian church since the first century toward involvement in war. Includes comments on the just war theory as well as on individual pacifists throughout Christian history.

Peachey, Paul L. *Why Be a Christian.* N.p.: Mennonite General Conference Peace Problems Committee, 1956. 17 pages. The Christian Youth and War Pamphlets No. 2. Directed to young men approaching draft age, this pamphlet discusses the significance of Christian commitment and alternatives to it, and the meaning of following Christ.

Peachey, Paul L. *Why Men Fight.* N.p.: Mennonite General Conference Peace Problems Committee, 1956. 16 pages. The Christian Youth and War Pamphlets, No. 1. Directed to young men approaching draft age, this pamphlet discusses sin—the presence of evil in the human spirit created good—as the root cause of war.

Peachey, Shem. "Peacetime Military Training." *GH* 41 (Feb. 3, 1948), 100-102. The Christian must put God first and government second. Unless the Christian is allowed to say what work he will do, conscription puts government first and God second.

Penner, Gus. Letter to the Editor. *ChrLead* 42 (July 17, 1979), 14. Responds to a letter from a person who said they would not register for the military (*Leader*, May 8). Cautions this person against being disruptive and disrespectful.

Platt, Dwight. "An Open Letter to President Truman." *Menn* 66 (Mar. 27, 1951), 206-209. Platt refused to register for the draft as a witness against war, which he sees as contrary to the way of Jesus.

Preheim, Loren. "The Draft: Will It Be Abolished?" *GH* 58 (June 1, 1965), 466-67. A review of the draft, its present status, and its possible future.

Prieb, Wesley. "Prophet, Priest, and Mortar." *MCC PS Newsletter* 10 (Mar.-Apr., 1980), 5-6. Reflects on the differing viewpoints on responses to the draft present at the Mar., 1980, Assembly on the Draft by using the images of prophet and priest.

"Resistance Is Discussed." *GH* 64 (Apr. 27, 1971), 385. Draft resisters are lauded for promoting a discussion on the corporate church's attitude to the military system.

"Response to Conscription and Militarism." *CanMenn* 17 (Aug. 29, 1969), 5. A statement consisting of ten articles adopted by the Mennonite General Conference (MC) at Turner, Oregon, Aug. 18, 1969, as a response to young people expressing their convictions on the evils of conscription.

(Review). *Sourcebook on Peacetime Conscription.* American Friends Service Committee. 1944. Pp. 52. *CPS Bull* 3 (Feb. 22, 1945), 2. Recommends the book as a good presentation of arguments for and against peacetime draft.

Ratzlaff, Don. "Affirming a Doctrine, Exploring a Witness." *MBH* 19 (Apr. 25, 1980), 17-19; *ChrLead* 43 (Apr. 8, 1980), 2-5. Exploratory Peace Study Conference examined various forms of response to military conscription, from nonregistrant to noncombatant.

Ratzlaff, Don. "How Should I Respond?" *Lifework* 3 (1979), 8-11. Reviews the options available to Christians in the event of registering for Selective Service and urges young people to begin evaluating their convictions before reinstatement of draft registration. Includes a response by a young Mennonite committed to peacemaking and possible nonregistration.

Redekop, John H. "Penner vs. Beaver County Draft Board." *MBH* 9 (Aug. 21, 1970), 8. MCC assists a CO from Oklahoma to make his stand before the courts. Article discusses how one can learn from this encounter.

Redekop, John H. "The Dodgers." *MBH* 7 (June 14, 1968), 2. Those who migrate because of conscientious objection to conscription merit our sympathetic understanding and assistance.

Redekop, John H. "The New Conscientious Objectors." *MBH* 14 (Mar. 21, 1975), 8. Although Canadian youths do not face the draft, other forms of conscientious objection are being practiced, such as noncooperation with unions or forced tax evasion.

Regier, Austin. "Christianity and Conscription As Viewed by a Non-Registrant." *Menn* 63 (Nov. 30, 1948), 13-15. The Christian's sense of vocation should be determinitive, rather than any contrary demand by the state (e.g., conscription). Regier urges "doing the will of God" without reference to the demands of the state.

Regier, Austin. "The Faith of a Convict." *Menn* 64 (Feb. 15, 1949), 8-10. Text of the statement made by Regier to the federal court, Jan. 10, 1949, in which he said that he perceived his Christian duty as being dissociated from the war machine as much as possible.

Regier, Pearlmarie. "He Was Against Peacetime Conscription." Student paper for Our Christian Heritage, Feb., 1957. Pp. 5. About Austin Regier. MLA/BeC.

Rempel, John. "Why Young Mennonites Resist the Draft." *CanMenn* 18 (May 22, 1970), 7; *EV* 83 (June 25, 1970), 13. Mennonite youth consider themselves part of a 400-year tradition of faithfulness to an Anabaptist witness of love and peace when worldly governments contrarily seek their allegiance.

Rempel, Wendell. "Is Noncooperation a Responsible Christian Witness?" *Menn* 85 (May 19, 1970), 338-42. Responds to the confusion in Mennonite circles regarding noncooperation with Selective Service by emphasizing the positive contribution of a valid peace witness.

Rensberger, David. "My Testimony." *GH* 64 (Feb. 2, 1971), 96-97. In response to an earlier article opposing draft resistance, the writer argues that draft registration is indeed an example of the state demanding service it has no right to demand, and that Christians ought, therefore, to obey God rather than human authorities.

Rensberger, David and Lois. "The Case of David Rensberger, 22." *ChrLiv* 18 (Sept., 1971), 2-6. Draft resister and his mother speak on the eve of his sentencing.

Richert, P. H. "Why Conscription in Peacetime . . ." *Menn* 55 (July 30, 1940), 5. Peacetime conscription has more propaganda value than military value and should be opposed as a totalitarian measure.

"Statement on Peacetime Military Conscription." *Menn* 59 (Oct. 31, 1944), 1. Statement adopted by the Western District Conference (GCMC) on Oct. 19, 1944, at North Newton, Kansas, opposing a militaristic totalitarian peacetime military conscription.

"Statement on Position and Practices of the Church of the Brethren in Relation to War." *GH* 42 (May 17, 1949), 475, 484. The Church of the Brethren statement adopted in 1948 presents the church's position on war, freedom of conscience, conscription, and Christian citizenship.

"Students Puzzled by Views of Revolution." *Menn* 84 (Apr. 15, 1969), 252-54. Differing theologies and political theories are presented in order to find an answer to the problems of our time: injustice, war, poverty, inequality, conscription, and violence.

Schloneger, Weldon. "Would Shadrach Register for the Draft?" *GH* 73 (Nov. 4, 1980), 890-91. Examines the decision of Shadrach as one example of obeying God rather than the false gods of conformity, legality, and survival.

Schmidt, Linda. "Peace Section (US) Opposes Registration; Less Clear About Nuclear Issues." *Menn* 94 (June 26, 1979), 438. MCC Peace Section (US) annual meeting agenda includes proposed draft registration legislation, discussion of various peace education projects, and debate on nuclear energy.

Schrag, Don. "On the Serious Side: A Study of the Templin Incident and a College Under Pressure." Social Science Seminar paper, Apr., 1971. Pp. 18. Bethel College and community relations in World War II—issue of registration. MLA/BeC., BfC.

Schrag, Martin H. "The New Call to Peacemaking—Hearing and Heeding the Call." *EV* 91 (Dec. 25, 1978), 5-7. A report on the national meeting of the New Call to Peacemaking held at Green Lake, Wis. Although the US is presently not engaged in a war, the threat of a nuclear holocaust, the possibility of conscription, and the build-up of arms, among other things, all urge us to heed the call to peacemaking.

Schrock, T. E. Letter to the Editor. *GH* 62 (Dec. 9, 1969), 1061. Interprets draft resisters to be misunderstanding the "sorting" function of the Selective Service system when they attribute only military motivations to the system. Questions whether Mennonites want to change from a nonresistant church into a resisting church.

*

Shank, Duane. "Amnesty Activity Increases." *RepConsS* 33 (Dec., 1976), 1, 3. Summarizes efforts by the amnesty movement to urge President-elect Carter to include more categories of war resisters in his plan to pardon draft law violators.

Shank, Duane. "An Open Letter to Selective Service." *RepConsS* 27 (May, 1970), 1. An eighteen-year-old refuses to register with the SSS on the grounds that to accept any classification from Selective Service indicates participation in the "war machine."

Shank, Duane. "COs and the Draft." *RepConsS* 32 [*sic,* 33] (May, 1976), 5. Ford Foundation "Information Paper" provides data on inequities and inconsistencies in handling of CO applications by local Selective Service personnel.

Shank, Duane. "House Backs SSS Cut." *RepConsS* 32 [*sic,* 33] (May, 1976), 1, 3. Discusses House decision to cut appropriations for the Selective Service System and the effects of this cut on noncooperation with the draft.

Shank, Duane (Editorial). "Now That the Draft Is Over . . . ?" *RepConsS* 32 [*sic,* 33] (Mar., 1976), 2. The draft over, NISBCO will work on such issues as military recruitment for the all-volunteer force and war taxes.

Shank, J. Ward. "Regarding Military Registration." *ST* 48 (May, 1980), 8-9. Resisting the draft is confusing national policy with the interests of the church.

Shank, J. Ward (Editorial). "Noncooperation and Resistance." *ST* 38 (Feb., 1970), 1. The church has always stood in support of sincere expressions of conscience, even where individuals have stood alone upon their convictions. But to expect public support of an act designed to stir reaction has about it something of dubious ethical quality.

Shellenberger, Eunice. *Wings of Decision.* Scottdale: Herald Press, 1951. Pp. 240. Fictional account of a young man facing the draft in World War II, his decision to seek conscientious objector status, and his experiences in Civilian Public Service.

Shelly, Maynard. "Draft Resistance Makes the Scene." *With* 3 (May, 1970), 28. In addition to alternate service, in 1969 the Mennonite traditions of civil disobedience and martyrdom

have come back to take their place as new options in the Mennonite protest against war.

Shelly, Maynard. "Mennonite Ghetto Faces Eviction into the World." *CanMenn* 17 (Oct. 24, 1969), 9. Western District Mennonite conference (GCMC) delegates vote to recognize total noncooperation with the Selective Service System as a meaningful witness of one's belief and as a peace witness compatible with the historical traditions of the Mennonite church.

Shelly, Maynard. "Two Mennonites Convicted of Selective Service Violations." *Menn* 86 (May 11, 1971), 309. Mennonites individually and collectively are judged for lack of cooperation with draft requirements and tested in their peace position.

Shenk, Gerald E. "Motives Behind Presidential Reforms Probably Mixed." *RepConsS* 27 (June, 1970), 4. Discusses motivation behind President Nixon's executive order eliminating most II-A and III-A deferments.

Shenk, Gerald E. "The President's Continuing Power." *RepConsS* 28 (June, 1971), 5. Explains that a vote against the extension of the draft would leave the President with power to induct all previously deferred, physically fit registrants under 35.

Shenk, Jerry. "Selling a System." *IPF Notes* 17 (Nov.-Dec., 1970), 2-3. Describes the Selective Service campaign to win public acceptance of the draft.

Shenk, Phil M. "The Power and Penalty of Moral Dissent." *Sojourners* 9 (July, 1980), 10. Reviews the approved Selective Service draft registration program and the possibilities and penalties of noncooperation.

Sherk, J. Harold. "Draft Prospects and Problems." *RepConsS* 22 (Oct., 1965), 1, 4. Assesses CO situation for US citizens in light of the draft call increase announced by President Johnson on July 28.

Sherk, J. Harold. "The Alternative Service Law and Its Operation." *MennLife* 13 (July, 1958), 103-105. An explanation of the Universal Military Training Act of 1951 and the place of NSBRO in relation to its operation.

Sherk, J. Harold (Editorial). "From Where I Sit." *RepConsS* 20 (Feb., 1963), 2. Decries the religious test for COs and conscription as infringements of religious freedom.

Shisler, Barbara. "Peace Teachers: The Mike Rhode File." *Builder* 31 (Jan., 1981), 17-18. Mike Rhode, formerly in the US Navy, has joined with four other Mennonite men with military experience to act out the role of the draft board

---

*For additional listing, see Supplement, pp. 717-719.

in order to help Mennonite youth think more seriously about their responses to militarism.

Simpkins, Sean Ozzie. Letter to the Editor. *Menn* 91 (June 8, 1976), 393. Goshen College student and former military enlistee publishes a letter he sent to the military announcing a stance of noncooperation, based on radical Christian commitment which forbids killing and exploitation of others.

Smucker, Donovan E. "A Statement of Position to the Armed Services Committee of the US Senate Concerning Peacetime Conscription and the Christian Conscience Against War." *Menn* 63 (May 4, 1948), 6-7. Statement made at public hearing Mar. 31, 1948, on behalf of MCC, vigorously opposing peacetime conscription and witnessing against war itself.

Smucker, Donovan E. "Registration Without Resignation." *Fellowship* 6 (Oct., 1940), 123. Reviews the reasons why he, a Christian pacifist, intends to register.

Smucker, Donovan E. "Some Reflections on Peacetime Conscription." Outline of lecture given at Mulberry, Fla., 1945. Pp. 4. MHL.

Stauffer, John L. "Government Plans for the Next War and How They May Affect Us." *The Eastern Mennonite School Journal* 18 (Apr., 1940), 36-41. Speculates as to what form conscription might take should the US enter the war and calls young people to live lives consistent with nonresistant principles in anticipation of confrontations with draft boards.

Steiner, Sam. "I Could Not Tolerate the War Machine." *With* 2 (Mar., 1969), 34. Any cooperation with a military system is a violation of one's moral responsibility to humanity.

Steiner, Sam. Letter to the Editor. *GH* 61 (Aug. 20, 1968), 762. Draft resister explains why he and other resisters choose noncooperation instead of alternative service. Reasons cited include the discrimination of the Selective Service system against blacks and just-war protesters.

Steiner, Sam and Zeoli, Leonard F. "Two Draft Resisters React to Earned Reentry." *Forum* 8 (Oct., 1974), 5. Two draft resisters living in Canada state their reasons for refusing to accept the earned reentry program as outlined by President Ford.

Steiner, Susan Clemmer. "We Could Not Go Home." *With* 8 (June, 1975), 6. Description of the radical changes in the lives of four Mennonite draft dodgers in Canada.

Stone, Oliver. "Draft Classifications." *YCC* 30 (Jan. 30, 1949), 453. There seems to be some confusion about draft classifications. The conscientious objector should assert his CO claim and should take whatever appeal may be necessary to secure his IV-E classification.

Stoner, John K. "Consultation Planned on Draft, National Service." *ChrLead* 40 (Sept. 27, 1977), 15. Notice of the inter-Mennonite "Consultation on the Draft and National Service" to be held Nov. 11 and 12, 1977.

Stoner, John K. "MCC Testifies on Draft." *EV* 92 (July 10, 1979), 14. K. B. Hoover, a representative of the Brethren in Christ Church to MCC, appeared May 21 before the Senate Armed Services Subcommittee on Manpower and Personnel to testify for MCC Peace Section against the renewal of draft registration.

Studer, Gerald C. Letter to the Editor. *GH* 63 (Aug. 25, 1970), 706-707. Expresses regret that the Mennonite Church approved paying jobs in I-W assignments as alternative service, instead of remaining with nonsalaried PAX or VS work. Supports all forms of draft resistance as valid witnesses to the state.

Suderman, David H. "The Returning Civilian Public Service Men." *MennLife* 1 (Jan., 1946), 5-7, 21. An analysis of the CPS camper: discusses pre-camp decision about conscription, camp influences, and adjustment to home community after camp experience.

Suderman, Jacob. "The Origin of Mennonite State Service in Russia." *MQR* 17 (Jan., 1943), 23-46. A review of the history of Mennonite resistance to the draft in Russia, together with a translation of key documents in that history.

"The Church and Selective Service." *Menn* 84 (Oct. 28, 1969), 646. Mennonites support both noncooperation with Selective Service and established alternative service programs as possible and appropriate expressions of their peace witness, says resolution adopted by the Western District Conference (GCMC) on Oct. 11, 1969.

"The Draft Law and Your Choices." *With* 2 (Mar., 1969), 4. Explanation of four responses, three of which are recognized as legitimate by Selective Service, that can be made to the draft law.

"The Refugee American. . ." *Forum* (Jan., 1971), A4-A5. Several Mennonites dialogue about their work with American draft dodgers in Ottawa and the problems and attitudes of these Americans.

"Trudeau on Violence." *CanMenn* 18 (Apr. 10, 1970), 1. The prime minister's positive attitude to nonviolence and the draft dodgers is cited.

"Two Draft Resisters—Where Are They Now?"

*Menn* 88 (Apr. 17, 1973), 254-55. Dennis Koehn and David Rensberger, Mennonite draft resisters sentenced to prison, reflect on their decisions not to cooperate with Selective Service and their experiences in prison.

Teichroew, Allan. "The Flight to Canada: Mennonites Dodge the Draft in the First World War." Social Science Seminar paper, May, 1969. Pp. 28. MLA/BeC.

Teichroew, Allan. "World War I and the Mennonite Migration to Canada to Avoid the Draft." *MQR* 45 (July, 1971), 219-49. A report on motives and experiences of draft age men going to Canada. "The war and all its manifestations—conscription, anti-German sentiment, bond drives, and unabated government efforts to mobilize America physically, spiritually, and emotionally— dictated the response of Mennonites who went to Canada."

Thierstein, J. R. "A Momentous Battle On." *Menn* 55 (Sept. 17, 1940), 1. "We should not let up imploring those in authority to stem the tide away from conscription."

Toews, John A. (Review). *Broken Promises: A History of Conscription in Canada*, by J. L. Granatstein and J. M. Hitsman. Toronto: Oxford Univ. Press, 1977. Pp. 281. *MQR* 53 (Oct., 1979), 333. Based on extensive research, the authors cite conscription as the single issue which has "done more to destroy the unity of the nation." Reviewer expresses disappointment that Mennonites and other conscientious objectors are mentioned only in passing.

Toews, John B. "The Russian Mennonite Migrations of the 1870s and 1880s—Some Background Aspects." *ChrLead* 37 (Apr. 2, 1974), 4. A czarist decree intorduced universal military conscription in 1870s with no provisions for exempting the Mennonites. The question of their historic pacifism became a watershed in the history of the Russian Mennonites.

Unrau, Neil. "American Moravian Noncombatancy: A Study in Changing Attitudes." Paper for War, Peace, and Revolution class, AMBS, Elkhart, Ind., n.d. Pp. 17. AMBS.

Unruh, Wilfred J. "An Evaluation of Mennonite Service Programs." *PCMCP Sixteenth*, 143-59. N.p. Held at Hesston College, Hesston, Kansas, June 8-9, 1967. An examination of the philosophy, history, and empirical data of the service programs. The conclusion includes the statement that conscription is probably the single most significant influence in service programs.

Unruh, Wilfred J. *Parents and the Draft*. [Newton,

Ks.]: Faith and Life Press, 1966. Pp. 7. MHL. Offers parents counsel on how to guide their draft age children toward authentic, mature decisions on the issue and how to work through their own parental feelings so that they may truly support their children in these decisions.

Unsigned. "Symposium on Post-War Conscription." *CPS Bull* 3 (Oct. 22, 1944), 5-6. Most of the seven CPS respondents encourage the Mennonite church to continue an alternative service program whether or not peacetime conscription becomes a reality.

Urry, James. "Division and Emigration: The Reasons Were Complex." *MennRep* 4 (Nov. 25, 1974), 10-11. Examines reasons for migrations from southern Russia to North America, including the threat of military conscription. Observes that a possible draft threatened the colonists in two ways: violating pacifist principles, and removing young men from congregational authority.

US Board of Reference and Counsel of the Mennonite Brethren Churches. "A Recommendation on Peace and the Draft." *ChrLead* 43 (Apr. 8, 1980), 4. Statement clarifying the conference peace position.

Vogt, J. W. "Won the War—But Lost the Peace?" *ChrLead* 12 (Apr. 1, 1948), 2. War cannot produce peace. Preparations for war—such as the proposal for universal military training— usually result in actual war.

"When You Fill Out Form 150." *With* 2 (Mar., 1969), 28. Because the decision of the local draft board depends on the information given on the Form 150, one should avoid oversimplified answers.

"Witness in Washington." *CanMenn* 3 (Feb. 25, 1955), 2. Comments on the witness of US Mennonites to the state regarding draft alternatives.

"Witnessing to God's Will for Peace." *CanMenn* 18 (July 17, 1970), 16. Purpose, organization, and action of the MCC Peace Section are outlined. The draft, the Washington office, the Middle East, and International relationships are topics receiving special emphasis.

Weaver, Henry, Jr. "The Permanent Draft." *GH* 48 (June 7, 1955), 533. Christians should work to abolish the permanent draft. But as long as it exists it may be used as a means of furthering the peace witness.

Weinbrenner, Reynold (Editorial). *Menn* 60 (July 17, 1945), 3, 12. Advocates abolition of peacetime conscription.

Wert, Jim and Epp, Leonard. " . . . Some Churches and Their Leaders Are Calling for Help." *I Would Like to Dodge the Draft-dodgers But . . . .* Ed. Frank H. Epp. Waterloo and Winnipeg: Conrad Press, 1970, 69-75. Pp. 95. In this two-part treatment, Wert describes the Canadian Council of Churches' involvement with the US draft dodgers and Epp describes the estimated 60,000 young Americans in Canada for reasons of conscientious objection and makes some suggestions as to how the church leadership might deal constructively with this phenomenon.

Wiebe, Katie Funk. "Caught in the Draft." *GH* 72 (Aug. 21, 1979), 667; *ChrLead* 42 (June 19, 1979), 19. With impending conscription, we are urged to be more prepared than we were for the World War II crisis. Peacemaker registration through MCC Peace Section is one suggestion for getting ready.

Wiebe, Katie Funk. "The Breeze Before the Draft." *GH* 73 (Feb. 12, 1980), 135; *Menn* 95 (Mar. 4, 1980), 161; *ChrLead* 43 (Feb. 12, 1980), 22. Comment on the reinstatement of draft registration and the need for young people to be articulate about their peace stance.

Wiebe, Rudy H. "Conscription for Military Service." *MBH* 1 (May 11, 1962), 4. The MB Youth Service Program is a most significant witness as an alternative to military service.

Wittlinger, Carlton O. (Review). *Twas Seeding Time: A Mennonite View of the American Revolution,* by John L. Ruth. Scottdale, Pa. and Kitchener, Ont.: Herald Press, 1976. Pp. 224. *MQR* 52 (July, 1978), 271-72. Reviewer considers this book of stories of Mennonite noncooperation in the Revolution a good, and informal, contribution to the subject of Mennonite history during the Revolution.

World War I. 302 interviews: over half are transcribed. Emphasis is on CO's from many Mennonite branches and other churches. Also includes several regulars and civilians (women, pastors). Some very dramatic stories of abuse in army camps, courts-martial, prison, personal testimonies about nonresistant stances, moving to Canada to escape conscription, community war fervor. Guide to interviews published as Sprunger, *et al., Voices Against War,* 1973. MLA/ BeC.

Yake, C. F. "Conscription." *YCC* 21 (Oct. 6, 1940), 316, 320. General survey of the issue of conscription, information on the Burke-Wadsworth Conscription Bill.

Yake, C. F. "Selective Service." *YCC* 31 (Mar. 26, 1950), 100. Keeping updated on the status of the selective service act.

Yake, C. F. "Universal Military Training." *YCC* 29 (May 23, 1948), 164. Discussion of peacetime conscription in the form of universal military training. Caution about fundamentalists who teach it is the Christian's duty to fight.

Yoder, Edward. "Permanent Conscription." *GH Supplement* 37 (Aug., 1944), 392. Questions the desirability of permanent conscription.

Yoder, Edward. "The Christian's Attitude Toward Participation in War Activities." *MQR* 9 (Jan., 1935), 5-19. Mennonites have consistently chosen a moderate position between total noncooperation with the military and a willingness to engage in noncombatant duty in their witness against war.

Yoder, Edward and Smucker, Donovan. *The Christian and Conscription: An Inquiry Designed as a Preface to Action.* Akron: MCC, 1945. Pp. 124. An evaluation of the alternative service experience in World War II and a guide to witness against conscription.

Yoder, Gideon G. "My Faith and Military Conscription." *GH* 65 (Mar. 7, 1972), 220-24. A late professor and pastor shares in one of his last sermons the pilgrimage of events in his life, and his reflections on those events, which led him to affirm noncooperation with military conscription.

Yoder, J. Otis (Editorial). "The Church and the 'New Left'." *ST* 39 (July, 1971), 7. The language and concepts of the "new left" are affecting the Old Mennonite nonresistant stance. An example is the Mennonite Draft Resisters at Turner, Oregon, 1969.

Yoder, John. "Peace Is Our Business." *Intercom* 10 (Mar.-Apr., 1970), 1. VS worker in Atlanta describes his job as a draft counselor, especially his work with conscientious objectors from non-pacifist backgrounds.

Yoder, Samuel A. "Caught in a Draft?" *YCC* 34 (Aug. 30, 1953), 694. Warnings against the reality that dissipation and indulgence are normal reactions to times of great uncertainty.

Yutzy, Homer E. "Conscription as Experienced by Mennonites in the US During World War II." Paper prepared for Anabaptist-Mennonite History class, [AMBS, Elkhart, Ind.], Dec. 20, 1976. Pp. 9. MHL.

Zehr, Albert. "Deserter-Evangelist in Tradition of Menno." *CanMenn* 18 (May 22, 1970), 8. John Webb tells a Mennonite congregation in Ontario why he left the army and then, with his wife, fled to Canada. He is disillusioned by a "system which is built on, and nourished by, war and bloodshed, containing a church . . . which blesses the state and prays, 'God grant our men safety, and may they bring back many dead.'"

Zercher, John E. "I Feel a Draft." *EV* 92 (Apr. 25, 1979), 15. With present efforts in Congress to reinstate the military draft, special emphasis needs to be given to the biblical teaching on peace in times of peace in order for the youth to be prepared for times of war or near war.

Zook, Gordon. "Militarism and Conscription, an Introduction." *GH* 72 (Oct. 2, 1979), 777. The Mennonite Church statement on militarism

and conscription grew from at least four influences: the Acts of the Apostles; the arms race; international fellowship; efforts to reactivate military conscription.

"1979 Mennonite Church General Assembly Statement on Militarism and Conscription." *GH* 72 (Oct. 2, 1979), 778-79. Seeking to be a faithful witness in a militaristic world, the Mennonite Church speaks out on peace and obedience, the use of material resources, Christian service and conscription, militarism and taxation.

# C. Amnesty

"Amnesty: A Peace Church Concern." [Elkhart, IN]: Mennonite Board of Congregational Ministries, 1973. Pp. 11. MHL

Barrett, Lois [Janzen]. "Clemency—Now He Sees It; Now He Doesn't." *Menn* 90 (Mar. 11, 1975), 162-63. Relates the story of Steve Trimm, a draft resister who had been refused conscientious objector status and sought to obtain clemency; shows the difficulties inherent in President Ford's "conditional amnesty" program.

Boers, Arthur Paul. "Speaking for the Imprisoned." *MBH* 18 (Apr. 27, 1979), 18-19. Part of Amnesty International's concern for those unjustly imprisoned includes a special concern for conscientious objectors to war.

Brenneman, Virgil J. "A Parent's Reflection on Amnesty." *GH* 67 (Oct. 1, 1974), 748-49. A parent whose son is a draft refugee in Canada favors amnesty in order to restore civil liberties denied for conscience' sake, and to further heal the wounds of war.

Cook, J. Patrick. "Amnesty Must Provide Total Restoration, Says Exile." *Menn* 87 (Apr. 11, 1972), 252; "Is Amnesty the Word?" *GH* 65 (May 16, 1972), 440-41. Reflects on the immorality of war and the commitment of war objectors to label it as such. Does not ask for amnesty but for totally nonpunitive restoration of civil liberties for these war objectors.

Dueck, Allan. Letter to the Editor. *ChrLead* 40 (Dec. 6, 1977), 15. Urges support for Amnesty International, an organization whose special concern is political prisoners.

"Earned Reentry Has Many Weaknesses." *Forum* 8 (Oct., 1974), 3. Reaction to President Ford's earned reentry program has been mixed and many are determined to refuse anything less than full amnesty which an MCC Peace Section statement supports.

Franz, Delton, ed. "Amnesty: Will Reconciliation

Occur?" *MCC PS Wash. Memo* 7 (May-June, 1975), 5-6. Discusses alternatives Congress is considering with regard to amnesty for Vietnam draft evaders.

Gaede, Don H. Letter to the Editor. *ChrLead* 36 (Dec. 11, 1973), 22. Mennonite Brethren should come out in full support of amnesty.

"Historic Peace Churches Seek Amnesty." *RepConsS* 32 (June, 1975), 1. One outcome of two-day meeting in New Windsor, Maryland, is a letter to President Ford urging amnesty.

"Human Rights in Our World." *Menn* 94 (June 5, 1979), 386-87. Table listing by country the number of prisoners of conscience identified by Amnesty International.

Hackman, Walton. "A Christian Declaration on Amnesty." *ChrLead* 36, (May 15, 1973), 14. A description and history of the recipients of a possible amnesty. Mennonites should support universal amnesty which is consonent with the Mennonite theology of peacemaking and reconciling.

Hackman, Walton. Letter to the Editor. *MennRep* 3 (Feb. 5, 1973), 6. Executive Secretary of the Peace Section clarifies the statement on amnesty published in the Jan. 22 issue; presents revised version of the final section of the statement.

Hackman, Walton. "The Issue Now Is Amnesty." *GH* 65 (Jan. 4, 1972), 9-10. Reprinted from MCC Peace Section *Newsletter*. After World War II, only 10 percent of Selective Service violators were pardoned. Writer wonders whether present society has enough latitude to respect and accept the estimated 100,000 Vietnam War resisters.

Harms, Orlando. "Our Peace Position." *ChrLead* 36 (Oct. 30, 1973), 28. The major argument for amnesty is reconciliation. There is indication that the more evangelical and fundamental a person is, the more he/she is against amnesty.

This includes many Mennonite Brethren people.

Hershberger, Guy F. "Conscientious Objectors in Prison." *GH Supplement* 39 (Aug., 1946), 460. There is growing support for the policy of granting amnesty to the war objectors still in prison. Many of these persons have been imprisoned unjustly.

Koontz, Ted. "Few Benefit from Earned Reentry." *Menn* 89 (Oct. 22, 1974), 612. Lists the vast differences between President Ford's clemency program and universal amnesty for draft resisters, which include assuming moral and legal guilt on the part of resisters, and overlooking all who received less than honorable military discharges for protesting the war.

Kroeker, David. "Torture, Prison, Rats, and Hunger." *MennRep* 9 (Jan. 22, 1979), 6. Relating numerous incidents of persons maltreated for political and/or religious beliefs, the writer urges the reader to contact Amnesty International and become involved in the campaign to free those unjustly treated.

Landis, Jim. "Clemency Program Ends; Amnesty Still Urged." *Menn* 90 (May 27, 1975), 336. President Ford's clemency program for draft evaders was a poorly designed program, rejected by many resisters for its punitive measures and because it ignored large groups of people needing amnesty.

Landis, Maurice W. "The Secularization of the Church and Civil Religion, Part 2." *GfT* 8 (Nov.-Dec., 1973), 10-11, 15. By advocating amnesty for those who broke the Selective Service law, the church is violating the principle of separation of church and state and becoming an instrument of lawlessness.

Lapp, John A. "The Case for a Universal Amnesty." *ChrLiv* 20 (Apr., 1973), 16, 35. Discussion of possible amnesty for the 500,000 facing criminal charges for draft resistance, military desertion, or less than honorable discharge.

"MCC (Canada) Annual Meeting." *MBH* 12 (Jan. 26, 1973), 8-9. Among other agenda items, the MCC Canada board discussed capital punishment, amnesty for US war resisters, and ecumenical relations at its annual meeting.

"MCC (Canada) Endorses Resolution on Amnesty." *MennRep* 3 (Jan. 22, 1973), 11. Publishes the working draft of the MCC Peace Section statement on the necessity of amnesty for US war resisters.

Mennonite Central Committee Peace Section. "A Christian Declaration on Amnesty." *GH* 66 (May 15, 1973), 413-14; *Menn* 88 (Apr. 24, 1973), 268-69. Based on the belief that peace and reconciliation are at the heart of the gospel, the Peace Section urges adopting a "general amnesty" to cover all types of conscientious objectors, an action that would help to bind up the wounds of the Vietnam war.

Mennonite Central Committee Peace Section. "The Contemporary Scene. Amnesty: A Christian Declaration." *EV* 86 (July 25, 1973), 16. This statement represents the consensus of the MCC Peace Section which has attempted to state with clarity and precision the position which it feels reflects the Mennonite theology of peacemaking and reconciliation.

Mennonite Church General Conference. "Letter to the President." *GH* 62 (Oct. 7, 1969), 870. Reprints letter from the Mennonite General Conference to Richard Nixon, expressing concern over the Vietnam war, requesting discontinued conscription as well as amnesty for draft dodgers, and urging the president to set human need as the national priority. Includes reply from Nixon.

Monke, Lowell. *A Report on Amnesty.* Newton, Ks.: Commission on Home Ministries, GCMC, 1975. Pp. 100. MHL. Defines the concept of amnesty, surveys the history of its practice, summarizes the situations and circumstances of those eligible for amnesty as a result of war resistance, explains the laws governing amnesty, and discusses the moral, religious, and political implications of the issue.

Monke, Lowell. "Amnesty: Who Needs It?" *Menn* 89 (Apr. 16, 1974), 254-57. Encourages Christians to support amnesty for not only the conscientious objectors, but also for the possibly 150,000 draft dodgers and deserters living as fugitives in the US, and the nearly 560,000 Vietnam-era veterans with less-than-honorable discharges, many of whose problems in the military centered on their unarticulated opposition to the war.

"NIBSCO Council Members Respond." *RepConsS* 31 (Oct., 1974), 3. Peace and Social Concerns Committees of the General Conference Mennonite Church and the Mennonite Church offer five suggestions as to how congregations can respond to the government's program of earned reentry.

Ortman, David. Letter to the Editor. *Menn* 92 (Jan. 25, 1977), 61. Reprints letter written to President Carter on "deeply troubling" issues such as development of the Trident undersea missile system, production of the B-1 bomber, and absence of amnesty for war resisters.

"Religious Statements on Amnesty." *RepConsS* 30 (Apr., 1973), 3-8. Prints the MCC Peace Section statement on amnesty (Mar. 31, 1973) alongside a number of similar statements from other religions and peace groups.

"Responses to Amnesty." *Menn* 88 (Apr. 24, 1973), 269-71. Seven persons share their responses to "A Declaration on Amnesty," a statement by the Mennonite Central Committee Peace Section. Responses range from unconditional support of the document's call for universal amnesty for war resisters, to disagreement with the statement, to discouragement that amnesty will in fact become a reality.

Shank, Duane. "Amnesty Activity Increases." *RepConsS* 33 (Dec., 1976), 1, 3. Summarizes efforts by the amnesty movement to urge President-elect Carter to include more categories of war resisters in his plan to pardon draft law violators.

Shank, Duane. "Amnesty for Vice-President." *RepConsS* 32 [*sic,* 33] (June, 1976), 1, 3, 4. Reports successful efforts to bring the issues of amnesty before the Democratic National Convention.

Shank, Duane. "Amnesty Raised in Campaign." *RepConsS* 33 (Aug.-Nov., 1976), 1, 5. Analyzes how, where, and why the issues of amnesty were discussed in the recent presidential campaign.

Shank, Duane. "Carter Pardons Some; Amnesty Movement Continues." *RepConsS* 34 (Feb., 1977), 2, 4, 5. Describes the amnesty movement's reactions to Carter's partial pardon and its plans to continue working for "a real and total amnesty."

Shank, Duane. "Catholics Recommend Amnesty." *RepConsS* 33 (Dec., 1976), 3. Excerpts recommendations resulting from a two-year study process initiated by US Catholic bishops.

Shank, Duane. "Congress Limits Carter Program; Boycott Urged." *RepConsS* 34 (Sept., 1977), 1, 4. Denounces two pieces of legislation currently before Congress as efforts to undermine Carter's already limited amnesty program.

Shank, Duane. Letter to the Editor. *GH* 67 (Aug. 6, 1974), 605-606. Agrees with the writer of "A Letter to My Son" (July 2, 1974), that amnesty for the war resisters is needed, but he asserts that amnesty in a moral sense is not forgiveness, but rather recognition that the offenders' actions were not wrong.

Shank, Duane. "Light Response to Discharge Program." *RepConsS* 34 (May, 1977), 2. Update on the amnesty movement and President Carter's discharge program.

Shank, Duane. "Pardons for Some." *RepConsS* 32 [*sic,* 33] (May, 1976), 1, 3. Discusses the Democratic Party plank favoring pardons for those whose conscientious objection to the Vietnam War resulted in Selective Service violations.

Shank, Duane. "Pentagon Announces Discharge Review." *RepConsS* 34 (Apr., 1977), 1, 6. Explains and responds to President Carter's policies dealing with military deserters and veterans receiving other than honorable discharges from the amnesty movement's point of view.

Shank, Duane (Editorial). "The Convention and the Campaign." *RepConsS* 32 [*sic,* 33] (June, 1976), 2. Despite the publicity given amnesty at the Democratic National Convention, the rhetoric of the presidential campaign tends toward treating the Vietnam War as a mistake rather than a crime against humanity.

Shank, J. Ward (Editorial). "Amnesty and Indemnity." *ST* 41 (Nov., 1973), 7. Questions the right of alternative service workers to veteran's benefits, and thus to amnesty as well.

Shank, J. Ward (Editorial). "The Question of Amnesty." *ST* 41 (May, 1973), 4. The church should recognize that the president's options with amnesty may be limited; and it should be slow in pressing for any specific line of action, especially on grounds other than the recognition of Christian conscience.

"Women Respond to Clemency." *RepConsS* 32 (Mar., 1975), 2. Women students at Goshen College write President Ford volunteering themselves as substitutes for the draft resisters in exile required to earn re-entry through labor. Willems, Malcolm. Letter to the Editor. *ChrLead* 36 (June 26, 1973), 13. The question of amnesty deals with the most complex matters of conscience, ethics, and morality in the Christian's dual role as citizen of both kingdom and state. It is an intensely personal question.

Worth, David (Review). *The Amnesty of John David Herndon,* by James Reston, Jr. McGraw-Hill, 1973. Pp. 46. *RepConsS* 30 (Mar., 1973), 2, 3. Describes book as avoiding sensationalism to speak powerfully for the cause of universal amnesty.

Young, Robert T. "A Letter to My Son." *GH* 67 (July 2, 1974), 529-31. Letter to a fictitious son, a draft resister who fled the country, reflects on the enormous and varied costs of the Vietnam war and calls for amnesty for the 70,000 who refused to fight.

Zercher, John E. "In Honor of Conscience." *EV* 87 (Sept. 10, 1974), 3. The church should be on the side of leniency and mercy and support President Ford in his effort to consider amnesty for draft evaders and military deserters.

Ziegler, Donald. "Leamington Hosts MCC Annual Meeting." *MBH* 12 (Feb. 23, 1973), 2-3. Among other concerns, the MCC annual meeting adopted in principle a working draft on amnesty and a resolution on reconstruction in Indochina.

Ziegler, Donald. "MCC Examines Self and Issues." *EV* 86 (Mar. 10, 1973), 5, 6. MCC met for its annual meeting in Leamington, Ont., to discuss the progress of the MCC self-study, to adopt guidelines on the use of government funds, to resolve interest in reconstruction in Indochina, to consider a working draft statement on universal amnesty for conscientious objectors, and to recognize four dynamic leaders of past inter-Mennonite activites.

# 12

# Nationalism

## A. General

Augsburger, David W. "Who Said Americans Are Christian?" *YCC* 48 (July 2, 1967), 3. Looks at the myth that being Christian and being American are one and the same thing.

*Bicentennial Studies for the Church.* Akron, Pa.: Congregational Peace Education Program, 1976. Pp. 31. MHL. Study guide with the option of four or thirteen sessions on such themes as church and state relations, civil religion and evangelism.

Bieber, Doreen. "Nationalism vs. the Kingdom of God." *GH* 71 (Jan. 24, 1978), 68-69. Speech, which won second place in the C. Henry Smith Peace Oratorical Contest, suggests that nation-worship leads to war, and war is sin. Also in MHL.

Born, Daniel (Review). *Twilight of the Saints: Biblical Christianity and Civil Religion in America,* by Robert D. Linder and Richard V. Pierard. Downers Grove, IL: Inter Varsity, 1978. In *ChrLead* 41 (Aug. 15, 1978), 17. Examines the spectrum of attitudes on Christianity vis-a-vis patriotism steeped in religious rhetoric.

Brubacher, Glenn. "The Strange Gods in the Land." *GH* 65 (Jan. 18, 1972), 56-57. Militarism and nationalism are mentioned as false gods to whom Christians are paying homage, as well as materialism and sensuousness.

Burkhalter, Sheldon, et al. *A Mennonite Response, 1776-1976.* Souderton, Pa.:" Franconia Mennonite Conference, 1975. Pp. 16. MHL. Discussion on Mennonite responses during the Revolutionary War and what being citizens in Christ's kingdom means for today. Also includes suggestions for Bible study and congregational action.

Burkholder, J. Lawrence. "Our Attitude Toward Communism." *GH* 44 (May 1, 1951), 409-410. The Christian evaluates communist structures and persons in a spirit of fairness and love, ready to admit that not all of our institutions

are beyond reproach. Communism can only be stopped by fighting poverty and oppression.

"Christ Is Not Enough." *GH* 47 (Feb. 16, 1954), 153. Growing militarism and nationalism call people to put their trust in armies rather than in God.

"Civil Religion Packet." MCC, 1976. MHL. Mennonite contributions include: Lapp, John A., "Understanding Civil Religion," pp. 4; Hackman, Walton, "The Old Time Religion or a New Civil Religion," pp. 2; Franz, Delton, "Mennonites and Civil Religion," pp. 4; Augsburger, David, "In Civil Religion We Trust?" pp. ?; MacMaster, Richard K., *Christian Obedience in Revolutionary Times,* Akron: MCC US Peace Section, 1976, pp. 26 [MHL, annotated separately]; Longacre, James C., "Mennonites and the Bicentennial," pp. 3; Faith and Life Commission, Southern District Conference of Mennonite Brethren Churches, "A Bicentennial Statement for Mennonite Brethren," p. 1; "Christians and the Bicentennial," MCC US Peace Section, [1976], brochure; Detweiler, Richard, *et al.,* "The Bicentennial and the Mennonite Church," Mennonite Church Board of Congregational Ministries, May 13, 1975, pp. 1; "Mennonites and Bicentennial Celebrations," statement adopted by Lancaster Conference, Sept. 18, 1975, pp. 1; "Resolution on the Bicentennial," statement of the Western District Conference of the General Conference Mennonite Church, n.d., pp. 1; Burkholder, Sheldon, *et al., A Mennonite Response, 1776-1976,* Souderton: Franconia Mennonite Conference, 1975, pp. 16 [annotated separately]; Stoner, John K., *Bicentennial Studies for the Church,* Akron: Congregational Peace Education Program, n.d., pp. 31 [annotated separately].

"Conflict of Loyalties." *CanMenn* 8 (Jan. 29, 1960), 2. Anonymous letter to the editor responds to earlier article "Conflict of Loyalties" by Walter Waetkau in the vein that Paetkau didn't take a clear enough stand against nationalism.

Christner, Walter. Letter to the Editor. *GH* 69 (May 4, 1976), 393. Disagrees with the writer of "The Christian and the US Bicentennial" (Apr. 13, 1976), claiming that such uncritical participation in celebrating the Bicentennial denies Mennonite understandings of peace.

*Citizens and Disciples: Christian Essays on Nationalism.* Akron, Pa.: MCC Peace Section, [1974]. Pp. 30. MHL. Includes, annotated separately: Schroeder, David, "Nationalism and Internationalism: Ground Rules for a Discussion," 1-3; Lapp, John A., "The New Nationalism: A Pagan Cult or Man's Search for Meaning?" 4-9; Klaassen, Walter, "The Christian and the State: Biblical and Anabaptist Perspectives," 10-12; Longacre, James, "Religion and the State: the Contemporary American Scene," 13-17; Juhnke, James, "Mennonites and a Christian America," 18-20; Sawatsky, Rodney J., "Nationalism—Myths and Realities," 21-25; Redekop, John N., "Christians in a World of International Confrontation," 26-30.

Crouse, Susan Kay. "The Conscientious Objector: His Right to a Conscience." Research paper for American Religion: The Sacred and the Civil class, 1980. Pp. 12. BfC.

"Demonstrate Biblical Citizenship." *Menn 83* (Sept. 10, 1968), 566; "Resolution or [sic] Nationalism," *GH 61* (Nov. 5, 1968), 992-93. The 1968 resolution on nationalism as adopted by the GCMC at the Estes Park conference. A call to Christian internationalism which parallels our contribution to the welfare of the country we live in.

De Fehr, Albert William. "A Critique of 'An Analysis of Germanism and National Socialism in the Immigrant Newspaper of a Canadian Minority Group,' 1965." Student paper, AMBS, Elkhart, Ind., Feb., 1970. Pp. 12. AMBS.

Derstine, C. F. "Impressions of the Nazi Regime and its Effect on the Churches." *ChrMon 26* (Jan., 1934), 30-31. Support of U. S. Christians is due the church in Germany for its resistance to the race prejudice and nationalism of the Nazi state church.

Derstine, C. F. "Nationalism the Supreme Rival of Christianity." *ChrMon 30* (Feb., 1938), 61-62. Fascism, Nazism, and communism try to replace devotion to God with loyalty to the state.

Derstine, C. F. "The Great Controversy Between Christ and Antichrist." *ChrMon 34* (Oct., 1942), 318-20. Cites examples of Christians refusing to deify the state in seven countries.

Dick, Ernie (Review). *A Strategy for Peace*, by Frank H. Epp. Grand Rapids: Eerdmans, 1973. Pp.

128. "Essays 'Point Finger' at Exploitation and Injustice." *MennRep* 4 (Apr. 1, 1974), 8. Although the essays were delivered as addresses in the late 1960s and early 1970s, their message of striving after peace remains timely. Most helpful essays deal with themes of nationalism, dialogue between pacifists and nonpacifists, arms buildup, complicity of the Christian church in making war.

Drescher, John M. "Graham's Vietnam Visit." *GH* 60 (Feb. 1, 1967), 117. Drescher praises Graham's evangelistic work but seriously questions his identification, as an evangelist, with American nationalism and imperialism in Vietnam.

Dyck, Ernie. "The Border That Divides." *With* 4 (July, 1971), 30. Views on the problems of American influence and Canadian nationalism.

Eby, Omar. "Rhodesia Feels the Squeeze of a Religious Recipe of Nationalism." *CanMenn* 18 (July 24, 1970), 4, 9. A comprehensive review of the Rhodesian racial situation. Challenges the church to condemn the oppressive action of the Smith regime and to establish a work of reconciliation.

Ediger, Peter J. "Encounters at Explo." *Forum* (Oct., 1972), 4-5. The People's Christian Coalition and Mennonite Central Committee were represented at Explo, a Campus Crusade for Christ event, to wtiness for peace in the midst of Americanized civil religion.

Ediger, Peter J. "Here Comes Myth America." *With* 9 (Mar., 1976), 12. Explores many of the American myths which are especially highlighted in the bicentennial celebrations.

Epp, Frank H. "A New Nationalism." *CanMenn* 5 (Apr. 5, 1957), 2. Decries the new Canadian nationalism which renounces a world citizenship in favor of a narrower identity based on economics.

Epp, Frank H. "For Mennonites: A Place to Stand." *ChrLiv* 20 (Apr., 1973), 25-29, 33. Tenets for modern Mennonites include loyalty to God before loyalty to culture or nation.

Ewert, Mrs. D. P. Letter to the Editor. *Menn* 89 (Feb. 19, 1974), 126-27. The Christian church must not reduce itself to a position of nation-worship by overlooking corruption in high places or baptizing military strategies, since to be truly pro-American is to be a world citizen.

Flaming, E. W. Letter to the Editor. *ChrLead* 39 (July 20, 1976), 16. The Bicentennial is an opportunity and challenge to revive America with an injection of the same religious faith and dedication that brought about the birth of a great nation.

Franz, Delton. "Mennonites and Civil Religion." N.d. Pp. 4. MLA/BeC.

Friesen, LeRoy. "The Church and the Middle East (3): Palestinian Christians—People with an Uncertain Future." *MennRep* 6 (May 17, 1976), 7. Explores Palestinian Christian response to Palestinian nationalism and Jewish occupation, and the question of using violence.

Friesen, Tom (Review). *Our Star-Spangled Faith,* by Donald B. Kraybill. Scottdale: Herald Press, 1976. Pp. 216. *Menn* 92 (Mar. 1, 1977), 157. Kraybill's exposure of America's "God and country" religion helps Christians distinguish the symbols of the military and government from those of Christianity.

Gautsche, Charles. "'Sermons for 76.'" *GH* 69 (Jan. 13, 1976), 17-19. One of the three subjects presented for possible sermons in 1976 is the theme of nationalism and what it means to give primary loyalty to the Kingdom of God rather than to the state.

General Conference Mennonite Church. "Resolution or Nationalism." *GH* 61 (Nov. 5, 1968), 992-93. Calls for a spirit of internationalism in the face of advocated military solutions to exaggerated national threats.

Gingerich, Melvin. "Citizenship in the Kingdom of God." Sermon, College Mennonite Church, Goshen, Ind., July 1, 1973. Pp. 4. MHL.

Gingerich, Melvin. *Youth and Christian Citizenship.* Scottdale: Herald Press, 1949. Pp. 204. A collection of 50 essays written for high school age Christians on a variety of practical citizenship issues raised by the church and state relationship. Topics include nationalism, patriotism, political participation, racism, communism, community vitality, ecology, and more.

Good, I. Merle. "A Conscientious Objector's View of the Bicentennial." *FQ* 3 (May, June, July, 1976), 2. Reprinted from *The Washington Post,* (1976). Sketches Mennonite history of conscientious objection to war, and outlines the dilemma facing Mennonites condemned by wider society for not joining wholeheartedly in celebrating the American Revolution.

Hackman, Walton. "'Pursue What Makes for Peace.'" *GH* 66 (Feb. 6, 1973), 108-109. The growing civil religion in the US increasingly blesses national interests and policies, including military actions.

Harding, Vincent G. "Our Crisis of Obedience." *Menn* 81 (Feb. 15, 1966), 109-110. In response to President Johnson's prosecution of the war in Vietnam, the writer calls for rejection of war and nationalism as incompatible with the gospel of Jesus.

Hart, Lawrence H. "Two Hundred Years of Dishonor." *Menn* 91 (May 18, 1976), 334-35; "The Native American: Two Hundred Years of Dishonor." *With* 9 (Feb., 1976), 20. A Cheyenne Mennonite takes the occasion of the US Bicentennial to reflect on Native American efforts to live at peace with a white government that has reciprocated with broken treaties and massacres.

Hatfield, Mark O. "Civil Religion." *EV* 86 (Aug. 10, 1973), 4, 5, 11. Senator Hatfield, in his commencement address at Messiah College, warns that the Christian, like every citizen, cannot avoid being political in some sense, but the political realm must be under the authority of Jesus Christ and not of the surrounding culture.

Hatfield, Mark O. "If Christ Be Lord." *EV* 89 (June 10, 1976), 16. Transcript of Senator Hatfield's remarks at the National Association of Evangelicals meeting, Feb. 24, 1976, in which he warned against encultured Christianity which makes God and Caesar one and the same.

Hatfield, Mark O. "Misplaced Allegiance." *Menn* 88 (Mar. 27, 1973), 216. Statement given by the Senator at the National Prayer Breakfast in Washington, D.C., calls Americans to distinguish between the god of American civil religion and the God revealed in Scriptures and in Jesus Christ who commands justice and peace.

Hatfield, Mark O. "Spiritual Revolution." *ChrLead* 39 (July 6, 1976), 2. "Obedience to Christ can exercise a vital influence in our corporate life as a nation and people, but only on His own terms" is the theme of these excerpts from a National Prayer Breakfast speech.

Hershberger, Guy F. "False Patriotism." *MQR* 1, Part 1, (Jan., 1927), 9-27; Part 2, (Apr., 1927), 29-45. An exposé of the attitudes and actions of earlier Americans together with an analysis of the dynamics of nationalism.

Hershberger, Guy F. "Nationalism and Internationalism: The Christian Witness to the State." (Part 4). *GH* 53 (Oct. 18, 1960), 913, 924. The Christian will witness for cooperative internationalism as opposed to competitive and conflicting nationalism.

Hershberger, Guy F. "Prophets, Priests, and Kings: Civil Religion, Then and Now." Sermon delivered at Trinity Mennonite Church, Mar. 3, 1974, in Glendale, Ariz. Typescript. Goshen: AMC Hist. MSS 1-171 Box 54. Defines civil religion as the form of idolatry in which men give their highest allegiance not to God but to Caesar, and then use worship and religious ceremony for the glorification of Caesar and the state. Traces civil religion from the Old Testament to the modern political situation.

Hershberger, Guy F. "The Mennonite Peace Witness Beyond North America." *GH* 58 (May 18, 1965), 427. In a time of the emergence of many new nations and growing nationalism, Mennonites must spend (and are spending) more time and money in peace witness around the world.

Hershberger, Guy F. "The People of God, Then and Now." *GH* 67 (Jan. 1, 1974), 6-8. Hershberger briefly recounts the history of the People of God from Abraham to the present noting that the church has taken on a subservient role of "spiritual advisor to power and prestige" and needs to once again assume the role of prophet to nationalism and the glorification of American interests.

Hess, James R. "The Christian and the Bicentennial Celebrations." *ST* 44 (Apr., 1976), 24-26. Reprinted from *Pastoral Messenger.* Among the positive aspects of life in the US is the fact that nearly 5 times as much of the Gross National Product goes for social services as for military expenditures.

Hess, James R. "The Christian and the US Bicentennial." *GH* 69 (Apr. 13, 1976), 306-307. Government is ordained by God, but not called to operate according to the Sermon on the Mount. Christians should neither endorse militarism nor excessively criticize the government.

Hess, James R. (Review). *Our Star-Spangled Faith,* by Donald B. Kraybill. Scottdale: Herald Press, n.d. Pp. 216. *ST* 45 (Sept., 1977), 22-23. The book calls for avoidance of all civil religion, but the reviewer cautions that this will mean that the state as well as the church will separate religious values from national business.

Hochstetler, Walter. "Albert B. Cleage, Jr. and Black Religious Nationalism." Paper for Church and Race class, AMBS, Elkhart, Ind., May, 1970. Pp. 11. AMBS.

Hurd, Menno B. "Menno's Opinion." *GH* 69 (Oct. 12, 1976), 782. Compares the 1975 celebration of Anabaptist heritage with the 1976 celebration of the national Bicentennial, and cautions Mennonites to "worship neither at the Liberty Bell in Philadelphia nor the Memorial Shaft in Witmarsum."

Jacobs, Donald R. *The Christian Stance in a Revolutionary Age.* Scottdale: Herald Press, Focal Pamphlet No. 14, 1968. Pp. 32. Describes the factors influencing social change in the

developing nations and the issues, such as tribalism, racism, and nationalism, which confront the church in these areas. Then, in this context, Jacobs contends that peace and development are two parts of the same issue—that any peace theology must necessarily speak to the issues of distributive justice.

Janzen, Gerald. "A Christian's Response to the Canada Question." *MBH* 17 (July 7, 1978), 5-6. Commitment to the gospel of peace means that Canadian Mennonites must abandon racism and ethnic self-interest in seeking reconciliation with French Quebec.

Jost, Connie. Letter to the Editor. *ChrLead* 39 (Mar. 2, 1976), 11. Does not support the *Christian Leader*'s opposition to Mennonites joining America's bicentennial celebration.

Juhnke, James C. *A People of Two Kingdoms: The Political Acculturation of the Kansas Mennonites.* Newton: Faith and Life Press, 1975. Pp. 215. Explains that this process of acculturation was fundamentally shaped by the "abrasive encounter of Mennonite nonresistance with American nationalism" and charts the encounter from the shadows cast on the civic role of the Mennonite German-Americans by the Spanish-American War, through the essential Mennonite-American compatibility of the Progressive Era, through the shattering of that easy course in World War I, through the efforts to bridge the conflict in the inter-war period, to the new phase—characterized by voting and alternative service—during World War II.

Juhnke, James C. "Freedom and the American Revolution." *Menn* 91 (June 22, 1976), 417-18. Bicentennial celebrations reinforce the idea that freedom is a military achievement, when in fact revolution may not have been the only alternative in 1775; similarly, political independence later became a license to oppress blacks and Native Americans.

Juhnke, James C. "Mennonite Benevolence and Civic Identity: the Post-War Compromise." *MennLife* 25 (Jan., 1970), 34-37. Examines the thesis that Mennonite relief and service efforts, historically most energetic during wartime, originate in American nationalism. Notes that these efforts may in fact grow from a Mennonite need to contribute "meaningfully and sacrificially toward national goals" in a time when others are offering their lives to the war effort.

Juhnke, James C. "Mennonites and a Christian America." *Citizens and Disciples: Christian Essays on Nationalism.* Akron: MCC Peace Section, [1974], 18-20. MHL. Suggests that, instead of vainly trying to escape participation in the political communities, Mennonites would do well to renew the affirmations that Jesus is Lord and that the kingdom of God takes precedence over all earthly nations, and to recover a prophetic witness to the powers more comprehensive than the refusal of military service.

Juhnke, James C. "Mennonites and Afrikaners." *MBH* 11 (Aug. 24, 1972), 4-5; *MennLife* 27 (Dec., 1972), 118-19; "Mennonites and Afrikaners: Losing Grip?" *Menn* 87 (May 30, 1972), 365, 366. Compares and contrasts the South African Afrikaners and the Mennonites on such issues as: nationalism, language and literature, acculturation, etc. within a larger consideration of the issues of acculturation and race relations.

Kauffman, Allen L. Letter to the Editor. *GH* 69 (Mar. 2, 1976), 188-89. Disagrees with the picture of American liberty painted by Benjamin Lapp ("The Bicentennial: Two Views," Feb. 10, 1976), and suggests Mennonites wait to celebrate freedom of religion until the anniversary of the Constitution or Bill of Rights, instead of celebrating the American Revolution in 1976.

Kauffman, Richard A. "Beggar to Beggar." *GH* 68 (May 20, 1975), 384-85. Urges Christians who separate the peoplehood of the nation from that of the church to witness to the Christian patriots in the upcoming celebration of the American Revolution.

Keeney, William E. (Review). *The Captain America Complex: The Dilemma of Zealous Nationalism,* by Robert Jewett. Philadelphia: Westminster Press, 1973. Pp. 286. *Menn* 89 (Oct. 29, 1974), 637. Summarizes the contents of this book, centered around the thesis that American people misread the realities of history and adopt means to save the world which result in destruction and defeat. Reviewer pays special attention to the author's view of the use and results of violence.

Kehler, Larry. "Evangelism, Militarism, and Nationalism." *Menn* 86 (June 22, 1971), 405-408. Relating the idolatry of nationalism and of militarism to the evangelistic message is an integral part of the proclamation of the gospel to repentance.

Kehler, Larry. "Mennonite Communities and the 1976 Dilemma." *Menn* 91 (Mar. 16, 1976), 182-83. Examines the responses of Mennonites in towns across the US to local Bicentennial celebrations.

Kehler, Larry. "Structures and Nationalism Looms [sic] Large at MCC Meeting." *MBH* 14 (Feb. 7, 1975), 10-12. At the annual meeting, the committee passed a resolution on world hunger calling for reduced military expenditure and increased food development.

Keim, Ray; Beechy, Atlee; and Beechy, Winifred. *The Church: The Reconciling Community.* Scottdale: Mennonite Publishing House; Newton: Faith and Life Press, 1970. Pp. 92. Examines the direction set for the church by the reconciling work of Jesus and looks at such issues as militarism, nationalism, human rights, racism, poverty, crime and violence as tasks for the church which embodies that reconciliation.

King, Martin Luther, Jr. "Transformed Nonconformist." *ChrLiv* 11 (Feb., 1964), 9-10, 38. Reprinted from *Strength to Love,* by King; Harper and Row, 1963. Urges nonconformity to the world in matters of nationalism, militarism, racism, and lifestyle.

Klaassen, Walter. "The Christian and the State: Biblical and Anabaptist Perspectives." *Menn* 89 (July 9, 1974), 428-29; *Citizens and Disciples: Christian Essays on Nationalism.* Akron: MCC Peace Section, [1974], 10-12. MHL. In both the Old and New Testaments the concepts of "people" and "nation" are distinguished with the concept of "people" taking priority. The majority of Anabaptists also expressed this biblical principle in the doctrine of the "two kingdoms." Finally, while neither the biblical nor Anabaptist traditions can be used as prescriptive law today, these perspectives present models with which to shape contemporary responses to the issues of church and state.

Klopfenstein, Janette K. "The Bicentennial in Archbold." *GH* 68 (Dec. 30, 1975), 926-27. Reflects on the visit of the Bicentennial Freedom Train to Archbold, and the various approaches Mennonites are taking to the celebration of revolution and history.

Kraus, C. Norman. "Christian Perspectives on Nationalism, Racism, and Poverty in American Life." *Peacemakers in a Broken World.* Ed. John A. Lapp. Scottdale: Herald Press, 1969, 30-42. Calls Christians to disassociate themselves from national selfishness and a "might makes right" mind set to understand the black power movement and to work for fair employment and aid policies.

Kraybill, Donald B. "Civil Religion vs. New Testament Christianity." *GH* 69 (May 11, 1976), 402-3. Kraybill draws distinctions between American civil religion, which uses religious language to legitimize national policies such as militarism, and New Testament Christianity, which follows the narrow way of Jesus.

Kraybill, Donald B. *Our Star-Spangled Faith.* Scottdale, Pa.: Herald Press, 1976. Pp. 216. An anthology of examples, quotations, slogans, photos that illustrate the historical and contemporary merger of religion and politics that has resulted in an American civil religion that is idolotrous by nature.

Krehbiel, Edward. *Nationalism, War, and Society.* New York: Macmillan, 1916. Pp. 276. A discussion of the history of nationalism and war including recent developments, together with suggestions for political alternatives.

Kreider, Alan. "The US Bicentennial." *GH* 68 (Oct. 21, 1975), 749-51; "The American Bicentennial: Historical Propaganda and Eternal Truths." *MennRep* 5 (Nov., 1975), 8-9; "The Bicentennial: Not to Be Ignored or Deplored—But No Occasion for Flagwaving." *Menn* 90 (Oct. 28, 1975), 602-604. Americans will celebrate the Bicentennial either authentically, by advocating revolution for all oppressed people, or fraudulently, by ignoring the violent nature of the American Revolution. Americans who give primary loyalty to Jesus should use the occasion to reflect on the history in which they have participated.

Landis, Maurice W. "The Secularization of the Church and Civil Religion, Part 2." *GfT* 8 (Nov.-Dec., 1973), 10-11, 15. By advocating amnesty for those who broke the Selective Service law, the church is violating the principle of separation of church and state and becoming an instrument of lawlessness.

Lapp, Alice W. (Review). *Our Star-Spangled Faith,* by Donald B. Kraybill. Scottdale: Herald Press, 1976. *FQ* 3 (May, June, July, 1976), 4. Kraybill's discussion of patriotism and biblical foundations for respecting government helps clear up the common confusion between loyalty to God and to country.

Lapp, Benjamin F. "The Bicentennial: Two Views. 2. My Attitude Toward My Country." *GH* 69 (Feb. 10, 1976), 103-104. While the Christian's allegiance is to the heavenly kingdom rather than the earthly country, the Christian is also called to be subject to the existing authorities, not to criticize the government in the name of peace.

Lapp, Helen and Sam, "Raising Children in a Bicentennial Year." *ChrLiv* 23 (Sept., 1976), 6-9. Conflict of loyalty experienced by people committed to peace in a year of patriotism.

Lapp, John A. *A Dream for America.* Scottdale, Pa.: Herald Press, 1976. Pp. 128. Bicentennial reflection calls the nation to attend to the issues of the moment—issues such as racial equality, disproportionate distribution of global resources, learnings from the Vietnam War, conflict resolution, honest government, civil religion, etc.—and decide to implement in our time the worthy goals of the Declaration of Independence.

Lapp, John A. "Bicentennial Choices." *ChrLiv* 23 (May, 1976), 17-18. Adapted from *A Dream for America,* John Lapp, Herald Press, 1976. American society today includes forces moving toward both revolution and counterrevolution.

Lapp, John A. "Civil Religion Is But Old Establishment Writ Large." *Kingdom, Cross, and Community.* Ed. John R. Burkholder and Calvin Redekop. Scottdale: Herald Press, 1976, 196-207. Lapp studies the definition of civil religion among scholars of society and religion, traces its rise in American society as the overarching political religion, and asserts the need for the church to act as a dissenting institution.

Lapp, John A. "The New Nationalism: A Pagan Cult or Man's Search for Meaning?" *Citizens and Disciples: Christian Essays on Nationalism.* Akron: MCC Peace Section, [1974], 4-9. MHL. Considers the historical context giving rise to western nationalism and then defines the essentials of the "new" nationalisms of Asia, Africa, and Latin America. Invites readers not to discount too quickly the idea of a nation. While there must be a tension between the people of God and the people of a nation, the church is properly concerned for the legitimate aspirations of a people to control their own lives in freedom and justice.

Lapp, John A. "Understanding Civil Religion." *ChrLiv* 20 (Oct., 1973), 15, 24-25. Essay traces the philosophical roots of civil religion, comments on its role in the social order, and attempts to separate the American Way of Life from authentic Christian claims.

Lefever, Harry G. (Review). *The Strange Tactics of Extremism,* by Harry and Bonaro Overstreet. W. W. Norton, 1964. Pp. 315. *ChrLiv* 12 (Aug., 1965), 24-26. Recommends the book as a review of the methods and assumptions of the Radical Right, and its status as a pseudo-religion.

Lehman, Celia. "The Middle Man." *Swords into Plowshares: A Collection of Plays About Peace and Social Justice.* Ed. Ingrid Rogers. Elgin: The Brethren Press, 1983, 109-124. A choral reading which explores the issue of civil religion as well as other aspects of the church and state relationship.

Lind, Millard C. "Israeli or Jacobi?" *GH* 62 (June 10, 1969), 514-16. The relevance of the Old Testament to the contemporary Middle East situation lies in the biblical witness to a new community which transcends nationalism.

Longacre, James C. "Mennonites and the Bicentennial." *ChrLead* 38 (July 8, 1975), 24. The bicentennial year provides an opportunity to witness to the Kingdom of God.

Longacre, James C. "Religion and the State: The Contemporary American Scene." *Menn* 89 (July 9, 1974), 430-32; *Citizens and Disciples: Christian Essays on Nationalism.* Akron: MCC Peace Section, [1974], 13-17. Pp. 30. MHL. The American church, by taking the symbols of God's people and relating them to the nation rather than the church, has limited the parameters of faith to personal piety and deprived itself of an identity, a vision, and a mission separate from that of the nation.

Longacre, James C. "The Kingdom and the US Bicentennial." *GH* 68 (July 1, 1975), 477-78; "The Bicentennial: Dilemma and Opportunity." *Menn* 90 (July 8, 1975), 410-11. Instead of participating in bicentennial celebrations, the church should witness to the Kingdom of God, since participation perpetuates the picture of the church baptizing national goals.

Lord, Charles R. "An Exercise in Integration: In *God* We Trust." Paper presented to War and Peace in the Bible class, AMBS, Elkhart, Ind., Jan. 25, 1980. Pp. 21. AMBS.

"Message from the Detroit Peace Conference." *Menn* 69 (Feb. 16, 1954), 105, 110. A call to reject nationalism, violence, and war as inconsistent with the missionary and universal character of the church.

Mason, Walter J. Letter to the Editor. *ChrLead* 41 (Jan. 31, 1978), 16. The testimony of peace and rejection of nationalism and warfare are so much of an absolute to the development of the perfect person that to try to take them from the Scriptures and reduce them to options based on rationalization seems to be a tragic development.

Mennonite Central Committee Peace Section. "Christians and the Bicentennial: Facing the Ambiguities." *Menn* 90 (July 8, 1975), 412-13. Statement for reflection focuses on distinguishing loyalty to the nation from loyalty to God.

Miller, Marlin E. "Degrees of Glory." *GH* 73 (Feb. 12, 1980), 129-32. Funeral sermon for Doris Janzen Longacre focuses in part on her concern for the false power of nationalism and military violence.

Mullet, James. "Nationalism—Blessing or Curse?" *GH* 68 (Feb. 25, 1975), 140. Nationalism in its place may be helpful, but out of control it builds walls of separation and tests Christians to see if their primary loyalty is to Caesar or Christ.

Nelson, Boyd N. "A Peaceful Look at Civil Religion." *GH* 64 (July 20, 1971), 620-21. Explores the benefits to be derived from a concept like "civil religion" as well as the liabilities of the concept.

Neufeld, Elmer. "Peace—the Way of the Cross." *ChrLiv* 7 (Jan., 1960), 6-7, 34. Prose poem relating peace to issues of militarism, nationalism, and racism.

Nigh, Paul A. "Internationally Speaking." *EV* 89 (Jan. 25, 1976), 5. A Canadian congratulates the United States on its bicentennial but at the same time cautions against national pride which uses violence to obtain freedom from oppression.

Nisimura, Umeno. "MCC Peace Section in Japan." Paper presented to Mennonite History class, AMBS, Elkhart, Ind., May, 1963. Pp. 8. MHL.

Ollenburger, Ben C. "Mennonites, 'Civil Religion,' and the American Bicentennial." An interview with James C. Juhnke. *Direction* 5 (July, 1976), 15-21. It is not the task of the church to abolish civil government and civil religion. Our task is to restore the integrity of the church's symbols as separate and distinct from those of the state.

"Proposed Resolution on Nationalism." *Menn* 83 (July 9, 1968), 462-63. A statement proposed for adoption at the 1968 conference of the GCMC. The state has a legitimate, limited function which is to be respected, but to equate the state's action with God's action is idolatrous. One's loyalty and commitment are given first to God who is the Lord of history.

Peachey, Paul L. *Your Church and Your Nation: An Appeal to American Churchmen.* Washington, DC: The Church Peace Mission, [1963]. Pp. 22. MHL. Contends that to construct a theological sanction of war just because conflict is inevitable in a fallen world is no more justifiable than to construct a theology of segregation because we have not achieved human equality.

Peachey, Paul L. (Review). *The War Myth,* by Donald A. Wells. Pegasus, n.d. and *Peace, Power and Protest,* ed. Donald Evans. Ryerson, n.d. *ChrCent* 85 (Apr. 17, 1968), 486-87. Discusses two books with themes pertinent to peacemaking—the first an analysis of the rationalizations for war and the second a Canadian perspective on nationalism.

Pierce, Glen. "Personal Reflections on the NAE Convention." *EV* 89 (June 10, 1976), 6. The National Association of Evangelicals convention in Washington, DC, showed a strong flavor or nationalism, even promoting militarism.

Ratzlaff, Vernon. "A Christian Thinks About His Nation: A Response to Eight Lectures in March." *MennRep* 4 (May 13, 1974), 7. Responding in part to MCC Peace Section Assembly lectures, Ratzlaff reflects on the dream of the American destiny, civil religion, and an appropriate Christian concern for the nation that does not idolize it.

Redekop, Calvin W. "The Church for the World." *ChrLiv* 12 (Jan., 1965), 15-17. Reflections on the nature of the free church tradition, including relationship to state and nationalism.

Redekop, John H. "Billy James Hargis' Perception of the American Constitution, Government, and Society." *JChSoc* 1 (Spring, 1965), 43. Survey of Hargis' political orientation and his place in the American tradition of civil religion.

Redekop, John H. "Christians in a World of International Confrontation." *Menn* 89 (July 9, 1974), 433-35. Describes international exploitation by firms based in North America, and the rise of nationalism which counters this colonialism. Concludes that the present nation-state system produces injustice and inequality, against which Christians must speak out.

Redekop, John H. "Civil Religion in Canada." *Direction* 5 (July, 1976), 10-14. By definition of the status of civil religion in the United States, civil religion is hardly discernible in Canada.

Redekop, John H. "How to Be Christian in Politics." *MBH* 16 (Oct. 28, 1977), 6-8. Anabaptist conservative Christianity parts company with political conservatism on such things as super-patriotism, militant nationalism.

Redekop, John N. "Christians in a World of International Confrontation." *Citizens and Disciples: Christian Essays on Nationalism.* Akron: MCC Peace Section, [1974], 26-30. Pp. 30. MHL. Contends that nationalism is neither primarily a blessing or a curse but a fact, a dynamic which can be used for good or evil. A constructive nationalism recognizes the nation-state system as sub-Christian, checks militant nationalism without becoming a crusading universalist, and listens to prophetic criticisms.

Sawatsky, Rodney J. "Nationalism—Myths and Realities." *Citizens and Disciples: Christian Essays on Nationalism.* Akron: MCC Peace Section, [1974], 21-25. Pp. 30. MHL. The distinctives between Canadian and American nationalism make clear that the issue of nationalism should not be oversimplified. Rather we should learn to differentiate between useful national mythologies and those which deny the place of prophetic religion and become idolatrous by deifying a certain social and political order.

Sawatsky, Rodney J. (Review). *A People of Two Kingdoms: The Political Acculturation of the Kansas Mennonites,* by James C. Juhnke. North Newton, Kansas: Faith and Life Press, 1975. Pp. 215. *MQR* 50 (Jan., 1976), 72-73. Juhnke defines the dualism of the title as "conflict between the ethic of modern nationalism and the ethic of traditional Mennonitism" characterized by pacifism, apoliticism, and German ethnic identity.

Schmidt, Jay. Letter to the Editor. *ChrLead* 39 (Apr. 13, 1976), 14. The Bicentennial ought to be a time to sense the need to return to the call of discipleship.

Schrag, James. *Gerald Burton Winrod: The Defender.* Unpublished seminar paper at Bethel College, N. Newton, 1966. Pp. 48. A study of the personality and organization of Winrod and his influence upon Mennonites, particularly in the areas of nationalism and anti-Semitism.

Schroeder, David. "Nationalism and Internationalism: Ground Rules for a Discussion." *Citizens and Disciples: Christian Essays on Nationalism.* Akron: MCC Peace Section, [1974], 1-3. MHL. Also in *Menn* 89 (July 9, 1974), 426-27. Suggests that there are basic biblical principles that can help to form a frame of reference within which the questions of nationalism and internationalism can be discussed constructively. Schroeder concludes that Christians are called to be citizens of the state also, discerning carefully among national policies which work for and against justice and goodness.

Shank, J. Ward. "Civil Religion and Anti-Nationalism." *ST* 44 (Feb., 1976), 8-10. Scriptures advise Christians to be neither pro-civil religion nor anti-nationalist, but subject to the authorities.

Shank, J. Ward. "The Christian and Nationalism." *ST* 38 (Nov., 1970), 4. The dedicated Christian should not be caught up in the wave of revolution. He or she should continue to express loyalty and appreciation to country with the limits of his higher duty to God.

Shank, J. Ward (Editorial). "Nationalism and Anti-Nationalism." *ST* 41 (Apr., 1973), 5. There is no inherent wrong in expressing loyalty and regard for one's country even in the face of its wrongdoing. Rather the sin is in the negativist and antinational attitudes.

Shenk, Dan; Lehman, Pauline; Kennel, Ron; Landis, Jim. "Doing It Differently July 4." *GH* 69 (Oct. 19, 1976), 797-99. Four Mennonite writers describe how their congregations observed the Bicentennial creatively through worship.

Shetler, Sanford G. "Churches in Bicentennial Swing." *GfT* 11 (Jan.-Feb., 1976), 20-21. Nonresistant Christians can still honor the founders of the nation because of the biblical mandate to pray for and obey those in authority.

Shetler, Sanford G. "'Civil Religion'—Let's Quit the Confusion." *ST* 44 (Oct., 1976), 8-9. From *Guidelines for Today.* Peace activists, while rejecting God-and-country ethics, are instead championing a new kind of civil religion in which the church may scrutinize the government, but not vice versa.

Sider, Ronald J. "Aside: Where Have All the Liberals Gone?" *The Other Side* 12 (May-June, 1976), 42-44. The essence of liberal theology can be described as when the current culture supplies the operational norms and values for a significant number of evangelicals and mainline church people. Concerns like racism, militarism, civil religion, and unjust economic structures are not spoken to because of the liberal context.

Sider, Ronald J. "Zeal, Zealot." *Baker's Dictionary of Christian Ethics,* ed. Carl F. H. Henry. Grand Rapids, MI: Baker Book House Co., 1973, 724. Jesus' ethic of love and nonresistance was developed in the face of and in tension with the Zealot nationalism.

Smith, Elbert. "Memorial Day Message, 1976— The Essence of Freedom." *EV* 90 (May 25, 1977), 5. This article, written in the bicentennial year, urges Americans to look again at the cause of freedom, those values for which our forebears died, and accept the challenge of the struggle for freedom today.

Steiner, Susan Clemmer. "Nationalism: Not Throwing Out the Baby with the Bathwater." *MennRep* 6 (Feb. 9, 1976), 7. Nationalism holds the pitfall of developing a primary identification with one's country rather than with the church of Jesus Christ which is international and relies on no given political system for existence.

Stoltzfus, Luke G. (Review). *A Strategy for Peace,* by Frank Epp. Grand Rapids: Wm. B. Eerdmans, 1973. *GH* 67 (Oct. 1, 1974), 758. Recommends the book for its fresh approach to issues of nationalism, North American militarism, separation of church and state, a biblical response to communism, evangelism and peace witness.

Stoner, John K. "Evangelicals Convene in Capitol; Resolve to Let Freedom Ring." *ChrLead* 39 (Mar. 30, 1976), 18. Comments on the Bicentennial Convocation, the joint conventions of the National Association of Evangelicals and the National Religious Broadcasters, Feb. 22-25, 1976.

Stoner, John K. (Review). *Between a Rock and a Hard Place,* by Mark Hatfield. Waco, Tex.: Word Books, 1976. Pp. 224. *Menn* 91 (Oct. 26, 1976), 633; *ChrLead* 39 (Aug. 17, 1976), 14. Hatfield prods the church to separate its vision from the destiny of America, examining questions of nuclear war, violence, and patriotism.

Studer, Gerald C. "The Bicentennial: Two Views. 1. Will a Christian Be a Patriot?" *GH* 69 (Feb. 10, 1976), 102-103; *Menn* 91 (June 22, 1976, 426-27. Christians cannot divide their loyalty between God and the state; they are called to live wholly according to God's kingdom.

Toews, John A. "Fly Your Flag but Not Too High." *CanMenn* 15 (June 13, 1967), 1, 26. An appeal to Mennonites to distinguish between nationality and nationalism and to subordinate nationalism to the kingdom of God.

Toews, Paul. "America's National Faith and the Bicentennial." *Direction* 5 (July, 1976), 3-9. American civil religion carries the historic sense of being special and chosen. The church must learn to distinguish loyalties and priorities in relationship to civil religion.

Toews, Paul. "Religion American Style." *ChrLead* 39 (Jan. 20, 1976), 2. Explores the background and hazards of civil religion, especially in the United States.

Toews, Paul (Review). *A Dream for America,* by John A. Lapp. Scottdale: Herald Press, 1976. In *ChrLead* 39 (Oct. 12, 1976), 7. The bicentennial provides the occasion for this discerning discussion of contemporary social/political, economic/religious ills confronting us.

Toews, Paul (Review). *Our Star-Spangled Faith,* by Donald B. Kraybill. Scottdale: Herald Press, 1976. In *ChrLead* 39 (Oct. 12, 1976), 7. A most revealing display of that phenomenon commonly known as civil religion.

Wiebe, Katie Funk. "Power and the Gospel." *GH* 73 (Dec. 30, 1980), 1045. On the dangers of identifying the Christian gospel with political power and force.

Wiebe, Katie Funk. "The Gospel and the Nation." *ChrLead* 39 (Apr. 13, 1976), 19. Reports on the MCC Peace Assembly on "Civil Religion and the American Empire" held Mar. 21-23, 1976 in Washington, DC.

Wiebe, Katie Funk. "Two Sides of a Counterfeit Coin." *ChrLead* 39 (Apr. 27, 1976), 19. Looks at how politics gets involved in church decision making. Civil religion in government and politics in church life are two sides of a counterfeit coin.

Wood, James E., Jr. *The Problem of Nationalism in Church-State Relationships.* Focal Pamphlet No. 18. Scottdale: Herald Press, 1969. Pp. 31. A paper read at the Evangelicals in Social Action Peace Witness Seminar at Eastern Mennonite College in 1967. Exposes the idolatrous nature of nationalism as a denial of the universalism of the gospel.

Yoder, Edward. "A New Statism: Peace Principles from a Scriptural Viewpoint." Part 1. *GH* 27 (Jan. 17, 1935), 914-15. Christians must beware of a growing mood of nationalism and prepare to witness against "modern Caesar worship."

Yoder, Edward. *Compromise with War.* Akron: MCC, 1943. Pp. 15. A critique of liberalism's capitulation to nationalism and violence, focusing particularly on the writings of Charles C. Morrison, editor of *The Christian Century.*

Yoder, Edward. "Nationalism—A False Faith." *GH Supplement* 37 (Feb., 1945), 942-43. Extreme nationalism neglects and destroys the values needed to preserve humankind.

Yoder, John H. "A Historic Free Church View." *Church Unity in North America: A Symposium.* Ed. J. Robert Nelson. St. Louis: The Bethany Press, 1958, 89-97. Pp. 208. Within a broader discussion of ecumenism, holds that one of the most formidable obstacles to Christian unity is the churches' "unhesitating consent to nationalism in its demonic military form."

Yoder, John H. "Our Nationality? Christian: The Way of Peace in a World at War." Part 2. *GH* 54 (July 25, 1961), 645-46. No political nation, no geographical homeland, can take precedence over the heavenly citizenship which is given a Christian in the new birth. Nationalism is testing many Christians on this point.

Yoder, John H. "The Christian Case for Democracy." *Journal of Religious Ethics* 5 (Fall, 1977), 209-223. To inflate the democratic claim to the point that faith becomes a civil religion is clearly wrong; however, if that sort of idolatry can be avoided we may indeed nurture and celebrate a relative democratization as "one of the prophetic ministries of a servant people in a world we do not control."

Zehr, Paul M. "After the Shouting." *GH* 69 (Nov. 23, 1976), 907-908. A post-mortem of the US Bicentennial observes its positive as well as negative effects on Mennonites. Among the latter is a greater confusion of church and state.

Zercher, John A. "The Need for Discernment." *EV* 88 (Oct. 10, 1975), 3. Recognizing that the history of the US entails much violence and destruction, our observances of the nation's bicentennial will call for discernment.

# B. Civil Defense

Bender, Harold S. "Civilian Defense: In the Midst of War—Thoughts for Nonresistants," (Part 8). *GH* 35 (Mar. 25, 1943), 1105-1106. The Peace Problems Committee recommends that nonresistant Christians not take part in Civilian Defense but find alternate ways of service.

"Church and Society Conference." Paper, reports, minutes, etc., of General Conference Mennonite Church conference, Chicago, Ill., Oct. 31-Nov. 3, 1961. Two volumes. MHL. Some pertinent commission papers include: "The Christian Church and Civil Defense;" "Christian Labor and Management Relations;" "The Christian in Race Relations;" "The Christian Church and the State;" "The Church, the State, and the Offender."

"Civil Defense and Christian Responsibility." *Menn* 77 (Mar. 20, 1962), 178-180. The MCC Peace Section's position statement on civil defense and preparation for nuclear war stresses the call to be a community of faith rather than of fear, one which witnesses against the false securities of preparation for war.

Driedger, Leo. "Fallout Shelters: A Discussion." Newton: Board of Christian Service, 1962. Pp. [27]. MHL. Presents arguments for and against shelters. Includes responses which a number of Mennonite churches in Kansas made to the government when Civil Defense officers investigated, sometimes without permission, their buildings to determine their utility as shelters. These responses deal directly with the issue of whether preparing for war is, to some extent, participation in warfare.

Ediger, Elmer. "Facing Civil Defense." *Menn* 70 (Dec. 6, 1955), 758, 765. Discusses the dilemma of Mennonite participation in Civil Defense, i.e., it is not purely military in purpose, but includes welfare service. Several guidelines for action are suggested.

Epp, Frank H. "Civil Defense Moves." *CanMenn* 7 (Apr. 10, 1959) 2. It is of paramount importance that changes in the Civil Defense structure be watched closely. A specific point of concern is whether the military or the civil authorities will assume top authority in an emergency.

Epp, Frank H. "Civil Defense or Civil Disaster." *CanMenn* 4 (May 11, 1956), 2. While the Health Minister defines disaster service as outside the scope of civil defense, Mennonites are primarily interested in civil disaster, not civil defense.

Epp, Frank H. "Confusion Re: Civil Defense." *CanMenn* 5 (Mar. 8, 1957), 2. Clarifies the official Mennonite stance on Civil Defense. Mennonites cooperate with Civil Defense in specific areas but give their greatest support to parallel church programs such as Mennonite Disaster Service.

Epp, Frank H. "Guidance Concerning Civil Defense." *CanMenn* 4 (May 4, 1956), 2. Support is expressed for the statement drafted by MCC Peace Section concerning Mennonite participation in Civil Defense. We must be ready to minister to human needs at all times, yet look first to our Lord for protection in any emergency.

Epp, Frank H. "The Church and Canadian Civil Defense." *CanMenn* 5, Part 1, (Nov. 1, 1957), 2; Part 2, (Nov. 8, 1957), 2; Part 3, (Nov. 15, 1957), 2, 7. Analyzes the civil defense program and Mennonite captivation with it. The church's response to human need does not mean compromising its central doctrine of love.

Epp, Frank H. "What About Civil Defense." *CanMenn* 3 (Feb. 4, 1955), 2. Civil defense is at best second to Christian service. It may, however, be a civil obligation which Mennonites should not seek to escape and in which a service to others can be given.

Epp, Lorene F. "Civil Defense and the Mennonite Viewpoint." Student paper, 1957. Pp. 16. MLA/ BeC.

Erb, Paul. "Is Civilian Defense War Participation?" *GH* 44 (Feb. 6, 1951), 123. A clarification of a previous editorial regarding civilian defense. There should be trained Mennonite emergency units which could be loaned to the parts of the civilian defense programs not inconsistent with a nonresistant faith.

"Guiding Principles in Special Emergencies." *Menn* 71 (June 19, 1956), 396, 398. At a time when nationwide preparation for war emergencies is at a height, MCC and MDS urge clear distinction between relief ministries and activities of Civil Defense which "support the war effort."

Gingerich, Orland. "Peace Churches Position on Civil Defense Is Clarified." *CanMenn* 5 (Apr. 5, 1957), 1, 5. Confusion over Mennonites assisting the armed forces by endorsing participation in Civil Defense programs is clarified in accordance with the official statement of the historic peace churches. Civil defense is seen as "organized self-help in case of disaster."

Hein, Marion [*sic, Marvin*]. "Basic Christian Principles Involved in the Problem of Civil Defense." Consultation on Civil Defense, Newton, KS, Feb. 7, 1961. Pp. 7. MLA/BeC.

Hein, Marvin. "Basic Principles Involved in Civil Defense." *ChrLead* 24 (Apr. 18, 1961), 12-14. Because Civil Defense intends to "preserve maximum civilian support of the war effort," Christians should work primarily through more positive channels, e.g. Mennonite Disaster Service.

Hershberger, Guy F. "Civil Defense: Guest Editorial." *GH* 55 (1962), 995-96. Commendation to those churches who have refused the use of their property as public shelters and have expressed their desire to save life by working through Mennonite Disaster Service in the event of a disaster.

"In This Time of Cold War." *CanMenn* 9 (Sept. 29, 1961), 2, 11. A reaffirmation of MDS and "A Plan of Action" to be used instead of complete, unconditional cooperation with Civil Defense.

Kauffman, Daniel. "Defense Drives." *GH* 34 (July 10, 1941), 313. Nonresistant Christians should not buy war bonds or contribute scrap aluminum to the defense aluminum drive.

Lehman, Milton. "Civil Defense—'Our Sure Defense'?" *GH* 55 (June 19, 1962), 561. We must realize that Civil Defense is an integral part of the national defense. The Peace Section statement on Civil Defense is a good guide for Mennonites.

Lind, Loren. "War or Peace?" *YCC* 43 (Mar. 18, 1962), 2. An examination of the real meaning of words used to describe the function of the military, e.g., civil defense, peace, strength.

Mennonite Central Committee. "Civil Defense." *GH* 49 (June 12, 1956), 558-59. A statement made by MCC and MDS suggests that Mennonites should not become integrally involved in Civilian Defense.

Mennonite Central Committee. "Civil Defense: A Statement of Guiding Principles," *GH* 52 (Aug. 11, 1959), 695. Mennonites should refrain from membership in Civil Defense organizations.

Mennonite Central Committee. "Civil Defense and Disaster Services," *GH* 55 (Feb. 20, 1962), 169. A position statement indicates that Mennonites will support those efforts which make war less likely and avoid a hysterical war spirit.

Metzler, Edgar. "The Church and the Civil Defense Dilemma." *CanMenn* 10 (Nov. 9, 1962), 5-6; "The Church and the Fallout Shelter Program." *GH* 55 (Nov. 13, 1962), 997-99. Presents the challenge the church faces in the increasing interest in fallout shelters and similar preparations for nuclear war. See also "Biblical Nonresistance, Christian Concern, and Civil Defense" in "Articles and Lectures for and about Mennonite Disaster Service." 1960-1966. Topic 13c.

"New Civil Defense Order Challenges Peace Churches." *CanMenn* 7 (July 3, 1959), 1, 6. Description of Canada's approach to Civil Defense and the cooperation possible with the Disaster Service organizations of the Mennonite church.

Neufeld, Elmer. "Alternative to Civil Defense." *GH* 54 (Apr. 4, 1961), 321; "MDS Meets Civil Defense." *Menn* 76 (May 23, 1961), 342, 346; "Alternative to Civil Defense." *CanMenn* 9 (Mar. 31, 1961), 5. Mennonites are encouraged to refrain from membership in Civil Defense organizations; MDS should be recognized as an alternative.

Neufeld, Elmer. "Mennonite Disaster Service and Civil Defense." *CanMenn* 9 (June 9, 1961), 2. Mennonite Disaster Service is a more appropriate Mennonite response to urgent need than full fledged cooperation with the Civil Defense program.

"Peace, War, and Social Issues: A Statement of the Position of the Amish Mennonite Churches." Officialy adopted by the ministerial body of the Beachy Amish Mennonite constituency . . . at Wellesley, Ont., Apr. 18-19, 1968. [n.p., 1968]. Pp. 16. MSHL. Topics include the role of government, military service, civil defense, the Christian's role in race relations, unions, etc.

"Position on Civil Defense Clarified." *CanMenn* 4 (Aug. 24, 1956), 2. The General Conference Mennonite Church recommends cooperation with Civil Defense and other disaster organizations according to certain guiding principles.

"Statement on Civil Defense Lists Guiding Principles." *CanMenn* 4 (May 4, 1956), 2. A statement of faith in terms of love and peace.

Schwartzentruber, Dorothy M. "Canadian Civil

Defense Consults Our Clergymen." *CanMenn* 5 (Aug. 16, 1957), 1, 6. Consultation urges the peace churches to speak with one voice and to be properly prepared for eventual disaster.

Snyder, John. "On the Civilian Bond Question." *GH* 36 (Sept. 23, 1943), 538-41. The nonresistant witness may be inconsistent and compromised if one buys civilian bonds.

"Two Men to Visit Arnprior Civil Defense College." *CanMenn* 4 (June 15, 1956), 1. Representatives of the historic peace churches of Ontario are appointed to visit the college near Ottawa.

"Two Ontario Men Attend Civil Defense Course." *CanMenn* 5 (Apr. 19, 1957), 1. Attenders are representatives of the historic peace churches of Ontario.

Toews, John A. "Do We Need an Alternative to Civil Defense?" *CanMenn* 2 (May 14, 1954), 7. A cautious aproval of the thesis that some areas of a nation's civil defense program may be acceptable to the Christian.

Vogt, Virgil. "A Nonresistant Christian Looks at Civil Defense." *ChrLiv* 2 (Dec., 1955), 4-5, 38-39. The Civil Defense system is intimately linked to the military in both its motivation and its tasks.

Von Wijk, Hein. "French Conscientious Objectors Under Military Jurisdiction." *CanMenn* 14 (Jan. 4, 1966), 3. A report on French CO's and their plight in camps under military jurisdiction. French law of July 9, 1965, introduced four kinds of service: the armed services; civil defense; technical aid (in overseas territories); and cooperation (in underdeveloped foreign countries). The last two (non-military) types of service are closed to CO's.

"What About Civil Defense." *CanMenn* 3 (Feb. 4, 1955), 2. An analysis of the Canadian Civil Defense program and its relationship to the Mennonite church.

# C. Flag

Brunk, George R., II. "The Flag Salute Problem." *ST* 12 (Mar., 1944), 123. Examines the position of the church, Supreme Court, and the War Department on the issue of saluting the flag.

Derstine, C. F. "The Flag Salute." *ChrMon* 33 (Aug., 1943), 255. Continued debate on the appropriateness of the flag salute for nonresistant Christians.

Derstine, C. F. "The Nonresistant Christian and the Flag Salute." *ChrMon* 35 (June, 1943), 191. The flag salute is a gesture of respect for the symbol of this land; article includes part of the General

Conference statement on saluting the flag.

Friesen, Chimo. Letter to the Editor. *ChrLead* 36 (Aug. 21, 1973), 13. The American flag does not belong in Mennonite Brethren churches because of what it symbolizes in the world.

Landis, Ira D. "A New Chapter on the Flag Salute." *GH* 36 (July 29, 1943), 363. Mennonites should be thankful for recent court decisions against the obligatory flag salute.

Shelly, Maynard. "Are the Stars and Stripes in a Different Class?" *Builder* 32 (Nov., 1982), 32-34.

Reflects on question asked by Bruno and Ruth Schottstaedt, East German Christians, while on a visit to the United States: "Why is there an American flag in a Mennonite church?"

Smucker, J. N. "Flags in Church." *Menn* 91 (Apr. 27, 1976), 294. Reprinted from *Menn* 68 (Dec. 1, 1953), 739. To reflect the priority of God's kingdom over the nation, Mennonite churches should not display an American flag in the sanctuary.

Stoda, Kevin. "Why Does a Nation in This Century Invade Another Nation When That Other Nation Refuses to Salute Its Flag?" Social Science Seminar paper, Apr., 1985. Pp. 49. MLA/BeC.

Stoltzfus, Grant M. "When the Flag Goes By."

*ChrLiv* 18 (Oct., 1971), 3-9. Review of national and state policies regarding flag display and salute, with the accompanying dissent from conscientious objectors.

"The Nonresistant Christian and the Flag Salute." *GH* 34 (Nov. 13, 1941), 706-707. As long as the salute does not involve a militaristic commitment, and as long as it is not an act of worship, the nonresistant Christian may participate, says the Mennonite Peace Problems Committee.

Wenger, J. C. "A Leader Faces Civil Powers." *ST* 46 (Sept., 1978), 1. Relates the story of George R. Brunk facing the Board of Education for the Commonwealth of Virginia about the right of a boy not to salute the flag for conscience' sake.

# 13

# Peace

## A. General

"A Message to Our Canadian Churches." *CanMenn* 2 (May 14, 1954), 2. Statement emerging from Winnipeg Peace Study Conference, Apr. 9-10, 1954, urges recommitment to the way of love and a stronger peace program.

*A Christian Declaration on the Way of Peace.* Newton: Faith and Life Press, 1972. Pp. 24. MHL. Resolution adopted by the GCMC at its triennial session at Fresno, Cal., Aug., 1971. Presented in two sections. The first deals with biblical perspectives on peace; the second with issues of practical application such as the use of resources, citizenship, conscription and military service, and social change.

Alderfer, Helen and Cutrell, Dorothy. "18 Books that Make for Peace." *ChrLiv* 25 (July, 1978), 15-18. Abstracts of books for children and parents promoting peace.

Andrews, Sharlene (Review). *Is There No Peace?*, by Lauren Friesen. Seattle: Crockett and Howe, 1979. Pp. 37. *MBH* 19 (May 9, 1980), 31-32. Recommends this play dramatizing the problem of global poverty.

Archibald, Bill. "Peace: It Can Only Be Given." *GH* 73 (Aug. 5, 1980), 615. Criticizes the world's concept of peace, abundance without denial, because it views peace as a possession instead of a relationship.

Arnett, Ronald D. "Conflict from the Peace Tradition, by Ronald C. Arnett." Dept. of Interpersonal Communication, Ohio Univ., Fall, 1976. Pp. 33. MLA/BeC.

Barrett, Lois. "Stand for What You Believe." *With* 13 (Oct., 1980), 14-15. Conscientious objector from World War I and active peace advocate counsels young people to be able to articulate their peace position.

Bartel, Verlin Paul. "The Contribution of Rev. H. B. Schmidt to the Peace Effort." Student paper for Christian Heritage, June, 1961. Pp. 24. MLA/BeC.

Basinger, Carlus. "Education as a Solution for Peace." *Menn* 53, Part 1, (July 12, 1938), 10-11; Part 2, July 19, 1938), 9. Peace education includes disassociation of war from patriotism, a sense of national humility, and a knowledge of the real causes and results of war.

Beachy, Ezra P. "Enduring Peace." *YCC* 32 (Mar. 4, 1951), 490. Before any one person can contribute anything toward establishing peace in the world he or she must have it in his or her own heart and life. Prize-winning oration on peace.

Beck, Carl. "Students in Japan Talk Peace." *CanMenn* 13 (Aug. 24, 1965), 3. Report on first Student Christian Peace Seminar, held in Osaka, Japan. Seminar sponsored by MCC Peace Section, Japan.

Bergmann, Frank. "Talking About Peace." *MBH* 14 (Jan. 10, 1975), 12-13. MCC (BC) Peace and Service Committee consulted on such topics as peace education, conflict resolution, distribution of wealth, and family ties as compared with Christian fellowship ties.

Bohn, Ernest J. "Our Peace Objectives." *Menn* 57 (Mar. 24, 1942), 1-4. Outlines the objectives of peace churches in a time of war and calls for clarity about our procedures when others are going off to war.

Brenneman, George. "Can We Have Peace and the Automobile?" *GH* 71 (Nov. 14, 1978), 893-97. Compares statistically American Mennonite monetary involvement in the auto and military industries and raises ethical questions about the dehumanizing and destructive tendencies of automobiles.

Brubaker, Darrel J. and Sider, Ronald J., eds. *Preaching on Peace.* Philadelphia: Fortress Press, 1982. Pp. 95. A collection of addresses and sermons reflecting the broadening variety of theological perspectives being brought to bear upon such issues of peace as disarmament, attitudes which create peace and the biblical basis for peace.

Brunk, S. H. "What Price Peace?" *ChrMon* 45 (July, 1953), 202. Discusses peace with God, with ourselves, and with others.

Bryoki, Al. Letter to the Editor. *ChrLead* 42 (Nov. 6, 1979), 9. Supports the *Leader's* direction in identifying various issues for discussion like peace and business ethics.

Burkholder, J. Lawrence. "The Peace Churches as Communities of Discernment." *Christian Century* 80 (Sept. 4, 1963), 1072-75. Discusses the relationship between the structure of the local congregation and its ability to make vital ethical decisions about peace and other issues.

Burkholder, John D. "Peace Through Friendship and Love." *GH Supplement* 38 (June, 1945), 215. Peace cannot come as long as selfishness destroys human relationships.

Burkholder, Oscar. "Peace." *ChrMon* 22 (July, 1930), 202. Poem illustrating the difference between the peace won through war and the peace given by God.

Charles, Howard H. (Review). *Biblical Realism Confronts the Nation*, edited by Paul Peachy. Fellowship Publications, 1963. Pp. 224. "Biblical Imperatives on the Question of War and Peace." *CanMenn* 12 (Apr. 28, 1964), 8. Book points out the stimulating contributions of both pacifists and non-pacifists to the current discussion of the church's responsibility in a nuclear age.

Claassen, Willard. "Being Christian Together." *Builder* X [sic, I] (Nov., 1960), 10, 11. Interpersonal relationships within the congregation ought to reflect what we say we believe about peace.

Clemens, J. C. (Review). *For Conscience Sake*, by Sanford Calvin Yoder. Goshen: The Mennonite Historical Society, 1940. Pp. 320. *MHB* 1 (Oct., 1940), 4. Recommends the book as a valuable history of Mennonite searchings for a place of peace, and as a means of encouraging Mennonites in such continued commitment.

Cowan, Roger A. "God's Peace and Man's Pieces." *ChrLiv* 7 (June, 1960), 24-25. Reprinted from *Social Progress*. Peace is possible, not through human organization, but through acceptance of God's action in Christ.

Derstine, C. F. "Permanent Universal Peace." *ChrMon* 39 (Feb., 1947), 62-63. True peace will come only through turning away from false gods of military security, liberalism, and Marxism.

Derstine, C. F. "Vague Dreams of World Peace." *ChrMon* 37 (May, 1945), 126-27. Peace is won

only through change in the human heart, thus conquering sin.

Dettwiler, Alma W. "'In the Name of Christ.' " *ChrLiv* 15 (Aug., 1968), 22-23. Explanation of the MCC label illustrating peace and worldwide friendship.

Dick, Ernie (Review). *Peace in the Family of Man*, by Lester B. Pearson. Oxford U. Press, n.d. "Creative Leadership for Peace." *CanMenn* 17 (Nov. 21, 1969), 6, 11. Cites the former prime minister's discussion of peace within the context of the nuclear bi-polar balance, the needs of the developing nations, and the efforts of the United Nations.

Dirks, Virgil R. "Peace and the Future." An original oration, n.d. Pp. 8. MLA/BeC.

Dyck, A. A. "Peace." *MBH* 16 (Jan. 21, 1977), 32. Christians can have inner peace with God even when there is no peace in the world.

Dyck, A. A. "War Will Always Be With Us." *CanMenn* 18 (Jan. 16, 1970), 5. Participation in the March Against Death (Washington) or in other demonstrations is questioned. Rather than working towards peace in far-off places one must seek to help those who lack peace in one's own neighborhood.

Dyck, Walter H. "Our Peace Stand." *Menn* 54 (Sept. 26, 1939), 4-6. In contrast to war, the nonresistant position is a reasonable, rightful, and realistic stand and there are concrete examples of things which can be done to further the peace testimony.

Ediger, Peter J. "Human Welfare, or Humanity, Farewell." Student address prepared for peace oratorical contest, Mar., 1950. Pp. 5. MLA/BeC.

Enz, Jacob J. "Christ, the Bond of Peace: A Study of the Epistle to the Ephesians." Paper prepared for the 1945 Pastoral Visitation Program, Newton, Kansas, [1945]. Pp. 12. AMBS.

Epp, Dick H.; Giesbrecht, P. U.; Lehn, Cornelia; Willms, Alfred. "In My Opinion: The Significance of the Canadian Peace Study Conference." *CanMenn* 2 (Apr. 23, 1954), 7. Four letters assessing the Apr. 9-10 Winnipeg peace conference.

Epp, Frank H. "Frontiers for Peace." *CanMenn* 11 (Nov. 5, 1963), 5. The MCC Peace Section lists frontiers on which it is working to advance Christ's gospel of peace.

Epp, Frank H. "Joy, Peace, Love." *CanMenn* 1 (Dec. 18, 1953), 2. "Peace is the miracle of Christmas . . . . Personal and social peace will come to us if we do God's will as revealed in Jesus. This task involves denying one's self and not demanding one's rights, dying to one's self and not exploiting others, personal martyrdom and not mass murder."

Epp, Frank H. "United Nations Day." *CanMenn* 3 (Oct. 21, 1955), 2. Only as the United Nations allows God to use it as an instrument of peace will it attain its goal of international unity and understanding.

Epp, Frank H. (Editorial). "Mobilizing Youth for Peace." *CanMenn* 2 (July 23, 1954), 2. In World War II, Canadians put 7 percent of their human resources toward the war effort while Canadian Mennonites put .2 percent of their human resources toward the peace effort. Encourages, in light of this disparity, more involvement with PAX and other service programs.

Epp, Henry P. "There Is Our Peace." *CanMenn* 9 (Nov. 3, 1961), 6. A sermon for Peace Sunday. It is in Jesus that true peace is to be found. The insights given by this peace must be instilled into the world.

"Food for Peace." *CanMenn* 7 (July 31, 1959), 15. Describes the government's Food for Peace program. MCC, as a voluntary agency, has given over $1.5 million worth of US government surplus to eleven foreign countries.

Foreman, Dennis W. "Preparation for Peace." *ChrMon* 40 (Aug., 1948), 235, 243. Guidelines for promoting peace in the face of militaristic propaganda.

Fosburgh, Lacey, "Some Find a Taste of Peace." *ChrLiv* 19 (July, 1972), 20-21. Fresh Air children experience the peacefulness of Amish lifestyle and theology.

Franz, Delton. "Peace Shall Reign on Earth." *Menn* 69 (Aug. 17, 1954), 500-501. War continues in spite of humanity's best efforts and wisdom. Peace will come only as Christians learn to "resist not evil with evil, but overcome evil with good."

Franz, Delton. "US Senators Propose Department of Peace." *CanMenn* 16 (Dec. 31, 1968), 1, 2. The proposal is for an umbrella organization for the Agency for International Development, the Peace Corps, and the Arms Control and Disarmament Agency.

Friesen, Bert, *Where We Stand: An Index of Peace and Social Concern Statements by Mennonites and Brethren in Christ in Canada, 1787-1982.* Winnipeg: MCC Canada and Akron, PA: MCC U.S., 1986. Pp. 300. Distributed by Mennonite Heritage Center, 600 Shaftesbury Blvd., Winnipeg. This publication lists and indexes approximately 2000 statements by church conference (GCMC, MC, MB, BIC) and by general topic. The topics

include peace and war, military service, conscription, relief, immigration and emigration, and church and social problems. The texts of these statements are available on microfilm from the MCC Canada office.

Friesen, Norris. Letter to the Editor. *ChrLead* 41 (May 23, 1978), 15. Appreciates *Leader's* articles on peace to help raise children in the way of peace.

Fry, A. Ruth. "The Laws of Peace." Address given to the National Peace Conference, London, June 28, 1935. Pp. 10. AMBS.

Galle, R. W. "The Way of Peace." *Menn* 57 (Sept. 29, 1942), 13-14. There cannot be permanent peace on earth until Christ returns, but there can be peace in the heart. It is this kind of peace which Christ gives.

Garber, Ruth M. "The Gift of Peace." *YCC* 11 (Apr. 6, 1930), 110. God gives peace to every person who is saved by grace through Jesus Christ.
*

Gingerich, John M. "Peace Concerns at Goshen College, 1905-1935." Paper presented to history seminar, Goshen College, Goshen, Ind., Feb 20, 1980. Pp. 41. MHL.

Gingerich, Melvin. "Peace Notes." *GH* 52 (Mar. 17, 1959), 249. A selection of news items pertaining to the peace concern. Includes world news and letters and speeches by prominent Americans.

Gingerich, Melvin. "Practicing Peace in a Hostile World." *Builder* 12 (June, 1962), 52-53. Worship and sermon suggestions to use in conjunction with patriotic holidays that emphasize peace.

Gingerich, Melvin. "The Price of Peace." *ChrLiv* 4 (June, 1957), 28, 37. True peace is not merely the absence of war, but the presence of God in the lives of people committed to Jesus as Lord.

Glick, Del. "The Search for Shalom in Mennonite Interscholastic Athletics." Paper for War, Peace, and Revolution class, AMBS, Elkhart, Ind., Dec. 20, 1978. Pp. 32. AMBS.

Glockner, Michael W. "The Peace Thought of Robert McAfee Brown." Paper for War, Peace, and Revolution class, AMBS, Elkhart, Ind., Apr. 10, 1969. Pp. 3. AMBS.

Goering, Mabel. "Our Peace Teaching." *Menn* 51 (Mar. 3, 1936), 4-5. As nonresistant Christians we must speak out against those who contribute to the killing and slaughter of people in war, viz., the munitions makers. It is not enough to hold to an individual ideal and assert, "I will not fight," if we do nothing to bring about peace.

Goering, Terence R. "A History of the Bethel

---

*For additional listing, see Supplement, pp. 717-719.

College Peace Club." Social Science Seminar paper, May, 1975. Pp. 59. MLA/BeC.

Hacker, Cheryl R. "Lancaster County Peace Churches Struggle to Retain Their Consciousness During the Revolution." Pp. 20. BfC.

Hackman, Walton. "Giving for Peace." *Menn* 88 (Dec. 18, 1973), 734. Encourages alternative giving for Christmas to people such as families of civilian prisoners in South Vietnam, imprisoned conscientious objectors, war resisters exiled in Canada, and political refugees from Chile.

Harder, Geraldine. "Teaching Pilgrim Children Peace and Love." *Builder* 24 (May, 1974), 21-23. Suggestions to help juniors and junior highs focus on peace concerns. Examples from Mennonite history and contemporary Mennonite service programs are used.

Harder, Geraldine, "Time Is Running Out." *ChrLiv* 16 (Nov., 1969), 26-27. Being present to those hurt by war and teaching the way of peace are two important tasks.
*
Harder, Kurt. "A Concrete Commitment." *Forum* 12 (Dec., 1978), 6-7. Writer supports and discusses the proposal of a National Peace Academy as a viable and concrete alternative to violence as a means of resolving conflict.

Harding, Vincent G. "Peace in Our Time?" *Menn* 73 (Nov. 11, 1958), 699. There will not be any peace until we actively "seek peace and pursue it" more than we pursue cash and comfort and crops.

Harms, Orlando. "Peace, Peace; When There Is No Peace." *ChrLead* 23 (Nov. 1, 1960), 2. Christians should support only a redemptive answer to the issue of war, since they are committed to the Prince of Peace.

Hartzler, Levi C. "Building for Peace." *ChrMon* 28 (Feb., 1936), 50-51. Love from God conquers fear and hate and builds a foundation for true peace.

Hershberger, Guy F. "A Call to Peace from the Cotswold Bruderhof." *YCC* 19 (Dec. 25, 1938), 414c. Excerpts from a message issued by the Cotswold Bruderhof, officially recognized as a Hutterian Bruderhof, entitled, "A Call: The Way to True Peace."

Hershberger, Guy F. "Memorials of Peace and Memorials of War." *YCC* 19 (July 3, 1938), 216. The majority of national memorials are memorials of war. Christians should build memorials that promote the ways of love and peace.

Hertzler, Daniel (Editorial). "The Hard Way of Peace." *Builder* 18 (May, 1968), 1. The motivation for a peace position is neither political nor pragmatic but consists of belief in the God revealed through Jesus.

Hiebert, Paul. "Peace, Today's Problem." *ChrLead* 24 (Oct. 31, 1961), 5. Christian peace is a gift of God, intended to permeate our total life-style, replacing force, violence, and hostility with reconciling, suffering love.

Hochstedler, Eli and Hochstedler, Jim. "Peace, Freedom, Love." *With* 2 (Sept., 1969), 14. A discussion about cooperation/noncooperation with a system set up for war between two Christian brothers.

Hofer, Phil. "Peace Wins a Battle." *Intercom* 9 (May-June, 1969), 5. Reflections on interpersonal and national peace by an MCCer in Nigeria.

Holderman, George. "A Sure Foundation for Peace." *ChrMon* 27 (June, 1935), 171-72. Cites examples of conflict settled through trust and goodwill to show that New Testament principles do work.

Horsch, John (Archival). Boxes 20-29—Contains notebooks of clippings on war and peace, religion and peace. Goshen, Ind. AMC. Hist. Mss. 1-8.

Horst, John L. (Editorial). "Peace." *ChrMon* 37 (June, 1945), 136. Comments on the end of the war in Europe and the postwar negotiations.

Hostetler, John Andrew. "The Christian Challenge to Peace." *GH* 38 (Aug. 31, 1945), 412-13. Peace and salvation are inseparable. The CPS program offers an opportunity for true peace testimony to those whose lives are filled with the Spirit of Christ.

Hostetler, John Andrew. "The Peace Challenge of Civilian Public Service." *ChrMon* 37 (Sept., 1945), 230. The CPS program attempts to communicate to society that the personal experience of peace with God affects one's response to war.

Hostetler, Nancy Gingrich. "War of Words Destroying Peace." *ChrMon* 23 (Sept., 1931), 268. Verbal conflict destroys peace as surely as armed conflict.

Jacks, Ethel Andrews. "Promote Peace Where You Are." *ChrLiv* 1 (Nov., 1954), 15. The military machine can be halted only if each person contributes something to the cause of peace where he or she is.

Janzen, A. E. "Patriotism, Peace, and War." *ChrLead* 13 (July 1, 1949), 3-4. Christians are devoted to the welfare of all people; because they believe peace is the will of God, they renounce the use of force and violence.

Janzen, Rodney. "Big Bear, Peaceful Plains Cree." Peace Research Essay, Aug. 31, 1975. Pp. 18. CGCL.

Just, L. R., ed. "Peace Conference Lectures." Papers presented at Peace Conference, Tabor College, Mar. 12-13, 1953. Pp. 45. MHL. Includes: Peters, Frank C., "Principles of Peace," 5-14; _____, "The Maladjusted Christian," 15-24; Waltner, Erland, "God's Love and Our Peace," 25-36; Kaufman, Milo, "The Challenge of the Second Mile," 37-45.

Kauffman, Daniel. "Jesus Christ the Prince of Peace." *GH* 32 (Oct. 26, 1939), 641-42. In times of trial on earth one should look to Jesus Christ, who lived and taught the way of nonresistant love and peace.

Kauffman, Daniel. "Let Us Pray for Peace." *GH* 32 (Nov. 30, 1939), 737-38. Pray for peace in the hearts of individuals, in homes, in congregations, in home communities, in nations, and in Europe where the war rages.

Kaufman, Donald D. "Mothers Work for Peace." *Menn* 85 (May 5, 1970), 306, 307. There are exceptions to the complacency of many mothers about war. Cites examples and makes suggestions of what mothers can do to work for peace.

Keeney, William E. "European Christian Peace Activities Expand. *Menn* 89 (Jan. 22, 1974), 56-57; *MennRep* 4 (Feb. 18, 1974), 7. Examines the disparate, yet growing, peace groups in Europe, the status of conscientious objection in various European countries, areas of concern among peace groups, and the progress of peace educational research, suggesting possible Mennonite contributions to these efforts.

Keeney, William E. "What Peace and Which Prince?" *GH* 65 (Dec. 19, 1972), 1028-29. An appropriate celebration of the coming of the Prince of Peace who rules by love, not coercion, would be to give aid to the innocent victims of war, especially to those labelled national enemies.

Keeney, William E. (Review). *Hoe leren we de vrede* (How Do We Teach Peace), by S. C. Derksen. Groningen: J. B. Wolters, 1967. Pp. 140. "Teaching Peace in the Nuclear Age." *MennLife* 27 (June, 1972), 47-48. The book has been well accepted in the Netherlands and is in its third printing.

Kehler, Larry. "In Times of Crisis." *CanMenn* 9 (July 28, 1961), 2. Even in times of crisis we must continue to testify to our country of the futility of war, continue to pray for peace and demonstrate our firm conviction that Jesus Christ is the answer to the world's problems.

Kehler, Larry. "What Local Pastors Did for Peace." *CanMenn* 10 (Mar. 30, 1962), 3, 10. History of the Lombard, Illinois, Ministerial Association's peace statement "Peace or War." The text of the statement is included.

King, Martin Luther, Jr. "Peace on Earth." *Menn* 93 (Apr. 4, 1978), 226-28. World peace will necessitate people working nonviolently for loyalties which transcend racial and national boundaries, said King in this Christmas Eve sermon.

Klaassen, Walter. "The Christian and Peace." Lectures given for Conrad Grebel College Adult Education Programme, Apr.-May, 1968. Pp. 63. CGCL.

Klingelsmith, Sharon and Springer, Kenneth, comps. "A Bibliography of the Writings of Melvin Gingerich." *MQR* 52 (Apr., 1978), 170-82. Exhaustive bibliography of historian Gingerich's published work includes a significant amount of writing on peace themes.

Krahn, David. "The Treaty of Versailles." *CanMenn* 17 (Nov. 14, 1969), 7. Insists that "territorily the Treaty (of Versailles) was not unusually severe; but economically, financially, militarily, and especially morally it was intolerable." Quotes George Goldberg as saying that "the Peace Conference of 1919 . . . was the peace to end peace."

Kreider, Carl. "Does the 'Threat' of Peace Mean Economic Collapse for the United States?" *MennComm* 5 (Aug., 1951), 30, 32. Reprint of a statement by Quaker economist Kenneth Boulding on peacetime economic policies that stimulate growth and prevent depression.

Kreider, Carl. "The Christian Message of Peace." *Japan Christian Quarterly* 18 (Autumn, 1952), 293-99. Both the teachings of Jesus and his own example call us to practice the way of love and peace, as an answer to those who trust in military power.

Kreider, Carl (Review). *The Perils of Peace,* by Donald W. Cox. Chilton Books, 1965. Pp. 215. *ChrLiv* 12 (Sept., 1965), 34. Recommends the book as a discussion of the disproportionately high percentage of manufacturing for defense purposes.

Kroeker, Albert. "This Diminishing World." *Peace Orations: Winners in National Speech Contests.* Hillsboro: Tabor College Bulletin, Mar., 1950, 7-12. Pp. 15. MHL. Because our world is becoming increasingly interdependent, our hope for future survival depends on establishing new economic and social stability through permanent world peace.

"Less Than 20 Percent Pray, Speak or Work for Peace." *CanMenn* 13 (Nov. 2, 1965), 1, 13. Reports results of a survey of a cross-section of Mennonite ministers.

"Loss of Peace Position Possible. . ." *CanMenn* 7 (Dec. 18, 1959), 5, 11. A news report of discussions at a meeting of the Association of Mennonite Students in Winnipeg. A student, Hans-Jürgen Goertz, expressed concern over the loss of the peace position among German Mennonites and noted increased interest from non-Mennonite groups now being attracted to this position.

Lantz, Russell. "The Mennonite Peace Position and the Present Crisis." *Menn* 56 (Apr. 1, 1941), 7-8. Mennnites are committed, historically and biblically, to a program of peace. Today that means doing alternate service even if it becomes very costly for them.

Lapp, John A. "A Treaty, But No Peace." *ChrLiv* 26 (May, 1979), 33-35. President Carter's peace mission to Egypt and Israel has resulted in a treaty but not peace because negotiations did not include other essential Arab voices.

Lapp, John A. "Brazil's Peace Pilgrim." *ChrLiv* 19 (June, 1972), 18-19. Sketch of Archbishop Dom Helder Camara, spokesman for peace and nonviolent social change.

Lapp, John A. "Disengagement Is Not Peace." *ChrLiv* 21 (July, 1974), 15, 29. Review of deeper issues affecting Israeli-Arab negotiations.

Lapp, John A. "JFK—in Life and Death." *ChrLiv* 11 (Feb., 1964), 18-19. The late JFK's statesmanship is evidenced in a speech excerpt on war and peace.

Lapp, John A. "Peace Section Not Political." *CanMenn* 19 (Feb. 2, 1971), 2. A concern that the MCC Peace Section not be a political unit but inspire to a life of peace that has political dimensions.

Lapp, John A. "Vignettes from Russia." *ChrLiv* 23 (Dec., 1976), 15-16. One aspect of Soviet life is the emphasis on peace.

Lapp, John E. (Review). *The Peace Calendar*, by Dr. Lowell H. Coate. Humanist Friend Publishers, 1968. Pp. 88. *ChrLiv* 16 (Jan., 1969), 36. Reviewer gives this calendar of daily meditations on peace a limited recommendation because its quotations are helpful to the political pacifist, but not necessarily to the biblical pacifist.

Lehman, Chester K. "Peace in the Heart." *The Eastern Mennonite School Journal* 18 (Apr., 1940), 63-66. Two aspects of peace are peace with God and peace with one's fellow human beings. Two results of peace are the absence of strife and works of righteousness.

Leisy, Elva Krehbiel. "Henry Peter Krehbiel (1862-1946)." *MennLife* 9 (Oct., 1954), 162-66. Review of Krehbiel's life focuses on his convictions regarding war and peace.

Lichti, June. "Peace, But How?" Speech given at the Peace Oratorical Contest, St. Catharine's, Ont., Nov. 19, 1966. Pp. 3. CGCL.

Liechty, Sandra. Letter to the Editor. *Menn* 94 (May 1, 1979), 316. A new publication, "Agora" (in Japanese and English) has been started in Japan to coordinate Mennonite-related groups working on peace issues and activities, including camps for Vietnamese refugees.

Lind, Miriam Sieber. "Coals of Fire and Gettysburg." *ChrLiv* 4 (Jul., 1957), 12-15. Family visit to the battlesite inspires conversation about war and peace.

Loewen, Harry. "Significance of Peace Is Heart of Christmas Message." *MennRep* 10 (Dec. 22, 1980), 5. Calls for Mennonites to actively reclaim their heritage of a peace position, which is at the heart of the gospel.

Lohrentz, Vernon. "Peace: The Hope of Humanity." Student paper for Our Christian Heritage, Feb., 1950. Pp. 12. MLA/BeC.

McPhee, Arthur G. "How Christians Can Show Gratitude for Their Heritage." *GfT* 11 (Jan.-Feb., 1976), 5-6. Christians can hope for peace and a better world because through Christ humankind and creation have already begun to be redeemed.

Mennonite Central Committee (Archival). Papers related to peace and social concerns, 1920 to present. Goshen, IN. AMC. MCC Peace Section Materials IX.

*
Metzler, Edgar. "Who Really Sing." *ChrMon* 39 (Dec., 1947), 360-61. Christians must be channels to bring about that peace made possible through Jesus' coming.

Mifflin, Lloyd. "Pioneer of Peace: The Mennonite Farmer." *MennComm* 4 (Mar., 1950), 4. Poem about the peaceful life and convictions of Mennonite farmers.

Miller, D. D. "Thou Wilt Keep Him in Perfect Peace, Whose Mind Is Stayed on Thee." *The Eastern Mennonite School Journal* 18 (Apr., 1940), 90-93. Real, genuine, perfect peace is the result of settling the sin question.

Miller, Fred. "Peace Teachers: He Begins at Home." *Builder* 31 (Jan., 1981), 14-15. Jim Swartzentruber, Kidron, Ohio, believes the peace journey begins when the strength of one's relationship to God filters into one's commitments and relationships with others.

Miller, Levi (Editorial). "Paul's Letters of Peace." *Builder* 29 (June, 1979), inside front cover. Introduces a new Sunday School peace emphasis utilizing the theme of "Jesus Christ Our Lord" focused by the epistles of Philippians, Ephesians, and Colossians.

Miller, Levi (Editorial). "The Professionalization of Peace Teaching." *Builder* 29 (November, 1979), 1. While peace professionals are needed and can provide deeper understanding of issues, the message and work of peace must be seen in a biblical context and be considered a task or mission in which every congregational member participates in some measure.

Miller, Orie O. (Archival). Boxes 1-80: collection contains MCC and various peace related materials; Committee on Economic and Social Relations; Mennonite Relief Commission on War Sufferers; Peace Problems Committee. Goshen, IN. AMC. Hist. Mss. 1-45.

Moore, John V. "How Did Your Children Become Involved in People's Temple?" *ChrLiv* 26 (Nov., 1979), 12-14. Methodist minister describes his children's sharing in concern for peace and social justice.

Moore, Ruth Nulton. *Peace Treaty.* Scottdale: Herald Press, 1977. Pp. 153. Juvenile fiction about a young Moravian boy, captured by Indians near Fort Duquesne, who learns he can use his faith to promote peace.

Mosemann, John H. "World Peace." *ST* 5 (July, 1933), 21. World peace will not be a reality until Christ comes to rule on earth.

"Nuclear Energy, Hot Topic at Peace Section Meeting." *GH* 72 (June 19, 1979), 504-505. Agenda items at the annual MCC Peace Section Meeting in Washington, DC, June 1-2, included proposed draft registration legislation, various peace education projects, and nuclear energy.

Neufeld, Elmer. "Peace—the Way of the Cross." *ChrLiv* 7 (Jan., 1960), 6-7, 34. Prose poem relating peace to issues of militarism, nationalism, and racism.

Niemoeller, Martin. "The Way of Peace." *GH* 48 (Feb. 15, 1955), 153; *CanMenn* 5 (July 19, 1957), 2. The author talks with three leading German nuclear physicists. The destructive power of the bomb cannot be exaggerated; war is madness. The New Testament's teaching of peace is the only answer.

Niggle, Gail. "Art: War and Peace." 1966. Pp. 31. BfC.

Nigh, Harry. "Our Father's Zeal." Speech given at the Peace Oratorical Contest, St. Catharine's, Ont., Nov. 19, 1966. Pp. 3. CGCL.

Nord, Randy. Letter to the Editor. *ChrLead* 40 (Dec. 20, 1977), 14. Concerned about Mennonite Brethren's lack of concern for social problems, including peace and justice.

Olson, Arnold T. "Peace for Export." *EvVis* 93 (Apr. 10, 1980), 3-5. As both a capital city and a symbol for three major world religions, peace in Jerusalem would have international and interfaith implications.

"Peace, War, and Social Issues: A Statement of the Position of the Amish Mennonite Churches." Officialy adopted by the ministerial body of the Beachy Amish Mennonite constituency . . . at Wellesley, Ont., Apr. 18-19, 1968. [n.p., 1968]. Pp. 16. MSHL. Topics include the role of government, military service, civil defense, the Christian's role in race relations, unions, etc.

"Peace and Social Concerns." *CanMenn* 13 (June 22, 1965), 3. Report on meeting in Chicago of MCC Peace Section, which consists of two MC peace committees and one GC peace committee. Enthusiasm was expressed at the meeting for coordinated effort between these committees.

"Peace Conference in Fraser Valley." *CanMenn* 7 (Feb. 20, 1959), 1, 3. F. C. Peters and Erland Waltner gave input to the meeting: love in action was a central theme.

"Peace Promotion Program." *MCE* 2 (Sept. 17, 1935), 9-11. From any perspective peace is the most desirable state of all—we must do all we can in the world to bring peace.

"Prospects and Programs for Peace in 1937." *Menn* 52 (Jan. 26, 1937), 9. The Peace Committee of the GCMC proposes a peace education program; included is a brief description of peace issues likely to be confronted by Congress in 1937.

Peace Lecture Series. 28 interviews by 1984. Taped lectures beginning in 1977 of the Bethel College Peace Lectures which address a variety of issues relating to war and peace. Includes lectures by Daniel Ellsberg, Pete Seeger, and Elise Boulding. MLA/BeC.

Peachey, J. Lorne. "Every One Wants Peace." *ChrLiv* 13 (Mar., 1966), 11. People promoting peace meet with opposition from government, manufacturer.

Peachey, Paul L. "Love, Justice, and Peace." *GH* 49,

Part 1, (Feb. 21, 1956), 177, 189; Part 2, (Mar. 20, 1956), 273, 287; Part 3, (Apr. 17, 1956), 369; Part 4, (May 15, 1956), 465; Part 5, (July 17, 1956), 680. Love is interpersonal, relational. It cannot be a principle on which to build society. Mennonites have seriously compromised the love community they profess.

Peachey, Urbane, ed. *Mennonite Statements on Peace and Social Concerns, 1900-1978.* Akron: Mennonite Central Committee US Peace Section, 1980. Pp. 262. Statements and actions of major Mennonite general conferences and a few district conferences, arranged topically according to conference.

Peters, Frank C. "Christ's Principle of Peace." *ChrLead* 23 (Nov. 1, 1960), 4-5, 9. Christian love will not necessarily be reciprocated; rather obedience to the Way of Jesus may lead to suffering. Even then the disciple "actively forgives."

Preheim, Lynn, ed. *The Voice of Peace.* CPS yearbook, CPS Camp No. 57, Hill City, SD, 1946. Pp. 56. MSHL.

Preheim, Marion Keeney. "The People of Peace." *ChrLiv* 23 (July, 1976), 34-35. How the author first learned about conscientious objection and how it affected her life.

Rasker, A. J. "The German Question and the Quest for Peace." *MennLife* 20 (July, 1965), 122, 123. ". . . The basic Christian views of repentance and willingness to be reconciled are not only essential for a personal Christian life, but are also relevant in the realm of the political life."

Reed, Kenneth. *Joseph, Put That Gun Down.* Lancaster, Pa.: Good Enterprises, Ltd., 1973. Pp. 34. Two-act play dramatizing the story of the Hochstetler family caught in the French, English, and Indian war of 1754. Contrasts the values of war and peace found in both the Amish and native American cultures.

Ritschl, Dietrich. "The Political Misuse of the Concern for Peace." *MennLife* 20 (July, 1965), 110-12. Our concern for peace must go beyond seeking to attain our own ends which often are not only politically based but also politically manipulated.

Ruth, Janet. "National Peace Academy." *MCC PS Wash. Memo* 12 (Nov.-Dec., 1980), 7-8. Description, background of, and possible problems with the establishment of a National Academy of Peace and Conflict Resolution.

Rutt, Clarence. "Peace, Peace, When There Is No Peace." *GH* 44 (Aug. 28, 1951), 829-31. The only solution to conflict is the spirit of Jesus. Mennonites have been negligent in teaching this principle.

Sawatsky, Walter W. "Piety Is not Enough." *MBH* 18 (Aug. 31, 1979), 16-17. Soviet Christians practice intense spiritual piety but are criticized for neglecting the social implications of following the Prince of Peace.

Shank, J. Ward. "First Righteousness and Then Peace." *ST* 48 (Sept., 1980), 6-8. Atonement and repentance bring about peace, not vice versa.

Shank, J. Ward (Editorial). "The Peace Issue." *ST* 47 (June, 1979), 5-6. Cautions against emphasizing peace teaching to the neglect of emphasis on redemption through the blood of Christ.

Shank, J. Ward (Editorial). "What Kind of Peace Education?" *ST* 41 (Sept., 1973), 9. Examines comments about peace education contained in a letter from Franconia Conference Peace and Social Concerns Task Force.

Shenk, Phil M. "A Sculptor of Justice and Peace." *Sojourners* 9 (Dec., 1980), 10-11. Describes the vision and work of Adolfo Perez Esquivel, human rights worker in Argentina and winner of the 1980 Nobel Peace Prize.

Sherk, J. Harold. "Looking Ahead." *RepConsS* 25 (Jan., 1968), 1, 2. Assesses the year ahead in terms of what it may mean for peace.

Sherk, J. Harold. "Reflections." *RepConsS* 25 (June, 1968), 1, 2. The assassination of Robert Kennedy reminds us of the pervasiveness of evil and calls us to a renewed commitment to the way of peace.

Sherk, J. Harold. "The Way to Peace." *RepConsS* 22 (Dec., 1965), 2. Short collection of peace quotations taken from biblical, historical, and literary sources.

Shetler, Sanford G. "Panel Discussion on Peace and War." *GfT* 6 (Sept.-Oct., 1971), 6-7. Collects writngs of Edward Yoder, Guy Hershberger, Henry A. Fast, and Thomas G. Sanders on war and peace and presents them in the form of a panel discussion.

Showalter, Richard and Jewel. *What Mennonites Believe about Peace and Service.* Scottdale, Pa.: Mennonite Publishing House, 1979. Pp. 8. MHL. The concepts of peace and service begin with the question of who is at the center of the universe—God or ourselves.

Smith, C. Henry. "Is the General Conference Losing Its Peace Testimony?" *Menn* 57 (July 28, 1942), 1-2. Because of a neglect of peace education the peace doctrine is being lost in the Mennonite churches.

Stahl, Mrs. Lawrence. Letter to the Editor. *Fellowship* 35 (Nov., 1969), 28. Suggests that less destructive measures be used in peace witnessing than destroying property.

Swartley, Willard M. "Cry for Peace." *Builder* 17 (Dec., 1967), 11-14. A dramatic reading utilizing the resources of Scripture, music, literature, and history to develop the concept of peace as an obedient response to a loving God.

Swartz, Carl J. Letter to the Editor. *GH* 65 (Dec. 5, 1972), 996. Since many Mennonites are uncertain of their peace stance, refusing to own guns would be a hypocritical action. Moreover, it would not guarantee that one were a peaceful person on the inside.

"The Christian Attitude on Peace: As Held by the Mennonites." *MCE* 2 (Dec. 3, 1935), 5-6. Because war is contrary to the teaching of Jesus, we renounce it and educate against it.

Teichroeb, Ruth. "Peace Conversion." Term paper for Peace and Conflict Studies course, Apr., 1978. Pp. 32. CGCL.

Tiessen, Erwin. "What Does Peace Really Mean?" Speech given at the Peace Oratorical Contest, St. Catharine's, Ont., Nov. 19, 1966. Pp. 3. CGCL.

"University Students Call for Peace Efforts." *CanMenn* 3 (Mar. 11, 1955), 1, 7. Winnipeg university and college students pass resolutions at peace conference calling for greater dissemination of peace literature and preparatory work for satisfactory alternative service in the event of war.

Unruh, John D. "Peace and War: Peace Conferences Transcend Political Barriers." *GH* 53 (Jan. 19, 1960), 57. Christians from all over the world are coming together to think about militarism and peace. Mennonites should be thankful and live lives that present a clear peace testimony.

Valette, Henri. "Peace Position." Senior Seminar, 1982. Pp. 32. MBBS.

Veenstra, Yt. "Peace As I See It." *IPF Notes* 1 (June, 1955), 3-4. Tabor College student from Holland reflects on scenes from World War II and the meaning of peace.

Vos, Peter. "Peace in Christian Endeavor." *MCE* 2 (Oct. 1, 1935), 5-6. War exists because Christianity has not been tried. If enough people would refuse to fight it would affect government decisions.

Voth, Cornelius, Jr. "Reverend P. H. Richert as a Peace Leader." Student paper, 1956. Pp. 6. MLA/BeC.

Waltner, Erland. "Peace and Your Health." *Menn* 95 (Nov. 25, 1980), 689. Discusses the close proximity of physical health, mental health, and right relationships with God and others in the biblical concept of shalom.

Waltner-Toews, David. "The Peaceable Kingdom: A Christian Position on Animal Welfare." *MennRep* 8 (Dec. 11, 1978), 7. The vision of peace on earth presented in Isaiah 11 indicates that the goal of peace and harmony includes the animal world. Veterinarian discusses faulty and adequate views toward human coexistence with animals.

Ward, Frank G. *Peace Is No Option*. Newton, Ks.: Faith and Life Press, 1975. Pp. 23. MHL. One-act play raises the questions of whether the complexity of complicity in our society's violence renders peace impossible or whether peace is so vital to Christianity that the Christian has no option but to work for peace. Designed to stimulate discussion about the relation of a peace commitment to one's lifestyle and use of money.

Wenger, Martha. "Black Kettle: His Way of Peace." Student paper for Humanities and Peace Studies, 1975. Pp. 33. Cheyenne Indians. MLA/BeC.

Wenger, Samuel S. "Peace and War: The Way of Love in This Atomic Age." *GH* 53 (Feb. 16, 1960), 145. The Christian follows Jesus, loves his or her fellow human beings, and witnesses to them. Killing people is inconsistent with all three of these vocations.

Weston, Stephen F., ed. *Prize Orations of the Intercollegiate Peace Association*. Boston: The World Peace Foundation, 1914. Pp. 185. MHL. First chapter summarizes the history of the Intercollegiate Peace Association crediting President Noah E. Byers of Goshen College with the conception of the association. But none of the prize-winning speeches, between 1907-1913, were from Goshen College contributions.

Widmer, Pierre. "Peace and War: International Mennonite Peace Conference at Luxembourg." *GH* 56 (May 21, 1963), 433. A report of the March 9 and 10, 1963, proceedings.

Wiebe, Bernie. "What Is the Price for Peace?" *The Abundant Life* (Nov., 1967). Altona, Man.: Mennonite Radio Mission. Pp. 15. Four brief radio talks entitled: 1) The War Game; 2) The Hawks and the Doves; 3) Prisoners of War, and 4) War and Peace.

Wiebe, Harvey. "Peace Is Love." Speech given at the Peace Oratorical Contest, St. Catharine's, Ont., Nov. 19, 1966. Pp. 2. CGCL.

Wingert, Norman A. "Japan Wants Peace and Education." *ChrLiv* 2 (Jan., 1955), 8-9, 35.

Japanese people are opposed to rearming the country.

"You Put Too Much Emphasis on Peace." *With* 3 (May, 1970), 34. A discussion with five young people from South America who think that North American Mennonites put too much emphasis on peace.

Yoder, Edward. "After Twenty-five Years: Peace Principles from a Scriptural Viewpoint." Part 31. *GH* 32 (Oct. 19, 1939), 639-40. The greed of the past war is leading us into another. The Christian must remain neutral and prepare to help those who suffer.

Yoder, Edward. "Conference on Peace and War." *GH* 27 (Mar. 7, 1935), 1038. Report of a peace conference held at Goshen College, Feb. 15-17, 1935.

Yoder, Edward. "Shall Christians Resist Aggressors? Peace Principles from a Scriptural Viewpoint." Part 49. *GH Supplement* 34 (Feb., 1942), 1014. Yoder looks at scripture frequently used to support the nonpacifist position. He concludes there is no justification for this sort of interpretation.

Yoder, Edward. "The Cry for Peace: Peace Principles from a Scriptural Viewpoint." Part 4. *GH* 28 (Oct. 17, 1935), 623. Many people say they want peace but they actually desire some things more than peace. The Spirit of Christ can overcome this selfishness and bring healing.

Yoder, Edward. "The Peace of God: Peace Principles from a Scriptural Viewpoint." Part 41. *GH Supplement* 34 (July, 1941), 356. God brings inner joy and peace, but also concern for the suffering and needs of the physicial world.

Yoder, Edward. "The Sins of Christendom: Peace Principles from a Scriptural Viewpoint." Part 11. *GH* 30 (July 15, 1937), 365-66. Christians must confess those times where they have been unfaithful and be prepared to suffer for the faith.

Yoder, Edward. "The Spirit of Hate: Peace Principles from a Scriptural Viewpoint." Part 8. *GH* 29 (Jan. 21, 1937), 926-27. The biblical attitude towards political issues was indifference instead of hate.

Yoder, Edward (Archival). Box 5: pacifism— indices, booklets, correspondence; Pax Christiana; peace articles, ideas. Goshen, IN. AMC. Hist. Mss. 1-47.

Yoder, John H. "Disarmed by God: The Way of Peace in a World at War." Part 3. *GH* 54 (Aug. 1, 1961), 661-62. God disarms us by taking away our selfishness. So, in the last analysis, the Christian lays aside carnal weapons not because they are too dangerous but because they are too weak.

Yoder, Perry B. "Toward a Shalom Theology." *CGR* 1 (Fall, 1983), 39-49. Notes that Mennonite theologians have, with the exception of Gordon Kaufman, not integrated the peace focus into their theological constructs. Proposes that shalom is a "deep structure" and outlines briefly how it might be integrated into main biblical theology topics such as creation, covenant, community, cult, cross, and consummation. Finally, raises two issues as problems with which Mennonites must work in order to formulate a solid shalom biblical theology: the meaning of shalom in the biblical materials, and the biblical relationship between shalom and the state.

Yoder, Perry B. "What the Bible Teaches About Peace." *With* 11 (Oct., 1978), 14. A Bible study that shows that the Bible has more to say about peace than speaking against war.

Yoder, S. A. "I Am Ill at Ease." *GH* 63 (Mar. 3, 1970), 197. Editorial laments the state of American society in seeking peace through war and harrassing those people who identify with the cause of peace.

# B. Peacemaking, Peace Witness, and Peace Movements

"A Declaration on Peace, War, and Military Service." *Menn* 68 (Oct. 13, 1953), 632-33, 640. The official statement adopted at the 1953 conference of the GCMC. The way of peace and suffering love is rooted in the biblical witness to the gospel of Jesus. On this basis all forms of military service are disapproved.

"A Good Year for MCC Manitoba." *MennMirror* 1 (Mar., 1972), 12. Among other agenda, the MCC (Manitoba) annual meeting featured John A. Lapp as the keynote speaker who spoke of peacemaking as a Christian discipline.

"A Message to the Churches." *GH* 52 (May 19, 1959), 465; "A Message to All Christians," *CanMenn* 7 (May 8, 1959), 2. A statement issued by the 1959 Church Peace Mission Conference calling the church to unequivocally renounce war and take decisive action to break the circle of armament and counter-armament. The use of nuclear weapons, particularly, should be completely renounced.

"A Prophetic Call—Evangelicals and Social Concerns." *EV* 86 (Dec. 25, 1973), 7. Evangelical Christian leaders met in Chicago to explore the importance of social concern for contemporary biblical faith and adopted a major document in which they stated their conviction that biblical faith and social concern are inseparable.

"A Statement of the Position of the General Conference of the Mennonite Church of North America on Peace, War, Military Service, and Patriotism." *Menn* 56 (Sept. 9, 1941), 7-8. The statement approved at the 1941 meeting. "We believe that war is altogether contrary to the teaching and spirit of Christ and the gospel . . . ."

"An Urgent Appeal to the Churches." *EV* 90 (May 25, 1977), 6. With this appeal, twenty-five persons at a workshop on the church and militarism call our attention to the surprising silence of the Christian church in the face of mass starvation and nuclear stockpiling and urge the church to respond to these atrocities.

"Appeal to Canada's Prime Minister." *CanMenn* 14 (Feb. 8, 1966), 1, 13. Conference of Mennonites in Canada encourage the prime minister "to become a messenger of peace" and to project plans for helping those in war-ravaged countries.

"Associated Seminaries Hold Study Day on Conflict Between US and Iran." *GH* 72 (Dec. 25, 1979), 1032. A special meeting, "Iran Day," held at the Associated Mennonite Biblical Seminaries to bring about a better understanding and a response in prayer to the current Iranian-US conflict.

Abileah, Joseph W. "Federation in the Middle East." *Menn* 84 (June 3, 1969), 376; *MBH* 8 (May 30, 1969), 8; "An Israeli's Proposal for Peace," *CanMenn* 17 (June 6, 1969), 1. An Israeli pacifist proposes a solution to bring about reconciliation between the Middle East countries of Jordan, Arab Palestine (West Bank), and Israel.

Adrian, Herman, "A Report on Witness at CNE Peace Booth." *CanMenn* 13 (Nov. 2, 1965), 10. At the Canadian National Exhibition in Toronto, Herman and Helen Adrian confronted many people with the peace witness through a peace booth. There was some negative but generally favorable reaction, much of which came from Catholic university students.

Alexander, John F. "A Politics of Love." *MBH* 11 (Oct. 20, 1972), 4-6. Contends that the "most important contribution of Christianity to an understanding of politics is its teaching on rebirth."

Alexander, John F. "Politics, Repentance, and Vision." *GH* 67 (July 23, 1974), 564-66. Reprinted from *The Other Side*. What American society needs is not a political program for social reform—since political gains are grossly inadequate—but a program of repentance to change people's priorities from material comforts to justice, peace, and healing.

Amstutz, D. "Dutch Mennonite Missions During the War." *MennLife* 3 (Jan., 1948), 16-19. How missions in Java fared during the German occupation of Holland and the Japanese occupation of Java.

Arnold, Eberhard C. H. "All Things in Common." *ChrLiv* 4 (Dec., 1957), 12-15. Description of the Society of Brothers, including their links to the historic peace churches.

Augsburger, David W. "Optimism Despite World War III." *YCC* 48 (July 23, 1967), 3. Individuals must be at peace with themselves, family, neighbors, and God before they can create peace in the world.

Augsburger, David W. *Peacemonger or Peacemaker.* Harrisonburg, VA: The Mennonite Hour, 1966. Pp. 24. MHL. Booklet in two parts: radio talks on peacemaking; and short statements on Vietnam War by persons representing a variety of disciplines.

Augsburger, David W. *The Love-Fight.* Scottdale: Herald Press, 1973. Pp. 128. Handbook on interpersonal conflict resolution. Includes chapter relating conflict resolution to biblical peacemaking.

Augsburger, Myron S. "Beating Swords into Plowshares." *ChrToday* 20 (Nov. 21, 1975), 7-9. Calls all Christians to a peace commitment on the basis of their participation in Christ's body, which must be a minority community separate from the ethics of a secular state and society.

Augsburger, Myron S. "Evangelism that Cares." *The Other Side* 8 (Mar.-Apr., 1972), 30-31. Evangelism is making faith in Christ a clear option. An example of this is where Christ is shared without being identified with Americanism and its militaristic expressions.

Augsburger, Myron S. "Facing the Problem." In *Perfect Love and War: A Dialogue on Christian Holiness and the Issues of War and Peace,* 11-20. Ed. Paul Hostetler. Nappanee, IN: Evangel Press, 1974. Outlines five basic points of a New Testament approach to the problem of peace and relates these issues to the underlying consideration, the church and state relationship.

Augsburger, Myron S. *Pilgrim Aflame*. Scottdale: Herald Press, 1967. Pp. 288. Novel portraying the life of Michael Sattler, early Anabaptist leader and probably drafter of the Schleitheim Confession. Discussions of the sword, the oath, and the church and state relationship are developed in the contexts, characters, relationships of the 16th century martyrs of the Radical Reformation.

"Blessed Are the Peacemakers in Every Community." *MennComm* 3 (June, 1949), 26-27. Dialogue between peace team member and community resident about peace education and practice in all areas of life.

Baechler, Gerald W. "Peace Begins with Christ." *GH* 72 (Aug. 28, 1979), 687. All the peace demonstrations and efforts will not be helpful unless peace begins within us and in our daily relationships.

Baerg, Henry R. "Our Peace Witness." Study paper, n.d. Box 8-N-3. Redekop, John H. "Some Aspects of the Expression of a Peace Witness." Study paper, n.d. Box 8-N-4. CMBS/Win.

Bainton, Roland H. "The Enduring Witness: The Mennonites." *MennLife* 9 (Apr., 1954), 83-90. Focus on the contribution of Menno Simons to the Anabaptist movement; reprints some of his teaching on war.

Barkman, Jerry W. "The Peace Issue in the Mennonite Brethren Church." Research paper for the Mennonite Brethren Church course, 1976. Pp. 53. MBBS.

Barrett, Lois. "Practicing Peace Cooperatively." *Menn* 93 (Mar. 7, 1978), 164. Reflections on New Call to Peacemaking activities in 1977 and 1978.

Bartel, Barry C. "Henry A. Fast: A Man with a Purpose." Student paper for Advanced Religious Studies Seminar, Apr. 25, 1983. Pp. 41. MLA/BeC.

Bartel, Lois Franz. "Peace Begins at Home." *Menn* 85 (Mar. 31, 1970), 236-38. Helping those in need in our own neighborhoods is a matter of being aware of needs and being open to possibilities of fulfilling those needs.

Bauman, Clarence. "Focal Elements in the Anabaptist-Mennonite Peace Position." *ChrLead* 22, Part 1, (Nov. 3, 1959), 4-5, 24; Part 2, (Nov. 17, 1959), 4-5. The dualism, tension, and paradox symbolized by Christ's cross are resolved by the radical obedience of faith that distinguishes the Community of Faith in a faithless world.

Bauman, Clarence. "Our Witness for Peace." *GH* 52 (June 16, 1959), 562, 573; *Menn* 74 (July 7, 1959), 404-405. A record of conversations in England between representatives of the historic peace churches and the International Fellowship of Reconciliation, Apr. 13-18, 1959. Summarizes points of unity and divergence among these groups; despite differences, a deep sense of unity can prevail as these groups share their common commitment to the way of love.

Bauman, Clarence. "Recovering the Anabaptist Movement." Paper, n.d. Pp. 17. AMBS.

Bauman, Clarence. "The Theology of 'The Two Kingdoms.' A Comparison of Luther and the Anabaptists." *MQR* 38 (Jan., 1964), 37-49, 60. For Luther the rule of Christ remained hidden in the world, whereas for the Anabaptists the realization of the Kingdom was a present reality in their covenant community.

Bauman, Harold E. "A Grieved but Wiser Patriot." *GH* 66 (Nov. 13, 1973), 857-59. Isaiah's vision of the Lord in the year of King Uzziah's death provides a model of personal cleansing and prophetic witness against the militaristic, oppressive, and corrupt structures of a fallen government.

Bauman, John. "Peace is Our Responsibility." *Menn* 66 (July 17, 1951), 447, 449. The winning oration on peace in a contest at Bluffton College states that "procuring peace" is the job of those who understand and live the biblical faith through witness, service, education, and clear obedience to God rather than the state.

Beachey, Duane. *Faith in a Nuclear Age*. Scottdale, PA: Herald Press, 1983. Pp. 128. Treats the issues of war and peace, issues such as the just war theory. The biblical bases for peacemaking, submission to authority, peace wtiness, etc., from the perspective of the contemporary nuclear situation.

Beachy, Alvin J. "Reflections After Minneapolis— On Legality, Anabaptists, and War Tax Refusal." *God and Caesar* 5 (Apr., 1979), 4-5. Challenges the prevailing assumption that since Anabaptists did not practice any kind of tax resistance, it would be "un-Anabaptist" for us to do so.

Beachy, Alvin J. *The Concept of Grace in the Radical Reformation*. Nieuwkoop: De Graaf, 1977. Pp. 238. In this theological study of the Anabaptist movement, the chapter entitled "Anabaptist or Radical Ethics and the Works of Grace," 153-72, outlines the major points of the Anabaptist ethic: discipleship in conformity with the example of Christ is only possible through the power of the Holy Spirit; while the state has a legitimate place and function, it is limited by the example of Christ which precludes violence; oath-taking is one area in which Christians must disobey the state, according to the example of Christ; military duty is another area demanding disobedience to the state.

Beaver, R. Pierce. *Envoys of Peace.* Grand Rapids: Wm. B. Eerdmans, 1964. Pp. 133. An indictment of the divisiveness of Christian missionary activity together with a plea for mission as a ministry of reconciliation. Some attention is also given to the history of the peace witness in the missionary situation.

Beaver, R. Pierce. "The Peace Witness in the Christian Mission." *MQR* 37 (Apr., 1963), 96-112. Missionaries are facing great difficulties in relating reconciliation to the cultures in which they work. In many ways "protestant missions today are anything but a witness to peace." Young Mennonite churches in Asia and Africa do not seem to be any more peace conscious than other churches.

Beck, Carl. "A Church of Peacemakers Is a Church in Mission." *CanMenn* 13 (May 18, 1965), 3, 11. A report on the 1965 Tokyo Christian Student Peace Seminar entitled "Reconciliation in East Asia" which included much discussion of Japanese-Korean relationships.

Beck, Carl. "Japanese and Korean Students Find Each Other in Fellowship." *CanMenn* 13 (Sept. 28, 1965), 3. Report on a Korean-Japanese reconciliation work camp at the Mennonite Vocational School near Taegu, Korea, July 23-Aug. 2, 1965.

Beck, Carl. "Justice Shall Roll Down." Sermon preached at College Mennonite Church, Goshen, Ind., Jan. 30, 1955. Pp. 9. MHL.

Beck, Carl. "Korea Church Leaders Ponder Peace." *CanMenn* 14 (Feb. 22, 1966), 1, 2. Report on first Korean Reconciliation Seminar held in Taegu, South Korea, in Oct., 1965, involving 34 pastors, seminary and university professors, elders, and lay leaders. The seminar discussed the history of Korean-Japanese hatred, industrial relations, and reconciliation as the object of Christian faith.

Beck, Carl. "Peace Witness Is Mission." *GH* 58 (June 1, 1965), 477-78. Report of the proceedings of the 1965 Tokyo Christian Student Peace Seminar, focusing on the resolution of conflict in Japanese-Korean relationships and in other tension spots of East Asia.

Beck, Carl. "Reconciliation Progress Surprises Workcampers." *CanMenn* 16 (Sept. 12, 1967), 1, 5. Report on the third MCC-sponsored Reconciliation Work Camp held in Taegu, Korea July 21 to Aug. 1 and involving thirteen young people from Japan as guests of Korean young people.

Beck, Carl C. "Japanese-Korean Encounter Brings Pleas for Reconciliation." *CanMenn* 14 (July 19, 1966), 1, 6. A report on the fifth MCC Peace Section-sponsored annual Christian Youth Peace Seminar held in Tokyo, May 13-15. Fifty-one participants (including eight Koreans) listened to Prof. Saburo Takahashi of Tokyo University and Prof. Kidong Chang of the graduate school of Taegu University. It was decided to invite Koreans into leadership positions of the seminar.

Becker, Palmer. "Ten Vigorous Years: On Being Servants . . . Commission on Home Ministries." *Menn* 94 (May 22, 1979), 353-55. For the past ten years, CHM has been involved in three general areas: evangelism, peace, and service.

Beechy, Atlee. "God's People—The Compassionate Community." *CanMenn* 14 (Aug. 16, 1966), 5; *GH* 59 (Oct. 18, 1966), 932-33. Excerpts from a sermon delivered in the Episcopal Church in Saigon on July 24, 1966. Calls upon the church, as the "compassionate community" to bind the wounds Vietnam.

Beechy, Atlee. "Help Fulfill a Dream." *YCC* 49 (June 23, 1968), 5. The ministry of reconciliation is entrusted to those who take seriously Christ's call. The road is difficult and risky but there is no alternative.

Beechy, Atlee. "MCC Contacts Affirm Peace Witness." *ChrLiv* 16 (Jan., 1969), 11, 34-35. MCC assistant secretary reports on his talks with the National Liberation Front of South Vietnam and the Democratic Republic of [North] Vietnam.

Beechy, Atlee. "Nurturing Peacemakers." *Builder* 33 (June, 1983), 2-5. Interview with Levi Miller. Originally printed in Feb., 1976, *Builder.*

Beechy, Atlee. "Peacemaking in Vietnam." *Peacemakers in a Broken World.* Ed. John A. Lapp. Scottdale: Herald Press, 1969, 54-63. Discusses the role of Vietnam Christian Service in working for peace in Vietnam and the importance of Mennonites taking their peace witness into the heart of militarism and conflict in order to witness to God's love.

Bender, Bertha Burkholder. "Youth, Church, and State." *YCC* 12, Part 1, (Jan. 4, 1931), 420-21; Part 2, (Jan. 11, 1931), 426-27; Part 3, (Jan. 18, 1931), 434-35; Part 4, (Jan. 25, 1931), 444-45; Part 5, (Feb. 1, 1931), 450, 451, 453; Part 6, (Feb. 8, 1931), 461-62; Part 7, (Feb. 15, 1931), 466-67; Part 8, (Feb. 22, 1931), 479-80; Part 9, (Mar. 1, 1931), 487, 488; Part 10, (Mar. 8, 1931), 491, 493; Part 11, (Mar. 15, 1931), 498, 499; Part 12,

(Mar. 22, 1931), 505, 506; Part 13, (Mar. 29, 1931), 515, 517; Part 14, (Apr. 5, 1931), 523, 525; Part 15, (Apr. 12, 1931), 534, 535; Part 16, (Apr. 19, 1931), 539, 541; Part 17, (Apr. 26, 1931), 545-47; Part 18, (May 3, 1931), 559, 560; Part 19, (May 17, 1931), 571, 573; Part 20, (May 31, 1931), 589; Part 21, (June 7, 1931), 595; Part 22, (June 21, 1931), 610; Part 23, (July 5, 1931), 627, 629; Part 24, (July 19, 1931), 645, 646; Part 25, (July 26, 1931), 650, 651; Part 26, (Aug. 2, 1931), 657-59; Part 27, (Aug. 16, 1931), 675-77. Written in a narrative style, the progression of peace-related topics include: the biblical story, the history of the church, issues about responding to government and militarism, e.g., CO status during Civil War and World War I, and Mennonite relief work.

Bender, Dale. "Relating to Authority—An Anabaptist-Existentialist Alternative." *Forum* (Jan., 1974), 14-15. Anabaptists rebelled against both civil and religious authorities, arguing that religious experience could not be separated from life.

Bender, Gladys K. "Living the Life of Peace in the World." *GH* 42 (Dec. 6, 1949), 1191. A call to a peaceable Christ-like attitude of subjection to government as part of the nonresistant stand.

Bender, Harold S. "Anabaptist Testimonies on Religious Liberty." *Liberty* 51 (1st quarter, 1956), 10-12. Part 2 of "The Anabaptists and Religious Liberty in the 16th Century," originally published in *Archiv für Reformationsgeschichte* 44 (1953), 32-50; reprinted in *MQR* 29 (Apr., 1955), 83-100. See either of latter sources for annotation.

Bender, Harold S. "Mennonite Peace Action Throughout the World." *MQR* 24 (Apr., 1950), 149-55. A report of activities together with a program proposal for vigorous peacemaking throughout the world.

Bender, Harold S. "Mennonites Testify at Hearings on Post-War Military Policy." *Menn* 60 (July 10, 1945), 5-6. The MCC statement made at the hearings of the House Select Committee on Post-War Military Policy. The statement recounts the history of the Mennonite peace witness, and witnesses against permanent peacetime conscription.

Bender, Harold S. "Peace Problems Committee." *The Mennonite Encyclopedia* IV:130, Scottdale-Newton-Hillsboro Mennonite Publishing Offices, 1959. This MC committee works in peace education, witness to government leaders, and a witness to other Christians. Cf. Bender's article on "Peace Section" (of MCC) on p. 131, *ibid.*

Bender, Harold S. "The Anabaptist Vision." *Church History* 8 (Mar., 1944), 3-24. It consisted of a

vision of the essence of Christianity as discipleship, a new concept of the church as believers, and the ethic of love applied to all human relationships.

Bender, Harold S. "The Anabaptists and Religious Liberty in the 16th Century." *Archiv für Reformationsgeschichte* 44 (1953), 32-50. Examines writings from 16th-century Anabaptists advocating religious liberty and concludes their views were grounded in commitments to voluntary church membership and the way of love and suffering instead of force and coercion. [Published as booklet in Facet Book Historical Series, No. 16. Ed. Charles S. Anderson. Philadelphia: Fortress Press, 1970. Pp. 27.]

Bender, John M. A narrative report of a workshop on "Third and First Worlds: Multinational Perspectives," sponsored by the Peace and Social Concerns Committee, College Mennonite Church, Goshen, Ind., Feb. 9, 1980. Pp. 8. AMBS.

Bender, John M. "Mediators in Paris." *GH* 68 (Oct. 7, 1975), 712-13. Outlines the history and present goals of a Mennonite presence in Paris, working with international students and communicating peace concerns.

Bender, Titus. "Peacemaking." *GH* 60 (June 6, 1967), 508-509. Peace is more than the absence of violence. It is actively relating to persons, especially to those oppressed by any form of injustice in the congregation, community, or world.

Berg, Ford. "Church and Peace Conference in Detroit." *GH* 46 (Dec. 22, 1953), 1217, 1230. A report of the proceedings which includes summary of the key address by André Trocmé—a "Plea for Repentance as an Answer to the World's Ills."

Bergen, Lois. "Youth Education: Peace Education Is Lifelong Growth." *Builder* 31 (Jan., 1981), 28-29. Lists resources and makes suggestions for helping youth think through their positions on militarism, registration, conscientious objection, biblical peacemaking, etc.

Bethel College Peace Activities. About 65 interviews. Emphasis is on the 1960's and 1970's, including news reports on Bethel's Moratorium Day protest, nonregistration, bellringing, student attitudes, and Women's International League for Peace and Freedom. MLA/BeC.

Bicksler, Harriet. "Fortunate Are Those Who Work for Peace." *EV* 91 (Jan. 10, 1978), 10-11. The Keystone Bible Institute's Seminar on Christian Peacemaking and New Call to Peacemaking consider the broader implications

---

*For additional listing, see Supplement, pp. 717-719.

of peacemaking now that the draft and Vietnam war are over.

Bilderbeek, H. van. "The Dutch Mennonite Peace Group." *MennLife* 18 (Oct., 1963), 172-73. Principles and activities of the Dutch Mennonite Peace Group reorganized after World War II.

Birmingham, Egla. "Una Declaracion Cristiana Sobre El Sendero De Paz." Pp. 7. BfC.

Bishop, Elaine L. "Quaker Youth Describes 200-Hour December Fast in Canadian Capital." *CanMenn* 15 (Jan. 17, 1967), 1, 2. Description of a fast in Ottawa from Dec. 23-31, 1966 by Young Friends appealing to Canadians to remember innocent war victims in Vietnam who suffer during the Christmas season.

Bittinger, Elmer E. "Peace Only Through Christ." *GH* 45 (Mar. 4, 1952), 222-23. While expressing gratitude for national and world peace-making efforts, the author points out that those efforts are doomed to fail which appeal to the noble nature of humanity and include no acknowledgement of sin and need for repentance.

Blancke, Fritz. "Anabaptism and the Reformation." *The Recovery of the Anabaptist Vision.* Ed. Guy F. Hershberger. Scottdale: Herald Press, 1957, 57-68. Describes the rise of Anabaptism, showing that it grew out of dissent from Zwingli's reform. Elaborates on the Anabaptist view of "free church," i.e., both the relationship of church and state and the concept of voluntary church membership.

Blosser, Don. "All in the Name of God." *GH* 64 (Feb. 16, 1971), 138-40. Citing the prophet Micah who decried economic oppression of the poor in the name of divinely ordained national defense, the writer calls Christians to witness against such policies found in American government.

Blosser, Don. "Coming to Terms with Our Mennonite Faith." *GH* 66 (Oct. 16, 1973), 785-88. The discipleship modeled by the Anabaptists implies that the church as a voluntary fellowship of adult believers follows the way of loving enemies rather than the way of warfare and killing.

Blosser, Don. "How Many Men Must Die?" *GH* 61 (July 9, 1968), 612-14. Sermon preached on the day of mourning for Sen. Robert Kennedy claims that American society shares responsibility for the slayings of Martin Luther King, Jr., and Robert Kennedy by promoting violent solutions to disputes. Calls for a more active Mennonite witness to peace, beginning at home by limiting the use of war toys.

Blosser, Don. "In Jail with the Apostle Paul." *GH* 69 (Apr. 20, 1976), 324-25; also "On Sharing a Jail Cell with Paul," *Menn* 91 (Mar. 9, 1976), 165-66. The "principalities and powers," about which Paul warned the Ephesians, express themselves today in corrupt institutions and military madness, evils which Christians are called to confront.

Blosser, Don. "The Selling of the Pentagon: A Response." *GH* 64 (July 27, 1971), 636-37. Expresses deep dismay over the ideas and values communicated by the Pentagon as seen in the CBS documentary *The Selling of the Pentagon*. Calls Mennonites to become aware of militaristic tactics and to protest the use of their tax dollars in the Pentagon's propaganda.

Blosser, Don. "What Would Jesus Say to Us This Christmas?" *GH* 68 (Dec. 9, 1975), 868-69. The message of Jesus, as found in Old Testament prophets, calls for living in love, justice, forgiveness, and peace.

Boers, Arthur Paul. "A Spirituality Primer for Activists." MA in Peace Studies thesis, AMBS, 1983. Pp. 93. An introduction to spirituality directed toward Christians who are concretely seeking to bring about God's Kingdom of peace and justice. The first perspective explored is the political nature of spirituality. The finding is that prayer without justice is false prayer; God rejects rites of spirituality that take place in contexts of oppression and injustice. The second perspective explored has to do with the metaphors of spirituality and how these dimensions affect the activist. The finding is that while prayer enriches us, prayer also offers no guarantees of effective activism.

Boese, Ronald. "Toward a Life of Peace." *Menn* 86 (Sept. 21, 1971), 561. An experiment in intentional community included some efforts to work at the issues of peacemaking.

Bohn, E. Stanley. "A Hard Look in the Vietnam Mirror." *Menn* 81 (Nov. 1, 1966), 658-61. Most Mennonite congregations have no way of coping with social issues, are not accustomed to the protagonist role, and are too afraid of conflict to engage in a clear peace witness.

Bohn, E. Stanley. "Does It Help to Write My Representative in Government?" *CanMenn* 14 (May 24, 1966) 7. An appeal to Mennonites to witness to government by writing to legislators expressing convictions about war and peace.

Bohn, E. Stanley. "More Peacemaker Audiovisuals." *Builder* 18 (May, 1968), 15-16. Listing of audio-visual resources prepared for use with series of Sunday school lessons on "Peacemakers in a Broken World." Subjects covered: "Extremism and Communism," "Race," and "Poverty."

Bohn, E. Stanley. "Peace in Action—Case Studies." *Builder* 18 (June, 1968), 13-15. Reports illustrating various ways groups of Christians have witnessed for peace. Three areas of witness are highlighted: sharing convictions with church groups, with communities, with governments.

Bohn, E. Stanley. "Resources for Peacemaking." *Builder* 18 (Apr., 1968), 15-16. Listing of audio-visual resources prepared for use with series of Sunday school lessons on "Peacemakers in a Broken World." Subjects covered in this listing are: "Introduction to Peacemaking," "Relief and Service as Peacemaking," and "The Peace Witness Itself."

Bohn, Ernest J. *Christian Peace According to the New Testament Peace Teachings Outside the Gospels.* Peace Committee, General Conference Mennonite Church, 1938. Pp. 53. Some New Testament passages, for example, Acts 10; 23:12-35; Rom. 13, might seem to sanction war. However, exegeted carefully and viewed in light of such New Testament themes as the evil nature of war, nonresistant love and the international body of Christ, these texts cannot constitute an argument for the rightness of war.

Boll, Noah S. "The Christian's Duty Toward the Election and Our Country in General." *GH* 30 (Dec. 30, 1937), 843, 846. The Christian's prayer is more powerful than his or her vote.

Bontrager, Robert. "Missiles or Missions." *YCC* 40 (July 19, 1959), 461. Challenges the idea that security can be guaranteed with military might. Prize-winning essay.

Born, Daniel. "Our Uneasy Peace Witness." *ChrLead* 41 (Apr. 25, 1978), 3. Recognizes the open debate about the peace witness in the Mennonite Brethren Church. Can MB's as a body come to terms with this debate that still divides the church?

Bowman, Rufus. "The Historic Peace Churches Face the Future." In "Kansas Institute of International Relations 1938 Lecture Notes," ed. Agnes Wiens and Pauline Schmidt. Kansas Institute of International Relations, Bethel College, North Newton, Kan., 1938, 34-35. Pp. 81. MHL.

Breneman, Rose; Good, Luke; Hershey, Mim; Hess, Dan. "An Open Letter to Pastors of College Students." *GH* 63 (Aug. 25, 1970), 700. College students explain their support of peace demonstrations as a witness to the government against war and killing, in response to minister's sermon declaring that Christians should remain separate from government structures.

Brenneman, George. "Abortion: Review of Mennonite Literature, 1970-1977." *MQR* 53 (Apr., 1979), 160-72. Written to challenge Mennonites to continue the abortion dialogue, this article summarizes what has been written on the issue in Mennonite literature. One of the nine questions addressed regarding abortion calls attention to the relationship of the issue of abortion to a "peace church" stance.

Brenneman, Virgil J. "A Voice from the Crowd." *GH* 63 (Jan. 6, 1970), 10-11. Author reflects on his participation in the mass peace demonstration in Washington, DC, and is disturbed that the administration tried to discourage people from participating and deliberately downplayed the size of the crowd and their totally nonviolent spirit. A critical evaluation of this mode of peace witness.

Brenneman, Virgil J. "Christ, Israel, and Palestine." *GH* 63 (Oct. 6, 1970), 832-34. Maintains that God's ethical and salvific requirements for Israel are not unique. Therefore, Christians cannot take sides in the present conflict, but should instead support reconciliation and justice for all involved.

Brenneman, Virgil J. "How a Christian Responds." *GH* 63 (July 14, 1970), 599-600. Calls attention to the violent rhetoric and actions of both law-and-order advocates and revolutionary activists, and challenges Christians to be active peacemakers and reconcilers.

Broaddus, Daryl. "Reconciliation: The Educational Agenda for the 80s." *Builder* 31 (July, 1981), 4-5. Calls Sunday school teachers to renewed commitment to reconciliation among different ethnic groups and offers suggestions on ways teachers might promote peaceful coexistence.

Brown, Dale W. "Peace and the Peace Churches." *ChrCent* 95 (Mar. 15, 1978), 266-70. "The . . . present push for ecumenical wholeness among the Friends, the increasing desire of Mennonites to be involved in mission, and the recent revival of their heritage among the Brethren may mean a *kairos* time for fresh examination of the theology of peacemaking."

Brown, Dale W. "The Free Church of the Future." *Kingdom, Cross, and Community,* ed. John R. Burkholder and Calvin Redekop. Scottdale: Herald Press, 1976, 259-72. Brown suggests guidelines for the free church of the future, including placing more emphasis on faithfulness to Christ's nonresistant way than on pragmatic concerns and greater compassionate, nonviolent involvement in the social order.

Brown, Dale W. "The Historic Peace Churches." *GH* 70 (Sept. 27, 1977), 714-16; also in *Menn* 93 (Jan. 3, 1978), 2-3. Traces the historical roots of Brethren, Mennonites, and Quakers, discussing their differences and their common commitment to discipleship within a community, proclaiming justice and peace.

Brown, Dale W. "Those 'Radical' Peace Churches." *ChrLead* 43 (July 15, 1980), 5-7. Historic connections and differences among Friends, Mennonites, and Church of the Brethren.

Brown, H. J. "The Christian Peace Witness in China." *Menn* 68, Part 1, (Dec. 8, 1953), 760-61; Part 2, (Dec. 15, 1953), 776-77. A history of Christianity in China, including Mennonite work there. Traces the missionary movement since the seventh century, with particular attention to that branch whose Gospel was truly a "peaceable Gospel."

Brown, Robert McAfee. "We Must Love One Another or Die." *GH* 66 (Dec. 25, 1973), 957-58. Reprinted from *California Living* (Dec. 24, 1967). Behind the manger lies the shadow of the cross, the brutal end of life for one who translated love into justice and refused to believe peace was only an ideal.

Brubaker, Suzanne. "The Joy of Touching." *The Other Side* 15 (Apr., 1979), 57-60. A discussion of how adults can teach children security, trust, love, and contentment.

Brunk, Conrad G. "Reflections on the Anabaptist View of Law and Morality." *CGR* 1 (Spring, 1983), 1-20. Law is never amoral; only within the church can law really reflect Christian justice and Christian love. While the church's ethic cannot truly be put into effect in the state, the ethic should, nevertheless, guide the law of the state because Christians live in both kingdoms and both are orders of law and morality.

Brunk, Conrad G. (Review). *On Earth Peace: Discussions on War/Peace Issues Between Friends, Mennonites, Brethren and European Churches, 1935-75*, by Durnbaugh, Donald F., ed. Elgin, Ill.: The Brethren Press, 1978. Pp. 412. *MQR* 53 (Oct., 1979), 331-33. Contains papers from the discussions between the minority pacifist churches and the larger ecumenical community of the World Council of Churches on the Christian basis of pacifism. Reviewer recognizes these papers as foundational in shaping the questions and the idiom for present discussion on the subject.

Brunk, George R., I. "Peace." *ST* 6 (July, 1934), 3. Examines how presence of peace is related to the strife and discord that must be dealt with in the church.

Brunk, George R., I. "Peace Witness." *ST* 3 (Apr., 1931), 5. Churches that want peace must strangle the demon-child, modernism. The church must leave to Caesar what belongs to Caesar and expend energies to keep the church separate from the world and, if possible, secure exemptions for religious nonresistants, a religious freedom which the constitution guarantees.

Brunk, Harry A. "True and False Peace Movements." *The Eastern Mennonite School Journal* 18 (Apr., 1940), 57-59. False peace movements are not founded on Scripture; are political; believe that war is the means to peace.

Brusewitz, C. F., *et al.* "A Dutch Peace Testimony." *Menn* 72 (Jan. 15, 1957), 37. In the context of military conflict in Egypt and Hungary, the Dutch Mennonite Peace Group issues a call to the total church to live in the Spirit of Jesus and to pray for peace.

Buckingham, Jamie. "If You Are for Peace, Don't Use This Symbol." *GfT* Series 2, 5 (Nov.-Dec., 1970), 12, 17. Reprinted from *Christian Life* (Sept., 1970). The popular peace symbol has its roots in satanic and other anti-Christ traditions.

Buckwalter, Clair. Letter to the Editor. *GH* 64 (July 6, 1971), 611. Criticizes *Gospel Herald* reporting of MDS repairing park benches at the Washington Monument because it incorrectly implies that the damage was done by peace demonstrators. Criticizes the MDS action for responding to a peace demonstration as an apparent blessing on Nixon's war policies, when it has not made similar gestures toward reconstruction after race riots.

Buckwalter, Ralph. "Japan Missionary Peace Conference Held." *CanMenn* 6 (Nov. 28, 1958), 4. Report of Dr. James Graham's message to the conference on "The Biblical Approach to Peace and War." Central is his distinction between God's "sovereign will" and his "absolute will."

Buckwalter, Ralph. "That They May Be One . . ." *GH* 54 (Oct. 3, 1961), 865, 878-79. A recounting of peace ventures in Japan, particularly the 1961 seminar on "the Ministry of Reconciliation in a World of Conflict" which brought together representatives of seven denominations active in Japan.

Burkhalter, Sheldon. "The Christian and Politics: A Proposal." *GH* 69 (Oct. 26, 1976), 818-19. Supports Christian participation in the voting process because of the Christian calling to witness to society. Presents criteria for judging among political candidates.

Burkhalter, Sheldon. "How to Pray for Government." *GH* 68 (Apr. 29, 1975), 325-27. Examining passages from Genesis, Romans, and 1 Timothy, Burkhalter concludes that to properly pray for government is to pray for international peace so that the gospel may advance, not to pronounce a blanket endorsement on government policies.

Burkholder, J. Lawrence. "Exercising the Ministry of Reconciliation." *GH* 48 (Aug. 2, 1955), 721-22, 741-42. Are there "unexplored avenues of nonpolitical influence" through which nonresistant Christians might work for peace and reconciliation between nations?

Burkholder, J. Lawrence. "Profile of a Conscientious Objector." *GH* 73 (Mar. 18, 1980), 217-19. Examines traditionally high expectations on the CO and calls for peacemakers who see the interconnection of all nations and who commit themselves to spiritual growth.

Burkholder, J. Lawrence. "The Mennonite Concept of the Church." *ChrLiv* 5, Part 1, "The Church," (Feb., 1958), 22-23, 40; Part 2, "The Community," (Mar., 1958), 22-23, 39. Rather than being known for its ethnic ties, the church should be known for its witness to peace and justice.

Burkholder, J. Richard. "Wars and Rumors . . ." *GH* 71 (Jan. 24, 1978), 62-64. Using statistics from global military and social expenditures, Burkholder challenges Christians to speak out against the worldwide armaments buildup.

Burkholder, J. Richard. "Witness to the State: A Mennonite Perspective." *GH* 69 (Aug. 17, 1976), 621-24. A sectarian version of witnessing to the state is to speak the truth about oppression, injustice, and evil, without succumbing to the temptation to impose one's faith on others.

Burkholder, J. Richard and Bender, John. *Children of Peace.* Elgin: The Brethren Press; Nappanee: Evangel Press; Newton: Faith and Life Press; Scottdale: Mennonite Publishing House, 1982. Pp. 160. Theme of book is that peace is a way as well as a goal. The first unit explores the biblical meanings of peace in both their Old Testament and New Testament contexts. The second unit deals with the practice of peace in various areas of life, such as home, community, politics, and the military. The third unit explores the church and state relationship and includes accounts of the ways some people are effectively and creatively witnessing to peace in militaristic and totalitarian countries.

Burkholder, Oscar. "Pray for Peace." *GH* 43 (Aug. 29, 1950), 849-50. A call to prayer for the peace which comes only from the Prince of Peace.

Burkholder, Oscar. "The Doctrine of Separation in Relation to the State." *ST* 19 (2nd Qtr., 1951), 24. The believer's attitude to the state should be one of intelligence, sympathy, concern, support, prayer, and obedience.

Burkholder, Peter. "Blessed Are the Peacemakers." Transl. by Joseph Funk. *GH* 34, Part 1, (May 22, 1941), 171-72; Part 2, (May 29, 1941), 187-88; Part 3, (June 5, 1941), 206. As the church, the kingdom of peace is already here. This kingdom, however, is defenseless and will be persecuted.

Burkholder, Richard. "Young Christians Consider War." *YCC* 33 (Aug. 24, 1952), 268. Description of the Christian Youth Conference on War held Apr. 25-27, 1952, in Columbus, Ohio.

Burnett, Kristina Mast. "Amidst Injustice Palestinian Teaches Resistance Based on Love." *Menn* 94 (Oct. 9, 1979), 600. Bishara Awad, headmaster of a school established by MCC in the West Bank, advocates a resistance based on love and reports that Palestinian Christian pacifists are looking for peaceful, nonviolent methods of protest.

Buttrick, George A. "Our Call and Cross." *MBH* 15 (Apr. 2, 1976), 5. The Christian cross is not private suffering but public risk-taking that confronts systems of war, poverty, unemployment, and racism.

Buzzard, Lynn and Kraybill, Ron, eds. *Mediation: A Reader.* Oak Park, Ill.: Christian Legal Society, 1980. Pp. various. MHL. Mennonite contributions include: Kraybill, "An Outline of the Biblical Basis for a Ministry of Reconciliation;" Kraybill, "Institutionalizing Mediations as an Alternative Dispute Mechanism: An Ethical Critique;" Kraybill, "The Mennonite Conciliation Service."

Byler, Raymond. Letter to the Editor. *GH* 64 (May 4, 1971), 410-11. Chastises church members and leaders for having no greater responsibility toward peace than the nonchurched, and Mennonites in particular for silently supporting warfare on the basis of Romans 13.

"Canadian Peace Churches Council Is Now a Reality." *CanMenn* 7 (Mar. 6, 1959), 1. Mennonite and Brethren in Christ representatives unite for peace and service witness by forming the Historic Peace Church Council of Canada.

"Central American Churches Approve Peace Statement." *MennRep* 9 (Sept. 3, 1979), 5. A Central American Consultation of Mennonite Churches approved a peace statement which had been prepared at a meeting of Central American Mennonites last year in Belize.

"Christian Theses of Peace." *CanMenn* 15 (Jan. 24, 1967), 5. A reprint from the publication of the All-Union Council of Evangelical Christians-Baptists in the USSR gives a description of what the Christian church should strive for—righteousness and peace on earth.

"Christians Ought to Warn Against War Everywhere." *CanMenn* 4 (Nov. 23, 1956), 8. Report of Martin Niemoeller's Menno Simons lectures at Bethel College in which he criticizes the just war theory as difficult to implement and describes the theological basis of peace as "an agreement with God's will."

"Christians to be Lambs, Not Hawks or Doves." *CanMenn* 14 (Dec. 13, 1966), 1, 8, 9. Report on an inter-Mennonite consultation in Minneapolis Dec. 2-4 called by MCC Peace Section to discuss the nature of the Mennonite witness to government.

"Christmas Gifts for Peace." *CanMenn* 10 (Nov. 23, 1962), 12. The MCC Peace Section staff offers an opportunity to give to the peace witness of MCC in lieu of giving Christmas gifts.

"Church Peace Mission Seminar Held in Virginia." *CanMenn* 10 (Sept. 7, 1962), 7. An interdenominational meeting to discuss "Kerygma and Ethos in the Nuclear Age," with Paul Peachey, William Klassen, and Norman Kraus participating.

"Church Peace Union." *GH* 28 (Apr. 18, 1935), 74. Argues that Christians should not participate in the Church Peace Union because it is supported not only by Christians but also by atheists and communists.

"Colloquy by Krister Stendahl, John Yoder, and Arthur Cohen." *Fellowship* 31 (May, 1965), 30-31. This three-way exchange is a response to Krister Stendahl's address at the Consultation for Leaders of Religion: Moral and Technological Implications of Peace on Earth. John Yoder discusses the role of the church in relation to decision making and political powers in an age of increasing cybernation.

"Conference Message to Christian Churches." *Menn* 68 (June 16, 1953), 375. Representatives at the 1953 conference on "The Church, the Gospel, and War" issue a strong call for reconciliation and the way of love and peace to the churches and to the nations.

"Conference on Church and War." *Menn* 65 (May 30, 1950), 380-81. Describes the key messages and summarizes the "affirmation and appeal" issued by the conference. Appeals to the Christian church throughout the world to repent of warmaking and to live the gospel of peace.

"Conscription Moves Accelerate." *GH* 72 (Mar. 27, 1979), 256. Three principal legislative approaches are being introduced in the Congress to reinstate military conscription; MCC has responded, speaking against the development.

Cepeda, Rafael. "The Church in Cuba." *ChrLiv* 11 (Nov., 1964), 22-24. Christians are called not to destroy communism, but to dialogue with Marxism in order to witness concerning true peace.

Charles, Bob, and Suderman, Dale. Letter to the Editor. *Menn* 89 (Apr. 23, 1974), 278. Peacemakers must decry the false peace of detente, which is bought at the price of oppression for small anad powerless nations.

Charles, Howard H. "Blessed Are the Peacemakers." *Builder* 31 (Jan., 1981), 31-35. The ongoing mission of peacemaking is set out in the context of the salt and light imagery of Matt. 5:13-16, which suggests the positive redemptive function of the new life in Christ.

Charles, Howard H. "The Kingdom Beyond Caste." *Builder* 14 (Feb., 1964), 17-18. What the Bible teaches about the way of the cross in group relations can and should be applied to the issues of racial conflict: the church "must reach agressively across all barriers with the call of the Gospel."

Chauvin, Jacques. "Peace and the Christian Church." *Menn* 93 (June 27, 1978), 420-21. Peace is inseparable from the struggle for justice. The church, in accumulating wealth, fails to live "shalom," because it separates itself from the struggle for justice.

*Christian Responsibility to Society.* Newton: Faith and Life Press. Church and Society Series No. 2, 1963. Because Jesus is Lord not only of the church but also of the world, some social ills may be partially corrected. Therefore we are mandated to labor toward the eradication of racial discrimination, capital punishment, war, etc.

Christner, Walter. Letter to the Editor. *GH* 69 (May 4, 1976), 393. Disagrees with the writer of "The Christian and the US Bicentennial" (Apr. 13, 1976), claiming that such uncritical participation in celebrating the Bicentennial denies Mennonite understandings of peace.

Claassen, Edith. "The Peace Movement in the Methodist Church." Student paper for Peace Principles, May, 1949. Pp. 28. MLA/BeC.

Clemens, Steve. Letter to the Editor. *God and Caesar* 4 (Nov., 1978), 9. Suggests "peace church" institutions should, at least, not withhold the war tax portion of the federal income tax for all employees. Discussion could then decide what should be done with those monies.

Coffman, S. F. *The Sixth Commandment: "Thou Shalt Not Kill."* Scottdale, Pa.: Peace Problems Committee of the Mennonite Church, n.d. Pp. 4. MHL. Excerpts statement prepared by

Mennonite General Conference, Goshen, Ind., Aug. 29, 1917, which addressed, among other matters, the reasons for nonparticipation in military service.

Coffman, S. F. "Bible Study: Christian Doctrine." ChrMon 39, Part 66: Peace," (Feb., 1947), 50-51; Part 67: "Peace," (Mar., 1947), 80-81; Part 68: "Peace—The Kingdom of Peace," (Apr., 1947), 114-115; Part 69: "The Kingdom of Peace," (May, 1947), 146-47; Part 70: "The Kingdom of Peace," (June, 1947), 176-77. Uses the Old Testament and the Lord's Prayer to show that the Kingdom of God is a kingdom of peace, personally, socially, and eternally. Because peace grows out of righteousness before God, Old Testament law is not a law of vengeance and judgment but a law of peace and goodwill.

Coffman, S. F. "Praying for Authorities (I Timothy 2)." GH 28 (JUne 20, 1935), 258-59. The Christian attitude toward government is respectful, quiet, and peaceable. A Christian should not voice criticism of the authorities but rather should pray for them, maintaining peace and good will toward all.

Companion Forum. "Does Christian Pacifism Help Our Witness to Christ?" YCC 44 (Sept. 1, 1963), 8. Students respond to the posed question, "Does Christian pacifism help our witness to Christ?"

Conant, Elizabeth Babbott. "Making Peace Possible." With 6 (Jan., 1973), 31. Analysis of the thirty-one-hour role play which tried to put peacemaking into practice on Grindstone Island, Canada.

Conrad, Tom. "Counsel Decides Against Military Chaplaincy." ChrLead 39 (Mar. 30, 1976), 10. The Board of Reference and Counsel decided that the US Mennonite Brethren Conference will not try to place men in the military chaplaincy because that might harm the church's historic position on peace and conscientious objection.

Cosby, Gordon. "Resting on Golgotha's Cross." GH 72 (Apr. 3, 1979), 268-69. The idolatry of our dependence on military expenditures for "national defense" negates our biblical faith and therefore we need to repent and pay the cost of repentance.

Cunningham, Spencer. "Rocky Flats: Denver's Three-Mile Island." Menn 94 (May 29, 1979), 376. The first anniversary protest attracts more than 10,000 who gathered Apr. 28 at the Rocky Flats nuclear weapons facility to call for an end to the manufacture of nuclear weapons.

"Dampen Fire in City of Man with Drops of Peace." CanMenn 16 (Mar. 26, 1968), 9. Walter Klaasen, in an interview, expresses belief that

an individual can make an important contribution to peace. He or she is not a mere "drop in the bucket" and, therefore, insignificant.

"Daniel Gerber Never Returned from His MCC Assignment." MennMirror 8 (Nov., 1978), 24. Gerber, captured in May, 1962, while on an MCC assignment in Vietnam and never again heard from, is a reminder that to follow Christ demands a willingness to sacrifice oneself.

"Day of Prayer for Peace." CanMenn 15 (Feb. 21, 1967), 12. Churches announce a day of prayer for peace.

"Declaration of Peace." Menn 53 (Nov. 29, 1938), 5. Official statement adopted by the Eighth Street Mennonite Church, Goshen, Indiana, in a time of increasing national militarism. "We cannot sanction war" nor lend our support to its implementation, states the document.

"Don E. Smucker Appointed to Peace Foundation." CanMenn 4 (Nov. 16, 1956), 11. Smucker's appointment as a director of the Robert Treat Payne Foundation adds an effective voice to the Mennonite church's peace witness in the broader Christian community.

"Dutch Church Expresses Interest in Civil Struggle." CanMenn 13 (Aug. 10, 1965), 1. Reports that the Rotterdam Mennonite Church has sent a letter of encouragement and appreciation to Martin Luther King, Jr.

Dalke, Robert E. "The Peace Witness of the Early Mennonites Compared to the Present." Student paper for Mennonite History, Feb. 25, 1968. Pp. 24. MLA/BeC.

DeFehr, Arthur. "A Proposal for an MCC Food Bank." MennMirror 4 (June, 1975), 7-8. Suggests ways MCC might become involved in an effort to stockpile a designated supply of food for humanitarian purposes.

Derstine, C. F. "Mennonite Group Against Military Service in Holland." ChrMon 26 (Dec., 1934), 380. Includes statement of principles by the Peace Committee of Dutch Mennonites and news of war resisters there.

Derstine, C. F. "Missions or Munitions." ChrMon 38 (Nov., 1946), 350-51. The futility of war should be an inspiration to devote greater attention to missions.

Derstine, C. F. "Our Testimony and a Wartorn World." ChrMon 28 (Aug., 1936), 254-55. Mennonites with a heritage of peace should witness publicly to the rising militarism.

Derstine, C. F. "'Seven Men Went Singing into Heaven.'" ChrMon 32 (July, 1940), 222-23. Story of seven Bolshevik soldiers who were converted underscores the idea that the Gospel must be preached also to military personnel.

Derstine, C. F. "The Atomic Bomb a Milestone or a Tombstone." *ChrMon* 38 (Jan., 1946), 30-32. The awful power of the atomic bomb should move Christians to greater prayer, repentance, and foreign mission work.

Derstine, C. F. "The High Cost of Killing." *ChrMon* 33 (Jan., 1941), 31. While the world pours time, money, and lives into the world war, conscientious objectors should be active in prayer and sacrificial living.

Derstine, C. F. "The Trail of Blood." *ChrMon* 45 (Oct., 1953), 319. Review of the sufferings of the Anabaptists for their break with the state church.

Derstine, C. F. "The Universal Inquiry into the Legitimacy of War." *ChrMon* 26 (July, 1934), 221-22. Mennonites, with a history of peace witness, have a contribution to make to present popular opinion which is becoming critical of war.

Derstine, C. F. "The War Ended, the Malady Lingering On." *ChrMon* 39 (Dec., 1947), 382-83. In the face of continued world tensions, evangelical Christians should pray, practice loving enemies, support European evangelism and relief work.

Derstine, Norman. "Peacemakers in a Broken World." *GH* 61 (Jan. 23, 1968), 82-84. Elaborating on the peacemaker beatitude, the author reviews Christian attitudes toward participation in war from the early church through the Reformation, citing also American Mennonite experiences with conscientious objection.

Detweiler, J. F. "Peace!" *GH* 36 (Sept. 30, 1943), 546-47, 555, 557. An examination of Old Testament prophetic writings as to their vision of future world peace. When the prophets spoke of peace they were foretelling the church of Jesus Christ rather than a national world peace.

Detweiler, Richard C. "God's Peace Action—and Ours." *YCC* 49 (Apr. 28, 1968), 7. Incarnation, atonement, resurrection, and community are four aspects of God's peace action. The Christian's peace action is to participate in the ministry of reconciliation.

Detweiler, Richard C. *Mennonite Statements on Peace, 1915-1966: A Historical and Theological Review of Anabaptist-Mennonite Concepts of Peace Witness and Church-State Relations.* Scottdale, Pa.: Herald Press, 1968. Pp. 71. Finds that the Mennonite peace witness has essentially affirmed and restated the historic Anabaptist understandings on these issues while (in the process of relating these concerns to the contemporary situations) intensifying, clarifying, and expanding the early articulations. Includes observations on some of the theological implications of these trends in the recent peace witness.

Detweiler, Richard C. "Peace Is the Will of God." *Peacemakers in a Broken World.* Ed. John A. Lapp. Scottdale: Herald Press, 1969, 67-74. Builds a peace theology on four scriptural assertions: that peace is God's will for humanity; that Jesus Christ is the locus of God's peace action; that Christians should be ministers of reconciliation; that God's action in Christ is the model for Christian peacemaking.

Detweiler, Richard C. "Peace Is the Will of God." *YCC* 49 (Apr. 21, 1968), 3. If peace is God's will, and strife or brokenness of life in any form reflects human sin, we have a powerful thrust and motivation toward peacemaking.

Detweiler, Richard C. "The Biblical Basis for Peace Action." Paper, Feb. 24, 1968. Pp. 5. MHL.

Detweiler, Richard C. "The Pattern for Christian Peacemaking." *YCC* 49 (May 5, 1968), 8. Describes several principles of peacemaking.

Dick, Ernie (Review). *A Strategy for Peace,* by Frank H. Epp. Grand Rapids: Eerdmans, 1973. Pp. 128. "Essays 'Point Finger' at Exploitation and Injustice." *MennRep* 4 (Apr. 1, 1974), 8. Although the essays were delivered as addresses in the late 1960s and early 1970s, their message of striving after peace remains timely. Most helpful essays deal with themes of nationalism, dialogue between pacifists and nonpacifists, arms buildup, complicity of the Christian church in making war.

Dick, La Verne J. "Peace, Our Shaft of Light." *Menn* 86 (Nov. 2, 1971), 646-49. Witnesses to those aspects in Mennonite faith and practice in history which spell out the message of peace.

Dick, Mervin. "Families in Pieces or Families at Peace?" *ChrLead* 42 (Mar. 27, 1979), 2. Looks at peacemaking in the context of the family.

Dick, N. S. *The Peacemaker.* Scottdale: Herald Press and Newton: Faith and Life Press, 1972. Pp. 63. A Bible study guide on peacemaking organized into 13 lessons. Topics include the Jesus way, Old Testament wars, the relationship between poverty and militarism, patriotism, servanthood, etc. Resources include films, music, poetry, discussion questions.

Dick, Nicholas W. "The Church Peace Mission." Paper presented to Mennonite Polity and Church Administration class, Mennonite

Biblical Seminary, Elkhart, Ind., Apr. 29, 1959. Pp. 16. AMBS.

Diener, Harry A. "Peace, Peaceable, Peacemakers." *ChrMon* 43, Part 1, (June, 1951), 169-70; Part 2, (July, 1951), 201-202; Part 3, (Aug., 1951), 233-34. Peace program based on Romans 12 discusses inner peace, peace with friends, peace with enemies, and overcoming evil with good.

Dirks, Sylvester (Review). *Mission and the Peace Witness*, by Robert L. Ramseyer. Kitchener: Herald Press, 1979. Pp. 134. *MBH* 19 (Feb. 1, 1980), 29. Reviewer criticizes the perceived tendency of Mennonite missiologists to accept tenets of liberation theology.

Dirks, Victor A. "'War, Peace, and Freedom' a Lutheran Confrontation." *CanMenn* 14 (Nov. 1, 1966), 1, 4. A Mennonite observes that Lutheran young people are confronting American Lutheran Church leadership with peace ideas from the New Testament. The writer recalls Conrad Grebel and the Anabaptists and then considers the peace witness of the present-day Mennonites.

Dirrim, Allen W. "Political Implications of Sixteenth Century Hessian Anabaptism." *MennLife* 19 (Oct., 1964), 179-83. The Anabaptists' striving for a free and separate church and their absolute New Testament ethic, plus real and alleged connections with the Peasants' Revolt in 1525, are reasons why they were not accepted by their contemporaries.

Doerksen, Victor. "The Peace Witness in an Age of Pacifism." *MBH* 1 (July 20, 1962), 5-7. The peace witness is not the center of the gospel but must grow out of the center of faith; it must be a fruit of the Spirit.

Doerksen, Victor. "The Peace Witness in an Age of Pacifism." Term paper, 1961. Box 10-H-5. CMBS/Win.

Dourte, Eber. "To Serve the Present Age." *EV* 92 (Jan. 25, 1979), 9. At the semi-annual meeting of the MCC Peace Section, the agenda included reports and discussion on the New Call to Peacemaking, peace education, the World Arms Race and our peace witness, and the possibility of draft for military service.

Drescher, James M. "Is the Peace Ethic Optional for Anabaptists?" *GH* 73 (Oct. 7, 1980), 789. Commitment to the peace ethic, central to the New Testament andn Anabaptist history, should be as much a prerequisite for Mennonite membership as baptism.

Drescher, James M. "Living and Passing on an Ethic." *Builder* 29 (July, 1979), 6-9. Calls the church to recapture a vision of peace as God's

way and to make a conscious, consistent and systematic effort to transmit that vision to our children and youth.

Drescher, John M. "Cuba and Christian Concern." *GH* 55 (Nov. 13, 1962), 995. Some concerns arising out of the Cuban crisis are expressed. It is time to declare and believe that Christ is the Prince of Peace, and to confess that the church has not cared enough about the oppressed people of the world. This unconcern has helped give rise to communism.

Drescher, John M. "Demonstration . . . Then Proclamation." *ChrLead* 42 (May 22, 1979), 24. Before one talks of love and reconciliation, one must make love and reconciliation visible.

Drescher, John M. "Force for Peace." *GH* 65 (Aug. 29, 1972), 673. Political involvement and a materialistic outlook hinder an effective peace witness and forceful proclamation of reconciliation.

Drescher, John M. "Kill Toys Teach the 'Game' of Killing." *MBH* 7 (Nov. 29, 1968), 4-5; *Menn* 83 (Dec. 3, 1968), 746-47. Since replicas of the "machines of violence" contradict the spirit of Jesus, Christians should boycott and protest vigorously against "war toys."

Drescher, John M. "Racism or Reconciliation." *GH* 58 (Apr. 27, 1965), 359. Racism and ill feelings on race lead to murder. Christians must as reconcilers seek to quench this spirit of hatred.

Drescher, John M. "Validating Our Peace Position." *MBH* 19 (Nov. 7, 1980), 2-3. A valid peace position must be rooted in Christology, supported by personal witness, and not jeopardized by wealth.

Drescher, John M. "We Talked About Peace." *GH* 62 (Jan. 7, 1969), 6. Describes issues surrounding peacemaking discussed by Friends, Brethren, and Mennonites at a Historical Peace Church Conference.

Drescher, John M. (Editorial). "Peacemaker Questions." *GH* 61 (July 2, 1968), 585. Interprets "separation of church and state" to mean that the church should be the conscience of society raising questions on issues of military service and payment of war taxes.

Driedger, Arthur. "Hostetter Addresses Historic Peace Churches in Ontario." *CanMenn* 3 (Nov. 4, 1955), 1. Report of the annual Conference of Historic Peace Churches at Leamington, Ontario. Harvey Toews and C. N. Hostetter addressed the conference on the themes of "Service and Missions" and "Rethinking Our Peace Position."

Driedger, Leo, ed. *School of Peace*. Newton: Board of

Christian Service, GCMC, [1961?]. MHL. Curriculum designed to emphasize peace as a basic teaching of the Bible and our Christian faith. Planned for four sessions. Dick, Nickolas, "Blessed Are the Peacemakers: A Manual for Leaders of Adults," pp. 39; Reusser, James, "Blessed Are the Peacemakers: A Manual for Leaders of Intermediates and Youth," pp. 22; Rich, Elaine Sommers, "Blessed Are the Peacemakers: A Manual for Teachers of Juniors," pp. 17; Harder, Geraldine Gross, "Loving All the Time: A Manual for Teachers of Primary Children," pp. 41; "Peace School Activity Sheets for Primaries;" "Peace Maker Packet: Juniors."

Driedger, Leo. "Peacemakers in Africa." *CanMenn* 10 (Nov. 9, 1962), 6. Africa is a continent in turmoil. The need for concerned and praying Christian peacemakers is paramount.

Driedger, Leo, *et. al.* "War and Rumors of War." *Menn* 78 (Nov. 5, 1963), 664-66. A symposium on war and its meaning for peacemakers. Subjects include children and the bomb, fallout shelters, disarmament, peace witness in service and evangelism, and alternatives to violence.

Driver, Bonita and John. "Peacemakers at Work in Spain." *GH* 73 (Mar. 4, 1980), 190-91. Describes the individual work assignments as well as the corporate life of the Christian community in Barcelona as it witnesses to peace.

Driver, John. "Jeremiah's Message for the Church." *GH* 68 (June 3, 1975), 416-18. Jeremiah's vision of living the future now, rather than succumbing either to quick revolutions or spiritualizing the gospel, is a peacemaking vision for Christians in Latin America.

Dueck, Allan. "Implications of the Early Anabaptist View of Economics for Hutterites and Mennonites Today." Paper entered in John Horsch Essay Contest, Goshen College, Goshen, Ind., May 15, 1972. Pp. 20. MHL.

Dueck, Allan. "Vision and Reality." *Direction* 8 (Oct., 1979), 21-27. Compares the Mennonite Brethren Confession of Faith (1975) to the Kauffman-Harder survey in *Anabaptists Four Centuries Later* (Scottdale: Herald Press, 1975) and concludes that while MBs agree on doctrinal beliefs, they disagree on moral practices such as participation in war, sensitivity to social injustices, etc.

Duhs, Lindsay. "Doing Things Never Imagined." *Forum* 10 (Feb., 1977), 10. A member of the Sojourner community reflects on her involvement with this group which seeks to bring about social change through the working out of their Christian faith and identifying with the poor.

Durnbaugh, Donald F. "Historic Peace Churches: Who Are They and What Do They Do?" *MennRep* 9 (Oct. 29, 1979), 5. The three historic peace churches—the Society of Friends, the Mennonites, and the Church of the Brethren— have held to a consistent peace position and a persistent willingness to reach out to those suffering from acts of war, social oppression, or natural catastrophe.

Dyck, C. J. "Curitiba as Discipline for Listeners." *Menn* 86 (Apr. 27, 1971), 283. How can society be changed? "We need to discover that not every social problem has a political solution, that many of the deepest social needs have personal, spiritual, and moral answers, before political answers."

Dyck, C. J. "No Politics Lid Put on Brazil Conference." *Menn* 86 (Feb. 23, 1971), 132, 133. Curitiba conversations on locating the Mennonite World Conference show how difficult it is to draw a clear line between religious and social concerns and their political implications.

Dyck, C. J. and Dick, Nicholas. "The Word of God in the Nuclear Age." *Menn* 74 (May 19, 1959), 308-309. Report of the Church Peace Mission's interdenominational peace conference. The biblical orientation was notable as was the outstanding unity across denominational boundaries.

Dyck, Cornelius J. "The Peace Witness of MCC." Chapter 1 in *Witness and Service in North America.* Vol. 3 in *The Mennonite Central Committee Story.* Scottdale and Kitchener: Herald Press, 1980. Pp. 9-79. Consists of eighteen MCC documents which describe various aspects of MCC's peace witness. Document 14 is a policy statement regarding the MCC Peace Section Washington Office, stating its purposes in relation to the Mennonite constituency and in relation to the U.S. government. It cites the topical content of the various Mennonite Testimonies presented to Congress, 1940-72.

Dyck, Peter J. "Our Peace Witness in Relation to Government." Revised from an address given at a Peace Conference, Eden Church, Moundridge, Kansas, June 17, 1956. Pp. 8. MLA/BeC., MHL.

Dyck, Peter J. "Service as Lifestyle." *GH* 67 (Dec. 31, 1974), 982-85. Dyck advocates a lifestyle of service and peacemaking rather than upward mobility.

"Evaluations by Delegates at Ontario Peace Retreat." *CanMenn* 13 (Oct. 5, 1965), 11. Fourteen evaluations by young people who participated in the inter-Mennonite Peace

Retreat held at Chesley Lake Camp Sept. 17-19.

Early, Richard K. "The Origin of Conflict." *GH* 73 (July 8, 1980), 539. Also in *The Menn* 95 (Oct. 14, 1980), 582-83. No one who believes Jesus destroyed Satan's power through the cross can justify the use of conflict as a method of peacemaking.

Eby, Omar. "Mennonites from Israel, Arab Territories Convene in Athens." *CanMenn* 17 (July 4, 1969), 1, 2. Report on a meeting of Mennonite personnel in Athens Apr. 10-12 to discuss peace and reconciliation in the Middle East. Participants came from the East Bank, the West Bank, Israel, Lebanon, the US, and Europe. Action was taken to see what could be done about repatriation and resettlement of Arab refugees. First step was for West Bank/Israel personnel to make concrete proposal to the Israeli government. Politics in the Old Testament, myths about Arab countries and Israel and the refugee problem in the Middle East were discussed.

Eby, Omar. "Turmoil Coming to South Africa." *Menn* 84 (Apr. 8, 1969), 236-38. Reflects on conditions in South African countries that could lead to increased race conflicts and guerrilla warfare. Would a Mennonite presence benefit the peace witness here?

Eby, Sarah Ann. "Delegates Explore Peace." *RepConsS* 34 (May, 1977), 1, 6. European and North American Christians meet in W. Germany to discuss how the form of a congregation, which defines the relation between church and state, affects the congregation's peace witness.

Ediger, Donovan. Letter to the Editor. *ChrLead* 39 (Feb. 3, 1976), 14. Should not get so wrapped up in trying to bring peace on earth that we forget to tell people of Jesus and how he can bring peace in one's heart.

Ediger, Max. Letter to the Editor. *MBH* 19 (Feb. 29, 1980), 8. Being peacemakers in Southeast Asia has meant, for the MCCers, trying to develop solutions deeper than the "bandaid" remedy of handouts.

Ediger, Peter J. "America! America!" *GH* 69 (June 29, 1976), 527-28; "America! America! A Litany of Love and Lamentation." *MennRep* 6 (June 28, 1976), 5; *Menn* 91 (June 22, 1976), 413-16. Poem intended for use during worship on July 4 includes allusions from the Declaration of Independence, national hymns, Old Testament prophets, and Martin Luther King, woven into an outcry against American militarism and exploitation, and a prayer for peace.

Ediger, Peter J. "Explo '72." *Post-American* 1 (Fall, 1972), 13. Reflections upon presenting a witness for peace at Campus Crusade for Christ's convention.

Ediger, Peter J. "Jonah Revisited . . . Unfinished (Still)." *God and Caesar* 6 (Jan., 1980), 7-8. Poem comparing Jonah's mission to the North American Mennonite mission to be a peace witness to US and Canadian governments.

Ediger, Peter J. "Prayer." *MennRep* 10 (May 12, 1980), 5. Prayer for peace prepared for a prayer service at Rocky Flats nuclear plant.

Ediger, Peter J. "Rocky Flats: 'The Light Keeps Coming On.' " *MennRep* 8 (June 12, 1978), 5. Reflections on the Rocky Flats nuclear weapons plant peace rally, and a call for further Mennonite awareness of the nuclear arms buildup and witness against it.

Ediger, Peter J.; Lang, Sue; Lawless, Patty; Roberts, Marge. "Witness at Air Force Academy Chapel." *God and Caesar* 5 (Feb., 1979), 3-4. Excerpts from statements made by these, among other people, who were arrested during a week of prayer and fasting at the Colorado Springs Air Force Academy Chapel.

Ediger, Viola and Ferd. "Peace Mission in Japan to Students and Pastors." *CanMenn* 10 (Feb. 23, 1962), 5. A summary of peace witness activities carried out by the Edigers in Japan. Inter-Mennonite projects such as work camps are central.

Enns, Mary M. "MCC: Honey and Money Help to Meet Human Needs." *MennMirror* 4 (June, 1975), 7-9. Spending a working day with Arthur Driedger, executive director of MCC (Manitoba), gives author a sense of the variety of activities with which MCC is involved.

Ens, Adolph [sic] (Review). *Kingdom, Cross, and Community*, ed. J. Richard Burkholder and Calvin Redekop. Scottdale: Herald Press, 1976. Pp. 323. *MennRep* 7 (June 13, 1977), 9. Adolf Ens finds this 80th birthday tribute to Guy F. Hershberger by peace church scholars less exciting than Hershberger's own groundbreaking work in twentieth-century Mennonite peace problems.

Epp, Albert H. "Positive Approach to Peace." *Menn* 94 (Nov. 27, 1979), 706-707. Writer sets forth four principles for a positive approach to a peace witness which is characterized by light and deed, by respecting authority and not condemning it.

Epp, Carl. "Our Peace Witness in Society." *CanMenn* 11 (May 31, 1963), 6, 8. Peace has an elusive quality about it and constant striving is necessary to maintain it. An individual relationship to the Prince of Peace leads to peace witness on other levels.

Epp, Dick H.; Giesbrecht, P. U.; Lehn, Cornelia; Willms, Alfred. "In My Opinion: The Significance of the Canadian Peace Study Conference." *CanMenn* 2 (Apr. 23, 1954), 7. Four letters assessing the Apr. 9-10 Winnipeg peace conference.

Epp, Frank H. "A Call to Repentance." *CanMenn* 3 (Aug. 12, 1955), 2. A statement of repentance drawn up by the Fellowship of Reconciliation and concerned individuals on the tenth anniversary of the dropping of the atomic bomb. The nation which developed atomic power for war has the responsibility to develop atomic power for peace.

Epp, Frank H. *A Strategy for Peace: Reflections of a Christian Pacifist.* Grand Rapids: Wm. B. Eerdmans, 1973. Pp. 128. Eleven essays on topics related to war and peace, such as pacifism, militarism, nationalism, social order. Includes essays previously published in other collections, for example: "The Unilateral Disarmament of the Church" (*Peacemakers in a Broken World,* 1969); "American Causes of World War III" (*The Star-Spangled Beaver,* ed. Redekop, 1971); "Evangelism and Peace" (*Probe,* ed. Fairfield, 1972).

Epp, Frank H. "A United Peace Witness of Churches Across Canada." *CanMenn* 5 (May 10, 1957), 5-6. Reports that the inter-Mennonite peace conference plans for the extension of the Conference of Historic Peace Churches to a Canada-wide organization.

Epp, Frank H. "CO's or PM's." *CanMenn* 5 (Dec. 13, 1957), 2. "We are called to actively engage in peacemaking, to act as shock absorbers to the evil of the world, to help relieve the pressures which generate war."

Epp, Frank H. Letter to the Editor. *MennRep* 8 (Jan. 23, 1978), 6. Candidate for Canadian federal nomination defends his decision on the basis of Anabaptist views of church and state and continuity with his own life of conscientious protest and involved activism.

Epp, Frank H. "Makers of Peace." *CanMenn* 6 (Oct. 3, 1958), 2. The United Church of Canada is lauded for its stand for peace. The church has as much to say to government today about nuclear bombs as John the Baptist had to say to Herod about having the wrong wife.

Epp, Frank H. *Mennonites in Canada, 1920-1940. A People's Struggle for Survival,* Vol. 2. Toronto: Macmillan of Canada, 1982. Pp. 640. The concluding chapter of this extensive historical survey is entitled "Facing the World" and includes discussion of the issues of war and peace, church and state, Germanism, communism, peace conferences and resolutions.

Epp, Frank H. "No War in the World." *CanMenn* 2 (July 23, 1954), 2. An editorial statement underscoring the cease-fire in Indo-China and a call for prayer support for world leaders. Prayer is needed that these leaders not resort to the weapons of war.

Epp, Frank H. "Peace Mission in Orient Should Be Escalated." *CanMenn* 14 (Apr. 5, 1966), 3. A report on the peace activity, history and present needs of the MCC peace section in Japan. Based on Mar. 1-Apr. 5 tour to Asia, Epp argues that with nationalism's threat to the church in Asia, MCC Peace Section should support more peace education activity in the Far East.

Epp, Frank H. "Peace on the Retreat." *CanMenn* 12 (Aug. 4, 1964), 4. "Unless our Mennonite churches will be better stewards of the special gift God has given us, our historic torch will be taken from us, and the gospel of peace will be given to others to preach."

Epp, Frank H. "Peace Witness as Evangelism." *Probe.* Ed. James Fairfield. Scottdale: Herald Press, 1972, 27-41. Also "Which Call?" *Evangelism: Good News or Bad.* Pamphlet of MCC Peace Section and MCC (Canada), n.d. [1973?], 1-9. Epp supports his thesis that evangelism and peace must go together by looking at the person of Christ, the human social condition, and effective communication.

Epp, Frank H. "The Church in the Nuclear Age." *CanMenn* 10 (Sept. 7, 1962), 2, 8. A ten-point peace position is set forth as a guide to the church in the nuclear age. Jesus Christ is the focal point for hope in this time.

Epp, Frank H. "The Church Peace Council." *CanMenn* 7 (Mar. 6, 1959), 2. The formation of the Historic Peace Church Council of Canada is seen as a positive venture in which all Mennonite groups should participate.

Epp, Frank H. "The Effort for Peace." *CanMenn* 9 (Sept. 8, 1961), 2. Mennonite peace conferences are a small but significant part of the work of peacemaking in the present time of crisis.

Epp, Frank H. "The Hard and Heavy Cross of the Christian Church." *CanMenn* 14 (Oct. 4, 1966), 7. The dangers of giving a peace witness in the war-ravaged country of Vietnam.

Epp, Frank H. "The Peace Witness." *CanMenn* 11 (Aug. 27, 1963), 5. A reprint of Dr. H. A. Fast's statement as secretary of the General Conference Board of Christian Service regarding the unique opportunities for the peace witness of the Christian gospel in today's world.

Epp, Frank H. "The Prince of Peace." *CanMenn* 10 (Dec. 14, 1962), 6. Like the prophet Isaiah, the church expects the time when all will be light and the darkness will have vanished. But "as we wait we may not become weary because we are coworkers in bringing it to pass."

Epp, Frank H. "The Unilateral Disarmament of the Church." *Peacemakers in a Broken World.* Ed. John A Lapp. Scottdale: Herald Press, 1969, 126-43. Unilateral disarmament is considered impractical by American society because the rich fear losing their wealth. Epp maintains that Christians must cultivate an understanding of property as a stewardship resource in order to free themselves from dependence on the military for security. The church's unilateral disarmament would be truly a form of peace witness to the state.

Epp, Frank H. "The World's Largest Peace Church." *Menn* 84 (Sept. 30, 1969), 578-80. The story of the origin and development of a three-million-member peace church in the Congo, the Kimbanguists.

Epp, Frank H. "Two Christian Peacemakers." *CanMenn* 9 (Dec. 15, 1961), 2. In their search for guidance in the work of peacemaking, Christians have the examples of Dag Hammarskjold and Albert John Luthuli, Nobel peace prize winners.

Epp, Frank H. "Witness to Government." *CanMenn* 11 (Feb. 22, 1963), 6. Supports the witness given by the Peace, Social and Economic Relations Committee of the Ontario Conference in its letters to government agencies. More such opportunities to witness should be taken.

Epp, Frank H. (Editorial). "A United Peace Witness of Churches Across Canada." *CanMenn* 5 (May 10, 1957), 5-6. A report of an organizational meeting for a Canadian peace witness.

Epp, Frank H. (Editorial). "CO's or PM's." *CanMenn* 5 (Dec. 13, 1957), 2. A call to be peacemakers today, not only CO's of World Wars I and II.

Epp, Frank H. (Editorial). "Evangelism and Revolution." *CanMenn* 14 (Sept. 13, 1966), 5. A call to "spearhead a world revolution" in which a rich society is called to adopt the way of the cross.

Epp, Frank H. (Editorial). "No War in the World." *CanMenn* 2 (July 23, 1954), 2. Urges prayer for world leaders that they may not once again resort to violent solutions to the problems of international relationships.

Epp, Frank H. (Editorial). "Non-Resistant Love and Evangelism." *CanMenn* 4 (Mar. 9, 1956), 2. Epp asks that the ethic of love in the New Testament not be diluted in the name of evangelism. He sees the two as inseparable.

Epp, Frank H. (Editorial). "Peace Sunday." *CanMenn* 8 (Nov. 4, 1960), 2. Contends that church cannot separate peace teaching from evangelistic outreach.

Epp, Frank H. (Editorial). "Witness in Ottawa." *CanMenn* 5 (May 10, 1957), 2. Epp urges the church to witness for peace before a major crisis occurs.

Epp, Frank H. (Editorial). "You Have the Button." *CanMenn* 6 (Oct. 31, 1958), 2; *ChrLiv* 6 (Mar., 1959), 3. Humankind has the "button" to destruction, but God has the ultimate weapon—love. If we profess Christ, we have the "button" of reconciliation.

Epp, Frank H. (Review). *Mission and the Peace Witness: The Gospel and Christian Discipleship,* ed. Robert L. Ramseyer. Scottdale: Herald Press, with the Institute of Mennonite Studies, 1979. Pp. 152. *FQ* 6 (Nov., Dec., 1979, Jan., 1980), 11. While the book's audience is not clearly targeted, the message that evangelizing and the peace witness go together is very important.

Epp, George K. (Review). *Peacemakers in a Broken World,* ed. John A. Lapp. Scottdale: Herald Press, 1969. *The Voice* 19 (Apr., 1970), 25-26. Applauds editor's choice of 12 essays representing a solid cross-section of views on the issues of reconciliation in a complex world. Urges readers to examine the essays critically in order to come to greater understanding of the issues.

Epp, George K. (Review). *Soldiers of Compassion,* by Urie Bender. Scottdale: Herald Press, 1969. Pp. 319. *The Voice* 19 (July, 1970), 27-28. This interesting and well-written book belongs in every Mennonite home because it helps young people to know that the alternatives to violence, while demanding, are also rewarding.

Epp, Henry H. "Making a Dynamic Witness Today." *CanMenn* 7 (June 5, 1959), 2, 7. Presents the problems and opportunities of peace churches in the twentieth century as emphasized at the Church Peace Mission conference. The peace churches' witness to other denominations is needed.

Erb, Paul. "A Call to Peacemakers." *GH* 48 (Aug. 2, 1955), 723-24. Mennonites should explore more fully the nonpolitical methods of peacemaking. "Why not be peacemakers in the international context where the peace of the world seems chiefly to be threatened?"

Erb, Paul. "Prayer for Our Government." *GH* 44 (May 8, 1951), 435-36. Even though Mennonites cannot agree with the militarism of the US, we must still pray for the leaders of the country.

Erb, Paul. "The Peace Corps." *GH* 54 (May 16, 1961), 443-44. Description of the newly initiated Peace Corps, a valuable supplement to the work the churches have been doing. Suggests there can be some cooperation between church agencies and the Peace Corps.

Erb, Paul. "World-Wide Peace Testimony." *GH* 48 (May 10, 1955), 435. What message does the Mennonite church preach in its evangelistic efforts? The peace testimony must be an integral part of the evangelistic and missionary emphasis.

Esau, Alvin (Review). *Christian Faith and Criminal Justice*, by Gerald Austin McHugh. Paulist Press, 1978. Pp. 234. *MBH* 18 (Sept. 14, 1979), 26-27. Reviewer observes that the book's thesis states that a Christian approach to the penal system must be based on love of enemies, forgiveness, and reconciliation.

Escobar, Samuel and Driver, John. *Christian Mission and Social Justice*. Institute of Mennonite Studies, Missionary Studies No. 5. Scottdale: Herald Press, 1978. Pp. 112. Four essays bring to bear biblical perspectives and a historical critique derived from a reappraisal of the distinctive Anabaptist experience in the Reformation on the issues of mission and justice today. The application of these perspectives results in seeing missions and justice as necessary complements rather than a polarity. Essays are: "The Need for Historical Awareness;" "The Gospel and the Poor;" "Reform, Revolution, and Missions;" "The Anabaptist Vision and Social Justice."

Estep, William R. "Separation as Sedition: America's Debt to the Anabaptists." *ChrToday* 20 (May 21, 1976), 872-74. Attempts a fair presentation of major Anabaptist tenets, including voluntary church membership, religious liberty, and the corresponding limitation of the state's authority to temporal affairs.

Ewert, Mrs. D. P. "What Should We Be Doing for Peace?" *Menn* 85 (Jan. 20, 1970), 42, 43. Suggests areas in which peacemaking is urgently needed: the search for true and reliable information; the chasm between youth and adult; poverty areas, race relations, and corrections.

"Five Peace Ambassadors to Speak for Church." *CanMenn* 12 (Jan. 28, 1964), 3. A report on the MCC Peace Section's annual meeting, focusing on race relations. Summary of a panel discussion on racial conflict.

"Food and Peace Traveler Visits Campuses." *Forum* 8 (Apr., 1975), 8. Ray Hamm has joined the MCC Peace Section as campus food and peace traveler, which will involve visiting various Mennonite, Brethren in Christ, evangelical colleges, and universities to share food crisis and peace concerns, to facilitate activities related to food crises and to make resource materials available.

"Friends, Brethren, and Mennonites Meet." *RepConsS* 5 (Mar., 1947), 3. Reports a two-day meeting of historic peace churches at Akron, Pa., on "Peace Education in the Home, Sunday School, and the Church."

"From the Press: A Journey for Peace." *MennRep* 7 (Nov. 28, 1977), 7. Editorial reprinted from *Christian Science Monitor* (Nov. 22, 1977). Tribute to Prime Minister Begin of Israel and President Sadat of Egypt for the courage to carry out their historic peacemaking meeting in Jerusalem.

Fast, Heinold. "The Anabaptists as Trouble Makers." Trans. John H. Yoder. Paper presented to annual meeting of the Doopsgezinde Vredesgroep, Utrecht, May 3, 1975. Pp. 11. MLA/BeC.

Finnerty, Adam. "Confessions of an Activist." *With* 12 (Sept., 1979), 32. Includes suggestions for a would-be activist.

Ford, Leighton. "The Church and Evangelism in a Day of Revolution." *GH* 62, Part 1, (Dec. 9, 1969), 1046-48; Part 2, (Dec. 16, 1969), 1076-78. Contemporary revolutions issue a crucial call to change, but only the Christian message will cause effective, lasting change, because revolutions must grapple with sin. The gospel deals with sin, but one must follow conversion with commitment to social change.

Foreman, Dennis W. "How to Get Along with One's Enemies." *ChrMon* 38 (Oct., 1946), 297-98. Comment on Jesus' teachings concerning overcoming evil with good.

Franken-Liefrinck, E. "The Work of the Dutch Mennonite Peace Group." *CanMenn* 5 (Sept. 13, 1957), 4. Dutch Mennonites participate in alternative service and discussion for the cause of peace. Explains provisions for Dutch conscientious objectors and the activities of the Mennonite Peace Group.

Fransen, Harold. "Cold War Thaw and Mennonite Response." *Menn* 95 (Apr. 1, 1980), 225. Interprets the Soviet invasion of Afghanistan as an attempt to inhibit the rise of a nationalist Islamic state, and calls on Mennonites to take a public peace stance during present cold war politics.

Fransen, Harold. "The Savor of SALT." *Menn* 94 (Oct. 30, 1979), 653. Writer attempts to show the complexities of the SALT II issue and raises the question of where we as Christians endorsing a peace postition give our voice.

Franz, Delton. "Peace Section Testifies at Senate's Hearings." *CanMenn* 19 (Feb. 19, 1971), 23. Peace witness before government expresses hope that the US will discontinue conscription. Includes short dialogue between Senator Goldwater and William Keeney.

Franz, Delton. "1976: An Appropriate Mennonite Celebration." *ChrLiv* 17 (Jan., 1970), 27-29. Mennnonite voice to government must become louder on issues of war, racism, and poverty.

Franz, Delton. "A Witness on Behalf of the Powerless. *MCC PS Wash. Memo* 9 (July-Aug., 1977), 3-4. Patty Erb's meeting with members of Congress alerted them to injustice being done to the poor and prisoners in a country supported by US military aid.

Franz, Delton. "Brazilian Bishop Works for Peace with Justice." *Menn* 89 (Dec. 17, 1974), 745; "Brazilian Bishop Helps the Poor." *MBH* 13 (Dec. 13, 1974), 21-22. Describes the work of Dom Helder Camara for peace and justice for the poor of Brazil.

Franz, Delton. "Exported to Latin America: Safe Religion or Costly Discipleship?" *Peace Section Newsletter* 9 (Aug.-Sept., 1979), 1-4. Personal visit to Latin America raises concern about the impact of Mennonite mission and development programs in those countries. Concludes the Mennonite mission and service/development programs in Latin America have tended to take a "safe" theological and tactical posture.

Franz, Delton. "The Washington Office: Reflections After Ten Years." *MCC PS Wash. Memo* 10 (July-Aug., 1978), 1-3. Reflects on the assignment of the Washington office to be an active peace witness, in light of earlier Mennonite quietistic tendencies.

Fretz, Clarence Y. "The Christian Hope Today." *ST* 26 (3rd Qtr., 1958), 4. The demoralizing effects of war also take their toll on the morals of church members, alarmed about the shifting ethical testimony of the church.

Fretz, J. Winfield. "Our Peace Witness During World War II." *The Power of Love; A Study Manual Adopted for Sunday School Use and for Group Discussion,* pp. 58-96. Ed. Peace Committee of the General Conference Mennonite Church. Newton: Board of Publication, 1947. MHL. Discusses the history and operation of the CPS program, the point of view of those Mennonites who entered military service as chaplains, etc., and the witness of the noncombatants. Concludes that the CPS program was the choice most consistent with Mennonite belief and practice and that the program was an effective witness for peace to the nation, to the community, and to the Mennonite churches.

Fretz, J. Winfield. "Peace Corps: Child of the Historic Peace Churches." *MennLife* 16 (Oct., 1961), 178-81. Summarizes the origin and nature of the US Peace Corps and compares and contrasts it to PAX.

Fretz, J. Winfield; Krahn, Cornelius; and Kreider, Robert. "Altruism in Mennonite Life." *Forms and Techniques of Altruistic and Spiritual Growth.* Ed. Pitirim A. Sorokin. Boston: Beacon Press, 1954, 309-328. A description of select examples of Mennonite altruism, including the peace witness, and an analysis of its roots in biblicism and nonconformity.

Friedmann, Robert. "The Anabaptist Genius and Its Influence on Mennonites Today." *PCMCP First,* 20-25. North Newton: The Bethel College Press. Held at Winona Lake, Indiana, Aug. 7-8, 1942. Early Anabaptists understood the obedience of true discipleship based on love and the cross. Through the years various social settings and theological currents have influenced Anabaptist theology.

Friesen, Abraham. *Reformation and Utopia: The Marxist Interpretation of the Reformation and its Antecedents.* Wiesbaden: Franz Steiner Verlag GmbH, 1974. Pp. 271. MHL. Explanation and critique of the Marxist interpretation includes discussion of the possible relationship between Anabaptism and the Peasant War. Concludes that although there may have been some merging of the two movements and some exchange of influence between Thomas Müntzer and Anabaptist leaders such as Hans Hut, Melchior Rinck, and Hans Denck, the Marxists fail to take account of the fact that Anabaptism appealed not only to the poor but to the wealthy and that Anabaptist pacifism developed prior to and concurrent with the Peasants' War rather than as a *result* of the peasants' defeat.

Friesen, Abraham. "Thomas Müntzer and the Old Testament." *MQR* 47 (Jan., 1973), 5-19. Thomas Müntzer, leader of the peasants' revolt, found inspiration for his vision of the military inauguration of the kingdom of God on earth in Old Testament accounts of God's elect conquering the Promised Land, and in the dispensational thought of medieval Joachim of Fiore.

Friesen, Abraham. "Wilhelm Zimmermann and Friedrich Engels: Two Sources of Marxist Interpretation of Anabaptism." *MQR* 55 (July, 1981), 240-54. Argues that Zimmermann's first study of Müntzer and the Anabaptists, which was skewed in the direction of idealistic and revolutionary tendencies, was the one cited by Engels for an interpretation of Anabaptism, while Zimmermann's second edition, written after his conversion, was disregarded.

Friesen, Dorothy. "Meet Trinidad Herrera." *The Other Side* 14 (July, 1978), 18-31. Story about a remarkable woman and the urban poor organizations with which she works in the manipulative world of the Philippines' repressive "New Society."

Friesen, Dorothy. "Prayer and Peacemaking." *The Other Side* 18 (Feb., 1982), 25-29. Reflects upon the discovery of the power of prayer for the work of peace and how these two aspects of discipleship relate.

Friesen, Dorothy and Stoltzfus, Gene. "Human Rights: Argument and Action." *Intercom* 17 (Apr., 1977), 6. Presents responses to some of the objections of church people and coworkers against confronting injustice.

Friesen, Duane K. "Peace Studies: What Is It?" Paper presented at the American Society of Christian Ethics, Chicago, Ill., Jan. 19, 1974. Pp. 35. MHL.

Friesen, Duane K. "Teachings on Peace and Social Concerns—Mennonite and Brethren in Christ Churches in the United States: 1900-1980." N.d. Various paginations, illustrations, charts. MLA/ BeC.

Friesen, Duane K. "Toward a Theology of Peacemaking." Lectures. North Newton, Kansas, 1977. Pp. 179. (Available, AMBS)

Friesen, George C. "Speakers Say Evangelism Gives Peacemaking Mandate." *CanMenn* 17 (Sept. 19, 1969), 1. Hatfield, Abernathy, and Myron Augsburger speak their mind on peace for the world. "The task of peacemaking includes the call to evangelism. The call to evangelism is a call to proclaim and to love; it is a call to respond to these needs, and it involves us totally in the mandate of peacemaking" (Hatfield).

Friesen, Jacob T. Letter to the Editor. *Menn* 94 (Feb. 6, 1979), 93. Writer outlines the steps he took to begin a dialogue on peace by withholding a portion of his 1977 income tax.

Friesen, Jake. Letter to the Editor. *Intercom* 5 (May-June, 1965), 2-3. Calls attention to inconsistencies in the Mennonite peace witness, such as accepting protection from American military personnel while working in a foreign country.

Friesen, John. "The Christian Community in Mission." *Menn* 88 (Dec. 11, 1973), 714-17. Friesen examines evangelism in the Anabaptist context, concluding that the "new community," the reconciling, sharing, pacifist community, should be the matrix of missions in a Mennonite perspective.

Friesen, Lyle. "Mennonite Interpretations of Anabaptism as Presented in the *Mennonite Quarterly Review*." MA thesis, Mar., 1974. Pp. 80. CGCL.

Friesen, Orly. Letter to the Editor. *MennMirror* 7 (Mar., 1978), 25. The "Quebec problem" calls for love and reconciliation rather than the prejudice and animosity with which we view the French-Canadians.

Froese, Jacob A. "An Emphasis on Love, Peace, and Justice." *ChrLead* 40 (July 5, 1977), 5. Report on the role of the Contemporary Concerns Committee in the Mennonite Brethren Church.

Froese, Jacob A. and Hofer, Phil. *The Church As Peace Witness: A Resource Manual.* Hillsboro, Ks.: Mennonite Brethren Publishing House, 1975. Pp. 60. MHL. Presents the Mennonite Brethren peace position and suggests ways that position might affect the church in its relations with contemporary society. Topics include biblical foundations, issues of church and state, history of MB peace position, etc.

Fry, A. Ruth. "The Laws of Peace." Address given to the National Peace Conference, London, June 28, 1935. Pp. 10. AMBS.

Funk, Herta. "Mennonite World Conference: Male Face for the World?" *Daughters of Sarah* 4 (Nov.-Dec., 1978), 8. Reports that some of the Dutch Mennonite women leaders, as well as women from other parts of the world, have questioned the unequal participation of men and women at the Mennonite World Conference.

"G. C. Board Discusses Black Manifesto." *CanMenn* 17 (Aug. 8, 1969), 3. Report on General Board (GCMC) meeting in Chicago June 23-25. Commission of Home Ministries and Commission on Overseas Missions proposed projects to be financed through the Million Dollar Fund of the General Conference.

Gaeddert, Albert M. "An Important Peace Meeting." *Menn* 66 (July 10, 1951), 424. Church agencies affiliated with NSBRO state their concerns to Washington officials and propose a list of the kinds of work they would be willing to do under the new conscription law.

Gaeddert, Albert M., sec., et al. (The Peace Committee of the General Conference Mennonite Church, eds.) *The Power of Love: A Study Manual Adapted for Sunday School Use and for Group Discussion.* Newton, Ks.: The Board of Publication, 1947. Pp. 136. MHL. Four essays prepared to help the churches place greater emphasis on the teaching of New Testament peace principles. Essays are: Dyck, Walter H., "The Scriptural Basis of Our Faith," 11-37; Smith, C. Henry, "The Historical Background,"

38-57; Fretz, J. Winfield, "Our Peace Witness During World War II," 58-96; Mast, Russell, "Living the Peace Testimony," 97-122.

Garber, Robert Bates. "Peace Churches Emphasize Peacemaking." *Forum* 12 (Nov., 1978), 14-15. The New Call to Peacemaking conference held in Oct., 1978, at Green Lake, Wis., issued the challenge that the historic peace churches should play a more active role in working for peace and justice. Such participation would mean a loss of some of the religio-ethnic distinctiveness of Mennonites which, the writer states, is a small price to pay in helping promote peace and social justice.

General Board of the Mennonite Church. "GB Response to Selective Service Registration." *GH* 73 (Feb. 26, 1980), 184. Statement urges Mennonites into active witnessing for peace and seeking legal alternatives to registration.

General Conference Mennonite Church. *A Christian Declaration on the Way of Peace.* Newton: Commission on Home Ministries, General Conference Mennonite Church, 1971. Pp. 20. Position statement maintains that peace is grounded in biblical perspectives of love, evangelism, and justice, and it applies to use of resources, views of citizenship and military service, and involvement in social change.

General Conference Mennonite Church. *Christian Responsibility to Society.* Newton: Faith and Life Press, 1963. Pp. 18. "Christ's work of creation, redemption, and consummation constitutes the biblical-theological basis for a total ministry to the total person, individual and social."

General Conference Mennonite Church. *Studies in Church Discipline.* Newton: Mennonite Publication Office, 1958. Pp. 241. Eighteen papers on the nature of the church and the meaning of church membership, together with tables on the practice of church discipline in General Conference congregations, and five appendices, including the Portland, Ore., 1953 statement of the General Conference on Peace, War, and Military Service.

General Conference Mennonite Church. *The Church, the Gospel, and War.* General Conference Peace Study Conference. Eden Mennonite Church, Moundridge, Kans., Apr. 10-11, 1953. Sixteen essays on the theme, together with a report of discussions and findings and two messages—to the congregations of the conference, and to the Christian church at large.

General Conference Mennonite Church. *The Church and Its Witness in Society.* Study Conference Report. Canadian Board of Christian Service, Winnipeg, Jan. 9-11, 1959. Sixteen papers on concerns central to the conference theme,

including the role of the church in peacemaking and in political action, together with a report of discussions and findings.

General Conferences of the Mennonite and Brethren in Christ Churches. "Industrial Relations—A Statement by the Church." *MennComm* 3 (Mar., 1949), 22-27. The gospel's way of peace commands both employers and employees to practice nonresistant love and fairness toward one another.

Gingerich, Melvin. "A Peace Witness." *Menn* 74 (Mar. 31, 1959), 197-98; "Concerning Military Conscription," *GH* 52 (Apr. 21, 1959), 369, 381. A statement presented to the Senate Armed Services Committee in behalf of the MCC Peace Section, protesting conscription and America's preoccupation with military superiority. Proposals are given for various programs of peace and goodwill.

Gingerich, Melvin. "Christian Youth and Law Observance; Christian Youth and the State." *YCC* 21, Part 3, (Dec. 29, 1940), 410. The observance of even "minor" laws during peacetime gives more credibility to our saying no, if asked, to laws that are a part of supporting war or war psychology.

Gingerich, Melvin. "Christian Youth As Humanitarians; Christian Youth and the State." *YCC* 22, Part 8, (May 11, 1941), 566. The biblical basis for humanitarianism calls Christians to be concerned about the social needs of all people. Response can be either by material/money or by giving one's life in service.

Gingerich, Melvin. "It Seems to Me." *YCC* 37 (Dec. 30, 1956), 424. American missionaries in Japan are faced with questions like "How can you justify the manufacture and use of atomic and hydrogen bombs by Christian America?"

Gingerich, Melvin. "Monasticism; Christian Youth and the State." *YCC* 23, Part 24, (Sept. 27, 1942), 309. Jesus did not model withdrawal from the world. Mennonite communities have the potential of being monasteries for people who should witness to peace during both war and peace.

Gingerich, Melvin. "Orthodoxy and Pietism; Christian Youth and the State." *YCC* 24, Part 27, (Feb. 7, 1943), 459. The Age of Orthodoxy overemphasized right thinking and Pietism overemphasized right feeling. Anabaptists emphasized both and added right living. All three of these should be in balance.

Gingerich, Melvin. "Peace Ambassadors in Japan." *ChrLiv* 6 (Sept., 1959), 12-15, 26. Description of the Gingerich's two years as peace representatives in Japan.

Gingerich, Melvin. "Prayer in War Time; Christian Youth and the State." *YCC* 23, Part 22, (May 31, 1942), 172. Biblical principles for prayer that apply to both times of war and times of peace.

Gingerich, Melvin. "The Early Church; Christian Youth and the State." *YCC* 23, Part 23, (Aug. 2, 1942), 242. The understanding we have about the time of Christ's return may affect how we live in our willingness to share and our willingness to be separated from the world.

Gingerich, Melvin. "The Mennonite Peace Witness in Japan." *MennLife* 12 (Oct., 1957), 185-88. Japan is the first nation in history to embody the principle of pacifism in its constitution. A revulsion against war has opened many doors to the Mennonite peace witness.

Gingerich, Melvin. "The Need for a Peace Witness in the Orient." *MennLife* 14 (July, 1959), 99-101. Asia longs for peace. While Buddhism and communism carry the banner of peace, "Christian" America, including many of its missionaries, are identified with militarism and conquest.

Gingrich, Paul M.; Taylor, Clyde W.; and Toews, J. B. (Review). *Envoys of Peace: The Peace Witness in the Christian World Mission*, by R. Pierce Beaver. Grand Rapids: Eerdmans, 1964. Pp. 133. "The Peace Witness and Missions." *CanMenn* 13 (May 25, 1965), 8. All three reviewers recommend the book because it contains vital information for the issues of peace and missions.

Gleysteen, Jan. "Of Mountains, Windmills, and Potatoes." *ChrLiv* 15 (Aug., 1968), 34-35. Reviews four children's books dealing with war, peace, and reconciliation.

Glick, Mildred. "Peace Teachers: He Puts Peace in the Total Framework of Christian Living." *Builder* 31 (Jan., 1981), 16-17. Pastor Keith Hostetler, Edmunton, Alberta, perceives the peace witness as not only attending to the issues of government and war but also to the dynamics of human interaction with others and God.

Godshall, Stanley M. "Peace: A Call to Selfless Living." *GH* 56 (Oct. 15, 1963), 905, 908. The world's attempts to bring peace fail because they are selfishly motivated. True peace is an inner condition which results when pride and egotism are overcome.

Goering, Jack. "Biblical Issues Raised by War Tax Workshop." *Menn* 86 (Mar. 23, 1971), 190-91. Christian stewardship and a simpler lifestyle must supplement the decision to withhold or reduce taxes as a witness to peace.

Goering, James A. (Review). *Peace Shall Destroy Many*, by Rudy Wiebe. McClelland and Steward, 1962. *ST* 32 (1st Qtr., 1964), 29. Although it is a novel of high literary calibre, the dramatization of the church's weaknesses mars its image in the world and diminishes its effectiveness.

Goering, Roland R. "Die Stillen im Lande." *MennLife* 14 (Jan., 1959), 29-32. Reflects on the term, "the quiet people of the land." The expression is sometimes used as a compliment, sometimes as a reproach.

Goertz, Hans-Jürgen. "Willy Brandt and the Nobel Peace Prize." *CMR* 1 (Dec. 13, 1971), 9. Reflections on German politics with the observation "that those political parties which have no historic kinship with Christianity have developed a concept of peace, which is more suitable to the radical world peace demands of the gospel of Jesus Christ than the political assumptions and apprehensions of the so-called Christian parties."

Goertzen, Don. "Everything's Going to Blow Up." *Menn* 92 (Oct. 11, 1977), 578-79. Discusses nuclear disarmament issues from the perspective of one involved in peace witness at Rocky Flats plutonium plant in Colorado.

Goertzen, Don. "We Studied Peace in the Arvada-Denver Area." *Menn* 91 (Nov. 9, 1976), 663-64. Reflections on the Mennonite Peace team work in Denver, Colorado, sponsored by General Conference peace and social concerns office, Mennonite Voluntary Service, and the Arvada Mennonite Church.

Goosen, Wally. Letter to the Editor. *MennRep* 8 (Feb. 20, 1978), 6. Interprets Mennonite peace stance as withholding aid from the injured on the battlefield in order to convert people to a peace stance. Maintains that the peace of Christ is available in the midst of flying bombs.

Goossen, Steve. Letter to the Editor. *ChrLead* 42 (May 22, 1979), 15. Asks how one can pay for the war while uttering a prayer for peace.

Graber, Edith Claassen. *Children and Peace*. Newton: Board of Christian Service, General Conference Mennonite Church, n.d. Pp. 15. MHL. Discusses teaching children the basic attitudes for peace. Describes techniques and methods, provides resources, etc.

Graber, Edith Claassen. "Preparing Children for Peace and Non-resistance." *Menn* 68 (June 2, 1953), 342, 347. Deals with tools and methods for teaching children principles of peace and love. Lists Church of the Brethren and Quaker materials already available.

Graber, J. D. "To Proclaim or to Serve?" *Mission-*

*Focus* 3 (Jan., 1975), 1-8. Argues that gospel proclamation needs to be in the forefront of missionary strategy, giving social services and charity a secondary place. Inner-motivated self-help will come through the new hope in Christ and will be more effective in solving social ills than the conventional institutional approach.

Graham, James R. *Strangers and Pilgrims*. Scottdale: Herald Press, 1951. Pp. 55. Christ's followers must be prepared to witness to his power also through suffering—the way of the cross.

Groh, H. D. "The Peace Witness of the Church." *GH* 51 (May 13, 1958), 452. An account of Mennonite Voluntary Service in the British Isles. There is a real need for the Mennonite church to share the Gospel of peace and goodwill in this part of the world.

Groh, Norman I. Letter to the Editor. *GH* 61 (June 18, 1968), 554. Questions a pure anti-war stance toward Vietnam because the cause of the war was the communist takeover of the north. Calls for greater respect for the government than is evidenced in the anti-war movement.

Gronwald, Manfred. "An Example for a Position of Peace in the German Protestant Church." Paper for Christian Attitutdes to War, Peace, and Revolution class, AMBS, Elkhart, Ind., n.d. Pp. 3. AMBS.

Groves, Esther. *Leader's Guide: Lordship as Servanthood, Thirteen Lessons on the Biblical Basis for Peacemaking*. Newton: Faith and Life Press and Scottdale: Mennonite Publishing House, 1976. Pp. 73. Geared for both youth and adults, teaching aids include student worksheets, stated goals, resource listings, lesson outlines, discussion guides, etc., as well as background information on content.

Gruber, Nancy H. "The Grindstone Experiment." *With* 6 (Jan., 1973), 20. A thirty-one-hour role play trying to put peacemaking into practice on Grindstone Island, Canada.

Guenther, Allen R. "A Dean Looks at Student Unrest." *The Voice* 18 (Oct., 1969), 2. Inquiry into the reasons for student unrest on college campuses. Christians should be activists who share Christ's vision of human need—spiritual, intellectual, social, emotional, and physical.

Gundy, Lloyd. "Message to the Churches from Our District Peace Committees." *Menn* 67 (Jan. 1, 1952), 14. An urgent plea for Mennonites to witness against the proposed Universal Military Training program. Outlines the provisions of the program and its possible harmful effects.

Gustafson, David L. "Shalom, the Dream and the Reality: Curriculum for Advent Through Easter." MA in Peace Studies thesis, AMBS, 1981. Pp. 58. While the shalom theme, one of the major Anabaptist distinctives, has been extensively discussed in academic circles, little of its message has filtered down to the congregations. This adaptation of a shalom lectionary seeks to bring peace teachings into the worship life of the congregation. Outlines the basic teachings for each Sunday and provides one fully developed lesson as an example.

"Historic Peace Church Council Members Meet." *CanMenn* 9 (May 26, 1961), 1, 8. Members of the Council meet in Winnipeg to discuss problems related to citizenship, oaths of allegiance, and Mennonite Disaster Service. A main topic of dicussion was the denial of Canadian citizenship to new Canadians due to their CO position.

"Historic Peace Church Council of Canada." *CanMenn* 7 (Oct. 9, 1959), 1, 4; *GH* 52 (Oct. 27, 1959), 909. Representatives of peace and service organizations from all the Mennonite groups in Canada participate in the historic peace church gathering in Winnipeg to consider matters of common interest and concern.

"Historic Peace Church Council Will Hold Annual Meeting in Winnipeg." *CanMenn* 10 (Nov. 23, 1962), 1. The annual meeting of the Council, which unites nine Mennonite member groups, focuses on citizenship and service.

"Historic Peace Churches Meet for Conference." *CanMenn* 1 (Oct. 30, 1953), 1, 3, 7. J. A. Toews presented two messages on discipleship and participation in war.

"Historic Peace Churches Meeting in Kitchener." *CanMenn* 2 (Oct. 29, 1954), 1. Topics include: Israel and Christianity, the power of love, relief and voluntary service.

"Hour of Decision." *CanMenn* 18 (Oct. 2, 1970), 5. Denver Mennonites summarize their reactions to distribution of peace tracts to delegates of a Southern Baptist Convention.

Habegger, David L. "Evaluations and Impressions of the Bluffton Peace Conference." *Menn* 69 (Aug. 24, 1954), 516. Basic unity in a biblical understanding of love and peace was experienced at the conference of Friends, Brethren, and Mennonites. Mennonites have a strong sensse of community but remain too weak in their witness to society.

Habegger, Howard J. "Toward Doing Justice in Christian Missions." *MissFoc* 8 (Mar., 1980), 1-9. Commitment to Christian mission must also mean commitment to justice, carried out through nonviolent activity. Paper includes general suggestions and cautions regarding procedure.

Hackman, Walton. "Prisoners of Peace." *GH* 66 (July 31, 1973), 587-88; *ChrLead* 36 (July 10, 1973), 7; "The Veteran—Another Victim." *Menn* 88 (July 10, 1973), 428-29. Describes the plight of 25,000 Vietnam veterans, who sacrificed their dreams to fight the nation's war, and who now suffer neglect and discrimination in peacetime. The church has an obligation to minister to the needs and concerns of Vietnam veterans whose lives have been severely or permanently damaged as a result of the Indochina War.

*

Hamm, Ray. "The Way of Peace in Times of War and Otherwise." *MennRep* 10 (Apr. 28, 1980), 5. Poem calling for lives of service and simplicity in peacetime as well as nonresistant witness in wartime.

Harder, Erwin D. Letter to the Editor. *MennRep* 10 (Dec. 22, 1980), 7. Contends that Jesus' purpose on earth was to bring spiritual peace only, and that primary Christian energies should be focused toward personal evangelism, not toward witnessing to peace on earth.

Harder, Gary. "An Evaluation of the 'Peacemaker' Series of Mennonite Sunday School Lessons, April 21-June 30, 1968." Paper for War, Peace, and Revolution class, AMBS, Elkhart, Ind., May 8, 1969. Pp. 3. AMBS.

Harder, Leland. "The Political Behavior of Northern Indiana Mennonites." *Indiana Academy of the Social Sciences.* (Third Series.) Proceedings, 1970, Vol. 5, 159-72. A statistical and interpretive study of political attitudes and activities, particularly voting and the political role of the church, compared with respondents in Glock, Ringer, and Babbie study of Episcopalians. Study shows that low political permissiveness on the part of Elkhart Mennonites correlates with high religious commitment, low income, and low education. It appears that "among those who take the Anabaptist vision most seriously are persons who have found some implications in it which lead to political involvement."

Harding, Vincent G. "The Experiment in Peace." *MBH* 1 (Nov. 2, 1962), 6-7. The peace Christians seek is a molding of human hearts and institutions to the will of God, i.e., to reconciliation between all people.

Harding, Vincent G. "The Peace Witness and Revolutionary Movements." *CanMenn* 15 (Aug. 15, 1967), 7, 11, 12; *MennLife* 22 (Oct., 1967), 161-65. Also in *The Witness of the Holy Spirit.* Ed. Cornelius J. Dyck. Elkhart: MWC, 1967, 337-44. Asks whether we can "recommend the way of powerlessness while we dwell comfortably among the powerful" and proposes dialogue with revolutionaries in order to learn the meaning of nonresistance in situations where people have been pressed by oppression into violent resistance. A peace witness has integrity only when its messengers participate in the quest for social justice also.

Harding, Vincent G. "Vietnam: What Shall We Do?" *Menn* 80 (Sept. 21, 1965), 582-85; "What Shall We Do About Vietnam?" *CanMenn* 13, Part 1, (Sept. 14, 1965), 6; Part 2, (Sept. 21, 1965), 6; *MBH* 4 (Sept. 17, 1965), 14 (shortened version). It is time that Mennonites' professed opposition to war be proclaimed as public dissent to American military policy. Response must begin with repentance and then seek to witness openly to the way of love and reconciliation.

Harding, Vincent G. "Voices of Revolution." *Menn* 82 (Oct. 3, 1967), 590-93; *YCC* 49 (May 19, 1968), 12. How should the peace witness address the movement for black liberation? Who commits the greatest sin—the desperate person or the complacent person?

Harshbarger, Emmett L. "A Mennonite Preparedness Program." *Menn* 53 (Dec. 20, 1938), 5-6. A peacemaking response to international strife demands a different sort of preparedness than a military response. Mennonites must prepare themselves for wartime individually, educationally, and by taking part in peace programs.

Harshbarger, Emmett L. "Delegates from Historic Peace Churches Visit the President." *Menn* 55 (Jan. 23, 1940), 3-4. Report on a delegation seeking to secure a satisfactory program for conscientious objectors. Included is a statement presented to the president.

Harshbarger, Emmett L. "Out of the Czech Crisis." *Menn* 53 (Nov. 8, 1938), 2. The myth of "collective security" has been shattered, providing the church with further challenge and opportunity for peace witness.

Harshbarger, Emmett L. "What Can I Do for Peace?" 52 (Mar. 2, 1937), 4. A list of activities for individuals and groups interested in working for peace.

Hart, Lawrence H. "Cheyenne, Custer, and Centennials." *Menn* 91 (June 22, 1976), 420-21. Relates the story of the unplanned reconciliation between Cheyenne and white which took place at a 1968 centennial commemoration of the Battle of Washita, in order to encourage reflections on peace on the upcomign centennial of Custer's Last Stand.

Hartman, Wilmer J. "Living Peaceably with Others." *Builder* 20 (Sept., 1970), 21-25. An adult Sunday school lesson utilizing the story of Isaac's conflict with the Philistine herders over

---

*For additional listing, see Supplement, pp. 717-719.

a well (Gen. 26) to focus discussion of peacemaking.

Hartzler, Levi C. "Missions and Our Peace Witness." *GH* 46 (Aug. 11, 1953), 769. The true peacemaker is motivated by inner compulsion. For him or her the peace witness is an integral part of the Christian life and witness.

Hartzler, Levi C. "Pax Service, a Church Responsibility." *GH* 45 (May 20, 1952), 496-97. Pax Service offers an opportunity for Christian service which may soon be accepted as alternate service for drafted men. The church can support the positive peace witness of Pax Service with financial contributions.

Hartzler, Robert. "Reconciliation—The Business of Getting Back Together." *GH* 63 (Dec. 15, 1970), 1036-37. Describes reconciliation as changed relations with God and other people made possible through Christ's death and resurrection, acts of God's love.

Hasek, K. Gary. "Art and the Peacemaking Church." MA in Peace Studies thesis, AMBS, 1981. Cassette, slides, script (i, 13). A multimedia presentation which utilizes music, slides, and a script to explore what aesthetic concepts such as balance, light, shape, and tension contribute to an understanding of biblical shalom.

Hatfield, Mark O. "Misplaced Allegiance." *Menn* 88 (Mar. 27, 1973), 216. Statement given by the Senator at the National Prayer Breakfast in Washington, D.C., calls Americans to distinguish between the god of American civil religion and the God revealed in Scriptures and in Jesus Christ who commands justice and peace.

Hatfield, Mark O. "Spiritual Revolution." *ChrLead* 39 (July 6, 1976), 2. "Obedience to Christ can exercise a vital influence in our corporate life as a nation and people, but only on His own terms" is the theme of these excerpts from a National Prayer Breakfast speech.

Hege, Nathan. "Building Bridges Across Barriers." *GH* 72 (Oct. 16, 1979), 809-811. A look at how Mennonites have responded to the situation in Israel and how they are continuing to work at reconciliation.

Heidebrink, John C. "The Peace Conference and the Future." *MennLife* 20 (July, 1965), 124-27. Lists the achievements of the Christian Peace Conference and suggests directions it might take in the future.

Hein, Marvin. "Peace—Part of a Package." *CanMenn* 13 (Nov. 2, 1965), 9. Peace cannot be separated from the rest of life. It is "part and parcel of a much larger, ¢un⅝unnatural way of life."

Hein, Marvin. "Peacemaking—A Work of the Spirit." *ChrLead* 40 (Aug. 16, 1977), 6. Mennonites feel strongly that the role of a peacemaker arises out of a spirit-motivated experience of new life in Jesus Christ.

Hein, Marvin. "The Holy Spirit and Peacemaking." *Menn* 93 (June 27, 1978), 418. Peacemaking is the result of a changed person. The Holy Spirit calls believers to deliver others from whatever may be destroying them.

Heisi, Evan. "Saskatchewan Peace Talk Attracts 200 Participants. *Menn* 94 (Mar. 20, 1979), 214. "Peace is not the absence of conflict, but the presence of the Creator," was the theme of the native and Mennonite "peace talk" held Feb. 23-24 at Tiefengrund Mennonite Church.

Heisy, D. Ray. "On Which Issues Should the Church Witness to the State." Paper, n.d. Pp. 3. MHL.

Hernandez, Armando. "Justice Versus Injustice." *GH* 67 (May 14, 1974), 303-95. In a world full of injustices ranging from high prices to war, Christians should call people to repentance and speak out against war and violence of every kind.

Herr, Edwin. "The Christian and Politics: A Query." *GH* 69 (Oct. 26, 1976), 815-16. When Mennonites believe the tasks of the church are reconciliation, redemption, and mercy, while the state's purpose is to administer justice by force, to what extent can Mennonites participate in the state?

Herr, Judy Zimmerman. "Christians to Share Pain in South Africa." *GH* 72 (Feb. 6, 1979), 111. Report of a meeting on Jan. 20, 1979, in Pittsburgh where a group met to discuss the current situation in South Africa and possible Christian response.

Hershberger, Guy F. "A Mennonite Office in Washington?" *GH* 61 (Feb. 27, 1968), 186. [No. 25] Lists reasons supporting the establishment of a Washington office representing Mennonite peace concerns, and describes the possible functions of such an office.

Hershberger, Guy F. "Are We Bold Enough? Our Peace Witness—In the Wake of May 18." (Part 11). *GH* 60 (Nov. 7, 1967), 1018. To prophetically proclaim what it means to be Christian in today's society, Mennonites must be as bold as the Old Testament prophets and early Anabaptists.

Hershberger, Guy F. "Christian Missions and Colonialism: The Christian Witness to the

State." (Part 3). *GH* 53 (Sept. 20, 1960), 826. The identification of missions with paternalistic colonialism is an area in which a stronger witness to the state has been needed in the past. The Christian mission today must still speak out against paternalism and colonialism in word and deed.

Hershberger, Guy F. "Christians the Conscience of Society." *Goshen College Bulletin* 61 (Feb., 1967), 3. Also in *GH* 60 (1967), 934-36. With the history of the church in perspective, the challenge is that people respond to the call of Christian discipleship to go forth to turn the world right side up.

Hershberger, Guy F. "Conscience of Society." *GH* 61 (Feb. 20, 1968), 150-51. [No. 24] In support of his position that the church is the conscience of society, the author lists and describes cases of Mennonite protest against the Vietnam war and efforts toward peacemaking in addressing the problem of segregated urban housing.

Hershberger, Guy F. "Harold S. Bender and His Time." *MQR* 38 (1964), 83-112. Also in *Harold S. Bender: Educator, Historian, Churchman*. Ed. Guy F. Hershberger. Scottdale: Herald Press, 1964. A biography of Harold S. Bender outlining his life and contributions, which include his role in the recovery of the Anabaptist vision and in its implementation within the life and work of the worldwide Mennonite community. His life is described as an important era in Mennonite history, uniting anabaptism and peace.

Hershberger, Guy F. "How Can Mennonites Use Their Freedom for the Performance of Greater Works Than They Are Now Doing? Our Peace Witness—In the Wake of May 18." (Part 15). *GH* 60 (Dec. 12, 1967), 1114. The church should support young men to go into VS rather than I-W service.

Hershberger, Guy F. "How Important Is the Peace Problems Committee?" *GH* 56 (Apr. 23, 1963), 346-47. An historical sketch of the PPC, giving witness to its importance and attempting to raise funds for this program as well as General Conference (MC) involvement in other projects such as PAX, I-W, MCC, etc.

Hershberger, Guy F. "Is Modern Religious Liberalism a Force for Peace?" *GH* 28 (Feb. 20, 1936), 994-95. Modernism asserts the basic autonomy of humanity and thereby becomes an agency for war rather than peace. Only a Christ-centered faith can unite those divided by national or racial barriers.

Hershberger, Guy F. "Is This the Time for the Church to Speak Out on the Issue of Capital Punishment? Questions of Social Concern for Christians," (Part 9). *GH* 53 (May 17, 1960), 444.

It is time that Mennonites speak out as part of their peace witness.

Hershberger, Guy F. "Mennonites and Conscription in the World War." Prepared for use by Peace Problems Committee in view of approaching conscription (Burke-Wadsworth Bill). Typescript, 1940. Goshen: MHL. The Mennonite church is an historic peace church, having maintained a consistent testimony against war and military service throughout its entire history. Surveys the experience of Mennonites under conscription and the effect of the war experience upon the Mennonite church.

Hershberger, Guy F. "Military Conscription and the Conscientious Objector: A World-Wide Survey, with Special Reference to Mennonites." Paper presented at the Seventh Mennonite World Conference, Kitchener, Ont., Aug. 7, 1962. Mimeographed. Goshen: MHL. Pp. 38. Reports on draft laws in the worldwide Mennonite experience. Concluding comments focus on the status of the nonresistant peace teaching on the mission field.

Hershberger, Guy F. "Peace Movements That Have Failed in Time of Need." *YCC* 17 (July 19, 1936), 248. A survey of many peace movements in America previous to the Civil War that did not meet the test. The test of any peace conviction is whether during the time of war people who believe in peace still oppose the war.

Hershberger, Guy F. "Protest Against Evil." *GH* 61 (Jan. 30, 1968), 104. [No. 22] Asserts that protest against social evils goes hand in hand with preaching the gospel, citing prophetic witness and demonstrations by early Anabaptists.

Hershberger, Guy F. "Questions Raised Concerning the Work of the Committee on Peace and Social Concerns (of the Mennonite Church) and Its Predecessors." Mimeographed, 1967. Goshen: MHL. Summary review of questions raised concerning the work of the CPSC and its predecessors, particularly concerning witness to other Christians, to the state, and to society, with respect to peace and the social implications of the gospel, and concerning inter-Mennonite and inter-denominational cooperation in carrying on this work, 1925-66.

Hershberger, Guy F. "Robert Friedmann: In Remembrance." *MQR* 48 (Apr., 1974), 197-200. A memorial tribute delivered at the graveside service for Friedmann on July 30, 1970, in Kalamazoo, Mich. It acknowledges some of his contributions to the knowledge about and interpretation of Anabaptism.

Hershberger, Guy F. "Social Behavior and a Clear Conscience." Address given ca. 1959 at Goshen College, Goshen, Ind. Typescript. Goshen: AMC Hist. MSS 1-171 Box 12. For thinking about social behavior a clear conscience toward God and toward men is prized as the most real—the most tangible benefit—than which all else fades into insignificance and unreality.

Hershberger, Guy F. "Social Science Textbooks in Mennonite Colleges." *PCMCP Tenth*, 9-22. N.p. Held at Mennonite Biblical Seminary, Chicago, Illinois, June 16-17, 1955. Educators need to approach their social science teaching with the Anabaptist vision. Some suggestions on specific examples once teaching ideas are offered.

Hershberger, Guy F. "The Christian Redemptive Approach to the World in the History of Christendom." Paper read at Theological Workship, Aug., 1958, Goshen College, Goshen, Ind. Duplicated. Goshen: AMC Hist MSS 1-171 Box 10. Survey of both the biblical roots of and the historical responses to Christian ethics. The prophetic presence of Anabaptists is being tested by the process of assimilation.

Hershberger, Guy F. "The Christian Witness, Catholicism, and a Presidential Year." *GH* 53 (1960), 841, 861. A recognition of the persecution and treatment of Catholics and a plea to be a witness and testimony to the Catholic people.

Hershberger, Guy F. "The Committee on Peace and Social Concerns and Its Predecessors: A Summary Review of the Witness of the MC to Other Christians, to the State, and to Peace, with Respect to Peace and the Social Implications of the Gospel (1915-1966)." Paper, 1966. Pp. 22. MHL.

Hershberger, Guy F. "The Current Upsurge of War Objection." *GH* 61 (Jan. 16, 1968), 57. [No. 20] Writer observes that the growth of anti-war sentiment during wartime is unusual, and that the burgeoning peace movement protesting activities in Vietnam is disturbing to government officials.

Hershberger, Guy F. "The Friendly Association." *Dictionary of American History* 3 (1976), 122. Organized by Quakers, this association functioned as mediator in a series of conferences between government and Indians during the years of 1756-64.

Hershberger, Guy F. *The Mennonite Church in the Second World War.* Scottdale: Mennonite Publishing House, 1951. Pp. 308. A history and evaluation of the Mennonite Church (MC) experience during World War II in relation to its witness for peace.

Hershberger, Guy F. "The Mennonite Conference on Peace and War." *Goshen College Record* 36 (Mar., 1935), 1. This conference on war and peace, held at Goshen, Ind., Feb. 15-17, 1935, was the first of its kind sponsored by the Mennonite Church in America in its entire 400-year-old history.

Hershberger, Guy F. "The Mennonite Peace Witness Beyond North America." *GH* 58 (May 18, 1965), 427. In a time of the emergence of many new nations and growing nationalism, Mennonites must spend (and are spending) more time and money in peace witness around the world.

Hershberger, Guy F. "The Methodist Church and the Conscientious Objector." *YCC* 21 (Sept. 15, 1940), 296. The Methodist Church is one of the many groups who are giving attention to and support for the CO position. The US government has taken into account the nonresistant stand of these churches not among the historic peace churches in the Bukke-Wadsworth military conscription bill.

Hershberger, Guy F. "The Modern Social Gospel and the Way of the Cross." *MQR* 30 (Apr., 1956), 83-103. A major analysis and critique of the Social Gospel. While Rauschenbusch's theology and "the way of the Cross" are similar in many respects, the Social Gospel emphasizes "demanding justice" more than doing justice or suffering injustice.

Hershberger, Guy F. "The New Birth: A New Life, A New Social Order." Sermon delivered at Trinity Mennonite Church, June 2, 1974, in Glendale, Ariz. Typescript. Goshen: AMC Hist. MSS 1-171 Box 54. Examines the life and the atoning ministry of Christ which enables Christians to enter into the life of the new social order.

Hershberger, Guy F. "The People of God, Then and Now." *GH* 67 (Jan. 1, 1974), 6-8. Hershberger briefly recounts the history of the People of God from Abraham to the present noting that the church has taken on a subservient role of "spiritual advisor to power and prestige" and needs to once again assume the role of prophet to nationalism and the glorification of American interests.

Hershberger, Guy F., ed. *The Recovery of the Anabaptist Vision.* Scottdale: Herald Press, 1957. Pp. 360. Twenty-five essays on Anabaptist and Mennonite life and thought, presented to Harold S. Bender as a sixtieth anniversary tribute. Essays on war and peace are annotated separately, listed by author.

Hershberger, Guy F. "The Role of Pacifism and Pacifism in the Church: The Outlook for Christian Pacifism." Paper at Conference on the

Church and Peace, Detroit, Mich., Dec. 7-10, 1953. Pp. 8. MHL.

Hershberger, Guy F. *The Way of the Cross in Human Relations.* Scottdale: Herald Press, 1958. Pp. 424. Having been crucified with Christ, Christians follow Jesus in the way of the cross: they love with a self-giving love. After examining many theological traditions, Hershberger concludes that the Anabaptists most closely approximated this ideal. He then analyzes the organizations that structure modern society, proposes conditions under which Christians can become involved in them, and advocates a role for the church as society's conscience. Yet, because Christians look forward to Christ's consummation of history to establish justice, they depend not upon human efforts.

Hershberger, Guy F. "What Did the Early Mennonites Say About War and Peace?" *YCC* 17 (Apr. 5, 1936), 112. At the end of the Middle Ages there were many Christians in Europe who questioned the church-state union and its use of warfare. Included in this group were the Waldensians and later the Anabaptists, who believed that the teachings of Jesus on war must be literally obeyed.

Hershberger, Guy F. "Why Does the MCC Peace Section Plan to Establish an Office in Washington? Our Peace Witness—In the Wake of May 18." (Part 25). *GH* 61 (Feb. 27, 1968), 186. Such an office would greatly enhance our peace witness.

Hershberger, Guy F. "Why Have Many Christians Forgotten the Bible Teachings on Peace?" *YCC* 17 (Mar. 8, 1936), 80. Under Constantine's rule, beginning in 313 A.D., Christianity became a state religion. The union of church and state and the heathen ways of war are still a part of the larger church today.

Hershberger, Guy F. "Why Is Our Peace Witness Today Performing 'Greater Works'? Our Peace Witness—In the Wake of May 18." (Part 13). *GH* 60 (Nov. 21, 1967), 1063. The Mennonite peace witness is greater today than fifty years ago because of those who suffered persecution in 1917-18.

Hershberger, Guy F. "Why Is the Mennonite Peace Position Respected in Government Circles Today? Our Peace Witness—In the Wake of May 18." (Part 10). *GH* 60 (Oct. 31, 1967), 983. The Mennonite witness is respected because of its message and form. Perhaps, however Mennonites have been too reluctant to witness prophetically.

Hershberger, Guy F. "You Are the Salt of the Earth." *GH* 62 (Jan. 7, 1969), 6-9. Calls Christians to act as society's salt in witnessing against idolatry of the state and against the US climate of violence.

Hershberger, Guy F. (Review). *The Church of the Brethren and War,* by Rufus D. Bowman. Elgin: Brethren Pub. House, 1944, pp. 352; *Seventy Times Seven,* by Rufus D. Bowman. Elgin: Brethren Pub. House, 1945, pp. 158. "The Church of the Brethren and War." *GH Supplement* 39 (Oct., 1946), 638-39. Recommends these books as helpful not only for understanding the Brethren point of view on the issues of war and peace but also for gaining insight into ways we, as Mennonites, might bolster our own peace program.

Hershberger, Guy F., Metzler, Edgar, and Meyer, Albert J. "Theses on the Christian Witness to the State." Sub-committee report to the Peace Problems Committee of the Mennonite Church, June 22, 1960. Pp. 32. MHL.

Hertzler, Daniel. "Author Says Peace Message Hard to Hear." *GH* 71 (July 4, 1978), 532-33. Editor interviews John Howard Yoder about public response to *Politics of Jesus,* and about his response to various forms of Mennonite peace witness.

Hertzler, Daniel. "Is Peace Naive?" *GH* 71 (Oct. 10, 1978), 788. In a society filled with war and violence, peacemaking appears naive, but it is the simple-mindedness of Jesus which set the example.

Hertzler, Daniel. "On the Death of a King." *ChrLiv* 15 (June, 1968), 40. Thoughts on being a peacemaker, professionally or "by proxy."

Hertzler, Daniel. "Peace Lessons Begin on Apr. 21." *Builder* 18 (Apr., 1968), 1. Gives rationale for departure from Uniform Series outlines in order to make available eleven Sunday school lessons for youth and adults on the issues of peacemaking.

Hertzler, Daniel. "Pietism, Social Gospel, and Time Enough." *Builder* 18 (June, 1968), 1. Suggests that churches divided on the role of the peacemaker may need to engage in a twelve-hour worship-study-discussion session in order to discern God's particular will for the congregation in these times.

Hertzler, Daniel. "Sending a Message to Russia." *GH* 73 (July 1, 1980), 536. Open letter to the Christians of the Soviet Union calling for cooperation in resisting US and Soviet governments' commitment to war-making.

Hertzler, Daniel. "To Be a Peacemaker." *GH* 73 (June 17, 1980), 504. Reflects on instances of peacemaking that go beyond merely establishing justice or staying out of trouble.

Hertzler, Daniel. "To Henry W. Pierce." *GH* 68
(June 10, 1975), 444. Comments on a local
newspaper column linking violence to
deprivation of affection during childhood and
advocating free sex and less modesty. Cites
Jesus as a pioneer in love without violence, and
the historic peace churches as upholders of love
and monogomy.

Hertzler, Daniel (Editorial). "Dear Jim Bowman."
*GH* 72 (Mar. 20, 1979), 248. "Love your
neighbor as yourself" means a reduced standard
of living for us in rich countries to help the
poor.

Hertzler, Daniel (Editorial). "Kicking Uncle Sam."
*GH* 69 (Apr. 6, 1976), 302. Asserts that since a
national government stands opposed to Christ's
teachings on selflessness, defenselessness, love,
and truth, Christians must separate loyalty to
the state from living the way of peace.

Hertzler, Daniel (Editorial). "The New Call." *GH*
71 (Feb. 21, 1978), 168. Editorial describes the
emergence of the New Call to Peacemaking
movement among Quakers, Brethren, and
Mennonites.

Hertzler, Daniel (Editorial). "The Politics of the
Gospel." *GH* 72 (Jan. 2, 1979), 16. Hertzler
suggests a new sense of loyalty is needed to
displace the old loyalties, one in which people
are willing to seek peace at great personal risk.

Hess, James R. "The Washington Peace Seminar."
*ST* 44 (July, 1976), 21-23. Criticizes the hostility
shown toward business and government
leaders, and traces it to those involved in
church institutions as compared with those
involved in the workday world.

Hiebert, Clarence. "What About Vietnam?"
*ChrLead* 29 (Mar. 15, 1966), 14-15. Since God
wills peace, reconciliation, justice, and
redemption, God's people will also share this
attitude and will work for justice, peace, and
love in our present world.

Hiebert, Clarence. [Interview with.] "When the
Body Hurts . . ." *ChrLead* 42 (Mar. 27, 1979), 10.
Looks at the role of peacemaking in the local
church.

Hiebert, Murray. "War Scraps Forged into Plows."
*FStP* 1 (Sept., 1976), 1-2. Foundry near
Vientiane, Laos, buys military scrap metal and
forges it into farm implements.

Hiebert, P. C. "God's Peacemaker Warriors." *Menn*
51 (May 26, 1936), 1-4. In Ephesians 5, Paul
describes the armor of God's peacemaker
warriors; this spiritual armor is needed for the
days ahead.

Hiebert, P. C. *Life and Service in the Kingdom of God.*

No. 6 in *Mennonites and Their Heritage*. Akron:
MCC, 1942. Prepared for use in CPS camps, this
study manual emphasizes how all of life is to be
a peace witness in kingdom service.

Hiebert, Paul G. "The Kingdom Reconciling
Humanity." *ChrLead* 41 (Oct. 10, 1978), 7; *MBH*
17 (Oct. 13, 1978), 6-8. Hope that a model of
church and mission centered on Christ and
God's message of incarnation and reconciliation
would focus on the kingdom and ministries to
the whole person.

Hilborn, Jean A. "Positive Protest Through
Involvement." *YCC* 49 (June 16, 1968), 2;
*CanMenn* 16 (Mar. 5, 1968), 1. Text of the speech
by Jean Hilborn which won the national peace
oratorical contest in Canada. A challenge to
protest: its positive function arises from
involvement in social justice issues. To work for
peace is to understand the roots of war.

Hill, Joyce. "Mission Work Isn't What It Used to
Be." *With* 2 (Dec., 1969), 34. Along with
understanding themselves, "new" missionaries
must be aware of the religious, social, and
political concerns of the people with whom
they work.

Historic Peace Church Council of Canada
(Archival). 1 foot. CGCL.

Historic Peace Churches, Conference of (Archival).
5.8 feet. CGCL.

Historic Peace Churches and the International
Fellowship of Reconciliation. *War Is Contrary to
the Will of God.* London: Friends Peace
Committee, 1951. Pp. 32. Statements
identifying the position of the Mennonites,
Friends, Brethren, and the FOR on war in
response to the WCC 1948 Amsterdam
statement, "We believe there is a special call to
theologians to consider the theological
problems involved.

Hochstetler, Walter. "Anabaptist Dreams and
Menno-Nite-Mares: Some Reflections on
Mennonite Attitudes Toward Peace." Paper,
1971. Pp. 5. AMBS.

Hofer, Shirley. "The Christian Conscience and
War Taxes." *God and Caesar* 2 (June, 1976), 10-
12. A whimsical dialogue between Moses and
the Lord by Art Hoppe illustrates the
inconsistencies in biblical and theological
interpretation regarding the sixth
commandment and the sanctity of human life.
The writer also shares results from a survey she
took on the war tax issue.

Honser, Gordon. "Peace Teachers: He Takes His
Nap, Fellowships, and Acts." *Builder* 31 (Jan.,
1981), 18-19. Peter Ediger, Arvada, Colorado,
chalenges the church by asking if there can be

peace education without peace action.

Horner, Glen A. (Review). *New Testament Basis for Peacemaking,* by Richard McSorley. Washington, DC: Center for Peace Studies, n.d. Pp. 167. "Deals with Biblical Texts on Quesions of War," *MennRep* 9 (Oct. 29, 1979), 11. This book seriously questions the apparent approval of war by the Christian church, examines the message of the New Testament, and looks at Christian history, refuting questions and theories that indicate war to be of God.

Horning, Emma. "How a Bomb Transformed Chang." *ChrMon* 23 (May, 1931), 141. Reprinted from *The Gospel Messenger.* Story of a Chinese soldier who leaves the army upon conversion to Christianity.

Horsch, John. "World Betterment and World Regeneration." *GH* 27 (Jan. 17, 1935), 907-911. Modernism, the Social Gospel, and pacifism are inadequate in the context of an impending war. The element of personal regeneration has been forgotten in this campaign to build a new world through social reform.

Horst, John L. "Maintaining Our Peace Testimony." *ChrMon* 34 (June, 1942), 169. As the size of the army and CPS camps increases, Mennonites should stand firm in their nonresistant witness.

Horst, John L. "Relief Work as a Testimony for Christ and the Church." *GH* 39 (Jan. 7, 1947), 869, 872. Address at the 1946 Mennonite General Conference. The relief of suffering is a task based on Scripture and is one way to provide a platform for giving a testimony of peace.

Horst, Samuel. *Mennonites in the Confederacy: A Study in Civil War Pacifism.* Scottdale: Herald Press, 1967. Pp. 148. Documents the variety of ways Mennonites responded to the issues raised by the crisis of the Civil War, such as reluctant cooperation with the military, desertion, flight, choosing prison, working with government officials for legal alternatives, etc. Concludes that the Mennonite witness for peace in this era was not faultless but, nevertheless, significant and sincere. Includes extensive bibliography.

Hostetler, Marian. *Journey to Jerusalem.* Scottdale: Herald Press, 1978. Pp. 126. On a trip to the Middle East with her mother, 12-year-old Miriam begins to understand the complexities of the Arab-Israeli conflict when she enters into friendship with an Arab girl whose village is destroyed by Israeli soldiers.

Hostetler, Marian. "Peace Witness in Algeria." *GH* 55 (July 17, 1962), 628-29. Relates experiences of nonresistant VSer's in a war situation with its atmosphere of hatred and fear.

Hostetter, B. Charles. "Christian Love Is Needed." *CanMenn* 2 (Feb. 26, 1954), 6. Humanity's basic need is spiritual. Christian love, not military strength, is needed for human salvation.

Hostetter, B. Charles. "Christian Love Is Redemptive." *CanMenn* 2 (Dec. 17, 1954), 8. A Christmas sermon on Christian love as shown by God for humanity. In turn, people are asked to love in the same manner.

Hostetter, B. Charles. "The Dynamic of Christian Love." *CanMenn* 2 (Feb. 26, 1954). A biblical analysis of Christian love.

Hostetter, C. N., Jr. "Spiritu l Resources for Peace." *GH* 42 (July 19, 1949), 700. The true peace witness is based upon peace within, union and communion with God, and the demonstration of Jesus' law of love.

Hostetter, David E. "The Church and SALT II." *GH* 72 (Nov. 6, 1979), 880. The Mennonite Church should take a strong position condemning nuclear weapons of any kind, anywhere. In particular the church needs to respond to SALT II.

Hostetter, Douglas. "How to Write to Congress." *ChrLead* 40 (Jan. 4, 1977), 10. Helpful guide to communicating to government officials.

Howard, Walden. "Pay Them Back with Good." *ChrLiv* 18 (Sept., 1971), 14-17. Feedmill owner's business nearly destroyed for supporting justice in the form of school integration.

Howland, Larry O. "Becoming Peacemakers." *GH* 69 (June 29, 1976), 530-31. Former Mennonite inmate testifies that Christians are called to be peacemakers, after the example of Jesus, who showed that conferring peace upon others means to be willing to suffer for them.

Hull, Robert. "Historical Roots of a Peace Church Witness." *Affirm Life: Pay for Peace,* ed. Maynard Shelly and Ron Flickinger. Newton: Historic Peace Church Task Force on Taxes, 1981, 13-17. Pp. [87]. MHL. Charts history of historic peace church responses and actions on war tax issues from the French and Indian war, 1754-1763 to the contemporary period—the Vietnam War era, the World Peace Tax Fund (1973), and the General Conference Mennonite Church experience with Cornelia Lehn's request.

Hull, Robert. "Peace Evangelism." *Menn* 95 (Sept. 30, 1980), 550-51. Peace evangelism should be active, prudent, and centered in the local congregation.

Hull, Robert and Eccleston, Alan. "A Peace

Church Style of Witness." In *Affirm Life: Pay for Peace.* 19-24. Ed. by Maynard Shelly and Ron Flickinger. Newton: Historic Peace Church Task Force on Taxes, 1981. Pp. [87]. MHL. Examines methodology of a variety of New Testament and historic peace church examples of witness to the state and urges that the methods used to frame the peace message be consonant with the message.

Hunsberger, Gordon. "View from Haiti (1): The Mennonite Church." *MennRep* 10 (Mar. 31, 1980), 8. Writer expresses appreciation for Mennonite emphases on peace and stewardship of resources.

Hunter, J. H. "The Christmas Message and Permanent Peace." *GH* 37 (Dec. 22, 1944), 761-62, 772. Permanent peace is of the Spirit, not of the hand or mind of humanity. It is not discovered apart from the incarnate Son of God.

"If There Be Peace—A New Film." *RepConsS* 32 (Apr., 1975), 2. Describes film produced by the Mennonite Church and Church of the Brethren which documents how people in four communities live peace.

"In My Opinion." *CanMenn* 2 (Apr. 23, 1954), 7. Four participants respond positively to the Canadian Peace Study Conference, the first such study group focusing on the teaching of the Bible and the church on peace.

"International 'Arms Bazaar' Hampered by Protesters." *MennRep* 9 (Apr. 2, 1979), 10. A report on the protest activities of more than 2,000 people at an international military conference and trade show in suburban Chicago.

"International Meeting for Peace Called for Labor Day, September 5." *CanMenn* 14 (Aug. 9, 1966), 1, 10. Announcement of a proposed mass meeting of Canadians and Americans at the International Peace Gardens on the North Dakota-Manitoba border, to be addressed by A. J. Muste.

IFOR Collective. "Letter from the IFOR Collective." *Fellowship* 40 (Mar., 1974), 4. This letter describes some of the recent travels and involvements of individual collective members.

IFOR staff. "International FOR Staff Letter." *Fellowship* 40 (Apr., 1974), 31. From Denmark, this letter mentions FOR activities that are taking place in various countries around the world.

Indiana-Michigan Mennonite Conference—Peace and Social Concerns Committee. (Archival). II-5-6, Box 4. Material on various peace and social concerns: labor relations; draft; capital punishment; witness to the state. Goshen, Ind. AMC.

Inja, C. "Dutch Peace Group Sponsors Witness and Action Program." *CanMenn* 13 (Oct. 26, 1965), 3. A report on the Dutch Mennonite Peace Group organized in 1922. MCC's work in post-war Europe taught this group that if a peace witness is to be effective, it must be accompanied by positive acts. The Peace Group has sent substantial aid to Algeria. Meetings are attended by Mennonites, Dutch Reformed, Lutherans, Baptists, Roman Catholics, and humanists.

International Christian Service for Peace in Morocco." *CanMenn* 6 (Aug. 8, 1958), 7. Historic peace churches sponsor a peace project in Morocco consisting of building cattle shelters.

Interview with Jake Epp, "Christian Witness Growing in Ottawa." *MBH* 18 (Apr. 27, 1979), 6-9. Mennonite Member of Parliament reflects on Christian service and witness in political office.

"Japanese Christian Peace Witness." *CanMenn* 7 (Aug. 21, 1959), 7. Because of continuing problems facing Japan, a Christian witness is definitely needed in our contemporary nuclear age.

Jacobs, Donald R. "Peacemaking in the Congregation." *Builder* 25 (Mar., 1975), 7-10. Speaks to pastors about way to help church members affirm each other as brother and sister when they find themselves at very different places in their pilgrimages.

Jacobs, Donald R. *The Christian Stance in a Revolutionary Age.* Scottdale: Herald Press, Focal Pamphlet No. 14, 1968. Pp. 32. Describes the factors influencing social change in the developing nations and the issues, such as tribalism, racism, and nationalism, which confront the church in these areas. Then, in this context, Jacobs contends that peace and development are two parts of the same issue—that any peace theology must necessarily speak to the issues of distributive justice.

Jantz, Harold. "Conscience Doesn't Count, Says Labor Board." *MBH* 13 (May 31, 1974), 16-17; *MennMirror* 3 (Summer, 1974), 22. Two nurses in Manitoba who requested exemption from membership and dues in the Nurses' Association on the basis of conscientious objection were turned down by the Labor Board. Includes a letter written by the editor to the Premier of Manitoba requesting him to investigate this decision.

Jantz, Hugo W. "Peace Through Service and Evangelism." *MBH* 1 (Nov. 13, 1962), 1001. True peace with God and fellow humen beings comes only in the context of servanthood and evangelism.

Jantz, Sylvia. "Peace Is . . ." *GH* 65 (Mar. 21, 1972), 266. Vignettes of inner turmoil and conflict with neighbors and friends present images of the meaning of peace and peacemaking in the local setting.

Janzen, David. "Mennonites Should Establish a Seminary Chair for Peace." *CanMenn* 17 (Nov. 21, 1969), 11. After a critical analysis of Ralph B. Potter's *War and Moral Discourse,* in which the just war concept is developed as the only hope for effective war morality, Janzen proposes the seminary at Elkhart establish a chair for peace.

Janzen, David. "The Anabaptists (4): What Is Happening to the Believers' Church?" *MennRep* 5 (Sept. 15, 1975), 5. Challenges Mennonites to remain faithful to prophetic Anabaptist stances on conscientious objection from killing, and discipleship practiced according to the Sermon on the Mount.

Janzen, David (Review). *Anabaptists and the Sword,* by James M. Stayer. Lawrence, Kansas: Coronado Press, 1972. Pp. 375. "Significant New Book on Meaning of the Sword." *MennRep* 3 (July 9, 1973), 8. Janzen discusses his disagreements with Stayer, such as with Stayer's contention that all force is basically of one kind, or Stayer's use of "apolitical" as one category in his typology, in which both Luther and the Anabaptists are placed.

Janzen, David and Janzen, Joanne. "A Bridge for Peacemakers." *Forum* (Jan., 1972), 4. "The Bridge" is an intentional community in Newton, Kans., seeking to give a more radical witness for peace and care for their families at the same time.

Janzen, David and Janzen, Joanne, "Our 3-Family Community." *ChrLiv* 19 (May, 1972), 16-17. Three families decide to live together on basis of their commitment to peace witness.

Janzen, David and Peters, Kay. "Students Protest in Washington." *MennLife* 17 (Apr., 1962), 63-65. "The Bethel [College] students' demonstration for peace in Washington is an example of an active attempt to ameliorate the condition facing the world."

Janzen, Deborah. "Henry Peter Krehbiel: A Mennonite Peacemaker, 1934-1940." Social Science Seminar paper, Apr. 4, 1974. Pp. 45. MLA/BeC.

Janzen, Gerald. "A Christian's Response to the Canada Question." *MBH* 17 (July 7, 1978), 5-6. Commitment to the gospel of peace means that Canadian Mennonites must abandon racism and ethnic self-interest in seeking reconciliation with French Quebec.

Janzen, Lester E. "Reconciliation Is Our Business." *Menn* 84 (Nov. 4, 1969), 672. The church is to be God's agent for reconciliation—for the building of relationships that make communication possible between nations, peoples, and individuals.

Janzen, Rudy H. P. "Can Mennonite Brethren with Anabaptist Peace Emphases and Fundamentalist Leanings Constructively Utilize Inherent Hostility." Thesis (MTS), Waterloo Lutheran Seminary, 1981. Pp. 55. MBBS.

Janzen, William. "MCC's Ottawa Listening Post." *MBH* 14 (Oct. 31, 1975), 9. Describes the MCC (Canada) Ottawa office as a "listening post" because it is an attempt by the church to neither dominate nor withdraw from the state.

Jeschke, Marlin. "Scapegoats for Our Hate." *CanMenn* 5 (Jan. 4, 1957), 2. The gospel is at work in all lands with all people. We must not be led to think that Christian equals American. To fall prey to the hate campaign spirit is to misunderstand the universal nature of sin, the love of God, and the divine power working in history.

Johns, O. N. "The Church's Responsibility to the Returning Serviceman." *GH* 39 (Dec. 3, 1946), 757. The church must, with Christian love, find out where each of these men stands, and then accept him and help him.

Jost, Arthur. "An Interpretation of the Doctrine of Peace." *ChrLead* 17 (Nov. 1, 1953), 5, 7. The heart of the peace witness is relational; the love of Christ characterizes the mature Christian's attempt to communicate constructively, even with the enemy.

Juhnke, James C. "Anabaptists: Then and Now." *GH* 68 (May 13, 1975), 362-64; *Menn* 90 (May 13, 1975), 298-99; "Anabaptists Today: Comfortable, Middle Class, at Peace with the World." *MennRep* 5 (May 12, 1975), Section A 12. Comments on the findings of the Kauffman-Harder survey in *Anabaptists Four Centuries Later,* expressing concern that present Mennonite churches have accommodated themselves to the powers that be, rather than challenging loyalty to government as did the Anabaptists.

Juhnke, James C. "Mennonites and the Great Compromise." *Menn* 84 (Sept. 23, 1969), 562-64. "From the first World War through the 1960s, American Mennonites and the US government have made a compromise, a deal which has allowed church and state to coexist in peace, harmony, and productivity."

Juhnke, William. "Shall We Reverse Our Historic

Peace Stand?" *Menn* 56 (Aug. 12, 1941), 2. Mennonite tradition would seem to support alternate service. The church will not force young people into this position but should conduct a massive education program making this position clear.

Julian, Cheyne. Letter to the Editor. *ChrLead* 42 (June 19, 1979), 13. Questions an article on peacemaking on the job (*ChrLead*, Mar. 27, 1979) for it seems to put the burden of peacemaking on the employee rather than on the shareholders, company directors, etc.

*Justice and the Christian Witness: A Study Report and Study Guide.* Newton: Faith and Life Press; Scottdale: Mennonite Publishing House, 1982. Pp. 66. Discusses why and what issues of justice face the church, the character of biblical justice and how the Christian peace witness guides the church's efforts to speak to these issues.

Jutzi, Bruce. "Friends Peace Caravan Visits Kitchener-Waterloo Community." *CanMenn* 14 (July 12, 1966), 4. Report of a visit by a Quaker peace caravan to the Kitchener-Waterloo area June 15-22. The caravaners met daily at the offices of MCC (Ontario) for worship and planning and had several exchanges with Dan Zehr of MCC. They visited several Mennonite churches during their stay in the area and had other contacts as well.

Jutzi, Bruce. "Ten Thousand Gave Serious Consideration to Peace Message." *CanMenn* 14 (Nov. 22, 1966), 1, 3. Report on MCC (Canada) Peace Booth at the Toronto Exhibition with theme "Peace on Earth . . . Peace in Vietnam." While it is difficult to determine the success or failure of such a witness, the booth was an opportunity to take a necessary and unpopular position and defend its validity to a cross-section of society.

Kauffman, Daniel. "Our Evangelical Witness." *GH Supplement* 36 (June, 1943), 217. Bringing relief to physical suffering can open opportunities for ministering to spiritual needs.

Kauffman, Ivan. "Practicing the Peace We Preach." *GH* 73 (Dec. 2, 1980), 966. Suggestions for peacemaking and conflict resolution within the congregation.

Kauffman, Ivan. "Thereby Making Peace." *YCC* 48 (July 9, 1967), 2. Political protest can be a valid ministry of both proclamation and servanthood. But the church is the only place where the walls which create wars can be broken down, and only by making breaches in the walls can wars be either avoided or ended.

Kauffman, Ivan J. "Hawks, Doves, or the Cross?" *MBH* 6 (Apr. 19, 1967), 4-6. "The servant call of the Cross is a response to the real situation of

the real world—that is neither stupid nor naive."

Kauffman, Nelson E. "Giving Needed Witness." *GH* 64 (Aug. 24, 1971), 700. Calls Mennonites to greater peace witness in the public media, in light of the numbers of youth from other denominations searching for counsel on conscientious objection.

Kauffman, Ralph C. "The Philosophical Aspects of Mennonitism." *PCMCP Second,* 113-26. North Newton, Kansas: The Bethel College Press. Held at Goshen, Indiana, July 22-23, 1943. Philosophical aspects of Mennonitism are those aspects which can be rationally substantiated. Comments on separation of church and state, materialism as it relates to war, and the sovereignty of God as it relates to personal conscience.

Kauffmann, Joel. *The Weight.* Scottdale, Pa.: Herald Press, 1980. Pp. 146. Jon Springer, whose father is a Mennonite minister, turns eighteen during the summer after his high school graduation. The time is the Vietnam era and he must decide whether to register for conscientious objector status or to follow the example of some peers as well as community sentiment and register I-A. The questions with which he struggles as the peacemaker model of church and family teaching becomes his own choice are "the weight." Novel for young adults.

Kaufman, Donald D. "Cheyenne Soldier Testifies, Speaks for Way of Peace." *Menn* 84 (Jan. 21, 1969), 39. Having participated actively in World War II and the Korean War, Ted Risingsun maintains that anyone who is in the army no longer has self-possession. The army wants instant obedience. "How do I feel about it [army experience]? There is a better way."

Kaufman, Edmund G. "The Christian and Nuclear Warfare." *The Lordship of Christ (Proceedings of the Seventh Mennonite World Conference).* Ed. Cornelius J. Dyck. Elkhart: MWC, 1962, 536-44. Christians can work for peace by growing in faith, in their knowledge of world affairs, by supporting United Nations, by working together for peace, and by praying for peace.

Kaufman, Gordon D. "Comment on 'Peace Child,' " *Christian Theology: A Case Study Approach.* Ed. Robert A. Evans and Thomas D. Parker. New York: Harper & Row, 1976, 118-23. The story of the "peace child" ritual told by Don Richardson about a point of contact between tribal ritual and Christian message. Demonstrates that the meaning of Christ depends upon a quality of life, namely, reconciliation and love, rather than a set of intellectual beliefs.

Kaufman, Gordon D. "The Christian in a World of

Power." *MennLife* 21 (Apr., 1966), 65-67. Christ is central to the Christian understanding of humanity and history. The cross leads us to live lives of nonresistant love that only make sense in terms of God's Kingdom.

Kaufman, Maynard. "Where Peace Begins." *MennLife* 7 (Oct., 1952), 147-48. In regeneration, faith ought to displace anxiety, which is one of the causes for social conflict. Because regeneration does not achieve complete cessation of conflict, the realization of world peace comes through practicing Christian love.

Keener, Carl S. "Ten Issues Facing the Mennonite Church Today." *GH* 72 (Sept. 4, 1979), 698-701. The author lists "creative peacemaking" as one of ten issues that face Mennonites who are part of a culture of wealth, education, and modernity.

Keener, Carl S. (Review). *Unless Peace Comes,* ed. Nigel Calder. Viking, 1968. Pp. 243. *GH* 62 (July 15, 1969), 610. Book describes warfare techniques of the future, a spectacle the reviewer concedes is not pleasant, but necessary for intensifying peacemaking efforts.

Keeney, Lois. "Mennonite Attitudes in the North During the Civil War." Research paper for Anabaptist History class. 1972. Pp. 10. BfC.

Keeney, William E. "A Strategy for Waging a Battle for Peace." *CanMenn* 12 (Feb. 18, 1964), 6, 7. Address at MCC Peace Section Annual Meeting, 1964 which describes the motivation and task of the Peace Section.

Keeney, William E. "Conditions for a Revolutionary Century." *MennLife* 25 (Jan., 1970), 3-6. How the church in the 16th century responded to the conflicts arising in a changing society may guide the contemporary church responses to the revolutionary changes of the 20th century.

Keeney, William E. "Dutch Mennonites Discuss Problems of the Nuclear Era." *GH* 56 (July 16, 1963), 609. Report of a conference to consider the Dutch Reformed Church statement on nuclear weapons and the Mennonite response to the issue.

Keeney, William E. "European Christian Peace Activities Expand. *Menn* 89 (Jan. 22, 1974), 56-57; *MennRep* 4 (Feb. 18, 1974), 7. Examines the disparate, yet growing, peace groups in Europe, the status of conscientious objection in various European countries, areas of concern among peace groups, and the progress of peace educational research, suggesting possible Mennonite contributions to these efforts.

Keeney, William E. *Lordship as Servanthood: 13 Lessons on the Biblical Basis for Peacemaking.*

Newton: Faith and Life Press, 1975. Pp. 112. A series of lessons on the principles of Christian pacifism designed for either individuals or groups. Central premise: a Christ-centered view of the Bible yields an understanding that the way of the cross embodied by Jesus is to be normative for his disciples. Faithful disciples will take the effects of evil upon themselves and let the grace of God empower them to change evil into good. Other topics discussed within this framework include the kingdom and the church, Old Testament warfare, and the Christian's relation to government.

Keeney, William E. "Not By Fear." *GH* 56 (Apr. 16, 1963), 321; *MBH* 2 (Mar. 15, 1963), 10-11; "Great Opportunities for Real Message of Peace," *CanMenn* 11 (May 31, 1963), 6. In witnessing for peace in our world the Christian tactic is to begin with love and faith and not with fear. True peace is established by love and reconciliation through Jesus. Any other basis for pacifism is inadequate.

Keeney, William E. "Peace as Wholeness." *GH* 62 (Jan. 14, 1969), 37-38. Calls the church to act as a reconciling witness in society, even when such action involves the church in politics, because the church should bring a ministry of healing and peacemaking to the rest of the world.

Keeney, William E. "Peacemaking Is a Healing Ministry." *Menn* 83 (Apr. 16, 1968), 274-76. As the church has a healing ministry for bodies and souls of individuals, so peacemaking is a healing ministry for society.

Keeney, William E. "The Peace Witness in the Netherlands." *Menn* 64 (Oct. 11, 1949), 12-13. Various inter-Mennonite and inter-denominational conferences since the war have contributed to a resurgence of pacifism. The writer discusses pragmatic and religious bases for the pacifist stance.

Kehler, Larry. "A Profile of Mennonite Personnel Involved in International Experience." *PCMCP Sixteenth,* 9-39. Held at Hesston, Kansas, 1967. Statistics of Mennonites in service work abroad includes discussion of international service experience as peacemaking.

Kehler, Larry. "Christ's Lordship and Caesar's." *Menn* 86 (June 15, 1971), 390-93. Eight opinion leaders in the General Conference Mennonite Church in Canada discuss in a two-day encounter the relation between "the Lordship of Christ and our position on peace."

Kehler, Larry. "Conference Takes Fresh Look at Church-State Relationships." *CanMenn* 13 (Oct. 19, 1965), 1, 2, 14. Franklin Littel, Paul Peachey, Al Meyer, and Leo Driedger are represented in this detailed report.

Kehler, Larry. "David and Goliath." *Menn* 89 (June 25, 1974), 424. MCC representative reflects on a recent trip to the Mideast, concluding that while the area is highly polarized, voices of moderation and reconciliation are beginning to be heard from both sides.

Kehler, Larry. "Evangelism, Militarism, and Nationalism." *Menn* 86 (June 22, 1971), 405-408. Relating the idolatry of nationalism and of militarism to the evangelistic message is an integral part of the proclamation of the gospel to repentance.

Kehler, Larry. "Nine Minutes to Doomsday." *Menn* 89 (Oct. 29, 1974), 640. Lists reasons the specialists announce an increased threat of nuclear holocaust and calls Christians to be peacemakers in view of the impending doom.

Kehler, Larry. "Peace as Evangelism." Study paper, 1972. Box 13-A-15. CMBS/Win.

Kehler, Larry. "Peace Section of MCC Extends Witness into East Asia in 1963." *CanMenn* 11 (Jan. 25, 1963), 3. Roy Just plans to leave for a two-year assignment in East Asia as part of the Peace Section witness.

Kehler, Larry. "Peacemaking Efforts Fall Behind for Lack of Greater Financial Support." *CanMenn* 15 (Feb. 14, 1967), 1, 2. Expresses convictions on the urgency of the work of the MCC Peace Section and reports discussion "regarding the direction which its concern in the area of international conflict should take."

Kehler, Larry. "The Peace Corps and the Church." *GH* 54 (Dec. 5, 1961), 1040. This article outlines the history of the Peace Corps and traces the churches' reaction to it as it evolved.

Kehler, Larry. "The Way of Peace." *CanMenn* 15 (Nov. 7, 1967), 5. Practical suggestions for peace living on the level of the home and the neighborhood.

Kehler, Peter. "Fourth Southeast Asia Reconciliation Work Camp." *GH* 61 (Oct. 15, 1968), 937-38. Describes and reflects on a work camp hosted by Taiwan Mennonites for the purpose of building international cooperation in peacemaking while working on some worthy service project.

Kehler, Peter. "Responsibility to the State." *CanMenn* 6 (Jan. 31, 1958), 2. Christians are called to an active role in peacemaking and witnessing to the state.

Kehler, Peter. "Responsibility to the World." *CanMenn* 6 (Feb. 7, 1958), 2. The Christian's responsibility to the world lies both in evangelism and in loving service to the needy.

Kehler, Peter. "Southeast Asia Work Camp Builds Roads to Assist Refugees from Mainland China." *CanMenn* 16 (Sept. 17, 1968), 3. Report on the Fourth South East Asia Reconciliation Work Camp held in Taipei involving eleven participants from Japan (including two US citizens), one from Indonesia, one PAXperson from Korea, and twenty-two from Taiwan. Korean and Indian delegates could not attned due to government restriction.

Kehler, Peter. "The Mennonite Church in Peace and War." *CanMenn* 6 (Jan. 24, 1958), 2, 3. An argument based on following the God of love rather than the God of righteousness and justice. Kehler believes that God's greatest attribute is love. Stresses the need for the church to accept its responsibility to God and the Word both in peace and war.

Keidel, Levi O. "The Mennonite Credibility Gap." *GH* 68 (Oct. 7, 1975), 709-11; *MBH* 15 (July 9, 1976), 2-3; *ChrLead* 38 (Sept. 16, 1975), 2; *Menn* 90 (Dec. 23, 1975), 730-31. The Anabaptist lifestyle consisted of four major emphases—holy living, evangelical witness, attitude toward material wealth, and nonresistance—of which modern Mennonites emphasize only select parts, thus weakening their witness.

Keim, Ray; Beechy, Atlee; and Beechy, Winifred. *The Church: The Reconciling Community.* Scottdale: Mennonite Publishing House; Newton: Faith and Life Press, 1970. Pp. 92. Examines the direction set for the church by the reconciling work of Jesus and looks at such issues as militarism, nationalism, human rights, racism, poverty, crime and violence as tasks for the church which embodies that reconciliation.

Kelley, Mark. "Making Peace Public." *The Other Side* 14 (Dec., 1978), 36-39. The story of Robert Euler, the man behind the Nazareth-Bethlehem Christmas Peace Pilgrimage in Pennsylvania.

Kennel, LeRoy (Review). *The Demands of Freedom,* by Helmut Gollwitzer. Harper and Row, 1965. Pp. 176. *ChrLiv* 13 (Jan., 1966), 34-35. Reviews the author's thesis that freedom demands individual responsibility to call people and governments to peace.

King, Calvin J. "The Position of the Methodist Church Concerning War, Peace, and Revolution." Paper for War, Peace, and Revolution class, AMBS, Elkhart, Ind., n.d. Pp. 3. AMBS.

Kirk, Jack. "New Tides Running: The American Quaker Experience Since 1935." Address given at a meeting of the three historic peace churches, Bethel College Mennonite Church, North Newton, KS, Apr. 10, 1976. Pp. 8. MLA/BeC.

Kirkwood, Ronald. "Passive-ism or Pacifism." *Menn* 70 (Mar. 8, 1955), 150. The American government, in its very tolerance, is employing its most effective weapon against us. Our vigorous witness against militarism has become a passive witness to the way of love.

Klaassen, David. "Our Voice for Peace." *ChrLead* 30 (July 18, 1967), 7-8. We have been too indecisive; we must totally reject participation in war and totally endorse constructive service and the way of love.

Klaassen, Walter. "Anabaptism: So What?" *GH* 67 (Feb. 12, 1974), 129-33. Among the contemporary issues to which the sixteenth-century Anabaptist movement speaks are the issues of revolutionary change and the use of violence in working toward justice.

Klaassen, Walter. "The Meaning of Anabaptism." *MBH* 14 (Jan. 24, 1975), 6-7. Giving ultimate loyalty to God over social and political powers exercising violence was one of the marks of 16th-century Anabaptists.

Klaassen, Walter. "The Nature of the Anabaptist Protest," *MQR* 45 (Oct., 1971), 291-311. A delineation of the main features of the Anabaptist protest in the religious, social, and political context of the time, noting how Catholics and Protestants viewed the protest, and inquiring into Anabaptist consciousness of their protest.

Klaassen, Walter. "The Peace Churches and Social Revolution." *MennRep* 2 (May 29, 1972), 11. World Council of Churches representative and peace churches dialogue on the meaning of peace emphases, thoretical and practical, and alternatives to peace, the just revolution.

Klassen, Aaron. "DeBoer Speaks Bluntly to Canadian Mennonites." *CanMenn* 8 (June 17, 1960), 1, 2, 10. Reactions are mixed as Hans DeBoer challenges Canadian Mennonites to move out of their lethargy and witness for peace more actively.

Klassen, Aaron. "Peace Sunday." *CanMenn* 8 (Nov. 4, 1960), 2. The church might well ponder whether it can separate its peace teachings from its evangelistic outreach and whether or not Christ taught anything which speaks to the issue of war and peace.

Klassen, Aaron. "The Church Witnesses in the Market Place." *CanMenn* 10 (Sept. 7, 1962), 1, 4. An evaluation of the Peace Booth project at the Canadian National Exhibition.

Klassen, Bernard R. "Small Nations Are Pawns in Game of Political Chess." *CanMenn* 15 (Oct. 3, 1967), 1, 7. All through history the most advanced nations have felt that it was their prerogative to superimpose their "superior" culture on "less civilized peoples." To be a peacemaker, the Christian must condemn injustice, strive for the triumph of justice, and in the meantime show human compassion and understanding to all people, whether they are right or wrong.

Klassen, D. D. Letter to the Editor. *CanMenn* 4 (Dec. 28, 1956), 2, 9. A reply to John H. Redekop's "Non-Resistance and UN Police Action," (*CanMenn*, Dec. 7, 1956). Klassen reviews church history on church-state relations and asks for strong peace position through education.

Klassen, Don. "Reconcile. Reconcile! Reconcile!!: A Word Study." Paper for War, Peace, and Revolution class, AMBS, Elkhart, Ind., Apr., 1969. Pp. 3. AMBS.

Klassen, Frank S. "Reconciliation: Using the Resources of Music." *MennRep* 5 (July 7, 1975), 8. Reflects on the musical peace ministry of the Reconciliation Singers.

Klassen, Herbert. "Mennonites and World Peace." *CanMenn* 9 (July 14, 1961), 2, 12. We as Mennonites must become involved in cooperative activity with broader, worldwide agencies searching for peace.

Klassen, Mike. "The Draft as a Chance for Witness." *Forum* 13 (Apr., 1980), 1-3. Pastor of the Mennonite fellowship in Manhattan, Kansas, describes how potentially resumed draft registration became the vehicle for peace witnessing.

Klassen, Peter J. "L. B. Pearson—A Tribute." *MBH* 12 (Jan. 12, 1973), 11. Records some of the achievements of L. B. Pearson during his time as Prime Minister of Canada. Notes his international status as a peacemaker.

Klassen, William. "Christmas at Bethlehem, 1973." *MennMirror* 3 (Dec., 1973), 7, 8. In the midst of war, there are efforts and attempts at peacemaking between Jew, Moslem, and Christian in Bethlehem.

Klassen, William. "Mandate for Oneness." *Menn* 77 (Jan. 2, 1962), 4-5. A study of the biblical basis and Anabaptist precedent for the renewed concern for reconciliation and unity between Mennonite bodies.

Klassen, William. "To Be a Peacemaker." *YCC* 46 (July 4, 1965), 1. Survey of various "peacemaker" options young people must consider to make their decision their own and not just a decision that reflects their parents' belief.

Kliewer, John W. "A Sermon on Christian After

War Questions." Preached at Bethel College, Newton, Ks., Jan. 5, 1919. Pp. 12. MHL.

Kliewer, Marion W. "Delegates Study Meaning of Christian Love." *CanMenn* 2 (July 30, 1954), 1, 8. Reports historic peace church meeting at Bluffton College, July 15-18, 1954, where a large gathering studied commitment, love and justice.

Kliewer, P. A. "So Making Peace." *Menn* 53 (Oct. 4, 1938), 13-14. Peace is an idle dream so long as the Prince of Peace is rejected by most people.

Koehn, Brent A. "The Shalom Covenant and Peacemaking." Advanced Peace Studies Seminar paper, Mar. 28, 1979. Pp. 66. MLA/BeC.

Koehn, Dennis, ed. "Anabaptist Dreams and Menno-Nite-Mares." *IPF Notes* 18 (Jan., 1972), 5-6. Summary of a Michael Friedman paper on recovering Anabaptist peace church roots.

Kolb, Norman. "Nations on the Verge of Calamity." *ST* 47 (July, 1979), 24. A Bible study from which one learns that national preservation depends on national spirituality and not on national military might.

Koontz, Ted. "Join Now, Pay Later." *With* 7 (Sept., 1974), 12. The myths that operate behind the military recruitment efforts. Suggestions for positive peacemaking are offered.

Koontz, Ted. "Peace Groups Examine Development Strategies." *MBH* 12 (June 1, 1973), 14-15. Reports on the annual Intercollegiate Peace Fellowship Conference at the Church Center for the United Nations in New York which focused on "Third World Development and Exploitation."

Koontz, Ted. "Two Political Realisms and Christian Faith." *Menn* 94 (Apr. 24, 1979), 292-93. Presents the debate between two realisms—what can be expected of nations and what is required of humanity to avoid unprecedented disaster—and offers the resources of Christian faith as a response.

Koontz, Ted. "Urbana 73 Stresses Hope, Commitment—Reactions." *Forum* (Feb., 1974), 6. MCC Peace Section experienced many favorable responses to their peace witness at Urbana 73.

Kossen, Henk B. "The Peace Church in a World of Conflict." *CGR* 2 (Winter, 1984), 1-9. Reflects upon the church's mission in a society organized around economic, political, and ideological conflict. Concludes that the church is true to its mission to the degree it follows the example of Jesus, the Liberator, in identifying and repelling the powers operating within society.

Krahn, Cornelius. "Crossroads at Amsterdam." *MennLife* 22 (Oct., 1967), 153-56. A report on the Eighth Mennonite World Conference with an emphasis on Anabaptism, revolution, and radicalism.

Kraus, C. Norman. "A Theology for Action." *GH* 61 (June 18, 1968), 538-40; *ChrLead* 31 (June 18, 1968), 7-9. Historical and biblical definitions of the church. The church should be servant to the impoverished, witness against corrupt structures, and be a living demonstration of the new reality.

Kraus, C. Norman. "Confronting Revolutionary Change." *GH* 63 (June 23, 1970), 566-67. Defining "revolution" as "profound, irrevsersible change" of either a violent or nonviolent sort, the author cites Jesus and the Anabaptists as revolutionary and challenges Christians not to be threatened by those who call for change in the social structures.

Kraus, C. Norman. "Faint Not; Fight On." *GH* 39 (July 2, 1946), 289-90. The US fear of Russia, and the white attitude toward the blacks, are examples of attempts to overcome guilt through self-justification. Before reconciliation can take place one must admit his or her guilt and inability to solve the problem alone.

Kraybill, Donald B. "Bang-Bang." *ChrLiv* 21 (Jan., 1974), 32. Outlines his reasons for reconverting to hunting after having been convinced peacelovers should not kill or carry a gun in any circumstances.

Kraybill, Donald B. *Facing Nuclear War: A Plea for Christian Witness.* Scottdale and Kitchener: Herald Press, 1982. Pp. 307. Using the tragedy of Hiroshima as a reference point, Kraybill provides clear information on the effects of contemporary nuclear weapons. In light of this "chief moral issue," he analyzes the global political situation and interweaves, with these technological and political analyses, the pertinent biblical perspectives offering guidance to Christian responses to the threat of nuclear war. In the last part of the book he concretizes these responses by suggesting specific actions individuals can take toward peace and explodes some of the excuses commonly given for not taking action.

Kraybill, Donald B. "The Master Welder." *GH* 63 (Nov. 17, 1970), 962-64. Reconciliation with God and one another is the core of the gospel, and it must be worked out by people acting as ministers of reconciliation in all situations of conflict.

Kraybill, Paul N. "The Christian in Modern

Africa." Messages and Reports from the Limuru Study Conference, Limuru, Kenya, Mar. 28-Apr. 1, 1962. Pp. 45. MHL. Includes: Jacobs, Don, "The Spirit of the Lamb," 1-4; Neufeld, Elmer, "The Mighty Acts of God," 5-7; Neufeld, Elmer, "The Church—The Body of Christ," 8-11; Miller, Orie O., "Scriptural Position on War Participation—My Personal Testimony," 11-12; Mudenda, Sampson, "The Prophetic Christian in Relation to Local and National Politics," 13-15; Lemma, Daniel, "The Church and the State," 15-16; Kisare, Zedekiah, "Christians in a Newly Independent Country," 17-18; Kisanja, Elijah, "The Mau Mau and Christianity," 19-20; Weaver, Edwin I., "The Ministry of Reconciliation in Africa or Bridges of Forgiveness, Love, and Fellowship," 20-23.

Kraybill, Ron S. "Introducing Mennonite Conciliation Service." *Peace Section Newsletter* 9 (Dec., 1979), 9. Goal of this service is greater faithfulness to the biblical call to peacemaking through ministries in community conflicts. MSC aims to equip locally-based Mennonites for relating to disputes of various kinds in their surrounding communities.

Kraybill, Ron S. "Making Peace Out of Local Tensions." *MBH* 19 (Aug. 8, 1980), 16-17. Mennonite Conciliation Service works at peacemaking in local situations of conflict.

Kraybill, Ron S. *Repairing the Breach: Ministering in Community Conflict.* Scottdale, Pa.: Herald Press, 1980. Pp. 95. A manual providing suggestions and guidance for the art of Christian peacemaking based on the biblical emphasis of shalom. Reconciliation processes between groups, between individuals and within groups are discussed and illustrated by examples.

Krehbiel, H[enry]. P[eter]. "The Historic Mennonite Position on Peace." *Menn* 51 (June 16, 1936), 3-6. The pacifist position of Mennonites has been influential in the past and will be so in the future if its proponents expand their efforts.

Krehbiel, H[enry] P[eter] (Archival). Collection (12). Occupies 59 boxes. Collection contains extensive correspondence relating to Krehbiel's (1862-1940) many church and conference involvements and of special interest are letters regarding peace concerns. Included are a large number of peace pamphlets and minutes of General Conference and Western District peace committees. MLA/BeC.

Krehbiel, Olin A. "The Ministry of Reconciliation." *Menn* 65 (Apr. 4, 1950), 220, 224. Because of their peace tradition Mennonites are called to "lead out and show the way" to other groups of people.

Kreider, Alan, ed. "Thoughts from Conference Speakers." *IPF Notes* 6 (June, 1960), 3-10. Detailed summary of addresses on the topics of the Christian witness against militarism through politics, I-W program, and missions.

Kreider, Alan. "Witness in Washington." *YCC* 43 (May 13, 1962), 10. A group of Goshen students traveled to Washington, DC, with the belief that Christians can and should witness to government.

Kreider, Carl. "Peace Thought in the Mennonite Church from the Beginning of the World War in Europe, August, 1914, to the Establishment of the War Sufferer's Relief Commission, December, 1917." Paper presented to American History class, 1936. Pp. 34. MHL.

Kreider, Evelyn B. "It's Our Turn." *Lifework* 1 (1978), 3-5. Essay on peace outlines the biblical basis for shalom, the nonresistant convictions of Anabaptists, and the call to be peacemakers today as Christians.

Kreider, Evelyn B. "Shalom: God's Plan." *WMSC Voice* 54 (Dec., 1980), 3-4. Reprinted from *Lifework: Commitment to Christ and* peacemaking is a way of life that means working for peace and justice for all people and all social structures.

Kreider, Janet H. "Peacemakers in the Midst of War." *GH* 61 (Mar. 12, 1968), 218-19. Describes the activities and questions of Mennonite missionaries in Vietnam seeking to be peacemakers in the middle of the Vietnam war.

Kreider, Robert S. "A Litany of Violence and Reconciliation." *GH* 61 (Apr. 16, 1968), 346-47; *CanMenn* 16 (Aug. 13, 1968), 4-5; *MBH* 7 (Mar. 29, 1968), 4-5; *ChrLead* 31 (Mar. 26, 1968), 5, 12. Offsets scripture passages on hope and reconciliation against vignettes of the problems of war, violence, poverty, racial tensions.

Kreider, Robert S. "A Vision for Our Day." *MennLife* 3 (Jan., 1948), 5-7. A critical look at Mennonites followed by a statement of hope in the Mennonite vision as it calls people to be bridge builders of love and reconciliation.

Kreider, Robert S. "How Beautiful Are the Feet." *MBH* 14 (Oct. 31, 1975), 2-3. Peacemaking and peace education are central in the gospel and should be high in the church's priorities.

Kreider, Robert S. "How Do Mennonites View the Brethren and Friends?" *GH* 70 (Dec. 27, 1977), 966-68. Examines the relationships among the historic peace churches on peace issues, etc.

Kreider, Robert S. "Mennonites and the Historic Peace Churches." *Menn* 94 (Oct. 9, 1979), 593-95. An examination of the Mennonites' relationship to and cooperation with the

Brethren and Quakers, historically and currently.

Kreider, Robert S. "Mennonites Around the Rim of the Mediterranean." *Menn* 86 (Mar. 23, 1971), 186-89. The vice-chairman of MCC reports on the Mennonite witness for peace through projects around the Mediterranean.

Kreider, Robert S. "The Beautiful Feet." *GH* 68 (Apr. 15, 1975), 285-86; "How Beautiful Are the Feet: Taking Stock of Our Peacemaking Commitments When the Heat Is Off." *Menn* 90 (Apr. 15, 1975), 237-38. Discusses the need for congregational peace education programs, and the inseparability of peace and evangelism.

Kreider, Robert S. "The Gospel of Christ Is the Gospel of Peace." *CanMenn* 11 (Aug. 20, 1963), 6, 8. According to Colossians 1: 15, 20 and 3: 15, the motif of peace, love, and reconciliation is an essential part of the gospel.

Kreider, Robert S. "The Mennonite Vision for and in the World Today." Address at Elspeet, Netherlands, May 16, 1947. Pp. 5. MLA/BeC.

Kreider, Roy. "A Strategy of Witness in the Middle East." *GH* 62 (June 10, 1969), 519-20. "A demonstrated gospel blunts the attack against the gospel, shows the gospel to be superior love: through service projects, through the word of witness, through practical expressions of community."

Kroeker, David. "Delegates Vote for College Expansion; Adopt Peace Witness Policy Statement." *CanMenn* 17 (July 11, 1969), 1. At the annual Canadian MB conference delegates adopt a critical position toward MCC and specifically to the MCC peace section.

Kroeker, Walter.. "Concern Over Ethics, Pacifism." *ChrLead* 40 (Mar. 29, 1977), 9. Report from the Mennonite Brethren US Board of Reference and Counsel in which racism, peace/war attitudes, and alliance with New Call to Peacemaking were discussed.

Kroeker, Walter.. "Evangelism Without the Gospel." *ChrLead* 41 (Jan. 31, 1978), 24. A Christian proclamation that fails to include the making of disciples is failing to respond to the Great Commission. Some MB's use sound, doctrinal language to simply rationalize the existing social order.

Kroeker, Walter. "Influence in Politics." *The Voice* 20 (Oct., 1971), 15. If we let the force of clear Christian witness operate in and through our lives we will have a great impact on politicians and on legislation.

Kroeker, Walter.. "Justice and Relief Must Stay Together." *MBH* 18 (Feb. 16, 1979), 16-18.

Papers were presented at the MCC annual meeting on the relation of peace and reconciliation to Native American outreach, hunger concerns, and militarism.

Kroeker, Walter.. "Protecting Our Turf." *ChrLead* 41 (May 9, 1978), 24. Expresses concern that Mennonite Brethren spend more political energy crusading for the rights of others rather than only building walls around personal issues.

Kuitse, Roelf (Review). *Mission and the Peace Witness,* ed. Robert L. Ramseyer. Herald Press, 1979. Pp. 141. *MQR* 54 (Oct., 1980), 339. Recommends the book as a collection of essays centered around the theme of peace witness as an essential part of Mennonite missions.

Kurtz, Lydia. "Teaching Peace in Botswana." *MennRep* 7 (Apr. 4, 1977), 16. Mennonite teacher in Botswana describes incident with student that allowed her to reinforce peacemaking values.

"Lamb's Warriors Discuss Discipleship." *Menn* 87 (Sept. 12, 1972), 524, 525. Representatives from intentional communities and others share their involvements in the service for God, kingdom, and peace; envision future action; and establish a vehicle for communication; the *Post-American,* a radical, evangelical Christian newspaper.

"Letter from Vietnam to American Churches." *GH* 61 (Jan. 16, 1968), 65-66; *CanMenn* 16 (Mar. 5, 1968), 4. Mennonite missionaries in Vietnam speak for the perspective of Vietnamese people, pleading for greater awareness of the issues underlying the Vietnam war. Signed by James K. Stauffer, Everett G. Metzler, Luke S. Martin, James E. Metzler, Don M. Sensenig, S. Luke Beidler.

"Letters Call Young People to Become Makers of Peace." *CanMenn* 6 (Jan. 3, 1958), 1, 7. The Canadian Board of Christian Service sent peace literature to 4,000 youth. The literature includes reflections from a nonresistant Japanese Baptist and Erland Waltner.

"Living as Peacemakers." *Builder* 12 (Feb., 1962), 17-18. Four youth program ideas designed to help youth think through the implications of the church's peace theology with respect to practice and witness.

La Roque, Emma. *Defeathering the Indian.* Agincourt, Canada: The Book Society of Canada Limited, 1975. Pp. 82. A handbook for educators on Native Studies which deals with the ways cultures clash and offers suggestions for peacemakers on how to reverse such forces of psychological violence as stereotyping, denigrating language, and selective history.

Landes, Carl J. "A Call to Rural Fellowship Members." *Fellowship* 7 (Feb., 1941), 30. The Fellowship of Reconciliation Council has provided for a Rural Secretary for the next six months to serve rural pacifists in America.

Landes, Carl J. "A Mennonite Peace Program for Local Groups." *Menn* 51 (Apr. 14, 1936), 2-3. Individuals must not only have inner peace but must work for peace in the community and the nation. Specific suggestions are given.

Landes, Carl J. Letter to the Editor. *Fellowship* 16 (Mar., 1950), 31-32. Writes that it is necessary for pacifists to learn to work within the organized church and be willing to pay the price for reconciliation.

Lapp, Benjamin F. "The Bicentennial: Two Views. 2. My Attitude Toward My Country." *GH* 69 (Feb. 10, 1976), 103-104. While the Christian's allegiance is to the heavenly kingdom rather than the earthly country, the Christian is also called to be subject to the existing authorities, not to criticize the government in the name of peace.

Lapp, George J. "Helps and Hindrances to Peace." *GH* 37 (Sept. 22, 1944), 493. The Christian "stranger and pilgrim" does not participate in war because he or she is part of the kingdom of God and is engaged in spiritual, not carnal, warfare.

Lapp, James. "A Call to Prayer." *GH* 73 (Jan. 15, 1980), 48. In the face of the Iranian takeover of the US embassy and the Soviet invasion of Afghanistan, prayer is a powerful and peaceful response.

Lapp, John A. "Mennonites Discuss Peace at Curitiba." *Menn* 87 (Sept. 5, 1972), 509. Representatives from the Netherlands, Africa, Japan, etc., speak on the meaning of a peace position as it relates to economics, politics, racism, etc., and plan for ways of relating the peace message in the context of Mennonite World Conference.

Lapp, John A. "Missions, Missionaries, and the Political Process." Paper presented at the GCMC Commission on Overseas Missions, Missionary Retreat, June 26, 1976. Pp. 11. MHL.

Lapp, John A. "Peacemaking: the Way of Discipleship." *Menn* 87 (Oct. 31, 1972), 630-32. Since the meaning of peacemaking has been distorted, there is a need to reexamine what it means to be a peace church.

Lapp, John A. "The Christian Historian as Prophet." Paper presented at the Mennonite Graduate Fellowship, 1966. Pp. 13. MHL.

Lapp, John A. "The Church and the Social Question." *GH* 66 (July 17, 1973), 553-55. The church as a re-created community extends the message of reconciliation by rooting out racism and militarism within itself and thus becoming able to address these structures in society.

Lapp, John A. (Review). *Letters of a CO from Prison*, by Timothy W. L. Zimmer. The Judson Press, 1969. *GH* 63 (May 19, 1970), 460. Earlham College student imprisoned for refusing induction into the army or alternative service reflects on the topics of government, faith, revolution, protest, love. Recommended for its insight into the thinking of young American idealists.

Lapp, John E. "How Should I Witness to the State?" *GH* 59 (July 26, 1966), 659-61. A witness is given in due recognition of the authorities. The way of witnessing includes prayer, obedience when civil laws do not conflict with God's laws, paying taxes, personal witnessing, writing letters to officials and newspapers, and service in love.

Lapp, John E. "The Christian—A Servant of Reconciliation." *GH* 63 (Dec. 15, 1970), 1034-35. God calls all Christians to follow Jesus in becoming servants of reconciliation, a conviction the author arrives at through examining New Testament passages.

Lapp, John E. "The Committee on Peace and Social Concerns and its Work." *GH* 60 (Nov. 7, 1967), 1016-18. A brief historical review of the committee's work, concluding with projections for the future of this effort.

Lapp, John E. "The Gospel from Words to Deeds." *GH* 61 (Mar. 19, 1968), 249-50. Living as Christ lived means following the commands of the Sermon on the Mount regarding love, reconciliation, and nonresistance, taking positive action against social evils of war and poverty.

Lapp, John E. "The Gospel in Reconciliation of Men." *GH* 61 (Mar. 12, 1968), 228-29. The social implications of the gospel include economic and racial equality and opposition to war.

Lapp, John E. (Review). *Mennonite Statements on Peace, 1915-1966*, by Richard C. Detweiler. Scottdale: Herald Press, 1968. Pp. 71. *GH* 62 (Apr. 15, 1969), 353. Describes the contents of the booklet, which include an evaluation of the peace witness documents and a review of Mennonite scholarship on views of church and state and Anabaptist historiography in this century.

Lapp, John E. (Review). *The New Left and Christian Radicalism*, by Arthur G. Gish. Grand Rapids: Eerdmans, 1970. Pp. 158. *GH* 64 (May 18,

1971), 451. The author draws parallels between the Anabaptist wing of the Reformation and the New Radicalism of the twentieth century. Calls Christians to be nonviolently revolutionary.

Lawless, Mary Patricia. Letter to the Editor. *Menn* 94 (Feb. 20, 1979), 134. Author was arrested for unlawful conduct and criminal trespassing while trying to maintain a prayer vigil and fast in the cadet's chapel of the US Air Force Academy in Colorado Springs. Includes the statement she read to the judge before sentencing.

Leatherman, Dan. "Mennonite Youth and the New Peace Corps." *YCC* 42 (June 18, 1961), 386. Description of the Peace Corp program. Mennonite response to this program should be cautious while generating enthusiam for own church programs.

Lee, Nancy (Review). *Through the Valley of the Kwai*, by Ernest Gordon. Harper, 1962. Pp. 257. *ChrLiv* 10 (Feb., 1963), 33. Recommends the book as a testimony of reconciliation from soldiers in a Japanese prisoner of war camp who learned of love and forgiveness toward enemies.

Lehman, Carl M. "Has CPS Enlarged Our Concept of Missions?" *CPS Bull Supp* 5 (June 20, 1946), 2, 6. Since all of Christian life has been transformed by Christ, Christian missions is expressing the complete Christian life to other people.

Lehman, Celia. "The Middle Man." *Swords into Plowshares: A Collection of Plays About Peace and Social Justice*. Ed. Ingrid Rogers. Elgin: The Brethren Press, 1983, 109-124. A choral reading which explores the issue of civil religion as well as other aspects of the church and state relationship.

Lehman, Emmett R. "'Revolution,' the Theme of Intercollegiate Peace Conference." *GfT* Series 2, 4 (Mar.-Apr., 1969), 13-14. Comment on the militant spirit present at the conference.

Lehman, Ernest. "Establishing Peace Within." *GH Supplement* 40 (Apr., 1947), 95. Peace within and without begins with a personal commitment to Christ.

Lehman, Ernest. "Not Against Flesh and Blood." *GH Supplement* 39 (Feb., 1947), 1035. Spiritual weapons overcome Satan whereas carnal weapons only overcome the agents of Satan who are committing evil deeds prompted by Satan.

Lehman, Melvin L. (Review). *Who Burned the Barn Down?*, drama by I. Merle Good. *ChrLiv* 18 (May, 1971), 36-37. Reviewer observes the play explores the problem of peacemaking in the context of pacifism in personal relations. Lind, Loren. "One Thing to Do About It." *ChrLiv* 11 (Apr., 1964), 2. Editorial suggests books on war, nonviolent racial revolution, nuclear arms, cold war, and poverty, in order to help our minds keep pace with our bodies living in a modern world.

Lehman, Titus. Letter in "Our Readers Say." *GH* 52 (Dec. 22, 1959), 1074. Praises Edgar Metzler's article (Nov. 17) as prophetic. A peace witness should generate more reaction than the Mennonite Church's is now doing.

Leichty, Bruce. "IPF Assembly Reveals 'Folly' of Values." *Forum* 13 (Nov., 1979), 14, 15. The annual Intercollegiate Peace Fellowship assembly, meeting in Hesston, Kans., Oct. 25-27, confronted the participants with the "folly" of the peace witness.

Leichty, Daniel. "Grace and the Peace Question." *GH* 72 (Sept. 25, 1979), 754-55. The peace issue is central to Mennonite faith and must be kept at the center of discussion with other Christians because the gospel cannot be communicated through coercion and violence.

Leis, Vernon. "Our Mandate to Be Peacemakers." *GH* 65 (Feb. 29, 1972), 186-87. Underscoring biblical references, the writer asserts that peacemaking is central to the gospel, based on: Jesus' teaching and ministry; biblical evidence indicating that conversion produces ethical changes; and the fellowship of Christians around the world.

Levellers (corporate student project). "Peace Activities of 1969 at Bethel College or a Peace of the Rebellion." A series of student papers for a History of Civilization project, Dec. 15, 1972. Pp. 94. MLA/BeC.

Lichti, Jürgen. "Peace Seminar in Frankfurt." *Menn* 66 (June 19, 1951), 398. Report and summary of MCC's seminar for German Mennonite youth, Mar. 19-25, 1951, on biblical and historical perspectives of radical discipleship.

Lind, Loren. "A Time to March." *YCC* 47 (Jan. 23, 1966), 6. A description of participating in the march on Washington for Peace in Vietnam.

Lind, Loren. "They Walked for Peace." *YCC* 43, Part 1, (July 8, 1962), 13; Part 2, (July 15, 1962), 12; Part 3, (July 22, 1962), 12. An account of the "Walk for Peace—San Francisco to Moscow, Dec., 1960, to Oct., 1961."

Lind, Loren. "What Should We Do?" *YCC* 47 (July 3, 1966), 8. Survey of protest responses to the Vietnam War. What should Mennonites do to express their peace witness?

Lind, Marcus. "A Prophet of Grace and Peace." *ST* 47 (June, 1979), 10-13. Elisha's overcoming of evil with good in II Kings 6:23 is a paradigm for present day conflict.

Lind, Marcus. "Abigail, an Advocate of Peace." *ST* 47 (Mar., 1979), 12-14. Comment on I Samuel 25, where Abigail persuades David not to attack her husband Nabal.

Lind, Marcus. "From Carnal Sword to Peaceful Rod." *ST* 48 (May, 1980), 11-14. Moses led the children of Israel, not with a sword of violence, but with the more peaceful symbol of authority, a shepherd's rod.

Lind, Marcus. "Learning from the Bible's First War." *ST* 47 (Jan., 1979), 19-22. Abram's acceptance of Melchizedek's bread and wine instead of Bera's war spoils marked his choice of servanthood rather than violence.

Lind, Millard C. "The Gospel We Preach." *ChrLiv* 5 (Apr., 1958), 2. God's purposes for this world are unity and reconciliation in Christ.

Lind, Millard C. "Transformation of Justice: From Moses to Jesus." Paper presented to Lawbreaking and Peacemaking Workshop, Camp Assiniboia, Man., May 3, 1980. Pp. 25. AMBS.

Lockett, L. W. "Bridging Broken Walls." *Direction* 7 (Jan., 1978), 11-17. How can the church overcome the tendency to erect walls between itself and the world? Part of the answer is for the church to have an awareness of the nature of organizational behavior.

Loewen, Esko. "MCC in Europe Today." *Menn* 70 (Nov. 22, 1955), 728. MCC continues the peace witness via PAX, the Heerewegen Conference Center, the Puidoux conferences, and voluntary service projects.

Loewen, Les. "Love and Peace Emphasis Day Held at EMB Church." *CanMenn* 7 (May 29, 1959), 1, 4. F. C. Peters spoke on "The Biblical Basis of Non-Resistance" and "The Logic of Non-Resistance."

Long, Inez. "Unbroken Soldier for Peace." *ChrLiv* 7 (Oct., 1960), 16-17, 39-40. Church of the Brethren spokesman for peace who innocently kills three in a car accident rallies again to spread the message of reconciliation.

Longacre, Doris Janzen. *More-with-Less Cookbook.* Scottdale: Herald Press, 1976. Pp. 328. A cookbook which emphasizes the global perspective of MCC by offering recipes, based on economy of money, time, and energy, which express the spirit of a people "looking for ways to live more simply and joyfully, ways that grow out of our tradition but take their shape from living faith and the demands of our hungry world."

Longacre, James. "Agressive Peace." *GH* 56 (Oct. 15, 1963), 909. Real peace is embodied in the individual. It is an agressive love that absorbs hate via action.

Longacre, James C. "Letter of Concern to All." *GH* 66 (July 17, 1973), 556-57. A call for new peace education efforts for the Mennonite Church, in order to prevent Mennonite assimilation of the militaristic and economically oppressive values of US culture.

Longacre, James C., writer, and Martin, Lawrence, ed. *Citizens of Christ's Kingdom: A Peace Education Resource Guide for Congregational Leaders.* Scottdale, Pa.: Mennonite Publishing House, 1975. Pp. 16. MHL. Organized around 3 themes: biblical foundations for peacemaking; peacemaking in the family and congregation; and peacemaking in the social order.

Lord, Beverly Bowen and Lord, Charles R. Letter to the Editor. *ChrLead* 39 (Nov. 23, 1976), 14. Raises questions about the relationship of US foreign policy and the resulting stability in those countries with known human rights violations in terms of a hospitable environment for mission effort.

Lord, Charles R. "Building a Submarine for Peace." *Lifework* 4 (1979), 7-8. Describes a high school Sunday School class project of constructing a Trident submarine—a length of rope the length of the sub—as a witness against nuclear weapons.

Lord, Charles R. Letter to the Editor. *ChrLead* 41 (Jan. 17, 1978), 14. Relates peace concerns as generated by a missions weekend conference, books from Wilmington College Peace Resource Center, and *The Christian Leader.*

Luft, Murray. "'God Sides with the Poor' Says Seminar Leader in Calgary." *MennRep* 9 (Sept. 17, 1979), 4. Ron Sider, speaker at the MCC (Alberta)-sponsored seminar, presented two lectures calling the church to Christ's ongoing work of reconciliation in a suffering world.

Lutz, John A. "Eighteen." *YCC* 40 (Apr. 12, 1959), 235. Mennonite youth have to review seriously what they believe about peace and then make choices reflecting their belief. Prize-winning essay.

"Man and His World of War." *CanMenn* 14 (Nov. 1, 1966), 5. An essay on priorities and loyalties in the Christian life.

"MCC, Peace Conference Topics for Rev. G. Rempel." *CanMenn* 2 (Jan. 22, 1954), 8. Rempel reports on the Detroit Peace Conference and the annual meeting of the Mennonite Central Committee, encouraging the churches to continue their relief programs and peace witness. Strong statements on biblical nonresistance are reported. The problem of the fundamentalists and the peace witness is brought out in an example of the Old Fashioned Revival Hour refusing donations from Mennonite COs.

"MCC Opens Contacts with North Vietnam." *EV* 87 (Feb. 25, 1974), 16. Atlee Beechy, a member of the MCC executive committee returning from a visit to North Vietnam, reports that although MCC personnel will not be able to accompany material aid into North Vietnam, there is still possibility for a Christian peace witness there.

"MCC to Establish Washington Office." *CanMenn* 16 (Feb. 13, 1968), 1. The "office in Washington is not for lobbying. It shall serve as an *observer*, particularly with reference to developments in the federal government, but also in liaison with other church, welfare, and professional agencies. It would analyze and interpret trends which may affect peace, religious liberty, social welfare, education, and related fields."

"'Meals of Reconciliation' at Bethel College." *CanMenn* 15 (Nov. 7, 1967), 1, 11. The BC Peace Club conducted a week of frugal meals, and sent the money saved for relief in North and South Vietnam. The purpose of the meals was: to identify with war sufferers; to search for new methods of peace witness; repentance for personal involvement in situations making for war; and commitment and rededication to search for a peaceful world.

"Mennonite-Brethren Peace Caravan Tours England." *CanMenn* 2 (May 28, 1954), 7; "Mennonite and Brethren Peace Caravan." *Menn* 69 (Aug. 3, 1954), 474. Mennonites, Brethren, and Quakers share their peace positions as the first two groups respond to the Friends' invitation to tour Great Britain.

"Mennonite Conference on War and Peace: A Report of the Conference, Including the Principal Addresses Given." Goshen College, Goshen, Ind., Feb. 15-17, 1935. Pp. 68. MHL. Includes: Yoder, Edward, "Introductory Note," 1; Coffman, S. F., "The Teaching of the Scriptures on War and Peace," 3-9; Gingerich, Melvin, "Non-Religious Peace Movements," 9-16; Horsch, John, "Program of Other Religious Peace Movements," 16-20; Yake, C. F., "Our Peace Testimony: Goals and Methods within the Church," 20-31; Bender, H. S., "Our Peace Testimony to the World—Goals and Methods," 31-40; Yoder, Edward, "The Christian's Attitude Toward Participation in War Activities," 40-49; Hershberger, Guy F., "Is Alternative Service Desirable and Possible?" 49-59; Stoltzfus, Eli,

"Experiences of a Relief Worker During the World War," 59-61; Stauffer, J. L., "The Non-Resistant in the Next War," 61-63; Martin, Jesse B., "Non-Resistance in Peace Times," 63-66; Kauffman, Daniel, "Christian Peace vs. World Peace," 66-68.

"Mennonites Call for Prayer, Repentance, Action on War." *Menn* 87 (May 30, 1972), 364. Repentance as a prerequisite for entering the kingdom of God is seen "as a continued need for Christians, as a condition for national survival, and as more an act than words."

"Mennonites Co-operate at Peace Booth." *CanMenn* 8 (Sept. 16, 1960), 1. Mennonites in the Toronto area cooperate wtih other pacifist groups in helping with a peace booth at the Canadian National Exhibition.

"Mennonites Urged to Enter South Africa." *GH* 63 (July 28, 1970), 630-31. Study tour of five southern African countries reveals a need for an expression of peace in word and deed in view of the presence of acute human problems threatening international peace there.

"Message from the Detroit Peace Conference." *Menn* 69 (Feb. 16, 1954), 105, 110. A call to reject nationalism, violence, and war as inconsistent with the missionary and universal character of the church.

"Minneapolis Church Witnesses Against War Toys." *CanMenn* 12 (Dec. 15, 1964), 1. Churches act under the sponsorship of the Women's International League for Peace and Freedom and the Minnesota Council of Churches.

"Minneapolis Consultation on Faithfulness to Christ in Situations of International Conflict." *GH* 60 (Jan. 17, 1967), 67-68. The statement is an outline for Mennonite response to Vietnam and other conflict situations. The Christian obligation to call people to repentance and reconciliation includes an obligation to witness to the state.

"Muggers Express Victim Recovers from Assault." *GH* 72 (Apr. 3, 1979), 272. Report of the assault and recovery of Carl Smucker, young Mennonite director of operations for a new volunteer auxiliary patrol along a New York City subway line which tries to stop violence in a nonresistant manner.

"Muted Voices." *CanMenn* 16 (Jan. 30, 1968),m 4. Where and how should the Mennonite church voice the peace witness?

MacDonald, Dennis. "The Order of the Shovel." *Post-American* 1 (Fall, 1971), 6. An ethically self-conscious community which is militant in its refusal to be co-opted by the American war involvement, racism, and materialistic values, can be a basis for penetrating society with the message of total redemption in Jesus Christ.

Mann, Cleo A. "Our Testimony for Love and Peace." *ChrMon* 40 (Mar., 1948), 83-84. Love in action is a primary form of Christian witness.

Marr, Lucille. "Analysis of Peter Riedemann's Account of our Religion, Doctrine, and Faith." Term paper for History 348G course (and MCC Peace Section), 1974. Pp. 30. CGCL.

Marr, Lucille. "The Peace Witness of the Brethren in Christ." MCC Canada Scholarship paper, 1973. Pp. 29. CGCL.

Martens, Harry E. "Volunteers Are Peacemakers." *CanMenn* 17 (June 6, 1969), 4. "The most forceful, meaningful and acceptable way of serving as a 'peacemaker' is to serve and witness as a Christian volunteer." Serving in the Middle East, the author believes identification with the Arab refugees provides an "opportunity to talk, walk, and to work with them, and to demonstrate what the great love of Christ means."

Martens, Larry. Letter to the Editor." *ChrLead* 42 (Nov. 20, 1979), 14. Sees the conflict over recent articles on Amway, materialism, peace, taxes as beneficial to the integrity of the church.

Martin, Earl S. "Tough Enough for Peace." *Lifework* 5 (1981), 7-9. MCC worker in Vietnam describes peacemaking work as requiring as much, if not more, strength and courage than military work

Martin, Earl S. "Vietnam—Mennonite Testimony for Peace." *MBH* 15 (Mar. 19, 1976), 11. Mennonite aid to Vietnam, labeled an "enemy" by the US government, is a clear witness for peace and reconciliation.

Martin, J. Herbert. "An Agency for Reconciliation in a Broken World." *CanMenn* 11 (June 21, 1963), 6. The Church Peace Mission addresses itself to the task of uniting the work of the Christian pacifist forces in the church.

Martin, John R. and Roth, Willard E. "Peace, Not a Sword." *Builder* 14 (June, 1964), 17-18. A series of six ideas for youth programs designed to help young people grow in their understanding of Christian peace and acquire information about church service programs. Plans include texts, hymn selections, audiovisual resources, etc.

Martin, Luke S. "Implications of the Vietnam Experience for World Mission." *Mission-Focus* 6 (Nov., 1977), 9-15. Deals with the implications of the Vietnam experience for a North American Christian presence and witness in Asia and other parts of the world, focusing primarily on the task of communicating the gospel but also discussing service ministries.

Mast, Russell L. "Living the Peace Testimony." *The Power of Love: A Study Manual Adapted for Sunday School Use and for Group Discussion.* Newton: GCMC Peace Committee, 1947, 97-122. Discipleship demands not only working for a peaceful world but also establishing and maintaining reconciled relationships to others.

Mast, Russell L. "The Church and Conscription." *Menn* 67 (Mar. 11, 1952), 164-65. The church has a vital stake in the proposed universal military training bill because the bill would jeopardize the spiritual influence of the home, would militarize America, and would block any adequate peace efforts.

Matsuo, Hilda. "Can We Handle All Those Boat People?" *MennMirror* 9 (Sept., 1979), 10. The writer looks at the varying attitudes of Canadians towards Indochinese refugees and points out what two MCC employees have advised—that Canadians should act as peacemakers rather than continuing the more popular route of polarizing the situation in Southeast Asia.

Mayer, Robert. "At the Grass Roots—The Quest for an Alternative Community: An Historical and Contemporary Model." *Forum* (Oct., 1972), 1-2. Just as the early Anabaptists emphasized small, voluntary human communities which separated themselves from the state and witnessed to the state's injustices, we need to develop a life-style alternative to that of the present, where humanitarian values are primary.

McNamara, Francis J. "Capitol Peace Rally Successful 'Red Move.' " *GfT* Series 2, 5 (Jan.-Feb., 1970), 12, 9. Reprinted from *The Johnstown* [PA] *Tribune Democrat,* December 8, 1969. Claims anti-Vietnam war demonstrations are essentially communist operations.

McPhee, Arthur G. "Towards A Theology of Communication." *Mission-Focus* 6 (Nov., 1978), 1-3. Communication of the gospel can only be done effectively if it is incarnate in a person. The necessary result will be a ministry that models pacifism and love.

Mennonite Brethren Church. "Report to the Committee of Reference and Counsel . . . in Relation to the Question of Non-combatant Service." *Yearbook of the 46th General Conference of the Mennonite Brethren Church of North America.* Hillsboro: M.B. Publishing House, 1954, 115-21. A report of intensive study of the issues and conversation with government authorities in Washington. Noncombatant service is to be rejected in favor of alternative service. The report was adopted.

Mennonite Central Committee Peace Section. "A Guide to Peace Resources." 1977 pamphlet. Pp. 3. (Located in MCC Peace Section Official Statements folder in MHL.) Bibliography of books, study guides, periodicals, church statements, and visual aids on peace and war. (Located in MCC Peace Section Official Statements folder in MHL.)

Mennonite Church General Assembly. "Letters to the US and Canadian Governments." *GH* 70 (July 12, 1977), 542-43. Letters drafted at the Mennonite Church General Assembly in 1977 call the national leaders to pursue peace and human rights.

Mennonite Church Peace Problems Committee (Archival). Indexed materials. Goshen, IN. AMC. I-3-5. Boxes 1-75.

Mennonite General Conference. "A Letter to the President." *GH* 54 (Sept. 19, 1961), 825. General Conference (MC) relates to President Kennedy Mennonite prayer support and petitions him to work for peace by easing the tensions contributing to the cold war.

Mennonite General Conference. "General Conference Sends Letter to the President." *GH* 60 (Sept. 5, 1967), 807-808; "Turn Back from Vietnam." *Menn* 82 (Sept. 12, 1967), 546. General Conference (MC) pleads with President Johnson to "turn back from the immoral course on which the nation is now embarked in Vietnam."

Mennonite General Conference. "Letter to the President of the United States, Aug. 26, 1941." *GH* 34 (Nov. 13, 1941), 711. General Conference (MC) expression of gratitude for the possibility of the CPS program.

Mennonite General Conference. "Resolutions of General Conference IV-VII." *GH* 60 (Sept. 19, 1967), 845. Describes General Conference (MC) resolutions which deal with witness against war, the relation of personal and social concerns to Christian faith, and urban riots.

Mennonite General Conference. "Telegram to the President." *GH* 58 (Sept. 14, 1965), 813. General Conference (MC) calls upon the president to reverse the trend of increasing militarism and war policies.

Metzler, Edgar. "Christians Open to Peace Witness, Says Physics Professor." *CanMenn* 8 (Feb. 12, 1960), 7. Albert Meyer presents the needs and challenges of a world-wide peace witness to the MCC Peace Section meeting at Chicago.

Metzler, Edgar. "Is Alternate Service a Witness for Peace." *GH* 55 (Dec. 11, 1962), 1060; "Editorial." *Menn* 78 (Apr. 2, 1963), 240. The connection

between service and our peace witness has not been clearly seen. The I-W program is very often no peace witness at all but simply a government program administered by Selective Service.

Metzler, Edgar. "New Name for Peace Is World Development." *CanMenn* 15 (Apr. 18, 1967), 1, 11. Pope John encyclical "Peace on Earth" is reviewed with implications for our own churches: service ministries must be integral part of total mission and witness of the church; the churches should make sacrifices to provide for greatly increased service opportunities.

Metzler, Edgar. "Why I Oppose the War in Vietnam." *GH* 60 (Jan. 17, 1969), 62-63. Metzler outlines four reasons for opposing the war, including the fact that he is concerned about the cause of missions in Asia which is being harmed by this war.

Metzler, Edgar (Review). *At the Heart of the Whirlwind*, by John P. Adams. Harper & Row, 1976. Pp. 160. *MennRep* 7 (Oct. 3, 1977), 8. Adams' reference to Mennonite Disaster Service work following the 1973 Wounded Knee conflict accurately depicts the Mennonite contribution as "post-peace patching" rather than peacemaking in the center of conflict.

Metzler, Edgar (Review). *Envoys of Peace: The Peace Witness in the Christian World Mission*, by R. Pierce Beaver. "Christian Missions and Peace." *CanMenn* 12 (May 19, 1964), 8. The book deals in an original way with the question of how the gospel of peace and reconciliation should be made known in the church's total witness.

Metzler, Eric E. "Peacemaking Today." *GH* 73 (July 1, 1980), 524-26. Reflects on American values and Mennonite commitments and compares them with New Testament exhortations to peacemaking.

Metzler, James E. "Menno Speaks to Me." *GH* 67 (Mar. 26, 1974), 257-58. The Anabaptist vision of peace, equality, and justice still calls contemporary Mennonites to discipleship.

Metzler, James E. "Missions and Communism in Asia." *GH* 69 (Feb. 10, 1976), 100-101. Urges Mennonites to carefully evaluate the effect of "missions-by-proxy" carried on through radio broadcasts into communist countries. Maintains evangelical missionaries lost the confidence of the Vietnamese people when they evacuated Vietnam with the rest of the Americans.

Metzler, James E. "Shalom and Mission." MA in Peace Studies thesis, AMBS, 1977. Pp. 127. Reviews the biblical concept of Shalom from both OT and NT perspectives and evaluates Mennonite missions in light of the concept in an effort to suggest a model that integrates shalom as mission.

Metzler, James E. "Shalom Is the Mission." *Mission and the Peace Witness.* Ed. Robert L. Ramseyer. Scottdale and Kitchener: Herald Press, 1979, 36-51. The biblical vision of shalom presents a more holistic approach to missions than the Protestant evangelical model. Metzler calls for communities of mission inviting others into living shalom.

Metzler, James E. "Vietnam: I Wouldn't Do It Again." *Mission-Focus* 6 (Nov., 1977), 1-3; *GH* 70 (Dec. 13, 1977), 930-32. Because of his association with the political-military machine and American religiosity, the writer states that he would never again serve in an American organization in an area like Vietnam where the United States is involved. He raises critical issues, such as: how mission work aided the South, prolonging war and suffering; how the Mennonite Church in Vietnam did not distinguish itself from other Protestant groups through its peace witness.

Meyer, Albert J. "Conference Discusses the Problems of War and Peace." *CanMenn* 3 (Sept. 30, 1955), 6. A report on meeting between theologians from Lutheran and Reformed churches in Europe and representatives of the historic peace churches.

Meyer, Albert J. "Puidoux Theological Conference." *GH* 48 (Sept. 20, 1955), 897, 907; "Conference Discusses the Problems of War and Peace." *CanMenn* 3 (Sept. 30, 1955), 6, 7. Thirty-three Lutheran, Reformed, and peace church delegates discuss nonresistance as the International Fellowship of Reconciliation meets at Puidoux, Switzerland.

Mezynski, Kasimierz. "The Road of the Mennonites to Reconciliation with Poland." 1974. Pp. 9. MLA/BeC.

Miller, Ella May. *The Peacemakers: How to Find Peace and Share It.* Old Tappan, New Jersey: Fleming H. Revell Company, 1977. Pp. 179. Practical suggestions for living peacefully—with one's self, one's family, one's community, one's nation, one's world, and one's God.

Miller, Larry. "Rediscovering Christianity: Reason for Hope." *Peace Section Newsletter* 9 (Sept.-Oct., 1979), 1-3. Notes that in Europe there is evidence to suggest that several currents of Christianity are emerging which push not only towards renewal but towards radical reformation of the churches and radical reformulation of Christian theology and ethics.

Miller, Levi. "A Conversation on Nurturing Peacemakers." *Builder* 26 (Feb., 1976), 1-4. An interview with Atlee Beechy in which he says

that church people need to begin regarding conflict as having potential for growth and to teach Sunday School children to deal with conflict creatively in order to prepare them for discipleship in our competitive, violent world.

Miller, Levi. "Who Speaks for the Church?" *GH* 73 (May 13, 1980), 390-91. Urges the Mennonite church to spend less energy in professional political activism and to present a more unified peace witness by listening more closely to the wisdom of less vocal consituents.

Miller, Marlin E. "A Meeting with Professor Jürgen Moltmann of Tübingen." *GH* 73 (Jan. 15, 1980), 37-39. Mennonite representatives for the European Church and Peace organization converse with Moltmann on church renewal and peace witness.

Miller, Marlin E. "Degrees of Glory." *GH* 73 (Feb. 12, 1980), 129-32. Funeral sermon for Doris Janzen Longacre focuses in part on her concern for the false power of nationalism and military violence.

Miller, Marlin E. "The Basis and Development of Dialogue Between the Historic Peace Churches and Others: Christian and Non-Christian." *The Witness of the Holy Spirit.* Ed. Cornelius J. Dyck. Elkhart: MWC, 1967, 330-36. " . . . Genuine dialogue involves the challenge to submit all positions to the will and purposes of God. Such a dialogue is one form of witnessing to the God of peace . . . "

Miller, Marlin E. "The Gospel of Peace." *Mission Focus* 6 (Sept., 1977), 1-5. Also in *Mission and the Peace Witness,* ed. Robert L. Ramseyer. Scottdale and Kitchener: Herald Press, 1979, pp. 9-23. The gospel of peace, in which peace is both a social and structural reality as well as an inner tranquility and future promise, is integral to the Good News of Jesus Christ and has far-reaching consequences for missions today.

Miller, Marlin E. "Why Urbana?" *Forum* 10 (Feb., 1977), 6-7. Several reasons for Mennonite involvement and participation in Urbana are given, one of which is the growing social justice and peace concerns from which Mennonites can learn and to which they can contribute.

Miller, Mary Alene Cender. "The Yin/Yang Potential for Discipleship: Can Yin/Yang Be Normative for Peacemaking/Mission?" MA in Peace Studies thesis, AMBS, May 10, 1983. Pp. 87. This interpretation and critique of Yin/Yang philosophy in light of its peacemaking potential begins by noting that the Christian mission has often taken an oppressive yang position in relation to Oriental culture and that fact requires repentance. Next, the socio-historical development is explored with particular attention to the way gender has been assigned to yin/yang and other applications of the philosophy to the social structure. Finally, consideration is given to some specific theological dimensions of yin/yang such as God, Creator and creature, and Jesus. Concludes that while yin/yang symbol is not adequate according to the logic of systematic theological formulations, the yin/yang concept of wholeness—harmony, balance, peace, and rest—is a profound comment on Western materialistic perspectives.

Miller, Mary. "Christianity in Action." *ChrLiv* 1 (Sept., 1954), 4-7. The Mennonite Service Organization's response to disasters is an active witness to peace and goodwill.

Miller, Orie O. "Holland Mennonites on Peace." *GH* 27 (Mar. 7, 1935), 1030. Most Dutch Mennonites do not hold to the nonresistant principle, but it is encouraging to note that a growing number of younger groups are advocating it.

Miller, Orie O. "Our Peace Policy." *MQR* 3 (Jan., 1929), 26-32. An address delivered to World War I CO's deals with the problem of the ill preparedness of the CO's and puts forth the 1924 three-point program for peace education in the Mennonite Church.

Miller, Orie O. "Our Witness to the Government." *GH* 41 (Mar. 30, 1948), 294-95. In addition to obeying, respecting, and praying for governments, Mennonites should proclaim to governments God's word regarding the national and social sins of the day.

Miller, Orie O. "The Peace Witness Then and Now." *RepConsS* 23 (Feb., 1966), 2. Briefly reviews the history of the relationship between COs and governments in England, Canada, and the US in order to give thanks for current freedoms.

Miller, Orie O. "The Present World Situation and Our Peace Witness." *ChrMon* 23 (Feb., 1931), 1-2. Recent interest in the world peace movement shows that the Mennonite peace position is relevant and should be shared widely.

Miller, Orie O. "True and False Peace Movements." *The Eastern Mennonite School Journal* 18 (Apr., 1940), 55-56. Movements not based on Scripture, or whose attitude toward Scripture is not orthodox, or which are motivated by fear of war are not, perhaps, false, but they are certainly less true than those of which the opposite is true.

Miller, S. Paul. "Peace Literature for the Mennonite Church in India." Paper presented to Mennonite Seminar and Seminar in Christian Education, AMBS, Elkhart, Ind., 1964.

Pp. 35. MHL. With this is bound "Christ's Teaching About War, an Adaptation of the Book *Christ and War* by Millard Lind." Pp. 13.

Miller, Vern. "Christian Theology for Our Time." *Builder* 18 (June, 1968), 10-12. In an article designed to serve as a resource, the last of a series of lessons focused on peacemaking issues, the author suggests relevant Christian theology must be mission-oriented, community-oriented, and people-oriented.

Miller, Vern. "The Church and Public Policy (Another View)." *GH* 66 (May 15, 1973), 412-13. In response to an earlier article (Apr. 3), pessimistic of Christian influence on social conditions, Miller argues that government programs such as the Peace Corps have a positive moral quality compared to expenditures related to war.

Miller, William Robert. "An Epitaph for Adolf Eichmann." *ChrLiv* 9 (Aug., 1962), 26-28. Used by permission of the *United Church Herald*. Adolf Eichmann's sin is shared by all, and his death represents a lost opportunity for reconciliation.

Mohler, Allen R. "Caesar or God?" *GH* 68 (Apr. 8, 1975), 269-70. Christians preserve social morality, not by becoming involved in politics, but by leading people to accept Jesus as Lord.

Mojonnier, Rick. "From Protest to Professionalism." *Forum* 12 (Dec., 1978), 16. Challenges us to "turn from a self-preoccupation with career, professionalism, and social development to a life motivated by servanthood expressed in acts of peacemaking."

Moyer, John. "Upholding the Spiritual Revolution." *Forum* 13 (Oct., 1979), 12-13. Among the issues addressed at the Waterloo 1979 Assembly of the Mennonite Church was that of peace. The Assembly accepted a statement on "Militarism and Conscription," addressing the topics of peace and obedience, Christian service and conscription, and militarism and taxation.

Mumaw, John R. "A Response to the New Call to Peacemaking Second National Conference." *ST* 48 (Dec., 1980), 8-11. Summary of conference conclusions with questions about some of the assumptions behind them.

Mumaw, John R. (Review). *The Cost of Discipleship*, by Dietrich Bonhoeffer. Macmillan, 1959. *ST* 30 (4th Qtr., 1962), 16. This book will do much to strengthen the faith of Anabaptists and to challenge them to a deeper devotion to Christ.

Mumaw, Martha. "How May Christians Live Peaceably?" *GH* 28 (Sept. 5, 1935), 491. Peace, whether in an individual, in the church, among nations, or in the family is a gift of God.

"New Call to Peacemaking." *EV* 91 (Nov. 10, 1978), 16. The New Call to Peacemaking, a coalition of the historic peace churches, agreed to carry its concern about military spending, nuclear weapons, arms sales, and related matters to President Carter.

"News from the Peace Front." *Fellowship* 25 (Oct. 15, 1959), 3-4. News statement reporting that the 31st biennial General Conference of the Mennonite Church (MC) meeting at Goshen, Indiana, told President Eisenhower that totalitarian domination would be preferable to "assuming responsibility for a nuclear holocaust."

Neufeld, Elmer. "Opposing Forces Are Struggling for Dominance." *CanMenn* 11 (Nov. 19, 1963), 8. A call to throw our lives into the warfare of the world, that by using peaceful means we may usher in the Kingdom.

Neufeld, Elmer. "PEACE—the Way of the Cross." *Menn* 74 (June 16, 1959), 374-75. From an address to the MCC annual meeting; calls for consistent witness regarding the way of suffering love.

Neufeld, Elmer. "The Lordship of Christ in a Desperate World." *MennLead* 14 (Oct., 1959), 147-49, 171-76. Mennonites are called to be a prophetic voice in the world, but a radical change in life style is called for in order to be heard.

Neufeld, Elmer and Habegger, David. "Mission to Washington, DC." *Menn* 70 (Aug. 9, 1955), 486-87. Report of peace committee representatives concerning their witness against the reserve bill, which seems to be a preliminary step toward UMT.

Neufeld, Elmer *et al.* "A Christian Pacifist Witness Is Needed." *Menn* 74 (Dec. 1, 1959), 746-47. Mennonites must work aggressively for social justice within the Anabaptist framework, i.e., the way of the cross. This way grows out of faith in Christ.

Neufeld, Tom (Review). *Beyond the Rat Race,* by Arthur G. Gish. Scottdale: Herald Press, 1973. Pp. 192. *Direction* 3 (Apr., 1974), 179-80. While the book contains some profound insights (along with some "hopelessly trite suggestions for simple living"), simplicity as "the central category of value and criticism" is not an adequate approach toward the problems of poverty, violence, and technology to which Gish applies it.

Newcomer, Peggy Kilborn. "Peacemaking and Ownership: An Unstable Pair." *Menn* 94 (Feb. 6, 1979), 90; "Ownership/Peacemaking Antithetical." *MennRep* 9 (Feb. 19, 1979), 14; "Peacemaking and Ownership: An Unstable Couple." *MBH* 18 (Feb. 2, 1979), 18; *GH* 72 (Feb. 6, 1979), 113-14. Report of an annual College/Career Seminar at Camp Squeah, BC, in Dec., 1978. Perry Yoder, keynote speaker at the MCC-sponsored annual college/career seminar, lectured on the incompatibility of ownership of material possessions and peacemaking.

Newcomer, Peggy Kilborn. "Seattle Mennonites Participate in Anti-Trident March." *Menn* 94 (Dec. 4, 1979), 728. At Bangor, Washington, 20 members of the South Seattle Mennonite Church joined hundreds of others on Oct. 28 in a peaceful protest march against the proliferation of nuclear weapons.

Nickel, Arnold. "Peace Committee." *The Mennonite Encyclopedia* IV:130, Scottdale-Newton-Hillsboro Mennonite Publishing Offices, 1959. This committee of the General Conference Mennonite Church promoted peace education and peace witness from World War I until 1950, when it merged with other service committees to form the Board of Christian Service.

Nisley, Weldon D. "Nuclear Power and Sin." *Menn* 92 (Oct. 11, 1977), 580-81. Using "nuclear power" to mean the power accompanying possession and use of nuclear weapons, Nisly discusses the morality of nuclear weapons when compared with Jesus' teachings on peacemaking.

Nissly, Donovan E. "Peacemaking in Africa: Some Encouraging Steps." *Peace Section Newsletter* 8 (Aug., 1977), 3-5. Notes the involvement of Roman Catholics and Mennonites in peacemaking efforts in southern Africa.

Nofziger, Jan. Letter to the Editor. *ChrLead* 42 (July 17, 1979), 15. Weary of having Christian morality and character rest on whether or not a person believes in the national accumulation of weapons and the possibility of war.

Nyce, Howard G. "Rumors of Wars." *Menn* 54 (Apr. 18, 1939), 7-8. Peace will not come in this age but we must continue to work for it, emphasizing Jesus as Prince of Peace.

"Office Restructured, Clearer Witness Urged at Peace Section Meeting." *GH* 72 (Jan. 2, 1979), 8-9. Report from the annual MCC Peace Section (International) meeting at Hesston, Kansas, in Dec., 1978, where a statement was accepted calling North American Mennonites to give clearer witness to government and other bodies against militarism and the arms race.

"On TV Violence." *EV* 90 (Feb. 10, 1977), 16. Reprinted from *Release.* Television violence has increased and encourages behavior and solutions that run contrary to the Christian calling to be peacemakers.

"Our Position on Peace." *Menn* 54 (Jan. 17, 1939), 5. A resolution adopted by the Grace Mennonite Church, Lansdale, Pa., in the face of increasing armaments and international tensions. "We cannot sanction war nor conscientiously lend our support to the taking of human life."

Oliver, John. "Jesus and Subversives." *GH* 64 (Oct. 5, 1971), 820-21. Society in Jesus' day responded to subversives with "undisguised contempt." Jesus, however, responded differently. Perhaps, then, the followers of Jesus ought to reach out to those practicing civil disobedience and other forms of dissent with sensitivity and reconciliation.

Ollenburger, Ben C. "What Is Peace?" *ChrLead* 38 (Dec. 23, 1975), 2. Examines both the OT and NT views of peace. The biblical model for peacemaking is to be the church of Jesus Christ.

"Pacifists Are Peacemakers Before War Breaks Out." *CanMenn* 11 (Nov. 5, 1963), 6, 7. Hans de Boer addresses a meeting of the University of Waterloo's Student Christian Movement on the subject "Is Pacifism the Answer to the Problems in the World?"

"Peace Body to Seek Audience with Diefenbaker." *CanMenn* 6 (Dec. 12, 1958), 4. The committee of the Conference of Historic Peace Churches of Ontario attempts to meet with the prime minister.

"Peace Booth at CNE." *CanMenn* 10 (July 13, 1962), 1. The Historic Peace Churches Council of Canada sponsors a booth at the Canadian National Exhibition in Toronto; theme of the peace booth is "The Church in the Nuclear Age."

"Peace Church Seminar." *RepConsS* 32 (June, 1975), 5. Delegations of Brethren, Friends, and Mennonites meet to discuss coordination of their respective Washington offices.

"Peace Churches Challenge Conscription by New Government in Nicaragua." *GH* 72 (Sept. 11, 1979), 728. The peace churches in Nicaragua are assuming a positive peace witness by challenging the government's decree for conscription.

"Peace Committee Asks Witness Against War Toys." *CanMenn* 12 (Dec. 8, 1964), 1, 2. A letter from inter-Mennonite Ontario Peace, Social, and Economic Relations Committee to Mennonite clergy.

"Peace Emphasis Week at Goshen." *CanMenn* 7 (Nov. 27, 1959), 11. Dr. Henry Hitt Crane and Pastor André Trocmé speak at Goshen College's annual Peace Emphasis Week. They commend the Mennonite church for its peace efforts but advocate more vigorous and effective measures.

"Peace Groups Affirm SALT, Caution President." *Menn* 94 (June 19, 1979), 424. Thirty national organizations, including MCC Peace Section and individuals, urge President Carter not to use promises of new weapons to win Senate votes for the approval of the SALT II Treaty.

"Peace in the Middle East, Assembly Concern." *MBH* 12 (Dec. 28, 1973), 18. The MCC Peace Section semi-annual meeting discussed the current Middle East situation and the need to help reconcile not only Israel and the Arab states but also North Americans who have become polarized over the situation.

"Peace Play Presented by Markham Players." *CanMenn* 15 (Jan. 10, 1967), 4. Members of the Markham (Ill.) Mennonite Church presented a play, "Which Way the Wind?" in lieu of the church's Sunday morning worship service. The play was about atomic war and world peace.

"Peace Section Meeting Centers on European Witness." *CanMenn* 9 (Mar. 31, 1961), 7. Need in Europe is for greater integration of the peace witness with other biblical and theological issues.

"Peace Tent at Fair." *RepConsS* 20 (Nov., 1963), 2, 3. Eighteen Brethren and Mennonite congregations of Wayne Co., Ohio, sponsor and operate a multi-media peace witness at the county fair.

"Peace Workers to Make Two-Month Visit.," *CanMenn* 8 (Jan. 29, 1960), 8. Paul Peachey, peace worker in Tokyo, will itinerate in India to strengthen Christian conviction and initiative on the peace witness.

"Peacemaker in Revolution." *CanMenn* 17 (Apr. 1, 1969), 1. Norman Kraus addresses the Intercollegiate Peace Fellowship conference in Washington: "Although Jesus operated with agape love, God is not a pacifist. According to Revelation, the lamb that was slaughtered was the one who poured out vengeance and judgment. Revolution may be God's way of judging our sin.

"Peacemaker Workshop Stimulating." *CanMenn* 16 (May 14, 1968), 10. Hugo Jantz makes statement about "Positive Non-Resistance."

"Peacemakers Sense Urgency, Agree to Meet in 1980. *Menn* 94 (June 12, 1979), 411. A second national New Call to Peacemaking Conference has been recommended for Oct., 1980, out of a sense of urgency that peace churches move toward a deeper level of discipleship in the face of growing militarization in our world.

"Peacemaking Should not Wait till Hostilities

Begin." *CanMenn* 15 (Nov. 14, 1967), 1, 11. On Nov. 11 there was a one-day peace conference at the Portage Avenue MB Church in Winnipeg sponsored by MCC. John Howard Yoder was the guest speaker. He said that the Christian life is the normal life and we misunderstand the gospel if we think it is a call to a difficult life. Definitions of the life of peace in Christ, the meaning of bearing the cross, and the meaning of rediscovering discipleship.

"Positive Peace Action Discussed in Switzerland." *CanMenn* 10 (May 4, 1962), 3. The historic peace churches and the International Fellowship of Reconciliation met at the Bienenberg Apr. 10-13. Hugo Jantz, John Thiessen, John Howard Yoder, and Peter J. Dyck participated.

"Prepare Draft, Peace Materials for Spanish Speaking." *GH* 65 (Sept. 26, 1972), 787. Puerto Rican Mennonites are requesting materials in the Spanish language because of an admitted passive and dormant peace witness.

"Probe Military Recruitment in High Schools." *Forum* 13 (Oct., 1979), 11. As a result of a survey of military recruitment practices which included eight Mennonite students in Indianapolis, the local New Call to Peacemaking group recommends, among other things, elimination of military recruitment on school grounds or equal time for peacemaking recruitment.

"Protestors Convicted of Rocky Flats Trespass." *GH* 72 (Jan. 2, 1979), 9. A Report of the eleven-day trial of the Rocky Flats nuclear protestors, involving ten defendants, two of whom are Mennonites.

"Protests Force Curtailment of Chicago Weapons Fair." *GH* 72 (Mar. 20, 1979), 240. Report on the peace witness of Mennonites and Church of the Brethren, among others, at the international weapons trade show Feb. 18-21 in a Chicago suburb.

"Puidoux Theological Conference." *GH* 49 (Jan. 17, 1956), 57. Includes a declaration adopted by the Puidoux Conference and summary of the study of theological problems involved in saying that Christ is Lord over both church and world.

Pannabecker, S. F. "Some Effects of 1938 on Missions." *Menn* 54 (June 13, 1939), 2-3. Partly due to the climate of political and social tensions, the missionaries are receiving a new welcome in China.

*Peace Is the Will of God: A Testimony to the World Council of Churches/A Statement Prepared by the Historic Peace Churches and the Fellowship of Reconciliation.* Geneva: Brethren Service Commission, 1953. Pp. 23. MHL. Concludes that the church must reject war, not only because of the confusion and suffering it causes but because it is a negation of the gospel itself.

*Peace or Pieces: Leader's Guide.* Salunga, Pa.: Eastern Mennonite Board of Missions, Voluntary Service Office, 1968. Pp. 18. MHL. Suggestions for leading a Bible study on peace. Includes structures for working with the biblical materials, stimulating group discussion, group action, individual creative expression, and prayer experience.

Peacemakers. Letter to the Editor. *MBH* 18 (Dec. 7, 1979), 8. Group of Mennonites and others in Vancouver urging the editor to deal further with the issue of nuclear madness.

Peachey, J. Lorne. "Community News and Trends." *ChrLiv* 15 (Aug., 1968), 11. Mennonites in Iowa City and Ottawa respond to war and violence through a public letter and through assisting draft evaders.

Peachey, J. Lorne. "How Do You Teach Peace to Children?" *GH* 73, Part 1, (Apr. 22, 1980), 329-30; Part 2, (Apr. 29, 1980), 353-55; Part 3, (May 6, 1980), 373-75. Encourages a broad definition of peace as a reconciling lifestyle. Suggests ways in which both home and church can contribute to children's appreciation for peace.

Peachey, J. Lorne. "How Should a Christian Speak to His Government?" *ChrLiv* 13 (July, 1966), 12, 44. Report of discussions concerning Christian dialogue with the state, as in the case of demonstrations against war

Peachey, J. Lorne. *How to Teach Peace to Children.* Scottdale and Kitchener: Herald Press, 1981. Pp. 32. MHL. Surveys historic peace church writing since World War II on peace education and condenses this wisdom into 20 suggestions for parents and other caretakers. Addresses such issues as war toys, entertainment glorifying violence, competitive vs. cooperative play, international experience, peace projects, etc. Other resources included in the book are a discussion guide and reading list.

Peachey, J. Lorne. "Hup—Left, Right, Left, Right . . . " *ChrLiv* 14 (May, 1967), 11. Report on a peace march organized by Bethel College Peace Club for Armistice Day, 1966.

Peachey, J. Lorne. "Intercollegiate Peace Fellowship Discusses the Christian and National Government." *CanMenn* 13 (Apr. 20, 1965), 3, 10. Report on the IPF meeting in Washington, Mar. 25-27, 1965.

Peachey, J. Lorne. "Speaking Out." *ChrLiv* 16 (Apr., 1969), 11. Joe Hertzler, pastor in Iowa City, wrote of his conscientious objector position in *The Daily Iowan,* student newspaper of the University of Iowa.

Peachey, Paul L. "A Decade of the Peace of Fear." *GH* 50 (Mar. 19, 1957), 273. Persons are beginning to realize that the real problem in the atomic age is a moral and spiritual one. What does this mean for those of us who have supposedly known this tragic fact all along?

Peachey, Paul L., ed. *Biblical Realism Confronts the Nation.* New York: Fellowship Publications, 1963. Pp. 224. Ten Christian scholars summon the church to the discipleship of peace. I. *The Problem:* 1. Paul Peachey, "Church and Nation in Western History;" 2. John Edwin Smylie, "The Christian Church and National Ethos." II. *Old Testament Perspectives:* 3. Lionel A. Whiston, Jr., "God and the Nations: A Study in Old Testament Theology;" 4. Norman K. Gottwald, "Prophetic Faith and Contemporary International Relations." III. *New Testament Perspectives:* 5. George R. Edwards, "Christology and Ethics;" 6. Clinton Morrison, "The Mission of the Church in Relation to Civil Government;" 7. Otto A. Piper, "Conflict and Reconciliation." IV. *Some Proposed Solutions:* 8. Krister Stendahl, "Messianic License;" 9. William Klassen, "Love Your Enemy: A Study of New Testament Teaching on Coping with an Enemy;" 10. John J. Vincent, "Christ's Ministry and Our Discipleship." Summary by the editor, "Toward Recovery."

Peachey, Paul L. "Brethren, Friends, and Mennonites Converse." *GH* 49 (Aug. 14, 1956), 777. A report of the July, 1956, peace conference at Manchester College, including the conference statement. In spite of theological differences, a growing sense of mutuality among members of the peace churches was noted.

Peachey, Paul L. "Church and Peace." *GH* 50 (Aug. 27, 1957), 751. A report on the proceedings of the July, 1957, conference at Iserlohn, Germany, on the lordship of Christ over church and state.

Peachey, Paul L. "Dare We Work for Peace?" *The Japan Christian Quarterly* 24 (Oct., 1958), 283-89. As the Japanese church struggles to understand its role in the world's yearning for peace, it faces such issues as the ideological differences between East and West, the strengths and weaknesses of the various peace theories, and the meaning of Japan's experience with atomic war.

Peachey, Paul L. "Hiroshima: Mecca of World Peace?" *ChrLiv* 6 (Dec., 1959), 12-14. The city is dedicated to peace, but the effects of the atomic bomb remain. Also as paper, n.d. Pp. 4. MLA/BeC.

Peachey, Paul L. "Intercollegiate Peace Fellowship." *GH* 50 (Apr. 16, 1957), 369. A report on the March, 1957, IPF seminar held in Washington, DC. The conference gave students an opportunity to see the problems of government first-hand.

Peachey, Paul L. "Interreligious Conference on Peace." *ChrCent* 83 (Apr. 13, 1966), 476-78. Author reflects on the interfaith dialogue at the conference on such issues as US military involvement in Vietnam, and a model for religious peace witness to a pluralistic society in which the religious community's primary role is to produce a moral climate in society conducive to peacemaking.

Peachey, Paul L. "Our Peace Witness in Europe." *Menn* 65 (June 20, 1950), 439. Mennonite witness can be something of a beacon to other Protestants. Witness must be rooted in the concept of conversion, in which peace characterizes all relationships.

Peachey, Paul L. "Our Peace Witness to Christendom." N.d. Pp. 5. MLA/BeC.

Peachey, Paul L., ed. *Peace Is the Will of God: A Testimony to the World Council of Churches.* Amsterdam: J. H. De Bussy Ltd., 1953. Pp. 23. The second of the peace statements addressed to the WCC by representatives of the historic peace churches and the International Fellowship of Reconciliation.

Peachey, Paul L. "Peace or Revolution: The Coming Struggle." *MennLife* 20 (July, 1965), 99-101. Change, not peace, is the task at hand; the question of how change occurs is of importance—is it by evolution or revolution? The answer lies in the healing of the broken community of faith—the church.

Peachey, Paul L. "Peacemakers in the Pacific." *GH* 52 (Feb. 17, 1959), 153. Peachey pays tribute to Reiji Oyama, a Japanese evangelist working to alleviate Japanese-Filipino conflict.

Peachey, Paul L. "The Challenger of Europe." *Menn* 66, Part 1, (Apr. 10, 1951), 236-37; Part 2, (Apr. 17, 1951), 250-51, 253. History has vindicated "the Anabaptist Vision;" qualified American Mennonites should be sent to Europe to strengthen the peace witness.

Peachey, Paul L. "The Christ and the Atom." *GH* 49 (Dec. 20, 1955), 1209. "War is the final result of the breakdown of worship." Especially at Christmas, Christians choose between worship and contributing to war.

Peachey, Paul L. *The Churches and War.* N.p.: Mennonite General Conference Peace Problems Committee, 1956. Pp. 19. The Christian Youth and War Pamphlets No. 5. Directed toward young men approaching draft age, pamphlet traces the attitudes of the Christian church since the first century toward involvement in war. Includes comments on the just war theory as well as on individual pacifists throughout Christian history.

Peachey, Paul L. "The Peace Churches as Ecumenical Witness." *Kingdom, Cross, and Community.* Ed. John R. Burkholder and Calvin Redekop. Scottdale: Herald Press, 1976, 247-58. Peachey discusses the relationship of the minority or sectarian peace churches to the wider Christian community, calling for continued dialogue between them.

Peachey, Paul L. "The Relevancy of the Peace Witness of the Prophetic Christian Community." Paper presented at Church Peace Mission Consulation on the Relevance of Christian Pacifism, New Windsor, Md., Sept. 23-24, 1954. Pp. 5. MHL. Published Akron: MCC, 1953. Pp. 5. MHL, MLA/BeC.

Peachey, Shem. "Christian Ethics and State Ethics." *GfT* 6 (Jan.-Feb., 1971), 17-18. Love, peace, and holiness characterized the early church for the first several centuries, before they began to confuse national interests with Christian commitment.

Peachey, Shem. "Peace Witness in the Orient." *GH* 53 (Jan. 19, 1960), 53-54. The Mennonite Church has the opportunity to witness for God's love and peace in the Orient, but does it have the human desire and resources?

Peachey, Shem. *Shall America Fight Herself Into Extinction?* Quarryville, Pa.: By the Author, n.d. Pp. 15. MHL. Laments warfare's destruction and calls America's Christians to commit themselves to the teachings of the Sermon on the Mount as a basis for living peacefully with one's neighbors and other nations.

Peachey, Shem. "The Scriptural Alternative to War." *GH* 43 (Oct. 24, 1950), 1044. Mennonites should give their peace testimony "in the name of Christ" via church organizations and not first of all through CPS camps as an alternative to military service.

Peachey, Urbane. "Hope Reborn in Middle East." *MennRep* 8 (Feb. 20, 1978), 7. Analyzes Egyptian president Sadat's peacemaking visit to Israel.

Peachey, Urbane. "Perspective for Contacts in the Soviet Union." *MCC PS Newsletter* 10 (July-Aug., 1980), 1-2. Suggestions for beginning steps of peacemaking between the people of the Soviet Union and the people of North America.

Peachey, Urbane (Review). *Mission and the Peace Witness*, ed. Robert L. Ramseyer. Herald Press, 1979. Pp. 141. *MissFoc* 8 (June, 1980), 40-41.

Reviewer considers the book "an important theological corrective to the historical evangelism-ethics dichotomy."

Penner, Archie. "Christ the Prince of Peace." *The Lordship of Christ (Proceedings of the Seventh Mennonite World Conference).* Ed. Cornelius J. Dyck. Elkhart: MWC, 1962, 252-60. Jesus calls us to unconditional obedience, including peacemaking and suffering love, as a condition for participation in the kingdom of peace.

Penner, Edith. "A Winnipeg Youth Talks About the Exhibit at the World's Fair." *CanMenn* 13 (Nov. 2, 1965), 11. Reports experience of working as an attendant at the Mennonite exhibit of the World's Fair, which was an interesting peace witness.

Penner, I. P. "The One Task for Mennonites." *CanMenn* 13 (July 6, 1965), 4. Letter to the editor points out the discrepancy between belief and practice concerning the peace witness among Mennonites.

Penner, Lydia. "The Peacemaker." *EV* 89 (Aug. 25, 1976), 11. Rev. E. J. Swalm, a bishop of the Brethren in Christ Church in Ontario and minister for fifty-six years, has dedicated his life to teaching conscientious objection and opposition to war.

Penner, Peter (Review). *That There Be Peace: Mennonites in Canada and World War II*, ed. Lawrence Klippenstein. Winnipeg, Man.: The Manitoba CO Reunion Committee, 1979. Pp. 104. *MQR* 55 (July, 1981), 271. Recalls the Christian witness of young Manitobans whose unpopular stance benefited themselves and their fellow Canadians.

Peters, Robert V. "In the Big Apple." *Menn* 94 (July 10, 1979), 461. Two current movements struggling to promote life and justice are the Catholic Worker Movement and Mobilization for Survival. The writer participates in both.

Peters, Robert V. Letter to the Editor. *Menn* 91 (July 6, 1976), 440. Justice for all is the precursor of peace, made possible through discipleship, not through accepting instant salvation.

Peters, Robert V. "Marching with Mobe." *Menn* 94 (May 15, 1979), 349. On May 26, 1978, the Mobilization for Survival (Mobe) held the International Religious Convocation for Human Survival around the theme, "Therefore choose life, so that you and your children will live" (Deut. 30:19).

Petkau, Brian T. "Reconciliation in the Joseph Narrative." Paper presented to Hebrew Exegesis: Law in the Old Testament class,

AMBS, Elkhart, Ind., spring, 1981. Pp. 16. AMBS.

Platt, Dwight. "An Open Letter to President Truman." *Menn* 66 (Mar. 27, 1951), 206-209. Platt refused to register for the draft as a witness against war, which he sees as contrary to the way of Jesus.

Poettcker, Henry. "The Christian and National Loyalties." *CanMenn* 16, Part 1, (Oct. 29, 1968), 4, 5, 8; Part 2, (Nov. 5, 1968), 5. The church is torn between serving Caesar and Christ. Some solutions that have been suggested are inadequate. The author seeks to emphasize those solutions that have their roots in an acceptance of the lordship of Christ.

Powell, John. "Out of the Voices of the Oppressed—God." *Menn* 86 (Jan. 21, 1971), 18, 19. A black Christian interprets God and Jesus Christ and what the call "Follow me" by Jesus signifies in view of poverty, racism, and injustice.

Powers, Jim. "A Plea for Peace and Love." *GH* 73 (July 22, 1980), 573. Former Marine now committed to Christ asks Mennonites to examine inconsistencies others see in the Mennonite peace witness.

Preheim, Marion Keeney. "Send Us Young Men Without Guns." *CanMenn* 17 (Aug. 22, 1969), 6. Interview with Lucien Luntadila, a Kimbanguist leader visiting American Mennonite communities.

Preheim, Vern. "Service Frontiers in Community Development." *PCMCP Fourteenth,* 83-91. Held at Harrisonburg, Virginia. Discusses community development as peacemaking.

Prieb, Wesley. "A Call for Renewal." *ChrLead* 41 (Apr. 25, 1978), 11. Examines some problems that may explain why the Mennonite Brethren are hesitant to preach and teach about peace and reconciliation.

Puidoux Secretariat. *The Sources of Christian Social Ethics. Report on the Puidoux IV Conference.* Oud Poulgeest, Holland, July 9-14, 1962. N.p.: Puidoux Secretariat, 1963. Pp. 34. Continues the series of conversations between continental churches and historic peace churches begun in 1955 at Puidoux, Switzerland. Includes 4 papers, with one response by John H. Yoder, and reports on the discussions.

"Questions on Alternative Service." *CanMenn* 10 (Nov. 16, 1962), 7, 11. Can I-W be considered a witness for peace?

"Reconciliation in North America and Vietnam." *Forum* 8 (Jan., 1975), 4-6. An interview with Max Ediger, assistant director of MCC programs in Vietnam, focusing on his work in Vietnam and his perceptions of his mediator role in Vietnam and now in North America.

"Religious Community: The Way of the Reba Place Fellowship." *Fellowship* 40 (Apr., 1974), 10-12. Extracts from an interview published last year in the *Post-American* with three members of the Reba Place Fellowship. The interview centers on their understanding and experience of community as they have known it at Reba Place.

"Resolutions and Decisions of Conference." *Menn* 65 (Sept. 12, 1950), 608-609. GCMC vigorously reaffirms 1941 peace statement regarding reconciliation and war. Encourages expansion of VS program and cooperation with other Christian peace movements.

"Resolutions of the Western District Christian Endeavor Convention Held at Memorial Hall, Bethel College, July 26, 1942." *Menn* 57 (Sept. 8, 1942), 10. Includes resolutions pertaining to the peace witness.

(Review). *It Is Not Lawful for Me to Fight,* by Jean-Michel Hornus. Trans. Alan Kreider. Scottdale: Herald Press, 1980. *MCC PS Newsletter* 10 (June-July), 9. Recommends the book as a historical and theological study of documents from the early church on war and peace, indicating that pacifism was the accepted practice of the early church.

(Review). *Peacemakers in a Broken World,* by John A. Lapp. Scottdale: Herald Press, 1969. *GfT* 6 (Sept.-Oct., 1971), 13. Notes that the book presents views held by contemporary Mennonites which do not necessarily represent the historic Mennonite peace position.

(Review). *The Mennonite Church in the Second World War,* by Guy F. Hershberger. Scottdale: Mennonite Publishing House, 1951. Pp. 308. *Fellowship* 18 (Nov., 1952), 28. This book is "not only an account of the direct relation of the church to the war, but includes as well chapters on missions, education, relief, voluntary service, and intergroup relations both within and without the Mennonite family."

(Review). *War—Peace—Amity,* by Henry P. Krehbiel. Berne: Mennonite Book Concern. *Fellowship* 3 (Sept., 1937), 19. Summarizes the thesis of this book which sketches the history of warfare, shows how the church abandoned its earlier pacifism and must now take up the struggle for peace.

Ramalingam, Mrs. M. P. Letter to the Editor. *Menn* 92 (June 21, 1977), 412. Indian Christian calls western missionaries to distinguish allegiance to Christ from allegiance to the economic and political structures of their countries, since western dominance feeds the arms race and breeds dependence.

Ramseyer, Robert L. "Mennonite Missions and the Christian Peace Witness." *Mission and the Peace Witness.* Ed. Robert L. Ramseyer. Scottdale and Kitchener: Herald Press, 1979, 114-34. Ramseyer examines reasons for the separation of salvation and peace witness in Mennonite missions. Shows that salvation and the way of peace are inseparable and makes suggestions about what this means for missions.

Ramseyer, Robert L. "The Christian Peace Witness and Our Missionary Task: Are Mennonites Evangelical Protestants with a Peace Witness?" Paper presented at the GCMC Commission on Overseas Missions, Missionary Retreat, June 26, 1976. Pp. 13. MHL.

Ramseyer, Robert L. "The Gospel of Peace in Christian Missions." *Menn* 91 (Nov. 16, 1976), 672-74. Mennonite mission churches must recover the vision of peace as an integral part of salvation.

Ratzlaff, Don. "Affirming a Doctrine, Exploring a Witness." *MBH* 19 (Apr. 25, 1980), 17-19; *ChrLead* 43 (Apr. 8, 1980), 2-5. Exploratory Peace Study Conference examined various forms of response to military conscription, from nonregistrant to noncombatant.

Ratzlaff, Don. "How Should I Respond?" *Lifework* 3 (1979), 8-11. Reviews the options available to Christians in the event of registering for Selective Service and urges young people to begin evaluating their convictions before reinstatement of draft registration. Includes a response by a young Mennonite committed to peacemaking and possible nonregistration.

Ratzlaff, Don. "Speakers Probe the Shape of the Kingdom." *ChrLead* 41 (Aug. 15, 1978), 5. Report on the Mennonite World Conference and the issues facing the changing world of the Mennonite church.

Ratzlaff, Peter. "Not in the Bomb." *CanMenn* 5 (Aug. 16, 1957), 2. Hope is found in God as international scientific group issues statement against nuclear war.

Ratzlaff, Vernon. "Blessed Are Those Who Bring Peace." *MBH* 10 (May 28, 1971), 8-9. In a meditation on the beatitude in Matthew 5:9, the emphasis is on the meaning of being a peacemaker, how peacemaking can be practical, and why peacemakers are fortunate.

Ratzlaff, Vernon (Review). *A Strategy for Peace,* by Frank Epp. Grand Rapids: Eerdmans, 1973. Pp. 128. *Direction* 4 (Oct., 1975), 392. Says Epp's essays focus two pacifist motifs—the motifs of obedience and pragmatism.

Raud, Elsa. "Jesus Was Not a Revolutionary." *ST* 37 (Sept., 1969), 19. In all his teaching Jesus stressed faith in God as a basic element of human life. Not revolution to overthrow the economic, or the political, or the religious establishment, but faith was the path he appointed for his followers.

Redekop, Calvin W. "Christian Responsibility in a World of Change." *JChSoc* 4 (Spring, 1968), 2. Description of the changes in the contemporary world. The "free church" offers an alternative mode of human existence: community, morality, mutuality, authority, and brotherhood.

Redekop, Calvin W. "Peace Resources and People." *ChrLiv* 6 (Aug., 1959), 32-33, 37. Witness to peace through education and living should be the work of local congregations.

Redekop, Calvin W. "The Marketplace—Where Tension Often Reigns." *ChrLead* 42 (Mar. 27, 1979), 8. By using case studies, looks at what is involved in being a peacemaker in the job, business, or professional position.

Redekop, John H. "A Call to Consistency." *MBH* 16 (Aug. 5, 1977), 10. Concerned about MCC personnel identification with black resistance movements in Africa, author cannot reconcile pacifism with terrorism.

Redekop, John H. "A Christian Pacifist Looks at the Expression of Our Peace Witness." *MBH* 7 (Nov. 1, 1968), 7-10. Mennonites have been too hesitant to engage in lobbying or demonstrating for peace; they have not seen peace as integrally related to love and justice.

Redekop, John H. "How to Be Christian in Politics." *MBH* 16 (Oct. 28, 1977), 6-8. Anabaptist conservative Christianity parts company with political conservatism on such things as super-patriotism, militant nationalism.

Redekop, John H. "The Middle East." *MBH* 12 (Nov. 2, 1973), 10. Mennonite reaction to the Middle East conflict has not been one of peacemaking, loving the enemy, and identifying with the poor and oppressed.

Reed, Kenneth; Pawling, Jim; and Rhodes, James. "Setting Our Faces Toward Lockheed." *GH* 73 (June 17, 1980), 491-93. Three Mennonite participants in demonstrations against weapons manufacture explain how their actions relate to their Christian commitment.

Reedy, Stan. "Peace Action Movement at Goshen." *GH* 55 (Apr. 3, 1962), 309-310. A report of GC students' peace concerns and a Washington trip in which students expressed these concerns to government officials.

Regehr, Ernie. "African Anabaptists: Confronting a Continent at War." *MennRep* 10 (July 21, 1980), 7. African Mennonites and Brethren in Christ grapple with the peace tradition in countries embroiled in struggles against repressive political and economic structures.

Regehr, Ernie. "Edgar Epp's Prison Riot." *ChrLiv* 19 (Apr., 1972), 20-23. Mennonite warden opposed to capital punishment disarmed the prison and dealt effectively with a subsequent riot.

Regehr, Ernie and Thomson, Murray. "Appeal to US and Soviet Leaders." *MCC PS Newsletter* 10 (Sept.-Oct., 1980), 9. Reprinted from *PlMon* (Feb.-Mar., 1980), 2. Letter to Presidents Jimmy Carter and Leonid Brezhnev urging detente and nuclear weapons freeze.

Regier, C. C. "A Christian Witness in War and Peace." *MennLife* 4 (Jan., 1949), 17-20. Describes the work of the historic peace churches in setting up the CPS program with Selective Service. Includes history and statistics of the Civilian Public Service program during World War II and post-war relief work.

Regier, Harold R. "Group Initiates Peace Pledge." *God and Caesar* 5 (Feb., 1979), 11-12. The article encourages others to follow the example of a group of persons from the Bethel College Mennonite Church, North Newton, Kans., who have developed a "Peace Pledge" and considered other personal actions to protest war taxes.

Reimer, Dalton. Letter to the Editor. *ChrLead* 41 (June 6, 1978), 9. There are many responses that the church can give to controversial concerns like the issue of "peace."

Reimer, Jim (Review). *The Odyssey of the Bergen Family,* by Gerhard Lohrenz. Winnipeg: Gerhard Lohrenz, 1978. *Thy Kingdom Come: The Diary of Johann J. Nickel,* ed. John P. Nickel. Saskatoon: John P. Nickel, 1978. "Two Books Focus on Revolutionary Russia," *MennRep* 9 (Mar. 5, 1979), 8. These two books attempt to tell the Mennonite story of what happened in revolutionary and post-revolutionary Russia, depicting both the glory and the shame which the reviewer suggests is as much a part of the essence of "Mennonitism" as is "ideal Anabaptism."

Reimer, Keith. "The Mennonite Church: Do We Have a Message?" Student paper for Anabaptist-Mennonite Seminar, Apr. 1, 1967. Pp. 24. MLA/BeC.

Reimer, Margaret Loewen. "Vietnam: Did Mennonites Belong There?" *MennRep* 8 (Jan. 23, 1978), 6. Summarizes James E. Metzler's critique of Mennonite missions and witness in Vietnam presented in Dec. 13, 1977 issue of *Gospel Herald.*

Reimer, Roland. "Does Love Really Conquer?" *ChrLead* 26 (Feb. 5, 1963), 14, 19. Love conquers (evil) if it is genuine (i.e., issuing from a regenerated heart), if it takes the initiative, and if it looks beyond the cross and the grave.

Reimer, Vic. "Catholic Peace Movement Initiates Contacts with Mennonites; Opposes SALT." *Menn* 94 (Nov. 20, 1979), 697. Pax Christi USA, the US branch of the international Roman Catholic peace movement, initiated formal contacts with Mennonite peace spokespersons at their sixth annual convention.

Reimer, Vic. "More Than a Gripe." *Menn* 93 (Apr. 4, 1978), 240. The madness of nuclear weapons calls all Christians to witness against evil powers. Writer encourages Mennonites to participate in the national peaceful demonstration at Rocky Flats against nuclear weapons.

Reimer, Vic. "Peacemakers Shy Away from Shocking Anyone." *Menn* 93 (Oct. 24, 1978), 614-15. Extended report on the New Call to Peacemaking conference at Green Lake, Wisconsin. Reflects on the discussion there among Mennonites, Brethren, and Friends concerning peacemaking strategies.

Reimer, Vic. "The Gospel, Marxism, and Christian Mission: A View from Latin America." *Menn* 92 (Oct. 11, 1977), 584-85. Interview with Orlando Costas, Latin American theologian, discussing evangelization and challenging Mennonites to place their peace witness behind ratification of the Panama Canal treaty and other Latin American human rights issues, as they did in the struggle against the Vietnam War.

Reitz, Herman R. "Evangelism in the Shadow of Peace." *ST* 47 (Mar., 1979), 27. After describing a spiritual conversion, Reitz notes that this pattern seems less and less common in mainstream Mennonite thinking. Attributes this to Mennonite scholars like John H. Yoder and his book *The Politics of Jesus,* which, while not discounting conversion experience, does not place it sequentially before the working out of human reconciliation.

Reitz, Herman R. "Prayer and the Selective Conscience." *ST* 47 (Nov., 1979), 6. Examines the implications of responding to concerns with only prayer or of responding to concerns with a selective conscience.

Rempel, C. J. "Mennonite Delegation Visits Canadian Prime Minister." *Menn* 74 (Mar. 17, 1959), 167-68. Canadian Historic Peace Church Council representatives issue statements reiterating historical peace position and pledge continued service for peace.

Rempel, John. Letter to the Editor. *MennRep* 9 (Nov. 26, 1979), 6. In response to the editorial, "Remembrance Day and the Peace Witness" (*MennRep* 9 [Oct. 29, 1979], 6), questions are raised about our strong identification with society rather than placing ourselves in a framework in which Christ and culture are opposed to each other.

Rempel, John. "Why Young Mennonites Resist the Draft." *CanMenn* 18 (May 22, 1970), 7; *EV* 83 (June 25, 1970), 13. Mennonite youth consider themselves part of a 400-year tradition of faithfulness to an Anabaptist witness of love and peace when worldly governments contrarily seek their allegiance.

Rempel, Peter H. and Miller, Larry. "Church Life in Russia: Two Impressions by North Americans." *MennRep* 9 (Dec. 10, 1979), 5. These reports from a study tour to Russia include concern over the arms race and the need for sincere peace initiatives by the United States.

Rempel, Ron. "Disarmament—Urgent Agenda for Christians." *MennRep* 10 (Nov. 10, 1980), 6. Urges Mennonites to become actively involved into the disarmament movement, not to allow a two-kingdom theology to lead to passive resignation to nuclear arms buildup.

Rempel, Ron. "Remembrance Day and the Peace Witness." *MennRep* 9 (Oct. 29, 1979), 10. How we observe Remembrance Day provides one indicator of how we understand the peace position which we have inherited.

Rempel, Wendell. "Concerning the Swearing of Oaths." Paper presented to the Anabaptist Theology class, MBS, Elkhart, Ind., May 13, 1963. Pp. 31. AMBS.

Rempel, Wendell. "Is Noncooperation a Responsible Christian Witness?" *Menn* 85 (May 19, 1970), 338-42. Responds to the confusion in Mennonite circles regarding noncooperation with Selective Service by emphasizing the positive contribution of a valid peace witness.

Ressler, J. A. "The Beatitudes." *GH* 29, Part 8 (Sept. 17, 1936), 530-31. Sin broke man's peace with God. If one is to be a peacemaker, he or she must first again be at peace with God.

Rich, Ronald. Letter to the Editor. *Menn* 92 (Jan. 11, 1977), 29-30. Quotes Andrei Sakharov and two persecuted Russian Christians to call attention to the responsibility of peacemakers to speak for prisoners of conscience in the Soviet Union.

Rich, Ronald. Letter to the Editor. *Menn* 93 (Apr. 4, 1978), 237. Calls peacemakers not to use editorial power to cover up reports of violence and repression in communist countries, while exposing such violations of human rights in fascist countries.

[Richards], Emma Sommers. "Peace Section: Peace in the Gathering Storm." *GH* 42 (Apr. 19, 1949), 371. The individual with a "new heart" will practice the love ethic at any cost.

Richert, P. H. "Our Post-War Youth Problem." *Menn* 58 (Aug. 10, 1943), 6-7. Those who participated in the military voluntarily should receive some disciplining action when they return. Yet the church must find a way to deal with the individual conscience.

Richert, P. H. "The Way to Peace They Have Not Known." *Menn* 56 (Mar. 25, 1941), 3-4. The way of peace is to follow Jesus all the way.

Riddick, Ed. "An Anabaptist View of Social Protest." Paper presented to the Mennonite Graduate Fellowship, Waterloo, Ont., Dec., 1962. Pp. 6. MHL, MLA/BeC.

Rise, Emil R. (Review). *The Chrysanthemum and the Rose,* by Ruth Benedict. NY: H. Mifflin, 1946; pp. 324; *Meeting of East and West,* by F. S. C. Northrop. MY: Macmillan, 1946; pp. 531; *The Logic of the Sciences and the Humanities,* by F. S. C. Northrop. NY: Macmillan, 1947; pp. 399. "Pathways to Peace." *MennLife* 4 (Jan., 1949), 20-21. Feels these books will add an intellectual dimension to an approach to peacemaking and thereby balance the emotional and practical dimensions which we have more often considered.

Roberts, Marge. Letter to the Editor. *Menn* 94 (Sept. 25, 1979), 574. The writer was sentenced to pay a fine of $1000 for trespassing against the Rocky Flats nuclear weapons plant; she explains in the letter her ongoing participation in a peace witness.

Root, Robert. "European Relief Needs." *ChrMon* 39 (Feb., 1947), 37. Church World Service peace correspondent outlines the needs present in war torn Europe.

Rosenberger, A. S. "Conference on Historic Peace Churches." *Menn* 54 (Feb. 25, 1936), 2-3. A report of the proceedings which includes the conference statement against militarism.

Roth, John. "Call for a Church-Centered Peace Witness." *GH* 72 (June 2, 1979), 467-69. Plea for a quiet but constructive, active, church-centered peace witness.

Roth, Nadine S. "Ship's Acquaintance." *ChrMon* 28 (Mar., 1936), 67-69. Story about a young Mennonite woman on a cruise who witnesses about the peace position to fellow passengers.

Roth, Willard E. "Ireland and Mennonites." *GH* 71 (June 13, 1978), 470-71. Visitor to Ireland reviews the complexity of the Irish conflict, searching for ways Mennonites might contribute to peacemaking there.

Roth, Willard E., ed. *Is There a Middle Road?* Scottdale: Herald Press, 1964. Pp. 15. Peacemaker Pamphlet No. 5. Bob Baker describes his experience in noncombatant service during World War II to show that such service is not an acceptable alternative to either military duty or a rejection of military duty if one wants to follow Christ's way of love.

Roth, Willard E., ed. *What About Church History?* Scottdale: Herald Press, 1964. Pp. 15. Peacemaker Pamphlet No. 4. Reviews Christian church history up to the Reformation to show that nonparticipation in war, the early church's position, changed to approval of war when the church was joined with the state.

Roth, Willard E., ed. *What Is Christian Citizenship?* Scottdale: Herald Press, 1964. Pp. 15. Peacemaker Pamphlet No. 6. Calls for Christian obedience to government except in those situations where it conflicts with loyalty to God. Identifies peacemaking as practicing true Christian citizenship.

Roth, Willard E., ed. *Why Be a Christian?* Scottdale: Herald Press, 1964. Pp. 15. Peacemaker Pamphlet No. 2. Calls young people to commitment to Christ, resulting in a life of fellowship with God and others, freedom from guilt and false gods, and service to others.

Roth, Willard E., ed. *Why Do Men Fight?* Scottdale: Herald Press, 1964. Pp. 15. Peacemaker Pamphlet No. 1. Written for young people, this pamphlet sees the roots of war in human sin and challenges readers to commit themselves to Christ's way of love.

Royer, Kathy. "Journey of an Aspiring Peacemaker." *With* 13 (Sept., 1980), 28-29. Author reviews formative decisions inspired by her commitment to Christ's way of peace.

Ruh, Hans. "The Second All-Christian Peace Assembly." Part 2. *MennLife* 20 (July, 1965), 118-22. Conference was an "unusual experience" of growing in understanding and awareness for participant.

Ruth, John L., ed. "Mennonite Petition to the Assembly." *GH* 68 (Nov. 4, 1975), 800; *Menn* 91 (Jan. 13, 1976), 21. A 1775 Mennonite petition to the Pennsylvania Assembly requesting respect for the position of those who cannot, in good conscience, bear arms.

Ruth, John L. "Mennonites: Rooted in Discipleship." *ChrLead* 43 (July 29, 1980), 8-9. Varieties of Mennonites are tied together in part by their vision of discipleship and radical love that emphasizes peacemaking.

"Saskatchewan Peace Vigil to Call for Disarmament." *CanMenn* 13 (June 1, 1965), 1, 2. Report on a Doukhobor peace witness at the Dana radar base in Saskatchewan, led by Peter Makaroff. Makaroff wanted to involve the Mennonites but found them too apathetic.

"Settling the Peace of the World." *CanMenn* 1 (Nov., 1953), 2. Christian peace motives must go beyond political advantage. Christians need to give of themselves—materially and spiritually—in order that peace will come on earth.

"Seven Arrested at Rocky Flats: Felony Charge Leveled." *Menn* 94 (Oct. 16, 1979), 617. On Sept. 26, seven persons, all members of Christian communities, trespassed onto the property surrounding the Rocky Flats nuclear weapons plant near Denver, Colo.

"Some MB Impressions." *ChrLead* 41 (Nov. 7, 1978), 12. Reactions of several Mennonite Brethren who attended the New Call to Peacemaking conference at Green Lake, Wisconsin, Oct. 5-8, 1978.

"Speakers Say: Peace Witness Goes Beyond Secular Pacifism and 'Christian Militarism.' " *CanMenn* 9 (Oct. 20, 1961), 1, 10. Elmer Neufeld and Paul Peachey speak to peace conferences in Manitoba.

"Statement to the Naval Affairs Committee." *Menn* 53 (Mar. 1, 1938), 3-4. From a Mennonite and biblical perspective the Mennonite Peace Society Executive Committee speaks against war in general and naval expansion specifically.

"Student Council Co-sponsors Race March." *CanMenn* 13 (Apr. 6, 1965), 4. Report on the reconciliation walk in Elkhart on Mar. 15 in which MBS students and faculty participated. The walk was from Canaan Baptist church to First Presbyterian.

"Suggest World Peace Conference." *CanMenn* 14 (Oct. 11, 1966), 3. United Church of Canada leaders give reasons for a suggested world peace conference.

Sattler, Michael. "Concerning the Sword . . ." *IPF Notes* 24 (Mar., 1978), 5-6. Part of Sattler's Confession of Faith presented at Schleitheim, 1535.

Sauder, Menno. *A Suggestion.* [Elmira, Ont.: By the Author, 1942.] Pp. 18. MHL. Formulates a proposal for a worldwide anti-war peace movement and offers one thousand dollars to the Canadian or Allied governments for distribution of his article by plane throughout Germany.

Sawadsky, Hedy. "Scream, Adopt, or Move." *CanMenn* 14 (Apr. 26, 1966), 1, 2. Report of speech given by Marian Franz at the Women's Mission Conference. She asks that we scream out against war, adopt a homeless child, and move to areas of need.

Sawatsky, Rodney J. (Review). *Anabaptists and the Sword*, by James M. Stayer. Lawrence, Kansas: Coronado Press, 1972. Pp. 375. *Menn* 89 (Oct. 29, 1974), 636. Reviewer considers the book a significant contribution to Anabaptist historiography, because it documents differing positions among Anabaptists on the use of force. One possible shortcoming is his typology, the use of categories that intrude upon the historical situation.

Schellenberg, Ed. "Reconciliation: One of the Great Words of Salvation." *ChrLead* 11 (Apr. 1, 1947), 3-4. Jesus' death on a cross removed the cause of offense and reconciled humanity to God. We need only appropriate this reconciliation by faith.

Schload, Mary L. "The Peace of God in the Midst of Strife." *GH* 34 (Dec. 4, 1941), 746-47. Spiritual peace precedes every effective peace witness.

Schmidt, David H. Letter to the Editor. *MBH* 17 (Aug. 18, 1978), 32. Criticizes use of war imagery as analogy for missions work.

Schmidt, Dwight R. "The Contribution of the Tabor Mennonite Church to the Mennonite Commitment to Peace." Social Science Seminar paper, May 1, 1980. Pp. 69. MLA/BeC.

Schmidt, George. "Blessed Are the Peacemakers." *Menn* 95 (Mar. 11, 1980), 177. Meditation on the fifth beatitude stresses beginning peacemaking by making the conditions of the first four beatitudes present in one's personal life.

Schmidt, Steven G. Letter to the Editor. *Menn* 88 (Feb. 6, 1973), 93-94. Writer mourns the American bombing of Vietnam, speaking out in order to disassociate himself from the terrible acts.

Schowalter, Max. "Our Hope  The Fulfillment of Reconciliation in Glory." *ChrLead* 36 (June 12, 1973), 2. Although there should be some sympathy with the efforts of people and organizations who work at reconciliation with other people, the Christian should never forget that the final solution is in Jesus Christ alone.

Schrag, Dale R. "The Key in Reconciliation." *Menn*

85 (Nov. 3, 1970), 678. The nature of reconciliation as it relates to our peace witness and our attitudes toward other races or minority groups.

Schrag, Martin H. "The New Call to Peacemaking—Hearing and Heeding the Call." *EV* 91 (Dec. 25, 1978), 5-7. A report on the national meeting of the New Call to Peacemaking held at Green Lake, Wis. Although the US is presently not engaged in a war, the threat of a nuclear holocaust, the possibility of conscription, and the build-up of arms, among other things, all urge us to heed the call to peacemaking.

Schrag, Myron. "Proclaiming the Gospel of Peace." *Builder* 31 (July, 1981), 10-12. Reports ways in which the Faith Mennonite Church in Minneapolis has witnessed concerning the issues of peace in their community and their city.

Schrag, Robert M. "Peace Fellowship Hears Reappraisal of China." *CanMenn* 14 (Apr. 12, 1966), 3; *YCC* 47 (May 22, 1966), 5. Report on the March 17-19 IPF conference at Bethel College under the theme "China and Christian Concern." S. F. Pannabecker spoke at the conference as did George Beckmann of KU. Participants saw a US State Department film on China and a color documentary by Felix Greene, a British producer.

Schroeder, David. "A Call to Consider Peace." *CanMenn* 16 (Nov. 5, 1968), 1, 2. A speech given at anti-war protest rally held at Winnipeg's Memorial Park on Oct. 26, 1968.

Schroeder, David. "Dare to Be a Jeremiah." *CanMenn* 4 (May 11, 1956), 6. A call for people like Jeremiah who will speak out in this world of revolution.

Schroeder, David. "Not Heroes of the Dagger But Soldiers of the Cross." *CanMenn* 1 (Nov., 1953), 6. A creative, active peace will only come about when we give of ourselves. Harmony between Christians with peace emphasis is essential.

Schroeder, David. "The Church Representing the Kingdom." *MBH* 17 (Sept. 29, 1978), 4-6. The church is a sign of the kingdom when it speaks against injustice and manifests in its life the liberating action of God.

Schroeder, P. R. "The First World Peace Meeting of Mennonites." *Menn* 51 (Oct. 27, 1936), 1-2. A favorable report on the formation of an International Mennonite Peace Committee.

Schroeder, Richard J. "The Cutting Edge." *ChrLead* 37 (Feb. 5, 1974), 15. Compares the goals and means of the Watergate conspirators with those of various peace activists.

Schultz, Harold J. "A Christian College: Vision for Peacemaking." *Menn* 88 (Apr. 24, 1973), 266-67. The central focus of a small, Mennonite, liberal arts college on peacemaking and conflict resolution can inform its other commitments: reconciling a fractured Christianity; genuine community with the campus; a philosophy of continuing education.

Schultz, J. S. "Contributions to World Peace by the Historic Peace Churches." Paper, Bluffton, Ohio, [1957]. Pp. 15. MLA/BeC., MHL.

Schurz, Franklin D. "Love and Shame." *Menn* 86 (June 29, 1971), 433. Reprinted from *South Bend Tribune*, June 2, 1971. An editor of an Indiana daily commends the peace witness of Mennonite Disaster Service personnel who cleaned up after the peace demonstrators who left the space they ocupied in the capital a "shambles."

Schwartz, David. "A Gesture of Reconciliation." *MBH* 12 (Apr. 20, 1973), 2. An evening in Paris, where the two South Vietnamese parties formally meet, is seen as a demonstration of national accord and reconciliation among the South Vietnamese.

Schwartzentruber, Dorothy M. "Historic Peace Churches Meet 22nd Time in Ontario." *CanMenn* 5 (Dec. 6, 1957), 1, 4-5. Participants included: Edgar Metzler, Frank C. Peters, C. J. Rempel, and E. J. Swalm.

Schwartzentruber, Dorothy M. "Will Appoint Men to Attend Canadian Defense College." *CanMenn* 4 (Nov. 23, 1956), 1, 8. A report of historic peace church meeting in Kitchener on Nov. 17 where A. J. Metzler, J. Harold Sherk, and J. J. Toews were a few of the featured speakers.

Schwartzentruber, Hubert. "A Foundation for the Urban Church." *GH* 72 (Jan. 30, 1979), 76-77. Proposes some essential elements that belong to a biblical foundation for urban and social justice concerns identified at Estes '77.

Seibel, D. Lamar. Letter to the Editor. *GfT* Series 2,4 (Sept.-Oct., 1969), 17. Reprinted from *Intelligencer Journal*, Lancaster, Pa., Aug. 25, 1969. Differentiates between opposition to war and nonparticipation in war, and claims the latter as the historical Anabaptist stance.

Seitz, Blair. "Another Look at Peacemaking in Indochina." *GH* 73 (Apr. 8, 1980), 298-301. In light of the US role in the Indochina conflicts, peace churches should promote support for socialist reconstruction that has begun to take place.

Seitz, Ruth. "Agony and Ecstacy in Uganda." *Menn* 92 (Oct. 11, 1977), 589-90. Bishop Festo Kivengere of Uganda discusses Archbishop Luwum's martyrdom for speaking out for human rights and challenges Mennonites to bring their peace witness to bear actively on situations of oppression in the world.

Sensenig, Donald E. "A Church and the Search for Peace." *GH* 68 (Jan. 28, 1975), 56-57; *Menn* 90 (Jan. 28, 1975), 51. While Christians in Vietnam, both Protestant and Catholic, contribute little to making peace between communism and South Vietnam, the United Buddhist Church promotes a peace campaign.

Sensenig, Donald E., and Sensenig, Doris, *et al.* "Letter from Saigon." *GH* 65 (June 20, 1972), 530-31. Mennonite missionaries and MCC workers in Vietnam send letter to President Nixon describing the hopelessness of the US involvement and appealing for cessation of hostile action by all US military forces.

Shank, David A. "King Jesus' Call to Mission in '74." *GH* 67 (Mar. 5, 1974), 193-95. Translates the call to Christian mission into the language of a subversive movement, "infiltrating" countries with the good news of peace and justice, and establishing "cells of loyalists" to King Jesus "in exile."

Shank, David A. Letter to the Editor. *Mission-Focus* 6 (May, 1978), 13-15. Reflecting on the suffering servant role discussed in the Vietnam issue of *Mission-Focus* 6 (Nov., 1977), the reader states that missions need to live out loyalty to Christ and opposition to those things at "home" which work against the good of people abroad.

Shank, Duane (Editorial). "There Will Be Peace." *RepConsS* 33 (Dec., 1976), 2. After reviewing events of the previous four years, Shank concludes that the work of peace movements such as NISBCO will grow in importance in the future.

Shank, J. R. "'Blessed Are the Peacemakers.'" *ChrMon* 25 (June, 1933), 184-85. Young People's Meeting study guide focuses on living in peace with all people.

Shank, J. R. "'Blessed Are the Peacemakers.'" *ChrMon* 31 (June, 1939), 188. Young People's Meeting study guide for a lesson on peacemaking.

Shank, J. R. "Loyalty to the Prince of Peace." *ChrMon* 34 (June, 1942), 1889. Young People's Meeting study guide focuses on peace with God and love toward enemies.

Shank, J. R. "The Promotion and Practice of Peace." *ChrMon* 26 (June, 1934), 186-87. Young People's Meeting study guide focuses on peace living.

Shank, J. R. "The Way of Peace." *ChrMon* 29 (June, 1937), 189. Young People's Meeting study guide for a lesson on peace with self, others, and God.

Shank, J. Ward. "Ambassadors of Reconciliation." *ST* 40 (Jan., 1972), 28. Discusses how the function and role of ambassador is an appropriate concept to associate with the ministry of reconciliation.

Shank, J. Ward. "Authentic Protest." *ST* 39 (Apr., 1971), 7. Protest should be kept within the bounds of morality and propriety. Within the church we need to distinguish carefully between what is authentic protest and what may be rebellion.

Shank, J. Ward. "Fighting the Vietnam War." *ST* 40 (Mar., 1972), 8. The conviction of Christians against participation in all war, like the Vietnam war, should be clearly given, but let it be in terms of personal commitment to Christ and of influence exerted on a nonpartisan level.

Shank, J. Ward. "Focus on Revolution." *ST* 38 (Sept., 1970), 10. Report on a seminar on "Peacemaking in a World of Revolution" at Eastern Mennonite College, June 15-26, 1970.

Shank, J. Ward. "For a Better World." *ST* 47 (Aug., 1979), 8. Christians should not wait to preach salvation through the blood of Christ until the human problems are settled or until they have found a better world.

Shank, J. Ward. "For God and Country." *ST* 38 (June, 1970), 5. Preoccupation with social and political affairs is producing a variety of near-revolutionary Mennonites.

Shank, J. Ward. "Frustrations of the Peace Movement." *ST* 39 (Apr., 1971), 6. While seeking to draw together on the biblical ground of peace, people of the church should recognize the temporary and sometimes temporal aspects of the peace movement so much in vogue.

Shank, J. Ward. "How Should We Pray for the President?" *ST* 41 (Sept., 1973), 8. Even with the Watergate affair, Christians should pray for the President. Suggests several areas for prayer.

Shank, J. Ward. "Ideals of the Mennonite Church." *ST* 19 (2nd Qtr., 1951), 6. Among the many ideals of the Mennonite Church, peace and service are included. The basic form of peace is within the heart.

Shank, J. Ward. "In Time of Peace Prepare for War." *ST* 43 (Jan., 1975), 7. Christians must work to salt the war-prone earth now with the Gospel of peace.

Shank, J. Ward. "The Meaning of Peace." *ST* 46 (Dec., 1978), 8-10. The essence of peace is peace

with God, and it first comes to reality in our justification before God. Harmony in the social and political order is one manifestation of true peace. Cautions about the many ways that "peace" and "peacemaking" ideas are used.

Shank, J. Ward. "The Ministry and Word of Reconciliation." *ST* 46 (Jan., 1978), 8. Reconciliation involves both ministry and word. Especially important as it relates to philosophy of missions.

Shank, J. Ward. "'The Ministry of Reconciliation.'" *ST* 39 (Nov., 1971), 25. The point of beginning in healing for humankind is for people first to be reconciled to God. This is the real ministry of reconciliation.

Shank, J. Ward. "The Reconciling Ministry." *ST* 38 (Dec., 1970), 20. The reconciling ministry is based upon the new creation, or new birth. The beginning aspect of reconciliation is that of the reconciler himself or herself to God.

Shank, J. Ward. "The Society of Friends Issues a 'New Call to Peacemaking.'" *ST* 45 (July, 1977), 6-8. Briefly reports the origins of the New Call to Peacemaking movement and questions its strategy and the existing doctrinal disagreements among the founding groups.

Shank, J. Ward. "The Word of Reconciliation." *ST* 39 (Dec., 1971), 22. God has committed to his followers the vital "word" of reconciliation. Nonverbal; communication is not sufficient in the ministry of reconciliation.

Shank, J. Ward (Editorial). "Herald Youth Bible Studies." *ST* 36 (May, 1968), 20. Critiques the Sunday school lesson quarterly, published by Herald Press, Scottdale, entitled "Peacemakers in a Broken World."

Shank, J. Ward (Editorial). "Militant Communism Today." *ST* 43 (June, 1975), 7-9. Christians should not advocate direct, violent opposition of militant communism, but they should rather preach the gospel of reconciliation.

Shank, J. Ward (Editorial). "On Vietnam." *ST* 34 (1st Qtr., 1966), 1. We should seriously question the obligation, or even the competency, of the church, as such, to pronounce upon matters like the Vietnam War and international policy. We should pursue avenues of relief and service as opportunities to relieve the sufferings of war.

Shank, J. Ward (Editorial). "Peace Makes Strange Bedfellows." *ST* 35 (Apr., 1967), 3. Notes how groups concerned about "peace" begin with "dialogue" and end with joint social and political action.

Shank, J. Ward (Editorial). "Peace Moratoriums." *ST* 37 (Dec., 1969), 8. Nonresistant Christians need to examine everything that may be advocated in the name of peace. The use of a device like the peace moratorium is the politics of force and contradiction, not of reasoned judgment and orderly appeal.

Shank, J. Ward (Editorial). "Political Effect." *ST* 36 (Jan., 1968), 1. One may not be able to avoid the consequences (political effect) of one's activities, but the test comes in one's purposes and designs. When actions are calculated for their maximum political impact, it may well be that the Spirit of God is not in them.

Shank, J. Ward (Editorial). "Prayer for Rulers." *ST* 47 (Oct., 1979), 6. Should never criticize or oppose a person in office without having prayed for that person. Prayer for rulers does not imply that Christians must articulate policy.

Shank, J. Ward (Editorial). "Repentance— Personal and Corporate." *ST* 46 (Apr., 1978), 6. Notes the lack of distinctions in the call to repentance and that this is a significant shift in Mennonite thought, from Anabaptist piety and discipleship to neo-evangelical social action.

Shank, J. Ward (Editorial). "The New War." *ST* 37 (Sept., 1969), 4. With renewed interest in the Middle East, the task of the church is to preach reconciliation to both Jews and Arabs.

Shank, J. Ward (Editorial). "The Religion of Peace." *ST* 38 (Jan., 1970), 10. Wave of agitation and political protest has its particular appeal to certain people who have been brought up in the nonresistant tradition.

Shank, J. Ward (Editorial). "To Join or Not to Join." *ST* 48 (Jan., 1980), 4-6. Cautions against policies of both liberal peacemaking groups and conservative lobbying groups trying to influence the state to operate by Christian principles.

Shank, J. Ward (Editorial). "To the Streets." *ST* 46 (Oct., 1978), 7. Concern expressed about the renewed interest and support for "prophetic witness." The influence for peace comes through the preaching of the gospel in every community.

Shank, J. Ward (Editorial). "Voice in the Streets." *ST* 37 (Apr., 1969), 4. Questions the Christian legitimacy of demonstrations and other public forms of protest.

Shank, J. Ward (Editorial). "Was Jesus a Hippie Type?" *ST* 37 (Nov., 1969), 7. Strenuously objects to the deliberate identification of Jesus with the hippie cult, or of the hippies with the Lord.

Shank, J. Ward (Editorial). "What Is Political?" *ST* 39 (June, 1971), 6. Politics has to do with things relating to human government. Christians should be careful with the use of political tools—protests, lobbying, group pressures, party identification, and the like.

Shank, J. Ward (Editorial). "Which Way to Peace." *ST* 38 (Aug., 1970), 5. The Christian makes his most fundamental contribution to peace neither in conjunction with the military nor in fighting against it.

Shank, J. Ward (Review). *Let Justice Roll Down*, by John Perkins. Regal Publications, n.d. Pp. 223. *ST* 45 (Apr., 1977), 32-33. While reviewer appreciates Perkins' emphasis on spiritual conversion in combating racism, he raises questions about Perkins' involvement in forms of active resistance such as boycotts.

Shank, J. Ward (Review). *Pioneers for Peace Through Religion*, by Charles S. McFarland. Fleming H. Revell Co., 1946. Pp. 256. *ChrMon* 39 (Apr., 1947), 119. Study of the religious organizations promoting peace through political channels leads the reviewer to criticize this cooperation of church and state.

Sheats, Ladon. *God and Caesar* 4 (June, 1978), 4-5. A poem reflecting on the nonviolent peace witness in which the writer was involved at the Pentagon and describing the three days of action and vigils.

Sheley, Griselda. "Mennonite Farmer Sees Progress in Vietnam." *MBH* 17 (June 23, 1978), 14. Mennonite wheat farmer who helped present a shipment of wheat to the Vietnamese people saw the trip as one step toward peacemaking between the US and Vietnam.

Shelly, Andrew R. "COMBS to Step Up Peace Witness." *CanMenn* 16 (Jan. 16, 1968), 3. At a joint MCC-COMBS meeting in Akron on Dec. 13 it was decided to make Peace Section resources available to all missionaries. It was also felt that new ways must be found to respond to the desire of new churches for resources and help in stimulating peace teaching.

Shelly, Andrew R. "The Mennonite Witness Today." *Menn* 94 (Jan. 16, 1979), 36-37. There is a large gap between our profession of the peace and sharing witness and our performance.

Shelly, Maynard. "Becoming Reconciled." *Builder* 25 (Nov., 1975), 98-103. A Sunday school lesson for adult students which uses the conflict between Joseph and his brothers, Genesis 45-50, to focus contemporary peacemaking concerns.

Shelly, Maynard. "Finding the Boat in History's Mainstream." *GH* 62 (Jan. 7, 1969), 13-15. Reflects on papers about the historic peace church role in peacemaking, discussed at the recent Conference of Historic Peace Churches. Reports at length on John H. Yoder's presentation, which highlighted the failure of the peace churches to take leadership in facing the problems of race relations and the Vietnam war.

Shelly, Maynard. "Mennonite Ghetto Faces Eviction into the World." *CanMenn* 17 (Oct. 24, 1969), 9. Western District Mennonite conference (GCMC) delegates vote to recognize total noncooperation with the Selective Service System as a meaningful witness of one's belief and as a peace witness compatible with the historical traditions of the Mennonite church.

Shelly, Maynard. *New Call for Peacemakers: A New Call to Peacemaking Study Guide.* Newton: Faith and Life, 1979. Pp. 109. Ten lessons on various aspects of living peacefully such as the biblical bases for peace, the roots of violence, the relationship of evangelism and peacemaking, the politics of servanthood, etc. Each lesson contains a Bible study guide and concludes with items for discussion and further study.

Shelly, Maynard. "New Definitions for Evangelism." *Menn* 84 (Oct. 7, 1969), 597-99. Participants in the Congress on Evangelism in Minneapolis were introduced to the connections between evangelism and such issues of social concern as race relations.

Shelly, Maynard. "Peace Churches Polarized by Peace Witness." *Menn* 86 (Feb. 16, 1971), 102, 103. Questions are being raised about the geographic area of witness, home or abroad, and about the content of the peace witness, the theological or also the political dimension.

Shelly, Maynard. "Peacemakers in a Guerilla Tent?" *CanMenn* 17 (July 11, 1969), 1. During a Middle East tour, 21 American and Canadian Mennonites met an al-fateh leader in a refugee camp in Jordan. Refugees have tried nonviolent means for 20 years, and no one has listened. Now they will fight to the death to regain their homeland. The tour was sponsored by the MCC peace section.

Shelly, Maynard. "Peacemakers In Spite of Ourselves." *MennRep* 8 (Oct. 16, 1978), 6. Senator Bob Dole's visit to an MCC relief sale in Kansas gave this fundraising event for peace the appearance of condoning militaristic government policies.

Shelly, Maynard. "Peacemakers Need a Lot of Love, Too." *MennRep* 10 (Oct. 27, 1980), 6. Reflections on the New Call to Peacemaking statement requesting support for peacemakers and peacemaking.

Shelly, Maynard. "Pioneers for Peace:

Nonregistrants Lead the Field." *Builder* 32 (Oct., 1982), 15-18. Contends that we should acknowledge the risk nonregistrants have taken for the cause of peace and recognize the quality of their witness, whether or not we fully approve their stand.

Shelly, Maynard. "Songs of Men and of Angels." *GH* 70 (Dec. 20, 1977), 944-45; *EV* 90 (Dec. 25, 1977), 4; *MennRep* 7 (Dec. 26, 1977), 6. Describes the vision of peace as the new order of salvation, outlined by the songs of peace sung at Jesus' birth. The biblical use of the word peace carries the idea of a new order, a whole new way of life for people now living on earth, but when we want to escape the way of the cross on earth we twist it to mean "peace in heaven."

Shelly, Maynard. "The Peace Witness: A Dying Minority View?" *CanMenn* 16 (Dec. 10, 1968), 1, 15-16. Consultation of nine groups representing the three historic peace church traditions at New Windsor, Md. John Howard Yoder and Walter Klaassen represented Mennonites.

Shelly, Maynard. "Vietnamese Ask Church Help in Peace Drive." *Menn* 86 (Mar. 16, 1971), 172, 173. Buddhists from Vietnam and Mennonites in the USA correspond and encourage each other to make every effort for peace in Vietnam count.

Shelly, Maynard. "World Conference Site Being Questioned," *Menn* 85 (Sept. 15, 1970), 556, 558; "Militarism Blocks Social Reform in Brazil." *Menn* 85 (Oct. 6, 1970), 604, 605; "Church Can Shape Revolution in Brazil." *Menn* 85 (Oct. 13, 1970), 620. North Americans comment on the situation in Brazil and how the church ought to witness to it for change and peace.

Shenk, Charles B. "Fourth of July Peace Vigil." *GH* 65 (Oct. 3, 1972), 795. Relates the story of involvement in a small, low-key peace presence at a local Fourth of July celebration, and the progress made in conversations about peace.

Shenk, David W. *Peace and Reconciliation in Africa.* Nairobi, Kenya: Uzima Press Limited, 1983. Pp. 180. The first part of the book provides background on peace themes and conflict resolution in traditional African religion. The 2nd part of the book comments on the ways African Christianity has interacted with these traditional concepts and, in that process, created a unique contribution to the whole of Christianity.

Shenk, Norman G. "Reconciliation Through Forgiveness." *GH* 64 (Feb. 2, 1971), 94-95. Outlines forgiveness as the first step toward reconciliation and peace.

Shenk, Phil M. "Faith in the Works." *GH* 72 (Oct. 30, 1979), 851-52. A plea to the Mennonite

Church to respond to our present perilous situation, and in particular to the SALT II treaty.

Shenk, Phil M. and Bicksler, Harriet. "Blessed Arc the Peacemakers." *EV* 91 (June 25, 1978), 6. Peacemakers met together in Pennsylvania, Apr. 8 and 9, to lift up hunger, militarism, and self as three issues in need of peacemaking attention by the historic peace churches.

Shenk, Wilbert R. "Authoritarian Governments and Mission." *Mission-Focus* 5 (May, 1977), 6-8. Looks at theological, strategic, policy, and training questions in discussing the problem of missions in a world rapidly moving toward more authoritarian patterns of government.

Shenk, Wilbert R. "The Middle East: A World on Trial." *GH* 60 (Oct. 3, 1967), 888. The situation is difficult. The Christian church is hardly in a position to preach peace here but it can at least live peaceably and in a reconciling way.

Shenk, Wilbert R. (Editorial). "Missions and Politics." *Mission-Focus* 6 (Nov., 1977), 15-16. Briefly discusses some of the positions concerning the relationship between the missionary and the political order, and lessons to learn about it.

Sherk, J. Harold. "COs in the News." *RepConsS* 25 (Feb., 1968), 1, 2. Summarizes the plights of several COs with various religious orientations who have attempted to witness for peace in a variety of ways.

Sherk, J. Harold. "My Peace I Give to You." Address given at Conference of Brethren, Friends, and Mennonites, Chicago, Ill., Dec. 5-7, 1952. Pp. 4. MHL. Christ and peace. MLA/BeC.

Sherk, J. Harold (Editorial). "From Where I Sit." *RepConsS* 21 (Jan., 1964), 1, 2. Deplores the violence that felled John F. Kennedy and Lee Oswald. Sherk calls for a renewed commitment to peacemaking.

Shetler, Jan Bender. "Admonitions from a Fellow Traveler." *IPF Notes* 24 (Mar., 1978), 3-4. Humility in peacemaking means being content with showing compassion in small ways.

Shetler, Sanford G. "America Criticized in Washington Peace Conference." *ST* 44 (June, 1976), 9-11. Briefly summarizes conference proceedings and criticizes the anti-American rhetoric and political activism of speakers and participants alike.

Shetler, Sanford G. "Disarming America—A Real Cause for Alarm." *GfT* Series 2, 4 (May-June, 1969), 2. Efforts of liberal pacifists to disarm America are dangerous, because the adversary, Russia, is a nation without moral conscience.

Shetler, Sanford G. "God's Sons Are Peacemakers." *Peacemakers in a Broken World.* Ed. John A. Lapp. Scottdale: Herald Press, 1969, 75-84. The process of peacemaking involves first individual reconciliation to God, followed by Christian activity as salt in all areas of society. God's children can have no part in war activities.

Shetler, Sanford G., ed. "Is the Mennonite Central Committee Peace Section Becoming Political?" *GfT* 9 (Sept.-Oct., 1974), 15, 20. Questions whether the church should tell the government how to run its business, as the Mennonite lobby in Washington does.

Shetler, Sanford G., ed. "Mennonite and Quaker Delegations Give Glowing Report of Hanoi, Saigon Visit." *GfT* 11 (Mar.-Apr., 1976), 12. Questions the conclusion that the spirit of the victorious Vietnamese can be likened to the reconciliation of Jesus.

Shetler, Sanford G., ed. "Mennonite Peace Mission to Hanoi." *GfT* 6 (Jan.-Feb., 1971), 7. The delegation of Mennonite students visiting Hanoi and Saigon is doomed to failure, since such missions have not been successful in other wars, and since peace will not come without change in human hearts.

Shetler, Sanford G. "Pacifism and the War in Vietnam." *GfT* Series I, No. 5 (May, 1967), 1-8. Truly biblical objectors to war and evil should refrain from participating in activities that complicate a peace witness, such as the popular anti-Vietnam war protests.

Shetler, Sanford G. "Peace and War: The Hydrogen Bomb and Our Peace Testimony." *GH* 48 (Jan. 18, 1955), 57. The witness should be not only against the hydrogen bombs but against all war, all weapons. The world should know we are fighting a spiritual battle.

Shetler, Sanford G. "Personal Observations on November Peace Rally—Washington." *GfT* Series 2, 5 (Jan.-Feb., 1970), 10-11, 14, 16. Evaluates positive and negative aspects of the peace rally.

Shetler, Sanford G. "The Triumphant Tactic." *ST* 35 (Feb., 1967), 5. Examines the politico-social actionism in the churches. For Mennonite actionists historical Anabaptism is lined up behind the politico-social actionist view.

Shetler, Sanford G. "Universal Peace—That Elusive Dream." *GfT* 10 (July-Aug., 1975), 14-15. Peace rhetoric in the 20th century shows the truth of the biblical idea that lasting peace will not be won until the Prince of Peace comes.

Shetler, Sanford G. "What Should Be Our Attitude Toward the Modern Social Interpretation of the Gospel?" *ST* 34, Part 1, (2nd Qtr., 1966), 6; Part 2, (3rd Qtr., 1966), 23. Notes the main fallacies of the modern social interpretation of the Gospel—its warped teachings and its spurious methods.

Shive, Glenn. "Teenager Testifies Before Congress." *YCC* 49 (June 2, 1968), 2-7. The church participates in congressional hearings as part of its witness to the secular problems of the modern age. Personal reflections on a testimony before House Armed Services Committee Hearings.

Showalter, Stuart W., ed. "Peacemaking in a World of Revolution." Seminar lectures delivered at EMC, Harrisonburg, VA, June 15-26, 1970. Pp. 88. MSHL. Includes: Lapp, John A., "Revolution as a Political Event," 1-8; Yutsy, Daniel, "Revolution in the Economic Struggle," 9-15; Epp, Frank, "Revolution in the Middle East," 16-23; Skinner, Tom, "Revolution in Racial Relationships," 24-36; Jacobs, Donald R., "Revolution Amid Social Change," 37-42; Augsburger, Myron, "Revolution in the Church," 43-52; Yoder, John H., "Peacemaking Amid Political Revolution," 53-60; Miller, John W., "Steps Toward Peace in a World of Economic Conflict," 61-71; Haynes, Michael, "Peacemaking in Race Relations," 72-82; Trueblood, Elton, "Peacemaking Through the Church," 83-88.

Shrock, Simon. "On Being Kind in a Rude World." *GH* 72 (Oct. 23, 1979), 834-35. Christians can use the rudeness in our world as a unique opportunity to respond with witness of kindness and love.

Shutt, Joyce M. Letter to the Editor. *Menn* 94 (Apr. 17, 1979), 285. The midtriennium conference has shown us that we are not a peace church and that we view peacemaking as incidental to and irrelevant to the preaching and doing of Christ.

Shutt, Kristel S. "Blessed Are the Peacemakers." Research paper for Christian Ethics class. 1981. Pp. 9. BfC.

Sider, Ronald J. "Christ and Power." *International Review of Mission* 69 (Jan., 1980), 8-20. Author appeals to New Testament passages to support his thesis that power is not inherently evil but becomes compatible with the way of the cross when it is exercised for the other's good. Calls the church to actively witness to and resist the evil in government.

Sider, Ronald J. "Lifestyles a Christian Can Live With." *GH* 72 (Feb. 6, 1979), 106-109. Sider outlines the need for a simple lifestyle, suggests general criteria, provides supportive contexts, and describes a process for discerning the specifics of a simple lifestyle; shares some

models and sample guidelines on lifestyles as well.

Sider, Ronald J. "The Christian as Peacemaker: A Response." *Perfect Love and War: A Dialogue on Christian Holiness and the Issues of War and Peace,* ed. Paul Hostetler. Nappanee, IN: Evangel Press, 1974, 83-88. Responds to an article by free Methodist Paul N. Ellis by explaining why a biblical pacifism based on loyalty to God's Kingdom is neither unrealistic nor irresponsible.

Sider, Ronald J. "The Peace of Christ." *Preaching on National Holidays,* ed. Alton M. Motter. Philadelphia: Fortress, 1976, 99-104. The occasion of Veterans Day is a reminder that the peace of Christ involves the vertical dimension of right relationship to God and the horizontal dimension of reconciliation with one's enemies.

Sider, Ronald J. "Watching Over One Another . . . in Love." *The Other Side* 11 (May-June, 1975), 13-19, 58-60. Discusses church discipline as a component of proclaiming the gospel, a component necessitated by the nature of the church as a body called out of a greedy, materialistic, adulterous, warmongering society.

Sider, Ronald J. "Words and Deeds." *Journal of Theology for South Africa* 29 (Dec., 1979), 31-50. Discusses the biblical basis for both evangelism and social justice as well as the interrelationship between the two in formulating a vision for the church today.

Siebert, Allan J. "Mennonites and Political Power: Yoder Gives Lectures in Winnipeg." *MennRep* 9 (Oct. 1, 1979), 13. John Howard Yoder gave a series of three lectures at the Univ. of Winnipeg, each centering around political themes: "An Anabaptist View of Political Power;" "Mennonite Political Conservatism: Paradox or Contradiction;" and "An Anabaptist View of Liberation Theology."

Siebert, Allan J. "Saying No, and Being Heard." *MBH* 19 (Nov. 7, 1980), 6-7. Mennonites engaged in peaceful protest against a proposed nuclear reactor.

Siebert, John. "Editorial." *IPF Peace Notes* 25 (Apr., 1979), 1-2. Tribute to J. A. Toews and his commitment to church work and the peace witness.

Siebert, John. "New Call to Peacemaking." *MBH* 17 (Oct. 27, 1978), 18-19. Consensus from the New Call to Peacemaking conference includes commitments to local peace education, peacemaking lifestyle, confronting militarism, and continued witness to peace and justice.

Siemens, Mark. "The Mennonite Brethren Peace

Position." Research paper for the Mennonite Brethren Church History course, Dec., 1982. Pp. 24. MBBS.

Simons, Menno. "An Early Mennonite Appeal to Government." *Builder* 18 (June, 1968), 2-3. Reprinted from *The Complete Writings of Menno Simons*, ed. J. C. Wenger. Scottdale: Herald Press, 1956, 528-30. An example of Menno Simons' approach to those in civil authority. Reprinted as a resource for adult lesson on peacemaking.

Smith, Ann Henry. "Sitting in Communion with the Warlords." *CanMenn* 13 (Apr. 13, 1965), 7. A television critic finds the church fearful, compromising and misunderstanding Jesus. The church must speak to social evils although most often its message will be rejected.

Smucker, Barbara Claassen. "Fellowship Conference at Haverford." *Fellowship* 5 (Oct., 1939), 7-8. Report on the 24th annual Fellowship of Reconciliation conference at Haverford College on Sept. 8-10. The theme of the conference was "Pacifism: A Faith and a Program."

Smucker, Carl F. "Social Work as a Christian Profession." In *Proceedings of the Ninth Conference on Mennonite Educational and Cultural Problems*, pp. 61-72. North Newton: The Mennonite Press. Held at Hesston College, Hesston, Kans., June 18-19, 1953. Social work is a professional service whose principles and objectives arise from and are closely identified with the basic objectives of the church, including peacemaking.

Smucker, Donovan E. "A Critique of Mennonites at Mid-Century." *PCMCP Ninth*, 99-113. Held at Hesston, Kansas. Evaluates the Mennonite peace witness as part of the prophetic function of the church.

Smucker, Donovan E. "A Mennonite Critique of the Pacifist Movement." *MQR* 20 (Jan., 1946), 81-88. The peace movement is too optimistic about the possibility of world peace; it compromises by using coercion and seeks to use the state to "Christianize" the social order.

Smucker, Donovan E. "A Statement of Position to the Armed Services Committee of the US Senate Concerning Peacetime Conscription and the Christian Conscience Against War." *Menn* 63 (May 4, 1948), 6-7. Statement made at public hearing Mar. 31, 1948, on behalf of MCC, vigorously opposing peacetime conscription and witnessing against war itself.

Smucker, Donovan E. "FOR Welcomes Youth Secretary." *Fellowship* 5 (Sept., 1939), 14. Smucker, newly-appointed youth secretary for the Fellowship of Reconciliation, shares his visions for expanded participation and organization of youth in working for nonviolent change.

Smucker, Donovan E. "Pacifist Youth in Action." *Fellowship* 5 (Dec., 1939), 13. Reports on Fellowship of Reconciliation activities and commitments among youth in both Protestant and Catholic circles.

Smucker, Donovan E. "Pacifist Youth in Action." *Fellowship* 6 (Jan., 1940), 13. Reports on some of the events, available movies, publications, and conferences in the area, including a meeting of the historic peace church colleges in Bluffton, Ohio.

Smucker, Donovan E. "Peace and War: Christian Responsibility in the Face of National and International Problems." *GH* 43 (Mar. 21, 1950), 275. The Christian must witness to government if Christ is King. The Christian can become involved in government to the degree which does not force him or her to disobey Christ.

Smucker, Donovan E.; Miller, Orie O.; Swalm, E. J. et al. *The Christian Conscience and War.* Washington: Church Peace Mission Pamphlet No. 1. 1963. Pp. 48. A delineation of the common ground on which both pacifists and nonpacifists can agree to reject war.

Smucker, Donovan E. and Shelly, Paul. "Echoes of Evanston." *Menn* 69 (Sept. 19, 1954), 568-69. Themes of Christian hope and evangelism emphasized. WCC recognizes two major moral barriers to evangelism: race prejudice and war.

Snyder, John M. "Social Evils and Christian Action." *ST* 38, Part 1, (Apr., 1970), 16; Part 2, (May, 1970), 11. Examines scriptural principles for responding to social evils which result from human failure to live according to the righteous standards of God's law.

Snyder, John M. (Review). *The New Left and Christian Radicalism*, by Arthur G. Gish. Grand Rapids: Eerdmans, 1970. *ST* 39 (Nov., 1971), 11. Well-written book analyzing the New Left and sixteenth century Anabaptism in the first part. The second part discusses biblical faith, radicalism, and hope. The weakness lies in the author's lack of commitment to evangelical Christian faith.

Spalding, Blanche. "The Library." *Builder* 31 (Jan., 1981), 30. Encourages church librarians to update their peace education resources and makes several recommendations.

Sprunger, Timothy W. (Review). *Mission and the Peace Witness*, ed. Robert L. Ramseyer. Herald Press, 1979. Pp. 134. *Menn* 95 (Nov. 11, 1980), 656. Recommends the book for its discussion of mission as calling peopel to faithful discipleship, which includes peacemaking and justice.

Sprunger-Froese, Mary. Letter to the Editor. *Forum* 13 (Nov., 1979), 16. One of the defendants in the Rocky Flats trial provides some detail on the trial proceedings and thoughts about this kind of peace witness.

Staff (Review). *New Call for Peacemakers,* by Maynard Shelly. Newton: Faith and Life Press, 1980. *MCC PS Newsletter* 10 (Jan.-Feb., 1980), 9. Reviewer highlights the book's thesis that Jesus witnessed to a violent world through active, suffering love.

Steiner, Susan Clemmer. *Joining the Army that Sheds No Blood.* Scottdale: Herald Press, 1982. Pp. 155. Written to help youth make responsible and informed decisions about peacemaking, the book explores such questions as why wars and other kinds of violence exist, what Jesus' response to violence was and how followers of Jesus can live as peacemakers. Other issues addressed are the classic arguments against pacifism and some practical ways people can become involved in the creation of peace.

Stobbe, Leslie H. "Anabaptist Distinctives." *MBH* 1 (Dec. 14, 1962), 6-7. Anabaptists responded nonviolently to persecution, yet vigorously opposed capital punishment and participation in any form of violence.

Stoesz, Edgar. "Holy Living and Structural Evil." *EV* 89, Part 1, (Aug. 25, 1976), 5-6; Part 2, (Sept. 10, 1976), 6. America's dependence on military might, international trade policies, national indifference to the poor, and disproportionate consumption of the world's resources embody structural evil, but the responsible Christian can respond through alternative structures.

Stoltzfus, Edward. "Peace and War: The Church's Responsibility in War." *GH* 49 (June 19, 1956), 585. The church's responsibility to society is viewed in the light of its responsibility to Christ. Thus ethical instructions come from Christ and not from what seems to work in society.

Stoltzfus, Eldon Roy. "Power and Intervention: Reflections on the Ethics of Power in Development." MA in Peace Studies thesis, AMBS, 1982. Pp. 63. Suggests that power, as the ability to influence behavior, is an entity in and of itself—and can be either disintegrative or integrative. Further suggests that the character and quality of the power identified from within the story of the people of God, the power most concretely expressed in Jesus, is unique and can be integrated toward creative participation in the church and in the world.

Stoltzfus, Luke G. (Review). *A Strategy for Peace,* by Frank Epp. Grand Rapids: Wm. B. Eerdmans,

1973. *GH* 67 (Oct. 1, 1974), 758. Recommends the book for its fresh approach to issues of nationalism, North American militarism, separation of church and state, a biblical response to communism, evangelism and peace witness.

Stoltzfus, Victor. "A History of the Peace Section of the Mennonite Central Committee." Paper presented to Mennonite History and Church History classes, Goshen College Biblical Seminary, Goshen, Ind., 1959. Pp. 57. MHL.

Stoltzfus, Victor. "'Beloved Community.' " *ChrLiv* 10 (Mar., 1963), 2. The presence of God's kingdom means that we are called to be reconcilers and peacemakers here and now.

Stoltzfus, Victor, comp. "Color Bar Draws Protest Letter." *ChrLiv* 9 (Nov., 1962), 11, 33. Letter of protest written to Scottdale newspaper expressing dismay at racial discrimination and calling Christians to be peacemakers.

Stoner, John K. "Beloved, Do Not Be Surprised: Anabaptists and the State." *Peace Section Newsletter* 8 (Sept.-Oct., 1977), 1-9. Develops the biblical and theological basis for actions and words which witness to the state.

Stoner, John K. "Loving Confrontation in the Life of Jesus." *Affirm Life: Pay for Peace.* Ed. Maynard Shelly and Ron Flickinger. Newton: Historic Peace Church Task Force on Taxes, 1981, 11-12. Pp. [87]. MHL. The instances in which Jesus confronted the political, religious, and satanic powers of his day reveal that Jesus: did not compromise truth for tranquility; was clear that evil had both cosmic and human dimensions; regarded the law highly but right more highly; took initiative in confronting evil.

Stoner, John K. "New Call to Peacemaking Moves Ahead." *RepConsS* 34 (Jan., 1977), 1, 2. Goals for this cooperation effort of the historic peace churches emphasize a balance between spiritual rededication and active peacemaking.

Stoner, John K. "Peace and Evangelism." *EV* 86 (Jan. 25, 1973), 5. Three major New Testament themes show the inseparable unity of evangelism and peace: the kingdom, the cross, and the resurrection.

Stoner, John K. "Peace and Evangelism . . . Are They Related?" *ChrLead* 42 (June 19, 1979), 5; *MBH* 18 (Oct. 26, 1979), 8-9 An evangelistic message can speak to people's hunger for peace and freedom from the idolatry of militarism.

Stoner, John K. "Peace Churches Launch New Witness." *RepConsS* 32 [*sic,* 33] (June, 1976), 6. Representatives of the historic peace churches, meeting in Elgin, Ill., propose that the Quaker-initiated "New Call to Peacemaking" become a cooperative project.

Stoner, John K. "Pieces of Peacemaking for 1976." *ChrLead* 39 (Jan. 6, 1976), 8. Thirty suggestions of specific things to do in Christian peacemaking during 1976.

Stoner, John K. "Shalom Means 'The Extra Thing'." *CanMenn* 18 (Dec., 11, 1970), 6. An interpretation of "the extra thing," taken from the Sermon on the Mount, as that which "moves Christian ethics beyond legalistic justice toward positive reconciliation."

Stoner, John K. "Thirty Peacemaking Actions." *GH* 69 (Jan. 6, 1976), 5. Thirty suggestions for specific actions in Christian peacemaking, ten in each of the categories, "large," "medium," and "small."

Stoner, John K. "Why a New Call to Peacemaking?" *ChrLead* 40 (Apr. 12, 1977), 7. Describes the historical basis and the biblical mandate for New Call to Peacemaking.

Stoner, John K. (Review). *Does the Bible Teach Pacifism?*, by Robert E. D. Clark. England: Fellowship of Reconciliation, 1976. Pp. 70. *Fellowship* 43 (Sept., 1977), 22. Provides a summary of the contents of the book which gives an affirmative response to its title as well as examining why most of Christendom is not pacifist. Recommends this book for its timely subject and persuasive, original handling of the subject.

Strubhar, Roy. "Peace—Whence?" *GH* 40 (Oct. 28, 1947), 657. Peace is more than the absence of strife; it is active, positive, and brings personal happiness to people.

Stucky, Peter. "Survey of Attitudes Held by I-W Fellows Toward the Witness Value of I-W Service." Paper for War, Peace, and Revolution class, AMBS, Elkhart, Ind., May 8, 1969. Pp. 3. AMBS.

Studer, Gerald C. "That Controversial Peace Symbol." *GH* 63 (Aug. 11, 1970), 662-63; *CanMenn* 18 (Aug. 21, 1970), 5. Presents the findings of his research into the origins of the inverted broken cross within a circle, research which shows no demonic or communist connections. Also discusses the meanings of the MCC peace symbol.

Suderman, Carole J. "The Basis for Radical Discipleship Within the Anabaptist Vision." Student paper Mennonite History, May 5, 1978. PP. 31. MLA/BeC.

Suderman, Jacob. "Peace and Good Will." *MennLife* 12 (Jan., 1957), 3. Responding to God's gift of incarnation brings peace with God and then with fellow humans.

Suderman, Jacob. "The Climber." *ChrLiv* 2 (Jan., 1955), 4-5, 42-45; (Feb., 1955), 6-7, 41-45; (Mar., 1955), 8-9, 41-44; (Apr., 1955), 12-13, 34-35, 44-46; (May, 1955), 32-33, 41-45; (June, 1955), 28-29, 41-43. Six-part fictional serial about Zacchaeus focuses on the justice and reconciliation brought about by the coming of God's kingdom in Jesus.

Swalm, E. J. "Ontario Conference of Historic Peace Churches." *CanMenn* 7 (Nov. 6, 1959), 5. Some highlights in the history of the conference.

Swarr, John. "What College Students Taught Me About Peace." *ChrLiv* 19 (Oct., 1972), 26-29. Author travelled to colleges and universities to discuss war and peace with students.

Swarr, John. "Passivism or Pacifism?" *GH* 65 (Sept. 5, 1972), 697. Calls Mennonites to active peacemaking, overcoming evil with good, instead of passivism, giving silent consent to injustice.

Swarr, John. "Peacemaking as a Lifestyle." *Forum* (Nov., 1971), 2-3. Jesus does not call us to a "peaceful" lifestyle, but to a lifestyle of "peacemaking" which means building community and being agents of reconciliation in a violent world.

Swartley, Willard M. "Peacemakers: The Salt of the Earth." *Peacemakers in a Broken World.* Ed. John A. Lapp. Scottdale: Herald Press, 1969, 85-100. Studies biblical teachings on incarnation, atonement, church, government, and morality, concluding that Jesus' life, death, and resurrection are the bases for a peace witness; that the international church is the locus for this witness; and that war is politically as well as morally wrong.

Swartley, Willard M. "What Does the New Testament Say About War Taxes?" Condensed by Lois Barrett. *Affirm Life: Pay for Peace.* Ed. Maynard Shelly and Ron Flickinger. Newton: Historic Peace Church Task Force on Taxes, 1981, 7-9. Pp. [87]. MHL. Brief exegetical comments on the tax texts: Matt. 17:24-27; Mark 12:13-17; Luke 23:2; Rom. 13:6-7. Concludes that while these particular texts cannot be used as a rulebook for the issue, application of the basic moral principles of the New Testament determines that such witnessing as nonpayment can speak a word faithful to the gospel.

Swartley, Willard M. and Barrett, Lois. "God's Government and Human Government: The Christian's Relationship to Power and Peace." *MCC PS Newsletter* 12,6 (Nov.-Dec.), 1982.

Biblically oriented, the article focuses on the kingship of Yahweh and Jesus and what this means for the way to peace. With exposition of Romans 12—13 and other texts, the call to overcome evil with good becomes the guiding vision in witness to government.

Swartz, Herbert L. "The Church and Social Issues." *The Voice* 17 (Sept.-Oct., 1968), 3. A probe into the responsibility of the Christian and his or her church for a witness, which can be properly called mission, in the world—a witness that is different from, and separate from, our usual understanding of proclamation.

Swartzendruber, A. Orley. "The Piety and Theology of the Anabaptist Martyrs in van Bracht's *Martyr's Mirror.*" *MQR* 38, Part 1, (Jan., 1954), 5-26; Part 2, (Apr., 1954), 128-42. A softening of eschatological and pneumatic motifs is observed after the first generation of martyrs in favor of an ethical and legalistic emphasis which inevitably sowed the seed for later divisions.

Swartzendruber, Fred. "A Mennonite Lobby in Washington?" *Forum* 12 (Dec., 1978), 1-3. Describes the functions of the MCC Peace Section office in Washington, DC, and the difficult task of relating to a very diverse Mennonite constituency, from those offering strong resistance to a Mennonite presence in Washington to those who are strong supporters.

Swartzendruber, Fred. "The Christian, Militarism, and the State." *Forum* 10 (Dec., 1976), 6-7. A report on the Intercollegiate Peace Fellowship conference at Tabor College, Hillsboro, Kans., Oct. 28-30, 1976, which focused on militarism and the Christian response.

"Talks on Peace." *CanMenn* 4 (Mar. 2, 1956), 8. Arlan Gaufman takes first place honors in the peace oratorical contest held under the Julius and Olga L. Stucky Peace Oration Fund at Bethel College.

"Tent Dwellers Witness at Arms Show." *EV* 92 (Apr. 10, 1979), 13. A group protests "Defense Technology '79," an international military conference and trade show, in Rosemont, Ill., and one member of this group, Doug Wiebe, contributes a poem, "The Second Nativity," which expresses his reflections on nuclear weapons

"The Atomic Bomb Is No Fun Anymore." *CanMenn* 17 (Mar. 25, 1969), 1, 2. Report of a teach-in on war held in Winnipeg on Mar. 22. Walter Dinsdale, M.P., was one speaker. Frank Epp, William Eichhorst who is dean of the faculty at the Winnipeg Bible Institute, and David Schroeder spoke as well.

"The Brethren Peace Witness." *GH* 55 (Aug. 21, 1962), 737. A report on the Brethren "Peace Action Project" in Washington. By taking this opportunity to witness, they have assumed a Christian responsibility.

"'The Church and Radical Peace Action' is Student Conference Theme." *CanMenn* 10 (Apr. 6, 1962), 1, 8. Albert Meyer addresses the Intercollegiate Peace Conference at Tabor College. Focusing on the nature of the church, he points out that "direct peace action, for Christians, can be considered only in the context of the church."

"The Church and Selective Service." *Menn* 84 (Oct. 28, 1969), 646. Mennonites support both noncooperation with Selective Service and established alternative service programs as possible and appropriate expressions of their peace witness, says resolution adopted by the Western District Conference (GCMC) on Oct. 11, 1969.

"The Church in the German Democratic Republic." *GH* 72 (July 17, 1979), 562-63. Disillusionment and spiritual and theological disorientation are problems in the GDR churches but they show strength in issues of war and peace.

"The Difference Between Our Peace Program and the Program of Other Religious Peace Movements." Author unknown, term paper, n.d. Pp. 9. MHL.

"The Dilemma of Christian Involvement." *ChrLead* 28 (Nov. 9, 1965), 14-15. MCC relief operations, as a part of the Mennonite peace witness, must be expanded in spite of the danger of being identified with American military violence.

"The Expression of Our Peace Witness." *MBH* 7 (July 26, 1968), 8-9. A clear peace witness must be given to the state; though we support our government generally, civil disobedience may sometimes be necessary.

"The Gospel and Group Egoism Discussed at European Peace Conference." *CanMenn* 14 (Apr. 19, 1966), 4. Historical notes on the International Mennonite Peace Committee (European Mennonite) and a report on its activities.

"The Lordship of Christ over Church and State." *Menn* 70 (Oct. 11, 1955), 632-33. Summary of the Puidoux Theological Conference and its statement on "The Church and Peace."

"The Prayer by Elders in the Nabo (meeting place of elders) of Gob Wambile, Kenya." (From the film, *The Rendille* by Granada Television.) *FStP* 3 (July, 1978), 1-2. Prayer for peaceful life and guidance from God by a nomadic cattle herding people. Poem.

"The Symbol of the Clenched Fist." *GH* 45 (Dec. 16, 1952), 1225. Not the clenched fist but the cross has been the mighty force in history.

"The Way of Peace." *CanMenn* 15 (Nov. 7, 1967), 5. Looks at day by day decisions that lead to peace or hostility.

"Three Hundred Peace Plays to Choose From." *CanMenn* 8 (Sept. 2, 1960), 10. The Board of Christian Service office at Newton makes peace play kits available on a loan basis.

"To Place 'Peace Person' with World Council of Churches." *MennRep* 9 (Jan. 8, 1979), 2. Mennonites of the Netherlands are ready to finance the salary of one staff worker in the World Council of Churches program to combat militarism.

"Two Men to Visit Arnprior Civil Defense College." *CanMenn* 4 (June 15, 1956), 1. Representatives of the historic peace churches of Ontario are appointed to visit the college near Ottawa.

"Two Ontario Men Attend Civil Defense Course." *CanMenn* 5 (Apr. 19, 1957), 1. Attenders are representatives of the historic peace churches of Ontario.

"Two Peace Conferences Slated for Early April." *CanMenn* 4 (Mar. 30, 1956), 1. Winnipeg and Clearbrook are the hosts for spring conferences.

Taber, Charles R. "No More 'Crusades.' " *MBH* 17 (Sept. 29, 1978), 7. The despicable militarism of the Crusades has resulted in fierce rejection of Christianity by Muslims.

Tanimoto, Kiyoshi. "The Youth of Hiroshima." *YCC* 37 (Feb. 5, 1956), 45, 48. Acts of reconciliation and rebuilding in both Japan and America after the bombing of Hiroshima and Nagasaki.

Taves, Harvey. "The Church Makes Peace in a World at War." *GH* 58 (Aug. 17, 1965), 714-17. The Mennonite church needs to be a more aggressive and prophetic voice and actor for peace. We need to move into actual conflict areas.

Teichroeb, Ruth. "From Trident to Life for Humankind." *Menn* 92 (Sept. 27, 1977), 557. Describes nonviolent resistance efforts in Seattle protesting the Trident submarine and nuclear weapons, and challenges Mennonites to take risks in their peace witness.

Teichroew, Lowell (Review). "The Christian and War: A Theological Discussion of Justice, Peace, and Love." Historic peace churches and the FOR, 1958, *CanMenn* 7 (Aug. 21, 1959), 2. Peace

dialogue bewtween the historic peace churches and the World Council of Churches.

*The Christian and War: A Theological Discussion of Justice, Peace, and Love.* Amsterdam: Historical Peace Churches and Fellowship of Reconciliation, 1958. Pp. 47. MHL. Sequel to *Peace Is the Will of God* makes a greater effort to take seriously the nonpacifist position by including chapter entitled "God Wills Both Peace and Justice," written by Angus Dun and Reinhold Niebuhr at the invitation of the historic peace churches and FOR. Grapples with the questions of pacifism and social responsibility in the context of this dialogue.

*The Christian Conscience and War;* A Church Peace Mission Pamphlet. Scottdale, Pa.: Herald Press, 1971. Pp. 48. MHL. First outlines the points upon which pacifists and nonpacifists agree and disagree and then proposes how the love ethic, as constraint, guide, and grace, may be utilized in working at the problem of war.

"'The Church and Radical Peace Action' Is Student Conference Theme." *CanMenn* 10 (Apr. 6, 1962), ', 8. Intercollegiate Peace Conference held at Tabor College, Mar. 23-24, with Al Meyer one of the keynote speakers.

Thierstein, J. R. "Blessed Are the Peacemakers." *Menn* 54 (Dec. 12, 1939), 1. The church must rise in peaceful resistance against war so that politicians and militarists will take notice.

Thierstein, J. R. "Keep America Out of War." *Menn* 54 (June 6, 1939), 1-2. Persons should inform their congresspersons that they are against war. Examples of appropriate telegrams and letters are given.

Thiessen, John H. "Peace: From Words to Deeds." *MBH* 3 (Nov., 6, 1964), 4-6. When Christ is truly present, the reconciled congregation becomes a "redemptive community of peacemakers."

Toews, J. J. "Towards a Simplicity of Christian Ethics." *The Voice* 15 (Jan.-Feb., 1966), 1. Christian ethics demands a Christian approach, calls for a biblical analysis, and demands a divine purpose. Discusses basic principles of Christian ethics.

Toews, John A. "Jesus Christ Reconciles." *GH* 64 (Sept. 28, 1971), 805. Reconciliation with God and other humans was central to Jesus' ministry, a proclamation and task now given to the church.

Toews, John A. "The Expression of Our Peace Witness." Study paper, n.d. Box 8-N-2. CMBS/ Win.

Toews, John A. "Why Witness for Peace?" *MBH* 7 (Nov. 1, 1968), 4-6. Peace and reconciliation are at the heart of the gospel; dissent (e.g., regarding war and discrimination) is the church's prophetic responsibility.

Toews, John B. *Czars, Soviets, and Mennonites.* Newton: Faith and Life Press, 1982. Pp. 221. Analytical and interpretive study of the history of the Mennonites in Russia. While this examination of parochial Mennonitism in the wider socio-political context discusses the church's peace witness, including the church and state relationship, at various points, chapters which deal more explicitly with war/peace issues are: "The Russian Mennonites and World War I," 63-78; "Response to Anarchy," 79-94; "Communism and the Peace Witness," 95-106.

Toews, John E. "A Theology and Strategy of Evangelism from the Peace Perspective." *ChrLead* 35 (Oct. 3, 1972), 4, 5, 19. Tests the theology and strategy of evangelism from the peace perspective of the early Christians.

Toews, John E. "Response: The Theology and Strategy of Peace as Evangelism." *Direction* 3 (Apr., 1974), 173-76. Evangelism from the peace perspective must be rooted in the voluntary confession of Jesus as Christ, in the formation of disciple counter-cultural communities in the world, and in the fact that it is not for all people nor does it promise success.

Troutt, Margaret. "Army of Salvation." *ChrLiv* 7 (Apr., 1960), 20-23. Introductory sketch of the Salvation Army, the military system that wars against evil.

"US Missionaries in Japan Protest Vietnam Policy." *CanMenn* 15 (Nov. 7, 1967), 1, 11. Text of a letter addressed to the "Reader's Forum" of Japan's *The Mainichi Daily News* by 11 American missionaries (including Carl Beck). The letter calls for an American expression of contrition for mistakes in the past and a willingness to take greater risks in the quest for peace by negotiation in the future.

Umble, Roy H. (Review). *Clash by Night,* by Wallace Hamilton. Pendle Hill Pamphlet No. 23. Wallingford, PA: Pendle Hill Publications, 1945. Pp. 58. *CPS Bull* 4 (Aug. 8, 1945), 3. Recommends the pamphlet and encourages conscientious objectors to direct educational efforts to the public to explain their peace position.

Unrau, Neil. "Peace Themes in General Conference Mission Work with the Cheyenne and Hopi Tribes, 1880-1960." MA in Peace Studies thesis, AMBS, May, 1983. Pp. 130. Explores the extent to which GCMC missionaries recognized and responded to the Hopi and Cheyenne peace traditions as well as the extent of the peace message communicated

to these tribes from the beginning of the mission work in 1880 until approximately 1960. After study of the histories of the Mennonite mission work among these two tribes concludes that, ironically, the peace church mission work proceeded for over 80 years among people with significant peace ideals of their own before the issues of peace actually became a point of cross-cultural dialogue. Suggests that as we probe the distinctives of an anabaptist mission effort the Cheyenne and Hopi situations will continue to raise questions about the role of the peace witness in missions.

Unruh, John D. "Concerning the Nuclear Test-Ban." *MBH* 2 (Aug. 20, 1963), 2, 5. Mennonites should vigorously support the test-ban treaty proposal, in spite of massive national opposition.

Unruh, John D. "Mass Suicide." *Menn* 74 (Dec. 8, 1959), 761-62. Discusses the threat of chemical, biological, radiological warfare and urges Mennonites to protest against these weapons.

Unruh, John D. and Loewen, Esko. "Is This Our Revolution?" *Menn* 78 (Sept. 10, 1963), 534-36. Mennonites need to give a clearer peace witness to government in the context of struggle for constructive action and change at the grass roots.

Unruh, John D. and Preheim, Loren. "Now Is the Time." *YCC* 44 (Oct. 20, 1963), 5. Personal experience of participating in the "March on Washington for Jobs and Freedom."

Unruh, Mark. "E. L. Harshbarger: Mennonite Activist." Social Science Seminar paper, May 6, 1982. Pp. 42. MLA/BeC.

Unruh, Verney. "The Christian Peace Testimony in Japan." *CanMenn* 3 (Aug. 5, 1955), 2. In spite of its constitution, Japan has not renounced the use of force completely. A strongly coordinated peace witness is still necessary.

Unruh, Verney. "The Peace Position and Decision in Taiwan." *Menn* 87 (Sept. 5, 1972), 505, 506. The training of nurses in Taiwan involves participating in bayonet practices, etc. The Mennonite church has chosen to continue the teaching of the Mennonite peace position and a compromise solution to training, too, has been reached.

Unsigned. "Probing the Issues of Peace." *ChrLead* 43 (Sept. 9, 1980), 10-12. Reports on five papers dealing with peace issues prepared for the MB convention at Minneapolis.

Unsigned. "Straddling the Middle East Fence." *Intercom* 16 (Sept., 1976), 1-2. Returned MCCers

LeRoy and Carol Friesen reflect on their peacemaking efforts in the Middle East.

"Vietnam Personnel Write to the President." *GH* 63 (June 2, 1970), 504. Prints a letter written by 62 American workers in Vietnam, including Mennonite missions and service workers, protesting the deployment of US troops in Cambodia and the repression of the student movement in Saigon, and calling for a political rather than military solution to the conflict.

"Vietnam Workers Urge Cut in Arms Flow." *GH* 67 (July 2, 1974), 536. Reprints the text of a letter from 22 MCC and Eastern Board of Missions workers to congressional committees responsible for military funding in Vietnam. Letter calls for drastic reductions in military hardware to Vietnam.

"Vigil at Cape Canaveral." *ChrLiv* 6 (July, 1959), 12. Reprinted from *Gospel Messenger* (Sept. 6, 1958). The effect of a silent protest against missile warfare held by the Fellowship of Reconciliation.

"Visitors from Hiroshima Share Vision for Peace." *MennRep* 9 (Sept. 17, 1979), 3. Four Japanese from Hiroshima, sponsored by the World Friendship Center in Hiroshima, engaged in a speaking tour in the US, advocating peace education.

Van der Wissel, Felix. "Peace and War: The Dutch Mennonite Peace Group." *GH* 42 (June 21, 1949), 594-95. A report on the motivation and activities of this group.

Vogt, Reinhard. "The Church and Non-Pacifists." *CanMenn* 10 (Jan. 19, 1962), 6. In answer to the question of the congregation's attitude toward those who wish to become members but do not hold the "peace position," Vogt says that the only question is whether the inquirer wishes to be saved through Jesus Christ. If so, the congregation's doors must be open to them.

Vogt, Roy. "Art Defehr's Proposal for an MCC Food Bank." *MennMirror* 4 (June, 1975), 14. Urges farmers and others to support Defehr's proposal.

Vogt, Roy. "Mennonites and the Strike." *MennMirror* 9 (June, 1980), 42. Suggests that traditional Mennonite nonparticipation in unions is less redemptive than a potential Mennonite participation characterized by witness against militancy and for constructive processes of reconciliation.

Vogt, Roy. "Mennonites in Politics: No Radicals." *MennMirror* 9 (Apr., 1980), 22. Calls upon the growing number of Canadian Mennonites in politics to risk radical Christian action even if

that action requires "engaging in unsafe or unpopular politics."

Vogt, Roy. "Our Word: Questions Raised by the Death of a Mennonite Terrorist." *MennMirror* 9 (Sept., 1979), 22. Elizabeth von Dyck's death during a bank robbery in West Germany raises questions of the church's relationship both to an unjust society and to its youth.

Vogt, Roy. "Response to Henk B. Kossen, 'The Peace Church in a World of Conflict,' *Conrad Grebel Review* 2 (Winter, 1984), 1-9." *CGR* 2 (Spring, 1984), 149-51. Agrees with Kossen's basic assumptions that the church must simultaneously identify with society and distinguish itself from society but criticizes Kossen's hyperbolic reasoning for producing simplistic and misleading conclusions about the capitalist system.

Vogt, Ruth (Review). *Lest Innocent Blood Be Shed,* by Philip Haillie. New York: Harper & Row, 1979. "Leader With Conviction Is Light in Evil World." *MennMirror* 9 (Dec., 1979), 15. Reports on the main content of this book, which tells the story of André Trocmé, a remarkable spiritual leader who started the work of harboring Jewish refugees during World War II in the French village of Le Chambon. Recommends the book, particularly for those who believe pacifism to be an essential part of the Christian gospel.

Vogt, Virgil. "A Concern." *ChrLead* 25 (Aug. 7, 1962), 3. Worship and Christian service activities have real integrity only when brothers and sisters have developed a relationship of openness, harmony, and love.

Voolstra, Sjouke. "The Search for a Biblical Peace Testimony." *Mission and the Peace Witness.* Ed. Robert L. Ramseyer. Scottdale and Kitchener: Herald Press, 1979, 24-35. An adequate peace theology will interpret the Bible in its social and political context, paying special attention to Old Testament visions of shalom and justice. An authentic peace witness must be active (not merely nonresistant) and community-oriented. Also available as paper, 1977. Pp. 6. MLA/BeC.

"Waging Peace . . ." *ChrLead* 41 (Nov. 7, 1978), 11. Faithfulness to the life and teachings of Christ and the New Testament necessitates active involvement—perhaps to the point of civil disobedience. This is a conclusion reached at the national New Call to Peacemaking conference held in Green Lake, Wis., Oct. 5-8, 1978.

"We Encourage You to Help Our Country to Become a Messenger of Peace." *CanMenn* 14 (Feb. 8, 1966), 1, 13. Text of a letter from the Conference of Mennonites in Canada to Canada's Prime Minister urging the government to declare its opposition to the

Vietnam war and to engage in steps to build up rather than destroy Vietnam.

"When War Clouds Hang Low." *CanMenn* 3 (Jan. 28, 1955), 2. A reminder of the Christian's role in a tense world situation.

"Why Glamorize War?" *CanMenn* 16 (June 25, 1968), 1. Bergtaler Mennonite Church sends a note of dissatisfaction to the Canadian Broadcasting Corporation: "We the undersigned urge you as those responsible for our public communication media, to use our common resources to promote not the causes of war and violence, but rather those of peace and internationalism."

"Will Appoint Men to Attend Canadian Defense College." *CanMenn* 4 (Nov. 23, 1956), 1, 8. Noted speakers address the twenty-first session of the Conference of Historic Peace Churches in Kitchener.

"World Conference Message." *GH* 65 (Oct. 24, 1972), 860-61. Statement adopted at the conclusion of the Ninth Mennonite World Conference focuses on reconciliation as the primary task of the church—reconciliation in situations of war, violent repression, racism, economic oppression.

Wagler, Harley. "The Peace Churches in Nicaragua (2): Mixed Reaction to Revolution." *MennRep* 10 (Oct. 13, 1980), 6-7. Review of the Catholic, evangelical, and Mennonite church responses to the Sandinista revolution and attitudes toward the new government.

Wagler, Mark. "White Guilt and Black Power." *Menn* 83 (Apr. 30, 1968), 306-308. Mennonites, unfaithful to the Anabaptist dream of true community, are feeling too guilty to be able to effectively cope with the black situation.

Waltner, David. "Mennonites and Overpopulation." *Forum* (Jan., 1974), 2-3. The problem of overpopulation demands a response, and the writer suggests we re-claim two responses from our Anabaptist heritage, the concept of a caring community and a distrust of materialism.

Waltner, Erland. "Centennial Conversation and Repentance." *Menn* 76 (Jan. 17, 1961), 39-41. Texts and commentary on conversation pieces, i.e., expressions of repentance and desire for reconciliation, between the Mennonite Brethren and the General Conference Mennonites.

Waltner, Orlando A. "A Ministry of Reconciliation." *MennLife* 22 (Jan., 1967), 35, 36. The ministry of reconciliation is a mission of peace to a people who are at war within and among themselves. We ought to undertake this ministry on behalf of the blacks and the whites of the South.

*War Is Contrary to the Will of God: Statements by the Historic Peace Churches and the International Fellowship of Reconciliation.* Amsterdam: J. H. de Bussy, July, 1951. Pp. 32. MHL. Introductory statement contends that Christ's call to overcome evil with good will be more effective in the long run than any kind of violent response to problems. The Christian's task is to rediscover and reconstruct in modern language and concrete situations the New Testament kind of warfare against evil. From this central tenet, each of the historic peace churches and the IFOR offers a separate statement emerging from its own tradition and in its own idiom.

Wasser, Myrtle. "The Evils of Wars and the Methods of Preventing Future Wars." *Menn* 60 (Sept. 18, 1945), 9-11. Stresses the need for international cooperation in the task of peacemaking.

Weaver, Beth. "Peacemaking Is Theme for Fall Course." *MennRep* 9 (Dec. 24, 1979), 15. A description of "The Call to Peacemaking," a course offered in Christian education at the Valleyview Mennonite Church, London, Ont.

Weaver, Edwin L. "Instruments of His Peace." *YCC* 25 (Oct. 8, 1944), 323, 324. An amplification of Francis of Assisi's prayer for peace. Describes the Christian's response to war in the contemporary setting.

Weaver, Edwin L. "Reflections of a Civilian Public Service Man." *ChrMon* 38 (July, 1946), 209-11, 213. Relates nonparticipation in war to missions effectiveness, spiritual maturity, and respect for the natural environment.

Weaver, Edwin L. "The Peacemakers." *YCC* 26 (Nov. 11, 1945), 681, 688. The Christians are the true peacemakers, for they are the children of God. Examination of Benjamin Franklin's peacemaking philosophy.

Weaver, Edwin L. "Working for Peace." *YCC* 24 (Dec. 26, 1943), 827, 830. Only the nonresistant Christian, with deep convictions against the sinfulness of war, is qualified to make a permanent contribution toward peace on earth.

Weaver, Edwin L. (Review). *Pathways of Peace,* by Leslie Eisan. Elgin: Brethren Publishing House, 1948. Pp. 480. *ChrMon* 41 (July, 1949), 215. Recommends the book as a history of the Civilian Public Service program from the Church of the Brethren perspective.

Weaver, Edwin L. (Review). *Power for Peace,* by O. Frederick Nolde. Muhlenberg Press, 1946. Pp. 138. *ChrMon* 39 (June, 1947), 182. The author describes how Christians can promote world peace by supporting the United Nations Organization, but the reviewer is skeptical of such political activity.

Weaver, Henry, Jr. "The Permanent Draft." *GH* 48 (June 7, 1955), 533. Christians should work to abolish the permanent draft. But as long as it exists it may be used as a means of furthering the peace witness.

Weaver, John W. "Presidents, Prayers, and Breakfasts." *GH* 64 (June 1, 1971), 492-93. Criticizes presidential prayer breakfasts for reinforcing values of militarism and oppressive economic policies, and calls Mennonites to greater courage in "speaking truth to power."

Weaver, William B. "Peace Be Unto You." *GH* 29 (Oct. 8, 1936), 594-95. True peace is spiritual. Desire for any other sort is folly.

Weber, Ralph K. "Peace and War: Presenting Our Peace Position." *GH* 50 (Nov. 19, 1957), 993. Our approach must be evangelical, spiritual, and historical.

Weber, Ralph K. "Peace Teaching in the Local Church." *Menn* 72 (May 7, 1957), 296-97. The peace position is central to the gospel; it must be woven into the very fabric of the church's ministry.

Wedel, Delmar. "Rehabilitation of Prisoners of War." *MennLife* 4 (Jan., 1949), 35-37. Physical and spiritual needs of people displaced and broken by war, including Mennonite prisoners of war, and the response of the YMCA.

Wendling, Woody and Zimmerman, Diane. "The Peaceful Warrior: A One-act Play Based on the Story of Michael Sattler, an Anabaptist Martyr, Living in the 16th Century in Germany." 1972. Pp. 17. MHL.

Wenger, J. C. *The Way of Peace.* Scottdale, Pa.: Herald Press, [1977]. Pp. 70. MHL. Examines peace teachings of Old and New Testaments and traces the history of the doctrine of peace as well as its present status in the larger church. In the last chapter, Wenger summarizes the case for the way of peace along the lines of the sovereignty of God, cross-bearing, internationalism, evangelism, the permissiveness of God, the divine institution of government, the separation of church and state, etc.

Wenger, Malcolm. "Core Issues Considered by Indians and Mennonites." *Menn* 94 (Apr. 10, 1979), 263. Foundational issues about missions were discussed at the "peace talks" between non-native Mennonites and native leaders at Tiefengrund Mennonite Church, Saskatchewan, Feb. 23-24, 1979.

Wenger, Malcolm. "Hard Thinking Done at Native/Mennonite Peace Talk." *MennRep* 9 (Mar. 19, 1979), 14. "Peace talks" between Mennonites and native leaders focused on issues concerning missions.

Wentland, Theodore. Letter to the Editor. *GH* 61 (Mar. 19, 1968), 262-63. Calls attention to Mennonite acts of violence toward one another in conflict situations and schisms, and calls for a spirit of forgiveness and peacemaking in congregations.

Widmer, Pierre. "International Mennonite Peace Committee Met for Biblical Studies in Luxembourg." *CanMenn* 11 (Mar. 29, 1963), 3-4; *GH* 56 (May 21, 1963), 433. Meeting emphasized church and christocentric pacifism.

Wiebe, Bernie. "Making Peace." *Menn* 93 (Jan. 3, 1978), 16. Calls attention to two peacemaking events of 1977: Egyptian President Sadat's visit to Israel, and the conversion of the Aldridge family of California from nuclear weapons development to nonviolent resistance to arms buildup.

Wiebe, Bernie. "Peace and Social Concerns." *Menn* 95 (Apr. 29, 1980), 278-82. Interview with Harold Regier and Hubert Schwarzentruber reveals their reflections on Mennonite peace and social concerns stances in the 1970s and projections for the 1980s.

Wiebe, Bernie. "Peacemaking Is a Lifestyle." *Menn* 94 (Oct. 9, 1979), 608. Peacemaking is a lifestyle involving the total person, and not just a wartime response.

Wiebe, Bernie. "The Forces of Diversity." *Menn* 94 (Apr. 24, 1979), 304. There is diversity and interdependency in the General Conference Mennonite Church but we resist the peaceful and peacemaking process of reciprocal listening and learning.

Wiebe, Bernie (Editorial). "Love and Peace." *Menn* 95 (Apr. 29, 1980), 292. Calls for continued dual emphases on right beliefs and the right action of peacemaking.

Wiebe, Christine (Review). *Agenda for Biblical People,* by Jim Wallis. New York: Harper and Row, 1976. Pp. 145. *ChrLeader* 40 (Jan. 18, 1977), 13-14. Applauds Wallis' challenge to the established church on such issues as money, power, violence, etc., while lamenting that the book is too abstract and "intellectual" for the average reader.

Wiebe, Don (Review). *Agenda for a Biblical People,* by Jim Wallis. Harper and Row, 1976. Pp. 145. *MBH* 15 (Dec. 24, 1976), 21. Wallis attacks the peace between the Christian church and present economic and military goals of Western capitalism; reviewer labels his ethics "utopian."

Wiebe, Dwight. "Christian Unity for a Divided World?" *GH* 48 (Nov. 20, 1955), 1133. The Christian hope for the future does not lie in the acceptance of a divided world.

Wiebe, Dwight. "Redemption or Retaliation?" *ChrLead* 21 (Nov. 4, 1958), 4-5. We are to overcome the world through the witness of love and servanthood rather than through the use of force and retaliation.

Wiebe, Eric, and Letkemann, Jake. "Peacemaker Workshop Stimulating." *CanMenn* 16 (May 14, 1968), 10. Report on a workshop in British Columbia designed to assist the teaching of the peacemaker Sunday school series.

Wiebe, Herb. "Draft-Age Canadian Gives Impressions of Peace Work." *CanMenn* 4 (July 6, 1956), 3, 4. A PAX worker relates his experience and impressions and also assesses the peace witness being made by PAX workers abroad.

Wiebe, Katie Funk. "A Search for Abigail." *ChrLead* 43 (Sept. 23, 1980), 17. Reflections on women and peacemaking.

Wiebe, Katie Funk. "To Arm or Not to Arm." *ChrLead* 43 (Apr. 8, 1980), 19; *MBH* 19. (May 9, 1980), 36. Reflections on the Exploratory Peace Study sponsored by the US Board of Reference and Counsel of the Mennonite Brethren churches.

Wiebe, Katie Funk. "Who Are the Mennonite Brethren?" *ChrLead* 41 (Nov. 7, 1978), 13. Explores the question of why there were not more Mennonite Brethren present at the national New Call to Peacemaking conference held Oct. 5-8, 1978.

Wiebe, Menno. "Mitgefühl Plus Theory—A Theology of Missions and the Indian." *Forum* (Nov., 1972), 3-4. A theology of missions to the Indian people requires that the church pursue both a thorough understanding by intense involvement and a properly guided theoretical consideration.

Wiens, Marie K. "Hiroshima: In Search of Peace." *MBH* 16 (Sept. 16, 1977), 7. Hiroshima, a city speaking to peace through shrines and organizations, needs the true peace found through Christ, say two missionaries.

Wiens, Marie K. Letter to the Editor. *ChrLead* 43 (May 20, 1980), 12-13. Relates the gospel of peace and reconciliation to maintaining integrity in missions.

Wiens, P. B. "Protest Marches Are Not Good." *CanMenn* 14 (May 17, 1966), 5, 7. Lists reasons for believing anti-war protest marches are not doing the Mennonites nor their cause of peace any good.

Wiggers, Arverd. *History and Report of the 1-W Program of the Church of God in Christ (Mennonite): Covering Nearly Ten Years of Activity from the Fall of 1950-July 1, 1960.* Galva, Ks.: Christian Public Service, Inc., [1960?] Pp. 112. MHL. In addition to summary statement of the work of various units, the report addresses such topics as the relationship with MCC, spirituality in the units, improving our peace witness, etc.

"Youth Sounds Off on War, Peace." *YCC* 48 (July 16, 1967), 13. Findings of a 20-question form filled out by young people from across the Mennonite church in Canada and the United States.

Yake, C. F. "What If War Should Come?" *YCC* 20 (Nov. 5, 1939), 772. Reflections on the proposed Neutrality Legislation and the work of the Mennonite Church Peace Committee.

Yake, Lois. "The Social Message of the New Testament: The Social Gospel; Growth of a Social Consciousness in the Mennonite Church." Paper presented to Sociology Seminar, Goshen College, Goshen, Ind., Aug., 1947. Pp. 81. MHL.

Yamada, Takashi. "The Anabaptist Vision and Our World Mission (II)." *Mission-Focus* 4 (Mar., 1976), 7-14. In this discussion of the Anabaptist movement and vision as an attitude of confrontation in world missions, the writer also considers the nonresistant position of Mennonites in world mission.

Yoder, Bill. "Being the Church in Eastern Europe." *The Other Side* 15 (Mar., 1979), 15-20. An American living in a socialist country suggests that Christians must think in terms of long-range, daily, person-to-person involvement in Marxist societies as an alternative to evangelical "missions to the communist world."

Yoder, Edward. "A New Statism: Peace Principles from a Scriptural Viewpoint." Part 1. *GH* 27 (Jan. 17, 1935), 914-15. Christians must beware of a growing mood of nationalism and prepare to witness against "modern Caesar worship."

Yoder, Edward. "A Peace Meditation." *GH Supplement* 36 (Apr., 1943), 78. Those who live against the law of God have no peace.

Yoder, Edward. "Blessed Are the Peacemakers: Peace Principles from a Scriptural Viewpoint." Part 47. *GH Supplement* 34 (Dec., 1941), 821-22. The peacemaker realizes his or her helplessness apart from God and lives a life of peace and helpfulness to others.

Yoder, Edward. "God Is the Ruler." *GH Supplement* 36 (June, 1943), 278. God rules the world even in times of war.

Yoder, Edward. "Harvest of the Spirit." *GH Supplement* 36 (Oct., 1943), 638. The work of the Spirit in the believer is largely that of producing right social attitudes and relationships.

Yoder, Edward. "New Books." *GH Supplement* 37 (Dec., 1944), 760. A brief review of Guy F. Hershberger, *War, Peace, and Nonresistance* (1944) and Rufus D. Bowman, *The Church of the Brethren and War, 1708-1941* (1944).

Yoder, Edward. "Not By Might." *GH Supplement* 36 (Aug., 1943), 447. The right kind of victory cannot be attained by material forces.

Yoder, Edward. "Of One Blood All Nations." *GH Supplement* 36 (June, 1943), 178-79. All people belong to the same "family." Whatever divisions there are—race, class, etc.—are evidence of the sinfulness of humanity.

Yoder, Edward. "On 'Perish with the Sword'." *GH Supplement* 37 (Feb., 1945), 943. All works and institutions founded on the sword are subject to destruction.

Yoder, Edward. "Peace and War: What the Bible Teaches About War." *GH* 46 (Jan. 20, 1953), 56-57. War is contrary to the teachings of Christ.

Yoder, Edward. "Prayer in Wartime: Peace Principles from a Scriptural Viewpoint." Part 45. *GH Supplement* 34 (Oct., 1941), 629-30. Names groups of persons that ought to be prayed for in this time of war.

Yoder, Edward. "The Cry for Peace." *GH Supplement* 37 (Dec., 1944), 758-59. The church cannot outline specifics for postwar peace treaties but, because it recognizes the sinfulness of people and nations, it must tell the state what Christ has said about the value of persons.

Yoder, Edward. "The Obligation of the Christian to the State and Community—'Render to Caesar'." *MQR* 13 (Apr., 1939), 104-22. The Christian community, as a loving fellowship, is "a light to the world" and in its scattered life is "a salt to the earth," while committed to the way of love, it also works through direct social action to improve society.

Yoder, Edward. "The Peacemakers." *GH Supplement* 35 (Feb., 1943), 1022. Those people who are most like God in character work to remove strive and the causes of strife from among people.

Yoder, Edward. "Times That Try Men's Souls: Peace Principles from a Scriptural Viewpoint." Part 36. *GH* 33 (July 18, 1940), 366-67. In troubled times persons look everywhere for answers. The Christian looks to God and commits him- or herself to costly obedience.

Yoder, Edward. "War Is Sin: Peace Principles from a Scriptural Viewpoint." Part 3. *GH* 28 (July 18, 1935), 366-67. War is contrary to the teachings of the New Testament. Mennonites should witness to the truth that Jesus Christ has abrogated the Mosaic provision for revenge.

Yoder, Edward (Editorial). "An Unusual Peace Testimony." *GH* 30 (Apr. 15, 1937), 80. Reports an interview between the historic peace churches and President Franklin Roosevelt.

Yoder, Glee. "Who Are the Brethren?" *Menn* 93 (Sept. 19, 1978), 532-33. Outlines the historical origins of the Church of the Brethren and its central emphases, including peacemaking and reconciliation.

Yoder, J. Otis. "Eschatology and Peace." *ST* 34 (4th Qtr., 1966), 29. Christians should penetrate the twentieth-century world with a positive proclamation of the reconciling gospel that offers peace with God on the individual level.

Yoder, John H. "A People in the World: Theological Interpretation." *The Concept of the Believers Church.* Ed. James Leo Garrett Jr. Scottdale: Herald Press, 1969, 250-83. Pp. 342. Differentiates the believers' church understanding of the church from the theocratic, or Puritan, and the spiritualist, or Pietist, understanding and contends that the distinctness of the church is essential to the gospel. Then reinterprets Menno Simons' marks of the church—holy living, love, witness, and suffering—and speculates as to how the church might better meet human need by utilizing the believers' church as a model.

Yoder, John H. "Adventures in Fellowship." *Menn* 69 (Aug. 24, 1954), 518-19; "An Adventure in Fellowship." *CanMenn* 2 (Aug. 6, 1954), 2, 7. Mennonite and Brethren Peace Caravan among English Quakers discovers similarity in peace church origins, the effect peace witness has on a nation's life, and the importance of experiencing the meaning of Christian fellowship.

Yoder, John H. "Anabaptist Vision and Mennonite Reality." *Consultation on Anabaptist-Mennonite Theology.* Ed. by A. J. Klassen. Fresno: Council of Mennonite Seminaries, 1970, 1-46. Pp. 147. The way of the cross, components of which are the renunciation of power and refusal of war, is one of the criteria Yoder uses to analyze and describe the history of Mennonitism in the last century.

Yoder, John H. "'Anabaptists and the Sword' Revisited: Systematic Historiography and

Undogmatic Nonresistants." *Zeitschrift für Kirchengeschichte* 85 (1974), 126-39. Challenges reformation historiography in setting up a systematic polarization between "nonresistant separatism" of the Anabaptists and "responsible participation" of the reformers in relation to the state. Analyzes the weaknesses of this dualism and offers a model for a more pluralistic historiography recognizing the middle option of prophetic witness to the state.

Yoder, John H. ". . . And on Earth Peace . . . ." *MennLife* 20 (July, 1965), 108-110. Avoiding the "assumption shared by all kinds of men in our time, that peace can be *made,* the Bible peace is a promise, a practice, a person and a prayer."

Yoder, John H. "Continental Theology and American Social Action." *Religion in Life* (Spring, 1961), 225-30. The fundamental structure of ethical thought is quite similar in Europe and America; European theologians (e.g., Barth), may again teach us the authority of revelation and the dignity of the church as a totally new kind of community. Discusses the necessary and interdependent relationship between revelation as faith's content and the work of the church for social change as faith's act.

Yoder, John H. "Echoes from Nairobi: An Unfinished Debate." *Menn* 91 (Apr. 6, 1976), 239-40. Reports and analyzes World Council of Churches discussion on the five-year-old Program to Combat Racism and its controversial policy of funding organizations engaged in armed independence campaigns.

Yoder, John H. "Evangelism and Latin American Politics: A Document." *GH* 66 (Jan. 2, 1973), 4-5. J. S. Coffman's speech at the dedication of the Elkhart Institute building in 1896 shows that Mennonites of that era were concerned about peace issues, and specifically the ethics of government, and that such concern is not the sign of the loss of Mennonite identity, as some contemporaries claim.

Yoder, John H. "How Do Christians Witness to the State?" *GH* 56, Part 1, (May 28, 1963), 461; Part 2, (June 4, 1963), 475; Part 3, (June 11, 1963) 506; Part 4, (June 18, 1963), 522; Part 5, (June 25, 1963), 542. The Christian peace witness is characterized by the inner life of the church, by the service the church renders to people in need, by a human concern for people in government, and by formal testimony at congressional hearings. Whether the exercise of the franchise is or is not an appropriate Christian witness to the state is less clear.

Yoder, John H. "Living the Disarmed Life." *Sojourners* 6 (May, 1977), 16. If God's strategy for dealing with his enemies was to love them and give himself for them, it must be ours as well. Christians have been disarmed by God.

Yoder, John H. "Our Witness to the State." *Menn* 81 (Jan.25, 1966), 58-59. We witness to the lordship of Jesus; God is on the side of humanity, especially the poor; the state cannot be trusted to be its own judge; violence is no basis for social peace.

Yoder, John H. *Peace Without Eschatology?* Scottdale: Herald Press, [1959]. Pp. 25. Places the Christian peace witness into its essential eschatological setting.

Yoder, John H. "Question for Now, Forever." *GH* 41 (Aug. 17, 1948), 763. Selfless love is the only ultimate answer to war.

Yoder, John H. "The Anabaptist Dissent—The Logic of the Place of the Disciple in Society." *Concern* 1 (June, 1954), 45-68. An elaboration of a doctrine of social responsiility logically consistent with the concept of discipleship as understood and interpreted within the Anabaptist-Mennonite tradition. Issues relating to violence and war are discussed.

Yoder, John H. *The Christian and Capital Punishment.* (Institute of Mennonite Studies, No. 1.) Faith and Life Press, 1961. Pp. 24. MHL. Both biblical reasons, such as that to deprive persons of their lives denies them the possibility of reconciliation with God and others, and logical reasons, such as the lack of correlation between the crime rate and the death penalty, indicate that Christians should support efforts to abolish the death penalty as a legal way to deal with offenders.

Yoder, John H. *The Christian Witness to the State.* Newton: Faith and Life Press, IMS Series No. 3, 1964. Pp. 90. Examines the question of whether a Christian pacifist position rooted in christological considerations is relevant to the social order. Concludes that such relevancy is supported by a view of the church and state relationship which recognizes a duality of response—faith or unbelief—but which upholds a unity of norm; God's will for all is the love revealed in Christ. Thus the Christian should speak critically about specific ways the state is misusing its ordination while not presupposing the faith of the person or persons involved in such evils.

Yoder, John H. "The Peace Issue from the Historic Peace Church Perspective." Paper read at the spring conference of the Inter Seminary Movement, Apr., 1965 (St. Paul, Minn.). Pp. 31. MHL. Dialogue with Lutheran James Burtness and Roman Catholic Father Terrence Murphy.

Yoder, John H. "The Peace Testimony and Conscientious Objection." *GH* 51 (Jan. 21, 1958), 57. "The church living in true discipleship, devoted to her Lord in service and witness, love and suffering for both neighbors and strangers, be they friend or foe, will find no time for carnal warfare."

Yoder, John H. "The Place of the Peace Message in Missions." Condensation of an address given at the Mission Board Meeting, Lansdale, Pa., 1960. Pp. 7. MHL.

Yoder, John H. "The Unique Role of the Historic Peace Churches." *Brethren Life and Thought* 14 (Summer, 1969), 132-49. Published separately by Shalom Publishers (Elkhart, Ind.), n.d. Pp. 18. Brethren, Friends, and Mennonites, with other older and younger "historic peace churches" should accept a distinct mission arising out of their distinct identity. A certain imbalance at the point of peace witness is justified by the special need of today's world and by the key place of the violence/servanthood issue at the heart of the gospel.

Yoder, John H. "The Unity We Have." *Menn* 77 (Mar. 13, 1962), 165; (Mar. 20, 1962), 181-82; (Mar. 27, 1962), 213-14. Unity is not primarily negotiated but received as a gift of God.

Yoder, John H. "The Way of the Peacemaker." *Peacemakers in a Broken World.* Ed. John A. Lapp. Scottdale: Herald Press, 1969, 111-25. Outlines major criteria of the "just war" theory, contrasts it with Jesus' example of loving enemies. Argues that Jesus' authority and humanity are to be taken at full value, so that he is the peacemaking example for Christians.

Yoder, John H. "The Wrath of God and the Love of God." Address delivered at the Historic Peace Churches and International Fellowship of Reconciliation Conference, Beatrice Webb House, England, Sept. 11-14, 1956. Pp. 11. MHL.

Yoder, John H. "What Do Ye More Than They?" *GH* 66 (Jan. 23, 1973), 72-75. Yoder maintains that the beatitudes, including reconciliation and peacemaking, are not moral demands. They are rather the good news, signs of the wholeness of the kingdom.

Yoder, John H. "Which Ranks First?" *GH* 39 (June 11, 1946), 229. Missions and relief are both part of Christian witness.

Yoder, John H. "Why Should a Christian Witness to the State?" *GH* 56, Part 1, (Apr. 30, 1963), 373; Part 2, (May 7, 1963), 381; Part 3, (May 14, 1963), 407; Part 4, (May 21, 1963), 434. Because of concern for the state and the welfare of its people; to be helpful to misguided Christians in government; because the church has been given the ministry of prophecy; because in modern life whatever we do is already a form of witness. Therefore, Christians should endeavor to make their witness positive, intelligent, and scriptural.

Yoder, John H. "Why Speak to Government." *CanMenn* 14 (Dec. 13, 1966), 10; *GH* 59 (Jan. 25, 1966), 73-74. Background paper for the MCC consultation in Minneapolis. We should speak to government because: we love our neighbor; we reject idolatry; the statespersons in North America are church people; we are Christian missionaries; we live in a democracy; we are already involved. In so speaking, what do we say? That God is on the side of humanity; that human beings cannot be trusted to be their own judges; that violence is no basis for social peace.

Yoder, John H. with Miller, Donald E. "Does Natural Law Provide a Basis for a Christian Witness to the State? (A Symposium)." *Brethren Life and Thought* 7 (Winter, 1962), 8-22. In this Brethren-Mennonite dialogue, Yoder takes issue with Miller's delineation of natural law tendencies as a basis for Christian witness to the state and suggests, as an alternative, that we seek moral constants in the themes of covenant and incarnation, and, then, base moral dialogue with the state on the assumption that both the realm of unbelief and the church have, by the work of Christ, been subjugated to his lordship.

Yoder, Orrie D. "'Politics' in the Church." *ST* 17 (1st Qtr., 1949), 26. The tactics of worldly politics have no place in the church of Jesus Christ.

Yoder, Sol and Hertzler, Daniel. "The Heerewegen Vision." *ChrLiv* 3 (Feb., 1956), 24-25. Dutch Mennonite campground houses a Peace Center and Library, publishes a monthly *Peace Letter,* and holds an annual International Peace Seminar.

Yordy, Richard. "Unshakeable Peace." *GH* 38 (Nov. 23, 1945), 641. The only way to make peace is by leading people to Christ.

*

Yutzy, Norman. "Always, Everywhere . . . Religious Groups Must Work for Peace." *CanMenn* 14 (Apr. 12, 1966), 1, 2. John Howard Yoder, Paul Peachey, Edgar Metzler, and the author took part in the first National Inter-Religious Conference for Peace held in Washington, DC, Mar. 15-17, 1966. Four hundred representatives of Catholic, Jewish, and Protestant faiths attended.

Zehr, Daniel. "Discipleship Includes Peacemaking." *Menn* 92 (July 12, 1977), 433-34; *EV* 90 (Aug. 25, 1977), 10; "Discipleship Includes Peacemaking: Example from the Biblical Record." *MennRep* 7 (Aug. 8, 1977), 5. Jesus' life shows peacemaking to be a daily commitment. Jesus' death and resurrection provide the strategy for the new kingdom, nonviolent peacemaking under Christ's kingship.

---

*For additional listing, see Supplement, pp. 717-719.

Zehr, Daniel. "Inter-Mennonite Peace Retreat Conducted by MCC (Ontario)." *CanMenn* 13 (Sept. 28, 1965), 1, 2, 14. A synopsis of messages and talks on the teaching of peace as portrayed in the Bible and through Christ with an application to the current situation. Edgar Metzler and Frank C. Peters were the main speakers.

Zehr, Daniel. Letter to the Editor. *MennMirror* 7 (May, 1978), 17-19. In response to the editorial (*MennMirror* 7 [Apr., 1978], 26) on Mennonite pacifism, the writer expresses concern about Mennonites becoming comfortable with the compromises and rationalizations made for the use of force in certain instances. Contains a response from the editor which points out the ambiguous nature of peace and reconciliation.

Zehr, Daniel. "Special Committee Advises on Peace." *CanMenn* 16 (Mar. 5, 1968), 4. Peace witness apologetic by Zehr on his appointment as MCC (Canada) peace secretary.

Zehr, Daniel. "Teach-In Looks at Religion and International Affairs." *CanMenn* 15 (Oct. 31, 1967), 1, 10. Reflections of attitudes on revolution, war, and the church by prominent leaders in theology, education, and the church from South America, North America, and Africa.

Zehr, Daniel. "The Cross and Peacemaking." *MBH* 16 (Oct. 28, 1977), 36. The peace of Jesus is not only inner peace but also nonviolent peacemaking that takes its strategy from the cross.

Zehr, Howard. "The Case of the Wilmington 10." *GH* 70 (Nov. 1, 1977), 814-15. Summarizes events leading to the conviction of the "Wilmington 10," and appeals to Mennonites as a peacemaking people to become aware of the miscarriage of justice in this racial issue, and to play a reconciling role.

Zehr, Howard. "To Remove the Walls." *YCC* 45 (June 14, 1964), 5. Personal commitment to work on reconciliation between whites and blacks led the author to enter Morehouse College in Atlanta, as one of the two white students enrolled at that time.

Zercher, John E. "Violence." *EV* 85 (Mar. 10, 1972), 3. An examination of the significance of the cross against the dark background of violence.

Zook, J. Kore. "Peace and War: A Letter to I-W Men." *GH* 46 (June 16, 1953), 569. I-W personnel have a great responsibility to uphold the Mennonite peace witness.

"1979 Mennonite Church General Assembly Statement on Militarism and Conscription." *GH* 72 (Oct. 2, 1979), 778-79. Seeking to be a faithful witness in a militaristic world, the Mennonite Church speaks out on peace and obedience, the use of material resources, Christian service and conscription, militarism and taxation.

# C. Nonresistance, Nonviolence, and Pacifism

"A Message from the Peace Problems Committee." *GH* 32 (Oct. 5, 1939), 570. The committee reports their activities as they relate to the war in Europe and encourages Mennonites to seriously study the doctrine of nonresistance.

"A Message to Nonresistant Christians." *GH* 34 (Jan. 15, 1942), 898. Principles for nonresistant Christians to follow in times of war outlined by PPC.

"A Nearly Non-existent Nonresistance." *CanMenn* 11 (Mar. 8, 1963), 6. Mennonites would rather have war with nuclear weapons than experience communism. In their fear of communism the Mennonites have become followers of Carl McIntire, Billy James Hargis, etc., instead of carrying the peaceful cross of Christ.

"A Statement of Concerns: Adopted at a Study Conference on Christian Community Relations." *GH* 44 (Aug. 14, 1951), 780-81. Contains sections on: 1) Doctrine and practice; 2) Nonresistance in daily life; 3) Christian ethics in business and professions; 4) Organized labor; 5) Race and minority group relations; and 6) other related concerns.

"Applied Nonresistance." Papers read at the Mennonite Conference on Applied Nonresistance, Goshen, Indiana, Apr., 1939. Reprinted from *MQR* 13 (Apr., 1939), 75-154. MHL. Published by Peace Problems Committee, Mennonite General Conference, Scottdale, 1939. Includes Erb, Paul, "Nonresistance and Litigation," 75-82; Bender, H. S., "Church and State in Mennonite History," 83-103; Yoder, Edward, "The Obligation of the Christian to the State—'Render to Caesar,'" 104-122; Gingerich, Melvin, "The Menace of Propaganda and How to Meet It," 123-34; Hershberger, Guy F. "Nonresistance and Industrial Conflict," 135-54.

Adams, Paul. "The Mennonite Doctrine of Nonresistance Under Test During World War II in Canada: Special Attention Given to Mennonites of Kitchener-Waterloo." Term paper for 20th Century Canadian History course (MCC Peace Scholarship paper), Mar., 1978. Pp. 22. CGCL.

Alderfer, Helen (Review). *Peace Shall Destroy Many*, by Rudy Wiebe. McClelland and Stewart, 1962. Pp. 239. *ChrLiv* 10 (Nov., 1963), 33. Reviewer considers the book a probing novel of a young man struggling to understand Mennonite faith, including nonresistance.

*Arthur Jost, Petitioner v. United States of America.* Petition [to the Supreme Court of the United States, October Term, 1953] for a Writ of Certiorari to the District Court of Appeal for the Fourth Appellate District of California. By Dean Acheson and others, attorneys for the petitioner, Covington and Burling, of Counsel. [Washington, DC: Supreme Court, 1953.] Pp. 39. MHL. This petition, to review the denial of naturalization to Arthur Jost on grounds that his request to take the conscientious objector's oath was unconvincing, includes summary of Mennonite teachings on nonresistance as well as the questions, perceptions, and arguments emerging from the opposition in a legal context.

Augsburger, David W. "The Mennonite Dream." *GH* 70 (Nov. 15, 1977), 855-57. Reprinted from pamphlet #147, The Mennonite Hour, Harrisonburg, VA. The Mennonite dream of radical discipleship to Jesus Christ includes emphasis on nonviolent, suffering, reconciling love for all, even enemies.

Augsburger, Myron S. "An Answer for Nonresistance." *MBH* 14 (Oct. 31, 1975), 32. Five simple explanations for conscientious objection based on biblical texts.

Augsburger, Myron S. "Christian Pacifism." *War: Four Christian Views*, ed. Robert G. Clouse. Downers Grove, Ill.: InterVarsity Press, 1981, 81-97. Pp. 210. Outlines the evangelical premises and perspectives leading to the conclusion that, while Christians may participate in government as long as they do not create a state church, they may not participate in war. The book is composed of articulations of four positions on war: nonresistance, Christian pacifism, the just war, and the crusade or preventive war. Then each of the presenters comments on the other three discussions. So, in addition to Augsburger's essay on Christian pacifism, he responds from that point of view to the other three views: to nonresistance, 58-63; to just war, 141-45; to the crusade, 175-80.

Augsburger, Myron S. "Nonresistance Clarified."

*GH* 66 (Nov. 20, 1973), 883-84. Outlines five basic and biblical reasons why evangelical Christians should be pacifists: priority of membership in the kingdom of Christ; the Great Commission, which extends to enemies; Jesus' command to love; the sacredness of human life; the materialistic causes of war.

Augsburger, Myron S. "What Do Mennonites Believe?" *MBH* 18 (Nov. 9, 1979), 5-7. Nonresistant love (pacifism) is one of the external marks of the church.

"Biblical Teaching on Nonresistance." *GH* 35 (Nov. 12, 1942), 706. A review of New Testament passages supporting nonresistance, including the sayings of Jesus and the writings of Paul and Peter.

"Brethren in Christ Fellowships Meet." *EV* 91 (Aug. 25, 1975), 8, 9, 11. Persons from Brethren in Christ fellowships around the world met in Pennsylvania to fellowship and discuss areas of need; one area is the failure in some of the younger churches to teach the nonresistance position held by the Brethren in Christ Church.

Baerg, Henry R. Letter to the Editor. *MBH* 15 (Feb. 20, 1976), 9, 28-29. Supporter of capital punishment builds his case from biblical passages and criticizes contemporary understandings of nonresistance that would tend to prohibit the use of the death penalty.

Bainton, Roland H. "Christian Pacifism Reassessed." *CanMenn* 8, Part 1, (Oct. 7, 1960), 2, 11; Part 2, (Oct. 14, 1960), 2, 8. Also in *ChrLiv* 6 (Feb., 1959), 16-17, 39-40. Reprinted from *Christian Century.* 1958. A realistic look at atomic warfare in the light of the Christian ethic. Christian pacifism is a witness, not a political strategy for preventing a third world war.

Bainton, Roland H. "The Churches and War: Historic Attitudes Toward Christian Participation." *Social Action* 11 (Jan. 15, 1945), 5-71. Reviews the three positions of pacifism, just war, and crusade from the first through the twentieth centuries, including World War II. Examines especially 20th-century attitudes. Refers to Anabaptist views in the Reformation, as well as the treatment of conscientious objectors and Civilian Public Service.

Bainton, Roland H. (Review). *Pacifism, An Historical and Sociological Study,* by David A. Martin. New York: Schocken, 1966. Pp. 249. "Modern Pacifism Under the Glass." *Fellowship* 32 (Sept., 1966), 29. Summarizes the contents of the book which offers an analysis of pacifism from many angles with reference to ideas, forms of church structure and sociological situations.

Bargen, Ralph. "This Is the Sorrow." *Fellowship* 15 (May, 1949), 7-9. Statement which a young

Mennonite nonregistrant presented to the FBI at the time of his arrest; statement outlines the convictions which have led him to a stance of nonresistance.

Barrett, Lois. "Living Nonviolently." *Menn* 91 (Sept. 21, 1976), 556. Discusses nonviolence on the interpersonal level, suggesting that loving the enemy breaks the circle of fear and hate.

Barrett, Lois. "Nonviolence and the National Defense." *Menn* 91 (Feb. 3, 1976), 75. Interpretive report on lectures by Gene Sharp, advocate of nonviolent civilian national defense.

Barrett, Lois. "Varieties of Christian Pacifism." *Menn* 91 (Sept. 7, 1976), 518. Interpretive report on the Fellowship of Reconciliation conference, where pacifists gathered to discuss nuclear arms, Christian participation in the political system.

Bauman, Clarence. "Christainity [sic] and Non-Violence." *CanMenn* 7 (Mar. 20, 1959), 2. Reflections on the political relevance of non-Christian nonviolence and its distinctiveness from Christian pacifism. Concludes that since part of the mystery of God's grace is the evidence that God works through evil for good, we should not "exclude the 'lower levels' of political, economic, and social involvement from our redemptive concern."

Bauman, Clarence. *Gewaltlosigkeit im Täufertum.* Vol. III in *Studies in the History of Christian Thought.* Heiko A. Oberman, ed. Leiden: E. J. Brill, 1968. Pp. 401. A study of the theological ethics of sixteenth-century Anabaptism, with particular reference to their understanding of nonresistance as a central ethical concern.

Bauman, Clarence. "The Meaning of the Cross: The Essence of Mennonite Way of Life," (Part 1). *CanMenn* 4 (Nov. 16, 1956), 2. A statement of the centrality of biblical nonresistance in Anabaptism and Mennonitism.

Beachy, Alvin J. "Conscription: The Pacifist View." *ChrCent* 73 (Sept. 26, 1956), 1097-98. Responds to a previous writer's assertion that military service is not incompatible with discipleship by recommending Christian pacifism and its commitment to the lordship of Christ and the call to make disciples in all nations.

Beard, Ruth. "The Fading Out of Nonresistance in the Early Christian Church." Paper prepared for church history class, [Goshen College], Goshen, Ind., n.d. Pp. 10. MHL.

*

Becker, Henry. "Don't Take Nonresistance Too Far!" *CanMenn* 14 (Jan. 4, 1966), 15. Letter to the Editor denouncing *CanMenn* for its criticism of Canadian and US governments.

Becker, Paul. "Practical Nonresistance." Student paper for Mennonite History, Life, and Principles, May, 1953. Pp. 33. MLA/BeC.

Beechy, Atlee. "My Response to Vietnam." *GH* 60 (Aug. 15, 1967), 736-37. As a Christian who believes in nonresistance, Beechy takes a stand against the war in Vietnam and calls for concrete action to bring it to an end.

Beidler, Hoke. "No Rights for Mennonites." Offprint from *The Lincoln Times,* Lincoln, Ill., Sept. 6, 1900. Pp. 1. MHL.

Bender, Harold S. "A Message to Nonresistant Christians: Preparatory Statement by the Peace Problems Committee." *GH* 34 (Jan. 15, 1942), 898-99; *Menn* 57 (Jan. 27, 1942), 2-4. Summary of the Peace Problems Committee's work in searching for constructive ways for the nonresistant Christian to contribute to his or her nation while making the least possible contribution to war and defense efforts.

Bender, Harold S. "Forward Into the Postwar World with our Peace Testimony." *GH Supplement* 39 (June, 1946), 213. A challenge to move forward into a hostile world with the message of "love your enemies." The peace testimony is biblical and central to Christianity, not something extra or peripheral.

Bender, Harold S. "Money and War: In the Midst of War—Thoughts for Nonresistants," (Part 4). *GH* 35 (Feb. 18, 1943), 1002-1003. The nonresistant Christian should use money sacrifically and try to keep it out of the war effort by refusing to purchase war bonds and by donating excess profits to relief and mission work.

Bender, Harold S. "One Program of Christian Pacifism." Pp. 9. In "Study Materials." Adopted documents of the Conference on the Church and War, Detroit, May 8-11, 1950. Various pagination. MHL.

Bender, Harold S. "The Pacifism of the Sixteenth-Century Anabaptists." *Church History* 24 (June, 1955), 119-31. Presents the views of nonresistant Anabaptists in Switzerland and the Netherlands, then analyzes the distinctions between their two-kingdom theology and the theologies of Calvin and Luther, and the difference between their biblically-oriented pacifism and the humanistic pacifism of Erasmus.

Bender, Harold S. "Rationing: In the Midst of War—Thoughts for Nonresistants," (Part 6). *GH* 35 (Mar. 11, 1943), 1074-75. The nonresistant Christian should cheerfully cooperate in

---

rationing efforts by reducing consumption and complying with all regulations.

Bender, Harold S. "The High School Victory Corps: In the Midst of War—Thoughts for Nonresistants," (Part 2). *GH* 35 (Feb. 4, 1943), 954. The nonresistant Christian high school student should not participate in this organization.

Bender, Harold S. Letter to the Editor. *Fellowship* 26 (Nov., 1960), 35-36. In response to A. J. Muste's article "Their Church and Ours" (*Fellowship*, Nov., 1959), which cites a statement by Jacob Zhidkov about the Russian Mennonites abandoning their nonresistance after World War I, H. S. Bender points out that this is greatly exaggerated and only a small minority joined the Selbstschutz.

Bender, John M. "Youth Attacked Twice in Subway Mercy Mission." *MennRep* 9 (Apr. 30, 1979), 10. A new volunteer around-the-clock patrol along a New York subway line is meeting violence with nonviolence.

Bender, Philip. "The Schleitheim Confession: Its Background, and an Interpretation of its Significance." *MHB* 38 (Apr., 1977), 1-7. Comment on the articles of the 1527 confession deals in part with Anabaptist convictions on nonresistance found in article six.

Bender, Wilbur J. "Pacifism Among the Mennonites, Amish Mennonites, and Schwenkfelders of Pensylvania to 1783." *MQR* 1, Part 1 (July, 1927), 23-40; Part 2 (Oct., 1927), 21-48. Until 1776 these groups succeeded in observing strict nonresistance without too much difficulty. Even during the War of Independence there was general tolerance for them, though many paid fines for not bearing arms and refusing to pay war taxes.

Berg, Ford. "A Pardon for Wittman." *ChrLiv* 1 (Oct., 1954), 30, 40. Story of a Seventh Day German Baptist nonresistant Peter Miller who won a pardon for his enemy from George Washington.

Berg, Ford. "Let Us Tell." *GH Supplement 40* (Aug., 1947), 463. The Mennonite church should be more aggressive in proclaiming the doctrine of nonresistance. Too often this testimony has been "hidden under a bushel," when it could have been helpful, especially to CO's of other denominations.

Berg, Ford. "Mennonites to Participate in Church and War Conference." *GH* 43 (Apr. 18, 1950), 371. The Detroit "Church and War" conference offers an opportunity for Mennonites to clarify to the wider church the basis of their nonresistant stand.

Berg, Ford. "Nonresistance Stories Which Are Open to Question." *GH* 43 (Feb. 21, 1950), 179. One needs to proceed with caution when attempting to validate the nonresistant position by an appeal to certain Old Testament stories which have, at first glance, "the nonresistant flavor."

Berg, Ford. "Peace Study Conference at Winona Lake." *GH* 44 (Jan. 16, 1951), 59. A report of the MCC peace conference of Nov., 1950; summarizes the study papers dealing with "the problems of nonresistance in its implications with the world."

Berg, Ford. "Second Conference on the Church and Peace at Detroit." *GH* 46 (Nov. 17, 1953), 1097. Announcement of the conference, which is being called to study the basis of Christian pacifism in Scripture and its application to contemporary problems.

Berkey, E. J. "Bible Teaching on Nonresistance." *GH Supplement* 34 (Oct., 1941), 627-28, 632. Presents the Biblical basis of nonresistance. Israel was blessed in war only when it fought under the direct command of God. The dispensation of the New Testament makes it clear that Christians are called to be nonresistant.

Berkey, Esther. "Actions of the Indiana-Michigan Mennonite Conference in Reference to Nonconformity and Nonresistance." Term paper for a Social Science seminar, Goshen College, Goshen, Ind., Mar. 12, 1953. Pp. 36. MHL.

Bethel College in World War Two. 29 interviews. Covers Bethel's stance on nonresistance and hostile community response. MLA/BeC.

Birky, Luke. "When Is Life?" *GH* 61 (Jan. 30, 1968), 98-99. Raises complex questions related to abortion and euthanasia in the context of Mennonite belief in the sacredness of life, seen in the practice of nonresistance.

Bohn, E. Stanley. "Black Power and Nonviolence." *Menn* 81 (Sept. 13, 1966), 557. Board of Christian Service sends a fraternal letter to the Congress of Racial Equality (CORE) urging continuation of "courageous nonviolent" action.

Bohn, E. Stanley. "Toward a New Understanding of Nonresistance." *Peacemakers in a Broken World.* Ed. John A. Lapp. Scottdale: Herald Press, 1969, 103-110. Reprinted from *MennLife* (Jan., 1967). Nonresistance is possible only for those who take sides in a conflict, not for those who act only as "go-betweens" or "umpires." Based on the incarnation, it means siding with the oppressed. Bohn describes his experience as a reconciler amid racial tensions.

Bontreger, Eli J. "Nonresistance." *GH* 41 (Jan. 6, 1948), 5. The Christian does not participate in carnal conflict because he or she is under the new dispensation.

Bontreger, Eli J. "Nonresistance in Daily Practice." *GH* 41 (June 1, 1948), 511. Many parents and other church members who oppose participation in war fail to live a truly nonresistant daily life. Consequently many young men choose military service.

Bordeaux, Michael. "Baptists and Other Protestants." *MBH* 13 (Jan. 25, 1974), 4-7. Mennonites in the Soviet Union give up pacifism through official ties with Baptists, an arrangement made necessary by Soviet policies toward evangelical Christians.

Boserup, Anders and Mack, Andrew. "Nonviolence in National Defense." *PlMon* 2 (Nov., 1979), 5. Reprinted from the introduction to *War Without Weapons: Non-violence in National Defense*, by the same authors. New York: Schocken Books, 1975. Reviews military strategy since the advent of nuclear weapons to show that national security through military means in the nuclear age is a fallacy.

Bowman, David. "Mennonite Nonresistance: A Comparison of Practices in the American Revolution and the War Between the States." Term paper for Anabaptist and Mennonite History, Apr. 6, 1978. Pp. 22. MHL.

Bowman, Randall J. "From World War II Until Vietnam: Societal Influence on the Mennonites." Term paper for Mennonite History and Thought course, Feb. 17, 1978. Pp. 15. MSHL.

Boyer, Dave. Letter to the Editor. *God and Caesar* 5 (Apr., 1979), 8-9. A Catholic pacifist expresses his appreciation to the Mennonite community for support and guidance in taking a pacifist stance and his feeling of isolation in the Caholic community.

Brackbill, Milton. "The Fruit of Righteousness Is Sown in Peace of Them that Make Peace." *The Eastern Mennonite School Journal* 18 (Apr., 1940), 51-55. Nonresistance is rooted in the person of Jesus and must be expressed as peace among nations, peace among individuals, and peace with God.

Brandt, Diana (Review). *No King But Caesar? A Catholic Lawyer Looks at Christian Violence*, by William R. Durland. Scottdale: Herald Press, 1975. Pp. 182. Also, *A People of Two Kingdoms: The Political Acculturation of the Kansas Mennonites*, by James C. Juhnke. Newton: Faith and Life Press, 1975. Pp. 215. *Menn* 90 (Oct. 28, 1975), 611-12. Durland, a Catholic lawyer, makes a strong plea for Christian nonviolence, based on Jesus'

demand to love neighbors and enemies. Juhnke's study demonstrates that Mennonite nonresistance and apoliticism has persisted to the present, in spite of thorough political acculturation.

Bremer, Henk. "Rise Up and Walk." *MennLife* 22 (Oct., 1967), 150-51. Nonviolent involvement with the beggar and the oppressed is the only hope for the world.

Brengle, Colonel S. L. "The Sheathed Sword. A Law of the Spirit." *EV* 88 (Feb. 25, 1975), 4. Human beings are fighters by nature, but the Christian is a citizen of God's kingdom and conquers not by fighting but by submitting.

Brenneman, John M. "Christianity and War: A Sermon Setting Forth the Sufferings of Christians, the Origin and Import of the Christian Name, Christianity and War." 1863. Pp. 52. MHL.

Brock, Peter, ed. and trans. "A Polish Anabaptist Against War: The Question of Conscientious Objection in Marcin Czechowic's *Christian Dialogues* of 1575." *MQR* 52 (Oct., 1978), 279-93. Dialogue on nonresistance written by a Polish Anabaptist presents the first detailed and systematic treatment of the subject from a pacifist point of view. Introductory essay describes the development of Polish Anabaptism and the contemporary debate over nonresistance.

Brock, Peter. "The Nonresistance of the Hungarian Nazarenes to 1914." *MQR* 54 (Jan., 1980), 53-63. Documents the suffering of Hungarian Nazarenes for the sake of nonresistance during the nineteenth century and reflects upon why the authorities were harsher with them than with the Mennonites of the same time period.

Brown, Dale W. Letter to the Editor. *ChrLead* 43 (Nov. 4, 1980), 13. Contends that Christ's teachings, not church growth or the lack of it, must be the motivation and criteria for teaching nonresistance.

Brown, Dale W. (Review). *Karl Barth and the Problem of War*, by John H. Yoder. Nashville: Abingdon, 1970. Pp. 141. *MQR* 46 (Apr., 1972), 168-70. Calling the book a "superb study in theological ethics," the reviewer outlines Yoder's questions to Barth's views on war, calling for a future biblical and systematic work on pacifism by Yoder.

Brubacher, Donald L. "Nonresistance and Industrial Conflict." *YCC* 40 (April 5, 1959), 218. With more Mennonites moving to urban industrial areas, the application of nonresistance to the concerns associated with this type of work are needed. Prize-winning essay.

Brubacher, Dwight. "Mennonite Nonresistance in Ontario, World War I: The Persecution of a Separate People." Paper presented to Social Science Seminar, Goshen College, Goshen, Ind., May 13, 1976. Pp. 23. MHL.

Brubaker, Dean M. "From Biblical Nonresistance to Religious Pacifism." ST 29 (3rd Qtr., 1961), 1. Documents how the Church of the Brethren drifted from a position of biblical nonresistance to a position of religious pacifism.

Brubaker, Dean M. "To Resist or Not to Resist, That Is the Question." GH 63 (Dec. 8, 1970), 1012-14. Discusses biblical passages related to the subject of Christian obedience to government, and questions whether draft registration is really part of the military system. Opposes nonviolent resistance because he considers it foreign to biblical nonresistance.

Brunk, Conrad G. "'Active' Nonresistance." GH 63 (Oct. 27, 1970), 902-904. Part three of a college baccalaureate address calls nonresistant Christians to witness against the violence of dissenter and patriot and to embrace a pacifism that strikes at the roots of violence and hate.

Brunk, Conrad G. (Review). On Earth Peace: Discussions on War/Peace Issues Between Friends, Mennonites, Brethren and European Churches, 1935-75, by Durnbaugh, Donald F., ed. Elgin, Ill.: The Brethren Press, 1978. Pp. 412. MQR 53 (Oct., 1979), 331-33. Contains papers from the discussions between the minority pacifist churches and the larger ecumenical community of the World Council of Churches on the Christian basis of pacifism. Reviewer recognizes these papers as foundational in shaping the questions and the idiom for present discussion on the subject.

Brunk, George R., I. "Nonresistance." ST 2 (Oct., 1930), 20. Examination of "nonresistance" in both the Old Testament and New Testament, based on the premise that God is the same in nature and attributes forever but His law and government have changed with changed conditions.

Brunk, George R., I. "Nonresistance Not the Law of the Old Testament." ST 46 (July, 1978), 9-12. Reprinted from ST (Oct., 1930), p. 20. Mennonite belief in nonresistance is grounded in the difference between the two covenants represented by the Old and New Testaments.

Brunk, Harry A. Life of Peter S. Hartman, Including His Lecture: Reminiscences of the Civil War. By the Hartman Family, 1937. Pp. 73. MHL. Relates the temptations, failures, and triumphs experienced by the Virginia Mennonite Church

as its members struggled with the meaning of nonresistance during the turbulent years of the Civil War.

Buckwalter, Anna M. "Practical Nonresistance." GH 42 (Mar. 1, 1949), 199. Our nonresistant witness does not apply only to wartime but must be lived daily. There must be a readiness to suffer for Christ.

Buller, Harold. "Why I Am a Conscientious Objector to War." GH 42 (Feb. 15, 1949), 155, 165-66; Menn 65 (Oct. 24, 1950), 702-703, 711. Seven reasons, with many biblical references, are advanced in support of the CO position. Nonresistance is the heart of the Good News since the nonresistant love of God, the example of Jesus, and the life of the early church all affirm this way of love. Also in BfC., MLA/BeC.

Burck, Lois C. "How Vital Is the Doctrine of Nonresistance." ChrMon 36 (Aug., 1944), 233, 245. Nonresistance in the home, community life, and nation.

Burkholder, H. D. The Blessed Fruit of the Gospel: An Address Presented at the Quarterly Conference of the Eastern District General Conference of Mennonites by H. D. Burkholder, DD, President of Grace Bible Institute, Omaha, Neb. Henderson: Service Press, 1954. Pp. 5. MHL. Author relates personal story of his early rejection of nonresistance because those who were preaching the doctrine also denied the Virgin Birth, and his subsequent conversion to biblical pacifism through the arguments presented in Theodore Epp's "Should God's People Partake in War?" Also in MSHL.

Burkholder, J. Lawrence. "An Examination of the Mennonite Doctrine of Nonconformity to the World." ThM thesis, Princeton Theological Seminary, 1951. Pp. 221. MHL. Thesis discusses the distinctive Mennonite doctrine and practice of nonconformity to the world in the life of the Swiss Brethren of the Reformation period, the Hutterites and Amish, the Mennonite Church in America. A fourth major section deals with the doctrine and practice of nonresistance as the most essential aspect of nonconformity. Included in this section are such topics as the biblical basis of nonresistance, Mennonite nonresistance in the Revolutionary War, Civil War, World War I and World War II, a comparison of nonresistance with modern religious pacifism, nonresistance and industrial conflict. Concludes that the doctrine of nonconformity has hindered Mennonites from accepting social responsibility and produced a sectarianism which can only be judged theologically, on the basis of whether God has designed the church to lose itself in the world by accepting responsibility for the world.

Burkholder, J. Lawrence. "Nonresistance,

Nonviolent Resistance, and Power." *Kingdom, Cross, and Community.* Ed. John R. Burkholder and Calvin Redekop. Scottdale: Herald Press, 1976, 131-37. Burkholder contends that Guy F. Hershberger's wedge between biblical nonresistance and nonviolenct resistance undercuts the kind of social conflict which leads to the cross. Advocates active nonviolence as an alternative to violent social change.

Burkholder, J. Lawrence. "Social Implications of Mennonite Doctrines." *PCMCP Twelfth,* 91-111. N.p. Held at Mennonite Biblical Seminary, Elkhart, Indiana, June 16-17, 1959. States main doctrines of the Mennonite tradition which bear on the problem of social structures. Inquires into the kind of social order these doctrines logically call for and discusses alternative approaches.

Burkholder, J. Lawrence. "Some Early Nineteenth Century Pacifists." Term paper, n.d. Pp. 13. MHL.

Burkholder, J. Lawrence. "The Anabaptist Vision of Discipleship." *The Recovery of the Anabaptist Vision.* Ed. Guy F. Hershberger. Scottdale: Herald Press, 1957, 135-51. In Anabaptism the ambiguous term "discipleship" meant correlating the demands of the kingdom with the demands of society in an ethic of nonresistance which led logically to withdrawal from society.

Burkholder, J. Lawrence. "The Problem of Social Responsibility from the Perspective of the Mennonite Church." ThD dissertation, Princeton Theological Seminary, 1958. Pp. 369. MHL. Examines, from a sociology of religion perspective, the acute challenge which the ecumenical doctrine of the responsible society poses for Mennonites caught between a tradition of nonresistant noninvolvement and the pressures of modern culture. After outlining what is meant by social responsibility and why responsibility ethics underscore the fundamental conflict between the absolutism of the way of the cross and the relativities of the social order, the author reviews the relevant theological and ethical themes found in the early Anabaptist formulation of Christianity as discipleship. In subsequent chapters, attention is given to Anabaptism as dissent from the corpus christianum, to the types of social structures promoted by Mennonites historically, and to a summary of Mennonite social outreach. In the final chapters, the author lists the sociological, ethical, and theological factors which the Mennonite Church should consider in constructing an adequate social policy. Concludes that Mennonites must come to understand the inevitability of power in the ethical demand for justice, to recognize the inadequacy of nonresistance as a norm and to include nonviolent resistance in the Mennonite ethic.

Burkholder, J. Lawrence. "The Relation of Agape, the Essential Christian Ethic to Social Structure and Political Action." Term paper, n.d. Pp. 13. MHL.

Burkholder, J. Lawrence. "Violence, Nonviolent Resistance, and Nonresistance in Revolutionary Times." *CanMenn* 17 (June 27, 1969), 8, 9. Analyzes in 1969 CMPA lecture the distinction between nonviolent resistance and nonresistance and then raises question of how to use power in Christian way. Suggests concept of "Mennonite power" based on simplicity of heart, honesty, forgiveness, etc. but does not spell out what form this kind of power should take.

Burkholder, J. Richard. *Continuity and Change: A Search for a Mennonite Social Ethic.* Akron, Pa.: MCC Peace Section, 1977. Pp. 31. MHL. Explores, in dialogue with Yoder's *Politics of Jesus,* the adequacy of the central principle of nonresistance as a foundation for ethical thinking. Concludes that justice is the goal of the kingdom order and the love ethic of the Sermon on the Mount the means to the goal.

Burkholder, J. Richard. "Forms of Christian Witness to the State: A Mennonite Perspective." Convocation address given at Goshen College, Goshen, Ind., Mar. 12, 1976. Pp. 7. MHL.

Burkholder, J. Richard. (Review). *Mennonite Statements on Peace, 1915-1966,* by Richard C. Detweiler. Scottdale: Herald Press, 1968. Pp. 71. Also *The Christian and Warfare,* by Jacob J. Enz. Scottdale: Herald Press, 1972. Pp. 95. Also *Christian Pacifism in History,* by Geoffrey F. Nuttall. Berkeley: World Without War Council, 1971. Pp. 84. Also *Nevertheless,* by John H. Yoder. Scottdale, Herald Press, 1971. Pp. 144. *MQR* 48 (Apr., 1974), 269-72. Describes, with limited analysis, these four books presenting distinctive perspectives on Christian peace concerns.

Burkholder, John D. "War a Delusion." *GH* 37 (Sept. 8, 1944), 454. To believe that the sword can bring peace is is a delusion. Only the spirit of love can transform an enemy and bring life instead of death.

Burkholder, Roy (Review). *The Original Revolution,* by John H. Yoder. Scottdale: Herald Press, 1972. Pp. 189. *GH* 66 (Nov. 6, 1973), 855. A helpful collection of Yoder's articles and lectures articulating the conviction that pacifism as practiced by the disciple community is a key to Christian faithfulness and social change.

Burrell, Curtis E., Jr. "Nonresistance: 'For

Mennonites Only'?" *GH* 59 (Aug. 16, 1966), 731. Our call to preach and witness includes the call to nonresistant living. Mennonites are careful to limit nonresistance to themselves in order not to lose their privileges.

Byler, Frank. "A History of the Nonresistant People of Logan and Champaign Counties, 1917-1918." Paper presented to Social Science Seminar, Goshen College, Goshen, Ind., n.d. Pp. 32. MHL.

Byler, Raymond. "The Nature of Christianity." *GH* 52 (Dec. 15, 1959), 1057, 1069. Understanding Christianity as "a life to be lived" rather than as only a "story to be believed" leads followers to forsake all activities which result in the destruction of human lives.

"Cheyenne Leader Switches from Military to Ministry." *CanMenn* 9 (Dec. 1, 1961), 4. Laurence Hart discusses the Cheyenne and the doctrine of nonresistance.

"Conference on Nonresistance and Political Responsibility." Papers presented and discussion summaries, Laurelville, PA, Sept. 21-22, 1956. Pp. 54. MHL.

Capuano, Thomas M. "The Nightmare." *With* 11 (Feb., 1978), 16. Because of his efforts in working with the poor as a Mennonite Central Committee volunteer, Capuano was imprisoned.

Charles, Howard H. "Paul and the Way of Love." *Builder* 29 (Oct., 1979), 28-32. Focuses Paul's teachings on the way of love by examining three areas: love and the Christian community; love and the state; love and the enemy.

Chatfield, Charles. "Nonviolence and the Peace Movement: the Americanization of Gandhi." *MennLife* 25 (Oct., 1970), 155-59. As a result of Gandhi's nonviolent opposition to injustice and strife, Martin Luther King, Jr., and many others, including some Mennonites, followed his example in a nonviolent stance.

Claassen, Edith. "The History of the Doctrine of Nonresistance Among Mennonites During the Revolutionary and Civil Wars." Student paper for Constructive English, Nov. 20, 1944. Pp. 22. MLA/BeC.

Coon, Helen C. *The House at the Back of the Lot.* Newton: Faith and Life Press, 1982. Pp. 147. Thirteen-year-old Ellen Schmidt lives with her family in the city of Chicago. The time is 1944 and, because her family believes in nonresistance, she must struggle with feelings of alienation as her school class competes to buy war bonds. Through her parents' example and patient explanation, as well as other experiences of growth, she comes to a better understanding of her heritage and a greater appreciation for it.

Crous, Ernst. "The Mennonites in Germany Since the Thirty Years War." *MQR* 25 (Oct., 1951), 235-62. In the 18th and 19th centuries, German Mennonites became increasingly acculturated, thus losing almost completely the principle of nonresistance.

Culp, Richard. "Comparison of Mennonite-Related Groups." *ST* 21 (3rd Qtr., 1953), 24. A study of groups of Mennonite origin focusing on the factors that influence nonresistance.

Culp, Richard. "The Relationship of Calvinism to Nonresistance." *ST* 21 (3rd Qtr., 1953), 14. The difference between people who embrace Calvinism and people who embrace nonresistance is cradled in the different viewpoints concerning the Scriptures.

"Delegates Agree Bible Teaches Non-Resistance." *CanMenn* 2 (Apr. 16, 1954), 1, 3. Issues discussed at GCMC Peace Study Conference in Winnipeg on Apr. 9-10, 1954, included absolutism, non-combatant service, positive alternatives to war, and the biblical basis of nonresistance.
*

"Dr. H. Bender Speaks to Peace Conference." *CanMenn* 1 (July 3, 1953), 1, 4. J. A. Toews and H. S. Bender address conference sponsored by the Canadian Conference and MB churches. Toews spoke of the purpose of the church as the proclaimation of the salvation of the cross. Bender gave a summary of the history of Mennonite nonresistance and the Christian view of the state.

"Dutch Mennonites Return to Non-Violence." *Fellowship* 14 (Jan., 1948), 25. Half of Holland's Mennonite ministers have indicated their willingness to return to the principles of nonresistance.

"Dwight L. Moody and War." *ChrMon* 43 (Feb., 1951), 43-44. Discusses the little-known fact of Moody's nonresistance to war.

"Dwight L. Moody and War." *GH* 43 (Apr. 18, 1950), 371, 382. Describes Dwight L. Moody as a nonresistant Christian and quotes extensively from his famous sermon on forgiveness, "Good News."

"Dwight L. Moody and War." *GH Supplement* 35 (Feb., 1943), 1022-23. Reprint of tract. The story of Moody's nonresistant faith.

Dabit, Raji Joseph. "The Doctrine of Nonresistance." Research paper for Anabaptist History class. 1970. Pp. 12. Bfc.

DeKoster, Lester. "Anabaptism at 450: A Challenge, A Warning." *ChrToday* 20 (Oct. 24,

---

*For additional listing, see Supplement, pp. 717-719.

1975), 75-78. Commends Anabaptist courage and emphasis on practical consequences of faith, while criticizing consistent pacifism as undermining the state's legitimate use of force to maintain order.

Derstine, C. F. "Fertile Soil for our Peace Testimony." *ChrMon* 29 (Apr., 1937), 126. Suggests sending traveling peace teams from city to city to teach nonresistance.

Derstine, C. F. "THe Greatest Battle a Colonel Ever Lost, But Really Won It." *ChrMon* 33 (Aug., 1941), 254. Story of nonresistant people in the Tyrol meeting the Austrian army demonstrates that nonresistant Christians do not depend on the "powers that be" for protection.

Derstine, C. F. "The New Army—The New War for the Old War." *ChrMon* 28 (Oct., 1936), 319-20. Nonresistance has both a negative side, opposing war, and a positive side, overcoming evil with good.

Derstine, Kenton M. "The Nonresistance of the Mennonites in Southeastern Pennsylvania During the Revolutionary War." Term paper for Mennonite History and Thought course, Feb. 15, 1972. Pp. 44. MSHL.

Derstine, Mark M. "A Comprehensive Survey of the *Christian Exponent* on the Themes of Nonresistance, Peace, and War." Term paper for Mennonite History and Thought course, Nov., 1970. Pp. 21. MSHL.

Doerbaum, Lloyd A. "A Biblical Critique of War, Peace, and Nonresistance." Thesis paper for Dallas Theological Seminary. 1969. Pp. 64. BfC.

Drescher, John M. "Approach to Peace." *GH* 56 (Oct. 15, 1963), 907; *ChrLead* 26 (Oct. 29, 1963), 2. In contrast to humanistic, Gandhian, moralistic, and political pacifism, Christian pacifism is rooted in Jesus and his teaching. The Christian's peace testimony depends upon the presence of the Prince of Peace.

Drescher, John M. "Why Christians Shouldn't Carry the Sword." *Christianity Today* 24 (Nov. 7, 1980), 15-17, 20-23. Discusses the theological components of a biblical pacifism, claiming that concepts such as the cosmic Christ, the global appeal of the gospel, and the internationalism of the church imply that a proper national loyalty is a limited loyalty. Bible and peace

Drescher, John M. *Why I Am a Conscientious Objector.* Scottdale: Herald Press, 1982. Pp. 73. Introductory chapter provides brief overview of the different kinds of pacifism, different approaches used to sanction war and a comparison of the just war theory with the principles of nonresistance. Subsequent chapters provide brief discussions of such

pacifist rationale as the example of Christ, the global nature of the Gospel, an understanding of the church as universal, biblical limitation of governmental authority, and the church's nonresistant tradition.

Drescher, John M. "Would Revival Bring Peace?" *GH* 63 (July 21, 1970), 617. Why a real spiritual revival cannot guarantee peace but possibly ought to result in persecution, ostracism, and suffering.

Drescher, John M. (Editorial). "Will We Awake?" *GH* 61 (Apr. 30, 1968), 385. Editorial reflects on the violence and hate bred into American society and its effects on a person of nonviolence such as Martin Luther King.

Driedger, Leo. "Acceptable and Non-Acceptable Forms of Witness: A Special Study Report on Nonviolence and Civil Disobedience." Leaflet printed by the Canadian Board of Christian Service, Winnipeg, Manitoba, 1966. Pp. 2. Also in *CanMenn* 14 (May 31, 1966), 7-8. Discusses and evaluates the trends in nonviolent protest stimulated by the civil rights movement and the Vietnam war. Analysis includes consideration of Mennonite youth involvement in these trends.

Driedger, Leo. "Native Rebellion and Mennonite Invasion: An Examination of Two Canadian River Valleys." *MQR* 46 (July, 1972), 290-300. A focus on the Red River Valley in Manitoba in 1869-74 and on the Saskatchewan River Valley in 1884-95 in order to determine in what sense peace-loving Mennonites cooperated with a government using force to drive away native Canadians so that the Mennonites could settle.

Driedger, Leo. "Non-Violence and Civil Disobedience: Acceptable and Non-acceptable Forms of Witness." *CanMenn* 14 (May 31, 1966), 7, 8. A discussion of several prominent leaders of nonviolence, nonviolent methods used today, new trends in nonviolence etc.

Dueck, Abe (Review). *Kingdom, Cross, and Community,* ed. J. R. Burkholder and Calvin Redekop. Scottdale: Herald Press, 1976. Pp. 323. *Direction* 7 (July, 1978), 44-46. This collection of essays is both a fitting tribute to Guy F. Hershberger on his 8th birthday and a laudable attempt to "consciously engage in dialogue with the twentieth century" on such issues as fundamentalism, nonresistance and nonviolence, and church and state relations.

Dueck, John. "Forsake 400-Year Tradition; Mennonites Enter Politics by the Dozen." *MennRep* 6 (Jan. 12, 1976), 10-11. Dueck reflects on Mennonite tradition of expressing nonresistance through refusing public office; interviews Canadian Mennonite politicians.

Durland, William R. *No King But Caesar?* Scottdale: Herald Press, 1975. Pp. 182. Catholic lawyer urges Christians to assume the risk of nonviolence through faith and hope. Argument proceeds in three sections: an examination of the pacifist and nonresistant ethic of the biblical materials, especially the Sermon on the Mount and Isaiah; an historical overview of Christian responses to state violence, from the apostolic peace gospel and the pacifism of the early church, through the Constantinian synthesis to the contemporary confusion; an analysis of that contemporary confusion concerning the demands of God and Caesar, particularly in the context of the Roman Catholic church.

Dyck, C. J. (Review). *The Doctrine of Love and Nonresistance,* by Harley J. Stucky. N.p.: By the Author, 1955. Pp. 60. *MennLife* 10 (Oct., 1955), 192. Booklet places nonresistance in its historical setting in Palestine of Jesus' time and the church of the first three centuries.

Dyck, Gary A. "Test of Faith." Student paper for Church History, Hesston College, May 19, 1965. Pp. 8. MLA/BeC.

Dyck, Peter J. "Entering Holland." *MCC WSRB* 1 (Sept., 1945), 1-2. Describes conditions in Holland as a result of the war, and the stance of Dutch Mennonites toward nonresistance.

Dyck, Walter H. "Lasting Peace." *Menn* 51 (Mar. 10, 1936), 3-4. Before forsaking Christian nonresistance for the liberal "Peace Program," Mennonites should remember that lasting peace comes only to those who have accepted Jesus as Savior and Lord.

Dymond. "The Opinions of the Primitive Christians on the Lawfulness of War." *GH* 44 (Mar. 20, 1951), 274-75, 285. Reprinted from *Herald of Truth* (Dec., 1866). Christ, the disciples, and the first Christians disavowed any part in the military. Quotations from early church sources show numerous incidences of this stand.

Ediger, Donovan. Letter to the Editor. *ChrLead* 40 (July 5, 1977), 21. Understands the Mennonite Brethren church position on nonresistance to be a position that sets the MBs apart from other evangelical churches.

Ediger, Elmer. "Christian Discipleship in Time of War and Peace." *CanMenn* 2 (May 7, 1954), 6, 7. The Christian's nonresistant stand is to be expressed both in times of war and in times of peace. Whether we choose voluntary service, prison, or some other alternative requires the guidance of the Spirit and the Christian community.

Ediger, Elmer. "Nonviolence and Nonresistance." *Menn* 72 (May 28, 1957), 342. Points out the difference between nonviolence, as practiced by Gandhi and Martin Luther King, and New Testament nonresistance. What is the Christian way of dealing with the oppressor?

Ediger, Elmer and Waltner, Erland, eds.; Wiebe, Willard; Gundy, Wilma; and Dyck, C. J., writers; Jost, Norma and Duerkesen, Roland, assistants. *Youth and Christian Love.* Newton: Mennonite Publication Office, n.d. Pp. 69. Thirteen study lessons for young people on nonresistance as a way of life.

Ediger, Peter J. (Review). *The Politics of Nonviolent Action,* by Gene Sharp. Boston: Porter Sargent Publisher, 1973. Pp. 1,000. *Menn* 88 (Dec. 11, 1973), 724. Reviewer expresses hope in the power of nonviolent actions, as documented by Sharp, and dismay in Sharp's perspective of viewing nonviolence as a political strategy apart from a faith or worldview.

Edwards, George R. (Review). *The Politics of Jesus,* by John H. Yoder. Grand Rapids: Eerdmans, 1972. Pp. 260. *MQR* 48 (Oct., 1974), 537-38. Commends Yoder's contribution to studies in Christian pacifism and political responsibility, but disagrees with Yoder's conclusions regarding the Year of Jubilee and "revolutionary subordination" in the household codes.

Eller, Vernard. *King Jesus' Manual of Arms for the 'Armless.* Nashville: Abingdon Press, 1973. Pp. 205. Revised and reprinted by Scottdale: Herald Press, *War and Peace from Genesis to Revelation,* 1981. Makes a case for scriptural unity on pacifism by saying that the Old Testament holy war and Zion traditions, rightly understood, provide the framework within which the New Testament Christians understood Jesus' life, death, and resurrection. The last few chapters apply this concept to the contemporary scene.

Enns, Alvin. "Can We Love Our Enemies?" *MBH* 14 (Oct. 31, 1975), 6-7, 31. God's love means redemption for, not vengeance on, enemies of the state, enemies of society, and individual enemies.

Ens, Henk. "The History of Nonresistance in the Netherlands." 1948. Pp. 12. MLA/BeC.

Enz, Jacob J. *The Christian and Warfare. The Roots of Pacifism in the Old Testament.* Scottdale: Herald Press, 1972. Pp. 95. Given originally as the Menno Simons Lectures at Bethel College, North Newton, Kans., in 1957. An exegetical-theological analysis of the roots of biblical pacifism in such concepts as creation, covenant, kingdom, incarnation, substitution, proclamation, and messianic hope. From the compassion of Joseph, through the literature of the Suffering Servant, and "the quiet pacifist cosmogony of Genesis 1 and 2" and Isaiah 53, the implicit pacifism in the Old Testament prepares for the explicit pacifism in the New Testament.

Epp, Bryan. "History and Nonresistant Doctrine of *The Sword and Trumpet.*" Student paper for Mennonite History, Life, and Thought, Jan. 28, 1985. Pp. 14.

*
Epp, Edgar W. "Prisons Must Help People, and Not Only Hold Them." *CanMenn* 13 (Mar. 9, 1965), 3. Letter from Epp to his friends upon his appointment as superintendent of the Provincial Correctional Institution at Prince Albert, Sask. Letter reflects Epp's thinking on the nonresistant position and his conclusion that if good people do not serve in government institutions bad people will.

Epp, Edgar W. "The Church and the Offender." *MBH* 11 (Feb. 11, 1972), 3-5. Analyzes various methods of dealing with offenders and considers what might be the outcome if practices of nonresistant love were applied to the system of corrections.

Epp, Frank H. "Japan Pacifist Leanings Being Put to the Test." *CanMenn* 14 (Mar. 22, 1966), 1, 2. Pressures from the USA and from other sources to have Japan become militarily involved are being objected to by the press and the churches (not all) and by society on the whole.

Epp, Frank H. "A Nearly Non-existent Non-resistance." *CanMenn* 11 (Mar. 8, 1963), 6. Concludes that evidence is strong that nonresistance among Mennonites is nearly nonexistent.

Epp, Frank H. "Non-Resistant Love and Evangelism." *CanMenn* 4 (Mar. 9, 1956), 2. Christian love and nonresistance cannot and must not be separated from evangelism since they are both fundamental elements in the biblical message; nonresistance is not a cultural appendage.

Epp, Frank H. "Primary and Secondary Doctrines." *CanMenn* 3 (Aug. 5, 1955), 2. Nonresistance is called a secondary doctrine by some people. To distinguish between primary and secondary doctrines is both dangerous and unbiblical. Christ did not separate love of God from love of humans, and it is wrong for the church to do so.

Epp, Frank H. "The Christian Response to the Communist Advance: Four Radio Talks." Mennonite Radio Mission, Sept., 1961. Pp. 16. MHL.

Epp, George K. (Review). *No Strangers in Exile,* by Hans Harder. *MennLife* 34 (Dec., 1979), 28. Describes the content and intent of this book which tells the experience of Mennonite martyrs in the Russian labor camps in order to draw the attention of the world to this unbelievable suffering. Commends the book and its excellent translation.

Epp, Henry H. "The Word of God in the Nuclear Age." *CanMenn* 7 (May 29, 1959), 2. An interpretation of the Church Peace Mission conference at Evanston, Ill. The military chaplaincy, civil disobedience, and nonviolence as a means of social change were among the topics discussed.

Epp, J. B. "Refusing to Go to War." *Menn* 52 (Nov. 23, 1937), 1. Nonresistance does not even allow for participation in wars that are only "defensive" in nature.

Epp, Theodore H. *Should God's People Partake in War? A Study on Nonresistance in the Old and New Testaments.* Inman, Kans.: By the Author, n.d. Pp. 25. MHL. While war will continue as long as there is sin, the only warfare permitted to the people of God is spiritual warfare. Material warfare is to be left to those who are not God's people because only God fights for the people of God.

Epp, Theodore H. "The Attitude of the Early Christians Toward War." *GH* 30 (Oct. 21, 1937), 649-50. Historical survey of the early church concludes that the church held to the nonresistance principle only to drift away from it after several centuries.

Erb, Elizabeth. " 'Bless, and Curse Not.' " *ChrMon* 36 (July, 1944), 194, 198. Story about a schoolteacher's nonresistant attitude toward an angry parent.

Erb, Paul. "A Call to Prayer." *GH* 43 (Aug. 29, 1950), 851. Comments on plans for a day of prayer for peace. Calls for prayer that people will realize that faults lie on both sides of the Korean conflict, and that Mennonites will have the courage to preach and live nonresistance.

Erb, Paul. "Discipleship of Love." *GH* 47 (May 4, 1954), 411. The negative emphasis of nonresistance is not totally sufficient to deal with class conflicts, racial tensions, and military rivalries. There must also be a positive demonstration of love.

Erb, Paul. "Love the Russians." *GH Supplement* 40 (Oct., 1947), 643-44. The Christian is not called to struggle against any political or economic order. Rather, the Christian tries to understand the enemy, to see where one's own failures, and to be helpful to the enemy as opportunity occurs.

Erb, Paul. "Nonresistance and Litigation." *MQR* 13 (Apr., 1939), 75-82. Nonresistance is to be integrated into the Christian's total life-style;

---

*For additional listing, see Supplement, pp. 717-719.

going through law courts to settle conflicts is foreign to the spirit of the loving fellowship.

Erb, Paul. "The Nonresistant Personality." *ChrLiv* 1 (July 1954), 7, 41. The truly nonresistant person is one who cultivates a character of love and meekness.

Erb, Paul. "Pacifism vs. Nonresistance." *GH* 37 (May 12, 1944), 107. It is increasingly evident that the only valid ground for refusal to participate in war is that God has forbidden Christian participation. Pacifism based on human reason usually disintegrates under the pressures of wartime.

Erb, Paul. "Preparing for the Next War." *GH* 39 (June 18, 1946), 243. Mennonites must preach and teach clearly the principles of nonresistance to the young people. Such peace teaching is the best possible preparation for a future war.

Esau, John A. "The Congressional Debates on the Coming of the Russian Mennonites." Paper presented to the Anabaptist-Mennonite History class, MBS, Elkhart, Ind., June 2, 1961. Pp. 31. AMBS.

Evert, J. G. "The Other Side: A Plea for Fair Play to the COs by a Mennonite." Paper, n.d. Pp. 4. MHL.

Ewert, Alden H. "Why Alternate Service." *ChrLead* 17 (Aug. 1, 1953), 4. Love of neighbors and enemies necessitates total rejection of participation in violence and suggests instead constructive service, e.g., in mental health services or in ministry to war-torn Korea.

"Fifteen Goshen Students Marched in Alabama." *CanMenn* 13 (Apr. 20, 1965), 3, 11. Goshen students and Civil Rights demonstrators have common belief in the uses of nonviolence in the search for justice in race relations.

Farrell, Frank. "Mennonites Reaffirm Biblicism and Pacifism." *ChrToday* 3 (Sept. 28, 1959), 23, 24, 29. Reports on General Conference and Mennonite Church conferences, summarizing pertinent issues and describing the theological position of the denominations regarding their views of the Bible and ethics of nonresistance.

Fast, G. H. "Nonviolence as Focused in and Around Joan Baez and Ira Sandperl." Paper for War, Peace, and Revolution class, AMBS, Elkhart, Ind., n.d. Pp. 5. AMBS.

Fencil, Jeannine. "Some Questions on Resistance and Nonresistance." *GH* 71 (July 4, 1978), 530-31. Within the context of a congregational study of nonresistance, Fencil poses probing questions to adherents of both resistance and

nonresistance on the consistency of their convictions.

Ferguson, John. "The Christian Necessity of Pacifism." Chapel address, Goshen College, Goshen, Ind., Jan. 27, 1969. Pp. 3. MHL, MLA/BeC.

Fieguth, Wolfgang G. "The Rise and Decline of the Principle of Nonresistance Among the Mennonites in Prussia." Paper presented to the Mennonite History and Peace Principles classes, Bethel College, North Newton, Ks., July, 1948. Pp. 73. MHL, MLA/BeC.

Fisk Student Panel. "The Protest Movement." *IPF Notes* 7 (May, 1961), 5-9. Panel at IPF conference discusses nonviolence and the race protest movement.

Fransen, Herta. "J. W. Fretz Sees Loss of Nonresistance." *CanMenn* 6 (Feb. 7, 1958), 1. Fretz lectures in Ontario churches and points out the decline of interest in nonresistance. Statistics are cited and stages in this decline are outlined.

Freed, Sara Ann. "Violence: A Way into the Inner City." *With* 2 (Oct., 1969), 17. The discussion of two experiences that answer the question, "What happens when Mennonites are exposed to the violence and aggression of city living?"

Fretz, Clarence Y. "Nonresistance Is More Than a Mennonite Doctrine." *ST* 13 (May, 1945), 303. States that nonresistance was taught by Christ and the apostles long before Mennonites existed. Surveys the many groups that have or embrace a nonresistant doctrine.

Fretz, J. Winfield. "CO's—Hold On!" *YCC* 37 (Apr. 15, 1956), 125. Evidence that principles of pacifism are growing in larger society while among historic peace churches pacifist philosophy is declining.

Fretz, J. Winfield. "Mennonites Are Losing Their Biblical Nonresistance." *Menn* 66 (June 12, 1951), 376, 385. Compares statistics from World War I and World War II and then attributes the erosion of conviction on nonresistance more to forces from within the church than to external factors.

Fretz, J. Winfield. "Nonresistance and the Social Order." N.d. Pp. 37. MLA/BeC.

Fretz, J. Winfield. "The Church's Attitude Toward Organized Labor." *Menn* 61 (June 18, 1946), 5-6. The church must be concerned to break down class warfare; it must teach ethical sensitivity regarding exploitation and adhere to love and nonviolence in the midst of "industrial warfare."

Fretz, J. Winfield. "Why Mennonite Boys Choose Military Service." (Part 2) *Menn* (July 31, 1945), 5-6. The position of drafted men generally reflects the attitudes of their pastors. The census as a whole indicates that the General Conference is losing its doctrine of biblical nonresistance.

Fretz, Mark J. "Nonresistance During World War II: A Comparison of the (Old) Mennonites and General Conference Mennonite Positions." Term paper for Mennonite History and Thought Course, Feb. 20, 1978. Pp. 17. MSHL.

Frey, Philemon L. "Lessons from the World War: for Conscientious Objectors." *The Eastern Mennonite School Journal* 18 (Apr., 1940), 42-45. Twelve "lessons"—all the way from "In time of war it is best to keep our eyes and ears open and our mouths shut" to "It is best to stay out of politics" to "Nonresistance should be practiced in times of peace as well as in time of war," etc.

Frey, Philemon L. "Nonresistance Taught in the Scriptures." *The Eastern Mennonite School Journal* 18 (Apr., 1940), 18-21. Despite the fact that God permitted the Israelites to practice warfare, the divine intention was, from the very beginning, that God's people should live by the principles of nonresistance.

Friedmann, Robert. "An Anabaptist Ordinance of 1633 on Nonresistance." *MQR* 25 (Apr., 1951), 116-27. Text and commentary on an ordinance on self-defense in the *Smaller Chronicle* of the Hutterites. Provides a simple, authoritative statement on the Anabaptist way of discipleship.

Friesen, Ivan. "Springtime and Death in the Jordan Valley." *CanMenn* 17 (Apr. 8, 1969), 3. Perhaps the best contribution of Mennonites in the Middle East is to live the nonviolence which they profess.

Friesen, Lauren. *Is There No Peace?* Seattle: Crockett and Howe Press, 1979. Pp. 37. MHL. When Caroline Miller's return flight from a study tour in Athens is hijacked, her family must decide whether to cooperate with the state department's "get tough with terrorists" stance or whether their beliefs about peace and nonviolence lead them to respond to the hijackers' demands in another way. One-act play for eight actors.

Friesen, Lyle. "The Russian Mennonite Selbstschutz in its Historical Perspective." MCC Canada Scholarship paper, Apr. 30, 1973. Pp. 29. CGCL.

Friesen, Mrs. Dee. Letter to the Editor. *ChrLead* 41 (Jan. 31, 1978), 16. Pacifism is a very privileged position. There are many members of the military who are just as devout and sincere Christians as the "best" Mennonites.

Friesen, Steven K. "The Rise of Mennonite Social Consciousness, 1899-1905." Paper presented to Seminar in Political and Social History, Bethel College, Newton, Ks., Dec. 9, 1973. Pp. 44. MHL, MLA/BeC.

Froese, Peter J. "The Problem of Nonresistance as the Mennonites of Russia Dealt with It." N.d. Pp. 21. MLA/BeC.

Froese, Richard J. Letter to the Editor. *MennRep* 8 (Mar. 20, 1978), 6. Mennonite nonresistance has degenerated into legalistic practices of nonparticipation in war and ministering to material needs, rather than loving enemies and ministering to people spiritually as Jesus did.

Fundenburg, Harry C. "Military Training Unchristian." *GH* 28 (Nov. 14, 1935), 706-707. Military training, war, and killing of any sort are not sanctioned by the New Testament. The Church of the Brethren has since its beginning opposed war and maintained the principle of nonresistance.

Funk, John F. "A Centennial." *GH* 69 (May 4, 1976), 384-85. Reprints an article from an 1876 issue of the *Herald of Truth*, apparently written by the editor Funk, which calls nonresistant and nonconformed Mennonites to use the nation's centennial as an opportunity to pray for the government, instead of taking part in the festivities.

Funk, John F. *Warfare. Its Evils Our Duty. Addressed to the Mennonite Churches Throughout the United States, and All Others Who Sincerely Seek and Love the Truth.* Chicago: By the Author, 1863. Pp. 16. MHL. Despite the pressures of society and the lure of military glory, let us remain faithful to the example of Jesus, who lived the nonresistant life in every way.
*
"Graduates Ask, What Is Nonviolence." *Menn* 87 (Jan. 18, 1972), 40. Mennonite graduate students conference on nonviolence includes such topics as: testing a fifth-grade history curriculum; applying nonviolent problem solving models to government and organizations; and critical analyses of MCC involvement in the Middle East.
*
Gaeddert, Albert M. and Lehman, Carl M. "Towards Understanding." *Menn* 61 (Nov. 5, 1946), 3-5. An attempt by two nonresistant Christians to articulate the stance of both the "militaristic Christian" and that of the "nonresistant Christian." Each writes first from the militarist's point of view and then states why he himself as a nonresistant Christian cannot take part in war.

Gaeddert, Albert M. "Turning the Other Cheek."

---

*For additional listing, see Supplement, pp. 717-719.

*Menn* 66 (Jan. 23, 1951), 57. Nonresistance is the spirit that characterized Jesus' whole life and teaching and that spirit must also characterize the witness and service that is needed today.

Gascho, Timothy N. "A Survey of Articles on Nonresistance in the *Gospel Herald* (1909-1913) and (1919-1924)." Term paper for Mennonite History and Theology course, 1970. Pp. 10. MSHL.

Geissinger, Marjorie. "TV—Is Your Family Turned On?" *Menn* 91 (Feb. 10, 1976), 92-93. Examines the prevalence of violence on television, especially during children's shows, and urges nonresistant parents to carefully monitor TV use.

General Conference Mennonite Church. *The Gospel, Discipleship, and Nonresistance.* Winnipeg: Canadian Peace and Service Committee, n.d. Fifteen papers read at the conference in Winnipeg, Apr. 9-10, 1954.

General Conferences of the Mennonite and Brethren in Christ Churches. "Industrial Relations—A Statement by the Church." *MennComm* 3 (Mar., 1949), 22-27. The gospel's way of peace commands both employers and employees to practice nonresistant love and fairness toward one another.

George, Albert. "The VS Scandal." *GH* 64 (Apr. 20, 1971), 354-55. Reprinted from *Agape* (Nov.-Dec., 1970). Raised a Methodist, the writer was converted to Anabaptist nonresistance through Mennonite writings and relationships. Maintains that just as nonresistance is a scandal when considered pragmatically, so VS service is based on the scandal of the uniqueness of Christian conversion and love.

Gerber, Ellis J. Letter to the Editor. *ChrLiv* 26 (Mar., 1979), 2-3. Nonviolence and pacifism must be instilled into coming generations through limiting children's use of toy guns.

Giesbrichet, H. (Review). *True Nonresistance Through Christ,* by J. A. Toews. Board of General Welfare and Public Relations of the Mennonite Brethren Church of North America, 1955. *The Voice* 4 (Sept.-Oct., 1955), 18. The fundamental thesis of this book is that Christ, in his life as well as in his teachings, constitutes the most compelling reason for holding so firmly to the doctrine of nonresistance.

Gingerich, David. "The Reform Movement in Civilian Public Service, 1941-1947." Paper presented to Social Science Seminar, Goshen College, Goshen, Ind., May, 1977. Pp. 64. MHL.

Gingerich, Melvin. "The Anabaptist Vision in Japan." *MennLife* 12 (Oct., 1957), 189-92. Well-trained missionaries are needed, with a vision of the church as a peoplehood. A knowledge of Japanese history and culture will help bridge the many barriers to nonresistance; there is a longing for peace.

Gingerich, Melvin (Archival). Box 18—Peace Committees: General Conference Mennonite, 1935-48; MCC, 1944-48; CPS history, 1938-49. Box 20—Peace Deputation trips. Box 39—Draft; Committee on Armed Service hearing, 1959. Box 40—Civilian Public Service. Box 51—Civil Defense; communism; Congressional Record (debate on universal military training), Feb. 5, 1959; conscientious objectors; Japan Anti-A & H Bomb Conference; Japan and peace. Box 52—peace clippings; peace conferences; Peace Problems Committee reports Puidoux Theological Conference. Box 53—peace and Mennonites. Box 62—"The Christian and Revolution;" church-state relations; communism. Box 64—"Nonresistance and Social Justice;" Peace Institutes; Peace/War. Box 91—Service for Peace; CPS history and correspondence. Goshen, Ind., AMC Hist. Mss. 1-129.

Gingerich, Melvin. "Ye Are the Salt of the Earth; Christian Youth and the State." *YCC* 22, Part 4 (Jan. 12, 1941), 432. True Christians are the "salt of the earth." While other people may say that nonresistant Christians are not contributing to society, the truth is that nonresistant Christians are those preserving society.

Gingerich, Ray C. "The Sword in the Disputations Between the Swiss Anabaptists and Zwinglian Reformers, 1531-1538." Paper presented to the History of Christian Thought class, AMBS, Elkhart, Ind., spring, 1969. Pp. 24. AMBS.

Gish, Arthur G. "Sacrificial Love." *Post-American* 3 (Nov., 1974), 9-11. A proper understanding of Jesus' life, death, and resurrection leads to a commitment to nonviolence.

Gleijsteen, Jan, Sr. "A Nonresistance Movement." *GH* 52 (Dec. 15, 1959), 1057. Report on the formation of a group of persons in Amsterdam who want to donate their time and energy to promoting nonresistance and its application to daily living.

Glick, Jesse B. Letter to the Editor. *GH* 61 (May 7, 1968), 418. Eulogizes Martin Luther King and his commitment to love and nonviolence, drawing a parallel between the treatment accorded King and that given to Jesus.

Godshalk, Jacob, *et al.* "An Appeal from Pennsylvania Mennonites to the Mennonites of Holland for Aid in Maintaining the Principles of Nonresistance in the Face of Approaching War." Skippack, Pa., Oct. 19, 1745. Pp. 3. MHL. (Typewritten copy, in English, n.d.)

Goering, James A. "Martin Luther King and the Gandhian Method of Nonviolent Resistance." *ST* 36 (Oct., 1968), 1. The philosophy of nonviolent resistance embodies enough Christian truth and has done enough good in the past decade in rectifying social ills, that well-meaning but undiscerning Christians may find themselves not only sympathetic to the movement, but actively supporting it without really being aware of its merely semi-Christian aspects.

Goering, James A. (Review). *Martin Luther King, Jr.,* by William Robert Miller. New York: Weybright and Talley, 1968. *ST* 38 (Mar., 1970), 17. Both a biography and an interpretation of his role in the movement in which King played the leading role.

Goering, Paul L. and Fretz, J. Winfield (Review). *The Theological Basis of Christian Pacifism,* by Charles E. Raven. New York: Fellowship Pub., 1951, pp. 87; *The Dagger and the Cross,* by Culbert G. Rutenber. New York: Fellowship Pub., 1950, pp. 134; *Conscientious Objection,* Special Monograph No. 11 by Selective Service. Washington, DC: Government Printing Office, n.d., Vol. I, pp. 342, Vol. II, pp. 288; *Conscription of Conscience: the American State and the Conscientious Objector, 1940-1947,* by Mulford Q. Sibley and Philip E. Jacob. Ithaca: Cornell U. Press, 1952, pp. 580. "The Conscientious Objector in Recent Literature." *MennLife* 8 (Jan., 1953), 43-46. Reviewers recommend these four books on pacifism and the conscientious objector as "significant."

Goertzen, Gaylord L. "A Survey of the Beliefs and Teachings on Nonresistance of Mennonite Brethren Pastors in the USA." Research project (MDiv), 1978. Pp. 49. MBBS.

Goertzen, Gaylord L. "What Our Pastors Believe and Teach." *ChrLead* 41 (Apr. 25, 1978), 8. A survey that studies the beliefs of MB church pastors concerning nonresistance.

Good, I. Merle. *Who Burned the Barn Down? A Play in One Act.* Lancaster: Good Enterprises, Ltd., 1970. Pp. 51. MHL. The doctrine and practice of nonresistance are sources of tension and disagreement in the King family as the members are caught up in the issues and struggles of the Civil War and its destructive effects on their eastern Pennsylvania community.

Good, Noah G. "Applying Nonresistance in Agriculture, Business, and Industry in Peacetime and Wartime." *MennComm* 6 (Jan., 1952), 17-19, 32. Author relates biblical principles of nonresistance to everyday practices.

Graber, Eldon W. "What Do You Mean?—

Nonresistance." *Menn* 52 (May 11, 1937), 9-10. Nonresistance is a sound doctrine and could have great implications if it were not hidden, as a great light, under a bushel.

Graber, J. D. "Nonresistance and Missions." Elkhart, IN, n.d. Pp. 4. MLA/BeC.

Graber, Ralph. "Evaluation of the McCrackin Case as Related to Radical Pacifism." Paper for War, Peace, and Revolution class, AMBS, Elkhart, Ind., Jan., 1961. AMBS.

Groff, Weyburn W. *Nonviolence: a Comparative Study of Mohandas K. Gandhi and the Mennonite Church on the Subject of Nonviolence.* Unpublished doctoral dissertation, New York Univ., Dept. of Education, 1963. Pp. 242. Using twentieth century sources representing the (Old) Mennonite Church and the collected writings of M. K. Gandhi, the research demonstrates similarities and differences in concept and application in respect to social and political action.

Gross, Harold H. "The Christian Dilemma. The Politics of Morality." *MennLife* 23 (Apr., 1968), 59-63. A discussion of conscience, politics, pacifism, and patriotism. The need for sharpening Christian moral sensitivity must be a major concern.

Gross, Leonard, ed. "The First World War and Mennonite Nonresistance." *MHB* 33 (July, 1972), 4-10. Series of government and private documents traces Mennonite experiences in the war: correspondence with the Secretary of War on conscientious objection; procedures for military induction and discharge; treatment of COs in detention; public pressure to buy war bonds; government suspicion of tract on nonresistance; germinal ideas for alternative service in reconstruction.

Gross, Leonard; Hill, J. W.; and Steiner, M. S. "Is War Justifiable?" *MHB* 37 (Jan., 1976), 2-6. Steiner takes issue with the expansionist viewpoint of Hill's article, responding in a lengthy essay recommending nonresistance. Gross introduces the dialogue and comments on it.

Gross, Wesley. Letter to the Editor. *GH* 66 (July 31, 1973), 596-97. Calls Mennonites to refrain from criticizing governmental policies, since the state "stems the tide of lawlessness" and encourages Christians to spread the gospel. Mennonites should instead simply practice nonresistance.

"Hold Peace Conference." *CanMenn* 2 (Mar. 12, 1954), 8. A number of speakers address the Didsbury Peace Conference, stressing the centrality of regeneration through Jesus as the mainspring of nonresistance.

Habegger, David L. "How Is the Present Day Nonresistance Related to 16th-Century Martyrdom?" Student paper for Mennonite History, May 25, 1945. Pp. 11. MLA/BeC.

Habegger, David L. "'Nonresistance and Responsibility'—a Critical Analysis." *Concern* 7 (July, 1959), 33-40. Identification of a failure to see that "love is righteous" is an apparent weakness of Kaufman's article "Nonresistance and Responsibility" (*Concern* [Nov., 1958]).

Harder, Geraldine. "Through Children's Eyes: A Report of Discussions on Nonconformity and Nonresistance as Perceived by a Class of Fifth-Graders." *Builder* 18 (Jan., 1968), 6-8. Children's answers to "How are Christians different?" and "Is it wrong to fight back?"

Harder, Hans; trans. Reimer, Al. "The Wind Blows North." *MennMirror* 8 (Nov., 1978), 13-16. Reprinted from the opening pages of Hans Harder's novel, *In Wologdas Weissen Wälder* (1934), which tells the tragic story of Mennonite families who were transported to Russia's Far North by freight train in 1930.

Harder, Leland. "Mennonites and Contemporary Cultural Change." *The Lordship of Christ (Proceedings of the Seventh Mennonite World Conference.* Ed. Cornelius J. Dyck. Elkhart: MWC, 1962, 440-51. Includes a study of conscientious objection in the General Conference Mennonite Church. An inverse correlation was found to exist between evangelism and nonresistance. Includes three tables and one graph.

Harder, Leland. "Zwingli's Reaction to the Schleitheim Confession of Faith of the Anabaptists." *Sixteenth Century Journal* 11 (Winter, 1980), 51-66. Discussion on Zwingli's objections to article six concludes that Zwingli did not adequately appreciate the legitimacy assigned to the sword "outside the perfection of Christ," he did not fully believe the Anabaptist claim of nonresistance because he thought they had used violence, at times, for their own ends; he considered the rejection of political power *not* to be the issue in the biblical passages cited by the Confession.

Harder, Teresa. "The Political Relevance of Pacifism." Senior Honours Paper for Peace and Conflict Studies course, Sept., 1980. Pp. 37. CGCL.

Harding, Vincent G. "Black Power and the American Christ." *Christian Century* 84 (Jan. 4, 1967), 10-13. Suggests that the Black Power movement may bear God's message for the church. One part of that message is the movement's identification of the blasphemous

use of Christ's name to call angry black youth trapped in American ghettos to nonviolence while, at the same time and in the same name, to offer these youth no future except military service, where they must kill other dark-skinned, poor people in order to preserve white America's way of life. Black Power is a repudiation of the American culture-religion and its white Christ; it is a quest for a religious reality more faithful to the black experience.

Harding, Vincent G. "Conscientious Objection: Is It a Christian Response to Vietnam?" *Builder* 17 (Oct., 1967), 12-13. Questions the adequacy of the I-W program as a response to Jesus' call to love the enemy. Identifies a lack of congruence between objecting to war and accepting military protection of that right to object.

*

Hartzler, Jonas S. *Mennonites in the World War or Nonresistance Under Test.* Scottdale: Mennonite Publishing House, 1922. Pp. 246. MHL. Treatment of the World War I conscientious objector experience includes analysis of the issues, summaries of meetings and position papers, descriptions of camp life and life in the disciplinary barracks, congregational reaction, and relief work.

Hartzler, Jonas S. *Nonresistance in Practice.* Scottdale: Mennonite Publishing House, 1930. Pp. 47. Pamphlet includes summary of nonresistance in the early church, Articles 13 and 14 of the Dordrecht confession, a brief history of Mennnonite nonresistance in American wars as well as some more general statements. Intended to inform government officials as well as the youth and other members of the church.

Hartzler, Jonas S. and Kauffman, Daniel. *Mennonite Church History.* Scottdale, Pa.: Mennonite Book and Tract Society, 1905. Pp. 422. MHL. Topics listed in the index under "nonresistance" include nonresistance as taught by Christ, as practiced by the Albigenses, as a doctrine of Waldenses, as an issue which divided the Anabaptists, as a cause for emigration, etc.

Hartzler, Robert W. "What the Layman Can Do for Non-Resistance." *Menn* 66 (Feb. 13, 1951), 106. Encourages a number of activities to promote nonresistance, including discussing it in the public arena, practicing the spirit of nonresistance, and self-education through the study of peace literature.

Hasek, K. Gary. "A Goyim Examines the Religious Basis for Jewish Pacifism." Paper presented to the Theology of Warfare in the Old Testament class, AMBS, Elkhart, Ind., spring, 1981. Pp. 24. AMBS.

*

Henry, Glennys. "Martin Luther, John Calvin, Menno Simons and Nonresistance." Student

---

paper for History of Christianity, Mar. 1, 1946. Pp. 22. MLA/BeC.

Hernley, Elam R. "What It Meant to Be a Conscientious Objector in the World War." *YCC* 20 (Nov. 5, 1939), 769. Among some of the things shared: to be a conscientious objector in the World War meant a testing of nonresistance, an opportunity to witness for Christ, and an appreciation for Christian fellowship.

Hershberger, Guy F. "A Baptist Minister on Nonresistance." *GH* 39 (Oct. 15, 1946), 639. Excerpts from a letter received from a Baptist minister responding to the book *War, Peace, and Nonresistance.*

Hershberger, Guy F. "A Mennonite Analysis of the Montgomery Bus Boycott." Paper presented to the Intercollegiate Peace Fellowship, 1962. Pp. 12. MHL.

Hershberger, Guy F. "Biblical Nonresistance and Modern Pacifism." *MQR* 17 (July, 1943), 115-35. Although biblical nonresistance and modern pacifism seek similar goals (peace and justice), there are important differences. Modern pacifism, based on humanitarian ideals, primarily seeks specific forms of social change; nonresistance expresses, first of all, obedience to the will of God.

Hershberger, Guy F. "Biblical Nonresistance and Modern Pacifism." *GH* 39 (1946), 416. Brief introduction to Franklin H. Littell's article "The Inadequacy of Modern Pacifism" stating that a more sympathetic attitude is developing toward the nonresistant position.

Hershberger, Guy F. *Can Christians Fight? Essays on Peace and War.* Scottdale, Pa.: Mennonite Publishing House, 1940. Pp. 180. Compilation of essays originally written for the readers of *Youth's Christian Companion.* Broad range of topics on the issues of war and peace such as the biblical bases of nonresistance, wars in American history, peace and war in Mennonite history, Mennonite peace work and nonresistance in wartime.

Hershberger, Guy F. "Christian Nonresistance: Its Foundation and its Outreach." *MQR* 24 (Apr., 1950), 156-62; *GH* 44 (Oct. 16, 1951), 1002-1003, 1013. The doctrine of love and nonresistance is an integral part of the Gospel. It has consequences for all areas of life including race, labor, family, community, and nation. If Mennonites are to recover the dynamic of sixteenth century Anabaptism it will be on this biblical basis.

Hershberger, Guy F. "Committee on Economic and Social Relations." *ME* I (1955), 650-51. Major task of this committee has been to assist Mennonite labor employees to maintain the stand of the church (on grounds of nonresistance) against joining labor unions.

Hershberger, Guy F. "How Can We Witness Against the Spirit of Hate Directed Against Russia By Certain Preachers and Church Leaders? Questions of Social Concern for Christians," (Part 17). *GH* 53 (Aug. 2, 1960), 660. A conference resolution on living the nonresistant life.

Hershberger, Guy F. "John Horsch, a Proponent of Biblical Nonresistance." *MQR* 21 (1947), 156-59; *John Horsch Memorial Papers,* Harold S. Bender and others. Scottdale: Mennonite Publishing House, 1947. Pp. 28-31. Hershberger shows how Horsch, throughout his lifetime, used his writings to promote the cause of Biblical peace and nonresistance and to argue against militarism and unscriptural forms of pacifism. A bibliography of his extensive writings on peace. See also the bibliography of all his writings in the same issue of *MQR,* pp. 205-228.

Hershberger, Guy F. "Litigation in Mennonite History." Paper presented at the Laurelville, Pa., conference on "Nonresistance and Political Responsibility," 1956. N.p.: Peace Problems Committee, 1956, 32-35. MHL. Those Mennonites who have been most consistent in rejecting military service have also been most consistent in their refusal to seek legal redress.

Hershberger, Guy F. "Mennonites and the Negro Revolution." *PCMCP Fifteenth,* 112-22. North Newton, Kansas: The Mennonite Press. Held at Bluffton College, Bluffton, Ohio, June 10-11, 1965. Present racial crisis in America presents a ringing challenge to every Mennonite. The Christian view of race relations is based on the way of the Cross, on love and justice.

Hershberger, Guy F. "Nonresistance." *ME* III (1957), 897-906. Surveys of the anabaptist-Mennonite history which has come to use the term "nonresistance" to denote the faith and life of those who believe that the will of God requires the renunciation of warfare and other compulsive means for the furtherance of personal or social ends.

Hershberger, Guy F. "Nonresistance, the Christian Witness, and Communism." Paper, n.d. Pp. 12. MHL.

Hershberger, Guy F. "Nonresistance, the Mennonite Church, and the Race Question." *GH* 53 (June 28, 1960), 577-78, 581-82. Mennonites should not participate in or support discrimination in any way. They should support Martin Luther King although they should guard against accepting all of his theology. They must also guard against confusing nonresistance with obedience to all laws.

Hershberger, Guy F. "Nonresistance and Industrial Conflict." *MQR* 13 (Apr., 1939), 135-54. The industrial conflict is a fight for power with which to achieve social justice, whereas biblical nonresistance enjoins submission even to injustice rather than engage in conflict.

Hershberger, Guy F. "Nonresistance in Time of War." *YCC* 21 (Jan. 7, 1940), 8. It is much easier to talk about nonresistance during times of peace. Lists six things necessary to ensure a nonresistant stance during war.

Hershberger, Guy F. "Nonviolence." *ME* III (1957), 908. Distinguishes between nonviolence and New Testament nonresistance.

Hershberger, Guy F. "On Being True to the Faith of Their Fathers." *YCC* 19 (Sept. 11, 1938), 296. Changing conditions constantly test our faith. Do we have a faith like "the faith of our fathers" and mothers to enable us to remain true to the nonresistant lifestyle?

Hershberger, Guy F. "Pacifism." *Encyclopedia Americana* 21 (1968), 93-96. Definition and historical survey of pacifism.

Hershberger, Guy F. "Pacifism." *ME* IV (1959), 104-105. Lists some of the chief criticisms of modern pacifism from the viewpoint of New Testament nonresistance interpreted by the anabaptist tradition.

Hershberger, Guy F. "Pacifism and the State in Colonial Pennsylvania." *Church History* 8 (Mar., 1939), 54-74. Analyzes William Penn's "holy experiment" and concludes that pacifism, even if necessarily detached from the political order, contributes to society by establishing a moral witness.

Hershberger, Guy F. "Peace and War in the New Testament." *MQR* 17 (Apr., 1943), 59-72. The nonresistant way of life is integral to God's purpose for the church; it corresponds with the whole tenor of the Gospel and is to be practiced in our day.

Hershberger, Guy F. "Quaker Pacifism and the Provincial Government of Pennsylvania, 1682-1756." *University of Iowa Studies in the Social Sciences, Abstracts in History III* 10 (Feb. 15, 1938), 7-18. By combining the ethical position of the Anabaptists with the Calvinist attitude toward the social order, the Society of Friends in the seventeenth century challenged the idea that a given moral order required a particular attitude toward the social order to meet its peculiar needs.

Hershberger, Guy F. "Report on My Term of Service for the Peace Section of the Mennonite Central Committee, June 10, 1949, to Aug. 21, 1950." Mimeographed. Goshen: MHL. Study of pacifism in Europe, the peace attitudes of European Mennonites and the legal status of conscientious objectors in Europe.

Hershberger, Guy F. "Some Religious Pacifists of the Nineteenth Century." *MQR* 10 (Jan., 1936), 73-86. A discussion of the pacifist thought of Jonathan Dymond, Noah Worcester, William Ellery Channing, David Low Dodge, and Adin Ballou.

Hershberger, Guy F. "The Christian's Accommodation to the Organized Industrial Order." *ChrLiv* 3 (Dec., 1956), 22, 32. Summary of guidelines for nonresistant Christian presence in industry.

Hershberger, Guy F. "The Cross in Personal Relations." *ChrLiv* 6 (July, 1959), 27-29. An unloving spirit among church members invalidates a witness to nonresistance.

Hershberger, Guy F. "The Main Point: Doing What Is Right." *ChrLiv* 8 (Apr., 1961), 11-13. The primary emphasis of Mennonite community is not sociological, but ethical: nonresistance, simplicity, etc.

Hershberger, Guy F. "The Role of Pacifism and Pacifism in the Church: The Outlook for Christian Pacifism." Paper at Conference on the Church and Peace, Detroit, Mich., Dec. 7-10, 1953. Pp. 8. MHL.

Hershberger, Guy F. "The Significance of the Mennonite World Conference." *MennComm* 2 (Sept., 1948), 24-25. Review of Mennonites around the world focuses on their commitment to or rejection of nonresistance to war.

Hershberger, Guy F. "Types of Modern Pacifism." Paper read at Indiana Academy of the Social Sciences, 1950. Typescript. Goshen: AMC Hist. MSS 1-171 Box 11. Classifies modern pacifism into three general types: nonresistant tradition, liberal protestant pacifism, and revolutionary tradition of nonviolent coercion. Treats each type historically and shows the role of each in the twentieth century.

Hershberger, Guy F. *War, Peace, and Nonresistance.* Scottdale: Herald Press, 1944. Pp. 375. For many years the standard work in the field. God has one eternal plan for human conduct: love for God and neighbor. This law forbids one to compel another. One rather meets force with nonresistance. In the Old Testament covenant with Israel, God made a concession to the hardness of human hearts by permitting warfare. In the New Testament, Jesus initiates a new covenant in which believers receive a new heart, enabling them to keep God's fundamental moral law. By going to the cross rather than retaliating, Jesus indeed modeled nonresistance perfectly. The early church at first followed Jesus' nonresistant example but gradually applied it less strictly. After Constantine's conversion, the church abandoned nonresistance as an ideal for all Christians. Small Christian sects however retained it, of whom the Mennonites provide a history extending from the sixteenth century to the present. Because nonresistance renounces all coercion, finds its authority in God's will, and takes sin seriously, one should not confuse it with other types of pacifism. Nonresistance implies that Christians will not take part in coercive state functions, will search for alternatives in the complex industrial, agricultural, and economic conflicts of modern life, and will nurture an attitude of brotherhood toward other races. By bringing healing to society, nonresistance serves society in a more essential way than those who take responsibility for running it.

Hershberger, Guy F. "What Did the Early Christians Think About War and State?" *YCC* 17 (Feb. 2, 1936), 40. The first two hundred years of the Church after Christ show that most Christians believed that killing was wrong. There were many martyrs for peace.

Hershberger, Guy F. "What Is the Relationship of Our Peace Message to the Gospel? Our Peace Witness—In the Wake of May 18." (Part 16). *GH* 60 (Dec. 19, 1967), 1134. The New Testament teaching on nonresistance is an integral part of the gospel message.

Hershberger, Guy F. "Why I Am a Nonresistant Christian." Typescript. Address given frequently ca. 1943ff. Goshen: AMC Hist. MSS 1-171 Box 11. Lists several reasons why he takes the nonresistant position.

Hershberger, Guy F. "Why Is the Mennonite Church Doing Relief Work in Spain?" *YCC* 18 (Dec. 5, 1937), 808. There are many relief needs in Spain. Nonresistance is a readiness to sacrifice and to suffer for the sake of Christ, and for the welfare of people.

Hershberger, Guy F. (Review). *Christian Attitudes Toward War and Peace: A Historical Survey and Critical Re-evaluation,* by Roland H. Bainton. New York and Nashville: Abingdon Press, 1960. Pp. 299. *MQR* 35 (1961), 322-24. Hershberger summarizes this book and credits it with giving an excellent analysis of the various attitudes to war and peace in the history of Christendom, as well as of the varieties of pacifism.

Hershberger, Guy F. (Review). *For Peace and Justice: Pacifism in America, 1914-1941,* by Charles Chatfield. Knoxville: Univ. of Tennessee Press, 1971. In *CH* 41 (1972), 418-19. This is the story

of the new Christian (social gospel) pacifism which emerged during World War I and its encounter both with the older (non-pacifist) peace movement and with secular forces working for social justice as all labored together in a kind of unofficial grand alliance for the abolition of war.

Hershberger, Guy F. (Review). *George Fox and the Purefeys: A Study of the Puritan Background in Jenny Drayton in the 16th and 17th Centuries,* by T. Joseph Pickvance. London, Friends' Historical Society, 1970. Pp. 350. *MQR* 45 (1971), 389-90. Hershberger summarizes Pickvance's study of the emergence and roots of Quakerism and Quaker pacifism and raises the question whether more of an explanation is not necessary to explain the leap from Puritan regicide to Quaker pacifism.

Hershberger, Guy F. (Review). *Mennonites in the World War, or Nonresistance Under Test,* by J. S. Hartzler. Scottdale: Mennonite Publishing House, 1921. *MQR* 25 (1951), 229-30. A brief review of Hartzler's book, an eyewitness account of the Mennonite war experience in World War I. It is written by a church leader who writes from his own experience and draws upon the records in his care.

Hershberger, Guy F. (Review). *Pacifist's Progress: Norman Thomas and the Decline of American Socialism,* by Bernard K. Johnpoll. Chicago: Quadrangle Books, 1970. In *AAAPSS* 397 (1971), 185-86. The story of Norman Thomas (1884-1968), Presbyterian pacifist, social gospel miniter turned socialist, operating within the political structure itself for the building of a just and peaceable social order.

Hershberger, John Kenneth. "A Comparative Study of the Relationship of Hans Hut to Thomas Müntzer and Nonresistance in Recent Anglo-American Writings." Paper presented to the Mennonite History class, AMBS, 1974. Pp. 23. MHL.

Hertzler, Daniel. "Going to Church . . . " *GH* 70 (May 10, 1977), 400. Beginning from a medical report stating that church attendance is good for your health, editor comments on medical ethics for the unborn, linking nonresistance to protecting fetal life.

Hertzler, Daniel. "How Responsible Are We?" *ChrLiv* 6 (July, 1959), 2. Nonresistance and social and political responsibility

Hertzler, Daniel. "Nonresistance Tested." *GH* 73 (Oct. 28, 1980), 888. Tells the story of peaceable Palestinians whose village was confiscated by Jewish soldiers and who responded nonviolently.

Hess, James R. "Did Mennonite Conservatives Meet Their Waterloo at Assembly '79?" *ST* 47 (Nov., 1979), 8. In analyzing the Mennonite Church General Assembly at Waterloo, Ont., in Aug., 1979, the following are among the concerns raised: the role of women, nonconformity, nonresistance, relationship to minorities, and the relationship between word and deed.

Hess, James R. "Estes Assembly—Symbol of Spiritual Progress or Social Accommodation." *GfT* 12 (Sept.-Oct., 1977), 14-16. Includes comment on Mennonite movement toward political pacifism and away from nonresistance.

Hewett, James S. "Disillusioned Pacifists." *JChSoc* 4 (Spring, 1968), 57. Analysis of the relationship between the peace movement and Christian pacifism.

Hildebrand, Fred. "The Rockpile." *Fellowship* 21 (Mar., 1955), 15. Poem describing the strength of the will of the prisoner and of good people in facing difficult odds.

Hinshaw, Cecil. "The Relevance of Non-Violence." *MennLife* 17 (Apr., 1962), 59-63. Considers how the techniques and practice of nonviolence might be relevant to both the political and religious aspects of life.

Hirstine, Ed. "What Choice Shall I Make?" *Menn* 54 (Jan. 31, 1939), 9-10. Mennonites should not compromise with the military regarding a possible draft, by accepting a kind of alternative to drilling with guns. Only total nonresistance is sufficient.

Hobbs, William O. "Maintaining Scriptural Discipline and the Nonresistant Faith." *GH* 35 (Mar. 18, 1943), 1092. Those in the Mennonite church who do not hold to the nonresistant principle should be disciplined so that the church's witness remains clear. Half-hearted attitudes will not maintain this testimony.

Hochstetler, Paul. "Nonresistance." Research paper for Mennonite history class. 1963. Pp. 3. BfC.

Hofer, Michael. "The Martyrdom of Joseph and Michael Hofer, 1918." Pp. 4. BfC.

Hofer, Rodney. "Sour Grapes, the Modest Mind, and the Idealist." *Intercom* 10 (July-Aug., 1970), 1-2. MCC worker in Yugoslavia reflects on the idealism of not participating in war.

Hornus, Jean-Michel. *It Is Not Lawful for Me to Fight: Early Christian Attitudes Toward War, Violence, and the State,* trans. Alan Kreider and Oliver Coburn. Rev. ed. Scottdale and Kitchener: Herald Press, 1980. Pp. 367. Hornus studies the social, political, and theological framework and extant writings from the first 3 centuries of Christianity to show: Christian teaching consistently opposed military participation; this position was based in commitment to nonviolence, not merely the rejection of idolatry in emperor worship; why this position was abandoned in the 4th century.

Horsch, John. "An Historical Survey of the Position of the Mennonite Church on Nonresistance." *MQR* 1, Part 1, (July, 1927), 5-22; Part 2, (Oct., 1927), 3-20. On the basis of original source materials it appears that almost all Mennonites held to absolute nonresistance until the nineteenth century; during that century most European Mennonites lost the principle.

Horsch, John. "Balthasar Hubmaier, the Outstanding Defender of Believers' Baptism." *ChrMon* 26 (Oct., 1934), 293-94; edited reprint, *ChrMon* 29 (July, 1937), 197-98. Although he did not preach nonresistance, Hubmaier broke with Zwingli on the issue of infant baptism and rejected a state church model.

Horsch, John. "Menno Simons on the Principle of Nonresistance." *GH* 31 (Jan. 12, 1939), 874-75. A collection of Menno's writings supporting nonresistance. It is clear that no one familiar with Menno's writings could say he approved of military service.

Horsch, John. *Mennonites in Europe.* Scottdale: Herald Press, 1942. Pp. 427. A comprehensive history of the life and thought of sixteenth-century anabaptist-Mennonites, describing among other aspects of doctrine their nonresistance and peace position.

Horsch, John. "Nonresistance and the Service of the Army Chaplain." *ChrMon* 31 (Jan., 1939), 5-6; *Menn* 53 (Dec. 13, 1938), 12-13. Answers a booklet written to quell soldiers' doubts about the rightness of their actions.

Horsch, John. "Nonresistance Under Difficulties." *GH* 28 (Oct. 24, 1935), 650. The Hutterite Brethren of Germany have settled in Liechtenstein to avoid military conscription but their colonies have encountered financial difficulties. They have, nevertheless, remained faithful to the principle of nonresistance.

Horsch, John. "Observations Concerning a Live Issue." *GH* 32 (Nov. 9, 1939), 698. A recitation of some opinions on the question of absolute nonresistance and an expression of the conviction that this principle must be maintained.

Horsch, John. "The Difference Between Our Peace Program and the Program of Other Religious Peace Movements." *GH* 28, Part 1, (July 4, 1935), 291-92; Part 2, (July 11, 1935), 322-23.

American Mennonites are almost the only defenders of nonresistant principles. Other Christians are either pacifists only in peace time or hold to a humanistic sort of pacifism.

Horsch, John. "The Earliest Protestant Leaders on the Principle of Nonresistance." *GH* 31 (Aug. 11, 1938), 426. Both Luther and Zwingli were advocates of nonresistance in the earliest period of the Reformation. This position was lost when they accepted the establishment of a state church.

Horsch, John. "The Hutterian Brethren." *ChrMon* 30 (June, 1938), 164-165. Reviews Hutterite history, including their nonresistant stand.

Horsch, John. "The Life of the Mennonites of Switzerland as Seen by an Opponent Two and a Half Centuries Ago." *ChrMon* 30 (Dec., 1938), 360-61. Loyalty to the principle of nonresistance was one of the distinguishing marks.

Horsch, John. "The Position of the Early Mennonites as Regards the Principle of Nonresistance." *GH* 31 (Nov. 3, 1938), 666-67, 677-78. Speaks to the assertion that the early leaders of the Mennonite church were disunited about nonresistance from the beginning. Balthasar Hubmaier, who did not hold to nonresistance, cannot truly be considered an early leader of the Mennonite church.

Horsch, John. *The Principle of Nonresistance as Held by the Mennonite Church.* Scottdale: Herald Press, 1927, 1939, 1940, 1951. Pp. 60. A review of the Anabaptist-Mennonite position on nonresistance, including numerous quotations and an extended bibliography.

Horsch, John. "The Principle of Nonresistance Compared with Popular Pacifism." *GH* 31 (Sept. 1, 1938), 475, 485-87. A brief history of pacifist movements in America. Popular pacifism contends that there is war because people are ignorant; nonresistance says there are wars because they are sinful.

Horsch, John. "The Relation of the Old Testament Scriptures to the New Testament." *ChrMon* 30 (Nov., 1938), 329. The Anabaptists' distinction between the Testaments was basic to their convictions on nonresistance, separation of church and state, etc.

Horsch, John. "The Spread and Persecution of the Evangelical Baptists." *ChrMon* 25, Part 1, (Aug., 1933), 230-31; Part 2, (Sept., 1933), 260-61, 263; Part 3, (Oct., 1933), 292-94. The progress of the Anabaptist movement threatened the existence of the state church. Briefly mentions nonresistance as a factor in the persecutions.

Horst, Amos S. "Implications of Living the Nonresistant Life in Our Times." *GH* 36 (May 13, 1943), 138-39. Specifies twelve issues with which nonresistant Christians must deal.

Horst, Irvin B. "Mennonite Position on Relief and Service." *Menn* 65 (Nov. 7, 1950), 734. Social concern flows spontaneously from the life of discipleship and includes the practice of nonresistance, service, and mutual aid.

Horst, John L. (Editorial). "The Next War." *ChrMon* 26 (Feb., 1934), 41. Encourages preaching nonresistance during peacetime so that the church may stand firm in its convictions during the next war.

Hostetler, Adelia L. and Shank, J. R. "The Christian Principle of Peace." *ChrMon* 22 (Dec., 1930), 376-77. Young People's Meeting lesson study guide and comment on the principles of peace and nonresistance.

Hostetler, John Andrew. "Farmers Organizations and the Nonresistant Conscience." *MennComm* 6 (Feb., 1952), 17-19, 32. Implications of nonresistance for involvement in farmers organizations, farm technology, and farm business practices.

Hostetler, John Andrew. "Peace Teams: Current Work of the Peace Problems Committee." (Part 1). *GH* 42 (June 28, 1949), 614. The peace teams sent out by the Peace Problems Committee have worked to teach nonresistance and to assist congregations in learning to carry on this teaching ministry.

Hostetler, John Andrew. *The Sociology of Mennonite Evangelism.* Scottdale, Pa.: Herald Press, 1954. Pp. 287. MHL. Includes: "Rules and Discipline: Nonparticipation in the Affairs of Government," 28-29; "Unanticipated Evangelistic Interaction: Relief and Peace Activities," 128-30; "Religious Experience and Values Discovered: Nonresistance," 207; "Out-Group Social Attractions: Military Service," 236-37.
*

Hostetter, B. Charles. "Love that Wins." *ChrLiv* 1 (Nov., 1954), 10-11, 39-40. Love for enemies as taught in the Sermon on the Mount is the only remedy for war.

Hostetter, B. Charles. "Our Witness to Christendom." Address on passive resistance. n.d. Pp. 5. MLA/BcC.

Hostetter, C. N., Jr. "The Christian and His Enemies." *EV* 81 (Jan. 29, 1968), 3, 4. Love for enemies is the test of a nonresistant faith.

Hostetter, C. N., Jr. "The Christian and War." *EV* 82 (Dec. 1, 1969), 3, 4, 13. Summarizes the historical development of the church's

---

*For additional listing, see Supplement, pp. 717-719.

changing attitude to war and the relevant teaching of the New Testament on war and discipleship.

Hübner, Harry. "Pacifism, Non-Pacifism— Indistinguishable." *CanMenn* 17 (Nov. 28, 1969), 4. Letter to the editor asks counsel concerning some of the difficult issues of pacifism as it relates to President Nixon's actions in Vietnam.

Huebert, Helmut, Dr. (Review). *Mennonites in Canada, 1786-1920: The Story of a Separate People*, by Frank H. Epp. Toronto: Macmillan of Canada, 1974. Pp. 480. *MBH* 14 (Feb. 7, 1975), 24-25. Reviewer praises Epp's historical analysis, but suggests he overemphasized the principle of nonresistance.

Hunsberger, Arthur G. "According to the 'Teaching of the Twelve Apostles'." *GH* 72 (Aug. 14, 1979), 645-46. Two items, biblical nonresistance and baptism of believers, are lifted out of the Didache (or "Teaching of the Twelve Apostles") because of their similarity to Anabaptist principles.

Hunsicker, Ronald J. and Neufeld, John H. "Pacifism in *The Christian Century*." Paper for War, Peace, and Revolution class, AMBS, Elkhart, Ind., Apr. 10, 1969. Pp. 5. AMBS.

Hurd, Menno B. "Menno's Opinion." *GH* 69 (Feb. 3, 1976), 86. Encourages Mennonites to see the relationship between nonresistance and the abortion issue, and to be consistent in respecting human life.

"Is Nonviolent Resistance for Mennonites?" *CanMenn* 7 (Jan. 23, 1959), 1, 9. A detailed report of a debate with David Falk and Dr. John Dirks taking the affirmative and Leslie Stobbe and Allen Labun the negative.

Ilunga, Makanza; Weaver, Dale; Muller, Willy. "Nonresistance." *FQ* 7 (Nov., Dec., 1980, Jan., 1981), 20-21. Three people, from Africa, the US, and France, respectively, respond to the question of the meaning of nonresistance in their cultural setting, and their responding stances.

Isaak, George P. Letter to the Editor. *ChrLead* 36 (Apr. 3, 1973), 12. The doctrinal position of the Mennonite Brethren conference on the issue of nonresistance needs a thorough reevaluation. Desires more openness to equal time to military participation.

Jackson, Dave. *Dial 911: Peaceful Christians and Urban Violence*. Scottdale: Herald Press, 1981. Pp. 150. Recounts experiences that Reba Place Fellowship members have had with different sorts of violent crime in their Evanston neighborhood. These stories are interspersed with reflections upon different aspects of a

Christian response to urban violence such as making distinctions between different kinds of crimes, deterrents to crime, attitudes toward persons who commit crimes, and what the scriptures have to say to the issue.

Jantz, Harold. "Love Your Enemies." *MBH* 5 (Mar. 18, 1965), 3. Christians confess that evil will be overcome by good rather than through further violence.

Jantz, Hugo W. "Dietrich Bonhoeffer: Theologian, Disciple, Martyr." *MBH* 14 (July 11, 1975), 1-3. Tribute to the theologian and pacifist who participated in the plot to kill Hitler.

Janzen, David. "Attitude to Our Enemies: A Call to Repentance." *MennRep* 3 (Jan. 8, 1973), 7-8. Expresses disappointment over Mennonite failure to love communists in Russia. Reprints article from *Der Bote* giving thanks for Mennonite escape from Russia with "an anti-communist attitude that evades repentance."

Janzen, David. "On Politics and Immorality, Communism and Democracy." *CanMenn* 5 (Jan. 4, 1957), 7. In debate with John H. Redekop, Janzen tries to define terms for understanding of nonresistance and the Christian's involvement with the state.

Janzen, David. "Tolstoy and Nonresistance." *CanMenn* 5 (Feb. 22, 1957), 2. Janzen points out that Tolstoy, although he based his nonresistance on the Sermon on the Mount, failed to acknowledge grace as a factor in his moral teachings. His moralism was too rational and secular. It lacked Christian mysticism and the concept of revelation. Biblical nonresistance is an active love that permeates the whole of Christian morality.

Janzen, Edmund. "The Practical Application of Love and Nonresistance." *ChrLead* 43 (Jan. 15, 1980), 12-13. Analyzes Mennonite Brethren ambivalence toward the doctrine of nonresistance and contends that nonresistance is central to the person and teachings of Christ.

Janzen, Gerald. "Student: War Is Sin; PBI Principal: 'Peace Is Communist Plot'." *CanMenn* 18 (Apr. 17, 1970), 6, 7. An exchange of letters on pacifism between a Mennonite Brethren student, who supports the pacifist position, and Mr. Maxwell, president of Prairie Bible Institute, who does not.

*

Jeschke, Marlin (Review). *Brethren and Pacifism*, by Dale W. Brown. Elgin, Ill.: The Brethren Press, 1970. Pp. 152. *MQR* 46 (July, 1972), 314-15. Reviewer summarizes Brown's outline of popular varieties of pacifism and his cautions against pacifism as merely a political strategy or a legal right to request exemption from the

---

*For additional listing, see Supplement, pp. 717-719.

military. Faults the book for uneven tone and style.

Jost, Jerrold. "Pacifism of the Sixteenth Century Anabaptists." Student paper for Mennonite History, Life and Thought, May 6, 1974. Pp. 9. MLA/BeC.

Juhnke, James C. *A People of Two Kingdoms: The Political Acculturation of the Kansas Mennonites.* Newton: Faith and Life Press, 1975. Pp. 215. Explains that this process of acculturation was fundamentally shaped by the "abrasive encounter of Mennonite nonresistance with American nationalism" and charts the encounter from the shadows cast on the civic role of the Mennonite German-Americans by the Spanish-American War, through the essential Mennonite-American compatibility of the Progressive Era, through the shattering of that easy course in World War I, through the efforts to bridge the conflict in the inter-war period, to the new phase—characterized by voting and alternative service—during World War II.

Juhnke, James C. "Pax Peace Through Love." *MennLife* 16 (July, 1961), 102-104. PAX is welcome outgrowth of the principles of nonresistance, conscientious objection, etc. because it measures success by what is accomplished rather than what is not done.

Juhnke, James C. "The Victories of Nonresistance: Mennonite Oral Tradition and World War I." *Fides et Historia* 7 (Fall, 1974), 19-25. Mennonite oral tradition from World War I, as collected in taped interviews in the Schowalter Oral History Collection at Bethel College, contains a strain of "triumph tales," which reveal how nonresistant people maintained their self-respect and responded to the testing of their religious faith during that time of public humiliation.

Juhnke, James C. "What Does the Profile Say?" *MBH* 14 (June 27, 1975), 5-6. The *Anabaptists, Four Centuries Later* (J. Howard Kauffman and Leland Harder) study shows that 10-20 percent of present church members disagree with Anabaptist principles of church and state separation, nonresistance, etc.

Juhnke, James C. and Moyer, J. Harold. *The Blowing and the Bending: A Musical Drama in Two Acts.* By the authors, 1975. Pp. 60. Copy in AMBS library. The Unruhs, a Kansas Mennonite family, struggle with what being nonresistant means in 1918. Pressure to buy war bonds, anti-German, anti-pacifist sentiment in the community, and scant but frightening information concerning the harrassment of Mennonite young men in the military camps are some of the issues dramatized in this musical.

Kauffman, Beulah. "Family Life Education." *Builder* 31 (Jan., 1981), 24-25. Column focuses on topics such as peace for families in distress, parenting for peace and justice, nonviolence and children, etc.

Kauffman, Daniel. "Attitudes of Nonresistant People Toward War." *GH* 35 (May 21, 1942), 161. As nonresistant people, we are against war because God has commanded us to be peaceful and holy.

Kauffman, Daniel. "Biblical Nonresistance: Oldfashioned Mennonitism." (Part 8). *GH* 32 (Sept. 21, 1939), 529-30. Mennonites have held to the principle of nonresistance through war and peace because it is a biblical doctrine.

Kauffman, Daniel. "Militarism, Pacifism, Nonresistance." *GH* 35 (Oct. 22, 1942), 641-42. The militarist supports war; the pacifist opposes it because of its physical and spiritual destructiveness; the nonresistant opposes it out of obedience to Christ.

Kauffman, Daniel. "Nonresistance." *GH* 32 (Sept. 28, 1939), 546-47. Nonresistance as the way of Christ demands submission to the powers that be but, first of all, submission to God as the Supreme Ruler of heaven and earth.

Kauffman, Daniel. "Scriptural Principles Underlying the Doctrine of Nonresistance." *GH* 34 (May 1, 1941), 97-98. The sacredness of human life, the blessedness of peace, the constraining power of love, and the passion for saving lost souls are some of the principles outlined.

Kauffman, Daniel. "The European War Situation." *GH* 31 (Oct. 13, 1938), 601-602. In war time the Christian must live according to civil law until the point he or she is forced to disobey it in order to obey God, love the enemy, and pray for the authorities.

Kauffman, Daniel. "We Adhere to the Nonresistant Faith: Ten Reasons Why." (Part 6). *GH* 35 (Feb. 11, 1943), 977-78. Biblical, historical, and practical reasons are stated for the nonresistant position.

Kauffman, Ivan and Francis, Dale. "A Mennonite and a Catholic in Dialogue." *CanMenn* 15 (Feb. 21, 1967). Exchange of letters discussing pacifism. Francis, editor of the *Operation Understanding* edition of *Our Sunday Visitor* asks how Mennonites acquit themselves of responsibility for others; Kauffman argues that Mennonite pacifism is theologically, not politically, motivated and points out the conflict between service under Christ and service under the state involved in war.

Kauffman, J. Howard. "Pacifism and Political

Interpretation: The Case of the Mennonites."
Pp. 29. Presented at Society for the Scientific
Study of Religion, Savannah, Ga., 1985.
Correlates pacifism with political activism,
utilizing data on the Mennonites from
*Anabaptism: Four Centuries Later.*

Kauffman, Ralph C. "Satyagraha and Christian
Pacifism." *Menn* 61 (Feb. 12, 1946), 3-6. Hindu
pacifism is legalistic and simply a means to an
end; Christian pacifism arises out of the Spirit
of Jesus and is based on the sacredness of the
human personality.

Kaufman, Gordon D. "Nonresistance and
Responsibility." *Concern* 6 (Nov., 1958), 5-29.
Challenges the assumption that a Christian
ethic founded in nonresistant love leads
inevitably to withdrawal from the social order
and failure to take responsibility for it in the
name of love. Reprinted in book by same title,
1979.

Kaufman, Gordon D. *Nonresistance and Responsibility,
and Other Mennonite Essays.* Newton: Faith and
Life Press, 1979. Pp. 144. Reprints of essays by
Kaufman formerly published in Mennonite
periodicals or presented as speeches at special
occasions. Discusses Mennonite interpretation
of nonresistance and Christian participation in
secular society.

Kaufman, Gordon D. "Some Theological
Emphases of the Early Swiss Anabaptists." *MQR*
25 (Apr., 1951), 75-99. From the beginning
radical Anabaptists believed discipleship
involves an ethic of love and nonresistance
which grows out of the words of Jesus and the
spirit of yieldedness (Gelassenheit).

Kaufman, Gordon D. *Systematic Theology: A
Historicist Perspective.* New York: Scribners, 1968.
Pp. 543. Part of God's perfection is nonresistant
love (pp. 219-22); Jesus' acceptance of the cross
and his call for followers to "take up the cross"
results from the Christian ethic of nonresistant,
reconciling love (pp. 493ff., 510).

Kaufman, Gordon D. *The Context of Decision: A
Theological Analysis.* New York: Abingdon Press,
1961. Pp. 126. Studies theological foundations
of decisionmaking in Christian etgucsm
aoktubg tge duscyssuib especially in the
question of pacifism and nonviolence. Includes
essays published later in Kaufman;s *Nonresistance
and Responsibility* (1979); "The Church and the
World," "The Problem of Decision," and "God
and Man."

Kaufmann, F. Wilhelm. "And the Second Is Like
Unto It." *Fellowship* 21 (Nov., 1955), 19-20.
Meditation based on Matt. 22 in which the two
great commandments of love are given equal
rank and are to be universally applied.

Kautz, Bernard. "Nonresistance." *GH* 33 (June 6,
1940), 202. A brief review of the biblical basis
for nonresistance.

Keeney, William E. "Calling the World Council of
Churches to a Nonviolent Position." *MennRep* 4
(Jan. 7, 1974), 7. Examines Mennonite
interaction with the WCC on peace issues,
especially WCC's study on violence and
nonviolence.

Keeney, William E. "The Martin Luther King
Legacy." *Menn* 93 (Apr. 4, 1978), 229-30. On the
ten-year anniversary of King's death, Keeney
examines the Mennonite response to King's
active nonviolence and his impact on peace
theology.

Keeney, William E. "WCC Called to Nonviolent
Position." *Menn* 89 (Jan. 1, 1974), 11.
Summarizes the statement, "Violence,
Nonviolence, and the Struggle for Social
Justice," prepared by the historic peace church
representatives for the World Council of
Churches discussion. Reviews the history of
peace church-WCC discussions on the issue of
war, and alludes to the broader issues which it
touches: christology, biblical interpretation, the
relationship of church and state.

Keeney, William E. "What Peace and Which
Prince?" *GH* 65 (Dec. 19, 1972), 1028-29. An
appropriate celebration of the coming of the
Prince of Peace who rules by love, not coercion,
would be to give aid to the innocent victims of
war, especially to those labelled national
enemies.

Kehler, Marvin. "Observations at Koinonia."
*ChrLiv* 6 (Mar., 1959), 32-33. Brief description of
the integration, pacifist community.

King, Calvin. "The Nonresistance Credibility Gap."
*ChrLiv* 14 (July, 1967), 11. Nonresistant
Christians must live and die for eternal, not
earthly, values.

Kingsley, Keith. "Politics and the Kingdom of
God." *GH* 65 (Oct. 24, 1972), 857-59. Calls
Christians to focus their attention on the
politics of God's Kingdom, which might be
characterized by communities of people
committed to nonresistance, economic sharing,
marital fidelity, and spiritually and
psychologically interdependent relationships,
instead of focusing attention on national
politics.

Klaassen, David. "Now Is the Time to Speak for
Peace." *CanMenn* 15 (July 25, 1967), 1, 2. A
Mennonite Brethren Christian Service worker
discovers the element of peace in the gospel
message which Christians have been called to
proclaim. Discovery results in contention that
nonresistance must be a way of life and a

strategy in all situations; that social evils and peace are intimately related; that the total love strategy has much to do with civil rights and evangelism.

Klaassen, Walter. "For a Man to Be Remembered He Must Kill His Fellow Man." *CanMenn* 19 (Jan. 22, 1971), 6. In a "letter" to Jacob Hutter, the author looks at some contemporary questions of nonviolence in light of Hutter's point of view.

Klaassen, Walter. "Nature Bats Last." *With* 3 (July, 1970), 5. Caring for the natural environment of which we are a part is a basic way of practicing the nonviolence which is part of the history of Mennonites.

Klaassen, Walter. "The Biblical Basis of Nonresistance." *MennLife* 17 (Apr., 1962), 51, 52. The biblical basis of nonresistance is established "not on the basis of a collection of prooftexts" but on the "basis of the total relationship of the Christian to God."

Klaassen, Walter. *What Have You to Do with Peace?* Altona: D. W. Friesen and Sons, Ltd., 1969. Pp. 74. Originally given as lectures designed to help Sunday school teachers teach the basic principles of nonviolence. Covers subjects such as the biblical use of the language of "principalities and powers," the church as the agency of peace, just war doctrine, nuclear war and disarmament issues, and church and state relations.

Klaassen, Walter (Review). *Anabaptists and the Sword,* by James M. Stayer. Lawrence, Kansas: Coronado Pr., 1972. Pp. 375. *MQR* 47 (Apr., 1973), 160. Recommends the author's painstaking and well-documented research which reveals, among other things, a surprising amount of disagreement on nonresistance by the Swiss Brethren prior to Schleitheim.

Klaassen, Walter (Review). *Pacifism in Europe to 1914,* by Peter Brock. Princeton: Princeton Univ. Press, 1974. Pp. 556. *MQR* 50 (Jan., 1976), 69. Highly recommends this exhaustive work on varieties of pacifism existing in Europe, with a major amount of space devoted to Mennonites from the 16th century to 1914.

Klaassen, Aaron. "Peace Is the Will of God." *CanMenn* 7 (Nov. 6, 1959), 2. The pragmatic pacifist asks whether it will work, but the Christian pacifist is primarily concerned with doing the will of God.

Klassen, D. D. "UN Police Action and Nonresistance." *CanMenn* 4 (Dec. 28, 1956), 2, 9. A reply to John H. Redekop's article, "Nonresistance and UN Police Action." Redekop's questions are based on a confusion over the nature of the separation of church and state.

Klassen, James R. "There Is Another Way." Student peace oration, 1966. Pp. 7. MLA/BeC.

Klassen, William. "Coals of Fire: Sign of Repentance or Revenge?" *NT Studies* 9 (July, 1963), 337-50. "Heaping coals of fire" in Rom. 12:20 is a sign of repentance brought about by an act of love. It is an image, not for nonresistance of evil, but for overcoming evil with good.

Klassen, William. "Love Your Enemy: A Study of the New Testament Teaching on Coping with an Enemy." *MQR* 37 (July, 1963), 147-71 and in *Biblical Realism Confronts the Nations,* ed. Paul Peachey (Fellowship Publications, 1963), 153-83. Surveys briefly the history of interpretation of "love of enemy," then studies its meaning as against the Old Testament and Qumran backgrounds, and assesses its meaning in the gospels and Pauline uses. Article then examines the church's faithfulness in light of this teaching.

Klassen, William. "Revenge of Love." *GH* 55 (Apr. 12, 1962), 361. Christ gave us a way to relate to enemies—the way of love. Christians have perverted discipleship as they have watered down this truth.

Klassen, William. "The Choice Is Now Between Nonviolence and Nonexistence." *CanMenn* 16 (Feb. 17, 1968), 3, 4. Describes Feb. 5 and 6 march on Washington by clergy and lay people concerned about Vietnam and summerizes M. L. King's speech as well as that of Chaplain Coffin. Learnings from the expericne include a sense of the value of working within church structure even when many people in churches may not take positions against the Vietnam war.

Klassen, William. "The Two Swords in Luke 22:35-38." *CanMenn* 2 (Nov. 19, 1954), 2. An interpretation of Luke 22:35-38 in support of nonresistance. Klassen makes the point that we should concentrate on "absolute love" not the negative term nonresistance.

Klassen, William (Review). *On Violence,* by Hannah Arendt. Harcourt, Brace, and World, 1970. Pp. 106. *GH* 64 (Apr. 20, 1971), 362. Recommends the book for its careful analysis of the distinction and relation between power and violence, the utility of violence when used to dramatize grievances, and the power of nonviolence in building a new order.

Kliewer, John D. Letter to the Editor. *ChrLead* 40 (Dec. 20, 1977), 15. If nonresistance is really the all-important goal of our church, then civilians are already ideal in life-style, and our ministry should be on military bases all over the world.

Kliewer, Warren. "The Berserkers." Play, 14 Dorann Avenue, Princeton, NJ, 1973. Pp. 101. MHL.

Knagy, Ruth. "The Price of Nonresistance." YCC 17 (July 12, 1936), 218-19. To be a nonresistant person means to be willing to suffer the consequences. Each war has its own stories of how people who followed Christ's way suffered for their choice not to participate in the war effort.

Kniss, Lloy A. "The Meaning of Redemptive Dealing." GH 63 (Apr. 14, 1970), 340-41. Urges Christians to show forgiveness and humility toward both non-Christians and fellow believers, because God's way is the way of love which dies for another, even the enemy.

Kniss, Mark. "The Other Side of Nonresistance." GH 42 (Apr. 26, 1949), 388. Mennonites have placed too much emphasis on the sacrifice involved in nonresistance and not enough on the motivating factor—love.

Knoop, Faith Yingling. "The Persecuted: Rejoice!" ChrLiv 6 (July, 1959), 8-9. The nonresistant response of a group of Pennsylvania Indians forced to become refugees in 1763.

Koehn, Dennis. "Peace and Anabaptist Studies at IPF Colleges and Seminaries." IPF Notes 19 (Feb. 8, 1973), 3-8. Course offerings at Intercollegiate Peace Fellowship schools on war, peace, nonviolence, etc.

Koontz, Ted. "Call to Draft Marks End of a Peculiar Era." Menn 95 (Mar. 11, 1980), 176. Resumed draft registration confronts Mennonites with the choice of continuing to focus peace concern on the broader question of government policy, or retaining pacifism merely as a personal response to military service.

Koontz, Ted. "Hard Choices: Abortion and War." Menn 93 (Feb. 28, 1978), 132-34. Analyzes the inconsistency of Mennonite prohibition of killing in war, without a corresponding prohibition on abortion. Concludes that rethinking both issues will lead to a less simplistic formulation of Mennonite pacifism.

Koshy, Kochu. "Nonresistance as a Biblical Principle as Expounded and Practiced by Sixteenth-Century Anabaptists." Term paper for Anabaptist Theology course, May, 1972. Pp. 15. MSHL.

Krady, Ruth M. "The Law Supreme." ChrMon 36 (May, 1944), 130, 133. Story about a college student challenged by the principle of nonresistance.

Krahn, Cornelius. "The Christian's Responsibility." MennLife 13 (Jan., 1958), 31-33. A review of Martin Niemoeller's Menno Simons lectures on the "Relevance of Christian Nonresistance in Our Present World Situation" delivered at Bethel College in 1956.

Krause, James R. Letter to the Editor. Menn 92 (Apr. 26, 1977), 285. Christian obedience to government is limited, because those in power, being human, carry out God's will only imperfectly. Primary loyalty is to God, who commands love to enemies, even national enemies.

Kreider, Alan. "The Arms Race: The Defense Debate—Nuclear Weaponry and Pacifism." The Year 2000, ed. John R. W. Stott. Downers Grove: InterVarsity Press, 1983, 27-55. Pp. 179. Since the security afforded by deterrence policy is neither adequate nor real, and since pacifists and just war theorists agree that nuclear war is indefensible, we ought to unite, despite other differences, in order to search for viable alternatives for conflict resolution.

Kreider, Alan. "Why the Christian Church Must Be Pacifist." Ireland and the Threat of Nuclear War, ed. Bill McSweeney. Dublin: Dominican Publications, 1985. Pp. 83-103. Pacifism is now growing in the Church for several reasons: people have seen the futility of military violence in attaining its objectives; new biblical and theological insights undermine former justifications for violence; because attempts to control modern events have had unanticipated results, Christians are abandoning consequential ethics for principled, prophetic nonconformity; and Christians have discovered that violence does not exhaust the possibilities for relevant involvement in the world.

Kreider, Alan (Review). It Is Not Lawful for Me to Fight: Early Christian Attitudes Toward War, Nonviolence, and the State, by Jean-Michel Hornus. Revised, ed., trans. A. Kreider and O. Coburn. Scottdale: Herald Press, 1980. Pp. 367. "The Early Church and Warfare." GH 73 (Dec. 2, 1980), 964-65. The experience of the early Christians was more nearly pacifist than not.

Kreider, Alan and John H. Yoder. "Christians and War." Eerdman's Handbook to the History of Christianity. Ed. Tim Dowley. Grand Rapids: Eerdmans Publ. Co., 1977, 24-27. Pp. 656. Traces the development of the three approaches to the relationship between war and the gospel: the crusade, just war theory, and pacifism.

Kreider, Carl. "Defense Against H Bomb." ChrLiv 1 (Jan., 1954), 39-40. Military, political, and economic defenses are discussed, as well as some practical suggestions for the Christian nonresistant.

Kreider, Carl. "Some Questions About Business Principles." *MennComm* 1 (Sept., 1947), 6-7. Nonresistance and obedience to the government when not conflicting with obedience to God are two biblical principles relating to business ethics.

Kreider, Robert S. "Anabaptism and Humanism." *MQR* 26 (Apr., 1952), 123-41. Anabaptism went beyond Erasmian pacifism to nonresistance, a concept derived from a radicalization of the love ethic and the concept of a suffering church.

Kreider, Robert S. "Do We Take a Stand on Nonresistance?" *Menn* 60 (May 8, 1945), 6. We have not taken a clear or unanimous stand on nonresistance. The issue and its implication should be honestly faced at General Conference (GCMC) meetings.

Kreider, Robert S. "The Ethics of Nonviolence in American Trade Unionism." MA Thesis, Divinity School, Univ. of Chicago, Chicago, Ill., Aug., 1941. Pp. 98. MHL. Examines the ethics of the ends sought and the means employed by different types of American unionism. Includes a chapter on nonviolent unionism, analyzing such examples of peaceful arbitration as the Quaker-led effort at the Berkshire Knitting Mills, Pa., and the Oklahoma coal miners who simply prayed, audibly, fervently, and by name, for their employers and the strike-breakers who violated the picket lines until negotiations were concluded. Concludes, in light of this examination, that the church ought to establish relationships with such social movements as unionism and then pursue its historic role of being prophetically critical and ethically constructive in social change.

Kremer, Russell. "Nonresistance to Nonviolence: The Mennonite Story." Student paper [Goshen College, Goshen, Ind.], Dec. 6, 1974. Pp. 12. MHL.

Kunjam, Shantkumar S. "An Exploratory Examination of the Ethics of Gandhiji in the Light of Biblical Teachings." MA in Peace Studies thesis, AMBS, 1982. Pp. 94. A critical discussion of the theological and moral bases that guided Gandhi's effort to ease class conflicts and win liberation for the Indian people by nonviolent means. Includes statement of what Christians may learn from Gandhi.

Laag, Albertina van der. "Nonresistance Among Dutch Mennonites." Paper presented at the Church History class, Goshen College, Goshen, Ind., June, 1949. Pp. 21. MHL.

Landers, Bertha M. "Fools, Cabbages, and Christ." *Builder* 26 (Apr., 1977), 2-6. A short play portraying how one family puts the principles of nonresistance into practice in a neighborhood dispute that develops when the cows get into the garden.

Landes, Carl J. "Keep the Unity of the Spirit." *Menn* 56 (Jan. 14, 1941), 8. Pacifist Christians and non-pacifist Christians, Christian registrants and Christian non-registrants should not judge one another, but encourage each other to follow conscience.

Landis, John E. "The Nonresistant Faith and Life." *GH* 32 (Sept. 28, 1939), 554-55. If Mennonites are to effectively witness to the nonresistant way during war time, they must have the principle of peace in their hearts.

Lanting, Esther. "Nonresistance in Anabaptism and Bonhoeffer." Thesis (MA), 1977. Pp. 121. MBBS.

Lapp, George J. "Is Mr. Gandhi Nonresistant?" *GH Supplement* 38 (Dec., 1945), 697. Gandhi is a nonviolent revolutionist and an obstructionist and can therefore not be considered nonresistant.

Lapp, George J. "Nonresistance." *GH* 33 (Sept. 5, 1940), 482. God's people were to be ministers of peace from beginning times. The principle of peace and nonresistance must be made practical by individual conviction.

Lapp, John A. (Review). *Faith and Violence,* by Thomas Merton. U. of Notre Dame, 1968. Pp. 291. *ChrLiv* 16 (Aug., 1969), 28-29. Recommends this collection of Merton's essays on the ethics of nonviolence.

Lapp, John A. (Review). *For Peace and Justice: Pacifism in America, 1914-1941,* by Charles Chatfield. Knoxville: The University of Tennessee Press, 1971. Pp. 447. *MQR* 47 (Jan., 1973), 73-75. Reviewer considers the book a "masterful account" of the American peace movement in the early part of this century, emphasizing liberal Protestant pacifists and treating too lightly the impacts of the "Red Scare" and Reinhold Niebuhr on the pacifist community.

Lapp, John A. (Review). *Gandhi on Non-Violence,* ed. Thomas Merton. New Directions, 1965. Pp. 81. *ChrLiv* 13 (Sept., 1966), 35-36. Recommends this collection of Gandhi's writings on nonviolence, with an introductory essay by Merton.

Lapp, John A. (Review). *No King But Caesar? A Catholic Lawyer Looks at Christian Violence,* by William R. Durland. Scottdale: Herald Press, 1975. *FQ* 2 (Winter, 1975), 14. Lapp observes the book's strength lies in Durland's sincere wrestling with the violence of the church through the centuries. Calls the Christian church to lay down its weapons of war.

Lapp, John A. (Review). *Nonresistance and Responsibility and Other Mennonite Essays,* by Gordon D. Kaufman. Newton: Faith and Life Press, 1979. Pp. 144. *FQ* 7 (Aug., Sept., Oct., 1980), 9. Kauffman develops issues of biblicism, church witness, and modernity in light of his conviction that Mennonite distinctiveness lies in commitment to nonresistance.

Lapp, John A. (Review). *Protest: Pacifism and Politics,* ed. James Finn. Random House, 1968. Pp. 528. *ChrLiv* 16 (Mar., 1969), 36. Recommends this collection of interviews with 38 leading people who address themselves to issues of war and peace.

Lapp, John A. (Review). *Violence: Reflections from a Christian Perspective,* by Jacques Ellul, Seabury Press, 1969. Pp. 179. *ChrLiv* 17 (Dec., 1970), 37. Supports Ellul's appeal for a Christian ethic that represents the rights of the poor and oppressed without resorting to violence.

Lapp, John E. "Maintaining Nonresistance in Doctrine and Practice." *GH* 36 (Sept. 9, 1943), 498-99. Mennonites need to understand both the Old and New Testaments, their relationship, and their teachings on nonresistance. Then practice of these teachings is required.

Lapp, John [E.]. "Nonresistance: In Domestic Relations." *The Eastern Mennonite School Journal* 18 (Apr., 1940), 75-79. Three principles are vital to the practice of nonresistance in the home: proper marital relationships; Christian child training; avoidance of the spirit of jealousy.

Lapp, John E. *Studies in Nonresistance: An Outline for Study and Reference.* Akron, Pa.: Peace Problems Committee, 1948. Pp. 35. MHL. Outlines a study course for MYF in 12 lessons. Topics covered include Old Testament and New Testament teachings on war and peace, nonresistance in the early church, Anabaptist concepts of nonresistance, the Mennonite experience in America, World War I, World War II, and church and state.

Lapp, John E. "The Church Speaking in Our Time." *ChrLiv* 4 (Sept., 1957), 16-17. The prophetic voice of the Mennonite church, which has centered on nonresistance, should also include economics.

Leatherman, John D. "The Story of Non-Resistant Peoples During the World War as Told in the *Goshen Daily Democrat.*" Paper presented to Peace and War Seminar, Goshen College, Goshen, Ind., June, 1940. Pp. 22. MHL.

Lederach, John Paul. "The So-Called Pacifists: A Study of Nonviolence in Spain." Social Science Seminar paper, Mar., 1980. Pp. 97. MLA/BeC.

Lee, Nancy (Review). *The Waiting People,* by Peggy Billings. Friendship Press, 1965. Pp. 127. *ChrLiv* 11 (Apr., 1964), 33. Reviewer observes that stories of people in East Asia address questions such as the meaning of nonresistance, suffering, and violence.

Lehman, Chester K. "Biblical Perspectives on Christianity and the State." Conference on "Nonresistance and Political Responsibility," Peace Problems Committee (1956), 2-11. The state has no allegiance to God. Christians obey the state in things not contrary to the law of God, but as aliens and exiles.

Lehman, Chester K. "Nonresistance Practical Today." *The Eastern Mennonite School Journal* 18 (Apr., 1940), 27-31. Lists reasons why many people think nonresistance is impractical and then counters this list with a list of reasons why nonresistance is practical. Offers examples.

Lehman, Emmett R. "Basic Concerns in the Anabaptist Position." *GfT* Series 2, 4 (Jan.-Feb., 1969), 15. Discusses three tenets: separation of church and state; nonresistance as the refusal to judge actions of the state; and the difference between nonresistance and pacifism.

Lehman, Emmett R. "Nonresistance and the State." *GH* 59 (Aug. 30, 1966), 774. States three tenets which must be kept particularly clear in every discussion of government policy.

Lehman, Emmett R. "War and Killing in Both Testaments." *GfT* Series 2, Vol. 3, Part 1, (Oct., 1968), 6-7; Part 2, (Dec., 1968), 15. Supports a two-covenant view by citing Old Testament divine commands for warfare as evidence that nonresistance was not part of God's plan for that time. Roots nonresistance in commitment to Christ and differentiates nonresistance from pacifism.

Lehman, Ernest. "Strengthening the Nonresistant Faith." *GH Supplement* 39 (Feb., 1947), 1035. The Mennonite record of nonresistance in the last war was not good. The church must do better.

Lehman, J. Irvin. "Holding Nonresistance." *ST* 19 (1st Qtr., 1951), 1. The doctrine of nonresistance must be kept in proper ratio to all the other doctrines of the Bible, must be related to every area of life, and must be applicable to all people.

Lehman, J. Irvin. "Questions and Answers on Nonresistance." *ST* 18 (4th Qtr., 1950), 21. Nonresistance is discussed between an inquiring conscientious objector and a minister.

Lehman, J. Irvin. "Wars and Persecutions in Prophetic Prospect." *The Eastern Mennonite School Journal* 18 (Apr., 1940), 82-90. Speaks of the persecution of Christians, the prophetic view of wars among the nations, and the wars and persecutions which came upon Israel.

Lehman, J. Irvin. "Weakening the Military Defenses." *ST* 16 (1st Qtr., 1949), 22. Comparison between a pacifist stance and a biblical nonresistant Christian position on war.

Lehman, J. Irvin (Editorial). "Biblicist Nonresistance." *ST* 21 (1st Qtr., 1953), 27. Outlines Matthew 5:17-48 as it relates to nonresistance.

Lehman, Melvin L. "Jury Duty." *GH* 73 (July 8, 1980), 540-42. Discusses his experience in being called for jury duty against the backdrop of his commitment to nonviolence and justice.

Lehn, Cornelia and P. U. Geisbrecht. "The Gospel, Discipleship, and Nonresistance." *Menn* 69 (May 11, 1954), 294-95. Canadian Peace Study Conference emphasizes the biblical basis of nonresistance and declares that discipleship to Jesus leaves no other choice.

Leinbach, Nola C. "A World War Episode." *ChrMon* 22 (Oct., 1930), 290, 320. Story of the attempted murder of an advocate of nonresistance during World War I, based on a true story.

Lepp, Jack Randolph. "A Study of the Principle of Nonresistance in the Mennonite Tradition." Term paper for Comprehensive Seminar at Waterloo Lutheran Seminary, 1981. Pp. 62. CGCL.

Liau, Timothy Y. S. "Christian Responsibility to the Future of Taiwan." MA in Peace Studies thesis, AMBS, 1979. Pp. 133. Analyzes the role of the Taiwanese Christians in the contemporary struggle for justice in Taiwan from the perspectives of both the biblical attitude toward the principalities and powers and the classic peace tradition of nonviolence.

Liechty, C. Daniel. "Political Nonresistance: A Thesis in Christian Ethics." MA in Peace Studies thesis, AMBS, 1978. Pp. 71. An exploration of the OT anti-kingship tradition, a comparison of the political views of Hegel and Marx, and a summary of Christian thinking on the relationship of church and state contribute to a Christian understanding of the political organism.

Liechty, C. Daniel. "War in the Old Testament: Three Views." *GH* 71 (May 23, 1978), 408-409; *Menn* 94 (Nov. 6, 1979), 658-59. Examines three types of Mennonite writers on the subject of war in the Old Testament: 1)Those who posit discontinuity between the Old and New Testaments; 2) those who find nonresistance as an ideal presesnt in the Old as well as New Testaments; 3) those who see Israel's trust in a

warrior-God instead of a warrior-king as a challenge to military action.

Lind, Ivan Reuben. *The Labor Union Movement in the Light of Nonresistance as Held by the Mennonite Church*. Unpublished MA thesis, Dept. of Commerce, the State Univ. of Iowa, 1941. Pp. 69. Mennonites see unions as power groups organized for coercion in which nonresistant Christians cannot participate. Compromises are being made, however, as well as new attempts to find alternate solutions, including migration to rural areas.

Lind, Loren. "Nonresistance and You." *Builder* 14 (Jan., 1964), 59-61. A planning guide for a youth program designed to help the participants become enthusiastic about the principle of nonresistance and to find new ways of making the concept meaningful in life.

Lind, Marcus. "'The Just Shall Live.' " *ST* 48 (Aug., 1980), 24-27. Justification by faith, which results in nonresistance, is God's reply to violence.

Lind, Millard C. *Christ and War*. Ed. Paul Peachey, n.p.: Mennonite General Conference Peace Problems Committee, 1956. Pp. 19. The Christian Youth and War Pamphlets No. 3. Pamphlet directed to young men approaching draft age enjoins them to follow Christ by following the way of nonresistant love, even toward national enemies.

Lind, Millard C. "Nonresistance." *ChrMon* 42 (Feb., 1950), 41-42. Marks of a nonresistant faith include love, concern for the lost, and willingness to suffer.

Lind, Millard C. "Nonresistance." *ChrMon* 42 (Mar., 1950), 72-73. The footwashing ordinance is a reminder that Christians are to serve one another.

Lind, Millard C. (Review). *The Way to Peace*, by L. John Topel, S.J. Maryknoll: Orbis Books, 1979. Pp. 199. *MissFoc* 8 (Mar., 1980), 19-20. Reviewer discusses Topel's biblical theology and pacifism in his approach to liberation theology.

Lindsay, Vachel. "Where Is the Real Nonresistant?" *ChrLiv* 9 (June, 1962), 27. Poem reprinted from *Collected Poems* by Vachel Lindsay. Macmillan, 1917.

Littell, Franklin H. "The Inadequacy of Modern Pacifism." *GH Supplement* 39 (Aug., 1946), 461-64. Modern pacifism is based on false assumptions and is an inadequate philosophy for Christian action.

Loepp, Franzie. "Nonresistance." Student paper for Mennonite History, 1959. Pp. 12. MLA/BeC.

Loewen, Harry (Review.) *With Courage to Spare: The Life of B. B. Janz (1877-1964),* by John B. Toews. Winnipeg: The Board of Christian Literature of the General Conference of the Mennonite Brethren Churches of North America, 1978. *MQR* 53 (Oct., 1979), 327-28. The story of B. B. Janz, who assisted Russian Mennonites in settling in North America, built up congregations in Canada, and fought to preserve the Mennonite principles of peace and nonresistance during World War II.

Loewen, Theodore W. "Mennonite Pacifism: The Kansas Institute of International Relations." Social Science Seminar paper, Apr., 1971. Pp. 33. MLA/BeC.

Lohrenz, Gerhard. "Nonresistance Tested." *MennLife* 17 (Apr., 1962), 66-68. The story of Nester Makhno, who after the Russian Revolution in 1917 roamed the countryside with his band, plundering, murdering, and raping the populace, including many Mennonites.

Lord, Charles R. Letter to the Editor. *ChrLead* 41 (May 9, 1978), 10. Reason for joining Mennonite Brethren was an understanding of the position on peace and nonresistance. Urges a statement of concern on the arms race.

Mack, Noah H. "Nonresistance: In Church Differences." *The Eastern Mennonite School Journal* 18 (Apr., 1940), 79-82. The Jerusalem conference and the relationship of Paul and Barnabas are models of nonresistance operating in church disputes.

MacMaster, Richard K. *Christian Obedience in Revolutionary Times: The Peace Churches and the American Revolution.* Akron, Pa.: MCC (US) Peace Section, 1976. Pp. 26. MHL. Demonstrates that Mennonites and other Christians committed to peace during the Revolutionary War times conflicted with the government on issues of military service, war taxes, and oaths of allegiance. Discusses their stance and resulting persecution within the context of differing concepts of religious liberty; the sectarian concept of discipleship as a separate and distinct way of life was not understood by a government to whom religious freedom meant the freedom to worship according to the dictates of conscience, not the freedom to live by conscience.

Markley, W. O. "Do Pacifists Help Cause War?" *EV* 77 (Apr. 13, 1964), 5, 28. Each individual pacifist is responsible for living his or her life in a way that helps prevent war.

Martens, Harry E. "Graduated from Civilian Public Service." *CPS Bull Supp* 6 (Jan. 30, 1947), 1, 3. Nonresistance must be a way of life, not confined to the Civilian Public Service camp.

Martin, Brenda. "The Relation Between the Historic Peace Churches and the Government of Pennsylvania from 1775 to the Beginning of the Revolutionary War." Paper for History Seminar, Goshen College, Goshen, Ind., Apr. 15, 1975. Pp. 55. MHL.

Martin, Harold S. "Anabaptist Thought Today." *ST* 38 (Dec., 1970), 12. Examination of the Anabaptist themes of discipleship, voluntary church membership, and the practice of love and nonresistance.

Martin, Harold S. "Safeguarding the Doctrine of Nonresistance." *ST* 47 (June, 1979), 13-14. Reprinted from *Bible Helps.* Nonresistance is based on scriptural mandate, while pacifism stems from the desire for survival.

Martin, Lewis. "Nonresistance: In Industrial Problems." *The Eastern Mennonite School Journal* 18 (Apr., 1940), 71-75. Christians involved in labor problems should remember: Christians have a place in the world; they have a testimony in the world; they should be steadfast in suffering wrong rather than doing wrong.

Martin, Mark J. "Our Responsibility to the Germans and the Japanese." *GH* 38 (Jan. 25, 1946), 820. The nonresistant Christian must take food and the Christian message to the defeated "enemy."

Martin-Adkins, Ron. "Why Christian Pacifism?" *Menn* 95 (Dec. 2, 1980), 694-95. Roots Christian pacifism in God who creates life, Christ's suffering love on the cross, and Christian commitment to the kingdom of God.

McPhee, Arthur G. "Scriptural Guidelines on the Way of Peace." *GfT* 6 (Mar.-Apr., 1971), 10-11. Sermon on Matthew 5:43-48 extols love as the way to peace with God and humans.

Mennonite General Conference. "A Declaration of Christian Faith and Commitment with Respect to Peace, War, and Nonresistance." *GH* 44 (Oct. 16, 1951), 992-93 All carnal strife is wrong in spirit and method as well as in purpose. General Conference (MC) statement deals with numerous implications of this position.

Metzler, Alice Marie. "The Challenge of Nonresistance." *YCC* 33 (Nov. 9, 1952), 355, 360. A true understanding of nonresistance brings with it the realization that this is something which must become a part of our everyday life. Prize winning essay in contest sponsored by Peace Problems Committee.

Metzler, Edgar. "Deeds of Love." *ChrMon* 39 (July, 1947), 202-3. The principle of nonresistance should be reinterpreted to mean active love in all areas of life.

Metzler, Edgar, "I Talked with a Man of God." *ChrLiv* 12 (Aug., 1965), 18-19, 29. Mennonite leader in Russia reports on the status of Mennonite churches there, including the stance on war and nonresistance.

Metzler, Edgar. "Six Questions About Peace." *GH* 59 (Mar. 23, 1965), 249; "Students and Leaders in India Ask Six Questions About Peace." *CanMenn* 12 (Dec. 29, 1964), 7. Report by the MCC Peace Missioner to India about the growing interest in nonresistance in India. Outlines six questions frequently asked there about nonresistance.

Meyer, Albert J. "A Second Look at Responsibility." *Concern* 6 (Nov., 1958), 30-39. Responding to Kaufman's article "Nonresistance and Responsibility" (printed in same issue), Meyer defends the uniqueness of Christian love and the kind of loyalty it demands of the Christian as citizen.

Miller, Albert. Letter to the Editor. *ChrLead* 41 (June 6, 1978), 10. Raising the concern that a "re-emphasis" of biblical nonviolence falls short if it is only a response to a draft.

Miller, D. D. "Lessons from the World War: for Church Officials." *Eastern Mennonite School Journal* 18 (Apr., 1940), 46-49. One important learning for church leaders from the World War I experience is that the church needs more teaching on the doctrine of nonresistance.

Miller, D. D. "Nonresistance: In Litigation Provocations." *The Eastern Mennonite School Journal* 18 (Apr., 1940), 67-75. Describes policies and experiences of the Elkhart Mission Board in regards to various kinds of legal procedures.

Miller, John W. "Letter in Response to 'A General Speaks on War' by Paul Peachey." *GH* 48 (July 12, 1955), 650. Peachey's use of the term "institutionalized murder" fails to distinguish between the just state and the lawless state. It also reveals that Peachey grounds his nonresistance in the sacredness of life instead of in Christ's teaching about the coming of his kingdom.

Miller, John W. (Review). *The Christian and Warfare: The Roots of Pacifism in the Old Testament,* by Jacob J. Enz. Herald Press, 1972. Pp. 95. "Pacifism: A Stream in the Ocean of History." *MennRev* 4 (Jan. 21, 1974), 8. The unifying theme of these essays on biblical theology is biblical pacifism, on which Enz focuses in order to demonstrate the unity and direction of biblical materials.

Miller, Leo J. "The Pacifism of Leo Tolstoy." Paper for War, Peace, and Revolution class, AMBS, Elkhart, Ind., Apr. 10, 1969. Pp. 3. AMBS.

Miller, Leo J. "Pentecostalism and the Pacifist Position." Paper for War, Peace, nd Revolution class, AMBS, Elkhart, Ind., n.d. Pp. 3. AMBS

Miller, Orie O. "Lessons from the World War: For the Nonresistant Laity." *The Eastern Mennonite School Journal* 18 (Apr., 1940), 49-51. World War I experience has taught us that there is a need for greater clarity and consistency in our nonresistant peace witness.

Mills, C. Wright. "A Pagan Sermon." *ChrLiv* 7 (Apr., 1960), 16-18. Reprinted from *The Causes of World War Three,* Mills, Simon and Schuster, 1958. Non-Christian author challenges the church to greater faithfulness in the areas of nonconformity and nonresistance.

Mininger, J. D. "Nonresistance." *GH Supplement* 35 (Oct., 1942), 635. An outline of the basis for nonresistance in the Old and New Testaments, and the Christian's relationship to civil government.

Mohr, Roberta. "I Resisted Nonresistance." *ChrLiv* 16 (Apr., 1969), 20-21. Wife of conscientious objector faces her disagreement with his position.

Moomaw, Benjamin F. "A Dialogue on the Doctrine of Nonresistance." *Discussion on Trine Immersion by Letter Between Elder Benj. F. Moomaw . . . and Dr. J. J. Jackson . . . ,* by Benjamin F. Moomaw. Singer's Glen, Va.: Joseph Funk's Sons, 1867, 220-74. Using the form of a dialogue between an advocate and an opponent of Christian pacifism, the Brethren author deals with such arguments on nonresistance issues as the New Testament passages on submission to authority, Old Testament warfare, and natural law.

Mumaw, David K. Letter to the Editor. *GH* 65 (Dec. 12, 1972), 1020-21. Argues that gun ownership can be consistent with a profession of nonviolence if the gun is used only on animals, not people. Disagrees with the idea that guns breed violence.

Mumaw, John R. "Nonresistance and Pacifism." *GH Supplement* 37 (June, 1944), 220-23. A comparison of the two positions with the conclusion that they are very different; the Christian must be more than a pacifist.

Mumaw, Lloyd I. "Hans Hut and the Sword." Paper, n.d. Pp. 2. AMBS.

Musser, Daniel. *Nonresistance Asserted: Or the Kingdom of Christ and the Kingdom of This World Separated, and No Concord Between Christ and Belial.* Lancaster: Elias Barr and Co., 1864. Pp. 74. MHL. Argues the biblical basis of nonresistance and contends, in regard to the pending draft, that to pay another person to go to war in one's place is just as wrong as actually going to war one's self.

"New Nonresistance Book Published." *CanMenn* 3 (July 15, 1955), 1. Announces the publication of J. A. Toews' *True Nonresistance Through Christ* and outlines the contents of this book.

"Nonresistance and Church Membership." *Builder* 29 (Oct., 1979), 4-8. Document prepared by study committee for discussion and response in the Franconia Conference congregations reviews historical and biblical perspectives, restates a position on the centrality of peace and nonresistance to the gospel, and offers guidelines for congregational practice.

"Nonresistance in the Mennonite Church." Panel discussion presented to the Roger Williams Fellowship by members of the Mennonite Fellowship, Kansas State Univ., Oct. 24, 1965. Pp. 7. MLA/BeC.

"Nonresistance Talks in Leamington Area." *CanMenn* 6 (Feb. 14, 1958), 9. J. W. Fretz delivers a number of speeches on different areas of nonresistant love.

"Nonresistant Way of Life." *GH* 32 (Sept. 7, 1939), 483. A reprint of an editorial which appeared in a local paper during Mennonite General Conference (MC) held at Allensville, Pa. Mennonite reiteration of the "will to peace" is seen as a sigh of hope in light of the tensions in Europe.

"Nonviolence and Civil Disobedience." *CanMenn* 14 (Feb. 8, 1966), 8. Report on the reading of a paper by Leo Driedger during Council of Board (GCMC) meeting on Jan. 21. Driedger's paper reviewed biblical and contemporary leaders who practiced civil disobedience, including Hosea, Jesus, and Martin Luther King, and noted that Mennonites in general have not participated in radical civil disobedience. Paper concludes that positive ways to bind society's wounds should be found but that occasional radical action is needed.

Nachtigall, Wilbur. "What the Mennonite Church in Puerto Rico Is Doing about Nonresistance." *GH* 44 (Feb. 20, 1951), 179. A record of efforts by Mennonites to explain the nonresistant position to Selective Service personnel in Puerto Rico.

Nase, Elva. "Nonresistance at Zion Mennonite Church, Souderton, Pensylvania." Student paper for Our Churcistian Heritage, Bethel College, 1957. Pp. 13. MLA/BeC.

Nation, Mark. "The Politics of Compassion: A Study of Christian Nonviolent Resistance in the Third Reich." MA in Peace Studies thesis, AMBS, 1981. Pp. 115. Summarizes the variety of nonviolent resistance offered by German Christians to both the ideology of the Nazi regime and to Nazi practices such as the persecution of the Jews, euthanasia, and war in order to dispel the notions that violence is inherent in the word "resistance" and that pacifists can be nothing but "passivists" in the face of tyranny.

Nelson, Boyd N. "New Look in I-W Services: Love, Peace, Nonresistance, or What." (Part 6) *GH* 53 (Mar. 29, 1960), 281-82. Until all our lives are filled daily with love the I-W program will be a mere mockery.

Nelson, Boyd N. "The Plus Side of Nonresistance." *ChrLiv* 5 (July, 1958), 3-5. Outlines the constructive service work done by people opposed to war.

Nelson, Boyd N. "War and God's Work." *GH* 59 (Apr. 12, 1966), 326-27. One's reasons for being nonresistant need to shift from a desire to remain pure to a positive concern for the total welfare of humanity.

Nelson, John Olwir (Review). *Nevertheless: The Varieties of Religious Pacifism,* by John H. Yoder. Scottdale: Herald Press, 1971. Pp. 144. *Fellowship* 38 (Apr., 1972), 6. Describes the author's attempt to differentiate the many varieties of religion-based nonviolence. Recommends the book and praises it for its nonpartisan and nonpatronizing irenicism.

Neuenschwander, A. J. "Can We Do Anything to Advance the Cause of Peace?" *MCE* 2 (Apr. 16, 1935), 1-2. During times of preparation for war such as the present, Mennonites must look again at their nonresistant heritage. We must also tell others, including the government, of our position.

Neuenschwander, A. J. "Representatives from Historic Peace Churches Present Position to Government." *Menn* 52 (Mar. 9, 1937), 4-6. Three letters presented to President Roosevelt along with a summary of Mennonite principles of nonresistance.

Newberry, Loren. "Areas of Co-operation and Conflict Between the Communities of Newton and North Newton." Social Science Seminar paper, May, 1962. Pp. 11. Includes nonresistance as cause for conflict. MLA/BeC.

Newcomer, Frank C. "Nonresistance under Test— Experiences of CO's During the World War." *YCC* 21 (Feb. 25, 1940), 58, 59, 64. The World War was a time of severe testing of the Mennonite doctrine of nonresistance. Present conditions are moving toward a possible US involvement in the war. Are Mennonite youth ready to respond?

Nickel, J. W. "The Canadian Conscientious Objector." *MennLead* 3 (Jan., 1948), 24-28. A picture of Canadian camp life. The problems and frustrations of the CO's are related with an emphasis on the inadequate instruction on nonresistance.

Nickeson, Walter. "Menno Simons and John Calvin: Pacifism or Just War?" Research paper for the Christian Faith class. 1978. Pp. 8. BfC.

Nidever, Rodney J. "Nonresistance: A Traditional and Personal Perspective." A paper for the Mennonite Brethren Church course, 1979. Pp. 17. MBBS.

North, Wayne. "Peacemakers—God's True Sons." *Builder* 18 (Apr., 1968), 54-56. Commentary on youth Sunday School lesson which clarifies the theological link between the lordship of Christ and nonresistance as a human response.

Ollenburger, Ben C. Letter to the Editor. *ChrLead* 36 (June 26, 1973), 13. One of the broadest avenues of witness open to Mennonite churches is provided by a stance of nonresistance.
*

Ovensen, Barney. "Why It Is NOT Right for a Christian to Fight." *GH* 45, Part 1, (June 17, 1952), 592-93, 605; Part 2, (July 15, 1952), 696-97. Argues against Robert C. McQuilkin's position (*Why It Is Right for a Christian to Fight*) on the grounds that McQuilkin bases too much on the Old Testament and fails to consider sufficiently Christ's command to love the enemy.

Oyer, John S. "The Reformers Oppose the Anabaptist Theology." *Recovery of the Anabaptist Vision.* Ed. Guy F. Hershberger. Scottdale: Herald Press, 1957, 202-216. Oyer examines the views of Zwingli, Bullinger, Luther, and Melanchthon toward the Anabaptists. Discusses an objection common to the reformers: the Anabaptist threat to religious and civil order in their commitment to nonresistance.

"Peace Position Studied at Winnipeg Conference." *CanMenn* 4 (Apr. 13, 1956), 1, 4. Leaders were Elmer Ediger, D. D. Klassen, Ted Friesen, Henry Poettcker, and George Groening.

"Prison Is No Picnic." *With* 2 (Mar., 1969), 14. A look at some of the men and their reasons of conscience serving time in a United States federal prison.

"Prisoner for Christ." *With* 11 (Feb., 1978), 4. Patty Erb tells about being imprisoned and tortured in Argentina for the "crime" of working with poor people.

Pacifism (since 1945). 12 interviews. Includes Historic Peace Churches Consultation (1975), MCC involvement, National Service Board for Religious Objectors, and draft counselling. MLA/BeC.

*Pacifist Handbook: Questions and Answers Concerning the Pacifist in Wartime, Prepared as a Basis for Study and Discussion.* Peace Section, AFSC; Brethren Board of Christian Ed.; FOR; Friends Book Committee; General Conference Commission on World Peace, Methodist Church; The Mennonite Peace Society; War Resisters League; Women's International League for Peace and Freedom, June, 1939. Pp. 48. MHL. Presents problems pacifists are likely to face in a time of war, explores the various courses of action open to them and suggests activities which pacifists may do in peace times.

Paetkau, Walter. "Conflict of Loyalties." *CanMenn* 8 (Jan. 15, 1960), 2, 11. A student paper presented in a political science class at the University of Alberta elucidating the active Christian pacifist position.

Pankratz, Harland. "Pacifism in the Churches." Student paper for Our Christian Heritage, Nov. 22, 1948. Pp. 10. MLA/BeC.

Pauls, Jacob F. "A Theology of Separation: A Study in the Writings of Michael Sattler and Peter Rideman." Paper presented to theology of Anabaptist Classics class, AMBS, Elkhart, Ind., May 10, 1971. Pp. 15. MHL.

Peachey, J. Lorne. "Community News and Trends." *ChrLiv* 16 (Feb., 1969), 11. Two subjects highlighted: a Mennonite family responds to armed intruders; violence portrayed on TV.

Peachey, Paul L. "Nonresistance and Pacifism." *MennLife* 17 (Apr., 1962), 53-55. Anabaptist nonresistance was rooted in the Bible; it was agressive in word and deed. Among Mennonites nonresistance has come to mean non-involvement in the agony of society. It is a clear judgment upon them that many modern prophetic movements stem from secular roots.

Peachey, Paul L. "Nonviolence in the South." *GH* 50 (Feb. 19, 1957), 177. An account of the growing black self-conscious nonviolent resistance movement in the South.

Peachey, Paul L. "Pacifism in Germany." *GH* 50 (Jan. 15, 1957), 57. A historical review of the growth of pacifism in Germany since World War II and the part Mennonites played in it.

Peachey, Paul L. "The Cost of Conscience." *GH* 50 (Aug. 6, 1957), 703. A collection of items pertaining to CO's and pacifism from many countries.

Peachey, Paul (Review). *The New Testament Basis of*

---

*For additional listing, see Supplement, pp. 717-719.

*Pacifism,* by G. H. C. Macgregor. NY: FOR, 1954; *The Early Christian Attitude to War,* by C. John Cadoux. London: Headly Bros. Publ., 1919; *The State in the New Testament,* by Oscar Cullmann. NY: Chas. Scribner's Sons, 1956; *The Sword and the Cross,* by Robert M. Grant. NY: MacMillan, 1955; *Church and State from Constantine to Theodosius,* by S. L. Greenslade. London: SCM Press, 1954. "Some New Books on the Early Church and War." *GH* 49 (Sept. 18, 1956), 897, 911. Recommends these books as helpful in identifying the practices of the early church on the issues of church and state.

Peachey, Shem. "Nonresistance." *GH* 37 (Mar. 9, 1945), 993-94. Summarizes the biblical texts referring to the theme of nonresistance.

Peachey, Shem. "Our Present Nonresistant Status." *GH* 37 (Mar. 16, 1945), 1012. The Mennonites are in grave danger of losing their nonresistant faith.

Peachey, Urbane (Review). *Christ and Violence,* by Ronald J. Sider. Scottdale: Herald Press, 1979. Pp. 108. *MissFoc* 8 (June, 1980), 40. Reviewer considers the book's strength its direct connection between commitment to biblical nonviolence and life within modern society dominated by violent structures.

Penner, Helen. "Have a Heart in a World of Need." *ChrMon* 34 (Nov., 1942), 338-39. Describes MCC relief work in France and the motivating belief in nonviolence and aggressive good will.

Penner, Jeanne. "Routes and Application of Anabaptist Nonresistance." Student paper for Mennonite History, May, 1984. MLA/BeC.

Peters, Frank C. "The Scriptural Basis for Nonresistance." *ChrLead* 22 (Oct. 20, 1959), 4-5, 18. While Israel was, in a sense, the carrier and promoter of divine justice, the church is clearly the carrier of divine grace and redemptive love.

Peters, Gerhard M. "Hermeneutics and Nonresistance." Paper presented to Mennonite History and Nonresistant Theology classes, [AMBS], Elkhart, Ind., 1962. Pp. 25. MHL.

*
Peters, Peter H. (Review). *Christ and Violence,* by Ron Sider. Herald Press, 1979. Pp. 105. *MennRep* 10 (Aug. 18, 1980), 8. The book locates Christ's love and suffering for enemies at the heart of the gospel and examines the relationship of subjection to government and nonviolent resistance to governmental injustice.

Plett, Harvey. "Nonresistance in the Gospel and in Church History." Paper presented to Mennonite History class, GBS, Elkhart, Ind., May 17, 1962. Pp. 51. MHL.

*
Preheim, Marion Keeney. "Wrongly Imprisoned: Riding It Out with a Purpose." *GH* 72 (Oct. 23, 1979), 825-26. Opher Hinton, a black Mennonite from Philadelphia, was wrongly accused of a crime in July 1975 but has been serving his prison sentence believing that "the Lord had a reason for me to be in prison."

Preheim, Naomi. "In the World but Not of It." History 31, Carleton College, Minn., Mar. 3, 1972. Pp. 16. MLA/BeC.

Prieb, Wesley. "What Are Our Racial Attitudes?" *Menn* 64 (Jan. 25, 1949), 13-14. As in the area of nonresistance, Mennonites must bring together theology and practice regarding racial attitudes.

Purves, John H. "My Decision on Militarism." *Menn* 67 (Jan. 1, 1952), 11-12. An account of a pilgrimage from the militaristic point of view to persuasion that nonresistance is God's will and way.

(Review). *Gewaltlosigkeit im Täufertum,* by Clarence Bauman. "New Book on Nonviolence in Anabaptism Recommended." *CanMenn* 17 (Sept. 19, 1969), 3. MCC Peace Section recommends book as an investigation of the theological ethic of North German Anabaptism during the Reformation which focuses on the theology underlying the Anabaptist concern with nonviolence.

(Review). *It Is Not Lawful for Me to Fight,* by Jean-Michel Hornus. Trans. Alan Kreider. Scottdale: Herald Press, 1980. *MCC PS Newsletter* 10 (June-July), 9. Recommends the book as a historical and theological study of documents from the early church on war and peace, indicating that pacifism was the accepted practice of the early church.

(Review). *War—Peace—Amity,* by Henry P. Krehbiel. Berne: Mennonite Book Concern. *Fellowship* 3 (Sept., 1937), 19. Summarizes the thesis of this book which sketches the history of warfare, shows how the church abandoned its earlier pacifism and must now take up the struggle for peace.

(Review). *War, Peace, and Nonresistance,* by Guy F. Hershberger. Scottdale: Herald Press, 1944. Pp. 415. *CPS Bull* 3(Dec. 22, 1944), 3. Recommends the book for reading by every CPS worker.

(Review). *Why I Couldn't Fight,* by Lloy A. Kniss. N.p., n.d. *GfT* 10 (Jan.-Feb., 1975), 14-15. World War I conscientious objector explains his position. Reviewer recommends the book because it distinguishes between pacifism and biblical nonresistance.

Ramseyer, Lloyd L. "The Pacifist in a National Emergency." 1942. Pp. 9. BfC.

---

*For additional listing, see Supplement, pp. 717-719.

Redekop, Calvin W. "Instutions, Power, and the Gospel." *Kingdom, Cross, and Community.* Ed. John R. Burkholder and Calvin Redekop. Scottdale: Herald Press, 1976, 138-50. Religious movements use power and create institutions, thus emphasizing the goal-oriented or "doing" side of life rather than the relationship-oriented, or "being" side. Institutional power in itself is a neutral entity, but it becomes contrary to the gospel when it is used to solidify status differences and domination. Nonresistant or "free" churches have tended to ignore rather than analyze their use of power.

Redekop, Calvin W. "Why a True-Blue Nonresistant Christian Won't Waste Natural Resources." *FQ* 4 (Aug., Sept., Oct., 1977), 14-15. Christian nonresistance means refusing to do violence to life—human, animal, or natural environment.

Redekop, John H. "A Call to Consistency." *MBH* 16 (Aug. 5, 1977), 10. Concerned about MCC personnel identification with black resistance movements in Africa; author cannot reconcile pacifism with terrorism.

Redekop, John H. "Limitless Christian Love." *ChrLead* 36 (Oct. 30, 1973), 4; *MBH* 12 (Nov. 2, 1973), 2-3, 8. Although an integral part of the confession of the church, Christian nonresistance is not really understood or practiced. Suggests the use of "limitless Christian love" instead of "nonresistance."

Redekop, John H. "Non-Resistance and UN Police Action." *CanMenn* 4 (Dec. 7, 1956), 3. Calls nonresistant Christians to take a stand on the issues of an international police force, armed forces, local police, etc.

Redekop, John H. "On Capital Punishment." *MBH* 5 (Jan. 7, 1966), 2. To advocate capital punishment while also endorsing biblical nonresistance is fundamentally inconsistent.

Redekop, John H. "Prince of Peace and Pacifism." *MBH* 15 (Nov. 26, 1976), 10. Disturbed by attitudes displayed during a peace conference, author urges pacifism as a lifestyle affecting all relationships.

Redekop, John H. "The Full Gospel." *MBH* 16 (Feb. 4, 1977), 10. While "full gospel" groups display enthusiasm and conviction, they ignore Jesus' teachings on discipleship and nonresistance.

Redekop, John H. "Where Do We Stand on Pacifism?" *MBH* 17 (May 12, 1978), 17. The Kauffman-Harder survey in *Anabaptists Four Centuries Later* reveals that Mennonite Brethren need a greater emphasis on peace teaching.

Redekop, John H. (Review). *Twentieth-Century Pacifism,* by Peter Brock. New York: Van Nostrand Reinhold, 1970. Pp. 274. *MQR* 46 (Apr., 1972), 173-74. Faults the book for uneven analysis, failure to define various types of pacifism, and overstating Gandhi's contribution to peace. Still, considers the book a significant contribution to peace studies.

Reed, Paul E. "The Non in Biblical Nonresistance." *ST* 37 (Mar., 1969), 22. The heart of Biblical nonresistance involves confronting sin and changing human lives.

Reeser, Ethel. "The Significance of Relief Work in the Program of the Mennonite Church." Paper presented to Sociology Seminar, Goshen College, Goshen, Ind., May 20, 1949. Pp. 43. MHL.

Regier, Dwight. "The Biblical Basis of Dutch Anabaptist Nonresistance." Student paper for Mennonite History, Nov. 29, 1976. Pp. 20. MLA/BeC.

Regier, Paul S. "Mennonite Nonresistance in Prussia, 1740-1815." Social Science Seminar paper, May, 1967. Pp. 41. MLA/BeC.

Reimer, Vic. "Irish Peace People Build Confidence in Nonviolence." *Menn* 94 (May 1, 1979), 312-13. An interview with Nobel Peace Prize co-winner Mairead Corrigan who is optimistic about the prospect of peace in Northern Ireland.

Rempel, John. "The Age of the Spirit: A Study of the Temptation Among Anabaptists to Try to Make History Come Out Right." Paper presented to Theology of History class, AMBS, Elkhart, Ind., n.d. Pp. 28. AMBS.

Rempel, John G. "A Catechism on Nonresistance: A Short Set of Questions and Biblical Answers for the Instruction of Young People." Paper, n.d. Pp. 4. MHL.

Rempel, Peter H. "Nonresistance Without Privilege: The Dilemma of the Russian Mennonites, 1917-1927." Term paper for Modern Russian History course, Aug., 1976. Pp. 35. CGCL.

Ressler, Dale. "Nonresistance from 1914-1918." Term paper for Mennonite History course, Nov. 9, 1970. Pp. 7. MSHL.

Rich, Elaine Sommers. Langenwalter, J. H., as told to Elaine Rich, "Keep Your Mouth Shut and Saw Wood." *ChrLiv* 6 (Jan., 1959), 32-33. Author shares this advice, which helped him in tight places, such as his nonresistant position in the Spanish-American War.

Richardson, Lonnie L. "A Limited Survey of the *Gospel Herald* on the Teaching of Nonresistance from 1939 to 1945." Term paper for Mennonite History course, Nov., 1969. Pp. 13. MSHL.

Rohrer, Charles. *When and Where the Church Met Three Disastrous Defeats.* Elkhart: By the Author, 3140 Idelwild St., 1973. Pp. 23. MHL. The three "defeats" named in the title are the abandonment of pacifism for just war theory in the time of Constantine, the unification of church and state in the Edict of Intolerance at Nicea, and the exchange of immersion water baptism for the sprinkling of babies baptism at the Church Council of Carthage, 418 BCE.

Roy, Prodipto, "A Hindu Shames Us." *ChrLiv* 1 (Mar., 1954), 15, 41-42. The apostle of Gandhi, Acharya Vinoba Bhave, fights communism in India by preaching nonviolence and voluntary giving of land by wealthy landowners.

Ruth, Carl. "Is Nonresistance Enough?" *GH* 56 (Oct. 15, 1963), 909. We are in danger of losing the validity of our nonresistance because we do not operate on the basis of love and peace.

Ruth, Merle. "Affirmative Aspects of Nonresistance." *ST* 38 (Jan., 1970), 1-4. Nonresistance is sometimes regarded as a negative term, but both the doctrine and the consequent practice are positive as expressions of Christian love.

"Statement of Concerns." *MennComm* 5 (Nov., 1951), 17-19. Statement resulting from Study Conference on Christian Community Relations links the doctrine of nonresistance to war to issues of business ethics, organized labor, race and minority relations, and standard of living.

Sanger, S. F. and Hays, D. *The Olive Branch of Peace and Good Will to Men: Anti-War History of the Brethren and Mennonites, the Peace People of the South, During the Civil War 1861-1865.* Elgin: Brethren Publishing House, 1907. Pp. 232. Compilation of personal accounts from Brethren and Mennonites in the Confederacy who refused to participate in the war. Includes treatises on church and state, and the basis for nonresistance; reprints Exemption Act of Confederate Congress.

Santiago, Lydia Esther. "Peace and War: A Personal Experience with Nonresistance." *GH* 43 (Nov. 21, 1950), 1147. Santiago explains how she encountered nonresistance and conscientious objectors in World War II in Puerto Rico.

Sauder, Menno. *An Introduction to the Pamp[h]let "The Peaceful Kingdom of Christ: An Exposition on the Twentieth Chapter of Revelations [sic]" by Peter Twisk and a Treatise by Several Other Authors Bearing on the Same Subject.* Elmira, Ont.: By the Author, 1943. Pp. 40. MHL. Believes an interpretation of apocalyptic literature that envisions Christ's kingdom as a physical entity can lead to an abandonment of nonresistance in the effort to "help" the vision to fulfillment and, thus, to violation of a basic biblical principle.

Sawatsky, Rodney J. "History and Ideology: American Mennonite Identity Definition Through History." PhD dissertation, Princeton University, Princeton, NJ, May, 1977. Pp. 332. MHL. Contends that the American Mennonites, from their first expressions of identity in the early 18th century, have always tried to explain who they are and what they are about by means of their history both among themselves and with their neighbors. Sawatsky traces this usage through the ""owning" of the *Martyrs' Mirror*, the work of C. Henry Smith and John Horsch and the identity crisis of the 1920s to the work of Harold S. Bender and the reformation captioned as the ""Anabaptist vision." Within this context, the issues of war and peace receive substantive treatment in two sections: the chapter entitled, "Two Wars: The Context of Identity," 122-69; the chapter entitled, "Biblical Nonresistance: An Acceptable Denominational Distinctive," 211-60.

Sawatsky, Rodney J. *The Influence of American Fundamentalism on Mennonite Nonresistance, 1908-1945.* Unpublished MA thesis, Dept. of History, U. of Minnesota, 1971. Pp. 200. The Mennonite Church (MC), following its nineteenth-century awakening, adopted much of the Fundamentalist stance during the Modernist-Fundamentalist controversy. This association with an often militaristic theology subtly weakened the political implications of the Mennonite nonresistant stance.

Sawatsky, Rodney J. (Review). *A People of Two Kingdoms: The Political Acculturation of the Kansas Mennonites,* by James C. Juhnke. North Newton, Kansas: Faith and Life Press, 1975. Pp. 215. *MQR* 50 (Jan., 1976), 72-73. Juhnke defines the dualism of the title as "conflict between the ethic of modern nationalism and the ethic of traditional Mennonitism" characterized by pacifism, apoliticism, and German ethnic identity.

Sayre, John Nevin (Review). *Christian Pacifism,* by Edgar W. Orr. Ashingdon, England: C. W. Daniel Co. Pp. 161. *Fellowship* 25 (Sept., 1959), 31-32. A critical response to this handbook which presents Christian pacifist history with excellent bibliography and references to literature on pacifism. Points out its omissions and limitations as well as its strengths, recommending it for its wide range of pacifist events touched on in brief compass.

Scheifele, Nelson. "Pacifism." Speech given at the Peace Oratorical Contest, St. Catharine's, Ont., Nov. 19, 1966. Pp. 3. CGCL.

Schellenberg, Tim. "Nonresistance Stand in the Krimmer Mennonite Brethren Church in World War I." Research paper for the Mennonite Brethren Church course, May 27, 1981. Pp. 25. MBBS.

Schlabach, Theron F. "To Focus a Mennonite Vision." *Kingdom, Cross, and Community.* Ed. John R. Burkholder and Calvin Redekop. Scottdale: Herald Press, 1976, 15-50. Reviews Guy F. Hershberger's intellectual development and life work of interpreting Mennonite nonresistance in relation to war, industrial relations, church-state relations, community life and mutual aid, and race relations.

Schmidt, Daryl Dean. "The Roots of Early Anabaptist Nonresistance." Student paper for Anabaptist-Mennonite Seminar, Feb., 1966. Pp. 22. MLA/BeC.

Schmidt, John F. "To Fight or Not to Fight." Student paper for Mennonite History Seminar, Mar. 5, 1965. Pp. 14. MLA/BeC.

Schmidt, Vyron L. "A Historical and Biblical Review of the Mennonite Stand on War, Peace, and Nonresistance." Social Science Seminar paper, May, 1970. Pp. 34. MLA/BeC.

Schrag, Duane. "Two Twentieth-Century Mennonite Martyrs." *Menn* 90 (Oct. 28, 1975), 613. Quotes from Werner Forssmann's *Experiments on Myself* (St. Martin's Press), which tells of the execution of two Mennonite men by Nazis for conscientious objection.

Schrag, Martin H. "Pacifism's Small Band." *EV* 79 (Mar. 28, 1966), 3-5. Throughout the past 2000 years a small minority of people have sought to practice pacifism. Anabaptists and Quakers have given a particularly clear witness to the power of love.

Schrock, Marion D. Letter in "Our Readers Say." *GH* 58 (Jan. 19, 1965), 52. We need to enter into more dialogue with other Protestants on the topic of pacifism.

Schrock, Paul M. "Peace and War: Atomic Love." *GH* 47 (July 20, 1954, 681. The greatest power in the universe is nonresistant love. It is required of the New Testament believer in all aspects of life.

Schrock, T. E. Letter to the Editor. *GH* 62 (Dec. 9, 1969), 1061. Interprets draft resisters to be misunderstanding the "sorting" function of the Selective Service system when they attribute only military motivations to the system. Questions whether Mennonites want to change from a nonresistant church into a resisting church.

Schroeder, Ardith. "Nonviolence Begins at Home." Paper, entry in C. Henry Smith Peace Contest, Bethel College, North Newton, Ks., May 19, 1977. Pp. 5. MHL.

Schroeder, Lorraine. "Pacifism in Action." Student paper for Mennonite History Seminar, n.d. Pp. 43. MLA/BeC.

Schwartz, G. "The Two Resistances." *Fellowship* 13 (Nov., 1947), 169-71. "One is born to resistance as one is born male or female, but there are two resistances, and only one is the way to lasting peace"which is God. This statement was delivered in summer of 1946 at Le Chambou.

Schwartzentruber, Hubert. " 'Schleitheim,' a Peace Document." *MHB* 38 (Apr., 1977), 7. Author takes inspiration from 16th-century Anabaptists who risked death to counter the principalities and powers, and he calls for a similar commitment to justice and righteousness through nonviolence among Mennonites today.

Schwarzschild, Steven S. "The Basis of Jewish Pacifism." *GH* 42 (Jan. 17, 1950), 59. Jewish pacifists hold that pacifism is the logical direction of the internal dynamic of Jewish faith and history.

Seifert, Harvey (Review). *The More Excellent Way,* by Lloyd L. Ramseyer. Newton: Faith and Life Press, 1965. Pp. 122. "Sermons on Pacifism." *Fellowship* 32 (Jan., 1966), 29. Describes the tone and message of this book which contains short meditations on biblical themes in the form of thoughtful statements on the motive and method of love as a total way of life.

Sensenig, Kenneth L. "Why Study the Doctrine of Nonresistance?" *ST* 48 (Sept., 1980), 22-23. Discusses why nonresistance is receiving renewed support, and differentiates between nonresistance and pacifism.

Shank, Aaron M. *Studies in the Doctrine of Nonresistance: A Study Guide.* Myerstown, Pa.: Publication Board of the Eastern Pennsylvania Mennonite Church, [ca. 1974]. Pp. 42. MHL. Series of ten reading and memorization assignments plus detailed lesson outlines includes such topics as Jesus and nonresistance, the Old Testament and nonresistance, the state and nonresistance, etc.

Shank, Henry. "Turn the Other Cheek." *GH* 71 (Jan. 10, 1978), 17-19. Examines Jesus' command in Luke 6:29 to "turn the other cheek," concluding that a contemporary application calls for prophets of God's way to love the enemy of God's truth.

Shank, J. M. *"A Time to Kill and a Time to Heal:" A Treatise on the Sanctity of Human Life, War and Human Government, and Nonresistance.* N.p.:

Mennonite Messianic Mission, 1967. Pp. 24. Citing examples and stories from Genesis to Samuel, the author contends that God in the Old Testament commanded war and capital punishment. As a new dispensation, however, the New Testament forbids both, commanding instead love and nonresistance.

Shank, J. R. "Applied Nonresistance." *ChrMon* 32 (June, 1940), 188. Young People's Meeting study guide focuses on nonresistance in daily living.

Shank, J. R. "Bible Nonresistance, as Applied to Our Present Day." *ChrMon* 28 (June, 1936), 188-89. Young People's Meeting study guide for a lesson on this topic.

Shank, J. R. "Nonresistance in Practice." *ChrMon* 38 (Sept., 1946), 279. Young People's Meeting study guide focuses on overcoming evil with good.

Shank, J. Ward. "Applied Nonresistance." *ChrMon* 32 (June, 1940), 168-69. Advocates nonresistance in the home and church as foundations for nonresistance in time of war.

Shank, J. Ward. "Christian Principles Applied in Business Relations." *ST* 26 (1st Qtr, 1958), 28. Examines several Christian principles that are involved in business relations which includes nonresistance.

Shank, J. Ward. "How Ethical Is the Boycott?" *ST* 38 (Apr., 1970), 9. The use of the boycott, as a means of social pressure, is a weapon. One who joins a boycott is compelling another to go the second mile.

Shank, J. Ward. "Is the Mennonite Faith Epitomized in Nonresistance?" *ST* 29 (4th Qtr., 1961), 1. The application of the doctrine of nonresistance must be accompanied by a faithful representation of discipleship in all its phases.

Shank, J. Ward. "Listening In on the Anabaptist Dialogue." *ST* 45 (June, 1977), 7-10. Nonresistance to war is one issue interpreted differently among Mennonites.

Shank, J. Ward. "Nonviolent Resistance." *ST* 28 (2nd Qtr., 1960), 1. Should not confuse the social weapon of nonviolent resistance with the ideal of Christian love and nonresistance.

Shank, J. Ward. "Teaching the Doctrine of Love and Nonresistance." *ST* 43 (July, 1975), 9-10. Love and nonresistance should be translated into action, but not the militant political action that characterizes much of the peace movement.

Shank, J. Ward. "The Christian Doctrine of

Peace." *ST* 47 (Feb., 1979), 22-24. Comment on Romans 12:17-21 and its contribution to the concepts of peace and nonresistance.

Shank, J. Ward. "The Death of Martin Luther King, Jr." *ST* 36 (June, 1968), 1. Comments on the implications and assessment of the death of King.

Shank, J. Ward. "The Pursuit of Justice." *ST* 47 (Apr., 1979), 8-10. The former Mennonite emphasis on love and nonresistance is changing to emphasis on peace and justice through social programs and reform.

Shank, J. Ward (Editorial). "A New Legalism?" *ST* 40 (Oct., 1972), 5. Raises the possibility that there may be a new legalism in the church related to nonresistance or the doctrine of "peace."

Shank, J. Ward (Editorial). "Militant Nonresistance." *ST* 38 (Jan., 1970), 7. The phrase "militant nonresistance" is a contradiction in terms. We rather need new emphasis upon the essence of the biblical doctrine of nonresistance.

Shank, J. Ward (Editorial). "Nonviolence a la King." *ST* 33 (4th Qtr., 1965), 1. We should recognize that King's nonviolence is not of the gospel, whatever its good intentions or laudable objectives.

Shearer, Jon (Review). *Jesus and the Nonviolent Revolution,* by André Trocmé. Scottdale: Herald Press, 1971. Pp. 173. "The Ministry of Jesus: Justice and Redemption Inseparable." *MennRep* 4 (Apr. 29, 1974), Section A, 8. Book focuses on Jesus' ministry of active nonviolence rooted in his inauguration of the Year of Jubilee. Shearer observes it is foundational work for John H. Yoder's *Politics of Jesus.*

Shearer, Vel. " 'Make Us Builders of Peace': The Meaning of Discipleship." *MennRep* 4 (Apr. 15, 1974), 5. Address given at World Day of Prayer focuses on Jesus' teachings on discipleship and his practice of nonresistance, even to the cross.

Shelly, Andrew R. "The Biblical Basis for Nonresistance." *Fourth Mennonite World Conference Proceedings.* Aug. 3-10, 1948. Akron: MCC, 1950, 159-65. Nonresistance is not a human doctrine but part of the whole message of the Bible. It must not be taken out of that context.

Shelly, Maynard. "South African Police Met with Nonviolence." *Menn* 92 (Apr. 12, 1977), 249-50. Describes the nonviolent witness of a South African church leader to security police raiding church headquarters in reprisal for the church's opposition to apartheid.

Shelly, Maynard. "Suffering Servant and King (3):

Weakness as a Way of Life." *MennRep* 7 (Apr. 4, 1977), 6. In Jesus' nonviolence and suffering we see that God works through weakness, not strength.

Shelly, Maynard. "50-450." Convocation address, 1967. Pp. 8. Revolution, nonviolence, response to Communism. MLA/BeC.

Shenk, Coffman S. "Mennonite Youth and Nonresistance." *GH* 38 (Sept. 28, 1945), 489-90. When approximately fifty percent of drafted Mennonite youth enter the military, the fact that Mennonites have been too unconcerned with spiritual matters is exposed.

Shenk, R. J. "Nonresistance." *GH* 42 (Jan. 18, 1949), 53-55. The Mennonite Church can maintain a nonresistant witness only if it is willing to live the faith and make sacrifices daily.

Shenk, Stanley C. *Youth and Nonresistance.* Scottdale: Herald Press, 1953. Pp. 63. A series of thirteen lessons for group discussion prepared for the Mennonite Commission for Christian Education.

Shenk, Wilbert R. (Review). *The Original Revolution,* by John H. Yoder. Scottdale: Herald Press, 1972. Pp. 189. *GH* 66 (Jan. 2, 1973), 13. Comments primarily on the title essay, in which Yoder sets forth the model of the "messianic community"a community of committed believers living out the ethics of Jesus, including pacifism.

Shetler, Sanford G. "Is This Our Task?" *GH* 58 (July 20, 1965), 629-30. The racial problem is first of all a spiritual problem which will not be solved by nonviolent coercive methods. These methods are not congruent with biblical pacifism.

Shetler, Sanford G. "Pacifism and the Vietnam War." *GfT* 6 (Sept.-Oct., 1971), 14, 18, 13. War is evil yet inevitable, and those who profess to follow Christ should not participate in it.

Shetler, Sanford G. "The Theory of Direct Nonviolent Action." *GfT* Series I, No. 8 (Apr.-June, 1968), 1-8. (Stapled between pp. 8-9 of *GfT* Series 2, Vol. 3 (Apr.-June, 1968). Quotes Mennonite thinkers on nonresistance to show that nonviolent resistance is not biblical agape but rather a humanistic political movement.

Shetler, Sanford G., comp. "Three Views on War and Peace and Related Issues." *GfT* 6 (Sept.-Oct., 1971), 16-17. Compares a militarist-fundamentalist, a liberal-pacifist (humanistic pacifism), and an Anabaptist-nonresistant (Biblical pacifism) on 20 points.

Showalter, Bernard. "Nonresistance in the Early

Church." Research paper for History Seminar, Goshen College, Goshen, Ind., May, 1951. Pp. 29. MHL, BfC.

Showalter, Dennis. "References to Nonresistance and Militarism in the Virginia Mennonite Conference Minutes (1835-1966)." Term paper for Menonite History and Thought course, Feb. 14, 1973. Pp. 20. MSHL.

Sider, E. Morris. "Nonresistance in the Early Brethren in Christ Church in Ontario." *MQR* 31 (Oct., 1957), 278-86. Although they strongly uphold the practice of nonresistance, Brethren in Christ often paid a "tax" for the privilege of exemption from militia duty.

Sider, Ronald J. *Christ and Violence.* Scottdale: Herald Press, 1979. Pp. 108. Four essays which speak both exegetically and practically to the thesis that the concept of active nonviolence is a more adequate expression of the way of Jesus than the concept of nonresistance.

Sider, Ronald J. "Reconciling Our Enemies." *Sojourners* 8 (Jan., 1979), 14. Jesus' vicarious death for sinful enemies of God lies at the very heart of a Christian's commitment to nonviolence.

Sider, Ronald J. "Zeal, Zealot." *Baker's Dictionary of Christian Ethics,* ed. Carl F. H. Henry. Grand Rapids, MI: Baker Book House Co., 1973, 724. Jesus' ethic of love and nonresistance was developed in the face of and in tension with the Zealot nationalism.

Smith, C. Henry. *Christian Peace: Four Hundred Years of Mennonite Peace Principles and Practice.* N.p., 1938. Pp. 32. A summary statement of the anabaptist-Mennonite experience with nonresistance.

Smith, C. Henry. *Menno Simons, Apostle of the Nonresistant Life.* Berne: Mennonite Book Concern, n.d. Pp. 76. Brief, readable biography of Menno Simons, paying particular attention to his teachings.

Smith, C. Henry. *Smith's Story of the Mennonites.* Fifth edition revised and enlarged by Cornelius Krahn. Newton: Faith and Life Press, 1981. (First edition copyright 1941.) Pp. 589. A comprehensive overview of Mennonites from the 16th century to the present. The theme of nonresistance is woven into the story, while the final chapter, "Witnessing in War and Peace," discusses church-state issues in early America and the World Wars.

Smith, C. Henry. "The Historical Background." *The Power of Love: A Study Manual Adapted for Sunday School User and for Group Discussion.* Ed. Peace Committee of the GCMC. Newton: Board of Publication, 1947, 38-57. MHL. Brief summary of the belief and practice of nonresistance from the New Testament church through World War I.

Smith, Wayne LaVelle. "Rockingham County Nonresistance and the First World War." MA thesis, Madison College, Harrisonburg, Va., 1967. Pp. 160. A study of Mennonite and Brethren experiences, attitudes, and activities during World War I. Includes summary of the nonresistant position dating from the Reformation, and a brief look at Mennonite experiences during the Civil War. MSHL.

Smucker, Donovan E. "Christian Love: Its Four Dimensions as a Resolution of the Ancient Conflict Between Faith and Works." *Mission-Focus* 5 (Jan., 1977), 4-9. A discussion of various dimensions of agape love includes a section on the nonviolence of Martin Luther King, Jr., which was rooted in love going beyond the demands of the law.

Smucker, Donovan E. "Mennonite Critique of Modern Pacifism." Paper, n.d. Pp. 3. MHL.

Smucker, Donovan E. "The Influence of Public Schools on Mennonite Ideals and Its Implications for the Future." *PCMCP Second,* 44-66. North Newton, Kansas: The Bethel College Press. Held at Goshen, Indiana, July 22-23, 1943. A survey of the impact of the public school system on Mennonite ideals as interpreted by Mennonites who have graduated from Mennonite colleges. Nonresistance is cited as the most frequently abused ideal.

Smucker, Donovan E. "The Theological Basis for Christian Pacifism." *MQR* 27 (July, 1953), 163-86 and at BfC, pp. 21. A delineation of discipleship as the difference between pacifist and non-pacifist Christians.

Smucker, Donovan E. "Whither Christian Pacifism." *MQR* 23 (Oct., 1949), 256-68 and at MHL, pp. 7. A review and evaluation of pacifism outside of the historic peace churches and a plea for involvement with them and all who work for peace.

Smucker, Donovan E. and Smucker, Barbara Claassen. *A Catechism of Peace in a World at War with a Casebook in Non-violence.* Philadelphia: American Friends Service Committee, n.d. Pp. 24. Presents theses on the evil of war and discusses the role of work camps in modeling peaceful social structures. Reprints case studies in nonviolence, with bibliography.

Smucker, John I. "Martin Luther King, Jr. and Nonviolence." Paper prepared for Social Development of the Negro in America class, Union Theological Seminary, New York, NY, May 8, 1968. Pp. 10. MHL.

Smucker, John I. "The New Mennonites." *GH* 61 (Jan. 30, 1968), 104-105. Reviews Mennonite belief in nonresistance which led to a retiring, nonaggressive stance toward the rest of society. Calls for a renewal of aggressive gospel preaching which meets people's needs, in order to face outbreaks of evil adequately and nonviolently.

Smucker, Joseph. "Pacifism and Nonviolence in the Colonial United States Before and During the Revolutionary War." Student paper for Mennonite History, Life and Thought, Dec. 9, 1980. Pp. 15. MLA/BeC.

Snider, Marie Gingerich. "LoveA Business Deal?" *ChrLiv* 2 (Dec., 1955), 23. True Christian love is nonresistant and leads to the cross.

Snider, Miriam. "The Way of Peace." *YCC* 31 (Oct. 15, 1950), 334, 335. Nonresistance is not the gospel, it is a fruit of the gospel. Christians' peace testimony will manifest itself in a positive, active way of life.

Snyder, C. Arnold. "The Relevance of Anabaptist Nonviolence for Nicaragua Today." *CGR* 2 (Spring, 1984), 123-37. In comparing the Peasants' War of 1525 and the Nicaraguan Revolution of 1979, one notes that both produced theologies of social justice allowing for armed resistance. However, in response to the 16th century peasant revellion, the Anabaptists (Schleitheim, 1527) specifically rejected armed resistance as a response to injustice. Is this sort of response relevant to the situation in Central America? Concludes that the Anabaptists not only rejected violence but reinterpreted and preserved a vision of justice in their ecclesiology. Concludes that this reinterpreted vision of justice can be relevant to Nicaragua if we abandon the strict dichotomy between church and world and try to be the church in the middle of the world, acting for justice. Also "The Relevance of Anabaptist Nonviolence for Nicaragua Today." Pp. 21. BfC.

Snyder, James C. "Peace and War: Nonresistance in School Life." *GH* 42 (Oct. 18, 1949), 1027. High School age students need support in their efforts to present the nonresistant faith to classmates.

Snyder, John. "On the Civilian Bond Question." *Gh* 36 (Sept. 23, 1943), 538-41. The nonresistant witness may be inconsistent and compromised if one buys civilian bonds.

Stauffer, Ethelbert. "The Anabaptist Theology of Martyrdom." *MQR* 19 (July, 1945), 179-214. The basic conception of the Anabaptist theology of history is that the true church has always been a suffering church; the Anabaptists were the heirs of this martyrs' tradition.

Stauffer, Ethelbert. "The Anabaptist Theology of Martyrdom, Part II." *ChrMon* 38 (Apr., 1946), 116-20. Reprinted from *MQR*. Relates nonresistance to martyrdom.

Stauffer, J. L. "Nonresistance in War-Time." *GH* 28 (Nov. 7, 1935), 675-76. Excerpts from a pastoral letter to the Lower District in Virginia outline the biblical basis for abstaining from direct or indirect contribution to the war effort. The Christian citizen should continue to pay taxes.

Stauffer, John L. "Can We Agree on Nonresistance?" *ST* 47 (June, 1979), 1-3, 26-29. Eight propositions on biblical hermeneutics and the nature of God form the basis of his defense of nonresistance. We must have unity on the philosophy of peace. A major point of disagreement on the basis of nonresistance arises from the question of warfare in the Old Testament. Paper, Harrisonburg, Va., n.d. Pp. 5. MHL.

Stauffer, John L. "Ninety to One." *ST* 27 (3rd Qtr., 1959), 37. The New Testament does not recommend nonresistance as a way of life for the nations of the world.

Stauffer, John L. "Peace Section: Can We Agree?" *GH* 42 (Mar. 15, 1949), 247-48. Nonresistant suffering is a New Testament doctrine. In the Old Testament there are warrior saints, in the New Testament there are martyr-saints.

Stauffer, John L. "The Error of Old Testament Nonresistance." *ST* 6 (2nd Qtr., 1960), 6. The line of argument that nonresistance must have been God's way of life for Israel in the Old Testament brings confusion to an understanding of law and grace.

Stauffer, John L. *The Message of the Scriptures on Nonresistance.* Harrison, Va.: Tract Press, n.d. Pp. 15. MHL. Summarizes New Testament and Old Testament views on war, church and state, etc., as well as the differences between the Testaments on these issues.

Stauffer, John L. "Was Nonresistance God's Plan for Old Testament Saints?" *ST* 13 (May, 1945), 352. Examines the premises of *War, Peace, and Nonresistance* by Guy F. Hershverger. Stauffer's critical response is based on the belief that there is a radical difference between the Old and the New Covenants, which Hershberger does not sufficiently recognize.

Stauffer, John L. "Will Our Young Brethren Retain Bible Nonresistance?" *GH* 44 (Apr. 17, 1951), 364-65. Pacifism, Fundamentalism, and conformity to the world are undercutting nonresistant faith.

Stauffer, John L. (Review). *War, Peace, and Nonresistance,*" by Guy F. Hershberger. Herald Press, 1944. *ST* 13 (May, 1945), 377. This book should furnish much evidence to honest inquirers who are perplexed in their attempts to reconcile the Christian's participation in carnal warfare according to the teaching by both fundamentalists and modernists in the religious world.

Stayer, James M. "Anabaptist Nonresistance and the Rewriting of History: On the Changing Historical Reputation of the Schleitheim Articles and the Four Hundred Fiftieth Anniversary of Hans Denck's "Concerning Genuine Love'." Presented at the Schleitheim Seminar, Goshen College, June 29, 1977. Pp. 19. MHL.

Stayer, James M. "Anabaptists and the Sword." *MQR* 44 (Oct., 1970), 371-75. Argues that Anabaptist nonresistance originated because "sects without a real possibility of revolution, and with a very real experience of the misuse of power, arrived with compelling historical and religious logic at this most radical form of apolitical thought."

Stayer, James M. *Anabaptists and the Sword.* Lawrence, Ks.: Coronado Press, 1972; reprint edition including "Reflections and Retractions," Lawrence, Ks., 1976. Pp. 375. The larger Reformation developments, within which Anabaptist discussions took place regarding the legitimacy and limits of coercive force as a means for preserving society, provided three options: moderate apoliticism, represented by Luther; realpoliticism, represented by Zwingli; the crusade, represented by Müntzer. Stayer reviews the histories of the Swiss Brethren, the Upper German sects, and the Melchiorites in light of the three options and concludes that the Anabaptists pursued all three of these options and developed a position of nonresistant apoliticism only over a period of time.

Stayer, James M. "Melchior Hofmann and the Sword," *MQR* 45 (July, 1971), 265-77. Research notes with reference to an examination of previous interpretations as to who the real descendant of Melchior Hofmann was: Menno Simons or Jan van Leyden and David Joris.

Stayer, James M. "The Doctrine of the Sword in the First Decade of Anabaptism." *MQR* 41 (Apr., 1967), 165-66. Abstract of dissertation which argues that an absolute renunciation of violence and coercion was regarded by the majority of the Anabaptists of this period as an essential of the Christian life.

Steiner, Susan Clemmer. "The Hermeneutics of the Sword: An Investigation into Sattler, Denck, and Hubmaier." Term paper for Religious Studies course, Sept. 11, 1980. Pp. 49. CGCL.

Stobbe, Leslie H. "Anabaptist Distinctives." *MBH* 1 (Dec. 14, 1962), 6-7. Anabaptists responded nonviolently to persecution, yet vigorously opposed capital punishment and participation in any form of violence.

Stoesz, Edgar. "A Mennonite Reflects on Martin Luther King." *GH* 61 (May 14, 1968), 437; *Intercom* 8 (May-June, 1968), 2-3. Eulogizes King and his commitment to nonviolence, relating incidents from his life which underscored his message and challenging Mennonites to uphold justice as bravely.

Stoltzfus, Ed. "An Historical Survey of Nonresistance from the New Testament Times to the Present." Paper presented to Church History class, [Goshen College, Goshen, Ind.], n.d. Pp. 28. MHL.

Stoltzfus, Edward. "A Statement Relating to the Local Ground Observers Corps." *Gh* 48 (Nov. 15, 1955), 1089. Since GOC is basically part of the military program, nonresistant Christians should not participate in it. Alternate proposals are outlined.

Stoltzfus, Edward. "Where "On the Way' Is the Mennonite Church?" *GH* 70 (July 12, 1977), 522-25. Mennonite Church moderator urges Mennonites to use power nonviolently to confront evil in the world instead of advocating absolute nonresistance and cultural separation from the world.

Stoltzfus, Grant M. "Peace and War: Now Is the Time." *GH* 44 (Aug. 21, 1951), 811. Comments on the application of nonresistance to vocation, specifically nursing.

Stoltzfus, Grant M. "Virginia Mennonites in the Civil War." *MennLife* 18 (Jan., 1963), 27-29. How the Mennonites of Virginia met the tests of nonresistance during the Civil War in the US.

Stoltzfus, Grant M. "Where Have All the Russian Brothers Gone?" *ChrLiv* 19 (May, 1972), 25-30. Discussion of the book *Mennonity* by Russian W. F. Krestyaninov and his treatment of their attitudes toward war and nonresistance.

Stoltzfus, Victor. "Return Love for Hate, Says Martin Luther King." *ChrLiv* 7 (Aug., 1960), 11. Comparison of descriptions of nonviolence and nonresistance by King and Guy Hershberger, respectively.

Stoner, John K. "Jesus, Are You Really Serious?" *Lifework* 2 (1979), 3-5. Places Jesus' ministry in the context of national oppression by Rome, emphasizing Jesus' nonviolence as seen through eyes of Peter who hoped for a national revolution.

*
Strunk, Stephen. Letter to the Editor. *Menn* 92

(Oct. 18, 1977), 604. Questions the practice of war tax resistance, using Matthew 5:39 to show that refusal to pay war taxes is a form of resistance, contradicting Jesus' command to nonresistance.

Stucky, Frank. "Anabaptist Martyrs Their Nonviolent Reaction." Student paper for Mennonite History, Life and Thought, Nov., 1969. Pp. 22. MLA/BeC.

Stucky, Harley J. *The Doctrine of Love and Nonresistance.* N. Newton: Mennonite Press, 1955. Pp. 60. A discussion of Jewish nationalism, the historic roots of nonresistance, early Christian peace witness, and reasons for the decline of the peace witness in our day.

Stucky, Harley J. (Review). *War, Peace, and Nonresistance,* by Guy Franklin Hershberger. Scottdale: Herald Press, 1953. Pp. 375. *MennLife* 9 (Apr., 1954), 94-95. Reviews the revised edition of Hershberger's history and interpretation of Mennonite nonresistance.

Studer, Gerald C. "Conscripts of Christ." *GH* 43 (Sept. 19, 1950), 1. Mennonites hold to the nonresistant faith because Christ, the Apostles, and the early church taught and practiced it. The Old Testament teaching on nonresistance is valid only insofar as it is not contradicted by the New Testament.

Studer, Gerald C. (Review). *Death Row Chaplain,* by Byron Eshelman with Frank Riley. Prentice Hall, 1962. Pp. 252. *ChrLiv* 19 (Mar., 1963), 33. Recommends the book as a probing discussion of prison life, capital punishment, and nonresistance.

Swalm, E. J. "The Prince of Peace in the Gospels." *CanMenn* 13 (Sept. 7, 1965), 9, 15. A Bible study on nonresistance.

Swarr, David. "Pacifism in the Mennonite Church in the 20th Century." Term paper for Mennonite History and Thought course, Mar. 17, 1978. Pp. 12. MSHL.

Swartzendruber, A. Orley. "The Piety and Theology of the Anabaptist Martyrs in van Bracht's *Martyr's Mirror.*" *MQR* 38, Part 1, (Jan., 1954), 5-26; Part 2, (Apr., 1954), 128-42. A softening of eschatological and pneumatic motifs is observed after the first generation of martyrs in favor of an ethical and legalistic emphasis which inevitably sowed the seed for later divisions.

Swartzentruber, Ruth Ann. "By Love Serve One Another." *YCC* 40 (Mar. 29, 1959), 202. The Christian's fulfillment of positive nonresistance is found in the statement "by love serve one another." Prize-winning essay in church-wide contest.

---

*For additional listing, see Supplement, pp. 717-719.

"The Position of the Mennonite Brethren Church on Nonresistance." In *Guiding Principles and Policies of the Board of General Welfare and Public Relations*. Hillsboro: Board of General Welfare and Public Relations of the Mennonite Brethren Church, 1963, 28-29. Pp. 32. MHL. States basic assumptions of position and urges young men to accept the provision of civilian service as offered by the government.

"The Position of the Mennonite Church of North America on Peace, War, Military Service, and Patriotism." *Menn* 63 (Oct. 12, 1948), 5-6. The official statement of the GCMC on this subject. Appeals to the biblical basis for love and nonviolence. While refusing military service, Mennonites have shown genuine willingness to render service of national importance in alternative programs.

"Theologian Advocates Mennonite Power." *CanMenn* 17 (Mar. 11, 1969), 1. J. Lawrence Burkholder speaks on "Nonresistance and Nonviolence" on a lecture tour in Canada. After distinguishing the major differences between the two and advocating the second, he points out some of the limits and dangers of this response.

"Trudeau on Violence." *CanMenn* 18 (Apr. 10, 1970), 1. The prime minister's positive attitude to nonviolence and the draft dodgers is cited.

Tallack, William. "The Peace Loving Mennonites." Youngstown, Ohio, *Telegram*. n.d., n.p. Briefly reviews the social history of Mennonites from the sixteenth century through the late 1800s, focusing especially on Mennonite simplicity, gentleness, and nonresistance. Depicts Menno Simons as the founder and originator of Mennonite convictions on nonresistance. Typescript. Pp. 6. MLA/BeC.

*The Christian Nonresistant Way of Life*. Scottdale: Mennonite Publishing House, 1940. Also issued by Peace Problems Committee and Tract Editors of Lancaster Conference District, 1940, and Weaverland Conference, Menn., 1968. Pp. 48. MSHL. Pamphlet on the biblical basis for the doctrine of nonresistance. Includes such topics as "Christ Our Example under Test," "The Christian and Government" and "The Christian Conscience."

Thiessen, Elmer. Letter to the Editor. *MBH* 18 (Nov. 9, 1979), 13. One issue underlying the movement to change the Mennonite Brethren name may be the desire not to identify with the Anabaptist vision of radical discipleship and nonresistance.

Thiessen, Jake. Letter to the Editor. *ChrLead* 40 (Nov. 22, 1977), 20. Voices concern about Mennonite Brethren lack of willingness to support a nonresistant position on the grassroots level.

Thiessen, Mary. "Nonresistance in Canada During World War I and II." Student paper for Mennonite History, Nov., 1960. Pp. 17. MLA/BeC.

Toews, J. B. "Nonresistance and the Gospel." N.d. Pp. 5. MLA/BeC. MBBS.

Toews, John A. "Conference on the Church and Peace." *The Voice* 2 (Nov.-Dec., 1953), 13. Report on a conference sponsored by Church Peace Mission in 1950. Mennonite Brethren must distinguish themselves from "liberal pacifism" and "fighting fundamentalists."

Toews, John A. "American Religious Pacifism Prior to World War II." *The Voice* 16 (Mar.-Apr., 1967), 3. A study of the views of representative liberal theologians in the United States during the inter-war period.

Toews, John A. "NonresistanceA Matter of Discipleship." *MBH* 4 (Mar. 19, 1965), 8, 18. The "way of the cross" is inseparable from the meaning of the work of Jesus Christ.

Toews, John A. "Nonresistance or Pacifism?" *MBH* 4 (Feb. 19, 1965), 8-9. Utopian pacifism, having only ideological roots, tends to collapse during times of crisis, but biblical nonresistance stands because it is rooted in the gospel of Jesus.

Toews, John A. "The Christian and Armed Combat." Paper. n.d. Pp. 10. MHL.

Toews, John A. *True Nonresistance Through Christ*. Winnipeg: Board of General Welfare and Public Relations of the MB Church of North America, 1955. Pp. 63. A study of biblical teachings on nonresistance in relation to the teaching, life, cross, and church of Jesus Christ.

Toews, John B. "The Origin and Activities of the Mennonite *Selbstschutz* in the Ukraine (1918-1919)." *MQR* 46 (Jan., 1972), 5-40. Describes the rise and consequences of Russian Mennonite self-defense units (Selbstschutz) armed against the violence of Bolshevik and bandit forces, their strategies, and ensuing revenge. Traces the rise of such units to the credal, separatist, and largely untested pacifism of the Mennonite settlers, and to the threat of violence against Mennonite women, more than the threat of property loss.

Toews, John B. "The Russian Mennonite Migrations of the 1870s and 1880sSome Background Aspects." *ChrLead* 37 (Apr. 2, 1974), 4. A czarist decree intorduced universal military conscription in 1870s with no provisions for exempting the Mennonites. The question of their historic pacifism became a watershed in the history of the Russian Mennonites.

Trocmé, André. "Christian Nonresistance Only Alternative to Communism." *CanMenn* 7 (Oct. 16, 1959), 1, 10. Discussion with MCC personnel at Akron, Pa.

Trocmé, André. *Jesus and the Nonviolent Revolution.* Trans. Michael H. Shank and Marlin E. Miller. Introduction by Marlin E. Miller. Scottdale: Herald Press, 1973. Pp. 211. Develops the thesis that the social, economic, and political revolution based upon the jubilary law of Moses was central to Jesus' vision and led to the conflict which ended on the cross. The second part of the book surveys the history of violence and nonviolence from Elijah to Herod and identifies a prophetic concept of nonviolent resistance within the broader stream of nationalism and messianism. The last section traces Jesus' expansion of contemporary religious thought by transforming messianic expectations through the choice of nonviolent resistance as his kingdom method.

Unger, P. A. "Testing Non-Resistance." *CanMenn* 2 (May 14, 1954), 6-7. Analyzes of nonresistance from both a historical and biblical viewpoint. Strong encouragement for the church to be prepared to stand the test.

Unrau, Albert. "What I Expect from a Mennonite Minister." *MBH* 13 (May 31, 1974), 5, 8. Simplicity, separateness, pacifism, and a scriptural orientation.

Unrau, Ed (Review). *The Mennonite Brotherhood in Russia,* by P. M. Friesen. Mennonite Brethren, 1978. "Russian Mennonites Created a Brotherhood in Name Only," *MennMirror* 8 (Nov., 1978), 9, 10. Provides a summary of this book, which is a detailed and critical summary of the Mennonites of Russia, and gives a brief statement of the author's view on military service and nonresistance. Describes the book as "overwhelming in its scope and shattering in its impact."

Unruh, Abraham Heinrich. "Die Mennonitischen Wehrlosigkeit?" MBBS.

Unruh, B. H. "Nonresistance." Address, June 15, 1917. Pp. 16. MLA/BeC.

Unruh, Duane. "The Alexanderwohl Church and Nonresistance." Student paper for Mennonite History, Life and Thought, May 11, 1979. Pp. 26. MLA/BeC.

van der Zijpp, Nanne. "Experiences of the Dutch Mennonites During the Last World War." *MennLife* 1 (July, 1946), 24-27. Gives insight into the involvement of the Dutch Mennonite Church in the areas of Jewish persecution, nonresistance, and mutual aid.

Vogt, Roy. "Are Mennonites Pacifists?" *MennMirror* 7 (Apr., 1978), 26. Argues that very few Mennonites actually believe in an absolute pacifist position because we are sometimes forced to use force in our containment of evil. The Christian faith urges us to explore other ways.

Vogt, Roy. "Strikes Symbolize Union Power But You Wield Power Too." *MennMirror* 4 (May, 1975), 7-8. While sympathetic to view of Henry Funk, who is fighting a legal battle over his refusal to join a union on the grounds of conscientious objection to violent union tactics, Vogt urges Christians to think critically and analytically about the way we ourselves are involved with the uses of power. We must then exercise this power with care and responsibility to Christian ethics of nonviolence, etc., rather than withdrawing from situations simply because there is use of power.

Vogt, Roy. "Toews Explores Mennonite Pacifism." *MennMirror* 10 (Nov., 1980), 17, 19. Reports a series of lectures in which John B. Toews developed the thesis that the Russian Mennonites, while committed to "positive action in the midst of suffering," did not formulate a theology of nonresistance or pacifism.

Vogt, Roy (Editorial). "Who Is a Mennonite?" *MennMirror* 10 (Sept., 1980), 30. Assesses various components of the Mennonite identity, including aspects such as principles of peace and nonviolence, church and state relations.

Vogt, Virgil. "A Study of Balthasar Hubmaier's Conception of the Church." Paper presented to Anabaptist Theology Seminar, 1959. Pp. 55. AMBS.

Voolstra, Sjouke. "Dutch Mennonites Review Peace Vision." *GfT* 13 (May-June, 1978), 17, 19. Reviews the Dutch Mennonite position on peace since the 16th century and the difference of opinion in the 1960s between the advocates of nonresistance and of justice.

Voolstra, Sjouke. "Love Your Enemies: Called to Be Citizens of a New World." *MennRep* 7 (Dec. 26, 1977), 5. Love for enemies is part of the new way of Jesus which comes into conflict with the old world. Christian love must cross boundaries or it is an enemy of the new world.

Voth, Harold W. "Nonresistance in the Alexanderwohl Church." Student paper for Our Christian Heritage, Nov. 11, 1946. Pp. 17. MLA/BeC.

"War, Peace, and Nonresistance." *RepConsS* 5 (Feb.,

1947), 1, 3, 4. Briefly reports content, publication history, and reviewers' comments in regard to Guy F. Hershberger's *War, Peace and Nonresistance.*

Wall, C. "My Concept of Biblical Nonresistance." *The Voice* 9, Part 1, (Mar.-Apr., 1960), 4; Part 2, (July-Aug., 1960), 5; Part 3, (Sept.-Oct., 1960), 11. A personal testimony to the belief in biblical nonresistance as it was tested in both Russia and the United States.

Waltner, Emil J. "Difficulties in Applying Non-Conformity in Modern Life." *PCMCP Third,* 53-67. North Newton, Kansas: n.p. Held at North Newton, Kansas, Aug. 18-19, 1944. As people attempt to live a life of nonconformity in modern times, the issue of post-war military training is one of the most challenging.

Waltner, Emil J. "The Conscientious Objector in History and Now." *Menn* 57 (Mar. 31, 1942), 4-6. A brief review of nonresistance from the time of the Roman Empire to the present.

Waltner, Erland. "From Sword-Bearing to Cross-Bearing." *CanMenn* 1 (Dec. 4, 1953), 6. A sermon illustrating the development of the Apostle Peter's nonresistant position and how this position is paralleled in Paul and John.

Waltner, Erland. *The Apostle Peter: A Pilgrimage to Nonviolence.* [Newton: Faith and Life Press, 197__]. Pp. 7. MHL. Jesus both taught and practiced nonviolence himself; his early followers, with some difficulty and in time, came to understand that nonviolence was Jesus' way for them as well.

Waltner, Gary. "Nonconformist Practices Among the Swiss Volhynian Mennonites from their Anabaptist Beginnings to the Present." Social Science Seminar paper, Apr., 1962. Pp. 31. MLA/BeC.

Waltner, James. "Pacifist Witness at Omaha." *Menn* 74 (Aug. 11, 1959), 453-94. Mennonite critique of "Omaha Action," a pacifist protest of the arms race and particularly of construction of ICBM bases. Lists "nonresistant" reservations about such a witness.

Waltner, Orlando A. "Mahatma Gandhi and World Peace." *MennLife* 17 (Apr, 1962), 55-58. A brief article highlighting the man and his message.

Warkentin, B. Alf. "More on Non-Resistance." *CanMenn* 8 (Oct. 21, 1960), 2, 7. With references to Hans DeBoer and Henry Krueger, Warkentin holds out some hope that the elders of the Mennonite church might yet be moved into active pacifism.

Warkentin, B. Alf. "Test War Tax in the Courts." *CanMenn* 10 (Nov. 23, 1962), 6. If Mennonites sincerely believe in nonresistance, they should take every step to bring their belief to the attention of others.

Warkentin, Irvin. "Peace Conference Begins with Youth Rally." *CanMenn* 14 (Nov. 29, 1966), 9. At Inter-Mennonite Peace Conference youth rally J. B. Toews says acceptance of nonresistance because it is a Mennonite tradition is not enough; nonresistance must be re-evaluated in the context of the individual and her or his relationship to Jesus Christ.

Warkentin, Irvin. "Seminary Prof Predicts Loss of Nonresistance, Unless . . ." *CanMenn* 14 (Nov. 22, 1966), 1, 11. J. B. Toews re-evaluates Mennonite principle of nonresistance. Toews sees nonresistance as having its basis in an individual relationship to Jesus Christ. The syncretism of faith and culture is breaking down true biblical nonresistance.

Warkentin, Melvin. "Nonresistance and the Mennonite Brethren Church." Research paper for the Mennonite Brethren Church course, Dec., 1982. Pp. 24. MBBS.

Weaver, Jerry. "Nonresistant Robots." Student essay presented to Mennonite Contributions Contest, May, 1963. Pp. 4. MLA/BeC.

Weaver, William B. "The Need of Nonresistance in the Light of Present Day Conditions." *GH* 29 (Jan. 21, 1937), 920-22. The effectiveness of the nonresistant message in war time depends on whether or not it was lived well in peace time.

Webb, Jon. "Why I Choose Canada." *With* 4 (Mar., 1971), 10. The story of one man's experience in military prison. When he was unable to get a CO classification, he again went AWOL to Canada.

Weber, M. Alice. "Peace and War: Nonresistance in Eighteenth-Century Pennsylvania." *GH* 45 (Apr. 15, 1952), 369. A historical sketch of Mennonites in the time of the Revolutionary War.

Wedel, James. "Origins of American Pacifism." Student paper for Mennonite History, Dec. 2, 1969. Pp. 15. MLA/BeC.

Wellcome, I. C. *Should Christians Fight?* Scottdale, Pa.: Mennonite Publishing House, 1951. Pp. 53. MHL. Format is a debate between "Demi," representative of those "half-christianized by the Gospel," and "Christian," representative of those to whom Christ's law is supreme—and, who, consequently, believe in nonresistance. Topics discussed within this polemic are Christ's teaching on warfare, obedience to civil law, Old Testament warfare, the standards of the early church, etc.

Wendling, Woody and Zimmerman, Diane. "The Peaceful Warrior: A One-act Play Based on the Story of Michael Sattler, an Anabaptist Martyr, Living in the 16th Century in Germany." 1972. Pp. 17. MHL.

Wenger, A. Grace. "Anabaptist Perspectives on Education." *GH* 68 (Feb. 25, 1975), 137-39. Among distinctive emphases of Anabaptism which must be communicated to each generation is the emphasis on love and nonresistance, which translates in part into "vocation as servanthood."

Wenger, J. C. *History of the Mennonites of the Franconia Conference.* Telford: Franconia Mennonite Historical Society, 1937. Pp. 523. Includes a chapter on nonresistance and relief activities.

Wenger, J. C., ed. *Mennonite Handbook: Indiana-Michigan Conference.* Scottdale: Mennonite Publishing House, 1956. Pp. 159. MHL. Articles pertinent to peace issues include: "A Declaration of Christian Faith and Commitment with Respect to Peace, War, and Nonresistance," 105-114; "The Way of Christian Love in Race Relations," 127-36. In addition to these items, the various constitutions and by-laws reproduced here have articles on the issues of peace and nonresistance.

Wenger, J. C. "Nonresistance and the Gospel." *ChrMon* 43 (Mar., 1951), 80. Basis of nonresistance is in the doctrine of love.

Wenger, J. C. "Nonresistant and Nonpolitical." *GH* 59 (Mar. 15, 1966), 229. The nonresistant Christian will not become involved in political functions or offices that employ coercion. However we must speak out against injustice.

Wenger, J. C. "Our Threefold Calling." *ChrMon* 44 (May, 1952), 152. Address to the Mennonite Publication Board includes the call to support nonresistance to war.

Wenger, J. C. *Pacifism and Biblical Nonresistance.* Focal Pamphlet No. 15. Scottdale: Herald Press, 1968. Pp. 28. A definition of both pacifism and nonresistance in relation to their understanding of Christ, sin, society, power, etc. with the latter emerging as the preferred biblical teaching.

Wenger, J. C. "Regaining the Early Anabaptist Peace Testimony." *GH* 43 (Aug. 1, 1950), 777-78. A renewed educational effort is needed to revitalize the Mennonite position on nonresistance.

Wenger, J. C. "Revolutionaries or Reconcilers?" *GH* 64 (Mar. 9, 1971), 217. Reprinted from *Sword and Trumpet.* Cites the contrasting examples from the 16th century of Jan Matthijs, who espoused a revolutionary theocracy, and Obbe Philips, committed to nonresistance, to show the error of setting up the rule of God through violent coercion.

Wenger, J. C. *Separated unto God.* Scottdale: Mennonite Publishing House, 1951. Pp. 350. A plea for Christian simplicity of life and for a scriptural nonconformity to the world. Nonconformity functions as the context for separation from the worldly military nature of political rule, and for nonresistance specifically church and state.

Wenger, J. C. "The Message of the Mennonite Church." *GH* 63 (Aug. 25, 1970), 697. Summarizes major tenets of Anabaptist leaders, including statements on the relationship of church and state, baptism, and nonviolence.

Wenger, James. "Nonresistance: What College Students Think." *ChrLiv* 15 (June, 1968), 9-10. Report on a survey of 150 Mennonite juniors and seniors in college.

Wenger, Samuel S. "Mennonites and the Law." *ChrLiv* 5 (Feb., 1958), 6-8, 33. Guidelines regarding nonresistance and litigation.

Wenger, Warren M. "Peace—The Vine or the Grape?" *GH* 63 (Jan. 20, 1970), 60-62. While the question of how Mennonites with a peace position rooted in love for the enemy should relate to the popular peace movement is an important one, Mennonites should be giving greater attention to providing adequate structures for conscientious objectors in I-W service.

Wengerd, Carolyn. "Nonresistance of the Mennonites in Pennsylvania During the Revolution." Research paper for American Colonial and Revolutionary History class. 1970. Pp. 23. BfC.

Werkema, G. Frank. "Dutch Resistance (1940-1945)." Term paper for Nonviolence Seminar, 1975. Pp. 14. CGCL.

Werscham, Mary. Letter to the Editor. *God and Caesar* 3 (Nov., 1977), 5-6. A summary of how the writer has tried to witness to her commitment to nonviolence through non-payment of taxes.

*

Widjaja, Albert. "The Kingdom Renewing the Environment." *MBH* 17 (Oct. 27., 1978), 6-8. The deepest motive of nonresistance is care for people as God's created beings. This means challenging oppressive environments.

Widmer, Pierre. "From Military Service to Christian Nonresistance: the Testimony of a Former French Army Officer." *MQR* 23 (Oct., 1949), 245-56. The history of French Mennonite attitudes toward nonresistance, together with

---

*For additional listing, see Supplement, pp. 717-719.

an autobiographical account of renewed peace concern.

Widmer, Pierre. "International Mennonite Peace Committee Met for Biblical Studies in Luxembourg." *CanMenn* 11 (Mar. 29, 1963), 3-4. Meeting emphasized church and christocentric pacifism.

Wiebe, Arns. "The Principle of Love." *ChrLead* 31 (Oct. 22, 1968), 6, 7, 12. Love is to be exercised toward God, brothers and sisters, and the enemy. When that love becomes militant and political, however, it has lost its base in the experience of the love of God in our hearts.

Wiebe, Bernie. "Martyrs Mirror." *Menn* 93 (June 27, 1978), 432. In the season of national celebration, Wiebe reminds readers of Christian martyrs who died for giving first allegiance to God, not the state.

Wiebe, Esther C. "Nonresistance on the Mission Field." Student paper for Mennonite History, Life and Principles, Nov., 1957, Pp. 19. MLA/BeC.

Wiebe, Karen. Letter to the Editor. *ChrLead* 37 (Jan. 22, 1974), 14. Explores the possibility that Mennonite "limitless love" still has many limits.

Wiebe, Katie Funk. "Taboo Religion." *ChrLead* 36 (Aug. 7, 1973), 19. Looks at a questionnaire that indicates that Mennonite Brethren and Brethren in Christ lean more toward fundamentalism than other Mennonite groups tested, and therefore rank lower in nonresistance, race relations, and social witness.
*

Wiens, Jacob B. "The Mennonite Position on Nonresistance." Trans. J. H. Jansen. *MCE* 2 (Sept. 3, 1935), 1-2. Our faith and nonresistance is based on the Word of God, history, and our own experience.
*

Wiens, Karen. "The Tabor Mennonite Church in its Historical Pacifist Position." Student paper for Mennonite History, Life and Thought, Dec. 14, 1971. Pp. 30. MLA/BeC.

"Youth Are Committed to Nonresistance." *CanMenn* 17 (July 18, 1969), 3. Report of results of a research project in the Mennonite Church (MC) showing Mennonite youth are committed to nonresistance but are troubled by lack of parental understanding and by the gap between profession and practice in adults.

Yake, C. F. "'Peace, Peace' When There Is No Peace." *YCC* 12, Part 1, (June 21, 1931), 612; Part 2, (June 28, 1931), 620. Encouragement for youth to keep guard in the interest of true peace and the biblical principle of nonresistance. Reports on the current promotion of militarism in the United States. Also the forces opposing this militarism and promoting peace are mentioned.

Yoder, Bruce (Review). *Christ and Violence,* by Ronald Sider. Scottdale: Herald Press, 1979. Pp. 104. *FQ* 6 (Nov., Dec., 1979, Jan., 1980), 9. Filled with unanswered questions, Sider's book sensitizes readers to violent social structures, calling for activist nonviolence based in God's work in Christ on the cross.

Yoder, Delmar R. "A Plea for Nonresistance and Nonconformity." *GH* 72 (Aug. 28, 1979), 696. A questioning of the conservative rank of the "Smoketown 20" over the issue of all Scripture being of equal importance which would put an end to the Mennonite doctrines of nonresistance and nonconformity.

Yoder, Edward. "Are Nonresistant Christians Parasites? Peace Principles from a Scriptural Viewpoint" Part 15. *GH* 31 (Apr. 21, 1938), 78-79. While nonresistant Christians may not contribute directly to social justice, they are not parasites on society if they are living and preaching the gospel of Christ.

Yoder, Edward. "Beware of False Prophets." *GH Supplement* 35 (Apr., 1942), 78-80. Points on which Mennonites need to be clear include: the state is provisional, human, and lower than the church. The Christian, therefore, gives all of his or her obedience to the church; Christ taught nonresistance; Christ is superior to the Old Testament; nonresistant Christians will suffer reproach.

Yoder, Edward. "Can Nonresistant Christians Cooperate with a Government at War? Peace Principles from a Scriptural Viewpoint." Part 7. *GH* 29 (Oct. 15, 1936), 638. Knowing the interrelatedness of modern society, should one refuse induction into the army?

Yoder, Edward. "Christians in a World at War: Peace Principles from a Scriptural Viewpoint." Part 40. *GH Supplement* 34 (Apr., 1941), 78-79. In the confusion of war the doctrines of love and nonresistance are in danger. The Christian must continually look to God and his word.

Yoder, Edward. "Citizenship and War Service: Peace Principles from a Scriptural Viewpoint." Part 25. *GH* 32 (Apr. 20, 1939), 78-79. Some totalitarian trends in this and other countries should make it clear to nonresistant Christians that in times of war their position may well depend on the clearness of their own personal conviction.

Yoder, Edward. "Did Jesus Get Politicaly Involved?" *GfT* 6 (Sept.-Oct., 1971), 2-3. Reprinted from *Mennonites and Their Heritage,* No. 3, Mennonite Central Committee, 1942. Also reprinted in *GfT* 9 (Mar.-Apr., 1974), 18-19, 3, under the title "Jesus in a World of Strife!" Jesus practiced nonresistance and nonparticipation in politics because his kingdom was not of this world.

Yoder, Edward. "Kinds of Pacifists: Peace Principles from a Scriptural Viewpoint." Part 42. *GH Supplement* 34 (July, 1941), 358. There are many kinds of pacifists and several kinds of Christian pacifists. The nonresistant Christian pacifist has no particular advice to give government; the liberal Christian pacifist tries to apply Christ's teaching to politics.

Yoder, Edward. "Love Your Enemies." *GH Supplement* 36 (Feb., 1944), 1006. The love ethic is the only principle which will work in human relationships.

Yoder, Edward. "Old Testament Nonresistance." *GH Supplement* 37 (Oct., 1944), 591. David was nonresistant toward his personal enemies and militant only against God's enemies.

Yoder, Edward. *Our Mennonite Heritage: Mennonites and Their Heritage.* No. 3. Akron: MCC, 1942. This booklet is third in a series of six studies on Mennonite heritage prepared for use in CPS camps. It focuses specifically on doctrinal beliefs with major emphasis on peace and nonresistance.

Yoder, Edward. "The Patience of the Saints: Peace Principles from a Scriptural Viewpoint." Part 38. *GH* 33 (Jan. 16, 1941), 909-911. The Bible and history teach that nonresistant suffering is the way of the Christian.

Yoder, Edward. "Peace Principles: An Armistice Day Address." *Hesston College and Bible School Bulletin* 17 (Jan., 1931), 3-7. Discusses false foundations for nonresistance, such as weakness or cowardice, then examines the distinction between pacifism based on humanitarian ideals and pacifism based on Christian faith in the power of God to deal with the root of war—sin.

Yoder, Edward. "Peter Cheltschizki." *GH Supplement* 37 (Dec., 1944), 759-60. Cheltschizki is a little-known fifteenth-century Czechoslovakian who wrote about and upheld the Christian principles of love and nonresistance.

Yoder, Edward. "The Power of Love—A Notable Testimony: Peace Principles from a Scriptural Viewpoint." Part 2. *GH* 28 (Apr. 18, 1935), 78-79. The nonresistant love ethic can successfully deal with the threat of danger or violence. Examples are given.

Yoder, Edward. "Special Peace Meetings: Peace Principles from a Scriptural Viewpoint." Part

30. *GH* 32 (Oct. 19, 1939), 638. Mennonites who do not normally work together have been comparing notes on the meaning of nonresistance in wartime.

Yoder, Edward. "Teaching Nonresistance: Peace Principles from a Scriptural Viewpoint." Part 34. *GH* 33 (Apr. 18, 1940), 77-79. A review of Mennonite self-education on nonresistance, a brief study of Luke 12:49-53 which warns Christians to prepare for suffering, and selected news items relating to the war.

Yoder, Edward (Review). *Nonresistance and Pacifism,* by John R. Mumaw. Mennonite Publishing House, 1944. Pp. 28. "Nonresistance and Pacifism." *GH Supplement* 37 (1945), 943. Recommends booklet because it contains precise definitions of nonresistance and pacifism.

Yoder, Edward (Review). *Pacifist Handbook—Questions and Answers Concerning the Pacifist in Wartime, Prepared as a Basis for Study and Discussion,* "by a number of peace societies," n.d. *ChrMon* 32 (Oct., 1940), 305. Observes that the book stimulates conscientious objectors to war to consider the fuller implications of nonresistance.

Yoder, Edward (Review). *War and the Christian Conscience,* by John Horsch. Scottdale: Mennonite Publishing House, n.d. *ChrMon* 32 (October, 1940), 305. Recommends the book for its demonstration of the scriptural basis for and the reasonableness of nonresistance.

Yoder, Edward and others. *Must Christians Fight? A Scriptural Inquiry.* Akron: MCC, 1943. Pp. 68. MHL. Fifty-six questions and answers on nonresistance, ranging from definition of principles, biblical teaching, the essential, nonresistant character of Christ, apostolic practice of nonresistance, etc., to payment of taxes, relationship to pacifism, separation of church and state, etc.

Yoder, John H. "Karl Barth and Christian Pacifism." Work paper prepared for the Second Puidoux Conference, Iserlohn, Germany, 1957. Pp. 47. AMBS.

Yoder, John H. "Karl Barth and Non-Resistance." *Menn* 66 (Feb. 27, 1951), 143. Barth acknowledges nonresistance as "the way to serve God," but sets aside, in specific situations, the strict demands for suffering obedience.

Yoder, John H. *Karl Barth and the Problem of War.* Nashville: Abingdon, 1970. Pp. 141. A critique of Barth for stopping short of the Christian pacifism implicit in his work.

Yoder, John H. *Nevertheless: The Varieties of Religious Pacifism.* Scottdale: Herald Press, 1971. Pp. 141.

"Pacifism is not a single position, clearly defined, to which all pacifists adhere." This book identifies over twenty types of pacifism and remarks upon their similarities as well as their differences, their weaknesses as well as their strengths. Some of the types are well known, such as the pacifism of nonviolent social change and the pacifism of the categorical imperative. Others are less familiar such as the pacifism of cultic law and non-pacifist nonresistance of the Mennonite "Second Wind."

Yoder, John H. "Portraits of Christ: The Way of Peace in a World at War." Part 1. *GH* 54 (July 25, 1961), 617-18. Christ's strategy in dealing with his enemies was to love them and give himself for them. The Christian must do likewise.

Yoder, John H. "Questions on the Christian Witness to the State; What Should Christians Say to the State?" *GH* 56, Part 1, (July 2, 1963), 560; Part 2, (July 9, 1963), 586-87; Part 3, (July 16, 1963), 611-12; Part 4, (July 23, 1963), 633; Part 5, (Aug. 13, 1963), 698-99; Part 6, (Aug. 20, 1963), 720-21. We speak in favor of humanity. Concerning the prosecution of war: no war is acceptable to the nonresistant Christian but some kinds of warfare are even worse than others. We witness in favor of legality. The state should be a good steward of nature. The Christian should present a testimony against idolatry. The Christian calls the state to religious neutrality.

Yoder, John H. *Reinhold Niebuhr and Christian Pacifism.* Scottdale: Herald Press, n.d. Pp. 19. A critique of the presuppositions underlying Niebuhr's rejection of pacifism as a viable option.

Yoder, John H. "Reinhold Niebuhr and Christian Pacifism." *MQR* 30 (Apr., 1955), 101-17. We agree with Niebuhr that the New Testament teaches nonresistant love as the ultimate ethical norm, but we challenge his concepts of "impossibility," "necessity," and "responsibility."

Yoder, John H. "The Christian and War." *United Evangelical Action* 13 (Oct. 1, 1954), 434, 445 [sic. 455]. Just as Jesus did not defend himself but suffered unto death, so we are to love those who treat us unjustly; we share in the triumph of the cross by walking in the way of the cross. Distinguishes between the religious liberal peace position and the biblical peace position.

Yoder, John H., ed. *The Legacy of Michael Sattler.* Scottdale: Herald Press, 1973. Pp. 191. This collection of the early Anabaptists' writings with editorial comment includes not only article No. 6 of the Schleitheim Confession, from which much of the Mennonite tradition

of nonresistance derives, but also references to such related subjects as government, the oath, the sword, etc. See indices, pp. 183ff.

Yoder, John H. *The Pacifism of Karl Barth.* Washington, DC: The Church Peace Mission, 1964. Pp. 30. A discussion of Barth's "almost pacifist" position and the place of the "limiting case" in his ethics.

Yoder, John H. *The Politics of Jesus.* Grand Rapids: Wm. B. Eerdmans Publ. Co., 1972. Pp. 260. Yoder shows that Jesus and his proclamation of the Kingdom of God are normative for present social and political ethics. Focuses the discussion especially on pacifism as normative for Christians. Represents a scholarly landmark in the interconnections between biblical studies and theological-ethical methodological reflection.

Yoder, John H. "The Politics of the Messiah." Memorandum to the AMBS faculty. AMBS, Elkhart, Ind., Oct. 18, 1965. Pp. 7. AMBS.

Yoder, John H., ed. and trans. "The Schleitheim Text." *GH* 70 (Feb. 22, 1977), 153-56. Reprinted from *The Legacy of Michael Sattler* (Scottdale: Herald Press, 1973). Reprinted text of the Schleitheim Confession of Faith includes among its articles beliefs about nonresistance and the use of the sword.

Yoder, John H. "The Search for a Nonresistant Historiography." Memorandum to Mennonite Historians, Dec. 21, 1965. Pp. 6. MHL.

Yoder, John H. "The War in Algeria." *GH* 51 (Mar. 18, 1958), 254-56. Reviews the Algerian war and considers how a nonresistant Christian may respond to it. Concludes the nonresistant Christian will witness against injustice and oppression on both sides of the conflict.

Yoder, John H. "The Wrath of God and the Love of God." Address delivered at the Historic Peace Churches and International Fellowship of Reconciliation Conference, Beatrice Webb House, England, Sept. 11-14, 1956. Pp. 11. MHL.

Yoder, John H. "What Do You Think of Capital Punishment?" *ChrLiv* 11 (Sept., 1964), 22-26. Relating nonresistance to the role of government and capital punishment.

Yoder, John H. *What Would You Do?* Scottdale: Herald Press, 1983. Pp. 119. Takes seriously the question frequently asked pacifists of what action is right should a violent person threaten to harm a loved one. Considers the assumptions behind the question, how this hypothetical situation differs from the questions of war, and what the options for response to the situation might be. Subsequent sections of the book excerpt thinking other pacifists have done on the topic and offer examples of how nonviolent responses to threatening situations have functioned to defuse the violence.

Yoder, John H. (Review). *Pacifism in the United States*, by Peter Brock. Princeton: Princeton University Press, 1968. Pp. 1005. *GH* 63 (Feb. 3, 1970), 103. Carefully documented, thoroughly researched study of American pacifism which illumines problems of Mennonite self-understanding. Highly recommended.

Yoder, Kermit. "A Pax Man's Purpose and Motivation." *GH* 55 (Jan. 16, 1962), 57. Reports conversation between a PAX person and Greek villager on the subject of nonresistance.

Yoder, Lloyd. "Nonresistance of Today." *YCC* 17 (Aug. 9, 1936), 249, 250, 255-56. To stand for one's convictions on nonresistance against the majority opinion is an example of a true soldier of Christ. Even with all the peace activity and education, each individual has to search their own heart for this courage.

Yoder, Marcus. "The Roots of Swiss Brethren Nonresistance." Mennonite History, Feb., 1963. Pp. 13. MLA/BeC.

Yoder, Mervin. "A Study of the Church Status of Mennonites Who Accepted Military Service." Paper prepared for Mennonite Seminar, [1949]. Pp. 22, plus charts. MHL.

Yoder, Orrie D. Letter in "Our Readers Say." *GH* 58 (Oct. 26, 1965), 951. If we are to be nonresistant then we must also maintain a strict separation of church and state.

Yoder, Orrie D. "What Nonresistance Is Not." *ST* 27 (1st Qtr., 1959), 27. Nonresistance is not an isolated doctrine of the New Testament. Nonresistance must be taught and believed in conjunction with other fundamental doctrines of the Christian faith.

Yoder, Richard B. "Nonresistance Among Peace Churches of Southern Somerset County, Pa., During the Civil War." Paper prepared for Mennonite History class, Goshen College Biblical Seminary, Goshen, Ind., 1959. Pp. 30. MHL, MSHL.

Yoder, Roy F. "Peace and War: Spiritual Foundations of the Nonresistant Principle." *GH* 41 (Nov. 16, 1948), 1091. The principle of nonresistance is founded in the basic principle that Christ is head of the church and serves as the Christians' head, example, and leader.

Yoder, Sanford Calvin. "Migratory Movements Among the Mennonites as a Result of the World War." MA in Religion thesis, Winona Lake School of Theology, Winona Lake, Ind., 1933. Pp. 112. MHL. Historical overview of the way the practice of nonresistance has been the source of tension between Mennonites and their governments, leading in most cases to Mennonite migration in search of lands more open to their peculiarities. Emphasizes the Mennonite migration from Russia to Canada, Mexico, and Latin America during World War I.

Zercher, John E. "Thoughts on Memorial Day." *EV* 86 (May 25, 1973), 3. The Christian response on the occasion of a country honoring its war dead needs to be the way of nonresistant love.

# D. Evangelicals, Social Action

"A Prophetic Call—Evangelicals and Social Concerns." *EV* 86 (Dec. 25, 1973), 7. Evangelical Christian leaders met in Chicago to explore the importance of social concern for contemporary biblical faith and adopted a major document in which they stated their conviction that biblical faith and social concern are inseparable.

Anderson, John B. and Penner, Archie. "Get Active Politically: Two Views." *Chr Today* 20 (March 26, 1976), 10-12. Anderson urges evangelical Christians to become politically involved with the issues of economic injustice while Penner insists that any such involvement must find expression within the limits imposed by the concept of agape love exemplified by Christ.

Augsburger, Myron S. "The Renewal of Social Conscience Among Evangelicals." *GH* 63 (Apr. 14, 1970), 344-45. Comments on the growing phenomenon of evangelicals who remain conservative in their theology but liberal in their political and social concerns. Asserts the need for a pacifist witness among these groups.

Bartel, Lawrence. Letter to the Editor. *Menn* 88 (April 3, 1973), 231. Defends Richard Nixon and Billy Graham against attacks from "partisan political criticisms" by stating that Nixon is keeping his pledge to seek an honorable peace in Vietnam, and that previously hostile nations are now friendly to the US.

Buhr, Martin. "On Graham's War Stand: Leaders Talk with Evangelist Ford at Kitchener-Waterloo Crusade." *CanMenn* 14 (May 10, 1966), 1-2. A verbatim on a meeting between

Mennonite leaders in Ontario and Evangelist Ford on the proclamation of the gospel of peace and resultant peace action.

"Christians Belong in Politics, Says Speaker." *ChrLead* 33 (June 16, 1970), 12. An evangelical Christian sees the need for Christians in politics because political issues have moral or spiritual dimensions and Christians "need to show support of the decision-making process by becoming involved."

Darby, George. "The Church and Social Action." *ST* 43 (Apr., 1975), 1. Analysis draws that the early forms of the social gospel made social reconstruction a substitute for individual salvation. More recent manifestation consists in adding to the personal appropriation of Christ an involvement in social reform as part and parcel of the Christian life and of the church's ministry. The Christian must stay away from both forms.

Drescher, John M. (Editorial). "Remember the Prisoners . . . ." *GH* 65 (Jan. 11, 1972), 29. Editorial which considers the historical correlation between spiritual renewal and prison reform in this call for social action.

Driedger, Leo; Currie, Raymond; and Linden, Lick. "Dualistic and Wholistic Views of God and the World." *Review of Religions Research* 24 (March, 1983), 225-44. Findings support the posited correlation between a dualistic view of God and less interest in social action, and a wholistic view of God and more interest in social action.

"Evangelicals in Social Action Peace Witness Seminar." Papers presented at EMC, Nov. 30- Dec. 2, 1967. Pp. 71. MSHL. Includes: Hostetter, C. N. Jr., "What Is the Christian Attitude Toward Those Who Are Considered Enemies?"; Hoyt, Herman A., "Is Warfare a Denial of the World-wide Nature of the Church?"; Wenger, J. C., "Pacifism and Biblical Nonresistance;" King, Lauren A., "The Effect of War on Preaching the Gospel;" Wood, James E., Jr., "The Problem of Nationalism in Church-State Relations;" Grounds, Vernon D., "Evangelism and Social Responsibility;" Shenk, Wilbert R., "Christian Responsibility: National and International."

Erb, Paul. "Militarism as Social Service." *GH* 39 (July 16, 1946), 339. The evangelical fundamentalists are inconsistent when they so greatly emphasize participation in war as a Christian form of service to the world.

Evangelicals for Social Action. "Can My Vote Be Biblical?" *ChrLead* 43 (Oct. 21, 1980), 2-5. Guidelines for making Christ lord of our politics include emphasis on peacemaking and justice for the poor.

Fransen, Harold. "The North American Military— I." *Menn* 93 (Mar. 21, 1978), 206. Comments on the exorbitant defense budget and the high incidence of drug and alcohol use in the volunteer army. Laments the fact that the evangelical community is one of the strongest supporters of the military.

Franz, Delton. "Will We Conform or Overcome?" *GH* 63 (Sept. 22, 1970), 782-83. Expresses concern for the solid evangelical backing of a July 4 "Honor America Day" celebration and the equation of Christianity with the war in Southeast Asia. Calls Mennonites to begin dialogue with evangelicals on the local level about Jesus' way of peace.

Friesen, Dorothy and Stoltzfus, Gene. "Philippino Christians Question Graham Crusade." *The Other Side* 13 (Oct., 1977), 78-79. Concludes that the Billy Graham Metro Manila Crusade will be seen as a symbol of the church's collusion with continued American influence and affluence in the Philippines.

Gerig, Joan and Sawatsky, Sharon. "An Ethical Analysis of Operation PUSH—An Alternative Social Action Structure." Paper for New Testament Ethics class, AMBS, Elkhart, Ind., Jan. 24, 1975. Pp. 34. AMBS.

Graham, Billy. "A Change of Heart." *ChrLead* 42 (Aug. 28, 1979), 5. An interview with Billy Graham where he states his belief that the nation and the world face their own hour of decision about halting the escalation of nuclear weapons.

Graham, Billy. "From the Press: Graham on Vietnam and Watergate." *MennRep* 3 (June 11, 1973), 7. Reprinted from *Christianity Today* (Jan. 19, 1973), 416 and *New York Times* (May 6, 1973), 17. Evangelist Graham states that while the Bible indicates there will always be wars, he has never advocated war. Denies his publicized role as "White House chaplain."

Graham, Billy, and Tçth, Karçly. "Breaking the Dividing Wall of Hostility . . . ' " *God and Caesar* 6 (Sept., 1980), 9-11. Reprints of letters between two religious leaders on Christian witness against the arms race.

Harms, Orlando. "Our Peace Position." *ChrLead* 36 (Oct. 30, 1973), 28. The major argument for amnesty is reconciliation. There is indication that the more evangelical and fundamental a person is, the more he/she is against amnesty. This includes many Mennonite Brethren people.

Harms, Orlando. "Social Implications." *ChrLead* 23 (June 28, 1960), 2. When Christian discipleship does not express the social implications of the gospel, the church has betrayed the Gospel of Jesus.

Hatfield, Mark O. "A Senator's Message to Evangelicals." *GH* 63 (Sept. 15, 1970), 764-65. The task of the evangelical community is to develop a responsible social and political ethic, to reevaluate the faith in the office of the presidency, and to regain sensitivity to the corporateness of human life.

Hatfield, Mark O. "If Christ Be Lord." *EV* 89 (June 10, 1976), 16. Transcript of Senator Hatfield's remarks at the National Association of Evangelicals meeting, Feb. 24, 1976, in which he warned against encultured Christianity which makes God and Caesar one and the same.

Hershberger, Guy F. "Church and State: The Mennonite View." Paper presented at the National Association of Evangelicals, 1952. Pp. 6. MHL.

Janzen, David. "Anabaptist View Is No Accident." *CanMenn* 18 (Nov. 6, 1970), 7. Letter criticizing Victor Adrian's "Anabaptist or Evangelical?" (Oct. 16) for not taking the doctrine of nonresistance as an Anabaptist distinctive seriously enough.

Janzen, David. "Billy Graham's War Stand." *CanMenn* 14 (June 21, 1966), 5, 6. Critical analysis of Walter Klaassen's evaluation of Billy Graham's attitude to war, with an additional criticism of Billy Graham's attitude.

Jeschke, Marlin. "The Evangelical Christian and Modern War." *CanMenn* 11 (Sept. 24, 1963), 7. An analysis of a three-day meeting of some thirty teachers, ministers, writers, and others at Winona Lake to discuss the relationship between the evangelical Christian and modern war.

Juhnke, James C. "Recently in South Africa." *MBH* 12 (May 4, 1973), 32. Both Billy Graham and a group of American sportsmen recently visited South Africa. Though both visits were clouded by controversy and sensationalism, Graham in some measure communicated the gospel's critique to the white South Africans while the sportsment were completely "duped" by their white hosts.

Klaassen, Walter. "Once More: Graham's War Stand." *CanMenn* 14 (July 12, 1966), 5. Indicates difficulty of being critical and, at the same time, remaining open to communication, love, and peace.

Klaassen, Walter. "Setting the Record Straight on Billy Graham's War Stand." *CanMenn* 14 (June 7, 1966), 1, 2. Reflections and conclusions on Billy Graham's attitude to war in Vietnam on the basis of discussions and reports of statements made at the Houston crusade.

Klassen, Peter J. "Evangelicals and the Vietnam War" and "The Silence of Billy Graham." *MBH* 12 (Feb. 23, 1973), 11. With the end of the Vietnam war at hand, the editor reflects and comments that it has brought home to humankind the utter futility of trying to solve serious questions through violence. He also comments on the tacit approval Billy Graham gave to the president's actions in the war.

Kreider, Alan. "An International Call to Simpler Living." *MBH* 19 (Apr. 25, 1980), 20-21; *ChrLead* 43 (Apr. 22, 1980), 17; *EvVis* 93 (May 10, 1980), 16. An international gathering of evangelical leaders near London, England, makes a commitment to a simple lifestyle in recognition that wealth and militarism contribute to poverty and powerlessness.

Kroeker, David. "American Military Men in Vietnam Dedicated and Highly Motivated." *CanMenn* 15 (Jan. 10, 1967), 1, 2. Commentary on the Graham Team's view of the war in Vietnam based on the Jan. 8 radio broadcast of *The Hour of Decision,* a first-hand report of the Graham Team's 9-day visit in Vietnam. Graham and Co. praised efforts of American soldiers in Vietnam and encouraged listeners to write to the soldiers in a show of support.

Kroeker, David. "Graham on Peace and Revival." *CanMenn* 15 (May 30, 1967), 1, 2. At a press conference in Winnipeg, B. Graham makes some pessimistic statements on his hopes for peace.

Kroeker, Walter.. "Crying 'Wolf' in Washington." *ChrLead* 39 (Mar. 2, 1976), 24. The Christian image in Washington is being smudged by the impulsive and ill-advised way some evangelicals have reacted to recent Congressional bills.

Lohrenz, Gerhard. "The Church and Social Questions." *CanMenn* 14 (May 24, 1966), 5. The church agrees that Christianity should be practical, but does not agree on the form this praxis should take. This issue, too, ought to be reconciled with the word of God.

"Mennonite Leaders Meet with Billy Graham." *GH* 54 (Sept. 19, 1961), 824. Some Mennonite leaders meet with Billy Graham to share with him their understanding of the New Testament ethic of love and nonresistance.

*
Metzler, James E. "Shalom Is the Mission." *Mission and the Peace Witness.* Ed. Robert L. Ramseyer. Scottdale and Kitchener: Herald Press, 1979, 36-51. The biblical vision of shalom presents a more holistic approach to missions than the Protestant evangelical model. Metzler calls for

---

*For additional listing, see Supplement, pp. 717-719.

communities of mission inviting others into living shalom.

Miller, Marlin E. "Evangelical Pacifism in Southern Germany." *GH* 57 (Dec. 15, 1964), 1065; "A Report on a Movement Which Began in 1934." *CanMenn* 12 (Dec. 15, 1964), 5. Evangelical pacifism in southern Germany is rooted in the confession that Jesus is Lord of life. It challenges both East and West to pay attention to the claims of Christ.

Miller, Marlin E. "The Church in the World: A Mennonite Perspective." *The Covenant Quarterly: Lutheran-Conservative Evangelical Dialogue*, ed. Joseph A. Burgess. Chicago: North Park Theol. Seminary, Aug., 1983, 45-50. Some foundational components of a theological understanding of the church's relationship to the world are grace as God's creating love, discipleship as inclusive of both personal and social dimensions, and the distinctive reality of the Christian community.

Mumaw, John R. "The New Call to Peacemaking." *ST* 46 (June, 1978), 9-11. Shares personal reflections on the New Call to Peacemaking movement. The social action called for by the movement represents not only an erosion of nonresistance but a stretching of the definition of "peace."

Pannell, William. "An Evangelical Speaks for Negroes." *ChrLiv* 11 (July, 1964), 8-11. Among the signs that blacks belong in North America is the fact that black soldiers fought alongside whites in the Revolutionary and Civil Wars.

Peachey, Paul L. "Billy Graham on Nonresistance." *GH* 50 (Oct. 22, 1957), 896-97. Billy Graham's acceptance of war and the military is inconsistent with the Gospel. The writer urges him to seriously study this topic.

Peachey, Paul L. "Evangelical Christianity and Atomic War." *United Evangelical Action* 14 (Oct. 15, 1955), 467-68, 472, 474. Argues that the union of evangelicalism and pacifism is not only theologically compatible but necessary as well. Also as paper, n.d. Pp. 7. AMBS.

Peachey, Paul L. "Evangelicals and War." *GH* 48 (Aug. 16, 1955), 777. Those evangelicals who support war usually read the New Testament in the perspective of the Old. The nonresistant Christian reads the Old by way of the New.

Peachey, Paul L. "The Relation of Agape, the Essential Christian Ethic to Social Structure and Political Action." Paper, n.d. Pp. 27. AMBS.

Pierce, Glen. "Personal Reflections on the NAE Convention." *EV* 89 (June 10, 1976), 6. The National Association of Evangelicals convention in Washington, DC, showed a strong flavor or nationalism, even promoting militarism.

Pinnock, Clark. "A Statement for Disciples in Society." *MBH* 15 (Feb. 20, 1976), 2-3, 29. Evangelical Christians need a systematic theology dealing with Christian concern for injustice, racism, and militarism.

"Racial Tension Eased by Peace Representative." *CanMenn* 15 (Mar. 21, 1967), 3. Titus Bender brings blacks and whites together for Billy Graham film and initiates interracial pastoral meetings.

Ramseyer, Robert L. "The Christian Peace Witness and Our Missionary Task: Are Mennonites Evangelical Protestants with a Peace Witness?" Paper presented at the GCMC Commission on Overseas Missions, Missionary Retreat, June 26, 1976. Pp. 13. MHL.

Ratzlaff, Vernon. "A Problem of Stance." *CanMenn* 15 (Feb. 28, 1967), 4. In view of the (Billy) Graham crusade in Winnipeg, the question of allying with those who do not preach a gospel including the peace witness becomes acute.

Ratzlaff, Vernon. "How About Caesar?" *The Voice* 12 (Sept.-Oct., 1968), 8. A biblical assessment of social action and political involvement.

Redekop, John H. "Evangelical Christianity . . . and Political Ideology." *ChrLead* 27 (Nov. 10, 1964), 4-5. True Christianity cannot be equated with either the liberal or conservative political orientation. It stands in tension with both.

Redekop, John H. "Getting Through." *MBH* 12 (Apr. 20, 1973), 10. Writer expresses his concern about the pressure evangelical churches are placing on government to vote for capital punishment.

Regehr, Rudy A. "Director Feels Most Mennonites Do Not Hold to Position on Peace." *CanMenn* 15 (Mar. 28, 1967), 1, 7. Charleswood Mennonite Church presented a peace brief to Harry B. Williams, director of the Billy Graham Crusade in Winnipeg which expressed concern for Graham's stand on the Vietnam war. Williams said he felt most Mennonites would not agree with the brief.

Rinks, Riley. Letter to the Editor. *Menn* 88 (Feb. 13, 1973), 110-111. Criticizes the voices faulting Billy Graham for not speaking out against American bombing of Vietnam, since the writer believes government efforts toward a settlement of the war are being hampered by meddling and criticism from "peace" advocates.

Ruth, Merle. "Should the Mennonite Church Become More Deeply Engaged in Social Action?" *ST* 35 (Aug., 1967), 8. Raises several concerns about the subtle call to Mennonites for deeper involvement in social action.

"Setting the Record Straight on Billy Graham's War Stand." *CanMenn* 14 (June 7, 1966), 1, 2. Although Billy Graham in a Texas Crusade did *not* appeal to his listeners to support the war in Vietnam, he did contrast those who "protest sin and moral evil" by attending his meeting and the "noisy minority" which protests against the war. This distinction is either careless rhetoric or moral confusion.

Sawatsky, Walter W. *Soviet Evangelicals Since World War II.* Scottdale and Kitchener: Herald Press, 1981. See especially Chapter 4, "Preaching and Peace."

Schrag, Martin H. "Graham and Stott on Nuclear Weapons." *Menn* 95 (Dec. 2, 1980), 705; *EvVis* 93 (Sept. 10, 1980), 4-5. Comment on recent conclusions by John R. W. Stott and Billy Graham that the nuclear weapons race is madness and that Christians are called to seek salvation, not destruction.

Schrag, Myron. "Dear Jerry Falwell." *Menn* 95 (Nov. 4, 1980), 642. Questions Falwell's stance on a strong American military and challenges him to preach a gospel of peace.

Shank, J. Ward. "Anything and Anybody in the Name of Peace." *ST* 39 (June, 1971), 5. A whole new generation of Mennonites is being schooled in pacifism and social action which is in contrast to the basic principle of nonresistance, based on agape love as set forth in the New Testament.

Shank, J. Ward. "Issues the Church Faces in Conference and College." *ST* 33 (2nd Qtr., 1965), 26. One of the issues noted is the crisis in service. Interest in social service leads almost invariably into demands for social action, going from forms of actual service into messianic pursuit of social reform.

Shank, J. Ward. "Recent Landmark Policy Decisions by the United Presbyterian Church." *ST* 48 (Oct., 1980), 24-26. The Presbyterian peacemaking program is essentially main line social action.

Shank, J. Ward. "The Church and Social Action." *ST* 40 (May, 1972), 8. To take the church into the arena of the materialistic and political in order to create a climate through which the Gospel can supposedly work is social action.

Shank, J. Ward (Editorial). "Peace Makes Strange Bedfellows." *ST* 35 (Apr., 1967), 3. Notes how groups concerned about "peace" begin with "dialogue" and end with joint social and political action.

Shank, J. Ward (Editorial). "Repentance—Personal and Corporate." *ST* 46 (Apr., 1978), 6. Notes the lack of distinctions in the call to repentance and that this is a significant shift in Mennonite thought, from Anabaptist piety and discipleship to neo-evangelical social action.

Shank, J. Ward (Editorial). "The Peace Dialectic." *ST* 38 (Sept., 1970), 7. What many people are now promoting is not a positive biblical statement of belief, but a dialectic of peace which relates it to worldly philosophies, confuses its eschatalogical content, and applies it almost solely in areas of social action.

Shank, J. Ward (Editorial). "The Pursuit of Justice." *ST* 47 (Spr., 1979), 8. Notes the growing emphasis on justice along with peace. Examines biblical justice and concludes that the common usage is more in line with the concepts and techniques of social action.

Shank, J. Ward (Editorial). "What Is Social Action?" *ST* 37 (May, 1969), 3. Social action translates Christian benevolence or social service into militancy, or into a movement for reform. The problem with social action is that it is so far removed from the heart of the gospel.

Shank, J. Ward (Review). *The Worldly Evangelicals,* by Richard Quebedeaux. Harper and Row, 1978. In *ST* 47 (Jan., 1979), 23. This book focuses upon evangelicals and the evolution of their thought; it helps one to note that the Mennonite church is allowing a liberal, advanced scholarship to reinterpret the Anabaptist vision and in many parts is adopting the program of social radicals.

Sherk, J. Harold (Review). *The Theological Basis for Christian Pacifism,* by Don E. Smucker. MCC, n.d.; *Peace Is the Will of God,* WCC, n.d.; *Reinhold Niebuhr and Christian Pacifism,* by John H. Yoder. MCC, n.d.; *Mennonite Origins in Europe,* by Harold S. Bender. MCC, n.d. "New Booklets on Christian Peace." *Menn* 69 (Feb. 9, 1954), 90. Recommends these "evangelical and theological position" papers and statements on pacifism.

Sider, Ronald J. "A Call for Evangelical Nonviolence." *Christian Century* 93 (Sept. 15, 1976), 753-57. Also in *Mission and the Peace Witness.* Ed. Robert L. Ramseyer. Scottdale and Kitchener: Herald Press, 1979, 52-67. Contends that the biblical understandings of the ministry, cross, and resurrection of Jesus of Nazareth both lead to and are the only proper basis for nonviolent action.

Sider, Ronald J. "An Evangelical Theology of Liberation." *Perspectives on Evangelical Theology,* ed. Kenneth S. Kantzer and Stanley N. Gundry. Grand Rapids: Baker Book House, 1979, 117-33. Claims evangelical theology's failure to take seriously the biblical teaching that God identifies with the poor is evidence that evangelicals have fallen into the heresies of theological liberalism.

Sider, Ronald J. "An Evangelical Witness for Peace." *Preaching on Peace,* ed. Darrel J. Brubaker and Ronald J. Sider. Philadelphia: Fortress Press, 1982, 25-28. Finds theological basis for evangelical position on peace in the themes of creation and the redemptive work of Jesus of Nazareth.

Sider, Ronald J. "Aside: Where Have All the Liberals Gone?" *The Other Side* 12 (May-June, 1976), 42-44. The essence of liberal theology can be described as when the current culture supplies the operational norms and values for a significant number of evangelicals and mainline church people. Concerns like racism, militarism, civil religion, and unjust economic structures are not spoken to because of the liberal context.

Sider, Ronald J. "At Arm's Length." *United Evangelical Action* 42 (Mar.-Apr., 1983), 7-8. Supports the nuclear freeze movement because the proposed new weapons systems complicate verification and because the hope that the superpowers can continue to possess nuclear weapons without using them is based on the shaky premises of humanism.

Sider, Ronald J. "Corporate Guilt and Institutionalized Racism." *United Evangelical Action* 36 (Spring, 1977), 11-12, 26-28. Because the Bible calls us to live apart from the wrong doings of society, evangelical Christians should look at the ways individuals share responsibility for racism and seek practical expressions of repentance. Includes selected bibliography.

Sider, Ronald J. "Evangelical Influence Felt." *EV* 89 (Apr. 25, 1976), 5-6. A report on the Fifth Assembly of the World Council of Churches which met in Nairobi, Kenya, Nov. 23-Dec. 10, 1975, where, among other concerns, peace, justice, and human rights were discussed.

Sider, Ronald J., ed. *Evangelicals and Development: Toward a Theology of Social Change.* Philadelphia: Westminster Press, 1981. A collection of articles addressing the ethical issues of justice and social change from an evangelical Christian point of view.

Sider, Ronald J. "Evangelism, Salvation and Social Justice." *International Review of Mission* 64 (July, 1975), 251-67; reprint ed., Bramcote Notts: Grove Books, 1977. Evangelism and social action are distinct but inseparable aspects of the church's mission. Not only does evangelism often lead to greater social justice, and vice versa, but those who follow Jesus' example must seek liberty for the oppressed as well as announce the good news.

Sider, Ronald J. "God and the Poor: Toward a Theology of Development." *The Ministry of Development in Evangelical Perspective: A Symposium on the Social and Spiritual Mandate,* ed. Robert Lincoln Hancock. Pasadena: William Carey Library, 1979, 35-59. Uses biblical themes to critique an understanding of development as GNP growth and of development as structural change via revolutionary violence. Concludes by proposing that the church's contribution to development is the concept of the new community.

Sider, Ronald J. "Is Racism as Sinful as Adultery?" *GH* 65 (Apr. 4, 1972), 315; *EV* 84 (Sept. 25, 1971), 5, 6. Calls evangelicals to concern over social evils of racism and militarism equal to concern about personal evils such as adultery.

Sider, Ronald J. "Response to the Question, 'Does Your Evangelical Heritage and Theology Create Radical Christian Commitment?' " *Sojourners* 5 (Apr., 1976), 16. The word "evangelical" is a useful label to designate clusters of traditions. The evangelical commitment to scriptural authority means that they are always peculiarly vulnerable to the biblical summons to radical discipleship as the way to peace.

Sider, Ronald J. "Resurrection and Liberation: An Evangelical Approach to Social Justice." *The Recovery of Spirit in Higher Education,* ed. Robert Rankin. New York: Seabury Press, 1980, 154-77. Develops three biblical themes as central to the pursuit of justice: the prophetic model, God's identification with the poor, and the bodily resurrection of Jesus of Nazareth as the foundation of hope.

Smedes, Lewis B. "Who Will Answer?" *Menn* 88 (Jan. 9, 1973), 32. Calls for evangelist Billy Graham, who "has the heart of evangelical middle America in his hands" to speak out on the moral and spiritual issues involved in the massive bombing of Vietnam.

Snyder, John M. "Social Evils and Christian Action." *ST* 38, Part 1, (Apr., 1970), 16; Part 2, (May, 1970), 11. Examines scriptural principles for responding to social evils which result from human failure to live according to the righteous standards of God's law.

Snyder, John M. (Review). *The New Left and Christian Radicalism,* by Arthur G. Gish. Grand Rapids: Eerdmans, 1970. *ST* 39 (Nov., 1971), 11. Well-written book analyzing the New Left and sixteenth century Anabaptism in the first part. The second part discusses biblical faith, radicalism, and hope. The weakness lies in the author's lack of commitment to evangelical Christian faith.

Stauffer, James K. "Vietnam Churches Struggle with New Trials." *Menn* 93 (Sept. 19, 1978), 537; *MennRep* 8 (Sept. 18, 1978), 7. Describes freedoms and limitations of the evangelical church in Vietnam since the change in government. Reflects on the church's previous sanctioning of American military policies and its present compromise of church and state separation by allowing some pastors to work on local government committees.

Stoner, John K. "Evangelicals Convene in Capitol; Resolve to Let Freedom Ring." *ChrLead* 39 (Mar. 30, 1976), 18. Comments on the Bicentennial Convocation, the joint conventions of the National Association of Evangelicals and the National Religious Broadcasters, Feb. 22-25, 1976.

Stoner, John K. (Review). *Between a Rock and a Hard Place*, by Mark Hatfield. Waco, Tex.: Word Books, 1976. Pp. 224. *Menn* 91 (Oct. 26, 1976), 633; *ChrLead* 39 (Aug. 17, 1976), 14. Hatfield prods the church to separate its vision from the destiny of America, examining questions of nuclear war, violence, and patriotism.

Swartz, Herbert L. (Review). *The Social Conscience of the Evangelical*, by Sherwood Eliot Wirt. New York: Harper and Row, Pub., 1968. *The Voice* 19 (Oct., 1970), 31-32. The way the author deals with the question of war, particularly the Vietnam war, is exemplary of a more general idealization of American values that aborts deep thinking about the issues.

"Thirty Evangelicals to Discuss War Attitudes." *CanMenn* 11 (July 19, 1963), 1, 9. MCC Peace Section arranges a summer seminar at Winona Lake, Ind.

"To the NAE Point of View." *Menn* 81 (Feb. 15, 1966), 117. A letter of appeal from the Mennonites in Canada to the National Association of Evangelicals to reconsider their support of "unjust and unchristian methods of resisting communism." This is a response to the NAE's apparent endorsement of the Vietnam war.

Thiessen, John H. "Evangelical Leaders Discuss Peace at NAE Convention." *CanMenn* 14 (May 10, 1966), 1, 2. John Howard Yoder led discussion on "War, Peace, and the Evangelical Challenge" at the anual meeting of the National Association of Evangelicals in Denver.

Wagler, Harley. "The Peace Churches in Nicaragua (2): Mixed Reaction to Revolution." *MennRep* 10 (Oct. 13, 1980), 6-7. Review of the Catholic, evangelical, and Mennonite church responses to the Sandinista revolution and attitudes toward the new government.

Walters, LeRoy. "The Vietnam Situation. An Open Letter to the Brotherhood." *EV* 79 (Jan. 17, 1966), 19-20. The Christian's first loyalty is to the international community of faith. Therefore we must protest both the Vietnam War itself and recent statements by Billy Graham and President Johnson.

Wiebe, Katie Funk. "While Making Gravy." *ChrLead* 37 (July 23, 1974), 19. Thoughts on the role of an "advocate" and social action. Advocates are people who speak and act on Christ's behalf for the person who has no courage or power to keep going.

Wiebe, Katie Funk (Review). Moberg, David O. *The Great Reversal: Evangelism Versus Social Concern.* Evangelical Perspective Series, John Warwick Montgomery, ed. Philadelphia: Lippencott, 1972. In *Direction* 3 (Apr., 1974), 185. The division between traditional evangelism, which stresses preaching and personal evangelism, and social concern and action is unscriptural and the two must be brought together.

Wood, James E., Jr. *The Problem of Nationalism in Church-State Relationships.* Focal Pamphlet No. 18. Scottdale: Herald Press, 1969. Pp. 31. A paper read at the Evangelicals in Social Action Peace Witness Seminar at Eastern Mennonite College in 1967. Exposes the idolatrous nature of nationalism as a denial of the universalism of the gospel.

Yoder, John H. "Continental Theology and American Social Action." *Religion in Life* (Spring, 1961), 225-30. The fundamental structure of ethical thought is quite similar in Europe and America; European theologians (e.g., Barth), may again teach us the authority of revelation and the dignity of the church as a totally new kind of community. Discusses the necessary and interdependent relationship between revelation as faith's content and the work of the church for social change as faith's act.

Yoder, John H. "The Biblical Mandate." *Post-American* 3 (Apr., 1974), 21-25. (Address given at the Evangelical and Social Concern Workshop, Chicago, Ill., Nov. 23, 1973. Pp. 14. AMBS.) Discusses many strands of Christian faith that call for Christian responsibility for love and justice in the social order.

Yoder, John H. "The Contemporary Evangelical Revival and the Peace Churches." *Mission and the Peace Witness.* Ed. Robert L. Ramseyer. Scottdale and Kitchener: Herald Press, 1979, 68-103. It is the peace churches' duty to communicate their position on war and peace to evangelicals because peace theology is at the logical center of evangelicalism, if evangelicalism's emphases are followed consistently; more evangelicals are discussing the "suffering church" and the impact of the gospel on social change; ethical matters are "essential" to the gospel, not part of the "nonessentials" in which diversity is permissible.

# E. Women, Peace, and War

Alderfer, Helen. "Family News and Trends: Women and Peace." *ChrLiv* 17 (Jan., 1970), 40. Comments on gathering of women at Laurelville Church Center to discuss women's responsibility in the question of peace versus war.

Alderfer, Helen. "To Be a Peacemaker." *ChrLiv* 16 (July, 1969), 32-33. Seven women share their ideas on how mothers go about working for peace.

Alderfer, Helen. "Women in Peace." *ChrLiv* 13 (Apr., 1966), 31, 34. Description of some activities of the Women's International League for Peace and Freedom.

Bargen, Jan. "Pacifist Inclinations of the Woman's Movement." Social Science Seminar paper, Apr., 1975. Pp. 34 MLA/BeC.

Barrett, Lois [Janzen]. "Peace Assembly Looks at Male-Female Stereotypes." *Forum* (Dec., 1973), 12-13. The MCC Peace Section Assembly dealt with the theme of "the interdependence of men and women," noting that biblical peace is not only "the absence of war" but total well-being and the reconciliation of those who are separated from one another.

Barrett, Lois [Janzen]. "When They Draft Women." *Menn* 87 (May 9, 1972), 324. If and when women are drafted, there may be some benefits. Women will need to deal more directly with the issues of war and violence and with the formulation of clear positions on these issues.

Bartel, Lois Franz. "Peace Witness for Women." *ChrLiv* 15 (Dec., 1968), 22-23. Opportunities for peace witness include offering one's home to released mental patients, guiding children against playing with war toys, etc.

Beechy, Winifred Nelson. "The Impact of Militarism on the Chinese Women's Movement." *MCC PS TF on Women in Ch. and Soc. Report* 35 (Jan.-Feb., 1981), 7-9. Traces the evolving emphases of the Chinese women's movement in this century.

Beechy, Winifred Nelson. "Women and Peace Concerns." *GH* 64 (Jan. 12, 1971), 37. Urges women to become more involved and articulate about peace concerns and to take more initiative in ministries of reconciliation.

Berg, Ford. "Women and Nonresistance." *GH* 41 (May 18, 1948), 467. The peace witness is to be carried by the sisters as well as the brothers of the church. Teaching should be directed to them also so that they may take a strong stand.

Congressional Record—Senate. "Women in the Military Will Help Recruiting Crunch." *MCC PS TF on Women in Ch. and Soc. Report* 19 (Apr.-May, 1978), 7. Reprinted entry includes *New York Times* editorial describing the Defense Department's petition to Congress lifting the ban on women being assigned to combat zones.

Duvanel, Tammy. "Women and World War II: An Examination of Home Front Involvement Comparing Newton-Area Women with the National Trend." Social Science Seminar paper, 1984. Pp. 20. MLA/BeC.

Ebersole, Myron. "A History of Mennonite Central Committee Voluntary Service, 1944-1949." Paper presented to Mennonite History Class, n.d. Pp. 38. MHL.

Enns, Mary M. "Ingrid Rimland Turns to Face the Forces That Shaped Her Life." *MennMirror* 8 (Jan., 1979), 6, 7. Describes some of the forces that shaped Rimland's life and led her to write the novel *The Wanderers* which tells of three women who survived the Russian Revolution, World War II, and the hardships of Paraguay.

*Forum* staff. "A Random Sampling on Registration." *Forum* 13 (Apr., 1980), 3-5. Five undergraduates respond to questions on the appropriateness of the draft registration, military service, and the registering of women.

Frazer, Heather T. and O'Sullivan, John. "Forgotten Women of World War II: Wives of Conscientious Objectors in Civilian Public Service." *Peace and Change* 5 (Fall, 1978), 46-51. Documents the injustice of the CPS system in the absence of government pay or benefits granted to other enlisted men. Focuses especially on the economic and emotional plight of wives of CPS workers.

Glassburn, Lorene. "Our Sisters' Part in the Present World Crisis." *GH* 34 (July 10, 1941), 318. While the nonresistant witness falls most directly to young men, there are numerous ways that women can give their full cooperation and support. Moreover, it is not impossible that women will need to face the issue of conscription in the future as the men do now.

Gleysteen, Jan. "Käthe Kollwitz—An Artist's Protest to War." *YCC* 48 (July 9, 1967), 5. The story of Kollwitz, a famous woman artist, whose art reflects her social conscience and pacifist ideology.

Guest-Smith, Kathleen N. "The Militarization of Women." *Forum* 9 (Feb., 1976), 5. A growing number of women are entering the military and the Equal Rights Amendment would ensure their participation in registration and the draft. Women therefore must look critically at their role in the all-volunteer army.

Habegger, Luann. "Report from the Peace Section Task Force on Women in Church and Society." *MCC PS TF on Women in Ch. and Soc. Report* 1 (Aug., 1973), 1-5. Essay introduces the topic of women's concerns for peace and justice and outlines a brief history of men's and women's roles in the church.

Habegger, Luann. "Women and Peace." In "Persons Becoming: Project of MCC Peace Section Task Force on Women." Ed. Dorothy Yoder Nyce. Akron, Pa.: MCC Peace Section, 1974. Pp. 4.

Heinritz, Lotte. "Women's Odyssey." *MennLife* 3 (Apr., 1948), 19-22. Describes the horrors of war as experienced by women from Danzig, Poland, during World War II.

Kerigan, Florence. "Women Are Peacemakers." *ChrLiv* 16 (Dec., 1969), 32-33. Women exercise their peace loving nature in whatever roles they choose, whether as wives, mothers, or career women.

King, Mrs. Noah and Miller, Mrs. D. D. "Conditions in War-Stricken Countries and Relief Work." Papers read at Indiana-Michigan Branch of Sisters' Sewing Circle Meeting, June, 1918. Pp. 16.

Klaus, Marilyn. "The Draft and Women." *MCC PS TF on Women in Ch. and Soc. Report* 35 (Jan.-Feb., 1981), 5-6. While reasons for excluding women from registration are sexist, a greater evil is involving men in a system committed to violence and war.

Koontz, Gayle Gerber. "Peaceable Women: Feminism and Peacemaking in the Church." Address given at the Women in Ministry Conference, Kitchener, Ont., Oct. 16, 1982. Pp. 8. AMBS.

Koontz, Ted, comp. "Abortion: Resources for Study and Discussion." *Persons Becoming: Project of MCC Peace Section Task Force on Women.* Ed. Dorothy Yoder Nyce. Akron, Pa.: MCC Peace Section, 1974. Pp. 2.

Krehbiel, H[enry] P[eter]. *War, Peace, Amity.* Newton: Herald Publishing Co., 1937. Pp. 350. A historical study of the dynamics of war and peace, written in a time of fear of another war as a study guide for church and peace groups. Includes a chapter on "Women and Peace," by Elva Krehbiel Leisy (annotated separately).

Kreider, Connie. "Countering Militarism in the Schools." *MCC PS TF on Women in Ch. and Soc.*

*Report* 35 (Jan.-Feb., 1981), 6-7. Lists myths perpetuated by military recruiters, especially regarding opportunities for women, and counters them with facts.

Kreider, Rachel. *Key in Your Hand: Words to Girls on the Subject of Peace.* Newton: Faith and Life Press, 1961. Pp. 12. MHL. Advice directed to high school senior girls encourages them to think about peace issues because, as those who determine the atmosphere of future homes, they carry the major responsibility to transmit the basic beliefs about Christian peace to the next generation.

Leisy, Elva Krehbiel. "Women and Peace." *War, Peace, Amity,* by H. P. Krehbiel. Newton: Herald Publishing Co., 1937, 302-315. Reviews the beginnings of women's peace groups and the contributions of individual women around the world. Calls upon women to make their creative impulses felt against the destructiveness of war by working in peace education programs, or by instilling international awareness in their children.

Lord, Beverly Bowen. "Women and the Social Costs of Militarism." *MCC PS TF on Women in Ch. and Soc. Report* 35 (Jan.-Feb., 1981), 3-4. Compares national defense budget to social spending, especially those programs assisting women.

Lugibihl, Jan. "Feminism and Community at AMBS (1981-1983): Does Our Rhetoric Match Our Experiences?" MA in Peace Studies thesis, AMBS, Elkhart, Ind., July, 1984. Pp. 131. AMBS. 1981-83 was a period in which a great deal of the community process, both dialogical and conflictual, at AMBS had to do with the issues of women's and men's relationships. This thesis, employing a feminist interactive methodology, based on elements of story and personal experience, reflects upon the successes and failures of this particular peacemaking effort and offers, to the educational institution and to women who might enroll at AMBS in the future, some suggestions for continued process.

Mennonite Central Committee (US). "Statement on World Tensions and the Draft." Adopted Jan. 24, 1980. P. 1. (Located in MCC Peace Section Official Statements folder in MHL.) Urges young Mennonite men and women to register their conscientious objector convictions with the Peacemaker Registration Program in response to proposed military conscription.

Pennell, Christine Hamilton. "Women and Militarism." *Daughters of Sarah* 7 (Nov.-Dec., 1981), 3-10. Recognizing that the systematic dehumanization of males, which is an essential part of military training, has sinister implications for women as well. A growing number of feminist women are protesting militarism by becoming involved in the nonviolent struggle for a just world.

Poettcker, Henry. "Peace Witness with a Feminine Touch." *CanMenn* 16 (Nov. 5, 1968), 5. What part in the peace witness do women play? The author draws his response from *The Challenge of Good Will,* on the US Peace Corps; *Champions of Peace,* by Edith Patterson Meyer; *Tomorrow Is Now,* by Eleanor Roosevelt; and other articles in periodicals.

Reedy, Janet Umble. "Sexual Equality and Peace." *MCC PS TF on Women in Ch. and Soc. Report* 35 (Jan.-Feb., 1981), 1-3. Analysis of the polarization of men's and women's roles into dominance and passivity, leading to violence and militarism.

Reedy, Janet Umble. "Women Against Daddy Warbucks: Women Working for Peace." Chapel talk at Goshen College, Dec. 4, 1975. Pp. 5. MHL, MLA/BeC.

Regier, Harold R. "Tax Resister Named Arvada Woman of the Year." *God and Caesar* 3 (Jan., 1977), 6-7. Marge Roberts, a peace and social concerns activist who participates in the Arvada Mennonite Church, was named the city woman of the year.

Reimer, Al (Review). *The Wanderers: The Saga of Three Women Who Survived,* by Ingrid Rimland. St. Louis: Concordia Publishing House, 1977. Pp. 323. "Novel Proves Mennonite Russian Experience." *MennMirror* 7 (Feb., 1978), 14, 15. Describes and critiques this fictional novel which portrays the lives of three Mennonite women who manage, under incredible hardships, to survive the Russian Revolution, the Stalin era, World War II, and who finally emigrate to Paraguay. Concludes that it is a very worthwhile novel in spite of some technical flaws which he details.

Rempel, Ruth Yoder (Review). *Against Our Will: Men, Women, and Rape,* by Susan Brownmiller. Simon & Schuster, 1975. Pp. 480. *MCC PS TF on Women in Ch. and Soc. Report* 10 (Mar.-Apr., 1976), 5-7. Reviewer observes that one-half of the book is devoted to documenting the use of rape during war to prove dominance and power.

Roth, Nadine S. "On the Altar." *ChrMon* 27 (Feb., 1935), 35-36. Story about the friendship of two neighbor women strained over the issue of participation in war.

Sawatzky, Sharon R. "Rape: Keeping Women in Their Place." *Menn* 91 (Sept. 28, 1976), 558-60. Just as the church works against war, it must work against other violence such as rape, which demeans women. Limited resistance to an attacker is a response in line with Jesus' perfect love.

Schertz, Mary H. "For the Healing of the Nations." Paper presented to War and Peace in the Bible class, AMBS, Elkhart, Ind., Nov. 30, 1981. Pp. 21. AMBS.

Steele, Richard. "Rape—Male Violence: A Personal and Political Perspective." Paper presented to Women and Men: History and Vision, and War, Peace, and Revolution classes, AMBS, Elkhart, Ind., Dec., 1982. Pp. 73. AMBS.

Stucky, Diane Pearson. "Women Working for Peace: A Slice of Herstory." *Daughters of Sarah* 7 (Nov.-Dec., 1981), 15-16. Brief summary of women's work for peace from the World War I era to the present.

Swartley, Willard M. "The Bible and War" and "The Bible and Women." *Slavery, Sabbath, War, and Women: Case Issues in Biblical Interpretation.* Scottdale and Kitchener: Herald Press, 1983, 96-191. Shows how the Bible has been used in opposing ways for both the Christian's participation in war and the role of women in relation to men. In the final chapter the use of the Bible for both topics, war and women, is briefly compared (197-98). Swartley suggests several reasons why the World Wars had a negative impact upon the women's movement (271, n.4).

Swartzentruber, June. "Raising Children for Peace." *MCC PS TF on Women in Ch. and Soc. Report* 28 (Nov.-Dec., 1979), 3-4. Suggestions for effective peace teaching and parenting, including list of published resources.

"Women Respond to Clemency." *RepConsS* 32 (Mar., 1975), 2. Women students at Goshen College write President Ford volunteering themselves as substitutes for the draft resisters in exile required to earn re-entry through labor. Wengerd, Sara. "Some Behavioral Objectives for Women of Peace." *WMSC Voice* 54 (Dec., 1980), 4-6. Suggestions for peacemaking in the home and community.
*
Wiebe, Katie Funk. "The Conflict of Peace." *ChrLead* 35 (June 27, 1972), 19. Assesses what it means to be violent and to resolve conflict, how women can relate to peacemaking, and what it means for the proclamation of the gospel to believe in peace and reconciliation.

Wiebe, Katie Funk. "The Militarization of Women." *ChrLead* 41 (Apr. 25, 1978), 10; *GH* 71 (June 6, 1978), 451. ERA discussion is shattering the idea that nonresistance and nonviolence is a doctrine mainly for men. Just as many women are joining the military, so women of the historic peace churches should share with

*For additional listing, see Supplement, pp. 717-719.

men in the commitment to nonviolence and peacemaking.

World War I. 302 interviews: over half are transcribed. Emphasis is on CO's from many Mennonite branches and other churches. Also includes several regulars and civilians (women, pastors). Some very dramatic stories of abuse in army camps, courts-martial, prison, personal testimonies about nonresistant stances, moving to Canada to escape conscription, community war fervor. Guide to interviews published as Sprunger, *et al., Voices Against War,* 1973. MLA/BeC.

World War II. 134 interviews, some transcribed. Emphasis on Mennonite CO's who did CPS work. ALso includes some civilians (women, pastors) and regulars.MLA/BeC.

Yoder, Elizabeth (Review). *The Wanderers,* by Ingrid Rimland. St. Louis: Concordia, 1977. *MennLife* 34 (Mar., 1979), 30. Gives a summary of the story which depicts three generations of Russian Mennonite women from the Civil War of 1917-20 to the immigration to Paraguay in 1947. Describes it as a fictional portrait of a people. Comments that Mennonite theology and the theme of pacifism are given very ambiguous treatment.

# F. Peace Stories

Adrian, Walter. "A Thrilling Story from an Old Diary." *MennLife* 3 (July, 1948), 23-28, 39, 44. Narrative of one family's trek in the mid-1800's from Prussia into the Ukraine to settle in an area offering freedom from military service.

Banks, Louis. "Healing the Feud." *ChrLiv* 2 (Feb., 1955), 20-21. Reprinted from *Soul Winning Stories.* Making peace between a father and son-in-law made possible a revival in the community.

Bauer, Evelyn. "About Face." *YCC* 48, Part 1, (July 23, 1967), 12; Part 2, (July 30, 1967), 6. Story about a man who joined the army and then discovered inconsistencies between Christ's teachings and the program of training he had chosen.

Bauer, Evelyn. "Breaking Bottlenecks Around the World." *YCC* 44 (Nov. 24, 1963), 5. The story of Andrew W. Cordier, who for sixteen years was the executive assistant to the Secretary-General of the United Nations. Member of Church of the Brethren.

Bauman, Elizabeth Hershberger. *Coals of Fire.* Scottdale and Kitchener: Herald Press, 1954. Pp. 128. True stories of peace drawn from the experiences of Mennonites, Brethren, Quakers, early Christians, and others. The classic Mennonite collection of peace stories for children.

Beechy, Winifred Nelson. "André and the French City of Refuge, La Chambon." *GH* 72 (Nov. 13, 1979), 884-85. Philip Hallie, a Jewish philosopher, has written a book, *Lest Innocent Blood Be Shed,* about André Trocmé and the people of La Chambon, who took in fugitives, mostly Jewish, during World War II and risked their lives in so doing. Hallie, himself, experiences a renewal of spirit and optimism through their remarkable faith and courage.

Bender, Nevin and Swartzendruber, Emanuel.

*Nonresistance under Test.* Rosedale, Ohio: Keynote Series No. 1, 1969. Pp. 16. The stories of the two authors who refused to bear arms during World War I.

Berg, Ford. "A Pardon for Wittman." *ChrLiv* 1 (Oct., 1954), 30, 40. Story of a Seventh Day German Baptist nonresistant Peter Miller who won a pardon for his enemy from George Washington.

Berg, Nettie. "The Sausage Skins Did It." *MBH* 13 (Jan. 11, 1974), 29-30. Children's story about conscientious objector in army camp who appeased a sergeant's dog with table scraps and befriended the sergeant.

Bontrager, Marion. "Regan Savage and the Mennonite Dream." *GH* 71 (July 4, 1978), 521. Relates the story of a tank commander who, after six years in the Army, received discharge as a conscientious objector.

Braun, Jack D. "Bread of Forgiveness." Dramatic interpretation of Hugu Jantz short story by same title, n.d. Pp. 13. MHL.

Buchanan, Roy. "A Personal Testimony." *GH* 63 (May 5, 1970), 408-409. World War I conscientious objector disagrees with the position of draft resisters, describing his positive experiences in obtaining cooperation from the military to perform alternative service.

Conrad, Willard D. (Review). *Kagawa of Japan,* by Cyril J. Davey. Abingdon, 1961. Pp. 150. *ChrLiv* 9 (Aug., 1962), 33. Recommends this story of a Japanese Christian leader who espoused pacifism through reading about Jesus.

Dick, David. "Faith Put to the Test." *MBH* 16 (Apr. 15, 1977), 2-4. Mennonite family in the Ukraine refused to defend their estate by force during the Russian revolution.

Dyck, Anna Reimer. *Anna: From the Caucasus to*

*Canada*, trans. and ed. Peter J. Klassen. Hillsboro: Mennonite Brethren Publishing House, 1979. Pp. 216. The particular experience of one Russian Mennonite woman is a microcosm of the populations dislocated by the fury of war and revolution. The section describing the Russian revolution and civil war depicts not only the suffering caused by war but, in the simple accounting for friends and relatives, the variety of ways the Mennonite community responded to the Russian government's call to bear arms.

Dyck, Edna Krueger. "Peace Teachers: She Studies and Obeys." *Builder* 31 (Jan., 1981), 12-13. The consequences of Cornelia Lehn's commitment to "study the Bible seriously and then to obey the Word" have resulted in a General Conference study process on the issues of tax resistance and a collection of peace stories which she edited entitled *Peace Be With You* (Faith and Life, 1981).

Eash-Sutter, Ruth. "Continental Walk." *Lifework* 1 (1978), 6-8. Participant in four of the nine months of the Continental Walk for Disarmament and Social Justice in 1976 reflects on the experience as part of a lifetime commitment to peacemaking.

Eby, Omar. "Peace." *ChrLiv* 11 (Nov., 1964), 25-28. Story in which African pastor demonstrates love for his enemies and learns about love for his wife.

Enns, Mary M. "Ingrid Rimland Turns to Face the Forces That Shaped Her Life." *MennMirror* 8 (Jan., 1979), 6, 7. Describes some of the forces that shaped Rimland's life and led her to write the novel *The Wanderers* which tells of three women who survived the Russian Revolution, World War II, and the hardships of Paraguay.

Erb, Alta Mae (Review). *Prudence Crandall, Woman of Courage*, by Elizabeth Yates. Aladdin Books, 1955. *ChrLiv* 3 (Feb., 1956), 33. Recommends this story of a nineteenth-century woman who worked for justice for blacks, especially in education.

Fast, Henry A. (Review). *Voices Against War: A Guide to the Schowalter Oral History Collection on World War I Conscientious Objection*, by Keith L. Sprunger, James C. Juhnke, and John D. Waltner. N. Newton, Kansas: Bethel College, 1973. *Menn* 89 (Oct. 29, 1974), 628. A valuable guide to a priceless collection of conscientious objector experiences recorded on tape, the book and the collection should stimulate further research.

Finger, Reta (Review). *Peace Be with You*, by Cornelia Lehn. Faith and Life Press, 1980. Pp. 126. *Daughters of Sarah* 7 (Nov.-Dec., 1981), 20-21. Praises Lehn's collection of peacemaking

stories as a vivid portrayal of the power of forgiveness and active gentleness in the midst of suffering and violence.

Foster, Edith. "In Pursuit of Freedom." *ChrLiv* 5, Part 1, (Jan., 1958), 14-17, 34, 39; Part 2, (Feb., 1958), 14-17, 19, 37 and (Mar., 1958), 14-47, 19, 37; Part 3, (Apr., 1958), 24-29, (May, 1958), 24-29, and (June, 1958), 24-28. Story traces the migrations of the Pannabakker family through nearly 300 years. Includes the migration of a young Dutch man to Pennsylvania to escape military service, and the troubles of a Menonite family in Canada during the 1812 war.

Funk, Cornelius C. *Escape to Freedom*, trans. and ed. Peter J. Klassen. Hillsboro: Mennonite Brethren Publishing House, 1982. Pp. 124. Personal account of Russian young man who enlists in the medical corps of the Russian army. Describes horrors of war as well as the difficult task of sorting through the chaotic political situation in order to make ethical decisions about one's participation in a changing government.

Garber, John. "Nonresistance Exemplified in History." *The Eastern Mennonite School Journal* 18 (Apr., 1940), 21-26. Traces the theme of nonresistance from the early martyrs of the Roman era through the Reformation to the American wars. Concludes with several historical examples of nonresistant behavior.

Gerlach, Horst. "Through Darkness to Light." *ChrLiv* 3 (Aug., 1956), 6-9, 40-41; 3 (Sept., 1956), 12-15, 40; 3 (Oct., 1956), 14-17, 19, 34, 36; 3 (Nov., 1956), 19-22, 24, 34, 35-37; 3 (Dec., 1956), 24-29, 36; 4 (Jan., 1957), 24-29; 4 (Feb., 1957), 24-29. Life story of a young German man growing up in a pro-Nazi family during the Hitler and World War II era. Enemy occupation of home town; prisoner of war in northern Russia as slave laborer; conversion to Christianity from trust in military force while an MCC trainee serving in the US.

Gingerich, Melvin. "King Charles XII of Sweden and the Mennonite Preacher Stephen Funk." *GH* 51 (Oct. 21, 1958), 997. The story of Funk explaining nonresistance to the king, and the friendship between the two. From a manuscript written by John Funk.

Gingerich, Melvin. "Phocas of Asia Minor." *GH* 51 (May 20, 1958), 469, 479. An excerpt from Paul S. Rees' book *Prayer and Life's Highest* (Eerdmans, n.d.). Tells of Phocas, a fourth-century Christian who preferred to sacrifice his own life rather than endanger others.

Gingerich, Melvin (Review). *Through Tribulation to Crown of Life: The Story of a Godly Grandmother*, by Ethel Estella Cooprider Erb. n.p., n.d. Pp. 48. *MHB* 8 (Oct., 1947), 4. Reviewer observes that this tribute to Susanna Heatwole Brunk Cooprider contributes to the record of Mennonite experiences during the Civil War, because it describes in detail Susanna's search for her husband, who deserted the Confederate Army.

Glass, Esther Eby. "The Peacemaker in Cabin X." *ChrLiv* 1 (July, 1954), 18-19, 40. Story of a junior high school camper helping to make peace between two girls in her cabin who are competing with one another.

Goertz, Duane and Edwards, Carl, comp. "Court Martial Records of 131 Conscientious Objectors During World War I." Summer, 1975. MHL (microfilm, 3 rolls). Research project consisting of 98 case files, gathered from Army records and National Archives, documenting litigations involving CO's representing various branches of Mennonites. Materials include memorandae, forms, handwritten notes, transcripts of questioning, sentences, personal testimony, etc.

Gross, Leonard, comp. "Alternative to War: A Story Through Documents, Part 1." *GH* 65 (Nov. 7, 1972), 899-901; Part 2, (Dec. 26, 1972), 1046-47; 66, Part 3, (Jan. 2, 1973), 10-12; Part 4 (Jan. 9, 1973), 34-36; Part 5, (Jan. 16, 1973), 52-55. Uses contemporary documents to describe the difficulties Mennonites encountered during the Civil War and World War I, as well as the Mennonite response.

Hackman, Walton. "Penner Case Acquitted, and Prayers Answered." *GH* 63 (Aug. 11, 1970), 671; *EV* 83 (Aug. 25, 1970), 13. Reviews the story of an Oklahoma Mennonite conscientious objector who was refused CO status, prosecuted, convicted, and sentenced for refusing to comply with induction orders, and whose conviction was reversed on recommendation by the Solicitor General of the Supreme Court.

Heatwole, L. J. "Brother Christian Good, Whose Gun Was 'Out of Order.' " *MHB* 33 (July, 1972), 3. Letter written in 1918 recounts the story of Christian Good, who refused to fire a gun when inducted into the Confederate Army during the Civil War.

Heatwole, Reuben Joseph. "A Civil War Story." *MHB* 9 (Jan., 1948), 3-4; *ST* 40 (Oct., 1972), 12. Relates his experiences as a seventeen-year-old migrating north from Virginia to escape military duty during the Civil War. Written in 1919.

Hershberger, Guy F. "Do We Know Where We Stand on the War Question?" *YCC* 16 (Nov. 24, 1935), 792. This history of the Mennonite Church, including the most recent experience of World War I, is full of stories of people who believed in peace and declined to fight. Young people must continue to study and explore issues of peace to know where they stand.

Hershberger, Guy F. (Review). *"Hey! Yellowbacks!" The War Diary of a Conscientious Objector*, by Ernest L. Meyer. New York: John Day Co., 1930. In *MQR* 5 (1931), 72-77. This book contains the memoirs of a Univ. of Wisconsin undergraduate who was inducted into the United States Army against his will in 1918.

Hofer, David. "The Martyrdom of Joseph and Michael Hofer." Paper translated from the German by Franz Wiebe, 1974. Pp. 4. MHL.

Hofer, Joy. "Reality Brought Close to Home." *MBH* 19 (Dec. 5, 1980), 12. One family's story of suffering from the civil war in El Salvador.

Hooley, E. M. *The 1918 Christmas Eve Man of the Hour at Leavenworth: Written by a Mennonite Who Was Entrapped in that Riot.* n.p., [1960]. Pp. 13. MHL. World War I conscientious objector sentenced to 10 years at Leavenworth relates, with considerable awe, the story of how Col. Sedgwick Rice quelled a prison riot using no force other than the strength of his presence and the respect he had acquired among the prisoners.

Horst, Samuel L., ed. "The Journal of a Refugee." *MQR* 54 (Oct., 1980), 280-304. Journal of a young Mennonite refugee from Virginia fleeing military duty during the Civil War.

Hostetler, Marian. *African Adventure.* Scottdale: Herald Press, 1976. Pp. 124. Fiction, ages 10-14. In the course of an MCC-type assignment to Chad, 12-year-old Denise and her family begin to experience and understand the problems of hunger and violence in their relatedness. The story depicts a variety of ways church agencies work at the tasks of relief and mission.

"I Can Make Peace." Scottdale: Herald Press, [1983]. Record album of stories and songs for children about making peace. Some of the topics explored are peacemaking in the family, loving one's enemies, peacemaking in time of fear and war, etc. For kindergarten and early primary grades.

"I-Ws Narrowly Escape Death in the Congo." *RepConsS* 22 (Jan., 1965), 1, 3. Two Mennonite PAX persons resume duties in the Congo (Zaire) after a harrowing episode in Stanleyville in which Dr. Paul Carlson was fatally shot on Nov. 24.

Jantz, Harold. "Moros in the Peaceable Kingdom." *MBH* 18 (Aug. 10, 1979), 27-28. Christian conversion for the Moro tribe in Paraguay meant seeking peace with enemy groups within their tribe.

Keidel, Levi O. *Caught in the Crossfire.* Scottdale and Kitchener: Herald Press, 1979. Pp. 229. Account of the early years of Zaire's political independence, a period characterized by revolution and tribal warfare, and the ethical dilemmas the church had to face in regard to participation in violence or conscientious objection to it.

Keidel, Levi O. *War to Be One.* Grand Rapids: Zondervan, 1977. Pp. 239. An account of the Mennonite church in the Congo, now Zaire, during the turbulent years of famine and warfare from 1930-1960. The story is one in which both the African Mennonite leaders and the US missionaries participated in the processes of survival and reconciliation.

Kniss, Lloy A. *I Couldn't Fight: The Story of a CO in World War I.* Scottdale, Pa.: Herald Press, 1971. Pp. 47. Portrays the ridicule and hardship experienced by a World War I CO as a result of his steadfast refusal to cooperate with the military system in the military training camps into which he had been forced.

Kniss, Lloy A. *Why I Couldn't Fight.* Harrisonburg, Va.: Christian Light Publications, 1974. Pp. 72. Uses experiences as a World War I CO to explain and defend the nonresistant position.

Koehn, Dennis. "Draft Resistance: A Christian Response." *Lifework* 4 (1979), 3-6. Draft resister who spent 18 months in prison in the early 1970s relates the story of his decision, arrest, trial, sentencing, and reorientation to society after being released.

Kreider, Lucille. *The Friendly Way: A One-Act Play in Three Scenes.* Newton: Faith and Life Press, 1961. Pp. 22. Set in 1917, the drama depicts some of the struggles experienced by a Quaker family as the son refuses to join the military and, instead, volunteers for relief work in Beirut, where his nonresistant ideals are tested.

Kreider, Rachel. *Overcoming Evil: A One-Act Play in Two Scenes.* Newton: Faith and Life Press, 1961. Pp. 28. Dramatizes the Hochstetlers' encounter with the Indians in Berks Co., PA, in 1757. Emphases include the price this Amish family paid to follow the way of nonresistance as well as what the captured family members learned about peace in eight years of living with the Indian people.

Kroeker, David. "The Boys from CO Camps Remembered Harold Sherk." *MennRep* 4 (Apr. 1, 1974), 9. Tribute to peacemaker Sherk, outspoken advocate of conscientious objector legislation and pastor to CPS camps.

Landers, Bertha M. "The Battle on the Tyrol: A Children's Play on Peacemaking." Austrian soldiers are nonplussed when the mayor claims that no one will resist the soldiers because Christ is their leader and he has taught them another way.

Landers, Bertha M. "The Day the Wind Changed." *Builder* 26 (Apr., 1977), 7-11. When a pirate ship visits the Quaker community on Nantucket in 1778 for the purpose of plundering the island, the pirates are welcomed with nonresistant love. A short play suitable for Sunday School use as well as with intergenerational groups.

Leatherman, Noah H. *Diary Kept by Noah H. Leatherman While in Camp During World War I.* Linden, Alberta: Aaron L. Toews, 1951. Pp. 86. MHL. A day to day account gives a detailed portrait of life as a World War I CO including prison experience at Fort Leavenworth. Materials include journal reflections, menus, schedules, letters, and essays.

Lehman, Melvin L. "The Tent." *ChrLiv* 16 (May, 1969), 20-27. Story of young Amish men who refrained from playing a trick of revenge upon city tourists because it was not consistent with the way of peace.

Lehn, Cornelia. *Peace Be with You.* Newton: Faith and Life, 1980. Pp. 126. Fifty-nine stories about peace from the first through the 20th centuries. Intended as a resource for peace education with children.

Loewen, Harry (Review). *Die Rose von Wüstenfelde,* by Ernst Behrends. D-7762 Bodman/Bodensee: Hohenstaufen Verlag, 1973. Pp. 220. "A Worthwhile Novel in German." *MennMirror* 8 (Jan., 1979), 19. Summarizes this novel, telling of the hope, faith, and love of a woman in northern Germany during the horrors of the Thirty Years' War (1618-48). It is the second in a series of six novels dealing with the story of the Mennonites, and the reviewer finds the author's positive treatment of the Mennonites gratifying and refreshing.

Löwen, Peter H. As told to Peter Klassen, Jr., "An Unusual Business in Watermelons." *ChrLiv* 6 (Apr., 1959), 3. Mennonite farmer in the Chaco attempts to do business with the soldiers fighting the Chaco War in 1933.

Martin, Earl S. *Reaching the Other Side: The Journal of an American Who Stayed to Witness Vietnam's Post-War Transition.* New York: Crown Publishers, Inc., 1978. Pp. 281. Journal records actions and observations of an MCCer during the six-week period between the time the Provisional Revolutionary Government (Viet Cong) stages a peaceful takeover of Quang Ngai City and the fall of Saigon. An intimate view of the day to day ramifications of trying to live out the MCC philosophy of ministering beyond the boundaries of nationality and political ideology.

Miller, Korla, and Zuercher, Melanie. "Prepared?" *Lifework* 5 (1981), 12-13. Reprinted from *Goshen College Record*. Vietnam veteran turned pacifist and Mennonite describes the turning point in his life and his current peace activities.

Mueller, Peter (Review). *That There Be Peace,* by Lawrence Klippenstein. Winnipeg: The Manitoba C.O. Reunion Committee, 1979. Pp. 104. *MBH* 19 (Apr. 25, 1980), 28. Reviewer observes that this collection of memorabilia from Canadian conscientious objectors in alternative service during World War II reveals both courage and cowardice.

Northcott, Cecil. "Berlin's Dibelius—Watchman of East and West." *ChrLiv* 6 (June, 1959), 32-33, 34. Reprinted from *Presbyterian Life,* Philadelphia, Pa. The witness of Otto Dibelius through war and totalitarian regimes.

Penner, Lydia. "E. J. Swalm: A Life Dedicated to Peace." *MennRep* 6 (Aug. 23, 1976), 9. Describes the life and thoughts of this Brethren in Christ bishop who has devoted his life to teaching conscientious objection.

Preheim, Marion Keeney. "Lawrence Hart: Indian Chief in a Tradition of Peace." *MennRep* 10 (Nov. 24, 1980), 10. Reviews the pilgrimage of a native American from military service to affirming both Cheyenne and Christian commitments to peace.

Q[Anonymous]. "Letter from a I-A-O." *MCC Bull* 3 (Oct. 8, 1944), 5-6. This letter, written to CPS and AFSC, describes the hateful attitudes and military environment which he (Q) experienced in noncombatant service. Because of his resistance of these attitudes, his colonel rightly decided he belonged in CPS.

Ratzlaff, Vernon (Review). *The Struggle for Humanity,* by Marjorie Hope and James Young. Maryknoll: Orbis Books, 1977. Pp. 305. *MBH* 17 (Dec. 22, 1978), 31. Recommends this collection of the stories of seven people working nonviolently for reconciliation and justice.

Reimer, Al (Film Review). *"Hiding Place* Is Good Religious Cinema." *MennMirror* 6 (Dec., 1976), 16. This film dramatizes the life of Corrie ten Boom, who aided Jewish refugees in Holland during the Nazi occupation and was imprisoned in a concentration camp. It is especially good because it depicts faith and spiritual devotion; it teaches also about the nature of both evil and faith.

*Remembering: Stories of Peacemakers.* Akron, Pa.: MCC Peace Section, 1982. Pp. 59. MHL. Stories, readings, and short plays for use in churches and schools. Topics included are conscientious objection in World War I, World War II, and the Vietnam War, as well as an interview with a South African conscientious objector.

Rhodes, Samuel A. "The Rebellion, the Cause of My Traveling Adventures to the North." *MHB* 33 (July, 1972), 2-3. Excerpts from the diary of a young man during the Civil War who fled his Virginia home to escape induction in the Confederate Army.

Roth, Willard E., ed. *What Does Christ Say About War?* Scottdale: Herald Press, 1964. Pp. 15. Peacemaker Pamphlet No. 3. Shows that Jesus chose a way of love and nonviolence in his life; relates stories of contemporary Christians who chose love rather than hatred or violence.

Rubin, George. "The Making of a Pacifist." *With* 13 (May, 1980), 4-6. Allied bomber pilot in World War II describes his experience of the horror of war which led to his commitment to pacifism.

"Six Diener Brothers in Alternative Service." *RepConsS* 5 (Apr., 1947), 5. Six of Amanda and Harry A. Diener's seven sons, all members of the Mennonite Church near Hutchinson, Kan., have been involved with alternative service.

Samuel, Dorothy T. "Love Is a Self-Feeding Explosion." *Menn* 91 (Sept. 28, 1976), 561. Reprinted from *Safe Passages on City Streets,* by Dorothy T. Samuel (1975). Relates the story of two women accosted at night who responded with dignity and understanding love, transforming the scene of potential violence into a genuine human meeting.

Savage, Regan. "The Military is Not All It's Cracked Up to Be." *With* 11 (Nov., 1978), 4. Savage received a conscientious objector's discharge after six years as a tank commander in the United States Army.

Sawatsky, Walter W. "Prince Alexander N. Golitsyn (1773-1844): Tsarist Minister of Piety." PhD Dissertation, University of Minnesota, June, 1976. Pp. 552. MHL. The life and career of Alexander Golitsyn, whose tenure in high office (1803-24) spans almost the entire reign of Tsar Alexander I, offers an example of a concerted effort to apply Christian principles and a Christian experience, which encompassed both a Pietist-inspired personal conversion and an interest in mysticism, to his role as a government official. His career also represents, on another level, a major attempt by the state administration to establish and maintain a policy of tolerance toward a multi-confessional empire.

Schlabach, Theron F., ed. *"An Account* by Jakob Waldner: Diary of a Conscientious Objector in World War I." *MQR* 48 (Jan., 1974), 73-111. The diary of a Hutterite conscientious objector demonstrates belief in two strictly separate kingdoms, with unswerving loyalty to the kingdom of God rather than to the nation.

Schlich, Victor A. "A Service of Everyday Incidents." *ChrLiv* 18 (May, 1971), 10-12. Sketch of Heinrich Treblin, peace advocate in Hesse, West Germany, who served in the underground resistance movement during Hitler's rule.

Schmidt, Allen. *Experiences of Allen Schmidt During World War I.* Hesston, Ks.: Gospel Publishers, [1972]. MHL. Series of letters from a conscientious objector, sentenced to 25 years in Fort Leavenworth, to his family and friends.

Schmidt, Vernon. "Applied Peace." *ChrMon* 31 (Feb., 1939), 41. Recounts stories of Mennonite practice of nonresistance and love of enemies, from 1600s to the present.

Seitz, Ruth. "Peacemaking Is a Sensitive Matter." *With* 11 (Sept., 1978), 24. The story of Pat Hostetter Martin and her peacemaking efforts.

Seitz, Ruth. "There Is No Way to Peace." *With* 11 (Oct., 1978), 10. The story of Earl S. Martin and his peacemaking efforts in Vietnam.

Seitz, Ruth. "Where on Earth Is There Peace?" *With* 10 (Nov., 1977), 2. Six Mennonite youth say where they find peace in their lives.

Shank, J. Ward (Review). *A Russian Dance of Death,* by Dietrich Neufeld. Translated and edited by Al Reimer. Hyperion Press and Herald Press, 1977. Pp. 142. *ST* 46 (Nov., 1978), 22-24. Recommends this firsthand account of the violence and hardship experienced by Mennonite colonists during the Russian Revolution.

Shellenberger, Eunice. *Wings of Decision.* Scottdale: Herald Press, 1951. Pp. 240. Fictional account of a young man facing the draft in World War II, his decision to seek conscientious objector status, and his experiences in Civilian Public Service.

Shenk, Charles B. "Only One Voice." *GH* 67 (May 14, 1974), 399. The story of one Japanese soldier who continued for thirty years to carry out his mission is a lesson in absolute faithfulness and personal sacrifice.

Shenk, Stanley C. "It Has Been Ten Years." *GH* 65 (May 30, 1972), 478-79. On the ten-year anniversary of MCC Paxman Daniel Gerber's capture in Vietnam, the author reflects on Dan's witness, the home life which prepared him for difficult experiences, and the message he might have about American involvement in Southeast Asia if he did return.

Shisler, Barbara. "Peace Teachers: The Mike Rhode File." *Builder* 31 (Jan., 1981), 17-18. Mike Rhode, formerly in the US Navy, has joined with four other Mennonite men with military experience to act out the role of the draft board in order to help Mennonite youth think more seriously about their responses to militarism.

Showalter, Jewel. "War Has No Winners." *With* 2 (Mar., 1969), 20. The story of Art McPhee's change from military duty to a position of nonresistance.

Smith, Willard H. "The Pacifist Thought of William Jennings Bryan." *MQR* 45 Part 1 (Jan., 1971), 33-81; Part 2 (Apr., 1971), 152-81. Part 1 reviews the beginning of Bryan's pacifist thought after the Spanish-American War; Tolstoy's influence on him; Bryan's work as Secretary of State and resignation from that office over disagreement with President Wilson's preparations for war. Part 2 examines Bryan's vigorous support of US involvement in World War I once it had been declared, his thinking and strategies for peace following the war, and some of the inconsistencies of his thought.

Smucker, Barbara Claassen *Days of Terror* Scottdale: Herald Press, 1979. Pp. 152. Young Peter Neufeld and his family are Mennonites in Russia during the internal and external turbulence experienced by the Russian nation during the World War I era. A strong theme of this moving juvenile novel is the theme of how people of faith, people who have practiced nonresistance for four hundred years, respond to acts of violence committed against their persons and their possessions in their own homes and barnyards. Both the Mennonite Self-Defense movement and the connections between the economic and cultural distance maintained by the Mennonites and the violence inflicted upon them are sensitively portrayed. For ages 8-12 and up.

Steiner, Susan Clemmer. "We Could Not Go Home." *With* 8 (June, 1975), 6. Description of the radical changes in the lives of four Mennonite draft dodgers in Canada.

Thomas, Kobangu. "I Preach with Happiness and Power Because I Did Not Use My Gun." *CanMenn* 12 (Jan. 7, 1964), 8. Testimony of African pastor who takes pacifist position amidst the terrors and pressures of tribal warfare.

Toews, Monroe. *Why I Can't Take Part in Carnal Warfare Since I've Become a Christian.* Hesston: Free Tract and Bible Society, [1962]. Pp. 15. MHL. Argument against war in fulfillment of a promise the author made to God during his tour of duty as an American soldier in Germany during World War II—that if he lived he would spend his days speaking of the love of God and the horrors of war.

Vogt, Virgil. "Having Done All to Stand." *ChrLiv* 9 (June, 1962), 26-27. Army recruit is converted to pacifist Christianity.

"Who Can Postmark the Stamp of Liberty?" *Lifework* 4 (1979), 2-3. Summarized from articles by Richard K. MacMaster in *Purpose* (Scottdale: 1976). Relates stories of Eve Yoder and John Newcomer of Pennsylvania who stood for peace and liberty during the Revolutionary War.

Waltner, Edward J. B. "A CO in the First World War." Paper, Marion, SD, 1942. Pp. 39. MHL.

Waybill, Nelson. "No Return." *ChrLiv* 6 (Apr., 1959), 8-10, 13. Anabaptist sentenced to be a galley slave contemplates cooperation with a violent escape plan.

Weaver, H. Brent. "A Long and Windy Road." *With* 13 (Oct., 1980), 4-8. Former Air Force recruit tells of his personal journey from commitment to war to a pacifist stance.

Wiebe, Rudy H. *Peace Shall Destroy Many.* [Toronto]: McClelland and Steward, 1962. Pp. 239. As 20-year-old Thom Wiens struggles to understand the "traditions of the fathers" and formulate his own responses to life and faith, he finds he must recognize and face the incongruity of his Mennonite community—a community which insists upon a nonresistant position in relation to war while forcing the Indians and Mitis to sell their land to the Mennonites; a community where harsh words are repressed while tensions between the generations, between families, seethe under the surface.

Wiebe, Rudy H. *The Blue Mountains of China.* Grand Rapids: Eerdmans, 1970. Pp. 227. Epic novel explores the Russian Mennonite experience from several points of view, times, and places. While the themes are also multiple, the examination of the intersection of faith and survival is a compelling one as the novel asks how and what love and traditions of nonresistance *become* in such crises. The chapter entitled "The Vietnam Call of Samuel U. Reimer" is especially focused on the questions of war and peace, although these themes appear in many of the other episodes as well.

Wiens, Hartmut (Review). *Peace Child,* by Don Richardson. Glendale: Regal Books, 1974. Pp. 287. *MBH* 15 (May 14, 1976), 29-30. Reviewer recommends this narrative of a missionary who communicates the gospel of reconciliation through the indigenous symbol of the peace child.

Williams, Howard. *Let My People Go: A Peace Play in Three Acts, Using Three Episodes Based upon Historical Incidents in the History of the Oldest Group of People to Object to War for Religious Reasons, the People Called the Mennonites.* [North Newton]: Bethel College, ca. 1936. Pp. 49. MHL. A tale of modern martyrdom among the Mennonites in Paraguay frames three historical scenes—one from the period of the Reformation and two from the Mennonite experience in Russia—which portray elements of the nonresistant tradition.

Wittlinger, Carlton O. (Review). *Twas Seeding Time: A Mennonite View of the American Revolution,* by John L. Ruth. Scottdale, Pa. and Kitchener, Ont.: Herald Press, 1976. Pp. 224. *MQR* 52 (July, 1978), 271-72. Reviewer considers this book of stories of Mennonite noncooperation in the Revolution a good, and informal, contribution to the subject of Mennonite history during the Revolution.

Witucki, Carol Lawson. "He Saw the Star." *Menn* 92 (Dec. 20, 1977), 748-49. Fictional story of a soldier who surrenders his gun to a vision of the Christ child on Christmas Eve.

Yoder, Elizabeth (Review). *The Wanderers,* by Ingrid Rimland. St. Louis: Concordia, 1977. *MennLife* 34 (Mar., 1979), 30. Gives a summary of the story which depicts three generations of Russian Mennonite women from the Civil War of 1917-20 to the immigration to Paraguay in 1947. Describes it as a fictional portrait of a people. Comments that Mennonite theology and the theme of pacifism are given very ambiguous treatment.

Yoder, Henry P. "'I Hold Nothing Against You.'" *GH* 63 (Dec. 22, 1970), 1054-55. Story of Cuban immigrant physician overcoming hostilities and forgiving those who wronged him illustrates the love of Christ which absorbs hostilities and brings peace.

Yoder, John H. (Review). *In Solitary Witness,* by Gordon Zahn. Holt, Rinehart, and Winston, 1965. Pp. 278. *ChrLiv* 12 (Nov., 1965), 35-36. Recommends the book as the narrative of a Catholic conscientious objector beheaded under Nazism.

Yoder, John H. (Review). *In Solitary Witness: The Life and Death of Franz Jägerstätter,* by Gordon Zahn. Holt, Rinehart, and Winston, 1964. Pp. 278. *ChrLiv* 13 (June, 1966), 32-33. Recommends this narrative of a Catholic layperson beheaded under Nazism for conscientious objection to war.

Zehr, Rosemary. "Jacob R. Bender: A Servant of Christ and the Church." *MennRep* 4 (Dec. 9, 1974), 5. Tribute to minister who promoted nonresistance and nonconformity among Ontario Mennonites.

Zook, Al. "A Family Affair." *The Other Side* 103 (Apr., 1980), 24-27; "A Family's Faith Put into

Action." *ChrLiv* 27 (Apr., 1980), 23-25. One family's participation in a demonstration against the arms race at the Rocky Flats, Colorado, nuclear weapons plant.

Zuercher, Melanie. "Peace Teachers: He Recruits (for Peace) at the High Schools." *Builder* 31 (Jan.,

1981), 13-14. Vietnam veteran Vaughn Mareno, Goshen, Ind., has found the Mennonite peace position to be a viable Christian alternative to the just war theory and puts his faith into practice in committee work, by involvement with the housing problems of the poor, and by counterrecruiting in the high schools.

# G. Christian-Marxist Dialogue

Bauman, Clarence, comp. and trans. "Report of East-West Theological Peace Conference, Frankfurt/Main, Germany, Jan. 10-13, 1959." Pp. 50. AMBS.

Bender, Harold S. "Prague Peace Conference." *GH* 54 (Sept. 19, 1961), 825, 837-38; "A Significant Christian Movement for Peace." *CanMenn* 9 (Sept. 1, 1961), 2. Bender reports on the Prague Peace Conference, the purpose of which was to contribute to a reduction of tensions between East and West, and to promote understanding and reconciliation between peoples. Includes a summary and brief positive evaluation of this nonpacifist Christian conference which many Christian pacifists attended.

Borovoi, Vitali. "A 'Covenant of Life and Peace' Today." *MennLife* 20 (July, 1965), 135-37. The message of a Soviet, Orthodox Christian priest to the Peace Assembly in Prague.

"Christian Obedience in a Divided World: An East-West Student Encounter Between Mennonites and Persons from Czechoslovakia, Hungary, and the GDR." MCC Peace Section, June, 1965. Various pagings. MHL. Includes: Janz, Hugo. "The Eastern Setting of Christian Encounter." Pp. 8. Keeney, William. "Report of the Advisory Committee of the Christian Peace Conference, Prague, Czechoslovakia, June 4-8, 1963." Pp. 3. Miller, Marlin E. "An East-West Encounter." Pp. 8. Miller, Marlin E. "Interview on East-West Student Encounter." (Interview of John Howard Yoder.) Pp. 7.

*Christians Between East and West.* Winnipeg: Board of Christian Service, Conference of Mennonites in Canada. Ca. 1965. Pp. 55. Contains essays addressing the questions of communist and anticommunist ideologies and suggests Christian responses. Epp, Frank H., "Christians Between East and West," 7-16; Toews, John A., "The Christian Response to Communism," 17-24; Metzler, Edgar, "Christian Response to Communism and Anti-Communism," 25-39; Janzen, David, "Mennonites and the East-West Conflict," 40-53; bibliography, 54.

DeBoer, Hans A. "'I Must Disobey Laws Against Democracy and God'—Sibley. *CanMenn* 13, Part 1, (Apr. 13, 1965), 1, 11; Part 2, (Apr. 20, 1965),

11. A Quaker pacifist analyzes student protests, the US involvement in Vietnam, and the nature of the East-West cold war.

DeBoer, Hans A. (Editorial). "A Man Who Talked to the Viet Cong Suggests 15 Responses to Asian War." *CanMenn* 13 (Oct. 5, 1965), 6. Suggestions include taking a critical attitude toward information available through national news services, beginning serious Christian-Marxist dialogue, supporting demonstrations and peace protests against the Vietnam War, etc.

Dyck, Peter J. "Sixty Countries Represented at Second Peace Assembly Held in Prague." *CanMenn* 12 (Aug. 11, 1964), 1-2. Report on the second all Christian Peace Assembly held in Prague in 1964. Theme of the conference was "My Covenant is Life and Peace."

Eby, Omar. "Mennonites from Israel, Arab Territories Convene in Athens." *CanMenn* 17 (July 4, 1969), 1, 2. Report on a meeting of Mennonite personnel in Athens Apr. 10-12 to discuss peace and reconciliation in the Middle East. Participants came from the East Bank, the West Bank, Israel, Lebanon, the US, and Europe. Action was taken to see what could be done about repatriation and resettlement of Arab refugees. First step was for West Bank/ Israel personnel to make concrete proposal to the Israeli government. Politics in the Old Testament, myths about Arab countries and Israel and the refugee problem in the Middle East were discussed.

Epp, Frank H. "Christians Between East and West." *Christians Between East and West.* Christian Concerns Series No. 1. Winnipeg: Board of Christian Service, Conference of Mennonites in Canada, [ca. 1965], 7-16. Describes features of communist and anticommunist propaganda which have attracted Mennonites to both camps, then uses the image of Christ to critique the materialism, militarism, power, and propaganda of both perspectives.

Epp, Frank H. "The East-West Assignment." *CanMenn* 5 (July 5, 1957), 2. "The very essence of the Mennonite faith and principles will be put to the test" for all Mennonites as Elfrieda and Peter J. Dyck undertake a three-year MCC assignment in Europe. This assignment will focus on East-West relations and communication.

Epp, Frank H. (Editorial). "War and Man." *CanMenn* 5 (July 19, 1957), 2. Summarizes statements made by 20 East and West scientists who met in Nova Scotia to discuss the consequences of nuclear war.

Gaillard, Albert. "Christians and Marxists." *Concern* 10 (Nov., 1961), 13-20. The ambiguities between Christianity and Marxism are heightened if one attempts to analyze them as if they are spiritually comparable. With this in mind, Christians must seriously commit themselves to dialogue with communists.

Gingerich, Melvin. "Reflections on the Prague Conference." *GH* 57 (Nov. 17, 1964), 1001, 1012-13. A report on the second Prague peace conference. "It was good that Mennonites participated in this conference where they were free to witness to their understanding of the desire for Christian peace and the sinfulness of war."

Gingerich, Melvin. "The Prague Peace Assembly in the Press." *MennLife* 20 (July, 1965), 127-30. This report consists of quotes from secular press releases as well as from reports in religious journals and church papers, including those from Mennonite denominations.

Goering, Erwin C. "Christian Peace Conference." *Menn* 74 (Aug. 18, 1959), 502-503. Report of the second Christian Peace Conference held in Prague. Includes the complete text of the conference's *Message to All Christians* summarizing the goals of the conference.

"How Some US Mennonite Leaders Reacted to the East-West Crisis Over Cuba." *CanMenn* 10 (Nov. 2, 1962), 1, 3, 10. Reactions include feelings that the US as well as Soviets must be held to account for actions leading to the crisis and that both nations must be reminded of the sovereignty of God.

Hackman, Walton. "Peace Seminar Encounters Communism in Eastern Europe." *CanMenn* 15 (Nov. 7, 1967), 7, 8. Report on MCC Peace Section study tour of Eastern Europe to speak with both Christians and Marxists in order to transcend some of the barriers which have divided for so long.

Harding, Vincent G. "The Prague Peace Conference: An Opportunity for Encounter." *CanMenn* 12 (Aug. 11, 1964), 5. A black Mennonite's response to the All Christian Peace Assembly held in Prague in 1964.

Hershberger, Guy F. "August 6: A Day of Intercession." *GH* 52 (1959), 663. On Apr. 16-

19, 1959, an international Christian peace conference, held in Prague, designated Aug. 6, the anniversary of the destruction of Hiroshima, as a day of confession, penitence, and intercession for the world. A copy of the summons to intercession is included.

Hiebert, Erwin N. "The Role of the Scientist as Reconciliator." *PCMCP Fourteenth*, 92-98. N.p. Held at Eastern Mennonite College, Harrisonburg, Virginia, June 6-7, 1963. Evaluation of the position of the scientist to be a potential reconciler between East and West. Modern science can provide a new language and new tools that might adapt to a new formulation of the Christian ethos in various non-Western cultures.

Hromadka, J. L. "On the Threshold of a Dialogue." *MennLife* 20 (July, 1965), 102-106. Considers where and how the issues of Christian faith intersect with the Christian Marxist dialogue.

Jantz, Hugo W. "Our Encounter in the East." *CanMenn* 13 (Aug. 3, 1965), 5. Report of 1965 Christian Peace Conference and MCC Peace Section talks in East Germany and Czechoslovakia.

Janzen, David. "Mennonites and the East-West Conflict." *Christians Between East and West.* Winnipeg: Board of Christian Service, Conference of Mennonites in Canada, [ca. 1965], 40-53. Links the rise of Communism with rejection of a false Christianity identifying with the exploiting class. Calls Mennonites to reject anticommunist propaganda as well as trust in nuclear weapons, in order to engage in deeper dialogue with communist people. Paper presented at the Canadian Conference Sessions, Altona, Man., July 20, 1963. Pp. 11. AMBS, MLA/BeC.

Kehler, Larry. "The Challenge of Peace Witness Is Very Close to Home." *CanMenn* 13 (Feb. 9, 1965), 3. Report on MCC Peace Section's annual meeting in Chicago on Jan. 14. Crucial issue for 1965 is the local church's involvement in peacemaking. Continuation of participation in Prague Peace Conference was proposed and a major study conference on church-state relations, in which MCC Peace Section would be involved, was discussed.

Kloppenburg, H. "The All-Christian Peace Conference." *MennLife* 20 (July, 1965), 112-14. The origin of the Peace Conference and the four elements which seem to be characteristic of the work of the Peace Conference.

Krahn, Cornelius. "The Prague Peace Assembly in the Eastern Press." *MennLife* 20 (July, 1965), 130-31. The Eastern press tended to report the Peace Assembly without debating its merits or demerits.

Kroeker, David. "Berlin: The Wall That Separates Is Built at from Both Sides!" *CanMenn* 15 (Aug. 29, 1967), 5. Report of an Aug. 7 tour of East Berlin in which author recalls the 8th Mennonite World Conference appeal to Christians to stand between East and West rather than on one side or the other. It was not only communism that built the Berlin wall but the West as well. The wall is a judgment of God on everyone.

Metzler, Edgar. "Christian Response to Communism and Anti-Communism." *Christians Between East and West*. Winnipeg: Board of Christian Service, Conference of Mennonites in Canada, [ca. 1965], 25-39. Criticizes communist opposition based on "Christian nationalism" because it confuses religious and political critiques. Analyzes characteristics of right-wing groups espousing such opposition, and outlines responses to both communism and anticommunism which could deepen the church's understanding and critique of both.

Miller, Marlin E. "Christian Obedience in a Divided World to be Subject of East-West Encounter." *CanMenn* 13 (Apr. 13, 1965), 1, 2. Preliminary report of 1965 Christian Peace Conference and MCC Peace Section talks with East German and Czechoslovakian theology students.

Northcott, Cecil. "Berlin's Dibelius—Watchman of East and West." *ChrLiv* 6 (June, 1959), 32-33, 34. Reprinted from *Presbyterian Life*, Philadelphia, Pa. The witness of Otto Dibelius through war and totalitarian regimes.

Peachey, Paul L. "Dare We Work for Peace?" *The Japan Christian Quarterly* 24 (Oct., 1958), 283-89. As the Japanese church struggles to understand its role in the world's yearning for peace, it faces such issues as the ideological differences between East and West, the strengths and weaknesses of the various peace theories, and the meaning of Japan's experience with atomic war.

Peachey, Paul L. "Peacemaking, a Church Calling." *ChrCent* 80 (July 31, 1963), 952-54. Reflects on an ecumenical peace colloquium which discussed such topics as church-state separation, the church's position toward possession of nuclear weapons, and the church's contribution to the resolution of the East-West conflict.

Peachey, Paul L. "The Christian Peace Conference and the Czech Crisis." *GH* 61 (Dec. 31, 1968), 1147-48; *CanMenn* 16 (Dec. 31, 1968), 5. Describes the process followed by the ecumenical Christian Peace Conference in responding to the Soviet movement into Czechoslovakia. Asserts that the same "demons of war and hate" are behind the Soviet action and American military activities in Vietnam.

Peachey, Paul L. "The Intellectual Ferment in Central Europe." *MennLife* 20 (July, 1965), 102. An introduction to an East-West dialogue report. God and human realities are stronger than any ideology; dialogue is possible and imperative for Christians.

Peachey, Paul L. (Review.) *Varieties of Christian-Marxist Dialogue*, ed. Paul Mojzes. Philadelphia: The Ecumenical Press, 1978. Pp. iv and 210. *MQR* 53 (July, 1979), 259-60. Eighteen essayists contribute to this discussion, representing a variety of European and American writers, both Marxist and Christian; they reflect a rich variety of sometimes conflicting views and approaches.

Redekop, John H. "Communism Versus Christianity." *CanMenn* 4 (Feb. 10, 1956), 3. A spokesman for the Evangelische Kirche in Deutschland states that Christianity and communism can only exist side by side if the church compromises its principles.

Redekop, John H. "Peace with Honour." *MBH* 12 (Feb. 9, 1973), 10. Although an imminent Vietnam truce has been announced, several disquieting aspects remain: the millions of refugees, orphans, cripples, etc.; the possibility of continued guerilla warfare; and the threat of communism and east-west distrust.

Rise, Emil R. (Review). *The Chrysanthemum and the Rose*, by Ruth Benedict. NY: H. Mifflin, 1946; pp. 324; *Meeting of East and West*, by F. S. C. Northrop. MY: Macmillan, 1946; pp. 531; *The Logic of the Sciences and the Humanities*, by F. S. C. Northrop. NY: Macmillan, 1947; pp. 399. "Pathways to Peace." *MennLife* 4 (Jan., 1949), 20-21. Feels these books will add an intellectual dimension to an approach to peacemaking and thereby balance the emotional and practical dimensions which we have more often considered.

Shelly, Maynard. "Is Peace Possible? Prague Conference Thinks So." *CanMenn* 16 (Mar. 26, 1968), 6, 7. An introduction to the history and ideology of the Christian Peace Conference in Prague. The conference began in 1958 with a series of small yearly international meetings for church people from Eastern Europe. In 1961 and 1964 there were two large assemblies with Christians from around the world. The article discusses the third assembly to be held from Mar. 31 to Apr. 5, 1968.

Shelly, Maynard. "Prague Discusses Involvement in the Long Fight for Peace." *CanMenn* 16, Part 1, (Apr. 16, 1968), 1, 2. Reports on the Christian Peace Conference held in Prague. Issues of war and peace were discussed (especially Vietnam)but the issue of the tension between the rich nations and the poor nations was also given serious attention. The conference motto was "Save man—peace is possible."

Shelly, Maynard. "Prague Fails to Get Down to Business." *CanMenn* 16, Part 2, (Apr. 23, 1968), 1, 4. Reports on the Christian Peace Conference held in Prague. The conference showed that it is easy enough to condemn the other person's war but difficult to condemn one's own. Shelly feels that this difference may begin to change because the Czech theologian Josef Smolik called for a study of the abuses of power by countries of both the East and West and the proposal was passed by the conference.

Shelly, Maynard. "The Peace That Fails Us." *GH* 61 (May 28, 1968), 479-80. Reports and reflects on an ecumenical Christian Peace Conference held in Prague in which Christians from western nations seemed more able to criticize their governments' actions than Christians from Eastern European countries.

Stahl, Omar. "A Christian Encounter in East Berlin." *CanMenn* 14 (Mar. 22, 1966), 7. A report on an exchange of views by representatives of East and West churches on church and state relationships and an agreement to do something for peace together.

Toews, John A. "The Christian Response to Communism." *Christians Between East and West.* Winnipeg: Board of Christian Service, Conference of Mennonites in Canada, [ca. 1965], 17-24. Outlines ingredients of a Christian response to communism, such as belief in the unity of humankind, a Christian spirit of humility and redemptive concern, and an evangelical strategy that demonstrates Christ's love on a personal level.

Tomin, Julius. "A Marxist Speaks." *MennLife* 20 (July, 1965), 106-108. A Marxist seeks to lay the philosophical foundations of true dialogue between Marxists and Christians. "Discussion becomes real dialogue" only when: it strikes and transforms the person in the very ground of their being; when it makes a person more humane, more open to real human values; and when it in turn stimulates both partners to deepen their own inner life.

Unruh, John D. "Peace Conferences Transcend Political Barriers." *CanMenn* 7 (Dec., 11, 1959), 2, 10. A discussion of East-West theological dialogue of recent years and how Mennonites should relate to it.

West, Charles C. "The Second All-Christian Peace Assembly." Part 1. *MennLife* 20 (July, 1965), 115-18. Christians from East and West meet to converse not only about peace but about Christian faith and life on both sides of the Iron Curtain.

# 14
# Race Relations

"A Statement of Concerns: Adopted at a Study Conference on Christian Community Relations." *GH* 44 (Aug. 14, 1951), 780-81. Contains sections on: 1) Doctrine and practice; 2) Nonresistance in daily life; 3) Christian ethics in business and prpfessions; 4) Organized labor; 5) Race and minority group relations; and 6) other related concerns.

Augsburger, David W. "Prejudice—What Has It Done for You Lately?" *GH* 65 (May 9, 1972), 418-19. A treatment of the origins and the nature of prejudices as they relate to other races and what to do about them.

"Bible Principles Governing Race Relations in Church and Industry." Paper, n.d. Pp. 10. AMBS.

"Black Group Asks $500 Million in Reparations." *Menn* 84 (June 3, 1969), 378. The National Black Economic Development Conference in Detroit feels strongly that the white churches owe the black community reparations and requests a large sum of money for which projects have been designated.

"Bombers and Arsonists Are Hastening Integration and Freedom in the South." *CanMenn* 13 (Mar. 30, 1965), 3, 10. Points out that the very violence of those resisting integration is defeating their cause, as the church is roused from apathy to sympathy for the victims of the violence.

Banman, James. "Denver Mennonites Tackle Hispano Minority Problem." *CanMenn* 17 1 (Sept. 5, 1969), 6. Mennonite churches in the Denver area seek to meet the needs of blacks and Hispanics. The article includes some of the seven objectives and goals

Bender, Don. "Whites in Black Community." *CanMenn* 17 (Apr. 29, 1969), 5; *GH* 62 (May 13, 1969), 428. Bender makes five suggestions about black-white relations: 1) whites who work in black communities should be under black supervision; 2) whites cannot and should not try to lose their identity by becoming too

completely absorbed in the black poverty ghetto; 3) our main mission is to the white community; 4) we must keep in communication with the black people; 5) we should support the political candidates and measures which call for massive federal aid to the ghettos and control by black leadership in the use of those funds.

Bender, John M. "Longeneckers Work for Indians' Rightful Pride." *CanMenn* 18 (Apr. 24, 1970), 4, 12. Seeking to help Canadian Indians, a Mennonite couple discovers history, a people, and opportunities for meaningful service.

Berg, Ford. "Their Blood Is Upon Us." *GH* 45 (Oct. 28, 1952), 1057, 1069-70. An historical overview of anti-Semitism in Christendom, showing how the attitude of the Christian church during the past 19 centuries made possible the massacre of six million Jews under Hitler in this century.

Berthrong, Donald J. "Indian Policy: a Need for Change." *GH* 65 (Nov. 14, 1972), 921-25. "Politically powerless, demographically decimated, economically impoverished, and physically uprooted, but still maintaining dignity, the Native American defied total destruction and has survived," making a new Native American policy necessary.

Bishop, Jim. "'Accept Us as Brothers,' Minority Speakers Say." (open quotes) *GH* 64 (May 11, 1971), 418-19. Summarizes what an Apache Indian, a Spanish pastor, a Japanese schoolteacher, and a black pastor have to say to the whites in the Mennonite church.

Bohn, E. Stanley. "Black Power and Nonviolence." *Menn* 81 (Sept. 13, 1966), 557. Board of Christian Service sends a fraternal letter to the Congress of Racial Equality (CORE) urging continuation of "courageous nonviolent" action.

Bohn, E. Stanley. "Many Vacant Houses While Negroes Live in Slums." *CanMenn* 14 (Sept. 6, 1966), 3. Report of participation by Chicago

Mennonites in a march into a Lithuanian-Polish neighborhood led by Martin Luther King on Aug. 1. Bohn comments on the white residents who hurled obscenities at the marchers and warns how easy it is to become like the persecutors from whom Mennonites fled.

Brandt, Laurie. "South African Crisis Stirs Action in United Nations and Congress." *MCC PS Wash. Memo* 9 (Nov.-Dec., 1977), 4, 9. The UN arms embargo to South Africa is insufficient protest against the apartheid system.

Braun, Theodore. "Racism's Last Stand." *Fellowship* 23 (May, 1957), 16-21. A Kentucky minister probes the reaction of people reared in white supremacy customs to the moral onslaught of desegregation and the last-ditch harangues of racist agitators.

Brown, Hubert L. *Black and Mennonite: A Search for Identity.* Scottdale: Herald Press, 1976. Pp. 124. Brown examines the racial conflict in the Mennonite Church from the viewpoints of personal experience, black theology, and Anabaptist theology. Proposes, as an alternative to both white integration and an either/or model with implications for separatism, a diunital approach embracing both blackness and Anabaptism.

Brown, Hubert L. "Let America Be America Again." *With* 9 (Sept., 1976), 30. America should be an America of the people, by the people, for the people, rather than being two Americas, white and black.

Brown, Hubert L. "Mennonites Are Guilty." *GH* 62 (Nov. 4, 1969), 968. The need for corporate guilt feelings in the church for sins against the blacks and what to do about them.

Buhr, Martin. "A Dream Deferred Is Like a Dried-Up Raisin." *CanMenn* 16 (Mar. 19, 1968), 1, 2. Report of Vincent Harding speech on Mar. 9, 1968 at Conrad Grebel College. Deferred dreams, said Harding, explode like a grape in a winepress.

Burrell, Curtis E., Jr. "A Primer on the Urban Rebellion." *Menn* 83 (June 18, 1968), 418-20; *ChrLead* 31 (June 18, 1968), 4-6; *GH* 61 (June 18, 1968), 534-36; *EV* 81 (June 17, 1968), 5, 13-14. The judgment of God which cries "let my people go" is at the heart of the current urban "riots." Years of injustice and white racism are the cause of the cities' upheavals. White Christians must repent of their racism and follow new black leadership if America is to be reformed.

Burrell, Curtis E., Jr. "How My Mind Has Changed About Whites." *ChrLiv* 13 (Sept., 1966), 28-29. The deep injustice of racism is the supposed superiority of the white value system.

Buttrick, George A. "Our Call and Cross." *MBH* 15 (Apr. 2, 1976), 5. The Christian cross is not private suffering but public risk-taking that confronts systems of war, poverty, unemployment, and racism.

"Canadians Claim US Imperialism." *CanMenn* 18 (Mar. 13, 1970), 3. Fifty-three American and Canadian Mennonites join to conduct a Christian Citizenship Seminar in New York City. Focusing on each nation's problems (imperialism, poverty, native American policies, external affairs, bureaucracy), an attempt is made to pinpoint the Christian's responsibility as the member of a nation and of the world community.

"Cheyenne Leader Switches from Military to Ministry." *CanMenn* 9 (Dec. 1, 1961), 4. Laurence Hart discusses the Cheyenne and the doctrine of nonresistance.

"Church and Society Conference." Paper, reports, minutes, etc., of General Conference Mennonite Church conference, Chicago, Ill., Oct. 31-Nov. 3, 1961. Two volumes. MHL. Some pertinent commission papers include: "The Christian Church and Civil Defense," "Christian Labor and Management Relations," "The Christian in Race Relations," "The Christian Church and the State," "The Church, the State, and the Offender."

"Conference Resolutions on Race Relations." *ChrLead* 26 (Aug. 20, 1963), 3. The text of a resolution adopted at the 1963 convention of the Mennonite Brethren Conference. Since the Christian gospel is universal, congregations should serve and witness to all people. MB congregations are urged to work actively to eliminate all forms of discrimination.

Cardinal, Harold. "To Survive Indian Must Become Good Little Brown White Man." *CanMenn* 18 (Feb. 6, 1970), 6, 8. An excerpt from "The Unjust Society" criticizes the Canadian government's treatment of Native Americans and makes several suggestions as to the steps necessary before Native Americans can begin to develop their full potential.

Charles, Howard H. "Do CO's Have Civil Rights?" *GH Supplement* 38 (Aug., 1945), 407-408. A description of recent attempts to deprive CO's of their personal and civil rights and a number of court cases crucial to the definition of the legal basis of the civil rights of religious objectors.

Coates, Paul V. "He Broke the Color Barrier." *YCC* 44 (May 5, 1963), 11. The story about John Howard Griffin, a white, who changed his physical features enough to pass for a black for a study project.

Cornell, David L. "Is the World Moving into 'Promised Land' or Nightmare?" *ST* 36 (Dec., 1968), 4. With the senseless killing of Martin Luther King as a reference point, the writer examines social change and personal change from a biblical perspective.

"Dutch Church Expresses Interest in Civil Struggle." *CanMenn* 13 (Aug. 10, 1965), 1. Reports that the Rotterdam Mennonite Church has sent a letter of encouragement and appreciation to Martin Luther King, Jr.

Davis, Abraham. "Ethnic Integration." *The Other Side* 10 (Sept.-Oct., 1974), 48-49. Failure to implement ethnic integration throughout a liberal arts education not only academically and psychologically damages the disadvantaged minority, but it also perpetuates ignorance among American students.

De Leon, Lupe. "The Church and the Mexican American People: The Nation's Second Largest Minority." Paper for Church and Race class. AMBS, Elkhart, Ind., Mar. 11, 1974. Pp. 10. AMBS.

Derstine, C. F. "The Black Blotch on American Civilization." *ChrMon* 23 (Mar., 1931), 92. The mob violence and lynchings of blacks and other foreigners is a terrible injustice.

Dirks, Carole, ed. ["Conference Addresses."] *IPF Notes* 7 (May, 1961), 2-4. Summaries of IPF conference speeches on the topic of race relations.

Dirks, Otto. "By Way of Salvation." *CanMenn* 9 (May 12, 1961), 2. The church must not only generate a spirit of love and cooperation but must also give active support to anti-discrimination measures and movements.

Drescher, John M. "Racism or Reconciliation." *GH* 58 (Apr. 27, 1965), 359. Racism and ill feelings on race lead to murder. Christians must as reconcilers seek to quench this spirit of hatred.

Driedger, Leo. "Acceptable and Non-Acceptable Forms of Witness: A Special Study Report on Nonviolence and Civil Disobedience." Leaflet printed by the Canadian Board of Christian Service, Winnipeg, Manitoba, 1966. Pp. 2. Also in *CanMenn* 14 (May 31, 1966), 7-8. Discusses and evaluates the trends in nonviolent protest stimulated by the civil rights movement and the Vietnam war. Analysis includes consideration of Mennonite youth involvement in these trends.

Driedger, Leo. "Christian Witness in Race Relations." *MennLife* 15 (Apr., 1960), 81-86. A survey of the beginnings and the development of witness in race relations by the General Conference Mennonite Church.

Driedger, Leo. "Louis Riel and the Mennonite Invasion." *CanMenn* 18 (Aug. 28, 1970), 6. A reflection on what happened when Mennonites moved onto land taken away from native Canadians and what the consequences were for both groups of people.

Driedger, Leo. "Native Rebellion and Mennonite Invasion: An Examination of Two Canadian River Valleys." *MQR* 46 (July, 1972), 290-300. A focus on the Red River Valley in Manitoba in 1869-74 and on the Saskatchewan River Valley in 1884-95 in order to determine in what sense peace-loving Mennonites cooperated with a government using force to drive away native Canadians so that the Mennonites could settle.

Dyck, Ernie, "College Peace Fellowship Probes Social Revolution." *CanMenn* 16 (Mar. 19, 1968), 1, 12. Report on the IPF meeting in Chicago which discussed the black social revolution.

"Eight Conferences, 100 Delegates Attended Race Conference." *CanMenn* 12 (Mar. 17, 1964), 3, 11. "It is a sin to prevent a Christian brother, whatever his color, from worshipping with us." This theme was emphasized at an MCC Peace Section conference on race relations.

"Elkhart Board Approves Interracial Council." *CanMenn* 16 (Aug. 13, 1968), 1, 4. In a July meeting, the Mennonite Board of Missions and Charities formed a Council for Interracial Concerns related to evangelism and church development in urban churches. This decision was made partly because representatives of interracial churches at the meeting called for more black participation in the decisionmaking processes affecting them.

"Elmer Neufeld Begins As Peace Section Exec.-Sec." *CanMenn* 7 (Sept. 18, 1959), 5. The appointment of Elmer Neufeld as full-time executive secretary of MCC Peace Section will make possible intensified witness in the areas of militarism and race relations.

Eby, Omar. "Turmoil Coming to South Africa." *Menn* 84 (Apr. 8, 1969), 236-38. Reflects on conditions in South African countries that could lead to increased race conflicts and guerrilla warfare. Would a Mennonite presence benefit the peace witness here?

Epp, Frank H. "Canada's Second Class Citizens." *CanMenn* 4 (Sept. 28, 1956), 2. Indians and Eskimos also were created in the image of God and have a right to first class citizenship. Canadians must repent of their kind of racism.

Epp, Frank H. "Civil Disobedience." *CanMenn* 11

(May 10, 1963), 6. Expresses support for the practice of civil disobedience in desegregation demonstrations in the American South. "It is better to break the law and be right than to keep the law and be wrong."

Epp, Frank H. "Forgive Us, Black Brothers." *CanMenn* 3 (Nov. 4, 1955), 2. Reprint of and commentary on the statement of confession and repentance of a Mennonite pastor for Christian involvement in the sin of racial intolerance.

Erb, Paul. "Discipleship of Love." *GH* 47 (May 4, 1954), 411. The negative emphasis of nonresistance is not totally sufficient to deal with class conflicts, racial tensions, and military rivalries. There must also be a positive demonstration of love.

Erb, Paul. "Nonconformity in Race Relations." *GH* 48 (June 7, 1955), 531. It is time that the Mennonites declare themselves against racism—a major cause of war. We have too long conformed to the world's sin of racism.

Ewert, David. "The Church in a Racially Changing Community." *MennLife* 22 (Jan., 1967), 44-45. A report of a Mennonite conregation's attempt to accept a neighborhood and a church that was no longer white.

Ewert, Mrs. D. P. "What Should We Be Doing for Peace?" *Menn* 85 (Jan. 20, 1970), 42, 43. Suggests areas in which peacemaking is urgently needed: the search for true and reliable information; the chasm between youth and adult; poverty areas, race relations, and corrections.

"Fifteen Goshen Students Marched in Alabama." *CanMenn* 13 (Apr. 20, 1965), 3, 11. Goshen students and Civil Rights demonstrators have common belief in the uses of nonviolence in the search for justice in race relations.

"Five Peace Ambassadors to Speak for Church." *CanMenn* 12 (Jan. 28, 1964), 3. A report on the MCC Peace Section's annual meeting, focusing on race relations. Summary of a panel discussion on racial conflict.

Fairfield, James G. T. "Mennonites and the Black Manifesto." *CanMenn* 17 (Nov. 7, 1969), 3. Does the Black Manifesto speak to the shortcomings of the Mennonite church? Concludes that we may not have exploited black people, but we have stood beside those who have; that the Mennonite church may not have the blood of slavery on its hands, but we are unquestionably guilty of repression and paternalism.

Fast, Darrell. "Mennonites Will Have to Deal With Racism." *CanMenn* 18 (July 31, 1970), 9. Defines racism and its symptoms. Suggests ways of combating racism, especially white racism.

Franz, Delton. "1976: An Appropriate Mennonite Celebration." *ChrLiv* 17 (Jan., 1970), 27-29. Mennnonite voice to government must become louder on issues of war, racism, and poverty.

Fretz, Herbert. "The Germantown Anti-slavery Petition of 1688." *MQR* 23 (Jan., 1959), 24-59. Prints the text of the petition and comments on its origin—mostly of Quaker origin with some possible Mennonite connections.

Friesen, George C. "Minorities Urge Nonracial Image for Christianity." *CanMenn* 17 (Sept. 26, 1969), 1. Blacks and Native Americans challenge US Congress on evangelism. In a statement, blacks call for church war against prejudice and discrimination. Native Americans confront delegates with a challenge to repent for what whites have done to native people.

Funk, John F. "A Terrible Massacre." *GH* 69 (June 22, 1976), 515. Reprint from the *Herald of Truth* of 1876 views the massacre of Custer's army as the fruit of deception and injustice done by the white people. Asserts the relations with Native Americans would have been different if whites had followed Jesus' way of peace.

Gerig, Joan and Sawatsky, Sharon. "An Ethical Analysis of Operation PUSH—An Alternative Social Action Structure." Paper for New Testament Ethics class, AMBS, Elkhart, Ind., Jan. 24, 1975. Pp. 34. AMBS.

Gingerich, Melvin. "Christianity Versus Racism; Christian Youth and the State." *YCC* 22, Part 9 (June 1, 1941), 587. The theory and methods of racism are totally un-Christian. Youth can use their influence to combat the growth of racism.

Gingerich, Melvin. "Negroes and the Mennonites." *Menn* 64 (June 14, 1949), 4, 9. Mennonite contacts with blacks have been infrequent, partly because of accidents of history and partly because of Mennonite unwillingness. Inter-racial service and fellowship must increase.

Gingerich, Melvin. "The Race Revolution in America." *GH* 62 (Apr. 1, 1969), 292-93. Links the civil rights movement to the growing worldwide consciousness among people of color that they need not be second-class citizens. Urges nonresistant people to work at the injustice of racial discrimination in order to become reconcilers.

Gingerich, Melvin. *Youth and Christian Citizenship.* Scottdale: Herald Press, 1949. Pp. 204. A collection of 50 essays written for high school age Christians on a variety of practical citizenship issues raised by the church and state relationship. Topics include nationalism, patriotism, political participation, racism, communism, community vitality, ecology, and more.

Gingerich, Melvin (Review). *The Bridge Is Love,* by Hans de Boer. Grand Rapids: Eerdmans, n.d. *GH* 52 (Jan. 20, 1959), 57, 69. Recommends this "travel" book for its emphasis on issues of apartheid, economic disparity, and nuclear war.

Gingerich, Paul M. "'Black Manifesto': A Study of Reaction by Some Christian Churches." Paper presented to History of Christian Thought class, AMBS, Elkhart, Ind., Nov. 21, 1969. Pp. 11. AMBS.

Gingerich, Ray C. "Jesse Jackson: The Prophet in Politics." Paper presented to the Church and Race class, AMBS, Elkhart, Ind., spring, 1970. Pp. 28. AMBS.

Goertzen, Arlean L. "Study of Violence Draws New Attention." *Menn* 84 (May 6, 1969), 301. Examines opposing views on the application of violence in order to bring about justice in the US racial situation.

Goldsmith, Katy, and Huebert, Hans. "They Went to Alabama." *ChrLiv* 12 (July, 1965), 23-25, 27. Reflections of people who participated in the Selma to Montgomery civil rights march.

Hamm, Peter M. "Overcoming Racism." *MBH* 17 (Apr. 28, 1978), 30-31. Presents guidelines for recognizing racism and seeking to act fairly in light of the fact that a majority of Mennonite Brethren believe there is biblical basis for separation of races.

Harder, Leland. "Plockhoy and Slavery in America." *MennLife* 7 (Oct., 1952), 187-89. Examines the implications of condemning slavery absolutely and uncompromisingly as an institution.

Harder, Leland. "Thy People Shall Be My People." *Menn* 63 (Feb. 3, 1948), 3-4. A comparison of the experience of Mennonites in Russia who, in 1873, petitioned the US Senate for a large tract of land for a colony (denied), with that of blacks in America who, in the same year, were struggling to get the 1873 Civil Rights Bill passed.

Harding, Rosemarie. "Sing a Song for Freedom." *ChrLiv* 11 (Aug., 1964), 22-24. Comment on the songs coming out of the civil rights movement and the struggle for justice.

Harding, Vincent G. "Black Power and the American Christ." *Christian Century* 84 (Jan. 4, 1967), 10-13. Suggests that the Black Power movement may bear God's message for the church. One part of that message is the movement's identification of the blasphemous use of Christ's name to call angry black youth trapped in American ghettos to nonviolence while, at the same time and in the same name, to offer these youth no future except military service, where they must kill other dark-skinned, poor people in order to preserve white America's way of life. Black Power is a repudiation of the American culture-religion and its white Christ; it is a quest for a religious reality more faithful to the black experience.

Harding, Vincent G. "Build on Christ in the City." *Menn* 74 (Oct. 20, 1959), 644-45, 655. A call to break down the walls of fear and hostility which prevent Christian ministry in the urban situation.

Harding, Vincent G. "Do We Have an Answer for Black Power?" *Menn* 82 (Feb. 7, 1967), 82-83; "What Answer to Black Power?" *GH* 59 (Dec. 27, 1966), 1114-15. Are the Mennonites ready to follow Jesus even if it means breaking with the church? Are they really ready to help the poor and the oppressed, to extend their fellowship to these?

Harding, Vincent G. "The Beggars Are Rising . . . Where Are the Saints?" *MennLife* 22 (Oct., 1967), 152-53. Also in "The Beggars Are Marching . . . Where Are the Saints?" *The Witness of the Holy Spirit.* Ed. Cornelius J. Dyck. Elkhart: MWC, 1967, 128-29. Sermon response to Henk Bremer's "Rise Up and Walk" at the Eighth Mennonite World Conference, Amsterdam, 1967. The poor and disinherited are rising to accuse the rich and indifferent, including the Mennonites, of using Christ's name in vain.

Harding, Vincent G. "The Experiment in Peace." *MBH* 1 (Nov. 2, 1962), 6-7. The peace Christians seek is a molding of human hearts and institutions to the will of God, i.e., to reconciliation between all people.

Harding, Vincent G. "The History of a Wall." *GH* 61 (June 18, 1968), 543-45. Reprinted from *Must Walls Divide?* New York: Friendship Press. Briefly traces the history of white racism in America from slavery through the Civil War, segregation policies, racial revolution, and the nonviolent change proposed by Martin Luther King.

Harding, Vincent G. "To My Fellow Christians: An Open Letter to Mennonites." *Menn* 73 (Sept. 30, 1958), 597-98. Mennonites can no longer afford to be *die Stillen im Lande.* They need to renounce white power, privilege, and seclusion in order to serve people in need.

Harding, Vincent G. "Voices of Revolution." *Menn* 82 (Oct. 3, 1967), 590-93; *YCC* 49 (May 19, 1968), 12. How should the peace witness address the movement for black liberation?

Who commits the greatest sin—the desperate person or the complacent person?

Harding, Vincent G. "Walls of Bitterness." *Menn* 83 (June 18, 1968), 424-26; *ChrLead* 31 (June 18, 1968), 3-4. Deep bitterness is resulting from the largely ineffective struggles against the barriers imposed betwen the races by slavery, the Civil War, and segregation.

Harding, Vincent G. "What Answer to Black Power?" *YCC* 48 (Feb. 19, 1967), 2. Black power's critical interpretation of the affluent, complacent Anabaptists.

Harding, Vincent G. "When Stokely Met the Presidents: Black Power and Negro Education." *Motive* 27 (Jan., 1967), 4-9. The confrontation of Stokely Carmichael and the presidents of 2 Atlanta black colleges focuses an analysis of several key educational issues of race relations.

Harding, Vincent G. "Where Have All the Lovers Gone?" *MennLife* 22 (Jan., 1967), 5-13. An analysis of the hopelessness and seeming failure of the nonviolent movement in the black-white crisis.

Harding, Vincent G. (Review). *Why We Couldn't Wait*, by Martin Luther King, Jr. Harper and Row, 1963. Pp. 178. *ChrLiv* 12 (Feb., 1965), 33-35. Recommends the book as revealing reflections on King's struggles with himself, white America, the church, and his commitment to nonviolent change.

Harding, Vincent G., *et al.* "Church and Race in Six Cities." *Menn* 78 (Feb. 12, 1963), 98-101. Mennonite leaders in Chicago outline specific concerns and proposals regarding the Mennonite presence in various cities.

Harms, Orlando. "In Christ There Is No Black or White." *ChrLead* 33 (Sept. 22, 1970), 24. Outlines what the Mennonite Brethren Church can do "to see the issue of race in the right perspective and to help bring justice" to the blacks.

Harshbarger, Emmett Leroy. "African Slave Trade in Anglo-American Diplomacy." PhD dissertation, Ohio State University, 1933.

Hart, Lawrence H. "Two Hundred Years of Dishonor." *Menn* 91 (May 18, 1976), 334-35; "The Native American: Two Hundred Years of Dishonor." *With* 9 (Feb., 1976), 20. A Cheyenne Mennonite takes the occasion of the US Bicentennial to reflect on Native American efforts to live at peace with a white government that has reciprocated with broken treaties and massacres.

Hatfield, Mark O. "Piety and Patriotism." *MBH* 13 (Aug. 9, 1974), 1-4. Since ultimate loyalty belongs to God, not the state, Christians must confront militarism, materialism, and racism. Cites cases of third century pacifist stances.

Heimichs, Alfred. "The Indian and the Canadian Mennonites." *MennLife* 22 (Jan., 1967), 27-28. Calls upon the Mennonite churches in Canada to become as supportive of the cause of the native Americans who live within a half hour's drive of many Mennonite communities as they are of the cause of the blacks in the US south.

Heinrichs, Alfred. "Problem of Discrimination." *CanMenn* 9 (May 5, 1961), 2. There is racial discrimination in Canada. What is the church's response to it.

Heisey, Marion J. "Whose Teeth Are Set on Edge?" *EV* 88 (June 25, 1975), 5. Violence and injustice have been done to the traditionally peaceful Navajo tribe and have implications for continuing ministries to the Navajo people.

Heisi, Evan. "Saskatchewan Peace Talk Attracts 200 Participants. *Menn* 94 (Mar. 20, 1979), 214. "Peace is not the absence of conflict, but the presence of the Creator," was the theme of the native and Mennonite "peace talk" held Feb. 23-24 at Tiefengrund Mennonite Church.

Hershberger, Guy F. "A Christian Witness on Race Relations Now." *GH* 57 (May 19, 1964), 425. The Committee on Economic and Social Relations of the Mennonite Church believes that it is again time that we speak out clearly on the issue of race relations. Included is a letter sent to the 100 US senators.

Hershberger, Guy F. "A Mennonite Analysis of the Montgomery Bus Boycott." Paper presented to the Intercollegiate Peace Fellowship, 1962. Pp. 12. MHL.

Hershberger, Guy F. "A Senator Speaks to the Churches." *GH* 57 (Aug. 4, 1964), 666. A letter from Senator Gaylord Nelson reminding the churches that the Civil Rights Act does not solve the race problem. The church must be prepared to meet the even greater challenges ahead.

Hershberger, Guy F. "Conscience of Society." *GH* 61 (Feb. 20, 1968), 150-51. [No. 24] In support of his position that the church is the conscience of society, the author lists and describes cases of Mennonite protest against the Vietnam war and efforts toward peacemaking in addressing the problem of segregated urban housing.

Hershberger, Guy F. "From Words to Deeds in Race Relations." *GH* 58 (Feb. 16, 1965), 121, 130. Suggestions to help churches put into practice their principles on race relations.

Hershberger, Guy F. "How Can We Witness to Business Establishments Which Discriminate

Against Minority Groups in Their Services? Questions of Social Concern for Christians," (Part 15). *GH* 53 (July 5, 1960), 600. A letter from Goshen College students to the Woolworth Company, New York.

Hershberger, Guy F. "Islands of Sanity." *GH* 45 (Mar. 25, 1952), 293-94. Are Mennonite communities islands of sanity in our society on issues of race, peace, etc.?

Hershberger, Guy F. "Lessons from Anabaptist History for the Church Today." Paper presented at the Mennonite Conference on Race Relations, Atlanta, Ga., Feb. 24-25, 1964. Mimeographed. Goshen: MHL. An address on lessons from anabaptist history that provide insightful principles on race relations and the related concern of the threat of "being called a communist."

Hershberger, Guy F. "Martin L. King: Professor's View." *Elkhart Truth* 65 (Mar. 17, 1960), 15. AMC Hist. MSS 1-171 Box 54. A commentary on Dr. Martin Luther King, who spoke at Goshen College and on the issues discussed in the King lecture.

Hershberger, Guy F. "Mennonites and the Current Race Issue: Observations, Reflections, and Recommendations Following a Visitation to Southern Mennonite Churches, July-Aug., 1963, with a Review of Historical Background." Paper, [1963]. Pp. 25. AMBS.

Hershberger, Guy F. "Mennonites and the Negro Revolution." *PCMCP Fifteenth*, 112-22. North Newton, Kansas: The Mennonite Press. Held at Bluffton College, Bluffton, Ohio, June 10-11, 1965. Present racial crisis in America presents a ringing challenge to every Mennonite. The Christian view of race relations is based on the way of the Cross, on love and justice.

Hershberger, Guy F. "Nonresistance, the Mennonite Church, and the Race Question." *GH* 53 (June 28, 1960), 577-78, 581-82. Mennonites should not participate in or support discrimination in any way. They should support Martin Luther King although they should guard against accepting all of his theology. They must also guard against confusing nonresistance with obedience to all laws.

Hershberger, Guy F. "Race Relations." *ME* IV (1959), 241. Brief introduction to how Mennonites have worked on better race relations, although prejudice and discrimination are still exhibited in Mennonite groups.

Hershberger, Guy F. "What Are False Prophets Doing to Confuse the Public with Respect to the Race Question and Other Issues? Questions of Social Concern for Christians." (Part 16). *GH* 53 (July 19, 1960), 620. A warning against Dan Smoot, Carl McIntire, and others.

Hershberger, Guy F. "What Can Be Learned About Race Relations on an Observation Tour? Questions of Social Concern for Christians." (Part 10). *GH* 53 (May 31, 1960), 492. A description of the southern itinerary of several Mennonite leaders.

Hershberger, Guy F. "What Is the American Negro Doing to Change the Segregation Pattern? Questions of Social Concern for Christians," (Part 12). *GH* 53 (June 14, 1960), 532. Blacks are resisting the evils of segregation with courage and patience, using economic forces such as lunch counter sit-ins as primary weapons.

Hershberger, Guy F. "What Is the Role of the Church in the Desegregation Struggle? Questions of Social Concern for Christians." (Part 14). *GH* 53 (June 28, 1960), 580. The church must lead in speaking out against segregation.

Hershberger, Guy F. "What Is the White Response to the Negro's Bid for Equal Rights? Questions of Social Concern for Christians." (Part 13). *GH* 53 (June 21, 1960), 556. Some are glad, some fearful, some violently opposed.

Hershberger, Guy F. "What Was Learned About Segregation on the Southern Tour? Questions of Social Concern for Christians." (Part 11). *GH* 53 (June 7, 1960), 508. There is much segregation, even in the churches.

Hershey, Lynford. "Does Silence Mean Consent for Violence?" *GH* 65 (Jan. 11, 1972), 28. Offers evidence that the church has not really been loving toward the minorities.

Hershey, Lynford. "God's Altar and Race Relations." *GH* 64 (Aug. 17, 1971), 682-83. The article challenges the sincerity of the faith of the Mennonite church, which too often reveals negative attitudes to minorities completely in opposition to Mt. 5:23, 24.

Hershey, Lynford. "Probe 'Guilty' Verdict Gives Hope." *Menn* 87 (June 13, 1972), 393. The "guilty" verdict handed down by a mock trial of the Mennonite church on charges of neglect of social issues is a mandate to leaders in Mennonite churches to give more positive leadership in alleviating the suffering which is experienced most often by the minority people.

Hershey, Lynford. "Sowing (White) and Weeping." *GH* 65 (May 23, 1972), 460-61. Article holds white Christians responsibile for their ever-showing racist attitudes.

Hershey, Lynford. "What Is the Mennonite Attitude on Race Relations?" *GH* 64 (Mar. 23, 1971), 262-64. A questionnaire, results, and evaluation of data concerning attitudes towards other races in 58 Mennonite churches.

Hertzler, James R. "Slavery in the Yearly Sermons Before the Georgia Trustees." *The Georgia Historical Quarterly* 59, 1975 Supplement, 118-25. Summarizes the emphases regarding slavery of fifteen sermons preached and published before the Georgia Trustees between 1731 and 1750. These sermons did not promote anti-slavery but rather the evangelization of the Negroes and that Christian slaves should be submissive.

Hiebert, David. Letter to the Editor. *ChrLiv* 18 (Dec., 1971), 43. Maintains that the article entitled "Goshen's Bridgebuilder, Vernon Schertz (*ChrLiv*, Aug., 1971) assumes that whites will retain their position of dominance by making blacks pacifist.

Hiebert, Edna. "King's Example." *CanMenn* 16 (May 28, 1968), 4. Letter to the editor by a woman asking some introspective questions about her identification with the native Americans whom she came to serve.

Hiebert, Susan. "Heated Red-White Debate in Manitoba." *Menn* 87 (May 16, 1972), 332. Alleged misuse of funds puts native Americans in bad light and strains race relations in Manitoba. The church is called to advocacy for the native Americans who bear the brunt of the reaction.

Hiebert, Susan. "Indian-White Relations." *CanMenn* 16 (Mar. 5, 1968), 5. Reflects on how Mennonites, as a minority with experiences in two world wars, might utilize this experience in our understanding and treatment of the native Americans, another minority group.

Hiebert, Susan. "The Street that Leads in Two Directions." *CanMenn* 16 (Mar. 5, 1968), 5-7. A native American woman, having become a Christian at a Mennonite mission, receives a cool welcome in a Winnipeg Mennonite church and is hurt by the inconsistency between the gospel which she believes and the feeling she is not welcome in this church.

Hochstetler, Walter. "Albert B. Cleage, Jr. and Black Religious Nationalism." Paper for Church and Race class, AMBS, Elkhart, Ind., May, 1970. Pp. 11. AMBS.

Holsinger, Justus G. "The False Worship of Race." *Menn* 64 (Nov. 8, 1949), 4, 9. Sharp indictment of white American egocentrism; likens racial superiority to a false god of the present civilization.

Horst, Samuel L. "Education for Manhood: the Education of Blacks in Virginia During the Civil War." PhD dissertation: University of Virginia, 1977. Examines the educational situation of blacks in Virginia during the Civil War; finds that churches played a significant role in trying to provide religious instruction for blacks.

Hostetler, John Andrew. (Review). *The Quaker Approach to Contemporary Problems,* ed. by John Kavanaugh. G. P. Putnam's Sons, 1953. Pp. 243. *ChrLiv* 1 (May, 1954), 27. Recommends the book as a compilation of Quaker views on social problems such as war, civil liberties, prisons, etc.

Hostetter, B. Charles. "Race Is Only Skin Deep." *MBH* 2 (Nov. 22, 1963), 5-6. Racial differences are basically unimportant; all people must seek to "create social solidarity and brotherhood."

Hostetter, J. N. "Concern or Protest; Which?" *EV* 78 (Apr. 12, 1965), 2-3. Although Mennonites tend toward "non-involvement," their concerns regarding social evils must find expression in vigorous protest against racial exploitation and discrimination.

Hostetter, B. Charles. "The Christian and Race Relations." *CanMenn* 4 (Aug. 10, 1956), 6. The church was intended to be a world-wide fellowship incorporating all races. "It is the church's task to take the 'torn tissues of fellowship' and help repair them."

Houston, Stephen (Review). *Perceptions of Apartheid,* by Ernie Regehr. No publisher, n.d. *Intercom* 24 (Apr., 1980), 3, 12. Discusses the issues of the injustice and violence of apartheid raised by the book.

Iutzi, Donna. "Ontario Youth Go 'Beyond Words'" *CanMenn* 16 (Oct. 22, 1968), 1, 2. Report on a peace action retreat at Chesley Lake, Oct. 4-6. The retreat dealt with welfare, drugs, the draft, and the native American.

"Judge Rules Indian Case Dismissed." *GH* 65 (July 18, 1972), 582. A native American of the Chippewa tribe makes successful case for CO status on basis of his tribal religious beliefs and the fact that the US-Chippewa treaty requires the tribe to "live in peace."

Jackson, Hugh. "Civil Rights and Race Relations." Convocation address, Jan. 23, 1967. Pp. 4. MLA/BeC.

Jacobs, Donald R. "Race, an International Problem." *MennLife* 22 (Jan., 1967), 23-25. Blacks today "understand the intricate machinery of the power structures and see these structures almost hopelessly rigged against them. The important fact is that they now feel they know the facts earlier denied them."

Jacobs, Donald R. "South Africa Assembly: The Yeast in the Dough?" *MennRep* 9 (Aug. 6, 1979), 2. The South Africa Christian Leadership Assembly (SACLA) met against a backdrop of racism and division to encourage ongoing fellowships of various races and denominations to commit themselves anew to Christ and one another.

Jacobs, Donald R. *The Christian Stance in a Revolutionary Age.* Scottdale: Herald Press, Focal Pamphlet No. 14, 1968. Pp. 32. Describes the factors influencing social change in the developing nations and the issues, such as tribalism, racism, and nationalism, which confront the church in these areas. Then, in this context, Jacobs contends that peace and development are two parts of the same issue—that any peace theology must necessarily speak to the issues of distributive justice.

Jacobs, Donald R., and Yoder, John Howard. "Historic Multiracial Meeting in South Africa's Capital." *Menn* 94 (Aug. 21, 1979), 503. A report on the South Africa Christian Leadership Assembly held July, 1979, in Pretoria, South Africa, which was a major religious event profoundly affecting the policy of apartheid.

Jantz, Harold. "God's Kingdom in the Twentieth Century." *MBH* 17 (Sept. 1, 1978), 2-3. Speakers at Mennonite World Conference in Wichita centered their talks around the theme of the peaceable kingdom's response to militarism, oppression, and racism.

Janzen, Gerald. "A Christian's Response to the Canada Question." *MBH* 17 (July 7, 1978), 5-6. Commitment to the gospel of peace means that Canadian Mennonites must abandon racism and ethnic self-interest in seeking reconciliation with French Quebec.

Jordan, Clarence. "The Good Samaritan." *MennLife* 22 (Jan., 1967), 17-18. A retelling of the "Good Samaritan" story, which makes a point about race relations.

Jost, Dean. "The Christian and Campus Ferment." *GH* 63 (July 14, 1970), 598-99. Given the division in American society between "establishment" and "radical" cultures, the church must act as a reconciler and as a prophet witnessing against the violence of both cultures: the sexism, racism, and militarism of the establishment, and the drugs, sexual mores, and individualism of the radicals.

Juhnke, James C. "Freedom and the American Revolution." *Menn* 91 (June 22, 1976), 417-18. Bicentennial celebrations reinforce the idea that freedom is a military achievement, when in fact revolution may not have been the only alternative in 1775; similarly, political independence later became a license to oppress blacks and Native Americans.

Juhnke, James C. "Mennonites and Afrikaners." *MBH* 11 (Aug. 24, 1972), 4-5; *MennLife* 27 (Dec., 1972), 118-19; "Mennonites and Afrikaners: Losing Grip?" *Menn* 87 (May 30, 1972), 365, 366. Compares and contrasts the South African Afrikaners and the Mennonites on such issues as: nationalism, language and literature, acculturation, etc. within a larger consideration of the issues of acculturation and race relations.

Juhnke, James C. "New Black Consciousness in South Africa." *Menn* 87 (Nov. 28, 1972), 700, 701. The black separatism movement still is in its infancy; however, it is showing remarkable vigor in its quest for political power, in its anticipated organization of an African workers' union, and in the emergence of a "black theology" movement.

Kauffman, Ellen B. (Review). *The Desegregated Heart,* by Sarah Patton Boyle. Marrow Co. *ST* 35 (Apr., 1967), 37. On the whole the book is readable, informative, and stimulating. One must respect the author for assuming Christian responsibility for the social evil of segregation.

Kauffman, Ivan. "Are We the Problem?" *GH* 61 (June 18, 1968), 545-47; *ChrLead* 31 (June 18, 1968), 9-11. Summarizes the US Riot Commission Report which attributed most of the violence and riots in American cities to white racism.

Kauffman, J. Howard. "Are We All Brothers?" *ChrLiv* 1 (Mar., 1954), 38. The Mennonite church and the problem of racial discrimination.

Kauffman, J. Howard and Harder, Leland. *Anabaptists Four Centuries Later: A Profile of Five Mennonite and Brethren in Christ Denominations.* Scottdale: Herald Press, 1975. Pp. 399. Reports a survey of 3,591 church members. Chapter 8, entitled "Social Ethics," probes participants' adherence to a nonresistant ethic in relation to a variety of issues such as war, race relations, labor-management relations, concern for the poor, capital punishment, etc. Chapter 9, entitled "Political Participation," explores attitudes concerning the church and state relationship as well as other related topics.

Kaufman, Donald D. "Cheyenne Soldier Testifies, Speaks for Way of Peace." *Menn* 84 (Jan. 21, 1969), 39. Having participated actively in World War II and the Korean War, Ted Risingsun maintains that anyone who is in the army no longer has self-possession. The army wants instant obedience. "How do I feel about it [army experience]? There is a better way."

Kehler, Larry. "Racism Darkens a Beautiful Continent." *Menn* 87 (Mar. 21, 1972), 190-93;

*MennRep* 2 (Apr. 17, 1972), 2. Defines apartheid, what it is and how it influences attitudes within the borders of South Africa and beyond.

Kehler, Larry. "Southern Africa: What to Do?" *Menn* 87 (Mar. 21, 1972), 212. Although the solution to the tragic suppression of the Africans will have to come from within, there are things that concerned people from North America can do to help the cause.

Kehler, Larry. "Sympathetic Ear Needed for Community Development Work." *CanMenn* 16 (Jan. 16, 1968), 6. A report on a MCC community development project on the Beardy Indian Reserve near Rosthern, Saskatchewan. The project headed by Bill Siemens involves listening to the people, teaching leathercraft to a paraplegic, and attending meetings in an effort to relate meaningfully in a non-governmental manner to the native American population.

Keim, Ray; Beechy, Atlee; and Beechy, Winifred. *The Church: The Reconciling Community.* Scottdale: Mennonite Publishing House; Newton: Faith and Life Press, 1970. Pp. 92. Examines the direction set for the church by the reconciling work of Jesus and looks at such issues as militarism, nationalism, human rights, racism, poverty, crime and violence as tasks for the church which embodies that reconciliation.

King, Martin Luther, Jr. "Transformed Nonconformist." *ChrLiv* 11 (Feb., 1964), 9-10, 38. Reprinted from *Strength to Love,* by King; Harper and Row, 1963. Urges nonconformity to the world in matters of nationalism, militarism, racism, and lifestyle.

Klaassen, David. "Now Is the Time to Speak for Peace." *CanMenn* 15 (July 25, 1967), 1, 2. A Mennonite Brethren Christian Service worker discovers the element of peace in the gospel message which Christians have been called to proclaim. Discovery results in contention that nonresistance must be a way of life and a strategy in all situations; that social evils and peace are intimately related; that the total love strategy has much to do with civil rights and evangelism.

Klassen, Aaron. "Racial Discrimination." *CanMenn* 9 (May 5, 1961), 2. As Christians, our stance must be that all people are to have equal rights and opportunities.

Klassen, Peter J. "Ironic Developments." *MBH* 12 (Mar. 23, 1973), 11. Using the situation at Wounded Knee to illustrate, the author suggests that Christians in Canada and the US demonstrate to the government with deeds of justice and mercy in holding to the promises that have been made with the Indians.

Klassen, William. "Man of Courage, Martin Luther King." *Menn* 85 (Apr. 7, 1970), 242-44. The way this one man interpreted the New Testament and what that meant for the civil rights movement can be seen as a standard or test for Mennonite faith and practice.

Klassen, William. "Walking with Dr. King." *MBH* 7 (Apr. 12, 1968), 8-9. The church is called to be "a remnant of renewal, a remnant of dissent from suicidal national policies," living in the freedom of the gospel.

Koehn, Robert. "Indian Awareness: Another Look at Wounded Knee." Paper for Church and Race class, AMBS, Elkhart, Ind., May 20, 1973. Pp. 20. AMBS.

Koop, Robert. "Native Rights Campaign Moves Across Canada." *MennRep* 9 (Apr. 16, 1979), 9. Native leaders from northern Canada have begun a two-week campaign across Canada to plead their case for recognition of aboriginal rights and against the construction of the Alaska Highway pipeline.

*

Kraus, C. Norman. "Christian Perspectives on Nationalism, Racism, and Poverty in American Life." *Peacemakers in a Broken World.* Ed. John A. Lapp. Scottdale: Herald Press, 1969, 30-42. Calls Christians to disassociate themselves from national selfishness and a "might makes right" mind set to understand the black power movement and to work for fair employment and aid policies.

Kraus, C. Norman. "Faint Not; Fight On." *GH* 39 (July 2, 1946), 289-90. The US fear of Russia, and the white attitude toward the blacks, are examples of attempts to overcome guilt through self-justification. Before reconciliation can take place one must admit his or her guilt and inability to solve the problem alone.

Kraus, C. Norman (Review). *Diary of a Sit-in,* by Merrill Proudfoot. U. of N. Carolina Press, 1962. Pp. 204. *ChrLiv* 10 (Sept., 1963), 35. Recommends the book as a discussion of the nonviolent witness to human relations by a Presbyterian minister and leader in the sit-in movement.

Kreider, Carl. "Civil Rights Here and Abroad." *ChrLiv* 7 (June, 1960), 18, 23, 39. Racial discrimination in violent form, such as in South Africa, or in the more subtle form of granting voting rights on the basis of race, denies the gospel of Jesus Christ.

Kreider, Carl. "Ferment in Africa." *ChrLiv* 6 (June, 1959), 18, 34. Rising nationalist tendencies and white racism contribute to sometimes violent ferment across the continent.

Kreider, Carl. "Strife at the University of

---

*For additional listing, see Supplement, pp. 717-719.

Mississippi." *ChrLiv* 9 (Dec., 1962), 18, 34-35. Racism and riots at the Univ. of Mississippi.

Kreider, Carl. "The Civil Rights Bill." *ChrLiv* 4 (Nov., 1957), 18, 40. Passage of the Civil Rights bill is another step forward in dealing fairly with all.

Kreider, Carl. "The United Nations and the Congo." *ChrLiv* 9 (Mar., 1962), 18, 34. Background of the present civil strife in the Congo.

Kreider, Carl (Review). *The Church and Social Responsibility,* by J. Richard Spann. Abingdon-Cokesbury, 1953. Pp. 272. *ChrLiv* 1 (Nov., 1954), 31. Recommends this collection of essays on social problems such as war, church and state, crime, civil rights, etc.

Kremer, Russell. "Nonresistance to Nonviolence: The Mennonite Story." Student paper [Goshen College, Goshen, Ind.], Dec. 6, 1974. Pp. 12. MHL.

Kroeker, Walter.. "Concern Over Ethics, Pacifism." *ChrLead* 40 (Mar. 29, 1977), 9. Report from the Mennonite Brethren US Board of Reference and Counsel in which racism, peace/war attitudes, and alliance with New Call to Peacemaking were discussed.

Kroeker, Walter.. "Justice and Relief Must Stay Together." *MBH* 18 (Feb. 16, 1979), 16-18. Papers were presented at the MCC annual meeting on the relation of peace and reconciliation to Native American outreach, hunger concerns, and militarism.

Kunjam, Shantkumar S. "An Exploratory Examination of the Ethics of Gandhiji in the Light of Biblical Teachings." MA in Peace Studies thesis, AMBS, 1982. Pp. 94. A critical discussion of the theological and moral bases that guided Gandhi's effort to ease class conflicts and win liberation for the Indian people by nonviolent means. Includes statement of what Christians may learn from Gandhi.

"Love Will Change a Lot of Things." *CanMenn* 13 (Apr. 6, 1965), 3, 11. Report of urban-racial concerns meetings in Youngstown, Ohio, where Guy Hershberger spoke on "The Role of the Mennonite Church in Civil Rights Concerns."

La Roque, Emma. "Did the Devil Make You Do It?" *The Other Side* 13 (May, 1977), 73-74. Examines how Christianity and imperialism have affected the native American world.

La Roque, Emma. "Savage Indian, Noble Red Man." *With* 9 (Feb., 1976), 4. Stereotypes of Indians need to be demythologized. Sketches of three different Indian tribes.

La Roque, Emma. "Secular Struggles." *MBH* 12, (July 13, 1973), 8. A Metis Cree Indian woman writes about the need for the Mennonite church to be involved in the struggle that the Indians face rather than continuing to hide behind the mask of meekness.

La Roque, Emma. "The Ethnic Church and the Minority." ¢i⅜Kingdom, Cross, and Community. Ed. John R. Burkholder and Calvin Redekop. Scottdale: Herald Press, 1976, 208-218. La Rocque studies the relationship between a Mennonite ethnic religious minority and the Native American minority, noting that the Mennonites hold the power in their relationships with other minority people.

Landes, Henry D. "Marriage and Institutional Racism in the Mennonite Church: . . . But Would You Want Your Daughter to Marry One?" Paper for Church and Race class, AMBS, Elkhart, Ind., May 20, 1974. Pp. 19. AMBS.

Landis, Paul G. "Tribute Lauds King's Life, Work." *GH* 61 (Apr. 23, 1968), 374. A tribute to Martin Luther King on the national day of mourning after his death, calling others to follow King's way of nonviolent love.

Lapp, John A. "Allan Bakke and Reverse Discrimination." *ChrLiv* 24 (Dec., 1977), 11-12. The Bakke case challenges affirmative action, a process of redressing social injustice.

Lapp, John A. "Confrontation in Southern Africa." *ChrLiv* 17 (Oct., 1970), 18-19. Peaceful change is increasingly impossible in the apartheid states of South Africa and neighboring nations.

Lapp, John A. "Mennonites Discuss Peace at Curitiba." *Menn* 87 (Sept. 5, 1972), 509. Representatives from the Netherlands, Africa, Japan, etc., speak on the meaning of a peace position as it relates to economics, politics, racism, etc., and plan for ways of relating the peace message in the context of Mennonite World Conference.

Lapp, John A. "The Church and the Social Question." *GH* 66 (July 17, 1973), 553-55. The church as a re-created community extends the message of reconciliation by rooting out racism and militarism within itself and thus becoming able to address these structures in society.

Lapp, John A. "The Greatness of Martin Luther King, Jr." *ChrLiv* 15 (June, 1968), 18-19. Reflections on a man who worked for peace both at home and abroad.

Lapp, John A. "The Negro Revolution: Year Two." *ChrLiv* 12 (Feb., 1965), 18-19. Comment on the search for justice in race relations in 1964.

Lapp, John E. "Social Issues the Church Can Not

Ignore." *Builder* 21 (Oct., 1971), 10-12. Some issues demanding the attention of the church are: communism, war, poverty, racism, Zionism, drugs, sex, abortion, wealth and popularity.

Lapp, John E. *et al.* "Moral Issues in the Election of 1964." *GH* 57 (Sept. 22, 1964), 826. Mennonites who vote should give especially serious consideration to the candidates' positions on civil rights and nuclear warfare.

Lapp, John E.; Hernley, H. Ralph; and Hershberger, Guy F. "Moral Issues in the Election of 1964." *GH* 57 (1964), 826. Christians who vote in the 1964 election must endeavor to find those issues important from the viewpoint of Christian morals and to discover which candidates are most responsive to the claims of Christ. Civil rights and nuclear warfare are two issues considered.

Leatherman, Paul. "Vietnams in the US." *GH* 63 (Feb. 3, 1970), 97-98. Uses the image of violence and injustice in Vietnam as a metaphor for injustice toward poor and blacks in the US.

Lind, Loren. "The Problem of Malcolm X." *YCC* 46 (Nov. 28, 1965), 2. A description of Malcolm X is a description of our own history and a mirror of our own hatred.

Lind, Loren. "Which Way Freedom?" *YCC* 47 (Sept. 11, 1966), 7. The movement toward force in the Civil Rights movement may be a reflection of an adaptation of the white man's tactics.

Lind, Loren (Review). *The Day They Marched,* ed. Doris E. Saunders. Johnson Publ. Co., 1963. Pp. 88. *ChrLiv* 11 (Aug., 1964), 33. Recommends the book as a recap of the civil rights march on Washington, D.C.

Lind, Marcus. "The Gospel of God." *ST* 36, Part 1, (Aug., 1968), 14; Part 2, (Dec, 1968), 11; Part 3, (Dec, 1968), 11. A Bible study in the book of Romans on the Christian and the state. Accents the difference between the Christian way of love and governmental force. Shows also how Romans provides an answer to racial prejudice.

Lind, Millard C. "Bible Principles Governing Race Relations in the Church." *GH* 47 (Oct. 12, 1954), 960-61. The governing principle is the principle of love (agape). The denial of interracial fellowship in the church is a denial of God's unmerited grace in Christ.

Lord, Charles R. "An Exercise in Integration: In *God* We Trust." Paper presented to War and Peace in the Bible class, AMBS, Elkhart, Ind., Jan. 25, 1980. Pp. 21. AMBS.

"MCC Gives a Voice for the Voiceless." *EV* 91 (Oct. 10, 1978), 10. MCC volunteer, Jan Curry, is completing the history of the Houma Indians in Dulac, Louisiana, which will enable the now "unrecognized" tribe to begin the process for official recognition by the US government.

"MDS Converses with Black Front Leaders." *CanMenn* 16 (Dec. 31, 1968), 1, 2. Conversation centers on possibility of MDS working with blacks to rehabilitate urban housing.

"Mennonite Race Relations Still at Low." *CanMenn* 18 (Aug. 14, 1970), 4, 12. A report on a study of Mennonite attitudes toward blacks by Denny Weaver includes a historical survey over the last hundred years, an evaluation, and a listing of resources for improving race relations.

MacDonald, Dennis. "The Order of the Shovel." *Post-American* 1 (Fall, 1971), 6. An ethically self-conscious community which is militant in its refusal to be co-opted by the American war involvement, racism, and materialistic values, can be a basis for penetrating society with the message of total redemption in Jesus Christ.

MacMaster, Richard K.; with Horst, Samuel L. and Ulle, Robert F. *Conscience in Crisis: Mennonites and other Peace Churches in America, 1739-1789; Interpretation and Documents.* Scottdale and Kitchener: Herald Press, 1979. Pp. 576. Sourcebook of Mennonites in 18th-century America, focusing especially on Mennonite experience in the Revolutionary War. Includes documents on relations with Native Americans, conscientious objection, nationalism, religious liberty, etc.

Martin, E. K. *The Mennonites.* Philadelphia: Everts and Peck, 1883. Pp. 17. MHL. A history which discusses at some length the struggles of the Mennonites and other peace sects to maintain a nonresistant stance in relation to the conflicts between the colonists and native Americans as well as in relation to the government's demands for support for the military in the pre-Revolutionary and Revolutionary War periods.

Martin, Patricia Hostetter. "Teaching in a Segregated School." *MennLife* 22 (Jan., 1967), 37-39. Explains why segregated schools in a predominantly black community are not equal with other segregated or integrated schools.

Mast Burnett, Kristina. "Canada-US Relations, Vietnam, Issues at Reedley Meetings." *GH* 72 (Feb. 13, 1979), 128. MCC's annual meeting in Reedley, Jan. 25-27, addressed such issues as Canada-US relations, aid to Vietnam, justice and human rights overseas, Native American outreach, hunger concerns, and militarism.

Mennonite Board of Missions. "Resolution Approved by Mission Board at Kidron, Ohio, July 3-7." *GH* 61 (July 16, 1968), 647-48.

Resolution II states that Mennonites must recognize and respond to their participation in white racism and the hostilities and tensions that it creates.

Mennonite Church General Conference Statements (Archival). Goshen, IN. AMC. 1-1-1, Box 5. File 5/12: the way of Christian love in race relations, 1955.

Metzler, Edgar. "Selective Conscientious Objectors." *GH* 60 (Mar. 14, 1967), 233. NSBRO and MCC Peace Section support the concern for the civil rights of religious selective objectors. This support was declared on Nov. 19-20, 1965.

Metzler, Edgar. "The Mennonite Churches and the Current Race Crisis." *CanMenn* 11 (July 30, 1963), 6; *GH* 56 (Aug. 6, 1963), 863-64. An outline of concrete action taken by the Mennonite churches in order to gain a better understanding of the racial crisis and to witness to the common humanity of all races.

Metzler, Edgar. "The Road Through Jericho Led Through Selma." *CanMenn* 13 (Mar. 23, 1965), 6-7. Commentary on the death of James Reeb. Metzlar could have but didn't go to Selma and he sees his decision as "passing by on the other side."

Metzler, Edgar (Review). *Segregation and the Bible,* by Everett Tilson. Abingdon, 1958. Pp. 176. *The Bible and Race,* by T. B. Maston. Broadman, 1959. Pp. 117. *Segregation and Desegregation,* by T. B. Maston. Macmillan, 1959. Pp. 178. *The Racial Problem in Christian Perspective,* by Kyle Haseldon Harper, 1959. *Christian Ethics and the Sit-in,* by Paul Ramsey. Association, 1961. *Structures of Prejudice,* by Carlyle Marney. Abingdon, 1961. *ChrLiv* 9 (Aug., 1962), 33-34. Briefly reviews and compares these six works on racism and nonviolent action for racial equality.

Metzler, James E. and Rachel. "The Confession of a Southerner." *GH* 57 (Feb. 18, 1964), 120. A letter of confession of failure to really love the people in the South.

Miller, Marlin E. "Studied Integration at Fisk." *ChrLiv* 8 (Oct., 1961), 22-24. Summary of Intercollegiate Peace Fellowship conference in Nashville on "Problems of Interracial Relations."

Miller, Paul M. "21 Ways to Oppose the Soft Violence of Apartheid." *GH* 70 (Aug. 23, 1977), 638-39. Calls nonresistant Christians to greater awareness of "soft" violence—structural violence sanctioned by law and order—by suggesting 21 ways for nonresistant Christians to witness against apartheid.

Miller, Vern. "The Peace Churches and Racial Justice." *CanMenn* 13 (Mar. 9, 1965), 1, 2.

Friends, Mennonites, and Brethren met in Elgin, Ill., Feb. 15-17 to reexamine historic peace church role in bringing about racial justice. Article points to absence of Mennonite funds to help blacks to help themselves.

Miller, Vern. "We Shall Overcome." *GH* 61 (May 14, 1968), 425. Sermon focuses on the death of Martin Luther King and the truth and efficacy of overcoming evil with good.

Miller, Vern (Review). *The Long Freedom Road,* by Janet Harris. McGraw Hill, 1967. Pp. 150. *ChrLiv* 15 (Jan., 1968), 35. Reviewer considers this book a historical and readable account of the struggle for justice during the 1960s civil rights movement.

Moore, Warren. "Ethnic Mennonites?" *MennLife* 22 (Jan., 1967), 25-26. Mennonite communities reveal a survival tactic, "the disavowal of values in alien groups and institutions." ". . . What would happen to the concepts, customs, and language of Mennonite-styled Christianity" if Mennonites decided to live in all-black neighborhoods?

Mpanya, Mutombo. "Apartheid In South Africa." *Forum* 11 (Oct., 1977), 2-3. Discusses aspects of apartheid exploitation and urges Western churches to seek justice by refusing to identify with apartheid systems.

Mumaw, John R. (Review). *Rising Above Color,* ed. Henry Lantz. Association Press, 1943. Pp. 112. *ChrMon* 36 (May, 1944), 147. Reviewer observes that the book presents the life stories of 13 outstanding blacks appealing for justice and racial equality.

"Native Concerns Are Significant." *EV* 92 (July 25, 1979), 8, 9. MCC US Ministries is seeking to support US Indian rights and trying to build an understanding between immigrant Americans and native Americans.

Naylor, Phyllis Rehnolds. "First But Now Forgotten." *With* 5 (Apr., 1972), 25; *GH* 65 (Nov. 14, 1972), 926-28. Political, sociological, economic, and educational situation of the native American with a good deal of historical background.

Neufeld, Elmer. "Peace—the Way of the Cross." *ChrLiv* 7 (Jan., 1960), 6-7, 34. Prose poem relating peace to issues of militarism, nationalism, and racism.

*Of All Nations One People: A Study Guide on Race Relations.* Salunga, Pa.: Peace Committee of the Lancaster Conference of the Mennonite Church, 1972. Pp. 24. MHL. Three lessons designed to help persons recognize their attitudes and work toward greater understanding and empathy with all people—whatever their race.

"Peace, War, and Social Issues: A Statement of the Position of the Amish Mennonite Churches." Officialy adopted by the ministerial body of the Beachy Amish Mennonite constituency . . . at Wellesley, Ont., Apr. 18-19, 1968. [n.p., 1968]. Pp. 16. MSHL. Topics include the role of government, military service, civil defense, the Christian's role in race relations, unions, etc.

"Peace Conference Discusses Northern Race Relations." *CanMenn* 12 (Mar. 31, 1964), 4, 12. A report on the Goshen meeting of the Mennonite Intercollegiate Peace Fellowship where delegates from Mennonite colleges discussed "Race Relations and the Northern Churches."

"Press Bob Jones U. on Ban of Blacks." *GH* 65 (Oct. 31, 1972), 895. The university is contending that separation of the races is ordained of God and that the government's attempt to penalize the university for this conviction is a violation of religious freedom.

Paetkau, Walter. "An Albertan in Atlanta." *CanMenn* 12, Part 1, (Feb. 25, 1064); Part 2, (Mar. 3, 1964), 7; Part 3, (Mar. 10, 1964), 7; Part 4, (Mar. 17, 1964), 7. A series of four articles on the church's responsibility to achieve racial equality and justice in our society.

Pannell, William. "An Evangelical Speaks for Negroes." *ChrLiv* 11 (July, 1964), 8-11. Among the signs that blacks belong in North America is the fact that black soldiers fought alongside whites in the Revolutionary and Civil Wars.

Peachey, Paul L. "Nonviolence in the South." *GH* 50 (Feb. 19, 1957), 177. An account of the growing black self-conscious nonviolent resistance movement in the South.

Peachey, Paul L. "Travail in the South." *GH* 50 (June 18, 1957), 585. In some instances the racial situation is improving in the South; in other situations it is getting worse. Koinonia Farm seems to light the way to true Christian evangelism in this sort of situation.

Peachey, Urbane, comp. "Mennonite Peace Theology Colloquium II: Theology of Justice, Bethel Mennonite Church, North Newton, Ks., Nov. 15-18, 1978, [Papers]." Akron, Pa.: MCC Peace Section, 1979. MHL. Includes: Brubacher, Ray, "Case Study of Southern Africa," pp. 9; Keeney, William, "Reactions to Case Study of Southern Africa," pp. 3; Friesen, LeRoy, "A Brief on the Southern Africa Case Study," pp. 3; Lind, Millard, "Programmatic Decision/Action in Southern Africa: Implications of the Decision from the Viewpoint of Biblical Theology," pp. 4; Rempel, Henry, "Response to the South Africa

Case Study," pp. 4; Wiebe, Menno, "Canadian Northern Development, An Account of the Churchill-Nelson River Diversion Project," pp. 18; Schroeder, David, "Case Study: Native Concerns, The Frame of Reference from the Standpoint of Biblical Theology," pp. 2; LaRogne, Emma, "Response to Menno Wiebe," pp. 3; Klassen, A. J., "Response to Northern Development Case Study," pp. 2; Vogt, Roy, "Response to Menno Wiebe's Case Study of Canadian Northern Development," pp. 4; Defehr, Art, "Northern Development and Justice: The Business Perspective," pp. 3; Kraus, C. Norman, "Toward a Biblical Perspective on Justice," pp. 17; Stoltzfus, Edward, "Response to Study Paper 'Toward a Biblical Perspective on Justice' by C. Norman Krause," pp. 3; Gajardo, Joel V., "The Latin American Situation: The Challenge of Liberation Theology," pp. 12; Lind, Millard, review, *Marx and the Bible* by José Miranda (Maryknoll, NY: Orbis, 1974. Pp. 338), pp. 9.

Peters, Robert V. "Speaking Out." *Menn* 94 (Mar. 27, 1979), 237. Mennonite involvement in the take-over of native American lands in Kansas and Manitoba calls us to repentance, to side with the poor, and to speak out against injustice.

Powell, John. "Out of the Voices of the Oppressed—God." *Menn* 86 (Jan. 21, 1971), 18, 19. A black Christian interprets God and Jesus Christ and what the call "Follow me" by Jesus signifies in view of poverty, racism, and injustice.

Preheim, Loren and Unruh, John. "Now Is the Time." *CanMenn* 11 (Sept. 10, 1963), 7. An analytical look at the "March on Washington for Jobs and Freedom" on Aug. 28, 1963. The success of the march demonstrates the strength of the civil rights movement led by Martin Luther King.

Preheim, Lyle. "Which Way—Cleaver or King." Paper presented to Church and Race class, AMBS, Elkhart, Ind., spring, 1970. Pp. 23. AMBS.

Preheim, Marion Keeney. "Lawrence Hart: Indian Chief in a Tradition of Peace." *MennRep* 10 (Nov. 24, 1980), 10. Reviews the pilgrimage of a native American from military service to affirming both Cheyenne and Christian commitments to peace.

Preheim, Vern. "No Turning Back, We Are on the Move." *CanMenn* 13 (Apr. 6, 1965), 1-2. Reports on trip to Montgomery to participate in freedom march.

Prieb, Wesley. "What Are Our Racial Attitudes?" *Menn* 64 (Jan. 25, 1949), 13-14. As in the area of nonresistance, Mennonites must bring together theology and practice regarding racial attitudes.

Proceedings of the Conference on Christian Race Relations, Goshen, Ind., Apr. 22-24, 1955. Pp. 111. MHL. Sponsored by the Committee on Economic and Social Relations of the Mennonite Church and by the Mennonite Community Association. Includes: Kraus, C. Norman, "Scriptural Teachings on Race Relations," 31-44; Graber, J. D., "Problems and Challenges in Building Christian Human Relations," 45-51; Schulze, Andrew, "Progress in Race Relations in the United States Since World War I," 52-57; Offutt, Garland K., "Social and Psychological Factors in Prejudice and Discrimination," 58-66; Peachey, Paul, "What Can Be Done to Improve Race Relations in the Mennonite Church?" 67-72; Offutt, Garland K., "The Church, a Fellowship of the Redeemed of All Races," 92-99; Lind, Millard, "Bible Principles Governing Race Relations in the Church," 100-105; Moseman, John H., "Right Answers: Wrong Living," 106-111.

"Race Is Major Issue at Annual Peace Meetings." *CanMenn* 12 (Jan. 14, 1964), 1. MCC Peace Section's annual meeting in Chicago discusses race as priority item.

"Racial Tension Eased by Peace Representative." *CanMenn* 15 (Mar. 21, 1967), 3. Titus Bender brings blacks and whites together for Billy Graham film and initiates interracial pastoral meetings.

"Racial Wall Traps Indians." *CanMenn* 15 (Dec. 12, 1967), 1, 2. Statistical information on the plight of native Americans in Canada, together with a report on what is being done and what might be done to make them first-class citizens.

"Racism Is 'Most Serious Domestic Evil' Says Conference on Religion and Race." *CanMenn* 11 (Feb. 8, 1963), 2. The National Conference on Religion and Race meeting in Chicago issues an emphatic call for racial justice.

"Report Calls for Mennonite Presence in Southern Africa." *CanMenn* 18 (June 5, 1970), 1, 2. After a COMB and MCC-sponsored study tour of the southern African states, Don Jacob and James Bertsche suggest Mennonite involvement there because of the evils of apartheid, the political scheme of separate development of the races, and the opportunities for growth and nurture of the kingdom of heaven within the situation.

"Report of a Seminar on Christ, the Mennonite Churches and Races, Woodlawn Mennonite Church, Chicago, Illinois, April 17-19, 1959." Akron, Pa.: MCC, Peace Section, n.d. Pp. 60. MHL. Includes: Loewen, Jacob, "The Gospel and Race Relations," 7-15; Abernathy, Ralph, "Race as a Challenge to the Christian Church," 17-25; Harding, Vincent, "The Task of the Church in Establishing Racial Unity," 27-36; Graber, J. D., "Race Relations in World Evangelism," 37-44.

(Review). "Integration: Who's Prejudiced?" by C. Norman Kraus. Scottdale: Herald Press. Pp. 31. *Fellowship* 24 (Sept., 1958), 34. Describes the contents of this pamphlet which gives a fact-filled presentation of both the biblical and the scientific case for integration and refutes many of the common theories and arguments of segregationists.

(Review). *Shall We Overcome?* by Howard O. Jones. Fleming H. Revell Co., Westwood, NJ, 1966. Pp. 146. *GfT* Series 2, 3 (Dec., 1968), 16. Commends the book for its view that violence and racism will be answered only by a spiritual revival among all Christians.

Redekop, John H. "Looking Backward . . . and also Ahead." *MBH* 17 (Dec. 22, 1978), 10. Ominous signs of the future include stockpiling weapons, Mideast conflict, racism in Africa.

Redekop, John H. "Race Consciousness Generates World Tension." *CanMenn* 3 (Mar. 4, 1955), 2. "One of the best ways to prevent communism or any other despicable 'ism' from exploiting anti-West, anti-Christian attitudes is to eliminate and eradicate the factors which give rise to those attitudes."

Redekopp, Orlando. "Rhodesia/Zimbabwe Elections: The Future Is Not Bright." *MennRep* 9 (Apr. 16, 1979), 7. Although an election is possible, it is not known what form it will take. Churches in Zimbabwe have been only minimally involved and are not unified on issues of racism, violence, rich and poor relations, or minority domination.

Redekopp, Orlando (Review). *Biko,* by Donald Woods. New York and London: Paddington Press, 1978. Pp. 288. And *Steve Biko,* by Hilda Bernstein. London: International Defense and Aid Fund for Southern Africa, 1978. Pp. 147. *MennRep* 9 (Feb. 5, 1979), 11. Both books recount the life and death of Steve Biko, a founder and respected leader in the South African Black consciousness movement. They reveal a world where the ideology of apartheid cruelly crushes eighty percent of South Africa's population.

Redekopp, Orlando (Review). *Perceptions of Apartheid: The Churches and Political Change in South Africa,* by Ernie Regehr. Toronto: Between the Lines, 1979. Pp. 280. *MBH* 19 (Feb. 15, 1980), 32. Book's theme is the role of the churches in creating and maintaining apartheid in South Africa. Reviewer considers it "indispensable to any Christian concerned with justice and peace."

Reed, Kenneth. *Joseph, Put That Gun Down.* Lancaster, Pa.: Good Enterprises, Ltd., 1973. Pp. 34. Two-act play dramatizing the story of the Hochstetler family caught in the French, English, and Indian war of 1754. Contrasts the values of war and peace found in both the Amish and native American cultures.

Regehr, Ernie. "Conscientious Objection in South Africa." *GH* 68 (Dec. 9, 1975), 872-73; *MennRep* 5 (May 12, 1975), A7. Examines a resolution by the South African Council of Churches to consider conscientious objection as a means of refusing to support apartheid. Considers the resolution a "modest beginning," since it denounces violence only when supporting an unjust cause.

Regehr, Ernie. *Perceptions of Apartheid: The Churches and Political Change in South Africa.* Scottdale: Herald Press; Kitchener: Between the Lines, 1979. Pp. 309. Detailed analysis of racial violence in South Africa. Includes extensive discussion of the church and state relationship in that context as well as a final chapter entitled "Violence/Nonviolence and the Dilemma of the Churches" in which the issues of conscientious objection, as well as other issues of war and peace, are raised.

Regier, Harold R. "The Black Manifesto and Christ's." *Menn* 84 (Sept. 2, 1969), 514-16. A Mennonite response to the *Black Manifesto*: We need to listen; we need to repent; we need to let black people act. Christ's manifesto was Luke 4:16-18.

Riddick, George E. "Black Power in the White Perspective." *MennLife* 22 (Jan., 1967), 29-34. The black community will organize. For the church it becomes necessary to ally with this organization as much as possible in order to break the strangle hold of the corporate structure.

"Seminary Receives Citation for Inter-Racial Work." *CanMenn* 13 (Feb. 23, 1965), 1. On Feb. 8 MBS received a citation from the Elkhart Urban League for volunteer service (tutors of potential dropouts) and inter-racial teamwork.

"Social Values are Key to Assimilation." *CanMenn* 15 (Nov. 14, 1967), 4. Report of Lawrence Hart's recent visit to the Elkhart seminary. Greatest contributing factor to lack of understanding between native Americans and their white fellow citizens is the divergence in thinking about social values.

"Statement from the Black Delegates of US Congress on Evangelism." *EV* 83 (Jan. 25, 1970), 6. Statement deals with what it means to be committed to evangelism and seriously concerned about attitudes of prejudice in race relations.

"Statement of Concerns." *MennComm* 5 (Nov., 1951), 17-19. Statement resulting from Study Conference on Christian Community Relations links the doctrine of nonresistance to war to issues of business ethics, organized labor, race and minority relations, and standard of living.

"Student Council Co-sponsors Race March." *CanMenn* 13 (Apr. 6, 1965), 4. Report on the reconciliation walk in Elkhart on Mar. 15 in which MBS students and faculty participated. The walk was from Canaan Baptist church to First Presbyterian.

Sauder, Bill. "Employment Regardless of Race or Religion." *ChrLiv* 12 (Sept., 1965), 18-19. Provisions of Title VII of the Civil Rights Act of 1964 will affect job discrimination because of conscientious objection to war.

Schlabach, Theron F. "To Focus a Mennonite Vision." *Kingdom, Cross, and Community.* Ed. John R. Burkholder and Calvin Redekop. Scottdale: Herald Press, 1976, 15-50. Reviews Guy F. Hershberger's intellectual development and life work of interpreting Mennonite nonresistance in relation to war, industrial relations, church-state relations, community life and mutual aid, and race relations.

Schmidt, Edgar. "Bannock and Borscht and Justice in the North." *MennRep* 9 (May 28, 1979), 10. An interchurch task force in Manitoba has assisted Indian people in getting a hearing from the powers that want to flood their land.

Schrag, Dale R. "The Key in Reconciliation." *Menn* 85 (Nov. 3, 1970), 678. The nature of reconciliation as it relates to our peace witness and our attitudes toward other races or minority groups.

Schwartzentruber, Hubert. Letter to the Editor. *Sojourners* 8 (Oct., 1978), 38. As awareness of Native American justice concerns grows, the writer hopes that the same errors of neglect that many Christians made in the 1960s will not be made again.

Schwartzentruber, Hubert. "The Brokenness of the City." *Peacemakers in a Broken World.* Ed. John A. Lapp. Scottdale: Herald Press, 1969, 20-29. Also in "The Broken People of the City." *ChrLiv* 17 (Dec., 1970), 30-33. Outlines problems of poverty, unemployment, depression, racism, violence in city ghettos and rural areas, and calls Christians to help relieve these conditions as part of spreading the gospel.

Shank, J. Ward (Review). *Christianity and the Class Struggle,* by Harold O. J. Brown. Arlington House, 1970. *ST* 39 (Mar., 1971), 15. The central political reality in the world today is that of class struggle for which the only answer is the Christian message.

Shank, J. Ward (Review). *Let Justice Roll Down,* by John Perkins. Regal Publications, n.d. Pp. 223. *ST* 45 (Apr., 1977), 32-33. While reviewer appreciates Perkins' emphasis on spiritual conversion in combating racism, he raises questions about Perkins' involvement in forms of active resistance such as boycotts.

Shelly, Maynard. "Christians Still Reflect a Racist Society." *Menn* 85 (Sept. 29, 1970), 587, 588. Reports on a study on Mennonite attitudes toward other races from 1886 to 1969 by Denny Weaver, a graduate student in church history at Duke University.

Shelly, Maynard. "Finding the Boat in History's Mainstream." *GH* 62 (Jan. 7, 1969), 13-15. Reflects on papers about the historic peace church role in peacemaking, discussed at the recent Conference of Historic Peace Churches. Reports at length on John H. Yoder's presentation, which highlighted the failure of the peace churches to take leadership in facing the problems of race relations and the Vietnam war.

Shelly, Maynard. "New Definitions for Evangelism." *Menn* 84 (Oct. 7, 1969), 597-99. Participants in the Congress on Evangelism in Minneapolis were introduced to the connections between evangelism and such issues of social concern as race relations.

Shelly, Maynard. "South African Police Met with Nonviolence." *Menn* 92 (Apr. 12, 1977), 249-50. Describes the nonviolent witness of a South African church leader to security police raiding church headquarters in reprisal for the church's opposition to apartheid.

Shenk, Phil M. "God Owns, We Tend." *Sojourners* 9 (Nov., 1979), 3. As stewards of God's creation, Christians should be very concerned about land use. The Native American people of North America can provide some viable options and models emerging out of their culture and history.

Shenk, Phil M. "The Frontier Days Are Here Again." *Sojourners* 7 (Jan., 1978), 20. Explores the impact of the energy crisis on Native Americans.

Shenk, Phil M. "The Longest Walk." *Sojourners* 8 (July, 1978), 10. Examines the anti-Indian legislation being proposed in the US Congress. The purpose of the Longest Walk is to bring attention to this legislation.

Shenk, Susan E. S. "Israel's Settlement: Conquest, Immigration, or Revolt? An Overview of Gottwald's Critique." Paper presented to War

and Peace in the Bible class, AMBS, Elkhart, Ind., 1980. Pp. 23. AMBS.

Shetler, Sanford G. "Is This Our Task?" *GH* 58 (July 20, 1965), 629-30. The racial problem is first of all a spiritual problem which will not be solved by nonviolent coercive methods. These methods are not congruent with biblical pacifism.

Shetler, Sanford G. "Martin Luther King, Five Years Later." *GfT* 8 (Mar.-Apr., 1973), 15-16; (May-June, 1973), 7, 17; (July-Aug., 1973), 14-15; (Sept.-Oct., 1973), 12-13; (Nov.-Dec., 1973), 13-14; 9 (Jan.-Feb., 1974), 12-13; (Mar.-Apr., 1974), 13-14; (May-June, 1974), 14-15; (Jul.-Aug., 1974), 13-14. Evaluation of King's leadership and teachings on nonviolence and his position within the nonviolent civil rights movement; traces King's tactics to Thoreau, the Fellowship of Reconciliation, and especially Gandhi; describes civil disobedience; distinguishes between nonviolence and nonresistance. Author claims that the writers King picked as mentors—Kirkegaard, Heidegger, Sartre, Tillich—led him in the direction of humanism rather than toward a theology of salvation through the atonement of Christ.

Shetler, Sanford G. "Our Peace Witness and Civil Rights Activities." *GfT* Series I, No. 1 (Jan., 1966), 1-4. Mennonite nonresistance and peace witness are weakened by cooperation with civil rights activities which base their pacifism on other than biblical grounds.

Showalter, Stuart W., ed. "Peacemaking in a World of Revolution." Seminar lectures delivered at EMC, Harrisonburg, VA, June 15-26, 1970. Pp. 88. MSHL. Includes: Lapp, John A., "Revolution as a Political Event," 1-8; Yutsy, Daniel, "Revolution in the Economic Struggle," 9-15; Epp, Frank, "Revolution in the Middle East," 16-23; Skinner, Tom, "Revolution in Racial Relationships," 24-36; Jacobs, Donald R., "Revolution Amid Social Change," 37-42; Augsburger, Myron, "Revolution in the Church," 43-52; Yoder, John H., "Peacemaking Amid Political Revolution," 53-60; Miller, John W., "Steps Toward Peace in a World of Economic Conflict," 61-71; Haynes, Michael, "Peacemaking in Race Relations," 72-82; Trueblood, Elton, "Peacemaking Through the Church," 83-88.

Shutt, Kristel S. "Blessed Are the Peacemakers." Research paper for Christian Ethics class. 1981. Pp. 9. BfC.

Sider, Arbutus. Letter to the Editor. *The Other Side* 10 (May-June, 1974), 71-72. Shares personal struggles with integration by recognizing the problem "how to have unity without destroying blackness."

Sider, Arbutus. "White in a Black School." *The Other Side* 10 (Sept.-Oct., 1974), 27-31. White parents struggle with what it means to have pre-school children in public school education in a predominantly black neig¹.borhood.

Sider, Ronald J. "Aside: Where Have All the Liberals Gone?" *The Other Side* 12 (May-June, 1976), 42-44. The essence of liberal theology can be described as when the current culture supplies the operational norms and values for a significant number of evangelicals and mainline church people. Concerns like racism, militarism, civil religion, and unjust economic structures are not spoken to because of the liberal context.

Sider, Ronald J. "Corporate Guilt and Institutionalized Racism." *United Evangelical Action* 36 (Spring, 1977), 11-12, 26-28. Because the Bible calls us to live apart from the wrong doings of society, evangelical Christians should look at the ways individuals share responsibility for racism and seek practical expressions of repentance. Includes selected bibliography.

Sider, Ronald J. "Is Racism as Sinful as Adultery?" *GH* 65 (Apr. 4, 1972), 315; *EV* 84 (Sept. 25, 1971), 5, 6. Calls evangelicals to concern over social evils of racism and militarism equal to concern about personal evils such as adultery.

Sider, Ronald J. "Rendezvous with History in South Africa." *EV* 92 (Nov. 10, 1979), 10. The South African Christian Leadership Assembly which met in Pretoria, S. Africa, on July 5-15, 1979, was called to offer the church perhaps its last chance to take a stand for fundamental, peaceful change in South Africa.

Sider, Ronald J. "Spirituality and Social Concern." *The Other Side* 9 (Sept.-Oct., 1973), 8-11, 38-41; *GH* 67 (Apr. 23, 1974), 337-40. Spirituality and social concern are a unity—regeneration involves changed attitudes toward poverty, racism, and war; the disciplines of the spirit are essential to social change.

Sider, Ronald J. "What If Ten Thousand . . ." *The Other Side* 15 (Nov., 1979), 14-15. Report on the South African Christian Leadership Assembly (SACLA) which has prompted hundreds of South African Christians to ask in a new and urgent way what biblical faith demands of them.

Smiley, Glenn E. "They Do Not Walk Alone." *ChrLiv* 3 (Nov., 1956), 13. Description of the beginning of Martin Luther King's nonviolent protest against racism in Montgomery, Alabama.

Smucker, Donovan E. and Shelly, Paul. "Echoes of Evanston." *Menn* 69 (Sept. 19, 1954), 568-69.

Themes of Christian hope and evangelism emphasized. WCC recognizes two major moral barriers to evangelism: race prejudice and war.

Smucker, John I. "Can Christians Purge Themselves of Racism?" *MBH* 12 (July 13, 1973), 2-3. Out of his own experience working as a Mennonite pastor in the Bronx, Smucker writes that white racism is an individual sickness even though it is expressed and nurtured by groups. We must deal with it personally, allowing Jesus Christ to purge us from it in repentance.

Smucker, John I. "Martin Luther King, Jr. and Nonviolence." Paper prepared for Social Development of the Negro in America class, Union Theological Seminary, New York, NY, May 8, 1968. Pp. 10. MHL.

Soden, Ruth Ann. "Church Has Color Bias, Too." *YCC* 47 (Nov. 13, 1966), 7. Describes the work of Hubert and June Swartzentruber in a poor, black neighborhood in St. Louis, Mo.

Sommer, John P. "Prejudice, Mistreatment, and the Mennonites: The Japanese-Americans During World War II." Paper presented to Church and Race class, AMBS, Elkhart, Ind., May 20, 1974. Pp. 17. AMBS.

Sprunger, Joseph (Review). *Bury My Heart at Wounded Knee, An Indian History of the American West,* by Dee Brown. Bantam Press, 1972. Pp. 419. "History Rewritten," *Forum* (Nov., 1972), 7. Reflects on the main theme of the book—the destruction and deception of the North American Indian people by white men. Concludes that the book reads well and elicits much feeling about this ugly part of history.

Stoesz, Edgar. "A Mennonite Reflects on Martin Luther King." *GH* 61 (May 14, 1968), 437; *Intercom* 8 (May-June, 1968), 2-3. Eulogizes King and his commitment to nonviolence, relating incidents from his life which underscored his message and challenging Mennonites to uphold justice as bravely.

Stoltzfus, Brenda. "Feminism: Classism, Racism, or Sisterhood?" Paper presented to Women and Men: History and Vision class, AMBS, Elkhart, Ind., Dec. 1, 1983. Pp. 16. AMBS.

Studer, Gerald C. (Review). *Black Like Me,* by John Howard Griffin. Houghton Mifflin, 1961. Pp. 176. *ChrLiv* 8 (Dec., 1961), 32-33. Reviewer urges Mennonites to direct nonresistant witness to the problem of racism as well as to war.

Swartley, Willard M. "The Bible and Slavery." In *Slavery, Sabbath, War and Women.* Scottdale and Kitchener: Herald Press, 1983. Pp. 31-66. Shows how the Bible was used to support both pro-slavery and anti-slavery positions. Exposes how religion has often been an ally of racism; presents also biblical and theological teachings to counter racism.

"The Christian and Race Relations." *Menn* 74 (Sept. 1, 1959), 540. A statement adopted by the General Conference Mennonite Church which calls on individuals, congregations, and church institutions to purge themselves of racial prejudice and exclusiveness.

"The Church Must Solve Race Problem." *CanMenn* 7 (May 8, 1959), 1, 7. Rev. Ralph Abernathy addresses a Chicago seminar on "Christ, the Mennonite Churches, and Race." Since the end of slavery, the Mennonite church's voice against injustice has grown silent.

"The First Protest Against Slavery: Germantown, 1688." *CMR* 1 (Sept. 15, 1971), 5. Statement sent from the Germantown Monthly Meeting to the Monthly Meeting at Richard Worrell's on Feb. 18, 1688.

"The Way of the Cross in Race Relations." *GH* 48 (June 7, 1955), 529-30, 549. A statement adopted by the 1955 Conference on Christian Community Relations. Emphasizes that God has called us into a ministry of reconciliation. Only as we rise above class and race differences will this ministry be fulfilled.

Tiessen, Daniel. "Ahab and Naboth: Some Lessons About Land." *MennRep* 9 (June 25, 1979), 5. The Old Testament story of Ahab and Naboth is strikingly similar to the way in which the white society has claimed the land of the Indians.

Tiessen, Daniel. "Dividing Up the Land: Lessons from the Old Testament." *MennRep* 9 (July 9, 1979), 5. Referring to several of the Old Testament laws regarding the possession of land, this article addresses the issue of Indians being allowed to exercise control over the resources of their land.

Umble, Diane Z. *Choices for Human Justice: How to Care About the Poor, Disabled, Abused, Oppressed.* Harrisonburg, Va.: Choice Books, 1978. Pp. 111. A collection of articles, reprinted from a variety of sources such as *Sojourners,* the *Gospel Herald,* and *The Mennonite,* which focus various justice issues such as the exploitation of native Americans, the penal system, racism, rape and the battering of women, and the arms race.

Unrau, Ed. "Native People: The Tragedy Is Why White Folks Can't See Variety and Value in Native Culture." *MennMirror* 9 (May, 1980), 9-10. Summarizes Menno Wiebe's views of what white people need to learn in order to become able to "reach out, not down" to native American people.

Unrau, Harlan D. "Institutional Racism and the Military-Industrial Complex." *Forum* (Mar., 1972), 5. The military-industrial complex which has direct bearing on the welfare of the minority worker is a form of racism that is no less destructive of human values than physical violence.

Unrau, Harlan D. "Institutional Racism in America." *Menn* 87 (Feb. 15, 1972), 112-14. Current conditions that perpetuate discrimination can be changed, not with endless ghetto surveys, church conference resolutions, and foundations-sponsored investigative research but with "substantive action."

Unrau, Neil. "American Moravian Noncombatancy: A Study in Changing Attitudes." Paper for War, Peace, and Revolution class, AMBS, Elkhart, Ind., n.d. Pp. 17. AMBS.

Vogt, Virgil. "The Implications of Christian Ethics for Modern Business." Paper presented to social science seminar, Goshen College, Goshen, Ind., 1953-54. Pp. 66. MHL.

"World Conference Message." *GH* 65 (Oct. 24, 1972), 860-61. Statement adopted at the conclusion of the Ninth Mennonite World Conference focuses on reconciliation as the primary task of the church—reconciliation in situations of war, violent repression, racism, economic oppression.

Wagler, Mark. "White Guilt and Black Power." *Menn* 83 (Apr. 30, 1968), 306-308. Mennonites, unfaithful to the Anabaptist dream of true community, are feeling too guilty to be able to effectively cope with the black situation.

Waltner, Orlando A. "A Ministry of Reconciliation." *MennLife* 22 (Jan., 1967), 35, 36. The ministry of reconciliation is a mission of peace to a people who are at war within and among themselves. We ought to undertake this ministry on behalf of the blacks and the whites of the South.

Weaver, Edwin L. "With Negroes in the Deep South." *YCC* 31, Part 1, "Negroes in the United States," (May 28, 1950), 172, 173; Part 2, (June 4, 1950), 180, 181; Part 3, "Colored Quarters and Homes," (June 11, 1950), 188, 189; Part 4, "Making a Living," (June 18, 1950), 196, 197; Part 5, "Family Life," (June 25, 1950), 204, 207; Part 6, (July 2, 1950), 212-14; Part 7, "Negro Traits," (July 16, 1950), 231, 232; Part 8, "Negroes as Individuals," (July 23, 1950), 239, 240; Part 9, "Negro Schools," (July 30, 1950), 243, 244; Part 10, "Negro Churches," (Aug. 6, 1950), 249; Part 11, "Helping the Colored People," (Aug. 13, 1950), 258, 259. The sociology of comtemporary blacks in the Deep

South. Draws on personal observations made in Polk County, Florida, where a CPS public health project established contact with the black community.

Weaver, Edwin L. (Review). *Racism a World Issue,* by Edmund Davison Soper. Abingdon-Cokesbury Press, 1947. Pp. 304. *Menn Comm* 2 (Dec., 1948), 26. In recommending the book, the reviewer asks if Mennonites are as aware of the destructiveness of racism as they are of war.

Wenger, J. C., ed. *Mennonite Handbook: Indiana-Michigan Conference.* Scottdale: Mennonite Publishing House, 1956. Pp. 159. MHL. Articles pertinent to peace issues include: "A Declaration of Christian Faith and Commitment with Respect to Peace, War, and Nonresistance," 105-114; "The Way of Christian Love in Race Relations," 127-36. In addition to these items, the various constitutions and by-laws reproduced here have articles on the issues of peace and nonresistance.

Wenger, Malcolm. "Core Issues Considered by Indians and Mennonites." *Menn* 94 (Apr. 10, 1979), 263. Foundational issues about missions were discussed at the "peace talks" between non-native Mennonites and native leaders at Tiefengrund Mennonite Church, Saskatchewan, Feb. 23-24, 1979.

Wenger, Malcolm. "Hard Thinking Done at Native/Mennonite Peace Talk." *MennRep* 9 (Mar. 19, 1979), 14. "Peace talks" between Mennonites and native leaders focused on issues concerning missions.

Wenger, Malcolm. "Indians and Whites Meet Together." *Menn* 85 (June 16, 1970), 414, 415. A native American chief and pastor of Mennonite churches speaks at a workers' conference about what can be done in the future as whites and native Americans relate to each other.

Wenger, Martha. "Black Kettle: His Way of Peace." Student paper for Humanities and Peace Studies, 1975. Pp. 33. Cheyenne Indians. MLA/BeC.

Wenger, Martha, *et al.* "Wounded Knee: Four Papers by Bethel College Students in Interterm Class on Causes of Human Conflict, January, 1974." Pp. 75 total. MLA/BeC.

West, James Lee. "A Native American's Reflections on Thanksgiving." *GH* 65 (Nov. 14, 1972), 931-32, 943. Makes critical connections between the 200-year-old exploitation of the native Americans and contemporary situations in Vietnam and Central America.

Wiebe, Katie Funk. "Taboo Religion." *ChrLead* 36 (Aug. 7, 1973), 19. Looks at a questionnaire that indicates that Mennonite Brethren and

Brethren in Christ lean more toward fundamentalism than other Mennonite groups tested, and therefore rank lower in nonresistance, race relations, and social witness.

Wiebe, Menno. "Indian Doll." *EV* 92 (July 10, 1979), 9; "The Indian Doll: Cast Aside and Rejected." *MennRep* 9 (July 9, 1979), 5. The church is faced with the challenge of accepting native peoples as full-fledged brothers and sisters in Christ rather than continuing to relate with a paternalistic attitude.

Wiebe, Menno. "Mitgefühl Plus Theory—A Theology of Missions and the Indian." *Forum* (Nov., 1972), 3-4. A theology of missions to the Indian people requires that the church pursue both a thorough understanding by intense involvement and a properly guided theoretical consideration.

Wiebe, Menno. "The Real Rita Joe." *MBH* 12 (July 13, 1973), 9. Describing the degradation of the Indian people of Winnipeg, Wiebe urges that rebuilding a people belongs to the heart of the Christian message.

Wiens, Erwin. "Racism on the Receiving End." *ChrLead* 40 (May 24, 1977), 18. A multiracial family's experience traveling in South Africa.

Wingert, Norman. "Wounded Knee: Symbol of the Indian Problem." *MBH* 14 (Oct. 17, 1975), 19-20. Recounts the confusion and violence of the two-month-long occupation of Wounded Knee in 1973 and the continuing conflict between Native Americans and white officials.

Yake, C. F. "A Benighted People in Our Own Midst—The American Indian." *YCC* 30 (Mar. 20, 1949), 508. In spite of increased awareness about the American Indian, we remain ignorant of the material and spiritual needs of these people.

Yoder, Edward. "Of One Blood All Nations." *GH Supplement* 36 (June, 1943), 178-79. All people belong to the same "family." Whatever divisions there are—race, class, etc.—are evidence of the sinfulness of humanity.

Yoder, Edward. "On Overcoming Class Enmity and Hatred: Peace Principles from a Scriptural Viewpoint." Part 22. *GH* 31 (Jan. 19, 1939), 917-19. The way to overcome race and class conflict is to unite persons on the higher level of Christian society.

Yoder, Edward. "The Tyranny of Fear: Peace Principles from a Scriptural Viewpoint." Part 27. *GH* 32 (July 20, 1939), 351-52. There is a great deal of fear in the world causing people to become irrational regarding race relations, class relations, and relations between nations. Be on guard against those who denounce any particular segment of the world's population.

Yoder, Howard. "Reflections on Riots." *GH* 60 (Oct. 3, 1967), 894-95. Riots are the harvest of violence whites have been sowing for years. Christians must comdemn all violence, recognize our part in it, and stand with the poor and the oppressed.

Yoder, John H. "Clarifying the Gospel." *Builder* 23 (Aug., 1973), 1-2. Faithfulness to the Jesus of the gospel demands disavowal of the Jesus in whose name Christians have sanctioned colonialism, racism, militarism, and anti-communism.

Yoder, John H. "Echoes from Nairobi: An Unfinished Debate." *Menn* 91 (Apr. 6, 1976), 239-40. Reports and analyzes World Council of Churches discussion on the five-year-old Program to Combat Racism and its controversial policy of funding organizations engaged in armed independence campaigns.

Zehr, Albert. "Urban Racial Committee Presents Recommendations." *CanMenn* 17 (Sept. 5, 1969), 3. Mennonites at their conference in Oregon (MC) respond positively to the Black Manifesto.

Zehr, Howard. "The Case of the Wilmington 10." *GH* 70 (Nov. 1, 1977), 814-15. Summarizes events leading to the conviction of the "Wilmington 10," and appeals to Mennonites as a peacemaking people to become aware of the miscarriage of justice in this racial issue, and to play a reconciling role.

Zehr, Howard. "To Remove the Walls." *YCC* 45 (June 14, 1964), 5. Personal commitment to work on reconciliation between whites and blacks led the author to enter Morehouse College in Atlanta, as one of the two white students enrolled at that time.

# 15

# Refugees

## A. General

"But I Say Unto You, 'Love Your Enemies'—Jesus." *EV* 90 (Nov. 25, 1977), 11. Christians are experienceing much suffering in Uganda; MCC and the Mennonite mission boards are working on the problems which refugees from Uganda and several other African states face.

Baker, Robert J. "From Chile with Love." *GH* 72 (May 29, 1979), 436-37. A Chilean family, exiled for political reasons, is assisted by the First Mennonite Church of Fort Wayne, Indiana, as they make the US their home.

Barnett, Kenneth. Letter to the Editor. *ChrLead* 39 (May 11, 1976), 9. Difficult to know who are the illegal aliens since employers ask for only a social security number.

Bender, Harold S. "Russian Relief." Address to the General Conference, Aug. 24, 1933. Pp. 3. MHL.

Brenneman, Helen Good. "But Not Forsaken." *ChrLiv* 1 (Apr., 1954), 4-5, 42-43, 45-46; 1 (May, 1954), 6-7, 41-42, 44-45, 47-48; 1 (June, 1954), 6-8, 43, 45-48; 1 (July, 1954), 8-10, 42-48; 1 (Aug., 1954), 12-13, 39-44; 1 (Sept., 1954), 18-19, 39-43; 1 (Oct., 1954), 16-17, 42-45; 1 (Nov., 1954), 18-19, 41-45; 1 (Dec., 1954), 18-19, 40-45. Nine-part serial on refugees after World War II. Published as book, *But Not Forsaken,* Scottdale: Herald Press, 1954.

Brenneman, Helen Good. "Farewell to the Heintzelman." *ChrMon* 40 (May, 1948), 144-45. Departure of the ship *Heintzelman* from Germany carrying Russian Mennonite refugees to Paraguay.

Brenneman, Virgil J. "A Parent's Reflection on Amnesty." *GH* 67 (Oct. 1, 1974), 748-49. A parent whose son is a draft refugee in Canada favors amnesty in order to restore civil liberties denied for conscience' sake, and to further heal the wounds of war.

Brunk, Emily. *Espelkamp: The MCC Shares in Community Building in a New Settlement for German Refugees.* Frankfurt, Germany: MCC, 1951. Pp. 42. MHL. Relates the story of Espelkamp, an initial experiment in resettlement of the refugees of World War II in which both American and European Mennonite youth participated on a Voluntary Service basis.

Brunk, Marie and Friesen, Magdalen. "The Sailing of the S. S. Volendam." *ChrMon* 39 (Mar., 1947), 78-79, 85. Dramatic story of the last-minute departure of Russian Mennonite refugees out of Berlin.

Buhr, Mildred. "Welcome 'Mennonitas'." *ChrMon* 40 (June, 1948), 176-77. Arrival of the second group of Russian Mennonite refugees in Paraguay.

Burnett, Kristina Mast and Rennei, Amy. "The 'Boat People'—Why They Are Leaving and How to Be a Sponsor." *Menn* 94 (Jan. 16, 1979), 40-41. MCC gives an explanation for why people are leaving Vietnam and how to sponsor the refugees for resettlement.

"Church Completion Ends Project." *RepConsS* 17 (Oct., 1960), 3, 4. The dedication of the Mennonite Church in Bechterdissen, Germany, completes another community for refugees built by PAX persons.

Dick, Henry H. "Peace Has Not Come to South Vietnam." *ChrLead* 36 (Apr. 17, 1973), 13. The lack of peace in Vietnam is most clearly seen in the refugee problem and the unexploded ordinance still buried in the farm land.

Dueck, Dora. "Mexico Mennonites Return to Canada." *MBH* 14 (Jan. 10, 1975), 22. Mennonites who left Canada to preserve religious and ethnic freedom (including nonparticipation in the military) are returning to Canada for the same reasons.

Dyck, Anne Konrad. "Refugee Sponsorship: Toronto Church Led the Way." *MennRep* 9 (Aug. 6, 1979), 16. The Toronto United Mennonite Church has assisted several refugee families and couples from Vietnam and provided assistance to other non-Mennonite groups wishing to do the same.

Dyck, Cornelius J. *From the Files of MCC.* Vol. 1 in *The Mennonite Central Committee Story.* Scottdale and Kitchener: Herald Press, 1980. Pp. 159. The documents in this volume tell the story of MCC's beginning intertwined with relief work in Russia and refugee settlements in Paraguay. Later reports on immigrations to and settlements in Uruguay, Brazil, and Mexico are also included.

Dyck, Harvey L. "Despair and Hope in Moscow— A Pillar, A Willow Trunk, and a Stiff-Backed Photograph." *MennLife* 34 (Sept., 1979), 16-23. Recalling his uncle's disappearance during the flight from Russia, Dyck tells the story of the many refugees who finally succeeded in leaving Russia.

Dyck, Peter J. "Peter Dyck's Story." *MennLife* 3 (Jan., 1948), 8-11. Story in words and photos of the evacuation of Mennonite refugees from Berlin and the sailing to South America.

Dyck, Peter J. "South Meadow: A Service of Love 'Unto the Least of These'." *ChrMon* 34 (Oct., 1942), 309-10. Describes an MCC-sponsored children's convalescent home in North Wales as part of the war relief work.

Dyck, Peter J. "'The Woodlands': A Symbol of Love and Service to Aged War Sufferers." *ChrMon* 34 (July, 1942), 209-10. Description of the MCC home in England for elderly people evacuated from war zones.

Eby, Omar. "Mennonites from Israel, Arab Territories Convene in Athens." *CanMenn* 17 (July 4, 1969), 1, 2. Report on a meeting of Mennonite personnel in Athens Apr. 10-12 to discuss peace and reconciliation in the Middle East. Participants came from the East Bank, the West Bank, Israel, Lebanon, the US, and Europe. Action was taken to see what could be done about repatriation and resettlement of Arab refugees. First step was for West Bank/Israel personnel to make concrete proposal to the Israeli government. Politics in the Old Testament, myths about Arab countries and Israel and the refugee problem in the Middle East were discussed.

Ediger, Max. "Handles for Lending a Hand." *Menn* 88 (July 10, 1973), 440. Outlines tasks in which MCC could participate in reconstructing Vietnam after the ceasefire, such as encouraging refugees to move back to their lands, helping to clear the land of unexploded ordnance, continuing with missions and medical programs.

Epp, Frank H. ". . . My Own History Allows Me No Escape." *I Would Like to Dodge the Draft-Dodgers But . . . ,* ed. Frank H. Epp. Waterloo and Winnipeg: Conrad Press, 1970, 8-19. Pp. 95. Reminds readers that the 1967 movement of

American war resisters to Canada has an antecedent in the 1917 movement of Mennonite conscientious objector families to Canada in order to escape persecution and harrassment in the US.

Epp, Frank H., ed. *I Would Like to Dodge the Draft-dodgers But . . .* Waterloo and Winnipeg: Conrad Press, 1970. Pp. 95. Includes: Epp, Frank H., ". . . My Own History Allows Me No Escape," 8-19; Lapp, John A. ". . . The New Militarism Makes Its Harsh Demands," 21-26; Lott, John C., ". . . A Man's Conscience Must Be Respected," 29-38; Webb, Jon M., ". . . The Jails Are Already Too Full," 41-47; Wilcox, Jim, ". . . They Are Up Against the Canadian Border," 49-59; Klaassen, Walter, ". . . Christianity Demands A Positive Response," 61-67; Wert, Jim and Epp, Leonard, ". . . Some Churches and Their Leaders Are Calling for Help," 69-75; Neufeld, Bob, ". . . They Are Coming to Our Chapel Looking for Jobs," 77-85.

Epp, Frank H. "War Compounds the Problems It Was Meant to Solve." *CanMenn* 14 (Aug. 9, 1966), 7; *GH* 59 (Oct. 4, 1966), 878-79. Describes such consequences of the Vietnam War as corruption in Saigon government; prostitution; the effects of defoliation; refugees; death.

Epp, Leonard. "Canada: Refuge from Militarism?" *CanMenn* 18 (May 22, 1970), 1, 2. Draft refugees coming to Canada from the United States are often denigrated. In describing a number of cases, the author describes them as draft resisters, deserters, frustrated and confused, of extraordinary caliber, and less politically and mre religiously inclined.

Esau, Elmer. "A Day in a Refugee Camp." *MCC WSRB* 2 (July, 1946), 1-2. Describes life in Danish refugee camp housing war evacuees.

Fieguth, Margot. "How One Church Looked After Its Refugees." *MennMirror* 10 (Oct., 1980), 11-12. Outlines experiences of a Toronto-area congregation's involvement with MCC's effort to resettle Southeast Asia refugees.

Fransen, David Warren (Review). *Canada's Refugee Policy: Indifference or Opportunism,* by Gerald Dirks. McGill-Queen's Univ. Press, 1977. "Immigration Policies Based on Economic and Political Concerns." *MennRep* 9 (Dec. 10, 1979), 8. Canadian immigration policies are based on economic and political concerns rather than human need.

Frantz, Margarete. "Last Ship to Freedom." *MBH* 13 (Nov. 29, 1974), 26-28. Russian Mennonite refugee in Germany tries to obtain exit visa by lying about his service in Hitler's army.

Franz, Delton, ed. "The 'Winding Down' of a War!" *MCC PS Wash. Memo* 2 (Nov.-Dec., 1970),

1-3. Even though American involvement in Vietnam has decreased, a massive refugee problem in Indochina remains.

Fretz, Clarence Y. "Helping the Needy in Spain." *ChrMon* 31 (Apr., 1939), 108. Report of the relief work being done among Spanish war refugees.

Gingrich, John E. "I Heard Their Cry." *GH* 61 (Apr. 2, 1968), 293. Visitor to South Vietnam is appalled by the destruction and suffering caused by US policies that force people into becoming refugees, and he urges a settlement in the war involving the National Liberation Front.

Hackman, Walton. "Giving for Peace." *Menn* 88 (Dec. 18, 1973), 734. Encourages alternative giving for Christmas to people such as families of civilian prisoners in South Vietnam, imprisoned conscientious objectors, war resisters exiled in Canada, and political refugees from Chile.

Harms, Orlando. "What I Learned in California." *ChrLead* 39 (May 25, 1976), 2. Report on a trip made to California to investigate the practices Mennonite Brethren and others were employing regarding legal and illegal immigrants.

Haury, David A. "German-Russian Immigrants to Kansas and American Politics." *Kansas History: A Journal of the Central Plains* 3 (Winter, 1980), 226-37. Compares two groups of German-Russian immigrants, one Catholic and one Mennonite, on issues of political participation in government. Concludes that a variety of cultural and religious factors plus influences from the local environment and its leadership have given shape to the Mennonite and Catholic political experience in Kansas.

Headrick, Betsy. "Status of Undocumented Aliens." *MCC PS Newsletter* 8 (June, 1977), 5-7. Examines the issue of undocumented persons in the United States and what the church is doing to respond.

Hershberger, Guy F. "Mennonite Relief Commission for War Sufferers." *ME* III (1957), 636-37. Organized in 1917 to distribute funds and supplies for the relief of war sufferers.

Hertzler, Daniel (Editorial). "The Year of the Refugee." *GH* 72 (July 3, 1979), 544. Describes the plight of African, Middle East, and especially Southeast Asian refugees; congregations are encouraged to consider sponsorship.

Hess-Yoder, Beulah and John. "Refugees from Laos: Why Do They Leave Their Homeland?" *MennRep* 9 (Oct. 15, 1979), 7. A report outlining some of the reasons and circumstances

prompting the 180,000 refugees to flee since the communist government came to power in 1975 in Laos.

Hiebert, Linda Gibson. "Report from Indochina: Why Are People Fleeing?" *MennRep* 9 (Sept. 17, 1979), 7. A report on the severe hardships that refugees are experiencing in Laos, Vietnam, and Kampuchea and what the Canadian response has been.

Hiebert, Murray and Hiebert, Linda Gibson. "Future Dim on Refugee Road." *Menn* 90 (May 6, 1975), 288. Description of the suffering and chaos experienced by refugees fleeing with the retreating South Vietnamese army, many of whom begin to regret their decision.

Hiebert, Robert. Letter to the Editor. *MBH* 18 (Mar. 2, 1979), 10-11. Peace in the Middle East will be found only through divine action. Arabs hold the lion's share of responsibility for the plight of the West Bank refugees.

Hofer, Joy. "When Violence Becomes Real." *ChrLead* 43 (Nov. 4, 1980), 10. The plight of a refugee family in Guatemala illustrates the suffering caused by violence in Central America.

Horst, Samuel L., ed. "The Journal of a Refugee." *MQR* 54 (Oct., 1980), 280-304. Journal of a young Mennonite refugee from Virginia fleeing military duty during the Civil War.

"I-Ws Build Block Upon Block at Enkenbach." *RepConsS* 18 (Nov., 1961), 1. One hundred fifty I-Ws have spent 624,000 work hours to build forty-four houses for refugees in Enkenbach, Germany.

Jansen, Curtis, "Building for Eternity." *ChrLiv* 1 (Feb., 1954), 4-5, 42-43. The PAX program began as a system for building houses for refugees in Europe.

Jantz, Harold. "Aid to Vietnam/ese Major Agenda Item in Calgary." *MennRep* 9 (Feb. 5, 1979), 1. At an MCC (Canada) meeting in Jan., considerable discussion revolved around aid to Vietnam and the Vietnamese boat refugees. Among other decisions, it also supported the intention of the Peace and Social Concerns Committee to issue a statement on militarism in Canada.

Jantz, Harold. "Workers Caution About Babylift." *MBH* 14 (May 2, 1975), 16. MCC and Mission Board personnel are concerned that many children being evacuated from Vietnam may not be true orphans.

Jantz, Harold (Editorial). "Vietnam Orphans." *MBH* 14 (Apr. 18, 1975), 11. Comments on the irony of the American concern for war orphans as compared with the earlier support for continued aggression in the war.

Joy, Charles R. "The Lost Parents of Europe." *MennComm* 5 (Aug., 1951), 12-14. Documents the plight of orphans and children separated from their parents in war-torn Europe.

"King Hussein Lauds Mennonite Work in Jordan." *RepConsS* 17 (Oct., 1960), 1, 3. King Hussein expresses appreciation for MCC aid to 63,000 Jordanian refugees.

Kehler, Peter. "Southeast Asia Work Camp Builds Roads to Assist Refugees from Mainland China." *CanMenn* 16 (Sept. 17, 1968), 3. Report on the Fourth South East Asia Reconciliation Work Camp held in Taipei involving eleven participants from Japan (including two US citizens), one from Indonesia, one PAXperson from Korea, and twenty-two from Taiwan. Korean and Indian delegates could not attned due to government restriction.

Klaassen, Walter. ". . . Christianity Demands a Positive Response." *I Would Like to Dodge the Draft-Dodgers But . . .*, ed. Frank H. Epp. Waterloo and Winnipeg: Conrad Press, 1970, 61-67. Pp. 95. Contends that Mennonite resistance to supporting draft-dodgers is both inconsistent with our history as conscientious objectors and incompatible with the words and attitudes of Jesus.

Klaassen, Walter. "Why Should We Care About Draft Resisters?" *CanMenn* 18 (May 22, 1970), 5. Analyzes the dynamics of Mennonite attitudes to the draft refugee and suggests a positive response to the resisters on the basis of Mennonite history.

Klassen, James R. Letter to the Editor. *Menn* 94 (Dec. 11, 1979), 750. Describes how the US deliberately helped create Vietnamese refugees. The US now is only offering assistance to boat people who represent a very small fraction of the population. Much more aid needs to be given to help Vietnamese in Vietnam.

Knoop, Faith Yingling. "The Persecuted: Rejoice!" *ChrLiv* 6 (July, 1959), 8-9. The nonresistant response of a group of Pennsylvania Indians forced to become refugees in 1763.

Krabill, Willard S. "Vietnam: Soulsick, War-weary, and Divided." *CanMenn* 14 (Feb. 8, 1966), 9; *ChrLead* 29 (Mar. 15, 1966), 3-5. A condensed version of Krabill's report to Elkhart Mennonite churches about the extent and solution of the refugee problem in Vietnam. Includes discussion of the question of Vietnamese national identity and how that question relates to questions of politics, government, and war.

Krahn, Cornelius. "Can These Bones Live?" *MennLife* (July 1, 1946), 3-4. An appeal to American Mennonites to rescue the dry bones of the "Menno Valley," the destitute of Europe particularly.

Kreider, Robert S. "Mennonite Refugees in Germany." *MCC WSRB* 2 (July, 1946), 4. Describes MCC efforts to make possible the migration of Russian Mennonite refugees in Berlin.

Kreider, Thomas Edmund. "J. E. Brunk, Mennonite Relief Worker in Constantinople, 1920-21." Paper presented to History Seminar, Goshen College, Goshen, Ind., Jan. 6, 1979. Pp. 27. MHL.

Kurtz, Karen B. "The Uprooted, Continuing Problem." *GH* 72 (Dec. 4, 1979), 937-38. A historical overview on refugees, noting that there have been thirteen million in our contemporary world.

Landis, Marian. "The Horn of Africa: World's Worst Refugee Problem." *MCC PS Newsletter* 10 (June July, 1980), 5-6. Information and statistics on the flow of refugees into Somalia from the Somali-Ethiopian conflict.

Lapp, John A. "Stop the Killing in East Pakistan." *MBH* 10 (Aug. 27, 1971), 12, 13. Describes the problems of the refugees in East Pakistan and makes suggestions about what North American Christians can do to bring relief to the situation.

Lapp, John A. "The Personal Face of Displacement: 'To Lose My Land Is to Lose My Life.' " *MennRep* 8 (Dec. 25, 1978), 7. Relates story of one displaced Palestinian refugee in an attempt to draw attention to the plight of Palestinians removed from their homes by illegal Israeli settlements.

Lapp, John A. "The Problem of Illegal Aliens." *ChrLiv* 24 (May, 1977), 19-20. Outlines the complexity of the issue and calls for Christians to speak up for the powerless.

Lapp, John A. "The United Nations in the Middle East." *ChrLiv* 26 (Aug., 1979), 15, 25. Description of UN peacekeeping operations in the Middle East, from relief for Palestinian refugees to troops stationed in demilitarized zones.

Lapp, John A. "Two Land Deals: Ancestral Homeland Returned in New York . . . and Seized in Occupied West Bank." *Menn* 94 (Jan. 9, 1979), 24-25. Report on MCC's involvement with two different groups of people, the Mohawk Indians of New York and the Palestinians, as they each struggle for land. While the Mohawks succeed in claiming part of their ancestral homeland in NY, many Palestinian refugees have been scattered throughout the Middle East as their land is lost or destroyed.

*
Lehman, M[artin] C[lifford]. "Uprooted People; Needs and Conditions in Europe." ChrMon 37, Part 2, (Aug., 1945), 205-6. The war has created millions of refugees and prisoners.

Leiper, Henry Smith. "The Effect of War on the Refugee Problem." GH 32 (Oct. 12, 1939), 603. Hopes that Americans will respond to the refugees, especially the German ones, created by the war.

Liechty, Sandra. Letter to the Editor. Menn 94 (May 1, 1979), 316. A new publication, "Agora" (in Japanese and English) has been started in Japan to coordinate Mennonite-related groups working on peace issues and activities, including camps for Vietnamese refugees.

Lubosch, Lore. "The Mennonites in Brazil—They Did It Almost Without Help . . .' " MennMirror 1 (Jan., 1972), 10-14. Dr. Boruszenko, economic historian in Curitiba, Brazil, gives a detailed report on the history of Brazil's Mennonites from the emigration from Russia in 1929 to the present, including such aspects as education, economics, and conscription.

"MCC (Canada) Answers Queries re Draft Evaders." CanMenn 18 (Apr. 17, 1970), 1, 2. Six of the most frequently asked questions about the draft refugee situation are clarified.

Mark, Leslie E. and Moneypenny, Rene. "Christian Employers and Illegal Immigrants." ChrLead 39 (Apr. 13, 1976), 8. Identifies some of the problems associated with the illegal alien situation. Notes that hundreds of illegal aliens are hired by Mennonite Brethren employers.

Martens, Harry E. "Bitterness and Hopelessness— the Changing Mood in Refugee Camps." CanMenn 17 (Oct. 24, 1969), 1, 2. After 13 months of work among the refugees in Jordan, Martens quotes a high official of the UNRWA organization: "The physical conditions . . . have slightly improved the lot of the refugee, but the psychological and emotional conditions have greatly deteriorated and are much worse as compared to a year ago."

Martens, Harry E. "Houses on Cold Amman Hills." GH 61 (Nov. 12, 1968), 1028. Describes the plight of Palestinian war refugees facing a cold winter with only tents, and challenges North American Christians to share out of their abundance to construct makeshift shelters.

Martens, Harry E. "Volunteers Are Peacemakers." CanMenn 17 (June 6, 1969), 4. "The most forceful, meaningful and acceptable way of serving as a 'peacemaker' is to serve and witness as a Christian volunteer." Serving in

the Middle East, the author believes identification with the Arab refugees provides an "opportunity to talk, walk, and to work with them, and to demonstrate what the great love of Christ means."

Martin, Alice S. "Nothing the Grass Said." ChrLiv 20 (Dec., 1973), 13-14. Thoughts of a Vietnamese refugee on hate and war.

Martin, Earl S. "Bombs Wait for Viet Farmers." ChrLead 36 (July 10, 1973), 4; Menn 88 (July 10, 1973), 431; MennRep 3 (July 9, 1973), 9; GH 66 (July 31, 1973), 589. There is a serious problem for Vietnamese refugees as they move back to the farmland which is littered with live bombs, dud artillery shells, and undetonated mines and booby traps.

Martin, Earl S. "Who Speaks for Indochina?" ChrLiv 17 (Sept., 1970), 18-19, 35-37. Relates personal experiences from work with Vietnamese refugees, and pleads for an end to the war.

Martin, Luke S. (Review). Vietnam, by Mary McCarthy. Harcourt, Brace and World, 1967. Pp. 106. ChrLiv 15 (July, 1968), 37. Recommends this critic's description of the US government policy of creating refugees and her simple and radical suggestions for change.

Matsuo, Hilda. "Can We Handle All Those Boat People?" MennMirror 9 (Sept., 1979), 10. The writer looks at the varying attitudes of Canadians towards Indochinese refugees and points out what two MCC employees have advised—that Canadians should act as peacemakers rather than continuing the more popular route of polarizing the situation in Southeast Asia.

Mennonite Central Committee Annual Meeting. "Christian Love and Faith Transform Problems into Opportunities." EV 89 (Mar. 10, 1976), 5. MCC ministries in 1976 will include responses to victims of war and political tensions.

Miller, Robert W. "Reflections on Vietnam." GH 64 (Oct. 19, 1971), 867-68. Director of Vietnam Christian Service for three years describes the death and corruption caused largely by the involvement of the US government. Focuses especially on the plight of refugees.

Miller, Robert W. and Hutchison, Frank L. "The Vietnam Refugee Program: A Report." [Akron, Pa.: MCC, 1965.] Pp. [22.] MHL.

Moyal, Maurice. "Father to the Orphans of Europe." ChrLiv 6 (Sept., 1959), 20-22. Doctor establishes home for war orphans in Austria after World War II.

"New Project in Salzburg." RepConsS 18 (July,

1961), 2. MCC will assist Nazarene refugees, who have been living in wooden barracks for fifteen years, with new housing construction.

Neufeld, Bob. ". . . They Are Coming to Our Chapel Looking for Work." *I Would Like to Dodge the Draft-dodgers But . . . .* Ed. Frank H. Epp. Waterloo and Winnipeg: Conrad Press, 1970, 77-85. Pp. 95. Relates experiences as an employment counselor working with US war resisters having sought refuge in Canada.

Neufeld, Bob. "Those Refugee Americans." *With* 4 (Mar., 1971), 4. A discussion of the hopes and frustrations in dealing with American immigrants to Canada.

Peachey, Urbane. "Refugees Flee Israeli Forces." *Intercom* 22 (May, 1978), 1, 4. Describes the plight of refugees from Israel's invasion of Lebanon and outlines the issues involved in the conflict.

Pertusio, Carolyn E. "For One Vietnamese Refugee, It's Been a Journey from Despair to Hope." *EV* 92 (Dec. 10, 1979), 9-10. Report describing the helpless, homesick, and hopeful feelings which were all part of one man's experience in resettling in America after escaping from Vietnam by boat.

Preheim, Marion Keeney. "For Toni Neufeld: No More Yesterdays." *Menn* 91 (May 4, 1976), 298-300. Traces the life of Antonette Neufeld, German-Russian war refugee child who has served many years as a foster parent for other homeless children.

Quiring, Paul. "Camp David: A Commentary." *MennRep* 8 (Oct. 2, 1978), 7. The peace agreements between Egypt's President Sadat and Israel's Prime Minister Begin fail to speak to both the problem of Palestinian refugees and a bilateral agreement, but they do buy additional time for negotiating peace.

(Review). *Vietnam: Who Cares?,* by Atlee and Winifred Beechy. Scottdale: Herald Press, 1968. Pp. 154. *Fellowship* 36 (May, 1970), 27. Brief summary of the book which is a compilation of the reports from six months of working with the Church World Service's relief and refugee service program in Vietnam. Recommended for its detail, excellent historical outline, and bibliography.

Redekop, John H. "Peace with Honour." *MBH* 12 (Feb. 9, 1973), 10. Although an imminent Vietnam truce has been announced, several disquieting aspects remain: the millions of refugees, orphans, cripples, etc.; the possibility of continued guerilla warfare; and the threat of communism and east-west distrust.

Redekop, John H. "Refugees." *MBH* 14 (May 20,

1975), 8. Love for neighbor means receiving Vietnam refugees with concern, not self-interested excuses.

Reimer, Al. "A New Life Half Way Around the World." *MennMirror* 4 (Dec., 1974), 7-10. "A dramatized meditation on the journey of the first group of Russian Mennonites to Manitoba in 1874, presented at a special centennial ceremony held at the original landing site on July 31, 1974."

Reimer, Al (Film Review). "*Hiding Place* Is Good Religious Cinema." *MennMirror* 6 (Dec., 1976), 16. This film dramatizes the life of Corrie ten Boom, who aided Jewish refugees in Holland during the Nazi occupation and was imprisoned in a concentration camp. It is especially good because it depicts faith and spiritual devotion; it teaches also about the nature of both evil and faith.

Reimer, Otto B. Letter to the Editor. *ChrLead* 39 (May 25, 1976), 13. Comments on the article "Christian Employers and Illegal Immigrants" (*Leader,* Apr. 13), claiming it contains several erroneous statements.

Reimer, Vic. "MCC (US) Promoting Refugee Sponsorship." *Menn* 94 (Oct. 2, 1979), 582. Interest by US Mennonites in sponsoring refugees from Southeast Asia is increasing.

Rempel, Ron. "Response to the Refugees: Feeding the Problems or Making Peace?" *MennRep* 9 (Oct. 1, 1979), 6. The Mennonite Church's response in Canada to southeast Asian refugees has been notable but the next step calls for a new round of homework to enlarge understandings and respond in ways that make for peace.

*Report of American Mennonite Relief to Holland, 1945-1947.* Druk de Bussy, Amsterdam: MCC, [1947]. Pp. 14. MHL. Text and photos recount the story of the post-war service project. Describes distribution of clothes and food, reconstruction efforts, caring for the Mennonite refugees, etc.

Rich, Elaine Sommers. "A Danzig Mennonite, as Told to Elaine Sommers Rich, 'I Was a Refugee.' " *ChrLiv* 2 (Dec., 1955), 20-21. Unforgettable horrors of war are still etched in the refugee's memory ten years later.

Roth, Willard E. "Refugee: Statistic or Brother?" *ChrLiv* 7 (June, 1960), 8-10, 34. Focus on the estimated 15 million victims of war, persecution, or natural disaster.

"Sponsorship Rises to 2,500; Over 200 Have Arrived." *MennRep* 9 (Sept. 3, 1979), 1. MCC (Canada) reports on the Canadian Mennonite churches' response to the refugees coming from Southeast Asia.

Samson, Hugh. "No Room, No Inn." *ChrLiv* 15 (Nov., 1968), 31-32. Plight of refugees from the 1967 Arab-Israeli war.

Schloneger, Florence. *Sara's Trek.* Newton: Faith and Life Press, 1981. Pp. 105. Sara Friesen and Liese Rempel become separated from their families during the flight from Russia during World War II. In the year of separation spent in a German children's home and, upon being reunited with their families to live as refugees, the girls must not only cope with the logistics of survival amid the ravages of war but struggle to discover the meaning of these experiences for their lives and their faith. Fiction for ages 10-14.

Seals, Eugene. "Asian Refugees: a Two-Congregation Response." *GH* 72 (Aug. 21, 1979), 668-69. The experience of two congregations—Huber and First Dayton Mennonite churches—in assisting a southeast Asian refugee family to resettle in their community.

Shelly, Maynard. "Peacemakers in a Guerilla Tent?" *CanMenn* 17 (July 11, 1969), 1. During a Middle East tour, 21 American and Canadian Mennonites met an al-fateh leader in a refugee camp in Jordan. Refugees have tried nonviolent means for 20 years, he said, and no one has listened. Now they will fight to the death to regain their homeland. The tour was sponsored by the MCC peace section.

Shenk, Susan E. S. "Israel's Settlement: Conquest, Immigration, or Revolt? An Overview of Gottwald's Critique." Paper presented to War and Peace in the Bible class, AMBS, Elkhart, Ind., 1980. Pp. 23. AMBS.

Siebert, Allan J. "Response to Refugees Criticized as 'Cautious and Restrained'." *MennRep* 9 (Dec. 10, 1979), 1, 3. MCC (Canada) refugee assistance program has encountered criticism in recent weeks over its limited response to the refugee crisis in Southeast Asia.

Steiner, Susan Clemmer. "We Could Not Go Home." *With* 8 (June, 1975), 6. Description of the radical changes in the lives of four Mennonite draft dodgers in Canada.

Stoltzfus, Gene. Letter to the Editor. *MennRep* 9 (Aug. 6, 1979), 6. A warning to the churches to look beyond the stories of the refugees to try to determine the realities in Indochina and make some meaning out of this chapter of history.

Stoltzfus, Gene. "Philippine War Refugees Face Difficult Life." *Intercom* 22 (Apr., 1978), 4. Describes the plight of refugees from the fighting between the Filipino military and Muslim secessionist groups.

Stoltzfus, Gene. "Report from Southeast Asia: From a CIA Jungle to Mennoland." Part 4. *MennRep* 9 (Dec. 10, 1979), 7. The movement of refugees from Laos raises a number of spiritual and ethical issues for Christians which this writer attempts to address.

Stoltzfus, Gene. "What the War Is Doing to the Vietnamese People." *GH* 61 (Feb. 20, 1968), 153-54; *CanMenn* 16 (Feb. 6, 1968), 1, 5. Identifies five levels of traditional Vietnamese society: people who are educated (monks, teachers, ruling people)—many of whom are going abroad because they have no future in Vietnam; farmers—instability in rural areas means not enough rice even for the people of Vietnam; laborers—composed of refugees; businesspeople—many have made poor investments in hotels and living quarters for foreigners; soldiers. As a result of the war, the Vietnamese society has been tipped upside down with the soldiers on top and the educated on the bottom.

"The Refugee American. . ." *Forum* (Jan., 1971), A4-A5. Several Mennonites dialogue about their work with American draft dodgers in Ottawa and the problems and attitudes of these Americans.

Toews, Susanna. *Trek to Freedom: The Escape of Two Sisters from South Russia During World War II.* Winkler, Man.: Heritage Valley Publication, 1976. Pp. 43. MHL. Part 1 offers a vivid description of life as experienced by the Mennonites in Russia before and during World War II. Part 2 describes the flight from Russia as refugees caught in the confusion of the advances and retreats of both the Russian and German armies. A unifying theme is the maintenance of faith in the turbulance of war.

Vogt, Ruth (Review). *Lest Innocent Blood Be Shed,* by Philip Haillie. New York: Harper & Row, 1979. "Leader With Conviction Is Light in Evil World." *MennMirror* 9 (Dec., 1979), 15. Reports on the main content of this book, which tells the story of André Trocmé, a remarkable spiritual leader who started the work of harboring Jewish refugees during World War II in the French village of Le Chambon. Recommends the book, particularly for those who believe pacifism to be an essential part of the Christian gospel.

Wert, Jim and Epp, Leonard. " . . . Some Churches and Their Leaders Are Calling for Help." *I Would Like to Dodge the Draft-dodgers But . . . .* Ed. Frank H. Epp. Waterloo and Winnipeg: Conrad Press, 1970, 69-75. Pp. 95. In this two-part treatment, Wert describes the Canadian Council of Churches' involvement with the US draft dodgers and Epp describes the estimated 60,000 young Americans in Canada for reasons of conscientious objection and makes some suggestions as to how the church leadership might deal constructively with this phenomenon.

Wiebe, Bernie. "Chapter on Vietnam Refuses to Close." *Menn* 94 (Aug. 7, 1979), 487. Plea for more families and congregations to become personally involved in the plight of the Vietnamese refugees.

Wiebe, Bernie. "The Homeless Ones." *Menn* 94 (May 29, 1979), 384. There are over ten million refugees in the world who test the concern and compassion of the western world and the church.

Woodruff, Lance. "Vietnamese Aid in Constructing Housing." *GH* 61 (June 4, 1968), 503-504. Describes the refugee shelters under construction by Vietnam Christian Service to house refugees from Saigon rendered homeless by the Tet New Year offensive.

Yoder, Henry P. "'I Hold Nothing Against You.'" *GH* 63 (Dec. 22, 1970), 1054-55. Story of Cuban immigrant physician overcoming hostilities and forgiving those who wronged him illustrates the love of Christ which absorbs hostilities and brings peace.

Yoder, Samuel A. *Middle-East Sojourn.* Scottdale, Pa.: Herald Press, 1951. Pp. 310. Reminisces and reflects on travels and work undertaken on eighteen-month assignment to relief work in the Sinai Desert following World War II. Appendices offer specific information about the various efforts of this one refugee project.

# B. Russian story

"Baptist Delegation from Russia Meets Mennonites." *CanMenn* 4 (June 1, 1956), 1, 7. Russian Baptists visiting the Mennonite Biblical Seminary in Chicago describe Mennonite-Baptist cooperation in the Soviet Union and discuss the status of conscientious objection in their country.

Bender, Harold S. "Russian Relief." Address to the General Conference, Aug. 24, 1933. Pp. 3. MHL.

Bender, Harold S. Letter to the Editor. *Fellowship* 26 (Nov., 1960), 35-36. In response to A. J. Muste's article "Their Church and Ours" (*Fellowship*, Nov., 1959), which cites a statement by Jacob Zhidkov about the Russian Mennonites abandoning their nonresistance after World War I, H. S. Bender points out that this is greatly exaggerated and only a small minority joined the Selbstschutz.

Brenneman, Helen Good. "Farewell to the Heintzelman." *ChrMon* 40 (May, 1948), 144-45. Departure of the ship *Heintzelman* from Germany carrying Russian Mennonite refugees to Paraguay.

Brunk, Marie and Friesen, Magdalen. "The Sailing of the S. S. Volendam." *ChrMon* 39 (Mar., 1947), 78-79, 85. Dramatic story of the last-minute departure of Russian Mennonite refugees out of Berlin.

Buhr, Mildred. "Welcome 'Mennonitas'." *ChrMon* 40 (June, 1948), 176-77. Arrival of the second group of Russian Mennonite refugees in Paraguay.

Claassen, Jack G. "When Christmas Came." *RepConsS* 7 (Dec., 1949), 2. The dialectic between church and state is concretized in two anecdotes concerning Russian Mennonite children's efforts to honor Christmas in spite of pressure from peers and teachers.

Clemens, Rachel. "Mennonites as the Military: The Selbstschutz Experience." 1984. Pp. 10. BfC.

"Disaster Ends Russian Mennonite Settlements." *MennLife* 4 (Jan., 1949), 22-23, 26-27. Upheavals suffered by Russian Mennonite villagers through wars and purges from the Revolution to World War II.

Dick, David. "Faith Put to the Test." *MBH* 16 (Apr. 15, 1977), 2-4. Mennonite family in the Ukraine refused to defend their estate by force during the Russian revolution.

Dyck, Anna Reimer. *Anna: From the Caucasus to Canada,* trans. and ed. Peter J. Klassen. Hillsboro: Mennonite Brethren Publishing House, 1979. Pp. 216. The particular experience of one Russian Mennonite woman is a microcosm of the populations dislocated by the fury of war and revolution. The section describing the Russian revolution and civil war depicts not only the suffering caused by war but, in the simple accounting for friends and relatives, the variety of ways the Mennonite community responded to the Russian government's call to bear arms.

Dyck, Arnold; trans. Reimer, Al. "A Tale of Bullets, Rifles, Red Rif-Raf, and Shooting Only 'So High'." *MennMirror* 8 (Apr, 1979), 6, 7. A translated excerpt from Arnold Dyck's Low German "Koop enn Bua" writings. In this skit a "Russian" Mennonite defends and justifies the Mennonite Selbstschutz with self-deprecating irony.

Dyck, Harvey L. "Despair and Hope in Moscow—A Pillar, A Willow Trunk, and a Stiff-Backed Photograph." *MennLife* 34 (Sept., 1979), 16-23.

Recalling his uncle's disappearance during the flight from Russia, Dyck tells the story of the many refugees who finally succeeded in leaving Russia.

Dyck, Peter J. "A Twentieth Century Miracle." *ChrMon* 39 (Oct., 1947), 305-7. Relates the story of MCC efforts to bring Russian Mennonite refugees out of Berlin.

Dyck, Peter J. "New Wind Blowing in US-Soviet Relations?" *ChrLead* 36 (Aug. 7, 1973), 14. A survey of the history of the church in Russia supports the idea that communism can be defined as a judgment upon the church.

Dyck, Peter J. "The Beginning of Project 483." *ChrMon* 41, Part 1, (Feb., 1949), 50-52; Part 2, (Mar., 1949), 80-81. The second voyage of the *Volendam* to South America with European Mennonite refugees and the arrival of Mennonite immigrants in Uruguay.

Ediger, Amand. "The Russian Mennonites During World War II." Student paper for Mennonite History, May 23, 1946. Pp. 16. MLA/BeC.

Enns, Frank F. (Review). *Einer von Vielen,* by Olga Rempel. CMBC Publications, 1979. Pp. 201. *MennLife* 34 (Dec., 1979), 31. Gives a summary of the book which is divided into three parts: a biography of Aron P. Toews, who suffered and perished in Siberia, his diary in exile, and some of his poems and stories.

Enns, Mary M. "Christians on Both Sides of the Iron Curtain Need Each Other." *MennMirror* 6 (Mar., 1977), 7, 8. Dr. Henry D. Wiebe, as part of an MCC delegation to Russia, shares his perceptions of the visit which sought to strengthen previous contacts with believers and to learn from them.

Enns, Mary M. "Ingrid Rimland Turns to Face the Forces That Shaped Her Life." *MennMirror* 8 (Jan., 1979), 6, 7. Describes some of the forces that shaped Rimland's life and led her to write the novel *The Wanderers* which tells of three women who survived the Russian Revolution, World War II, and the hardships of Paraguay.

Enns, Mary M. "Keeping the Faith Alive Behind the Iron Curtain." *MennMirror* 5 (Mar., 1976), 9, 10. A report on the research Walter Sawatsky is doing under MCC in Russia and East European countries with particular attention to the current religious situation.

Epp, Frank H. "Mass Migration from Russia to Manitoba: The Choice Wasn't Easy." *MennRep* 4 (Nov. 25, 1974), 12-16. Detailed account of circumstances leading to the decision of thousands of Russian Mennonites to migrate to Canada, including the impact of threatened compulsory military service.

Epp, Frank H. (Editorial). "Do Communists Save Souls?" *CanMenn* 2 (Feb. 26, 1954), 2. Mennonites should not let memories of bitter experiences in Russia blind them to the humanness of the Russian people.

Epp, Frank H. (Review). *A Russian Dance of Death: Revolution and Civil War in the Ukraine,* by Dietrich Neufeld. Winnipeg: Hyperion Press, 1977. Pp. 142. "A Russian Dance Should be Read by All Under 50." *MennMirror* 7 (Jan., 1978), 15. Summarizes the contents of this book which is a personal narrative arising out of the author's experience during the civil war in the Ukraine and the terror inflicted by anarchist Nestor Makhno. Describes the book as valuable because of the author's personalized account and critical assessment of the events and tragedies that befell the Mennonites.

Epp, George K. (Review). *No Strangers in Exile,* by Hans Harder. *MennLife* 34 (Dec., 1979), 28. Describes the content and intent of this book which tells the experience of Mennonite martyrs in the Russian labor camps in order to draw the attention of the world to this unbelievable suffering. Commends the book and its excellent translation.

Epp, Jacob P. "Nonresistance—Selbstschutz." Pp. 30. MBBS.

Epp, Jacob. P. "The Mennonite Selbstschutz in the Ukraine: an Eyewitness Account." *MennLife* 26 (July, 1971), 138-42. A report on the emergence of the Selbstschutz (self-protection), its involvement as a protective force, and its disbanding.

Esau, John A. "The Congressional Debates on the Coming of the Russian Mennonites." Paper presented to the Anabaptist-Mennonite History class, MBS, Elkhart, Ind., June 2, 1961. Pp. 31. AMBS.

Fast, Henry A. "Mennonite Response to the Russian Revolution." *JChSoc* 6 (Fall, 1970), 8. An evaluation of the Russian Mennonite response, which was largely ethnic, cultural, and narrowly religious, to the Russian Revolution of 1917.

Fast, Peter G. "The Russian Mennonites and the State." Paper presented to the Social Science Seminar, Goshen College, Goshen, Ind., May 31, 1949. Pp. 39. MHL.

Frantz, Margarete. "Last Ship to Freedom." *MBH* 13 (Nov. 29, 1974), 26-28. Russian Mennonite refugee in Germany tries to obtain exit visa by lying about his service in Hitler's army.

Friesen, Lyle. "The Russian Mennonite Selbstschutz in its Historical Perspective." MCC

Canada Scholarship paper, Apr. 30, 1973. Pp. 29. CGCL.

Froese, Peter F. "Die Oktoberrevolution in Ruʃʃland und ihre Auswirkungen." 1950. Pp. 405. BfC.

Froese, Peter J. "The Problem of Nonresistance as the Mennonites of Russia Dealt with It." N.d. Pp. 21. MLA/BeC.

Funk, Cornelius C. *Escape to Freedom,* trans. and ed. Peter J. Klassen. Hillsboro: Mennonite Brethren Publishing House, 1982. Pp. 124. Personal account of Russian young man who enlists in the medical corps of the Russian army. Describes horrors of war as well as the difficult task of sorting through the chaotic political situation in order to make ethical decisions about one's participation in a changing government.

Gerlach, Horst. "Through Darkness to Light." *ChrLiv* 3 (Aug., 1956), 6-9, 40-41; 3 (Sept., 1956), 12-15, 40; 3 (Oct., 1956), 14-17, 19, 34, 36; 3 (Nov., 1956), 19-22, 24, 34, 35-37; 3 (Dec., 1956), 24-29, 36; 4 (Jan., 1957), 24-29; 4 (Feb., 1957), 24-29. Life story of a young German man growing up in a pro-Nazi family during the Hitler and World War II era. Enemy occupation of home town; prisoner of war in northern Russia as slave laborer; conversion to Christianity from trust in military force while an MCC trainee serving in the US.

Goering, Terence R. "The Mennonites in Russia and Their Relations with the Political and Military Authorities of the Russian Government." Student paper for A Decade Relived, Jan. 25, 1974. Pp. 59. MLA/BeC.

Haendiges, Emil. "The Catastrophe of the West-Prussian Mennonites." Pp. 7. BfC.

Hampton, Peter J. "They Paid the Highest Price." *MennMirror* 6 (June, 1977), 25, 26. Describes how, during the Russian Revolution, his grandfather and uncle were killed by Russian bandits while they were on a mission of mercy.

Harder, Leland. "Thy People Shall Be My People." *Menn* 63 (Feb. 3, 1948), 3-4. A comparison of the experience of Mennonites in Russia who, in 1873, petitioned the US Senate for a large tract of land for a colony (denied), with that of blacks in America who, in the same year, were struggling to get the 1873 Civil Rights Bill passed.

Hershberger, Guy F. "Concerning the Reliability of Statements of Carl McIntire." *GH* 57 (1964), 602. Hershberger includes McIntire's protesting statements which he released when a Russian Baptist delegation came to Philadelphia on May 29, 1964, and a letter of response from Paul Verghese, associate secretary of the World Council of Churches, denying these statements.

Hershberger, Guy F. "How Can We Witness Against the Spirit of Hate Directed Against Russia By Certain Preachers and Church Leaders? Questions of Social Concern for Christians," (Part 17). *GH* 53 (Aug. 2, 1960), 660. A conference resolution on living the nonresistant life.

Horsch, John. "The Mennonites of Russia, Part III." *ChrMon* 28 (Aug., 1936), 230, 237. Experiences of the Rusasian Mennonites during World War I, when young men served in noncombatant posts.

Horsch, John. "The Mennonites of Russia, Part IV." *ChrMon* 28 (Sept., 1936), 262-63. Experiences of the colonists during the Russian Revolution, when Mennonites formed armed self-defense units

Hunter, Allan A. *Heroes of Good Will: Thirty-five Stories of Valor in Creative Living.* New York: Fellowship of Reconciliation, [1943]. Pp. 63. MHL. Compilation of illustrations of nonresistance include two from Mennonite experience in Russia: "Light in Russia that Overcame Darkness" and "Suppose He Had Not Tried Christian Force."

Janzen, David. "Attitude to Our Enemies: A Call to Repentance." *MennRep* 3 (Jan. 8, 1973), 7-8. Expresses disappointment over Mennonite failure to love communists in Russia. Reprints article from *Der Bote* giving thanks for Mennonite escape from Russia with "an anti-communist attitude that evades repentance."

Janzen, Wilhelm. "Deliverance." Part 2. *MennMirror* 2 (Apr., 1973), 11-13. An installment from Janzen's book which describes some of his experiences in Russia during World War II.

Janzen, Wilhelm. "The Arrest: Uncle Frank Is Taken." Part 1. *MennMirror* 2 (Mar., 1973), 7, 8. This installment from Janzen's book, which describes some of his experiences in Russia during World War II, tells of the arrest of his uncle and the fear and hope surrounding this event.

Klippenstein, La Verne (Review). *Anna: From the Caucasus to Canada,* by Anna Reimer Dyck. Mennonite Brethren Publishing House, 1979. Pp. 216. "From Steppe to Prairie." *MennMirror* 9 (Oct., 1979), 14. Provides a brief summary of this autobiographical account of Anna's journey from a wealthy Russian estate through peril to a small Manitoba community. Concludes that the book is unique and inspiring because it lacks the bitterness and hostility evident in other books covering this period.

Klippenstein, La Verna (Review). *Days of Terror,* by Barbara Claassen Smucker. Toronto: Clark, Irwin and Co., 1979. Pp. 156. *MennLife* 34 (Dec., 1979), 31. Summarizes this story which relates the experience of the Neufeld family during and after the Russian Revolution. Recommends this book especially for church librarians.

Krahn, Cornelius. "Mennonites in Russia and Their Exodus." *GH* 72 (Nov. 20, 1979), 897-900. The writer examines what has happened to Mennonites who remained in Russia following World War II and develops an understanding for the difficulties and adjustments they experience as Umsiedler in Germany.

Krahn, Cornelius. "Mennonites in Russia Today Gaining the Favor of the State." *MennRep* 9 (July 23, 1979), 6, 7. A description is given of the situation and conditions under which the Mennonite church in Russia is struggling to preserve its identity.

Krahn, Cornelius. "Mennonites the World Over." *MennLife* 1 (Jan., 1946), 29-30. Describes the fate of European and Russian Mennonites in World War II.

Kreider, Robert S. "Mennonite Refugees in Germany." *MCC WSRB* 2 (July, 1946), 4. Describes MCC efforts to make possible the migration of Russian Mennonite refugees in Berlin.

Kreider, Robert S. "The Anabaptist Conception of the Church in the Russian Mennonite Environment." *MQR* 25 (Jan., 1951), 17-33. In Russia the Mennonite church moved in the direction of a Volkskirche (state church type) away from a believers' church type, though renewal movements also countered the trend.

Lapp, Alice W. (Review). *A Russian Dance of Death: Revolution and Civil War in the Ukraine,* by Dietrich Neufeld. Ed. and Trans., Al Reimer. Winnipeg: Hyperion Press, 1977. Pp. 142. *FQ* 5 (May, June, July, 1978), 13. Chronicles the misery of war and anarchy experienced by Russian Mennonites in the Ukraine during the early part of the century.

Lapp, John A. "Fifty Years of Russian Revolution." *ChrLiv* 15 (January, 1968), 18-19. Review of 50 years of Russian life, beginning with the Revolution in 1917.

Lapp, John A. "Vignettes from Russia." *ChrLiv* 23 (Dec., 1976), 15-16. One aspect of Soviet life is the emphasis on peace.

Loewen, Harry (Review). *The Odyssey of the Bergen Family,* by Gerhard Lohrenz. Steinbach: Derksen Printers, 1978. Pp. 146. "Bergen Family Trials Explored." *MennMirror* 8 (Apr., 1979), 11. Encourages Canadian Mennonites, especially those under 40, to read this story of the Bergen family. It is the story of many Mennonites in Russia between 1930 and 1950.

Loewen, Harry (Review.) *With Courage to Spare: The Life of B. B. Janz (1877-1964),* by John B. Toews. Winnipeg: The Board of Christian Literature of the General Conference of the Mennonite Brethren Churches of North America, 1978. *MQR* 53 (Oct., 1979), 327-28. The story of B. B. Janz, who assisted Russian Mennonites in settling in North America, built up congregations in Canada, and fought to preserve the Mennonite principles of peace and nonresistance during World War II.

Loewen, Mary J. "Persecuted Optimists." Paper presented to Christianity in Russia class, MBS, [Chicago, Ill.], fall, 1951. Pp. 41. AMBS.

Lohrenz, Gerhard. "Nonresistance Tested." *MennLife* 17 (Apr., 1962), 66-68. The story of Nester Makhno, who after the Russian Revolution in 1917 roamed the countryside with his band, plundering, murdering, and raping the populace, including many Mennonites.

Lohrenz, Gerhard. "Rejection of Marxist Worldview." *CanMenn* 16 (Jan. 9, 1968), 5. Lohrenz criticizes Frank Epp's book review of "Lost Fatherland" on a number of counts. Concludes that "the Soviets . . . demand of every Soviet citizen that he accept their Weltanschauung unconditionally . . . Those who still think of themselves as Mennonites cannot do this . . . they reject the materialistic world view of communism. This—and this alone—is the source of tension between the Soviets and the Mennonites in Russia today."

Lohrenz, Gerhard (Review). *A Russian Dance of Death: Revolution and Civil War in the Ukraine,* by Dietrich Neufeld, trans. Al Reimer. Winnipeg: Man.: Hyperion Press and Scottdale, Pa.: Herald Press, 1977. Pp. 157. *MQR* 53 (Jan., 1979), 85-86. A personal account of the situation in the Ukraine during the stormy years of 1919-21.

Lohrenz, Gerhard (Review). *August 1914,* by Alexander Solzhenitsyn. New York: Farrar, Straus, and Giroux, 1972. Pp. 622. *Menn* 88 (Jan. 30, 1973), 77-78. Russian novel explores the reasons for the defeat of Russian forces by German in the battle of Tannenberg, during World War I. Reviewer observes that the book is a song of praise for the spirit of the Russian people, and that it also portrays the futility of war.

Lohrenz, Gerhard (Review). *Nestor Makhno: The Life of an Anarchist,* by Victor Peters. Winnipeg: Echo Books, n.d. "Anarchist: Nestor Makhno." *MennMirror* 1 (Oct., 1971), 13. Recommends this readable and well-documented biography of the Russian "bandit" who plundered Mennonites and others during the 1917 revolution.

Lubosch, Lore. "The Mennonites in Brazil—They Did It Almost Without Help . . . ' " *MennMirror* 1 (Jan., 1972), 10-14. Dr. Boruszenko, economic historian in Curitiba, Brazil, gives a detailed report on the history of Brazil's Mennonites from the emigration from Russia in 1929 to the present, including such aspects as education, economics, and conscription.

Matsuo, Hilda. "Siberian Camps Kept This Family Scattered." *MennMirror* 8 (Nov., 1978), 7-8. An elderly couple relates their experiences of being separated and sent to different prison camps in Siberia and their eventual move to Canada in 1963.

Metzler, Edgar, "I Talked with a Man of God." *ChrLiv* 12 (Aug., 1965), 18-19, 29. Mennonite leader in Russia reports on the status of Mennonite churches there, including the stance on war and nonresistance.

Miller, Alvin J. "The Beginning of American Mennonite Relief Work." *MennLife* 17 (Apr., 1972), 71-75. Mennonites of America heard of the need in Russia and in 1921 made contacts with the Mennonites there and provided aid for the starving.

Miller, Orrie L. "Mennonites of the Chaco." *Fellowship* 2 (Apr., 1936), 8-9. Reviews the German Mennonite trek to Russia for exemption from military service, then describes their migration to and settlement in the Argentine Chaco following the 1918 revolution.

"No Alternative Service for CO's in Soviet Russia." *CanMenn* 4 (Apr. 27, 1956), 2. Russia does not wish to make martyrs out of CO's. Hence many are ignored, although some are imprisoned.

Neufeld, Dietrich. *A Russian Dance of Death: Revolution and Civil War in the Ukraine.* Trans. and ed. Al Reimer. Scottdale: Herald Press and Winnipeg: Hyperion Press, 1977. This moving and well-written account contains three parts. Part I, "Under the Black Flag of Anarchy," consists of Neufeld's diary entries Sept. 15, 1919-March 5, 1920, relating the agonizing experiences of the Khortitza Mennonites under the brutal and plundering attacks of Makhno's Anarchists. Part II, "The Ordeal of Zagradovka," relates in the third person the bitter fate of this colony (the author's home colony until age 20). Here Mennonites had allowed themselves to serve as volunteers for the White army and had taken up weapons for self-defense. Makhno's Nov. 29-30, 1919, vengeful massacre destroyed the village completely, with much murder and rape. Part

III, "Escape from the Maze: by Horse Through the Ukraine," recounts the author's dramatic escape from Russia disguised as a German prisoner of war.

Neufeld, P. L. "Army Officer Played Key Role in Moving Mennonites to Prairies." *MennMirror* 8 (Jan., 1979), 9-10. Describes the efforts Col. J. S. Dennis, Jr., made to bring Mennonites across from Russia to settle on the Canadian prairies following the Russian Revolution.

"Origin of Alternative Service." *RepConsS* 5 (Mar., 1947), 1, 6-8. Credits the origin of the concept of CPS as an alternative to war to 19th century Russian Mennonites and discusses the Russian Mennonite CO movement.

Paetkau, Peter (Review). *Far Above Rubies,* by Nettie Kroeker. "One Story of Emigration from Russia to Manitoba." *MennMirror* 6 (Mar., 1977), 6. Describes the contents of this book, which is a "biographical novel" of the life of Helena Wiens, a Mennonite Brethren woman who immigrated to Canada in the 1870's. The book fills a void in the annals of Mennonite Brethren literature.

Paetkau, Peter (Review). *Wer nimmt uns auf?,* by Olga Rempel. "Seven Scenes from Mennonite History." *MennMirror* 5, (Apr., 1976), 16. Review of a Mennonite Theatre production. Describes the scenes from this documentary which traces the story of the Mennonites of certain areas of the Ukraine, in 1937, through World War II, and to their destination in Canada. Concludes that the documentary is an excellent and useful one.

Pauls, Helen Rose. "We Were Boat People Too." Story told to H. R. Pauls. *MBH* 19 (June 27, 1980), 40. Russian Mennonite refugees from World War II relate the story of their escape.

Peters, Gerald (Review). *A Russian Dance of Death,* by Diedrich Neufeld, trans. Al Reimer. Winnipeg, 1978. Pp. 142. *MennLife* 34 (Dec., 1979), 27. Briefly summarizes and critiques Neufeld's book which describes some of the worst agonies and ordeals faced by Mennonites during the Russian Civil War caused by Ukrainian anarchists. Although the style is somewhat biased, Peters concludes that it is an effective and personal way of presenting history.

Peters, Gerald (Review). *No Strangers in Exile,* by Hans Harder, trans. Al Reimer. Winnipeg, 1979. Pp. 123. *MennLife* 34 (Dec., 1979), 27. Provides a literary critique of this book which is a fictional account of life in forced labor camps in northern Russia and the struggle to survive under impossible conditions. Finds it worthwhile in terms of its intent to preserve the fate and labors of the Russian Mennonites during the 1930's.

Preheim, Marion Keeney. "A Miracle Sent by God." *EV* 92 (June 10, 1979), 14. An MCC release relating the imprisonment and release of the Russian dissident Baptist prisoner Georgi Vins.

"Russian Convert Killed?" *MBH* 12 (Feb. 9, 1973), 2-3. Further speculation on the mysterious death of Sergei Kourdakov, the Russian defector who later became a Christian. A previous article (*MBH* 12 [Jan. 26, 1973], 19) reports on his death.

"Russian Convert Killed?" *MBH* 12 (Jan. 26, 1973), 19. Reports on the mysterious death and enthusiastic faith of Sergei Kourdakov, a young Russian naval officer who defected to Canada and had become an ardent Christian convert.

Reimer, Al. "A Face in the Mud." *MennMirror* 4 (Nov., 1974), 13, 14. Inspired by the photo of a young woman, the writer tells a story of a Mennonite girl fleeing with her family from Russia to Germany.

Reimer, Al. "A New Life Half Way Around the World." *MennMirror* 4 (Dec., 1974), 7-10. "A dramatized meditation on the journey of the first group of Russian Mennonites to Manitoba in 1874, presented at a special centennial ceremony held at the original landing site on July 31, 1974."

Reimer, Al (Review). *Days of Terror,* by Barbara Claassen Smucker. Clark Irwin, 1979. Pp. 152. *River of Glass,* by Wilfred Martens. Herald Press, 1980. Pp. 223. "Two Novels Tell Tale of Russian Experience That's Much Needed." *MennMirror* 9 (Feb., 1980), 19-20. While *Days of Terror* is the stronger of the two novels, both stories of Mennonite experiences in war-torn Russia offer, together with other English fictive accounts, "exciting new perspectives" on aspects of our religious heritage.

Reimer, Al (Review). *The Wanderers: The Saga of Three Women Who Survived,* by Ingrid Rimland. St. Louis: Concordia Publishing House, 1977. Pp. 323. "Novel Proves Mennonite Russian Experience." *MennMirror* 7 (Feb., 1978), 14, 15. Describes and critiques this fictional novel which portrays the lives of three Mennonite women who manage, under incredible hardships, to survive the Russian Revolution, the Stalin era, World War II, and who finally emigrate to Paraguay. Concludes that it is a very worthwhile novel in spite of some technical flaws which he details.

Reimer, E. E. (Al). "Nun danket alle Gott Sets Tone at Alma Ata Reunion." Part 3. *MennMirror* 1 (Dec., 1971), 16-20. Excerpts from the writer's diary, depicting his experiences and impressions during a tour through some of the former Mennonite settlements in Russia.

Reimer, E. E. (Al). "Wrecked Mennonite Church a Powerful Symbol of Ruined Hopes." Part 2. *MennMirror* 1 (Nov., 1971), 9-11. Mennonite tourists explore their past by visiting Molotschna and observing the changes that have taken place in what used to be a Mennonite colony.

Reimer, Jim (Review). *The Odyssey of the Bergen Family,* by Gerhard Lohrenz. Winnipeg: Gerhard Lohrenz, 1978. *Thy Kingdom Come: The Diary of Johann J. Nickel,* ed. John P. Nickel. Saskatoon: John P. Nickel, 1978. "Two Books Focus on Revolutionary Russia," *MennRep* 9 (Mar. 5, 1979), 8. These two books attempt to tell the Mennonite story of what happened in revolutionary and post-revolutionary Russia, depicting both the glory and the shame which the reviewer suggests is as much a part of the essence of "Mennonitism" as is "ideal Anabaptism."

Rempel, D. D. "The Wonderful Ways of God." *MennMirror* 3 (May 1974), 9-10. Excerpt from a book, describing some of the difficult but interesting experiences encountered in trying to collect money owing on the travel debt of the 1920 immigration of the Russian Mennonites.

Rempel, David G. "A Response to the 'Lost Fatherland' Review." *CanMenn* 16 (Aug. 13, 1968), 7. An interpretation of the Mennonite involvement in the Russian famine and revolution during and after World War I.

Rempel, Peter H. "Mennonites and State Service in the USSR, 1917-1939." Term paper for 19th and 20th Century Russia course, Apr., 1975. Pp. 25. CGCL.

Rempel, Peter H. "Nonresistance Without Privilege: The Dilemma of the Russian Mennonites, 1917-1927." Term paper for Modern Russian History course, Aug., 1976. Pp. 35. CGCL.

Rich, Ronald. Letter to the Editor. *Menn* 92 (Jan. 11, 1977), 29-30. Quotes Andrei Sakharov and two persecuted Russian Christians to call attention to the responsibility of peacemakers to speak for prisoners of conscience in the Soviet Union.

Sawatsky, Walter W. *Soviet Evangelicals Since World War II.* Scottdale and Kitchener: Herald Press, 1981. See especially Chapter 4, "Preaching and Peace."

Schloneger, Florence. *Sara's Trek.* Newton: Faith and Life Press, 1981. Pp. 105. Sara Friesen and Liese Rempel become separated from their families during the flight from Russia during World War II. In the year of separation spent in a German children's home and, upon being reunited with their families to live as refugees, the girls must not only cope with the logistics of survival amid the ravages of war but struggle to discover the meaning of these experiences for their lives and their faith. Fiction for ages 10-14.

Schroeder, William. "Bergthal's Pilgrimage to Manitoba." *MennMirror* 3 (Jan.-Feb., 1974), 9-16. An account of the migration of the entire Bergthal colony in South Russia to Manitoba, beginning with the situation in Russia in the 1870's which prompted the emigration.

Shank, J. Ward (Review). *A Russian Dance of Death*, by Dietrich Neufeld. Translated and edited by Al Reimer. Hyperion Press and Herald Press, 1977. Pp. 142. *ST* 46 (Nov., 1978), 22-24. Recommends this firsthand account of the violence and hardship experienced by Mennonite colonists during the Russian Revolution.

Smucker, Barbara Claassen. *Days of Terror*. Scottdale: Herald Press, 1979. Pp. 152. Young Peter Neufeld and his family are Mennonites in Russia during the internal and external turbulence experienced by the Russian nation during the World War I era. A strong theme of this moving juvenile novel is the theme of how people of faith, people who have practiced nonresistance for four hundred years, respond to acts of violence committed against their persons and their possessions in their own homes and barnyards. Both the Mennonite Self-Defense movement and the connections between the economic and cultural distance maintained by the Mennonites and the violence inflicted upon them are sensitively portrayed. For ages 8-12 and up.

Smucker, Barbara Claassen. *Henry's Red Sea*. Scottdale: Herald Press, 1955. Pp. 108. Eleven-year-old Henry Bergen and his family are Mennonite refugees waiting in Berlin after having fled post-World War II Russia. Through the eyes of this family, Claassen Smucker provides a moving account of refugee experiences, the work of MCC and the dangerous trip across the Russian zone of Germany to meet the SS Volendam at Bremerhaven. For children ages 8-12.

Smucker, Donovan E. "Russian Christianity and Communism." *Menn Comm* 7 (Sept., 1953), 10-11, 34; *Menn* 68 (May 17, 1953), 312-13. Briefly discusses the relationship of church and state in Russia before the communist government, and considers communism a judgment on Christianity.

Stoltzfus, Grant M. "Where Have All the Russian Brothers Gone?" *ChrLiv* 19 (May, 1972), 25-30.

Discussion of the book *Mennonity* by Russian W. F. Krestyaninov and his treatment of their attitudes toward war and nonresistance.

Suderman, Jacob. "The Origin of Mennonite State Service in Russia." *MQR* 17 (Jan., 1943), 23-46. A review of the history of Mennonite resistance to the draft in Russia, together with a translation of key documents in that history.

"The Recollections of A. P." *MennMirr* 8, Part 1, "A Look at a Way of Life that Ended Forever," (Feb., 1979), 9-10; Part 2, "Waiting to Leave as Chaos Follows Chaos," (Mar., 1979), 16-18. Excerpts from the journal of an anonymous Russian Mennonite. Includes accounts of experiences in alternative service during World War I and the Russian Revolution.

The Reporter, extracted. "Russian CO Reports Alternate Service Still Possible in USSR." *ChrLiv* 3 (Sept., 1956), 11. Review of the status of alternate service in USSR since late 1800s.

Toews, John B. "A Voice of Peace in Troubled Times." *MennLife* 27 (Sept., 1972), 93, 94. A report on the discovery of a Russian Mennonite newspaper of 1918, the *Volksfreund*, in Stuttgart, Germany, and the insights it provides on the Mennonite editor's attitude to communism.

Toews, John B. *Czars, Soviets, and Mennonites*. Newton: Faith and Life Press, 1982. Pp. 221. Analytical and interpretive study of the history of the Mennonites in Russia. While this examination of parochial Mennonitism in the wider socio-political context discusses the church's peace witness, including the church and state relationship, at various points, chapters which deal more explicitly with war/peace issues are: "The Russian Mennonites and World War I," 63-78; "Response to Anarchy," 79-94; "Communism and the Peace Witness," 95-106.

Toews, John B. *Lost Fatherland*. Scottdale: Herald Press, 1967. Pp. 262. The story of the Mennonite migration from Soviet Russia, 1921-27, to Canada with particular attention to the situation in Russia.

Toews, John B. "The Halbstadt Volost 1918-1922: A Case Study of the Mennonite Encounter with Early Bolshevism." *MQR* 48 (Oct., 1974), 489-514. Documents Mennonite experience with the violence and terror of the early days of Red Army and anarchist rule in southern Russia. The ensuing disillusionment among Mennonites regarding future life in the Soviet Union led by 1922 to applications for mass exodus.

Toews, John B. "The Origin and Activities of the Mennonite *Selbstschutz* in the Ukraine (1918-1919)." *MQR* 46 (Jan., 1972), 5-40. Describes the rise and consequences of Russian Mennonite self-defense units (Selbstschutz) armed against the violence of Bolshevik and bandit forces, their strategies, and ensuing revenge. Traces the rise of such units to the credal, separatist, and largely untested pacifism of the Mennonite settlers, and to the threat of violence against Mennonite women, more than the threat of property loss.

Toews, John B. "The Russian Mennonite Migrations of the 1870s and 1880s—Some Background Aspects." *ChrLead* 37 (Apr. 2, 1974), 4. A czarist decree intorduced universal military conscription in 1870s with no provisions for exempting the Mennonites. The question of their historic pacifism became a watershed in the history of the Russian Mennonites.

Toews, John B. "The Russian Mennonites and the Military Question (1921-1927)." N.d. Pp. 28. MLA/BeC.

Toews, Susanna. *Trek to Freedom: The Escape of Two Sisters from South Russia During World War II.* Winkler, Man.: Heritage Valley Publication, 1976. Pp. 43. MHL. Part 1 offers a vivid description of life as experienced by the Mennonites in Russia before and during World War II. Part 2 describes the flight from Russia as refugees caught in the confusion of the advances and retreats of both the Russian and German armies. A unifying theme is the maintenance of faith in the turbulance of war.

Unrau, Ed (Review). *The Mennonite Brotherhood in Russia,* by P. M. Friesen. Mennonite Brethren, 1978. "Russian Mennonites Created a Brotherhood in Name Only," *MennMirror* 8 (Nov., 1978), 9, 10. Provides a summary of this book, which is a detailed and critical summary of the Mennonites of Russia, and gives a brief statement of the author's view on military service and nonresistance. Describes the book as "overwhelming in its scope and shattering in its impact."

Unsigned. "Mennonite Youth Abroad." *CPS Bull Supp* 5 (May 16, 1946), 3, 8. Story of Russian Mennonite defector into Germany who, pressed into service with the German army, was captured and sent to American POW camp.

Urry, James. "Division and Emigration: The Reasons Were Complex." *MennRep* 4 (Nov. 25, 1974), 10-11. Examines reasons for migrations from southern Russia to North America, including the threat of military conscription. Observes that a possible draft threatened the colonists in two ways: violating pacifist principles, and removing young men from congregational authority.

"Vins Says Western Campaigns Held Dissidents."

*Menn* 94 (June 5, 1979), 392. An interview with Russian dissident, Vins, points out that peaceful demonstrations arising out of Christian principles are important.

Vogt, Esther L. Anonymous, as told to Esther L. Vogt, "To Face Another Dawn." *ChrLiv* 12 (Oct., 1965), 16-17. Young Russian Mennonite woman during World War II regards the advancing Nazi army as liberators.

Vogt, Roy. "A Russian Sequel to My East German Visits." Part 6. *MennMirror* 6 (Summer, 1977), 9-11. Describes writer's visit to Russia, where he presented a paper on the East German economy at the International Congress of Economic Historians conference in Leningrad.

Vogt, Roy. "Toews Explores Mennonite Pacifism." *MennMirror* 10 (Nov., 1980), 17, 19. Reports a series of lectures in which John B. Toews developed the thesis that the Russian Mennonites, while committed to "positive action in the midst of suffering," did not formulate a theology of nonresistance or pacifism.

Vogt, Roy (Review). *A Russian Dance of Death: Revolution and Civil War in the Ukraine,* by Dietrich Neufeld. Winnipeg: Hyperion Press, 1977. Pp. 138. "Mennonite's Journal Captures Gripping Detail of Russian Revolution." *MennMir* 7 (Dec., 1977), 15. Describes the history and summarizes the contents of this book, which is an annotated and edited journal of Dietrich Neufeld's experiences in the Russian Revolution and Civil War.

Vogt, Roy (Review). *Storm Tossed,* by Gerhard J. Lohrenz. Winnipeg: The Christian Press, 1976. Pp. 204. "Lohrenz Writes of His Life in Russia." *MennMirror* 5 (Apr., 1976), 12. Briefly summarizes this personal narrative in which Lohrenz describes the tragic impact of the Russian Revolution on some of the Russian Mennonites through the telling of his own life story. Concludes that it is a valuable contribution to our understanding of past and present events.

Vogt, Ruth (Review). *The Fateful Years 1913-1923,* by Gerhard Lohrenz. Winnipeg: Christian Press, 1977. Pp. 141. "Historical, But No Novel." *MennMirror* 7 (Mar., 1978), 12. Points out the shortcomings of this book, which is an account of the Mennonite encounter with the Machnovsky anarchists and the subsequent formation of the Selbstschutz. Criticizes the lack of character development and descriptive detail and laments the author's difficulty with the English language.

Wall, C. "My Concept of Biblical Nonresistance." *The Voice* 9, Part 1, (Mar.-Apr., 1960), 4; Part 2, (July-Aug., 1960), 5; Part 3, (Sept.-Oct., 1960),

11. A personal testimony to the belief in biblical nonresistance as it was tested in both Russia and the United States.

Wiebe, Rudy H. *The Blue Mountains of China.* Grand Rapids: Eerdmans, 1970. Pp. 227. Epic novel explores the Russian Mennonite experience from several points of view, times, and places. While the themes are also multiple, the examination of the intersection of faith and survival is a compelling one as the novel asks how and what love and traditions of nonresistance *become* in such crises. The chapter entitled "The Vietnam Call of Samuel U. Reimer" is especially focused on the questions of war and peace, although these themes appear in many of the other episodes as well.

Wiebe, Rudy (Review). *No Strangers in Exile,* by Hans Harder, trans. Al Reimer. Scottdale: Herald Press, 1979. Pp. 123. *MennMirror* 9 (Nov., 1979), 4. Reflects on the main theme of this book, which is the struggle of Mennonite people to survive under unbelievable conditions in a Russian logging camp, stripped of everything but their raw humanity. Highly recommends the book, but questions the necessity of the editing and expanding that Al Reimer has done to the original 1934 version.

Yoder, Elizabeth (Review). *The Wanderers,* by Ingrid Rimland. St. Louis: Concordia, 1977. *MennLife* 34 (Mar., 1979), 30. Gives a summary of the story which depicts three generations of Russian Mennonite women from the Civil War of 1917-20 to the immigration to Paraguay in 1947. Describes it as a fictional portrait of a people. Comments that Mennonite theology and the theme of pacifism are given very ambiguous treatment.

Yoder, Sanford Calvin. "Migratory Movements Among the Mennonites as a Result of the World War." MA in Religion thesis, Winona Lake School of Theology, Winona Lake, Ind., 1933. Pp. 112. MHL. Historical overview of the way the practice of nonresistance has been the source of tension between Mennonites and their governments, leading in most cases to Mennonite migration in search of lands more open to their peculiarities. Emphasizes the Mennonite migration from Russia to Canada, Mexico, and Latin America during World War I.

# 16
## War*

## A. General

"A Message to the Churches." *GH* 52 (May 19, 1959), 465; "A Message to All Christians," *CanMenn* 7 (May 8, 1959), 2. A statement issued by the 1959 Church Peace Mission Conference calling the church to unequivocally renounce war and take decisive action to break the circle of armament and counter-armament. The use of nuclear weapons, particularly, should be completely renounced.

"A Statement of Christian Conviction with Reference to War." *Menn* 54 (Dec. 12, 1939), 4-5. An eight-point statement of position against war drafted and adopted by the Defenseless Mennonite Conference and the GCMC.

"An Urgent Message to Our Churches from the 1967 Council of Boards." *Menn* 82 (Dec. 12, 1967), 753-54. A statement by the GCMC Council of Boards to their constituency, urging more vigorous witness against the war in Vietnam. Part of this witness would be war tax resistance.

Alderfer, Edwin. "The Giving of the Mennonite Church to Missions, Charities, and Relief." Term paper, Apr. 24, 1945. Pp. 18 (handwritten, includes charts). MHL.

Alderfer, Helen. "Family News and Trends." *ChrLiv* 12 (June, 1965), 41-42. Comments on American manufacture of toys emphasizing war and violence.

Alderfer, Helen. "Grief." *ChrLiv* 1 (Feb., 1954), 14. Poem. Mother grieves, not for the death of her son, but because he went to war.

Amstutz, D. "Dutch Mennonite Missions During the War." *MennLife* 3 (Jan., 1948), 16-19. How missions in Java fared during the German occupation of Holland and the Japanese occupation of Java.

Atmosuwito, S. "The Desert: for Peace or War?" *ChrLiv* 8 (July, 1961), 36-37. Options for use of desert lands include development for food production or the testing of nuclear weapons.

*See also War Tax Resistance, Topic 6B.

Augsburger, David W. "A Just War, or Just a War?" *GH* 63 (June 23, 1970), 564-65. Message broadcast on the Mennonite Hour explores commonly used justifications for wars and challenges listeners to follow Christ's way of love instead of war.

Augsburger, Myron S. "Christian Pacifism." *War: Four Christian Views*, ed. Robert G. Clouse. Downers Grove, Ill.: InterVarsity Press, 1981, 81-97. Pp. 210. Outlines the evangelical premises and perspectives leading to the conclusion that, while Christians may participate in government as long as they do not create a state church, they may not participate in war. The book is composed of articulations of four positions on war: nonresistance, Christian pacifism, the just war, and the crusade or preventive war. Then each of the presenters comments on the other three discussions. So, in addition to Augsburger's essay on Christian pacifism, he responds from that point of view to the other three views: to nonresistance, 58-63; to just war, 141-45; to the crusade, 175-80.

Augsburger, Myron S. "The Basis of Christian Opposition to War." *GH* 63, Part 1, (Nov. 17, 1970), 960-71; Part 2, (Nov. 24, 1970), 990-91; also in *EV* 84 (Sept. 25, 1971), 4. Christians oppose war on the basis of Christ's revelatory commands. The Christian's loyalty is not to the state but to the Kingdom of Christ, in which Christians arm themselves only with love.

Aukerman, Dale. "God's Rogue." *ChrLiv* 10 (Dec., 1963), 3-5. Reprinted from *Gospel Messenger*. Sir George MacLeod, former moderator of the Church of Scotland, speaks out eloquently against war and injustice.

Bainton, Roland H. "The Churches and War: Historic Attitudes Toward Christian Participation." *Social Action* 11 (Jan. 15, 1945), 5-71. Reviews the three positions of pacifism, just war, and crusade from the first through the twentieth centuries, including World War II. Examines especially 20th-century attitudes. Refers to Anabaptist views in the Reformation, as well as the treatment of conscientious objectors and Civilian Public Service.

Bainton, Roland H. "The Enduring Witness: The Mennonites." *MennLife* 9 (Apr., 1954), 83-90. Focus on the contribution of Menno Simons to the Anabaptist movement reprints some of his teaching on war.

Barbosa, Carlos. "War, from the Social, Moral, and Religious Point of View." *ChrMon* 24 (June, 1932), 190. War is evil and Christians should not go to war, nor permit it to continue.

Barrett, Lois [Janzen]. "War Investments and Mennonites." *Menn* 87 (June 6, 1972), 378, 379. Mennonites are aware of problems other denominations have with investing stocks in military firms and are examining situations where they, too, may be involved.

Basinger, Carlus. "Education as a Solution for Peace." *Menn* 53, Part 1, (July 12, 1938), 10-11; Part 2, July 19, 1938), 9. Peace education includes disassociation of war from patriotism, a sense of national humility, and a knowledge of the real causes and results of war

Batstone, Donald R. "My Testimony Against War." *ChrLiv* 4 (Apr., 1957), 23. Reprinted from *Reconciliation*. Christians should pray and work for peace, because God's will is nonresistant love.

Bauman, Clarence. "An Introduction to Theological Discussion on Christian Participation in War and Related Concerns." Paper presented to Puidoux Theological Conference: The Lordship of Christ over Church and State, n.d. Pp. 9. AMBS.

Bauman, Clarence. "The Meaning of the Cross: Christ and His Disciples," (Part 5). *CanMenn* 4 (Dec. 14, 1956), 2. War is sin, and since the Christian believer is called to forsake sin, he or she cannot participate in war.

Bauman, Clarence. "The Meaning of the Cross: The Heart of the Gospel," (Part 2). *CanMenn* 4 (Nov. 23, 1956), 2, 5. The cross, the heart of the gospel, exemplifies Christian suffering for the purpose of reconciliation. It points to the impossibility of Christian war.

Beachey, Duane. *Faith in a Nuclear Age.* Scottdale, PA: Herald Press, 1983. Pp. 128. Treats the issues of war and peace, issues such as the just war theory. The biblical bases for peacemaking, submission to authority, peace witness, etc., from the perspective of the contemporary nuclear situation.

Beachy, Alvin J. "You Shall Not Kill." *Menn* 94 (Aug. 7, 1979), 493. A study of the sixth commandment with emphasis on the sacredness of human life.

Beechy, Atlee. "God's People Belong in Vietnam." *YCC* 48 (Mar. 5, 1967), 4. If the church belongs where human need is, it belongs in Vietnam. God's people must seek to eliminate those things which cause prejudice, hate, fear, and violence.

Beechy, Atlee. "When Peace?" *Lancaster Independent Press* (Dec. 29, 1972), 1. Poem lamenting the destructiveness of war.

Beechy, Atlee (Review). *Vietnam and Armageddon: Peace, War, and the Christian Conscience,* by Robert F. Drinnan. Sheed & Ward, 1970. Pp. 210. *GH* 64 (Apr. 6, 1971), 314. A Catholic priest writing on the morality of war concludes that US and Soviet possession of fantastically destructive nuclear, biological, and chemical weapons renders meaningless the concept of just war.

Bender, Harold S. "Farming and Fighting: In the Midst of War—Thoughts for Nonresistants," (Part 1). *GH* 35 (Jan. 28, 1943), 938. The farmer is not morally taking part in the war.

Bender, Harold S. "Marriage in the Midst of War: In the Midst of War—Thoughts for Nonresistants," (Part 7). *GH* 35 (Mar. 18, 1943), 1090-91. Various reasons are given why wartime marriages should be given especially careful deliberation, and even discouraged.

Bender, Harold S. "Money and War: In the Midst of War—Thoughts for Nonresistants," (Part 4). *GH* 35 (Feb. 18, 1943), 1002-1003. The nonresistant Christian should use money sacrificially and try to keep it out of the war effort by refusing to purchase war bonds and by donating excess profits to relief and mission work.

Bender, Harold S. "Our Duties and Privileges as Loyal Christian Citizens." *GH* 34 (Jan. 15, 1942), 893, 900; *Menn* 57 (Jan. 27, 1942), 1. Eight guidelines for Mennonite action in wartime which speak to issues of participation in the war effort.

Bender, Harold S. "War Hysteria: In the Midst of War—Thoughts for Nonresistants," (Part 5). *GH* 35 (Mar. 4, 1943), 1050. The Christian should not participate in any "propaganda or activity that tends to promote ill-will."

Bender, Titus. "Peace, Freedom, and Religion." *CanMenn* 15 (Feb. 14, 1967), 5. Letter to the editor makes point about the absurdity of war and the validity of conscientious objection via a short satire involving a father-son conversation.

Bender, Urie A. "Swords into Plowshares." *ChrMon* 39 (June, 1947), 169-70. The senselessness of war, and its opposition to biblical teachings.

Berg, Ford. "Do Some Clergymen Ride to War?" *GH Supplement* 40 (Dec., 1947), 846-48. The clergy has been instrumental in perpetuating war as a means to certain ends.

Berg, Ford. "Protesting Against Protestants on the Christian's Right to Warfare." *GH* 41 (Dec. 21, 1948), 1207-1208, 1221; *Menn* 64 (Jan. 4, 1949), 8-10, 16. Sharp indictment of Fundamentalist thinking and warning against its infiltration into the Mennonite Church. Because of its confusion regarding the Old and New Covenants, Fundamentalism not only allows but advocates participation in war.

Bergen, Norman D. "The Thirty Years' War." Paper for Survey of Church History class, MBS, Chicago, Ill., May, 1953. Pp. 18. AMBS.

Best, James S. "Jerusalem's Unaccomplished Warfare." *Menn* 86 (Mar. 30, 1971), 210-13. Reflecting on the complexity of the problem that surrounds and penetrates the Arab-Israeli community at odds with one another.

Bieber, Doreen. "Nationalism vs. the Kingdom of God." *GH* 71 (Jan. 24, 1978), 68-69. Speech, which won second place in the C. Henry Smith Peace Oratorical Contest, suggests that nation-worship leads to war, and war is sin. Also in MHL.

Blosser, Don. "How Many Men Must Die?" *GH* 61 (July 9, 1968), 612-14. Sermon preached on the day of mourning for Sen. Robert Kennedy claims that American society shares responsibility for the slayings of Martin Luther King, Jr., and Robert Kennedy by promoting violent solutions to disputes. Calls for a more active Mennonite witness to peace, beginning at home by limiting the use of war toys.

Blosser, Don. "What Did Jesus Say About Killing People?" *GH* 63 (Feb. 10, 1970), 121-23. Discusses passages from the Gospels showing that Jesus forbade armed resistance and killing. Implications of his teaching for today include actively seeking to correct injustices, refusing to trust the protection of the army, and offering sacrificial service.

Bohn, Ernest J. "Our Peace Objectives." *Menn* 57 (Mar. 24, 1942), 1-4. Outlines the objectives of peace churches in a time of war and calls for clarity about our procedures when others are going off to war.

Brenneman, John M. "Christianity and War: A Sermon Setting Forth the Sufferings of Christians, the Origin and Import of the Christian Name, Christianity and War." 1863. Pp. 52. MHL.

Brennen, Joseph M. "The Theology of Anti-War Thought in the Music of Bob Dylan." Paper for War, Peace, and Revolution class, AMBS, Elkhart, Ind., May 1, 1969. Pp. 5. AMBS.

Brown, Dale W. (Review). *Karl Barth and the Problem of War,* by John H. Yoder. Nashville: Abingdon, 1970. Pp. 141. *MQR* 46 (Apr., 1972), 168-70. Calling the book a "superb study in theological ethics," the reviewer outlines Yoder's questions to Barth's views on war, calling for a future biblical and systematic work on pacifism by Yoder.

Brunk, George R., I. "War." *ST* 47 (July, 1979), 22-23. Reprinted from *ST* (Oct., 1931). Short poem on war and peace.

Burkhard, Samuel. "Dependence and Morality." Paper presented at the annual meeting of the Far Western Philosophy of Education Society, Arizona State University, Tempe, Arizona, Dec. 3-5, 1971. Pp. 10. MHL.

Burkholder, J. Richard. "All the War That's Fit to Print." In "Reading the Times," 5-10. Addresses given during Perspectives Weeks, Goshen College, Goshen, Ind., Sept. 10-24, 1976. Pp. 27. AMBS.

Burkholder, John D. "War a Delusion." *GH* 37 (Sept. 8, 1944), 454. To believe that the sword can bring peace is is a delusion. Only the spirit of love can transform an enemy and bring life instead of death.

Burkholder, Richard. "Young Christians Consider War." *YCC* 33 (Aug. 24, 1952), 268. Description of the Christian Youth Conference on War held Apr. 25-27, 1952, in Columbus, Ohio.

Buttrick, George A. "American Protestantism and European War." *Menn* 54 (Oct. 3, 1939), 4-5. A radio address given one week after the outbreak of World War II explains the duty of American Protestant churches in the face of war.

"Can Conscientious Objectors Work in War Industry?" *GH* 35 (June 25, 1942), 282. PPC asserts that it is inconsistent for a person who claims conscientious objector status to participate in a war industry.

"Change Hearts on War." *GH* 65 (Sept. 26, 1972), 787. Maintaining that Americans have moved away from the gospel on the question of peace, a Roman Catholic bishop seeks to awaken the people to what is really happening under the guise of patriotism.

"Christians Are More Warlike." *CanMenn* 14 (Jan. 11, 1966), 2. A survey of the Canadian Peace Research Institute reveals that Christians as a whole are more warlike in their attitudes than atheists and agnostics. The news report draws other conclusions from the survey.

"Christians Ought to Warn Against War Everywhere." *CanMenn* 4 (Nov. 23, 1956), 8. Report of Martin Niemoeller's Menno Simons lectures at Bethel College in which he criticizes the just war theory as difficult to implement and describes the theological basis of peace as "an agreement with God's will."

"Conference Message to Christian Churches." *Menn* 68 (June 16, 1953), 375. Representatives at the 1953 conference on "The Church, the Gospel, and War" issue a strong call for reconciliation and the way of love and peace to the churches and to the nations.

"Conference on Church and War." *Menn* 65 (May 30, 1950), 380-81. Describes the key messages and summarizes the "affirmation and appeal" issued by the conference. Appeals to the Christian church throughout the world to repent of warmaking and to live the gospel of peace.

Claassen, Marlan. "The Causes and Cure of War." Student peace essay presented as an entry in the Julius and Olga Stucky Mennonite Contributions Contest, Apr., 1954. Pp. 11. MLA/BeC.

Cousins, Norman. "Peace Without Panic." *ChrLiv* 8 (Jan., 1961), 19, 35. Reprinted from *Saturday Review*. Questions the view that the American economy needs the threat of war to stabilize it.

Cunningham, Jim. "Putting Waste in Its Proper Perspective." *MBH* 16 (May 13, 1977), 32. The problem of household waste compared with national waste of war, abortion, drunk driving.

"Declaration of Peace." *Menn* 53 (Nov. 29, 1938), 5. Official statement adopted by the Eighth Street Mennonite Church, Goshen, Indiana, in a time of increasing national militarism. "We cannot sanction war" nor lend our support to its implementation, states the document.

"Dehumanized War." *GH* 64 (Dec. 7, 1971), 1000. An account of the way electronic weapons have been substituted for direct human involvement in killing.

"Dwight L. Moody and War." *ChrMon* 43 (Feb., 1951), 43-44. Discusses the little-known fact of Moody's nonresistance to war.

"Dwight L. Moody and War." *GH* 43 (Apr. 18, 1950), 371, 382. Describes Dwight L. Moody as a nonresistant Christian and quotes extensively from his famous sermon on forgiveness, "Good News."

"Dwight L. Moody and War." *GH Supplement* 35 (Feb., 1943), 1022-23. Reprint of tract. The story of Moody's nonresistant faith.

Dahl, Edward H. "The War Crisis of the Canadian Mennonites, 1930-1945." Paper for the MB Pacific District, 1966. Pp. 21. MBBS.

Derstine, C. F., ed. "Abolition Without War: How Latin America Got Rid of Slavery." *ChrMon* 36 (June, 1944), 191-92. Reprinted from *Worldover Press*. Review of emancipation pressures and practices in Latin American history.

Derstine, C. F. "'If Goods Do Not Cross Frontiers, Armies Will!'" *ChrMon* 35 (Dec., 1943), 381. Advocates free flow of food across national borders to lessen hunger and the subsequent risk of war.

Derstine, C. F. "Impressions of the Nazi Regime and its Effect on the Churches." *ChrMon* 26 (Jan., 1934), 30-31. Support of U. S. Christians is due the church in Germany for its resistance to the race prejudice and nationalism of the Nazi state church.

Derstine, C. F. "Jehovah's Judgments on Jew Jingo Nations." *ChrMon* 31 (Jan., 1939), 30. God will eventually punish those nations taking a warlike attitude to Jews.

Derstine, C. F. "Missions or Munitions." *ChrMon* 38 (Nov., 1946), 350-51. The futility of war should be an inspiration to devote greater attention to missions.

Derstine, C. F. "Our Testimony of Peace Amid a War-torn World." *ChrMon* 24 (June, 1932), 187-88. The folly of war may be seen in the extent of losses suffered by Japan and China during their recent conflict.

Derstine, C. F. "The Christian and War" *ChrMon* 35 (June, 1943), 190-91. Reprinted message advocating the conscientious objector position by J. A. Huffman, the Dean of Religion, Taylor University and President of the Winona Lake School of Theology.

Derstine, C. F. "The Crying Need for the Return of the Prince of Peace." *ChrMon* 24 (Sept., 1932), 285. The threat of war in Europe and Asia is matched by the spread of the peace movement in American churches.

Derstine, C. F. "The Disturbed Waters of the Political and Economic Sea." *ChrMon* 25 (Nov., 1933), 350-51. None of the three prevailing social systems—capitalism, socialism, communism—will attain social justice.

Derstine, C. F. "The Italo-Ethiopian Land Grab." *ChrMon* 27 (Nov., 1935), 350-51. Italy's invasion of Ethiopia is a modern case of coveting land.

Derstine, C. F. "The New Army—The New War for the Old War." *ChrMon* 28 (Oct., 1936), 319-20. Nonresistance has both a negative side, opposing war, and a positive side, overcoming evil with good.

Derstine, C. F. "The Spanish Volcano." *ChrMon* 28 (Nov., 1936), 350-51. Briefly examines the causes of the Spanish civil war.

Derstine, C. F. "The State—Absolute, Final, Supreme!" *ChrMon* 30 (Sept., 1938), 290. The great threat of fascism is its claim to total loyalty and obedience.

Derstine, C. F. "The United States and Japan, and the 'Scrap Iron'." *ChrMon* 34 (Feb., 1942), 61-62. Modernism as practiced in Germany and greed as seen in US arms trades with Japan helped precipitate the world war, and rejection of both will help the US get out of the war.

Derstine, C. F. "The Universal Inquiry into the Legitimacy of War." *ChrMon* 26 (July, 1934), 221-22. Mennonites, with a history of peace witness, have a contribution to make to present popular opinion which is becoming critical of war.

Derstine, C. F. "The War Question and the Coming Disarmament Conference." *ChrMon* 24 (Jan., 1932), 30. World disarmament is necessary because war wastes lives and economic resources, but the only absolute solution is the gospel.

Derstine, C. F. "Trotsky Finale—'This Time They Succeded.' " *ChrMon* 32 (Oct., 1940), 319. Review of the power struggles in the Soviet Union shows that "those who live by the sword will die by the sword."

Derstine, C. F. "Uncle Sam Building a War Machine." *ChrMon* 23 (July, 1931), 221-22. Documents public anti-war sentiment and contrasts it with the recent Supreme Court decision to deny citizenship to two conscientious objectors.

Derstine, C. F. "War, Pestilence, Famine, and Depression, the Scourges of God on a Sinful and Immoral World." *ChrMon* 23 (Mar., 1931), 93, 95. These social evils are acts of God to bring people to repentance.

Derstine, C. F. "World Trouble Spots." *ChrMon* 38 (Feb., 1946), 62. Lists six causes of war and observes that the only true solution to war is a change of heart throughout the world.

Derstine, C. F. "War! War! War!" *ChrMon* 32 (Dec., 1940), 381. God delegates the use of force to the state, while the church operates by love, so the two must be completely separate for the Christian.

Derstine, C. F. "What the Soldier Said." *ChrMon* 28 (Feb., 1936), 62-63. In the face of war's destructiveness, peaceloving Christians should take a firm stand against participating in war.

Derstine, C. F. "'What War Has Done to Shanghai to Awaken the Sleeping Giant.' " *ChrMon* 30 (May, 1938), 158-60. Changes in China brought about by the war with Japan.

Derstine, C. F. "Will the 'Son of Heaven' Keep War's Hell from Flaming the World?" *ChrMon* 29 (Nov., 1937), 350-51. Japan's aggression toward China is based on Japanese belief in divine destiny.

Drescher, John M. "Disturbing the War." *GH* 62 (Mar. 25, 1969), 269. The church is divided between those who believe it ought to be the conscience of the nation and those who believe it has nothing to say to the government.

Drescher, John M. "Kill Toys Teach the 'Game' of Killing." *MBH* 7 (Nov. 29, 1968), 4-5; *Menn* 83 (Dec. 3, 1968), 746-47. Since replicas of the "machines of violence" contradict the spirit of Jesus, Christians should boycott and protest vigorously against "war toys."

Drescher, John M. "The Game of Killing." *ChrLiv* 15 (Dec., 1968), 9-10. Urges Christians to protest the manufacture and sale of war toys.

Drescher, John M. *Why I Am a Conscientious Objector.* Scottdale: Herald Press, 1982. Pp. 73. Introductory chapter provides brief overview of the different kinds of pacifism, different approaches used to sanction war and a comparison of the just war theory with the principles of nonresistance. Subsequent chapters provide brief discussions of such pacifist rationale as the example of Christ, the global nature of the Gospel, an understanding of the church as universal, biblical limitation of governmental authority, and the church's nonresistant tradition.

Driedger, Leo. "Fallout Shelters: A Discussion." Newton: Board of Christian Service, 1962. Pp. [27]. MHL. Presents arguments for and against shelters. Includes responses which a number of Mennonite churches in Kansas made to the government when Civil Defense officers investigated, sometimes without permission, their buildings to determine their utility as shelters. These responses deal directly with the issue of whether preparing for war is, to some extent, participation in warfare.

Driedger, Leo, *et. al.* "War and Rumors of War." *Menn* 78 (Nov. 5, 1963), 664-66. A symposium on war and its meaning for peacemakers. Subjects include children and the bomb, fallout shelters, disarmament, peace witness in service and evangelism, and alternatives to violence.

Dueck, Abe (Review). *No King But Caesar? A Catholic Lawyer Looks at Christian Violence,* by William R. Durland. Scottdale: Herald Press, 1975. Pp. 182. *MBH* 15 (Nov. 12, 1976), 34-35. Recommends this book for its biblical exegesis on violence, its examination of the just war theory, and its review of the types of violence found in contemporary movements.

Dueck, Allan. "Vision and Reality." *Direction* 8 (Oct., 1979), 21-27. Compares the Mennonite Brethren Confession of Faith (1975) to the Kauffman-Harder survey in *Anabaptists Four Centuries Later* (Scottdale: Herald Press, 1975) and concludes that while MBs agree on doctrinal beliefs, they disagree on moral practices such as participation in war, sensitivity to social injustices, etc.

Durnbaugh, Donald F. "Historic Peace Churches: Who Are They and What Do They Do?" *MennRep* 9 (Oct. 29, 1979), 5. The three historic peace churches—the Society of Friends, the Mennonites, and the Church of the Brethren—have held to a consistent peace position and a persistent willingness to reach out to those suffering from acts of war, social oppression, or natural catastrophe.

Durnbaugh, Donald F., ed. *On Earth Peace: Discussions on War/Peace Issues Between Friends, Mennonites, Brethren, and European Churches, 1935-1975.* Elgin, Ill.: Brethren Press, 1978. Pp. 412. A collection of documents emphasizing the "Puidoux" Conferences held in Europe on the theme of "The Lordship of Christ Over Church and State" and the contributions made by the historic peace churches to the study processes sponsored by the WCC on the issues of peace and justice. Essays focused on or by Mennonites include: "Principles of Christian Peace and Patriotism—Historic Peace Churches," 30-32; "War Is Contrary to the Will of God—HPC and FOR," 46-72; "God Establishes Both Justice and Peace," (Paul Peachey and members of the Continuation Committee, 1955 and 1958), 108-21; "The Theological Basis of the Christian Witness to the State," John H. Yoder, 136-43; "Discipleship as Witness to the Unity in Christ as Seen by the Dissenters," Paul Peachey, 153-60; "On Divine and Human Justice," John H. Yoder, 197-210; "The Sixth Commandment: Its Significance for the Christian as Citizen and for the Statesman," Warren F. Groff, 211-22; "Church and State According to a Free Church Tradition," John H. Yoder, 279-88; "Response to the Cardiff Report by Brethren, Friends, Mennonites," 353-64; "Jesus and Power," John H. Yoder, 365-72; "Epilogue: The Way Ahead," John H. Yoder, 390-93.

Dyck, A. A. "War Will Always Be With Us." *CanMenn* 18 (Jan. 16, 1970), 5. Participation in the March Against Death (Washington) or in other demonstrations is questioned. Rather than working towards peace in far-off places one must seek to help those who lack peace in one's own neighborhood.

Dyck, Arthur J. *On Human Care: An Introduction to Ethics.* Nashville, Tenn.: Abingdon, 1977. Pp. 189. Considers the stringency of the obligation not to kill in the context of a general survey of the philosophical questions of ethics.

Dymond. "The Opinions of the Primitive Christians on the Lawfulness of War." *GH* 44 (Mar. 20, 1951), 274-75, 285. Reprinted from *Herald of Truth* (Dec., 1866). Christ, the disciples, and the first Christians disavowed any part in the military. Quotations from early church sources show numerous incidences of this stand.

Eastway, JoAnn. "Reflections." *Forum* (Nov., 1971), 4. War is not instinctive or inevitable, but begins in our minds and is part of our socialization. Individual, personal involvement in the needs of others is the key to building a defense of peace.

Eby, Ezra E. "The Eighteenth Century Story." *MHB* 35 (Apr., 1974), 2-4. Reprinted excerpts from an 1895 document describe North American Mennonite life from colonial times through the 1820s. Includes section on Mennonites and the War of 1812.

Eby, Omar. "A Time to Build." *GH* 63 (Feb. 3, 1970), 105. Reviews the events leading to the Nigeria/Biafra war and describes Mennonite and Quaker relief activities during the war.

Eichelberger, Roger A. "Christian Ethics and War." Student paper for Christians and World Peace Seminar, May 15, 1964. Pp. 27. MLA/BeC.

Eitzen, Ruth. "Can I Have a Part in Change?" *Lifework* 5 (1981), 14. Describes Mennonite protest against slavery which may be seen as "forerunner" of the later abolition movement, and suggests that war is another issue in which small protests could bring overarching change.

Engle, T. L. "Attitudes Toward War as Expressed by Amish and Non-Amish Children: A Follow-Up Study." *The Elementary School Journal* 53 (Feb., 1953), 345-51. Follow-up study indicates that the differences in the attitude toward war between Amish and non-Amish children are less marked than they were eight and a half years earlier.

Entz, Loren. "Jihad." Student paper, AMBS, Elkhart, Ind., n.d. Pp. 44. AMBS.

Entz, Margaret. "Free to Buy: American World War I Financing and the Mennonite Response."

Social Science Seminar paper, May 24, 1975. Pp. 31. MLA/BeC.

Epp, Frank H. "A Convict, a CO, and a Soldier." *CanMenn* 3 (Mar. 18, 1955), 2. A newspaper clipping illustrates an interesting paradox in our society, where killing is rewarded in some situations (war) and punished in others (murder), while CO's are imprisoned for refusing to kill!

Epp, Frank H. *A Strategy for Peace: Reflections of a Christian Pacifist.* Grand Rapids: Wm. B. Eerdmans, 1973. Pp. 128. Eleven essays on topics related to war and peace, such as pacifism, militarism, nationalism, social order. Includes essays previously published in other collections, for example: "The Unilateral Disarmament of the Church" (*Peacemakers in a Broken World,* 1969); "American Causes of World War III" (*The Star-Spangled Beaver,* ed. Redekop, 1971); "Evangelism and Peace" (*Probe,* ed. Fairfield, 1972).

Epp, Frank H. "American Causes of World War III." *The Star-Spangled Beaver.* Ed. John H. Redekop. Toronto: Peter Martin Assoc. Ltd., 1971, 118-33. While causes of World War III would be complex and widespread, American causes include a shift toward economic greed and international profiteering; dependence on an oversized military machine; and belief in a national religion that paints opponents as anti-Christs.

Epp, Frank H. "CO's or PM's." *CanMenn* 5 (Dec. 13, 1957), 2. "We are called to actively engage in peacemaking, to act as shock absorbers to the evil of the world, to help relieve the pressures which generate war."

Epp, Frank H. "In the Eleventh Hour of Civilization." *CanMenn* 6 (Aug. 15, 1958), 2, 4. War is terrible and absurd! Yet all of us are guilty of promoting war in some way. We must confess our corporate guilt and become guardians of peace.

Epp, Frank H. "War Over the Suez." *CanMenn* 4 (Sept. 21, 1956), 2. A commendation to US and Canadian statespersons who have announced that they will not cooperate with "shooting our way through the Suez."

Epp, Frank H. "'Wars and Rumors of Wars'." *CanMenn* 14 (Feb. 8, 1966), 5. One of a series of five letters written by Frank Epp to Henry Becker in response to Becker's denunciation of the *CanMenn* in the Jan. 4 issue. Epp argues that to justify participation in war because Jesus said there would always be "wars and rumors of wars" is to limit the Lordship of Christ to the church.

Epp, Frank H. "We Welcomed Armed Intervention." *CanMenn* 14 (Jan. 25, 1966), 5. Epp deplores the dualistic ethic of the Mennonites expressed in the belief that armies and wars are good for others but not for Mennonites who ought to refrain from participation.

Epp, Frank H. "When War Clouds Hang Low." *CanMenn* 3 (Jan. 28, 1955), 2. In times of tense international situations Christians must remember that God is still sovereign and they must remain true to their confession and calling.

Epp, Frank H. (Editorial). "No War in the World." *CanMenn* 2 (July 23, 1954), 2. Urges prayer for world leaders that they may not once again resort to violent solutions to the problems of international relationships.

Epp, Theodore H. "The Attitude of the Early Christians Toward War." *GH* 30 (Oct. 21, 1937), 649-50. Historical survey of the early church concludes that the church held to the nonresistance principle only to drift away from it after several centuries.

Erb, Paul. "Militarism as Social Service." *GH* 39 (July 16, 1946), 339. The evangelical fundamentalists are inconsistant when they so greatly emphasize participation in war as a Christian form of service to the world.

Erb, Paul. "Preparing for the Next War." *GH* 39 (June 18, 1946), 243. Mennonites must preach and teach clearly the principles of nonresistance to the young people. Such peace teaching is the best possible preparation for a future war.

Erb, Paul. "The Bloodiest Century in History." *GH* 43 (Oct. 10, 1950), 995. Christians must humbly confess to the part they have played in the wars of the twentieth century and pray for the opportunity to carry relief into Korea as the war there comes to an end.

Erb, Paul. "The War Is Not Over." *GH* 38 (Aug. 31, 1945), 411. The war seems to be over but the evils which it was to cure still exist. The Atomic bomb, enormous national debts, and continued conscription are part of the legacy of this war.

"Forces That Make for War." *Menn* 53 (Oct. 25, 1938), 10-11. A Young People's program suggested by the GCMC. Causes of war need to be dealt with if war is to cease. Some of these causes are economic rivalry, secret diplomacy, and large military establishments.

Failing, George E. "Could It Happen Before 1984?" *EV* 91 (Nov. 10, 1978), 15. Reflecting on George Orwell's book, *1984,* the writer suggests the US has chosen the alternative of war over peace probably on the presumption that no viable economy can survive without the sale of arms.

Fast, Gerhard. "Mennonites of the Ukraine Under Stalin and Hitler." *MennLife* 2 (Apr., 1947), 18-21, 44. Statistics concerning forced exiles and life during the Revolution and war years, by a native of one of the Mennonite settlements.

Fransen, Harold. "Cold War Thaw and Mennonite Response." *Menn* 95 (Apr. 1, 1980), 225. Interprets the Soviet invasion of Afghanistan as an attempt to inhibit the rise of a nationalist Islamic state, and calls on Mennonites to take a public peace stance during present cold war politics.

Franz, Arthur R. "What Should My Attitude as a Christian Be Toward War?" *MCE* 1 (Aug. 21, 1934), 2-4. The Mennonite church is not now taking an active part in the fight against war and militarism. Those who do not raise a voice of protest against the evils of war are guilty of these evils.

Franz, Delton. "Against the Wall in Latin America." *GH* 67 (Nov. 5, 1974), 846-47; "Washington Report: Latin America: A Look at North/South Relations." *MennRep* 4 (Sept. 30, 1974), 7. Multinational corporations in Latin America promote the increasing gap between rich and poor, while US military and torture procedures oppress those who work for change.

Franz, Delton. "From 1776 to 1976—the Changing Style of Oppression." *MBH* 15 (July 9, 1976), 14-15; *MennRep* 6 (June 28, 1976), 7. US economic policy contributes to the invisible violence of starvation, torture, and exploitation, while seeking to avoid the visible violence of war and revolution.

Franz, Delton, ed. "The Ninety-first Congress: End of an Era, a New One Beginning." *MCC PS Wash. Memo* 2 (Jan., 1970), 1-3. Evaluation of the 91st Congress shows it moved to limit defense spending and the power of the executive branch to wage war.

Franz, Delton, ed. "The Roots of War." *MCC PS Wash. Memo* 4 (July-Aug., 1972), 1-2. Comment on Richard Barnet's *Roots of War.*

Franz, Delton. "Washington Report: of Swords and Plowshares." *MennRep* 4 (Apr. 1, 1974), 7. American billions for "swords" compared with pennies for "plowshares"—peacemaking activities such as forestalling world famine—comes under the Isaiah prophecy of woe to those who trust in weapons of war.

Franz, Edward W. "Seeking the Mind of Christ in Our Attitude Toward War." *Menn* 51, Part 1, (May 26, 1936), 4-5; Part 2, (June 2, 1936), 2-6. Our tradition teaches that we must not only be of the mind of Christ in our opposition to war, but that we must apply this principle practically. It is not patriotism but selfishness which leads one into war. When one studies wars it is seen that they are foolish and do not accomplish their goals. Mennonites have numerous opportunities to work with others to bring peace.

Franz, Edward W. "The Fallacy of War Arguments." *MCE* 2 (May 7, 1935), 14. Criticizes the usual arguments used to defend war. Wars are the result of selfish desires and do not really settle any problem.

Franz, Marian Claassen. "National Turmoil, Our Children, Government." *Builder* 24 (May, 1974), 10-14. Reflects on ways adults can help children understand the world's problems, including war, from an appropriately global, international Christian perspective.

Fretz, Clarence Y. "The Christian Hope Today." *ST* 26 (3rd Qtr., 1958), 4. The demoralizing effects of war also take their toll on the morals of church members, alarmed about the shifting ethical testimony of the church.

Frey, Philemon L. "Lessons from the World War: for Conscientious Objectors." *The Eastern Mennonite School Journal* 18 (Apr., 1940), 42-45. Twelve "lessons"—all the way from "In time of war it is best to keep our eyes and ears open and our mouths shut" to "It is best to stay out of politics" to "Nonresistance should be practiced in times of peace as well as in time of war," etc.

Friesen, Isaac I. "What Will the War Teach Us?" *Menn* 60 (Sept. 11, 1945), 1-2. A series of lessons to be learned from the war. War is irreconcilable with the spirit and teaching of Jesus and therefore sinful; repentance is imperative.

Friesen, Louise. "God and War." Student paper for Our Christian Heritage, Feb., 1959. Pp. 15. MLA/BeC.

Friesen, Richard. "War Protest in Popular Music." Paper for War, Peace, and Revolution class, AMBS, Elkhart, Ind., n.d. Pp. 3. AMBS.

Friesen, Rudy. "CMBC Prof Calls for Creative Ways of Solving Human Conflict." *CanMenn* 18 (Feb. 27, 1970), 1, 2. During a one-day teach-in on "War and Peace" at the Univ. of Saskatchewan, David Schroeder outlines reasons why war is unrealistic as a problem-solving institution to an audience that challenges his point of view.

Fundenburg, Harry C. "Military Training Unchristian." *GH* 28 (Nov. 14, 1935), 706-707. Military training, war, and killing of any sort are not sanctioned by the New Testament. The

Church of the Brethren has since its beginning opposed war and maintained the principle of nonrèsistance.

Funk, Jacob. *War Versus Peace: A Short Treatise on War, Its Causes, Horrors, and Cost and Peace, Its History and Means of Advancement.* Elgin, Ill.: Brethren Publishing House, 1910. Pp. 175. Argues for the development of a universal court of arbitration, contending that the existing difficulties in such a proposition are outweighed by the potential savings, in money and morals, which will result.

Funk, John F. *Warfare. Its Evils Our Duty. Addressed to the Mennonite Churches Throughout the United States, and All Others Who Sincerely Seek and Love the Truth.* Chicago: By the Author, 1863. Pp. 16. MHL. Despite the pressures of society and the lure of military glory, let us remain faithful to the example of Jesus, who lived the nonresistant life in every way.

Gerber, Samuel (Review). *The Christian Attitude Toward War* by L. Boettner, for the War, Peace, and Revolution class, AMBS, Elkhart, Ind., n.d. Pp. 3. AMBS.

Gingerich, Melvin. "Four Great Political and Social Revolutions." *GH* 62 (Mar. 18, 1969), 246-47. Discusses the American, French, Russian, and Chinese revolutions as situations where the powerful ruling class refused to address the wrongs suffered by the masses, so that bloody revolution ensued. Author considers it a tragedy that the church has so often identified with the conservative privileged few against the cause of injustice.

Gingerich, Melvin. "Honesty; Christian Youth and the State." *YCC* 22, Part 13, (Aug. 17, 1941), 673. To be Christian is to be genuinely truthful. During war especially, there are many stories which are not true about which the Christian has an obligation to seek the truth.

Gingerich, Melvin. "Prayer in War Time; Christian Youth and the State." *YCC* 23, Part 22, (May 31, 1942), 172. Biblical principles for prayer that apply to both times of war and times of peace.

Gingerich, Melvin. "The Church of the Middle Ages; Christian Youth and the State." *YCC* 23, Part 25, (Nov. 1, 1942), 346. The church must remain separate from the world. Thus the church not only condemns war but the set of world conditions that make for war.

Gingerich, Melvin. "The Defense of Freedom; Christian Youth and the State." *YCC* 23, Part 21, (May 3, 1942), 138. War is a great enemy of freedom. Christ's approach to true freedom laid emphasis on the development of individual character.

Gingerich, Melvin. "The Life of Simplicity; Christian Youth and the State." *YCC* 23, Part 17, (Jan. 11, 1942), 10. Quality of life in a nation goes down during a war economy. There is a relationship between simple living and response to CPS.

Gingerich, Melvin. "War and Children; Christian Youth and the State." *YCC* 25, Part 33, (Apr. 30, 1944), 139. A secure home is essential to the development of "healthy children." War destroys the secure atmosphere of home life and also implants hatred for other peoples in the minds of children.

Gleysteen, Jan. "Käthe Kollwitz—An Artist's Protest to War." *YCC* 48 (July 9, 1967), 5. The story of Kollwitz, a famous woman artist, whose art reflects her social conscience and pacifist ideology.

Good, I. Merle. "Like War Is This Big Exciting Game . . ." *With* 3 (Sept., 1970), 34. Review of several war films.

Graham, Henry H. "The Tragedy of Hatred." *GH* 54 (Aug. 15, 1961), 713-14. Describes hatred as a tragedy so terrible it can lead to murder, either on a personal or national scale. Gives examples of the relationship between hatred and fear, and of how hatred is overcome.

Gross, Leonard; Hill, J. W.; and Steiner, M. S. "Is War Justifiable?" *MHB* 37 (Jan., 1976), 2-6. Steiner takes issue with the expansionist viewpoint of Hill's article, responding in a lengthy essay recommending nonresistance. Gross introduces the dialogue and comments on it.

Grove, Carolyn. "Congressional Opposition to the Mexican War." Paper presented to the Social Science Seminar, Goshen College, Goshen, Ind., n.d. Pp. 38. MHL.

Grubb, S. M. "When War Threatens." *Menn* 51 (Jan. 21, 1936), 1-2. A growing peace movement and peace consciousness among churches and in government quarters is encouraging. One wonders, however, how many will resist if the war spirit returns.

Guenther, Allen R. "God's Word to His Unjust People." *MBH* 14 (Feb.. 7, 1975), 6-7. "God's Word to Unjust Societies." *MBH* 14 (Jan. 24, 1975), 8,·29. "The Meaning of Justice." *MBH* 14 (Feb. 21, 1975), 6-7. Book study in Amos focuses on God's judgment through war of the injustice practiced by Israel and Judah; God's judgment upon the nations practicing injustice; justice and righteousness in their relationship to the oppressed.

"Historic Peace Churches Meet for Conference." *CanMenn* 1 (Oct. 30, 1953), 1, 3, 7. J. A. Toews presented two messages on discipleship and non-participation in war.

Hackman, Walton. "A Conscientious Objector Becomes a Military Chaplain—for a Day." *GH* 64 (Jan. 5, 1971), 18-19. Peace Section representative describes a day spent at Fitzsimmons Army Base: his discussions with army chaplains on the issue of just war, and his conversations with injured soldiers just returned from Vietnam.

Halteman, Jim. Letter to the Editor. *ChrLiv* 20 (Oct., 1973), 28-29. Maintains that distribution of income is as critical a problem to economic decision-making as is inflation caused by war expenditures.

Harder, Gary. "A Preliminary Summary Report on the Positions of Four Mennonite Scholars on the Question of War in the Old Testament." Paper for War, Peace, and Revolution class, AMBS, Elkhart, Ind., Apr. 10, 1969. Pp. 4. AMBS.

Harder, Geraldine, "Time Is Running Out." *ChrLiv* 16 (Nov., 1969), 26-27. Being present to those hurt by war and teaching the way of peace are two important tasks.

Harshbarger, Emmett L. "A Mennonite Program for Peace." *Menn* 51 (Apr. 7, 1936), 2-5. Mennonites must take a more active stand against war. Instead of merely professing love and peace they must work to destroy the war system.

Hartzler, Levi C. "For Whom the Bell Tolls." *ChrMon* 40 (Apr., 1948), 116-17. Argues against war because of the sacredness of human life and the futility of fighting evil with evil.

Hartzler, R. L. "A World in Need of Peace." *Menn* 83 (Nov. 26, 1968), 731. The glory of war has been stripped away; we need a world-wide youth movement for peace, to complete the abolition of war.

Hartzler, Robert. "A Parable of Unbrotherhood." *GH* 64 (Oct. 9, 1971), 862-64. Allegorizing the "white brother" and the "yellow brother" as Cain and Abel, the author makes a devastating comment on the effects of the war in Southeast Asia.

Helmuth, David. "Why (Some) Christians Fight for Their Country." *GH* 71 (July 4, 1978), 522-24. Discusses reasons Christians go to war, such as the US is a Christian nation, and answers with his personal reasons for not participating in war.

Hershberger, Guy F. *Can Christians Fight? Essays on Peace and War.* Scottdale, Pa.: Mennonite Publishing House, 1940. Pp. 180. Compilation of essays originally written for the readers of *Youth's Christian Companion.* Broad range of topics on the issues of war and peace such as the biblical bases of nonresistance, wars in American history, peace and war in Mennonite history, Mennonite peace work and nonresistance in wartime.

Hershberger, Guy F. "Current Antiwar Sentiment." *GH* 61 (Jan. 23, 1968), 86. [No. 21] Mennonites should support the anti-war sentiment but recognize that not all of the opposition is being expressed in a Christian manner. Cites England as an example of successful social criticism which has resulted in greater tolerance and freedom.

Hershberger, Guy F. "How Protest?" *GH* 61 (Feb. 6, 1968), 127. [No. 23] Author follows Senator Fulbright in asserting that because the American public is essentially a conservative one—shocked when freedom of speech is truly exercised—effective protest is calm and orderly protest.

Hershberger, Guy F. "How the American Churches Made Themselves Believe That the World War Was a Holy War." *YCC* 18 (Apr. 4, 1937), 528. Many preachers were misled into thinking that World War I was a "holy war." They failed because they were not rooted in the nonresistant teachings of the Bible.

Hershberger, Guy F. "Mennonites and Materialism." *GH* 37 (1945), 828-29. Mennonites must be on guard against materialism, which is one of the chief causes of war.

Hershberger, Guy F. "One War Leads to Another." *YCC* 20 (Nov. 26, 1939), 800. Reviews history to show that one war does lead to another. War is futile. Christians cannot make their contributions to the cause of peace by fighting in a war to destroy Hitlerism.

Hershberger, Guy F. "The Christian in a World at War." *YCC* 22, Part 1, (Jan. 19, 1941), 434; Part 2, (Jan. 26, 1941), 445. An address delivered on Armistice Day, 1940, at Goshen College, Goshen, Ind. To resist the blast of war one must have a clear conception of the requirements of God's moral law and one must maintain a way of life and a program of work which is in conformity to that law.

Hershberger, Guy F. "The Current Upsurge of War Objection." *GH* 61 (Jan. 16, 1968), 57. [No. 20] Writer observes that the growth of anti-war sentiment during wartime is unusual, and that the burgeoning peace movement protesting activities in Vietnam is disturbing to government officials.

Hershberger, Guy F. "The Mennonite Conference

on Peace and War." *Goshen College Record* 36 (Mar., 1935), 1. This conference on war and peace, held at Goshen, Ind., Feb. 15-17, 1935, was the first of its kind sponsored by the Mennonite Church in America in its entire 400-year-old history.

Hershberger, Guy F. "The Mennonite General Conference States Its Position on Peace and War." *YCC* 19 (Mar. 13, 1938), 87. Excerpts from the Mennonite General Conference statement on war and peace drawn together in Oregon.

Hershberger, Guy F. "War and the New Morality." *The Reformed Journal* 18 (Feb., 1968), 21-24. Response to an article "War and the New Morality" by Dewey J. Hoitenga, Jr., who writes that the Christian support of war is a prime illustration of the "new morality."

Hershberger, Guy F. "War Is a Maker of Hatred and Lies." *YCC* 18 (May 2, 1937), 560. War is also a violator of the ninth commandment about bearing false witness. Propaganda is used to stir up people's hatred of the other side.

Hershberger, Guy F. *War, Peace, and Nonresistance.* Scottdale: Herald Press, 1944. Pp. 375. For many years the standard work in the field. God has one eternal plan for human conduct: love for God and neighbor. This law forbids one to compel another. One rather meets force with nonresistance. In the Old Testament covenant with Israel, God made a concession to the hardness of human hearts by permitting warfare. In the New Testament, Jesus initiates a new covenant in which believers receive a new heart, enabling them to keep God's fundamental moral law. By going to the cross rather than retaliating, Jesus indeed modeled nonresistance perfectly. The early church at first followed Jesus' nonresistant example but gradually applied it less strictly. After Constantine's conversion, the church abandoned nonresistance as an ideal for all Christians. Small Christian sects however retained it, of whom the Mennonites provide a history extending from the sixteenth century to the present. Because nonresistance renounces all coercion, finds its authority in God's will, and takes sin seriously, one should not confuse it with other types of pacifism. Nonresistance implies that Christians will not take part in coercive state functions, will search for alternatives in the complex industrial, agricultural, and economic conflicts of modern life, and will nurture an attitude of brotherhood toward other races. By bringing healing to society, nonresistance serves society in a more essential way than those who take responsibility for running it.

Hershberger, Guy F. "Was the War of 1812 Justified?" *YCC* 17 (Nov. 1, 1936), 351. The real cause for the war was American desire to annex more territory rather than the defense of the merchants on the sea. The War of 1812 was a real blunder.

Hershberger, Guy F. "We Cannot Support War, Directly or Indirectly." *YCC* 19 (Aug. 7, 1938), 256. Nonresistant Christians must examine their lives to see if there are ways in which they support the war effort either directly or indirectly. The General Conference statement on war and peace is helpful in identifying some of these areas.

Hershberger, Guy F. "What About the Outlawry of War?" *MQR* 2 (July, 1928), 159-75. Outlines Dr. C. C. Morrison's thesis that war as an institution must be rejected and avoided by means of an international law code. Nonresistant Christians should support such anti-war movements.

Hershberger, Guy F. "What Did the Church Do to Help Our Young People During the World War?" *YCC* 18 (July 4, 1937), 632. The church issued strong resolutions against the war. They also sent a committee to Washington, DC, to speak with the Secretary of War about their position.

Hershberger, Guy F. "What Did the Early American Mennonites Do About War?" *YCC* 17 (April 26, 1936), 136. The early Mennonites who settled in Pennsylvania printed the *Ausbund* in 1742 and the *Martyr's Mirror* in 1748 to educate their people in the ways of peace.

Hershberger, Guy F. "What Did the Early Mennonites Say About War and Peace?" *YCC* 17 (Apr. 5, 1936), 112. At the end of the Middle Ages there were many Christians in Europe who questioned the church-state union and its use of warfare. Included in this group were the Waldensians and later the Anabaptists, who believed that the teachings of Jesus on war must be literally obeyed.

Hershberger, Guy F. "What Is the Meaning of the War in China?" *YCC* 18 (Oct. 31, 1937), 764a. The war in China has many roots in a variety of conflicts with Japan and the western countries. China has many resources and is vulnerable because of less development in relation to the other countries.

Hershberger, Guy F. "What Is the Significance of the Current Upsurge of War Objection? Our Peace Witness—In the Wake of May 18." (Part 20). *GH* 61 (Jan. 16, 1968), 57. Growth of anti-war sentiment in wartime is something new; this development is disturbing to some government officials.

Hershberger, Guy F. "What Shall We Think of the War with Mexico?" *YCC* 17 (Dec. 6, 1936), 392.

Chief cause of Mexican War in 1846 was westward expansion. The US provoked Mexico into a war so that the US could take Mexican land.

Hershberger, Guy F. "Why Did the United States Have a War with Spain?" *YCC* 18 (Feb. 7, 1937), 464. America's relation to Cuba led to a war with Spain in 1898 which was totally unjustified for several reasons.

Hershberger, Guy F. (Review). *To End War: The Story of the National Council for Prevention of War,* by Frederick J. Libby. Nyack, NY: Fellowship Publications, 1969. In *AAAPSS* 397 (1971), 184-85. Frederick J. Libby, Congregationalist minister turned Quaker, tells his own story as executive secretary (1921-1954) of the National Council for Prevention of War, the spearhead of the American peace movement in the twenties and thirties.

Hershberger, Guy F. (Review). *War and the Christian Conscience: How Shall Modern War Be Conducted Justly?* by Paul Ramsey. Durham: Duke University Press, 1961. *MQR* 38 (1964), 73-74. Also in *AAAPSS* 344 (1962), 144-45. This book presents an argument for a just war which Hershberger critiques and refutes.

Hertzler, Daniel. "Moral War on Moral Evil." *ChrLiv* 14 (July, 1967), 2. Editorial observing that Christians have not yet found a way to mobilize the church against evil as an alternative to war.

Hertzler, Daniel. "The War Hysteria." *GH* 73 (July 22, 1980), 592. Criticizes the atmosphere of aggression present in conservative political and religious circles.

Hester, Hugh B. "Can We Stop War?" *Menn* 76 (May 16, 1961), 324-25. Disarmament is absolutely essential to human survival, according to important American leaders. If nations do not learn to co-exist peacefully they will perish violently.

Hilty, Almeta. "The Christian's Attitude Toward War." *YCC* 21 (Sept. 1, 1940), 276, 280. Scripture teaches that the Christian should not participate in carnal warfare. Government and war are permitted by God to do His will.

Historic Peace Churches and the International Fellowship of Reconciliation. *War Is Contrary to the Will of God.* London: Friends Peace Committee, 1951. Pp. 32. Statements identifying the position of the Mennonites, Friends, Brethren, and the FOR on war in response to the WCC 1948 Amsterdam statement, "We believe there is a special call to theologians to consider the theological problems involved.

Holdeman, John. *A Treatise on Magistracy and War, Millenium, Holiness, and the Manifestation of Spirits.* Jasper, Mo.: By the Author, 1891. Pp. 303. MHL. Arguments against war based on Old Testament prophetic statements, the spirit of the gospel, the prohibition of Christ, the love commandment, and the two-kingdom theology.

Holsinger, Justus G. "Can I as a Christian Participate in War?" *GH* 44 (Apr. 17, 1951), 371, 381-82. If one hopes eventually to have a strong nonresistant faith, he or she must first look at both sides of the pro-war and anti-war argument. This consideration should include political, social, and theological viewpoints.

Horsch, John. *Symposium on War.* Scottdale: Mennonite Peace Problems Committee, 1927, 1940, 1944, 1956. Pp. 43. A compilation of quotations throughout history on the nature of war and the Christian imperative to love.

Horsch, John. "The Christian Conscience Against War." *GH* 31, Part 1, (Mar. 9, 1939), 1050-51, 1060; Part 2, (Mar. 15, 1939), 1066-67; Part 3, (Mar. 23, 1939), 1082-83; also in *Menn* 54, Part 1, (Feb. 14, 1939), 7-9; Part 2, (Feb. 21, 1939), 8-9. It is difficult to understand those Christians who frankly admit war is sin and yet have no conscience against participation in it. The conscience against war is a Christian one, not a Mennonite peculiarity. Most Christians, however, have not allowed this conscience to assert itself.

Horsch, John. *War and the Christian Conscience.* Scottdale: Mennonite Publishing House, [1938]. Pp. 16. MHL. Laments the fact that while most varieties of Christianity admit that war is sin, a conscience against participation in war is lacking. Contends, in contrast to these other denominations, that conscientious objection to war is a Christian essential.

Horsch, M. "He Maketh Wars to Cease." *Menn* 52 (Jan. 12, 1937), 4-5, 7. War is a product of fallen human nature which can be corrected only by the Prince of Peace.

Horsch, M. "War." *Menn* 53 (Apr. 19, 1938), 4-5. War is the prevailing characteristic of human history; it is proof of human depravity and will cease only according to God's will.

Horst, John L. "Large-Scale War Projects." *GH* 34 (Jan. 22, 1942), 909. Several Mennonite congregations are having homes and land taken by the government for defense projects. If one's land is taken for war projects, one looks peacefully for a new location.

Horst, John L. (Editorial). "Deepening World Shadows." *ChrMon* 42 (Aug., 1950), 232-33. Comments on the possibility of war in Korea.

Horst, John L. (Editorial). "'For Such a Time as This.' " *ChrMon* 29 (July, 1937), 201. Encourages nonresistant churches to give public testimony to peace, in light of world events pointing toward war.

Horst, John L. (Editorial). "War Production." *ChrMon* 35 (Feb., 1943), 40. Comments on the statistics of industrial output for the war.

Horst, Samuel L. "Mennonites in the Confederacy." *PCMCP Fifteenth,* 47-61. North Newton, Kansas: The Mennonite Press. Held at Bluffton College, Bluffton, Ohio, June 10-11, 1965. The Mennonites living in the Confederacy provide an impressive historical model of religiously-based opposition to war and conscription.

Hostetler, John Andrew, ed. *If War Comes.* Scottdale: Herald Press, 1949. Pp. 16. MHL. A condensation of *Must Christians Fight?* by Edward Yoder.

Hostetter, B. Charles. *The Christian and War.* Harrisonburg: The Mennonite Hour, 1957. Pp. 25. Argues that war is anti-Christian because its motivations, methods, and results are evil; it is contrary to Jesus' way of love; and the state is not the final authority for Christian faith and practice.

Hostetter, Robert D. "Cheyenne Jesus Buffalo Dream." Play presented at the 10th Assembly of Mennonite World Conference, Wichita, Kans., July 25-35, 1978. Pp. [78]. MHL.

Hübner, Harry (Review). *The Just War: A Summary,* by Walter Klaassen. Peace Research Reviews (Vol. 7, No. 6). Dundas, Ont.: Peace Research Institute, 1968. Pp. 70. "Helpful Booklet on Approaches to War." *MennRep* 9 (Jan. 22, 1979), 9. Summarizes this book which succinctly surveys the major historical positions on war. Recommended as helpful for Mennonites in understanding their own pacifism in relation to other positions on war. Concludes that there are no wars which are just, and working for peace should be our only agenda.

Jackson, C. E., Jr. "What Is Poverty?" *With* 2 (Nov., 1969), 30. Reflections on the relationship between poverty and quality of life.

Jantz, Harold. "A Place to Belong." *MBH* 16 (Dec. 9, 1977), 11. The longing for a world without war and broken relationships is evidence that there is a God.

Janzen, David. "Mennonites Should Establish a Seminary Chair for Peace." *CanMenn* 17 (Nov. 21, 1969), 11. After a critical analysis of Ralph B. Potter's *War and Moral Discourse,* in which the just war concept is developed as the only hope for effective war morality, Janzen proposes the

seminary at Elkhart establish a chair for peace.

Janzen, Jacob. "The War Is On." *Menn* 54 (Oct. 17, 1939), 5. We must confess our part in bringing about war and diligently work for peace.

Janzen, Wilhelm. "Christians Ought to Fight." *CanMenn* 14 (Aug. 30, 1966), 4. Letter to the editor states that Christians do not need carnal weapons but the weapons of truth, righteousness, gospel of peace, and faith.

Janzen, William and Koop, Robert. "Ottawa Report: Spending Cuts Affect the Wrong Things." *MennRep* 8 (Nov. 13, 1978), 8. Social services and valuable assistance programs are being cut from the Canadian federal budget, while the government is negotiating a huge deal to purchase new fighter aircraft.

Jenks, Philip E. "Holocaust." *GH* 71 (July 4, 1978), 540. Reprinted from *The American Baptist.* While the specter of the Nazi extermination of Jews troubles pacifist convictions, it should to a greater degree trouble the church that allows evildoers to feel they are justified in their actions until it is too late to stop them except through violence.

Jeschke, Marlin. "The Evangelical Christian and Modern War." *CanMenn* 11 (Sept. 24, 1963), 7. An analysis of a three-day meeting of some thirty teachers, ministers, writers, and others at Winona Lake to discuss the relationship between the evangelical Christian and modern war.

Kauffman, Benjamin K. "They Sound Out the Word." *GH* 60 (May 23, 1967), 458-59. There are so few in "Christian" America against war. Christ taught against all war, including the "just war"; he became a servant, not a fighter.

Kauffman, Daniel. "Christian Attitudes Toward War." *GH* 29 (Sept. 3, 1936), 482. The Gospel forbids any part in carnal warfare. Obedience to God, not disobedience to governments, determines our attitude towards war.

Kauffman, Daniel (Editorial). "Ever Since the Fall of Man . . . ." *GH* 34 (Aug. 14, 1941), 425. Explains how human greed is the basis of all wars.

Kauffman, Ralph C. "The Implications of Military Toys and Games for Children." *Menn* 63 (Dec. 21, 1948), 12-13. Though war games need not be regarded with alarm, more constructive games and activities should be encouraged.

Kauffman, Ralph C. "The Philosophical Aspects of Mennonitism." *PCMCP Second,* 113-26. North Newton, Kansas: The Bethel College Press. Held at Goshen, Indiana, July 22-23, 1943. Philosophical aspects of Mennonitism are those aspects which can be rationally substantiated. Comments on separation of church and state, materialism as it relates to war, and the sovereignty of God as it relates to personal conscience.

Kaufman, Maynard. "Where Peace Begins." *MennLife* 7 (Oct., 1952), 147-48. In regeneration, faith ought to displace anxiety, which is one of the causes for social conflict. Because regeneration does not achieve complete cessation of conflict, the realization of world peace comes through practicing Christian love.

Kaufmann, U. Milo. "Bunyan and the Christian Warfare." *ChrLiv* 10 (Dec., 1963), 22-24. Comment on Bunyan's likening of the Christian life to warfare.

Keen, Susan H. "The Futility of War." *ChrMon* 36 (Aug., 1944), 229. Comment on the horror of war and its incompatibility with the teachings of Jesus.

Keeney, William E. "WCC Called to Nonviolent Position." *Menn* 89 (Jan. 1, 1974), 11. Summarizes the statement, "Violence, Nonviolence, and the Struggle for Social Justice," prepared by the historic peace church representatives for the World Council of Churches discussion. Reviews the history of peace church-WCC discussions on the issue of war, and alludes to the broader issues which it touches: christology, biblical interpretation, the relationship of church and state.

Kehler, Larry. "In Times of Crisis." *CanMenn* 9 (July 28, 1961), 2. Even in times of crisis we must continue to testify to our country the futility of war, continue to pray for peace and demonstrate our firm conviction that Jesus Christ is the answer to the world's problems.

Kent, Katherine McElroy. "A Role for Christians in National Defense?" *CanMenn* 13 (Nov. 9, 1965), 6. Interview with Andrew Brewin, a lay leader of the Anglican church of Canada, delegate to the WCC at New Delhi and a member of Canada's Parliament and of its Special Committee on Defense, in which Brewin explains his interest in getting rid of war and of the arms race, and in national defense problems.

King, Calvin J. "The Position of the Methodist Church Concerning War, Peace, and Revolution." Paper for War, Peace, and Revolution class, AMBS, Elkhart, Ind., n.d. Pp. 3. AMBS.

King, Lauren A. "Better Buchenwald than Hiroshima." *GH* 45 (Aug. 19, 1954), 816-17. Analyzes the ancient question: "Can a follower of Christ take part in war?" The dilemma the pacifist faces in this world is the choice between inflicting injury on others and having injury inflicted on him- or herself and loved ones.

Klaassen, Walter. "The Just War: A Summary." *Peace Research Reviews* 7 (Sept., 1978), 1-70. Summarizes the major religious views in Western history which shaped the just war doctrine. Criticizes the doctrine in its justification of all forms of just war—holy war, crusade, and just revolution—because of its internal contradictions and ambiguities.

Klaassen, Walter. *What Have You to Do with Peace?* Altona: D. W. Friesen and Sons, Ltd., 1969. Pp. 74. Originally given as lectures designed to help Sunday school teachers teach the basic principles of nonviolence. Covers subjects such as the biblical use of the language of "principalities and powers," the church as the agency of peace, just war doctrine, nuclear war and disarmament issues, and church and state relations.

Klassen, D. D. "The Christian and War." *CanMenn* 18 (June 5, 1970), 6, 7, 8. Discusses the just war tradition, expecially the reluctance to designate any recent wars as "unjust." Concludes with a plea for primary allegiance to God and for peace.

Klassen, G[eorge] S[tanley]. *Practical Questions and Answers Concerning War.* Hillsboro, Ks.: By the Author, [1940]. Pp. 8. MHL. Sixteen questions and short answers ranging from simple definitions to more theoretical matters.

Klassen, Herbert. "Property: A Problem in Christian Ethics." *Concern* 4 (June, 1957), 42-56. Humankind's desire for material things can result in problems of exploitation, inequality, and poverty. A discussion of the biblical teaching concerning property.

Kliewer, Warren. Four war poems. N.d. Pp. 5. MLA/BeC.

Kliewer, Warren. "War and Rumors of War." *MennLife* 17 (Jan., 1962), 39-43. Death of a friend who was a soldier in Korea raises the issue of how we all share in violence.

Koontz, Ted. "The Logic of Noncooperation." *Menn* 95 (July 8, 1980), 432. Cautions Mennonites who contemplate not registering for Selective Service to do so from authentic pacifist motivations and not because of a selective just war theory.

Koop, Robert. "YHWH's War and the War of the Sons of Light: A Synergism of Holy War." Paper for Dead Sea Scrolls and Theology of War in the Old Testament classes, AMBS, Elkhart, Ind., May, 1977. Pp. 35. AMBS.

Kraybill, Donald B. "Why I Reject War." *With* 2

(Mar., 1969), 6. Various reasons for rejecting war.

Krehbiel, Edward. *Nationalism, War, and Society.* New York: Macmillan, 1916. Pp. 276. A discussion of the history of nationalism and war including recent developments, together with suggestions for political alternatives.

Krehbiel, Henry P[eter]. *War Inconsistent with the Spirit and Teaching of Christ.* Newton: Herald Publishing Co., 1934. Pp. 26. Examines Jesus' teachings and conduct and finds them opposing war, hatred, and resistance. Reprint of an 1894 essay.

Kreider, Alan. "An International Call to Simpler Living." *MBH* 19 (Apr. 25, 1980), 20-21; *ChrLead* 43 (Apr. 22, 1980), 17; *EV* 93 (May 10, 1980), 16. An international gathering of evangelical leaders near London, England, makes a commitment to a simple lifestyle in recognition that wealth and militarism contribute to poverty and powerlessness.

Kreider, Alan and John H. Yoder. "Christians and War." *Eerdman's Handbook to the History of Christianity.* Ed. Tim Dowley. Grand Rapids: Eerdmans Publ. Co., 1977, 24-27. Pp. 656. Traces the development of the three approaches to the relationship between war and the gospel: the crusade, just war theory, and pacifism.

Kreider, Carl. "Ferment in Africa." *ChrLiv* 6 (June, 1959), 18, 34. Rising nationalist tendencies and white racism contribute to sometimes violent ferment across the continent.

Kreider, Carl. "How Can We Respond to World Hunger?" *GH* 67 (Nov. 19, 1974), 891-94. Examines causes of hunger, from affluence to the energy crisis, and suggests seven responses, rooted in nonresistance, including cutting the defense budget.

Kreider, Carl. "India and China Again." *ChrLiv* 7 (Jan., 1960), 18, 39. Comment on the possibility of a major military clash between China and India.

Kreider, Carl. "India and China at War." *ChrLiv* 10 (Feb., 1963), 19, 38. Analysis of the border conflict.

Kreider, Carl. "Inflation: What It Does, Why It Happens." *GH* 71 (Aug. 1, 1978), 573-75. Discussion of the effects and causes of inflation concludes with reasons why excessive defense spending may be the major culprit.

Kreider, Carl. "Inflation and Recession." *ChrLiv* 22 (Mar., 1975), 15, 31. One of the causes of inflation is war and defense spending.

Kreider, Carl. "Internationalism or Isolationism?" *Menn Comm* 5 (Feb., 1951), 30, 32. Strongly advocates a Christian internationalism of increased foreign trade and aid, without rearmament and military intervention.

Kreider, Carl. "Tax or Borrow?" *MennComm* 5 (Mar., 1951), 28, 32. Why federal taxation is better than federal borrowing, especially for financing wars.

Kreider, Carl. "The Geneva Meeting of GATT." *ChrLiv* 2 (Feb., 1955), 22-23, 48. The General Agreements on Tariffs and Trade are important because they reduce world trade barriers, one of the causes of war.

Kreider, Carl. "The War in Korea." *MennComm* 4 (Sept., 1950), 30, 34. Analysis of the fighting in Korea concludes that the US is backing reactionary forces; the UN has turned into an anti-communist force; the war will strain the American economy.

Kreider, Carl. "Will the US Destroy the UN?" *MennComm* 7 (Aug., 1953), 29-31. Discussion of the difficulty of exercising effective police action toward heavily armed countries.

Landes, Carl J. "Mennonites and War." *MCE* 2 (May 21, 1935), 4-5. Mennonites don't take life but they profit from war. We must refuse to share in war profits.

Landis, Ira D. "When War Clouds Hover Low." *ChrMon* 34 (June, 1942), 171-72, 189. The experience of the children of Israel called to leave Babylon parallels Mennonite migrations and the calling out of Mennonite youth into CPS camps.

Lapp, John A. "'Openien, You Should Have Died Long Ago.'" *ChrLiv* 20 (Feb., 1973), 20, 25, 27. Unequal distribution of land and wealth and the imposition of martial law have created a setting of violence in the Philippines.

Lapp, John A. "The Roots of War." *ChrLiv* 25 (Apr., 1978), 14-15. Disarmament alone is not the key to peace; a new social order must be created.

Lapp, John A. "What Is Happening in Afghanistan? *ChrLiv* 27 (Mar., 1980), 15-16. Discussion of armed Russian movement into Afghanistan and the American response.

Lapp, John A. (Review). *No King But Caesar? A Catholic Lawyer Looks at Christian Violence,* by William R. Durland. Scottdale: Herald Press, 1975. *FQ* 2 (Winter, 1975), 14. Lapp observes the book's strength lies in Durland's sincere wrestling with the violence of the church through the centuries. Calls the Christian church to lay down its weapons of war.

Lapp, John A. (Review). *The Respectable Murderers: Social Evil and Christian Conscience,* by Paul Hanly Furfey. Herder and Herder, 1966. Pp. 192. *ChrLiv* 15 (Jan., 1968), 33-34. Recommends this discussion of four conspicuous social injustices: American slavery, German genocide of Jews, the mass bombing of noncombatants during World War II, and treatment of the poor.

Lapp, John E. "The Gospel in Reconciliation of Men." *GH* 61 (Mar. 12, 1968), 228-29. The social implications of the gospel include economic and racial equality and opposition to war.

Lasserre, Jean. "War and the Christian Ethic." *CanMenn* 11 (July 12, 1963), 7; *GH* 56 (Aug. 20, 1963), 720. In the New Testament there is no clear distinction between individual and collective, private and political ethics. The New Testament challenges the Christian consistently to a coherent and homogeneous kind of behavior without the duplicity of contradiction.

Lauver, Florence B. "The Church's Responsibility Concerning War." *GH* 29 (July 9, 1936), 330-31. The Christian should pray for rulers, pardon enemies, and preach the Gospel that saves souls.

Layman, Don Earl. "Christianity, the United States, and War." Term paper for War, Peace, and Revolution course, Nov. 7, 1974. Pp. 32. MSHL.

Leatherman, Mary. "When Your Child Wants to Play with Guns." *ChrLiv* 25 (July, 1978), 12-14. One family's attempts to deal with war toys and games.

Lehman, M[artin] C[lifford]. "Introductory; Needs and Conditions in Europe." *ChrMon* 37, Part 1, (July, 1945), 175, 177. Discusses the causes of war and its primary result, suffering.

Lind, Millard C. "The Christian and War." *GH* 52 (Oct. 20, 1959), 889. A summary of the booklet *The Christian and War* published in 1958 by the historic peace churches and the Fellowship of Reconciliation.

Lind, Millard C. "What About our Luxuries?" *ChrLiv* 1 (Sept., 1954), 3. There is a direct connection between luxury and oppression and war.

Loewen, Karin. "The Noise of War." Aug. 25, 1966. Pp. 49. Newton, KS in pre-World War II period. MLA/BeC.

"Man and His World of War." *CanMenn* 14 (Nov. 1, 1966), 5. An essay on priorities and loyalties in the Christian life.

"Mass Starvation or War Only Hope for Survival." *CanMenn* 16 (Feb. 27, 1968), 1. Report on a lecture by Georg Brogstrom, of Michigan State Univ., in special sessions at William Jewell College, Liberty, Missouri attended by the Population and Human Ecology class of Tabor College on Feb. 15 and 16. With 6 percent of the world's population controlling 40 percent of its resources, the six percent cannot afford to give up this control to help the underprivileged if their own high standard of living is to be maintained.

"Minneapolis Church Witnesses Against War Toys." *CanMenn* 12 (Dec. 15, 1964), 1. Churches act under the sponsorship of the Women's International League for Peace and Freedom and the Minnesota Council of Churches.

Markley, W. O. "Do Pacifists Help Cause War?" *EV* 77 (Apr. 13, 1964), 5, 28. Each individual pacifist is responsible for living his or her life in a way that helps prevent war.

Martens, Philip. "The Just War Theory: An Historical View." Research paper for Christian Faith class. 1981. Pp. 10. BfC.

Martin, Alice S. "Nothing the Grass Said." *ChrLiv* 20 (Dec., 1973), 13-14. Thoughts of a Vietnamese refugee on hate and war.

Mast, Russell L. "What Are We Doing to Prevent Another War?" *Menn* 58 (Nov. 2, 1943), 3-4. The Christian must work for those national policies that hold the greatest possibility for preventing another world war.

Mather, William G. "A Symptom, Not a Disease." *ChrLiv* 1 (Apr., 1954), 13. Reprinted by permission from *Penn State Alumni News.* Juvenile delinquency increases in time of war and economic depression.

McPhee, Arthur G. "Why Does God Allow War?" *ST* 42 (Aug., 1974), 1. Suggests that war as a revelation of sin, as a condemnation of sin, and as a manifestation of sin are helpful guides to understanding why God allows war.

Mennonite student in Yugoslavia. "My Concern for Yugoslav Christians." *MBH* 18 (Sept. 28, 1979), 36. Christians in Yugoslavia have to deal with the history of religious conflict, "the church at war with itself."

Metzler, Edgar. "I Talked with a Man of God." *ChrLiv* 12 (Aug., 1965), 18-19, 29. Mennonite leader in Russia reports on the status of Mennonite churches there, including the stance on war and nonresistance.

Metzler, Edgar. "War Is Not the Way to Peace." *CanMenn* 10 (Nov. 2, 1962), 1, 10. A historical perspective on the Cuban situation and a reminder that meeting an evil force with force is futile.

Meyer, Albert J. "Conference Discusses the Problems of War and Peace." *CanMenn* 3 (Sept. 30, 1955), 6. A report on meeting between theologians from Lutheran and Reformed churches in Europe and representatives of the historic peace churches.

Meyer, Jacob C. Letter to the Editor. *ChrLiv* 10 (Dec., 1963), 40. Comments on the large national defense budget which inhibits states from collecting adequate taxes to meet local social needs.

Miller, Carl S. "Background to American Intervention in Cuba, April, 1898." Paper presented to Social Science Seminar, Goshen College, Goshen, Ind., n.d. Pp. 20. MHL.

Miller, Dorcas S. "What If War Comes." *ChrLiv* 12 (Nov., 1965), 3. Mother faces child's questions about war.

Miller, William R., ed. and comp. *Bibliography of Books on War, Pacifism, Nonviolence, and Related Studies.* Nyack, NY: The Fellowship of Reconciliation, 1961. Pp. 37. General list of over 500 books and pamphlets plus a select, annotated list of outstanding books. Includes works by Mennonite authors. Mennonites participated on the bibliography selection committee.

Mills, C. Wright. "A Pagan Sermon." *ChrLiv* 7 (Apr., 1960), 16-18. Reprinted from *The Causes of World War Three,* Mills, Simon and Schuster, 1958. Non-Christian author challenges the church to greater faithfulness in the areas of nonconformity and nonresistance.

Nelson, Boyd N. "Blame George." *GH* 61 (Jan. 9, 1968), 39. Responding to an article criticizing I-W workers for their lack of sacrifice and commitment, author challenges all Mennonites to separate themselves from the unjust affluence of American life, instead of depending on drafted men to make this witness.

Nelson, Boyd N. "War and God's Work." *GH* 59 (Apr. 12, 1966), 326-27. One's reasons for being nonresistant need to shift from a desire to remain pure to a positive concern for the total welfare of humanity.

Nickeson, Walter. "Menno Simons and John Calvin: Pacifism or Just War?" Research paper for the Christian Faith class. 1978. Pp. 8. BfC.

Niggle, Gail. "Art: War and Peace." 1966. Pp. 31. BfC.

Oswald, Joseph. Letter to the Editor. *GH* 63 (July 14, 1970), 610. While opposing the war in Southeast Asia, the writer calls attention to the militant student spirit at Kent State which necessitated calling in the National Guards.

"Peace, War, and Social Issues: A Statement of the Position of the Amish Mennonite Churches." Officialy adopted by the ministerial body of the Beachy Amish Mennonite constituency . . . at Wellesley, Ont., Apr. 18-19, 1968. [n.p., 1968]. Pp. 16. MSHL. Topics include the role of government, military service, civil defense, the Christian's role in race relations, unions, etc.

"Peace Committee Asks Witness Against War Toys." *CanMenn* 12 (Dec. 8, 1964), 1, 2. A letter from inter-Mennonite Ontario Peace, Social, and Economic Relations Committee to Mennonite clergy.

Pannabecker, S. F. "Some Effects of 1938 on Missions." *Menn* 54 (June 13, 1939), 2-3. Partly due to the climate of political and social tensions, the missionaries are receiving a new welcome in China.

*Peace Is the Will of God: A Testimony to the World Council of Churches/A Statement Prepared by the Historic Peace Churches and the Fellowship of Reconciliation.* Geneva: Brethren Service Commission, 1953. Pp. 23. MHL. Concludes that the church must reject war, not only because of the confusion and suffering it causes but because it is a negation of the gospel itself.

Peachey, J. Lorne. "Army Men and Dart Guns." *ChrLiv* 22 (Apr., 1975), 39. Editorial recounts family search for a policy toward toys of war and violence.

Peachey, Paul L. "A General Speaks on War." *GH* 48 (June 21, 1955), 585. Fundamentalism and its support of war must be scrutinized by Mennonites with the same critical eye that examines liberalism.

Peachey, Paul L. "America and the Church." *ChrLiv* 9 (Dec., 1962), 28-29. Used by permission from *The Sunday School Times.* Institutional wealth is as great a peril to the Christian church as is the threat of communism.

Peachey, Paul L. *The Churches and War.* N.p.: Mennonite General Conference Peace Problems Committee, 1956. Pp. 19. The Christian Youth and War Pamphlets No. 5. Directed toward young men approaching draft age, pamphlet traces the attitudes of the Christian church since the first century toward involvement in war. Includes comments on the just war theory as well as on individual pacifists throughout Christian history.

Peachey, Paul L. *Why Men Fight.* N.p.: Mennonite General Conference Peace Problems Committee, 1956. Pp. 16. The Christian Youth and War Pamphlets, No. 1. Directed to young men approaching draft age, this pamphlet discusses sin—the presence of evil in the human spirit created good—as the root cause of war.

Peachey, Paul L. *Your Church and Your Nation: An Appeal to American Churchmen.* Washington, DC: The Church Peace Mission, [1963]. Pp. 22. MHL. Contends that to construct a theological sanction of war just because conflict is inevitable in a fallen world is no more justifiable than to construct a theology of segregation because we have not achieved human equality.

Peck, J. Richard. "Roast Beef and the B-1 Bomber." *Menn* 91 (Nov. 2, 1976), 652. Describes a talk given by a representative from Rockwell International, trying to sell B-1 bomber strategy to church leaders, since Rockwell had concluded church organizations are responsible for the opposition.

Preheim, Sheila. "The Hutterites During the World War Years." Student paper for Mennonite History, Life and Thought, Jan. 25, 1983. Pp. 10. MLA/BeC.

(Review). *Compromise with War,* by Edward Yoder. No publ., n.d. Pp. 14 (pamphlet). *CPS Bull* 2 (May 22, 1944), 3. Reviewer observes that the booklet is a critique of the position taken by *Christian Century* editors that God, as punishment, has condemned humans to fight wars.

Redekop, John H. "Warfare Be Limited?" *CanMenn* 4 (Feb. 17, 1956), 3. Five arguments against further nuclear testing.

Regehr, Ernie. "African Anabaptists: Confronting a Continent at War." *MennRep* 10 (July 21, 1980), 7. African Mennonites and Brethren in Christ grapple with the peace tradition in countries embroiled in struggles against repressive political and economic structures.

Reimer, Vic. "Easter Sunrise Service Planned for Kansas Missile Base." *God and Caesar* 5 (Apr., 1979), 6. A Titan II missile base near Rock, Kans., was chosen as the site of an Easter morning sunrise service by a group of citizens in the Newton/Wichita area, known as the Kansas Coalition for Peace and Justice.

[Richards,] Emma Sommers. "Mennonites and Materialism." *MennComm* 3 (Nov., 1949), 20-21. Relates materialism to war.

Richert, P. H. "The Root of the Peace Problem." *Menn* 52 (Feb. 13, 1937), 4. All war is rooted in the heart. Knowledge of Christ and his teachings will overcome war.

Rohrer, Charles. *When and Where the Church Met Three Disastrous Defeats.* Elkhart: By the Author, 3140 Idelwild St., 1973. Pp. 23. MHL. The three "defeats" named in the title are the abandonment of pacifism for just war theory in the time of Constantine, the unification of church and state in the Edict of Intolerance at Nicea, and the exchange of immersion water baptism for the sprinkling of babies baptism at the Church Council of Carthage, 418 BCE.

Roth, Willard E., ed. *Why Do Men Fight?* Scottdale: Herald Press, 1964. Pp. 15. Peacemaker Pamphlet No. 1. Written for young people, this pamphlet sees the roots of war in human sin and challenges readers to commit themselves to Christ's way of love.

"Soldiers Strong Spiritually and Not Opposed to War." *CanMenn* 14 (Feb. 8, 1966), 6. A report on the involvement in the church by generals in the army and their attitudes to war.

Sauder, Menno. *Christian Methods: Are Superior to Compulsory Social Legislation, Militarism, and War.* Elmira, Ont.: by the author, 1967. Pp. 8. MHL. A variety of comments, on these subjects as well as sundry others, interspersed with quotations from the Dordrecht confession and John Horsch's *Mennonites in Europe,* a summary of Jean Laserre's *War and the Gospel,* etc.

Sawatzky, Sharon R. "Rape: Keeping Women in Their Place." *Menn* 91 (Sept. 28, 1976), 558-60. Just as the church works against war, it must work against other violence such as rape, which demeans women. Limited resistance to an attacker is a response in line with Jesus' perfect love.

Schrag, Dale R. "Report on Student Services Pilot Project: Or, How Should the Christian Respond to War?" 1970? Pp. 13. MLA/DeC.

Schrag, Martin H. "Mars Rides Again." *GH* 62 (Apr. 15, 1969), 340-44. Relates statistics concerning burgeoning American military spending and production and its relation to domestic violence, and challenges Christians to bring Christian insights of internationality, forgiveness, and love to bear on this problem.

Schrag, Martin H. "The Cross on a Canteen." *GH* 69 (July 20, 1976), 562. Refers to the story of an MCC worker in Vietnam meeting a Christian North Vietnamese soldier with a cross on his canteen, and concludes that Christian commitment to God precludes rule by the sword.

Schroeder, Ardith. "An Alternative to War Bonds: The Mennonite Attempt to Establish Civilian Bonds for Humanitarian Purposes." Student paper for Mennonite History, Life and Thought, Nov. 29, 1976. Pp. 9. MLA/BeC.

Seitz, Blair. "Putting Words into Actions." *ChrLiv* 25 (Mar., 1978), 16-19. Working toward a simpler lifestyle in the concern for global justice.

Shank, J. Ward (Editorial). "The Case Against War." *ST* 48 (Aug., 1980), 6-8. Discourages Christians from participating in war but asserts that war is endemic to humanity and may sometimes be within God's will.

Shank, J. Ward (Editorial). "War as Sin." *ST* 35 (June, 1967), 1. War is sin not so much as a social phenomenon as in the sense that individuals sin who engage in warfare in any of its forms.

Shank, James. "The Character of War." *YCC* 23 (Aug. 16, 1942), 259. Several war experiences that describe the nature of war and what it does to people.

Sheats, Ladon. *God and Caesar* 4 (June, 1978), 4-5. A poem reflecting on the nonviolent peace witness in which the writer was involved at the Pentagon and describing the three days of action and vigils.

Shenk, Stanley C. "He Found No Peace." *YCC* 23 (May 31, 1942), 170-71. A plea to understand the reality of war. Webb Miller, a war correspondent, relates wartime experiences.

Showalter, Elizabeth A. (Review). *Christians and War,* by Llewelyn Harris. A Plough pamphlet, 1957. Pp. 12. *ChrLiv* 4 (Dec., 1957), 32. Recommends this short survey of Christian stands on war throughout Christian history, written by a member of the Society of Brothers in England.

Showalter, Jewel. "War Has No Winners." *With* 2 (Mar., 1969), 20. The story of Art McPhee's change from military duty to a position of nonresistance.

Sider, Burt. "Amid Civil Disorder—Nicaragua: A Suffering Church." *EV* 91 (Nov. 25, 1978), 8-9. Despite civil war and disruption in the political and economic sectors, the Nicaraguan church is showing remarkable strength.

Siebert, John (Review). *The Doctrine of the Just War in the West: A Summary,* by Walter Klaassen. Dundas, Ont.: Peace Research Institute, 1978. Pp. 70. *MBH* 18 (Apr. 27, 1979), 32. Recommends this tracing of the just war concept from its Judaic roots to modern discussions.

Smith, C. Henry. "God and War." *Menn* 57 (Dec. 15, 1942), 6. God is a universal God and therefore neither God nor the church can take part in war.

Smith, C. Henry. "Why Do Men Fight?" *Fellowship* 5 (Dec., 1939), 6. Seven FOR members, including Smith, respond to the question of why the people (not the rulers) fight. Smith contends that masses are driven into war by the misguided propaganda of the minority of leaders.

Smith, Gary. "Just War." Research paper for Christian Ethics class. Pp. 6. BfC.

Smucker, Barbara Claassen. "Are We Preparing for World War III?" *Menn* 59 (Jan. 4, 1944), 7. Our children should know the truth regarding the destructiveness of war and we should not provide them with war toys.

Smucker, Donovan E. "The Position of the Christian Soldier." *Menn* 62 (Jan. 21, 1947), 3. Most military personnel hate war and think it is evil but, at times, necessary.

Sprunger, Keith L. "Learning the Wrong Lessons." *MennLife* 23 (Apr., 1968), 64-68. An analysis of the psychology and history leading to Vietnam in an attempt to find a clearer understanding of revolution in our world.

Sprunger-Froese, Mary. "Peace—and All That Garbage." *WMSC Voice* 54 (Dec., 1980), 8-9. Reprinted from *Menn* 94 (Nov. 20, 1979), 692-93. Author confronted the enormity of American affluence and waste by living off edible garbage for one month.

Stafford, Chase. "The Anger of God." *ChrLead* 42 (Apr. 24, 1979), 2. Looks at the implications of the fact that even God frequently displayed anger.

Stauffer, Elam W. (ed.) "The Believer's Attitude Toward War." *GH* 34 (June 12, 1941), 234. Eleven reasons why the believer cannot participate in war.

Stauffer, Henry. "The Mennonite Conscience and War." *Religious Telescope 104* (Sept. 17, 1938), 11, 16. Author contends that forceful self-defense is an acceptable alternative when life and/or property are endangered. Cites the example of 16th-century Dutch Mennonites who financially supported William of Orange's Protestant defense against Catholic Spain's invasion.

Steiner, Susan Clemmer. "The Hermeneutics of the Sword: An Investigation into Sattler, Denck, and Hubmaier." Term paper for Religious Studies course, Sept. 11, 1980. Pp. 49. CGCL.

Stoda, Kevin. "Why Does a Nation in This Century Invade Another Nation When That Other Nation Refuses to Salute Its Flag?" Social Science Seminar paper, Apr., 1985. Pp. 49. MLA/BeC.

Stoltzfus, Grant M. (Review). *Preachers Present Arms,* by Ray H. Abrams. Scottdale: Herald Press, 1969. Pp. 354. *GH* 62 (Nov. 18, 1969),

1015-16. Discusses the book's impact when it was first published in 1933, and the continuing relevance of its study of the relationship of church and state during wartime.

Stoltzfus, Victor. "Just War Theology." *RepConsS* 23 (May, 1966), 2. The surprising agreement among America's top religious leaders that American involvement in Vietnam is immoral is based on the just war doctrine that guides the thinking of 90 percent of the world's Christians on the topic of war.

Stucky, Harley J. (Review). *Christianity, Diplomacy, and War,* by Herbert Butterfield. Abingdon-Cokesbury, 1953. Pp. 125. *MennLife* 9 (Oct., 1954), 189-90. Advocates making war more tolerable by removing ideological overtones and limiting objectives.

Stucky, Vernon. Letter to the Editor. *Menn* 90 (Feb. 11, 1975), 92. In "How to Live with Inflation" (Jan. 7, 1975), Leighton Ford's failure to mention the outrageous military budget as a source of inflation reveals a superficial understanding of the economy and of commitment to Christ.

Summer, Bob. "War Is Inevitable." *YCC* 47 (July 10, 1966), 8. The conclusion that war is inevitable is based on the human greed for power, opposition of communism, and lack of international power to control actions of modern societies.

Swartzendruber, Bill. "The Opposition to the Mexican War." Paper, n.d. Pp. 33. MHL.

"The Church Confronts War and Communism—Conference Concern." *CanMenn* 2 (Jan. 1, 1954), 1, 3. John C. Bennett and André Trocmé represented their respective positions at the Detroit Conference on the Church and Peace. Studied the basis of nonresistance in scripture, theology, and Christian experience. Major concerns were the Christian in the contemporary world, the church's confrontation with war and communism, and positive action for peace.

"The Church in the German Democratic Republic." *GH* 72 (July 17, 1979), 562-63. Disillusionment and spiritual and theological disorientation are problems in the GDR churches but they show strength in issues of war and peace.

"The Testimony of Josephus Against War." *GH* Supplement 39 (Apr., 1946), 95. Excerpt from Josephus' *Wars of the Jews* (5 : 818-20) in which he warns the Jews to refrain from war and fighting.

"Their Biblical Teaching Against War." *CanMenn* 2 (Aug. 20, 1954), 7. A personal testimony of how

this doctrine became the criteria for joining the Mennonite Church.

"Thirty Evangelicals to Discuss War Attitudes." *CanMenn* 11 (July 19, 1963), 1, 9. MCC Peace Section arranges a summer seminar at Winona Lake, Ind.

Taylor, James. "What Preparing for War Is Costing Us." *MBH* 19 (Nov. 7, 1980), 36. Statistics comparing the cost of defense spending with the cost of development and peace programs.

Teichroew, Lowell (Review). "The Christian and War: A Theological Discussion of Justice, Peace, and Love." Historic peace churches and the FOR, 1958, *CanMenn* 7 (Aug. 21, 1959), 2. Peace dialogue between the historic peace churches and the World Council of Churches.

*The Christian and War: A Theological Discussion of Justice, Peace, and Love.* Amsterdam: Historical Peace Churches and Fellowship of Reconciliation, 1958. Pp. 47. MHL. Sequel to *Peace Is the Will of God* makes a greater effort to take seriously the nonpacifist position by including chapter entitled "God Wills Both Peace and Justice," written by Angus Dun and Reinhold Niebuhr at the invitation of the historic peace churches and FOR. Grapples with the questions of pacifism and social responsibility in the context of this dialogue.
*

Thierstein, J. R. "Keep America Out of War." *Menn* 54 (June 6, 1939), 1-2. Persons should inform their congresspersons that they are against war. Examples of appropriate telegrams and letters are given.

Thiessen, Alvin (Review). *The Condemned of Altona,* by Jean-Paul Sartre. NT: Knopf, 1961. Pp. 178. "To Realize the Spiritual Horror of War." *CanMenn* 12 (Jan. 7, 1964), 8, 12. Recommends the play for its "razor-sharp dissection" of a war mentality.

Thut, John. "The World System Analyzed." *ChrMon* 26 (Mar., 1934), 74-76. One of the forces of evil active in the present world system is war.

Tochterman, Frank. "Jehovah's Witnesses and War." Paper for War, Peace, and Revolution class, AMBS, Elkhart, Ind., Apr. 10, 1969. Pp. 3. AMBS.

Toews, John A. "Just War, Fact or Fiction?" *MBH* 4 (Sept. 24, 1965), 6. "The just war is a strange theological fiction, but the unjust war is a stark historical fact." All war must be repudiated by disciples of Jesus.

Tutte, H. Charles. "Christ or War—Which?" *ChrMon* 29 (Aug., 1937), 254. Reprinted from

---

*For additional listing, see Supplement, pp. 717-719.

*War Cry.* The spirit of Jesus is the antithesis of war, says a non-Mennonite writer.

Vogt, Virgil. "Ethical Danger Zones." *ChrLiv* 3 (Aug., 1956), 12-14. One of the danger zones in the business world is competition, which some think can be a form of war.

Vogt, Virgil. "The Role of Well-Fed Mennonites in a Hungry World." *ChrLiv* 15 (Dec., 1968), 5-8. Comments on a Mennonite consultation on world hunger and calls Mennonites to confront wasteful militarism with greater witness against oppression and wealth.

*

"War Is Murder—Japanese Minister." *CanMenn* 5 (apr. 19, 1957), 7. Kunio Kodaira denounces war as robbery and murder.

"When War Clouds Hang Low." *CanMenn* 3 (Jan. 28, 1955), 2. A reminder of the Christian's role in a tense world situation.

"Why Glamorize War?" *CanMenn* 16 (June 25, 1968), 1. Bergtaler Mennonite Church sends a note of dissatisfaction to the Canadian Broadcasting Corporation: "We the undersigned urge you as those responsible for our public communication media, to use our common resources to promote not the causes of war and violence, but rather those of peace and internationalism."

*War Is Contrary to the Will of God: Statements by the Historic Peace Churches and the International Fellowship of Reconciliation.* Amsterdam: J. H. de Bussy, July, 1951. Pp. 32. MHL. Introductory statement contends that Christ's call to overcome evil with good will be more effective in the long run than any kind of violent response to problems. The Christian's task is to rediscover and reconstruct in modern language and concrete situations the New Testament kind of warfare against evil. From this central tenet, each of the historic peace churches and the IFOR offers a separate statement emerging from its own tradition and in its own idiom.

Weaver, Edwin L. "Loyalty to Christ in Wartime." *YCC* 25 (Apr. 23, 1944), 133, 136. The conscience against war is most frequently based on social, economic, or spiritual foundations. For the Christian, opposition to war is based on loyalty to Christ.

Weaver, Edwin L. "The Unnaturalness of War for the Christian." *YCC* 26 (Feb. 25, 1945), 449-50. Both the feelings aroused in warfare and the activities of the soldier are contrary to the example and teaching of Christ. Examples are included.

Weaver, Robert. "Comments on War." *Menn* 55 (July 30, 1940), 13-14. Love and kindness will break down a Hitler quicker than military means.

Wenger, A. D., selected by. "On Peace and War." *ChrMon* 27 (Aug., 1935), 235-36. Reprinted article by Thomas Lomax Hunter, in the *Richmond Times Dispatch*, on the inhumanity of war.

Wenger, Richard. "War and the Christian Ideal." *ChrMon* 37 (Mar., 1945), 57-58. Biblical basis for the nonparticipation of Christians in war, and debate with a contemporary writer allowing the use of force in resisting evil.

Wenger, Samuel S. "Peace and War: The Way of Love in This Atomic Age." *GH* 53 (Feb. 16, 1960), 145. The Christian follows Jesus, loves his or her fellow human beings, and witnesses to them. Killing people is inconsistent with all three of these vocations.

Wittmer, S. C. "War and You." *Menn* 53 (Jan. 18, 1938), 4-5. The proper time to express our opinion in opposition to war is before the war starts as we vote and participate in lawmaking.

World War I. 302 interviews: over half are transcribed. Emphasis is on CO's from many Mennonite branches and other churches. Also includes several regulars and civilians (women, pastors). Some very dramatic stories of abuse in army camps, courts-martial, prison, personal testimonies about nonresistant stances, moving to Canada to escape conscription, community war fervor. Guide to interviews published as Sprunger, *et al., Voices Against War,* 1973. MLA/ BeC.

"Youth Sounds Off on War, Peace." *YCC* 48 (July 16, 1967), 13. Finding of a 20-question form filled out by young people from across the Mennonite church in Canada and the United States.

Yoder, Edward. "Christian Thinking on War." *GH Supplement* 36 (Dec., 1943), 829-32. A critical examination of C. C. Morrison's position on war in the light of biblical doctrine.

Yoder, Edward. *Compromise with War.* Akron: MCC, 1943. Pp. 15. A critique of liberalism's capitulation to nationalism and violence, focusing particularly on the writings of Charles C. Morrison, editor of *The Christian Century.*

Yoder, Edward. "Compromise with War." *GH Supplement* 36 (Dec., 1943), 829-32. A criticism of Charles Clayton Morrison's position that the antiwar position is not in the interest of social welfare.

Yoder, Edward. "God Is the Ruler." *GH Supplement* 36 (June, 1943), 278. God rules the world even in times of war.

*For additional listing, see Supplement, pp. 717-719.

Yoder, Edward. "Jefferson and Franklin on War." *GH Supplement* 36 (Feb., 1944), 1006. Observations by two renowned men on the stupidity of war.

Yoder, Edward. "John Wesley on War." *GH Supplement* 36 (Oct., 1943), 638-39. Where there is war God is forgotten.

Yoder, Edward. "New Books." *GH Supplement* 37 (Dec., 1944), 760. A brief review of Guy F. Hershberger, *War, Peace, and Nonresistance* (1944) and Rufus D. Bowman, *The Church of the Brethren and War, 1708-1941* (1944).

Yoder, Edward. "Origen and War." *GH Supplement* 36 (Aug., 1943), 447. Origen defends the early Christian refusal to participate in warfare and politics.

Yoder, Edward. "Prayer in Wartime: Peace Principles from a Scriptural Viewpoint." Part 45. *GH Supplement* 34 (Oct., 1941), 629-30. Names groups of persons that ought to be prayed for in this time of war.

Yoder, Edward. "The Bitter Fruit of War." *GH Supplement* 35 (Oct., 1942), 638-39. The bitter fruit is the spirit of hatred and the thirst for revenge.

Yoder, Edward. "The Christian Conscience." *GH Supplement* 36 (Apr., 1943), 78-79. The Christian conscience does not allow participation in war, nor does it allow one to become calloused to the idea of destruction.

Yoder, Edward. "The Christian's Attitude Toward Participation in War Activities." *MQR* 9 (Jan., 1935), 5-19. Mennonites have consistently chosen a moderate position between total noncooperation with the military and a willingness to engage in noncombatant duty in their witness against war.

Yoder, Edward. "The Churches and the War: Peace Principles from a Scriptural Viewpoint." Part 43. *GH Supplement* 34 (July, 1941), 358-59. Often in times of war churches forget their testimony of peace. It is to be hoped that this will not happen in the present conflict.

Yoder, Edward. "The Early Christians and War: Peace Principles from a Scriptural Viewpoint." Part 12. *GH* 30 (Oct. 21, 1937), 651-56. The early Christians refused participation in war. A certain immaturity however, led to an increasing compromise with this stance.

Yoder, Edward. "The Madness of War: Peace Principles from a Scriptural Viewpoint." Part 16. *GH* 31 (July 21, 1938), 374-75. How does one guard against the irrational spirit of war? By knowing the Word, by realizing the bias of news agencies in wartime, and by recognizing propaganda for what it is.

Yoder, Edward. "The Mind to War: Peace Principles from a Scriptural Viewpoint." Part 5. *GH* 28 (Jan. 16, 1936), 910-11. Modern war is essentially conflict between whole populations. Governments employ propaganda techniques to arouse a populace against the enemy. The Christian must be alert to this.

Yoder, Edward. "The Peacemakers." *GH Supplement* 35 (Feb., 1943), 1022. Those people who are most like God in character work to remove strife and the causes of strife from among people.

Yoder, Edward. "The War Has Come: Peace Principles from a Scriptural Viewpoint." Part 28. *GH* 32 (Oct. 19, 1939), 637. In this time of confusion and despair we must be able to see God at work in the world.

Yoder, Edward. "War and Mental Breakdown." *GH Supplement* 37 (Aug., 1944), 392. Often war brings mental breakdown because of one's sense of guilt. The ethics of Jesus are the opposite of war.

Yoder, Edward. "Will Pastors Present Arms? Peace Principles from a Scriptural Viewpoint" Part 46. *GH Supplement* 34 (Oct., 1941), 631. So far preachers have been reluctant to support the war effort, but there are signs, unfortunately, that this sentiment is changing.

Yoder, Edward. "Worshipping Satan: Peace Principles from a Scriptural Viewpoint." Part 48. *GH Supplement* 34 (Dec., 1941), 822. Those who want America to defend religious liberty by war are deluding themselves; spiritual values cannot be defended with carnal weapons.

Yoder, Edward (Archival). Box 7: "The Christian's Attitude Toward Participation in War Activities;" 'Compromise with War." Goshen, IN. AMC. Hist. Mss. 1-47.

Yoder, J. Otis. "Is Love a Valid Basis for Ethics?" *ST* 34 (1st Qtr., 1966), 7. Concludes that divine holiness and not divine love is the valid basis of ethics.

Yoder, J. Otis. "The Awfulness of Divine Wrath." *ST* 40 (Mar., 1972), 29. The main reason for God's anger is sin, human rebellion and revolt against God.

Yoder, John H. "Christian Attitudes to War, Peace and Revolution: A Companion to Bainton." Study resource for War, Peace, and Revolution class, Goshen Biblical Seminary, Elkhart, Ind., 1983. Pp. 602. In 26 chapters presents class lectures on war and peace thought in historical perspective, from the biblical to the present periods.

Yoder, John H. *Karl Barth and the Problem of War.* Nashville: Abingdon, 1970. Pp. 141. A critique of Barth for stopping short of the Christian pacifism implicit in his work.

Yoder, John H. "The Christian and War." *United Evangelical Action* 13 (Oct. 1, 1954), 434, 445 [*sic.* 455]. Just as Jesus did not defend himself but suffered unto death, so we are to love those who treat us unjustly; we share in the triumph of the cross by walking in the way of the cross.

Distinguishes between the religious liberal peace position and the biblical peace position.

Yoder, John H. "What Does the Concept of the 'Just War' Mean?" *GH* 61 (June 4, 1968), 496-97. Instead of standing in judgment over just war critics of American policy, we should welcome this step forward as "an invitation to witness and a sign of potential capacity to make moral judgments on grounds other than patriotism or conformity." Explains the constraints of "just cause," "just means," and "just authority," which the just war theory places on the institution of war.

# B. Atomic War

"A Christian Approach to Nuclear War." *Menn* 77 (Nov. 6, 1962), 707-709. Adapted from the statement by the Church Peace Mission, this article calls on American Christians to renew their hope in the way of peace and to abandon reliance on military might. Includes an urgent plea for the discontinuation of stockpiling of nuclear armaments.

"A Message to the Churches." *GH* 52 (May 19, 1959), 465; "A Message to All Christians," *CanMenn* 7 (May 8, 1959), 2. A statement issued by the 1959 Church Peace Mission Conference calling the church to unequivocally renounce war and take decisive action to break the circle of armament and counter-armament. The use of nuclear weapons, particularly, should be completely renounced.

"A Nearly Non-existent Nonresistance." *CanMenn* 11 (Mar. 8, 1963), 6. Mennonites would rather have war with nuclear weapons than experience communism. In their fear of communism the Mennonites have become followers of Carl McIntire, Billy James Hargis, etc., instead of carrying the peaceful cross of Christ.

Alderfer, Helen. "Shelters for Pilgrims." *ChrLiv* 9 (Jan., 1962), 2. Editorial: calls for peace stance and concern for neighbors in an era of threatening nuclear war.

Atmosuwito, S. "The Desert: for Peace or War?" *ChrLiv* 8 (July, 1961), 36-37. Options for use of desert lands include development for food production or the testing of nuclear weapons.

Bainton, Roland H. "Christian Pacifism Reassessed." *CanMenn* 8, Part 1, (Oct. 7, 1960), 2, 11; Part 2, (Oct. 14, 1960), 2, 8. Also in *ChrLiv* 6 (Feb., 1959), 16-17, 39-40. Reprinted from *Christian Century.* 1958. A realistic look at atomic warfare in the light of the Christian ethic. Christian pacifism is a witness, not a political strategy for preventing a third world war.

Beachey, Duane. *Faith in a Nuclear Age.* Scottdale, PA: Herald Press, 1983. Pp. 128. Treats the issues of war and peace, issues such as the just war theory. The biblical bases for peacemaking, submission to authority, peace wtiness, etc., from the perspective of the contemporary nuclear situation.

Beyler, Betsy. "SALT II Not the Only Decision in SALT Debate." *MCC PS Wash. Memo* 11 (May-June, 1979), 1-2. The proposed SALT II agreements do not speak to the government's change in rhetoric from mutual deterrence to the concept of limited nuclear war.

Bicksler, Harriet S. Letter to the Editor. *EV* 92 (June 25, 1979), 2. An urgent plea for the church, and more particularly the Brethren in Christ Church, to speak out against war and the nuclear ams race.

Bleier, Brenton A. Letter to the Editor. *ChrLead* 42 (Sept. 25, 1979), 16. Asks for the politicization of *The Christian Leader* to stop. Explains that he would be willing to push the button in a nuclear exchange to protect our freedom.

Boyer, C. W. "Reflections on an Interview." *EV* 87 (Nov. 25, 1974), 5-6. Reflections on an interview, in which Albert Einstein states that the safety of humanity is dependent on "a reasonable or humane attitude or behavior" because, with atomic power, humanity holds the means for self-destruction.

Burnett, Kristina Mast. "Mennonites Threatened by Three Mile Incident." *ChrLead* 42 (Apr. 24, 1979), 16. Reports on the implications of the Three Mile Island near-tragic nuclear accident on Mar. 28, 1979, for Mennonites living in that area of Pennsylvania.

"Civil Defense and Christian Responsibility." *Menn* 77 (Mar. 20, 1962), 178-180. The MCC Peace Section's position statement on civil defense and preparation for nuclear war stresses the call to be a community of faith rather than of fear, one which witnesses against the false securities of preparation for war.

Charles, Howard H. (Review). *Biblical Realism Confronts the Nation,* edited by Paul Peachy. Fellowship Publications, 1963. Pp. 224. "Biblical Imperatives on the Question of War and Peace." *CanMenn* 12 (Apr. 28, 1964), 8. Book points out the stimulating contributions of both pacifists and non-pacifists to the current discussion of the church's responsibility in a nuclear age.

Derstine, C. F. "Is War with Russia Inevitable?" *ChrMon* 40 (May, 1948), 158. Analyzes the economic strength of the Soviet Union and exhorts believers to have faith in God in spite of the threat of nuclear war.

Derstine, C. F. "The Unnecessary War." *ChrMon* 42 (Aug., 1950), 254-55. Comment on World War II and the threat of nuclear war.

Enns, Elizabeth. Letter to the Editor. *MennRep* 10 (Mar. 31, 1980), 6. Registered nurse relates conscientious objection to the taking of fetal life to protesting war, nuclear weapons, and capital punishment.

Epp, Frank H. "A Call to Repentance." *CanMenn* 3 (Aug. 12, 1955), 2. A statement of repentance drawn up by the Fellowship of Reconciliation and concerned individuals on the tenth anniversary of the dropping of the atomic bomb. The nation which developed atomic power for war has the responsibility to develop atomic power for peace.

Epp, Frank H. "H-Bombs on H-Day." *CanMenn* 4 (May 25, 1956), 2. Condemns hydrogen bomb testing in general and the Pentecost Sunday test in particular. "All human and divine values, all sacredness in temporal living has suddenly been erased" when bombs are tested on holy days.

Epp, Frank H. "Our Hope Is in God." *CanMenn* 5 (July 19, 1957), 2. "God does not forsake the world or his children, but continues to woo them and to love them, so that they might yet turn to him." This is our only consolation as we face world destruction.

Epp, Frank H. "Sometimes I Pray for Nuclear War But I've Never Yet Said Amen!" Paper presented at Peace Days, Goshen College, Goshen, Ind., Oct. 20-23, 1968. Pp. 13. AMBS, BfC., CMBS/Win.

Epp, Frank H. "The Atomic Bomb Tests." *CanMenn* 3 (May 13, 1955), 2. Good cannot come from nations' testing weapons of mass destruction. While the physical results of atomic testing remain unknown, it is inevitable that this wrong use of resources will reap evil consequences.

Epp, Frank H. (Editorial). "War and Man." *CanMenn* 5 (July 19, 1957), 2. Summarizes statements made by 20 East and West scientists who met in Nova Scotia to discuss the consequences of nuclear war.

Erb, Paul. "The War Is Not Over." *GH* 38 (Aug. 31, 1945), 411. The war seems to be over but the evils which it was to cure still exist. The Atomic bomb, enormous national debts, and continued conscription are part of the legacy of this war.

Escalona, Sibylle. "Adolescence and the Threat of Nuclear War." *ChrLiv* 13 (Apr., 1966), 26-28. Reprinted from the pamphlet *Children and the Threat of Nuclear War,* 1962, Child Study Association and National Institute of Mental Health. Analysis of the threat of nuclear annihilation on adolescent development.

Franz, Delton. "A Time to Sound the Trumpet." *MCC PS Wash. Memo* 7 (July-Aug., 1975), 1-3. Discusses the White House and Pentagon's policy shift toward more freely considering limited nuclear war.

Franz, Delton. "The Carter Doctrine: A Blatant Gamble with 'Limited' Nuclear War." *MCC PS Wash. Memo* 12 (May-June, 1980), 1-4. Compares Carter's stance of military aggressiveness toward the Persian Gulf region with the more rational approach of trying to understand the grievances of adversaries in the region.

Gingerich, Melvin. "The Age of Terror." *GH* 51 (Sept. 16, 1958), 877, 889. An historical overview of war through the ages. Modern warfare makes the atomic age an age of terror. Peace will not come as long as humanity is sinful yet Christians must warn sinners of the consequences of their acts.

Gingerich, Melvin (Review). *The Bridge Is Love,* by Hans de Boer. Grand Rapids: Eerdmans, n.d. *GH* 52 (Jan. 20, 1959), 57, 69. Recommends this "travel" book for its emphasis on issues of apartheid, economic disparity, and nuclear war.

Gingerich, Ray C. "The Pacifist position of Helmut Gollwitzer." Paper presented to War, Peace, and Revolution class, AMBS, Elkhart, Ind., Apr. 10, 1969. Pp. 3. AMBS.

Graybill, Dave. "Mennonites Reflect on Values After Accident at Nuclear Plant." *GH* 72 (Apr. 24, 1979), 344-45. Individual responses of Mennonites in the area of the Three-Mile Island nuclear plant accident are presented.

Hassler, Alfred (Review). *The Voyage of the Lucky Dragon,* by Ralph E. Lapp. Harper, 1958. Pp.

200. "The Feel of Fallout." *Fellowship* 24 (July, 1958), 33. Describes how this book is able to personalize the horror and suffering caused by war by telling what happened to twenty-three fishermen when their boat was dusted with radioactive ashes from an American H-bomb test on Mar. 1, 1954. Recommends this book for its ability to awaken the conscience.

Haury, David A. "The Mennonite Congregation of Boston." *MennLife* 34 (Sept., 1979), 24-27. The birth and development of the Mennonite congregation of Boston including their concerns and mission regarding nuclear weapons, the Vietnam war, military service, and war taxes.

Hershberger, Guy F. "Christian Attitudes Toward Nuclear Warfare." In *Program Guide*, edited by Arnold Roth, pp. 104-106. Scottdale: Herald Press, 1967. General discussion about attitudes toward war which raise questions about responsible witness to the state.

Hershberger, Guy F., Metzler, Edgar, and Meyer, Albert J. "Theses on the Christian Witness to the State." Sub-committee report to the Peace Problems Committee of the Mennonite Church, June 22, 1960. Pp. 32. MHL.

Hershberger, Paul. "Editorial." *IPF Notes* 3 (May, 1957), 2, 5-6. Comment on the cold war and the nuclear arms race.

Hinshaw, Cecil. "The Relevance of Non-Violence." *MennLife* 17 (Apr., 1962), 59-63. Considers how the techniques and practice of nonviolence might be relevant to both the political and religious aspects of life.

"Japanese Christian Peace Witness." *CanMenn* 7 (Aug. 21, 1959), 7. Because of continuing problems facing Japan, a Christian witness is definitely needed in our contemporary nuclear age.

Klaassen, Walter. *What Have You to Do with Peace?* Altona: D. W. Friesen and Sons, Ltd., 1969. Pp. 74. Originally given as lectures designed to help Sunday school teachers teach the basic principles of nonviolence. Covers subjects such as the biblical use of the language of "principalities and powers," the church as the agency of peace, just war doctrine, nuclear war and disarmament issues, and church and state relations.

Koontz, Ted (Review). *The Fate of the Earth*, by Jonathan Schell. NY: Alfred A. Knopf, 1982. Pp. 244. *CGR* 1 (Winter, 1983), 67-72. Criticizes Schell's book first for focusing the extinction of the human race as the sole danger of nuclear war, a distortion of the multiple considerations which must inform a rounded perception of the nuclear situation. Secondly criticizes the secular

nature of Schell's discussion, saying that by prioritizing the survival of the race in his value structure, he has given humanity the place that belongs to God.

Koop, Robert. "Transfiguration." *Menn* 93 (Nov. 14, 1978), 671; *MennRep* 8 (Oct. 16, 1978), 8. Discusses the convergence of the church's celebration of Jesus' transfiguration, Aug. 6, with that day in 1945 when Hiroshima was transformed into a city of death by the atomic bomb.

Kraybill, Donald B. *Facing Nuclear War: A Plea for Christian Witness.* Scottdale and Kitchener: Herald Press, 1982. Pp. 307. Using the tragedy of Hiroshima as a reference point, Kraybill provides clear information on the effects of contemporary nuclear weapons. In light of this "chief moral issue," he analyzes the global political situation and interweaves, with these technological and political analyses, the pertinent biblical perspectives offering guidance to Christian responses to the threat of nuclear war. In the last part of the book he concretizes these responses by suggesting specific actions individuals can take toward peace and explodes some of the excuses commonly given for not taking action.

Kreider, Alan. "Biblical Perspectives on War." *Third Way* 4 (Nov., 1980), 13-14. Brings the Old Testament prophetic insistence—that Israel rely on Yahweh rather than numerical, technological or nonrestricted military strength—to bear upon our modern quest for security in nuclear weapons.

Kreider, Alan. "Swords into Plowshares." *Time to Choose: A Grass Roots Study Guide on the Nuclear Arms Race from a Christian Perspective.* Ed. Martha Keys Barker, et al. Dorset: Celebration Publishing, 1983, 54-88. Summarizes both the just war and pacifist positions and explains why adherents of both positions might together decry nuclear war.

Kreider, Alan. "The Arms Race: The Defense Debate—Nuclear Weaponry and Pacifism." *The Year 2000*, ed. John R. W. Stott. Downers Grove: InterVarsity Press, 1983, 27-55. Pp. 179. Since the security afforded by deterrence policy is neither adequate nor real, and since pacifists and just war theorists agree that nuclear war is indefensible, we ought to unite, despite other differences, in order to search for viable alternatives for conflict resolution.

Kreider, Alan. "Why the Christian Church Must Be Pacifist." *Ireland and the Threat of Nuclear War*, ed. Bill McSweeney. Dublin: Dominican Publications, 1985. Pp. 83-103. Pacifism is now growing in the Church for several reasons: people have seen the futility of military violence in attaining its objectives; new biblical and theological insights undermine former justifications for violence; because attempts to control modern events have had unanticipated results, Christians are abandoning consequential ethics for principled, prophetic nonconformity; and Christians have discovered that violence does not exhaust the possibilities for relevant involvement in the world.

Kreider, Carl. "US Resumes Atmospheric Nuclear Testing." *ChrLiv* 9 (July, 1962), 18, 34. Lay people have the right and responsibility to speak out about the drastic effects of nuclear testing and war.

Kreider, Carl (Review). *Peace or Atomic War?* by Albert Schweitzer. New York: Henry Holt and Co., 1958. Pp. 47. *ChrLiv* 6 (Sept., 1959), 33. Reviewer observes that Schweitzer presents his objections to testing and production of nuclear weapons simply and clearly.

Kreider, L. C. "The Atomic Age." *Menn* 60 (Aug. 28, 1945), 1-2. A brief description of the development of atomic power, its uses in peace and war, and the Christian attitude toward the atomic bomb.

Kreider, Robert S. "Deadly Force Authorized." *Menn* 94 (June 19, 1979), 418-19. Reports a visit to the Titan II installation of McConnell Air Force Base in Kansas, and the feelings evoked by the dangers of this weapon.

Kreider, Robert S. "Use of Deadly Force Authorized." *Sojourners* 9 (July, 1979), 36. Meditation on a visit to a Titan II installation of McConnell Air Force Base in Kansas.

Kroeker, Marvin (Review). *Between the Eagle and the Dove: The Christian and American Foreign Policy,* by Ronald Kirkemo. Downers Grove: InterVarsity, 1976. Pp. 215. *ChrLeader* 40 (Oct. 11, 1977), 11. This "Christian perspective" on such issues as war, nuclear armaments, and international relations is not distinguishable from a "strictly secular" perspective. Therefore the book is neither newly insightful nor compatible with an Anabaptist-Mennonite view.

"Let Us Renounce Nuclear War." *CanMenn* 7 (May 8, 1959), 2. Statement adopted at the Third National Conference of the Church Peace Mission, Apr. 20-23, 1959, at Evanston, Ill., by delegates from twenty denominations.

Lapp, John A. (Review). *Foreign Policy in Christian Perspective,* by John C. Bennett. Charles Scribner's Sons, 1966. Pp. 110. *ChrLiv* 13 (Nov., 1966), 28-29. Recommends this examination of the cold war, nuclear weapons, and Vietnam in light of Christian realism.

Mennonite Disaster Service. "Mennonite Disaster Service and Civilian Defense." *GH* 54 (Oct. 3,

1961), 873. In the event of nuclear war Mennonites should give service to save lives through MDS and without involvement in military aspects of Civilian Defense.

Metzler, Edgar. "The Church and the Civil Defense Dilemma." *CanMenn* 10 (Nov. 9, 1962), 5-6; "The Church and the Fallout Shelter Program." *GH* 55 (Nov. 13, 1962), 997-99. Presents the challenge the church faces in the increasing interest in fallout shelters and similar preparations for nuclear war.

Miller, Levi. "The Nuclear Threat." *Builder* 32 (Jan., 1982), 2-3. Although the historic peace churches have a long history of dealing with such war and peace issues as conscription, the issues of nuclear war are relatively new and require study and action.

Miller, Paul M. (Review). *This Atomic Age and the World of God,* by Wilbur M. Smith. Boston: W. A. Wilde Co., 1948. Pp. 363. *ChrMon* 41 (Mar., 1949), 86-87. Reviewer recommends the book for its study of the implications of releasing nuclear energy and its relating the effects of the bomb to select biblical passages.

Nelson, Boyd N. (Review). *The Irreversible Decision,* by Robert C. Batchelder. Macmillan, 1965. *ChrLiv* 13 (June, 1966), 34. Recommends this doctoral dissertation tracing the development of the atomic bomb and American military strategy in World War II.

Neufeld, Elmer. "Defense: Civilian, Military, or Spiritual." Paper read to MDS meeting, Chicago, Ill., Feb. 11, 1960.

Niemoeller, Martin. "The Way of Peace." *GH* 48 (Feb. 15, 1955), 153; *CanMenn* 5 (July 19, 1957), 2. The author talks with three leading German nuclear physicists. The destructive power of the bomb cannot be exaggerated; war is madness. The New Testament's teaching of peace is the only answer.

Ortman, David. Letter to the Editor. *Menn* 92 (Jan. 25, 1977), 61. Reprints letter written to President Carter on "deeply troubling" issues such as development of the Trident undersea missile system, production of the B-1 bomber, and absence of amnesty for war resisters.

"Peace Play Presented by Markham Players." *CanMenn* 15 (Jan. 10, 1967), 4. Members of the Markham (Ill.) Mennonite Church presented a play, "Which Way the Wind?" in lieu of the church's Sunday morning worship service. The play was about atomic war and world peace.

"Protestants, Jews, Catholics Discuss Nuclear Warfare." *CanMenn* 11 (Dec. 3, 1963), 4. John Howard Yoder, Clarence Bauman, and Paul Peachey were participants in the Nuclear War

Institute held at West Baden Jesuit Seminary in Indianapolis, Nov. 8-10, 1963.

Peachey, Paul L. "A Decade of the Peace of Fear." *GH* 50 (Mar. 19, 1957), 273. Persons are beginning to realize that the real problem in the atomic age is a moral and spiritual one. What does this mean for those of us who have supposedly known this tragic fact all along?

Peachey, Paul L. "Dare We Work for Peace?" *The Japan Christian Quarterly* 24 (Oct., 1958), 283-89. As the Japanese church struggles to understand its role in the world's yearning for peace, it faces such issues as the ideological differences between East and West, the strengths and weaknesses of the various peace theories, and the meaning of Japan's experience with atomic war.

Peachey, Paul L. "Evangelical Christianity and Atomic War." *United Evangelical Action* 14 (Oct. 15, 1955), 467-68, 472, 474. Argues that the union of evangelicalism and pacifism is not only theologically compatible but necessary as well. Also as paper, n.d. Pp. 7. AMBS.

Peachey, Paul L. (Editorial). "Is There Still Any Point to Conscientious Objection?" *RepConsS* 21 (June, 1964), 2. In order to meet the challenges presented by the threat of nuclear war, the CO position must be based on a less dubious premise than the hope that war will be eradicated through a popular adoption of the CO position.

Perry, Shawn, ed. *Words of Conscience: Religious Statements on Conscientious Objection.* Washington, DC: National Interreligious Service Board for Conscientious Objectors, 1980. 9th ed. Official and unofficial statements by Catholic, Protestant, Jewish, Krishna, Muslim, Buddhist, and American Indian groups. Includes essays on war and conscientious objection, and a section on nuclear pacifism. Some earlier editions have been edited by Mennonites (e.g., Michael L. Yoder, 4th ed.; J. Harold Sherk, 6th ed.; Gerald E. Shenk, 7th ed., etc.) and have included some Mennonite statements.

Ratzlaff, Peter. "Not in the Bomb." *CanMenn* 5 (Aug. 16, 1957), 2. Hope is found in God as international scientific group issues statement against nuclear war.

Reimer, Margaret Loewen. "The China Syndrome: Horrifying Coincidence." *MennRep* 9 (Apr. 30, 1979), 7. The story and timing of the movie, "The China Syndrome" coincides with the nuclear accident at Three Mile Island; despite the reassurances and manipulation of statistics, the dangers are frightening.

Reimer, Vic. "Nuclear Threat to World Stressed." *Menn* 94 (Jan. 2, 1979), 7. The first nuclear war conference held Dec. 7, 1978, in Washington, DC, discussed the inevitability of nuclear war, how it would start, where it would be fought, and its devastating effects.

Reimer, Vic. "The Arms Race: Playing Games with the Planet." *MennRep* 9 (Jan. 8, 1979), 3. The first nuclear war conference held Dec. 7, 1978, in Washington, DC, featured a panel of scientists, military men, and public affairs analysts, who discussed the threat of a nuclear holocaust.

Schrag, Martin H. "The New Call to Peacemaking—Hearing and Heeding the Call." *EV* 91 (Dec. 25, 1978), 5-7. A report on the national meeting of the New Call to Peacemaking held at Green Lake, Wis. Although the US is presently not engaged in a war, the threat of a nuclear holocaust, the possibility of conscription, and the build-up of arms, among other things, all urge us to heed the call to peacemaking.

Schrock, Paul M. "Peace and War: Atomic Love." *GH* 47 (July 20, 1954, 681. The greatest power in the universe is nonresistant love. It is required of the New Testament believer in all aspects of life.

Shetler, Sanford G. "Peace and War: The Hydrogen Bomb and Our Peace Testimony." *GH* 48 (Jan. 18, 1955), 57. The witness should be not only against the hydrogen bombs but against all war, all weapons. The world should know we are fighting a spiritual battle.

Sider, Ronald J. "Jesus' Resurrection and the Search for Peace and Justice." *Christian Century* 99 (Nov. 3, 1982), 1103-1108. Develops four theses explaining why the bodily resurrection of Jesus is important to the issues of nuclear war: 1) As the foundation for understanding the lordship of Jesus, 2) as source of strength for the struggle for justice, 3) as the clue to the relationship between our work for justice and the shalom of the second coming, and 4) as the base from which to confront the powers.

Sider, Ronald J. and Taylor, Richard K. "The Awesome Danger of Nuclear War." *The Other Side* 18 (Jan., 1982), 10-17. Questions both the logic and morality of the "deterrence" theory of national defense.

Smucker, Barbara Claassen. "And the Darkness Became Light." *MennLife* 1 (July, 1946), 28-32. Fantasy story about life in underground tunnels during nuclear war.

Stoner, John K. "A Parable." *EV* 91 (June 25, 1978), 11. A note of warning that we ought to pay attention to the threat of a nuclear war and not sit idly by.

Stoner, John K. "War Tax Dilemma: The Arms Race or the Human Race?" *Peace Section Newsletter* 9 (Dec., 1979), 7-8. War tax resistance is not the only way to say that nuclear deterrence is wrong, but it might be one way.

Stoner, John K. (Review). *Between a Rock and a Hard Place*, by Mark Hatfield. Waco, Tex.: Word Books, 1976. Pp. 224. *Menn* 91 (Oct. 26, 1976), 633; *ChrLead* 39 (Aug. 17, 1976), 14. Hatfield prods the church to separate its vision from the destiny of America, examining questions of nuclear war, violence, and patriotism.

"The Atomic Bomb Is No Fun Anymore." *CanMenn* 17 (Mar. 25, 1969), 1, 2. Report of a teach-in on war held in Winnipeg on Mar. 22. Walter Dinsdale, M.P., was one speaker. Frank Epp, William Eichhorst who is dean of the faculty at the Winnipeg Bible Institute, and David Schroeder spoke as well.

"The Christian and Nuclear Power." *Menn* 74 (Sept. 8, 1959), 549. The official statement of the 1959 conference of the GCMC earnestly urges government leaders to promote the peaceful uses of atomic energy and vigorously opposes the use of natural resources for purposes of war.

"The Empty Tomb at Hiroshima." *CanMenn* 6 (Nov. 28, 1958), 2. Little remains outwardly of the destruction and death caused by the bomb on Hiroshima, but the Memorial Peace Park with its flowers and monuments pleads that war should cease.

"The Possibility of a Nuclear Holocaust: Four Responses." *GH* 72 (May 29, 1979), 430-33.

Allen Brenneman, Stanley Shenk, John K. Stoner, and Patricia Lehman MacFarland write about the destruction of impending nuclear war.

van der Laag, Tina. "'By My Spirit.'" *ChrMon* 42 (Aug., 1950), 247. Goshen College student from Holland recounts memories of World War II and comments on the possiblity of nuclear war.

Voth, Orville L. "The Scientist and War." *MennLife* 23 (Apr., 1968), 84-87. Reports growing unease in the scientific community with regard to the Vietnam War and with regard to nuclear war.

Wald, George. "A Generation Unsure that It Has a Future." *MCC PS Wash. Memo* 1 (June, 1969), 7-9. Reprint from *Congressional Record* of an address on the Vietnam war and the threat of nuclear war.

Wenger, Samuel S. "Peace and War: The Way of Love in This Atomic Age." *GH* 53 (Feb. 16, 1960), 145. The Christian follows Jesus, loves his or her fellow human beings, and witnesses to them. Killing people is inconsistent with all three of these vocations.

Wiebe, Doug. "The Second Nativity." *God and Caesar* 5 (Apr., 1979), 7. A poem describing nuclear war ends on a note of hope, Jesus returning as a child, suffering from a war before its birth.

Williams, Melvin. "What's the Difference?" *YCC* 47 (Oct. 2, 1966), 2. In light of the universal question, "When will I be blown up?" critical comments are directed to those who don't care.

# C. Postwar*

Bender, Harold S. "Mennonites Testify at Hearings on Post-War Military Policy." *Menn* 60 (July 10, 1945), 5-6. The MCC statement made at the hearings of the House Select Committee on Post-War Military Policy. The statement recounts the history of the Mennonite peace witness, and witnesses against permanent peacetime conscription.

Beyler, Betsy. "Indochina Is Still on the Map—and on the Agenda." *MCC PS Wash. Memo* 10 (May-June, 1978), 6-7. US bombing during the war and deplorable post-war conditions have created severe problems for Vietnam, Laos, and Kampuchea.

Derstine, C. F. "Mennonite Ex-CPS Men Serve in Sixteen Nations." *ChrMon* 39 (Aug., 1947), 255-56. The MCC post-war relief programs have their roots in the Civilian Public Service program.

See also 10C, Relief.

Derstine, C. F. "The German and Japanese Nations from the Christian Viewpoint." *ChrMon* 37 (Nov., 1945), 302-3. Americans should forgive Germany and Japan and participate in the rebuilding of their physical and spiritual lives.

Derstine, C. F. "The NRA—The American Social Experiment." *ChrMon* 26 (Jan., 1934), 30. The National Recovery Act is an effort to correct an unjust situation, and it may have God's blessing, because God hears the cry of the poor.

Derstine, C. F. "The Palace of the Soviets." *ChrMon* 37 (Aug., 1945), 222-23. World War II did not solve problems; instead, the Soviet Union gathered power and influence.

Derstine, C. F. "The War Ended, the Malady Lingering On." *ChrMon* 39 (Dec., 1947), 382-83. In the face of continued world tensions, evangelical Christians should pray, practice loving enemies, support European evangelism and relief work.

Detweiler, Henry S. "Laying Bricks and Sawing Boards in the Name of Christ." *MCC WSRB* 2 (Sept., 1946), 1-3, 4. Describes the work of the MCC Reconstruction unit established in post-war Holland.

Ediger, Max. "Handles for Lending a Hand." *Menn* 88 (July 10, 1973), 440. Outlines tasks in which MCC could participate in reconstructing Vietnam after the ceasefire, such as encouraging refugees to move back to their lands, helping to clear the land of unexploded ordnance, continuing with missions and medical programs.

Epp, Hermann. "Mennonite Principles on Europe's Stage and Pulpit." *MennLife* 3 (Jan., 1948), 7, 21-22. The Mennonites have become a well-known group throughout much of post-war Europe due to their sacrificial service; now Mennonite principles are being expressed and debated by means of sermons and dramas written by non-Mennonites.

Esau, Elmer. "A Day in a Refugee Camp." *MCC WSRB* 2 (July, 1946), 1-2. Describes life in Danish refugee camp housing war evacuees.

Fretz, J. Winfield. "Post-War Problems Facing Mennonites." *Menn* 59 (May 9, 1944), 6-7; *ChrMon* 36 (July, 1944), 200. The post-war world will see great disillusionment and spiritual callousness on the part of the citizenry and increasing totalitarianism on the part of the government. Mennonites must not be complacent in the face of these pressures.

Fretz, J. Winfield. "Survey Men's Post-War Interests and Needs." *CPS Bull* 2 (Mar. 8, 1944), 3-4. Preliminary findings of the needs of CPS men after the war.

Gleysteen, Jan (Review). *Transfigured Night,* by Eileen Egan and Elizabeth Reiss. Livingston Pub. Co., 1964. Pp. 186. *ChrLiv* 12 (Dec., 1965), 37. Recommends this documented account of relief work done in Germany following World War II by eighteen relief agencies, including Mennonite work.

Goering, James A. (Review). *The Struggle for a Soul,* by William L. Hull. NY: Doubleday and Co., Inc., 1963. *ST* 33 (3rd Qtr., 1965), 23. A candid account of efforts to lead Adolf Eichmann, a man responsible for the extermination of six million Jews under Hitler, to a saving knowledge of Jesus Christ.

Hackman, Walton. "A Call for Concern and Action to Help Vietnamese Political Prisoners." *MennRep* 3 (Sept. 17, 1973), 7. Exposes the plight of South Vietnamese prisoners of war still held despite the cease-fire, and of the political prisoners not covered in the cease-fire who were detained for opposition to the war. Discusses US implication in their plight.

Hackman, Walton. "The Issue Now Is Amnesty." *GH* 65 (Jan. 4, 1972), 9-10. Reprinted from MCC Peace Section *Newsletter.* After World War II, only 10 percent of Selective Service violators were pardoned. Writer wonders whether present society has enough latitude to respect and accept the estimated 100,000 Vietnam War resisters.

Hiebert, Linda Gibson and Hiebert, Murray. "Laos Recovers from America's War." *Southeast Asia Chronicle* 61, special issue (Mar.-Apr., 1978), 1-20. Series of articles by MCCers discuss the political situation and possibilities in Laos, Laotian efforts to recover from the devastation of drought and bombing, the social problems created by the war, health needs, and economic problems.

Hiebert, Linda Gibson and Hiebert, Murray. "MCC Volunteer Describes Life in Vietnam." *Menn* 92 (Jan. 25, 1977), 55. Yoshihiro Ichakawa, MCC volunteer in Vietnam, describes post-war life in Saigon since the change in government, reporting on changes in local administration, land reform, reeducation centers, attitudes of church people.

Hiebert, Murray and Hiebert, Linda Gibson. "Laos Fights New War." *Menn* 92 (June 7, 1977), 377. Complicating Laotian attempts at postwar recovery are widespread disease, unexploded ordnance in fields, few surviving draft animals, and inadequate harvests.

Horst, J. Alton. "Peculiar Americans." *ChrMon* 40 (Mar., 1948), 82-83. Stories of Mennonite help given to war sufferers in Belgium and Poland.

Hostetter, J. J. "Notes from Belgium." *ChrMon* 40 (June, 1948), 178-79. Comment on the wartime destruction in Belgium and Mennonite efforts at reconstruction.

Hunsberger, Wilson. "Interesting Scenes in Europe; Warsaw—Life Among the Ruins." *ChrMon* 40, Part 5, (Oct., 1948), 308-9. Describes the German bombing of Poland and the present state of the city.

Hunsberger, Wilson. "Oswiecim, City of Death." *ChrMon* 40 (Sept., 1948), 278-79. Description of a Nazi concentration camp in southern Poland.

Hylkema, T. O. "To the Mennonites in America a Message from the Dutch Mennonites." *ChrMon* 40 (Jan., 1948), 5-7. A leader of the peace movement among Dutch Mennonites thanks American Mennonites for their relief work during and after the war.

"I-Ws Build Block Upon Block at Enkenbach." *RepConsS* 18 (Nov., 1961), 1. One hundred fifty I-Ws have spent 624,000 work hours to build forty-four houses for refugees in Enkenbach, Germany.

Inja, C. "Dutch Peace Group Sponsors Witness and Action Program." *CanMenn* 13 (Oct. 26, 1965), 3. A report on the Dutch Mennonite Peace Group organized in 1922. MCC's work in post-war Europe taught this group that if a peace witness is to be effective, it must be accompanied by positive acts. The Peace Group has sent substantial aid to Algeria. Meetings are attended by Mennonites, Dutch Reformed, Lutherans, Baptists, Roman Catholics, and humanists.

Jansen, Curtis, "Building for Eternity." *ChrLiv* 1 (Feb., 1954), 4-5, 42-43. The PAX program began as a system for building houses for refugees in Europe.

Janzen, Curtis. "Our PAX Boys in Europe." *MennLife* 9 (Apr., 1954), 80-82. Description of rebuilding and resettlement projects in post-war Europe.

Joy, Charles R. "The Lost Parents of Europe." *MennComm* 5 (Aug., 1951), 12-14. Documents the plight of orphans and children separated from their parents in war-torn Europe.

Juhnke, James C. "Mennonite Benevolence and Civic Identity: the Post-War Compromise." *MennLife* 25 (Jan., 1970), 34-37. Examines the thesis that Mennonite relief and service efforts, historically most energetic during wartime, originate in American nationalism. Notes that these efforts may in fact grow from a Mennonite need to contribute "meaningfully and sacrificially toward national goals" in a time when others are ofering their lives to the war effort.

Koontz, Gayle Gerber. "Vietnam Churches See Challenges, Pressures." *Menn* 90 (Sept. 16, 1975), 511. MCC volunteer returned from Vietnam discusses the change of government there and the challenges facing the church in helping to rebuild the country after the war.

Kreider, Carl. "The Berlin Crisis." *ChrLiv* 6 (May, 1959), 18, 29, 40. Summary of the events leading to the partitioning of Germany, and comment upon the possibility of world war.

Kreider, Carl. "The Changing Pattern of International Relations." *ChrLiv* 3 (July, 1956), 22, 32-33. Post-World War II assumptions about American policy and military strategy are being called into question by recent international developments.

Kreider, Carl. "The Japanese Election." *MennComm* 6 (Dec., 1952), 29-31. Japanese rearmament is one of the issues of the election disputes.

Kreider, Carl. "The Problem of Berlin." *ChrLiv* 8 (Sept., 1961), 18-19, 34. The divided city of Berlin is a symbol of the futility of war, as well as an explosive problem in the present Cold War.

Kreider, Carl. "The Schuman Plan." *MennComm* 6 (Mar., 1952), 30, 32. The Schuman Plan, integrating the coal and steel industries of Western Europe, is a constructive step toward world peace.

Kreider, Carl. "Underdeveloped Areas." *ChrLiv* 3 (April, 1956), 22, 43-44. Much of the post-war US economic aid is being diverted into military aid.

Kreider, Robert S. "Mennonite Refugees in Germany." *MCC WSRB* 2 (July, 1946), 4. Describes MCC efforts to make possible the migration of Russian Mennonite refugees in Berlin.

Lehman, Galen T. "What Price Glory?" *ChrMon* 29 (Jan., 1937), 17, 29. Adds up the cost of World War I in terms of lives, dollars, and moral lapse.

Lehman, M[artin] C[lifford]. "Diseases Incident to War Suffering; Needs and Conditions in Europe." *ChrMon* 37, Part 6, (Dec., 1945), 323. Post-war living conditions contribute to the spread of diseases.

Lehman, M[artin] C[lifford]. "Lack of Shelter; Needs and Conditions in Europe." *ChrMon* 37, Part 5, (Nov., 1945), 288. Civilians are most seriously affected by the lack of fiber for adequate clothing and fuel for heating.

Lehman, M[artin] C[lifford]. "Need of Shelter; Needs and Conditions in Europe." *ChrMon* 37, Part 4, (Oct., 1945), 256. Bombing and "scorched earth" policy destroy housing and shelter.

Lehman, M[artin] C[lifford]. "The Need for Food; Needs and Conditions in Europe." *ChrMon* 37, Part 3, (Sept., 1945), 233, 240. A majority of Europe's 30 million people are hungry because of the war.

Lehman, M[artin] C[lifford]. "Uprooted People; Needs and Conditions in Europe." *ChrMon* 37, Part 2, (Aug., 1945), 205-6. The war has created millions of refugees and prisoners.

Lind, Miriam Sieber, "A Time to Say No," as told by Roy Buchanan. *ChrLiv* 7 (Sept., 1960), 6-10, 34-35; 7 (Oct., 1960), 12-15, 34; 7 (Nov., 1960), 14-17, 19, 33-34; 7 (Dec., 1960), 22-25, 32-33; 8 (Jan., 1961), 24-27, 34. Experiences of a conscientious objector during World War I:

draft; imprisonment in guardhouse; discrimination ; persecution; reconstruction work in France.

Long, C. Warren. "Christian Service in Belgium." *ChrMon* 39 (Sept., 1947), 272. Although emergency relief in Belgium is no longer needed, rehabilitation from the effects of the war continues.

Martin, Earl S. *Reaching the Other Side: The Journal of an American Who Stayed to Witness Vietnam's Post-War Transition.* New York: Crown Publishers, Inc., 1978. Pp. 281. Journal records actions and observations of an MCCer during the six-week period between the time the Provisional Revolutionary Government (Viet Cong) stages a peaceful takeover of Quang Ngai City and the fall of Saigon. An intimate view of the day to day ramifications of trying to live out the MCC philosophy of ministering beyond the boundaries of nationality and political ideology.

Martin, Earl S. and Martin, Patricia Hostetter. "Interview: A Family's Account of Revolution and the Church in Post War Vietnam." *Sojourners* 5 (Jan., 1976), 29. Evaluation of the Revolution in Vietnam both before and after the change of government. Predicts that the church will grow smaller as government does a better job meeting the physical needs of the people.

Martin, Luke S. "How Does One Serve and Witness in a Marxist Society?" *Menn* 93 (Sept. 19, 1978), 536. Outlines new challenges for the evangelical church in Vietnam during post-war years under a communist government.

Martin, Luke S. "Vietnam Undergoing a Revolution." *Menn* 93 (Sept. 12, 1978), 520. Describes political changes in post-war Vietnam under communist government.

Mennonite Central Committee. "Mennonites Testify at Hearings on Post-War Military Policy," *Menn* 60 (July 10, 1945), 5-6; "A Statement of Position on Permanent Peacetime Conscription and the Christian Conscience Against War," *GH* 38 (July 20, 1945), 297-98. A statement presented to the House Select Committee on Postwar Military Policy opposes conscription from the perspective of biblical understandings, the nonresistant tradition, and a concern for freedom of conscience.

Morris, Edita. "Hiroshima Man." *ChrLiv* 12 (Oct., 1965), 6-7. Reprinted from *Liberation* magazine. The tragic economic and medical situation of the Hiroshima survivors.

Moyal, Maurice. "Father to the Orphans of Europe." *ChrLiv* 6 (Sept., 1959), 20-22. Doctor establishes home for war orphans in Austria after World War II.

Moyal, Maurice. "Introduction to Jesus." *ChrLiv* 4 (Aug., 1957), 20-21, 37. Neighborhood ministry to French children, victims of war and foreign occupation.

"News from the Peace Front." *Fellowship* 24 (June 1, 1958), 4. News statement reporting that Benjamin Kauffman, a 23-year-old Amish farmer, has been sentenced to eighteen months in prison for refusing to accept a civilian work assignment as a CO in an institution using modern conveniences.

Neufeld, David (Review). *Reaching the Other Side,* by Earl S. Martin. New York: Crown Publishers, Inc., 1978. Pp. 282. *MennRep* 9 (Sept. 17, 1979), 8. A journal written by an American working for MCC in Vietnam depicting the situation and people of Vietnam during the post-war transition.

Peachey, Paul L. "Rehabilitation in the Name of Christ." *ChrMon* 40 (Jan., 1948), 16-17. Outlines the plight of Belgian collaborators with the enemy and MCC efforts to provide help to their families.

Regehr, Lydia. "War's Aftermath." *MBH* 18 (Oct. 26, 1979), 7. Short poem on famine, the only victor in war.

Regier, C. C. "A Christian Witness in War and Peace." *MennLife* 4 (Jan., 1949), 17-20. Describes the work of the historic peace churches in setting up the CPS program with Selective Service. Includes history and statistics of the Civilian Public Service program during World War II and post-war relief work.

*Report of American Mennonite Relief to Holland, 1945-1947.* Druk de Bussy, Amsterdam: MCC, [1947]. Pp. 14. MHL. Text and photos recount the story of the post-war service project. Describes distribution of clothes and food, reconstruction efforts, caring for the Mennonite refugees, etc.

Rich, Elaine Sommers. "A Danzig Mennonite, as Told to Elaine Sommers Rich, 'I Was a Refugee.' " *ChrLiv* 2 (Dec., 1955), 20-21. Unforgettable horrors of war are still etched in the refugee's memory ten years later.

Richert, P. H. "Our Post-War Youth Problem." *Menn* 58 (Aug. 10, 1943), 6-7. Those who participated in the military voluntarily should receive some disciplining action when they return. Yet the church must find a way to deal with the individual conscience.

Root, Robert. "European Relief Needs." *ChrMon* 39 (Feb., 1947), 37. Church World Service peace correspondent outlines the needs present in war torn Europe.

Unsigned. "Symposium on Post-War

Conscription." *CPS Bull* 3 (Oct. 22, 1944), 5-6. Most of the seven CPS respondents encourage the Mennonite church to continue an alternative service program whether or not peacetime conscription becomes a reality.

Waltner, Emil J. "Difficulties in Applying Non-Conformity in Modern Life." *PCMCP Third,* 53-67. North Newton, Kansas: n.p. Held at North Newton, Kansas, Aug. 18-19, 1944. As people attempt to live a life of nonconformity in modern times, the issue of post-war military training is one of the most challenging.

# D. Communism and Anticommunism

"A Christian Declaration on Communism and Anti-Communism." *Menn* 79 (Apr. 28, 1964), 282. A condensed version of the statement adopted by the General Conference of the GCMC in 1962. While rejecting any ideology opposed to the gospel of Jesus, the church rejects also any holy war approach toward communism. The lived gospel of peace is the best answer.

"A Nearly Non-existent Nonresistance." *CanMenn* 11 (Mar. 8, 1963), 6. Mennonites would rather have war with nuclear weapons than experience communism. In their fear of communism the Mennonites have become followers of Carl McIntire, Billy James Hargis, etc., instead of carrying the peaceful cross of Christ.

"Anti-Communism on the Radio and in the Press." *GH* 57 (Apr. 21, 1964), 337-38. PPC notes that many of the anti-communist crusades in America use a manner of attack which is unchristian. We should not lend such movements our support.

Augsburger, David W. "Who Is Bringing Communism?" *MBH* 13 (Apr. 19, 1974), 2-3. Any society that preserves the status quo at any cost and sacrifices justice is ripe for communism.

Bauman, Clarence; Dyck, Peter; and Harms, Doreen. "Communist Youth Festival." *Menn* 74 (Sept. 15, 1959), 564-65; *GH* 52 (Nov. 17, 1959), 985. Report on the Seventh World Festival (communist) of Youth and Students in Vienna attended by Mennonites whose purpose was "to learn and to witness." Summarizes the presentations at the "International Meeting of Young Christians" on the subject "Religion and Peace."

Beechy, Atlee. "Courteous Reception by NLF, DRVN Representatives." *CanMenn* 16 (Oct. 8, 1968), 1, 2; (Oct. 15, 1968), 4. After a visit to North Vietnam, Beechy outlines his preparations for the contact with communist leaders, describes his contacts with North Vietnam government officials in various countries of Asia, Africa, and Europe, and cites his impressions of the mission sponsored by

MCC. Part 1 deals with the translated Mennonite documents given to all the representatives and the courteous reception given to Beechy.

Bohn, E. Stanley. "More Peacemaker Audiovisuals." *Builder* 18 (May, 1968), 15-16. Listing of audio-visual resources prepared for use with series of Sunday school lessons on "Peacemakers in a Broken World." Subjects covered: "Extremism and Communism," "Race," and "Poverty."

Bordeaux, Michael. "Baptists and Other Protestants." *MBH* 13 (Jan. 25, 1974), 4-7. Mennonites in the Soviet Union give up pacifism through official ties with Baptists, an arrangement made necessary by Soviet policies toward evangelical Christians.

Brunk, George R., I. "The World Revolution Idea." *ST* 4 (July, 1932), 11. Discusses the world-revolution idea which has the purpose of putting an end to wars and promoting humanitarianism which in reality leads to communism.

Burkholder, J. Lawrence. "Notes on the Theological Meaning of China." *Mission-Focus* 4 (Jan., 1976), 1-5. Writer points out the striking analogies and differences between Chinese Marxism and Christianity and discusses the theological problem of how China should be viewed in light of these contradictions.

Burkholder, J. Lawrence. "Our Attitude Toward Communism." *GH* 44 (May 1, 1951), 409-410. The Christian evaluates communist structures and persons in a spirit of fairness and love, ready to admit that not all of our institutions are beyond reproach. Communism can only be stopped by fighting poverty and oppression.

"Christian Nonresistance Only Alternative to Communism." *CanMenn* 7 (Oct. 16, 1959), 1, 10. André Trocmé addresses MCC personnel in Akron, Pennsylvania, stressing the church's responsibility for the Christian peace witness.

"Communism and Anti-communism." *Menn* 77 (June 5, 1962), 370-71. The statement of the General Conference Mennonite Church contends that our gospel of love, in word and deed, is for all people. Communism can only be overcome by peaceful witness to Christian truth, not by force and violence.

Cepeda, Rafael. "The Church in Cuba." *ChrLiv* 11 (Nov., 1964), 22-24. Christians are called not to destroy communism, but to dialogue with Marxism in order to witness concerning true peace.

*Christians Between East and West.* Winnipeg: Board of Christian Service, Conference of Mennonites in Canada. Ca. 1965. Pp. 55. Contains essays addressing the questions of communist and anticommunist ideologies and suggests Christian responses. Epp, Frank H., "Christians Between East and West," 7-16; Toews, John A., "The Christian Response to Communism," 17-24; Metzler, Edgar, "Christian Response to Communism and Anti-Communism," 25-39; Janzen, David, "Mennonites and the East-West Conflict," 40-53; bibliography, 54.

Davidson, Mike. Letter to the Editor. *MBH* 19 (Dec. 19, 1980), 11, 24. The disarmament movement is a humanistic venture. The best protection against Soviet attack is a strong defense.

Derstine, C. F. "Did We Deserve to Lose China?" *ChrMon* 43 (Feb., 1951), 62-63. In the fight against communism in China, Christian people relied on the sword instead of on love.

Derstine, C. F. "Nationalism the Supreme Rival of Christianity." *ChrMon* 30 (Feb., 1938), 61-62. Fascism, Nazism, and communism try to replace devotion to God with loyalty to the state.

Drescher, John M. "Cuba and Christian Concern." *GH* 55 (Nov. 13, 1962), 995. Some concerns arising out of the Cuban crisis are expressed. It is time to declare and believe that Christ is the Prince of Peace, and to confess that the church has not cared enough about the oppressed people of the world. This unconcern has helped give rise to communism.

Dyck, Peter J. "New Wind Blowing in US-Soviet Relations?" *ChrLead* 36 (Aug. 7, 1973), 14. A survey of the history of the church in Russia supports the idea that communism can be defined as a judgment upon the church.

Enns, Mary M. "Christians on Both Sides of the Iron Curtain Need Each Other." *MennMirror* 6 (Mar., 1977), 7, 8. Dr. Henry D. Wiebe, as part of an MCC delegation to Russia, shares his perceptions of the visit which sought to strengthen previous contacts with believers and to learn from them.

Epp, Frank H. "Christians Between East and

West." *Christians Between East and West.* Christian Concerns Series No. 1. Winnipeg: Board of Christian Service, Conference of Mennonites in Canada, [ca. 1965], 7-16. Describes features of communist and anticommunist propaganda which have attracted Mennonites to both camps, then uses the image of Christ to critique the materialism, militarism, power, and propaganda of both perspectives.

Epp, Frank H. "Communism, Anti-Communism, and the Mennonite Christian." Paper presented to MCC Peace Section Annual Meeting, Jan. 18, 1962. Pp. 9. MHL.

Epp, Frank H. "Errors of Anticommunism." *Menn* 76 (Aug. 8, 1961), 507. The triple alliance of democracy, Christianity, and capitalism distorts the Gospel of the Kingdom and reflects misunderstanding of communism and world revolution.

Epp, Frank H. "God's Word Stands Above Man's Opinions." *CanMenn* 2 (Oct. 1, 1954), 2. Human opinion must not be confused with biblical truth even as it relates to violence in war time. It is to be regreted that various Christian leaders have advocated "preventive war" against communism in recent times.

Epp, Frank H. "Man and the Missile." *CanMenn* 5 (Aug. 30, 1957), 2. Western Christendom is as missile-minded as atheistic communism. The missile race is a test because the true members of the church of Christ will die rather than take part in such a slaughter.

Epp, Frank H. *Mennonites in Canada, 1920-1940: A People's Struggle for Survival,* Vol. 2. Toronto: Macmillan of Canada, 1982. Pp. 640. The concluding chapter of this extensive historical survey is entitled "Facing the World" and includes discussion of the issues of war and peace, church and state, Germanism, communism, peace conferences and resolutions.

Epp, Frank H. "On Being Afraid of Communism." Paper presented at Peace Days, Goshen College, Goshen, Ind., Oct. 20-23, 1968. Pp. 11. AMBS.

Epp, Frank H. "Settling the Peace of the World." *CanMenn* 1 (Nov. 20, 1953), 2. "Guns, tanks, bombs have no place in the defense philosophy of a Christian and shouldn't be considered in a Christian nation." Our best defense is to share our material surpluses with those in need so that they need not turn to communism for an answer to their problems.

Epp, Frank H. "The Christian Attitude Toward Communism." *CanMenn* 3 (Jan. 14, 1955), 2. God created all people and wills that all should be saved. Christians, while hating the sins of communism, are called to love the sinners enslaved by these sins.

Epp, Frank H. *The Glory and the Shame.* Winnipeg: Canadian Mennonite Publishing Association, Inc., 1968. Pp. 79. A reprint of editorials appearing in *The Canadian Mennonite* in 1967 on the theme "The Past, Present, and Future of the Mennonite Church." N.b. chs. V on "Church and State" and VI on "Communism."

Epp, Frank H. (Editorial). "God's Word Stands Above Man's Opinions." *CanMenn* 2 (Oct. 1, 1954), 2. Editorial. Discussion of rightist evangelicals; statements on combating communism. World Council statements from Evanston are also reported.

Epp, Frank H. (Review). *The American Far Right: A Case Study of Billy James Hargis and Christian Crusade,* by John H. Redekop. Grand Rapids: Eerdmans, 1968. Pp. 232. *CanMenn* 16 (Feb. 27, 1968), 10. Lifts out major emphases concerning Billy James Harzis' interpretation of the Christian's stand against communism.

Erb, Paul. "The Korean War." *GH* 43 (Aug. 8, 1950), 779-80. Mennonites should not support the war against the communists but teach and demonstrate the life of Christian love against which communism cannot argue.

Erb, Paul. "Vengeance is Mine." *GH* 41 (Oct. 12, 1948), 947. It is not up to Christianity to destroy communism if vengeance is the Lord's. The self-assumed righteousness of one nation is not the way to set other nations right.

Erb, Paul. "World War III." *GH* 41 (Apr. 20, 1948), 363. It is not Christian to oppose communism by military pressure even though communism is anti-Christian. The Christian must remember that there is no righteous side in power politics.

Franz, Delton. "The Politics of Hostility and the Politics of Healing." *MCC PS Wash. Memo* 11 (Nov.-Dec., 1979), 1-2, 5. Cuba, Angola, and Vietnam might not have been driven into the Soviet camp if the US had not insisted on "cold war" foreign policy.

Gehman, Abraham, Jr. Letter in "Our Readers Say." *GH* 56 (Feb. 19, 1963), 143. Response to John Howard Yoder's "Why I Don't Pay All My Income Tax" [(Jan. 22, 1963), 81, 92.]. Disagrees with Yoder's implication that the US government has gone beyond the normal function of the state. The US government is trying to bring about world peace and defend itself from Russia. It does not have a philosophy of world domination as Marxist communism does.

Gingerich, Melvin. "Communism; Christian Youth and the State." *YCC* 24, Part 29, (May 23, 1943), 578. Description of the history and ideas of communism. Not all communists are of the Marxian type.

Gingerich, Melvin. "The Need for a Peace Witness in the Orient." *MennLife* 14 (July, 1959), 99-101. Asia longs for peace. While Buddhism and communism carry the banner of peace, "Christian" America, including many of its missionaries, are identified with militarism and conquest.

Gingerich, Melvin. *Youth and Christian Citizenship.* Scottdale: Herald Press, 1949. Pp. 204. A collection of 50 essays written for high school age Christians on a variety of practical citizenship issues raised by the church and state relationship. Topics include nationalism, patriotism, political participation, racism, communism, community vitality, ecology, and more.

Gingerich, Melvin (Archival). Box 51—includes communism. Goshen, Ind., AMC Hist. Mss. 1-129.

Gingerich, Melvin (Review). *Communism and the Churches,* by Ralph Lord Roy. New York: Harcourt, Brace, and Co., 1960. Pp. 495. "Communism and the Churches." *GH* 54 (July 18, 1961), 625, 637. Summarizes the author's conclusions about the extent to which communism has influenced American churches.

Hackman, Walton. "Peace Seminar Encounters Communism in Eastern Europe." *CanMenn* 15 (Nov. 7, 1967), 7, 8. Report on MCC Peace Section study tour of Eastern Europe to speak with both Christians and Marxists in order to transcend some of the barriers which have divided for so long.

Harms, Orlando. "What Can We Do?" *ChrLead* 25 (Mar. 6, 1962), 2. To thwart the advance of communism the church must be knowledgable about communism; rather than supporting extremist, rightist movements, it should counteract communism by applying the Gospel to all human needs.

Hershberger, Guy F. "Concerning the Reliability of Statements of Carl McIntire." *GH* 57 (1964), 602. Hershberger includes McIntire's protesting statements which he released when a Russian Baptist delegation came to Philadelphia on May 29, 1964, and a letter of response from Paul Verghese, associate secretary of the World Council of Churches, denying these statements.

Hershberger, Guy F. "Nonresistance, the Christian Witness, and Communism." Paper, n.d. Pp. 12. MHL.

Hershberger, Guy F. "The Tragedy of the Empty

House." *GH* 54 (1961), 733-35. Using Matt. 12:43-45, Hershberger identifies demons worse than communism which threaten the US because of the lack of dependence on God and growing dependence on wealth and power.

Hertzler, Daniel. "Sending a Message to Russia." *GH* 73 (July 1, 1980), 536. Open letter to the Christians of the Soviet Union calling for cooperation in resisting US and Soviet governments' commitment to war-making.

Horsch, John. *Communism: A Deadly Foe to the Christian Faith Assuming the Guise of Christianity.* Chicago: The Bible Institute Colportage Association, 1937. Pp. 28. MHL. Decries Russian communism as anti-Christian and Christian Marxism as "even more hideous." Also complains that religious liberalism, including social gospel ideology, has contributed to the success of these movements.

Jantz, Harold. Letter to the Editor. *ChrLead* 36 (Sept. 18, 1973), 14. A critical response to an article by Peter Dyck "New Wind Blowing in US-Soviet Relations" (*ChrLead*, Aug. 7, 1973).

Janzen, David. "A Program for the Mennonite Church." *CanMenn* 5 (Mar. 15, 1957), 2. Sets forth fifteen points toward an understanding of Christianity's encounter with communism. Also considers the role of pecifism in this encounter.

Janzen, David. "Attitude to Our Enemies: A Call to Repentance." *MennRep* 3 (Jan. 8, 1973), 7-8. Expresses disappointment over Mennonite failure to love communists in Russia. Reprints article from *Der Bote* giving thanks for Mennonite escape from Russia with "an anti-communist attitude that evades repentance."

Janzen, David. "Mennonites and the East-West Conflict." *Christians Between East and West.* Winnipeg: Board of Christian Service, Conference of Mennonites in Canada, [ca. 1965], 40-53. Links the rise of Communism with rejection of a false Christianity identifying with the exploiting class. Calls Mennonites to reject anticommunist propaganda as well as trust in nuclear weapons, in order to engage in deeper dialogue with communist people. Paper presented at the Canadian Conference Sessions, Altona, Man., July 20, 1963. Pp. 11. AMBS, MLA/BeC.

Janzen, David. "On Politics and Immorality, Communism and Democracy." *CanMenn* 5 (Jan. 4,1957), 7. In debate with John H. Redekop, Janzen tries to define terms for understanding of nonresistance and the Christian's involvement with the state.

Kreider, Carl. "Communists in Government Service." *Menn Comm* 4 (Aug., 1950), 30, 33.

Christians should work for peace and reconciliation, since communism feeds upon war and the confusion caused by events such as the recent McCarthy allegations.

Kreider, Carl. "The War in Indo-China." *ChrLiv* 1 (May, 1954), 35-36. Indo-China conflict is another example of the ineffectiveness of Western military intervention in dealing with communism.

Kreider, Carl. "The War in Korea." *MennComm* 4 (Sept., 1950), 30, 34. Analysis of the fighting in Korea concludes that the US is backing reactionary forces; the UN has turned into an anti-communist force; the war will strain the American economy.

Kreider, Carl. "Truce in Indo-China." *ChrLiv* 1 (Oct., 1954), 37-39. Comment on the partitioning of Vietnam and the effect of American military force in meeting communism.

Kreider, Carl (Review). *The Ultimate Weapon— Christianity,* by Paul M. Stevens. Thomas Nelson and Sons, 1961. Pp. 158. *ChrLiv* 8 (Aug., 1961), 33. Recommends the book for its emphasis on worldwide Christian witness as one response to the inability of military force to curb the spread of communism.

Kroeker, David. "Berlin: The Wall That Separates Is Built at from Both Sides!" *CanMenn* 15 (Aug. 29, 1967), 5. Report of an Aug. 7 tour of East Berlin in which author recalls the 8th Mennonite World Conference appeal to Christians to stand between East and West rather than on one side or the other. It was not only communism that built the Berlin wall but the West as well. The wall is a judgment of God on everyone.

Lapp, John A. "What Happened in Indonesia?" *ChrLiv* 13 (Aug., 1966), 18-19. Army coup launched brutal anti-communist purge in Indonesia, killing an estimated 300-500,000 people.

Lapp, John A. (Review). *Anatomy of Anti-Communism,* by Peace Education Committee of Friends Service Committee. Hill and Wang, 1969. Pp. 138. *GH* 63 (Dec. 29, 1970), 1075. Highly recommends the book for its analysis of the national ideology of Cold War and its effect on American life and foreign policy.

Lapp, John A. (Review). *Christianity and Communism,* by Russell L. Mast. Newton: Faith and Life Press, 1962. Pp. 32. *ChrLiv* 10 (Apr., 1963), 33. Recommends the book as a pacifist Christian approach to communism which calls the church to a greater concern for justice.

Lapp, John E. "Social Issues the Church Can Not

Ignore." *Builder* 21 (Oct., 1971), 10-12. Some issues demanding the attention of the church are: communism, war, poverty, racism, Zionism, drugs, sex, abortion, wealth and popularity.

Leach, Arthur B. "Militant Atheism in Our Schools." *ST* 20 (4th Qtr., 1952), 31. Christians remain ignorant of the fact that there is an organized attempt to educate school children to become communists in America.

Lind, Loren. "What Do You Think About Communism?" *YCC* 44 (May 19, 1963), 2. Includes comments from several of the resource people at an Inter-Collegiate Peace Fellowship conference on communism.

Lind, Tim C. Letter to the Editor. *Intercom* 23 (Jan., 1979), 2. The lack of knowledge of Yahweh in China is evidenced not in the absence of Christians but in the violence present in China's creation and the violence of dictated conformity.

Lochmann, Jan M. "Christian Thought in the Age of the Cold War." *Concern* 10 (Nov., 1961), 5-17 By faithful response to the peace of Jesus Christ, essential to the unabridged gospel, the Christian will find a way to reasonable political service to humankind in an age of cold war mentality and relationships.

Lohrenz, Gerhard. "Rejection of Marxist Worldview." *CanMenn* 16 (Jan. 9, 1968), 5. Lohrenz criticizes Frank Epp's book review of "Lost Fatherland" on a number of counts. Concludes that "the Soviets . . . demand of every Soviet citizen that he accept their Weltanschauung unconditionally . . . Those who still think of themselves as Mennonites cannot do this . . . they reject the materialistic world view of communism. This—and this alone—is the source of tension between the Soviets and the Mennonites in Russia today."

"Mennonites and Communism." *CanMenn* 12 (June 23, 1964), 5. Discusses Carl McIntire's attacks on the Mennonite Church for fellowshipping with the Russian Baptists.

Mast, Russell L. "Can Satan Cast Out Satan?" *Menn* 76 (Aug. 1, 1961), 485-86. The light of Christ must be brought to bear on both communism and anti-communism. Communism must be opposed by Christian means.

Mast, Russell L. *Christianity and Communism.* Newton, Ks.: Faith and Life Press, 1962. Pp. 32. Calls for a redemptive Christian response to communism—one that is not based on American nationalism, one that does not forget the humanity of persons holding a Communist

point of view and one that eliminates nuclear war as a valid "solution."

Mennonite Church General Conference Statements (Archival). File 5/12c: Resolution on Communism and Anti-communism, 1961. Goshen, IN. AMC. 1-1-1, Box 5.

Mennonite General Conference. "Communism and Anticommunism." *GH* 54 (Sept. 19, 1961), 817-18. Resolution adopted Aug. 24, 1961, at Johnstown, Pa., by General Conference (MC) asks Mennonites to continue to be nonresistant and loving people in face of the onslaught of communism and the strong anti-communist agitation.

Metzler, Edgar. "Christian Response to Communism and Anti-Communism." *Christians Between East and West.* Winnipeg: Board of Christian Service, Conference of Mennonites in Canada, [ca. 1965], 25-39. Criticizes communist opposition based on "Christian nationalism" because it confuses religious and political critiques. Analyzes characteristics of right-wing groups espousing such opposition, and outlines responses to both communism and anticommunism which could deepen the church's understanding and critique of both.

Metzler, Edgar. "War Is Not the Way to Peace." *CanMenn* 10 (Nov. 2, 1962), 1, 10. A historical perspective on the Cuban situation and a reminder that meeting an evil force with force is futile.

Metzler, James E. "Missions and Communism in Asia." *GH* 69 (Feb. 10, 1976), 100-101. Urges Mennonites to carefully evaluate the effect of "missions-by-proxy" carried on through radio broadcasts into communist countries. Maintains evangelical missionaries lost the confidence of the Vietnamese people when they evacuated Vietnam with the rest of the Americans.

Miller, John W. "Belligerence Is Blasphemy." *CanMenn* 10 (Nov. 2, 1962), 1, 3. What we fear in this dark moment of history is not what Russia may or may not do in Cuba, but what God certainly will do in judgment against the United States if it continues down this reckless path of blind, arrogant, and belligerent self-righteousness.

Neufeld, Elmer. "The Christian Church in the Cold War." *CanMenn* 11 (Jan. 25, 1963), 5, 10. The tendency of the church is to identify the cause of Christ with that of the western nations, something which is clearly a distortion of the church as God's covenant people.

Neufeld, Elmer. "The Church in the Balance of Terror." *Eternity* 12 (Sept., 1961), 9-13. Warns against the Western temptation to use God as a "fetish" to serve our own interests in the struggle against Communism. By contrast, the prophetic understanding is that Christ rules over all nations, judging all unfaithfulness.

Peachey, Paul L. "America and the Church." *ChrLiv* 9 (Dec., 1962), 28-29. Used by permission from *The Sunday School Times*. Institutional wealth is as great a peril to the Christian church as is the threat of communism.

Peachey, Paul L. "Beyond Christian-Communist Strife." *Christianity Today* 3 (Oct. 27, 1958), 15-17, 24. Exposes the theological errors resulting from the identification of Christianity with a particular political system which posits Christianity and communism as alternative world orders.

Peachey, Paul L. "Constantinian Christendom and the Marx-Engels Phenomenon." *MQR* 55 (July, 1981), 184-97. Identifies the Constantinian marriage of church and society and its remains in the 19th century as a necessary ingredient in Marx's intellectual development and critique of religion.

Peachey, Paul L. "The Intellectual Ferment in Central Europe." *MennLife* 20 (July, 1965), 102. An introduction to an East-West dialogue report. God and human realities are stronger than any ideology; dialogue is possible and imperative for Christians.

Redekop, John H. "Christianity and the Cold War." *CanMenn* 4 (Jan. 13, 1956), 5. Sees Christianity as only force that can displace communism.

Redekop, John H. "Comments on the Anti-Communist Movement." *ChrLead* 25 (May 4, 1962), 4-5. The movement, as a whole, has distorted Christianity into a religion serving the political goal of annihilating communism.

Redekop, John H. "Communism Versus Christianity." *CanMenn* 4 (Feb. 10, 1956), 3. A spokesman for the Evangelische Kirche in Deutschland states that Christianity and communism can only exist side by side if the church compromises its principles.

Redekop, John H. "Peace with Honour." *MBH* 12 (Feb. 9, 1973), 10. Although an imminent Vietnam truce has been announced, several disquieting aspects remain: the millions of refugees, orphans, cripples, etc.; the possibility of continued guerilla warfare; and the threat of communism and east-west distrust.

Redekop, John H. "Principles of Christian Anti-Communism." *MBH* 7 (Jan. 12, 1968), 4-6; *ChrLead* 31 (Feb. 13, 1968), 4, 5. Rejection of communism must be permeated with love for

all persons; it must be informed, reasoned, and appropriate to present political realities.

Redekop, John H. "Race Consciousness Generates World Tension." *CanMenn* 3 (Mar. 4, 1955), 2. "One of the best ways to prevent communism or any other despicable 'ism' from exploiting anti-West, anti-Christian attitudes is to eliminate and eradicate the factors which give rise to those attitudes."

Redekop, John H. "The Christian and Communism." *CanMenn* 15 (Oct. 10, 1967), 4, 6. Principles and general guidelines which will help Mennonites to be more Christian in their reaction to communism include: we must be informed about variations within communism; we must be able to evaluate and alter premises if necessary; Christian love must be central, not hate-motivated anti-communism; there must be a clear distinction between persons and ideas; a rejection of error must be reasoned and appropriate; we must be consistent in criticism; we must have a balanced perspective.

Rempel, Roy. Letter to the Editor. *MBH* 19 (Dec. 5, 1980), 8. Arms levels and defense spending must be kept where they are to insure against Soviet attack.

Robinson, James H. "The Revolution of Communism." *ChrLiv* 3 (July, 1956), 18-20, 41-42. Reprinted from *Tomorrow Is Today*, by James H. Robinson. Christian Education Press, 1954. Poverty and injustice alone do not motivate people to accept communism, as shown by the overwhelming rejection of communism by black Americans.

Roy, Prodipto, "A Hindu Shames Us." *ChrLiv* 1 (Mar., 1954), 15, 41-42. The apostle of Gandhi, Acharya Vinoba Bhave, fights communism in India by preaching nonviolence and voluntary giving of land by wealthy landowners.

"Speakers Recommend Dialogue wtih Communists and Joint Russian Studies Institute." *CanMenn* 13 (Feb. 2, 1965), 1, 12. J. A. Toews and Ed Metzler were main speakers at a Consultation on Communism and Anti-Communism.

Sawatsky, Rodney J. "The Attitudes of the Canadian Mennonites Toward Communism as Seen in Mennonite Weekly Periodicals." Social Science Sminar paper, Apr., 1965. Pp. 35. MLA/BeC.

Sawatsky, Walter W. "The Church in the Soviet Union." *MCC PS Newsletter* 9 (Jan.-Feb., 1978), 8-9. Describes the church in the Soviet Union.

Sawatzky, P. J. Letter to the Editor. *MennRep* 9 (July 9, 1979), 6. In response to the decision on war taxes made at the General Conference midtriennium, this writer stresses the need for military protection against communism and the biblical teachings to support the government and pay taxes.

Sawatzky, P. J. "The Question of War Taxes." *GfT* 14 (Sept./-Oct., 1979), 17-18. Reprinted "Letter to the Editor," *Mennonite Reporter* (July 9, 1979). Advocates paying all taxes in order to obey the government which preserves freedom by keeping a military check on Soviet communism.

Sensenig, Donald E. "A Church and the Search for Peace." *GH* 68 (Jan. 28, 1975), 56-57; *Menn* 90 (Jan. 28, 1975), 51. While Christians in Vietnam, both Protestant and Catholic, contribute little to making peace between communism and South Vietnam, the United Buddhist Church promotes a peace campaign.

Shank, J. Ward (Editorial). "Militant Communism Today." *ST* 43 (June, 1975), 7-9. Christians should not advocate direct, violent opposition of militant communism, but they should rather preach the gospel of reconciliation

Shank, J. Ward (Editorial). "Portents of Communism." *ST* 46 (May, 1978), 5. Examines the various ways that communism is the utter opposite of Christianity.

Shelly, Maynard. "50-450." Convocation address, 1967. Pp. 8. Revolution, nonviolence, response to Communism. MLA/BeC.

Shetler, Sanford G. "Disarming America—A Real Cause for Alarm." *GfT* Series 2, 4 (May-June, 1969), 2. Efforts of liberal pacifists to disarm America are dangerous, because the adversary, Russia, is a nation without moral conscience.

Smucker, Donovan E. "Russian Christianity and Communism." *Menn Comm* 7 (Sept., 1953), 10-11, 34; *Menn* 68 (May 17, 1953), 312-13. Briefly discusses the relationship of church and state in Russia before the communist government, and considers communism a judgment on Christianity.

Stoltzfus, Luke G. (Review). *A Strategy for Peace,* by Frank Epp. Grand Rapids: Wm. B. Eerdmans, 1973. *GH* 67 (Oct. 1, 1974), 758. Recommends the book for its fresh approach to issues of nationalism, North American militarism, separation of church and state, a biblical response to communism, evangelism and peace witness.

Stoner, John K. "The West Is Losing Ground." *Menn* 93 (Aug. 8, 1978), 480. Truth and justice, not bombs and weapons delivery systems, are the only adequate weapons against communism.

Stucky, Dean. "Communism—Antithesis or Parallel?" *Menn* 65 (Aug. 29, 1950), 580-81. Acknowledges certain parallels between communism and Christianity in aims (e.g., humanitarian concern for social justice) but challenges the church to be true to its uniqueness and to remain critical of whatever economic or political system within which it operates.

Summer, Bob. "War Is Inevitable." *YCC* 47 (July 10, 1966), 8. The conclusion that war is inevitable is based on the human greed for power, opposition of communism, and lack of international power to control actions of modern societies.

"The Christian Attitude Toward Communism." *CanMenn* 3 (Jan. 14, 1955), 2. Discussion of implications of Mennonite peace witness toward international communism.

"The Church Confronts War and Communism— Conference Concern." *CanMenn* 2 (Jan. 1, 1954), 1, 3. John C. Bennett and André Trocmé represented their respective positions at the Detroit Conference on the Church and Peace. Studied the basis of nonresistance in scripture, theology, and Christian experience. Major concerns were the Christian in the contemporary world, the church's confrontation with war and communism, and positive action for peace.

"The Church Makes Peace in a World Filled with War." *CanMenn* 7 (Jan. 23, 1959), 6. Papers given at Study Conference in Winnipeg on Jan. 9-11, 1959. Archie Penner looks at the problems of church and state, while Harvey Taves regards secularism, not communism, as the enemy.

"To the NAE Point of View." *Menn* 81 (Feb. 15, 1966), 117. A letter of appeal from the Mennonites in Canada to the National Association of Evangelicals to reconsider their support of "unjust and unchristian methods of resisting communism." This is a response to the NAE's apparent endorsement of the Vietnam war.

Toews, John A. "Confronting Communism with Love." *MBH* 16 (May 27, 1977), 17. Two-thirds of Mennonite Brethren support resisting communism by military force, while the church should be a messenger of peace.

Toews, John A. *People of the Way: Selected Essays and Adresses.* Ed. Abe J. Dueck, Herbert Giesbrecht, and Allen R. Guenther. Winnipeg, Man.: Historical Committee, Board of Higher Education, Canadian Conference of Mennonite Brethren Churches, 1981. Pp. 245. Memorial collection includes section entitled "Peace and Nonresistance: Crucial Issues for the Church."

Essays in this section include "The Christian Response to Communism."

Toews, John A. "The Christian Response to Communism." *Christians Between East and West.* Winnipeg: Board of Christian Service, Conference of Mennonites in Canada, [ca. 1965], 17-24. Outlines ingredients of a Christian response to communism, such as belief in the unity of humankind, a Christian spirit of humility and redemptive concern, and an evangelical strategy that demonstrates Christ's love on a personal level.

Toews, John B. "A Voice of Peace in Troubled Times." *MennLife* 27 (Sept., 1972), 93, 94. A report on the discovery of a Russian Mennonite newspaper of 1918, the *Volksfreund,* in Stuttgart, Germany, and the insights it provides on the Mennonite editor's attitude to communism.

Toews, John B. *Czars, Soviets, and Mennonites.* Newton: Faith and Life Press, 1982. Pp. 221. Analytical and interpretive study of the history of the Mennonites in Russia. While this examination of parochial Mennonitism in the wider socio-political context discusses the church's peace witness, including the church and state relationship, at various points, chapters which deal more explicitly with war/ peace issues are: "The Russian Mennonites and World War I," 63-78; "Response to Anarchy," 79-94; "Communism and the Peace Witness," 95-106.

Trocmé, André. "Christian Nonresistance Only Alternative to Communism." *CanMenn* 7 (Oct. 16, 1959), 1, 10. Discussion with MCC personnel at Akron, Pa.

van Drimmelen, Katharina. "Where Are the Firemen?" *Concern* 10 (Nov., 1961), 21-25. The popular response to communism and the Cold War is a very emotional, uninformed response. The discussion encourages the reader to respond to communism by "knowing and facing the facts" and confronting them with Christianity.

Vogt, Roy. "A Communist Talks of His Good Life in East Germany." Part 1. *MennMirror* 6 (Jan., 1977), 9, 10. The writer recounts some of his conversations with an East German communist in which they discuss the nature of communism in East Germany.

Vogt, Roy. "A Visit with an Older Couple in Leipzig Gives Yet Another View of Communism." Part 5. *MennMirror* 6 (June, 1977), 6-8. Writer describes his visit with an older East German couple as they discuss communism and its effects in their country.

Vogt, Roy. "As Usual, They Won't Have Everything Listed." Part 3. *MennMirror* 6 (Mar., 1977), 9, 10. Writer describes two encounters he has had during his visits to East Germany which reveal some of the conditions that exist under their socialist leadership.

Vogt, Roy. "Ideology Is Sometimes Only Skin Deep . . . Behind the Stone Faces Are Sensitive Hearts and Minds." Part 4. *MennMirror* 6 (Apr., 1977), 6-8. Writer describes two different encounters he has had with military personnel in East Germany when he has been able to penetrate their military mask and learn something about their personal experience in the military.

Wall, Elmer. "The Doctrine of Non-resistance and Communism." Student paper presented to Mennonite Contributions Contest, May 1, 1950. Pp. 30. MLA/BeC.

Yake, C. F. "Freedom for What?" *YCC* 32 (July 1, 1951), 628, 629. A discussion of freedom and liberty, e.g., the political sense, must not obscure the importance of freedom from sin. Destroying communism does not destroy bondage to sin.

Yake, C. F. "Parallel Thirty-eight!" *YCC* 31 (Oct. 28, 1950), 324. The implications of the situation in Korea for the Christian. When Christianity flourishes, communism cannot thrive.

Yoder, John H. "Clarifying the Gospel." *Builder* 23 (Aug., 1973), 1-2. Faithfulness to the Jesus of the gospel demands disavowal of the Jesus in whose name Christians have sanctioned colonialism, racism, militarism, and anti-communism.

Yoder, John H. "The Christian Answer to Communism." *Concern* 10 (Nov., 1961), 26-31. Much of the opposing behavior and attitudes directed toward communism are based on the provincial assumption that the United States is a Christian nation. The Christian answer to communism is repentance for the continuing failure of Christians to obey Christ.

# 17

# Wars

## A. Revolutionary War

Bender, Wilbur J. "Pacifism Among the Mennonites, Amish Mennonites, and Schwenkfelders of Pensylvania to 1783." *MQR* 1, Part 1 (July, 1927), 23-40; Part 2 (Oct., 1927), 21-48. Until 1776 these groups succeeded in observing strict nonresistance without too much difficulty. Even during the War of Independence there was general tolerance for them, though many paid fines for not bearing arms and refusing to pay war taxes.

Bowman, David. "Mennonite Nonresistance. A Comparison of Practices in the American Revolution and the War Between the States." Term paper for Anabaptist and Mennonite History, Apr. 6, 1978. Pp. 22. MHL.

Brunk, Gerald R. *A Guide to Select Revolutionary War Records Pertaining to Mennonties and Other Pacifist Groups in Southeastern Pennsylvania and Maryland, 1775-1800.* Harrisonburg, Va.: EMC, 1974. Pp. 49. MHL. Index of such militia records as fine lists, court appeals dockets, and delinquent returns.

Burkhalter, Sheldon, et al. *A Mennonite Response, 1776-1976.* Souderton, Pa.:" Franconia Mennonite Conference, 1975. Pp. 16. MHL. Discussion on Mennonite responses during the Revolutionary War and what being citizens in Christ's kingdom means for today. Also includes suggestions for Bible study and congregational action.

Burkholder, J. Lawrence. "An Examination of the Mennonite Doctrine of Nonconformity to the World." ThM thesis, Princeton Theological Seminary, 1951. Pp. 221. MHL. Included in section four is Mennonite nonresistance in the Revolutionary War.

Derstine, Kenton M. "The Nonresistance of the Mennonites in Southeastern Pennsylvania During the Revolutionary War." Term paper for Mennonite History and Thought course, Feb. 15, 1972. Pp. 44. MSHL.

Epp, Frank H. *Mennonites in Canada, 1786-1920: The History of a Separate People,* Vol. 1. Toronto: Macmillan of Canada, 1974. Pp. 480. History includes discussion of such pertinent war and peace topics as the effects of the American Revolution; the nonresistors and the militia in the War of 1812; World War I; and military exemptions. See table of contents.

Epp, Frank H. "The American Revolution and the Canadian Evolution." *GH* (Oct. 28, 1975), 771-72; *MennRep* 5 (Nov. 10, 1975), 8. Christian nonresistants in both the US and Canada need to reflect soberly on their national histories. While American revolutionary spirit has sought a violent solution to every problem, Canadian gradualism has meant being sucked into the military strategies of Britain and the US.

Funk, Christian. "A Mirror for All Mankind." *MHB* 35 (Jan., 1974), 3-11. Reprints this 1813 document describing the Revolutionary War era and the Funkite schism.

Good, I. Merle. "A Conscientious Objector's View of the Bicentennial." *FQ* 3 (May, June, July, 1976), 2. Reprinted from *The Washington Post,* (1976). Sketches Mennonite history of conscientious objection to war, and outlines the dilemma facing Mennonites condemned by wider society for not joining wholeheartedly in celebrating the American Revolution.

Haddad, Kathy (Review). *Conscience in Crisis,* by Richard K. MacMaster. Scottdale: Herald Press, 1979. *GH* 73 (Apr. 29, 1980), 347. Recommends the book for its historical study of Mennonite life and thought during the revolutionary and pre-revolutionary war period.

Harding, Vincent G. "The Revolution that Happened; The Revolution that Didn't Happen; The Revolution that Has to Happen." Paper presented at the American History and Christian Perspective Seminar, North Newton, Kansas, Jan. 23-24, 1976. Pp. 12. MHL.

Hershberger, Guy F. "Can the American Revolution Be Justified?" *YCC* 17 (Oct. 4, 1936), 320. History books do not always teach all the sides of the arguments in a war situation. The

American Revolution is a good example of a war that is only seen as a response on the part of the Americans to the British.

Hershberger, Guy F. "What Did the Mennonites Do in the American Revolution?" *YCC* 17 (May 31, 1936), 176. The Revolutionary War was a trying experience for nonresistant people. Mennonites did not take up arms, but they were willing to give aid to the suffering. The special war tax issues had a variety of responses.

Hershberger, Guy F. (Review). *War Comes to Quaker Pennsylvania, 1682-1756,* by Robert L. D. Davidson. New York: Columbia Univ. Press, Temple Univ. Publications, 1957. In *Bulletin of Friends Historical Association* 47 (1958), 113-15; also in *William and Mary Quarterly* 15 (1958), 532-34. A military history of colonial Pennsylvania.

Hertzler, James R. "The American Revolution in British Eyes." *GH* 69 (Jan. 27, 1976), 68-69. Examines the various opinions of British preachers and writers on the rebellion of the American colonies, and draws parallels between that conflict and the recent one in Vietnam.

Janzen, David (Review). *Conscience in Crisis: Mennonites and Other Peace Churches in America, 1739-1789,* by Richard K. MacMaster, with Samuel L. Horst and Robert F. Ulle. Herald Press, 1979. Pp. 575. *MennRep* 10 (June 23, 1980), 10. Recommends the book as a historical documentation of the response of peace churches to the wars of that period.

Juhnke, James C. "Freedom and the American Revolution." *Menn* 91 (June 22, 1976), 417-18. Bicentennial celebrations reinforce the idea that freedom is a military achievement, when in fact revolution may not have been the only alternative in 1775; similarly, political independence later became a license to oppress blacks and Native Americans.

Juhnke, James C. "Freedom and the American Revolution." Paper, Feb., 1976. Pp. 4. MHL.

Kauffman, Allen L. Letter to the Editor. *GH* 69 (Mar. 2, 1976), 188-89. Disagrees with the picture of American liberty painted by Benjamin Lapp ("The Bicentennial: Two Views," Feb. 10, 1976), and suggests Mennonites wait to celebrate freedom of religion until the anniversary of the Constitution or Bill of Rights, instead of celebrating the American Revolution in 1976.

Kauffman, Richard A. "Beggar to Beggar." *GH* 68 (May 20, 1975), 384-85. Urges Christians who separate the peoplehood of the nation from that of the church to witness to the Christian patriots in the upcoming celebration of the American Revolution.

Kauffman, S. Duane, comp. "Religious Pacifists and the American Revolution: Selected Readings and Suggested Student Activities." 1975. Pp. 15. MLA/BeC.

Kreider, Alan. "The US Bicentennial." *GH* 68 (Oct. 21, 1975), 749-51; "The American Bicentennial: Historical Propaganda and Eternal Truths." *MennRep* 5 (Nov., 1975), 8-9; "The Bicentennial: Not to Be Ignored or Deplored—But No Occasion for Flagwaving." *Menn* 90 (Oct. 28, 1975), 602-604. Americans will celebrate the Bicentennial either authentically, by advocating revolution for all oppressed people, or fraudulently, by ignoring the violent nature of the American Revolution. Americans who give primary loyalty to Jesus should use the occasion to reflect on the history in which they have participated.

Lapp, John A. "Bicentennial Choices." *ChrLiv* 23 (May, 1976), 17-18. Adapted from *A Dream for America,* John Lapp, Herald Press, 1976. American society today includes forces moving toward both revolution and counterrevolution.

Lapp, John A. "Why Didn't Mennonites Join the Revolution?" *GH* 69 (Aug. 3, 1976), 594-95. Mennonites objected to the Revolutionary War for three philosophical reasons: 1) The Mennonites were already a community, which the Revolution claimed to bring about; 2) The fall of the church was represented by the dominant churches' support of the war; 3) The revolution distorted good politics.

Lapp, John A. (Review). *Conscience in Crisis,* by Richard K. MacMaster with Samuel L. Horst and Robert F. Ulk. Scottdale: Herald Press, 1979. Pp. 576. *FQ* 7 (Feb., Mar., Apr., 1980), 11. Publishes and interprets documents from local history, revealing Mennonite responses to the Revolutionary War era.

Lehman, James O. "The Mennonites of Maryland During the Revolutionary War." *MQR* 50 (July, 1976), 200-229. Describes the geographical, cultural, religious, and political setting of Maryland Mennonites in the late 18th century, their responses to the Revolutionary War fermemt, and the conflict they faced as conscientious objectors during the war.

MacMaster, Richard K. *Christian Obedience in Revolutionary Times: The Peace Churches and the American Revolution.* Akron, Pa.: MCC (US) Peace Section, 1976. Pp. 26. MHL. Demonstrates that Mennonites and other Christians committed to peace during the Revolutionary War times conflicted with the government on issues of military service, war taxes, and oaths of allegiance. Discusses their stance and resulting persecution within the context of differing concepts of religious liberty; the sectarian concept of discipleship as a separate and distinct way of life was not understood by a government to whom religious freedom meant the freedom to worship according to the dictates of conscience, not the freedom to live by conscience.

MacMaster, Richard K. "'I'd as Soon Go into the War.'" *GH* 68 (Nov. 18, 1975), 832. Cites the refusal of Mennonites and Quakers in the 1770s to pay taxes intended for the Revolutionary War as an example for present-day Mennonites.

MacMaster, Richard K.; with Horst, Samuel L. and Ulle, Robert F. *Conscience in Crisis: Mennonites and other Peace Churches in America, 1739-1789; Interpretation and Documents.* Scottdale and Kitchener: Herald Press, 1979. Pp. 576. Sourcebook of Mennonites in 18th-century America, focusing especially on Mennonite experience in the Revolutionary War. Includes documents on relations with Native Americans, conscientious objection, nationalism, religious liberty, etc.

Martin, Brenda. "The Relation Between the Historic Peace Churches and the Government of Pennsylvania from 1775 to the Beginning of the Revolutionary War." Paper for History Seminar, Goshen College, Goshen, Ind., Apr. 15, 1975. Pp. 55. MHL.

Martin, E. K. *The Mennonites.* Philadelphia: Everts and Peck, 1883. Pp. 17. MIIL. A history which discusses at some length the struggles of the Mennonites and other peace sects to maintain a nonresistant stance in relation to the conflicts between the colonists and native Americans as well as in relation to the government's demands for support for the military in the pre-Revolutionary and Revolutionary War periods.

Mast, C. Z. "Imprisonment of Amish in the Revolutionary War." *ChrMon* 44 (May, 1952), 151; *MHB* 13 (Jan., 1952), 6-7. Relates the story of several nonresistant Amish men imprisoned in Reading, Pa. during the Revolutionary War, who were saved from execution by the intervention of a local minister of the German Reformed Church.

Mast, C. Z. "Releasing of Early Amish under Severe Trial." Unpublished paper, n.d. Pp. 4. MHL.

"Preparing for Revolution." *MHB* 35 (July, 1974), 2-7. Series of documents traces the tension caused in Lancaster County when nonresistant Mennonites refused to serve in military units being established in preparation for the Revolutionary War.

Ruth, John L., ed. "Mennonite Petition to the Assembly." *GH* 68 (Nov. 4, 1975), 800; *Menn* 91 (Jan. 13, 1976), 21. A 1775 Mennonite petition to the Pennsylvania Assembly requesting respect for the position of those who cannot, in good conscience, bear arms.

Ruth, John L. *'Twas Seeding Time: A Mennonite View of the American Revolution.* Scottdale and Kitchener: Herald Press, 1976. Pp. 224. An informal history of Mennonites in Pennsylvania during the Revolutionary War, focusing on the personalities and problems of the Mennonites of this period.

Smith, Daniel L. "The Exodus as Revolutionary Pedagogy: A Specific Critique of Aspects in Norman K. Gottwald's *The Tribes of Yahweh.*" Paper presented to War and Peace in the Bible class, AMBS, Elkhart, Ind., Jan., 1980. Pp. 21. AMBS.

Smucker, Joseph. "Pacifism and Nonviolence in the Colonial United States Before and During the Revolutionary War." Student paper for Mennonite History, Life and Thought, Dec. 9, 1980. Pp. 15. MLA/BeC.

Souder, John D. "Early Churches in the First Mennonite Conference District." *ChrMon* 25 (Feb., 1933), 46-47. History of churches in the Franconia (Pennsylvania) conference relates experiences of the settlers during the Revolutionary War.

Steinmetz, Rollin C. *Loyalists Pacifists and Prisoners.* Lititz, Pa.: Lancaster County Historical Society, 1976. Pp. 80. MHL. Discusses the circumstances and actions of Lancaster County's pacifists during the Revolutionary War in the context of the "underside" of the Revolution.

Ulle, Robert F. "The Approaching Revolution." *GH* 69 (Apr. 20, 1976), 329. Ulle examines the responses of Pennsylvania Mennonites to the rise of local colonial militia in the early 1770s.

"Who Can Postmark the Stamp of Liberty?" *Lifework* 4 (1979), 2-3. Summarized from articles by Richard K. MacMaster in *Purpose* (Scottdale: 1976). Relates stories of Eve Yoder and John Newcomer of Pennsylvania who stood for peace and liberty during the Revolutionary War.

Weber, M. Alice. "Peace and War: Nonresistance in Eighteenth-Century Pennsylvania." *GH* 45 (Apr. 15, 1952), 369. A historical sketch of Mennonites in the time of the Revolutionary War.

Wengerd, Carolyn. "Nonresistance of the Mennonites in Pennsylvania During the Revolution." Research paper for American

Colonial and Revolutionary History class. 1970. Pp. 23. BfC.

Wittlinger, Carlton O. (Review). *Twas Seeding Time: A Mennonite View of the American Revolution,* by John L. Ruth. Scottdale, Pa. and Kitchener,

Ont.: Herald Press, 1976. Pp. 224. *MQR* 52 (July, 1978), 271-72. Reviewer considers this book of stories of Mennonite noncooperation in the Revolution a good, and informal, contribution to the subject of Mennonite history during the Revolution.

# B. American Civil War

Beachy, Rosemary. "The Mennonites and the State." *MHB* 9 (Oct., 1948), 4. Focuses on separation of church and state as it has been expressed in Mennonite refusal to swear oaths and perform military duty. Reviews US government policies regarding such scruples from 1689 through the Civil War.

Bender, Bertha Burkholder. "Youth, Church, and State." *YCC* 12, Part 1, (Jan. 4, 1931), 420-21; Part 2, (Jan. 11, 1931), 426-27; Part 3, (Jan. 18, 1931), 434-35; Part 4, (Jan. 25, 1931), 444-45; Part 5, (Feb. 1, 1931), 450, 451, 453; Part 6, (Feb. 8, 1931), 461-62; Part 7, (Feb. 15, 1931), 466-67; Part 8, (Feb. 22, 1931), 479-80; Part 9, (Mar. 1, 1931), 487, 488; Part 10, (Mar. 8, 1931), 491, 493; Part 11, (Mar. 15, 1931), 498, 499; Part 12, (Mar. 22, 1931), 505, 506; Part 13, (Mar. 29, 1931), 515, 517; Part 14, (Apr. 5, 1931), 523, 525; Part 15, (Apr. 12, 1931), 534, 535; Part 16, (Apr. 19, 1931), 539, 541; Part 17, (Apr. 26, 1931), 545-47; Part 18, (May 3, 1931), 559, 560; Part 19, (May 17, 1931), 571, 573; Part 20, (May 31, 1931), 589; Part 21, (June 7, 1931), 595; Part 22, (June 21, 1931), 610; Part 23, (July 5, 1931), 627, 629; Part 24, (July 19, 1931), 645, 646; Part 25, (July 26, 1931), 650, 651; Part 26, (Aug. 2, 1931), 657-59; Part 27, (Aug. 16, 1931), 675-77. Written in a narrative style, the progression of peace-related topics include: the biblical story, the history of the church, issues about responding to government and militarism, e.g., CO status during Civil War and World War I, and Mennonite relief work.

Blosser, Don. "But, Daddy." *GH* 65 (June 27, 1972), 542-43. A family visit to Civil War battlefields provides the opportunity to talk with children about the incongruity of Christians believing in and financially supporting war.

Bowman, David. "Mennonite Nonresistance: A Comparison of Practices in the American Revolution and the War Between the States." Term paper for Anabaptist and Mennonite History, Apr. 6, 1978. Pp. 22. MHL.

Brunk, Harry A. *Life of Peter S. Hartman, Including His Lecture: Reminiscences of the Civil War.* By the Hartman Family, 1937. Pp. 73. MHL. Relates the temptations, failures, and triumphs experienced by the Virginia Mennonite Church as its members struggled with the meaning of

nonresistance during the turbulent years of the Civil War.

Brunk, Harry A. "Virginia Mennonites and the Civil War." *ChrLiv* 8 (July, 1961), 14-17. Experiences of conscientious objectors during the Civil War.

Burkholder, J. Lawrence. "An Examination of the Mennonite Doctrine of Nonconformity to the World." ThM thesis, Princeton Theological Seminary, 1951. Pp. 221. MHL. Included in section four is treatment of the biblical basis of nonresistance and Mennonite nonresistance in the Civil War.

Funk, John F. "A Terrible Massacre." *GH* 69 (June 22, 1976), 515. Reprint from the *Herald of Truth* of 1876 views the massacre of Custer's army as the fruit of deception and injustice done by the white people. Asserts the relations with Native Americans would have been different if whites had followed Jesus' way of peace.

Gingerich, Melvin. "The Military Draft During the American Civil War." *MHB* 12 (July, 1951), 3. Publishes official documents pertaining to the drafting of Samuel D. Guengerich of Pennsylvania in 1865 and the process he followed to be exempted from military duty.

Gingerich, Melvin (Review). *Through Tribulation to Crown of Life: The Story of a Godly Grandmother,* by Ethel Estella Cooprider Erb. n.p., n.d. Pp. 48. *MHB* 8 (Oct., 1947), 4. Reviewer observes that this tribute to Susanna Heatwole Brunk Cooprider contributes to the record of Mennonite experiences during the Civil War, because it describes in detail Susanna's search for her husband, who deserted the Confederate Army.

Good, I. Merle. *Who Burned the Barn Down? A Play in One Act.* Lancaster: Good Enterprises, Ltd., 1970. Pp. 51. MHL. The doctrine and practice of nonresistance are sources of tension and disagreement in the King family as the members are caught up in the issues and struggles of the Civil War and its destructive effects on their eastern Pennsylvania community.

Gross, Leonard, comp. "Alternative to War: A Story Through Documents, Part 1." *GH* 65 (Nov. 7, 1972), 899-901; Part 2, (Dec. 26, 1972),

1046-47; 66, Part 3, (Jan. 2, 1973), 10-12; Part 4 (Jan. 9, 1973), 34-36; Part 5, (Jan. 16, 1973), 52-55. Uses contemporary documents to describe the difficulties Mennonites encountered during the Civil War and World War I, as well as the Mennonite response.

Gross, Leonard, ed. "Civil War CO Documents." *MHB* 34 (Apr., 1973), 6. Publishes documents pertaining to Samuel Guengerich of Pennsylvania and his requested exemption from military duty.

Gross, Leonard, ed. "John M. Brenneman and the Civil War." *MHB* 34 (Oct., 1973), 1-3. Publishes the draft of a letter to President Lincoln written by a group of Ohio Mennonites, requesting exemption from military duty. Includes draft of a cover letter written by Brenneman.

Gross, William G. and Gross, Samuel G. "A Civil War Letter." *MHB* 23 (July, 1962), 5. Letter from twin brothers in Pennsylvania in 1862 describes provisions made by the North for conscientious objectors. The writers identified themselves with the American people as being punished by God for the sins of the nation.

Harding, Vincent G. "The History of a Wall." *GH* 61 (June 18, 1968), 543-45. Reprinted from *Must Walls Divide?* New York: Friendship Press. Briefly traces the history of white racism in America from slavery through the Civil War, segregation policies, racial revolution, and the nonviolent change proposed by Martin Luther King.

Harding, Vincent G. "Walls of Bitterness." *Menn* 83 (June 18, 1968), 424-26; *ChrLead* 31 (June 18, 1968), 3-4. Deep bitterness is resulting from the largely ineffective struggles against the barriers imposed betwen the races by slavery, the Civil War, and segregation.

Hartman, Peter S. "Civil War Reminiscences." *MQR* 3 (July, 1929), 203-19. A record of personal experiences and observations among the Mennonite objectors under the Confederate government in Virginia.

Hartman, Peter S. "The Bad Old Days of the Civil War." *ChrLiv* 11 (Oct., 1964), 24-28. Memories of the Civil War from the perspective of a Mennonite youth.

Heatwole, L. J. "Brother Christian Good, Whose Gun Was 'Out of Order.'" *MHB* 33 (July, 1972), 3. Letter written in 1918 recounts the story of Christian Good, who refused to fire a gun when inducted into the Confederate Army during the Civil War.

Heatwole, Reuben Joseph. "A Civil War Story." *MHB* 9 (Jan., 1948), 3-4; *ST* 40 (Oct., 1972), 12. Relates his experiences as a seventeen-year-old

migrating north from Virginia to escape military duty during the Civil War. Written in 1919.

Heatwole, Reuben Joseph. "Reminiscences of Civil War Days." *GH* 51 (Aug. 19, 1958), 782. Heatwole relates his boyhood memories of the experience of those opposed to fighting in the Civil War.

Hershberger, Guy F. "John M. Brenneman's Pamphlet on War." *YCC* 17 (July 5, 1936), 216. John M. Brenneman, an outstanding leader in the Mennonite Church, wrote a pamphlet *Christianity and War* in 1863. His arguments were based on scripture and were addressed to the issues of Christians and the Civil War.

Hershberger, Guy F. "Mennonites in the Civil War." *MQR* 18 (July, 1944), 131-44. Although Mennonites of the Civil War era were rooted deeply enough in their nonresistant faith to refuse conscription to combat duty, many either hired substitutes, paid a commutation fee which benefited the sick and wounded soldiers, or served in noncombatant roles.

Hershberger, Guy F. "Peace Movements That Have Failed in Time of Need." *YCC* 17 (July 19, 1936), 248. A survey of many peace movements in America previous to the Civil War that did not meet the test. The test of any peace conviction is whether during the time of war people who believe in peace still oppose the war.

Hershberger, Guy F. "Some Mennonite Experiences During the Civil War." *YCC* 17 (Sept. 13, 1936), 296. Most of the Mennonites who were tested during the Civil War remained true to their faith. Stories about many of these people are shared.

Hershberger, Guy F. "Was the Civil War Necessary to Free the Slaves?" *YCC* 18 (Jan. 3, 1937), 424. Both war and slavery are wrong, but it is never right for a Christian to violate one command of God in order that God's will be done in some other. By 1860 slavery was being abolished in the civilized world without war except in the United States.

Horst, Dale. "Mennonites and the Civil War." Student paper for Mennonite History, Nov., 1960. Pp. 12. MLA/BeC.

Horst, Samuel I. "Mennonites in the Confederacy." *PCMCP Fifteenth*, 47-61. North Newton, Kansas: The Mennonite Press. Held at Bluffton College, Bluffton, Ohio, June 10-11, 1965. The Mennonites living in the Confederacy provide an impressive historical model of religiously-based opposition to war and conscription.

Horst, Samuel. *Mennonites in the Confederacy: A Study in Civil War Pacifism.* Scottdale: Herald Press, 1967. Pp. 148. Documents the variety of ways Mennonites responded to the issues raised by the crisis of the Civil War, such as reluctant cooperation with the military, desertion, flight, choosing prison, working with government officials for legal alternatives, etc. Concludes that the Mennonite witness for peace in this era was not faultless but, nevertheless, significant and sincere. Includes extensive bibliography.

Horst, Samuel L., ed. "The Journal of a Refugee." *MQR* 54 (Oct., 1980), 280-304. Journal of a young Mennonite refugee from Virginia fleeing military duty during the Civil War.

Keeney, Lois. "Mennonite Attitudes in the North During the Civil War." Research paper for Anabaptist History class. 1972. Pp. 10. BfC.

Lehman, James O. "Conflicting Loyalties of the Christian Citizen: Lancaster Mennonites and the Early Civil War Era." *Pennsylvania Mennonite Heritage* 7 (Apr., 1984), 2-15. In the face of a growing war hysteria and the threat of the draft, the Lancaster Mennonites were not always clear on what position to take in that early period of the war. While most Mennonites tried to avoid entering military service, they also wanted to make clear their loyalty to the Union cause.

Pringle, Cyrus. "A Quaker Against the Civil War." *ChrLiv* 10, Part I: (Sept., 1963), 15-17, 38; Part II: (Oct., 1963), 24-25, 40. Adapted from *The Civil War Diary of Cyrus Pringle,* with foreword by Henry J. Cadbury, Pendle Hill Pamphlets, Wallingford, Pa. Experiences and thoughts of a conscientious objector who would not comply in the Union army camp.

Rhodes, Samuel A. "The Rebellion, the Cause of My Traveling Adventures to the North." *MHB* 33 (July, 1972), 2-3. Excerpts from the diary of a young man during the Civil War who fled his Virginia home to escape induction in the Confederate Army.

Rosenberger, Harleigh M. "A Brief Study of the Poetry of the Civil War Period." 1939. Pp. 15. BfC.

Sanger, S. F. and Hays, D. *The Olive Branch of Peace and Good Will to Men: Anti-War History of the Brethren and Mennonites, the Peace People of the South, During the Civil War 1861-1865.* Elgin: Brethren Publishing House, 1907. Pp. 232. Compilation of personal accounts from Brethren and Mennonites in the Confederacy who refused to participate in the war. Includes treatises on church and state, and the basis for nonresistance; reprints Exemption Act of Confederate Congress.

Schwarzendruber, Jacob. "An Essay [Against Warfare] Composed Before Pentecost, 1865, to be Presented to the Annual Dienerversammlung (Ministers' Meeting)." *MHB* 38 (Oct., 1977), 3-4. Speaks against either fighting or buying substitutes to fight in the Civil War. Calls for complete nonpartisanship among Mennonites, viewing the war as punishment from God upon the sins of all people.

Smith, Wayne LaVelle. "Rockingham County Nonresistance and the First World War." MA thesis, Madison College, Harrisonburg, Va., 1967. Pp. 160. A study of Mennonite and Brethren experiences, attitudes, and activities during World War I. Includes summary of the nonresistance position dating from the Reformation, and a brief look at Mennonite experiences during the Civil War. MSHL.

Steffen, Dorcas. "The Civil War and Wayne County Mennonites." *MHB* 26 (July, 1965), 1-3. Outlines provisions made by the North for conscientious objectors, then relates anecdotes from the war years concerning young men who did and did not fight, and the effects of the war on congregational life.

Stoltzfus, Grant M. "Conscientious Objection During the Civil War: Mennonites." *RepConsS* 19 (June, 1962), 3, 7. See also special issue devoted to same topic, by Stoltzfus. Describes Mennonite CO experience during the Civil War in its context—an emerging central government which had not completely established its primacy over the state governments.

Stoltzfus, Grant M. "Conscientious Objectors in the Civil War." *GH* 55 (Jan. 23, 1962), 81. Civil War CO's found more understanding with President Lincoln than in the Confederacy.

Stoltzfus, Grant M. "Virginia Mennonites in the Civil War." *MennLife* 18 (Jan., 1963), 27-29. How the Mennonites of Virginia met the tests of nonresistance during the Civil War in the US.

Wenger, Margaret. "Mennonites in the Civil War." Term paper for Anabaptist Theology course, 1973. Pp. 25. MSHL.

Wright, Edward Needles. *Conscientious Objectors in the Civil War.* Philadelphia: University of Pennsylvania Press, 1931. Pp. 274. While this discussion is focused more generally on CO's as a whole, there are numerous references to Mennonites. Topics include peace principles of the Mennonites, Mennonite experiences with both the North and the South, petitions and appeals, etc. Early standard work on conscientious objection in the Civil War.

Yoder, Mary Elizabeth. "Amish Settlers and the

Civil War." *ChrLiv* 9 (Jan., 1962), 28-29, 39-40. Amish families face the terrors of raiding soldiers.

Yoder, Richard B. "Nonresistance Among Peace Churches of Southern Somerset County, Pa., During the Civil War." Paper prepared for Mennonite History class, Goshen College Biblical Seminary, Goshen, Ind., 1959. Pp. 30. MHL, MSHL.

# C. World War I

*A Petition.* N.p., [1919]. Pp. 141. MHL. [Printed copy of a petition against universal military training presented to the United States Congress by approximately 20,400 Mennonites of various branches in 31 states.]

Baer, Isaac. "My Experience as a Conscientious Objector in World War I at Camp Meade, Maryland." Tape recording transcribed by John Kreider, 1962. Pp. 17. MSHL.

Barrett, Lois. "Stand for What You Believe." *With* 13 (Oct., 1980), 14-15. Conscientious objector from World War I and active peace advocate counsels young people to be able to articulate their peace position.

Bassinger, David W. Notebook of names, addresses (handwritten). World War I CO Records. Pp. 19. MSHLA.

Beery, Ward. Lists. World War I CO Records. COs of Camp Lee, Va., Sept., 1917-Dec., 1918; supplemental list to former, Dec. 5, 1918; "Jail Birds," Nov., 1917 (handwritten, xeroxed); and COs of Detachment CO, Jan. 24, 1918. MSHLA.

Beery, Ward. Notebook (handwritten, xeroxed copy). World War I CO Records. Pp. 53. Contains poems, lists of names and addresses, etc. Also list of birthday presents received in 1918, e.g., 1 penny, a ribbon, a pencil, and a safety pin. MSHLA.

Bender, Bertha Burkholder. "Youth, Church, and State." *YCC* 12, Part 1, (Jan. 4, 1931), 420-21; Part 2, (Jan. 11, 1931), 426-27; Part 3, (Jan. 18, 1931), 434-35; Part 4, (Jan. 25, 1931), 444-45; Part 5, (Feb. 1, 1931), 450, 451, 453; Part 6, (Feb. 8, 1931), 461-62; Part 7, (Feb. 15, 1931), 466-67; Part 8, (Feb. 22, 1931), 479-80; Part 9, (Mar. 1, 1931), 487, 488; Part 10, (Mar. 8, 1931), 491, 493; Part 11, (Mar. 15, 1931), 498, 499; Part 12, (Mar. 22, 1931), 505, 506; Part 13, (Mar. 29, 1931), 515, 517; Part 14, (Apr. 5, 1931), 523, 525; Part 15, (Apr. 12, 1931), 534, 535; Part 16, (Apr. 19, 1931), 539, 541; Part 17, (Apr. 26, 1931), 545-47; Part 18, (May 3, 1931), 559, 560; Part 19, (May 17, 1931), 571, 573; Part 20, (May 31, 1931), 589; Part 21, (June 7, 1931), 595; Part 22, (June 21, 1931), 610; Part 23, (July 5, 1931), 627, 629; Part 24, (July 19, 1931), 645, 646; Part 25, (July 26, 1931), 650, 651; Part 26, (Aug. 2, 1931), 657-59; Part 27, (Aug. 16, 1931), 675-77. Written in a narrative style, the progression of peace-related topics include: the biblical story, the history of the church, issues about responding to government and militarism, e.g., CO status during Civil War and World War I, and Mennonite relief work.

Bender, Harold S. Letter to the Editor. *Fellowship* 26 (Nov., 1960), 35-36. In response to A. J. Muste's article "Their Church and Ours" (*Fellowship*, Nov., 1959), which cites a statement by Jacob Zhidkov about the Russian Mennonites abandoning their nonresistance after World War I, H. S. Bender points out that this is greatly exaggerated and only a small minority joined the Selbstschutz.

Bender, Nevin and Swartzendruber, Emanuel. *Nonresistance under Test.* Rosedale, Ohio: Keynote Series No. 1, 1969. Pp. 16. The stories of the two authors who refused to bear arms during World War I.

Brenneman, Aldine. Diary, World War I CO Records. Handwritten, xeroxed copy. Pp. 37. MSHLA.

Brubacher, Dwight. "Mennonite Nonresistance in Ontario, World War I: The Persecution of a Separate People." Paper presented to Social Science Seminar, Goshen College, Goshen, Ind., May 13, 1976. Pp. 23. MHL.

Brubaker, Jack (Review). *Mennonite Soldier,* by Kenneth Reed. Scottdale: Herald Press, n.d. "Portrait of an Artist: Novel Tells of CO Dilemma in World War I." *MennRep* 5 (Mar. 3, 1975), 8. Reed reflects on his pilgrimage with conscientious objection to war.

Brunk, Harry A. *History of Mennonites in Virginia, 1900-1960.* Verona, Va.: by the author, 1972. Pp. 592. MHL. Contains chapter entitled "Conscientious Objectors in World Wars I & II," 451-66.

Buchanan, Roy. "A Personal Testimony." *GH* 63 (May 5, 1970), 408-409. World War I conscientious objector disagrees with the position of draft resisters, describing his positive experiences in obtaining cooperation from the military to perform alternative service.

Buchanan, Roy. Letter to the Editor. *GH* 62 (July 1, 1969), 594. World War I conscientious objector describes his experience of finding a response of positive action to the war in relief work in France. Written in response to Tom

Brubaker, "Don't Just Say No" (May 27, 1969).

Burkholder, J. Lawrence. "An Examination of the Mennonite Doctrine of Nonconformity to the World." ThM thesis, Princeton Theological Seminary, 1951. Pp. 221. MHL. Included in section four is Mennonite nonresistance in World War I.

Derstine, C. F. "CO's in World War I and World War II." *ChrMon* 36 (May, 1944), 158-59. Comparison of Selective Service regulations and penalties for refusing to comply in World Wars I and II.

Derstine, C. F. "Conscription and Conscientious Objectors." *ChrMon* 32 (May, 1940), 158-59. Reviews the government attitude toward conscientious objection during World War I and strongly advocates the position to youth in World War II.

Derstine, C. F. "The Holocaust of the Past War, and the Nightmare of the Next." *ChrMon* 23 (May, 1931), 158. Statistics of the destruction of · World War I, with projections of the shape of the next war.

Drange, E. R. "Reminiscences of War Experiences." *GH* 27 (Mar. 21, 1935), 1087. A recounting of one CO's personal opportunities for witness during wartime, and his conclusion that only a complete surrender of the will to God can lead one to live a highly Christian life in all times and situations.

Entz, Margaret. "Free to Buy: American World War I Financing and the Mennonite Response." Social Science Seminar paper, May 24, 1975. Pp. 31. MLA/BeC.

Epp, Frank H. *Mennonites in Canada, 1786-1920: The History of a Separate People,* Vol. 1. Toronto: Macmillan of Canada, 1974. Pp. 480. History includes discussion of such pertinent war and peace topics as the effects of the American Revolution; the nonresistors and the militia in the War of 1812; World War I; and military exemptions. See table of contents.

Epp, Henry H. "World War II Conscientious Objectors in Discussion with Church Leaders." *CanMenn* 11 (June 14, 1963), 3. A panel reviews the nature of the CO's relationship to the government and the community during World Wars I and II at the Ontario Ministers' Peace Retreat. Includes a summary of questions and answers about alternative service in World War II and the position of the Mennonite church today.

Ewert, Bruno. "Four Centuries of Prussian Mennonites." *MennLife* 3 (Apr., 1948), 10-18. Describes Prussian Mennonite stance on participation in war, and describes Prussian life during World War I and World War II.

Fast, Henry A. "Revisiting Camp Funston." *GH* 72 (Feb. 14, 1978), 129-30; *Menn* 92 (Aug. 9, 1977) 474. A World War I conscientious objector reflects on the witness he and others made against war at this military camp in Kansas.

Fast, Henry A. (Review). *Voices Against War: A Guide to the Schowalter Oral History Collection on World War I Conscientious Objection,* by Keith L. Sprunger, James C. Juhnke, and John D. Waltner. N. Newton, Kansas: Bethel College, 1973. *Menn* 89 (Oct. 29, 1974), 628. A valuable guide to a priceless collection of conscientious objector experiences recorded on tape, the book and the collection should stimulate further research.

Fretz, J. Winfield. "Mennonites Are Losing Their Biblical Nonresistance." *Menn* 66 (June 12, 1951), 376, 385. Compares statistics from World War I and World War II and then attributes the erosion of conviction on nonresistance more to forces from within the church than to external factors.

Goertz, Duane and Edwards, Carl, comp. "Court Martial Records of 131 Conscientious Objectors During World War I." Summer, 1975. MHL (microfilm, 3 rolls). Research project consisting of 98 case files, gathered from Army records and National Archives, documenting litigations involving CO's representing various branches of Mennonites. Materials include memorandae, forms, handwritten notes, transcripts of questioning, sentences, personal testimony, etc.

Graber, C. L. "Experiences of a Conscientious Objector." *GH* 28 (Apr. 18, 1935), 79-80. An address at the Conference on Peace and War. The writer recounts some of the persecutions he was subjected to in training camp during World War I.

Graber, Richard D. "The Evolution of the Treatment of the Conscientious Objectors by the War Department During the First World War." Paper presented to the Social Science Seminar, Goshen College, Goshen, Ind., June, 1957.

Gross, Leonard, comp. "Alternative to War: A Story Through Documents, Part 1." *GH* 65 (Nov. 7, 1972), 899-901; Part 2, (Dec. 26, 1972), 1046-47; 66, Part 3, (Jan. 2, 1973), 10-12; Part 4 (Jan. 9, 1973), 34-36; Part 5, (Jan. 16, 1973), 52-55. Uses contemporary documents to describe the difficulties Mennonites encountered during the Civil War and World War I, as well as the Mennonite response.

Gross, Leonard, ed. "The First World War and Mennonite Nonresistance." *MHB* 33 (July, 1972), 4-10. Series of government and private documents traces Mennonite experiences in the war: correspondence with the Secretary of War on conscientious objection; procedures for military induction and discharge; treatment of COs in detention; public pressure to buy war bonds; government suspicion of tract on nonresistance; germinal ideas for alternative service in reconstruction.

Habegger, Luann. "The Berne, Indiana, Mennonites During World War I." Paper presented to the Mennonite History class, Associated Mennonite Biblical Seminaries, Dec. 23, 1974. Pp. 15. MHL.

Harley, Isaiah Buckwalter. "Goshen's Attitude Toward Conscientious Objectors as Reflected in the News and Editorial Columns of the Goshen Daily News Times, Apr. 1, 1917-Nov. 11, 1918." Paper presented to the Peace and War Seminar, Goshen College, Goshen, Ind., n.d. Pp. 15. MHL.

Hartman, O. E. "An Original Draft Resister." ST 42 (June, 1974), 24. Taped interview of a personal account of someone who, when subject to the draft as a young man during World War I, solved his problem of conscientious objection to the war by living in the woods.

Hartzler, Jonas S. Mennonites in the World War or Nonresistance Under Test. Scottdale: Mennonite Publishing House, 1922. Pp. 246. MHL. Treatment of the World War I conscientious objector experience includes analysis of the issues, summaries of meetings and position papers, descriptions of camp life and life in the disciplinary barracks, congregational reaction, and relief work.

Hernley, Elam R. "My Experiences During the World War." ChrMon 31, Part 1, (Nov., 1939), 332-33; Part 2, (Dec., 1939), 363, 373; ChrMon 32, Part 3, (Jan., 1940), 10-11; Part 4, (Feb., 1940), 42-43; Part 5, (Mar., 1940), 75, 77; Part 6, (Apr., 1940), 105; Part 7, (May, 1940), 140-41. World War I CO reports his experience as a prisoner in the guardhouse of an army camp, his transfer to a CO detachment, his term on farm furlough, and his discharge from the camp.

Hershberger, Guy F. "Do We Know Where We Stand on the War Question?" YCC 16 (Nov. 24, 1935), 792. This history of the Mennonite Church, including the most recent experience of World War I, is full of stories of people who believed in peace and declined to fight. Young people must continue to study and explore issues of peace to know where they stand.

Hershberger, Guy F. "How the American Churches Made Themselves Believe That the World War Was a Holy War." YCC 18 (Apr. 4, 1937), 528. Many preachers were misled into thinking that World War I was a "holy war." They failed because they were not rooted in the nonresistant teachings of the Bible.

Hershberger, Guy F. "Reflections on Armistice Day." YCC 20 (Nov. 5, 1939), 776. The growing spirit of militarism shows how short our memories are in light of the cost (human, economic, social) of the World War.

Hershberger, Guy F. "The Origin of the Peace Problems Committee." YCC 18 (Aug. 1, 1937), 664. The Peace Problems Committee, as well as the earlier Military Problems Committee, concerned itself chiefly with problems arising out of World War I. The ongoing work of the Peace Problems Committee was to encourage the efforts to strengthen the nonresistant faith and stay in touch with government.

Hershberger, Guy F. "What Shall a Christian Youth Do in Time of War?" YCC 18 (June 6, 1937), 600. From the experience in World War I, there seem to be four possible courses of action a person might follow in time of war: regular military service; noncombatant service; complete refusal to participate in the military; alternative Christian service.

Hershberger, Guy F. "Why Did the United States Enter the World War?" YCC 18 (Mar. 7, 1937), 496. Outlines three reasons for US involvement in World War I. The case for World War I was so misleading that even some nonresistant people believed that the war was right.

Hershberger, Guy F. (Review). For Peace and Justice: Pacifism in America, 1914-1941, by Charles Chatfield. Knoxville: Univ. of Tennessee Press, 1971. In CH 41 (1972), 418-19. This is the story of the new Christian (social gospel) pacifism which emerged during World War I and its encounter both with the older (non-pacifist) peace movement and with secular forces working for social justice as all labored together in a kind of unofficial grand alliance for the abolition of war.

Hershberger, Guy F. (Review). Mennonites in the World War, or Nonresistance Under Test, by J. S. Hartzler. Scottdale: Mennonite Publishing House, 1922. MQR 25 (1951), 229-30. A brief review of Hartzler's book, an eyewitness account of the Mennonite war experience in World War I. It is written by a church leader who writes from his own experience and draws upon the records in his care.

Hershberger, Guy F. (Review). Opponents of War, 1917-1918, by H. C. Peterson and Gilbert C. Fite. Madison: Univ. of Wisconsin Press, 1957. In AAAPSS 313 (1957), 154-55; also in MQR 31 (1957), 302-303. An account of the various types of nonconformity to World War I and of its treatment at the hands of the government and of the public.

Hirsch, Charles B. "The Civilian Public Service Camp Program in Indiana." *Indiana Magazine of History* 46 (1950), 259-81. CPS program in Indiana, with all its inadequacies, was a distinct imporvement over World War I treatment of COs. Innovations included the recognition of COs of all faiths and an alternative program of military service.

Hofer, David. "The Martyrdom of Joseph and Michael Hofer." Paper translated from the German by Franz Wiebe, 1974. Pp. 4. MHL.

Hooley, E. M. *The 1918 Christmas Eve Man of the Hour at Leavenworth: Written by a Mennonite Who Was Entrapped in that Riot.* n.p., [1960]. Pp. 13. MHL. World War I conscientious objector sentenced to 10 years at Leavenworth relates, with considerable awe, the story of how Col. Sedgwick Rice quelled a prison riot using no force other than the strength of his presence and the respect he had acquired among the prisoners.

Horsch, John. "The Mennonites of Russia, Part III." *ChrMon* 28 (Aug., 1936), 230, 237. Experiences of the Rusasian Mennonites during World War I, when young men served in noncombatant posts.

Horsch, John (Review). *Preachers Present Arms*, by Dr. Ray H. Abrams. Round Table Press, n.d. *ChrMon* 26 (Feb., 1934), 37-39. The book documents the spiritual and moral losses of denominations which supported involvement in World War I.

Jantzen, Dave. "The Effect of World War I on the Mennonites in Beatrice." Social Science Seminar paper, 1968. Pp. 22. MLA/BeC.
*
Juhnke, James C. *A People of Two Kingdoms: The Political Acculturation of the Kansas Mennonites.* Newton: Faith and Life Press, 1975. Pp. 215. Explains that this process of acculturation was fundamentally shaped by the "abrasive encounter of Mennonite nonresistance with American nationalism" and charts the encounter from the shadows cast on the civic role of the Mennonite German-Americans by the Spanish-American War, through the essential Mennonite-American compatibility of the Progressive Era, through the shattering of that easy course in World War I, through the efforts to bridge the conflict in the inter-war period, to the new phase—characterized by voting and alternative service—during World War II.

Juhnke, James C. "CO's and Chemical Warfare in the First World War." *MHB* 30 (1969), 4. Quotes from and comments upon documents

from the Office of the Chief of Staff which show certain officials proposed that conscientious objectors be assigned to work in gas manufacturing plants instead of in agriculture.

Juhnke, James C. "Crisis of Citizenship: Kansas Mennonites in the First World War." *PCMCP Sixteenth*, 101-18. N.p. Held at Hesston College, Hesston, Kansas, June 8-9, 1967. There were many incongruities in nonresistant Mennonite attempts to validate American citizenship. During the early years of the war there was the identification with Germany; in later years, there was an emphasis on "Mennonite" as the primary source of identity for the community.

Juhnke, James C. "Mennonites in Militarist America: Some Consequences of World War I." *Kingdom, Cross, and Community.* Ed. John R. Burkholder and Calvin Redekop. Scottdale: Herald Press, 1976, 171-78. Juhnke discusses the effects of World War I on Mennonites in their search for a renewed identity and in their leanings toward fundamentalism. Calls for a comprehensive Mennonite historiography that recounts the diversity of Mennonite experience in World War I, not focusing only on what is assumed to have represented an "orthodox" Mennonite peace position. Also as paper, n.d. Pp. 11. MLA/BeC.

Juhnke, James C. "Mob Violence and Kansas Mennonites in 1918." *Kansas Historical Quarterly* 43 (Autumn, 1977), 334-50. Juhnke relates stories of local mob violence—tar and feathering, near lynching, and other coercion— toward war-resistant, German-American Mennonites of Kansas during World War I. Examines these incidents in light of the larger question of the history of American domestic violence. MLA/BeC.

Juhnke, James C. "The Agony of Civic Isolation: Mennonites in World War I." *MennLife* 25 (Jan., 1970), 27-33. World War I shattered the easy assumption many Mennonites held that they could be good citizens and good Mennonites at the same time. This experience was influential for clarifying the Mennonite self-identity.

Juhnke, James C. "The Victories of Nonresistance: Mennonite Oral Tradition and World War I." *Fides et Historia* 7 (Fall, 1974), 19-25. Mennonite oral tradition from World War I, as collected in taped interviews in the Schowalter Oral History Collection at Bethel College, contains a strain of "triumph tales," which reveal how nonresistant people maintained their self-respect and responded to the testing of their religious faith during that time of public humiliation.

Kauffman, Ivan. "Congress Decision on CO Provisions Influenced by Peace Section

Testimony." *CanMenn* 15 (June 6, 1967), 2. A proposed bill, which would have been a return to the provisions for CO's that were in effect in World War I, was changed to one with little difference from the present law. The change was due to MCC Peace Section testimony.

Knipscheer, L. D. G. "Renewal of the Doctrine of Nonresistance Among the European Mennonites." *The Witness of the Holy Spirit.* Ed. Cornelius J. Dyck. Elkhart: MWC, 1967, 328-30. Since World War I the Spirit of God is again bringing new life to Mennonites; false patriotism is rapidly giving way to radical obedience and reconciliation.

Kniss, Lloy A. *I Couldn't Fight: The Story of a CO in World War I.* Scottdale, Pa.: Herald Press, 1971. Pp. 47. Portrays the ridicule and hardship experienced by a World War I CO as a result of his steadfast refusal to cooperate with the military system in the military training camps into which he had been forced.

Kniss, Lloy A. *Why I Couldn't Fight.* Harrisonburg, Va.: Christian Light Publications, 1974. Pp. 72. Uses experiences as a World War I CO to explain and defend the nonresistant position.

Kreider, Carl. "Peace Thought in the Mennonite Church from the Beginning of the World War in Europe, August, 1914, to the Establishment of the War Sufferer's Relief Commission, December, 1917." Paper presented to American History class, 1936. Pp. 34. MHL.

Kreider, Robert S. "Discerning the Times." *Kingdom, Cross, and Community.* Ed. John R. Burkholder and Calvin Redekop. Scottdale: Herald Press, 1976, 65-85. A discussion of the cultural and political times of Guy Hershberger's life, including the effects of World War I and World War II on Mennonite ethos and institutions.

Landis, Cliff. "A Soldier for Christ." Paper entered in the Horsch History Essay Contest, [Kidron, Ohio], May 1, 1973. Pp. 5. MHL.

Lapp, John E. *Studies in Nonresistance: An Outline for Study and Reference.* Akron, Pa.: Peace Problems Committee, 1948. Pp. 35. MHL. Outlines a study course for MYF in 12 lessons. Topics covered include Old Testament and New Testament teachings on war and peace, nonresistance in the early church, Anabaptist concepts of nonresistance, the Mennonite experience in America, World War I, World War II, and church and state.

Lapp, Joseph L. "The United States vs. Mennonite Ministers." Term paper presented to EMC History Seminar, June 2, 1966. Pp. 28. MSHL.

Leatherman, John D. "The Story of Non-Resistant Peoples During the World War as Told in the *Goshen Daily Democrat.*" Paper presented to Peace and War Seminar, Goshen College, Goshen, Ind., June, 1940. Pp. 22. MHL.

Leatherman, Noah H. *Diary Kept by Noah H. Leatherman While in Camp During World War I.* Linden, Alberta: Aaron L. Toews, 1951. Pp. 86. MHL. A day to day account gives a detailed portrait of life as a World War I CO including prison experience at Fort Leavenworth. Materials include journal reflections, menus, schedules, letters, and essays.

Lehman, Eric. "Experiences of Mennonite Conscientious Objectors in Camp Sherman During World War I." Paper, Central Christian High School, Kidron, Ohio, May 30, 1977. MHL.

Lehman, Galen T. "What Price Glory?" *ChrMon* 29 (Jan., 1937), 17, 29. Adds up the cost of World War I in terms of lives, dollars, and moral lapse.

Leinbach, Nola C. "A World War Episode." *ChrMon* 22 (Oct., 1930), 290, 320. Story of the attempted murder of an advocate of nonresistance during World War I, based on a true story.

Lind, Miriam Sieber, "A Time to Say No," as told by Roy Buchanan. *ChrLiv* 7 (Sept., 1960), 6-10, 34-35; 7 (Oct., 1960), 12-15, 34; 7 (Nov., 1960), 14-17, 19, 33-34; 7 (Dec., 1960), 22-25, 32-33; 8 (Jan., 1961), 24-27, 34. Experiences of a conscientious objector during World War I: draft; imprisonment in guardhouse; discrimination; persecution; reconstruction work in France.

Lohrenz, Gerhard (Review). *August 1914,* by Alexander Solzhenitsyn. New York: Farrar, Straus, and Giroux, 1972. Pp. 622. *Menn* 88 (Jan. 30, 1973), 77-78. Russian novel explores the reasons for the defeat of Russian forces by German in the battle of Tannenberg, during World War I. Reviewer observes that the book is a song of praise for the spirit of the Russian people, and that it also portrays the futility of war.

"Mennonite Conference on War and Peace: A Report of the Conference, Including the Principal Addresses Given." Goshen College, Goshen, Ind., Feb. 15-17, 1935. Pp. 68. MHL. Includes: Stoltzfus, Eli, "Experiences of a Relief Worker During the World War." 59-61.

Malishchak, Richard (Review). *I Couldn't Fight,* by Lloy A. Kniss. Herald Press, 1971. Pp. 47. *RepConsS* 28 (Dec., 1971), 5. The testimony of a World War I CO lends perspective to the contemporary issues of conscientious objection.

Martin, Ernest H. Private papers and letters from

fellow imprisoned COs (Maurice Hess and Robert E. Fox). Lists: religious COs imprisoned at the US Disciplinary Barracks, Ft. Leavenworth, Ks., published by J. D. Mininger, 200 S. 7th, Kansas City, Ks., Mar. 10, 1919; Mennonite CO of World War I, reported to Mennonite Research Foundation. MSHLA.

Martin, Willard. "World War I Conscientious Objectors in Fort Leavenworth." Paper presented to History Seminar, Goshen College, Goshen, Ind., May 30, 1957. Pp. 44. MHL.

Miller, D. D. "Lessons from the World War: for Church Officials." *Eastern Mennonite School Journal* 18 (Apr., 1940), 46-49. One important learning for church leaders from the World War I experience is that the church needs more teaching on the doctrine of nonresistance.

Miller, Ernest H. "Experiences of a CO in World War I." Paper, Chesapeake, Va., Oct., 1972. Pp. 14. MSHLA.

Miller, Ernest H. "I Tried to Be Reasonable." *GH* 67 (Jan. 22, 1974), 72-74. Conscientious objector in World War I relates his experiences in Camp Funston, Kansas, and a short time in Leavenworth Prison.

Miller, Orie O. "Lessons from the World War: For the Nonresistant Laity." *The Eastern Mennonite School Journal* 18 (Apr., 1940), 49-51. World War I experience has taught us that there is a need for greater clarity and consistency in our nonresistant peace witness.

Miller, Orie O. "Our Peace Policy." *MQR* 3 (Jan., 1929), 26-32. An address delivered to World War I CO's deals with the problem of the ill preparedness of the CO's and puts forth the 1924 three-point program for peace education in the Mennonite Church.

Mumaw, Adam H. "My Experience as Conscientious Objector in World War I." Paper. Pp. 12. MSHLA.

Mumaw, John R. World War I papers. Lists names of CO's, Camp Lalor, Kentucky, 1918. MSHLA.

Mumaw, John R. (Archives). Archive box of papers labeled "World War I Conscientious objectors, Private Papers." Box includes materials (diaries, photographs, and miscellaneous records) from a variety of persons: Adam H. Mumaw from Ohio at Camp Taylor, Louisville, KY; Ernest H. Miller; Aldine Brenneman; Asa M. Hartzler; Lloy Kniss; David H. Ranck; Ward Beery; and John G. Meyers from Camp Lee, VA; and David W. Basinger (including a list of CO's imprisoned at Fort Leavenworth, Kansas, 1918-19). MSHL.

"Nebraska Amish Mennonites and War Bonds in World War I." *MHB* 30 (Jan., 1969), 4-5. Reprinted from the *Grand Island Daily Independent*, Oct. 17, 1918. Newspaper article relates the discussion between preacher Ammon Stoltzfus and the County Council of Defense about Stoltzfus' refusal to buy war bonds, and the understanding they reached on the problem.

Neufeld, Jean. "Experiences of Isaac T. Neufeld During World War I." Mar. 23, 1972. MLA/BeC.

Newcomer, Frank C. "Nonresistance under Test—Experiences of CO's During the World War." *YCC* 21 (Feb. 25, 1940), 58, 59, 64. The World War was a time of severe testing of the Mennonite doctrine of nonresistance. Present conditions are moving toward a possible US involvement in the war. Are Mennonite youth ready to respond?

Nickel, Arnold. "Peace Committee." *The Mennonite Encyclopedia* IV:130, Scottdale-Newton-Hillsboro Mennonite Publishing Offices, 1959. This committee of the General Conference Mennonite Church promoted peace education and peace witness from World War I until 1950, when it merged with other service committees to form the Board of Christian Service.

Penner, Lydia. "Never Made to Kill Each Other, Says Bishop." *MBH* 15 (Oct. 29, 1976), 15. Ontario bishop who was a CO in World War I negotiated with Canadian government in setting up alternative service during World War II.

(Review). *Why I Couldn't Fight*, by Lloy A. Kniss. N.p., n.d. *GfT* 10 (Jan.-Feb., 1975), 14-15. World War I conscientious objector explains his position. Reviewer recommends the book because it distinguishes between pacifism and biblical nonresistance.

Ranck, David H. Diary, World War I CO Records. Handwritten, xeroxed copy. Pp. 79. MSHLA. Contains extensive name, address list.

Reed, Kenneth. *Mennonite Soldier*. Scottdale, Pa.: Herald Press, 1974. Pp. 518. Novel uses the prodigal son motif to order this story of two brothers, Ira and Mastie Stoltzfus, and their different responses to the moral dilemmas posed for them by World War I. Ira, the older brother, remains true to the Mennonite Church position and endures camp life and a prison term as a CO. Mastie joins the army and is sent to fight on the French front. In addition to following these two stories, the novel also portrays the divisive effects of the war upon the Pennsylvania community that is home to the Stoltzfuses.

Reimer, George. "Canadian Mennonites and World War I." Winkler, Man., 1972. Pp. 50. MLA/BeC.

Reimer, Paul. "Conscientious Objectors at Fort Leavenworth Prison During World War I: A Mennonite Perspective." Social Science Seminar paper, Apr., 1973. Pp. 41. MLA/BeC.

*Remembering: Stories of Peacemakers.* Akron, Pa.: MCC Peace Section, 1982. Pp. 59. MHL. Stories, readings, and short plays for use in churches and schools. Topics included are conscientious objection in World War I, World War II, and the Vietnam War, as well as an interview with a South African conscientious objector.

Rempel, David G. "A Response to the 'Lost Fatherland' Review." *CanMenn* 16 (Aug. 13, 1968), 7. An interpretation of the Mennonite involvement in the Russian famine and revolution during and after World War I.

Rosenberger, David. "Were the Conscientious Objectors Fairly Treated in World War I?" Pp. 16. BfC.

Sawatsky, Rodney J. (Review). *Voices Against War: A Guide to the Schowalter Oral History Collection on World War I Conscientious Objection,* ed. Keith L. Sprunger, James C. Juhnke, and John D. Waltner. North Newton, Kansas: Bethel College, 1973. Pp. 100. *MQR* 50 (Jan., 1976), 69-70. Reviewer considers this book a valuable research aid to the important collection of Mennonite oral history, and he calls for greater historical analysis of the collected data.

Schellenberg, Tim. "Nonresistance Stand in the Krimmer Mennonite Brethren Church in World War I." Research paper for the Mennonite Brethren Church course, May 27, 1981. Pp. 25. MBBS.

Schlabach, Theron F., ed. "*An Account* by Jakob Waldner: Diary of a Conscientious Objector in World War I." *MQR* 48 (Jan., 1974), 73-111. The diary of a Hutterite conscientious objector demonstrates belief in two strictly separate kingdoms, with unswerving loyalty to the kingdom of God rather than to the nation.

Schmidt, Allen. *Experiences of Allen Schmidt During World War I.* Hesston, Ks.: Gospel Publishers, [1972]. MHL. Series of letters from a conscientious objector, sentenced to 25 years in Fort Leavenworth, to his family and friends.

Schmidt, John F. "Probing the Impact of World War I." *MennLife* 26 (Dec., 1971), 161, 162. Interviews with people who were CO's during World War I are being taped for preservation in the Bethel College Historical Library.

Schrag, Tim. "Mastered by Deceit: The Work of

the Exemption Committee of the Western District Conference." Paper presented to World War I Seminar, [Bethel College, North Newton, Ks.], Dec. 12, 1975. Pp. 18. MHL, MLA/BeC.

Shank, Clarence. "A Mennonite Boy's World War Experience." *YCC* 21, Part 1, "Preliminary Experiences, (Apr. 7, 1940), 106-107; Part 2, "My Trip to Camp Lee, Va," (Apr. 14, 1940), 117-20; Part 3, "First Events in Camp Lee;" (Apr. 21, 1940), 128; Part 4, "Going Through the Mustering Office," (Apr. 28, 1940), 135; Part 5, "Entering the 'Holy Hill';" (May 5, 1940), 142; Part 6, "The Six-Month Furlough," (May 19, 1940), 155; Part 7, "The Homeward Look," (May 26, 1940), 163, 168. A Mennonite describes his experience as a conscientious objector during World War I.

Shields, Sarah D. "The Treatment of Conscientious Objectors During World War I: Mennonites at Camp Funston." Student paper for History 801, University of Kansas, 1980. Pp. 26. MLA/BeC.

Showalter, John. "World War I Experiences." Paper, n.d. Pp. 4. MHL.

Smith, C. Henry. *Smith's Story of the Mennonites.* Fifth edition revised and enlarged by Cornelius Krahn. Newton: Faith and Life Press, 1981. (First edition copyright 1941.) Pp. 589. A comprehensive overview of Mennonites from the 16th century to the present. The theme of nonresistance is woven into the story, while the final chapter, "Witnessing in War and Peace," discusses church-state issues in early America and the World Wars.

Smith, C. Henry. "The Historical Background." *The Power of Love: A Study Manual Adapted for Sunday School User and for Group Discussion.* Ed. Peace Committee of the GCMC. Newton: Board of Publication, 1947, 38-57. MHL. Brief summary of the belief and practice of nonresistance from the New Testament church through World War I.

Smith, Wayne LaVelle. "Rockingham County Nonresistance and the First World War." MA thesis, Madison College, Harrisonburg, Va., 1967. Pp. 160. A study of Mennonite and Brethren experiences, attitudes, and activities during World War I. Includes summary of the nonresistant position dating from the Reformation, and a brief look at Mennonite experiences during the Civil War. MSHL.

Smith, Willard H. "The Pacifist Thought of William Jennings Bryan." *MQR* 45 Part 1 (Jan., 1971), 33-81; Part 2 (Apr., 1971), 152-81. Part 1 reviews the beginning of Bryan's pacifist thought after the Spanish-American War; Tolstoy's influence on him; Bryan's work as Secretary of State and resignation from that office over disagreement with President

Wilson's preparations for war. Part 2 examines Bryan's vigorous support of US involvement in World War I once it had been declared, his thinking and strategies for peace following the war, and some of the inconsistencies of his thought.

Smucker, Barbara Claassen. *Days of Terror.* Scottdale: Herald Press, 1979. Pp. 152. Young Peter Neufeld and his family are Mennonites in Russia during the internal and external turbulence experienced by the Russian nation during the World War I era. A strong theme of this moving juvenile novel is the theme of how people of faith, people who have practiced nonresistance for four hundred years, respond to acts of violence committed against their persons and their possessions in their own homes and barnyards. Both the Mennonite Self-Defense movement and the connections between the economic and cultural distance maintained by the Mennonites and the violence inflicted upon them are sensitively portrayed. For ages 8-12 and up.

Smucker, Donovan E. "Protestantism Faces the Peace." *Menn* 60 (Mar. 6, 1945), 6-7. The Protestant churches have come a long way towards Christian principles since the militarism of World War I but are still committed to a policy of willful compromise on the question of peace.

Smucker, Donovan E. "The Rauschenbusch Story." *Foundations* 2 (Jan., 1959), 4-12. A review of the influences on Rauschenbusch's theological development, closing with a brief discussion of the effect of World War I on his thinking.

Sprunger, Keith L. and Juhnke, James C. "Research Note: Mennonite Oral History." *MQR* 54 (July, 1980), 244-47. Publishes the questionnaire used for interviewing World War I people (primarily draftees) for Bethel College's oral history collection.

Sprunger, Keith L.; Juhnke, James C.; Waltner, John D. *Voices Against War: A Guide to the Schowalter Oral History Collection on World War I Conscientious Objection.* North Newton: Bethel College, 1973. Pp. 190. Alphabetical listing of 273 taped interviews with Mennonite men from the World War I era in 15 states and 4 provinces. Book includes 6 indices plus a selected bibliography on Mennonites and other pacifists during World War I.

Stucky, Gregory J. "Fighting Against the War: The Mennonite *Vorwärts* from 1914 to 1919," *The Kansas Historical Quarterly,* 38 (Summer, 1972), 169-86. Discusses the editorial attitude and coverage of World War I in the MB paper from Hillsboro, KS, including early support for Germany, war propaganda, the dilemma of being German-American during the war, and

the conflict encountered by nonresistant Mennonites who refused to buy war bonds. MLA/BeC.

Swalm, E. J. "Memories of an Old War." *ChrLiv* 16 (Dec., 1969), 7-10. From *My Beloved Brethren* by Ernest John Swalm, Evangel Press, 1969. Brethren in Christ minister tells of his experiences as a conscientious objector during World War I.

Swalm, E. J. *Nonresistance Under Test.* Nappanee, Ind.: E.V. Publishing House, 1938. Pp. 55. An account of the experiences of conscientious objectors during World War I.

Swalm, E. J. "Memories of an Old War." *ChrLiv* 16 (Dec., 1969), 7-10. From *My Beloved Brethren* by Ernest John Swalm, Evangel Press, 1969. Brethren in Christ minister tells of his experiences as a conscientious objector during World War I.

"The Recollections of A. P." *MennMirr* 8, Part 1, "A Look at a Way of Life that Ended Forever," (Feb., 1979), 9-10; Part 2, "Waiting to Leave as Chaos Follows Chaos," (Mar., 1979), 16-18. Excerpts from the journal of an anonymous Russian Mennonite. Includes accounts of experiences in alternative service during World War I and the Russian Revolution.

Teichroew, Allan, ed. "Military Surveillance of Mennonites in World War I." *MQR* 53 (Apr., 1979), 95-127. Publishes a report from the Military Intelligence Division of the War Department documenting government surveillance of Mennonites, Amish, and Hutterites between Mar., 1918 and Feb., 1919 and government pressure on them as conscientious objectors in World War I. The report concludes that their actions qualified as "treason."

Teichroew, Allan. "World War I and the Mennonite Migration to Canada to Avoid the Draft." *MQR* 45 (July, 1971), 219-49. A report on motives and experiences of draft age men going to Canada. "The war and all its manifestations—conscription, anti-German sentiment, bond drives, and unabated government efforts to mobilize America physically, spiritually, and emotionally— dictated the response of Mennonites who went to Canada."

Thiessen, Linda Dyck. "Mennonites and Military Exemption in Canada During World War I." Term paper, Feb. 21, 1978. Box 10-C-4. CMBS/ Win.

Thiessen, Mary. "Nonresistance in Canada During World War I and II." Student paper for Mennonite History, Nov., 1960. Pp. 17. MLA/ BeC.

Toews, John B. *Czars, Soviets, and Mennonites.* Newton: Faith and Life Press, 1982. Pp. 221. Analytical and interpretive study of the history of the Mennonites in Russia. While this examination of parochial Mennonitism in the wider socio-political context discusses the church's peace witness, including the church and state relationship, at various points, chapters which deal more explicitly with war/peace issues are: "The Russian Mennonites and World War I," 63-78; "Response to Anarchy," 79-94; "Communism and the Peace Witness," 95-106.

"War or Peace, What Shall It Be?" *GH* 32 (May 18, 1939), 146. Reprinted from *The Lutheran Witness* (May 2, 1939). As the possibility of another world war grows, the author urges persons not to forget the horrors of the last war. Perhaps they can teach us to denounce war and pray for peace. Warkentin, Bernard. Letter to the Editor. *MennRep* 8 (Aug. 7, 1978), 7. Relates personal experience of noncombatant duty in World War I, concluding that noninvolvement in war is an impossible dream given the interconnectedness of people and institutions in a society.

Warkentine, Kendal. "Military Justice in World War I: Court Martial Trials of Mennonite Conscientious Objectors." Social Science Seminar, Feb., 1983. Pp. 127. MLA/BeC.

Wenger, Martha. "Between Two Fires: A Study of War Department Policy Toward Conscientious Objectors in World War I." Paper presented to Seminar on World War I, [Bethel College, North Newton, Ks.], Dec. 14, 1975. Pp. 22. MHL, MLA/BeC.

World War I. 302 interviews: over half are transcribed. Emphasis is on CO's from many Mennonite branches and other churches. Also includes several regulars and civilians (women, pastors). Some very dramatic stories of abuse in army camps, courts-martial, prison, personal testimonies about nonresistant stances, moving to Canada to escape conscription, community war fervor. Guide to interviews published as Sprunger, *et al., Voices Against War,* 1973. MLA/BeC.

Yake, J. Stanley. "Treatment of Mennonite Conscientious Objectors in World War I Army Camps." Paper presented to History Seminary, Goshen College, Goshen, Ind., May 30, 1957. Pp. 43. MHL.

Yoder, Edward. "Twenty Years After: Peace Principles from a Scriptural Viewpoint." Part 10. *GH* 30 (Apr. 15, 1937), 78-79. Unreasonable war sentiment is being expressed again, only twenty years after the fiasco of World War I.

Yoder, Sanford Calvin. *For Conscience Sake.* Goshen: Mennonite Historical Society, 1940 (Scottdale, 1945). Pp. 300. A survey of Mennonite migrations resulting from World War I, together with a theological interpretation of their meaning.

Yoder, Sanford Calvin. "Migratory Movements Among the Mennonites as a Result of the World War." MA in Religion thesis, Winona Lake School of Theology, Winona Lake, Ind., 1933. Pp. 112. MHL. Historical overview of the way the practice of nonresistance has been the source of tension between Mennonites and their governments, leading in most cases to Mennonite migration in search of lands more open to their peculiarities. Emphasizes the Mennonite migration from Russia to Canada, Mexico, and Latin America during World War I.

# D. World War II

"America and the War in the East." *Menn* 52 (Sept. 21, 1937), 6-7. Exhorts Mennonites as Christian citizens to do all they can to support strict enforcement of the US neutrality law. The article explains the law as a deterrent to war; arguments for and against its full application are cited.

"Analysis of Draft Census of Five Mennonite Conferences." *GH* 49 (Nov. 20, 1956), 1105. Mennonite Research Foundation reports the CO record of the Mennonite Church in 1952-56 was better than it was in World War II.

Abrams, Ray H. *Preachers Present Arms.* Scottdale: Herald Press, 1969. Pp. 330. A revised edition of the 1933 volume documenting the active role of clergy in promoting war, with two additional chapters on World War II and later developments, including the Vietnam War.

Adams, Paul. "The Mennonite Doctrine of Nonresistance Under Test During World War II in Canada: Special Attention Given to Mennonites of Kitchener-Waterloo." Term paper for 20th Century Canadian History course (MCC Peace Scholarship paper), Mar., 1978. Pp. 22. CGCL.

Addinga, A. and Baumann, H. C. "Letter from Winschoten." *MCC WSRB* 1 (Sept., 1945), 7, 6. Mennonites in Holland describe sufferings during World War II.

Arms, George Wells. "The Bible and the War." *ChrMon* 32 (Nov., 1940), 336-37, 346. Reprinted from *The Presbyterian.* The war in Europe shows the failure of modernism, democracy, and Protestantism.

Bainton, Roland H. "The Churches and War: Historic Attitudes Toward Christian Participation." *Social Action* 11 (Jan. 15, 1945), 5-71. Reviews the three positions of pacifism, just war, and crusade from the first through the twentieth centuries, including World War II. Examines especially 20th-century attitudes. Refers to Anabaptist views in the Reformation, as well as the treatment of conscientious objectors and Civilian Public Service.

Barons, Kirk. "The Hutterite Experience in Alberta in World War II." Essay for History 363 course, Apr., 1975. Pp. 34. CGCL.

Beechy, Atlee. "The Civilian Public Service Experience." *GH* 68 (Dec. 9, 1975), 878-79. Beechy recounts personal remembrances of his CPS work during World War II in the US

Beechy, Winifred Nelson. "André and the French City of Refuge, La Chambon." *GH* 72 (Nov. 13, 1979), 884-85. Philip Hallie, a Jewish philosopher, has written a book, *Lest Innocent Blood Be Shed,* about André Trocmé and the people of La Chambon, who took in fugitives, mostly Jewish, during World War II and risked their lives in so doing. Hallie, himself, experiences a renewal of spirit and optimism through their remarkable faith and courage.

Bender, Harold S. *Mennonite Origins in Europe.* Akron: MCC, 1942. Pp. 72. First of a series of six studies published under the title *Mennonites and Their Heritage* for use in Civilian Public Service camps during World War II.

Bender, John E. "The Effect of the War on the Mennonites in Holland." *MCC WSRB* 1 (Sept., 1945), 3, 6. Describes destruction of life and property, along with the effect on religious life.

Bender, Urie A. *Soldiers of Compassion.* Scottdale: Herald Press, 1969. Pp. 320. The story of PAX, a service program of Mennonite Central Committee for conscientious objectors after World War II, told in first person and case history form.

Berg, Ford (Review). *Letters to My Son,* by Dagobert Runes. N.p., n.d.; *Etched in Purple,* by Frank J. Irgang. N.p., n.d. "Is He the Saviour?" *GH* 43 (Sept. 19, 1950), 930-31. Recommends these two indictments of war; the first is a Jewish perspective, the second an account of a medical noncombatant's experiences in World War II.

Bethel College in World War Two. 29 interviews. Covers Bethel's stance on nonresistance and hostile community response. MLA/BeC.

Bilderbeek, H. van. "The Dutch Mennonite Peace Group." *MennLife* 18 (Oct., 1963), 172-73. Principles and activities of the Dutch Mennonite Peace Group reorganized after World War II.

de Boer, M. "Flooding Walcheren Island." *MennLife* 1 (Jan., 1946), 35-37. Destruction wrought on a Dutch island to break the German position during World War II.

Bowman, Randall J. "From World War II Until Vietnam: Societal Influence on the Mennonites." Term paper for Mennonite History and Thought course, Feb. 17, 1978. Pp. 15. MSHL.

Brenneman, Helen Good. "But Not Forsaken." *ChrLiv* 1 (Apr., 1954), 4-5, 42-43, 45-46; 1 (May, 1954), 6-7, 41-42, 44-45, 47-48; 1 (June, 1954), 6-8, 43, 45-48; 1 (July, 1954), 8-10, 42-48; 1 (Aug., 1954), 12-13, 39-44; 1 (Sept., 1954), 18-19, 39-43; 1 (Oct., 1954), 16-17, 42-45; 1 (Nov., 1954), 18-19, 41-45; 1 (Dec., 1954), 18-19, 40-45. Nine-part serial on refugees after World War II. Published as book, *But Not Forsaken,* Scottdale: Herald Press, 1954.

Brenneman, Helen Good. "They Were Prisoners of War." *ChrLiv* 13 (June, 1966), 4-6. Marvin and Frieda Dirks' experiences as Japanese prisoners of war during World War II.

Brunk, Emily. *Espelkamp: The MCC Shares in Community Building in a New Settlement for German Refugees.* Frankfurt, Germany: MCC, 1951. Pp. 42. MHL. Relates the story of Espelkamp, an initial experiment in resettlement of the refugees of World War II in which both American and European Mennonite youth participated on a Voluntary Service basis.

Brunk, Harry A. *History of Mennonites in Virginia, 1900-1960.* Verona, Va.: by the author, 1972. Pp. 592. MHL. Contains chapter entitled "Conscientious Objectors in World Wars I & II," 451-66.

Burkholder, J. Lawrence. "An Examination of the Mennonite Doctrine of Nonconformity to the World." ThM thesis, Princeton Theological Seminary, 1951. Pp. 221. MHL. Section four includes Mennonite nonresistance during World War II.

Burkholder, Marie. "Alternative Service Programs Available for Mennonites During the Second World War." Term paper for History course, Dec. 4, 1973. Pp. 28. CGCL.

Buttrick, George A. "American Protestantism and European War." *Menn* 54 (Oct. 3, 1939), 4-5. A radio address given one week after the outbreak of World War II explains the duty of American Protestant churches in the face of war.

"Canadians Research Wartime Experiences." *RepConsS* 32 (June, 1975), 4. Conrad Grebel College has initiated an oral history project to preserve and deepen understanding of the Canadian Mennonite experience with alternative service in World War II.

"CO Confined in Mental Hospital for 29 Years." *GH* 65 (Jan. 11, 1972), 27. Reprinted from *The Reporter for Conscience Sake* (Nov., 1971). The story of a black CO who was wrongly institutionalized in a mental health facility as a result of the legal complications of his pacifist position on "Roosevelt's War."

Cattepoel, Dirk. "The Mennonites of Germany, 1936-1948, and the Present Outlook." *ChrMon* 40 (Sept., 1948), 261-63, 285. German Mennonite pastor describes church life in Nazi Germany and since the war.

Catton, Bruce. "Draft More Liberal Than in 1917 Toward Conscientious Objectors." *Goshen News* n.d., 16. Describes the Selective Service registration process for conscientious objectors (during World War II). Includes photo of a Mennonite from Pa. registering.

Charles, Howard H. "A Presentation and Evaluation of MCC Draft Status Census." *PCMCP Fourth*, 83-106. North Newton: Bethel College, 1945. Held at Bluffton, Ohio, Aug. 24-25, 1945. The purpose of the draft status census was to ascertain the number of men who had gone into military service and to learn why they did. Factual data revealed a variety of factors which influenced these decisions.

Claassen, Susan. "J. Lloyd Spaulding—Peace Witness in World War II." Student oral history project, May 11, 1973. Pp. 8. MLA/BeC.

Coon, Helen C. "A Flag Over His Grave." *Menn* 92 (June 28, 1977), 418-19. Tribute to the author's father, John T. Neufeld, a conscientious objector in World War II and pastor of Grace Mennonite Church in Chicago.

"Disaster Ends Russian Mennonite Settlements." *MennLife* 4 (Jan., 1949), 22-23, 26-27. Upheavals suffered by Russian Mennonite villagers through wars and purges from the Revolution to World War II.

Dahl, Edward H. "The War Crisis of the Canadian Mennonites 1930-1945." *JChSoc* 3 (Fall, 1967), 3. Survey of the historical background of the Mennonites, the situation in Canada between 1930-1945, and the effects of the war crisis on the Canadian Mennonites.

Derstine, C. F. "British Treatment of CO's." *ChrMon* 38 (May, 1946), 159-60. British laws governing conscientious objectors in World War II were tolerant by comparison to American laws.

Derstine, C. F. "Can the Allies Expect to Win the War?" *ChrMon* 34 (Nov., 1942), 350-51. Since neither the Allies nor the Axis is worthy to win, author uses scriptural passages to predict the outcome of the war.

Derstine, C. F. "CO's in World War I and World War II." *ChrMon* 36 (May, 1944), 158-59. Comparison of Selective Service regulations and penalties for refusing to comply in World Wars I and II.

Derstine, C. F. "Conscription and Conscientious Objectors." *ChrMon* 32 (May, 1940), 158-59. Reviews the government attitude toward conscientious objection during World War I and strongly advocates the position to youth in World War II.

Derstine, C. F. "England Calls the CO's 'Conchies.' " *ChrMon* 32 (Mar., 1940), 94-95. England takes lenient attitude toward conscientious objectors in World War II.

Derstine, C. F. "Fascism—Friend or Foe—Which?" *ChrMon* 25 (Oct., 1933), 318. Hitler's rise to power seems to mean the loss of liberties and perhaps even the advent of war.

Derstine, C. F. "Germany and Japan May Lose the War But Will We Save Ourselves?" *ChrMon* 35 (May, 1943), 159-60. Even if the US wins the war, its national moral debauchery will prevent the coming of true peace.

Derstine, C. F. "Hitler Starts Life Job as German Caesar." *ChrMon* 26 (Oct., 1934), 318. Hitler has won support by convincing Germans they are in danger of war from foreign aggression.

Derstine, C. F. "Hitler's Ten Commandments for the German Church." *ChrMon* 26 (Nov., 1934), 351. Deplores the close association of church and state in Germany.

Derstine, C. F. "Hitler's Triumphant Entry into His Native Austria." *ChrMon* 30 (Apr., 1938), 126. Report on Hitler's successful coup in Austria.

Derstine, C. F. "Impressions of the Nazi Regime and its Effect on the Churches." *ChrMon* 26 (Jan., 1934), 30-31. Support of U. S. Christians is due the church in Germany for its resistance to the race prejudice and nationalism of the Nazi state church.

Derstine, C. F. "Interned Mennonite Relief Worker Returns from Germany to America." *ChrMon* 34 (Aug., 1942), 254. Relief worker in Germany taken prisoner when war was declared with the US describes his experiences.

Derstine, C. F. "Is Europe Marching Back to 1914?" *ChrMon* 28 (June, 1936), 191. Tabulates the armies and airplanes amassed by European countries and decries the rising militarism.

Derstine, C. F. "Is the Shadow of the Beast Appearing Upon the Horizon." *ChrMon* 27 (Apr., 1935), 126-27. The buildup of armaments and the opposition to conscientious objection are signs of the Antichrist.

Derstine, C. F. "Man's Blackout God's Opportunity to Shine." *ChrMon* 33 (July, 1941), 222-23. The war and suffering in Europe are causing people to turn to God.

Derstine, C. F. "Our Testimony and a Wartorn World." *ChrMon* 28 (Aug., 1936), 254-55. Mennonites with a heritage of peace should witness publicly to the rising militarism.

Derstine, C. F. "'Seven Men Went Singing into Heaven.'" *ChrMon* 32 (July, 1940), 222-23. Story of seven Bolshevik soldiers who were converted underscores the idea that the Gospel must be preached also to military personnel.

Derstine, C. F. "State and Church in Nazi Germany." *ChrMon* 29 (June, 1937), 190. Cites magazine and newspaper articles showing Hitler's attempts to replace Christian faith with state loyalty.

Derstine, C. F. "The Canadian-United States Border a World Example." *ChrMon* 30 (Oct., 1938), 322. The peaceful relations and open border between US and Canada contrast with many of the European borders.

Derstine, C. F. "The Crying Need for the Return of the Prince of Peace." *ChrMon* 24 (Sept., 1932), 285. The threat of war in Europe and Asia is matched by the spread of the peace movement in American churches.

Derstine, C. F. "The Dark Side, the Brighter Side, and the Brightest Side of the War and Peace Problem in the World." *ChrMon* 26 (Feb., 1934), 58-59. The horrors of war as compared with the fact that 90 per cent of the European population does not want war, and the hope in Jesus, the Prince of Peace.

Derstine, C. F. "The Ethiopian Situation—Sixty-eight Words Twenty-one Years Ago Opened the World War." *ChrMon* 27 (Oct., 1935), 318-19. Italy's threatened invasion of Egypt might bring the world to the brink of another world war.

Derstine, C. F. "The Fall of the French Empire." *ChrMon* 32 (Sept., 1940), 287-88. France's defeat by Germany is another step to Armageddon.

Derstine, C. F. "The Four Grim, Deadly Horsemen Halted in Europe." *ChrMon* 30 (Nov., 1938), 353-54. Pact signed by Germany, England, Italy, and France has momentarily stayed the threat of war.

Derstine, C. F. "The German and Japanese Nations from the Christian Viewpoint." *ChrMon* 37 (Nov., 1945), 302-3. Americans should forgive Germany and Japan and participate in the rebuilding of their physical and spiritual lives.

Derstine, C. F. "The High Cost of Killing." *ChrMon* 33 (Jan., 1941), 31. While the world pours time, money, and lives into the world war, conscientious objectors should be active in prayer and sacrificial living.

Derstine, C. F. "The Holocaust of the Past War, and the Nightmare of the Next." *ChrMon* 23 (May, 1931), 158. Statistics of the destruction of World War I, with projections of the shape of the next war.

Derstine, C. F. "The Italo-Ethiopian Land Grab." *ChrMon* 27 (Nov., 1935), 350-51. Italy's invasion of Ethiopia is a modern case of coveting land.

Derstine, C. F. "'The Lull in the European Storm.'" *ChrMon* 31 (July, 1939), 222-23. Reviews the prospects for war in Europe.

Derstine, C. F. "The Palace of the Soviets." *ChrMon* 37 (Aug., 1945), 222-23. World War II did not solve problems; instead, the Soviet Union gathered power and influence.

Derstine, C. F. "The Royal Words of Hope for Our War-torn World." *ChrMon* 31 (Oct., 1939), 319. Report on the beginning of World War II.

Derstine, C. F. "The Threatening European Cataclysm." *ChrMon* 38 (Sept., 1936), 286-87. Cites the war preparations taking place in European countries and in the US.

Derstine, C. F. "The United States and Japan, and the 'Scrap Iron'." *ChrMon* 34 (Feb., 1942), 61-62. Modernism as practiced in Germany and greed as seen in US arms trades with Japan helped precipitate the world war, and rejection of both will help the US get out of the war.

Derstine, C. F. "The Unnecessary War." *ChrMon* 42 (Aug., 1950), 254-55. Comment on World War II and the threat of nuclear war.

Derstine, C. F. "War—Its Aim: To Stop One Man's March to Power." *ChrMon* 31 (Oct., 1939), 319-20, 315. Reviews Hitler's rise to power and Germany's movement toward war.

Derstine, C. F. "World War No. II Proves the Bible to Be True." *ChrMon* 34 (May, 1942), 158-59. The present worldwide conflict bears out the biblical prophecies of the presence of war in this dispensation.

Derstine, C. F. "Zero Hour." *ChrMon* 36 (July, 1944), 222. The occasion of the Allied invasion of Europe should serve as a reminder not to trust in military might.

Dettwiler, Alma W. and Stoltzfus, Grant M. "How Pearl Harbor Changed My Life." *ChrLiv* 13 (Dec., 1966), 12-13. Two Mennonites reflect on the way American involvement in the war shaped their lives.

Diggers, The (a corporate student group). "Rigorous, Regulated, Rowdy, Religious, and Radical: A Study of Bethel College During World War II." Oral history project for History of Civilization II, Mar. 6, 1974. Pp. 96. MLA/ BeC.

Driediger, Ab Douglas. Letter to the Editor. *MennRep* 9 (Sept. 3, 1979), 6. In response to the third part of John Friesen's series on church-state relations (Aug. 20, 1979), the writer argues that there were many more Mennonite men who accepted full military service in World War II than is commonly believed.

Dueck, Abe. "Church and State: Developments Among Mennonite Brethren in Canada Since World War II." Study paper, Nov. 22, 1980. Box 8-E-1.

Duvanel, Tammy. "Women and World War II: An Examination of Home Front Involvement Comparing Newton-Area Women with the National Trend." Social Science Seminar paper, 1984. Pp. 20. MLA/BeC.

Dyck, Anna. "We Experienced Hiroshima," story told by Setsuko Kokubu. *MBH* (Sept. 16, 1977), 6-8. Survivor describes the destruction, illness, and death during and following the bombing of Hiroshima.

Dyck, Peter J. "Entering Holland." *MCC WSRB* 1 (Sept., 1945), 1-2. Describes conditions in Holland as a result of the war, and the stance of Dutch Mennonites toward nonresistance.

Ediger, Amand. "The Russian Mennonites During World War II." Student paper for Mennonite History, May 23, 1946. Pp. 16. MLA/BeC.

Engle, T. L. "An Analysis of Themes on the Subject of War as Written by Amish and Non-Amish Children." *Journal of Educational Psychology* 35 (Apr., 1944), 267-73. Study finds that mention of rationing and shortages was the outstanding characteristic of themes written on the subject of "How the War Affects Me" and that the Amish children exhibited statistically significant less desire to help win the war than the non-Amish children.

Engle, T. L. "Attitudes Toward War as Expressed by Amish and Non-Amish Children." *Journal of Educational Psychology* 35 (Apr., 1944), 211-19. Evidence from two measurement instruments, children's essays, and an attitude-toward-war scale, indicates that the Amish children exhibited a statistically significant less favorable attitude toward war than non-Amish children.

Enns, Mary M. "Ingrid Rimland Turns to Face the Forces That Shaped Her Life." *MennMirror* 8 (Jan., 1979), 6, 7. Describes some of the forces that shaped Rimland's life and led her to write the novel *The Wanderers* which tells of three women who survived the Russian Revolution, World War II, and the hardships of Paraguay.

Epp, Arnold A. "Draft Status of Mennonite Men in American Wars from the French and Indian War to World War II." Student paper for Mennonite History course, May 24, 1949. Pp. 31. MLA/BeC.

Epp, Frank H. "How and When the USA Got Involved in Vietnam." *CanMenn* 14 (July 5, 1966), 10. Outlines the US involvement which began during World War II, USA support of the French, the Ngo Dinh Diem regime, AID, etc.

Epp, Frank H. Letter to the Editor, "Information on Military Experience Needed." *MennRep* 9 (Dec. 24, 1979), 6. A letter commenting on recent discussion in the *MennRep* on the subject of Mennonites in the armed forces during World War II and requesting assistance from readers in obtaining more information on military service.

Epp, Frank H. "Mobilizing Youth for Peace." *CanMenn* 2 (July 23, 1954), 2. Statistics show that Mennonites put far fewer human resources into service for the gospel than Canadians put into the armed forces during World War II. This trend must be reversed.

Epp, Frank H. (Editorial). "CO's or PM's." *CanMenn* 5 (Dec. 13, 1957), 2. A call to be peacemakers today, not only CO's of World Wars I and II.

Epp, Frank H. (Editorial). "Mobilizing Youth for Peace." *CanMenn* 2 (July 23, 1954), 2. In World War II, Canadians put 7 percent of their human resources toward the war effort while Canadian Mennonites put .2 percent of their human resources toward the peace effort. Encourages, in light of this disparity, more involvement with PAX and other service programs.

Epp, Henry H. "World War II Conscientious Objectors in Discussion with Church Leaders." *CanMenn* 11 (June 14, 1963), 3. A panel reviews the nature of the CO's relationship to the government and the community during World Wars I and II at the Ontario Ministers' Peace Retreat. Includes a summary of questions and answers about alternative service in World

War II and the position of the Mennonite church today.

Erb, Paul. "V-Day." *GH* 37 (Dec. 8, 1944), 699. Mennonites cannot help celebrate a military victory, but V-Day may be an appropriate time for prayers of thanksgiving, confession, and intercession.

Ewert, Bruno. "Four Centuries of Prussian Mennonites." *MennLife* 3 (Apr., 1948), 10-18. Describes Prussian Mennonite stance on participation in war, and describes Prussian life during World War I and World War II.

Fast, Henry A. (Review). *That There Be Peace: Mennonites in Canada and World War II,* ed. by Lawrence Klippenstein. Winnipeg: Manitoba CO Reunion Committee, 1979. *Menn* 95 (Feb. 12, 1980), 108. Recommends the book as a collection of reflections of alternative service workers.

Fransen, David Warren. "Canadian Mennonites and Conscientious Objectors in World War II." MA in History Thesis, Univ. of Waterloo, Waterloo, Ont., 1977. Pp. 204. MHL. Canadian Mennonites' experience on the CO issue in World War II involved internal and external struggle. The internal struggle was the effort to establish unity among the congregations on the nonresistant position. Fransen analyzes both the organizational development toward unity and the forces shaping this development—such as traditions, personalities, language, regionalism, etc. The external struggle was the effort to negotiate, with the government, an alternative to military service that had integrity for the Mennonite churches and for the government.

Fransen, David Warren. "Mennonites in World War II: The Beginnings of Cooperation and Social Conscience." *MennRep* 8 (July 10, 1978), 9. Traces differences that existed among Canadian Mennonite groups in considering alternative service programs prior to World War II, and their eventual cooperation in the formation of work camps.

Fransen, David Warren. "The Debate on Alternate Service During World War II." Paper presented to the Institute of Anabaptist-Mennonite Studies, Conrad Grebel College, Oct. 1, 1975. Pp. 28. CGCL.

Frantz, Margarete. "Last Ship to Freedom." *MBH* 13 (Nov. 29, 1974), 26-28. Russian Mennonite refugee in Germany tries to obtain exit visa by lying about his service in Hitler's army.

Frazer, Heather T. and O'Sullivan, John. "Forgotten Women of World War II: Wives of Conscientious Objectors in Civilian Public Service." *Peace and Change* 5 (Fall, 1978), 46-51.

Documents the injustice of the CPS system in the absence of government pay or benefits granted to other enlisted men. Focuses especially on the economic and emotional plight of wives of CPS workers.

Fretz, J. Winfield. "Mennonites Are Losing Their Biblical Nonresistance." *Menn* 66 (June 12, 1951), 376, 385. Compares statistics from World War I and World War II and then attributes the erosion of conviction on nonresistance more to forces from within the church than to external factors.

Fretz, J. Winfield. "Our Peace Witness During World War II." *The Power of Love; A Study Manual Adopted for Sunday School Use and for Group Discussion,* pp. 58-96. Ed. Peace Committee of the General Conference Mennonite Church. Newton: Board of Publication, 1947. MHL. Discusses the history and operation of the CPS program, the point of view of those Mennonites who entered military service as chaplains, etc., and the witness of the noncombatants. Concludes that the CPS program was the choice most consistent with Mennonite belief and practice and that the program was an effective witness for peace to the nation, to the community, and to the Mennonite churches.

Fretz, J. Winfield. "The Draft Status of General Conference Men in World War II." (Part 1) *Menn* 60 (July 24, 1945), 1-2. A summary, with tables, of the Peace Committee's census of draft-age men. Of the drafted men about 27 percent were CO's, 18 percent had I-AO status, and 55 percent enlisted as I-A's.

Fretz, Mark J. "Nonresistance During World War II: A Comparison of the (Old) Mennonites and General Conference Mennonite Positions." Term paper for Mennonite History and Thought Course, Feb. 20, 1978. Pp. 17. MSHL.

Frey, Virgil E. "The Relation of Bethel College Church to World War II." Student paper for Our Christian Heritage, Nov., 1949. Pp. 8. MLA/BeC.

Friesen, Paul A. "Relief Work, an Evangelical Witness." Seminary Paper, Goshen College, Goshen, Ind., 1947. Pp. 29. MHL.

Gerlach, Horst. "Through Darkness to Light." *ChrLiv* 3 (Aug., 1956), 6-9, 40-41; 3 (Sept., 1956), 12-15, 40; 3 (Oct., 1956), 14-17, 19, 34, 36; 3 (Nov., 1956), 19-22, 24, 34, 35-37; 3 (Dec., 1956), 24-29, 36; 4 (Jan., 1957), 24-29; 4 (Feb., 1957), 24-29. Life story of a young German man growing up in a pro-Nazi family during the Hitler and World War II era. Enemy occupation of home town; prisoner of war in northern Russia as slave laborer; conversion to

Christianity from trust in military force while an MCC trainee serving in the US.

Gingerich, Melvin. *Service for Peace*. Akron: MCC, 1949. Pp. 508. The standard history of Mennonite Civilian Public Service during World War II.

Gingerich, Melvin. "The Mennonite Church in World War II; A Review and Evaluation." *MQR* 25 (July, 1951), 183-200. A summary of the work of the Peace Problems Committee. In spite of intensive peace education between the World Wars, nearly half of the young men drafted in World War II served militarily; most others found it difficult to refrain from compromise.

Gleysteen, Jan (Review). *The Destruction of Dresden*, by David Irving. Holt, Rinehart, and Winston, n.d. Pp. 225. *ChrLiv* 11 (Nov., 1964), 33-34. Recommends the book as a reminder that the fire-bombing of Dresden during World War II shows that wartime atrocities are not committed only by "the other side."

Gleysteen, Jan (Review). *Transfigured Night*, by Eileen Egan and Elizabeth Reiss. Livingston Pub. Co., 1964. Pp. 186. *ChrLiv* 12 (Dec., 1965), 37. Recommends this documented account of relief work done in Germany following World War II by eighteen relief agencies, including Mennonite work.

Glick, Lester J. "How Starvation Would Affect You." *ChrLiv* 10 (Mar., 1963), 12-13. Thirty-five conscientious objectors volunteer for semi-starvation diet at the University of Minnesota in 1944.

Goering, James A. (Review). *The Struggle for a Soul*, by William L. Hull. NY: Doubleday and Co., Inc., 1963. *ST* 33 (3rd Qtr., 1965), 23. A candid account of efforts to lead Adolf Eichmann, a man responsible for the extermination of six million Jews under Hitler, to a saving knowledge of Jesus Christ.

Gorter, S. H. N. "Destruction and Reconstruction of Mennonite Churches in Holland." *MennLife* 1 (Jan., 1946), 31-35. Describes the suffering of the Mennonite churches in Holland during World War II.

Harris, Arthur S., Jr. "That's All You Need to Know." *ChrLiv* 4 (Mar., 1957), 16-17, 36. Conscientious objector learns a simple view of war and peace from a fellow worker in a CO camp during World War II.

Harshbarger, Emmett L. "Anti-semitism Before the World War: History Views the Jewish Persecutions" (Part 2). *Menn* 54 (Feb. 21, 1939), 3-4. A brief review of the course of anti-semitism from Old Testament times through the 19th century.

Harshbarger, Emmett L. "Concluding Statements from a Christian Point of View: History View the Jewish Persecutions" (Part 5). *Menn* 54 (May 2, 1939), 1-2. History says Christians can propagandize against and persecute the Jews. Mennonites who live by the Sermon on the Mount cannot join in nor condone this.

Harshbarger, Emmett L. "The Most Common Anti-semitic Arguments: History Views the Jewish Persecutions" (Part 4). *Menn* 54, Part 1, (Mar. 7, 1939), 4-5; Part 2, (Mar. 14, 1939), 8-9; Part 3, (Apr. 25, 1939), 5-6. Refutes the charge that the Jew is to blame for Germany's troubles since the World War; it is a half-truth to say that the Jews dominate the economics of the world; a common argument is that the Jew is the source of all kinds of radicalism.

Harshbarger, Emmett L. "The World War and Its Aftermath: History Views the Jewish Persecutions" (Part 3). *Menn* 54 (Feb. 28, 1939), 3-4. Describes the terrible persecutions during and after the war.

Harshbarger, Emmett L. "Why Jewish Persecutions? History Views the Jewish Persecutions" (Part 1). *Menn* 54 (Feb. 14, 1939), 2. The basis of anti-semitism is hatred of the foreigner, the person who is different.

Hartzler, R. L. Letter to the Editor. *Menn* 92 (July 12, 1977), 446. Commends General Lewis Hershey for his wise attitude toward conscientious objection in World War II, showing respect for the Civilian Public Service program and after the war reversing the ban on CO's going overseas, thus making possible the Mennonite contribution to European reconstruction.

Heinritz, Lotte. "Women's Odyssey." *MennLife* 3 (Apr., 1948), 19-22. Describes the horrors of war as experienced by women from Danzig, Poland, during World War II.

Hershberger, Guy F. "Conscientious Objectors in Prison." *GH Supplement* 39 (Aug., 1946), 460. There is growing support for the policy of granting amnesty to the war objectors still in prison. Many of these persons have been imprisoned unjustly.

Hershberger, Guy F. *The Mennonite Church in the Second World War*. Scottdale: Mennonite Publishing House, 1951. Pp. 308. A history and evaluation of the Mennonite Church (MC) experience during World War II in relation to its witness for peace.

Hershberger, Guy F. (Review). *Conscription of Conscience: The American State and the Conscientious*

*Objector, 1940-1947,* by Melford Q. Sibley and Philip E. Jacob. Ithaca: Cornell University Press, 1952. Pp. 580. *MQR* 27 (1953), 351-55. Summarizes the book's story of conscription and the CO in World War II as seen through the eyes of authors whose primary interest is in civil liberties rather than the New Testament way of nonresistant love. Harshberger raises the question of whether the two causes of social justice and nonresistant love can be served best by the more militant type of pacifist or the way of MCC. Considers this book helpful in raising this issue into sharp focus.

Hershberger, John Kenneth (Archival). "A Study of the Japanese Peace Movement: 1947-60." John Horsch Mennonite History Essay Contest 1971-72. Box 14. I-3-3.5. Examination of the Japanese peace movement that existed following World War II and which proved relatively ineffective in 1960, primarily as a result of pervasive disunity and factionalism. Goshen, Ind. AMC.

Hiebert, Susan. "In Time of Crisis: How Two Responded." *MennRep* 4 (Feb. 18, 1974), 9. Two Canadian conscientious objectors reflect on two major life crises: World War II and contracting polio.

Horst, Irvin B. *A Ministry of Goodwill. A Short Account of Mennonite Relief, 1939-1949.* Akron: MCC, 1949. Pp. 119. An account of Mennonite relief work around the world during and following World War II.

Horst, Irvin B. "Edward Yoder—A Tribute from Civilian Public Service." *GH Supplement* 38 (Aug., 1945), 407. Yoder's thought and writings were much appreciated by those in CPS camps during World War II; his book, *Our Mennonite Heritage,* brought inspiration and challenge to many.

Horst, John L. (Editorial). "America Enters the World War." *ChrMon* 34 (Jan., 1942), 8-9. Outlines the challenges present to nonresistant people with the US entry into World War II.

Horst, John L. (Editorial). "Another World War." *ChrMon* 31 (Oct., 1939), 297. Comments on the prospect of war breaking out in Europe.

Horst, John L. (Editorial). "'For Such a Time as This.'" *ChrMon* 29 (July, 1937), 201. Encourages nonresistant churches to give public testimony to peace, in light of world events pointing toward war.

Hostetler, Mervin J. "A Time to Remember: Civilian Public Service." *ChrLiv* 18 (May, 1971), 7-9. Impressions of years spent in CPS in World War II, and of the rejection faced as a conscientious objector after the war.

Hostetter, J. J. "Notes from Belgium." *ChrMon* 40 (June, 1948), 178-79. Comment on the wartime destruction in Belgium and Mennonite efforts at reconstruction.

Hunsberger, Willard. *The Franconia Mennonites and War.* Scottdale: Peace and Industrial Relations Committee of Franconia Mennonite Conference, 1951. After briefly surveying the experience of the Franconia Mennonites with the earlier American wars, their experience with World War II is discussed more fully. Some of the topics considered are community reactions to conscientious objectors, a typical day in a CPS camp, the activities of the church during and after the war.

Hunsberger, Wilson. "Interesting Scenes in Europe; Warsaw—Life Among the Ruins." *ChrMon* 40, Part 5, (Oct., 1948), 308-9. Describes the German bombing of Poland and the present state of the city.

Hunsberger, Wilson. "Oswiecim, City of Death." *ChrMon* 40 (Sept., 1948), 278-79. Description of a Nazi concentration camp in southern Poland.

Jantz, Hugo W. "Dietrich Bonhoeffer: Theologian, Disciple, Martyr." *MBH* 14 (July 11, 1975), 1-3. Tribute to the theologian and pacifist who participated in the plot to kill Hitler.

Janzen, Wilhelm. "Deliverance." Part 2. *MennMirror* 2 (Apr., 1973), 11-13. An installment from Janzen's book which describes some of his experiences in Russia during World War II.

Janzen, Wilhelm. "The Arrest: Uncle Frank Is Taken." Part 1. *MennMirror* 2 (Mar., 1973), 7, 8. This installment from Janzen's book, which describes some of his experiences in Russia during World War II, tells of the arrest of his uncle and the fear and hope surrounding this event.

Joy, Charles R. "The Lost Parents of Europe." *MennComm* 5 (Aug., 1951), 12-14. Documents the plight of orphans and children separated from their parents in war-torn Europe.

Juhnke, James C. *A People of Two Kingdoms: The Political Acculturation of the Kansas Mennonites.* Newton: Faith and Life Press, 1975. Pp. 215. Explains that this process of acculturation was fundamentally shaped by the "abrasive encounter of Mennonite nonresistance with American nationalism" and charts the encounter from the shadows cast on the civic role of the Mennonite German-Americans by the Spanish-American War, through the essential Mennonite-American compatibility of the Progressive Era, through the shattering of that easy course in World War I, through the efforts to bridge the conflict in the inter-war period, to the new phase—characterized by voting and alternative service—during World War II.

Juhnke, Roger. "One War—Three Fronts: Kansas General Conference Mennonite Response to World War II." Social Science Seminary paper, Mar., 1975. Pp. 85. MLA/BeC.

Juhnke, Roger. "The Perils of Conscientious Objection: An Oral History Study of a 1944 Event." *MennLife* 34 (Sept., 1979), 4-9. Juhnke tells and examines the story of an unusual bus ride to Fort Leavenworth in which six CO's were harrassed by a number of inductees in 1944.

Juhnke, William E., Jr. "A World Gone Mad: Mennonites View the Coming of the War, 1938-39." Student independent study, Jan. 20, 1966. Pp. 22. MLA/BeC.

Kauffman, Daniel. "Let Us Pray for Peace." *GH* 32 (Nov. 30, 1939), 737-38. Pray for peace in the hearts of individuals, in homes, in congregations, in home communities, in nations, and in Europe where the war rages

Kaufman, Donald D. "Cheyenne Soldier Testifies, Speaks for Way of Peace." *Menn* 84 (Jan. 21, 1969), 39. Having participated actively in World War II and the Korean War, Ted Risingsun maintains that anyone who is in the army no longer has self-possession. The army wants instant obedience. "How do I feel about it [army experience]? There is a better way."

Keim, Albert N. "John Foster Dulles and the Protestant World Order Movement on the Eve of World War II." *Journal of Church and State* 21 (Winter, 1979), 73-89. Documents Dulles's involvement—active between 1937 and 1949—in the ecumenical church movement to promote world order and his role as mediator in the disagreement on intervention in European affairs. Roots his later Cold War belligerency to the convictions formed in this period of ecumenical involvement.

Keim, Albert N. "Service or Resistance? The Mennonite Response to Conscription in World War II." *MQR* 52 (Apr., 1978), 141-55. Describes the development of an alternative service program during World War II, and stresses the degree to which such a plan was satisfactory to both nonresistant Mennonites and the Selective Service.

Klaassen, Walter. (Review). *Mennoniten im Dritten Reich: Dokumentation und Deutung*, by Diether Götz Lichdi. Weierhof/Pfalz: *Mennonitischer Geschichtsverein*, 1977. Pp. 248. *MQR* 53 (Jan., 1979), 87-88. An account of the Mennonite response and reaction to national socialism, beginning in 1933.

Klassen, D. D. Letter to the Editor. *Menn* 90 (Apr. 8, 1975), 230-31. Underscores the need to send Mennonite youth to Mennonite schools teaching peace theology, by citing situations from World War II, when Mennonites graduated from fundamentalist schools which preached going to war as a Christian duty.

Klippenstein, Lawrence. *That There Be Peace: Mennonites in Canada and World War II*. Winnipeg: Manitoba CO Reunion Committee, 1979. Pp. 104. Includes summary of the Canadian Mennonite experience of World War II, photographs of the projects and CPS camp life, newspaper clippings, and personal reminiscences.

Kokubu, Sersuko (as told to Anna Dyck). "I Experienced Hiroshima." *ChrLead* 40 (Sept. 13, 1977), 9. Personal experience of being bombed at Hiroshima.

Koop, Robert. "Transfiguration." *Menn* 93 (Nov. 14, 1978), 671; *MennRep* 8 (Oct. 16, 1978), 8. Discusses the convergence of the church's celebration of Jesus' transfiguration, Aug. 6, with that day in 1945 when Hiroshima was transformed into a city of death by the atomic bomb.

Krahn, Cornelius. "Can These Bones Live." *MennLife* (July 1, 1946), 3-4. An appeal to American Mennonites to rescue the dry bones of the "Menno Valley," the destitute of Europe particularly.

Krahn, Cornelius. "Mennonites in Russia and Their Exodus." *GH* 72 (Nov. 20, 1979), 897-900. The writer examines what has happened to Mennonites who remained in Russia following World War II and develops an understanding for the difficulties and adjustments they experience as Umsiedler in Germany.

Krahn, Cornelius. "Mennonites the World Over." *MennLife* 1 (Jan., 1946), 29-30. Describes the fate of European and Russian Mennonites in World War II.

Kreider, Carl. "Federal Reserve vs. Treasury." *MennComm* 5 (May, 1951), 30, 32. Comment on the Federal Reserve-Treasury debate over policies for financing World War II.

Kreider, Carl. "Foreign Aid." *ChrLiv* 5 (July, 1958), 18, 36-37. American foreign aid since World War II has tended toward military instead of economic aid.

Kreider, Carl. "Trade with Communist Countries?" *MennComm* 5 (Nov., 1951), 30, 32. Reviews trade policies during World War II and encourages peaceloving Christians to promote open trade with communist countries.

Kreider, Robert S. "Discerning the Times." *Kingdom, Cross, and Community.* Ed. John R. Burkholder and Calvin Redekop. Scottdale: Herald Press, 1976, 65-85. A discussion of the cultural and political times of Guy Hershberger's life, including the effects of World War I and World War II on Mennonite ethos and institutions.

Lang, Ehrhardt. "The Bomb." *YCC* 47 (Aug. 7, 1966), 2. Description of some of the events surrounding the bombing of Hiroshima.

Lapp, John A. (Review). *The Respectable Murderers: Social Evil and Christian Conscience,* by Paul Hanly Furfey. Herder and Herder, 1966. Pp. 192. *ChrLiv* 15 (Jan., 1968), 33-34. Recommends this discussion of four conspicuous social injustices: American slavery, German genocide of Jews, the mass bombing of noncombatants during World War II, and treatment of the poor.

Lapp, John E. *Studies in Nonresistance: An Outline for Study and Reference.* Akron, Pa.: Peace Problems Committee, 1948. Pp. 35. MHL. Outlines a study course for MYF in 12 lessons. Topics include the Mennonite experience in America during World War II.

Lind, Marcus. "What Made Joe Stalin Tick?" *ST* 34 (2nd Qtr., 1966), 28. Examines the home influence, schooling, social status, culture, and general environment that made Joe Stalin an inhumane brute once he came to a position of supreme power.

Loewen, Anna Falk. "Who Will Survive?" *MBH* 18 (Nov. 23, 1979), 2-5. Diary of the German-speaking settlers' flight from the Ukraine during World War II.

Loewen, Harry (Review.) *With Courage to Spare: The Life of B. B. Janz (1877-1964),* by John B. Toews. Winnipeg: The Board of Christian Literature of the General Conference of the Mennonite Brethren Churches of North America, 1978. *MQR* 53 (Oct., 1979), 327-28. The story of B. B. Janz, who assisted Russian Mennonites in settling in North America, built up congregations in Canada, and fought to preserve the Mennonite principles of peace and nonresistance during World War II.

Lord, Charles R. "The Response of the Historic Peace Churches to the Internment of the Japanese Americans During World War II." MA in Peace Studies thesis, AMBS, 1981. Pp. 115. Describes and assesses Quaker, Church of the Brethren, and Mennonite responses to the evacuation, relocation, and resettlement of Japanese Americans during World War II. The conclusion drawn from news stories, denominational minutes, as well as personal interviews and letters is that while Mennonites failed to raise a voice of protest in defense of the

Japanese Americans who were being treated unjustly, the Friends and the Church of the Brethren responded with greater concern and advocacy.

"Mennonites Lead in Alternate Service." *Fellowship* 30 (Nov., 1964), 12. According to a survey completed by the National Service Board of Religious Objectors, Mennonites had the largest total of men in draft age in alternative service of all major US denominations since 1951.

Meyer, Albert J. "Imprisoned for His Faith: A Report on Recent Experiences of André van der Mensbrugghe." Mar. 25, 1955. Pp. 12. MSHL. Account of trial and sentencing of a young Belgian Mennonite. Extensive bibliography chronicles media coverage.

Mezynski, Kasimierz. "The Road of the Mennonites to Reconciliation with Poland." 1974. Pp. 9. MLA/BeC.

Morris, Edita. "Hiroshima Man." *ChrLiv* 12 (Oct., 1965), 6-7. Reprinted from *Liberation* magazine. The tragic economic and medical situation of the Hiroshima survivors.

Moyal, Maurice. "Father to the Orphans of Europe." *ChrLiv* 6 (Sept., 1959), 20-22. Doctor establishes home for war orphans in Austria after World War II.

Mueller, Peter (Review). *Another Part of the War: The Camp Simon Story,* by Gordon C. Zahn. Amherst: U. of Mass. Press, 1979. Pp. 240. *MBH* 19 (Apr. 25, 1980), 28-29. Recommends this sociological study of Catholic conscientious objectors in a US forestry camp during World War II.

Mueller, Peter (Review). *That There Be Peace,* by Lawrence Klippenstein. Winnipeg: The Manitoba C.O. Reunion Committee, 1979. Pp. 104. *MBH* 19 (Apr. 25, 1980), 28. Reviewer observes that this collection of memorabilia from Canadian conscientious objectors in alternative service during World War II reveals both courage and cowardice.

Nation, Mark. "The Politics of Compassion: A Study of Christian Nonviolent Resistance in the Third Reich." MA in Peace Studies thesis, AMBS, 1981. Pp. 115. Summarizes the variety of nonviolent resistance offered by German Christians to both the ideology of the Nazi regime and to Nazi practices such as the persecution of the Jews, euthanasia, and war in order to dispel the notions that violence is inherent in the word "resistance" and that pacifists can be nothing but "passivists" in the face of tyranny.

*

Nelson, Boyd N. (Review). *The Irreversible Decision,* by Robert C. Batchelder. Macmillan, 1965.

*ChrLiv* 13 (June, 1966), 34. Recommends this doctoral dissertation tracing the development of the atomic bomb and American military strategy in World War II.

Northcott, Cecil. "Berlin's Dibelius—Watchman of East and West." *ChrLiv* 6 (June, 1959), 32-33, 34. Reprinted from *Presbyterian Life*, Philadelphia, Pa. The witness of Otto Dibelius through war and totalitarian regimes.

Oniga, Akiko. "The Sea of Flames." *YCC* 49 (May 12, 1968), 12. A personal tragedy is shared by an eyewitness of the bombing of Hiroshima.

Oral History Projects (Alternative Service, World War II) (Archival). Twenty-three oral interviews, cassette tape, not transcribed.

Oswald, Walter E. (Review). *The Mennonite Church in the Second World War*, by Guy F. Hershberger. Mennonite Publishing House, 1951. Pp. 308. *MHB* 14 (Jan., 1953), 7. Enthusiastic recommendation for Hershberger's careful research and clarity of style in documenting Mennonite activities and vision during World War II.

Paetkau, Peter (Review). *Wer nimmt uns auf?*, by Olga Rempel. "Seven Scenes from Mennonite History." *MennMirror* 5, (Apr., 1976), 16. Review of a Mennonite Theatre production. Describes the scenes from this documentary which traces the story of the Mennonites of certain areas of the Ukraine, in 1937, through World War II, and to their destination in Canada. Concludes that the documentary is an excellent and useful one.

Patton, Avery. "The American Mennonites and Their Reaction to World War II." Research paper for American History class. 1982. Pp. 6. BfC.

Pauls, Helen Rose. "We Were Boat People Too." Story told to H. R. Pauls. *MBH* 19 (June 27, 1980), 40. Russian Mennonite refugees from World War II relate the story of their escape.

Penner, Helen. "Have a Heart in a World of Need." *ChrMon* 34 (Nov., 1942), 338-39. Describes MCC relief work in France and the motivating belief in nonviolence and aggressive good will.

Penner, Lydia. "Never Made to Kill Each Other, Says Bishop." *MBH* 15 (Oct. 29, 1976), 15. Ontario bishop who was a CO in World War I negotiated with Canadian government in setting up alternative service during World War II.

Penner, Peter (Review). *That There Be Peace: Mennonites in Canada and World War II*, ed. Lawrence Klippenstein. Winnipeg, Man.: The Manitoba CO Reunion Committee, 1979. Pp. 104. *MQR* 55 (July, 1981), 271. Recalls the Christian witness of young Manitobans whose unpopular stance benefited themselves and their fellow Canadians.

Penner, William. *My Experiences in Camp Life*. Ste. Anne, Manitoba: By the Author, RR 1, Box 91, n.d. Pp. 15. MHL. Reflects upon the CO experience in a CPS camp on Vancouver Island where the men worked on various forestry projects including fire fighting.

Peters, Victor. "Era of Political Ferment Marks Pre-War Years." *MennMirror* 6 (June, 1977), 9, 10. Describes the emergence of the Canadian Nationalist party and the growing strength of the communist party in southern Manitoba just prior to World War II.

Purvis, Ralph B. "Shall the Terrible War Which Is Threatening Be the End of the World?" *GH* 32 (Apr. 20, 1939), 70. A biblical study of the problem, with the conclusion that the war will not likely bring the end of the world.

(Review) *That There Be Peace*, ed. Lawrence Klippenstein. Manitoba CO Reunion Committee, 1979. *MCC PS Newsletter* 10 (June-July, 1980), 9. The book reports on the alternative service activities of Canadian Mennonite conscientious objectors during World War II.

(Review). *The Mennonite Church in the Second World War*, by Guy F. Hershberger. Scottdale: Mennonite Publishing House, 1951. Pp. 308. *Fellowship* 18 (Nov., 1952), 28. This book is "not only an account of the direct relation of the church to the war, but includes as well chapters on missions, education, relief, voluntary service, and intergroup relations both within and without the Mennonite family."

Reddig, Kenneth W. "A Crisis of Conscience: Manitoba Mennonites and Their Response to World War II." Term paper, Mar. 4, 1985. Box 13-D-10. CMBS/Win.

Regier, Austin. "The General Conference and World War II." Student paper for Mennonite History, Life and Principles, May 24, 1948. Pp. 19. MLA/BeC.

Regier, C. C. "A Christian Witness in War and Peace." *MennLife* 4 (Jan., 1949), 17-20. Describes the work of the historic peace churches in setting up the CPS program with Selective Service. Includes history and statistics of the Civilian Public Service program during World War II and post-war relief work.

Regier, Hilda. "A Study of Some of the Publications Produced within CPS Camps During World War II." Student paper for Our

Christian Heritage, May 14, 1954. Pp. 18. MLA/
BeC.

Reimer, Al. "The War Brings Its Own Conflict to
Steinback." Part 1. *MennMirror* 3 (June, 1974),
15, 16. The writer reflects on his emergence
into the difficult years of adolescence, which
coincided with the onset of the grim years of
World War II.

Reimer, Al. "The War Imposes Its Brand of
Change." Part 2. *MennMirror* 3 (Summer, 1974),
11, 12. Describes the impact and influence of
the World War II years on the small, inward-
looking Mennonite community of Steinbach.

Reimer, Al (Film Review). "*Hiding Place* Is Good
Religious Cinema." *MennMirror* 6 (Dec., 1976),
16. This film dramatizes the life of Corrie ten
Boom, who aided Jewish refugees in Holland
during the Nazi occupation and was
imprisoned in a concentration camp. It is
especially good because it depicts faith and
spiritual devotion; it teaches also about the
nature of both evil and faith.

Reimer, Al (Review). *The Wanderers: The Saga of
Three Women Who Survived,* by Ingrid Rimland.
St. Louis: Concordia Publishing House, 1977.
Pp. 323. "Novel Proves Mennonite Russian
Experience." *MennMirror* 7 (Feb., 1978), 14, 15.
Describes and critiques this fictional novel
which portrays the lives of three Mennonite
women who manage, under incredible
hardships, to survive the Russian Revolution,
the Stalin era, World War II, and who finally
emigrate to Paraguay. Concludes that it is a
very worthwhile novel in spite of some
technical flaws which he details.

*Remembering: Stories of Peacemakers.* See Topic 17c,
World War I.

Rempel, John G. "The War and the Mennonites in
Canada." *Menn* 60 (June 19, 1945), 6-7.
Mennonites have not achieved consensus: some
received farm deferments, others entered the
Medical Corp, and many enlisted for active
combat in war.

Rempel, Peter H. "Attitudes to Jews and Nazi
Germany in the *Christian Science Monitor,* 1922-
1953." Term paper for Canadian minorities
course, Dec., 1974. Pp. 24. CGCL.

Richardson, Lonnie L. "A Limited Survey of the
*Gospel Herald* on the Teaching of Nonresistance
from 1939 to 1945." Term paper for Mennonite
History course, Nov., 1969. Pp. 13. MSHL.

Rohrer, James. "Why America Fought." Paper
presented to the Social Science Seminar,
Goshen College, Goshen, Ind., 1949. Pp. 31.
MHL.

Roth, Willard E., ed. *Is There a Middle Road?*
Scottdale: Herald Press, 1964. Pp. 15.
Peacemaker Pamphlet No. 5. Bob Baker
describes his experience in noncombatant
service during World War II to show that such
service is not an acceptable alternative to either
military duty or a rejection of military duty if
one wants to follow Christ's way of love.

Rubin, George. "The Making of a Pacifist." *With* 13
(May, 1980), 4-6. Allied bomber pilot in World
War II describes his experience of the horror of
war which led to his commitment to pacifism.

Santiago, Lydia Esther. "Peace and War: A
Personal Experience with Nonresistance." *GH*
43 (Nov. 21, 1950), 1147. Santiago explains how
she encountered nonresistance and
conscientious objectors in World War II in
Puerto Rico.

Schlich, Victor A. "A Service of Everyday
Incidents." *ChrLiv* 18 (May, 1971), 10-12. Sketch
of Heinrich Treblin, peace advocate in Hesse,
West Germany, who served in the
underground resistance movement during
Hitler's rule.

Schloneger, Florence. *Sara's Trek.* Newton: Faith
and Life Press, 1981. Pp. 105. Sara Friesen and
Liese Rempel become separated from their
families during the flight from Russia during
World War II. In the year of separation spent
in a German children's home and, upon being
reunited with their families to live as refugees,
the girls must not only cope with the logistics of
survival amid the ravages of war but struggle to
discover the meaning of these experiences for
their lives and their faith. Fiction for ages 10-14.

Schmidt, Daryl Dean. "'War Is Sin?' Mennonite
Preaching on War, 1940-1945." Social Science
Seminar paper, May, 1966. Pp. 22. MLA/BeC.

Schmidt, Linda. "Somewhat Cool but Sometimes
Boiling: World War II's Effect on Bethel-
Newton Relations." Paper presented to History
of Civilization class, Bethel College, North
Newton, Ks., 1974. Pp. 12. MHL.

Scholl, Otto. Letter to the Editor. *ChrLead* 41 (June
6, 1978), 10. Recounts personal experiences in
World War II. Concludes that God does not
want a Christian to help and to take part in
war.

Sera, Megumi. "Child of the A-Bomb." *ChrLiv* 10
(July, 1963), 28-29. Reprinted from *Children of the
A-Bomb,* compiled by Arata Osada. G. P.
Putnam's Sons, 1959. A woman from
Hiroshima who was a sixth grader when the
bomb was dropped describes that day.

Shellenberger, Eunice. *Wings of Decision.* Scottdale:
Herald Press, 1951. Pp. 240. Fictional account of

a young man facing the draft in World War II, his decision to seek conscientious objector status, and his experiences in Civilian Public Service.

Shetler, Sanford G. "'Americans Are Stupid Diplomats.'" *GfT* 6 (Mar.-Apr., 1971), 18. American concessions to communist countries since World War II show that Christians cannot place their hopes for peace in diplomacy or "peace schemes."

Shetler, Sanford G. "Rethinking Civilian Public Service." *ChrMon* 34 (Dec., 1942), 366; *Menn* 58 (Mar. 2, 1943), 9-10. The US entry into World War II caused CPS men to rethink their reasons for participating in the program.

Smith, C. Henry. *Smith's Story of the Mennonites.* See Topic 17c, World War I.

Sommer, John P. "Prejudice, Mistreatment, and the Mennonites: The Japanese-Americans During World War II." Paper presented to Church and Race class, AMBS, Elkhart, Ind., May 20, 1974. Pp. 17. AMBS.

Sprunger, Keith L. "The Most Monumental Mennonite." *MennLife* 34 (Sept., 1979), 10-15. The story of the construction of the Mennonite monument in Newton, Kans., including the difficulties encountered due to the nonresistant stance of Mennonites during World War II.

Sprunger, Mark. "The Mennonites in World War II." Student paper, n.d. Pp. 18. MLA/BeC.

Stoltzfus, Glen. "The Origins of Civilian Public Service: A Review of the Negotiations During the Period 1936-1940 Between Government Officials and Representatives of the Historic Peace Churches." Paper for History Seminar, Goshen College, Goshen, Ind., 1956. Pp. 35. MHL.

Stoltzfus, Ruth Ann (Review). *Poor Elephants,* by Yukio Tsuchiya. Tokyo: Kin-no-Hoshi-Sha Company, 1979. *Sojourners* 9 (June, 1980), 33. Observes that the book illustrates for children the horrors of war by describing the killing of Tokyo zoo animals during World War II to prevent them from straying in case of bombing.

Stoltzfus, Victor. "A History of the Peace Section of the Mennonite Central Committee." Paper presented to Mennonite History and Church History classes, Goshen College Biblical Seminary, Goshen, Ind., 1959. Pp. 57. MHL.

Tanimoto, Kiyoshi. "The Youth of Hiroshima." *YCC* 37 (Feb. 5, 1956), 45, 48. Acts of reconciliation and rebuilding in both Japan and America after the bombing of Hiroshima and Nagasaki.

Thierstein, J. R. "If War, Will the US Be In It?" *Menn* 54 (May 2, 1939), 2. The US will likely be drawn into the war, particularly because of the propaganda for war in our nation.

Thiessen, Mary. "Nonresistance in Canada During World War I and II." Student paper for Mennonite History, Nov., 1960. Pp. 17. MLA/BeC.

Toews, John A. *Alternative Service in Canada During World War II.* Winnipeg: Publishing Committee of the Canadian Conference of the MB Church, 1959. Pp. 127. A study of the legal status and actual experiences of all conscientious objectors, including Mennonites, in Canada.

Toews, John A. "American Religious Pacifism Prior to World War II." *The Voice* 16 (Mar.-Apr., 1967), 3. A study of the views of representative liberal theologians in the United States during the inter-war period.

Toews, Susanna. *Trek to Freedom: The Escape of Two Sisters from South Russia During World War II.* Winkler, Man.: Heritage Valley Publication, 1976. Pp. 43. MHL. Part 1 offers a vivid description of life as experienced by the Mennonites in Russia before and during World War II. Part 2 describes the flight from Russia as refugees caught in the confusion of the advances and retreats of both the Russian and German armies. A unifying theme is the maintenance of faith in the turbulance of war.

Unsigned. "Mennonite Youth Abroad." *CPS Bull Supp* 5 (May 16, 1946), 3, 8. Story of Russian Mennonite defector into Germany who, pressed into service with the German army, was captured and sent to American POW camp.

Unsigned. "Tales of French Relief Told by Brother J. N. Byler." *CPS Bull* 1 (Dec. 7, 1942), 3-4. Describes living conditions in France during the war and includes letters of thanks from children who received help through Mennonite relief work.

van der Laag, Tina. "'By My Spirit.'" *ChrMon* 42 (Aug., 1950), 247. Goshen College student from Holland recounts memories of World War II and comments on the possiblity of nuclear war.

van der Zijpp, Nanne. "Experiences of the Dutch Mennonites During the Last World War." *MennLife* 1 (July, 1946), 24-27. Gives insight into the involvement of the Dutch Mennonite Church in the areas of Jewish persecution, nonresistance, and mutual aid.

Veenstra, Yt. "Peace As I See It." *IPF Notes* 1 (June, 1955), 3-4. Tabor College student from Holland reflects on scenes from World War II and the meaning of peace.

Vogt, Esther L. Anonymous, as told to Esther L. Vogt, "To Face Another Dawn." *ChrLiv* 12 (Oct., 1965), 16-17. Young Russian Mennonite woman during World War II regards the advancing Nazi army as liberators.

Vogt, Ruth (Review). *Lest Innocent Blood Be Shed,* by Philip Haillie. New York: Harper & Row, 1979. "Leader With Conviction Is Light in Evil World. *MennMirror* 9 (Dec., 1979), 15. Reports on the main content of this book, which tells the story of André Trocmé, a remarkable spiritual leader who started the work of harboring Jewish refugees during World War II in the French village of Le Chambon. Recommends the book, particularly for those who believe pacifism to be an essential part of the Christian gospel.

"War in Experience." *CanMenn* 7 (July 17, 1959), 12. Report includes excerpts from eye-witness accounts of Hans and Antoinette Neufeld of Prussia.

"War or Peace, What Shall It Be?" *GH* 32 (May 18, 1939), 146. Reprinted from *The Lutheran Witness* (May 2, 1939). As the possibility of another world war grows, the author urges persons not to forget the horrors of the last war. Perhaps they can teach us to denounce war and pray for peace.

Weaver, Edwin L. "The Destructiveness of War." *YCC* 25 (Jan. 23, 1944), 27, 32. A survey of the destructiveness of World War II.

Weaver, Edwin L. (Review). *How Stands Our Press?* by Oswald Garrison Villard. Hinsdale, Ill.: Henry Regrery Company, n.d. Pamphlet. *MennComm* 2 (June, 1948), 15. Reviewer observes that the author criticizes the silence and misinformation of the American press during World War II.

Werkema, G. Frank. "Dutch Resistance (1940-1945)." Term paper for Nonviolence Seminar, 1975. Pp. 14. CGCL.

Wherry, Neal M. *Conscientious Objection.* Washington, D.C.: Government Printing Office, 1950. Vol. I, pp. 364. Vol. II, pp. 288. MHL. Chronicles World War II conscientious objection from the government's point of view. Mennonite documents and summaries of Mennonite practices and teachings are found in chapters entitled: "Church Backgrounds of CO's," "Conscientious Objection in American History," "Legislative Provisions on Conscientious Objection." Other chapters offer extensive information about the CPS program—history, assignments, administration, discipline, statistics, etc.

Wiebe, Katie Funk. "Caught in the Draft." *GH* 72 (Aug. 21, 1979), 667; *ChrLead* 42 (June 19, 1979),

19. Witn impending conscription, we are urged to be more prepared than we were for the World War II crisis. Peacemaker registration through MCC Peace Section is one suggestion for getting ready.

Wiens, Marie K. "A City in Search of Peace." *ChrLead* 40 (Sept. 13, 1977), 8. Introduction to Mennonite Brethren mission work in Hiroshima.

Wiens, Marie K. "Hiroshima: In Search of Peace." *MBH* 16 (Sept. 16, 1977), 7. Hiroshima, a city speaking to peace through shrines and organizations, needs the true peace found through Christ, say two missionaries.

World War II. 134 interviews, some transcribed. Emphasis on Mennonite CO's who did CPS work. ALso includes some civilians (women, pastors) and regulars.MLA/BeC.

Yoder, Edward. "After Twenty-five Years: Peace Principles from a Scriptural Viewpoint." Part 31. *GH* 32 (Oct. 19, 1939), 639-40. The greed of the past war is leading us into another. The Christian must remain neutral and prepare to help those who suffer.

Yoder, Edward and Smucker, Donovan. *The Christian and Conscription: An Inquiry Designed as a Preface to Action.* Akron: MCC, 1945. Pp. 124. An evaluation of the alternative service experience in World War II and a guide to witness against conscription.

Yoder, Orrie D. "The Awful Gravity of These Perilous Times." *GH* 42 (July 5, 1949), 634. Are the nonresistant Christians doing all they should in helping the world, spiritually and physically, to make amends for the sins of the last war?

Yutzy, Homer E. "Conscription as Experienced by Mennonites in the US During World War II." Paper prepared for Anabaptist-Mennonite History class, [AMBS, Elkhart, Ind.], Dec. 20, 1976. Pp. 9. MHL.

Zook, Mervin D. "Measurement of Attitudes Toward Religious Conscientious Objectors in Selected Magazines of World War II Years by Evaluative Assertion." MA in Journalism thesis, Indiana University, May, 1969. Pp. 114. BfC., MHL. Concludes that religious magazines treated COs slightly more favorably than nonreligious ones; letters to the editor tended to disagree with favorable view of COs presented in secular magazines but in the religious magazines, which also presented a favorable view of COs, the letters to the editor tended to be supportive; generally the COs choosing noncombatant service were rated higher than those choosing alternative service.

# E. Southeast Asia*

"A Letter of Concern." *ChrLead* 28 (July 6, 1965), 5. Letter from Reba Place Fellowship connects recent natural disasters in Mississippi and Indiana to US national sin in Vietnam and the Dominican Republic. Calls for national repentance.

"An Urgent Message to Our Churches from the 1967 Council of Boards." *Menn* 82 (Dec. 12, 1967), 753-54. A statement by the GCMC Council of Boards to their constituency, urging more vigorous witness against the war in Vietnam. Part of this witness would be war tax resistance.

Abrams, Ray H. *Preachers Present Arms.* See Topic 17d, World War II.

Arndt, Bill. Letter to the Editor. *ChrLead* 36 (Jan. 23, 1973), 17. Encouragement for Mennonites to express outrage at the violence in Southeast Asia, especially if the church is going to take stands on issues like abortion.

Augsburger, David W. *Peacemonger or Peacemaker.* Harrisonburg, VA: The Mennonite Hour, 1966. Pp. 24. MHL. Booklet in two parts: radio talks on peacemaking; and short statements on Vietnam War by persons representing a variety of disciplines.

Barrett, Lois [Janzen]. "After Getting Out of Vietnam." *Menn* 89 (Jan. 15, 1974), 48. Prints a letter from an MCC worker in Vietnam detailing the plight of a civilian prisoner tortured by South Vietnamese police trained in America.

Barrett, Lois [Janzen]. "Delegation Sees Continuation of Vietnam War." *Menn* 90 (Mar. 25, 1975), 190-91; also "Torture and Harrassment Keeps Thieu in Power," *MennRep* 5 (Mar. 31, 1975), 2. Gene Stoltzfus, former service worker in Vietnam, reports on the continued war and repression of South Vietnamese people, as he witnessed it during a recent visit.

Bartel, Lawrence. Letter to the Editor. *Menn* 88 (April 3, 1973), 231. Defends Richard Nixon and Billy Graham against attacks from "partisan political criticisms" by stating that Nixon is keeping his pledge to seek an honorable peace in Vietnam, and that previously hostile nations are now friendly to the US.

Bauer, Evelyn (Review). *The Bitter Fruit of Kom-Pawi,* by Taiwon Koh. John C. Winston Co., 1959. Pp. 148. *ChrLiv* 7 (Sept., 1960), 33. Recommends the book as a narrative of a Korean woman's personal experience with Japanese occupation and the war years.

Beachy, Alvin J. "Called to be Faithful." *MennLife* 23 (Apr., 1968), 51-53. A sermon crying out against the brutality of the Vietnam war with a plea to continue loving and pressing for an end to the war.

Beachy, Alvin J. "Lost in Vietnam—America's Soul." *Menn* 84 (Nov. 11, 1969), 674-75. America is losing its soul in the degradation that results from raping and destroying Vietnamese society.

Beck, Carl. "Korea Church Leaders Ponder Peace." *CanMenn* 14 (Feb. 22, 1966), 1, 2. Report on first Korean Reconciliation Seminar held in Taegu, South Korea, in Oct., 1965, involving 34 pastors, seminary and university professors, elders, and lay leaders. The seminar discussed the history of Korean-Japanese hatred, industrial relations, and reconciliation as the object of Christian faith.

Beck, Carl, *et al.* "The Credibility of Our Witness." *Menn* 83 (Jan. 2, 1968), 16. American involvement in the war in Indochina is a moral crisis that makes our Christian witness incredible unless we engage in prophetic protest.

Beechy, Atlee. "Courteous Reception by NLF, DRVN Representatives." *CanMenn* 16 (Oct. 8, 1968), 1, 2; (Oct. 15, 1968), 4. After a visit to North Vietnam, Beechy outlines his preparations for the contact with communist leaders, describes his contacts with North Vietnam government officials in various countries of Asia, Africa, and Europe, and cites his impressions of the mission sponsored by MCC. Part 1 deals with the translated Mennonite documents given to all the representatives and the courteous reception given to Beechy.

Beechy, Atlee. "God's People—The Compassionate Community." *CanMenn* 14 (Aug. 16, 1966), 5; *GH* 59 (Oct. 18, 1966), 932-33. Excerpts from a sermon delivered in the Episcopal Church in Saigon on July 24, 1966. Calls upon the church, as the "compassionate community" to bind the wounds in Vietnam.

Beechy, Atlee. "God's People Belong in Vietnam." *YCC* 48 (Mar. 5, 1967), 4. If the church belongs where human need is, it belongs in Vietnam. God's people must seek to eliminate those things which cause prejudice, hate, fear, and violence.

---

*Includes Vietnam, Sino-Japanese, Korean, and Cambodian wars

Beechy, Atlee. "Impressions on Vietnam." *CanMenn* 16, Part 2, (Oct. 15, 1968), 4, 5. Continuation of a report following Beechy's month-long trip to talk with NLF and DRVN representatives includes the following points: 1) DRVN and NLF are separate entities; 2) we cannot comprehend the suffering in Vietnam caused by the war; 3) DRVN and NLF see themselves in a relatively strong political and military position in Vietnam and want their goals and programs understood; 4) DRVN insists US must stop all bombing in the north as a condition for discussing other subjects; 5) NLF sees itself as the legitimate government in the south; 6) DRVN and NLF see the Saigon government as a puppet government; 7) DRVN and NLF representatives believe that world opinion is against the US; 8) DRVN and NLF interpret the war as an American militarists' war; 9) when peace comes, individuals, groups, and governments will be welcome to help rebuild but without strings; 10) NLF sees "Alliance of National, Democratic, and Peace Forces" as hopeful nationalistic movement; 11) possibility of Mennonite personnel visiting DRVN and NLF areas is marginal at this time; 12) DRVN and NLF are aware of Mennonite work in the south; 13) due to the military situation, continued interpretation of MCC purposes and program to DRVN and NLF representatives as well as to the US and Saigon governments is important; 14) DRVN and NLF representatives are able, articulate, dedicated to their cause. While they are not all communists, they are all nationalists.

Beechy, Atlee. "In Hanoi: The Wounds of War." *GH* 67 (Mar. 26, 1974), 262-63; "Journey to Hanoi: How Do We Heal the Wounds of War?" *MennRep* 4 (Mar. 4, 1974), 7; "Hanoi—Wounds of War," *MBH* 13 (Mar. 8, 1974), 18-19. MCC representative visiting Hanoi to assess the effects of the war reports on the destruction and continued suffering of the Vietnamese people, as well as their friendliness and determination to rebuild the country.

Beechy, Atlee. "Learning: The Lessons of Vietnam." *The Future of the Missionary Enterprise.* International Documentation and Communication Center (Nov. 18, 1976), 54-56. Reflects upon the history and ponders the future of voluntary agencies in Indochina.

Beechy, Atlee. "MCC Contacts Affirm Peace Witness." *ChrLiv* 16 (Jan., 1969), 11, 34-35. MCC assistant secretary reports on his talks with the National Liberation Front of South Vietnam and the Democratic Republic of [North] Vietnam.

Beechy, Atlee. "My Response to Vietnam." *GH* 60 (Aug. 15, 1967), 736-37. As a Christian who believes in nonresistance, Beechy takes a stand against the war in Vietnam and calls for concrete action to bring it to an end.

Beechy, Atlee. "Our Relief in a Country at War (Vietnam)." *The Witness of the Holy Spirit.* Ed. Cornelius J. Dyck. Elkhart: MWC, 1967, 199-207. A discussion of Vietnam Christian Service and the place of the Mennonite Church in a country at war.

Beechy, Atlee. "Our Vietnam Witness." *GH* 60 (Feb. 21, 1967), 144-46. Discusses various positions Mennonites are supporting on Vietnam and advocates effort to relieve suffering there as well as to end the conflict.

Beechy, Atlee. "Peacemaking in Vietnam." *Peacemakers in a Broken World.* Ed. John A. Lapp. Scottdale: Herald Press, 1969, 54-63. Discusses the role of Vietnam Christian Service in working for peace in Vietnam and the importance of Mennonites taking their peace witness into the heart of militarism and conflict in order to witness to God's love.

Beechy, Atlee. "Report from Vietnam." *Saturday Review* 49 (Dec. 3, 1966), 26, 81. Discusses discrepancy between stated objectives of US policy and the devastating effects strategies for achieving those objectives are having on the Vietnamese people, culture, economy, etc.

Beechy, Atlee. "The Needs in Vietnam and How We Meet Them." *CanMenn* 14 (Sept. 20, 1966), 7. A summary of the needs in Vietnam which are being met by Vietnam Christian Service.

Beechy, Atlee. "The Unfinished Peace Task in Indochina." *Menn* 89 (May 28, 1974), 360. m In spite of the ceasefire, the US continues to be involved in the Vietnamese conflict in the form of military advisers, equipment, and money. Beechy gives seven suggestions for speaking out against continued US support of the war effort.

Beechy, Atlee. "To Aid or Not to Aid? Some Reflections on Voluntary Agencies and Vietnam." Paper presented at Pendle Hill, Pa., Aug. 14, 1975. Pp. 18. MHL.

Beechy, Atlee. "What Will Happen to the Church When the Troops Leave?" *Christian Herald* 92 (Nov., 1969), 16-18, 23-25. Examines consequences of church and state identification for the missionary-supported church in Vietnam as the US military withdraws.

Beechy, Atlee (Review). *Anatomy of Error,* by Henry Brandon. Gambit, 1969. Pp. 178. *GH* 63 (Dec. 29, 1970), 1075. Highly recommends the book for its penetrating analysis of the forces and ideas behind American decision making about policy in Vietnam.

Beechy, Atlee (Review). *Reaching the Other Side,* by

Earl S. Martin. Crown Publishing Co., 1978. *Sojourners* 8 (Jan., 1979), 33. Personalized report of the events that took place during the transition period, March to May, 1975, when Thieu's government was replaced by the new revolutionary government in Vietnam.

Beechy, Atlee (Review). *The New Legions*, by Donald Duncan. Random House, 1967. Pp. 275. *ChrLiv* 15 (July, 1968), 36. Recommends this account by a highly decorated Vietnam veteran, tracing his uneasiness with US policy there.

Beechy, Atlee (Review). *The Vietnam War: Christian Perspectives*, ed. by Michael P. Hamilton. Grand Rapids: Eerdmans, 1967. *ChrLiv* 15 (July, 1968), 35-36. Reviewer observes that this collection of sermons by prominent Christian leaders reflects a wide range of positions on the Vietnam War.

Beechy, Atlee and Beechy, Winifred. *Vietnam: Who Cares?* Scottdale: Herald Press, 1968. Pp. 160. A first hand report on the war in Vietnam, including particularly its effects on the people of Vietnam, and the activities of Vietnam Christian Service.

Beidler, Luke. "Vietnam Missionaries State Position on War." *GH* 60 (Dec. 19, 1967), 1136. A statement prepared by missionaries in Vietnam and addressed to their Vietnamese friends: "We are not here as representatives of any government or government agency . . . . We affirm that the church of Jesus Christ is universal and should not be identified with any particular people or political system."

Bender, Urie A. "Earl Martin: PAXman with an Impulse to Kick." *With* 2 (Apr., 1969), 28. Martin is a PAXman working with others on the Mennonite Central Committee team under Vietnam Christian Service.

Beyler, Betsy. "Indochina Is Still on the Map—and on the Agenda." *MCC PS Wash. Memo* 10 (May-June, 1978), 6-7. US bombing during the war and deplorable post-war conditions have created severe problems for Vietnam, Laos, and Kampuchea.

Bishop, Elaine L. "Quaker Youth Describes 200-Hour December Fast in Canadian Capital." *CanMenn* 15 (Jan. 17, 1967), 1, 2. Description of a fast in Ottawa from Dec. 23-31, 1966 by Young Friends appealing to Canadians to remember innocent war victims in Vietnam who suffer during the Christmas season.

Bohn, E. Stanley. "A Hard Look in the Vietnam Mirror." *Menn* 81 (Nov. 1, 1966), 658-61. Most Mennonite congregations have no way of coping with social issues, are not accustomed to the protagonist role, and are too afraid of conflict to engage in a clear peace witness.

Bohn, E. Stanley. "US Bombing of Hospitals Adds Fuel to Vietnam Fire." *CanMenn* 14 (May 3, 1966), 3, 11. Bohn's claim that the US is bombing hospitals in North Vietnam is based on a letter from Duane Friesen, a student at the University of Berlin, in which Friesen cites information from Dr. Herbert Landmann, an MD in East Berlin who served in North Vietnam for several years setting up a state health program.

Bohn, E. Stanley. "Withdrawal Date is Key to Vietnam Peace." *Menn* 86 (Apr. 6, 1971), 230-32. A report on the Paris conference of 170 Americans with representatives of the four sides of the Vietnam peace talks.

Bowman, Randall J. "From World War II Until Vietnam: Societal Influence on the Mennonites." Term paper for Mennonite History and Thought course, Feb. 17, 1978. Pp. 15. MSHL.

Burnett, [Kris]Tina Mast and Kroeker, Wally. "Affluent People Who Neglect the Poor Are Not the People of God." *Menn* 94 (Feb. 20, 1979), 128-29. MCC (International) annual meeting discussed issues of justice and human rights, aid to Vietnam, native American outreach, hunger concerns, and militarism.

Burnett, Kristina Mast and Rennei, Amy. "The 'Boat People'—Why They Are Leaving and How to Be a Sponsor." *Menn* 94 (Jan. 16, 1979), 40-41. MCC gives an explanation for why people are leaving Vietnam and how to sponsor the refugees for resettlement.

Byrne, Kevin. "Significantly Involved." *GH* 64 (Jan. 12, 1971), 32-33. MCC volunteer in Vietnam writes a letter to his parents describing the suffering and destruction in which the US is very significantly involved.

"CO Kidnapped by Vietnamese Communists." *RepConsS* 19 (July, 1962), 1, 3. Describes the kidnapping of Daniel Gerber, member of the Kidron Mennonite Church, along withg two other American church workers from a leprosarium near Banmethnot, Vietnam.

"Continued Ties with Vietnam Urged by Delegation." *MennRep* 9 (July 9, 1979), 3. Despite difficulties with the Vietnamese government, the Canadian delegation urged that MCC continue to relate in creative ways to the Vietnamese people.

Chastain, Thane E. "The Media and Vietnam Peace Protests: Actual or Acted? A Small Campus Case Study." Social Science Seminar paper, Apr., 1982. Pp. 39. Includes transcript of videotape and questionnaire used in research and bibliography. Videotape available at Bethel College. MLA/BeC.

Clemens, Steve. "A Post-Indochina Foreign Policy?" *MCC PS Wash. Memo* 7 (May-June, 1975), 1-2. Congressional action since the defeat in Vietnam shows the US will continue to base its foreign policy on military might rather than humanitarian concern.

"Daniel Gerber Never Returned from His MCC Assignment." *MennMirror* 8 (Nov., 1978), 24. Gerber, captured in May, 1962, while on an MCC assignment in Vietnam and never again heard from, is a reminder that to follow Christ demands a willingness to sacrifice oneself.

DeBoer, Hans A. "'I Must Disobey Laws Against Democracy and God'—Sibley. *CanMenn* 13, Part 1, (Apr. 13, 1965), 1, 11; Part 2, (Apr. 20, 1965), 11. A Quaker pacifist analyzes student protests, the US involvement in Vietnam, and the nature of the East-West cold war.

DeBoer, Hans A. (Editorial). "A Man Who Talked to the Viet Cong Suggests 15 Responses to Asian War." *CanMenn* 13 (Oct. 5, 1965), 6. Suggestions include taking a critical attitude toward information available through national news services, beginning serious Christian-Marxist dialogue, supporting demonstrations and peace protests against the Vietnam War, etc.

DeFehr, Arthur. "Is God for the Poor and Homeless?" *MBH* 19 (Oct. 10, 1980), 2-5. A volunteer who helped set up a relief project in Southeast Asia in the middle of three competing armies reflects on response to human need.

Derstine, C. F. "A Lull in the Sino-Japanese Storm." *ChrMon* 24 (Apr., 1932), 126. The treaty between Japan and China has averted the immediate threat of conflict on a larger scale.

Derstine, C. F. "Our Testimony of Peace Amid a War-torn World." *ChrMon* 24 (June, 1932), 187-88. The folly of war may be seen in the extent of losses suffered by Japan and China during their recent conflict.

Derstine, C. F. "The American Paradox of Building Colleges and Bombs to Blow Them Up." *ChrMon* 31 (Mar., 1939), 94. Comment on the devastation of the Sino-Japanese war and the fact that bombs used by Japan were made in the US.

Derstine, C. F. "The Investigation of the China-Japanese Feud." *ChrMon* 24 (Nov., 1932), 349. Report on the findings of the Lytton Commission and its recommendations for peaceful settlement.

Derstine, C. F. "The Sino-Japanese Affair." *ChrMon* 24 (Mar., 1932), 94. Japan seems to be the aggressor in the conflict with China.

Derstine, C. F. "'What War Has Done to Shanghai to Awaken the Sleeping Giant.' " *ChrMon* 30 (May, 1938), 158-60. Changes in China brought about by the war with Japan.

Derstine, C. F. "Will the 'Son of Heaven' Keep War's Hell from Flaming the World?" *ChrMon* 29 (Nov., 1937), 350-51. Japan's aggression toward China is based on Japanese belief in divine destiny.

Devadoss, M. B. "A Talk with Little Lien." *GH* 63 (Oct. 6, 1970), 837. MCC worker in Vietnam describes his short friendship with a seven-year-old girl orphaned by the war.

Dick, Henry H. "Peace Has Not Come to South Vietnam." *ChrLead* 36 (Apr. 17, 1973), 13. The lack of peace in Vietnam is most clearly seen in the refugee problem and the unexploded ordinance still buried in the farm land.

Diggers, The (a corporate student group). "The Vietnam War and Its Effect on a Small Town." Project for History and Civilization II, Spring, 1980. Pp. 104. MLA/BeC.

Drescher, John M. "Dare We Pay Taxes for War?" *GH* 60 (Oct. 10, 1967), 909. A call for guidance on the question of war taxes in light of the uses of war tax revenues in Vietnam.

Drescher, John M. "Graham's Vietnam Visit." *GH* 60 (Feb. 1, 1967), 117. Drescher praises Graham's evangelistic work but seriously questions his identification, as an evangelist, with American nationalism and imperialism in Vietnam.

Drescher, John M. (Editorial). "Atrocities on Trial." *GH* 63 (Jan. 13, 1970), 29. In light of the fact that the essence of war is violence and the denial of all that is sacred in life, questions the sense of trying soldiers for committing "atrocities."

Drescher, John M. (Editorial). "Bombing, Law and Order, and the Press." *GH* 66 (Jan. 16, 1973), 64. Expresses outrage at the Christmas bombing in Vietnam and the president's efforts to stifle news reporting of such atrocities.

Drescher, John M. (Editorial). "Draft Resisters at General Conference." *GH* 62 (Oct. 7, 1969), 865. Outlines the resolution adopted by the Mennonite General Conference in support of the draft resisters and comments on the difficulty Mennonites had in showing love toward the resisters who presented their position.

Driedger, Leo. "Acceptable and Non-Acceptable Forms of Witness: A Special Study Report on Nonviolence and Civil Disobedience." Leaflet printed by the Canadian Board of Christian

Service, Winnipeg, Manitoba, 1966. Pp. 2. Also in *CanMenn* 14 (May 31, 1966), 7-8. Discusses and evaluates the trends in nonviolent protest stimulated by the civil rights movement and the Vietnam war. Analysis includes consideration of Mennonite youth involvement in these trends.

Driedger, Leo. "Doctrinal Belief: A Major Factor in the Differential Perception of Social Issues." *Sociological Quarterly* 15 (Winter, 1974), 66-80. This survey of clergy (including Mennonite clergy) to determine the correlation between doctrine and positions on social issues includes questions concerning military readiness, bombing of Vietnam, rights of communists, and racial integration.

Dyck, Anne Konrad. "Refugee Sponsorship: Toronto Church Led the Way." *MennRep* 9 (Aug. 6, 1979), 16. The Toronto United Mennonite Church has assisted several refugee families and couples from Vietnam and provided assistance to other non-Mennonite groups wishing to do the same.

"Escalation of Compassion for Vietnam." *Menn* 80 (June 22, 1965), 420. Text of a letter sent to President Johnson by the Mennonite Central Committee. MCC urges the president to turn from the military solution to the way of compassion and peace.

Eby, John W. "January 27, 1973; Will Peace Last?" *GH* 66 (Mar. 20, 1973), 254. Eby's joy in the Vietnam peace agreement is tempered by realization of the moral costs of the war; such as expanded power of the military over national priorities, and neglect of the problem of poverty.

Eby, Omar. "Vietnam: Compassion Provokes Conflict." *CanMenn* 15 (Dec. 5, 1967), 1, 2. Reports that Vietnam service worker Doug Hostetter felt he could not form any close associations with American AID officials or the US Armed Forces in Vietnam. Instead, he identified closely with the Vietnamese people in order to communicate Christian love and to understand Vietnamese feelings.

Edgar, Max. "April 30, 1975." *RepConsS* 32 (July, 1975), 2. Poem reflecting the jubilation of an MCC worker in Vietnam at war's end.

Ediger, Max. *A Vietnamese Pilgrimage.* Newton, Ks.: Faith and Life Press, 1978. Pp. 79. Poems, essays, biographical comments, short stories written by an MCC worker in Vietnam for five years of the Vietnam war. Also included are the art work of a Vietnamese prisoner and poems written by Vietnamese people.

Ediger, Max. "Handles for Lending a Hand." *Menn* 88 (July 10, 1973), 440. Outlines tasks in which

MCC could participate in reconstructing Vietnam after the ceasefire, such as encouraging refugees to move back to their lands, helping to clear the land of unexploded ordnance, continuing with missions and medical programs.

Ediger, Max. Letter to the Editor. *MBH* 19 (Feb. 29, 1980), 8. Being peacemakers in Southeast Asia has meant, for the MCCers, trying to develop solutions deeper than the "bandaid" remedy of handouts.

Ediger, Max. "Mennonites Urge Congressmen to End Vietnam War." *MBH* 12 (Jan 26, 1973), 2. Describes how Mennonites and Brethren in Christ spontaneously gathered with other peace advocates in Washington, DC, Jan. 3-4, 1973, to petition congresspersons to terminate funds for military operations in Vietnam, unless a negotiated peace settlement is reached by the end of January.

Ediger, Max. "No Celebration in Saigon." *ChrLead* 36 (July 10, 1973), 14. Explores the needs of Vietnam to which the church must respond.

Ediger, Max. "Profile of a Vietnam Mennonite." *GH* 67 (Oct. 1, 1974), 739; also in *Menn* 89 (Oct. 1, 1974), 268. Describes a young male Vietnamese Mennonite employed by MCC, whose future is threatened by the continuation of the war.

Ediger, Max. "Two Funerals in Vietnam." *MBH* 12 (Jan. 26, 1973), 2-3. Two funerals on the same day in the same family are used to illustrate the evil and destruction of the Vietnam war and to explain how American Christians are part of this destruction.

Ediger, Max, comp. and Longacre, Doris, ed. *Release Us from Bondage: Six Days in a Vietnam Prison.* Akron, Pa.: MCC Peace Section, 1974. Pp. 28. MHL. Materials for group use in six sessions include information about conditions in Vietnam prisons, poetry and art work done by some of the prisoners, Bible readings, and suggestions for action.

Ediger, Peter J. "An Urgent Call for Prophets." *Menn* 82 (Aug. 15, 1967), 490-92. Calls for emergence of a prophetic Mennonite witness regarding the atrocities being perpetrated in Vietnam.

Enns, Mary M. "Meet Harold of the Herald." *MennMirror* 6 (May, 1977), 7-10. An interview with Harold Jantz, editor of the *Mennonite Brethren Herald,* in which he discusses and shares, among other things, his perceptions after a visit to Vietnam as part of an MCC delegation.

Epp, Frank H. "A Brief History of Vietnam." Jan. 17, 1968. Pp. 17. MHL.

Epp, Frank H. "A Land of Beauty and Plenty Ravaged by Generation of War." *CanMenn* 14 (May 10, 1966), 7. Report on Epp's Asian tour.

Epp, Frank H. "How and When the USA Got Involved in Vietnam." *CanMenn* 14 (July 5, 1966), 10. Outlines the US involvement which began during World War II, USA support of the French, the Ngo Dinh Diem regime, AID, etc.

Epp, Frank H. "No War in the World." *CanMenn* 2 (July 23, 1954), 2. An editorial statement underscoring the cease-fire in Indo-China and a call for prayer support for world leaders. Prayer is needed that these leaders not resort to the weapons of war.

Epp, Frank H. "Socialism in Southeast Asia Is Traditional and Practical Way." *CanMenn* 13 (Sept. 21, 1965), 6. Concludes on basis of interview with Peter Fast, who recently returned from a 3-year theological teaching assignment with MCC in Indonesia, that Indonesia has a tribal tradition of mutual aid which is in agreement with socialism.

Epp, Frank H. "The Hard and Heavy Cross of the Christian Church." *CanMenn* 14 (Oct. 4, 1966), 7. The dangers of giving a peace witness in the war-ravaged country of Vietnam.

Epp, Frank H. "The Methods and Goals of the War in Vietnam." *CanMenn* 14 (July 12, 1966), 8. Reports on the involvement of the USA, the South Vietnam government, the Vietcong, North Vietnam, and the people of Vietnam in the war.

Epp, Frank H. "The Moratorium and Its Message." *CanMenn* 17 (Oct. 24, 1969), 3. Both supporters and critics of the Oct. 15 Vietnam Moratorium in the USA are cautioned lest they evaluate it too positively or, likewise, too negatively.

Epp, Frank H. "War and Economy." *CanMenn* 15 (Jan. 31, 1967), 4. Describes Canada's contribution to the conflagration in Vietnam and the ever-rising costs of the military machine there.

Epp, Frank H. "War Compounds the Problems It Was Meant to Solve." *CanMenn* 14 (Aug. 9, 1966), 7; *GH* 59 (Oct. 4, 1966), 878-79. Describes such consequences of the Vietnam War as: corruption in Saigon government; prostitution; the effects of defoliation; refugees; death.

Erb, Gordon. Letter to the Editor. *ChrLiv* 20 (Sept., 1973), 29-30. Responds to Carl Kreider's "The Fall of the Almighty Dollar," (May, p. 15), by observing that American economic problems cannot be the result of the Vietnam war, since the war consumes only one percent of the Gross National Product.

Erb, Paul. "A Call to Prayer." *GH* 43 (Aug. 29, 1950), 851. Comments on plans for a day of prayer for peace. Calls for prayer that people will realize that faults lie on both sides of the Korean conflict, and that Mennonites will have the courage to preach and live nonresistance.

Erb, Paul. "The Bloodiest Century in History." *GH* 43 (Oct. 10, 1950), 995. Christians must humbly confess to the part they have played in the wars of the twentieth century and pray for the opportunity to carry relief into Korea as the war there comes to an end.

Erb, Paul. "The Korean War." *GH* 43 (Aug. 8, 1950), 779-80. Mennonites should not support the war against the communists but teach and demonstrate the life of Christian love against which communism cannot argue.

Esau, John A. "Sermons in a Coffee House." *ChrLiv* 14 (Feb., 1967), 11. Coffeehouse setting provides opportunity to exchange ideas on American policy in Vietnam.

Ewert, Alden H. "Why Alternate Service." *ChrLead* 17 (Aug. 1, 1953), 4. Love of neighbors and enemies necessitates total rejection of participation in violence and suggests instead constructive service, e.g., in mental health services or in ministry to war-torn Korea.

Ewert, Claire. "Weapons of Death." *MennRep* 4 (Sept. 16, 1974), 9. Also "Canadian Weapons of Death." *Intercom* 14 (Aug., 1974), 6. Discusses Canada's role in the Vietnam war through its arms sales to the US.

Fast, Margaret. "A Doctor in Vietnam." *MennMirror* 3 (Nov., 1973), 9, 10. Dr. Margaret Fast reports on her experiences during the two years she practiced medicine under the auspices of MCC in a Vietnam hospital.

Fast, Victor. "The March on Washington." *CanMenn* 13 (Dec. 14, 1965), 5. Letter to the editor from participant in the March on Washington in the fall of 1965 for peace in Vietnam. Fast felt that the mass protest was justified because one voice can often not be heard.

Fieguth, Margot. "How One Church Looked After Its Refugees." *MennMirror* 10 (Oct., 1980), 11-12. Outlines experiences of a Toronto-area congregation's involvement with MCC's effort to resettle Southeast Asia refugees.

Franz, Delton. "Information Gap." *MCC PS Wash. Memo* 3 (Mar.-Apr., 1971), 1-2. Examines reasons American people do not speak out against the war in Indochina.

Franz, Delton. "The Politics of Hostility and the Politics of Healing." *MCC PS Wash. Memo* 11 (Nov.-Dec., 1979), 1-2, 5. Cuba, Angola, and Vietnam might not have been driven into the Soviet camp if the US had not insisted on "cold war" foreign policy.

Franz, Delton. "Will We Conform or Overcome?" *GH* 63 (Sept. 22, 1970), 782-83. Expresses concern for the solid evangelical backing of a July 4 "Honor America Day" celebration and the equation of Christianity with the war in Southeast Asia. Calls Mennonites to begin dialogue with evangelicals on the local level about Jesus' way of peace.

Franz, Delton, ed. "A Week of Witnesses on the War." *MCC PS Wash. Memo* 3 (May-June, 1971), 1-2. Returned MCC worker and Vietnam veteran both testify to the anguish of the Indochina war.

Franz, Delton, ed. "Civilian Victims of Indochina War Rank Low in US Government Priorities." *MCC PS Wash. Memo* 4 (May-June, 1972), 1-2. While the Indochina war is being escalated, humanitarian aid programs for the casualties are being phased out.

Franz, Delton, ed. "Review of Congress in 1972." *MCC PS Wash. Memo* 4 (Nov.-Dec., 1972), 4-5. Evaluates congressional action on topics such as the Vietnam War, military spending, the draft, etc.

Franz, Delton, ed. "The 'Winding Down' of a War!" *MCC PS Wash. Memo* 2 (Nov.-Dec., 1970), 1-3. Even though American involvement in Vietnam has decreased, a massive refugee problem in Indochina remains.

Franz, Roberta C. "Mennonite Preaching on the Vietnam War." Student paper for independent study, Dec., 1972. Pp. 37. MLA/BeC.

Friesen, Dorothy (Review). *Letters from South Korea.* T. K. Idoc/North America. *Sojourners* 6 (July, 1977, 35. A collection of anonymous letters sparked by a declaration of martial law by Korea's President Park in late 1972.

Gehman, Linford. "A Message from Mennonite General Conference to the Congregations Concerning the War in Vietnam. *CanMenn* 13 (Oct. 5, 1965), 6. A statement on Vietnam accepted at 34th biennial Mennonite General Conference (MC) appealing to Mennonite congregations and Christians in America to repent of our unfaithfulness and to work and pray for peace.

Gehman, Linford. "Life Goes On—and Death." *YCC* 48 (July 3, 1967), 10. Description of some of the work at the Evangelical Clinic at Whatrang, Vietnam.

Gehman, Linford. "Maybe War Is an Accident." *YCC* 47 (July 10, 1966), 2. Description of the activity at the Evangelical Christian Hospital on the day a bomber crashed into downtown Whatrang.

Gering, William. *I Must Go: A Play in One Act.* Newton: Faith and Life Press, 1961. Pp. 22. Jim, a college sophomore in a state school, struggles with what it means to be a conscientious objector in an environment that is neither sympathetic nor supportive. Setting is the era of the Korean conflict.

Gingerich, Melvin. "Mennonite Central Committee Assignment in Japan, 1955-57." Reports of MCC Peace Section representative, Goshen, Ind., 1962. Pp. 57. MHL. Sixfold mission included working with Mennonite and Brethren missionaries to correlate the peace message with the Gospel; making contact with the Japanese Christian peace movement; production of peace literature; building a peace library; studying the problem of legal recognition for the CO position in Japan; and visiting Formosa and Korea to evaluate potential for similar peace-oriented work there.

Gingrich, John E. "I Heard Their Cry." *GH* 61 (Apr. 2, 1968), 293. Visitor to South Vietnam is appalled by the destruction and suffering caused by US policies that force people into becoming refugees, and he urges a settlement in the war involving the National Liberation Front.

Goshen College. "Ad Hoc Committee for Aiding Victims of the War in North Vietnam." Clippings from *Goshen News,* 1966. Pp. 13. MHL. File of letters received in response to news story entitled "Suffering North Viets Subject of Meeting at GC," n.d.

Graham, Billy. "From the Press: Graham on Vietnam and Watergate." *MennRep* 3 (June 11, 1973), 7. Reprinted from *Christianity Today* (Jan. 19, 1973), 416 and *New York Times* (May 6, 1973), 17. Evangelist Graham states that while the Bible indicates there will always be wars, he has never advocated war. Denies his publicized role as "White House chaplain."

Groh, Norman I. Letter to the Editor. *GH* 61 (June 18, 1968), 554. Questions a pure anti-war stance toward Vietnam because the cause of the war was the communist takeover of the north. Calls for greater respect for the government than is evidenced in the anti-war movement.

"Harder Reflects on His Task in the External Affairs Department." *MennRep* 9 (Nov. 26, 1979), 10. In an interview, Peter Harder, special assistant to Flora MacDonald, Canadian Minister for External Affairs, responds to questions on foreign policy, international peace, and more specifically, the Canadian response to Southeast Asia.

"How the War Came to Mountain Lake." *With* 3 (Feb., 1970), 4. Forty students from Mountain Lake High School had a procession to observe Vietnam Moratorium Day on Oct. 15, 1969.

Habegger, Luann. "The Forgotten POWs." *GH* 66 (June 19, 1973), 505-506; *MennRep* 3 (July 9, 1973), 7. Documents the plight of an estimated 200,000 political prisoners in South Vietnam who continue to be held and tortured in tiger cages, while American prisoners-of-war return to the States.

Hackman, Walton. "A Conscientious Objector Becomes a Military Chaplain—for a Day." *GH* 64 (Jan. 5, 1971), 18-19. Peace Section representative describes a day spent at Fitzsimmons Army Base: his discussions with army chaplains on the issue of just war, and his conversations with injured soldiers just returned from Vietnam.

Hackman, Walton. "Accepting Defeat and Resolving Guilt." *Menn* 88 (Mar. 13, 1973), 184; *ChrLead* 36 (Mar. 6, 1973), 24. The lack of public celebration on the announcement of a peace settlement in Vietnam and the return of GI's indicates a national guilt about involvement in Vietnam

Hackman, Walton. "Giving for Peace." *Menn* 88 (Dec. 18, 1973), 734. Encourages alternative giving for Christmas to people such as families of civilian prisoners in South Vietnam, imprisoned conscientious objectors, war resisters exiled in Canada, and political refugees from Chile.

Hackman, Walton. "Out of Sight, Out of Mind in Vietnam." *MBH* 12 (Sept. 7, 1973), 32. MCC Peace Section is urging Mennonite congregations to make Sept. 23 a special concern because it is being declared an International Day of Concern and Action for the thousands of civilians imprisoned in South Vietnam.

Hackman, Walton. "Prisoners of Peace." *GH* 66 (July 31, 1973), 587-88; *ChrLead* 36 (July 10, 1973), 7; "The Veteran—Another Victim." *Menn* 88 (July 10, 1973), 428-29. Describes the plight of 25,000 Vietnam veterans, who sacrificed their dreams to fight the nation's war, and who now suffer neglect and discrimination in peacetime. The church has an obligation to minister to the needs and concerns of Vietnam veterans whose lives have been severely or permanently damaged as a result of the Indochina War.

Hackman, Walton. "The Issue Now Is Amnesty." *GH* 65 (Jan. 4, 1972), 9-10. Reprinted from MCC Peace Section *Newsletter*. After World War II, only 10 percent of Selective Service violators were pardoned. Writer wonders whether present society has enough latitude to respect and accept the estimated 100,000 Vietnam War resisters.

Hackman, Walton (Editorial). "No Victory Parades, No Peace Marches." *Intercom* 13 (Nov., 1973), 4. Observes the change in public sentiment from protesting the war in Vietnam to supporting the Middle East war.

Hamm, Ray. "Canada: Is Independence Possible?" *Menn* 88 (Mar. 13, 1973), 180-81. Hamm expresses the desire that Canada be freed from the intimate US presence there because of, among other reasons, US domination of other peoples through multinational corporations and because the US profiteered on the war in Vietnam.

Harder, John A. (Review). *A Vietnamese Pilgrimage*, by Max Ediger. Newton: Faith and Life Press, 1979. Pp. 79. *MennRep* 9 (Sept. 17, 1979), 8. Through poetry, prose, and illustrations, this book records the Vietnam drama from 1971-76 and the painful struggle of the author and his Vietnamese friends to understand and interpret these events.

Harder, Kurt. "A History of Kansans Concerned About Vietnam." Social Science Seminar paper, Apr. 30, 1981. Pp. 94. MLA/BeC.

Harding, Vincent G. "Conscientious Objection: Is It a Christian Response to Vietnam?" *Builder* 17 (Oct., 1967), 12-13. Questions the adequacy of the I-W program as a response to Jesus' call to love the enemy. Identifies a lack of congruence between objecting to war and accepting military protection of that right to object.

Harding, Vincent G. "Our Crisis of Obedience." *Menn* 81 (Feb. 15, 1966), 109-110. In response to President Johnson's prosecution of the war in Vietnam, the writer calls for rejection of war and nationalism as incompatible with the gospel of Jesus.

Harding, Vincent G. "Vietnam: What Shall We Do?" *Menn* 80 (Sept. 21, 1965), 582-85; "What Shall We Do About Vietnam?" *CanMenn* 13, Part 1, (Sept. 14, 1965), 6; Part 2, (Sept. 21, 1965), 6; *MBH* 4 (Sept. 17, 1965), 14 (shortened version). It is time that Mennonites' professed opposition to war be proclaimed as public dissent to American military policy. Response must begin with repentance and then seek to witness openly to the way of love and reconciliation.

Harms, Orlando. "Watergate and the Bible." *ChrLead* 36 (June 26, 1973), 24. The lessons of Vietnam and Watergate should be lessons to repent, confess, and turn away from evil.

Hartzler, Robert. "A Parable of Unbrotherhood." *GH* 64 (Oct. 9, 1971), 862-64. Allegorizing the "white brother" and the "yellow brother" as Cain and Abel, the author makes a devastating comment on the effects of the war in Southeast Asia.

Hatfield, Mark O. "Senator Mark Hatfield's 'End the War' Bill." *MCC PS Wash. Memo* 2 (May-June, 1970), 1-3. Reprint of a speech by Mark Hatfield urging support of an amendment withholding funds for military expenditures in Vietnam.

Heinrichs, Alfred. "Another Look at Vietnam." *CanMenn* 12 (Sept. 8, 1964), 4. Discusses church's attitude on Vietnam in letter to the editor.

Hershberger, Guy F. "Conscience of Society." *GH* 61 (Feb. 20, 1968), 150-51. [No. 24] In support of his position that the church is the conscience of society, the author lists and describes cases of Mennonite protest against the Vietnam war and efforts toward peacemaking in addressing the problem of segregated urban housing.

Hershberger, Guy F. "The Current Upsurge of War Objection." *GH* 61 (Jan. 16, 1968), 57. [No. 20] Writer observes that the growth of anti-war sentiment during wartime is unusual, and that the burgeoning peace movement protesting activities in Vietnam is disturbing to government officials.

Hershberger, Guy F. "Washington Visitation on Vietnam." *GH* 58 (June 15, 1965), 520. A report of religious groups, including Mennonites, which met in Washington for consultation on the Vietnam War. Emphasis was on witnessing to the powers that be about the righteousness which God requires of all people.

Hershberger, Guy F. "What Must We Do if Our Function as the Conscience of Society, and Our Obligation to Protest Against Evil, Is to Be Implemented? Our Peace Witness—In the Wake of May 18." (Part 24). *GH* 61 (Feb. 20, 1968), 150-51. Lists seven ways that Mennonites have protested the Vietnam war, poverty, and racial discrimination.

Hertzler, Daniel. "A Minority View on Vietnam." *ChrLiv* 14 (Feb., 1967), 2. Editorial expressing the opinion that US should get out of Vietnam, based on the editor's position against war.

Hertzler, Daniel. "No Cause but Others' Good." *ChrLiv* 13 (Nov., 1966), 2. Editorial commends three people whose cause is humanitarian and contrasts their cause with the one motivating the Vietnam war.

Hertzler, Daniel (Review). *The Korea Story*, by John

C. Caldwell in collaboration with Lesley Frost. Henry Regnery Co., 1952. Pp. 180. *MennComm* 7 (Feb., 1953), 27. Recommends the book as the candid reflections of a "civil information specialist" for the American Army of Occupation in Korea and its program for US propaganda.

Hertzler, James R. "The American Revolution in British Eyes." *GH* 69 (Jan. 27, 1976), 68-69. Examines the various opinions of British preachers and writers on the rebellion of the American colonies, and draws parallels between that conflict and the recent one in Vietnam.

Hertzler, Richard, and Lasserre, Jean. "Vietnam, Seen from Abroad." *ChrLiv* 14 (July, 1967), 29. A Frenchman and a German comment on US policy in Vietnam.

Hiebert, Clarence. "What About Vietnam?" *ChrLead* 29 (Mar. 15, 1966), 14-15. Since God wills peace, reconciliation, justice, and redemption, God's people will also share this attitude and will work for justice, peace, and love in our present world.

Hiebert, Linda Gibson. "Report from Indochina: Why Are People Fleeing?" *MennRep* 9 (Sept. 17, 1979), 7. A report on the severe hardships that refugees are experiencing in Laos, Vietnam, and Kampuchea and what the Canadian response has been.

Hiebert, Linda Gibson. "The Indochina Project." *Peace Section Newsletter* 9 (June-July, 1979), 3-5. The Indochina Project began in mid-1978 as a cooperative effort between the Mennonite Central Committee and the American Friends Service Committee, with the Center for International Policy joining later. Explains the role and concerns of the project.

Hiebert, Linda Gibson and Hiebert, Murray. "In the Wake of Revolution." *Sojourners* 8 (Sept., 1978), 15. Description of the conflicts and challenges facing Vietnam. A call for a spirit of reconciliation between Americans and Vietnamese.

Hiebert, Linda Gibson and Hiebert, Murray. "Laos: The Enemy at Home." *Sojourners* 6 (June, 1977), 35. The war in Laos continues as a war against sickness and hunger. The US has some responsibility since it spent billions of dollars financing twenty years of warfare.

Hiebert, Linda Gibson and Hiebert, Murray. "Laos' Plain of Jars Slowly Rebuilds." *Intercom* 22 (Jan., 1978), 2-3. Describes Laotians rebuilding after the war.

Hiebert, Linda Gibson and Hiebert, Murray. "MCC Volunteer Describes Life in Vietnam." *Menn* 92

(Jan. 25, 1977), 55. Yoshihiro Ichakawa, MCC volunteer in Vietnam, describes post-war life in Saigon since the change in government, reporting on changes in local administration, land reform, reeducation centers, attitudes of church people.

Hiebert, Linda Gibson and Hiebert, Murray. "My Lai: After the Massacre." *Sojourners* 5 (Sept., 1976), 12. A painful visit to My Lai. Christians must lead the way toward healing and reconciling with the wartorn people of Vietnam.

Hiebert, Linda Gibson and Hiebert, Murray. "Philippines: The Next Indochina?" *Menn* 90 (Apr. 22, 1975), 256-57. MCC workers in the Philippines trace political history which approximates that of Vietnam and could lead to similar military confrontation.

Hiebert, Linda Gibson and Hiebert, Murray. "The Ravages of Our Secret War." *Sojourners* 7 (Feb., 1978), 28. Description of a visit to Laos for the purpose of evaluating past assistance programs, formulating new projects, and witnessing the destruction in one of the most severely bombed areas of Indochina.

Hiebert, Murray. "Indochina Conflicts: A Complex Web." *MCC PS Newsletter* 9 (June-July, 1979), 1-3. The explanation for the February Chinese invasion of Vietnam lies in a complex web of shifting in major power alliances, ideological conflicts, border disputes, and traditional antagonisms.

Hiebert, Murray. "War Scraps Forged into Plows." *FStP* 1 (Sept., 1976), 1-2. Foundry near Vientiane, Laos, buys military scrap metal and forges it into farm implements.

Hiebert, Murray. "Washington Report: War Continues in Vietnam." *MennRep* 9 (July 9, 1979), 7. A report and analysis of the Vietnamese conflict with Kampuchea and China and its alliance with the Soviet Union.

Hiebert, Murray and Hiebert, Linda Gibson. "A Response." *Sojourners* 8 (Nov., 1978), 38. A response to "Letters to the Editor" by Dan Berrigan and Jim Forest on a highly-polarized, two-year-old debate on human rights in Vietnam.

Hiebert, Murray and Hiebert, Linda Gibson. "Laos Fights New War." *Menn* 92 (June 7, 1977), 377. Complicating Laotian attempts at postwar recovery are widespread disease, unexploded ordnance in fields, few surviving draft animanls, and inadequate harvests.

Hiebert, Murray and Hiebert, Linda Gibson. "Laos Invites the World to View Damage Caused by War." *MennRep* 8 (Jan. 23, 1978), 2. MCC representatives describe destruction in Laos caused by bombing.

Higgins, James. "'You Never Know Who's Who in Vietnam.' " *ChrLiv* 13 (June, 1966), 40. Vietnam war veteran speaks cynically of adjusting to civilian life after learning war.

Hope, Sam R. "Personal Reflections on Our Experience in Vietnam." *GH* 62 (Apr. 8, 1969), 320-22; "Personal Reflection on Vietnamese Experience." *CanMenn* 17 (Mar. 4, 1969), 4. Text of a speech by a former director of personnel for Vietnam Christian Service to MCC annual meeting in Chicago on Jan. 24. Reflects on his deepened faith and anti-war convictions because of his work in war-torn Vietnam.

Horst, John L. (Editorial). "Deepening World Shadows." *ChrMon* 42 (Aug., 1950), 232-33. Comments on the possibility of war in Korea.

Hostetler, Doug. "Agent Orange." *Forum* (Mar., 1971), A-8. Discusses America's exploitation of the Vietnamese people in the Vietnam war.

Hostetler, John Andrew. "Mennonite Relief in China; Problems and Needs of China." *ChrMon* 38, Part 3, (Sept., 1946), 270-71, 278. The recent war with Japan intensified many of the already-existing problems of food and shelter shortages.

Hostetter, Douglas. "A Trip Through the Countryside." *GH* 68 (Jan. 28, 1975), 57-59. Visitor to North Vietnam and Vietcong-held areas in the South reports on reconstruction efforts, especially in medical facilities, and the continuing civil war in the South.

Hostetter, Douglas. "After the Debris Is Cleared." *Sojourners* 8 (Sept., 1978), 20. Describes the church in post-revolutionary Vietnam and Cuba.

Hostetter, Douglas. "In Search of Peace for Vietnam." *With* 4 (July, 1971), 15. A former Mennonite Central Committee worker was asked by the National Student Association to return to Vietnam to help draw up a peace treaty.

Hostetter, Douglas. "Joe." *Menn* 89 (Apr. 16, 1974), 264. Hostetter relates the story of his involvement with one draft resister, whose dilemma symbolizes that of thousands of Vietnam War objectors who need the support of church and government.

Hostetter, Pat. "The Children of Vietnam." *YCC* 48 (Mar. 19, 1967), 2. The children of Vietnam grow up as victims of war and poverty, hate and suspicion.

Hübner, Harry. "Pacifism, Non-Pacifism—

Indistinguishable." *CanMenn* 17 (Nov. 28, 1969), 4. Letter to the editor asks counsel concerning some of the difficult issues of pacifism as it relates to President Nixon's actions in Vietnam.

Hull, Robert. "Historical Roots of a Peace Church Witness." *Affirm Life: Pay for Peace,* ed. Maynard Shelly and Ron Flickinger. Newton: Historic Peace Church Task Force on Taxes, 1981, 13-17. Pp. [87]. MHL. Charts history of historic peace church responses and actions on war tax issues from the French and Indian war, 1754-1763 to the contemporary period—the Vietnam War era, the World Peace Tax Fund (1973), and the General Conference Mennonite Church experience with Cornelia Lehn's request.

Jacobszoon, J. P. "The Indefensible Beachhead in Vietnam." *ChrLiv* 14 (Mar., 1967), 32. Dutch Mennonite leader offers suggestions for US policy in Vietnam.

Jantz, Harold. "Aid to Vietnam/ese Major Agenda Item in Calgary." *MennRep* 9 (Feb. 5, 1979), 1. At an MCC (Canada) meeting in Jan., considerable discussion revolved around aid to Vietnam and the Vietnamese boat refugees. Among other decisions, it also supported the intention of the Peace and Social Concerns Committee to issue a statement on militarism in Canada.

Jantz, Harold. "Depoliticizing Our Aid." *MBH* 18 (Dec. 7, 1979), 10. Editorial expresses the opinion that MCC workers, especially in Southeast Asia, should refrain from becoming involved in political activity.

Jantz, Harold. "Protest Simmers in Vietnam." *MBH* 13 (Nov. 29, 1974), 16-17. Dissatisfaction with the leadership of Nguyen Van Thieu may lead to increased military activity.

Jantz, Harold. "Workers Caution About Babylift." *MBH* 14 (May 2, 1975), 16. MCC and Mission Board personnel are concerned that many children being evacuated from Vietnam may not be true orphans.

Jantz, Harold (Editorial). "Viet Nam Profile." *MBH* 5 (Feb. 25, 1966), 3. Critiques World Vision's promotional film, "Viet Nam Profile," which totally accepts and supports the American war effort in Vietnam.

Jantz, Harold (Editorial). "Vietnam Orphans." *MBH* 14 (Apr. 18, 1975), 11. Comments on the irony of the American concern for war orphans as compared with the earlier support for continued aggression in the war.

Jones, Brennon. "Paper Flowers and Stethoscope." *GH* 63 (June 2, 1970), 494-95. Describes the medical and rehabilitation work of a Vietnam Christian Service nurse, as her work is shaped by the presence of war.

Juhnke, James C. "Our Almost Unused Political Power." *GH* 61 (Jan. 9, 1968), 38-39. Reflects on Mennonite use of political power to defeat proposed changes in the draft laws that would have been unfavorable to conscientious objectors, and urges Mennonites to use this power to influence foreign policy toward de-escalation in Vietnam.

Juhnke, James C. "Vietnam and the Politics of Repentance." *Lutheran Forum* (Feb., 1971), 16-27. Excerpts from Juhnke's opening congressional campaign address call for renewed commitment to American ideals of democracy and humane politics, which translate for Juhnke into withdrawal from Vietnam.

Jutzi, Bruce. "Ten Thousand Gave Serious Consideration to Peace Message." *CanMenn* 14 (Nov. 22, 1966), 1, 3. Report on MCC (Canada) Peace Booth at the Toronto Exhibition with theme "Peace on Earth . . . Peace in Vietnam." While it is difficult to determine the success or failure of such a witness, the booth was an opportunity to take a necessary and unpopular position and defend its validity to a cross-section of society.

"Korea: Victim of Repression and World Politics." *MennRep* 9 (Sept. 17, 1979), 2. Yoon Goo Lee, formerly of Korea, speaks to the Akron MCC staff about the situation in Korea, stressing that the main problem is the infringement of human rights in South Korea.

"Korean Protestant Leaders Speak Against Death Penalty." *CanMenn* 10 (Feb. 9, 1962), 9. Report of an appeal to the Korean government against the use of the death penalty for political prisoners.

Kaiser, Ward L. "Who's Winning?" *YCC* 47 (Oct. 30, 1966), 5. Analysis of the war on poverty and the Vietnam War.

Kauffman, Carl. "A Pacifist in a War Country." *YCC* 49 (June 2, 1968), 8. Reflections on what it means for a pacifist to live in a war-torn country like Vietnam.

Kauffman, Ivan. "War: A Necessary Evil and a Time for Tears." *CanMenn* 15 (Nov. 21, 1967), 3, 11. On Nov. 2, five MCC persons spoke with two members of President Johnson's staff about Vietnam. While there was agreement that war is evil, the Johnson people saw this evil as necessary to preserve the American way of life. Therefore the government officials asked for alternatives but quickly rejected those and were interested only in those alternatives capable of achieving the aims of the present war but without violence. Since the MCC personnel argued from totally different assumptions, there was little agreement beyond the basic affirmation that war is evil.

Kauffman, Nelson E. (Review). *P.O.W.: Two Years with the Vietcong,* by George E. Smith. Ramparts Press, 1971. Pp. 304. *IPF Notes* 20 (Oct. 18, 1973), 4. Reprinted from *Provident Book Finder* (Sept., 1973). Recommends this personal story of the training and brainwashing received as a soldier, contrasted with the morality and human decency of the Vietcong captors.

Kauffmann, Joel. *The Weight.* Scottdale, Pa.: Herald Press, 1980. Pp. 146. Jon Springer, whose father is a Mennonite minister, turns eighteen during the summer after his high school graduation. The time is the Vietnam era and he must decide whether to register for conscientious objector status or to follow the example of some peers as well as community sentiment and register I-A. The questions with which he struggles as the peacemaker model of church and family teaching becomes his own choice are "the weight." Novel for young adults.

Kaufman, Donald D. "Cheyenne Soldier Testifies, Speaks for Way of Peace." See Topic 17d, World War II.

Keener, Carl S. (Review). *The Ultimate Folly,* by Congressman Richard D. McCarthy. Knopf, 1969. Pp. 176. *GH* 63 (Dec. 29, 1970), 1075. Recommends the book for its documentation and discussion of American preparations for war by pestilence, by asphyxiation, and by defoliation.

Keeney, William E. "Not Yet Peace." *GH* 66 (July 3, 1973), 533-35; *ChrLead* 36 (July 10, 1973), 2; *Menn* 88 (July 10, 1973), 426-27. The ceasefire in Vietnam means only that American troops have withdrawn. It does not stop the Selective Service or decrease military expenditures or free South Vietnam's political prisoners or begin the immense reconstruction process. Concerns like amnesty, draft, and political prisoners need to be addressed.

Keeney, William E. "Serving a Nation in Agony." *MennLife* 23 (Apr., 1968), 54-58. Outlines the various kinds of problems the Vietnam people face in their war-torn country.

Kehler, Larry. "Do You Remember Vietnam?" *Menn* 91 (July 20, 1976), 460. The US must take responsibility for rebuilding Vietnam, a country it abused in war and is now rapidly forgetting.

Kehler, Larry. "Vietnamese Vignettes." *GH* 69 (Sept. 14, 1976), 685-91; *Menn* 91 (July 20, 1976), 446-47. MCC visitor to Vietnam describes the effects of war on the survivors and reports on the shape of Vietnamese society since liberation.

Kehler, Peter. "Fourth Southeast Asia Reconciliation Work Camp." *GH* 61 (Oct. 15, 1968), 937-38. Describes and reflects on a work

camp hosted by Taiwan Mennonites for the purpose of building international cooperation in peacemaking while working on some worthy service project.

Kehler, Peter. "Southeast Asia Work Camp Builds Roads to Assist Refugees from Mainland China." *CanMenn* 16 (Sept. 17, 1968), 3. Report on the Fourth South East Asia Reconciliation Work Camp held in Taipei involving eleven participants from Japan (including two US citizens), one from Indonesia, one PAXperson from Korea, and twenty-two from Taiwan. Korean and Indian delegates could not attned due to government restriction.

Klaassen, Walter. "Setting the Record Straight on Billy Graham's War Stand." *CanMenn* 14 (June 7, 1966), 1, 2. Reflections and conclusions on Billy Graham's attitude to war in Vietnam on the basis of discussions and reports of statements made at the Houston crusade.

Klassen, J. M. "'Operation North Vietnam' Slowed by Hanoi." *CanMenn* 16 (Mar. 5, 1968), 3. A report on efforts by Canadian Mennonites to send supplies to North Vietnam.

Klassen, James R. Letter to the Editor. *Menn* 94 (Dec. 11, 1979), 750. Describes how the US deliberately helped create Vietnamese refugees. The US now is only offering assistance to boat people who represent a very small fraction of the population. Much more aid needs to be given to help Vietnamese in Vietnam.

Klassen, James R. "To Push or Not to Push." *With* 10 (June, 1977), 32. A Mennonite Central Committee worker in Vietnam reflects on working for peace in that country.

Klassen, Peter J. "Evangelicals and the Vietnam War" and "The Silence of Billy Graham." *MBH* 12 (Feb. 23, 1973), 11. With the end of the Vietnam war at hand, the editor reflects and comments that it has brought home to humankind the utter futility of trying to solve serious questions through violence. He also comments on the tacit approval Billy Graham gave to the president's actions in the war.

Klassen, William. "The Choice Is Now Between Nonviolence and Nonexistence." *CanMenn* 16 (Feb. 17, 1968), 3, 4. Describes Feb. 5 and 6 march on Washington by clergy and lay people concerned about Vietnam and summarizes M. L. King's speech as well as that of Chaplain Coffin. Learnings from the expericne include a sense of the value of working within church structure even when many people in churches may not take positions against the Vietnam war.

Kliewer, Warren. "War and Rumors of War." *MennLife* 17 (Jan., 1962), 39-43. Death of a friend who was a soldier in Korea raises the issue of how we all share in violence.

Konkel, Gus. Letter to the Editor. *Menn* 88 (Apr. 10, 1973), 245. Calls *The Mennonite* to focus less attention on political issues, citing the examples of "copious verbiage on the Vietnam War" and the question of war tax payment as issues where poorly informed opinions fail to grasp the complexity of political issues.

Kooker, Harley M. "In the Heat of the Curfew." *ChrLiv* 19 (Mar., 1972), 2-5. MCCer in Vietnam recalls efforts to help a 12-year-old girl mutilated by Marine shelling.

Koontz, Gayle Gerber. "Moral Responsibility in Technological Warfare." *GH* 65 (Sept. 19, 1972), 762-63. Describes American warfare in Vietnam through dike bombing, forest burning, and cloud-seeding activities, and questions what responsibility Mennonites have to witness against such actions and withhold tax money from them.

Koontz, Gayle Gerber. "Vietnam—Testing Ground for a Way of Peace." *Intercom* 15 (Oct., 1975), 2, 7; *GH* 68 (Sept. 16, 1975), 659-60. Former MCCers Earl and Pat Martin discuss their decision that Earl stay temporarily in Vietnam during the change of government.

Koontz, Gayle Gerber. "Vietnam Churches See Challenges, Pressures." *Menn* 90 (Sept. 16, 1975), 511. MCC volunteer returned from Vietnam discusses the change of government there and the challenges facing the church in helping to rebuild the country after the war.

Krabill, Willard S. "Mennonites in Viet-Nam." *ChrLiv* 6 (May, 1959), 4-7, 34. Summary of the political and military conflict leading to South Vietnam's present independence.

Krabill, Willard S. "Vietnam: Soulsick, War-weary, and Divided." *CanMenn* 14 (Feb. 8, 1966), 9; *ChrLead* 29 (Mar. 15, 1966), 3-5. A condensed version of Krabill's report to Elkhart Mennonite churches about the extent and solution of the refugee problem in Vietnam. Includes discussion of the question of Vietnamese national identity and how that question relates to questions of politics, government, and war.

Kraus, C. Norman. Letter in "Our Readers Say." *GH* (Dec. 14, 1965), 1088. As we carry out our mission of mercy in Vietnam we must disassociate ourselves from the war effort. We must let the public and government officials know we are opposed to the war.

Kreider, Carl. "American Involvement in South Vietnam." *ChrLiv* 9 (May, 1962), 19, 39.

Background of the escalating military tension between North and South Vietnam.

Kreider, Carl. "Eisenhower's Trip to Korea." *MennComm* 7 (Mar., 1953), 29-32. List of reasons the Korean war must be settled, suggesting neutralization of the whole of the Far East as a peaceful solution.

Kreider, Carl. "Rhee's Forced Resignation in Korea." *ChrLiv* 7 (July, 1960), 18, 37. The events leading to Rhee's resignation include the Korean War of 1950-53 and its aftermath.

Kreider, Carl. "The MacArthur Dismissal." *MennComm* 5 (June, 1951), 28, 30. Analysis of disagreements between General Douglas MacArthur and President Truman over military policies in Korea.

Kreider, Carl. "The War in Indo-China." *ChrLiv* 1 (May, 1954), 35-36. Indo-China conflict is another example of the ineffectiveness of Western military intervention in dealing with communism.

Kreider, Carl. "The War in Korea." *MennComm* 4 (Sept., 1950), 30, 34. Analysis of the fighting in Korea concludes that the US is backing reactionary forces; the UN has turned into an anti-communist force; the war will strain the American economy.

Kreider, Carl. "Truce in Indo-China." *ChrLiv* 1 (Oct., 1954), 37-39. Comment on the partitioning of Vietnam and the effect of American military force in meeting communism.

Kreider, Janet H. "Peacemakers in the Midst of War." *GH* 61 (Mar. 12, 1968), 218-19. Describes the activities and questions of Mennonite missionaries in Vietnam seeking to be peacemakers in the middle of the Vietnam war.

Kreider, Robert S. (Review). *The Best and the Brightest*, by David Halberstam. New York: Random House, 1973. *GH* 67 (Feb. 5, 1974), 127; *Menn* 89 (Jan. 22, 1974), 61. Labels as "sad," "prophetic," and "readable" this book detailing the process of deceit and mistrust in the Kennedy and Johnson administrations that backed the country blindly into the Vietnam War.

Kreider, Robert S. and Kreider, Lois. "Little Peace, Less Honor." *Menn* 90 (Jan. 28, 1975), 50-51 Visitors to Vietnam report that fighting continues, supported by US money and political means, a picture far different from the official US news releases which approximate coverups.

Kroeker, David. "American Military Men in Vietnam Dedicated and Highly Motivated." *CanMenn* 15 (Jan. 10, 1967), 1, 2. Commentary on the Graham Team's view of the war in Vietnam based on the Jan. 8 radio broadcast of *The Hour of Decision,* a first-hand report of the Graham Team's 9-day visit in Vietnam. Graham and Co. praised efforts of American soldiers in Vietnam and encouraged listeners to write to the soldiers in a show of support.

Kroeker, Walter. "Justice and Rights Issues Occupy MCC Members in Reedley." *MennRep* 9 (Feb. 19, 1979), 1. Among the issues discussed at the MCC annual meeting was aid to Vietnam, justice and human rights overseas, and a paper on militarism calling the church to renounce the development of nuclear weapons and military exports.

Kroeker, Walter. "MCC—Wide-Ranging Agenda." *EV* 92 (Mar. 25, 1979), 8-9. At the MCC annual meeting, issues of justice, aid to Vietnam, the world food crisis, and militarism were addressed and a paper on militarism by Urbane Peachey was accepted.

"Lack of Concern for Rules of War." *Menn* 86 (Jan. 19, 1971), 36-38. Relief workers express their disapproval of the foreign military involvement in Vietnam and quote numerous articles from, for instance, the Nuremberg Tribunal, the Hague Convention, the Geneva Convention, and others, to point out the injustice of the USA.

"Letter from Saigon." *GH* 65 (June 20, 1972), 530-31. Letter to President Nixon signed by Mennonite church workers and missionaries in Vietnam sharply criticizes American backing of the unpopular and oppressive South Vietnamese government and calls for a US commitment to withdraw all forces from Southeast Asia.

"Letter from Vietnam to American Churches." *GH* 61 (Jan. 16, 1968), 65-66; *CanMenn* 16 (Mar. 5, 1968), 4. Mennonite missionaries in Vietnam speak for the perspective of Vietnamese people, pleading for greater awareness of the issues underlying the Vietnam war. Signed by James K. Stauffer, Everett G. Metzler, Luke S. Martin, James E. Metzler, Don M. Sensenig, S. Luke Beidler.

"'Love Works in Conflicts' Says Hostetter." *MBH* 10 (May 28, 1971), 18-19. Former MCC worker Doug Hostetter speaks of the effects of propaganda and the American military presence in war-torn Vietnam. Also speaks of the power of love at work in his relationships with the Vietnamese people.

Lapp, John A. *A Dream for America.* Scottdale, Pa.: Herald Press, 1976. Pp. 128. Bicentennial reflection calls the nation to attend to the issues of the moment—issues such as racial equality, disproportionate distribution of global

resources, learnings from the Vietnam War, conflict resolution, honest government, civil religion, etc.—and decide to implement in our time the worthy goals of the Declaration of Independence.

Lapp, John A. "Bullets Instead of Bodies: The New Indochina War." *ChrLiv* 19 (Apr., 1972), 18-19. Comment on the new automated and electronic techniques used by the US army in Vietnam.

Lapp, John A. "Conference Table or World War?" *ChrLiv* 12 (May, 1965), 18-19, 32-33. Background of the Vietnam conflict and the recent escalation of American military involvement there.

Lapp, John A. "'Confrontation' in Southeast Asia." *ChrLiv* 11 (Dec., 1964), 20-21. The longstanding Indonesia-Malaysia conflict disproves the theory that solving the Vietnam crisis will bring peace to the whole region.

Lapp, John A. "Credibility and the Democratic Process." *ChrLiv* 14 (Dec., 1967), 18-19. The conflicting government reports on the Vietnam War threaten the fabric of democracy.

Lapp, John A. "Denouement for Indochina." *ChrLiv* 22 (May, 1975), 15, 34. Review of Cambodia's role in the Southeast Asian conflict, and comment upon the US policy there.

Lapp, John A. "Dissent and American Consensus." *ChrLiv* 13 (Mar., 1966), 18-19. Vietnam war protesters are exercising their right to dissent, a long-standing tradition in both American and Mennonite histories.

Lapp, John A. "Inside South Vietnam." *ChrLiv* 18 (Mar., 1971), 18-19. Impressions of the continuing war and the Vietnamese people's desire for peace gained through a one-week trip to South Vietnam.

Lapp, John A. "Laos: Domino or Diversion?" *ChrLiv* 17 (May, 1970), 18-19. Military activity previously in Vietnam has been transferred to neighboring Laos.

Lapp, John A. "Nixon, Cambodia, and the Students." *ChrLiv* 17 (July, 1970), 14-15, 31. Student anti-war protests escalate upon receiving the news that Nixon ordered American troops into Cambodia.

Lapp, John A. "The Decade that Was." *ChrLiv* 27 (Jan., 1980), 11, 34. Review of 1970s events includes discussion of the Vietnam war.

Lapp, John A. "The Meaning of the Pentagon Papers." *ChrLiv* 18 (Sept., 1971), 18-19. Discussion of the revelations about American policy in Vietnam as found in the Pentagon study.

Lapp, John A. "The Search for Peace in Vietnam." *ChrLiv* 14 (Mar., 1967), 18-19, 37. Statistics of the Vietnam war during 1966 and conditions for peace put forth by each of the concerned parties.

Lapp, John A. "The Second Rebellion in South Vietnam." *ChrLiv* 10 (Nov., 1963), 18-19. Assessment of American involvement in the present conflict.

Lapp, John A. "The War Itself is the Atrocity." *ChrLiv* 17 (Feb., 1970), 18-19, 35. Although regulations governing war activities exist, the real crime is the Vietnam war itself and American involvement in it.

Lapp, John A. "Vietnam After Tet." *ChrLiv* 15 (Apr., 1968), 18-19. Vietcong offensive during the New Year holidays illustrates the fragile control held by South Vietnamese and Americans.

Lapp, John A. "Vietnam and Cambodia: What Can We Do?" *GH* 63 (May 26, 1970), 480. Calls churches to speak out against the extension of the Vietnam War into Cambodia; includes suggestions for action.

Lapp, John A. "Who Lost Indochina?" *ChrLiv* 22 (June, 1975), 15, 33. If the US lost the war in Indochina, it was because of backing the wrong side· allying with forces of reaction and corruption.

Lapp, John A. (Review). *Foreign Policy in Christian Perspective,* by John C. Bennett. Charles Scribner's Sons, 1966. Pp. 110. *ChrLiv* 13 (Nov., 1966), 28-29. Recommends this examination of the cold war, nuclear weapons, and Vietnam in light of Christian realism.

Lapp, John A. (Review). *In the Name of America,* by Seymour Melman. Clergy and Laymen Concerned About Vietnam, 1968. Pp. 422. *ChrLiv* 15 (Dec., 1968), 42. Recommends this documentation of American violations of international rules of war during the Vietnam War.

Lapp, John A. (Review). *Vietnam: Lotus in a Sea of Fire,* by Thich Nath-Hanh. Hill and Wang, 1967. Pp. 115. *ChrLiv* 15 (July, 1968), 36-37. Recommends this interpretation of the Vietnam War from the perspective of a Vietnamese Buddhist monk.

Lapp, John A. (Review). *Voices from the Plain of Jars,* compiled. Harper & Row, 1972. Pp. 160. *GH* 66 (Nov. 6, 1973), 855. Excerpts from interviews with Laotian peasants who fled the bombing of

the Plain of Jars in the 1960s graphically portray peasant life in wartime.

Lapp, John E. "Response to Letter Sent to President Johnson by Mennonite General Conference." *GH* 60 (Dec. 12, 1967), 1119. Lapp reports on response from the White House and urges Christians to give no support to the war in Vietnam in any way.

Leatherman, Paul. "Vietnams in the US." *GH* 63 (Feb. 3, 1970), 97-98. Uses the image of violence and injustice in Vietnam as a metaphor for injustice toward poor and blacks in the US.

Lehman, Frances (Review). *North Vietnam: A Documentary,* by John Gerassi. Bobbs-Merrill, 1968. Pp. 200. *ChrLiv* 16 (Nov., 1969), 33-34. Recommends this reporter's presentation of the reality of US bombing in Vietnam.

Lichti, Elda. Letter to the Editor. *Menn* 90 (June 24, 1975), 406-407. Defends the Christian and Missionary Alliance which had come under editorial fire (May 20, 1975) for identification with the American war effort in Vietnam. Criticizes Mennonites for being more concerned about opposition to war than about making disciples.

Lind, Loren. "A Time to March." *YCC* 47 (Jan. 23, 1966), 6. A description of participating in the march on Washington for Peace in Vietnam.

Lind, Loren. "Mennonites' Neutrality Recognized by Viet Cong." *CanMenn* 16 (Mar. 12, 1968), 1, 8. Betty Tiessen, who was in Vietnam during the Tet offensive, declares that Mennonite workers escaped harm because they tried not to be identified with US policy.

Lind, Loren. "Notes on the War." *YCC* 47 (Oct. 2, 1966), 9. Variety of notes and questions describing the Vietnam War.

Lind, Loren. "On Giving Aid to the Enemy." *YCC* 48 (May 7, 1967), 12. With a sense of responsibility, some people responded to the suffering on the "enemy" side with material aid during the Vietnam War.

Lind, Loren. "They Too Are Human." *YCC* 48 (Apr. 2, 1967), 12. Even the obvious acknowledgement that the Vietnamese are human does little to wear down the support for the Vietnam War.

Lind, Loren. "Toward Occupation." *YCC* 48 (Nov. 5, 1967), 10. A look at current strategies in the Vietnam War which include occupying the south while sealing off the north.

Lind, Loren. "What Should We Do?" *YCC* 47 (July 3, 1966), 8. Survey of protest responses to the

Vietnam War. What should Mennonites do to express their peace witness?

Linscheid, Ruth. "THe MCC in South Vietnam." Student paper for Anabaptist-Mennonite Seminar, May, 1967. Pp. 33. MLA/BeC.

Lohrentz, Vernon. Letter to the Editor. *Menn* 89 (Feb. 26, 1974), 150. The deceit and cover-up of US policies in Vietnam may have led to those practices in Watergate.

Longacre, Paul. "No Peace for the Vietnamese." *MBH* 12 (Apr. 6, 1973), 32; "Peace Not Yet at Hand for Vietnamese." *Menn* 88 (Apr. 3, 1973), 225. MCC representative visiting Vietnam after the ceasefire reports on the continuing struggle for control of contested areas and the likely continued military activity after the reduction of US forces.

Longacre, Paul. "Vietnam: The Church's Dilemma." *GH* 60 (Oct. 17, 1967), 939-40. MCC workers in Vietnam are not really free to speak out against the war; the church at home must do it for them.

Luce, Don. "Religious Resisters, Deserters Become Slaves of the Battlefield." *CanMenn* 18 (July 31, 1970), 4. Vivid description of inhumane treatment of those South Vietnam soldiers who resist or desert.

"MCC Opens Contacts with North Vietnam." *EV* 87 (Feb. 25, 1974), 16. Atlee Beechy, a member of the MCC executive committee returning from a visit to North Vietnam, reports that although MCC personnel will not be able to accompany material aid into North Vietnam, there is still possibility for a Christian peace witness there.

"MCC Plans for 1978." *EV* 91 (Mar. 10, 1978), 5. MCC's annual meeting held in Kitchener, Ont., included in its agenda discussion on MCC's response to need in Vietnam.

"MCC to Send Aid to Vietnam." *RepConsS* 33 (Feb., 1976), 3. In annual meeting, MCC approves million-dollar shipment of material aid and reconstruction supplies to Vietnam.

"MCC Workers Remain in Quang Ngai." *EV* 88 (Apr. 25, 1975), 15. Four of the MCC Vietnam volunteers have chosen to stay in Quang Ngai, which is being held by the Provisional Revolutionary Government.

"'Meals of Reconciliation' at Bethel College." *CanMenn* 15 (Nov. 7, 1967), 1, 11. The BC Peace Club conducted a week of frugal meals, and sent the money saved for relief in North and South Vietnam. The purpose of the meals was: to identify with war sufferers; to search for new methods of peace witness; repentance for

personal involvement in situations making for war; and commitment and rededication to search for a peaceful world.

"Mennonite Congregations Urged to Aid Vietnam Victims." *Fellowship* 34 (Jan., 1968), 16. The General Conference of the Mennonite Church (MC) has urged its congregations to send aid to war victims in North Vietnam, to study carefully the issues of the war, and to boycott companies manufacturing weapons.

"Minneapolis Consultation on Faithfulness to Christ in Situations of International Conflict." *GH* 60 (Jan. 17, 1967), 67-68. The statement is an outline for Mennonite response to Vietnam and other conflict situations. The Christian obligation to call people to repentance and reconciliation includes an obligation to witness to the state.

"Missionaries Speak Out." *GH* 65 (July 25, 1972), 597. Eastern Board missionaries send a letter to President Nixon calling attention to the horrible destruction wrought in Vietnam by American involvement, and challenging the government to halt war activities.

Martens, William. "Another Position on Vietnam in Support of USA Policy." *CanMenn* 14 (June 28, 1966), 6. Letter to the editor supporting US involvement in Vietnam.

Martin, Earl S. "A Sad Story." *GH* 68 (Jan. 28, 1975), 55-56. Story of a Vietnamese student whose family has been separated and killed in the saga of conflict in Vietnam since the 1950s.

Martin, Earl S. "Bombs Wait for Viet Farmers." *ChrLead* 36 (July 10, 1973), 4; *Menn* 88 (July 10, 1973), 431; *MennRep* 3 (July 9, 1973), 9; *GH* 66 (July 31, 1973), 589. There is a serious problem for Vietnamese refugees as they move back to the farmland which is littered with live bombs, dud artillery shells, and undetonated mines and booby traps.

Martin, Earl S. "Part of Me Died Today." *ChrLiv* 14 (Feb., 1967), 20. Poem mourning the deaths caused by American bombing in Vietnam.

Martin, Earl S. *Reaching the Other Side: The Journal of an American Who Stayed to Witness Vietnam's Postwar Transition.* New York: Crown Publishers, Inc., 1978. Pp. 281. Four Mennonite youths working for MCC in Vietnam (one Japanese and three Americans) were the only U.S. church personnel--with several individual exceptions--who deliberately stayed at the time of the exodus and collapse in 1975. In graphic descriptions and vivid photos, Earl has recorded his experiences, observations, and conversations during the transition to a new government in southern Vietnam. The book is a very personal encounter with a people at a moment of victory and defeat, written with warmth and empathy in the form of a journal. The author reflects a radically different attitude toward the Vietnamese and their crises than has been reflected by many mission and voluntary agency staff.

Martin, Earl S. "Tough Enough for Peace." *Lifework* 5 (1981), 7-9. MCC worker in Vietnam describes peacemaking work as requiring as much, if not more, strength and courage than military work.

Martin, Earl S. "Vietnam—Mennonite Testimony for Peace." *MBH* 15 (Mar. 19, 1976), 11. Mennonite aid to Vietnam, labeled an "enemy" by the US government, is a clear witness for peace and reconciliation.

Martin, Earl S. "Who Speaks for Indochina?" *ChrLiv* 17 (Sept., 1970), 18-19, 35-37. Relates personal experiences from work with Vietnamese refugees, and pleads for an end to the war.

Martin, Earl S. and Martin, Patricia Hostetter. "A Letter to Americans on Vietnam." *The Other Side* 15 (Mar., 1979), 27-36. A discussion about the debate between those calling for reconciliation and those calling for human rights in the new Vietnam.

Martin, Earl S. and Martin, Patricia Hostetter. "Interview: A Family's Account of Revolution and the Church in Post War Vietnam." *Sojourners* 5 (Jan., 1976), 29. Evaluation of the Revolution in Vietnam both before and after the change of government. Predicts that the church will grow smaller as government does a better job meeting the physical needs of the people.

Martin, Earl S. and Martin, Patricia Hostetter. "Who Are You Kidding, Brother?" *GH* 62 (Oct. 28, 1969), 938. Community development workers with Vietnam Christian Service reflect on giving aid to the Vietnamese when they resent the American military and economic presence.

Martin, Luke S. "A New Era for the Mennonite Church in Vietnam." *GH* 68 (Oct. 14, 1975), 729-31. It was probably a mistake for almost all the evangelical missionaries to leave South Vietnam at the time of the change in government, because it confirmed Protestant ties to the US, and it communicated a lack of support to the Vietnamese people in reconstruction following the war.

Martin, Luke S. "How Does One Serve and Witness in a Marxist Society?" *Menn* 93 (Sept. 19, 1978), 536. Outlines new challenges for the evangelical church in Vietnam during post-war years under a communist government.

Martin, Luke S. "Implications of the Vietnam Experience for World Mission." *Mission-Focus* 6 (Nov., 1977), 9-15. Deals with the implications of the Vietnam experience for a North American Christian presence and witness in Asia and other parts of the world, focusing primarily on the task of communicating the gospel but also discussing service ministries.

Martin, Luke S. Letter to the Editor. *Menn* 90 (Feb. 4, 1975), 75. MCC director in Vietnam reports recent events there: upsurge in fighting; public opposition to the policies and corruption of the South Vietnamese government; popular call for peace.

Martin, Luke S. "The War and Our Witness." *GH* 66 (July 3, 1973), 536; "The Gospel—Down But Not Out." *Menn* 88 (July 10, 1973), 430; "What the War Has Done to the Faith Witness." *MennRep* 3 (July 9, 1973), 5; "Vietnam War Makes Witness Hard." *MBH* 12 (Nov. 2, 1973), 14; "What War Has Done to Our Witness." *ChrLead* 36 (July 10, 1973), 4. Former missionary in Vietnam says that Christianity's entanglement with political and military power in that country has damaged the Christian witness, but the gospel must continue to be presented there in spite of past mistakes.

Martin, Luke S. "Vietnam Undergoing a Revolution." *Menn* 93 (Sept. 12, 1978), 520. Describes political changes in post-war Vietnam under communist government.

Martin, Patricia Hostetter. "Sometimes Family Has to Go." *ChrLiv* 22 (Aug., 1975), 4-7. As the Vietnam war progresses, MCC volunteers Earl and Pat Martin decide to separate as a family.

Mast Burnett, Kristina. "Canada-US Relations, Vietnam, Issues at Reedley Meetings." *GH* 72 (Feb. 13, 1979), 128. MCC's annual meeting in Reedley, Jan. 25-27, addressed such issues as Canada-US relations, aid to Vietnam, justice and human rights overseas, Native American outreach, hunger concerns, and militarism.

Matsuo, Hilda. "Can We Handle All Those Boat People?" *MennMirror* 9 (Sept., 1979), 10. The writer looks at the varying attitudes of Canadians towards Indochinese refugees and points out what two MCC employees have advised—that Canadians should act as peacemakers rather than continuing the more popular route of polarizing the situation in Southeast Asia.

Mennonite Central Committee. "A Letter to the President." *GH* 58 (June 29, 1965), 567. The text of a letter sent to President Johnson. MCC describes relief work in Vietnam and calls the president to an escalation of compassion rather than an escalation of conflict.

Mennonite Central Committee. "MCC Peace Commissioner Visits India and Vietnam," *GH* 53 (May 17, 1960), 449. A report on the churches in these countries and their successes and problems.

Mennonite Central Committee. "MCC Presents Vietnam Letter," *GH* 60 (Nov. 21, 1967), 1069-70. The letter, presented to President Johnson, questions US activities in Vietnam.

Mennonite Central Committee. "Telegram Commends President's Efforts," *GH* 61 (Apr. 23, 1968), 375-76. A telegram commending President Johnson for stopping the bombing of North Vietnam.

Mennonite Central Committee. "Vietnam Study: Relief Often Tied to Politics, Military." *MennRep* 2 (Oct. 2, 1972), 1. Relief agencies enjoy the benevolences of a government because the latter recognizes a potential in the former to realize its political and military ends.

Mennonite Central Committee. "White House Hears Mennonite Concern on War." *Menn* 82 (Nov. 21, 1967), 704-705. MCC message to the president deplores the present US policy in Vietnam and calls for a radical reversal of military policy.

Mennonite Central Committee News Service. "Church Still Active in Vietnam." *ChrLead* 38 (Sept. 30, 1975), 18. Earl Martin, MCC volunteer returning from Vietnam, reports that there are signs of hope amid the upheaval for the church in Vietnam.

Mennonite Central Committee News Service. "Dateline: Veintiane, Laos-Vietnam Delegation Receives Aid Report." *EV* 89 (Feb. 25, 1976), 10, 11. The aid that MCC gives to Vietnam is an important contribution in healing the wounds of war and demonstrating the desire to reconcile and share resources despite the US policy of continuing hostility.

Mennonite Central Committee News Service. "Mennonites Report No Bloodbath in Vietnam." *ChrLead* 38 (July 8, 1975), 14. Letters from Mennonite Central Committee workers indicate no apparent slaughter took place when the Provisional Revolutionary Government took control of Saigon.

Mennonite Church General Conference. "Letter to the President." *GH* 62 (Oct. 7, 1969), 870. Reprints letter from the Mennonite General Conference to Richard Nixon, expressing concern over the Vietnam war, requesting discontinued conscription as well as amnesty for draft dodgers, and urging the president to set human need as the national priority. Includes reply from Nixon.

Mennonite General Conference. "General Conference Sends Letter to the President." *GH* 60 (Sept. 5, 1967), 807-808; "Turn Back from Vietnam." *Menn* 82 (Sept. 12, 1967), 546. General Conference (MC) pleads with President Johnson to "turn back from the immoral course on which the nation is now embarked in Vietnam."

Mennonite General Conference. "The Church Speaks." *GH* 59 (Jan. 25, 1966), 75-76. A series of statements adopted by various Mennonite conferences regarding the war in Vietnam. The US must reverse the trend of events in Vietnam and the church must seek to find its responsibility in Vietnam.

Metzger, Dennis. "Letters from Vietnam." *With* 4 (July, 1971), 23. A volunteer working with Vietnam Christian Service describes the nature of his work in Vietnam.

Metzler, Edgar. "Still More Lessons from Indochina." *ChrLiv* 22 (Aug., 1975), 15, 26. Review of Laotian politics and American intervention there.

Metzler, Edgar. "Why I Oppose the War in Vietnam." *GH* 60 (Jan. 17, 1969), 62-63. Metzler outlines four reasons for opposing the war, including the fact that he is concerned about the cause of missions in Asia which is being harmed by this war.

Metzler, Edgar (Review). *The Politics of Escalation in Vietnam,* by Franz Schurmann, Peter Dale Scott, and Reginald Zelnik. Beacon Press, 1966. Pp. 160. *ChrLiv* 14 (Aug., 1967), 35. The author's thesis is that the US government desires military victory, not political settlement in Vietnam.

Metzler, Everett G. *et al.* "Letter to American Christians." *Menn* 83 (Jan. 30, 1968), 71-72. Christianity must be distinguished from our national (military) purposes; a change of heart and a change of policy and tactics is called for in Vietnam.

Metzler, James E. *From Saigon to Shalom* (The Pilgrimage of a Missionary in Search of a More Authentic Mission). IMS Missionary Studies No. 11. Scottdale: Herald Press, 1985. The author reflects on his experience in Vietnam (1962-70) as an American church worker during the U.S. involvement in the Vietnam civil war. He probes the liability of citizenship in such situations, calling on missions and relief agencies to recognize the impact of their associations with national interests and war efforts. These reflections serve as a case study for the need for a new approach in missions based on the biblical concept of shalom. Focusing on Jesus' blueprint for missions in Luke 10, the book shows how the shalom of

God's rule offers stirring yet realistic hope in a broken and confused world.

Metzler, James E. "Is It Nothing to You . . . Who Pass By?" *GH* 65 (Jan. 11, 1972), 38-39. Urges Mennonites to put forth gestures of acceptance toward and cooperation with North Vietnam, in order to become more involved in easing the suffering of the people caused by the protracted war.

Metzler, James E. "Meditation at the Morgue." *ChrLiv* 13 (Jan., 1966), 3. Mennonite missionary in Saigon meditates on war and the war dead.

Metzler, James E. "Missions and Communism in Asia." *GH* 69 (Feb. 10, 1976), 100-101. Urges Mennonites to carefully evaluate the effect of "missions-by-proxy" carried on through radio broadcasts into communist countries. Maintains evangelical missionaries lost the confidence of the Vietnamese people when they evacuated Vietnam with the rest of the Americans.

Metzler, James R.[*sic.*, E.] "This Is War!" *GH* 59 (June 14, 1966), 526-27. Describes war's horror, illusion, propaganda, and selfishness; we must represent the concern of Christ in our involvement in the Vietnam war and renounce our attitude of isolation.

Metzler, James E. "Vietnam, American Tragedy." *GH* 60 (May 2, 1967), 393. The identification of Christianity with Americanism (i.e., western ideologies, colonialism, war, anti-communism, white racism) has alienated much of the nonwestern world from the Christian message. Vietnam is our symbol of failure and a call to repentance.

Metzler, James E. "Vietnam: I Wouldn't Do It Again." *Mission-Focus* 6 (Nov., 1977), 1-3; *GH* 70 (Dec. 13, 1977), 930-32. Because of his association with the political-military machine and American religiosity, the writer states that he would never again serve in an American organization in an area like Vietnam where the United States is involved. He raises critical issues, such as: how mission work aided the South, prolonging war and suffering; how the Mennonite Church in Vietnam did not distinguish itself from other Protestant groups through its peace witness.

Meyers, Willie "Why I Left Vietnam." *ChrLiv* 15 (Aug., 1968), 6-7. International Voluntary Service worker left Vietnam in order to disassociate himself from the American military presence there.

Miller, Bernice and Berdella. "Justice Shall Roll Down." *Builder* 15 (July, 1965), 10-13. A choral reading arranged from a sermon by Carl Beck

that relates the message of Amos to the situation in war-torn Asia.

Miller, Korla, and Zuercher, Melanie. "Prepared?" *Lifework* 5 (1981), 12-13. Reprinted from *Goshen College Record*. Vietnam veteran turned pacifist and Mennonite describes the turning point in his life and his current peace activities.

Miller, Melissa and Shenk, Phil M. *The Path of Most Resistance*. Scottdale: Herald Press, 1982. Pp. 239. Accounts of ten young people who, during the turbulent Vietnam years, resisted cooperating with the draft. The stories relate not only the conflict with the government concerning these illegal actions, but also the conflicts in the church as the generations struggled to understand the demands of faithfulness for their concrete situations.

Miller, Robert W. "Reflections on Vietnam." *GH* 64 (Oct. 19, 1971), 867-68. Director of Vietnam Christian Service for three years describes the death and corruption caused largely by the involvement of the US government. Focuses especially on the plight of refugees.

Miller, Robert W. "What Is MCC Doing in Vietnam?" *ChrLead* 36 (July 10, 1973), 6; *MBH* 12 (Aug. 24, 1973), 17; "What Is Mennonite Central Committee Doing in Vietnam?" *GH* 66 (July 3, 1973), 538; *MennRep* 3 (July 9, 1973), 9.. From 1966-72, MCC was part of Vietnam Christian Service (VNCS), a joint effort of Church World Service, Lutheran World Relief, and MCC, but since Jan., 1973, MCC has been operating its own programs in cooperation with the national church and VNCS. These programs are described in this article.

Miller, Robert W. and Hutchison, Frank L. "The Vietnam Refugee Program: A Report." [Akron, Pa.: MCC, 1965.] Pp. [22.] MHL.

Naylor, Phyllis Reynolds. "To Continue Was to Condone." *With* 2 (Feb., 1969), 16. Discusses the resignation of Gene Stoltzfus from International Voluntary Service in Vietnam because he could no longer associate himself with American war policies.

Neufeld, David. "Attitude Toward Vietnam: As Found in *Christianity Today*." Paper for War, Peace, and Revolution class, AMBS, Elkhart, Ind., Apr. 4, 1969. Pp. 3. AMBS.

Neufeld, David. "On Leaving Vietnam." *GH* 61 (Apr. 23, 1968), 371. Reflects on his work with leprosy patients within a setting of war.

Neufeld, David (Review). *Reaching the Other Side*, by Earl S. Martin. New York: Crown Publishers, Inc., 1978. Pp. 282. *MennRep* 9 (Sept. 17, 1979), 8. A journal written by an American working for MCC in Vietnam depicting the situation and people of Vietnam during the post-war transition.

Neufeld, Roger C. Letter to the Editor. *ChrLead* 36 (Apr. 3, 1973), 13. People who have applied for the conscientious objector classification should not have to feel any guilt for the Vietnam war.

Nofziger, Ralph. Letter to the Editor. *ChrLiv* 17 (Nov., 1970), 35. Questions Earl Martin's ("Who Speaks for Indochina?," Sept., 1970) portrayal of the US as the aggressor, with no attention given to the activities of the other side.

Omura, Isamu. "A Letter from Japanese Christians Concerning Vietnam." *CanMenn* 13 (Sept. 14, 1965), 6. The letter serves as an introduction of a peace mission to American Christians, focusing on the folly of military involvement on the part of the USA in Vietnam.

Oswald, Joseph. Letter to the Editor. *GH* 63 (July 14, 1970), 610. While opposing the war in Southeast Asia, the writer calls attention to the militant student spirit at Kent State which necessitated calling in the National Guards.

"Peace in Vietnam Calls for Escalation of Compassion, Not of Conflict and War." *CanMenn* 13 (June 8, 1965), 1. Text of a letter from the MCC Executive Committee to President Lyndon B. Johnson urging him to escalate compassion in Vietnam rather than conflict.

"Presbyterians Reject War Criticism." *GH* 65 (Aug. 29, 1972), 678. Refusal of Presbyterians "to approve a plea for national repentance over the killing in Indochina and to condemn racist, inhuman acts against poor, nonwhite people in Southeast Asia.

"Protest Simmers in Vietnam." *Forum* 8 (Dec., 1974), 3. MCC volunteers in Vietnam report that political movements are mushrooming and there is dissatisfaction with the leadership of Nguyen Nan Thieu and his government's corruption.

Pasemand, Lloyd. "Double Standard!" *GH* 61 (Mar. 12, 1968), 230. Reprinted from the *Eugene Register-Guard* (Eugene, Ore.). Discusses a former military photographer's experiences of being ordered to photograph the Vietcong atrocities and ignore American ones.

Peachey, J. Lorne. "Aid to the 'Enemy'?" *ChrLiv* 14 (Dec., 1967), 11. MCC workers in Vietnam face the dilemma of trying to remain neutral in a country at war.

Peachey, J. Lorne. "Atrocities—1966 Style." *ChrLiv* 13 (June, 1966), 11, 37. Reprinting of a press release from the Council of the Society for the

Psychological Study of Social Issues condemning American torture of prisoners of war in Vietnam.

Peachey, J. Lorne. "For the Good of the People." *ChrLiv* 15 (Feb., 1968), 11, 32. Report of a Pentagon briefing with 45 editors of religious magazines attempting to gain access to facts about Vietnam.

Peachey, J. Lorne. "To Heal the Scars of War." *ChrLiv* 15 (June, 1968), 11. Activities of Vietnam Christian Service volunteers in Southeast Asia.

Peachey, J. Lorne. "'We Burned Every Hut.'" *ChrLiv* 14 (Sept., 1967), 11. Letter from GI in Vietnam detailing atrocities committed by American army.

Peachey, Paul L. "Interreligious Conference on Peace." *ChrCent* 83 (Apr. 13, 1966), 476-78. Author reflects on the interfaith dialogue at the conference on such issues as US military involvement in Vietnam, and a model for religious peace witness to a pluralistic society in which the religious community's primary role is to produce a moral climate in society conducive to peacemaking.

Peachey, Paul L. "The Christian Peace Conference and the Czech Crisis." *GH* 61 (Dec. 31, 1968), 1147-48; *CanMenn* 16 (Dec. 31, 1968), 5. Describes the process followed by the ecumenical Christian Peace Conference in responding to the Soviet movement into Czechoslovakia. Asserts that the same "demons of war and hate" are behind the Soviet action and American military activities in Vietnam.

Peachey, Urbane. "Human Rights in South Korea." *Peace Section Newsletter* 8 (June, 1977), 4-5. Examines the involvement of the many American Christian enterprises in South Korea. Notes that there seems to be a contradiction between the presence of so many Christians and the very repressive environment.

Pertusio, Carolyn E. "For One Vietnamese Refugee, It's Been a Journey from Despair to Hope." *EV* 92 (Dec. 10, 1979), 9-10. Report describing the helpless, homesick, and hopeful feelings which are all part of one man's experience in resettling in America after escaping from Vietnam by boat.

Preheim, Gayle O. "Letter from Vietnam." *RepConsS* 25 (Feb., 1968), 3, 4. In a letter to his parents, an alternative service worker in Vietnam reflects upon his work and the war with which he lives.

Preheim, Gayle O. "South Vietnam's Highlanders: An Oppressed People." Paper presented to Church and Race and Cultural Anthropology classes, AMBS, Elkhart, Ind., spring, 1971. Pp. 80. AMBS.

Presley, Michael. "The New MX Missile System." *GH* 72 (July 17, 1979), 567. A personal statement supporting Senator McGovern's statements against the missile system, the Vietnam war, and the increased defense spending.

"Reconciliation in North America and Vietnam." *Forum* 8 (Jan., 1975), 4-6. An interview with Max Ediger, assistant director of MCC programs in Vietnam, focusing on his work in Vietnam and his perceptions of his mediator role in Vietnam and now in North America.

"Resign Vietnam Service Posts to Protest War." *CanMenn* 15 (Sept. 26, 1967), 1. Increased suffering on the part of the Vietnamese and the self-interest of the USA in the area are reasons given for resignation from relief agency.

"Rockway Students Fast for War Sufferers Relief." *CanMenn* 14 (Jan. 4, 1966), 1, 16. During the week of Dec. 13-17 about thirty-five students of Rockway Mennonite School fasted for the innocent sufferers of Vietnam. The students gave up their noon lunches and gave the equivalent value of the food to a relief fund for Vietnam. During the lunch periods when they did not eat, they informed themselves on the war.

(Review). *Home from the War*, by Robert J. Lifton. Simon and Schuster, 1973. Pp. 478. *IPF Notes* 20 (Oct. 18, 1973), 4. Reprinted from *Provident Book Finder* (Sept., 1973). Reviewer notes that the book documents the psychological journey of Vietnam veterans, especially members of Vietnam Veterans Against the War.

(Review). *Vietnam: Who Cares?*, by Atlee and Winifred Beechy. Scottdale: Herald Press, 1968. Pp. 154. *Fellowship* 36 (May, 1970), 27. Brief summary of the book which is a compilation of the reports from six months of working with the Church World Service's relief and refugee service program in Vietnam. Recommended for its detail, excellent historical outline, and bibliography.

Redekop, John H. "Indochina." *MBH* 14 (Apr. 18, 1975), 10. In light of the worsening military situation and the massive American military aid, western churches ought to increase humanitarian aid.

Redekop, John H. "Peace with Honour." *MBH* 12 (Feb. 9, 1973), 10. Although an imminent Vietnam truce has been announced, several disquieting aspects remain: the millions of refugees, orphans, cripples, etc.; the possibility of continued guerilla warfare; and the threat of communism and east-west distrust.

Redekop, John H. "Refugees." *MBH* 14 (May 20, 1975), 8. Love for neighbor means receiving Vietnam refugees with concern, not self-interested excuses.

Redekop, John H. "Vietnam, 1976." *MBH* 15 (Mar. 5, 1976), 12. Calls peace-preaching Christians to give massive economic aid for the destruction caused by US bombing.

Regehr, Rudy A. "Director Feels Most Mennonites Do Not Hold to Position on Peace." *CanMenn* 15 (Mar. 28, 1967), 1, 7. Charleswood Mennonite Church presented a peace brief to Harry B. Williams, director of the Billy Graham Crusade in Winnipeg which expressed concern for Graham's stand on the Vietnam war. Williams said he felt most Mennonites would not agree with the brief.

Reichart, Elmer C. Letter to the Editor. *Menn* 88 (Sept. 4, 1973), 502-503. Response to the TV documentary, "The Sins of Our Fathers," which depicted US soldiers in Vietnam deserting their offspring and the children's mothers. The writer pleads for the blame to be placed with the US military, which drafted the young men, taught them to kill, and separated them from their loved ones by sending them overseas.

Reimer, Margaret Loewen. "Vietnam: Did Mennonites Belong There?" *MennRep* 8 (Jan. 23, 1978), 6. Summarizes James E. Metzler's critique of Mennonite missions and witness in Vietnam presented in Dec. 13, 1977 issue of *Gospel Herald*.

Reimer, Vic. "MCC (US) Promoting Refugee Sponsorship." *Menn* 94 (Oct. 2, 1979), 582. Interest by US Mennonites in sponsoring refugees from Southeast Asia is increasing.

*Remembering: Stories of Peacemakers.* See Topic 17c, World War I.

Rempel, John. "Aid Victims of War in North Vietnam." *CanMenn* 14 (Dec. 13, 1966), 20. Reports that Goshen College students collected $428 for war sufferers in North Vietnam.

Rempel, Ron. "A Time Comes When Silence Is Betrayal." *CanMenn* 16 (Feb. 20, 1968), 1. A participant's reflections on the gathering of over 2,000 clergy and lay people concerned about Vietnam in Washington on Feb. 5 and 6.

Rinks, Riley. Letter to the Editor. *Menn* 88 (Feb. 13, 1973), 110-111. Criticizes the voices faulting Billy Graham for not speaking out against American bombing of Vietnam, since the writer believes government efforts toward a settlement of the war are being hampered by meddling and criticism from "peace" advocates.

Rosenberger, Elaine. "Viet Vet's March." *ChrLiv* 18

(Oct., 1971), 27. Poem on encountering a Vietnam veteran.

Royer, Howard E. "Life Was Good for This Boy." *GH* 64 (Oct. 12, 1971), 848-49. By permission of *Brethren Messenger*. Tribute to a 25-year-old Brethren Voluntary Service worker in Vietnam who refused to participate in war and died a victim of war.

"Setting the Record Straight on Billy Graham's War Stand." *CanMenn* 14 (June 7, 1966), 1, 2. Although Billy Graham in a Texas Crusade did *not* appeal to his listeners to support the war in Vietnam, he did contrast those who "protest sin and moral evil" by attending his meeting and the "noisy minority" which protests against the war. This distinction is either careless rhetoric or moral confusion.

"Sponsorship Rises to 2,500; Over 200 Have Arrived." *MennRep* 9 (Sept. 3, 1979), 1. MCC (Canada) reports on the Canadian Mennonite churches' response to the refugees coming from Southeast Asia.

"Students Fast, Pray, and Protest." *CanMenn* 13 (May 18, 1965), 1. Report on a fast at MBS to show concern for American bombing of North Vietnam.

Schmidt, Steven G. Letter to the Editor. *Menn* 88 (Feb. 6, 1973), 93-94. Writer mourns the American bombing of Vietnam, speaking out in order to dissassociate himself from the terrible acts.

Schmidt, Steven G. Letter to the Editor. *ChrLiv* 20 (Mar., 1973), 28. Speaks out against US military destruction in Vietnam; suggests that opposers of war refuse payment of war taxes.

Schrag, Martin H. "The Cross on a Canteen." *GH* 69 (July 20, 1976), 562. Refers to the story of an MCC worker in Vietnam meeting a Christian North Vietnamese soldier with a cross on his canteen, and concludes that Christian commitment to God precludes rule by the sword.

Schrock, Paul M. "Sheets for South Vietnam Saturday." *ChrLiv* 11 (May, 1964), 20-23. One community's effort to collect sheets for medical use in South Vietnam.

Schroeder, Richard J. "The Cutting Edge." *ChrLead* 38 (June 10, 1975), 19. The impact of Vietnam on the US will continue even though the Saigon government has surrendered to the Viet Cong.

Seitz, Blair. "Another Look at Peacemaking in Indochina." *GH* 73 (Apr. 8, 1980), 298-301. In light of the US role in the Indochina conflicts, peace churches should promote support for socialist reconstruction that has begun to take place.

Seitz, Ruth. "There Is No Way to Peace." *With* 11 (Oct., 1978), 10. The story of Earl S. Martin and his peacemaking efforts in Vietnam.

Sensenig, Donald E. "A Church and the Search for Peace." *GH* 68 (Jan. 28, 1975), 56-57; *Menn* 90 (Jan. 28, 1975), 51. While Christians in Vietnam, both Protestant and Catholic, contribute little to making peace between communism and South Vietnam, the United Buddhist Church promotes a peace campaign.

Sensenig, Donald E., and Sensenig, Doris, *et al.* "Letter from Saigon." *GH* 65 (June 20, 1972), 530-31. Mennonite missionaries and MCC workers in Vietnam send letter to President Nixon describing the hopelessness of the US involvement and appealing for cessation of hostile action by all US military forces.

Shank, David A. Letter to the Editor. *Mission-Focus* 6 (May, 1978), 13-15. Reflecting on the suffering servant role discussed in the Vietnam issue of *Mission-Focus* 6 (Nov., 1977), the reader states that missions need to live out loyalty to Christ and opposition to those things at "home" which work against the good of people abroad.

Shank, Duane. "Pardons for Some." *RepConsS* 32 [*sic,* 33] (May, 1976), 1, 3. Discusses the Democratic Party plank favoring pardons for those whose conscientious objection to the Vietnam War resulted in Selective Service violations.

Shank, Duane (Editorial). "The Convention and the Campaign." *RepConsS* 32 [*sic,* 33] (June, 1976), 2. Despite the publicity given amnesty at the Democratic National Convention, the rhetoric of the presidential campaign tends toward treating the Vietnam War as a mistake rather than a crime against humanity.

Shank, J. Ward. "Aftermath of the Vietnam War." *ST* 48 (Jan., 1980), 6-7. Comment on and questions about the American military involvement in Vietnam.

Shank, J. Ward. "Collective Guilt." *ST* 36 (Sept., 1968), 10. Examination of corporate sin and collective guilt as they pertain to situations like the death of Martin Luther King and the Vietnam War.

Shank, J. Ward. "Fighting the Vietnam War." *ST* 40 (Mar., 1972), 8. The conviction of Christians against participation in all war, like the Vietnam war, should be clearly given, but let it be in terms of personal commitment to Christ and of influence exerted on a nonpartisan level.

Shank, J. Ward. "This Immoral War." *ST* 35

(June, 1967), 2. Instead of being overly concerned about the national justification for the Vietnam War (the question of its morality or immorality), the nonresistant Christian should proceed upon his or her basic principle that all war is immoral in the sense of spiritual reality.

Shank, J. Ward (Editorial). "On Vietnam." *ST* 34 (1st Qtr., 1966), 1. We should seriously question the obligation, or even the competency, of the church, as such, to pronounce upon matters like the Vietnam War and international policy. We should pursue avenues of relief and service as opportunities to relieve the sufferings of war.

Sheley, Griselda. "Mennonite Farmer Sees Progress in Vietnam." *MBH* 17 (June 23, 1978), 14. Mennonite wheat farmer who helped present a shipment of wheat to the Vietnamese people saw the trip as one step toward peacemaking between the US and Vietnam.

Shelly, Maynard. "Church Bell and Shuffling Feet Rattle Chains of Chauvinism." *CanMenn* 17 (Oct. 31, 1969), 1, 2. Bethel College students and faculty protest the continuation of the Vietnam War. In addition to a 4-day vigil and a march through the streets of Newton, KS, 11 ministers published a letter in the local paper calling on fellow Christians to join in a renewed effort to live as peacemakers.

Shelly, Maynard. "Finding the Boat in History's Mainstream." *GH* 62 (Jan. 7, 1969), 13-15. Reflects on papers about the historic peace church role in peacemaking, discussed at the recent Conference of Historic Peace Churches. Reports at length on John H. Yoder's presentation, which highlighted the failure of the peace churches to take leadership in facing the problems of race relations and the Vietnam war.

Shelly, Maynard. "Prague Discusses Involvement in the Long Fight for Peace." *CanMenn* 16, Part 1, (Apr. 16, 1968), 1, 2. Reports on the Christian Peace Conference held in Prague. Issues of war and peace were discussed (especially Vietnam)but the issue of the tension between the rich nations and the poor nations was also given serious attention. The conference motto was "Save man—peace is possible."

Shelly, Maynard. "Vietnamese Ask Church Help in Peace Drive." *Menn* 86 (Mar. 16, 1971), 172, 173. Buddhists from Vietnam and Mennonites in the USA correspond and encourage each other to make every effort for peace in Vietnam count.

Shenk, Stanley C. "It Has Been Ten Years." *GH* 65 (May 30, 1972), 478-79. On the ten-year anniversary of MCC Paxman Daniel Gerber's capture in Vietnam, the author reflects on Dan's witness, the home life which prepared him for difficult experiences, and the message he might have about American involvement in Southeast Asia if he did return.

Sherk, J. Harold. "Viet-nam War Protesters." *RepConsS* 24 (Nov., 1967), 1. Reports on various forms of protest against the war including a letter to President Johnson from Gene Stoltzfus and other International Voluntary Service workers in Vietnam.

Shetler, Sanford G. "Comment on Calley Case." *GfT* 6 (May-June, 1971), 17. Lieutenant Calley's massacre of civilians was a brutal act, but it was only an extension of war which, while never honorable, can still be an instrument of divine judgment.

Shetler, Sanford G., ed. "Mennonite Peace Mission to Hanoi." *GfT* 6 (Jan.-Feb., 1971), 7. The delegation of Mennonite students visiting Hanoi and Saigon is doomed to failure, since such missions have not been successful in other wars, and since peace will not come without change in human hearts.

Shetler, Sanford G. "Pacifism and the Vietnam War." *GfT* 6 (Sept.-Oct., 1971), 14, 18, 13. War is evil yet inevitable, and those who profess to follow Christ should not participate in it.

Shetler, Sanford G. "Pacifism and the War in Vietnam." *GfT* Series I, No. 5 (May, 1967), 1-8. Truly biblical objectors to war and evil should refrain from participating in activities that complicate a peace witness, such as the popular anti-Vietnam war protests.

Showalter, Stuart W. "Coverage of Conscientious Objectors to the Vietnam War: An Analysis of the Editorial Content of American Magazines, 1964-1972." PhD dissertation, Univ. of Texas at Austin, 1975. Pp. 163. MSHL. Study finds that the nation's most widely read and respected popular magazines took seriously their responsibility to defend individual rights because they portrayed COs, certainly an ideological minority during the Vietnam War, positively most of the time.

Showalter, Stuart W. "Six Opinion Magazines' Coverage of Conscientious Objectors to the Vietnam War." Paper presented to the Association for Education in Journalism, San Diego State University. Aug. 18-21, 1974. Pp. 22. MHL.

Siebert, Allan J. "Response to Refugees Criticized as 'Cautious and Restrained'." *MennRep* 9 (Dec. 10, 1979), 1, 3. MCC (Canada) refugee assistance program has encountered criticism in recent weeks over its limited response to the refugee crisis in Southeast Asia.

Smedes, Lewis B. "Dissent and Disruption." *GH* 61 (Apr. 16, 1968), 337. Reprinted from *The Reformed Journal.* Affirms the right to protest unjust American policies in the Vietnam war, but denounces protesters who refuse to respect another's opinion.

Smedes, Lewis B. "Who Will Answer?" *Menn* 88 (Jan. 9, 1973), 32. Calls for evangelist Billy Graham, who "has the heart of evangelical middle America in his hands" to speak out on the moral and spiritual issues involved in the massive bombing of Vietnam.

Smith, Kelly. "Home Is a Sidewalk." *ChrLiv* 15 (Apr., 1968), 20-21. From the Associated Press. Families uprooted and separated by war live on the streets in Saigon, Vietnam.

Snyder, William T. "Conflict in Asia." *GH* 61 (Aug. 20, 1968), 757. Our mission in conflict-ridden Vietnam must be to help the Vietnmese accomplish the goals they have established for themselves.

Snyder, William T. and Beechy, Atlee. "A Message from Vietnam Lists Needs." *GH* 61 (Mar. 12, 1968), 236. After a recent visit to Vietnam, these two men call nonresistant Christians to speak and live the reconciling word with renewed clarity and urgency.

Sprunger, Joseph. "'What's It Like to Live in Vietnam?' . . . Some Reflections." *Forum* (Mar., 1972), 4. A former MCC worker reflects on his experiences in Vietnam, the physical, cultural, and sociological destruction of the war, and his growing appreciation of the Vietnamese people.

Sprunger, Keith L. "Learning the Wrong Lessons." *MennLife* 23 (Apr., 1968), 64-68. An analysis of the psychology and history leading to Vietnam in an attempt to find a clearer understanding of revolution in our world.

Stauffer, James K. "Vietnam Churches Struggle with New Trials." *Menn* 93 (Sept. 19, 1978), 537; *MennRep* 8 (Sept. 18, 1978), 7. Describes freedoms and limitations of the evangelical church in Vietnam since the change in government. Reflects on the church's previous sanctioning of American military policies and its present compromise of church and state separation by allowing some pastors to work on local government committees.

Stauffer, James K. "War Taxes Questioned." *GH* 63 (June 2, 1970), 505. Death and destruction of the innocent in Vietnam raises the question of whether Christians should pay the taxes supporting this war.

Stauffer, James K. *et al.* "Letter from Vietnam to American Christians." *GH* 61 (Jan. 16, 1968), 65-66. American Christians' participation in the Vietnam War will result in many nations and people rejecting God's call. There must be repentance and a change of heart.

Stoltzfus, Gene. Letter to the Editor. *MennRep* 9 (Aug. 6, 1979), 6. A warning to the churches to look beyond the stories of the refugees to try to determine the realities in Indochina and make some meaning out of this chapter of history.

Stoltzfus, Gene. "Report from Southeast Asia: Economic Questions Dominate in Vietnam." Part 3. *MennRep* 9 (Nov. 26, 1979), 7. Because the economic situation in Vietnam is prompting many to leave the country, the normalization of US-Vietnam government and trade relations would be most helpful.

Stoltzfus, Gene. "Report from Southeast Asia: From a CIA Jungle to Mennoland." Part 4. *MennRep* 9 (Dec. 10, 1979), 7. The movement of refugees from Laos raises a number of spiritual and ethical issues for Christians which this writer attempts to address.

Stoltzfus, Gene. "Report from Southeast Asia: Will Kampuchea Survive?" Part 1. *MennRep* 9 (Oct. 15, 1979), 7. A report on the war and social upheaval in Kampuchea, emphasizing the need for food.

Stoltzfus, Gene. "Vietnam: Everyone's Tragedy." *GH* 60 (Oct. 17, 1967), 937-38. It is time to make clear to the world and to fellow Americans our condemnation of the Vietnam war.

Stoltzfus, Gene. "Vietnam Revisited." *Post-American* 4 (Apr., 1975), 18. Description of a visit to Vietnam which showed that the war was still going on with political prisoners and conditional relationships with countries like the United States.

Stoltzfus, Gene. "What the War Is Doing to the Vietnamese People." *GH* 61 (Feb. 20, 1968), 153-54; *CanMenn* 16 (Feb. 6, 1968), 1, 5. Identifies five levels of traditional Vietnamese society: people who are educated (monks, teachers, ruling people)—many of whom are going abroad because they have no future in Vietnam; farmers—instability in rural areas means not enough rice even for the people of Vietnam; laborers—composed of refugees; businesspeople—many have made poor investments in hotels and living quarters for foreigners; soldiers. As a result of the war, the Vietnamese society has been tipped upside down with the soldiers on top and the educated on the bottom.

Stoltzfus, Gene and [Janzen], Lois Barrett. "Vietnam Revisited." *Post-American* 4 (Apr., 1975), 18-23. Documents the harrassment and torture inflicted on opponents of the corrupt

Thieu regime in South Vietnam who are not pro-Communist.

Stoltzfus, Gene and Friesen, Dorothy. "Working for Human Rights." *Peace Section Newsletter* 8 (June, 1977), 1-3. Biblical words on justice are firm and consistent throughout the Old and New Testament. People who work for justice are sometimes the object of much criticism. Lists common objections voiced during the Vietnam era that continue to surface.

Stoltzfus, J. Letter to the Editor. *GH* 66 (Feb. 20, 1973), 169. Responding to the Jan. 16 editorial decrying American bombing in Vietnam, the writer attributes the editor's views to a political attempt to smear the newly re-elected president, instead of relying on the gospel of Christ to bring peace.

Stoltzfus, Victor. "Just War Theology." *RepConsS* 23 (May, 1966), 2. The surprising agreement among America's top religious leaders that American involvement in Vietnam is immoral is based on the just war doctrine that guides the thinking of 90 percent of the world's Christians on the topic of war.

Stoltzfus, Victor. "You Make Beggars, Prostitutes, and Communists." *CanMenn* 14 (Apr. 19, 1966), 7, 10. A paper presented at the Faculty Forum of the Social Science Club, Youngstown University on Mar. 25. Stoltzfus, a conscientious objector to war in any form, discusses three categories of objectors to the war in Vietnam: just war theorists; secular humanists; and military personnel who have turned against this war.

Stoltzfus, Victor (Review). *Peace in Vietnam,* report prepared for AFSC, NY: Hill and Wang, 1966. Pp. 112.. "An Eleventh Hour Appeal for Sanity." *CanMenn* 14 (May 3, 1966), 6. Summarizes the history of US involvement in Vietnam, defines "pacification attempts," and lists the steps on how the USA might disengage militarily from the area.

Stringfellow, William. "An American Tragedy." *ChrLiv* 14 (Jan., 1967), 32. The American conscience, and more importantly, the Christian church, is paralyzed by the Vietnam war.

Suderman, Dale. "One Week in Saigon." *Menn* 85 (May 12, 1970), 332. A member of the US Army in Saigon writes about facts and feelings as he and others become responsible for killing people even though he knows of a different vision of helping them.

Suderman, Elmer F. "Mennonites, Poets, and the Vietnam War." *JChSoc* V (Spring, 1969), 15. Discusses the interaction between anti-war poetry and Mennonites.

Swartz, Herbert L. (Review). *The Social Conscience of the Evangelical,* by Sherwood Eliot Wirt. New York: Harper and Row, Pub., 1968. *The Voice* 19 (Oct., 1970), 31-32. The way the author deals with the question of war, particularly the Vietnam war, is exemplary of a more general idealization of American values that aborts deep thinking about the issues.

"The Time for Negotiation Is Now." *CanMenn* 15 (Apr. 4, 1967), 1. Excerpts from a letter by Paul Longacre, associate director of VNCS, to friends stating that the US should withdraw from Vietnam.

"To the NAE Point of View." *Menn* 81 (Feb. 15, 1966), 117. A letter of appeal from the Mennonites in Canada to the National Association of Evangelicals to reconsider their support of "unjust and unchristian methods of resisting communism." This is a response to the NAE's apparent endorsement of the Vietnam war.

Thiessen, John H. "Action for Peace." *YCC* 48 (July 23, 1967), 6. Survey of Mennonite and other anti-war responses to the Vietnam War.

Thu, Bui Boanh and Nakajima, John. "Churches Active in North Vietnam According to Pastor." *MennRep* 5 (Jan. 20, 1975), 2; "Hanoi Minister Tells of Church's Vitality." *Menn* 90 (Jan. 14, 1975), 23. Reprinted from *Japan Christian Activity News.* Reflects on the life of the Protestant church in North Vietnam during 20 years of war since 1954. Conceives of the church's mission as evangelism and social service, and contribution to the country as sending young people to the front lines and growing produce.

Thuan, "Vietnam." *MBH* 14 (May 30, 1975), 4. Two poems express sadness for the war-torn desolation of a homeland.

Toews, David. "In Washington Love Was Realistic." *CanMenn* 17 (Nov. 28, 1969), 5. Notes ironically that Washington officials are dismayed by the violence of fringe groups in the March Against Death, which is hardly to be compared with the violence being done by American forces in Vietnam.

Toews, Ron. "Capital Punishment and Vietnam." *CanMenn* 14 (May 3, 1966), 5. Letter to the Editor against the abolition of capital punishment in Canada and against peace marches.

"US Missionaries in Japan Protest Vietnam Policy." *CanMenn* 15 (Nov. 7, 1967), 1, 11. Text of a letter addressed to the "Reader's Forum" of Japan's *The Mainichi Daily News* by 11 American missionaries (including Carl Beck). The letter calls for an American expression of contrition for mistakes in the past and a willingness to take greater risks in the quest for peace by negotiation in the future.

Unrau, Ruth. "How Many Heard at Bethel?" *ChrLiv* 17 (Feb., 1970), 17. Bethel College protested the war in Vietnam by reading aloud the names of all the American war dead, a reading which lasted 31 hours.

Unsigned. "Food to Aid Drought-Stricken Laos." *Intercom* 22 (Apr., 1978), 1. Describes the need for food in Laos, which suffered the fallout of the Vietnam War, as well as its own civil war.

"Vietnam: A Resource Collection of Statements, Clippings, and Other Documents." Akron, PA.: MCC Peace Section, [1968]. Pp. 7. MHL.

"Vietnam Challenges the Christian Conscience." *CanMenn* 14 (Jan. 18, 1966), 1. Mennonite leaders express their feelings about the cruelty of war.

"Vietnam Personnel Write to the President." *GH* 63 (June 2, 1970), 504. Prints a letter written by 62 American workers in Vietnam, including Mennonite missions and service workers, protesting the deployment of US troops in Cambodia and the repression of the student movement in Saigon, and calling for a political rather than military solution to the conflict.

"Vietnam Study: Relief Often Tied to Politics, Military." *MennRep* 2 (Oct. 2, 1972), 1. Relief agencies enjoy the benevolences of a government because the latter recognizes a potential in the former to realize its political and military ends.

"Vietnam Veterans Against the War." *GH* 64 (June 22, 1971), 572. 13,000 members of the veterans organization come out with their reasons for opposing US involvement in Vietnam.

"Vietnam Veterans Against the War." *GH* 65 (Apr. 4, 1972), 316. Denied a part in a Veterans' Parade in Denver, the VVAW's witness to the cruelty of war "becomes effective as they stand in silence, the majority in uniform, many with combat decorations on their jackets, hands behind their heads, which makes their presence quickly and disturbingly recognizable."

"Vietnam Voice: Go Home and Leave Us Alone." *Menn* 85 (June 9, 1970), 388-90. Why most of the fifty foreign voluntary agencies working in South Vietnam do more harm than good.

"Vietnam Workers Urge Cut in Arms Flow." *GH* 67 (July 2, 1974), 536. Reprints the text of a letter from 22 MCC and Eastern Board of Missions workers to congressional committees responsible for military funding in Vietnam.

Letter calls for drastic reductions in military hardware to Vietnam.

"Volunteer to Defuse Vietnam Bombs." *MBH* 12 (Oct. 19, 1973), 15-16. MCC volunteers will be doing exploratory work in the Vietnamese countryside to find ways to help local farmers clear their land of unexploded bombs.

Vietnam. 49 interviews. On effects of Vietnam War on Newton, KS, and area communities, including attitudes in Newton High School, Bethel College, churches, Mexican-American community, Halstead, Moundridge, Goessel, Lorraine Ave. Mennonite Church in Wichita. MLA/BeC.

Voth, Orville L. "The Scientist and War." *MennLife* 23 (Apr., 1968), 84-87. Reports growing unease in the scientific community with regard to the Vietnam War and with regard to nuclear war.

"We Encourage You to Help Our Country to Become a Messenger of Peace." *CanMenn* 14 (Feb. 8, 1966), 1, 13. Text of a letter from the Conference of Mennonites in Canada to Canada's Prime Minister urging the government to declare its opposition to the Vietnam war and to engage in steps to build up rather than destroy Vietnam.

Wald, George. "A Generation Unsure that It Has a Future." *MCC PS Wash. Memo* 1 (June, 1969), 7-9. Reprint from *Congressional Record* of an address on the Vietnam war and the threat of nuclear war.

Walters, LeRoy. "The Vietnam Situation. An Open Letter to the Brotherhood." *EV* 79 (Jan. 17, 1966), 19-20. The Christian's first loyalty is to the international community of faith. Therefore we must protest both the Vietnam War itself and recent statements by Billy Graham and President Johnson.

West, James Lee. "A Native American's Reflections on Thanksgiving." *GH* 65 (Nov. 14, 1972), 931-32, 943. Makes critical connections between the 200-year-old exploitation of the native Americans and contemporary situations in Vietnam and Central America.

Wiebe, Bernie. "Chapter on Vietnam Refuses to Close." *Menn* 94 (Aug. 7, 1979), 487. Plea for more families and congregations to become personally involved in the plight of the Vietnamese refugees.

Wiebe, Rudy H. *The Blue Mountains of China.* Grand Rapids: Eerdmans, 1970. Pp. 227. Epic novel explores the Russian Mennonite experience from several points of view, times, and places. While the themes are also multiple, the examination of the intersection of faith and survival is a compelling one as the novel asks how and what love and traditions of nonresistance *become* in such crises. The chapter entitled "The Vietnam Call of Samuel U. Reimer" is especially focused on the questions of war and peace, although these themes appear in many of the other episodes as well.

Wiebe, Rudy H. "The Vietnam Call of Samuel U. Reimer." Adapted by Frank Bueckert for readers theatre from a chapter in Wiebe's novel *The Blue Mountains of China.* Pp. 23. MHL.

Winsor, Richard J. "The Automobile: Unguided Missile." *GH* 64 (June 29, 1971), 586-88. Traffic safety is a religious concern, since there is more highway violence than in Vietnam, ghettos, or on university campuses.

Woodruff, Lance. "Vietnamese Aid in Constructing Housing." *GH* 61 (June 4, 1968), 503-504. Describes the refugee shelters under construction by Vietnam Christian Service to house refugees from Saigon rendered homeless by the Tet New Year offensive.

Yake, C. F. "Parallel Thirty-eight!" *YCC* 31 (Oct. 28, 1950), 324. The Implications of the situation in Korea for the Christian. When Christianity flourishes, communism cannot thrive.

Yoder, Galen. "The Moratorium and Priorities." *GH* 63 (Feb. 17, 1970), 145-46. The potential hypocrisy of the Vietnam Moratorium is its single-issue approach, when in fact the deeper problem is the misdirection of American priorities toward a military-industrial-educational complex.

Yoder, John H. "The Christian Witness and Current Events." *GH* 47 (Aug. 17, 1954), 777. The prophetic aspect of the Christian witness involves a proclamation of God's judgment on the life of non-Christian society and the nation. American involvement in Indo-China and Guatemala prompts this kind of witness.

Yoder, John H. "Vietnam: A Just War?" *His* 28 (Apr., 1968), 1-3. Complete article also reprinted in *This Day* (July, 1968), 4-7, 30. First of a two-part series on the just war examines US involvement in Vietnam on the basis of the criteria for a just war: fought by a just authority, having a legitimate cause, using just means. Concludes that US participation is morally questionable.

Yoder, John H. "Vietnam: Another Option." *His* 28 (May, 1968), 8-11. Complete article reprinted in *This Day* (July, 1968) 4-7, 30. In addition to the options of holy crusade, just war, and handing government a blank check of authority in waging war, the author offers the option of following Jesus' example in giving one's life for one's enemies.

Yordy, Franz W. Letter to the Editor. *GH* 65 (Dec. 19, 1972), 1037. Takes issue with the use Art Gish made (Sept. 19, 1972) of the soldier who was "saved" before he went to Vietnam and died in combat as an example of phony salvation. Maintains that all who accept Christ are saved, but their stance on war and peace is a matter of their spiritual maturity.

Young, Robert T. "A Letter to My Son." *GH* 67 (July 2, 1974), 529-31. Letter to a fictitious son, a draft resister who fled the country, reflects on the enormous and varied costs of the Vietnam war and calls for amnesty for the 70,000 who refused to fight.

Zehr, Daniel (Review). *Reaching the Other Side,* by Earl S. Martin. Crown Pub., 1978. Pp. 282. *MBH* 18 (Mar. 16, 1979), 29. Recommends this journal of the author's and a co- worker's experiences in Vietnam during the war and following the surrender of Saigon.

Ziegler, Donald. "Leamington Hosts MCC Annual Meeting." *MBH* 12 (Feb. 23, 1973), 2-3. Among other concerns, the MCC annual meeting adopted in principle a working draft on amnesty for Indochina and a resolution on reconstruction in Indochina.

Ziegler, Donald. "MCC Examines Self and Issues." *EV* 86 (Mar. 10, 1973), 5, 6. MCC met for its annual meeting in Leamington, Ont., to discuss the progress of the MCC self-study, to adopt guidelines on use of government funds, to resolve interest in reconstruction in Indochina, to consider a working draft statement on universal amnesty for conscientious objectors, and to recognize four dynamic leaders of past inter-Mennonite activites.

Zochert, Don. "Three for Vietnam." *ChrLiv* 14 (Jan., 1967), 34-35. Discussion of 3 books on Vietnam and the war: *The Truth About Vietnam,* ed. Frank M. Robinson and Earl Kemp; Greenleaf Classics, Inc., 1966. Pp. 414. *Here Is Your Enemy,* by James Cameron. Holt, Rinehart, and Winston, 1966. Pp. 144. *Peace In Vietnam,* by American Friends Service Committee; Hill and Wang, 1966. Pp. 112.

Zuercher, Melanie. "Peace Teachers: He Recruits (for Peace) at the High Schools." *Builder* 31 (Jan., 1981), 13-14. Vietnam veteran Vaughn Mareno, Goshen, Ind., has found the Mennonite peace position to be a viable Christian alternative to the just war theory and puts his faith into practice in committee work, by involvement with the housing problems of the poor, and by counterrecruiting in the high schools.

1970 Annual Mid Atlantic Brethren Conference. "A Hope for Peace." *IPF Notes* 17 (Oct., 1970), 5-6. Conference resolution deplores the war in Southeast Asia and calls for renewed commitment to peace witnessing.

# F. Middle East

"A Message from Participants of the 1969 MCC Peace Section Middle East Study Tour." *CanMenn* 17 (July 18, 1969), 4. Statement approved by study tour participants summarizing impressions received in the Middle East and urging others to become versed in the human struggle going on there.

Abileah, Joseph W. "Federation in the Middle East." *Menn* 84 (June 3, 1969), 376; *MBH* 8 (May 30, 1969), 8; "An Israeli's Proposal for Peace," *CanMenn* 17 (June 6, 1969), 1. An Israeli pacifist proposes a solution to bring about reconciliation between the Middle East countries of Jordan, Arab Palestine (West Bank), and Israel.

Anderson, Jack. "Armed Intervention Over Oil Eyed." *MCC PS Wash. Memo* 6 (Nov.-Dec., 1974), 8. Reprinted from *The Washington Post* (Nov. 8, 1974). Discusses government deliberations over using military action in the Mideast to secure US oil interests.

Best, James S. "Jerusalem's Unaccomplished Warfare." *Menn* 86 (Mar. 30, 1971), 210-13. Reflecting on the complexity of the problem that surrounds and penetrates the Arab-Israeli community at odds with one another.

Brenneman, Virgil J. "Christ, Israel, and Palestine." *GH* 63 (Oct. 6, 1970), 832-34. Maintains that God's ethical and salvific requirements for Israel are not unique. Therefore, Christians cannot take sides in the present conflict, but should instead support reconciliation and justice for all involved.

Burnett, Kristina Mast. "Amidst Injustice Palestinian Teaches Resistance Based on Love." *Menn* 94 (Oct. 9, 1979), 600. Bishara Awad, headmaster of a school established by MCC in the West Bank, advocates a resistance based on love and reports that Palestinian Christian pacifists are looking for peaceful, nonviolent methods of protest.

Derstine, C. F. "The Jews and the Arabs: Who Holds the Key to World Peace?" *ChrMon* 40 (Aug., 1948), 254-55, 253. Discusses the politics surrounding the establishment of Israel and urges evangelization of the Jews to hasten the return of the Prince of Peace.

"EMC Sponsors Mid-East Teach-In." *CanMenn* 17 (Apr. 22, 1969), 3. Report on an April 11 teach-in at EMC involving Rabbi Krinsky of the U. of Virginia, Fayez A. Sayegh, as a representative of Arab interests, and Frank Epp. Epp said Palestine does not belong to the Jews if it does not also belong to the Arabs and it does not belong to the Arabs if it does not also belong to the Jews.

Eby, Omar. "Mennonites from Israel, Arab Territories Convene in Athens." *CanMenn* 17 (July 4, 1969), 1, 2. Report on a meeting of Mennonite personnel in Athens Apr. 10-12 to discuss peace and reconciliation in the Middle East. Participants came from the East Bank, the West Bank, Israel, Lebanon, the US, and Europe. Action was taken to see what could be done about repatriation and resettlement of Arab refugees. First step was for West Bank/Israel personnel to make concrete proposal to the Israeli government. Politics in the Old Testament, myths about Arab countries and Israel and the refugee problem in the Middle East were discussed.

Eby, Sarah Ann. "Following Christ in a Cauldron of Tragedy." *ChrLead* 39 (Sept. 28, 1976), 18. Description of the work of LeRoy and Carol Friesen as a listening, mediating presence in the Middle East with MCC.

Epp, Frank H. "No Peace in the Promised Land." *Menn* 84 (Jan. 28, 1969), 50-56. A Middle East study trip and encounters with Middle East people in Geneva and Rome as well as at the Assembly of the WCC in Uppsala provide insights and impressions which are presented in the interests of the Mennonite contribution to peace there.

Epp, Frank H. "The Land of Promise Is a Land Without Peace." *CanMenn* 16 (Dec. 10, 1968), 1, 9, 10, 11, 12, 13, 14. Israel and Arabs are on a collision course due to contradictory cultures and incompatible political claims. Israel stresses historical need for Jewish national home, Palestinian Arabs say simply that they have been driven from their land. Christians have responsibility for seeking a solution to Middle East problems by witnessing to all parties involved.

Epp, Frank H. "The Mennonite Presence in the Middle East." *GH* 64 (Apr. 27, 1971), 378-80. Advances the thesis that since the root of the Mideast conflict is a religious/ideological conflict, Mennonite presence should incarnate the Word of peace found through Jesus the Messiah.

Epp, Frank H. "The Palestine Problem in Historical Perspective." *GH* 62 (June 10, 1969), 510-11; *CanMenn* 17 (June 6, 1969), 1, 2. Reviews Arab and Jewish historical claims to Palestinian soil, then describes the history of the conflict in this century, the role of the United Nations, the Arab perspective, and the wars following partitioning.

Epp, Frank H. *Whoses Land Is Palestine? The Middle East Problem in Historical Perspective.* Grand Rapids: Wm. B. Eerdmans, 1970. Pp. 283. In this work ". . . we hope to help overcome two weaknesses in the western approach to the world in general and the Middle East in particular, a historical view that is too short and a theological stance that is too narrow."

Epp, Frank H. and Goddard, John. *The Israelis: Portrait of a People in Conflict.* Scottdale: Herald Press, 1980. Pp. 205. Excerpts from interviews with ninety-six Israelis attempt to present their stories and feelings in the long conflict with Arabs.

Epp, Frank H. and Goddard, John. *The Palestinians: Portrait of a People in Conflict.* Toronto: McClelland and Stewart, 1976. Pp. 240. Based on interviews with 172 Palestinians in 1971 and 1974, the book attempts to make known the stories and feelings of Palestinian people caught in the longstanding conflict between Israelis and Arabs.

"Frank Epp May Have Lost But He's Not Done with Politics." *MennMirror* 9 (Sept. 1979), 7. Epp's effort to gain a Parliament seat, prompted by his concern that Canada find nonviolent ways to solve the unity issue, is an outgrowth of his interest in the Vietnam War and Mideast tensions.

"From the Press: A Journey for Peace." *MennRep* 7 (Nov. 28, 1977), 7. Editorial reprinted from *Christian Science Monitor* (Nov. 22, 1977). Tribute to Prime Minister Begin of Israel and President Sadat of Egypt for the courage to carry out their historic peacemaking meeting in Jerusalem.

Fransen, Harold. "The Middle East, 1977-78 (King James Version)." *Menn* 93 (June 27, 1978), 430. Allegorizes the Mideast conflict using Old Testament King James version language, characterizing Israel as trusting in weapons of war rather than in God.

Franz, Delton. "Administration's Initiatives for Middle East Peace Talks Need Support." *MCC PS Wash. Memo* 9 (Nov.-Dec., 1977), 1-2. Urges constituents to encourage the government to proceed with Israeli-Arab peace talks in Geneva in spite of opposition from American Jewish groups.

Franz, Delton. "Middle East a Proving Ground." *MCC PS Wash. Memo* 5 (Nov.-Dec., 1973), 1-2. The US is using Israel as testing ground for new weapons systems, thus threatening the military balance of power in the Mideast.

Franz, Delton. "Military Strike Force Planned to Safeguard Oil Supply." *MCC PS Wash. Memo* 11 (July-Aug., 1979), 1-2, 9. While publicly committed to nonintervention, the US is preparing a strike force of 110,000 to safeguard a continuous flow of oil from the Mideast.

Franz, Delton. "The Middle East: Concern for Palestinians Is Seldom Heard." *MennRep* 6 (Oct. 18, 1976), 7. Describes MCC efforts to encourage policymakers in Washington to hear Palestinian grievances and recognize their right to a homeland as well as Israeli rights.

Franz, Delton. "Washington Report: Middle East War: Lessons Not Learned." *MennRep* 3 (Nov. 12, 1973), 7. The superpowers contributed to resumption of open war in the Mideast by arming Egypt and Israel. Alternatives, such as economic development aid to lessen national insecurity, are feasible, in light of de-escalation strategies that have worked in the past.

Friesen, Ivan. "Springtime and Death in the Jordan Valley." *CanMenn* 17 (Apr. 8, 1969), 3. Perhaps the best contribution of Mennonites in the Middle East is to live the nonviolence which they profess.

Friesen, LeRoy. "The Church and the Middle East (1). Palestinian Christians—People with an Uncertain Future." *MennRep* 6 (May 17, 1976), 7. Explores Palestinian Christian response to Palestinian nationalism and Jewish occupation, and the question of using violence.

"Gift of Love Is Theme of Palestinian Worker." *GH* 72 (Oct. 9, 1979), 802. A Palestinian who is working as an MCC volunteer on the West Bank speaks of the suffering of the Palestinian people.

"Graduates Ask, What Is Nonviolence." *Menn* 87 (Jan. 18, 1972), 40. Mennonite graduate students conference on nonviolence includes such topics as: testing a fifth-grade history curriculum; applying nonviolent problem solving models to government and organizations; and critical analyses of MCC involvement in the Middle East.

George, Elias. "Ten Things I Wish North American Mennonites Knew About My People." *FQ* 6 (Nov., Dec., 1979, Jan., 1980), 15. Arab Mennonite social studies teacher clarifies misconceptions about Arabs and offers his perspective on the Arab-Israeli conflict and prospects for peace.

Goertzen, Don. Letter to the Editor. *ChrLead* 37 (Jan. 22, 1974), 15. Mennonites should not make the mistake of believing that America should support Israel because this fits a particular interpretation of prophecy.

Hackman, Walton (Editorial). "No Victory Parades, No Peace Marches." *Intercom* 13 (Nov., 1973), 4. Observes the change in public sentiment from protesting the war in Vietnam to supporting the Middle East war.

Haddad, Anis Charles. "Conflict in the Land of Peace." *ChrMon* 29 (Feb., 1937), 53. Describes attitudes of Arabs and Jews in Palestine and the recurring outbreaks of violence.

Hartzler, J. E. "The Middle East Encounter." Paper, Goshen, Ind., 1958. Pp. [9]. AMBS.

Hege, Nathan. "Building Bridges Across Barriers." *GH* 72 (Oct. 16, 1979), 809-811. A look at how Mennonites have responded to the situation in Israel and how they are continuing to work at reconciliation.

Hertzler, Daniel. "Nonresistance Tested." *GH* 73 (Oct. 28, 1980), 888. Tells the story of peaceable Palestinians whose village was confiscated by Jewish soldiers and who responded nonviolently.

Hertzler, Daniel (Editorial). "The Year of the Refugee." *GH* 72 (July 3, 1979), 544. Describes the plight of African, Middle East, and especially Southeast Asian refugees; congregations are encouraged to consider sponsorship.

Hiebert, Robert. Letter to the Editor. *MBH* 18 (Mar. 2, 1979), 10-11. Peace in the Middle East will be found only through divine action. Arabs hold the lion's share of responsibility for the plight of the West Bank refugees.

Hiebert, Robert. "The Middle East: A Moral Conflict." *MBH* 14 (Dec. 26, 1975), 2-3, 27. While Israel is concerned with maintaining its God-given right to the land, some Arabs have escalated the conflict to the level of a "holy war," determined to destroy all Jews.

Hiebert, Robert (Review). *The Palestinians: Portrait of a People in Conflict*, by Frank H. Epp. McClelland and Stewart, 1976. Pp. 240. *MBH* 15 (Nov. 12, 1976), 35. Reviewer maintains that the author paints too rosy a picture of the Palestinians, a perspective which will not further the cause of peace in the Mideast.

Hostetler, Marian. *Journey to Jerusalem*. Scottdale: Herald Press, 1978. Pp. 126. On a trip to the Middle East with her mother, 12-year-old Miriam begins to understand the complexities of the Arab-Israeli conflict when she enters into friendship with an Arab girl whose village is destroyed by Israeli soldiers.

Hyman, Sid and Susan. Letter to the Editor. *GH* 67 (Oct. 1, 1974), 756; *Menn* 89 (Oct. 22, 1974), 620-21. Jewish Mennonites protest the anti-Israel bias of Larry Kehler's articles on the Mideast, claiming Arab military offensives match Israeli actions.

"Israel Center Begins Expansion, Development." *GH* 72 (Oct. 16, 1979), 819. Immanual House and Center in Tel Aviv is working at encouraging closer links with other Hebrew-Christian congregations and developing its building and grounds to allow for a more expanded program.

"Jewish Pacifist Proposes Mid-East Confederation." *CanMenn* 17 (Sept. 19, 1969), 4. A conscientious objector to war, Mr. Abileah objects to the erection of a Jewish state with national sovereignty and proposes a confederation of three states, Jordan, Arab Palestine, and Israel—with a federal capital in Jerusalem. "Political solutions depend on economic solutions," says Abileah.

"Jewish Pacifist Urges Mid-East Federation." *CanMenn* 18 (Oct. 30, 1970), 1. Joseph Abileah of Israel presents his vision for peace in the Middle East to students and faculty at AMBS. This vision involves reconciliation between Arabs and Jews with the acceptance of the principles of nonviolence and mutual respect.

Jantz, Harold. "Origins of West Bank Tensions." *MBH* 15 (Aug. 6, 1976), 15-16. Illegal Israeli settlements in the West Bank contribute to tensions and outbreaks of violence with Palestinians.

Janzen, Waldemar. "Israel and the People of God." *CanMenn* 16 (May 7, 1968), 8. Janzen ascribes no special theological significance to the modern state of Israel. From Isaac on, he says, membership in Israel was based on standing under the promise, it was a matter of relationship to God, not of ethnic membership.

Janzen, Waldemar. "The Geography of Israel's Faith." *CanMenn* 17 (June 6, 1969), 1, 2. It is inconsistent with New Testament teaching to insist on a special theological importance for the area of Palestine. New Testament universals take priority over the specific geographical expectations which many Christians attach to Palestine. Church is always *somewhere* but that location is determined by where the Christian experiences God's leading.

Jeschke, Marlin. "The Middle East Crisis in Biblical Perspective." *CanMenn* 15 (Oct. 31, 1967), 6, 7. Jeschke defines Israel's right to exist as an eschatological community that leads humankind to unity. For Christians, Israel's future can be realized only by a return to the call to be a religious community, rather than yet another national state expressing a divided and hostile humanity.

Kehler, Larry. "America, Israel, and the Arabs." *GH* 67 (Aug. 20, 1974), 625-27; *Menn* 89 (July 9, 1974), 436-37; *MennRep* 4 (July 22, 1974), 6. MCC representative visiting the Mideast reports perspectives of both Arabs and Israelis and assesses the US role in the conflict.

Kehler, Larry. "Blossoms Amidst the Bursting Bombs." *Menn* 89 (June 25, 1974), 413-14; *MennRep* 4 (July 8, 1974), 7. Initial impressions of conflict-ridden Middle East by member of MCC delegation visiting there.

Kehler, Larry. "Churches of the Middle East." *GH* 67 (Sept. 10, 1974), 684-85; *MennRep* 4 (Sept. 2, 1974), 17; *Menn* 89 (Aug, 20, 1974), 486-87. Christians in the Arab countries of the Middle East urge American Christians to recognize their ties to other Christians as well as to the Jews, in order to further the cause of peace in the Mideast.

Kehler, Larry. "David and Goliath." *Menn* 89 (June 25, 1974), 424. MCC representative reflects on a recent trip to the Mideast, concluding that while the area is highly polarized, voices of moderation and reconciliation are beginning to be heard from both sides.

Kehler, Larry. "Israel Faces a New Reality." *GH* 67 (Sept 3, 1974), 664-65; *Menn* 889 (Aug. 6, 1974), 469-70; *MennRep* 4 (Aug. 19, 1974), 1; *EV* 87 (Oct. 10, 1974), 5, 6. Since Israel's military superiority over the Arabs was shaken in the 1973 Yom Kippur War, it should learn to build its security on the goodwill of its neighbors rather than on the strength of its borders.

Kehler, Larry. "People Without a Homeland." *GH* 67 (Aug. 27, 1974), 644-45; *MennRep* 4 (Aug. 5, 1974), 6, *Menn* 89 (July 23, 1974), 454 55. Describes the plight of the Palestinians as a politically naive peasant people used as pawns in an international conflict.

Klassen, William. "Christmas at Bethlehem, 1973." *MennMirror* 3 (Dec., 1973), 7, 8. In the midst of war, there are efforts and attempts at peacemaking between Jew, Moslem, and Christian in Bethlehem.

Klassen, William (Review). *The View from East Jerusalem,* by John A. Lapp. Herald Press, 1980. Pp. 124. *MennRep* 10 (Nov. 10, 1980), 9. Reviewer observes that the book presents the complexity of the Mideast conflict, giving special attention to the Palestinian perspective.

Koontz, Gayle Gerber. "Mennonite Peace in the Middle East Puzzle." *MBH* 13 (Aug. 23, 1974), 16-17. People-oriented MCC efforts, cooperation with Middle Eastern churches, and food and development programs will continue to receive Mennonite attention in the Mideast conflict.

Koontz, Gayle Gerber. "Palestinians Gain Confidence, Protest Israeli Occupation Policies." *MennRep* 6 (July 27, 1976), 2. Examines causes of recent outbreaks of Israeli-Palestinian violence, centering on Israel's occupation of the West Bank and expropriation of Palestinian property.

Koop, Robert. "Ottawa Report: Government Consults MCC on Mid-East Policy." *MennRep* 9 (Sept. 3, 1979), 7. Representatives from MCC and Robert Stanfield, the Canadian government's special representative to study Canada's relationship with the Middle East, met to discuss the vital role Canada could play in the future of Middle East peace negotiations.

Kreider, Carl. "Crises in the Middle East." *MennComm* 5 (Dec., 1951), 26, 32. Present crises in Iran and Egypt center on economic and military concerns.

Kreider, Carl. "Mistakes in the Middle East." *ChrLiv* 4 (Mar., 1957), 18, 34. Mistakes of the world powers in Middle East affairs include miscalculated military moves.

Kreider, Carl. "US Marines in Lebanon." *ChrLiv* 5 (Oct., 1958), 19, 33. Sending Marines to the Mid-east to quell rising tensions is a serious mistake.

Kreider, David. "Will Vengeance Bring Back Sweetness?" *With* 3 (May, 1970), 20. Peace and love and happiness are gone for a 16-year-old Arab of Gaza because of the June, 1967, war.

Kreider, Roy. "A Strategy of Witness in the Middle East." *GH* 62 (June 10, 1969), 519-20. "A demonstrated gospel blunts the attack against the gospel, shows the gospel to be superior love: through service projects, through the word of witness, through practical expressions of community."

"Lack of Security and Justice Key Issues of Mid-East Deadlock." *CanMenn* 20 (Sept. 11, 1970), 3. Observations gleaned from members of MCC Peace Section tour of the Middle East countries on Arab-Jewish relations.

Lapp, John A. "A New Equation in the Middle East." *ChrLiv* 25 (Feb., 1978), 12-13. Comment on peace negotiations between Egypt and Israel, spurred by Sadat's visit to Israel.

Lapp, John A. "Armenians Suffer Again." *MBH* 18 (Feb. 16, 1979), 24-25. Armenians, a Christian minority, are caught in the crossfire of the Lebanese civil war.

Lapp, John A. "'Chaos in the Middle East.'" *ChrLiv* 16 (Mar., 1969), 18-19. Background of and comment upon the escalating Arab-Israeli military conflict.

Lapp, John A. "Disengagement Is Not Peace."

*ChrLiv* 21 (July, 1974), 15, 29. Review of deeper issues affecting Israeli-Arab negotiations.

Lapp, John A. "Educators Protest Actions of Israel on West Bank." *GH* 72 (Jan. 9, 1979), 24. Report of harassment by Israeli military authorities at Bir Zeit University on the Israeli-occupied West Bank.

Lapp, John A. "Lebanon's Self-Destruction." *ChrLiv* 23 (Mar., 1976), 15-16. Description of the many-sided conflict in Lebanon.

Lapp, John A. Letter to the Editor. *Sojourners* 9 (Dec., 1979), 38. Acknowledges the difficulty of speaking a word for the Palestinians without appearing anti-Israel.

Lapp, John A. "Middle East Report: Why the Palestinians Hesitate." *MennRep* 8 (Nov. 27, 1978), 7. Explains eight reasons why Palestinians are suspicious of the Israeli-Egyptian peace accords signed at the Camp David summit.

Lapp, John A. "On the Spot in the Middle East." *ChrLiv* 16 (Sept., 1969), 18-19. Analysis of the demands of both sides in the Arab-Israeli political and military conflict.

Lapp, John A. "Personal Face of West Bank Displacement." *MBH* 18 (Jan. 5, 1979), 20. Camp David peace agreements are unsatisfactory to West Bank Palestinians, since Israel continues to expropriate land for illegal settlements.

Lapp, John A. "Round Four: The Arab-Israeli War." *ChrLiv* 21 (Feb., 1974), 15, 35. Review of the October, 1973, round of the war and the world-wide involvement in the conflict.

Lapp, John A. "The Arabian Powder Keg." *ChrLiv* 14 (Nov., 1967), 18-19. Description of military and political tensions among countries in the Arabian peninsula.

Lapp, John A. "The Middle East Cauldron." *ChrLiv* 14 (Aug., 1967), 18-19. Background of the Israeli-Arab conflicts, including a call for settlement of the Palestinian question.

Lapp, John A. "The New Environment for Mission/Service in the Middle East." *Peace Section Newsletter* 9 (Apr.-May, 1979), 1-8. Highlights the complexity of the Middle East. Western prejudice nurtured by the Christian-Muslim conflicts must be addressed.

Lapp, John A. "The Personal Face of Displacement: 'To Lose My Land Is to Lose My Life.' " *MennRep* 8 (Dec. 25, 1978), 7. Relates story of one displaced Palestinian refugee in an attempt to draw attention to the plight of Palestinians removed from their homes by illegal Israeli settlements.

Lapp, John A. "The United Nations in the Middle East." *ChrLiv* 26 (Aug., 1979), 15, 25. Description of UN peacekeeping operations in the Middle East, from relief for Palestinian refugees to troops stationed in demilitarized zones.

Lapp, John A. *The View from East Jerusalem.* Scottdale and Kitchener: Herald Press, 1980. Pp.122. Writing while living in East Jerusalem in 1978-79, Lapp addresses key topics in Palestinian-Israeli relations. These include the viability of and alternatives to a Palestinian state; the religious conflicts including the resurgence of Islam; Lebanon survival and the Iranian revolution; and the work of the United Nations in the Middle East. Lapp identifies five pillars of the new developing ecology of the region: rapid amassing of wealth, new vitality in Islam, militarism and totalitarian temptations, the denouement of the Arab-Israeli thirty years' war, and the critical U.S. role. The book concludes with a checklist of topics for educating oneself on the Middle East.

Lapp, John A. "Two Land Deals: Ancestral Homeland Returned in New York . . . and Seized in Occupied West Bank." *Menn* 94 (Jan. 9, 1979), 24-25. Report on MCC's involvement with two different groups of people, the Mohawk Indians of New York and the Palestinians, as they each struggle for land. While the Mohawks succeed in claiming part of their ancestral homeland in NY, many Palestinian refugees have been scattered throughout the Middle East as their land is lost or destroyed.

Lapp, John A. "Why Israel Does Not Give Up the West Bank." *ChrLiv* 27 (Aug., 1980), 15, 27. Comment on Israeli settlements in occupied territories and the subsequent wave of violence.

Lapp, John A. "Will Lebanon Survive?" *ChrLiv* 26 (Feb., 1979), 15, 25-26. Comment on factors contributing to instability in Lebanese government and society before and after the 1974 civil war.

Lapp, John A. (Review). *The Israelis: Portrait of a People in Conflict,* by Frank H. Epp. McClelland and Stewart and Herald Press, 1980. Pp. 208. *FQ* 7 (Feb., Mar., Apr., 1980), 10. Sequel to Epp's *The Palestinians: Portrait of a People in Conflict* contains a range of political opinion on war and peace through interviews with 99 people.

Lind, Loren. "Mideast in Fragile Hand." *YCC* 48 (Sept. 3, 1967), 6. An examination of the current Middle Eastern crisis.

Lind, Millard C. "Israeli or Jacobi?" *GH* 62 (June 10, 1969), 514-16. The relevance of the Old

Testament to the contemporary Middle East situation lies in the biblical witness to a new community which transcends nationalism.

"More Questions Than Answers on Middle East Situation." *CanMenn* 17 (Feb. 4, 1969), 1, 2. Reports on the MCC Peace Section annual meeting in Chicago on Jan. 23 where Frank Epp presented a 40-page paper entitled "Whose Land Is Palestine?" Respondents were Wilbert Shenk, Waldemar Janzen, and Elmer A. Martens. Theological and other issues stand at the root of a solution for the crisis in the Middle East and also affect the promotion of peace by MCC workers in the area.

Martens, Harry E. "Houses on Cold Amman Hills." *GH* 61 (Nov. 12, 1968), 1028. Describes the plight of Palestinian war refugees facing a cold winter with only tents, and challenges North American Christians to share out of their abundance to construct makeshift shelters.

Martens, Harry E. "Volunteers Are Peacemakers." *CanMenn* 17 (June 6, 1969), 4. "The most forceful, meaningful and acceptable way of serving as a 'peacemaker' is to serve and witness as a Christian volunteer." Serving in the Middle East, the author believes identification with the Arab refugees provides an "opportunity to talk, walk, and to work with them, and to demonstrate what the great love of Christ means."

Matar, Ibrahim. "Powers and Responsibilities of the Self-Governing Authority." *Peace Section Newsletter* 9 (Apr. May, 1979), 9-11. Notes the powers and responsibilities that will have to be present in order for the self-governing authority of the West Bank and Gaza, as proposed in the Camp David framework for peace in the Middle East, to be credible, acceptable, and effective in upholding the rights of the Palestinians.

Mennonite Central Committee Information Services. "Palestinian MCCer Discusses Middle East." *EV* 92 (Oct. 10, 1979), 16. Palestinian Bishara Awad, an MCC volunteer working as headmaster of a school established by MCC in the West Bank, is involved in a ministry of love in the Middle East conflict.

Olson, Arnold T. "Peace for Export." *EvVis* 93 (Apr. 10, 1980), 3-5. As both a capital city and a symbol for three major world religions, peace in Jerusalem would have international and interfaith implications.

"Palestinian Teacher Shares Agony of His People." *MennRep* 9 (Oct. 1, 1979), 13. Bishara E. Awad, an MCC volunteer as headmaster of a school in the West Bank, shares his concern and agony for the plight of the Palestinian people.

"Peace in the Middle East, Assembly Concern." *MBH* 12 (Dec. 28, 1973), 18. The MCC Peace Section semi-annual meeting discussed the current Middle East situation and the need to help reconcile not only Israel and the Arab states but also North Americans who have become polarized over the situation.

Peachey, Urbane. "Barriers Broken." *Menn* 93 (Jan. 24, 1978), 56-57. Analysis of Sadat's peace initiative in the Middle East and the prospects for peace.

Peachey, Urbane. "Hope Reborn in Middle East." *MennRep* 8 (Feb. 20, 1978), 7. Analyzes Egyptian president Sadat's peacemaking visit to Israel.

Peachey, Urbane. "Lebanon: The Roots of Conflict Are Complex." *MennRep* 6 (Jan. 26, 1976), 7. Reviews social history of Lebanese people, asserting that the civil war cannot be boiled down into a Moslem-Christian conflict.

Peachey, Urbane. "Refugees Flee Israeli Forces." *Intercom* 22 (May, 1978), 1, 4. Describes the plight of refugees from Israel's invasion of Lebanon and outlines the issues involved in the conflict.

Peachey, Urbane. "The Middle East Cauldron and Mennonite Involvement." *MennRep* 3 (Sept. 3, 1973), 7. Discusses Mideast conflict factors shaping MCC work in Jordan, and describes MCC projects there.

Peachey, Urbane. "The Sinai Fuse." *Intercom* 15 (Nov., 1975), 8. The Sinai pact, while recognizing grievances of both sides, does not touch the core issues of Israeli occupation of the West Bank, settlement of Palestinian claims, and mutual recognition of Arab and Israeli states.

Peachey, Urbane. "What Is a Military Occupation?" *MCC PS Newsletter* 8 (Aug., 1977), 6-7. Describes the treatment of West Bank inhabitants as military in every respect—labor exploitation, collective punishment, expulsion of leadership, land expropriation, arbitrary arrests, restrictions on place of residence, and restrictions on assembly and right of expression.

Pellman, Phyllis. "What I Heard the Arabs Say." *GH* 62 (Sept. 16, 1969), 806-807. Participant in MCC Middle East Study Tour heard Arabs calling for an end to Zionism and a homeland for Palestinians to end the present Mideast conflicts.

Preheim, Vern. "MCC's Efforts in the Middle East." *GH* 62 (June 10, 1969), 517-18. Describes MCC activities, primarily in Jordan, which range from war relief and reconstruction to education and crafts projects.

Quiring, Paul. "Camp David: A Commentary."
*MennRep* 8 (Oct. 2, 1978), 7. The peace
agreements between Egypt's President Sadat
and Israel's Prime Minister Begin fail to speak
to both the problem of Palestinian refugees and
a bilateral agreement, but they do buy
additional time for negotiating peace.

Quiring, Paul. "Israeli Peace Movement
Analyzed." *Menn* 93 (Sept. 12, 1978), 521.
Analyzes the objectives of the Peace Now
movement and its chances of influencing
Begin's hard-line military policy.

(Review). *The Israelis: Portrait of a People in Conflict,* by
Frank Epp. Herald Press and McClelland &
Stewart, 1980. *MCC PS Newsletter* 10 (Mar.-Apr.,
19800, 11. Recommends the book as a portrayal
of the Israeli point of view, and as a companion
volume to the author's earlier work on the
Palestinian people.

(Review). *The View from East Jerusalem,* by John A.
Lapp. Scottdale: Herald Press, 1980. *MCC PS
Newsletter* 10 (Jan.-Feb., 1980), 10. Reviewer
observes that the book presents the complexity
of the Middle East conflicts in language
understandable to the lay reader.

Redekop, John H. "Looking Backward . . . and
also Ahead." *MBH* 17 (Dec. 22, 1978), 10.
Ominous signs of the future include stockpiling
weapons, Mideast conflict, racism in Africa.

Redekop, John H. "The Middle East." *MBH* 12
(Nov. 2, 1973), 10. Mennonite reaction to the
Middle East conflict has not been one of
peacemaking, loving the enemy, and
identifying with the poor and oppressed.

Redekop, John H. "Think of the Arabs: Before You
Get Carried Away by the Victory of Israel."
*CanMenn* 15 (June 20, 1967), 1, 9. Expresses
concern for the fact that so much support is
given to the Israeli cause after the Six-Day War
and so little consideration for the Arab cause.

Samson, Hugh. "No Room, No Inn." *ChrLiv* 15
(Nov., 1968), 31-32. Plight of refugees from the
1967 Arab-Israeli war.

Schroeder, Richard J. "The Cutting Edge." *ChrLead*
36 (Dec. 11, 1973), 25. Analysis of the Arab-
Israeli conflict. US consumption of energy is
seemingly directing a more open foreign policy
toward the Arab side while lessening the
support of Israel.

Shank, J. Ward (Editorial). "The New War." *ST* 37
(Sept., 1969), 4. With renewed interest in the
Middle East, the task of the church is to preach
reconciliation to both Jews and Arabs.

Shank, J. Ward (Review). *Whose Land Is Palestine?,*
by Frank H. Epp. Grand Rapids: Eerdmans,

1970. *ST* 39 (Feb., 1971), 15. The question posed
is one of the central burdens of sacred history.
The apparent lack of certainty in the mind of
the author concerning the divine hand in these
events is reason for regret.

Shelly, Maynard. "Palestinian Arabs Tap Antiwar
Activists." *Menn* 94 (June 19, 1979), 422-23. A
national conference on human rights and the
Palestinian-Israeli conflict discussed efforts to
work for Palestinian freedom.

Shelly, Maynard. "Peacemakers in a Guerilla
Tent?" *CanMenn* 17 (July 11, 1969), 1. During a
Middle East tour, 21 American and Canadian
Mennonites met an al-fateh leader in a refugee
camp in Jordan. Refugees have tried nonviolent
means for 20 years, he said, and no one has
listened. Now they will fight to the death to
regain their homeland. The tour was sponsored
by the MCC peace section.

Shenk, Wilbert R. "The Middle East: A World on
Trial." *GH* 60 (Oct. 3, 1967), 888. The situation
is difficult. The Christian church is hardly in a
position to preach peace here but it can at least
live peaceably and in a reconciling way.

Shenk, Wilbert R. (Review). *The Israel-Arab Reader:
A Documentary History of the Middle East Conflict,* ed.
Walter Laqueur. Bantam, 1969. Pp. 371. *GH* 62
(Sept. 9, 1969), 786. Reviewer comments on the
level of complexity in the Mideast conflict
covered by twentieth-century documents
pertaining to the conflict published in the book.

Showalter, Stuart W., ed. "Peacemaking in a
World of Revolution." Seminar lectures
delivered at EMC, Harrisonburg, VA, June 15-
26, 1970. Pp. 88. MSHL. Includes Epp, Frank,
"Revolution in the Middle East," 16-23.

Siemens, Mark. Letter to the Editor. *ChrLead* 42
(Nov. 6, 1979), 9. The assumption that the areas
occupied militarily by Israel in 1967 are now
part of Israel legitimizes any powerful nation's
acquisition of property by force from its
neighbors.

Snyder, William T. "The Six-Day War Goes On."
*GH* 62 (Mar. 25, 1969), 279; *Intercom* 9 (Mar.-
Apr., 1969), 1-2. Two years after the Six-Day
War, hostilities and guerilla fighting between
Israelis and Arabs continue.

Sokoloff, B. (Review). *The Israelis; Portrait of a People
in Conflict,* by Frank H. Epp. Toronto:
McClelland and Stewart, 1980. Pp. 205. "Jewish
Reviewer Finds Epp's Book Worthwhile."
*MennMirror* 10 (Nov., 1980), 18. Appreciates
Epp's sensitivity to the issue of Jewish suffering
as well as Palestinian suffering in the Mideast
conflict entangling these peoples, but regrets
that too many of those interviewed by Epp for
the book "are simply not knowledgeable and

speak purely out of emotion and unsupported opinion."

Stoner, John K. "Jesus and the Middle East." *EV* 86 (Dec. 10, 1973), 5, 11. Will the church in America send its sons to deliver Israel by the sword or will it be willing to take the nonresistant path Jesus showed us?

Swarr, Bertha. "Sharing Faith in Israel." *GH* 61 (June 4, 1968), 490-92. Describes the political and religious atmosphere in Israel and the resulting challenge to a Christian witness. Describes also the needs resulting from the 1967 Six-Day War.

Swarr, Paul. "Working for Peace in the Middle East." *GH* 64 (Feb. 2, 1971), 90-91. Describes and reflects on various aspects of Mennonite mission work in the Mideast which attempt to share the gospel of peace, from peace conferences and programs to the joy of working with changed individuals.

Thomas, Everett. "What I Heard the Israelis Say." *GH* 62 (Sept. 16, 1969), 807-808. Participant in MCC Middle East Study Tour heard Israelis calling for the survival of the Jewish state at any military price.

Unsigned. "Straddling the Middle East Fence." *Intercom* 16 (Sept., 1976), 1-2. Returned MCCers LeRoy and Carol Friesen reflect on their peacemaking efforts in the Middle East.

"Witnessing to God's Will for Peace." *CanMenn* 18 (July 17, 1970), 16. Purpose, organization, and action of the MCC Peace Section are outlined. The draft, the Washington office, the Middle East, and International relationships are topics receiving special emphasis.

Wenger, Martha. "The Potential to Respond." *Forum* 11 (Dec., 1977), 4-5. Mennonite student enrolled in Palestinian Arab university on the West Bank reflects on the conflict and violence present in the Israeli-occupied West Bank.

Yoder, Edward. "No Peace in Palestine: Peace Principles from a Scriptural Viewpoint." Part 24. *GH* 32 (Apr. 20, 1939), 80. News report from the Middle East.

Yoder, J. Otis. "Biblical Light on the Middle East Crisis." *ST* 36, Part 1 (Apr., 1968), 27; Part 2 (May, 1968), 28; Part 3 (June, 1968), 22; Part 4 (July, 1968), 28; Part 5 (Aug., 1968), 27; Part 6 (Sept., 1968), 22; Part 7 (Oct., 1968), 24; Part 8 (Nov., 1968), 28; Part 9 (Dec., 1968), 20; *ST* 37, Part 10 (Jan., 1969), 29; Part 11 (Feb., 1969), 29; Part 12 (Apr., 1969), 27; Part 13 (May, 1969), 28; Part 14 (June, 1969), 26; Part 15 (July, 1969), 27; Part 16 (Aug., 1969), 25; Part 17 (Sept., 1969), 28; Part 18 (Nov., 1969), 25; Part 19 (Dec., 1969), 25; *ST* 38, Part 20 (Jan., 1970), 29; Part 31 (Feb., 1970), 28. A biblical and historical analysis of the then-current Middle East crisis.

Yoder, J. Otis. "Where Shall Justice in the Middle East Begin?" *GH* 63 (Mar. 10, 1970), 226-28. Author contends that the central question in the Mideast conflict is whether Arabs will learn to live in peace with Jews, or whether they will pursue a program of possible Jewish genocide.

Zerger, Sandra. "Martha Wenger: Go-Between." *Menn* 92 (Apr. 12, 1977), 246-47. Bethel College senior and peace intern reflects on her year of study in Israel and the occupied territories and the complexity of the Mideast conflict.

Ziegler, Donald (Review). *Whose Land Is Palestine?*, by Frank H. Epp. Grand Rapids: Wm. B. Eerdmans, n.d. *GH* 63 (Nov. 10, 1970), 950. Reviewer quotes extensively from the book's description of the meeting of a Palestinian man and a Jewish man, an event symbolizing the author's thesis that a Christian contribution toward Mideast peace means understanding both sides of the conflict.

# G. Latin and Central America

Born, Daniel (Review). *Christian Mission and Social Justice*, by Samuel Escobar and John Driver. Scottdale: Herald Press, 1978. In *ChrLead* 41 (Aug. 15, 1978), 16. The authors explore the range of theological attitudes toward social justice in Latin America.

"Central American Churches Approve Peace Statement." *MennRep* 9 (Sept. 3, 1979), 5. A Central American Consultation of Mennonite Churches approved a peace statement which had been prepared at a meeting of Central American Mennonites last year in Belize.

Driver, John. "Jeremiah's Message for the Church." *GH* 68 (June 3, 1975), 416-18. Jeremiah's vision of living the future now, rather than succumbing either to quick revolutions or spiritualizing the gospel, is a peacemaking vision for Christians in Latin America.

Franz, Delton. "Against the Wall in Latin America." *GH* 67 (Nov. 5, 1974), 846-47; "Washington Report: Latin America: A Look at North/South Relations." *MennRep* 4 (Sept. 30, 1974), 7. Multinational corporations in Latin

America promote the increasing gap between rich and poor, while US military and torture procedures oppress those who work for change.

Franz, Delton. "Exported to Latin America: Safe Religion or Costly Discipleship?" *MCC PS Newsletter* 9 (Aug.-Sept., 1979), 1-4. Personal visit to Latin America raises concern about the impact of Mennonite mission and development programs in those countries. Concludes the Mennonite mission and service/development programs in Latin America have tended to take a "safe" theological and tactical posture.

Franz, Delton. "Nicaragua: A Test Case for American Policy in Latin America." *MCC PS Wash. Memo* 10 (Sept.-Oct., 1978), 1-2. The Nicaraguan war can be attributed to the wealth and abuse of power by the ruling Somoza regime.

Franz, Delton. "Panama Canal Treaties: The Moral Questions for American Christians." *MCC PS Wash. Memo* 10 (Jan.-Feb., 1978), 7-8. Discusses the treaties in light of the question of justice for the Panamanians.

Franz, Delton. "Panama Canal Treaty: The Test for Future Inter-American Relations." *MCC PS Wash. Memo* 9 (Sept.-Oct., 1977), 1-2, 7. Exposes injustices present in the US administration of the Canal Zone and argues with the mythology of US military security insured by the US presence there.

Franz, Delton, ed. "'Third World' Concerns Focused with Plans for Mennonite World Conference in Brazil," *MCC PS Wash. Memo* 2 (Sept.-Oct., 1970), 1-4. Focuses on the economic injustice existing between the US and Latin American countries and raises the possibility of addressing this issue at the Mennonite World Conference in 1972.

Franz, Marian Claassen. "Central America." *Menn* 94 (Sept. 18, 1979), 552-53. Conditions are so bad in Central America that the people would rather die fighting for change than continue to live with the economic and political injustices done to them.

Friesen, Alida. Letter to the Editor. *MennMirror* 8 (Oct., 1978), 21. The writer, a former Argentinian, expresses disappointment in the Canadian attitude of indifference towards injustices, particularly in Latin America, and pleads for a response against injustices and violations of human rights.

Goertzen, Don. "Tightening the Vise." *Sojourners* 6 (Jan., 1977), 8. Notes recent events that indicate a clamping down on Latin American Christians.

Harder, Ernst. "To Hell with Good Intentions."

*Forum* (Mar., 1972), 1-2. More than good intentions, service in Latin America requires sympathetic understanding of the cultural and political situation and identification with a people struggling to establish their own liberation.

Hofer, Joy. "Reality Brought Close to Home." *MBH* 19 (Dec. 5, 1980), 12. One family's story of suffering from the civil war in El Salvador.

Hofer, Joy. "When Violence Becomes Real." *ChrLead* 43 (Nov. 4, 1980), 10. The plight of a refugee family in Guatemala illustrates the suffering caused by violence in Central America.

"I Was in Prison and You Visited Me—Jesus." *EV* 88 (Jan. 25, 1975), 16. Opportunities for involvement with offenders are increasing for Mennonite Central Committee volunteers in North America.

Jantz, Harold. "A Witness on Behalf of the Powerless." *MBH* 16 (Sept. 30, 1977), 16-17. Patty Erb and Thomas Capuano tell of their imprisonments and torture for their work among the poor in Latin American countries supported by US military aid.

Lapp, John A. "Upheaval in Central America." *ChrLiv* 27 (June, 1980), 15, 34. Review of recent events in Central American politics: victory of the Sandinistas in Nicaragua; murder of Archbishop Oscar Romero in El Salvador.

Mennonite Central Committee News Release. "Nicaragua Struggles to Recover." *EV* 92 (Sept. 25, 1979), 8-9. MCC cooperates with other Mennonite organizations in assessing needs and arranging for food shipments to Nicaragua in an effort to help the country recover from the pain and destruction of war.

Minnich, R. Herbert. "Hunger, Revolution, and the Church." *Peacemakers in a Broken World*. Ed. John A. Lapp. Scottdale: Herald Press, 1969, 43-53. Minnich predicts revolution in Latin America as poor and oppressed people begin to demand justice. Calls Christians to work nonviolently for greater socioeconomic equality.

Mullet, Steven L. "Nonviolent Latin American Liberation Theology: A Challenge to Modern-day Pacifists." Research paper for Biblical and Christian Perspectives on War and Peace class. Pp. 15. BfC.

Ollenburger, Ben C. (Review). *Christians and Marxists: The Mutual Challenge to Revolution*, by Jose Miguez Bonino. Grand Rapids: Eerdmans, 1976. In *ChrLead* 40 (Mar. 15, 1977), 18. Bonino's thesis is that both Christianity and Marxism provide challenges to the kind of revolution which may be necessary for the "correction" of injustice and oppression in Latin America.

"Peace Churches Challenge Conscription by New Government in Nicaragua." *GH* 72 (Sept. 11, 1979), 728. The peace churches in Nicaragua are assuming a positive peace witness by challenging the government's decree for conscription.

"People and Hunger." Papers presented to the Consultation on World Hunger and Population Pressures, Chicago, Ill., May 24-25, 1968. MHL. Sponsored by Council of Mennonite Colleges, Council of Mission Board Secretaries, Mennonite Central Committee. Includes: Klassen, William, "God's People and the Poor," pp. 9; Kreider, Carl, "Economic Factors Affecting Hunger," pp. 8; Blase, Melvin, "Programs for Economic Development in Latin America," pp. 16; Bishop, Franklin, "World Hunger: Reality and Challenge," pp. 11; Rhoades, J. Benton, "Programs of Agricultural Development in Latin America," pp. 7; Fretz, J. Winfield, "Population Pressures in Latin America: The Current Situation and Trends," pp. 9; Minnich, R. Herbert, "Hunger, Revolution, and the Church in Latin America," pp. 17; Hiebert, T. G., "Family Planning in Christian Relief Programs," pp. 7.

Peachey, Urbane, comp. "Mennonite Peace Theology Colloquium II: Theology of Justice, Bethel Mennonite Church, North Newton, Ks., Nov. 15-18, 1978, [Papers]." Akron, Pa.: MCC Peace Section, 1979. MHL. Includes: Gajardo, Joel V., "The Latin American Situation: The Challenge of Liberation Theology," pp. 12; Lind, Millard, review, *Marx and the Bible* by José Miranda (Maryknoll, NY: Orbis, 1974. Pp. 338), pp. 9.

Regehr, Ernie. "Civil War in El Salvador: North America Supports a Repressive Regime." *MennRep* 10 (Dec. 8, 1980), 8. Reports on North American military support of the violently repressive Salvadorian government, and calls for the right to self-rule by the people of El Salvador and an end to foreign arms shipments.

Reimer, Vic. "The Gospel, Marxism, and Christian Mission: A View from Latin America." *Menn* 92 (Oct. 11, 1977), 584-85. Interview with Orlando Costas, Latin American theologian, discussing evangelization and challenging Mennonites to place their peace witness behind ratification of the Panama Canal treaty and other Latin American human rights issues, as they did in the struggle against the Vietnam War.

Rennir, Amy. "MCC Helping Local Churches Respond to Nicaraguan Needs." *Menn* 94 (Sept. 4, 1979), 518. MCC is responding to various needs in Nicaragua resulting from nearly a year of intense fighting between the Nicaraguan National Guard and the Sandinista rebels.

Schlabach, Gerald. "Military Coup Leaves MCCers Uncertain." *MBH* 19 (Aug. 29, 1980), 19. Military coup in Bolivia halts progress toward a civilian-led democracy, challenging Bolivian Mennonites to define nonviolent processes of change.

Sider, Burt. "Amid Civil Disorder—Nicaragua: A Suffering Church." *EV* 91 (Nov. 25, 1978), 8-9. Despite civil war and disruption in the political and economic sectors, the Nicaraguan church is showing remarkable strength.

Sider, Burt. "I Was Hungry . . ." *EV* 92 (Feb. 25, 1979), 6. Life in Nicaragua under its oprressive dictatorship is described, and, more specifically, its effect on the Brethren in Christ family.

Snyder, C. Arnold. "The Relevance of Anabaptist Nonviolence for Nicaragua Today." *CGR* 2 (Spring, 1984), 123-37. In comparing the Peasants' War of 1525 and the Nicaraguan Revolution of 1979, one notes that both produced theologies of social justice allowing for armed resistance. However, in response to the 16th century peasant revellion, the Anabaptists (Schleitheim, 1527) specifically rejected armed resistance as a response to injustice. Is this sort of response relevant to the situation in Central America? Concludes that the Anabaptists not only rejected violence but reinterpreted and preserved a vision of justice in their ecclesiology. Concludes that this reinterpreted vision of justice can be relevant to Nicaragua if we abandon the strict dichotomy between church and world and try to be the church in the middle of the world, acting for justice. Also "The Relevance of Anabaptist Nonviolence for Nicaragua Today." Pp. 21. BfC.

"The Changing Church in Latin America." *CanMenn* 18 (Feb. 27, 1970), 4. The article represents a survey of what the church is and must be doing to meet the social needs of its people. Countries mentioned are: Colombia, Chile, Paraguay, Brazil, and Cuba.

"Visit to Nicaragua Launches Assistance Programs." *MennRep* 9 (Sept. 3, 1979), 2. Eight representatives from Mennonite churches and organizations met in Nicaragua to review the current situation, renew church contacts, and discuss relief efforts.

Wagler, Harley. "The Peace Churches in Nicaragua (2): Mixed Reaction to Revolution." *MennRep* 10 (Oct. 13, 1980), 6-7. Review of the Catholic, evangelical, and Mennonite church responses to the Sandinista revolution and attitudes toward the new government.

West, James Lee. "A Native American's

Reflections on Thanksgiving." *GH* 65 (Nov. 14, 1972), 931-32, 943. Makes critical connections between the 200-year-old exploitation of the native Americans and contemporary situations in Vietnam and Central America.

Wiebe, Katie Funk. "No-sweat Christianity." *ChrLead* 40 (Oct. 25, 1977), 17; *MBH* 16 (Oct. 28, 1977), 5. Reflections on hearing a Latin American evangelist challenge the church to break its ties to the state and the military.

Yoder, John H. "Evangelism and Latin American Politics: A Document." *GH* 66 (Jan. 2, 1973), 4-5. J. S. Coffman's speech at the dedication of the Elkhart Institute building in 1896 shows that Mennonites of that era were concerned about peace issues, and specifically the ethics of government, and that such concern is not the sign of the loss of Mennonite identity, as some contemporaries claim.

# Supplement to Bibliography

These entries were regretfully missed in the computer calls. Since page proofs and indexing were already done, they are included here as a supplement.

### 1B. Alternative Service: Civilian Public Service

Alderfer, Paul D. *et al. Camp Grottoes Director, 1941-42.* Pp. 40. MSHL. Includes name, address, photo, induction date, church affiliation.

### 3. Attitudes and Education

Graves. Mary Sue. "Non-resistance and Alternative Service—A Comparative Study of Goessel and Walton High School Juniors and Seniors." Student paper for Christian Heritage Day, 196l. Pp. 15. MLA/BeC.

### 5. Church and State

Burkholder, Marjorie V. "Ethical Aspects in Swearing of Oaths." *ST* 36 (Apr., 1968), 22. A study of the implications involved in the moral issue of the swearing of oaths.

Hershberger, Betty Ann. "A Pacifist Approach to Civil Government: A Comparison of the Participant Quaker and Non-Participant Mennonite View." BA Thesis, Swarthmore College, Swarthmore, Pa., 1951. Pp. 178. BfC.

Stucky, Mark E. "James C. Juhnke and Mennonite Political Involvement." Social Science Seminar paper, May, 1971. Pp. 33. MLA/BeC.

### 6A. Civil Disobedience: General

Tinker, Mary Beth. "The Case of the Black Armbands." *With* 3 (Oct. 1970), 22. A ruling of the United States Supreme Court on Feb. 24, 1969, said that peaceful, nondisruptive protest in US public high school was legal.

### 6B. Civil Disobedience: War Tax Resistance

Gerber, Mary. Letter to the Editor. *Menn* 94 (Apr. 17, 1979), 286. Warns against being led by the *Zeitgeist*—the spirit of the age—rather than the Holy Spirit in seeking God's will over the question of paying taxes that go to military purposes.

Kremer, Rich and Shank, Michael. "A Call for Tax Resistance." *GH* 73 (Apr. 8. 1980), 300-301. The character of modern warfare leads the defense department to depend more on financial support than on military service; thus peacelovers should withhold tax dollars.

Valentine, Lonnie. Letter to the Editor. *God and Caesar* 5 (Apr., 1979), 8. A reader gives his reason for refusing to pay taxes for military spending.

Zahn, Franklin. Letter to the Editor. *God and Caesar* 2 (June, 1976), 3-4. Writer offers his explanation for withholding all of his telephone tax unless requested by IRS for payment; he then will pay voluntarily all but the percentage which goes toward "current military expenses.'

### 9A. Justice: General

Wiedeman, Willi. Germans Support Brazil for Conference Site." *Menn* 85 (Dec. 29, 1970), 798. Asks that Mennonite World Conference be conducted according to the spirit of its theme: Jesus Christ reconciles.

### 9E. Justice: Corrections

Shand, Thomas M. "Prisoner Gets New Life. Thanks Church." *Menn* 87 (Mar. 28, 1972), 217, 218. A prisoner whose sentence of death was commuted to life imprisonment writes a letter of gratitude and exhortation to the Charleswood Mennonite Church which became instrumental in bringing about this commutation.

### 10B. Mennonite Central Committee: Development

Gingerich, Keith, E. "Journey Toward a Christian View of Development." MA in Peace Studies Thesis, AMBS, 1977. Pp. iii, 106. Critical discussion of development issues such as the history of the concept, liberation, the variety of typologies and pertinent theological themes. The concluding chapter outlines a biblical-based model of development both theoretically and by offering examples.

10C. **Mennonite Central Committee**: Relief (famine and hunger)

Sprunger, Cindy. "Food: The New Political Weapon." *Forum* 8 (Apr., 1975), 4. America needs to develop a national food policy that will respond to food needs here and abroad rather than using it in economic affairs as a political weapon.

11B. **Military Service**: Conscription, Registration and the Draft

Goering, Delbert D. "A Study of the Factors Which Influenced Our Drafted Men." Student paper for Our Christian Heritage, Nov. 19, 1949. Pp. 13. MLA/BeC.

Schroeder, Sue and Friesen, Michelle. "A Case of Non-registration—Dwight Platt." Students paper, Mar. 2., 1972. Pp. 12. MLA/BeC.

13A. **Peace**: General

Gerbrandt, Richard. Letter to the Editor. *ChrLead* 36 (May 1, 1973), 13. The implications of some editorial remarks explaining the Mennonite Brethren position on peace: "The Christian cannot participate in war:" War is destructive and divisive to the Body of Christ.

Harder, Helmut. "Response to Perry G. Yoder, 'Toward a Shalom Biblical Theology,'" *Conrad Grebel Review* 1 (Fall, 1983), 39-49." *CGR* 2 (Winter, 1984), 59-62. If Yoder's comments about the relevance of the shalom concept to biblical theology were applied to the task of systematic theology, that application, while fruitful in many ways, would restrict the discussion unnecessarily if the shalom concept must always provide the final touchstone.

Metzler, A. J. "A Post-Christmas Meditation." *ChrLiv* 7 (Feb., 1960), 2. Editorial describing the three phases of peace: peace with God, peace of God, and peace among humans.

13B. **Peace**: Peacemaking, Peace Witness and Peace Movements

Berkhof, Hendrik. *Christ and the Powers.* trans. by John H. Yoder, Scottdale: Herald Press, 1977. Pp. 79. By "powers" Paul means that "powers" are those hidden structures, created by God, which order human existence and which, when conceded authority apart from or beyond the Lordship of Christ, become demonic in human experience. This concept of the powers is an important component of Paul's construction of what being Christian means: ours is not to bring the powers "to their knees," an act already accomplished in the work of Christ, but to limit the powers by refusing their seductive enslavement and granting Lordship only to Christ.

Friesen, Donald G. "Ottawa Report: A Christian Witness to the Multinational Corporations." *MennRep* 9 (Jan. 8, 1979), 7. A workshop was convened in Ottawa to discuss the church's role with respect to multinational corporations, which support repressive regimes or show interest in their own profits only, causing needless suffering in other countries.

Haines, Leland M. Letter in "Our Readers Say." *GH* (June 11, 1963), 492. Response to "Why Should Christians Witness to the State (Part I of "Questions on the Christian Witness to the State, by John H. Yoder, *GH* 56 (May 21, 1963), 434. The concept of the two kingdoms means that Christians cannot and should not try to influence the state to operate on Christian values.

Yost, Don. "Alligator." *Swords into Plowshares: A Collection of Plays About Peace and Social Justice.* Ed. Ingrid Rogers. Elgin:The Brethren Press, 1983. Pp. 252-72. One-act play which explores the way people deal with the fear of nuclear warfare and its destruction. Asks the questions of what are bases for hope and how might we support each other in this situation.

13C. **Peace**: Nonresistance, Nonviolence, and Pacifism

Becker. Dennis. "Non-resistance." Research paper for the Mennonite Brethren History course, May, 1966. Pp. 14. MBBS.

Dettweiler, Kathleen. "Nonresister or Nonviolent Resister: Which Should it Be?" Student paper for Mennonite History, Dec. 2, 1975, pp. 7. MLA/BeC.

Eggers, Ernest. "'Love Your Enemies,'" *ChrMon* 33 (July, 1941), 194. Reprinted from *Cleveland Gospel Herald.* Story describes the change in one personal relationship when this principle was followed.

Epp, Duane. "Lutherans and Anabaptists— Concerning Nonresistance (*sic*)." Student paper for Mennonite History, Nov., 1955. Pp. 20. MLA/BeC.

Graber, Larry. "Non-resistance Practical?" Student paper for Our Christian Heritage, Feb., 1957. Pp. 14. MLA/BeC.

Graves, Mary Sue. "Non-resistance and Alternative Service—A Comparative Study of Goessel and Walton High School Juniors and Seniors." Student paper for Christian Heritage, May 1961. Pp. 15. MLA/BeC.

Harms, Dorothy. "Menno Simons and Non-resistance." Student paper for Our Christian Heritage, Feb. 23, 1959. Pp. 15. MLA/BeC.

Hathaway, Mary. "Opportunities for the Practice of Nonresistance." *GH Supplement* 39 (Apr., 1946), 95. The real test of nonresistance comes in daily living. Revenge, jealousy, and anger in personal contacts do not express Christian nonresistance.

Hostetler, Paul, ed. *Perfect Love and War.* Nappanee, IN: Evangel Press, 1974, pp. 170. A collection of essays dealing with the issues of war and peace from the perspective of the theological concept of perfect love shaped by the Wesleyan Holiness position. Both pacifist and nonpacifist views are represented.

Janzen, H. H. "Strengthening the Peace Witness." *MennLife* 7 (Jan., 1952), 3, 4. Suggests ways whereby the doctrine of nonresistance in the churches can be strengthened.

Orr, Hervé. "The Farmers from Larzac, the Gospel, and Non-Violence." *MCC PS Newsletter* 9 (May-June, 1978), 7-9. Describes the developments of a nonviolent resistance movement in opposition to the proposed expansion of a French military camp, a movement which has become known across Europe as a model of Christian resistance in a developed society.

Peters, Micael C. "Reinterpreting American History: A Mennonite Pacifistic Perspective." Social Science Seminar paper, May, 1984. Pp. 63. MLA/BeC.

Preheim, Emma Jean. "Professor Impressed by Emphasis on Non-Violence." *CanMenn* 12 (Apr. 21, 1964), 4. Report on talk given by Mulford Q. Sibley, professor of political science at the University of Minnesota to the Mennonite Student Fellowship on campus.

Schrag, Galen. "Mennonites: Agriculture and Non-resistance." Student paper for Our Christian Heritage, Feb. 27, 1959. Pp. 12. MLA/BeC.

Strausz, Arlene Joyce. "Mennonites and Non-resistance to War." Student paper for Mennonite History, Feb. 12, 1968. Pp. 20. MLA/BeC.

Whetstone, Bonnie. "Nonviolence or Nonresistance?" *Menn* 75 (Apr. 19, 1960), Research paper for Biblical and Christian Teachings on War and Peace class, 1984. Pp. 11. BfC.

Wiebe, Leonard. "Nonviolence or Nonresistance?" *Menn* 75 (Apr. 19, 1960), 250. Is nonviolent resistance too coercive? Has Mennonite nonresistance been replaced by Martin Luther King's nonviolence as the faithful peace witness for today?

Wiens, Dan E. "Non-resistance." *ChrLead* 13 (June 15, 1949), 7. The Gospel includes a renunciation of the use of force in the task of overcoming evil.

13D. **Peace**: Evangelicals, Social Action

Messner, David S. "Is It Better that a Christian Kill?" *ChrLiv* 15 (Feb., 1968), 28-29. Billy Graham's endorsement of war should warn Christians of the contradiction involved in loving and killing enemies at the same time.

13E. **Peace**: Women, Peace and War

Wengerd, Sara. "Some Behavioral Objectives for Women of Peace." *WMSC Voice* 54 (Dec., 1980), 4-6. Suggestions for peacemaking in the home and community.

14. **Race Relations**

Krall, C. Richard. "Why Is a Man?" *ChrLiv* 10 (July, 1963), 33-34, 40. Discusses four books on racial segregation and reconciliation.

Lee, Robert. "A Comparison of Martin Luther King and Guy F. Hershberger on the Race Problem in the US." Paper, n.d. Pp. 18. AMBS

16A. **War**: General

Templin, Mary. "The Beliefs of Menno Simons Concerning the Sword and the State." Research paper for Mennonite History class, 1977. Pp. 8. BfC.

Wall, Hugo. "Do We Want Peace." *Menn* 51 (Dec. 15, 1936), 8-10. War is not necessary or natural to humanity. The social scientist can help us avert war.

17C. **Wars**: World War I

Jong, Hielke de. "Some Experiences of the American Mennonites in the First World War." Student paper for Mennonite History, Nov., 1958. Pp. 34. MLA/BeC.

17D. **Wars**: World War II

Neufeld, I.G. "Mennonites and the War/WW II. "Neufeld papers, n.d. CMBS/Win.

# Author Index